CHARITY LAW HANDBOOK
(third edition)

Volume One: Statutes to 2000

Consultant edititors:
Michael Scott, MA (Hons)(Oxon), partner
Simon Wethered, MA (Hons)(Oxon), consultant
Charles Russell LLP

This (third) edition published by Spiramus Press Ltd,
102 Blandford Street, London, W1U 8AG.
www.spiramus.com
May 2012

ISBN

978 1907444 65 4	Book Set
978 1907444 49 4	Volume 1
978 1907444 50 0	Volume 2
978 1907444 66 1	Volume 3
978 1907444 63 0	CD-ROM
978 1907444 67 8	Book and CD-ROM

British Library Cataloguing-in-Publication Data.

A catalogue record for this book is available from the British Library.

This publication is based upon the law as at 15 March 2012.

Typeset by: Spiramus Press Ltd

Printed in Great Britain by: Berforts Information Press, Stevenage.

Preface to the third edition

We promised, in the Preface to our Second Edition of this Handbook, to put in hand the preparation of a Third Edition once the consolidating Charities Act had been passed. The Charities Act 2011 having come into force on the 14 March 2012, it forms the cornerstone of this work. The table of destinations should aid navigation.

Having also taken soundings from other practitioners, we have marginally increased the scope - and with it, we hope, the utility - of the Handbook by including a smattering of the most frequently used statutory provisions relating to housing, education and ecclesiastical law. A few omissions from the previous edition – some of venerable antiquity such as the Schools Sites Act 1841 – have also been remedied. The main provisions affecting charity law in Scotland and Northern Ireland will, we trust, mean that the work will be of use to charity law practitioners in those jurisdictions. These improvements have necessarily added to the bulk of the work which our publishers have sought to manage by not only dividing it into three handy volumes, but also making it available in CD-Rom form.

The previous Edition contained, in Part IV, some miscellaneous materials largely comprising HMRC Notices and Helpsheets. All these materials have been substantially updated by HMRC and the best source of such information is now their website, which is included amongst the list of useful addresses at the end of the work.

We are enormously grateful to Carl Upsall and his team at Spiramus for the care and patience with which they have tackled this project, and for undertaking the daunting task of providing an index.

The law here collated is that in force as at 14 March 2012.

Michael Scott
Simon Wethered
April 2012

Short table of contents – volume 1

PART I - STATUTES

Charitable Uses Act 1601

(43 Elizabeth I c. 4)

An Acte to redresse the Misemployment of Landes Goodes and Stockes of Money heretofore given to Charitable Uses

Whereas Landes Tenementes Rentes Annuities Profittes Hereditamentes, Goodes Chattels Money and Stockes of Money, have bene heretofore given limitted appointed and assigned, as well by the Queenes most excellent Majestie and her moste noble Progenitors, as by sondrie other well disposed persons, some for Releife of aged impotent and poore people, some for Maintenance of sicke and maymed Souldiers and Marriners, Schooles of Learninge, Free Schooles and Schollers in Universities, some for Repaire of Bridges Portes Havens Causwaies Churches Seabankes and Highwaies, some for Educacion and prefermente of Orphans, some for or towardes Reliefe Stocke or Maintenance of Howses of Correccion, some for Mariages of poore Maides, some for Supportacion Ayde and Helpe of younge tradesmen Handicraftesmen and persons decayed, and others for reliefe or redemption of Prisoners or Captives, and for aide or ease of any poore Inhabitantes concerninge paymente of Fifteenes, setting out of Souldiers and other Taxes; Whiche Landes Tenementes Rents Annuities Profitts Hereditaments Goodes Chattells Money and Stockes of Money nevertheles have not byn imployed accordinge to the charitable intente of the givers and founders thereof, by reason of Fraudes breaches of Truste and Negligence in those that shoulde pay delyver and imploy the same.

Schools Sites Act 1841

1841 CHAPTER 38 4 and 5 Vict

An Act to afford further Facilities for the Conveyance and Endowment of Sites for Schools.

[21st June 1841].

1. . . . . [1]

2 Landlords empowered to convey land to be used as sites for schools, &c. .

Any person, being seised in fee simple, fee tail, or for life, of and in any manor or lands of freehold, copyhold, or customary tenure, and having the beneficial interest . . . [2], may grant, convey, or enfranchise by way of gift, sale, or exchange, in fee simple or for a term of years, any quantity not exceeding one acre of such land, as a site for a school for the education of poor persons, or for the residence of the schoolmaster or schoolmistress, or otherwise for the purposes of the education of such poor persons in religious and useful knowledge; provided that no such grant made by any person seised only for life of and in any such manor or lands shall be valid, unless the person next entitled to the same in remainder, in fee simple or fee tail, (if legally competent,) shall be a party to and join in such grant: Provided also, that where any portion of waste or commonable land shall be gratuituously conveyed by any lord or lady of a manor for any such purposes as aforesaid, the rights and interests of all persons in the said land shall be barred and divested by such conveyance: Provided also, that upon the said land so granted as aforesaid, or any part thereof, ceasing to be used for the purposes in this Act mentioned, the same shall thereupon immediately revert to and become a portion of the said estate held in fee simple or otherwise, or of any manor or land as aforesaid, as fully to all intents and purposes as if this Act had not been passed, any thing herein contained to the contrary notwithstanding.

3 Chancellor and council of the duchy of Lancaster empowered to grant lands to the trustees of any existing or intended school..

And whereas it may be expedient and proper that the chancellor and council of her Majesty's duchy of Lancaster, on her Majesty's behalf, should be authorised to grant, convey, or enfranchise, to or in favour of the trustee or trustees of any existing or intended school, lands and hereditaments belonging to her Majesty in right of her said duchy, for the purposes of this Act: it shall and may be lawful for the chancellor and council of her Majesty's duchy of Lancaster for the time being, by any deed or writing under the hand and seal of the chancellor of the said duchy for the time being, attested by the clerk of the council of the said duchy for the time being, for and in the name of her Majesty, to grant, convey, or enfranchise, to or in favour of such trustee or trustees, any lands and hereditaments to be used by them for the purposes of this Act, upon such terms and conditions as to the said chancellor and council shall

seem meet; and where any sum or sums of money shall be paid as or for the purchase or consideration for such lands or hereditaments so to be granted, conveyed, or enfranchised as aforesaid, the same shall be paid by such trustee or trustees into the hands of the receiver general for the time being of the said duchy, or his deputy, and shall be by him paid, applied, and disposed of according to the provisions and regulations contained in the Duchy of Lancaster Act 1808, or any other Act or Acts now in force for that purpose: Provided always, that upon the said[If lands cease to be used for the purposes of the Act they shall revert.] land so granted as aforesaid, or any part thereof, ceasing to be used for the purposes in this Act mentioned, the same shall thereupon immediately revert to and become again a portion of the possessions of the said duchy, as fully to all intents and purposes as if this Act or any such grant as aforesaid had not been passed or made; any thing herein contained to the contrary notwithstanding.

4. . . . . [3]

5 Persons under disability empowered to convey lands for the purposes of this Act. .

Where any person shall be equitably entitled to any manor or land, but the legal estate therein shall be in some trustee or trustees, it shall be sufficient for such person to convey the same for the purposes of this Act without the trustee or trustees being party to the conveyance thereof; and where any married woman shall be seised or possessed of or entitled to any estate or interest, manorial or otherwise, in land proposed to be conveyed for the purposes of this Act, she . . . [4] may convey the same for such purposes by deed, without any acknowledgment thereof; and where it is deemed expedient to purchase any land for the purposes aforesaid belonging to or vested in any infant or [person of unsound mind], such land may be conveyed by the guardian or committee of such infant, or the committee of such [person of unsound mind][5], respectively, who may receive the purchase money for the same, and give valid and sufficient discharges to the party paying such purchase money, who shall not be required to see to the application thereof.

6 Corporations, justices, trustees, &c. empowered to convey lands for the purposes of this Act.

It shall be lawful for any corporation, ecclesiastical or lay, whether sole or aggregate, and for any officers, justices of the peace, trustees, or commissioners, holding land for public, ecclesiastical, parochial, charitable, or other purposes or objects subject to the provisions next herein-after mentioned, to grant, convey, or enfranchise, for the purposes of this Act, such quantity of land as aforesaid in any manner vested in such corporation, officers, justices, trustees, or commissioners: Provided always, that no ecclesiastical corporation sole, being below the dignity of a bishop, shall be authorised to make such grant without the consent in writing of the bishop of the diocese to whose jurisdiction the said ecclesiastical corporation is subject: Provided also, that no parochial property shall be granted for such purposes without the consent of . . . [6] the poor law commissioners, to be testified by their seal being affixed to the deed of conveyance . . . provided also, that where any officers, trustees, or commissioners, other than parochial trustees, shall make any such grant, it shall be sufficient if a majority or quorum authorised to act of such officers, trustees, or commissioners, assembled at a meeting duly convened, shall assent to such grant, and shall execute the deed of conveyance, although they shall not constitute a majority of the actual body of such officers, trustees, or commissioners: . . .[7]

7 Grants of land may be made to corporations or trustees, to be held by them for school purposes.

All grants of land or buildings, or any interest therein, for the purposes of the education of poor persons, whether taking effect under the authority of this Act or any other authority of law, may be made to any corporation sole or aggregate, or to several corporations sole, or to any trustees whatsoever, to be held by such corporation or corporations or trustees for the purposes aforesaid: Provided nevertheless, that any such grant may be made to the minister of any parish being a corporation, and the churchwardens or chapelwardens and overseers of the poor, or to the minister and kirk session of the said parish, and their successors; and in such case the land or buildings so granted shall be vested for ever thereafter in the minister, churchwardens, or chapelwardens, and overseers of the poor for the time being, or the minister and kirk session of such parish, but the management, direction, and inspection of the school shall be and remain according to the provisions contained in the deed of conveyance thereof: Provided also, that where any ecclesiastical corporation sole below the dignity of a bishop shall grant any land to trustees, other than the minister, churchwardens or chapelwardens, and overseers, for the purposes aforesaid, such trustees shall be nominated in writing by the bishop of the diocese to whose jurisdiction such corporation shall be subject; provided that where any school shall be intended for any ecclesiastical district not being a parish as herein-after

defined, it shall be sufficient if the grant be made to the minister and church or chapel warden or wardens of the church or chapel of such district, and to hold to them and their successors in office; and such grant shall enure to vest the land, subject to the conditions contained in the deed of conveyance, in such minister and the church or chapel warden or wardens for the time being.

8 Estates now vested in trustees for the purposes of education may be conveyed to the minister and churchwardens.

And whereas schools for the education of the poor in the principles of the Established Church, or in religious and useful knowledge, and residences for the masters or mistresses of such schools, have been heretofore erected, and are vested in trustees not having a corporate character: It shall be lawful for the trustees for the time being of such last-mentioned schools and residences, not being subject to the provisions of the Grammar Schools Act 1840, to convey or assign the same, and all their estate and interest therein, to such ministers and churchwardens and overseers of the poor of the parish within which the same are respectively situate and their successors as aforesaid, or, being situate within an ecclesiastical district not being a parish as herein after defined, then to the minister and church or chapel wardens of the church or chapel of such district, and their successors, in whom the same shall thereafter remain vested accordingly, but subject to and under the existing trusts and provisions respectively affecting the same.

9 Any number of sites may be granted for separate schools.

Any person or persons or corporation may grant any number of sites for district and separate schools, and residences for the master or mistress thereof, although the aggregate quantity of land thereby granted by such person or persons or corporation shall exceed the extent of one acre; provided that the site of each school and residence do not exceed that extent: Provided also, that not more than one such site shall be in the same parish.

10 Form of grants, &c..

All grants, conveyances, and assurances of any site for a school, or the residence of a schoolmaster or schoolmistress, under the provisions of this Act, in respect of any land, messuages, or buildings, may be made according to the form following, or as near thereto as the circumstances of the case will admit; (that is to say,)

"I [or we, or the corporate title of a corporation], under the authority of an Act passed in the year of the reign of her Majesty Queen Victoria, intituled "An Act for affording further facilities for the conveyance and endowment of sites for school," do hereby freely and voluntarily, and without any valuable consideration, [or do, in consideration of the sum of to me or us or the said paid], grant, [alienate,] and convey to all [description of the premises,] and all [my or our or the right, title, and interest of the] to and in the same and every part thereof, to hold unto and to the use of the said and his or their [heirs, or executors, or administrators, or successors,] for the purposes of the said Act, and to be applied as a site for a school for poor persons of and in the parish of and for the residence of the schoolmaster [or schoolmistress] of the said school [or for other purposes of the said school,] and for no other purpose whatever; such school to be under the management and control of [set forth the mode in which and the persons by whom the school is to be managed, directed, and inspected.] [In case the school be conveyed to trustees, a clause providing for the renewal of the trustees, and in cases where the land is purchased, exchanged, or demised, usual covenants or obligations for title, may be added.] In witness whereof the conveying and other parties have hereunto set their hands and seals, this day of Signed, sealed, and delivered by the said in the presence of of .'

And no bargain and sale or livery of seisin shall be requisite in any conveyance intended to take effect under the provisions of this Act, nor more than one witness to the execution by each party; . . [8]

11 Application of purchase money for land sold by any ecclesiastical corporation sole.

Where any land shall be sold by any ecclesiastical corporation sole for the purposes of this Act, and the purchase money to be paid shall not exceed the sum of twenty pounds, the same may be retained by the party conveying, for his own benefit; but when it shall exceed the sum of twenty pounds, it shall be applied for the benefit of the said corporation, in such manner as the bishop in whose diocese such land shall be situated shall, by writing under his hand, to be registered in the registry of his diocese, direct and appoint; but no person purchasing such land for the purpose aforesaid shall be required to see to the due application of any such purchase money.

12. . . . .[9].

13 Ecclesiastical corporations sole to procure a certificate as to the extent of the land conveyed.

When any ecclesiastical corporation sole below the dignity of a bishop shall grant any land belonging to him in right of his corporation for the purposes of this Act, he shall procure a certificate, under the hands of three beneficed clergymen of the diocese within which the land to be conveyed shall be situate, as to the extent of the land so conveyed, to be endorsed on the said deed; which certificate shall be in the form following; (that is to say,)

'We, A.B. clerk, rector[Form of certificate.] of the parish of C.D. clerk, rector of the parish of and E.F. clerk, vicar of the parish of , being three beneficed clergymen of the diocese of do hereby certify, that clerk, rector of the parish of within the said diocese of being about to convey a portion of land situate in the said parish of for the purposes of a school, under the powers of the Act passed in year of the reign of her Majesty Queen Victoria, intituled "An Act for affording further facilities for the conveyance and endowment of sites for schools," we have at his request inspected and examined the portion of land, and have ascertained that the same is situate at [here describe the situation], and that the extent thereof does not exceed acre . As witness our hands, this day of at in the county of and diocese of .

Witness of .'

And until such certificate shall have been signed no such conveyance shall have any force or validity.

14 Trustees empowered to sell or exchange lands or buildings.

When any land or building shall have been or shall be given or acquired under the provisions of the said first-recited Act or this Act, or shall be held in trust for the purposes aforesaid, and it shall be deemed advisable to sell or exchange the same for any other more convenient or eligible site, it shall be lawful for the trustees in whom the legal estate in the said land or building shall be vested, by the direction or with the consent of the managers and directors of the said school, if any such there be, to sell or exchange the said land or building, or part thereof, for other land or building suitable to the purposes of their trust, and to receive on any exchange any sum of money by way of effecting an equality of exchange, and to apply the money arising from such sale or given on such exchange in the purchase of another site, or in the improvement of other premises used or to be used for the purposes of such trust; provided that where the land shall have been given by any ecclesiastical corporation sole, the consent of the bishop of the diocese shall be required to be given to such sale or exchange before the same shall take place: Provided also, that where a portion of any parliamentary grant shall have been or shall be applied towards the erection of any school, no sale or exchange thereof shall take place [unless the Secretary of State consents.][10]

15. . . . . [11]

16. . . . .[12]

17 No schoolmaster to acquire a life interest by virtue of his appointment.

No schoolmaster or schoolmistress to be appointed to any school erected upon land conveyed under the powers of this Act shall be deemed to have acquired an interest for life by virtue of such appointment, but shall, in default of any specific engagement, hold his office at the discretion of the trustees of the said school.

18. . . . .[13]

19. . . . . [14]

20 Definition of the term "parish.".

The term "parish" in this Act shall be taken to signify every place separately maintaining its own poor, and having its own overseers of the poor and church or chapel wardens.

21 Act not to extend to Ireland.

This Act shall not extend to Ireland.

22. . . . .[15]

23. . . . .[16]

---

[1] Ss. 1, 4 repealed by Statute Law Revision Act 1874 (No. 2) (c. 96)

[2] Words repealed by virtue of Education (Scotland) Act 1945 (c. 37), Sch. 5

[3] Ss. 1, 4 repealed by Statute Law Revision Act 1874 (No. 2) (c. 96)

[4] Words repealed by Law Reform (Married women and Tortfeasors) Act 1935 (c. 30), Sch. 2

[5] Words substituted by Mental Treatment Act 1930 (c. 23), s. 20(5)

[6] Words repealed by Local Government Act 1929 (c. 17), Sch. 12 Pt. VII
[7] Words repealed by Local Government Act 1933 (c.51), Sch.11 Pt.IV and London Government Act 1939 (c.40), Sch.8
[8] Words repealed by virtue of Education (Scotland) Act 1945 (c. 37), Sch. 5
[9] S. 12 repealed by virtue of Education (Scotland) Act 1945 (c. 37), Sch. 5
[10] Words substituted by Statute Law (Repeals) Act 1978 (c. 45), Sch. 2 para. 1
[11] S. 15 repealed by Statute Law (Repeals) Act 1978 (c. 45), Sch. 1 Pt. V
[12] S. 16 repealed by Statute Law Revision Act 1874 (No. 2) (c. 96)
[13] S. 18 repealed by Rent Act 1965 (c. 75), Sch. 7 Pt. II
[14] S. 19 repealed by Statute Law (Repeals) Act 1978 (c. 45), Sch. 1 Pt. V
[15] S.22 repealed by Statute Law Revision Act 1874 (No.2) (c.96) and by virtue of Education (Scotland) Act 1945 (c.37),Sch.5
[16] S. 23 repealed by Statute Law Revision Act 1874 (No. 2) (c. 96)

Commons Act 1899

1899 CHAPTER 30 62 and 63 Vict

An Act to amend the Inclosure Acts 1845 to 1882 and the Law relating to Commons and Open Spaces.

[9th August 1899]

Part I Regulation of Commons

1 Power for district council to make scheme for regulation of common.

(1) The council of [a district][1] may make a scheme for the regulation and management of any common within their district with a view to the expenditure of money on the drainage, levelling, and improvement of the common, and to the making of bylaws and regulations for the prevention of nuisances and the preservation of order on the common.

(2) The scheme may contain any of the statutory provisions for the benefit of the neighbourhood mentioned in section seven of the Commons Act 1876.

(3) The scheme shall be in the prescribed form, and shall identify by reference to a plan the common to be thereby regulated, and for this purpose an ordnance survey map shall, if possible, be used.

2 Procedure for making scheme.

(1) Not less than three months before the making of a scheme under this Part of this Act the council shall give the prescribed notice of their intention to make it, and shall state thereby where copies of the draft of the scheme may be obtained, and where the plan therein referred to may be inspected...[2].

(2) During the three months aforesaid any person may obtain copies of the draft on payment of a sum not exceeding [2½p][3] per copy, and may inspect the plan at the prescribed place, and may make in writing to the [council][4] any objection or suggestion with respect to the scheme or plan.

(3) After the expiration of the said three months the [council][5] shall take into consideration any objections or suggestions so made, and for that purpose may, if they think fit, direct that an inquiry be held by an officer of the [council][6].

(4) The [council] may by order approve of the scheme, subject to such modifications, if any, as they may think desirable, and thereupon the scheme shall have full effect.

Provided that if, at any time before the [council][7] have approved of the scheme, they receive a written notice of dissent either—

(a) from the person entitled as lord of the manor or otherwise to the soil of the common; or

(b) from persons representing at least one-third in value of such interests in the common as are affected by the scheme,

and such notice is not subsequently withdrawn, the [council][8] shall not proceed further in the matter.

3 Management of regulated common.

The management of any common regulated by a scheme made by a district council under this Part of this Act shall be vested in the district council.

4 Provision for delegation of powers of district council to parish council.

A rural district council may delegate to a parish council any powers of management conferred by this part of this Act on the district council in relation to any commons within the parish, and thereupon the

Public Health Acts shall apply as if the parish council were a parochial committee.

5 Power for parish council to contribute to expenses.

A parish council may agree to contribute the whole or any portion of the expenses of and incidental to the preparation and execution of a scheme for the regulation and management of any common within their parish (including any compensation paid under this Act) . . . [9]

6 Provision for compensation.

No estate, interest, or right of a profitable or beneficial nature in, over, or affecting any common shall, except with the consent of the person entitled thereto, be taken away or injuriously affected by any scheme under this Part of this Act without compensation being made or provided for the same by the council making the scheme, and such compensation shall, in case of difference, be ascertained and provided in the same manner as if it were for the compulsory purchase and taking, or the injurious affecting, of lands under [Part I of the Compulsory Purchase Act 1965.][10]

7 Power for district council to acquire property in regulated common.

A district council may acquire the fee simple or any estate in or any rights in or over any common regulated by a scheme under this Part of this Act by gift or by purchase by agreement, and hold the same . . .[11] for the purposes of the scheme . . . [12]

8 Digging of gravel.

Section twenty of the Commons Act 1876 (which relates to the digging of gravel), shall apply to any common regulated by a scheme under this Part of this Act.

9 Power to amend scheme.

The power to make a scheme under this Part of this Act shall include power to amend or supplement any such scheme.

10 Provisions as to byelaws.

The provisions with respect to byelaws contained in [section two hundred and thirty-six of the Local Government Act 1972][13] shall apply to all byelaws made in pursuance of a scheme under this Part of this Act, and any fine imposed by any such byelaw shall be recoverable summarily and be payable to the council in whom the management of the common is vested.

[11 Expenses.

All expenses of and incidental to the preparation and execution of a scheme under this Part of this Act shall be paid by the district council.][14]

12 Power for urban district council to contribute towards expenses.

The council of any [district][15] may, with a view to the benefit of the inhabitants of their district, . [16] enter into an undertaking with any other council making or having made a scheme under this Part of this Act to contribute any portion of the expenses incurred by that council in executing the scheme.

13 Application to county boroughs.

This Part of this Act shall apply to the council of a county borough in like manner as if that council were the council of an urban district.

14 Saving for commons regulated under other Acts.

A scheme under this Part of this Act shall not apply to any common which is or might be the subject of a scheme made under the Metropolitan Commons Acts 1866 to 1878 or is regulated by a Provisional Order under the Inclosure Acts 1845 to 1882 or has been acquired, or managed as an open space, under the powers of the Corporation of London (Open Spaces) Act 1878 or any Act therein referred to, or is the subject of any private or local and personal Act of Parliament having for its object the preservation of the common as an open space, or is subject to byelaws made by a parish council under section eight of the Local Government Act 1894.

15 Definitions.

In this Part of this Act, unless the context otherwise requires,—

The expression "common" shall include any land subject to be inclosed under the Inclosure Acts 1845 to 1882, and any town or village green;

The expression "prescribed" shall mean prescribed by regulations made by the [Secretary of State.][17]

Part II Miscellaneous

16 Surplus rents from field gardens and recreation grounds.

(1) Surplus rents arising from field gardens may, in addition to the purposes for which they are now applicable, be applied for any of the purposes for which surplus rents arising from recreation grounds may be applied.

(2) Surplus rents arising from any field garden or recreation ground may be applied towards the redemption of any land tax, tithe rentcharge, or other charge on the garden or ground.

17 Amendment of 50 & 51 Vict. c. 32 as to open spaces.

(1) The powers exerciseable by the district council of a rural district under section five of the Open Spaces Act, 1887, may be exercised whether the council has been invested by an order of the Local Government Board with the powers of the Open Spaces Acts, 1877 to 1890, or not.

(2) A county council may invest a parish council with the powers of the Open Spaces Acts, 1877 to 1890, and thereupon those Acts shall apply in like manner as if the parish council were a district council, and the parish were the district thereof, except that any expenses incurred by the parish council shall be defrayed as expenses incurred under the Local Government Act, 1894, and be subject to the provisions of section eleven of that Act, and that byelaws made by a parish council need not be under common seal.

(3) Section seven of the Open Spaces Act, 1887, shall apply to a parish council in like manner as it applies to a district council.

(4) All the powers exerciseable by the London County Council and other local authorities under the Open Spaces Acts, 1877 to 1890, may also be exercises by the county council of any administrative county, and any expenses incurred by a county council under the said Acts shall be defrayed as expenses incurred under the Local Government Act, 1888.

18 Power to modify provisions as to recreation grounds, &c.

Any provisions with respect to allotments for recreation grounds, field gardens, or other public or parochial purposes contained in any Act relating to inclosure or in any award or order made in pursuance thereof, and any provisions with respect to the management of any such allotments contained in any such Act, order, or award, may, on the application of any district or parish council interested in any such allotment, be dealt with by a scheme of the Charity Commissioners in the exercise of their ordinary jurisdiction, as if those provisions had been established by the founder in the case of a charity having a founder

[For the purposes of this section the Broads Authority shall be treated as a district council.][18]

19 Amendment of 8 & 9 Vict. c. 118.

Section one hundred and fifty of the Inclosure Act, 1845, shall have effect as if "two successive weeks" were therein inserted instead of "three successive weeks," and as if "one month" were therein inserted instead of "three calendar months".

20 Amendment of law as to adjournment of meetings.

Where notice has been given of any sitting, whether original or by adjournment, to be held by an officer of the [Secretary of State][19] under the Metropolitan Commons Acts, 1866 to 1878, that officer may, by notice to be published in such manner as the [Secretary of State][20] direct, adjourn the sitting without attending for the purpose of the adjournment.

21 Annual report to Parliament.

. . . [21] The Secretary of State][22] shall include in an annual report to Parliament a statement of [his][23] proceedings under Part I. of this Act and under the Metropolitan Commons Acts 1866 to 1878 during the year ending the thirty-first day of December then last past, with such particulars as to [his][24] proceedings under the last-mentioned Acts as are required by section twenty-one of the Metropolitan Commons Acts 1866.

22 Restrictions on inclosures under scheduled Acts.

(1) A grant or inclosure of common purporting to be made under the general authority of any of the Acts mentioned in the First Schedule hereto or any Act incorporating the same, or any provisions thereof, shall not be valid unless it is either—

(a) specially authorised by Act of Parliament; or

(b) made to or by any Government Department; or

(c) made with the consent of the [Secretary of State.][25]

(2) The [Secretary of State][26], in giving or withholding [his consent][27] under this section, shall have regard to the same considerations, and shall, if necessary, hold the same inquiries as are directed by the Commons Act 1876 to be taken into consideration and held by the [Secretary of State][28] before forming an opinion whether an application under the Inclosure Acts shall be acceded to or not.

23 Repeal.

. . . [29] This repeal shall not affect the construction or effect of any local and personal Act of Parliament passed before the commencement of this Act, whereby any provisions of the said enactments are intended to be incorporated.

24 Short title.

This Act may be cited as the Commons Act 1899, and shall read with the Inclosure Acts 1845 to 1882.

SCHEDULES

Section 22.

FIRST SCHEDULE - Enactments relating to Inclosures subject to restriction under this Act.

Session and Chapter.	Title or Short Title.
43 Eliz. c. 2.	The Poor Relief Act, 1601.
. . . . . . [30]	. . . . . .
51 Geo. 3. c. 115.	The Gifts for Churches Act, 1811.
58 Geo. 3. c. 45.	The Church Building Act, 1818.
1 & 2 Will. 4. c. 42.	The Poor Relief Act, 1831.
1 & 2 Will. 4. c. 59.	The Crown Lands Allotments Act, 1831.
5 & 6 Will. 4. c. 69.	The Union and Parish Property Act, 1835.
4 & 5 Vict. c. 38.	The Schools Sites Act, 1841.
8 & 9 Vict. c. 18.	The Lands Clauses Consolidation Act, 1845.
17 & 18 Vict. c. 112.	The Literary and Scientific Institutions Act, 1854.
[1965 c. 56	Part I of the Compulsory Purchase Act, 1965.].

SECOND SCHEDULE[31]

. . . .

---

[1] Words substituted by virtue of Local Government Act 1972 (c. 70), s. 179(3)

[2] Words repealed by Local Government, Planning and Land Act 1980 (c. 65, SIF 81:1, 2), s. 194, Sch. 34 Pt. III

[3] Words substituted by virtue of Decimal Currency Act 1969 (c. 19), s. 10(1)

[4] Word substituted by virtue of Local Government, Planning and Land Act 1980 (c. 65, SIF 81:1, 2), s. 1(3), Sch. 3 para. 2(1)(b)

[5] Word substituted by Local Government, Planning and Land Act 1980 (c. 65, SIF 81:1, 2), s. 1(3), Sch. 3 para. 2(1)(c)

[6] Word substituted by Local Government, Planning and Land Act 1980 (c. 65, SIF 81:1, 2), s. 1(3), Sch. 3 para. 2(1)(c)

[7] Word substituted by Local Government, Planning and Land Act 1980 (c. 65, SIF 81:1, 2), s. 1(3), Sch. 3 para. 2(1)(c)

[8] Word substituted by Local Government, Planning and Land Act 1980 (c. 65, SIF 81:1, 2), s. 1(3), Sch. 3 para. 2(1)(c)

[9] Words repealed with savings by Local Government Act 1933 (c. 51), s. 307, Sch. 11 Pt. IV

[10] Words substituted by virtue of Compulsory Purchase Act 1965 (c. 56), s. 39(2)

[11] Words repealed by Statute Law Revision Act 1963 (c. 30)

[12] Words repealed with savings by Local Government Act 1933 (c. 51), s. 307, Sch. 11 Pt. IV

[13] Words substituted by virtue of Interpretation Act 1889 (c. 63), s. 38(1)

[14] S. 11 substituted by Local Government, Planning and Land Act 1980 (c. 65, SIF 81:1, 2), s. 1(3), Sch. 3 para. 2(2)

[15] Words substituted by virtue of Local Government Act 1972 (c. 70), s. 179(3)

[16] Words repealed by virtue of Local Government, Planning and Land Act 1980 (c. 65, SIF 81:1, 2), s. 194, Sch. 34 Pt. III

[17] Words substituted by virtue of Board of Agriculture and Fisheries Act 1903 (c. 31), s. 1(1), Ministry of Agriculture and Fisheries Act 1919 (c. 91), s. 1, S.I. 1955/554 (1955 I, p. 1200), 1965/143, 1967/156 and 1970/1681

[18] Paragraph added (E.W.) by Norfolk and Suffolk Broads Act 1988 (c. 4, SIF 81:1), s. 21, Sch. 6 para. 1

[19] Words substituted by virtue of Board of Agriculture and Fisheries Act 1903 (c. 31), s. 1(1), Ministry of Agriculture and Fisheries Act 1919 (c. 91), s. 1, S.I. 1955/554 (1955 I, p. 1200), 1965/143, 1967/156 and 1970/1681

[20] Words substituted by virtue of Board of Agriculture and Fisheries Act 1903 (c. 31), s. 1(1), Ministry of Agriculture

and Fisheries Act 1919 (c. 91), s. 1, S.I. 1955/554 (1955 I, p. 1200), 1965/143, 1967/156 and 1970/1681

[21] Words repealed by Statute Law Revision Act 1908 (c. 49)

[22] Words substituted by virtue of Board of Agriculture and Fisheries Act 1903 (c. 31), s. 1(1), Ministry of Agriculture and Fisheries Act 1919 (c. 91), s. 1, S.I. 1955/554 (1955 I, p. 1200), 1965/143, 1967/156 and 1970/1681

[23] Words substituted by virtue of Board of Agriculture and Fisheries Act 1903 (c. 31), s. 1(1), Ministry of Agriculture and Fisheries Act 1919 (c. 91), s. 1, S.I. 1955/554 (1955 I, p. 1200), 1965/143, 1967/156 and 1970/1681

[24] Words substituted by virtue of Board of Agriculture and Fisheries Act 1903 (c. 31), s. 1(1), Ministry of Agriculture and Fisheries Act 1919 (c. 91), s. 1, S.I. 1955/554 (1955 I, p. 1200), 1965/143, 1967/156 and 1970/1681

[25] Words substituted by virtue of Board of Agriculture and Fisheries Act 1903 (c. 31), s. 1(1), Ministry of Agriculture and Fisheries Act 1919 (c. 91), s. 1, S.I. 1955/554 (1955 I, p. 1200), 1965/143, 1967/156 and 1970/1681

[26] Words substituted by virtue of Board of Agriculture and Fisheries Act 1903 (c. 31), s. 1(1), Ministry of Agriculture and Fisheries Act 1919 (c. 91), s. 1, S.I. 1955/554 (1955 I, p. 1200), 1965/143, 1967/156 and 1970/1681

[27] Words substituted by virtue of Board of Agriculture and Fisheries Act 1903 (c. 31), s. 1(1), Ministry of Agriculture and Fisheries Act 1919 (c. 91), s. 1, S.I. 1955/554 (1955 I, p. 1200), 1965/143, 1967/156 and 1970/1681

[28] Words substituted by virtue of Board of Agriculture and Fisheries Act 1903 (c. 31), s. 1(1), Ministry of Agriculture and Fisheries Act 1919 (c. 91), s. 1, S.I. 1955/554 (1955 I, p. 1200), 1965/143, 1967/156 and 1970/1681

[29] Words repealed by Statute Law Revision Act 1908 (c. 49)

[30] Words repealed (1.4.1978) by Endowment and Glebe Measure 1976 (No. 4), Sch. 8

[31] Sch. 2 repealed by Statute Law Revision Act 1908 (c. 49)

Open Spaces Act 1906

1906 CHAPTER 25 6 Edw 7

3 Transfer to local authority of spaces held by trustees for purposes of public recreation.

(1) Where any land is held by trustees (not being trustees elected or appointed under any local or private Act of Parliament) upon trust for the purposes of public recreation, the trustees may, in pursuance of a special resolution, transfer the land to any local authority by a free gift absolutely or for a limited term, and, if the local authority accept the gift, they shall hold the land on the trusts and subject to the conditions on and subject to which the trustees held the same, or on such other trusts and subject to such other conditions (so that the land be appropriated to the purposes of public recreation) as may be agreed on between the trustees and the local authority with the approval of the Charity Commissioners.

(2) Subject to the obligation of the land so transferred being used for the purposes of public recreation, the local authority may hold the land as and for the purposes of an open space under this Act.

4 Transfer by charity trustees of open space to local authority.

(1) Where an open space is vested in trustees, other than such as are mentioned in the foregoing provisions of this Act, for any charitable purpose and as part of their trust estate, and it appears to the majority of the trustees that the open space is no longer required for the purposes of their trust, or may with advantage to the trust be dealt with under this section, the trustees may, in pursuance of a special resolution, [and with the sanction of an order of the Charity Commissioners or with that of an order of the court][1] to be obtained as hereinafter provided, convey or demise the open space to any local authority on such terms as they may agree, and the local authority shall thenceforth be entitled to hold the same as an open space on the terms and under the conditions specified in the conveyance or demise, or on such terms or under such conditions as may be so authorised or approved, or as the court may from time to time order, as the case may be.

(2) The court for the purposes of this section shall be either the High Court or the county court of the district in which the whole or any part of the open space is situate.

(3) An order of the court for the purposes of this section may be made upon application by the trustees, in manner directed by rules of court, and the court, before making any order, may direct such inquiries to be made, such consents to be obtained, and notice to be given to such persons, as to the court seem expedient, and may make such order thereon as in the discretion of the court appears proper.

[(4) Section 89 of the Charities Act 1993 (provisions as to orders under that Act) shall apply to any order of the Charity Commissioners under this section as it applies to orders made by them under that Act.][2]

....

8 Special resolutions and consents.

(1) A resolution shall for the purposes of this Act be a special resolution when it has been—

(a) passed by a majority of at least two-thirds of the persons present at a meeting summoned as herein-after provided; and

(b) confirmed by another resolution passed by a majority of at least two-thirds of the persons present at a meeting summoned as herein-after provided and held after an interval of not less than one month from the first meeting.

(2) A meeting of trustees for the purposes of this Act shall be summoned by a notice stating generally the object of the meeting, which notice shall be left at or sent by post, at least one month before the date of the meeting, to the last known or usual place of abode of each trustee.

(3) A meeting of owners and occupiers of houses under this Act shall be summoned by a notice stating generally the object of the meeting, which notice shall be left at, or sent through the post to, each of such houses, at least one month before the date of the meeting, and shall be inserted as an advertisement at least three times in any two or more papers circulating in the neighbourhood.

(4) If at any meeting of trustees or of owners and occupiers under this Act a resolution with respect to an open space is rejected, no meeting of the trustees, or, as the case may be, the owners or occupiers, shall be called or held with the same object and with respect to the same open space until the expiration of three years from the date of the rejection.

(5) A meeting of owners or occupiers of houses for the purposes of this Act shall not be held between the first day of August in one year and the thirty-first day of January in the following year.

Powers of Local Authorities with respect to Open Spaces and Burial Grounds

9 Power of local authority to acquire open space or burial ground.

A local authority may, subject to the provisions of this Act,—

(a) acquire by agreement and for valuable or nominal consideration by way of payment in gross, or of rent, or otherwise, or without any consideration, the freehold of, or any term of years or other limited estate or interest in, or any right or easement in or over, any open space or burial ground, whether situate within the district of the local authority or not; and

(b) undertake the entire or partial care, management, and control of any such open space or burial ground, whether any interest in the soil is transferred to the local authority or not; and

(c) for the purposes aforesaid, make any agreement with any person authorised by this Act or otherwise to convey or to agree with reference to any open space or burial ground, or with any other persons interested therein.

10 Maintenance of open spaces and burial grounds by local authority.

A local authority who have acquired any estate or interest in or control over any open space or burial ground under this Act shall, subject to any conditions under which the estate, interest, or control was so acquired—

(a) hold and administer the open space or burial ground in trust to allow, and with a view to, the enjoyment thereof by the public as an open space within the meaning of this Act and under proper control and regulation and for no other purpose: and

(b) maintain and keep the open space or burial ground in a good and decent state.

and may inclose it or keep it inclosed with proper railings and gates, and may drain, level, lay out, turf, plant, ornament, light, provide with seats, and otherwise improve it, and do all such works and things and employ such officers and servants as may be requisite for the purposes aforesaid or any of them.

15 Byelaws.

(1) A local authority may, with reference to any open space or burial ground in or over which they have acquired any estate, interest, or control under this Act, [[or in the case of the Greater London Council in relation to any other public park, heath, common, recreation ground, pleasure ground, garden, walk, ornamental enclosure or disused burial ground under the control and management of the said Council][3]][4] make byelaws for the regulation thereof, and of the days and times of admission thereto, and for the preservation of order and prevention of nuisances therein, and may by such byelaws impose penalties recoverable summarily for the infringement thereof, and provide for the removal of any person infringing any byelaw by any officer of the local authority or police constable.

(2) All byelaws made under this Act by any local authority shall be made—

(a) in the case of a county council . . . [5], subject and according to the provisions of section sixteen of the Local Government Act 1888; and

(b). . . . . [6]

(c) in the case of the Common Council of the City of London, subject and according to the Corporation of London (Open Spaces) Act 1878; and

(d). . . . . [7]

(e) in the case of a municipal borough or district or parish council, subject and according to the provisions with respect to byelaws contained in sections one hundred and eighty-two to one hundred and eighty-six of the Public Health Act 1875 and those sections shall apply to a parish council in like manner as if they were a local authority within the meaning of that Act, except that byelaws made by a parish council need not be under common seal.

(3) The trustees or other persons having the care and management of any open space, who in pursuance of this Act admit to the enjoyment of the open space any persons not owning, occupying, or residing in any house fronting thereon, shall have the same powers of making byelaws as are conferred on a committee of the inhabitants of a square by section four of the Town Gardens Protection Act 1863 and that section shall apply accordingly.

16 Power of local authorities to act jointly.

Any two or more local authorities may jointly carry out the provisions of this Act and may make any agreement on such terms as may be arranged between them for so doing and for defraying the expenses of the execution of this Act, and any local authority may defray the whole or any part of the expenses incurred by any other local authority in the execution of this Act.

20 Definitions.

In this Act, unless the context otherwise requires,—

The expression "open space" means any land, whether inclosed or not, on which there are no buildings or of which not more than one-twentieth part is covered with buildings, and the whole or the remainder of which is laid out as a garden or is used for purposes of recreation, or lies waste and unoccupied:

The expression "common council of the City of London" means the mayor, aldermen, and commons of the City of London in common council assembled:

The expression "owner"—

(a) used in relation to an open space (not being a burial ground), means any person in whom the open space is vested for an estate in possession during his life or for any larger estate;

(b) used in relation to a house, includes any person entitled to any term of years in the house;

(c) used in relation to a burial ground, means the person in whom the freehold of the burial ground is vested whether as appurtenant or incident to any benefice or cure of souls or otherwise:

The expression "occupier," used in relation to a house, means the person rated to the relief of the poor in respect of the house:

The expression "burial ground" includes any churchyard, cemetery, or other ground, whether consecrated or not, which has been at any time set apart for the purpose of interment:

The expression "disused burial ground" means any burial ground which is no longer used for interments, whether or not the ground has been partially or wholly closed for burials under the provisions of a statute or Order in Council:

The expression "building" includes any temporary or movable building.

22 Extent.

This Act shall not extend to Scotland.

---

[1] Words substituted by Charities Act 1960 (c. 58), Sch. 6

[2] S. 4(4) added (1.8.1993) by 1993 c. 10, s. 98(1), Sch. 6 para. 2

[3] Words inserted by S.I. 1965/654, art. 3(5)(a)

[4] Words repealed (E.W.) by S.I. 1986/1, arts. 2, 3(4), Sch. Pt. II

[5] Words repealed by London Government Act 1963 (c. 33), Sch. 18 Pt. II

[6] S. 15(2)(b) repealed by London Government Act 1963 (c. 33), Sch. 18 Pt. II

[7] S. 15(2)(d) repealed by London Government Act 1963 (c. 33), Sch. 18 Pt. II

Police, Factories, &c (Miscellaneous Provisions) Act 1916

1916 CHAPTER 31 6 and 7 Geo 5

An Act to amend the Enactments relating to the Police and certain other Enactments with the administration of which the Secretary of State for the Home Department is concerned.

PART I - POLICE

[1[1], 2[2], 3[3], 4[4]]

5 Regulations of street collections.

(1) [Each of the authorities specified in subsection (1A) below][5] may make regulations with respect to the places where and the conditions under which persons may be permitted in any street or public place, within [their][6] area, to collect money or sell articles for the benefit of charitable or other purposes, and any person who acts in contravention of any such regulation shall be liable on summary conviction to a fine not exceeding [level 1 on the standard scale][7] or in the case of a second or subsequent offence not exceeding [level 1 on the standard scale][8]:

Provided that—

(a) regulations made under this section shall not come into operation until they have been confirmed by the Secretary of State, and published for such time and in such manner as the Secretary of State may direct; and

(b) regulations made under this section shall not apply to the selling of articles in any street or public place when the articles are sold in the ordinary course of trade, and for the purpose of earning a livelihood, and no representation is made by or on behalf of the seller that any part of the proceeds of sale will be devoted to any charitable purpose.

[(1A) The authorities referred to in subsection (1) above are—

(a) the Common Council of the City of London,

(b) the police authority for the Metropolitan Police District, and

(c) the council of each district;

but any regulations made by a district council under that subsection shall not have effect with respect to any street or public place which is within the Metropolitan Police District as well as within the district.] [9]

(2) This section, except subsection (3) thereof, shall apply to Ireland with the following modifications:—

(a) references to the Secretary of State shall be construed as references to the Lord Lieutenant; and

(b) references to a police authority shall . [10] be construed as references to the Inspector General of the Royal Irish Constabulary.

(3)[11]

(4) In this section—

the expression "street" includes any highway and any public bridge, road, lane, footway, square, court, alley, or passage, whether a thoroughfare or not.

6 Extent of Part I.

This Part of this Act shall not apply, except where otherwise expressly provided, to Scotland or Ireland.

PART II

7—9[12]

PART III - MISCELLANEOUS AND GENERAL

10[13]

11[14]

12[15]

13 Short title

This Act may be cited as the Police, Factories, &c. (Miscellaneous Provisions) Act 1916.

SCHEDULE[16]

[1] s. 1 repealed by Police (Pensions) Act 1918 (c. 51), s. 3

[2] s. 2 repealed by Statute Law Revision Act 1927 (c. 42)

[3] s. 3 repealed by Statute Law (Repeals) Act 1973 (c. 39), Sch. 1 Pt. XIII

[4] s. 4 repealed by Local Government Act 1929 (c. 17), Sch. 12 Pt. VI

[5] Words substituted by Local Government Act 1972 (c. 70), Sch. 29 para. 22
[6] Words substituted by Local Government Act 1972 (c. 70), Sch. 29 para. 22
[7] Words substituted by virtue of Criminal Justice Act 1982 (c. 48, SIF 39:1), s. 46
[8] s. 5(1A) inserted by Local Government Act 1972 (c. 70), Sch. 29 para. 22
[9] Words substituted by virtue of Criminal Justice Act 1982 (c. 48, SIF 39:1), s. 46
[10] Words omitted by virtue of Statute Law Revision Act 1927 (c. 42), s. 3
[11] s. 5(3) repealed by Civic Government (Scotland) Act 1982 (c. 45, SIF 81:2), s. 119(15)
[12] ss. 7–9 repealed by Factories Act 1937 (c. 67), Sch. 4
[13] s. 10 repealed by Mines and Quarries Act 1954 (c. 70), Sch. 5
[14] s. 11 repealed by Mental Health Act 1959 (c. 72), Sch. 8 Pt. I
[15] s. 12 repealed by Criminal Justice Act 1948 (c. 58), Sch. 10 Pt. I
[16] Sch. repealed by Statute Law Revision Act 1927 (c. 42)

Trustee Act 1925

1925 CHAPTER 19 15 and 16 Geo 5

An Act to consolidate certain enactments relating to trustees in England and Wales.

[9th April 1925]

PART I - INVESTMENTS[1]

PART II - GENERAL POWERS OF TRUSTEES AND PERSONAL REPRESENTATIVES

General Powers

...

12 Power of trustees for sale to sell by auction, &c.

(1) Where[2] [a trustee has a duty or power to sell property], he may sell or concur with any other person in selling all or any part of the property, either subject to prior charges or not, and either together or in lots, by public auction or by private contract, subject to any such conditions respecting title or evidence of title or other matter as the Trustee thinks fit, with power to vary any contract for sale, and to buy in at any auction, or to rescind any contract for sale and to re-sell, without being answerable for any loss.

(2) A [duty][3] or power to sell or dispose of land includes a [duty][4] or power to sell or dispose of part thereof, whether the division is horizontal, vertical, or made in any other way.

(3) This section does not enable an express power to sell settled land to be exercised where the power is not vested in the tenant for life or statutory owner.

13 Power to sell subject to depreciatory conditions.

(1) No sale made by a trustee shall be impeached by any beneficiary upon the ground that any of the conditions subject to which the sale was made have been unnecessarily depreciatory, unless it also appears that the consideration for the sale was thereby rendered inadequate.

(2) No sale made by a trustee shall, after the execution of the conveyance, be impeached as against the purchaser upon the ground that any of the conditions subject to which the sale was made may have been unnecessarily depreciatory, unless it appears that the purchaser was acting in collusion with the trustee at the time when the contract for sale was made.

(3) No purchaser, upon any sale made by a trustee, shall be at liberty to make any objection against the title upon any of the grounds aforesaid.

(4) This section applies to sales made before or after the commencement of this Act.

14 Power of trustees to give receipts.

(1) The receipt in writing of a trustee for any money, securities, [investments][5] or other personal property or effects payable, transferable, or deliverable to him under any trust or power shall be a sufficient discharge to the person paying, transferring, or delivering the same and shall effectually exonerate him from seeing to the application or being answerable for any loss or misapplication thereof.

(2) This section does not, except where the trustee is a trust corporation, enable a sole trustee to give a valid receipt for—

[(a) proceeds of sale or other capital money arising under a trust of land;][6]

(b) capital money arising under the Settled Land Act, 1925

(3) This section applies notwithstanding anything to the contrary in the instrument, if any, creating the trust.

15 Power to compound liabilities.

A personal representative, or two or more trustees acting together, or, subject to the restrictions imposed in regard to receipts by a sole trustee not being a trust corporation, a sole acting trustee where by the instrument, if any, creating the trust, or by statute, a sole trustee is authorised to execute the trusts and powers reposed in him, may, if and as he or they think fit—

(a) accept any property, real or personal, before the time at which it is made transferable or payable; or

(b) sever and apportion any blended trust funds or property; or

(c) pay or allow any debt or claim on any evidence that he or they think sufficient; or

(d) accept any composition or any security, real or personal, for any debt or for any property, real or personal, claimed; or

(e) allow any time of payment of any debt; or

(f) compromise, compound, abandon, submit to arbitration, or otherwise settle any debt, account, claim, or thing whatever relating to the testator's or intestate's estate or to the trust;

and for any of those purposes may enter into, give, execute, and do such agreements, instruments of composition or arrangement, releases, and other things as to him or them seem expedient, without being responsible for any loss occasioned by any act or thing so done by him or them [if he has or they have discharged the duty of care set out in section 1(1) of the Trustee Act 2000][7].

16 Power to raise money by sale, mortgage, &c.

(1) Where trustees are authorised by the instrument, if any, creating the trust or by law to pay or apply capital money subject to the trust for any purpose or in any manner, they shall have and shall be deemed always to have had power to raise the money required by sale, conversion, calling in, or mortgage of all or any part of the trust property for the time being in possession.

(2) This section applies notwithstanding anything to the contrary contained in the instrument, if any, creating the trust, but does not apply to trustees of property held for charitable purposes, or to trustees of a settlement for the purposes of the Settled Land Act, 1925, not being also the statutory owners.

17 Protection to purchasers and mortgagees dealing with trustees.

No purchaser or mortgagee, paying or advancing money on a sale or mortgage purporting to be made under any trust or power vested in trustees, shall be concerned to see that such money is wanted, or that no more than is wanted is raised, or otherwise as to the application thereof.

18 Devolution of powers or trusts.

(1) Where a power or trust is given to or imposed on two or more trustees jointly, the same may be exercised or performed by the survivors or survivor of them for the time being.

(2) Until the appointment of new trustees, the personal representatives or representative for the time being of a sole trustee, or, where there were two or more trustees of the last surviving or continuing trustee, shall be capable of exercising or performing any power or trust which was given to, or capable of being exercised by, the sole or last surviving or continuing trustee, or other the trustees or trustee for the time being of the trust.

(3) This section takes effect subject to the restrictions imposed in regard to receipts by a sole trustee, not being a trust corporation.

(4) In this section "personal representative" does not include an executor who has renounced or has not proved.

19 Power to insure.[8]

(1) A trustee may—

(a) insure any property which is subject to the trust against risks of loss or damage due to any event, and

(b) pay the premiums out of the trust funds.

(2) In the case of property held on a bare trust, the power to insure is subject to any direction given by the beneficiary or each of the beneficiaries—

(a) that any property specified in the direction is not to be insured;

(b) that any property specified in the direction is not to be insured except on such conditions as may

be so specified.

(3) Property is held on a bare trust if it is held on trust for—

(a) a beneficiary who is of full age and capacity and absolutely entitled to the property subject to the trust, or

(b) beneficiaries each of whom is of full age and capacity and who (taken together) are absolutely entitled to the property subject to the trust.

(4) If a direction under subsection (2) of this section is given, the power to insure, so far as it is subject to the direction, ceases to be a delegable function for the purposes of section 11 of the Trustee Act 2000 (power to employ agents).

(5) In this section "trust funds" means any income or capital funds of the trust.

20 Application of insurance money where policy kept up under any trust, power or obligation.

(1) Money receivable by trustees or any beneficiary under a policy of insurance against the loss or damage of any property subject to a trust or to a settlement within the meaning of the Settled Land Act, 1925, [whether by fire or otherwise][9], shall, where the policy has been kept up under any trust in that behalf or under any power statutory or otherwise, or in performance of any covenant or of any obligation statutory or otherwise, or by a tenant for life impeachable for waste, be capital money for the purposes of the trust or settlement, as the case may be.

(2) If any such money is receivable by any person, other than the trustees of the trust or settlement, that person shall use his best endeavours to recover and receive the money, and shall pay the net residue thereof, after discharging any costs of recovering and receiving it, to the trustees of the trust or settlement, or, if there are no trustees capable of giving a discharge therefor, into court.

(3) Any such money—

(a) if it was receivable in respect of settled land within the meaning of the Settled Land Act, 1925, or any building or works thereon, shall be deemed to be capital money arising under that Act from the settled land, and shall be invested or applied by the trustees, or, if in court, under the direction of the court, accordingly;

(b) if it was receivable in respect of personal chattels settled as heirlooms within the meaning of the Settled Land Act, 1925, shall be deemed to be capital money arising under that Act, and shall be applicable by the trustees, or, if in court, under the direction of the court, in like manner as provided by that Act with respect to money arising by a sale of chattels settled as heirlooms as aforesaid;

(c) if it was receivable in respect of [land subject to a trust of land or personal property held on trust for sale][10], shall be held upon the trusts and subject to the powers and provisions applicable to money arising by a sale under such trust;

(d) in any other case, shall be held upon trusts corresponding as nearly as may be with the trusts affecting the property in respect of which it was payable.

(4) Such money, or any part thereof, may also be applied by the trustees, or, if in court, under the direction of the court, in rebuilding, reinstating, replacing, or repairing the property lost or damaged, but any such application by the trustees shall be subject to the consent of any person whose consent is required by the instrument, if any, creating the trust to the investment of money subject to the trust, and, in the case of money which is deemed to be capital money arising under the Settled Land Act, 1925, be subject to the provisions of that Act with respect to the application of capital money by the trustees of the settlement.

(5) Nothing contained in this section prejudices or affects the right of any person to require any such money or any part thereof to be applied in rebuilding, reinstating, or repairing the property lost or damaged, or the rights of any mortgagee, lessor, or lessee, whether under any statute or otherwise.

(6) This section applies to policies effected either before or after the commencement of this Act, but only to money received after such commencement.

21[11]

22 Reversionary interests, valuations and audit.

(1) Where trust property includes any share or interest in property not vested in the trustees, or the proceeds of the sale of any such property, or any other thing in action, the trustees on the same falling into possession, or becoming payable or transferable may—

(a) agree or ascertain the amount or value thereof or any part thereof in such manner as they may

think fit;

(b) accept in or towards satisfaction thereof, at the market or current value, or upon any valuation or estimate of value which they may think fit, any authorised investments;

(c) allow any deductions for duties, costs, charges and expenses which they may think proper or reasonable;

(d) execute any release in respect of the premises so as effectually to discharge all accountable parties from all liability in respect of any matters coming within the scope of such release;

without being responsible in any such case for any loss occasioned by any act or thing so done by them [if they have discharged the duty of care set out in section 1(1) of the Trustee Act 2000][12].

(2) The trustees shall not be under any obligation and shall not be chargeable with any breach of trust by reason of any omission—

(a) to place any distringas notice or apply for any stop or other like order upon any securities or other property out of or on which such share or interest or other thing in action as aforesaid is derived, payable or charged; or

(b) to take any proceedings on account of any act, default, or neglect on the part of the persons in whom such securities or other property or any of them or any part thereof are for the time being, or had at any time been, vested;

unless and until required in writing so to do by some person, or the guardian of some person, beneficially interested under the trust, and unless also due provision is made to their satisfaction for payment of the costs of any proceedings required to be taken:

Provided that nothing in this subsection shall relieve the trustees of the obligation to get in and obtain payment or transfer of such share or interest or other thing in action on the same falling into possession.

(3) Trustees may, for the purpose of giving effect to the trust, or any of the provisions of the instrument, if any, creating the trust or of any statute, from time to time (by duly qualified agents) ascertain and fix the value of any trust property in such manner as they think proper, and any valuation so made [.][13] shall be binding upon all persons interested under the trust [if the trustees have discharged the duty of care set out in section 1(1) of the Trustee Act 2000][14].

(4) Trustees may, in their absolute discretion, from time to time, but not more than once in every three years unless the nature of the trust or any special dealings with the trust property make a more frequent exercise of the right reasonable, cause the accounts of the trust property to be examined or audited by an independent accountant, and shall, for that purpose, produce such vouchers and give such information to him as he may require; and the costs of such examination or audit, including the fee of the auditor, shall be paid out of the capital or income of the trust property, or partly in one way and partly in the other, as the trustees, in their absolute discretion, think fit, but, in default of any direction by the trustees to the contrary in any special case, costs attributable to capital shall be borne by capital and those attributable to income by income.

23[15]

24 Power to concur with others.

Where an undivided share in [any][16] property, is subject to a trust, or forms part of the estate of a testator or intestate, the trustees or personal representatives may (without prejudice to the [trust][17] affecting the entirety of the land and the powers of the [trustees][18] in reference thereto) execute or exercise any [duty or][19] power vested in them in relation to such share in conjunction with the persons entitled to or having power in that behalf over the other share or shares, and notwithstanding that any one or more of the trustees or personal representatives may be entitled to or interested in any such other share, either in his or their own right or in a fiduciary capacity.

[25 Delegation of trustee's functions by power of attorney.

(1) Notwithstanding any rule of law or equity to the contrary, a trustee may, by power of attorney, delegate the execution or exercise of all or any of the trusts, powers and discretions vested in him as trustee either alone or jointly with any other person or persons.

(2) A delegation under this section—

(a) commences as provided by the instrument creating the power or, if the instrument makes no provision as to the commencement of the delegation, with the date of the execution of the instrument by the donor; and

(b) continues for a period of twelve months or any shorter period provided by the instrument creating the power.

(3) The persons who may be donees of a power of attorney under this section include a trust corporation.

(4) Before or within seven days after giving a power of attorney under this section the donor shall give written notice of it (specifying the date on which the power comes into operation and its duration, the donee of the power, the reason why the power is given and, where some only are delegated, the trusts, powers and discretions delegated) to—

(a) each person (other than himself), if any, who under any instrument creating the trust has power (whether alone or jointly) to appoint a new trustee; and

(b) each of the other trustees, if any;

but failure to comply with this subsection shall not, in favour of a person dealing with the donee of the power, invalidate any act done or instrument executed by the donee.

(5) A power of attorney given under this section by a single donor—

(a) in the form set out in subsection (6) of this section; or

(b) in a form to the like effect but expressed to be made under this subsection,

shall operate to delegate to the person identified in the form as the single donee of the power the execution and exercise of all the trusts, powers and discretions vested in the donor as trustee (either alone or jointly with any other person or persons) under the single trust so identified.

(6) The form referred to in subsection (5) of this section is as follows—

"THIS GENERAL TRUSTEE POWER OF ATTORNEY is made on [date] by [name of one donor] of [address of donor] as trustee of [name or details of one trust].

I appoint [name of one donee] of [address of donee] to be my attorney [if desired, the date on which the delegation commences or the period for which it continues (or both)] in accordance with section 25(5) of the Trustee Act 1925.

[To be executed as a deed]".

(7) The donor of a power of attorney given under this section shall be liable for the acts or defaults of the donee in the same manner as if they were the acts or defaults of the donor.

(8) For the purpose of executing or exercising the trusts or powers delegated to him, the donee may exercise any of the powers conferred on the donor as trustee by statute or by the instrument creating the trust, including power, for the purpose of the transfer of any inscribed stock, himself to delegate to an attorney power to transfer, but not including the power of delegation conferred by this section.

(9) The fact that it appears from any power of attorney given under this section, or from any evidence required for the purposes of any such power of attorney or otherwise, that in dealing with any stock the donee of the power is acting in the execution of a trust shall not be deemed for any purpose to affect any person in whose books the stock is inscribed or registered with any notice of the trust.

(10) This section applies to a personal representative, tenant for life and statutory owner as it applies to a trustee except that subsection (4) shall apply as if it required the notice there mentioned to be given—

(a) in the case of a personal representative, to each of the other personal representatives, if any, except any executor who has renounced probate;

(b) in the case of a tenant for life, to the trustees of the settlement and to each person, if any, who together with the person giving the notice constitutes the tenant for life; and

(c) in the case of a statutory owner, to each of the persons, if any, who together with the person giving the notice constitute the statutory owner and, in the case of a statutory owner by virtue of section 23(1)(a) of the Settled Land Act 1925, to the trustees of the settlement.][20]

Indemnities

26 Protection against liability in respect of rents and covenants.

(1) Where a personal representative or trustee liable as such for—

(a) any rent, covenant, or agreement reserved by or contained in any lease; or

(b) any rent, covenant or agreement payable under or contained in any grant made in consideration of a rentcharge; or

(c) any indemnity given in respect of any rent, covenant or agreement referred to in either of the foregoing paragraphs;

satisfies all liabilities under the lease or grant [which may have accrued and been claimed][21] up to the date of the conveyance hereinafter mentioned, and, where necessary, sets apart a sufficient fund to answer any future claim that may be made in respect of any fixed and ascertained sum which the lessee or grantee agreed to lay out on the property demised or granted, although the period for laying out the same may not have arrived, then and in any such case the personal representative or trustee may convey the property demised or granted to a purchaser, legatee, devisee, or other person entitled to call for a conveyance thereof and thereafter—

(i) he may distribute the residuary real and personal estate of the deceased testator or intestate, or, as the case may be, the trust estate (other than the fund, if any, set apart as aforesaid) to or amongst the persons entitled thereto, without appropriating any part, or any further part, as the case may be, of the estate of the deceased or of the trust estate to meet any future liability under the said lease or grant;

(ii) notwithstanding such distribution, he shall not be personally liable in respect of any subsequent claim under the said lease or grant.

[(1A) Where a personal representative or trustee has as such entered into, or may as such be required to enter into, an authorised guarantee agreement with respect to any lease comprised in the estate of a deceased testator or intestate or a trust estate (and, in a case where he has entered into such an agreement, he has satisfied all liabilities under it which may have accrued and been claimed up to the date of distribution)—

(a) he may distribute the residuary real and personal estate of the deceased testator or intestate, or the trust estate, to or amongst the persons entitled thereto—

(i) without appropriating any part of the estate of the deceased, or the trust estate, to meet any future liability (or, as the case may be, any liability) under any such agreement, and

(ii) notwithstanding any potential liability of his to enter into any such agreement; and

(b) notwithstanding such distribution, he shall not be personally liable in respect of any subsequent claim (or, as the case may be, any claim) under any such agreement.

In this subsection "authorised guarantee agreement" has the same meaning as in the Landlord and Tenant (Covenants) Act 1995.] [22]

(2) This section operates without prejudice to the right of the lessor or grantor, or the persons deriving title under the lessor or grantor, to follow the assets of the deceased or the trust property into the hands of the persons amongst whom the same may have been respectively distributed, and applies notwithstanding anything to the contrary in the will or other instrument, if any, creating the trust.

(3) In this section "lease" includes an underlease and an agreement for a lease or underlease and any instrument giving any such indemnity as aforesaid or varying the liabilities under the lease; "grant" applies to a grant whether the rent is created by limitation, grant, reservation, or otherwise, and includes an agreement for a grant and any instrument giving any such indemnity as aforesaid or varying the liabilities under the grant; "lessee" and "grantee" include persons respectively deriving title under them.

27 Protection by means of advertisements.

(1) With a view to the conveyance to or distribution among the persons entitled to any real or personal property, the trustees of a settlement[, trustees of land, trustees for sale of personal property][23] or personal representatives, may give notice by advertisement in the Gazette, and [in a newspaper circulating in the district in which the land is situated][24] and such other like notices, including notices elsewhere than in England and Wales, as would, in any special case, have been directed by a court of competent jurisdiction in an action for administration, of their intention to make such conveyance or distribution as aforesaid, and requiring any person interested to send to the trustees or personal representatives within the time, not being less than two months, fixed in the notice or, where more than one notice is given, in the last of the notices, particulars of his claim in respect of the property or any part thereof to which the notice relates.

(2) At the expiration of the time fixed by the notice the trustees or personal representatives may convey or distribute the property or any part thereof to which the notice relates, to or among the persons entitled thereto, having regard only to the claims, whether formal or not, of which the trustees or personal representatives then had notice and shall not, as respects the property so

conveyed or distributed, be liable to any person of whose claim the trustees or personal representatives have not had notice at the time of conveyance or distribution; but nothing in this section—

(a) prejudices the right of any person to follow the property, or any property representing the same, into the hands of any person, other than a purchaser, who may have received it; or

(b) frees the trustees or personal representatives from any obligation to make searches or obtain official certificates of search similar to those which an intending purchaser would be advised to make or obtain.

(3) This section applies notwithstanding anything to the contrary in the will or other instrument, if any, creating the trust.

28 Protection in regard to notice.

A trustee or personal representative acting for the purposes of more than one trust or estate shall not, in the absence of fraud, be affected by notice of any instrument, matter, fact or thing in relation to any particular trust or estate if he has obtained notice thereof merely by reason of his acting or having acted for the purposes of another trust or estate.

29[25]

30 Implied indemnity of trustees.[26]

Maintenance, Advancement and Protective Trusts

31 Power to apply income for maintenance and to accumulate surplus income during a minority.

(1) Where any property is held by trustees in trust for any person for any interest whatsoever, whether vested or contingent, then, subject to any prior interests or charges affecting that property—

(i) during the infancy of any such person, if his interest so long continues, the trustees may, at their sole discretion, pay to his parent or guardian, if any, or otherwise apply for or towards his maintenance, education, or benefit, the whole or such part, if any, of the income of that property as may, in all the circumstances, be reasonable, whether or not there is—

(a) any other fund applicable to the same purpose; or

(b) any person bound by law to provide for his maintenance or education; and

(ii) if such person on attaining the age of [eighteen years][27] has not a vested interest in such income, the trustees shall thenceforth pay the income of that property and of any accretion thereto under subsection (2) of this section to him, until he either attains a vested interest therein or dies, or until failure of his interest:

Provided that, in deciding whether the whole or any part of the income of the property is during a minority to be paid or applied for the purposes aforesaid, the trustees shall have regard to the age of the infant and his requirements and generally to the circumstances of the case, and in particular to what other income, if any, is applicable for the same purposes; and where trustees have notice that the income of more than one fund is applicable for those purposes, then, so far as practicable, unless the entire income of the funds is paid or applied as aforesaid or the court otherwise directs, a proportionate part only of the income of each fund shall be so paid or applied.

(2) During the infancy of any such person, if his interest so long continues, the trustees shall accumulate all the residue of that income [by investing it, and any profits from so investing it][28] from time to time in authorised investments, and shall hold those accumulations as follows:—

(i) If any such person—

(a) attains the age of [eighteen years][29], or marries under that age, and his interest in such income during his infancy or until his marriage is a vested interest or;

(b) on attaining the age of [eighteen years][30] or on marriage under that age becomes entitled to the property from which such income arose in fee simple, absolute or determinable, or absolutely, or for an entailed interest;

the trustees shall hold the accumulations in trust for such person absolutely, but without prejudice to any provision with respect thereto contained in any settlement by him made under any statutory powers during his infancy, and so that the receipt of such person after marriage, and though still an infant shall be a good discharge, and

(ii) In any other case the trustees shall, notwithstanding that such person had a vested interest in such income, hold the accumulations as an accretion to the capital of the property from which

such accumulations arose, and as one fund with such capital for all purposes, and so that, if such property is settled land, such accumulations shall be held upon the same trusts as if the same were capital money arising therefrom;

but the trustees may, at any time during the infancy of such person if his interest so long continues, apply those accumulations, or any part thereof, as if they were income arising in the then current year.

(3) This section applies in the case of a contingent interest only if the limitation or trust carries the intermediate income of the property, but it applies to a future or contingent legacy by the parent of, or a person standing in loco parentis to, the legatee, if and for such period as, under the general law, the legacy carries interest for the maintenance of the legatee, and in any such case as last aforesaid the rate of interest shall (if the income available is sufficient, and subject to any rules of court to the contrary) be five pounds per centum per annum.

(4) This section applies to a vested annuity in like manner as if the annuity were the income of property held by trustees in trust to pay the income thereof to the annuitant for the same period for which the annuity is payable, save that in any case accumulations made during the infancy of the annuitant shall be held in trust for the annuitant or his personal representatives absolutely.

(5) This section does not apply where the instrument, if any, under which the interest arises came into operation before the commencement of this Act.

32 Power of advancement.

(1) Trustees may at any time or times pay or apply any capital money subject to a trust, for the advancement or benefit, in such manner as they may, in their absolute discretion, think fit, of any person entitled to the capital of the trust property or of any share thereof, whether absolutely or contingently on his attaining any specified age or on the occurrence of any other event, or subject to a gift over on his death under any specified age or on the occurrence of any other event, and whether in possession or in remainder or reversion, and such payment or application may be made notwithstanding that the interest of such person is liable to be defeated by the exercise of a power of appointment or revocation, or to be diminished by the increase of the class to which he belongs:

Provided that—

(a) the money so paid or applied for the advancement or benefit of any person shall not exceed altogether in amount one-half of the presumptive or vested share or interest of that person in the trust property; and

(b) if that person is or becomes absolutely and indefeasibly entitled to a share in the trust property the money so paid or applied shall be brought into account as part of such share; and

(c) no such payment or application shall be made so as to prejudice any person entitled to any prior life or other interest, whether vested or contingent, in the money paid or applied unless such person is in existence and of full age and consents in writing to such payment or application.

[(2)This section does not apply to capital money arising under the Settled Land Act 1925.][31]

(3) This section does not apply to trusts constituted or created before the commencement of this Act.

33 Protective trusts.

(1) Where any income, including an annuity or other periodical income payment, is directed to be held on protective trusts for the benefit of any person (in this section called "the principal beneficiary") for the period of his life or for any less period, then, during that period (in this section called the "trust period") the said income shall, without prejudice to any prior interest, be held on the following trusts, namely:—

(i) Upon trust for the principal beneficiary during the trust period or until he, whether before or after the termination of any prior interest, does or attempts to do or suffers any act or thing, or until any event happens, other than an advance under any statutory or express power, whereby, if the said income were payable during the trust period to the principal beneficiary absolutely during that period, he would be deprived of the right to receive the same or any part thereof, in any of which cases, as well as on the termination of the trust period, whichever first happens, this trust of the said income shall fail or determine;

(ii) If the trust aforesaid fails or determines during the subsistence of the trust period, then, during the residue of that period, the said income shall be held upon trust for the application thereof for the maintenance or support, or otherwise for the benefit, of all or any one or more exclusively of

the other or others of the following persons (that is to say)—

(a) the principal beneficiary and his or her wife or husband, if any, and his or her children or more remote issue, if any; or

(b) if there is no wife or husband or issue of the principal beneficiary in existence, the principal beneficiary and the persons who would, if he were actually dead, be entitled to the trust property or the income thereof or to the annuity fund, if any, or arrears of the annuity, as the case may be;

as the trustees in their absolute discretion, without being liable to account for the exercise of such discretion, think fit.

(2) This section does not apply to trusts coming into operation before the commencement of this Act, and has effect subject to any variation of the implied trusts aforesaid contained in the instrument creating the trust.

(3) Nothing in this section operates to validate any trust which would, if contained in the instrument creating the trust, be liable to be set aside.

[(4) In relation to the dispositions mentioned in section 19(1) of the Family Law Reform Act 1987, this section shall have effect as if any reference (however expressed) to any relationship between two persons were construed in accordance with section 1 of that Act.][32]

PART III - APPOINTMENT AND DISCHARGE OF TRUSTEES

34 Limitation of the number of trustees.

(1) Where, at the commencement of this Act, there are more than four trustees of a settlement of land, or more than four trustees holding land on trust for sale, no new trustees shall (except where as a result of the appointment the number is reduced to four or less) be capable of being appointed until the number is reduced to less than four, and thereafter the number shall not be increased beyond four.

(2) In the case of settlements and dispositions [creating trusts of land][33] made or coming into operation after the commencement of this Act—

(a) the number of trustees thereof shall not in any case exceed four, and where more than four persons are named as such trustees, the four first named (who are able and willing to act) shall alone be the trustees, and the other persons named shall not be trustees unless appointed on the occurrence of a vacancy;

(b) the number of the trustees shall not be increased beyond four.

(3) This section only applies to settlements and dispositions of land, and the restrictions imposed on the number of trustees do not apply—

(a) in the case of land vested in trustees for charitable, ecclesiastical, or public purposes; or

(b) where the net proceeds of the sale of the land are held for like purposes; or

(c) to the trustees of a term of years absolute limited by a settlement on trusts for raising money, or of a like term created under the statutory remedies relating to annual sums charged on land.

35 Appointments of trustees of settlements and [and trustees of land].[34]

[(1) Appointments of new trustees of land and of new trustees of any trust of the proceeds of sale of the land shall, subject to any order of the court, be effected by separate instruments, but in such manner as to secure that the same persons become trustees of land and trustees of the trust of the proceeds of sale.][35]

(2) Where new trustees of a settlement are appointed, a memorandum of the names and addresses of the persons who are for the time being the trustees thereof for the purposes of the Settled Land Act, 1925, shall be endorsed on or annexed to the last or only principal vesting instrument by or on behalf of the trustees of the settlement, and such vesting instrument shall, for that purpose, be produced by the person having the possession thereof to the trustees of the settlement when so required.

[(3) Where new trustees of land are appointed, a memorandum of the persons who are for the time being the trustees of the land shall be endorsed on or annexed to the conveyance by which the land was vested in trustees of land; and that conveyance shall be produced to the persons who are for the time being the trustees of the land by the person in possession of it in order for that to be done when the trustees require its production.][36]

(4) This section applies only to settlements and dispositions of land.

36 Power of appointing new or additional trustees.

(1) Where a trustee, either original or substituted, and whether appointed by a court or otherwise, is dead, or remains out of the United Kingdom for more than twelve months, or desires to be discharged from all or any of the trusts or powers reposed in or conferred on him, or refuses or is unfit to act therein, or is incapable of acting therein, or is an infant, then, subject to the restrictions imposed by this Act on the number of trustees,—

(a) the person or persons nominated for the purpose of appointing new trustees by the instrument, if any, creating the trust; or

(b) if there is no such person, or no such person able and willing to act, then the surviving or continuing trustees or trustee for the time being, or the personal representatives of the last surviving or continuing trustee;

may, by writing, appoint one or more other persons (whether or not being the persons exercising the power) to be a trustee or trustees in the place of the trustee so deceased remaining out of the United Kingdom, desiring to be discharged, refusing, or being unfit or being incapable, or being an infant, as aforesaid.

(2) Where a trustee has been removed under a power contained in the instrument creating the trust, a new trustee or new trustees may be appointed in the place of the trustee who is removed, as if he were dead, or, in the case of a corporation, as if the corporation desired to be discharged from the trust, and the provisions of this section shall apply accordingly, but subject to the restrictions imposed by this Act on the number of trustees.

(3) Where a corporation being a trustee is or has been dissolved, either before or after the commencement of this Act, then, for the purposes of this section and of any enactment replaced thereby, the corporation shall be deemed to be and to have been from the date of the dissolution incapable of acting in the trusts or powers reposed in or conferred on the corporation.

(4) The power of appointment given by subsection (1) of this section or any similar previous enactment to the personal representatives of last surviving or continuing trustee shall be and shall be deemed always to have been exercisable by the executors for the time being (whether original or by representation) of such surviving or continuing trustee who have proved the will of their testator or by the administrators for the time being of such trustee without the concurrence of any executor who has renounced or has not proved.

(5) But a sole or last surviving executor intending to renounce, or all the executors where they all intend to renounce, shall have and shall be deemed always to have had power, at any time before renouncing probate, to exercise the power of appointment given by this section, or by any similar previous enactment, if willing to act for that purpose and without thereby accepting the office of executor.

[(6) Where, in the case of any trust, there are not more than three trustees—][37,38]

(a) the person or persons nominated for the purpose of appointing new trustees by the instrument, if any, creating the trust; or

(b) if there is no such person, or no such person able and willing to act, then the trustee or trustees for the time being;

may, by writing, appoint another person or other persons to be an additional trustee or additional trustees, but it shall not be obligatory to appoint any additional trustee, unless the instrument, if any, creating the trust, or any statutory enactment provides to the contrary, nor shall the number of trustees be increased beyond four by virtue of any such appointment.

[(6A) A person who is either—

(a) both a trustee and attorney for the other trustee (if one other), or for both of the other trustees (if two others), under a registered power; or

(b) attorney under a registered power for the trustee (if one) or for both or each of the trustees (if two or three),

may, if subsection (6B) of this section is satisfied in relation to him, make an appointment under subsection (6)(b) of this section on behalf of the trustee or trustees.

(6B) This subsection is satisfied in relation to an attorney under a registered power for one or more trustees if (as attorney under the power)—

(a) he intends to exercise any function of the trustee or trustees by virtue of section 1(1) of the

Trustee Delegation Act 1999; or

(b) he intends to exercise any function of the trustee or trustees in relation to any land, capital proceeds of a conveyance of land or income from land by virtue of its delegation to him under section 25 of this Act or the instrument (if any) creating the trust.

(6C) In subsections (6A) and (6B) of this section "registered power" means a power of attorney created by an instrument which is for the time being registered under section 6 of the Enduring Powers of Attorney Act 1985

(6D) Subsection (6A) of this section—

(a) applies only if and so far as a contrary intention is not expressed in the instrument creating the power of attorney (or, where more than one, any of them) or the instrument (if any) creating the trust; and

(b) has effect subject to the terms of those instruments.][39]

(7) Every new trustee appointed under this section as well before as after all the trust property becomes by law, or by assurance, or otherwise, vested in him, shall have the same powers, authorities, and discretions, and may in all respects act as if he had been originally appointed a trustee by the instrument, if any, creating the trust.

(8) The provisions of this section relating to a trustee who is dead include the case of a person nominated trustee in a will but dying before the testator, and those relative to a continuing trustee include a refusing or retiring trustee, if willing to act in the execution of the provisions of this section.

[(9) Where a trustee is incapable, by reason of mental disorder within the meaning of [the Mental Health Act 1983][40], of exercising his functions as trustee and is also entitled in possession to some beneficial interest in the trust property, no appointment of a new trustee in his place shall be made by virtue of paragraph (b) of subsection (1) of this section unless leave to make the appointment has been given by the authority having jurisdiction under [Part VII of the Mental Health Act 1983][41].][42]

37 Supplemental provisions as to appointment of trustees.

(1) On the appointment of a trustee for the whole or any part of trust property—

(a) the number of trustees may, subject to the restrictions imposed by this Act on the number of trustees, be increased; and

(b) a separate set of trustees, not exceeding four, may be appointed for any part of the trust property held on trusts distinct from those relating to any other part or parts of the trust property, notwithstanding that no new trustees or trustee are or is to be appointed for other parts of the trust property, and any existing trustee may be appointed or remain one of such separate set of trustees, or, if only one trustee was originally appointed, then, save as hereinafter provided, one separate trustee may be so appointed; and

(c) it shall not be obligatory, save as hereinafter provided, to appoint more than one new trustee where only one trustee was originally appointed, or to fill up the original number of trustees where more than two trustees were originally appointed, but, except where only one trustee was originally appointed, and a sole trustee when appointed will be able to give valid receipts for all capital money, a trustee shall not be discharged from his trust unless there will be either a trust corporation or at least two [persons][43] to act as trustees to perform the trust; and

(d) any assurance or thing requisite for vesting the trust property, or any part thereof, in a sole trustee, or jointly in the persons who are the trustees, shall be executed or done.

(2) Nothing in this Act shall authorise the appointment of a sole trustee, not being a trust corporation, where the trustee, when appointed, would not be able to give valid receipts for all capital money arising under the trust.

38 Evidence as to a vacancy in a trust.

(1) A statement, contained in any instrument coming into operation after the commencement of this Act by which a new trustee is appointed for any purpose connected with land, to the effect that a trustee has remained out of the United Kingdom for more than twelve months or refuses or is unfit to act, or is incapable of acting, or that he is not entitled to a beneficial interest in the trust property in possession, shall, in favour of a purchaser of a legal estate, be conclusive evidence of the matter stated.

(2) In favour of such purchaser any appointment of a new trustee depending on that statement, and any

vesting declaration, express or implied, consequent on the appointment, shall be valid.

39 Retirement of trustee without a new appointment.

(1) Where a trustee is desirous of being discharged from the trust, and after his discharge there will be either a trust corporation or at least two [persons][44] to act as trustees to perform the trust, then, if such trustee as aforesaid by deed declares that he is desirous of being discharged from the trust, and if his co-trustees and such other person, if any, as is empowered to appoint trustees, by deed consent to the discharge of the trustee, and to the vesting in the co-trustees alone of the trust property, the trustee desirous of being discharged shall be deemed to have retired from the trust, and shall, by the deed, be discharged therefrom under this Act, without any new trustee being appointed in his place.

(2) Any assurance or thing requisite for vesting the trust property in the continuing trustees alone shall be executed or done.

40 Vesting of trust property in new or continuing trustees.

(1) Where by a deed a new trustee is appointed to perform any trust, then—

(a) if the deed contains a declaration by the appointor to the effect that any estate or interest in any land subject to the trust, or in any chattel so subject, or the right to recover or receive any debt or other thing in action so subject, shall vest in the persons who by virtue of the deed become or are the trustees for performing the trust, the deed shall operate, without any conveyance or assignment, to vest in those persons as joint tenants and for the purposes of the trust the estate interest or right to which the declaration relates; and

(b) if the deed is made after the commencement of this Act and does not contain such a declaration, the deed shall, subject to any express provision to the contrary therein contained, operate as if it had contained such a declaration by the appointor extending to all the estates interests and rights with respect to which a declaration could have been made.

(2) Where by a deed a retiring trustee is discharged under [section 39 of this Act or section 19 of the Trusts of Land and Appointment of Trustees Act 1996][45] without a new trustee being appointed, then—

(a) if the deed contains such a declaration as aforesaid by the retiring and continuing trustees, and by the other person, if any, empowered to appoint trustees, the deed shall, without any conveyance or assignment, operate to vest in the continuing trustees alone, as joint tenants, and for the purposes of the trust, the estate, interest, or right to which the declaration relates; and

(b) if the deed is made after the commencement of this Act and does not contain such a declaration, the deed shall, subject to any express provision to the contrary therein contained, operate as if it had contained such a declaration by such persons as aforesaid extending to all the estates, interests and rights with respect to which a declaration could have been made.

(3) An express vesting declaration, whether made before or after the commencement of this Act, shall, notwithstanding that the estate, interest or right to be vested is not expressly referred to, and provided that the other statutory requirements were or are complied with, operate and be deemed always to have operated (but without prejudice to any express provision to the contrary contained in the deed of appointment or discharge) to vest in the persons respectively referred to in subsections (1) and (2) of this section, as the case may require, such estates, interests and rights as are capable of being and ought to be vested in those persons.

(4) This section does not extend—

(a) to land conveyed by way of mortgage for securing money subject to the trust, except land conveyed on trust for securing debentures or debenture stock;

(b) to land held under a lease which contains any covenant, condition or agreement against assignment or disposing of the land without licence or consent, unless, prior to the execution of the deed containing expressly or impliedly the vesting declaration, the requisite licence or consent has been obtained, or unless, by virtue of any statute or rule of law, the vesting declaration, express or implied, would not operate as a breach of covenant or give rise to a forfeiture;

(c) to any share, stock, annuity or property which is only transferable in books kept by a company or other body, or in manner directed by or under an Act of Parliament.

In this subsection "lease" includes an underlease and an agreement for a lease or underlease.

(5) For purposes of registration of the deed in any registry, the person or persons making the

declaration expressly or impliedly, shall be deemed the conveying party or parties, and the conveyance shall be deemed to be made by him or them under a power conferred by this Act.

(6) This section applies to deeds of appointment or discharge executed on or after the first day of January, eighteen hundred and eighty-two.

PART IV - POWERS OF THE COURT

Appointment of new Trustees

41 Power of court to appoint new trustees.

(1) The court may, whenever it is expedient to appoint a new trustee or new trustees, and it is found inexpedient difficult or impracticable so to do without the assistance of the court, make an order appointing a new trustee or new trustees either in substitution for or in addition to any existing trustee or trustees, or although there is no existing trustee.

In particular and without prejudice to the generality of the foregoing provision, the court may make an order appointing a new trustee in substitution for a trustee who .[46] is [incapable, by reason of mental disorder within the meaning of [the Mental Health Act 1983][47], of exercising his functions as trustee][48], or is a bankrupt, or is a corporation which is in liquidation or has been dissolved.

(2) The power conferred by this section may, in the case of a deed of arrangement within the meaning of the Deeds of Arrangement Act, 1914, be exercised either by the High Court or by the court having jurisdiction in bankruptcy in the district in which the debtor resided or carried on business at the date of the execution of the deed.

(3) An order under this section, and any consequential vesting order or conveyance, shall not operate further or otherwise as a discharge to any former or continuing trustee than an appointment of new trustees under any power for that purpose contained in any instrument would have operated.

(4) Nothing in this section gives power to appoint an executor or administrator.

42 Power to authorise remuneration.

Where the court appoints a corporation, other than the Public Trustee, to be a trustee either solely or jointly with another person, the court may authorise the corporation to charge such remuneration for its services as trustee as the court may think fit.

43 Powers of new trustee appointed by the court.

Every trustee appointed by a court of competent jurisdiction shall, as well before as after the trust property becomes by law, or by assurance, or otherwise, vested in him, have the same powers, authorities, and discretions, and may in all respects act as if he had been originally appointed a trustee by the instrument, if any, creating the trust.

Vesting Orders

44 Vesting orders of land.

In any of the following cases, namely:—

(i) Where the court appoints or has appointed a trustee, or where a trustee has been appointed out of court under any statutory or express power;

(ii) Where a trustee entitled to or possessed of any land or interest therein, whether by way of mortgage or otherwise, or entitled to a contingent right therein, either solely or jointly with any other person—

(a) is under disability; or

(b) is out of the jurisdiction of the High Court; or

(c) cannot be found, or, being a corporation, has been dissolved;

(iii) Where it is uncertain who was the survivor of two or more trustees jointly entitled to or possessed of any interest in land;

(iv) Where it is uncertain whether the last trustee known to have been entitled to or possessed of any interest in land is living or dead;

(v) Where there is no personal representative of a deceased trustee who was entitled to or possessed of any interest in land, or where it is uncertain who is the personal representative of a deceased trustee who was entitled to or possessed of any interest in land;

(vi) Where a trustee jointly or solely entitled to or possessed of any interest in land, or entitled to a contingent right therein, has been required, by or on behalf of a person entitled to require a conveyance of the land or interest or a release of the right, to convey the land or interest or to release the right, and has wilfully refused or neglected to convey the land or interest or release the right for

twenty-eight days after the date of the requirement;

(vii) Where land or any interest therein is vested in a trustee whether by way of mortgage or otherwise, and it appears to the court to be expedient;

the court may make an order (in this Act called a vesting order) vesting the land or interest therein in any such person in any such manner and for any such estate or interest as the court may direct, or releasing or disposing of the contingent right to such person as the court may direct:

Provided that—

(a) Where the order is consequential on the appointment of a trustee the land or interest therein shall be vested for such estate as the court may direct in the persons who on the appointment are the trustees; and

(b) Where the order relates to a trustee entitled or formerly entitled jointly with another person, and such trustee is under disability or out of the jurisdiction of the High Court or cannot be found, or being a corporation has been dissolved, the land interest or right shall be vested in such other person who remains entitled, either alone or with any other person the court may appoint.

45 Orders as to contingent rights of unborn persons.

Where any interest in land is subject to a contingent right in an unborn person or class of unborn persons who, on coming into existence would, in respect thereof, become entitled to or possessed of that interest on any trust, the court may make an order releasing the land or interest therein from the contingent right, or may make an order vesting in any person the estate or interest to or of which the unborn person or class of unborn persons would, on coming into existence, be entitled or possessed in the land.

46 Vesting order in place of conveyance by infant mortgagee.

Where any person entitled to or possessed of any interest in land, or entitled to a contingent right in land, by way of security for money, is an infant, the court may make an order vesting or releasing or disposing of the interest in the land or the right in like manner as in the case of a trustee under disability.

47 Vesting order consequential on order for sale or mortgage of land.

Where any court gives a judgment or makes an order directing the sale or mortgage of any land, every person who is entitled to or possessed of any interest in the land, or entitled to a contingent right therein, and is a party to the action or proceeding in which the judgment or order is given or made or is otherwise bound by the judgment or order, shall be deemed to be so entitled or possessed, as the case may be, as a trustee for the purposes of this Act, and the court may, if it thinks expedient, make an order vesting the land or any part thereof for such estate or interest as that court thinks fit in the purchaser or mortgagee or in any other person:

Provided that, in the case of a legal mortgage, the estate to be vested in the mortgagee shall be a term of years absolute.

48 Vesting order consequential on judgment for specific performance, &c.

Where a judgment is given for the specific performance of a contract concerning any interest in land, or for sale or exchange of any interest in land, or generally where any judgment is given for the conveyance of any interest in land either in cases arising out of the doctrine of election or otherwise, the court may declare—

(a) that any of the parties to the action are trustees of any interest in the land or any part thereof within the meaning of this Act; or

(b) that the interests of unborn persons who might claim under any party to the action, or under the will or voluntary settlement of any deceased person who was during his lifetime a party to the contract or transaction concerning which the judgment is given, are the interests of persons who, on coming into existence, would be trustees within the meaning of this Act;

and thereupon the court may make a vesting order relating to the rights of those persons, born and unborn, as if they had been trustees.

49 Effect of vesting order.

A vesting order under any of the foregoing provisions shall in the case of a vesting order consequential on the appointment of a trustee, have the same effect—

(a) as if the persons who before the appointment were the trustees, if any, had duly executed all proper

conveyances of the land for such estate or interest as the court directs; or

(b) if there is no such person, or no such person of full capacity, as if such person had existed and been of full capacity and had duly executed all proper conveyances of the land for such estate or interest as the court directs;

and shall in every other case have the same effect as if the trustee or other person or description or class of persons to whose rights or supposed rights the said provisions respectively relate had been an ascertained and existing person of full capacity, and had executed a conveyance or release to the effect intended by the order.

50 Power to appoint person to convey.

In all cases where a vesting order can be made under any of the foregoing provisions, the court may, if it is more convenient, appoint a person to convey the land or any interest therein or release the contingent right, and a conveyance or release by that person in conformity with the order shall have the same effect as an order under the appropriate provision.

51 Vesting orders as to stock and things in action.

(1) In any of the following cases, namely:—

(i) Where the court appoints or has appointed a trustee, or where a trustee has been appointed out of court under any statutory or express power;

(ii) Where a trustee entitled, whether by way of mortgage or otherwise, alone or jointly with another person to stock or to a thing in action—

(a) is under disability; or

(b) is out of the jurisdiction of the High Court; or

(c) cannot be found, or, being a corporation, has been dissolved; or

(d) neglects or refuses to transfer stock or receive the dividends or income thereof, or to sue for or recover a thing in action, according to the direction of the person absolutely entitled thereto for twenty-eight days next after a request in writing has been made to him by the person so entitled; or

(e) neglects or refuses to transfer stock or receive the dividends or income thereof, or to sue for or recover a thing in action for twenty-eight days next after an order of the court for that purpose has been served on him;

(iii) Where it is uncertain whether a trustee entitled alone or jointly with another person to stock or to a thing in action is alive or dead;

(iv) Where stock is standing in the name of a deceased person whose personal representative is under disability;

(v) Where stock or a thing in action is vested in a trustee whether by way of mortgage or otherwise and it appears to the court to be expedient;

the court may make an order vesting the right to transfer or call for a transfer of stock, or to receive the dividends or income thereof, or to sue for or recover the thing in action, in any such person as the court may appoint:

Provided that—

(a) Where the order is consequential on the appointment of a trustee, the right shall be vested in the persons who, on the appointment, are the trustees; and

(b) Where the person whose right is dealt with by the order was entitled jointly with another person, the right shall be vested in that last-mentioned person either alone or jointly with any other person whom the court may appoint.

(2) In all cases where a vesting order can be made under this section, the court may, if it is more convenient, appoint some proper person to make or join in making the transfer:

Provided that the person appointed to make or join in making a transfer of stock shall be some proper officer of the bank, or the company or society whose stock is to be transferred.

(3) The person in whom the right to transfer or call for the transfer of any stock is vested by an order of the court under this Act, may transfer the stock to himself or any other person, according to the order, and the Bank of England and all other companies shall obey every order under this section according to its tenor.

(4) After notice in writing of an order under this section it shall not be lawful for the Bank of England or any other company to transfer any stock to which the order relates or to pay any dividends thereon

except in accordance with the order.

(5) The court may make declarations and give directions concerning the manner in which the right to transfer any stock or thing in action vested under the provisions of this Act is to be exercised.

(6) The provisions of this Act as to vesting orders shall apply to shares in ships registered under the [Merchant Shipping Act 1995][49] as if they were stock.

52 Vesting orders of charity property.

The powers conferred by this Act as to vesting orders may be exercised for vesting any interest in land, stock, or thing in action in any trustee of a charity or society over which the court would have jurisdiction upon action duly instituted, whether the appointment of the trustee was made by instrument under a power or by the court under its general or statutory jurisdiction.

53 Vesting orders in relation to infant's beneficial interests.

Where an infant is beneficially entitled to any property the court may, with a view to the application of the capital or income thereof for the maintenance, education, or benefit of the infant, make an order—

(a) appointing a person to convey such property; or

(b) in the case of stock, or a thing in action, vesting in any person the right to transfer or call for a transfer of such stock, or to receive the dividends or income thereof, or to sue for and recover such thing in action, upon such terms as the court may think fit.

[54 Jurisdiction in regard to mental patients.

(1) Subject to the provisions of this section, the authority having jurisdiction under [Part VII of the Mental Health Act 1983][50], shall not have power to make any order, or give any direction or authority, in relation to a patient who is a trustee if the High Court has power under this Act to make an order to the like effect.

(2) Where a patient is a trustee and a receiver appointed by the said authority is acting for him or an application for the appointment of a receiver has been made but not determined, then, except as respects a trust which is subject to an order for administration made by the High Court, the said authority shall have concurrent jurisdiction with the High Court in relation to—

(a) mortgaged property of which the patient has become a trustee merely by reason of the mortgage having been paid off;

(b) matters consequent on the making of provision by the said authority for the exercise of a power of appointing trustees or retiring from a trust;

(c) matters consequent on the making of provision by the said authority for the carrying out of any contract entered into by the patient;

(d) property to some interest in which the patient is beneficially entitled but which, or some interest in which, is held by the patient under an express, implied or constructive trust.

The Lord Chancellor may make rules with respect to the exercise of the jurisdiction referred to in this subsection.

(3) In this section "patient" means a patient as defined by [section 94 of the Mental Health Act 1983][51], or a person as to whom powers are [exercisable under section 98 of that Act and have been exercised under that section or section 104 of the Mental Health Act 1959][52] of that Act.][53]

55 Orders made upon certain allegations to be conclusive evidence.

Where a vesting order is made as to any land under this Act or under [Part VII of the Mental Health Act 1983][54], as amended by any subsequent enactment, or under any Act relating to lunacy in Northern Ireland, founded on an allegation of any of the following matters namely—

(a) the personal incapacity of a trustee or mortgagee; or

(b) that a trustee or mortgagee or the personal representative of or other person deriving title under a trustee or mortgagee is out of the jurisdiction of the High Court or cannot be found, or being a corporation has been dissolved; or

(c) that it is uncertain which of two or more trustees, or which of two or more persons interested in a mortgage, was the survivor; or

(d) that it is uncertain whether the last trustee or the personal representative of or other person deriving title under a trustee or mortgagee, or the last surviving person interested in a mortgage is living or dead; or

(e) that any trustee or mortgagee has died intestate without leaving a person beneficially interested

under the intestacy or has died and it is not known who is his personal representative or the person interested;

the fact that the order has been so made shall be conclusive evidence of the matter so alleged in any court upon any question as to the validity of the order; but this section does not prevent the court from directing a reconveyance or surrender or the payment of costs occasioned by any such order if improperly obtained.

56 Application of vesting order to property out of England.

The powers of the court to make vesting orders under this Act shall extend to all property in any part of His Majesty's dominions except Scotland.

Jurisdiction to make other Orders

57 Power of court to authorise dealings with trust property.

(1) Where in the management or administration of any property vested in trustees, any sale, lease, mortgage, surrender, release, or other disposition, or any purchase, investment, acquisition, expenditure or other transaction, is in the opinion of the court expedient, but the same cannot be effected by reason of the absence of any power for that purpose vested in the trustees by the trust instrument, if any, or by law, the court may by order confer upon the trustees, either generally or in any particular instance, the necessary power for the purpose, on such terms, and subject to such provisions and conditions, if any, as the court may think fit and may direct in what manner any money authorised to be expended, and the costs of any transaction, are to be paid or borne as between capital and income.

(2) The court may, from time to time, rescind or vary any order made under this section, or may make any new or further order.

(3) An application to the court under this section may be made by the trustees, or by any of them, or by any person beneficially interested under the trust.

(4) This section does not apply to trustees of a settlement for the purposes of the Settled Land Act, 1925.

58 Persons entitled to apply for orders.

(1) An order under this Act for the appointment of a new trustee or concerning any interest in land, stock, or thing in action subject to a trust, may be made on the application of any person beneficially interested in the land, stock, or thing in action, whether under disability or not, or on the application of any person duly appointed trustee thereof.

(2) An order under this Act concerning any interest in land, stock, or thing in action subject to a mortgage may be made on the application of any person beneficially interested in the equity of redemption, whether under disability or not, or of any person interested in the money secured by the mortgage.

59 Power to give judgment in absence of a trustee.

Where in any action the court is satisfied that diligent search has been made for any person who, in the character of trustee, is made a defendant in any action, to serve him with a process of the court, and that he cannot be found, the court may hear and determine the action and give judgment therein against that person in his character of a trustee as if he had been duly served, or had entered an appearance in the action, and had also appeared by his counsel and solicitor at the hearing, but without prejudice to any interest he may have in the matters in question in the action in any other character.

60 Power to charge costs on trust estate.

The court may order the costs and expenses of and incident to any application for an order appointing a new trustee, or for a vesting order, or of and incident to any such order, or any conveyance or transfer in pursuance thereof, to be raised and paid out of the property in respect whereof the same is made, or out of the income thereof, or to be borne and paid in such manner and by such persons as to the court may seem just.

61 Power to relieve trustee from personal liability.

If it appears to the court that a trustee, whether appointed by the court or otherwise, is or may be personally liable for any breach of trust, whether the transaction alleged to be a breach of trust occurred before or after the commencement of this Act, but has acted honestly and reasonably, and ought fairly to be excused for the breach of trust and for omitting to obtain the directions of the court in the matter

in which he committed such breach, then the court may relieve him either wholly or partly from personal liability for the same.

62 Power to make beneficiary indemnify for breach of trust.

(1) Where a trustee commits a breach of trust at the instigation or request or with the consent in writing of a beneficiary, the court may, if it thinks fit,[55], make such order as to the court seems just, for impounding all or any part of the interest of the beneficiary in the trust estate by way of indemnity to the trustee or persons claiming through him.

(2) This section applies to breaches of trust committed as well before as after the commencement of this Act.

Payment into Court

63 Payment into court by trustees.

(1) Trustees, or the majority of trustees, having in their hands or under their control money or securities belonging to a trust, may pay the same into court; [56]

(2) The receipt or certificate of the proper officer shall be a sufficient discharge to trustees for the money or securities so paid into court.

(3) Where money or securities are vested in any persons as trustees, and the majority are desirous of paying the same into court, but the concurrence of the other or others cannot be obtained, the court may order the payment into court to be made by the majority without the concurrence of the other or others.

(4) Where any such money or securities are deposited with any banker, broker, or other depositary, the court may order payment or delivery of the money or securities to the majority of the trustees for the purpose of payment into court.

(5) Every transfer payment and delivery made in pursuance of any such order shall be valid and take effect as if the same had been made on the authority or by the act of all the persons entitled to the money and securities so transferred, paid, or delivered.

[63A Jurisdiction of County Court.

(1) The county court has jurisdiction under the following provisions where the amount or value of the trust estate or fund to be dealt with in the court does not exceed the county court limit—

section 41;
section 42;
section 51;
section 57;
section 60;
section 61;
section 62.

(2) The county court has jurisdiction under the following provisions where the land or the interest or contingent right in land which is to be dealt with in the court forms part of a trust estate which does not exceed in amount or value the county court limit—

section 44;
section 45;
section 46.

(3) The county court has jurisdiction—

(a) under sections 47 and 48 of this Act, where the judgment is given or order is made by the court;
(b) under sections 50 and 56, where a vesting order can be made by the court;
(c) under section 53, where the amount or value of the property to be dealt with in the court does not exceed the county court limit; and
(d) under section 63 (including power to receive payment of money or securities into court) where the money or securities to be paid into court do not exceed in amount or value the county court limit.

(4) Any reference to the court in section 59 of this Act includes a reference to the county court.

(5) In this section, in its application to any enactment, "the county court limit"means the amount for the time being specified by an Order in Council under section 145 of the County Courts Act 1984 as the county court limit for the purposes of that enactment (or, where no such Order in Council has been

made, the corresponding limit specified by Order in Council under section 192 of the County Courts Act 1959).][57]

PART V - GENERAL PROVISIONS

64 Application of Act to Settled Land Act Trustees.

(1) All the powers and provisions contained in this Act with reference to the appointment of new trustees, and the discharge and retirement of trustees, apply to and include trustees for the purposes of the Settled Land Act, 1925, and trustees for the purpose of the management of land during a minority, whether such trustees are appointed by the court or by the settlement, or under provisions contained in any instrument.

(2) Where, either before or after the commencement of this Act, trustees of a settlement have been appointed by the court for the purposes of the Settled Land Acts, 1882 to 1890, or of the Settled Land Act, 1925, then, after the commencement of this Act—

(a) the person or persons nominated for the purpose of appointing new trustees by the instrument, if any, creating the settlement, though no trustees for the purposes of the said Acts were thereby appointed; or

(b) if there is no such person, or no such person able and willing to act, the surviving or continuing trustees or trustee for the time being for the purposes of the said Acts, or the personal representatives of the last surviving or continuing trustee for those purposes,

shall have the powers conferred by this Act to appoint new or additional trustees of the settlement for the purposes of the said Acts.

(3) Appointments of new trustees for the purposes of the said Acts made or expressed to be made before the commencement of this Act by the trustees or trustee or personal representatives referred to in paragraph (b) of the last preceding subsection or by the persons referred to in paragraph (a) of that subsection are, without prejudice to any order of the court made before such commencement, hereby confirmed.

65[58]

66 Indemnity to banks, &c.

This Act, and every order purporting to be made under this Act, shall be a complete indemnity to the Bank of England, and to all persons for any acts done pursuant thereto, and it shall not be necessary for the Bank or for any person to inquire concerning the propriety of the order, or whether the court by which the order was made had jurisdiction to make it.

67 Jurisdiction of the "court."

(1) In this Act "the court" means the High Court,[59], or the county court, where those courts respectively have jurisdiction.

(2) The procedure under this Act in, county courts shall be in accordance with the Acts and rules regulating the procedure of those courts.

68 Definitions.

In this Act, unless the context otherwise requires, the following expressions have the meanings hereby assigned to them respectively, that is to say:—

(1) "Authorised investments" mean investments authorised by the instrument, if any, creating the trust for the investment of money subject to the trust, or by law;

(2) "Contingent right" as applied to land includes a contingent or executory interest, a possibility coupled with an interest, whether the object of the gift or limitation of the interest, or possibility is or is not ascertained, also a right of entry, whether immediate or future, and whether vested or contingent;

(3) "Convey" and "conveyance" as applied to any person include the execution by that person of every necessary or suitable assurance (including an assent) for conveying, assigning, appointing, surrendering, or otherwise transferring or disposing of land whereof he is seised or possessed, or wherein he is entitled to a contingent right, either for his whole estate or for any less estate, together with the performance of all formalities required by law for the validity of the conveyance; "sale" includes an exchange;

(4) "Gazette" means the London Gazette;

(5) "Instrument" includes Act of Parliament;

(6) "Land" includes land of any tenure, and mines and minerals, whether or not severed from the surface, buildings or parts of buildings, whether the division is horizontal, vertical or made in any other way, and other corporeal hereditaments; also a manor, an advowson, and a rent and other incorporeal hereditaments, and an easement, right, privilege, or benefit in, over, or derived from land.[60]; and in this definition "mines and minerals" include any strata or seam of minerals or substances in or under any land, and powers of working and getting the same .; and "hereditaments" mean real property which under an intestacy occurring before the commencement of this Act might have devolved on an heir;

(7) "Mortgage" and "mortgagee" include a charge or chargee by way of legal mortgage, and relate to every estate and interest regarded in equity as merely a security for money, and every person deriving title under the original mortgagee;

(8) [61]

(9) "Personal representative" means the executor, original or by representation, or administrator for the time being of a deceased person;

(10) "Possession" includes receipt of rents and profits or the right to receive the same, if any; "income" includes rents and profits; and "possessed" applies to receipt of income of and to any vested estate less than a life interest in possession or in expectancy in any land;

(11) "Property" includes real and personal property, and any estate share and interest in any property, real or personal, and any debt, and any thing in action, and any other right or interest, whether in possession or not;

(12) "Rights" include estates and interests;

(13) "Securities" include stocks, funds, and shares; [62] and "securities payable to bearer" include securities transferable by delivery or by delivery and endorsement;

(14) "Stock" includes fully paid up shares, and so far as relates to vesting orders made by the court under this Act, includes any fund, annuity, or security transferable in books kept by any company or society, or by instrument of transfer either alone or accompanied by other formalities, and any share or interest therein;

(15) "Tenant for life." "statutory owner," "settled land," "settlement," "trust instrument," "trustees of the settlement" . [63] "term of years absolute" and "vesting instrument" have the same meanings as in the Settled Land Act, 1925, and "entailed interest" has the same meaning as in the Law of Property Act, 1925;

(16) "Transfer" in relation to stock or securities, includes the performance and execution of every deed, power of attorney, act, and thing on the part of the transferor to effect and complete the title in the transferee;

(17) "Trust" does not include the duties incident to an estate conveyed by way of mortgage, but with this exception the expressions "trust" and "trustee" extend to implied and constructive trusts, and to cases where the trustee has a beneficial interest in the trust property, and to the duties incident to the office of a personal representative, and "trustee" where the context admits, includes a personal representative, and "new trustee" includes an additional trustee;

(18) "Trust corporation" means the Public Trustee or a corporation either appointed by the court in any particular case to be a trustee, or entitled by rules made under subsection (3) of section four of the Public Trustee Act, 1906, to act as custodian trustee;

(19) "Trust for sale" in relation to land means an immediate[64] trust for sale, whether or not exercisable at the request or with the consent of any person;

(20) "United Kingdom" means Great Britain and Northern Ireland.

[(2) Any reference in this Act to paying money or securities into court shall be construed as referring to paying the money or transferring or depositing the securities into or in the Supreme Court or into or in any other court that has jurisdiction, and any reference in this Act to payment of money or securities into court shall be construed—

(a) with reference to an order of the High Court, as referring to payment of the money or transfer or deposit of the securities into or in the Supreme Court; and

(b) with reference to an order of any other court, as referring to payment of the money or transfer or deposit of the securities into or in that court.][65]

69 Application of Act.

(1) This Act, except where otherwise expressly provided, applies to trusts including, so far as this Act applies thereto, executorships and administratorships constituted or created either before or after the commencement of this Act.

(2) The powers conferred by this Act on trustees are in addition to the powers conferred by the instrument, if any, creating the trust, but those powers, unless otherwise stated, apply if and so far only as a contrary intention is not expressed in the instrument, if any, creating the trust, and have effect subject to the terms of that instrument.

(3).[66]

70 Enactments repealed.

. .[67] without prejudice to the provisions of section thirty-eight of the Interpretation Act, 1889:

(a) Nothing in this repeal shall affect any vesting order or appointment made or other thing done under any enactment so repealed, and any order or appointment so made may be revoked or varied in like manner as if it had been made under this Act;

(b) References in any document to any enactment repealed by this Act shall be construed as references to this Act or to the corresponding enactment in this Act.

71 Short title, commencement, extent.

(1) This Act may be cited as the Trustees Act, 1925.

(2).[68]

(3) This Act, except where otherwise expressly provided, extends to England and Wales only.

(4) The provisions of this Act bind the Crown.

FIRST SCHEDULE[69]

---

[1] Pt. I (ss. 1-11) repealed (1.2.2001) by Trustee Act 2000, s. 40(1)(3), Sch. 2 Pt. II para. 18, Sch. 4 Pt. II (with s. 35, Sch. 3 paras. 2, 3); S.I. 2001/49, art. 2

[2] Words in s. 12(1) substituted (1.1.1997) by Trusts of Land and Appointment of Trustees Act 1996, s. 25(1), Sch. 3 para. 3(2)(a) (with ss. 24(2), 25(4)); S.I. 1996/2974, art.2

[3] Words in s. 12(2) substituted (1.1.1997) by Trusts of Land and Appointment of Trustees Act 1996, s. 25(1), Sch. 3 para. 3(2)(b) (with ss. 24(2), 25(4)); S.I. 1996/2974, art.2

[4] Words in s. 12(2) substituted (1.1.1997) by Trusts of Land and Appointment of Trustees Act 1996, s. 25(1), Sch. 3 para. 3(2)(b) (with ss. 24(2), 25(4)); S.I. 1996/2974, art.2

[5] Words in s. 14(1) inserted (1.2.2001) by Trustee Act 2000, s. 40(1), Sch. 2 Pt. II para. 19 (with s. 35); S.I. 2001/49, art. 2

[6] s. 14(2)(a) substituted (1.1.1997) by Trusts of Land and Appointment of Trustees Act 1996, s. 25(1), Sch. 3 para. 3(3) (with ss. 24(2), 25(4)); S.I. 1996/2974, art. 2

[7] Words in s. 15 substituted (1.2.2001) by Trustee Act 2000, s. 40(1), Sch. 2 Pt. II para. 20 (with s. 35); S.I. 2001/49, art. 2

[8] s. 19 substituted (1.2.2001) by Trustee Act 2000, s. 34(1)(3), (with s. 35); S.I. 2001/49, art. 2

[9] Words in s. 20(1) repealed (1.2.2001) by Trustee Act 2000, s. 34(2)(3), 40(3), 42(2), Sch. 4 Pt. II (with s. 35)

[10] Words in s. 20(3)(c) substituted (1.1.1997) by Trusts of Land and Appointment of Trustees Act 1996, s. 25(1), Sch. 3 para. 3(5) (with ss. 24(2), 25(4)); S.I. 1996/2974, art. 2

[11] s. 21 repealed (1.2.2001) by Trustee Act 2000, s. 40(1)(3), Sch. 2 Pt. II para. 21, Sch. 4 Pt. II (with s.35); S.I. 2001/49, art.2

[12] Words in s.22(1) substituted (1.2.2001) by Trustee Act 2000, s.40(1), Sch.2 Pt.II para. 22(a) (with s.35); S.I. 2001/49, art.2

[13] Words in s. 22(3) omitted (1.2.2001) by virtue of Trustee Act 2000, s. 40(1), Sch. 2 Pt. II para. 22(b) (with s. 35); S.I. 2001/29, art. 2

[14] Words in s. 22(3) inserted (1.2.2001) by Trustee Act 2000, s. 40(1), Sch. 2 Pt. II para. 22(b) (with s. 35); S.I. 2001/29, art.2

[15] s. 23 repealed (1.2.2001) by Trustee Act 2000, s. 40(1)(3), Sch. 2 Pt. II para. 23, Sch. 4 Pt. II (with s. 35, Sch. 3 para. 6); S.I. 2001/49, art. 2

[16] Words in s. 24 substituted (1.1.1997) by Trusts of Land and Appointment of Trustees Act 1996, s. 25(1), Sch. 3 para. 3(6)(a) (with ss. 24(2), 25(4)); S.I. 1996/2974, art.2

[17] Words in s. 24 substituted (1.1.1997) by Trusts of Land and Appointment of Trustees Act 1996, s. 25(1), Sch. 3 para. 3(6)(b) (with ss. 24(2), 25(4)); S.I. 1996/2974, art.2

[18] Words in s. 24 substituted (1.1.1997) by Trusts of Land and Appointment of Trustees Act 1996, s. 25(1), Sch. 3 para. 3(6)(c) (with ss. 24(2), 25(4)); S.I. 1996/2974, art.2

[19] Words in s. 24 substituted (1.1.1997) by Trusts of Land and Appointment of Trustees Act 1996, s. 25(1), Sch. 3 para. 3(6)(d) (with ss. 24(2), 25(4)); S.I. 1996/2974, art.2

[20] s. 25 substituted (1.3.2000) by the Trustee Delegation Act 1999, s. 5(1)(2); S.I. 2000/216, art. 2

[21] Words substituted by Law of Property (Amendment) Act 1926 (c. 11), Sch.

[22] s. 26(1A) inserted (1.1.1996) by Landlord and Tenant (Covenants) Act 1995, s. 30(1), Sch. 1 para.1 (with ss. 2(2), 26(1)(2)); S.I. 1995/2963, art.2

23 Words in s. 27(1) substituted (1.1.1997) by Trusts of Land and Appointment of Trustees Act 1996, s. 25(1), Sch. 3 para. 3(7) (with ss. 24(2), 25(4)); S.I. 1996/2974, art.2

24 Words substituted by Law of Property (Amendment) Act 1926 (c. 11), Sch.

25 s. 29 repealed by Power of Attorney Act 1971 (c. 27), Sch. 2

26 s. 30 repealed (1.2.2001) by Trustee Act 2000, s. 40(1)(3), Sch. 2 Pt. II para. 24, Sch. 4 Pt. II (with s. 35); S.I. 2001/49, art.2

27 Word substituted by Family Law Reform Act 1969 (c. 46), s. 1(3), Sch. 1 Pt. I

28 Words in s. 31(2) substituted (1.2.2001) by Trustee Act 2000, s. 40(1), Sch. 2 Pt. II para. 25 (with s. 35); S.I. 2001/49, art.2

29 Word substituted by Family Law Reform Act 1969 (c. 46), s. 1(3), Sch. 1 Pt. I

30 Word substituted by Family Law Reform Act 1969 (c. 46), s. 1(3), Sch. 1 Pt. I

31 s. 32(2) substituted (1.1.1997) by Trusts of Land and Appointment of Trustees Act 1996, s. 25(1), Sch. 3 para. 3(8) (with ss. 24(2), 25(4)); S.I. 1996/2974, art.2

32 s. 33(4) added by Family Law Reform Act 1987 (c. 42, SIF 49:7), s. 33(1)(2), Sch. 2 para. 2, Sch. 3 paras. 1, 6

33 Words in s. 34(2) substituted (1.1.1997) by 1996 c.47, s.25(1), Sch.3 para. 3(9) (with ss. 24(2), 25(4)); S.I. 1996/2974, art.2

34 Words "and trustees of land" substituted for "dispositions on trust for sale of land" (1.1.1997) by 1996 c. 47, s. 25(1), Sch. 3 para. 10(10)(c) (with ss. 24(2), 25(4)); S.I. 1996/2974, art.2

35 s. 35(1) substituted (1.1.1997) by 1996 c. 47, s. 25(1), Sch. 3 para. 3(10)(a) (with ss. 24(2), 25(4)); S.I. 1996/2974, art.2

36 s. 35(3) substituted (1.1.1997) by 1996 c. 47, s. 25(1), Sch. 3 para. 3(10)(b) (with ss. 24(2), 25(4)); S.I. 1996/2974, art.2

37 s. 36(6A)-(6D) inserted (1.3.2000) by 1999 c. 15, s. 8(1)(2); S.I. 2000/216, art. 2

38 Words before s. 36(6)(a) substituted (1.1.1997) by 1996 c. 47, s. 25(1), Sch. 3 para. 3(11) (with ss. 24(2), 25(4)); S.I. 1996/2974, art. 2

39 s. 36(6A)-(6D) inserted (1.3.2000) by 1999 c. 15, s. 8(1)(2); S.I. 2000/216, art. 2

40 Words substituted by Mental Health Act 1983 (c. 20, SIF 85), s. 148, Sch. 4 para. 4(a)

41 Words substituted by Mental Health Act 1983 (c. 20, SIF 85), s. 148, Sch. 4 para. 4(a)

42 s. 36(9) substituted by Mental Health Act 1959 (c. 72), Sch. 7 Pt. I

43 Word in s.37(1)(c) substituted (1.1.1997) by 1996 c.47, s.25(1), Sch.3 para.3(12) (with ss.24(2), 25(4)); S.I. 1996/2974,art.2

44 Word in s. 39(1) substituted (1.1.1997) by 1996 c.47, s.25(1), Sch. 3 para. 3(13) (with ss.24(2), 25(4)); S.I. 1996/2974, art.2

45 Words in s. 40(2) substituted (1.1.1997) by 1996 c.47, s.25(1), Sch.3 para.3(14) (with ss. 24(2), 25(4)); S.I. 1996/2974, art.2

46 Words repealed by Criminal Law Act 1967 (c. 58), Sch. 3 Pt. III

47 Words substituted by Mental Health Act 1983 (c. 20, SIF 85), s. 148, Sch. 4 para. 4(b)

48 Words substituted by Mental Health Act 1959 (c. 72), Sch. 7 Pt. I

49 Words in s. 51(6) substituted (1.1.1996) by 1995 c. 21, ss. 314(2), 316(2), Sch. 13 para.13 (with s. 312(1))

50 Words substituted by Mental Health Act 1983 (c. 20, SIF 85), s. 148, Sch. 4 para. 4(c)(i)

51 Words substituted by Mental Health Act 1983 (c. 20, SIF 85), s. 148, Sch. 4 para. 4(c)(ii)

52 Words substituted by Mental Health Act 1983 (c. 20, SIF 85), s. 148, Sch. 4 para. 4(c)(ii)

53 s. 54 substituted by Mental Health Act 1959 (c. 72), Sch. 7 Pt. I

54 Words substituted (with saving) by Mental Health Act 1983 (c. 20, SIF 85), s. 148, Sch. 4 para. 4(d)

55 Words repealed by Married Women (Restraint upon Anticipation) Act 1949 (c. 78), s. 1, Sch. 2

56 Words repealed by Administration of Justice Act 1965 (c. 2), Sch. 3

57 s. 63A inserted by County Courts Act 1984 (c. 28, SIF 34), s. 148(1), Sch. 2 Pt. I para. 1

58 s. 65 repealed by Criminal Law Act 1967 (c. 58), Sch. 3 Pt. I

59 Words repealed by Courts Act 1971 (c. 23), Sch. 11 Pt. II

60 Words in s. 68(6) repealed (1.1.1997) by 1996 c. 47, s. 25(2), Sch.4 (with ss. 24(2), 25(4)); S.I. 1996/2974, art.2

61 s. 68 para, (8) repealed by Administration of Justice Act 1965 (c. 2), Sch. 1

62 Words repealed by Administration of Justice Act 1965 (c. 2), Sch. 1

63 Words repealed by Mental Health Act 1959 (c. 72), Sch. 8 Pt. I

64 Words and definition of "trustees for sale" in s. 68(19) repealed (1.1.1997) by 1996 c. 47, s. 25(2), Sch.4 (with ss. 24(2), 25(4)); S.I. 1996/2974, art.2

65 S. 68(2) added by Administration of Justice Act 1965 (c. 2), Sch. 1

66 s. 69(3),Sch. 1 repealed by Statute Law (Repeals) Act 1978 (c. 45), s. 1, Sch. 1 Pt. XVII

67 Words repealed by Statute Law Revision Act 1950 (14 Geo. 6 c. 6)

68 s. 71(2), Sch. 2 repealed by Statute Law Revision Act 1950 (14 Geo. 6 c. 6)

69 Sch. 1 repealed by Statute Law (Repeals) Act 1978 (c. 45), s. 1, Sch. 1 Pt. XVII

House to House Collections Act 1939

1939 CHAPTER 44 2 and 3 Geo 6

An Act to provide for the regulation of house to house collections for charitable purposes; and for matters connected therewith.

[28th July 1939]

1 Charitable collections from house to house to be licensed.

(1) Subject to the provisions of this Act, no collection for a charitable purpose shall be made unless the requirements of this Act as to a licence for the promotion thereof are satisfied.

(2) If a person promotes a collection for a charitable purpose, and a collection for that purpose is made in any locality pursuant to his promotion, then, unless there is in force, throughout the period during which the collection is made in that locality, a licence authorising him, or authorising another under whose authority he acts, to promote a collection therein for that purpose, he shall be guilty of an offence.

(3) If a person acts as a collector in any locality for the purposes of a collection for a charitable purpose, then, unless there is in force, at all times when he so acts, a licence authorising a promoter under whose authority he acts, or authorising the collector himself, to promote a collection therein for that purpose, he shall be guilty of an offence.

(4) If the chief officer of police for the police area comprising a locality in which a collection for a charitable purpose is being, or is proposed to be, made is satisfied that that purpose is local in character and that the collection is likely to be completed within a short period of time, he may grant to the person who appears to him to be principally concerned in the promotion of the collection a certificate in the prescribed form, and, where a certificate is so granted, the provisions of this Act, except the provisions of sections five and six thereof and the provisions of section eight thereof in so far as they relate to those sections, shall not apply, in relation to a collection made for that purpose within such locality and within such period as may be specified in the certificate, to the person to whom the certificate is granted or to any person authorised by him to promote the collection or to act as a collector for the purposes thereof.

2 Licences.

(1) Where a person who is promoting, or proposes to promote, a collection in any locality for a charitable purpose makes to the [police][licensing][1] authority for the [police][2] area comprising that locality an application in the prescribed manner specifying the purpose of the collection and the locality (whether being the whole of the area of the authority or a part thereof) within which the collection is to be made, and furnishes them with the prescribed information, the authority shall, subject to the following provisions of this section, grant to him a licence authorising him to promote a collection within that locality for that purpose.

[(1A) In this section "licensing authority" means—

(a) in relation to the City of London, the Common Council;

(b) in relation to the Metropolitan Police District, the Commissioner of Police for the Metropolis; and

(c) in relation to a district exclusive of any part thereof within the Metropolitan Police District, the district council.][3]

(2) A licence shall be granted for such period, not being longer than twelve months, as may be specified in the application, and shall, unless it is previously revoked, remain in force for the period so specified:

Provided that, if it appears to a [police][licensing][4] authority to be expedient to provide for the simultaneous expiration of licences to be granted by them in respect of collections which in their opinion are likely to be proposed to be made annually or continuously over a long period, they may, on the grant of such a licence, grant it for a period shorter or longer than that specified in the application therefor, or for a period longer than twelve months (but not exceeding eighteen months), as may be requisite for that purpose.

(3) A [police][licensing][5] authority may refuse to grant a licence, or, where a licence has been granted, may revoke it, if it appears to the authority—

(a) that the total amount likely to be applied for charitable purposes as the result of the collection (including any amount already so applied) is inadequate in proportion to the value of the

proceeds likely to be received (including any proceeds already received);

(b) that remuneration which is excessive in relation to the total amount aforesaid is likely to be, or has been, retained or received out of the proceeds of the collection by any person;

(c) that the grant of a licence would be likely to facilitate the commission of an offence under section three of the Vagrancy Act 1824, or that an offence under that section has been committed in connection with the collection;

(d) that the applicant or the holder of the licence is not a fit and proper person to hold a licence by reason of the fact that he has been convicted in the United Kingdom of any of the offences specified in the Schedule to this Act, or has been convicted in any part of His Majesty's dominions of any offence conviction for which necessarily involved a finding that he acted fraudulently or dishonestly, or of an offence of a kind the commission of which would be likely to be facilitated by the grant of a licence;

(e) that the applicant or the holder of the licence, in promoting a collection in respect of which a licence has been granted to him, has failed to exercise due diligence to secure that persons authorised by him to act as collectors for the purposes of the collection were fit and proper persons, to secure compliance on the part of persons so authorised with the provisions of regulations made under this Act, or to prevent prescribed badges or prescribed certificates of authority being obtained by persons other than persons so authorised; or

(f) that the applicant or holder of the licence has refused or neglected to furnish to the authority such information as they may have reasonably required for the purpose of informing themselves as to any of the matters specified in the foregoing paragraphs.

(4) When a [police][licensing][6] authority refuse to grant a licence or revoke a licence which has been granted, they shall forthwith give written notice to the applicant or holder of the licence stating upon which one or more of the grounds set out in subsection (3) of this section the licence has been refused or revoked and informing him of the right of appeal given by this section, and the applicant or holder of the licence may thereupon appeal to the Secretary of State against the refusal or revocation of the licence as the case may be and the decision of the Secretary of State shall be final.

(5) The time within which any such appeal may be brought shall be fourteen days from the date on which notice is given under subsection (4) of this section.

(6) If the Secretary of State decides that the appeal shall be allowed, the [police][licensing][7] authority shall forthwith issue a licence or cancel the revocation as the case may be in accordance with the decision of the Secretary of State.

3 Exemptions in the case of collections over wide areas.

(1) Where the Secretary of State is satisfied that a person pursues a charitable purpose throughout the whole of England or a substantial part thereof and is desirous of promoting collections for that purpose, the Secretary of State may by order direct that he shall be exempt from the provisions of subsection (2) of section one of this Act as respects all collections for that purpose in such localities as may be described in the order, and whilst an order so made in the case of any person is in force as respects collections in any locality, the provisions of this Act shall have effect in relation to the person exempted, to a promoter of a collection in that locality for that purpose who acts under the authority of the person exempted, and to a person who so acts as a collector for the purposes of any such collection, as if a licence authorising the person exempted to promote a collection in that locality for that purpose had been in force.

(2) Any order made under this section may be revoked or varied by a subsequent order made by the Secretary of State.

4 Regulations.

(1) The Secretary of State may make regulations for prescribing anything which by this Act is required to be prescribed, and for regulating the manner in which collections, in respect of which licences have been granted or orders have been made under the last foregoing section, may be carried out and the conduct of promoters and collectors in relation to such collections.

(2) Without prejudice to the generality of the powers conferred by the foregoing subsection, regulations made thereunder may make provision for all or any of the following matters, that is to say:—

(a) for requiring and regulating the use by collectors, of prescribed badges and prescribed certificates of authority, and the issue, custody, production and return thereof, and, in particular,

for requiring collectors on demand by a police constable or by any occupant of a house visited to produce their certificates of authority;

(b) in the case of collections in respect of which licences have been granted, for requiring that the prescribed certificates of authority of the collectors shall be authenticated in a manner approved by the chief officer of police for the area in respect of which the licence was granted, and that their prescribed badges shall have inserted therein or annexed thereto in a manner and form so approved a general indication of the purpose of the collection;

(c) for prohibiting persons below a prescribed age from acting, and others from causing them to act, as collectors;

(d) for preventing annoyance to the occupants of houses visited by collectors;

(e) for requiring the prescribed information with respect to the expenses, proceeds and application of the proceeds of collections to be furnished, in the case of collections in respect of which licences have been granted, by the person to whom the licence was granted to the [police][8] authority by whom it was granted, and, in the case of collections in respect of which an order has been made, by the person thereby exempted from the provisions of subsection (2) of section one of this Act to the Secretary of State, and for requiring the information furnished to be vouched and authenticated in such manner as may be prescribed.

(3) Any person who contravenes or fails to comply with the provisions of a regulation made under this Act shall be guilty of an offence.

(4) Any regulations made under this Act shall be laid before Parliament as soon as may be after they are made, and if either House of Parliament, within the period of forty days beginning with the date on which the regulations are laid before it, resolves that the regulations be annulled, the regulations shall thereupon become void, without prejudice, however, to anything previously done thereunder or to the making of new regulations.

In reckoning any such period of forty days as aforesaid, no account shall be taken of any time during which Parliament is dissolved or prorogued or during which both Houses are adjourned for more than four days.

5 Unauthorised use of badges, &c.

If any person, in connection with any appeal made by him to the public in association with a representation that the appeal is for a charitable purpose, displays or uses—

(a) a prescribed badge or a prescribed certificate of authority, not being a badge or certificate for the time being held by him for the purposes of the appeal pursuant to regulations made under this Act, or

(b) any badge or device, or any certificate or other document, so nearly resembling a prescribed badge or, as the case may be, a prescribed certificate of authority as to be calculated to deceive,

he shall be guilty of an offence.

6 Collector to give name, &c. to police on demand.

A police constable may require any person whom he believes to be acting as a collector for the purposes of a collection for a charitable purpose to declare to him immediately his name and address and to sign his name, and if any person fails to comply with a requirement duly made to him under this section, he shall be guilty of an offence.

7 Delegation of functions.

(1). . [9] .

[(2) The functions conferred on a chief officer of police by this Act or regulations made thereunder may be delegated by him to any police officer not below the rank of inspector.][10]

8 Penalties.

(1) Any promoter guilty of an offence under subsection (2) of section one of this Act shall be liable, on summary conviction, to imprisonment for a term not exceeding six months or to a fine not exceeding [level 3 on the standard scale][11], or to both such imprisonment and such fine.

(2) Any collector guilty of an offence under subsection (3) of section one of this Act shall be liable, on summary conviction, in the case of a first conviction, to a fine not exceeding [£25][12], or in the case of a second or subsequent conviction, to imprisonment for a term not exceeding three months or to a fine not exceeding [£50][13], or to both such imprisonment and such fine.

(3) Any person guilty of an offence under subsection (3) of section four of this Act shall be liable on summary conviction, to a fine not exceeding [level 1 on the standard scale][14].

(4) Any person guilty of an offence under section five of this Act shall be liable, on summary conviction, to imprisonment for a term not exceeding six months or to a fine not exceeding [level 3 on the standard scale][15], or to both such imprisonment and such fine.

(5) Any person guilty of an offence under section six of this Act shall be liable, on summary conviction, to a fine not exceeding [level 1 on the standard scale][16].

(6) If any person in furnishing any information for the purposes of this Act knowingly or recklessly makes a statement false in a material particular, he shall be guilty of an offence, and shall be liable, on summary conviction, to imprisonment for a term not exceeding six months or to a fine not exceeding [level 3 on the standard scale][17], or to both such imprisonment and such fine.

(7) Where an offence under this Act committed by a corporation is proved to have been committed with the consent or connivance of, or to be attributable to any culpable neglect of duty on the part of, any director, manager, secretary, or other officer of the corporation, he, as well as the corporation, shall be deemed to be guilty of that offence and shall be liable to be proceeded against and punished accordingly.

9 Application to metropolitan police district.

(1) . . .[18].

(2) The functions which may be delegated by a chief officer of police by virtue of subsection (2) of section seven of this Act shall not include any functions conferred on the [Commissioner of Police for the Metropolis by virtue of his being a licensing authority within the meaning of section 2 of this Act.][19]

10 Application to Scotland.

This Act shall apply to Scotland subject to the following modifications:—

[(a) sections 1, 2 and 4 shall apply as if for references to the police authority for the police area comprising a locality and to the chief officer of police of such an area there were substituted respectively references to the islands or district council for the area comprising a locality and to the proper officer of such a council;][20]

(b) in paragraph (c) of subsection (3) of section two for references to section three of the Vagrancy Act 1824 there shall be substituted references to sections four hundred and eight or four hundred and ten of the Burgh Police (Scotland) Act 1892 or to the corresponding provisions of any local Act;

(c) in subsection (1) of section three of the word "England," there shall be substituted the word "Scotland";

(d) any offence against this Act for which the maximum penalty that may be imposed does not exceed ten pounds may be prosecuted in any court of summary jurisdiction within the meaning of the Summary Jurisdiction (Scotland) Act 1908, having jurisdiction in the place where the offence was committed;

(e). .[21]

11 Interpretation.

(1) In this Act the following expressions have the meanings hereby respectively assigned to them, that is to say:—

"charitable purpose" means any charitable, benevolent or philanthropic purpose, whether or not the purpose is charitable within the meaning of any rule of law;

"collection" means an appeal to the public, made by means of visits from house to house, to give, whether for consideration or not, money or other property; and "collector" means, in relation to a collection, a person who makes the appeal in the course of such visits as aforesaid;

"house" includes a place of business;

"licence" means a licence under this Act;

. .[22]

"prescribed" means prescribed by regulations made under this Act;

"proceeds" means, in relation to a collection, all money and all other property given, whether for consideration or not, in response to the appeal made;

"promoter" means, in relation to a collection, a person who causes others to act, whether for remuneration or otherwise, as collectors for the purposes of the collection; and "promote" and

"promotion" have corresponding meanings.

(2) For the purposes of this Act, a collection shall be deemed to be made for a particular purpose where the appeal is made in association with a representation that the money or other property appealed for, or part thereof, will be applied for that purpose.

12 Short title, commencement, interpretation and extent.

(1) This Act may be cited as the House to House Collections Act 1939.

(2) . . .[23]

(3) References in this Act to any enactment shall be construed as references to that enactment as amended by any subsequent enactment.

(4) This Act shall not extend to Northern Ireland.

Section 2.

SCHEDULE - Offences to which paragraph (d) of subsection (3) of section two applies

Offences under sections forty-seven to fifty-six of the Offences against the Person Act 1861.

[Robbery, burglary, and blackmail]

Offences in Scotland involving personal violence or lewd, indecent, or libidinous conduct, or dishonest appropriation of property.

Offences under the Street Collections Regulation (Scotland) Act 1915.

Offences under section five of the Police, Factories &c. (Miscellaneous Provisions) Act 1916.

---

[1] Word "licensing" substituted for word "police" by Local Government Act 1972 (c. 70), Sch. 29 para. 23(1)

[2] Word repealed by Local Government Act 1972 (c. 70), Sch. 30

[3] s. 2(1A) added by Local Government Act 1972 (c. 70), Sch. 29 para. 23(2)

[4] Word "licensing" substituted for word "police" by Local Government Act 1972 (c. 70), Sch. 29 para. 23(3)

[5] Word "licensing" substituted for word "police" by Local Government Act 1972 (c. 70), Sch. 29 para. 23(3)

[6] Word "licensing" substituted for word "police" by Local Government Act 1972 (c. 70), Sch. 29 para. 23(3)

[7] Word "licensing" substituted for word "police" by Local Government Act 1972 (c. 70), Sch. 29 para. 23(3)

[8] Word repealed by Local Government Act 1972 (c. 70), Sch. 30

[9] s.7(1) repealed by Local Government Act 1972 (c. 70), Sch. 30 and Local Government (Scotland) Act 1973 (c.65), Sch.29

[10] s. 7(2) repealed (S.) by Local Government (Scotland) Act 1973 (c. 65), Sch. 29

[11] Words substituted by virtue of Criminal Justice Act 1982 (c. 48, SIF 39:1), ss. 38, 46

[12] "£25" and "£50" substituted respectively by virtue of Criminal Law Act 1977 (c. 45, SIF 39:1), s. 31(5)(6) and as to substituted "£25" and "£50", Criminal Justice Act 1982 (c. 48, SIF 39:1), ss. 35 (in relation to liability on first and subsequent convictions) and 46 (substitution of references to levels on the standard scale) apply

[13] "£25" and "£50" substituted respectively by virtue of Criminal Law Act 1977 (c. 45, SIF 39:1), s. 31(5)(6) and as to substituted "£25" and "£50", Criminal Justice Act 1982 (c. 48, SIF 39:1), ss. 35 (in relation to liability on first and subsequent convictions) and 46 (substitution of references to levels on the standard scale) apply

[14] Words substituted by virtue of Criminal Justice Act 1982 (c. 48, SIF 39:1), s. 46

[15] Words substituted by virtue of Criminal Justice Act 1982 (c. 48, SIF 39:1), ss. 38, 46

[16] Words substituted by virtue of Criminal Justice Act 1982 (c. 48, SIF 39:1), s. 46

[17] Words substituted by virtue of Criminal Justice Act 1982 (c. 48, SIF 39:1), ss. 38, 46

[18] s. 9(1) repealed by Local Government Act 1972 (c. 70), Sch. 30

[19] Words substituted by Local Government Act 1972 (c. 70), Sch. 29 para. 23(5)

[20] s. 10(a) substituted by Local Government (Scotland) Act 1973 (c. 65), s. 188, Sch. 24 para. 37

[21] s. 10(e) repealed by Local Government (Scotland) Act 1973 (c. 65), s. 188, Sch. 24 para. 37, Sch. 29

[22] Definitions of "police area", "police authority" and "chief officer of police" repealed by Police Act 1964 (c. 48), Sch. 10 Pt. I and Local Government (Scotland) Act 1973 (c. 65) Sch. 29

[23] s. 12(2) repealed by Statute Law Revision Act 1950 (c. 6)

Charitable Trusts (Validation) Act 1954

1954 CHAPTER 58 2 and 3 Eliz 2

An Act to validate under the law of England and Wales, and restrict to charitable objects, certain instruments taking effect before the sixteenth day of December, nineteen hundred and fifty-two, and providing for property to be held or applied for objects partly but not exclusively charitable, and to enable corresponding provision to be made by the Parliament of Northern Ireland.

[30th July 1954].

1 Validation and modification of imperfect trust instruments.

(1) In this Act, "imperfect trust provision" means any provision declaring the objects for which

property is to be held or applied, and so describing those objects that, consistently with the terms of the provision, the property could be used exclusively for charitable purposes, but could nevertheless be used for purposes which are not charitable.

(2) Subject to the following provisions of this Act, any imperfect trust provision contained in an instrument taking effect before the sixteenth day of December, nineteen hundred and fifty-two, shall have, and be deemed to have had, effect in relation to any disposition or covenant to which this Act applies—

(a) as respects the period before the commencement of this Act, as if the whole of the declared objects were charitable; and

(b) as respects the period after that commencement as if the provision had required the property to be held or applied for the declared objects in so far only as they authorise use for charitable purposes.

(3) A document inviting gifts of property to be held or applied for objects declared by the document shall be treated for the purposes of this section as an instrument taking effect when it is first issued.

(4) In this Act, "covenant" includes any agreement, whether under seal or not, and "covenantor" is to be construed accordingly.

2 Dispositions and covenants to which the Act applies.

(1) Subject to the next following subsection, this Act applies to any disposition of property to be held or applied for objects declared by an imperfect trust provision, and to any covenant to make such a disposition, where apart from this Act the disposition or covenant is invalid under the law of England and Wales, but would be valid if the objects were exclusively charitable.

(2) This Act does not apply to a disposition if before the sixteenth day of December, nineteen hundred and fifty-two, property comprised in, or representing that comprised in, the disposition in question or another disposition made for the objects declared by the same imperfect trust provision, or income arising from any such property, has been paid or conveyed to, or applied for the benefit of, the persons entitled by reason of the invalidity of the disposition in question or of such other disposition as aforesaid, as the case may be.

(3) A disposition in settlement or other disposition creating more than one interest in the same property shall be treated for the purposes of this Act as a separate disposition in relation to each of the interests created.

3 Savings for adverse claims, etc.

(1) Subject to the next following subsection, where a disposition to which this Act applies was made before, and is not confirmed after, the commencement of this Act, the foregoing sections shall not prejudice a person's right, by reason of the invalidity of the disposition, to property comprised in, or representing that comprised in, the disposition as against the persons administering the imperfect trust provision or the persons on whose behalf they do so, unless the right accrued to him or some person through whom he claims more than six years before the sixteenth day of December, nineteen hundred and fifty-two; but the persons administering the imperfect trust provision, and any trustee for them or for the persons on whose behalf they do so, shall be entitled, as against a person whose right to the property is saved by this subsection, to deal with the property as if this subsection had not been passed, unless they have express notice of a claim by him to enforce his right to the property.

(2) No proceedings shall be begun by any person to enforce his right to any property by virtue of the foregoing subsection after the expiration of one year beginning with the date of the passing of this Act or the date when the right first accrues to him or to some person through whom he claims, whichever is the later, unless the right (before or after its accrual) either—

(a) has been concealed by the fraud of some person administering the imperfect trust provision or his agent; or

(b) has been acknowledged by some such person or his agent by means of a written acknowledgement given to the person having the right or his agent and signed by the person making it, or by means of a payment or transfer of property in respect of the right;

and if the period prescribed by this subsection for any person to bring proceedings to recover any property expires without his having recovered the property or begun proceedings to do so, his title to the property shall be extinguished.

This subsection shall not be taken as extending the time for bringing any proceedings beyond the period of limitation prescribed by any other enactment.

(3) For the purposes of the foregoing subsections, a right by reason of the invalidity of a disposition to property comprised in, or representing that comprised in, the disposition shall not be deemed to accrue to anyone so long as he is under a disability or has a future interest only, or so long as the disposition is subject to another disposition made by the same person, and the whole of the property or the income arising from it is held or applied for the purposes of that other disposition.

(4) [Subsections (2) to (6) of section thirty-eight of the Limitation Act 1980][1] (which define the circumstances in which, for the purposes of that Act, a person is to be deemed to be under a disability or to claim through another person), shall apply for the purposes of the foregoing subsections as they apply for the purposes of that Act.

(5) Where subsection (1) of this section applies to save a person's right to property comprised in, or representing that comprised in, a disposition, or would have so applied but for some dealing with the property by persons administering the imperfect trust provision, or by any trustee for them or for the persons on whose behalf they do so, the foregoing sections shall not prejudice the first-mentioned person's right by virtue of his interest in the property to damages or other relief in respect of any dealing with the property by any person administering the imperfect trust provision or by any such trustee as aforesaid, if the person dealing with the property had at the time express notice of a claim by him to enforce his right to the property.

(6) A covenant entered into before the commencement of this Act shall not be enforceable by virtue of this Act unless confirmed by the covenantor after that commencement, but a disposition made in accordance with such a covenant shall be treated for the purposes of this Act as confirming the covenant and any previous disposition made in accordance with it.

4 Provisions as to pending proceedings and past decisions and tax payments.

(1) Subject to the next following subsection, effect shall be given to the provisions of this Act in legal proceedings begun before its commencement, as well as in those begun afterwards.

(2) This Act shall not affect any order or judgment made or given before its commencement in legal proceedings begun before the sixteenth day of December, nineteen hundred and fifty-two, or any appeal or other proceedings consequent on any such order or judgment.

(3) Where in legal proceedings begun on or after the said sixteenth day of December, any order or judgment has been made or given before the commencement of this Act which would not have been made or given after that commencement, the court by which the order or judgment was made or given shall, on the application of any person aggrieved thereby, set it aside in whole or in part and make such further order as the court thinks equitable with a view to placing those concerned as nearly as may be in the position they ought to be in having regard to this Act:

Provided that proceedings to have an order or judgment set aside under this subsection shall not be instituted more than six months after the commencement of this Act.

(4) This Act shall not, by its operation on any instrument as respects the period before the commencement of the Act, impose or increase any liability to tax nor entitle any person to reclaim any tax paid or borne before that commencement, nor (save as respects taxation) require the objects declared by the instrument to be treated for the purposes of any enactment as having been charitable so as to invalidate anything done or any determination given before that commencement.

5. . . [2]

6 Application to Crown.

This Act, and (except in so far as the contrary intention appears) any enactment of the Parliament of Northern Ireland passed for purposes similar to the purposes of this Act, shall bind the Crown.

7 Short title.

This Act may be cited as the Charitable Trusts (Validation) Act 1954.

---

[1] Words substituted by Limitation Act 1980 (c. 58, SIF 79), s. 40(2) Sch. 3 para. 4

[2] S. 5 repealed by Northern Ireland Constitution Act 1973 (c. 36), Sch. 6 Pt. I

Recreational Charities Act 1958

1958 CHAPTER 17 6 and 7 Eliz 2

An Act to declare charitable under the law of England and Wales the provision in the interests of social welfare of facilities for recreation or other leisure-time occupation, to make similar provision as to certain trusts heretofore established for carrying out social welfare activities within the meaning of the Miners' Welfare Act 1952, to enable laws for corresponding purposes to be passed by the Parliament of Northern Ireland, and for purposes connected therewith.

[13th March 1958].

1 General provision as to recreational and similar trusts, etc.

(1) Subject to the provisions of this Act, it shall be and be deemed always to have been charitable to provide, or assist in the provision of, facilities for recreation or other leisure-time occupation, if the facilities are provided in the interests of social welfare:

Provided that nothing in this section shall be taken to derogate from the principle that a trust or institution to be charitable must be for the public benefit.

(2) The requirement of the foregoing subsection that the facilities are provided in the interests of social welfare shall not be treated as satisfied unless—

(a) the facilities are provided with the object of improving the conditions of life for the persons for whom the facilities are primarily intended; and

(b) either—

(i) those persons have need of such facilities as aforesaid by reason of their youth, age, infirmity or disablement, poverty or social and economic circumstances; or

(ii) the facilities are to be available to the members or female members of the public at large.

(3) Subject to the said requirement, subsection (1) of this section applies in particular to the provision of facilities at village halls, community centres and women's institutes, and to the provision and maintenance of grounds and buildings to be used for purposes of recreation or leisure-time occupation, and extends to the provision of facilities for those purposes by the organising of any activity.

2 Miners' welfare trusts.

(1) Where trusts declared before the seventeenth day of December, nineteen hundred and fifty-seven, required or purported to require property to be held for the purpose of activities which are social welfare activities within the meaning of the Miners' Welfare Act 1952 and at that date the whole or part of the property held on those trusts or of any property held with that property represented an application of moneys standing to the credit of the miners' welfare fund or moneys provided by the Coal Industry Social Welfare Organisation, those trusts shall be treated as if they were and always had been charitable.

(2) For the purposes of this section property held on the same trusts as other property shall be deemed to be held with it, though vested in different trustees.

3 Savings and other provisions as to past transactions.

(1) Nothing on this Act shall be taken to restrict the purposes which are to be regarded as charitable independently of this Act.

(2) Nothing in this Act—

(a) shall apply to make charitable any trust, or validate any disposition, of property if before the seventeenth day of December, nineteen hundred and fifty-seven, that property or any property representing or forming part of it, or any income arising from any such property, has been paid or conveyed to, or applied for the benefit of, the persons entitled by reason of the invalidity of the trust or disposition; or

(b) shall affect any order or judgment made or given (whether before or after the passing of this Act) in legal proceedings begun before that day; or

(c) shall require anything properly done before that day, or anything done or to be done in pursuance of a contract entered into before that day, to be treated for any purpose as wrongful or ineffectual.

(3) Except as provided by subsections (4) and (5) of this section, nothing in this Act shall require anything to be treated for the purposes of any enactment as having been charitable at a time before

the date of the passing of this Act, so as to invalidate anything done or any determination given before that date.

(4) For the purposes of income tax, this Act shall not require anything to be treated as having been charitable at a time before the date of the passing of this Act unless it would have been so treated in accordance with the practice applied by the Commissioners of Inland Revenue immediately before the eighteenth day of December, nineteen hundred and fifty-two; but, subject to that and to paragraphs (a) and (b) of subsection (2) of this section, there shall be made all such adjustments, whether by way of repayment of tax, additional assessment or otherwise, as are made necessary in relation to income tax by the retrospective operation of sections one and two of this Act, and nothing in the Income Tax Act 1952 shall preclude the repayment by virtue of this Act of tax for the year 1946–47 or a subsequent year of assessment if a claim is made in that behalf to the Commissioners of Inland Revenue within two years from the date of the passing of this Act.

(5) As respects stamp duty on any instrument executed before the date of the passing of this Act, this Act shall not require anything to be treated as having been charitable for the purposes of subsection (1) of section fifty-four of the Finance Act 1947 (which excepted instruments in favour of charities from certain increases of stamp duty under that Act), unless it would have been so treated in accordance with the practice applied by the Commissioners of Inland Revenue immediately before the eighteenth day of December, nineteen hundred and fifty-two; but subject to that and to paragraphs (a) and (b) of subsection (2) of this section, where more stamp duty has been paid on an instrument executed on or after the said eighteenth day of December and before the date of the passing of this Act than ought to have been paid having regard to sections one and two of this Act, the provisions of sections ten and eleven of the Stamp Duties Management Act 1891 shall apply as if a stamp of greater value than was necessary had been inadvertently used for the instrument, and relief may be given accordingly, and may be so given notwithstanding that, in accordance with the provisions of section twelve of the Stamp Act 1891, the instrument had been stamped before the passing of this Act with a particular stamp denoting that it was duly stamped.

An application for relief under the said section ten as applied by this subsection may be made at any time within two years from the date of the passing of this Act, notwithstanding that it is made outside the time limited by that section.

4. . .[1]

5 Application to Crown.

This Act, and (except in so far as the contrary intention appears) any enactment of the Parliament of Northern Ireland passed for purposes similar to section one of this Act, shall bind the Crown.

6 Short title and extent.

(1) This Act may be cited as the Recreational Charities Act 1958.

(2) Sections one and two of this Act shall affect the law of Scotland and Northern Ireland only in so far as they affect the operation of the Income Tax Acts or of other enactments in which references to charity are to be construed in accordance with the law of England and Wales [or, without prejudice to the foregoing generality, of the Local Government (Financial Provisions etc.) (Scotland) Act 1962][2].

---

[1] s. 4 repealed by Northern Ireland Constitution Act 1973 (c. 36), Sch. 6 Pt. I

[2] Words added by Local Government (Financial Provisions etc.) (Scotland) Act 1962 (c. 9), Sch. 2

Trustee Investments Act 1961

1961 CHAPTER 62 9 and 10 Eliz 2

An Act to make fresh provision with respect to investment by trustees and persons having the investment powers of trustees, and by local authorities, and for purposes connected therewith.

[3rd August 1961]

[1 New powers of investment of trustees.

(1) A trustee may invest any property in his hands, whether at the time in a state of investment or not, in any manner specified in Part I or II of the First Schedule to this Act or, subject to the next following section, in any manner specified in Part III of that Schedule, and may also from time to time vary any such investments.

(2) The supplemental provisions contained in Part IV of that Schedule shall have effect for the

interpretation and for restricting the operation of the said Parts I to III.

(3) No provision relating to the powers of the trustee contained in any instrument (not being an enactment or an instrument made under an enactment) made before the passing of this Act shall limit the powers conferred by this section, but those powers are exercisable only in so far as a contrary intention is not expressed in any Act or instrument made under an enactment, whenever passed or made, and so relating or in any other instrument so relating which is made after the passing of this Act.

For the purposes of this subsection any rule of the law of Scotland whereby a testamentary writing may be deemed to be made on a date other than that on which it was actually executed shall be disregarded.

(4) In this Act "narrower-range investment" means an investment falling within Part I or II of the First Schedule to this Act and "wider-range investment" means an investment falling within Part III of that Schedule.][1]

[2 Restrictions on wider-range investment.

(1) A trustee shall not have power by virtue of the foregoing section to make or retain any wider-range investment unless the trust fund has been divided into two parts (hereinafter referred to as the narrower-range part and the wider-range part), the parts being, subject to the provisions of this Act, equal in value at the time of the division; and where such a division has been made no subsequent division of the same fund shall be made for the purposes of this section, and no property shall be transferred from one part of the fund to the other unless either—

(a) the transfer is authorised or required by the following provisions of this Act, or

(b) a compensating transfer is made at the same time.

In this section "compensating transfer", in relation to any transferred property, means a transfer in the opposite direction of property of equal value.

(2) Property belonging to the narrower-range part of a trust fund shall not by virtue of the foregoing section be invested except in narrower-range investments, and any property invested in any other manner which is or becomes comprised in that part of the trust fund shall either be transferred to the wider-range part of the fund, with a compensating transfer, or be reinvested in narrower-range investments as soon as may be.

(3) Where any property accrues to a trust fund after the fund has been divided in pursuance of subsection (1) of this section, then—

(a) if the property accrues to the trustee as owner or former owner of property comprised in either part of the fund, it shall be treated as belonging to that part of the fund;

(b) in any other case, the trustee shall secure, by apportionment of the accruing property or the transfer of property from one part of the fund to the other, or both, that the value of each part of the fund is increased by the same amount.

Where a trustee acquires property in consideration of a money payment the acquisition of the property shall be treated for the purposes of this section as investment and not as the accrual of property to the trust fund, notwithstanding that the amount of the consideration is less than the value of the property acquired; and paragraph (a) of this subsection shall not include the case of a dividend or interest becoming part of a trust fund.

(4) Where in the exercise of any power or duty of a trustee property falls to be taken out of the trust fund, nothing in this section shall restrict his discretion as to the choice of property to be taken out.][2]

[3 Relationship between Act and other powers of investment.

(1) The powers conferred by section one of this Act are in addition to and not in derogation from any power conferred otherwise than by this Act of investment or postponing conversion exercisable by a trustee (hereinafter referred to as a "special power").

(2) Any special power (however expressed) to invest property in any investment for the time being authorised by law for the investment of trust property, being a power conferred on a trustee before the passing of this Act or conferred on him under any enactment passed before the passing of this Act, shall have effect as a power to invest property in like manner and subject to the like provisions as under the foregoing provisions of this Act.

(3) In relation to property, including wider-range but not including narrower-range investments,—

(a) which a trustee is authorised to hold apart from—

(i) the provisions of section one of this Act or any of the provisions of Part I of the Trustee Act, 1925, or any of the provisions of the Trusts (Scotland) Act, 1921, or

(ii) any such power to invest in authorised investments as is mentioned in the foregoing subsection, or

(b) which became part of a trust fund in consequence of the exercise by the trustee, as owner of property falling within this subsection, of any power conferred by subsection (3) or (4) of section ten of the Trustee Act, 1925, or paragraph (o) or (p) of subsection (1) of section four of the Trusts (Scotland) Act, 1921,

the foregoing section shall have effect subject to the modifications set out in the Second Schedule to this Act.

(4) The foregoing subsection shall not apply where the powers of the trustee to invest or postpone conversion have been conferred or varied—

(a) by an order of any court made within the period of ten years ending with the passing of this Act, or

(b) by any enactment passed, or instrument having effect under an enactment made, within that period, being an enactment or instrument relating specifically to the trusts in question; or

(c) by an enactment contained in a local Act of the present Session;

but the provisions of the Third Schedule to this Act shall have effect in a case falling within this subsection.][3]

4 Interpretation of references to trust property and trust funds.

(1) In this Act "property" includes real or personal property of any description, including money and things in action;

Provided that it does not include an interest in expectancy, but the falling into possession of such an interest, or the receipt of proceeds of the sale thereof, shall be treated for the purposes of this Act as an accrual of property to the trust fund.

(2) So much of the property in the hands of a trustee shall for the purposes of this Act constitute one trust fund as is held on trusts which (as respects the beneficiaries or their respective interests or the purposes of the trust or as respects the powers of the trustee) are not identical with those on which any other property in his hands is held.

(3) Where property is taken out of a trust fund by way of appropriation so as to form a separate fund, and at the time of the appropriation the trust fund had (as to the whole or a part thereof) been divided in pursuance of subsection (1) of section two of this Act, or that subsection as modified by the Second Schedule to this Act, then if the separate fund is so divided the narrower-range and wider-range parts of the separate fund may be constituted so as either to be equal, or to bear to each other the same proportion as the two corresponding parts of the fund out of which it was so appropriated (the values of those parts of those funds being ascertained as at the time of appropriation), or some intermediate proportion.

(4) In the application of this section to Scotland the following subsection shall be substituted for subsection (1) thereof:—

"(1) In this Act "property" includes property of any description (whether heritable or moveable, corporeal or incorporeal) which is presently enjoyable, but does not include a future interest, whether vested or contingent."

[5 Certain valuations to be conclusive for purposes of division of trust fund.

(1) If for the purposes of section two or four of this Act or the Second Schedule thereto a trustee obtains, from a person reasonably believed by the trustee to be qualified to make it, a valuation in writing of any property, the valuation shall be conclusive in determining whether the division of the trust fund in pursuance of subsection (1) of the said section two, or any transfer or apportionment of property under that section or the said Second Schedule, has been duly made.

(2) The foregoing subsection applies to any such valuation notwithstanding that it is made by a person in the course of his employment as an officer or servant.][4]

[6 Duty of trustees in choosing investments.

(1) In the exercise of his powers of investment a trustee shall have regard—

(a) to the need for diversification of investments of the trust, in so far as is appropriate to the circumstances of the trust;

(b) to the suitability to the trust of investments of the description of investment proposed and of the investment proposed as an investment of that description.

(2) Before exercising any power conferred by section one of this Act to invest in a manner specified in Part II or III of the First Schedule to this Act, or before investing in any such manner in the exercise of a power falling within subsection (2) of section three of this Act, a trustee shall obtain and consider proper advice on the question whether the investment is satisfactory having regard to the matters mentioned in paragraphs (a) and (b) of the foregoing subsection.

(3) A trustee retaining any investment made in the exercise of such a power and in such a manner as aforesaid shall determine at what intervals the circumstances, and in particular the nature of the investment, make it desirable to obtain such advice as aforesaid, and shall obtain and consider such advice accordingly.

(4) For the purposes of the two foregoing subsections, proper advice is the advice of a person who is reasonably believed by the trustee to be qualified by his ability in and practical experience of financial matters; and such advice may be given by a person notwithstanding that he gives it in the course of his employment as an officer or servant.

(5) A trustee shall not be treated as having complied with subsection (2) or (3) of this section unless the advice was given or has been subsequently confirmed in writing.

(6) Subsections (2) and (3) of this section shall not apply to one of two or more trustees where he is the person giving the advice required by this section to his co-trustee or co-trustees, and shall not apply where powers of a trustee are lawfully exercised by an officer or servant competent under subsection (4) of this section to give proper advice.

(7) Without prejudice to section eight of the Trustee Act, 1925, or section thirty of the Trusts (Scotland) Act, 1921 (which relate to valuation, and the proportion of the value to be lent, where a trustee lends on the security of property) the advice required by this section shall not include, in the case of a loan on the security of freehold or leasehold property in England and Wales or Northern Ireland or on heritable security in Scotland, advice on the suitability of the particular loan.][5]

7 Application of ss. 1–6 to persons, other than trustees, having trustee investment powers.

(1) Where any persons, not being trustees, have a statutory power of making investments which is or includes power—

(a) to make the like investments as are authorised by section one of the Trustee Act, 1925, or section ten of the Trusts (Scotland) Act, 1921, or

(b) to make the like investments as trustees are for the time being by law authorised to make,

however the power is expressed, the foregoing provisions of this Act shall with the necessary modifications apply in relation to them as if they were trustees:

Provided that property belonging to a Consolidated Loans Fund or any other fund applicable wholly or partly for the redemption of debt shall not by virtue of the foregoing provisions of this Act be invested or held invested in any manner specified in paragraph 6 of Part II of the First Schedule to this Act or in wider-range investments.

(2) Where, in the exercise of powers conferred by any enactment, an authority to which paragraph 9 of Part II of the First Schedule to this Act applies uses money belonging to any fund for a purpose for which the authority has power to borrow, the foregoing provisions of this Act, as applied by the foregoing subsection, shall apply as if there were comprised in the fund (in addition to the actual content thereof) property, being narrower-range investments, having a value equal to so much of the said money as for the time being has not been repaid to the fund, and accordingly any repayment of such money to the fund shall not be treated for the said purposes as the accrual of property to the fund:

Provided that nothing in this subsection shall be taken to require compliance with any of the provisions of section six of this Act in relation to the exercise of such powers as aforesaid.

(3) In this section "Consolidated Loans Fund" means a fund established under section fifty-five of the Local Government Act, 1958, and includes a loans fund established under [Schedule 3 to the Local Government (Scotland) Act 1975][6] and "statutory power" means a power conferred by an enactment passed before the passing of this Act or by any instrument made under any such enactment.

[8 Application of ss. 1–6 in special case.

(1) In relation to persons to whom this section applies—

(a) notwithstanding anything in subsection (3) of section one of this Act, no provision of any enactment passed, or instrument having effect under an enactment and made, before the passing of this Act shall limit the powers conferred by the said section one;

(b) subsection (1) of the foregoing section shall apply where the power of making investments therein mentioned is or includes a power to make some only of the investments mentioned in paragraph (a) or (b) of that subsection.

(2) This section applies to—

(a) the persons for the time being authorised to invest funds of the Duchy of Lancaster;

(b) any persons specified in an order made by the Treasury by statutory instrument, being persons (whether trustees or not) whose power to make investments is conferred by or under any enactment contained in a local or private Act.

(3) An order of the Treasury made under the foregoing subsection may provide that the provisions of sections one to six of this Act (other than the provisions of subsection (3) of section one) shall, in their application to any persons specified therein, have effect subject to such exceptions and modifications as may be specified.][7]

[9 Supplementary provisions as to investments.

(1) In subsection (3) of section ten of the Trustee Act, 1925, before paragraph (c) (which enables trustees to concur in any scheme or arrangement for the amalgamation of a company in which they hold securities with another company, with power to accept securities in the second company) there shall be inserted the following paragraph :—

"(bb) for the acquisition of the securities of the company, or of control thereof, by another company".

(2) It is hereby declared that the power to subscribe for securities conferred by subsection (4) of the said section ten includes power to retain them for any period for which the trustee has power to retain the holding in respect of which the right to subscribe for the securities was offered, but subject to any conditions subject to which the trustee has that power.][8]

10 Powers of Scottish trustees supplementary to powers of investment.

Section four of the Trusts (Scotland) Act, 1921 (which empowers trustees in trusts the execution of which is governed by the law in force in Scotland to do certain acts, where such acts are not at variance with the terms or purposes of the trust) shall have effect as if, in subsection (1) thereof, after paragraph (n), there were added the following paragraphs:—

"(o) to concur, in respect of any securities of a company (being securities comprised in the trust estate), in any scheme or arrangement—

(i) for the reconstruction of the company,

(ii) for the sale of all or any part of the property and undertaking of the company to another company,

(iii) for the acquisition of the securities of the company, or of control thereof, by another company,

(iv) for the amalgamation of the company with another company, or

(v) for the release, modification, or variation of any rights, privileges or liabilities attached to the securities or any of them,

in like manner as if the trustees were entitled to such securities beneficially; to accept any securities of any denomination or description of the reconstructed or purchasing or new company in lieu of, or in exchange for, all or any of the first mentioned securities; and to retain any securities so accepted as aforesaid for any period for which the trustees could have properly retained the original securities;

(p) to exercise, to such extent as the trustees think fit, any conditional or preferential right to subscribe for any securities in a company (being a right offered to them in respect of any holding in the company), to apply capital money of the trust estate in payment of the consideration, and to retain any such securities for which they have subscribed for any period for which they have the power to retain the holding in respect of which the right to subscribe for the securities was offered (but subject to any conditions subject to which they have that power); to renounce, to such extent as they think fit, any such right; or to assign, to such extent as they think fit and for the best consideration that can reasonably be obtained, the benefit of such right or the title thereto to any person, including any beneficiary under the trust."

11 Local Authority investment schemes.

(1) Without prejudice to powers conferred by or under any other enactment, any authority to which this section applies may invest property held by the authority in accordance with a scheme submitted to the Treasury by an association of local authorities . . [9] . . [10] and approved by the Treasury as enabling investments to be made collectively without in substance extending the scope of powers of investment.

(2) A scheme under this section may apply to a specified authority or to a specified class of authorities, may make different provisions as respects different authorities or different classes of authorities or as respects different descriptions of property or property held for different purposes, and may impose restrictions on the extent to which the power conferred by the foregoing subsection shall be exercisable.

(3) In approving a scheme under this section, the Treasury may direct that [the [Financial Services and Markets Act 2000][11]][12], shall not apply to dealings undertaken or documents issued for the purposes of the scheme, or to such dealings or documents of such descriptions as may be specified in the direction.

(4) The authorities to which this section applies are—

(a) in England and Wales [, the Greater London Authority,][13], the council of a county [a county borough,][14], a . . borough . . [15] a . . district or a [parish, [a river authority][16] the Common][17][parish, the Common][18] Council of the City of London [, a functional body (within the meaning of the Greater London Authority Act 1999),][19][the Broads Authority][20][a National Park authority][21][, a police authority established under [section 3 of the Police Act 1996][22]][23][, the Service Authority for the National Crime Squad][24][, [25], a joint authority established by Part IV of the Local Government Act 1985][26] . . and the Council of the Isles of Scilly;

(b) in Scotland, a local authority within the meaning of the Local Government (Scotland) Act, 1947;

(c) in any part of Great Britain, a joint board or joint committee constituted to discharge or advise on the discharge of the functions of any two or more of the authorities mentioned in the foregoing paragraphs (including a joint committee established by [those authorities acting in combination in accordance with regulations made under section 7 of the Superannuation Act 1972][27];

(d) in Northern Ireland, [a district council established under the Local Government Act (Northern Ireland) 1972][28], and the Northern Ireland Local Government Officers' Superannuation committee established under the Local Government (Superannuation) Act (Northern Ireland), 1950.

[(e) in any part of the United Kingdom, the Service Authority for the National Criminal Intelligence Service.][29]

[12 Power to confer additional powers of investment.

(1) Her Majesty may by Order in Council extend the powers of investment conferred by section one of this Act by adding to Part I, Part II or Part III of the First Schedule to this Act any manner of investment specified in the Order.

(2) Any Order under this section shall be subject to annulment in pursuance of a resolution of either House of Parliament.][30]

[13 Power to modify provisions as to division of trust fund.

(1) The Treasury may by order made by statutory instrument direct that, subject to subsection (3) of section four of this Act, any division of a trust fund made in pursuance of subsection (1) of section two of this Act during the continuance in force of the order shall be made so that the value of the wider-range part at the time of the division bears to the then value of the narrower-range part such proportion, greater than one but not greater than three to one, as may be prescribed by the order; and in this Act "the prescribed proportion" means the proportion for the time being prescribed under this subsection.

(2) A fund which has been divided in pursuance of subsection (1) of section two of this Act before the coming into operation of an order under the foregoing subsection may notwithstanding anything in that subsection be again divided (once only) in pursuance of the said subsection (1) during the continuance in force of the order.

(3) If an order is made under subsection (1) of this section, then as from the coming into operation of the order—

(a) paragraph (b) of subsection (3) of section two of this Act and sub-paragraph (b) of paragraph 3 of the Second Schedule thereto shall have effect with the substitution, for the words from "each" to the end, of the words "the wider-range part of the fund is increased by an amount which bears the prescribed proportion to the amount by which the value of the narrower-range part of the fund is increased";

(b) subsection (3) of section four of this Act shall have effect as if for the words "so as either" to "each other" there were substituted the words "so as to bear to each other either the prescribed proportion or"

(4) An order under this section may be revoked by a subsequent order thereunder prescribing a greater proportion.

(5) An order under this section shall not have effect unless approved by a resolution of each House of Parliament.][31]

14 Amendment of s. 27 of Trusts (Scotland) Act 1921.

So much of section twenty-seven of the Trusts (Scotland) Act, 1921, as empowers the Court of Session to approve as investments for trust funds any stocks, funds or securities in addition to those in which trustees are by that Act authorised to invest trust funds shall cease to have effect.

[15 Saving for powers of court.

The enlargement of the investment powers of trustees by this Act shall not lessen any power of a court to confer wider powers of investment on trustees, or affect the extent to which any such power is to be exercised.][32]

16 Minor and consequential amendments and repeals.

[(1)The provisions of the Fourth Schedule to this Act (which contain minor amendments and amendments consequential on the foregoing provisions of this Act) shall have effect.][33]

(2). . [34]

17 Short title, extent and construction.

(1) This Act may be cited as the Trustee Investments Act, 1961.

[(2) Section 11 of this Act extends to Northern Ireland, but, except as aforesaid and except so far as any other provisions of this Act apply by virtue of Northern Ireland legislation to trusts the execution of which is governed by the law of Northern Ireland, this Act does not apply to such trusts.][35]

(3) So much of section sixteen of this Act as relates to the [National Savings Bank][36] . . [37] shall extend to the Isle of Man and the Channel Islands.

(4) Except where the context otherwise requires, in this Act, in its application to trusts the execution of which is governed by the law in force in England and Wales, expressions have the same meaning as in the Trustee Act, 1925.

(5) Except where the context otherwise requires, in this Act, in its application to trusts the execution of which is governed by the law in force in Scotland, expressions have the same meaning as in the Trusts (Scotland) Act, 1921.

SCHEDULES

Section 1

FIRST SCHEDULE - Manner of Investment

PART I - NARROWER-RANGE INVESTMENTS NOT REQUIRING ADVICE

1. In Defence Bonds, National Savings Certificates and Ulster Savings Certificates [Ulster Development Bonds][38][National Development Bonds][39][British Savings Bonds][40][National Savings Income Bonds][41][National Savings Deposit Bonds][42][National Savings Indexed-Income Bonds.][43][National Savings Capital Bonds][44][National Savings FIRST Option Bonds][45][National Savings Pensioners Guaranteed Income Bonds][46].
2. In deposits in [the National Savings Bank][47] . . [48] and deposits in a bank or department thereof certified under subsection (3) of section nine of the Finance Act, 1956.

PART II - NARROWER-RANGE INVESTMENTS REQUIRING ADVICE

1. In securities issued by Her Majesty's Government in the United Kingdom, the Government of Northern Ireland or the Government of the Isle of Man, not being securities falling within Part I of this Schedule and being fixed-interest securities registered in the United Kingdom or the Isle of

Man, Treasury Bills or Tax Reserve Certificates [or any variable interest securities issued by Her Majesty's Government in the United Kingdom and registered in the United Kingdom.][49]

2. In any securities the payment of interest on which is guaranteed by Her Majesty's Government in the United Kingdom or the Government of Northern Ireland.

3. In fixed-interest securities issued in the United Kingdom by any public authority or nationalised industry or undertaking in the United Kingdom.

4. In fixed-interest securities issued in the United Kingdom by the government of any overseas territory within the Commonwealth or by any public or local authority within such a territory, being securities registered in the United Kingdom.

References in this paragraph to an overseas territory or to the government of such a territory shall be construed as if they occurred in the Overseas Service Act 1958.

4a [In securities issued in the United Kingdom by the government of an overseas territory within the Commonwealth or by any public or local authority within such a territory, being securities registered in the United Kingdom and in respect of which the rate of interest is variable by reference to one or more of the following:—

(a) the Bank of England's minimum lending rate;

(b) the average rate of discount on allotment on 91-day Treasury Bills;

(c) a yield on 91-day Treasury Bills;

(d) a London sterling inter-bank offered rate;

(e) A London sterling certificate of deposit rate.

References in this paragraph to an overseas territory or to the government of such a territory shall be construed as if they occurred in the Overseas Service Act 1958.][50]

5. In fixed-interest securities issued in the United Kingdom by [the African Development Bank, the Asian Development Bank, the Caribbean Development Bank, [the European Bank for Reconstruction and Development,][51]the International Finance Corporation, the International Monetary Fund or by][52] the International Bank for Reconstruction and Development, being securities registered in the United Kingdom.

[In fixed-interest securities issued in the United Kingdom by the Inter-American Development Bank.][53]

[In fixed-interest securities issued in the United Kingdom by [the European Atomic Energy Community, the European Bank for Reconstruction and Development, the European Economic Community,][54] the European Investment Bank or by the European Coal and Steel Community, being securities registered in the United Kingdom.][55]

[5A In securities issued in the United Kingdom by

(i) the International Bank for Reconstruction and Development or by the European Investment Bank or by the European Coal and Steel Community, being securities registered in the United Kingdom; or

(ii) the Inter-American Development Bank;

being securities in respect of which the rate of interest is variable by reference to one or more of the following:

(a) the Bank of England's minimum lending rate;

(b) the average rate of discount on allotment on 91-day Treasury Bills;

(c) a yield on 91-day Treasury Bills;

(d) a London sterling inter-bank offered rate;

(e) a London sterling certificate of deposit rate.][56]

[5B In securities issued in the United Kingdom by the African Development Bank, the Asian Development Bank, the Caribbean Development Bank, the European Atomic Energy Community, [the European Bank for Reconstruction and Development,][57] the European Economic Community, the International Finance Corporation or by the International Monetary Fund, being securities registered in the United Kingdom and in respect of which the rate of interest is variable by reference to one or more of the following:—

(a) The average rate of discount on allotment on 91-day Treasury Bills:

(b) a yield on 91-day Treasury Bills;

(c) a London sterling inter-bank offered rate;

(d) a London sterling certificate of deposit rate.][58]

6. In debentures issued in the United Kingdom by a company incorporated in the United Kingdom, being debentures registered in the United Kingdom.

7. In stock of the Bank of Ireland.
[In Bank of Ireland 7 per cent Loan Stock 1986/91.][59]

[8 In debentures issued by the Agricultural Mortgage Corporation Limited or the Scottish Agricultural Securities Corporation Limited.][60]

9. In loans to any authority to which this paragraph applies charged on all or any of the revenues of the authority or on a fund into which all or any of those revenues are payable, in any fixed-interest securities issued in the United Kingdom by any such authority for the purpose of borrowing money so charged, and in deposits with any such authority by way of temporary loan made on the giving of a receipt for the loan by the treasurer or other similar officer of the authority and on the giving of an undertaking by the authority that, if requested to charge the loan as aforesaid, it will either comply with the request or repay the loan.

This paragraph applies to the following authorities, that is to say—

(a) any local authority in the United Kingdom;
[(aa) the Greater London Authority;
(ab) any functional body, within the meaning of the Greater London Authority Act 1999;][61]
(b) any authority all the members of which are appointed or elected by one or more local authorities in the United Kingdom;
(c) any authority the majority of the members of which are appointed or elected by one or more local authorities in the United Kingdom, being an authority which by virtue of any enactment has power to issue a precept to a local authority in England and Wales, or a requisition to a local authority in Scotland, or to the expenses of which, by virtue of any enactment, a local authority in the United Kingdom is or can be required to contribute;
(d) ..[62] [a police authority established under [section 3 of the Police Act 1996][63];] [64];
[(da) the Service Authority for the National Criminal Intelligence Service or the Service Authority for the National Crime Squad;][65]
(e) the Belfast City and District Water Commissioners;
[(f) the Great Ouse Water Authority.][66]
[(g) any district council in Northern Ireland.][67]
[(h) ... [68].
(i) any residuary body established by section 57 of the Local Government Act 1985.][69]

[9A In any securities issued in the United Kingdom by any authority to which paragraph 9 applies for the purpose of borrowing money charged on all or any of the revenues of the authority or on a fund into which all or any of these revenues are payable and being securities in respect of which the rate of interest is variable by reference to one or more of the following:

(a) the Bank of England's minimum lending rate;
(b) the average rate of discount on allotment on 91-day Treasury Bills;
(c) a yield on 91-day Treasury Bills;
(d) a London sterling inter-bank offered rate;
(e) a London sterling certificate of deposit rate.].[70]

[10 In debentures or in the guaranteed or preference stock of any incorporated company, being statutory water undertakers within the meaning of the Water Act, 1945, or any corresponding enactment in force in Northern Ireland, and having during each of the ten years immediately preceding the calendar year in which the investment was made paid a dividend of not less than [½ per cent][71] on its ordinary shares.][72]

[10A In any units of a gilt unit trust scheme. A gilt unit trust scheme is an authorised unit trust scheme, or a recognised scheme, the objective of which is—

(a) to invest at least 90% of the property of the scheme in loan stock, bonds or other instruments creating indebtedness which—
(i) are transferable; and
(ii) are issued or guaranteed by the government of the United Kingdom or of any other country or territory, by a local authority in the United Kingdom or in a relevant state, or

by an international organisation the members of which include the United Kingdom or a relevant state;

(b) to invest the remainder of the property of the scheme in shares, debentures or other instruments creating or acknowledging indebtedness, certificates representing securities or units in a collective investment scheme.

Sub-paragraphs (a) and (b) must be read with—

(i) section 22 of the Financial Services and Markets Act 2000;

(ii) any relevant order under that section; and

(iii) Schedule 2 to that Act.][73]

11 . . .[74]

[12 In deposits with a building society within the meaning of the Building Societies Act 1986.].[75]

13 In mortgages of freehold property in England and Wales or Northern Ireland and of leasehold property in those countries of which the unexpired term at the time of investment is not less than sixty years, and in loans on heritable security in Scotland.

14 In perpetual rent charges charged on land in England and Wales or Northern Ireland and fee-farm rents (not being rent-charges) issuing out of such land, and in feu-duties or ground annuals in Scotland.

[15 In Certificates of Tax Deposit.][76]

[16 In fixed-interest or variable interest securities issued by the Government of a relevant state.][77]

[17 In any securities the payment of interest in which is guaranteed by the Government of a relevant state.][78]

[18 In fixed-interest securities issued in a relevant state by any public authority or nationalised industry or undertaking in any such state.][79]

[19 In fixed-interest or variable interest securities issued in a relevant state by the Government of any overseas territory within the Commonwealth or by any public or local authority within such a territory.

[For this purpose—

(a) "overseas territory" means any territory or country outside the United Kingdom, and

(b) the reference to the government of any overseas territory includes a reference to a government constituted for two or more overseas territories, and to any authority established for the purpose of providing or administering services which are common to, or relate to matters of common interest to, two or more such territories.][80]].[81]

[20 In fixed-interest or variable interest securities issued in a relevant state by—

(a) the African Development Bank;

(b) the Asian Development Bank;

(c) the Caribbean Development Bank;

(d) the International Finance Corporation;

(e) the International Monetary Fund;

(f) the International Bank for Reconstruction and Development;

(g) the Inter-American Development Bank;

(h) the European Atomic Energy Community;

(i) the European Bank for Reconstruction and Development;

(j) the European Economic Community;

(k) the European Investment Bank; or

(l) the European Coal or Steel Community.][82]

[21 In debentures issued in any relevant state by a company incorporated in that state.][83]

[22 In loans to any authority to which this paragraph applies secured on all or any of the revenues of the authority or on a fund into which all or any of those revenues are payable, in fixed-interest or variable interest securities issued in a relevant state by any such authority in that state for the purpose of borrowing money so secured, and in deposits with any authority to which this paragraph applies by way of temporary loan made on the giving of a receipt for the loan by the treasurer or other similar officer of the authority and on the giving of an undertaking by the authority that, if requested to charge the loan as aforesaid, it will either comply with the request or repay the loan. This paragraph applies to the following authorities, that is to say—

(a) any local authority in a relevant state; or

(b) any authority all the members of which are appointed or elected by one or more local authorities in any such state.][84]

[23 In deposits with a mutual investment society whose head office is located in a relevant state.][85]

[24 In loans secured on any interest in property in a relevant state which corresponds to an interest in property falling within paragraph 13 of this Part of this Schedule.][86]

PART III - WIDER-RANGE INVESTMENTS

[2 In shares in a building society within the meaning of the Building Societies Act 1986.][87]

[2A In any shares in an open-ended investment company within the meaning of the open-ended Investment Companies Regulations 2001][88]

[3 In any units of an authorised unit trust scheme. .[89].][90]

[4 In any securities issued in any relevant state by a company incorporated in that state or by any unincorporated body constituted under the law of that state, not being (in either case) securities falling within Part II of this Schedule or paragraph 6 of this Part of this Schedule.][91]

[5 In shares in a mutual investment society whose head office is located in a relevant state.][92]

[6 In any units of a recognised scheme which does not fall within Part 2 of this Schedule.][93]

PART IV - SUPPLEMENTAL

1 The securities mentioned in Parts I to III of this Schedule do not include any securities where the holder can be required to accept repayment of the principal, or the payment of any interest, otherwise than in sterling [, in the currency of a relevant state or in the european currency unit (as defined in article 1 of Council Regulation no. 3180/78/EEC).][94]

2 The securities mentioned in paragraphs 1 to 8 of Part II, other than Treasury Bills or Tax Reserve Certificates, securities issued before the passing of this Act by the Government of the Isle of Man, securities falling within paragraph 4 of the said Part II issued before the passing of this Act or securities falling within paragraph 9 of that Part, and the securities mentioned in paragraph 1 of Part III of this Schedule, do not include—

(a) securities the price of which is not quoted on [a recognised investment exchange. .[95]][96][or on an investment exchange which constitutes the principal or only market established in a relevant state on which securities admitted to official listing are dealt in or traded][97];

(b) shares or debenture stock not fully paid up (except shares or debenture stock which by the terms of issue are required to be fully paid up within nine months of the date of issue).

[2A The securities mentioned in paragraphs 16 to 21 of Part II of this Schedule, other than securities traded on a relevant money market or securities falling within paragraph 22 of Part II of this Schedule, and the securities mentioned in paragraph 4 of Part III of this Schedule do not include—

(a) securities the price for which is not quoted on a recognised investment exchange. . [98] or on an investment exchange which constitutes the principal or only market established in a relevant state on which securities admitted to official listing are dealt in or traded;

(b) shares or debenture stock not fully paid up (except shares or debenture stock which by the terms of issue are required to be fully paid up within nine months of the date of issue or shares issued with no nominal value).][99]

3 The securities mentioned in paragraph 6 [and 21][100] of Part II and paragraph 1 [or 4][101] of Part III of this Schedule do not include—

(a) shares or debentures of an incorporated company of which the total issued and paid up share capital is less than one million pounds;

[(ab) shares or debentures of an incorporated company of which the total issued and paid up share capital at any time on the business day before the investment is made is less than the equivalent of one million pounds in the currency of a relevant state (at the exchange rate prevailing in the United Kingdom at the close of business on the day before the investment is made);][102]

(b) shares or debentures of an incorporated company which has not in each of the five years immediately preceding the calendar year in which the investment is made paid a dividend on all the shares issued by the company, excluding any shares issued after the dividend was declared and any shares which by their terms of issue did not rank for the dividend for that year.

For the purposes of sub-paragraph (b) of this paragraph a company formed—

(i) to take over the business of another company or other companies, or

(ii) to acquire the securities of, or control of, another company or other companies,

or for either of those purposes and for other purposes shall be deemed to have paid a dividend as mentioned in that sub-paragraph in any year in which such a dividend has been paid by the other company or all the other companies, as the case may be.

[For the purposes of sub-paragraph (b) of this paragraph in relation to investment in shares or debentures of a successor company within the meaning of the Electricity (Northern Ireland) Order 1992 the company shall be deemed to have paid a dividend as mentioned in that sub-paragraph—

(iii) in every year preceding the calendar year in which the transfer date within the meaning of Part III of that Order of 1992 falls ("the first investment year") which is included in the relevant five years; and

(iv) in the first investment year, if that year is included in the relevant five years and that company does not in fact pay such a dividend in that year; and

"the relevant five years" means the five years immediately preceding the year in which the investment in question is made or proposed to be made.][103]

3A ...[104]

4 In this Schedule, unless the context otherwise requires, the following expressions have the meanings hereby respectively assigned to them, that is to say—

"debenture" includes debenture stock and bonds, whether constituting a charge on assets or not, and loan stock or notes;

"enactment" includes an enactment of the Parliament of Northern Ireland;

"fixed-interest securities" means securities which under their terms of issue bear a fixed rate of interest;

"local authority" in relation to the United Kingdom, means any of the following authorities—

(a) in England and Wales, the council of a county, [a county borough,][105] a . . [106] borough . . [107], an urban or rural district or a parish, the Common Council of the City of London [the Greater London Council][108] and the Council of the Isles of Scilly;

(b) in Scotland, a local authority within the meaning of the Local Government (Scotland) Act, 1947;

(c) . . . [109]

["mutual investment society" means a credit institution which operates on mutual principles and which is authorised by the appropriate supervisory authority of a relevant state;

"relevant money market" means a money market which is supervised by the central bank or a government agency of a relevant state;

"relevant state" means Austria, Finland, Iceland, [Liechtenstein,][110]Norway, Sweden or a member state other than the United Kingdom;][111]

. . .[112]

"securities" includes shares, debentures [units within paragraph 3 [or 6][113] of Part III of this Schedule][114], Treasury Bills and Tax Reserve Certificates;

"share" includes stock;

"Treasury Bills" includes . . [115] bills issued by Her Majesty's Government in the United Kingdom and Northern Ireland Treasury Bills.

[4A In this Schedule—.

"authorised unit trust scheme" and "recognised scheme" have the meaning given by section 237(3) of the Financial Services and Markets Act 2000;

"collective investment scheme" has the meaning given by section 235 of that Act; and

"recognised investment exchange" has the meaning given by section 285 of that Act.][116]

5 It is hereby declared that in this Schedule "mortgage", in relation to freehold or leasehold property in Northern Ireland, includes a registered charge which, by virtue of subsection (4) of section forty of the Local Registration of Title (Ireland) Act 1891, or any other enactment, operates as a mortgage by deed.

6 [In relation to the United Kingdom,][117] references in this Schedule to an incorporated company are

references to a company incorporated by or under any enactment and include references to a body of persons established for the purpose of trading for profit and incorporated by Royal Charter.

6 A .. [118]

7 .. [119]

Section 3

[SECOND SCHEDULE - Modification of s. 2 in relation to property falling within s. 3(3)][120]

[1 In this Schedule "special-range property" means property falling within subsection (3) of section three of this Act.][121]

[(1) Where a trust fund includes special-range property, subsection (1) of section two of this Act shall have effect as if references to the trust fund were references to so much thereof as does not consist of special-range property, and the special-range property shall be carried to a separate part of the fund.

(2) Any property which—

(a) being property belonging to the narrower-range or wider-range part of a trust fund, is converted into special-range property, or

(b) being special-range property, accrues to a trust fund after the division of the fund or part thereof in pursuance of subsection (1) of section two of this Act or of that subsection as modified by sub-paragraph (1) of this paragraph,

shall be carried to such a separate part of the fund as aforesaid; and subsections (2) and (3) of the said section two shall have effect subject to this sub-paragraph.][122]

[3 Where property carried to such a separate part as aforesaid is converted into property other than special-range property,—

(a) it shall be transferred to the narrower-range part of the fund or the wider-range part of the fund or apportioned between them, and

(b) any transfer of property from one of those parts to the other shall be made which is necessary to secure that the value of each of those parts of the fund is increased by the same amount.][123]

Section 3

[THIRD SCHEDULE - Provisions Supplementary to s. 3(4)][124]

[1 Where in a case falling within subsection (4) of section three of this Act, property belonging to the narrower-range part of a trust fund—

(a) is invested otherwise than in a narrower-range investment, or

(b) being so invested, is retained and not transferred or as soon as may be reinvested as mentioned in subsection (2) of section two of this Act,

then, so long as the property continues so invested and comprised in the narrower-range part of the fund, section one of this Act shall not authorise the making or retention of any wider-range investment.][125]

[2 Section four of the Trustee Act, 1925, or section thirty-three of the Trusts (Scotland) Act, 1921 (which relieve a trustee from liability for retaining an investment which has ceased to be authorised), shall not apply where an investment ceases to be authorised in consequence of the foregoing paragraph.][126]

Section 16

FOURTH SCHEDULE - Minor and Consequential Amendments

1[(1) References in the Trustee Act, 1925, except in subsection (2) of section sixty-nine of that Act, to section one of that Act or to provisions which include that section shall be construed respectively as references to section one of this Act and as including references to section one of this Act.][127]

(2) References in the Trusts (Scotland) Act, 1921, to section ten or eleven of that Act, or to provisions which include either of those sections, shall be construed respectively as references to section one of this Act and as including references to that section.

2. .[128].

[3 The following enactments and instruments, that is to say—

(a) subsection (3) of section seventy-four of the Third Schedule to the Water Act, 1945, and any order made under that Act applying the provisions of that subsection;

(b) any local and personal Act which, or any order or other instrument in the nature of any such

Act which, modifies paragraph (l) of subsection (1) of section one of the Trustee Act, 1925, shall have effect as if any reference to the said paragraph (l) there were substituted a reference to paragraph 10 of Part II of the First Schedule to this Act.][129]

4, 5 . .[130]

[6 For the reference in subsection (2) of section one of the House Purchase and Housing Act, 1959, to paragraph (a) of subsection (1) of that section there shall be substituted a reference to paragraph 12 of Part II and paragraph 2 of Part III of the First Schedule to this Act.][131]

FIFTH SCHEDULE . .[132]

---

[1] s. 1 repealed (with saving) (1.2.2001) by 2000 c. 29, s. 40(1)(3), Sch. 2 Pt. I para. 1(1), Sch. 4 Pt. I (with s. 35); S.I. 2001/49, art. 2

[2] s. 2 repealed (with saving) (1.2.2001) by 2000 c. 29, s. 40(1)(3), Sch. 2 Pt. I para. 1(1), Sch. 4 Pt. I (with s. 35); S.I. 2001/49, art. 2

[3] s. 3 repealed (with saving) (1.2.2001) by 2000 c. 29, s. 40(1)(3), Sch. 2 Pt. I para. 1(2), Sch. 4 Pt. I (with s. 35); S.I. 2001/49, art. 2

[4] s. 5 repealed (with saving) (1.2.2001) by 2000 c. 29, s. 40(1)(3), Sch. 2 Pt. I para. 1(1), Sch. 4 Pt. I (with s. 35); S.I. 2001/49, art. 2

[5] s. 6 repealed (with saving) (1.2.2001) by 2000 c. 29, s. 40(1)(3), Sch. 2 Pt. I para. 1(1), Sch. 4 Pt. I (with s. 35); S.I. 2001/49, art. 2

[6] Words substituted (S.) by Local Government and Planning (Scotland) Act 1982 (c. 43, SIF 81:2), s. 66(1), Sch. 3 para. 4

[7] s. 8 repealed (1.2.2001) by 2000 c. 29, s. 40(1)(3), Sch. 2 Pt. I para. 1(3)(a), Sch. 4 Pt. I (with s. 35);S.I. 2001/49, art. 2

[8] s. 9 repealed (1.2.2001) by 2000 c. 29, s. 40(1)(3), Sch. 2 Pt. I para. 1(3)(a), Sch. 4 Pt. I (with s. 35); S.I. 2001/49, art. 2

[9] Words repealed by Local Government Act 1985 (c. 51, SIF 81:1), s. 102, Sch. 17

[10] Words repealed by London Government Act 1963 (c. 33, SIF 81:1), Sch. 18 Pt. II

[11] Words in s. 11(3) substituted (1.12.2001) by S.I. 2001/3649, arts. 1, 268

[12] Words substituted by Financial Services Act 1986 (c. 60, SIF 69), s. 212(2), Sch. 16 para. 2(a)

[13] Words in s. 11(4)(a) inserted (8.5.2000 for the purposes of its application to the Authority and 3.7.2000 so far as it is not already in force) by 1999 c. 29, s. 387(2)(a) (with Sch. 12 para. 9(1)); S.I. 1999/3434, arts. 3, 4

[14] Words in s. 11(4)(a) inserted (1.4.1996) by 1994 c. 19, s66(6), Sch. 16 para. 19(1)(with ss. 54(7), 66(7), Sch. 17 paras. 22, 23(2)); S.I. 1996/396, art. 4, Sch. 2

[15] Words repealed by Local Government Act 1972 (c. 70, SIF 81:1), s. 273(1)–(3), Sch. 30

[16] Words inserted by Water Resources Act 1963 (c. 38, SIF 130), Sch. 13 para. 16

[17] Words "parish, the Common" substituted for words commencing "parish, [a river authority" by Water Act 1989 (c. 15, SIF 130), s. 190, Sch. 25 para. 29(1) (with ss. 58(7), 101(1), 141(6), 160(1)(2)(4), 163, 189(4)–(10), 190, 193(1), Sch. 26 paras. 3(1)(2), 17, 40(4), 57(6), 58)

[18] Words "parish, the Common" substituted for words commencing "parish, [a river authority" by Water Act 1989 (c. 15, SIF 130), s. 190, Sch. 25 para. 29(1) (with ss. 58(7), 101(1), 141(6), 160(1)(2)(4), 163, 189(4)–(10), 190, 193(1), Sch. 26 paras. 3(1)(2), 17, 40(4), 57(6), 58)

[19] Words in s. 11(4)(a) inserted (8.5.2000 for the purposes of its application to the Authority and 3.7.2000 so far as it is not already in force) by 1999 c. 29, s. 387(2)(b) (with Sch. 12 para. 9(1); S.I. 1999/3434, arts. 3, 4

[20] Words inserted by Norfolk and Suffolk Broads Act 1988 (c. 4, SIF 81:1), s. 21, Sch. 6 para. 3

[21] Words in s.11(4)(a) inserted (23.11.1995) by 1995 c.25, s.78, Sch. 10 para. 5(with ss.7(6), 115, 117); S.I. 1995/2950, art.2(1)

[22] Words in s. 11(4)(a) substituted (E.W.S.) (22.8.1996) by 1996 c. 16, ss. 103, 104(1), Sch. 7 Pt. I para. 2(a)

[23] Words in s. 11(4)(a) inserted (1.10.1994 for the purposes mentioned in S.I. 1994/2025, art. 6 and 1.4.1995 for all remaining purposes by S.I. 1994/3262) by 1994 c. 29, ss. 43, 94(1), Sch. 4 Pt. II para. 46; S.I. 1994/2025, art. 6(2)(g); S.I. 1994/3262, art. 4, Sch.

[24] Words in s. 11(4)(a) inserted (1.4.1998) by 1997 c. 50, s. 134(1), Sch. 9 para. 4(a); S.I. 1998/354, art. 2(2)(bb).

[25] Words repealed by Education Reform Act 1988 (c. 40, SIF 41:1), ss. 231(7), 235(6), 237, Sch. 13.

[26] Words inserted by Local Government Act 1985 (c. 51, SIF 81:1), s. 84, Sch. 14 Pt. II, para. 38

[27] Words substituted by Superannuation Act 1972 (c. 11, SIF 101A), Sch. 6 para. 40

[28] Words substituted by S.R.&O. 1973/256, art. 3, Sch. 2

[29] s. 11(4)(e) added (1.4.1998) by 1997 c. 50, s. 134(1), Sch. 9 para. 4(b); S.I. 1998/354, art. 2(2)(bb).

[30] s. 12 repealed (with saving) (1.2.2001) by 2000 c. 29, s. 40(1)(3), Sch. 2 Pt. I para. 1(1), Sch. 4 Pt. I (with s. 35); S.I. 2001/49, art. 2

[31] s. 13 repealed (with saving) (1.2.2001) by 2000 c. 29, s. 40(1)(3), Sch. 2 Pt. I para. 1(1), Sch. 4 Pt. I (with s. 35); S.I. 2001/49, art. 2. S. 13 applied (E.W.S.)(11.2.1997) by S.I. 1997/266, art. 10(4)

[32] s. 15 repealed (with saving) (1.2.2001) by 2000 c. 29, s. 40(1)(3), Sch. 2 Pt. I para. 1(1), Sch. 4 Pt. I (with s. 35); S.I. 2001/49, art. 2

[33] s. 16(1) repealed in so far as it relates to Sch. 4 para. 1(1) (1.2.2001) by 2000 c. 29, ss. 40(1)(3), Sch. 2 Pt. I para. 1(3)(c), Sch. 4 Pt. I (with s. 35); S.I. 2001/49, art. 2

[34] s. 16(2) repealed by Statute Law (Repeals) Act 1974 (c. 22), s. 1, Sch. Pt. XI

[35] s. 17(2) substituted (29.7.2002) by 2001 c. 14 (N.I.), ss. 44, Sch. 2 para. 20; S.R. 2002/253, art. 2
[36] Words repealed by Trustee Savings Banks Act 1985 (c. 58, SIF 110), ss. 4(3), 7(3), Sch. 4
[37] Words substituted by Post Office Act 1969 (c. 48, SIF 96), Sch. 6 Pt. III
[38] Words added by virtue of S.I. 1962/2611, art. 1
[39] Words added by virtue of S.I. 1964/703, art. 1
[40] Words added by virtue of S.I. 1968/470, art. 1
[41] Words added by virtue of S.I. 1982/1086, art. 2
[42] Words added by virtue of S.I. 1983/1525, art. 2
[43] Words added by virtue of S.I. 1985/1780, art. 2
[44] Words added by virtue of S.I. 1988/2254, art. 2
[45] Words added (13.8.1992) by virtue of S.I. 1992/1738, art. 2.
[46] Words in Sch. 1 para. 1 added (11.3.1994) by S.I. 1994/265, art.2
[47] Words substituted by Post Office Act 1969 (c. 48, SIF 96), Sch. 6 Pt. III
[48] Words repealed by Trustee Savings Banks Act 1976 (c. 4), s. 36(2), Sch. 6
[49] Words added by virtue of S.I. 1977/831, art. 3
[50] Para. 4A added by virtue of S.I. 1977/1878, art. 3
[51] Words in Sch. 1 Pt. II para. 5 added by virtue of S.I. 1991/999, art. 2
[52] Words added by virtue of S.I. 1983/772, art. 2(a)
[53] Para. added by S.I. 1964/1404
[54] Words added by virtue of S.I. 1983/772, art. 2(b)
[55] Para. added by S.I. 1972/1818
[56] Para. 5A added by virtue of S.I. 1977/1878, art. 3
[57] Words in Sch. 1 Pt. II para. 5B added by virtue of S.I. 1991/999, art. 2
[58] Para. 5B added by virtue of S.I. 1983/772, art. 2(c)
[59] Para. added by S.I. 1966/401
[60] Sch. 1 Pt. II para. 8 repealed (E.W.S.)(25.9.1991) by Agriculture and Forestry (Financial Provisions) Act 1991 (c. 33, SIF 2:2), s. 1(1)(5), SchedulePart IV; S.I. 1991/1978, art. 2
[61] Sch. 1 Pt. II para. 9(aa)(ab) inserted (8.5.2000 for the purposes of its application to the Authority and 3.7.2000 so far as it is not already in force) by 1999 c. 29, s. 387(3)(a) (with Sch. 12 para. 9(1)); S.I. 1999/3434, arts. 3,4
[62] Words in Sch. 1 Pt. II para. 9(d) shall cease to have effect (8.5.2000 for the purpose of its application to the Authority and otherwiseprosp.) and repealed (3.7.2000) by 1999 c. 29, s. 387(3)(b), 423, Sch. 34 Pt.I; S.I. 1999/3434, art.3; S.I. 2000/801, art. 2(2)(c), Sch. Pt. 3
[63] Words in Sch. 1 Pt. II para. 9(d) substituted (E.W.S.) (22.8.1996) by 1996 c. 16, ss. 103, 104(1), Sch. 7 Pt. I para. 2(a)
[64] Words in Sch. 1 Pt. II para. 9(d) substituted (1.10.1994 for the purposes mentioned in S.I. 1994/2025, art. 6 and 1.4.1995 for all remaining purposes by S.I. 1994/3262) by 1994 c. 29, ss. 43, 94(1), Sch. 4 Pt. II para. 47; S.I. 1994/2025, art. 6(2)(g); S.I. 1994/3262, art. 4, Sch
[65]Sch. 1 Pt. II para. 9(da) inserted (1.4.1998) by 1997 c. 50, s. 134(1), Sch. 9 para. 5; S.I. 1998/354, art. 2.
[66] Para. 9(f) added by S.I. 1962/658
[67] Para. 9(g) added by virtue of S.I. 1973/1332, art. 3
[68] Sch. 1 Pt. II para. 9(h) repealed by Education Reform Act 1988 (c. 40, SIF 41:1), ss. 231(7), 235(6), 237, Sch. 13
[69] Para. 9(h)(i) added by virtue of S.I. 1986/601, art. 2
[70] Para. 9A added by virtue of S.I. 1977/1878 art. 3
[71] Words substituted (in relation to dividends paid during any year after 1972) by virtue of S.I. 1973/1393, art. 3
[72] Sch. 1 Pt. II para. 10 ceased to have effect except in so far as it relates to the debentures or guaranteed or preference stock of a company which is a statutory water undertaker within the meaning of an enactment in force in Northern Ireland, by virtue of Water Act 1989 (c. 15, SIF 130), s. 190(1), Sch. 25 para. 29(2)(3) (with ss. 58(7), 101(1), 141(6), 160(1)(2)(4), 163, 189(4)–(10), 190, 193(1), Sch. 26 paras. 3(1)(2), 17, 40(4), 41(1), 57(6), 58)
[73] Sch. 1 Pt. II para. 10A substituted (1.12.2001) by S.I. 2001/3649, arts. 1, 269(2)
[74] Sch. 1 Pt. II para. 11 repealed by Trustee Savings Banks Act 1976 (c. 4, SIF 110), s. 36(2), Sch. 6
[75] Para. 12 substituted by Building Societies Act 1986 (c. 53, SIF 16), s. 120, Sch. 18 Pt. I para. 4(2)
[76] Para. 15 added by virtue of S.I. 1975/1710, art. 3
[77] Sch. 1 Pt. II paras. 16-24 inserted (22.8.1994) by S.I. 1994/1908 art. 2(2)
[78] Sch. 1 Pt. II paras. 16-24 inserted (22.8.1994) by S.I. 1994/1908 art. 2(2)
[79] Sch. 1 Pt. II paras. 16-24 inserted (22.8.1994) by S.I. 1994/1908 art. 2(2)
[80] Sch. 1 Pt. 2 para. 19; Words and (a) (b) substituted for words (17.6.2002) by International Development Act 2002 (c. 1), s. 19, Sch. 3 para. 1 (with Sch. 5 para. 5); S.I. 2002/1408, art. 2
[81] Sch. 1 Pt. II paras. 16-24 inserted (22.8.1994) by S.I. 1994/1908 art. 2(2)
[82] Sch. 1 Pt. II paras. 16-24 inserted (22.8.1994) by S.I. 1994/1908 art. 2(2)
[83] Sch. 1 Pt. II paras. 16-24 inserted (22.8.1994) by S.I. 1994/1908 art. 2(2)
[84] Sch. 1 Pt. II paras. 16-24 inserted (22.8.1994) by S.I. 1994/1908 art. 2(2)
[85] Sch. 1 Pt. II paras. 16-24 inserted (22.8.1994) by S.I. 1994/1908 art. 2(2)

86 Sch. 1 Pt. II paras. 16-24 inserted (22.8.1994) by S.I. 1994/1908 art. 2(2)
87 Para. 2 substituted by Building Societies Act 1986 (c. 53, SIF 16), s. 120, Sch. 18 Pt. I para. 4(3)
88 Sch. 1 Pt. III para. 2A substituted (1.12.2001) by S.I. 2001/1228, regs. 2(1), 84, Sch. 7 Pt. I para. 1; S.I. 2001/3538, art. 2
89 Words in Sch. 1 Pt. III para. 3 repealed (1.12.2001) by S.I. 2001/3649, arts. 1, 269(3)
90 Para. 3 substituted by Financial Services Act 1986 (c. 60, SIF 69), s. 212(2), Sch. 16 para. 2(b)
91 Sch. 1 Pt. III paras. 4-6 inserted (22.8.1994) by S.I. 1994/1908 art. 2(3)
92 Sch. 1 Pt. III paras. 4-6 inserted (22.8.1994) by S.I. 1994/1908 art. 2(3)
93 Sch. 1 Pt. III para. 6 substituted (1.12.2001) by S.I. 2001/3649, arts. 1, 269(4)
94 Words in Sch. 1 Pt. IV para. 1 inserted (22.8.1994) by S.I. 1994/1908, art. 3(2)
95 Words in Sch. 1 Pt. IV para. 2 repealed (1.12.2001) by S.I. 2001/3649, arts. 1, 269(5)
96 Words substituted by Financial Services Act 1986 (c. 60, SIF 69), s. 212(2), Sch. 16 para. 2(c)
97 Words in Sch. 1 Pt. IV para. 2(a) inserted (22.8.1994) by S.I. 1994/1908, art. 3(3)
98 Words in Sch. 1 Pt. IV para. 2A repealed (1.12.2001) by S.I. 2001/3649, arts. 1, 269(5)
99 Sch. 1 Pt. IV para. 2A inserted (22.8.1994) by S.I. 1994/1908, art. 3(4)
100 Words in Sch. 1 Pt. IV para. 3 inserted (22.8.1994) by S.I. 1994/1908, art. 3(5)(a)(b)
101 Words in Sch. 1 Pt. IV para. 3 inserted (22.8.1994) by S.I. 1994/1908, art. 3(5)(a)(b)
102 Sch. 1 Pt. IV para. 3(ab) inserted (22.8.1994) by S.I. 1994/1908, art. 3(5)(c)
103 Words in Sch. 1 Pt. IV para. 3 added (1.4.1992) by S.I. 1992/232, art. 4; S.R. 1992/117, art. 3(1)
104 Sch. 1 Pt. IV para. 3A as inserted by Housing (Consequential Provisions) Act 1985 (c. 71, SIF 61), s. 4(1), Sch. 2 para. 5(3) repealed by Building Societies Act 1986 (c. 53, SIF 16), s. 120, Sch. 19 Pt. I
105 Words in Sch. 1 Pt. IV para. 4 inserted (1.4.1996) by 1994 c. 19, s. 66(6), Sch. 16 para. 19(2)(with ss. 54(7), 66(7), Sch. 17 paras. 22, 23(2)); S.I. 1996/396, art. 4, Sch.2
106 Words repealed by London Government Act 1963 (c. 33, SIF 81:1), Sch. 18 Pt. II
107 Words repealed by Local Government Act 1972 (c. 70, SIF 81:1), s. 273(1)–(3), Sch. 30
108 Words inserted by London Government Act 1963 (c. 33, SIF 81:1), Sch. 17 para. 25
109 Sub-para. (c) repealed by Statute Law (Repeals) Act 1981 (c. 19), s. 1(1), Sch. 1 Pt. V
110 Words in Sch. 1 Pt. IV para. 4 inserted (18.4.1995) by S.I. 1995/768, art. 2
111 Definitions in Sch. 1 Pt. IV para. 4 inserted (22.8.1994) by S.I. 1994/1908, art. 3(6)(a)
112 Definitions repealed by Trustee Savings Banks Act 1976 (c. 4, SIF 110), s. 36(2), Sch. 6
113 Words in Sch. 1 Pt. IV para. 4 inserted (22.8.1994) by S.I. 1994/1908, art. 3(6)(b)
114 Words inserted by Financial Services Act 1986 (c. 60, SIF 69), s. 212(2), Sch. 16 para. 2(d)
115 Words repealed by National Loans Act 1968 (c. 13, SIF 99:3), Sch. 6 Pt. I
116 Sch. 1 Pt. IV para. 4A inserted (1.12.2001) by S.I. 2001/3649, arts. 1, 269(6)
117 Words in Sch. 1 Pt. IV para. 6 inserted (22.8.1994) by S.I. 1994/1908, art. 3(7)
118 Sch. 1 Pt. IV para. 6A repealed (1.12.2001) by S.I. 2001/3649, arts. 1, 269(7)
119 Sch. 1 Pt. IV para. 7 repealed by Building Societies Act 1986 (c. 53, SIF 16), s. 120, Sch. 19 Pt. I
120 Sch. 2 repealed (with saving) (1.2.2001) by 2000 c. 29, s. 40(1)(3), Sch. 2 Pt. I para. 1(2), Sch. 4 Pt. I (with s. 35); S.I. 2001/49, art. 2
121 Sch. 2 repealed (with savings) (1.2.2001) by 2000 c. 29, s. 40(1)(3), Sch. 2 Pt. I para. 1(2), Sch. 4 Pt. I (with s. 35); S.I. 2001/49, art. 2
122 Sch. 2 repealed (with savings) (1.2.2001) by 2000 c. 29, s. 40(1)(3), Sch. 2 Pt. I para. 1(2), Sch. 4 Pt. I (with s. 35); S.I. 2001/49, art. 2
123 Sch. 2 repealed (with savings) (1.2.2001) by 2000 c. 29, s. 40(1)(3), Sch. 2 Pt. I para. 1(2), Sch. 4 Pt. I (with s. 35); S.I. 2001/49, art. 2
124 Sch. 3 repealed (with saving) (1.2.2001) by 2000 c. 29, s. 40(1)(3), Sch. 2 Pt. I para. 1(2), Sch. 4
125 Sch. 3 repealed (with savings) (1.2.2001) by 2000 c. 29, s. 40(1)(3), Sch. 2 Pt. I para. 1(2), Sch. 4 Pt. I (with s. 35); S.I. 2001/49, art. 2
126 Sch. 3 repealed (with savings) (1.2.2001) by 2000 c. 29, s. 40(1)(3), Sch. 2 Pt. I para. 1(2), Sch. 4 Pt. I (with s. 35); S.I. 2001/49, art. 2
127 Sch. 4 para. 1(1) repealed (1.2.2001) by 2000 c. 29, s. 40(1)(3), Sch. 2 Pt. I para. 1(3)(b), Sch. 4 Pt. I (with s. 35); S.I. 2001/49, art. 2
128 Sch. 4 para. 2 repealed by Building Societies Act 1962 (c. 37, SIF 16), Sch. 10
129 Sch. 4 para. 3 repealed by Water Act 1989 (c. 15, SIF 130), s. 190(3), Sch. 27 Pt. II (with ss. 58(7), 101(1), 141(6), 160(1)(2)(4), 163, 189(4)–(10), 190, 193(1), Sch. 26 paras. 3(1)(2), 17, 40(4), 41(1), 57(6), 58)
130 Sch. 4 paras. 4 and 5 repealed by Trustee Savings Banks Act 1969 (c. 50), Sch. 3 Pt. I and National Savings Bank Act 1971 (c. 29, SIF 110), Sch. 2
131 Sch. 4 para. 6 repealed by Housing (Consequential Provisions) Act 1985 (c. 71, SIF 61), s. 3, Sch. 1 Pt. I
132 Sch. 5 repealed by Statute Law (Repeals) Act 1974 (c. 22), s. 1, Sch. Pt. XI

Perpetuities and Accumulations Act 1964

1964 CHAPTER 55

An Act to modify the law of England and Wales relating to the avoidance of future interests in property on grounds of remoteness and governing accumulations of income from property.

[16th July 1964]

Perpetuities

1 Power to specify perpetuity period.

(1) Subject to section 9(2) of this Act and subsection (2) below, where the instrument by which any disposition is made so provides, the perpetuity period applicable to the disposition under the rule against perpetuities, instead of being of any other duration, shall be of a duration equal to such number of years not exceeding eighty as is specified in that behalf in the instrument.

(2) Subsection (1) above shall not have effect where the disposition is made in exercise of a special power of appointment, but where a period is specified under that subsection in the instrument creating such a power the period shall apply in relation to any disposition under the power as it applies in relation to the power itself.

2 Presumptions and evidence as to future parenthood.

(1) Where in any proceedings there arises on the rule against perpetuities a question which turns on the ability of a person to have a child at some future time, then—

(a) subject to paragraph (b) below, it shall be presumed that a male can have a child at the age of fourteen years or over, but not under that age, and that a female can have a child at the age of twelve years or over, but not under that age or over the age of fifty-five years; but

(b) in the case of a living person evidence may be given to show that he or she will or will not be able to have a child at the time in question.

(2) Where any such question is decided by treating a person as unable to have a child at a particular time, and he or she does so, the High Court may make such order as it thinks fit for placing the persons interested in the property comprised in the disposition, so far as may be just, in the position they would have held if the question had not been so decided.

(3) Subject to subsection (2) above, where any such question is decided in relation to a disposition by treating a person as able or unable to have a child at a particular time, then he or she shall be so treated for the purpose of any question which may arise on the rule against perpetuities in relation to the same disposition in any subsequent proceedings.

(4) In the foregoing provisions of this section references to having a child are references to begetting or giving birth to a child, but those provisions (except subsection (1)(b)) shall apply in relation to the possibility that a person will at any time have a child by adoption, legitimation or other means as they apply to his or her ability at that time to beget or give birth to a child.

3 Uncertainty as to remoteness.

(1) Where, apart from the provisions of this section and sections 4 and 5 of this Act, a disposition would be void on the ground that the interest disposed of might not become vested until too remote a time, the disposition shall be treated, until such time (if any) as it becomes established that the vesting must occur, if at all, after the end of the perpetuity period, as if the disposition were not subject to the rule against perpetuities; and its becoming so established shall not affect the validity of anything previously done in relation to the interest disposed of by way of advancement, application of intermediate income or otherwise.

(2) Where, apart from the said provisions, a disposition consisting of the conferring of a general power of appointment would be void on the ground that the power might not become exercisable until too remote a time, the disposition shall be treated, until such time (if any) as it becomes established that the power will not be exercisable within the perpetuity period, as if the disposition were not subject to the rule against perpetuities.

(3) Where, apart from the said provisions, a disposition consisting of the conferring of any power, option or other right would be void on the ground that the right might be exercised at too remote a time, the disposition shall be treated as regards any exercise of the right within the perpetuity period as if it were not subject to the rule against perpetuities and, subject to the said provisions, shall be treated as void for remoteness only if, and so far as, the right is not fully exercised within that

period.

(4) Where this section applies to a disposition and the duration of the perpetuity period is not determined by virtue of section 1 or 9(2) of this Act, it shall be determined as follows:—

(a) where any persons falling within subsection (5) below are individuals in being and ascertainable at the commencement of the perpetuity period the duration of the period shall be determined by reference to their lives and no others, but so that the lives of any description of persons falling within paragraph (b) or (c) of that subsection shall be disregarded if the number of persons of that description is such as to render it impracticable to ascertain the date of death of the survivor;

(b) where there are no lives under paragraph (a) above the period shall be twenty-one years.

(5) The said persons are as follows:—

(a) the person by whom the disposition was made;

(b) a person to whom or in whose favour the disposition was made, that is to say—

(i) in the case of a disposition to a class of persons, any member or potential member of the class;

(ii) in the case of an individual disposition to a person taking only on certain conditions being satisfied, any person as to whom some of the conditions are satisfied and the remainder may in time be satisfied;

(iii) in the case of a special power of appointment exercisable in favour of members of a class, any member or potential member of the class;

(iv) in the case of a special power of appointment exercisable in favour of one person only, that person or, where the object of the power is ascertainable only on certain conditions being satisfied, any person as to whom some of the conditions are satisfied and the remainder may in time be satisfied;

(v) in the case of any power, option or other right, the person on whom the right is conferred;

(c) a person having a child or grandchild within sub-paragraphs (i) to (iv) of paragraph (b) above, or any of whose children or grandchildren, if subsequently born, would by virtue of his or her descent fall within those sub-paragraphs;

(d) any person on the failure or determination of whose prior interest the disposition is limited to take effect.

4 Reduction of age and exclusion of class members to avoid remoteness.

(1) Where a disposition is limited by reference to the attainment by any person or persons of a specified age exceeding twenty-one years, and it is apparent at the time the disposition is made or becomes apparent at a subsequent time—

(a) that the disposition would, apart from this section, be void for remoteness, but

(b) that it would not be so void if the specified age had been twenty-one years,

(2) Where in the case of any disposition different ages exceeding twenty-one years are specified in relation to different persons—

(a) the reference in paragraph (b) of subsection (1) above to the specified age shall be construed as a reference to all the specified ages, and

(b) that subsection shall operate to reduce each such age so far as is necessary to save the disposition from being void for remoteness.

(3) Where the inclusion of any persons, being potential members of a class or unborn persons who at birth would become members or potential members of the class, prevents the foregoing provisions of this section from operating to save a disposition from being void for remoteness, those persons shall thenceforth be deemed for all the purposes of the disposition to be excluded from the class, and the said provisions shall thereupon have effect accordingly.

(4) Where, in the case of a disposition to which subsection (3) above does not apply, it is apparent at the time the disposition is made or becomes apparent at a subsequent time that, apart from this subsection, the inclusion of any persons, being potential members of a class or unborn persons who at birth would become members or potential members of the class, would cause the disposition to be treated as void for remoteness, those persons shall, unless their exclusion would exhaust the class, thenceforth be deemed for all the purposes of the disposition to be excluded from the class.

(5) Where this section has effect in relation to a disposition to which section 3 above applies, the operation of this section shall not affect the validity of anything previously done in relation to the interest disposed of by way of advancement, application of intermediate income or otherwise.

(6) Section 163 of the Law of Property Act 1925 (which saves a disposition from remoteness arising out of a condition requiring the attainment of an age exceeding twenty-one years) is herby repealed.

The text of s. 4(6) is in the form in which it was originally enacted: it was not reproduced in Statutes in Force and does not reflect any amendments or repeals which may have been made prior to 1.2.1991.

5 Condition relating to death of surviving spouse.

Where a disposition is limited by reference to the time of death of the survivor of a person in being at the commencement of the perpetuity period and any spouse of that person, and that time has not arrived at the end of the perpetuity period, the disposition shall be treated for all purposes, where to do so would save it from being void for remoteness, as if it had instead been limited by reference to the time immediately before the end of that period.

6 Saving and acceleration of expectant interests.

A disposition shall not be treated as void for remoteness by reason only that the interest disposed of is ulterior to and dependent upon an interest under a disposition which is so void, and the vesting of an interest shall not be prevented from being accelerated on the failure of a prior interest by reason only that the failure arises because of remoteness.

7 Powers of appointment.

(a) in the instrument creating the power it is expressed to be exercisable by one person only, and

(b) it could, at all times during its currency when that person is of full age and capacity, be exercised by him so as immediately to transfer to himself the whole of the interest governed by the power without the consent of any other person or compliance with any other condition, not being a formal condition relating only to the mode of exercise of the power:

Provided that for the purpose of determining whether a disposition made under a power of appointment exercisable by will only is void for remoteness, the power shall be treated as a general power where it would have fallen to be so treated if exercisable by deed.

8 Administrative powers of trustees.

(1) The rule against perpetuities shall not operate to invalidate a power conferred on trustees or other persons to sell, lease, exchange or otherwise dispose of any property for full consideration, or to do any other act in the administration (as opposed to the distribution) of any property, and shall not prevent the payment to trustees or other persons of reasonable remuneration for their services.

(2) Subsection (1) above shall apply for the purpose of enabling a power to be exercised at any time after the commencement of this Act notwithstanding that the power is conferred by an instrument which took effect before that commencement.

9 Options relating to land.

(1) The rule against perpetuities shall not apply to a disposition consisting of the conferring of an option to acquire for valuable consideration an interest reversionary (whether directly or indirectly) on the term of a lease if—

(a) the option is exercisable only by the lessee or his successors in title, and

(b) it ceases to be exercisable at or before the expiration of one year following the determination of the lease.

(2) In the case of a disposition consisting of the conferring of an option to acquire for valuable consideration any interest in land, the perpetuity period under the rule against perpetuities shall be twenty-one years, and section 1 of this Act shall not apply:

provided that this subsection shall not apply to a right of pre-emption conferred on a public or local authority in respect of land used or to be used for religious purposes where the right becomes exercisable only if the land ceases to be used for such purposes.

10 Avoidance of contractual and other rights in cases of remoteness.

Where a disposition inter vivos would fall to be treated as void for remoteness if the rights and duties thereunder were capable of transmission to persons other than the original parties and had been so transmitted, it shall be treated as void as between the person by whom it was made and the person to whom or in whose favour it was made or any successor of his, and no remedy shall lie in contract or otherwise for giving effect to it or making restitution for its lack of effect.

11 Rights for enforcement of rentcharges.

(1) The rule against perpetuities shall not apply to any powers or remedies for recovering or compelling the payment of an annual sum to which section 121 or 122 of the Law of Property Act 1925 applies, or otherwise becoming exercisable or enforceable on the breach of any condition or other requirement relating to that sum.

(2) In section 121(6) of the Law of Property Act 1925 the words from "norto the same" onwards are hereby repealed.[1]

12 Possibilities of reverter, conditions subsequent, exceptions and reservations.

(1) In the case of—

(a) a possibility of reverter on the determination of a determinable fee simple, or

(b) a possibility of a resulting trust on the determination of any other determinable interest in property,

(2) Where a disposition is subject to any such provision, or to any such condition subsequent, or to any exception or reservation, the disposition shall be treated for the purposes of this Act as including a separate disposition of any rights arising by virtue of the provision, condition subsequent, exception or reservation.

Accumulations

13 Amendment of s. 164 of Law of Property Act 1925.

(1) The periods for which accumulations of income under a settlement or other disposition are permitted by section 164 of the Law of Property Act 1925 shall include—

(a) a term of twenty-one years from the date of the making of the disposition, and

(b) the duration of the minority or respective minorities of any person or persons in being at that date.

(2) It is hereby declared that the restrictions imposed by the said section 164 apply in relation to a power to accumulate income whether or not there is a duty to exercise that power, and that they apply whether or not the power to accumulate extends to income produced by the investment of income previously accumulated.

14 Right to stop accumulations.

Section 2 above shall apply to any question as to the right of beneficiaries to put an end to accumulations of income under any disposition as it applies to questions arising on the rule against perpetuities.

Supplemental

15 Short title, interpretation and extent.

(1) This Act may be cited as the Perpetuities and Accumulations Act 1964.

(2) In this Act—

(3) For the purposes of this Act a person shall be treated as a member of a class if in his case all the conditions identifying a member of the class are satisfied, and shall be treated as a potential member if in his case some only of those conditions are satisfied but there is a possibility that the remainder will in time be satisfied.

(4) Nothing in this Act shall affect the operation of the rule of law rendering void for remoteness certain dispositions under which property is limited to be applied for purposes other than the benefit of any person or class of persons in cases where the property may be so applied after the end of the perpetuity period.

(5) The foregoing sections of this Act shall apply (except as provided in section 8(2) above) only in relation to instruments taking effect after the commencement of this Act, and in the case of an instrument made in the exercise of a special power of appointment shall apply only where the instrument creating the power takes effect after that commencement:

(6) This Act shall apply in relation to a disposition made otherwise than by an instrument as if the disposition had been contained in an instrument taking effect when the disposition was made.

(7) This Act binds the Crown.

(8) Except in so far as the contrary intention appears, any enactment of the Parliament of Northern Ireland passed for purposes similar to the purposes of this Act shall bind the Crown.

(9) This Act shall not extend to Scotland or (apart from subsection (8) above) to Northern Ireland.

[1] The text of s. 11(2) is in the form in which it was originally enacted: it was not reproduced in Statutes in Force and does not reflect any amendments or repeals which may have been made prior to 1.2.1991.

Commons Registration Act 1965

1965 CHAPTER 64

An Act to provide for the registration of common land and of town or village greens; to amend the law as to prescriptive claims to rights of common; and for purposes connected therewith.

[5th August 1965]

1 Registration of commons and town or village greens and ownership of and rights over them.

(1) There shall be registered, in accordance with the provisions of this Act and subject to the exceptions mentioned therein,—

(a) land in England or Wales which is common land or a town or village green;

(b) rights of common over such land; and

(c) persons claiming to be or found to be owners of such land or becoming the owners thereof by virtue of this Act;

and no rights of common over land which is capable of being registered under this Act shall be registered under the Land Registration Acts 1925 and 1936.

(2) after the end of such period, not being less than three years from the commencement of this Act, as the Minister may by order determine—

(a) no land capable of being registered under this Act shall be deemed to be common land or a town or village green unless it is so registered; and

(b) no rights of common shall be exercisable over any such land unless they are registered either under this Act or under the Land Registration Acts 1925 and 1936.

(3) Where any land is registered under this Act but no person is registered as the owner thereof under this Act or under the Land Registration Acts 1925 and 1936, it shall—

(a) if it is a town or village green, be vested in accordance with the following provisions of this Act; and

(b) if it is common land, be vested as Parliament may hereafter determine.

2 Registration authorities.

(1) The registration authority for the purposes of this Act shall be—

(a) in relation to any land situated in any county . . . [1], the council of that county . . . [or, if the county is a metropolitan county, the council of the metropolitan district in which the land is situated][2];and

(b) in relation to any land situated in Greater London, the [council of the London borough in which the land is situated][3];

except where an agreement under this section otherwise provides.

(2) Where part of any land is in the area of one registration authority and part in that of another the authorities may by agreement provide for one of them to be the registration authority in relation to the whole of the land.

3 The registers.

(1) For the purpose of registering such land as is mentioned in section 1(1) of this Act and rights of common over and ownership of such land every registration authority shall maintain—

(a) a register of common land; and

(b) a register of town or village greens;

and regulations under this Act may require or authorise a registration authority to note on those registers such other information as may be prescribed.

(2) any register maintained under this Act shall be open to inspection by the public at all reasonable times.

4 Provisional registration.

(1) Subject to the provisions of this section, a registration authority shall register any land as common land or a town or village green or, as the case may be, any rights of common over or ownership of

such land, on application duly made to it and accompanied by such declaration and such other documents (if any) as may be prescribed for the purpose of verification or of proving compliance with any prescribed conditions.

(2) an application for the registration of any land as common land or as a town or village green may be made by any person, and a registration authority—

(a) may so register any land notwithstanding that no application for that registration has been made, and

(b) shall so register any land in any case where it registers any rights over it under this section.

(3) No person shall be registered under this section as the owner of any land which is registered under the Land Registration Acts 1925 and 1936 and no person shall be registered under this section as the owner of any other land unless the land itself is registered under this section.

(4) Where, in pursuance of an application under this section, any land would fall to be registered as common land or as a town or village green, but the land is already so registered, the registration authority shall not register it again but shall note the application in the register.

(5) A registration under this section shall be provisional only until it has become final under the following provisions of this Act.

(6) an application for registration under this section shall not be entertained if made after such date, not less than three years from the commencement of this Act, as the Minister may by order specify; and different dates may be so specified for different classes of applications.

(7) Every local authority shall take such steps as may be prescribed for informing the public of the period within which and the manner in which applications for registration under this section may be made.

5 Notification of, and objections to, registration.

(1) A registration authority shall give such notices and take such other steps as may be prescribed for informing the public of any registration made by it under section 4 of this Act, of the times and places where copies of the relevant entries in the register may be inspected and of the period during which and the manner in which objections to the registration may be made to the authority.

(2) The period during which objections to any registration under section 4 of this Act may be made shall be such period, ending not less than two years after the date of the registration, as may be prescribed.

(3) Where any land or rights over land are registered under section 4 of this Act but no person is so registered as the owner of the land the registration authority may, if it thinks fit, make an objection to the registration notwithstanding that it has no interest in the land.

(4) Where an objection to a registration under section 4 of this Act is made, the registration authority shall note the objection on the register and shall give such notice as may be prescribed to the person (if any) on whose application the registration was made and to any person whose application is noted under section 4(4) of this Act.

(5) Where a person to whom notice has been given under subsection (4) of this section so requests or where the registration was made otherwise than on the application of any person, the registration authority may, if it thinks fit, cancel or modify a registration to which objection is made under this section.

(6) Where such an objection is made, then, unless the objection is withdrawn or the registration cancelled before the end of such period as may be prescribed, the registration authority shall refer the matter to a Commons Commissioner.

(7) An objection to the registration of any land as common land or as a town or village green shall be treated for the purposes of this Act as being also an objection to any registration (whenever made) under section 4 of this Act of any rights over the land.

(8) A registration authority shall take such steps as may be prescribed for informing the public of any objection which they have noted on the register under this section and of the times and places where copies of the relevant entries in the register may be inspected.

(9) Where regulations under this Act require copies of any entries in a register to be sent by the registration authority to another local authority they may require that other authority to make the copies available for inspection in such manner as may be prescribed.

6 Disposal of disputed claims.

(1) The Commons Commissioner to whom any matter has been referred under section 5 of this Act shall inquire into it and shall either confirm the registration, with or without modifications, or refuse to confirm it; and the registration shall, if it is confirmed, become final, and, if the confirmation is refused, become void—

(a) if no appeal is brought against the confirmation or refusal, at the end of the period during which such an appeal could have been brought;

(b) if such an appeal is brought, when it is finally disposed of.

(2) On being informed in the prescribed manner that a registration has become final (with or without modifications) or has become void a registration authority shall indicate that fact in the prescribed manner in the register and, if it has become void, cancel the registration.

(3) Where the registration of any land as common land or as a town or village green is cancelled (whether under this section or under section 5(5) of this Act) the registration authority shall also cancel the registration of any person as the owner thereof.

7 Finality of undisputed registrations.

(1) If no objection is made to a registration under section 4 of this Act or if all objections made to such a registration are withdrawn the registration shall become final at the end of the period during which such objections could have been made under section 5 of this Act or, if an objection made during that period is withdrawn after the end thereof, at the date of the withdrawal.

(2) Where by virtue of this section a registration has become final the registration authority shall indicate that fact in the prescribed manner in the register.

8 Vesting of unclaimed land.

(1) Where the registration under section 4 of this Act of any land as common land or as a town or village green has become final but no person is registered under that section as the owner of the land, then, unless the land is registered under the Land Registration Acts 1925 and 1936, the registration authority shall refer the question of the ownership of the land to a Commons Commissioner.

(2) after the registration authority has given such notices as may be prescribed, the Commons Commissioner shall inquire into the matter and shall, if satisfied that any person is the owner of the land, direct the registration authority to register that person accordingly; and the registration authority shall comply with the direction.

(3) If the Commons Commissioner is not so satisfied and the land is a town or village green he shall direct the registration authority to register as the owner of the land the local authority specified in subsection (5) of this section; and the registration authority shall comply with the direction.

(4) On the registration under this section of a local authority as the owner of any land the land shall vest in that local authority and, if the land is not regulated by a scheme under the Commons Act 1899, section 10 and 15 of the Open Spaces Act 1906 (power to manage and make byelaws) shall apply in relation to it as if that local authority had acquired the ownership under the said Act of 1906.

[(5) Subject to subsection (6) of this section, the local authority in which any land is to be vested under this section is—

(a) if the land is in a parish or community where there is a parish or community council, that council, but, if the land is regulated by a scheme under the Commons Act 1899, only if the powers of management under Part I of that Act are, in accordance with arrangements under Part VI of the Local Government Act 1972, being exercised by the parish or community council;

(b) if the land is in a London borough, the council of that borough; and

(c) in any other case, the council of the district in which the land is situated.

(6) Where—

(a) any land has been vested in a district council in accordance with subsection (5)(c) of this section, and

(b) after the land has been so vested a parish or community council comes into being for the parish or community in which the land is situated (whether by the establishment of a new council or by adding that parish or community to a group of parishes or communities for which a council has already been established),

then, if the circumstances are such that, had the direction under subsection (3) of this section been given at a time after the parish or community council had come into being, the land would in

accordance with subsection (5)(a) of this section have been vested in the parish or community council, the district council shall, if requested to do so by the parish or community council, direct the registration authority to register the parish or community council, in place of the district council, as the owner of the land; and the registration authority shall comply with any such direction.

(7) The council of any district, parish or community affected by any registration made in pursuance of subsection (6) above shall pay to the other of those councils so affected such sum, if any, as may be agreed between them to be appropriate to take account of any sums received or to be received, or any expenditure incurred or to be incurred, in respect of the land concerned, and, in default of agreement, the question of what sum, if any, is appropriate for that purpose shall be determined by arbitration.][4]

9 Protection of unclaimed common land.

Where the registration under section 4 of this Act of any land as common land has become final but no person is registered under this Act or the Land Registration Acts 1925 and 1936 as the owner of the land, then, until the land is vested under any provision hereafter made by Parliament, any local authority in whose area the land or part of the land is situated may take such steps for the protection of the land against unlawful interference as could be taken by an owner in possession of the land, and may (without prejudice to any power exercisable apart from this section) institute proceedings for any offence committed in respect of the land.

10 Effect of registration.

The registration under this Act of any land as common land or as a town or village green, or of any rights of common over any such land, shall be conclusive evidence of the matters registered, as at the date of registration, except where the registration is provisional only.

11 Exemption from registration.

(1) The foregoing provisions of this Act shall not apply to the New Forest or Epping Forest nor to any land exempted from those provisions by an order of the Minister, and shall not be taken to apply to the Forest of Dean.

(2) The Minister shall not make an order under this section except on an application made to him before such date as may be prescribed.

(3) The Minister shall not make an order under this section with respect to any land unless it appears to him—

(a) that the land is regulated by a scheme under the Commons Act 1899 or the Metropolitan Commons Acts 1866 to 1898 or is regulated under a local Act or under an Act confirming a provisional order made under the Commons Act 1876; and

(b) that no rights of common have been exercised over the land for at least thirty years and that the owner of the land is known.

(4) The Minister shall, before dealing with any application under this section, send copies thereof to the registration authority and to such other local authorities as may be prescribed, and shall inform those authorities whether he has granted or refused the application; and those authorities shall take such steps as may be prescribed for informing the public of the application and its grant or refusal.

(5) If any question arises under this Act whether any land is part of the forests mentioned in subsection (1) of this section it shall be referred to and decided by the Minister.

12 Subsequent registration under Land Registration Act 1925 and 1936.

The following provisions shall have effect with respect to the registration under the Land Registration Acts 1925 and 1936 of any land after the ownership of the land has been registered under this Act, that is to say—

(a)..............................[5]

(b) if the registration authority is notified by the Chief Land Registrar that the land has been registered under the Land Registration Acts 1925 and 1936 the authority shall delete the registration of the ownership under this Act and indicate in the register in the prescribed manner that it has been registered under those Acts.

13 Amendment of registers.

Regulations under this Act shall provide for the amendment of the registers maintained under this Act where—

(a) any land registered under this Act ceases to be common land or a town or village green; or
(b) any land becomes common land or a town or village green; or
(c) any rights registered under this Act are apportioned, extinguished or released, or are varied or transferred in such circumstances as may be prescribed;

..................................[6]

14 Rectification of registers.

The High Court may order a register maintained under this Act to be amended if—

(a) the registration under this Act of any land or rights of common has become final and the court is satisfied that any person was induced by fraud to withdraw an objection to the registration or to refrain from making such an objection; or
(b) the register has been amended in pursuance of section 13 of this Act and it appears to the court that no amendment or a different amendment ought to have been made and that the error cannot be corrected in pursuance of regulations made under this Act;

and, in either case, the court deems it just to rectify the register.

15 Quantification of certain grazing rights.

(1) Where a right of common consists of or includes a right, not limited by number, to graze animals or animals of any class, it shall for the purposes of registration under this Act be treated as exercisable in relation to no more animals, or animals of that class, than a definite number.
(2) Any application for the registration of such a right shall state the number of animals to be entered in the register or, as the case may be, the numbers of animals of different classes to be so entered.
(3) When the registration of such a right has become final the right shall accordingly be exercisable in relation to animals not exceeding the number or numbers registered or such other number or numbers as Parliament may hereafter determine.

16 Disregard of certain interruptions in prescriptive claims to rights of common.

(1) Where during any period a right of common claimed over any land was not exercised, but during the whole or part of that period either—
  (a) the land was requisitioned; or
  (b) where the right claimed is a right to graze animals, the right could not be or was not exercised for reasons of animal health;

  that period or part shall be left out of account, both—
    (i) in determining for the purposes of the Prescription Act 1832 whether there was an interruption within the meaning of that Act of the actual enjoyment of the right; and
    (ii) in computing the period of thirty or sixty years mentioned in section 1 of that Act.
(2) For the purposes of the said Act any objection under this Act to the registration of a right of common shall be deemed to be such a suit or action as is referred to in section 4 of that Act.
(3) In this section "requisitioned" means in the possession of a Government department in the exercise or purported exercise of powers conferred by regulations made under the Emergency Powers (Defence) Act 1939 or by Part VI of the Requisitioned Land and War Works Act 1945; and in determining in any proceedings any question arising under this section whether any land was requisitioned during any period a document purporting to be a certificate to that effect issued by a Government department shall be admissible in evidence.
(4) Where it is necessary for the purposes of this section to establish that a right to graze animals on any land could not be or was not exercised for reasons of animal health it shall be sufficient to prove either—
  (a) that the movement of the animals to that land was prohibited or restricted by or under the Diseases of Animals Act 1950 or any enactment repealed by that Act; or
  (b) that the land was not, but some other land was, approved for grazing under any scheme in force under that Act or any such enactment and the animals were registered, or were undergoing tests with a view to registration, under the scheme.

17 Commons Commissioners and assessors.

(1) The Lord Chancellor shall—
  (a) appoint to be Commons Commissioners such number of [persons who have a 7 year general qualification, within the meaning of section 71 of the Courts and Legal Services Act 1990,][7] as he

may determine; and

(b) draw up and from time to time revise a panel of assessors to assist the Commons Commissioners in dealing with cases calling for special knowledge;

and shall appoint one of the Commons Commissioners to be Chief Commons Commissioner.

[(1A) a Commons Commissioner shall vacate his office on the day on which he attains the age of seventy years; but this subsection is subject to section 26(4) to (6) of the Judicial Pensions and Retirement Act 1993 (power of Lord Chancellor to authorise continuance in office up to the age of seventy-five years).][8]

(2) Any matter referred under this Act to a Commons Commissioner shall be dealt with by such one of the Commissioners as the Chief Commons Commissioner may determine, and that Commissioner may sit with an assessor selected by the Chief Commons Commissioner from the panel appointed under this section.

(3) If at any time the Chief Commons Commissioner is for any reason unable to act, the Lord Chancellor may appoint another Commons Commissioner to act in his stead.

(4) A Commons Commissioner may order any party to any proceedings before him to pay to any other party to the proceedings any costs incurred by that party in respect of the proceedings; and any costs so awarded shall be taxed in the county court according to such of the scales prescribed by county court rules for proceedings in the county court as may be directed by the order, but subject to any modifications specified in the direction, or, if the order gives no direction, by the county court, and shall be recoverable in like manner as costs awarded in the county court.

(5) The Minister shall pay to the Commons Commissioners and assessors appointed under this section such fees and such travelling and other allowances as the Minister may, with the approval of [the Minister for the Civil Service][9], determine, and shall provide the Commons Commissioners with such services and facilities as appear to him required for the discharge of their functions.

18 Appeals from Commons Commissioners.

(1) Any person aggrieved by the decision of a Commons Commissioner as being erroneous in point of law may, within such time as may be limited by rules of court, require the Commissioner to state a case for the decision of the High Court.

(2) So much of section 63(1) of the Supreme Court of Judicature (Consolidation) Act 1925 as requires appeals to the High Court to be heard and determined by a Divisional Court shall not apply to an appeal by way of case stated under this section, but no appeal to the Court of Appeal shall be brought against the decision of the High Court in such a case except with the leave of that Court or the Court of Appeal.

19 Regulations.

(1) The Minister may make regulations—

(a) for prescribing the form of the registers to be maintained under this Act and of any applications and objections to be made and notices and certificates to be given thereunder;

(b) for regulating the procedure of registration authorities in dealing with applications for registration and with objections;

(c) for prescribing the steps to be taken by registration authorities for the information of other local authorities and of the public in cases where registrations are cancelled or modified;

(d) for requiring registration authorities to supply by post, on payment of such fee as may be prescribed, such information relating to the entries in the registers kept by them as may be prescribed;

(e) for regulating the procedure of the Commons Commissioners and, in particular, for providing for the summoning of persons to attend and give evidence and produce documents and for authorising the administration of oaths, and for enabling any inquiry or proceedings begun by or before one Commons Commissioner to be continued by or before another;

(f) for enabling an application for the registration of rights of common attached to any land to be made either by the landlord or by the tenant and for regulating the procedure where such an application is made by both;

(g) for enabling the Church Commissioners to act with respect to any land or rights belonging to an ecclesiastical benefice of the Church of England which is vacant;

(h) for treating any registration conflicting with another registration as an objection to the other

registration;

(i) for requiring, before applications for registration are entertained, the taking of such steps as may be specified in the regulations for the information of persons having interests in any land affected by the registration;

(j) for the correction of errors and omissions in the registers;

(k) for prescribing anything required or authorised to be prescribed by this Act.

(2) The regulations may make provision for the preparation of maps to accompany applications for registration and the preparation, as part of the registers, of maps showing any land registered therein and any land to which rights of common registered therein are attached, and for requiring registration authorities to deposit copies of such maps with such Government departments and other authorities as may be prescribed.

(3) The regulations may prescribe the payment of a fee not exceeding five pounds on an application made after the end of such period as may be specified in the regulations.

(4) The regulation may make different provision with respect to different circumstances.

(5) Regulations under this Act shall be made by statutory instrument which shall be subject to annulment in pursuance of a resolution of either House of Parliament.

20 Orders.

(1) Any order made by the Minister under any provision of this Act may be varied or revoked by subsequent order made thereunder.

(2) Any such order, other than an order made under section 11 of this Act, shall be made by statutory instrument.

(3) Any statutory instrument made under this section shall be subject to annulment in pursuance of a resolution of either House of Parliament.

21 Savings.

(1) Section 1(2) of this Act shall not affect the application to any land registered under this Act of section 193 or section 194 of the Law of Property Act 1925 (rights of access to, and restriction on inclosure of, land over which rights of common are exercisable).

(2) Section 10 of this Act shall not apply for the purpose of deciding whether any land forms part of a highway.

22 Interpretation.

(1) In this Act, unless the context otherwise requires, "common land" means—

(a) land subject to rights of common (as defined in this Act) whether those rights are exercisable at all times or only during limited periods;

(b) waste land of a manor not subject to rights of common;

but does not include a town or village green or any land which forms part of a highway;

"land" includes land covered with water;

"local authority" means . . .[10] the council of a county, .[11], London borough or county district, the council of a parish . . . ;

"the Minister" means the [Secretary of State][12];

"prescribed" means prescribed by regulations under this Act;

"registration" includes an entry in the register made in pursuance of section 13 of this Act;

"rights of common" includes cattlegates of beastgates (by whatever name known) and rights of sole or several vesture or herbage or of sole or several pasture, but does not include rights held for a term of years or from year to year;

"town or village green" means land which has been allotted by or under any Act for the exercise or recreation of the inhabitants of any locality or on which the inhabitants of any locality have a customary right to indulge in lawful sports and pastimes [or which falls within subsection (1A) of this section][13].

[(1A) Land falls within this subsection if it is land on which for not less than twenty years a significant number of the inhabitants of any locality, or of any neighbourhood within a locality, have indulged in lawful sports and pastimes as of right, and either—

(a) continue to do so, or

(b) have ceased to do so for not more than such period as may be prescribed, or determined in accordance with prescribed provisions.

(1B) If regulations made for the purposes of paragraph (b) of subsection (1A) of this section provide for the period mentioned in that paragraph to come to an end unless prescribed steps are taken, the regulations may also require registration authorities to make available in accordance with the regulations, on payment of any prescribed fee, information relating to the taking of any such steps.][14]

(2) References in this Act to the ownership and the owner of any land are references to the ownership of a legal estate in fee simple in any land and to the person holding that estate, and references to land registered under the Land Registration Acts 1925 and 1936 are references to land the fee simple of which is so registered.

23 Application to Crown.

(1) This Act shall apply in relation to land in which there is a Crown or Duchy interest as it applies in relation to land in which there is no interest.

(2) In this section "Crown or Duchy interest" means an interest belonging to Her Majesty in right of the Crown or of the Duchy of Lancaster, or belonging to the Duchy of Cornwall, or belonging to a Government department, or held in trust for Her Majesty for the purposes of a Government department.

24 Expenses.

There shall be defrayed out of moneys provided by Parliament any expenses of the Minister under this Act and any increase attributable to this Act in the sums payable under any other Act out of moneys so provided.

25 Short title, commencement and extent.

(1) This Act may be cited as the Commons Registration Act 1965.

(2) This Act shall come into force on such day as the Minister may by order appoint, and different days may be so appointed for different purposes; and any reference in any provision to the commencement of this Act is a reference to the date on which that provision comes into force.

(3) This Act does not extend to Scotland or to Northern Ireland.

---

[1] Words repealed by Local Government Act 1972 (c. 70), Sch. 30

[2] Words inserted by Local Government Act 1985 (c. 51, SIF 81:1), s. 16, Sch. 8 para. 10(6)(a)

[3] Words substituted by Local Government Act 1985 (c. 51, SIF 81:1), s. 16, Sch. 8 para. 10(6)(b)

[4] S. 8(5)-(7) substituted by Local Government Act 1972 (c. 70), s. 189(2)

[5] S. 12(a) repealed (1.4.1998) by 1997 c. 2, s. 4(2), Sch. 2 Pt. I; S.I. 1997/3036, art. 2(c)

[6] Words repealed by Law of Property Act 1969 (c. 59), s. 16(2), Sch. 2 Pt. I as regards the Yorkshire deeds registries, their registers and areas

[7] Words substituted by Courts and Legal Services Act 1990 (c. 41, SIF 37), s. 71(2), Sch. 10 para. 26

[8] S. 17(1A) inserted (31.3.1995) by 1993 c. 8, s. 26, Sch. 6 para. 26 (with Sch. 7 paras. 2(2), 3(2), 4); S.I. 1995/631, art. 2

[9] Words substituted by virtue of S.I. 1968/1656

[10] Words repealed by Local Government Act 1985 (c. 51, SIF 81:1), s. 102, Sch. 17

[11] Words repealed by Local Government Act 1972 (c. 70), Sch. 30

[12] Words substituted by virtue of S.I. 1967/156 and 1970/1681

[13] S. 22(1): Words in definition substituted (30.1.2001) by 2000 c. 37, ss. 98(2), 103(2)

[14] S. 22(1A)(1B) inserted (30.1.2001) by 2000 c. 37, ss. 98(3), 103(2)

Industrial and Provident Societies Act 1965

1965 CHAPTER 12

An Act to consolidate certain enactments relating to industrial and provident societies, being those enactments as they apply in Great Britain and the Channel Islands with corrections and improvements made under the Consolidation of Enactments (Procedure) Act 1949.

[2nd June 1965]

Registered societies

1 Societies which may be registered.

(1) Subject to sections 2(1) and 7(1) of this Act, a society for carrying on any industry, business or trade (including dealings of any description with land), whether wholesale or retail, may be registered under this Act if—

(a) it is shown to the satisfaction of [the Authority][1] that one of the conditions specified in subsection

(2) of this section is fulfilled; and

(b) the society's rules contain provision in respect of the matters mentioned in Schedule 1 to this Act; and

(c) the place which under those rules is to be the society's registered office is situated in Great Britain or the Channel Islands.

(2) The conditions referred to in subsection (1)(a) of this section are—

(a) that the society is a bona fide co-operative society; or

(b) that, in view of the fact that the business of the society is being, or is intended to be, conducted for the benefit of the community, there are special reasons why the society should be registered under this Act rather than as a company under the [Companies Act 1985][2].

(3) In this section, the expression "co-operative society" does not include a society which carries on, or intends to carry on, business with the object of making profits mainly for the payment of interest, dividends or bonuses on money invested or deposited with, or lent to, the society or any other person.

2 Registration of society.

(1) Subject to subsection (2) of this section—

(a) no society shall be registered under this Act if the number of the members thereof is less than [three][3]; and

(b) an application for the registration of a society under this Act shall be signed by [three][4] members and the secretary of the society and shall be sent with two printed copies of the society's rules to [the Authority][5].

(2) A society whose members consist solely of two or more registered societies may be registered under this Act if the application for registration is signed by[6]. . the secretary of each [(or, if more than two, of each of any two)][7] of the constituent societies and is accompanied by two printed copies. . of the rules of the society sought to be registered.

(3) On being satisfied that a society has complied with the provisions of this Act as to registration thereunder, [the Authority][8] shall issue to the society an acknowledgment of registration [bearing the Authority's seal][9]

3 Registration to effect incorporation of society with limited liability.

A registered society shall by virtue of its registration be a body corporate by its registered name, by which it may sue and be sued, with perpetual succession and a common seal and with limited liability; and that registration shall vest in the society all property for the time being vested in any person in trust for the society, and all legal proceedings pending by or against the trustees of the society may be brought or continued by or against the society in its registered name.

4 Existing societies deemed to be registered.

Any society which at the date immediately before the commencement of this Act was registered or deemed to be registered under the Industrial and Provident Societies Act 1893 (hereafter in this Act referred to as "the Act of 1893"), being a society whose registered office was at that date in Great Britain or the Channel Islands, shall be deemed to be registered under this Act; and—

(a) any acknowledgment of registry of that society issued by virtue of section 5(4), 6 or 7(2) of the Act of 1893 shall be deemed to be an acknowledgment of the registration under this Act of that society and, by virtue of section 9 of this Act, of the rules of the society in force at the date of the acknowledgment;

(b) any acknowledgment of registry of an amendment of the society's rules issued by virtue of section 7(2) or 10(3) of the Act of 1893 shall be deemed to be an acknowledgment of the registration of that amendment under this Act;

(c) any change of the society's name duly made before the date of commencement of this Act in accordance with section 52 of the Act of 1893 as in force at the time of the change, and any change in the situation of the society's registered office of which notice was duly given before that date under section 11 of that Act, shall be deemed for the purposes of this Act to be a duly registered amendment of the society's rules;

(d) any rules of that society which, having been made before 1st January 1894, continued in force immediately before the commencement of this Act by virtue of section 3 of the Act of 1893 shall be deemed to be registered under this Act.

Name and maximum shareholding

5 Name of society.

(1) No society shall be registered under this Act under a name which in the opinion of [the Authority][10] is undesirable.

(2) Subject to subsection (5) of this section, [the last word in the name of every society registered under this Act shall be "limited" or, if the rules of the society state that its registered office is to be in Wales, either that word or the word "cyfyngedig"][11].

(3) A registered society may change its name in the following manner and in that manner only, that is to say—

(a) by a resolution for the purpose passed at a general meeting of the society after the giving of such notice as is required by the rules of the society of such a resolution or, if the rules do not make special provision as to notice of such a resolution, after the giving of such notice as is required by the rules of a resolution to amend the rules; and

(b) with the approval in writing [of the Authority][12].

(4) No change in the name of a registered society shall affect any right or obligation of the society, or of any member thereof, and any pending legal proceedings may be continued by or against the society notwithstanding its new name.

(5) If [the authority][13]is satisfied that the objects of a society applying for registration under this Act or of a registered society are wholly charitable or benevolent, [the Authority][14] may register the society by a name which does not contain the word "limited"[or the word "cyfyngedig"][15]or, as the case may be, permit the society to change its name to one which does not contain [either of those words][16]; but if it subsequently appears to [the Authority][17] that the society, whether in consequence of a change in its rules or otherwise, is not being conducted wholly for charitable or benevolent objects, [the Authority][18] may direct that the word "limited"[, or in an appropriate case the word "cyfyngedig",][19]be added as the last word in the name of the society and shall notify the society accordingly.

(6) Every registered society shall cause its registered name to be painted or affixed, and to be kept painted or affixed, in a conspicuous position and in letters easily legible, on the outside of its registered office and every other office or place in which the business of the society is carried on, and shall have that name engraven in legible characters on its seal and mentioned in legible characters—

(a) in all notices, advertisements and other official publications of the society;

(b) in all business letters of the society;

(c) in all bills of exchange, promissory notes, endorsements, cheques, and orders for money or goods, purporting to be signed by or on behalf of the society;

(d) in all bills, invoices, receipts, and letters of credit of the society.

(7) Any officer of a registered society, or any other person acting on such a society's behalf, who—

(a) uses any seal purporting to be a seal of the society which does not have the society's registered name engraven on it in legible characters; or

(b) issues or authorises the issue of any document such as is mentioned in subsection (6)(a) or (d) of this section in which that name is not mentioned in legible characters; or

(c) signs or authorises to be signed on behalf of the society any document such as is mentioned in subsection (6)(c) of this section in which that name is not so mentioned,

shall be liable on summary conviction to a fine not exceeding [level 3 on the standard scale][20] and, in the case of a conviction by virtue of paragraph (c) of this subsection, shall further be personally liable to the holder of any such document as is referred to in that paragraph for the amount specified in the document unless that amount is duly paid by the society.

6 Maximum shareholding in society.

(1) Where a society is, or is to be, registered under this Act, no member thereof other than—

(a) a registered society; or

(b) an authority who acquired the holding by virtue of [section [58][21]or 59(2) of the Housing Associations Act 1985 [or section 22 of the Housing Act 1996][22]][23] ;or

(c) a member who acquired the holding by virtue of paragraph 2 of Part I of the Schedule to the Agricultural Credits Act 1923 at a time when section 2 of that Act applied to the society,

shall have or claim any interest in the shares of the society exceeding [twenty thousand pounds][24]

(2) Where in the case of a society to which section 4 of this Act applies—

(a) immediately before 27th April 1952 the rules of the society provided for the maximum amount of the interest in the shares of the society permitted to be held by a member (other than a registered society) to be two hundred pounds; and

(b) no amendment of the rules of the society has been registered since that date; and

(c) on or after that date and before 22nd July 1961 the society's committee has by a resolution recorded in writing resolved that the said maximum amount shall be a specified amount greater than two hundred pounds but not greater than five hundred pounds,

then, subject to subsection (4) of this section, the registered rules of the society shall have effect subject to that resolution.

(3) Where in the case of a society to which section 4 of this Act applies—

(a) immediately before 22nd July 1961 the rules of the society provided for the maximum amount aforesaid to be five hundred pounds; and

(b) no amendment of the society's rules has been registered since that date; and

(c) on or after that date and before 22nd January 1963 the society's committee has by a resolution recorded in writing resolved that the said maximum amount shall be a specified amount greater than five hundred pounds but not greater than one thousand pounds,

then, subject to subsection (4) of this section, the registered rules of the society shall have effect subject to that resolution.

(4) Where subsection (2) or (3) of this section applies to any society, the society's committee shall not have power to vary or revoke the resolution referred to in that subsection; but upon the registration after the commencement of this Act under section 10 thereof of any amendment of the society's rules the registered rules of the society shall have effect as if the resolution had not been passed, so, however, that this subsection shall not affect any interest in the shares of the society held by a member immediately before the date of that registration.

Operations of registered society

7 Carrying on of banking by societies.

(1) A society which has any withdrawable share capital—

(a) shall not be registered with the object of carrying on, and

(b) if a registered society shall not carry on,

the business of banking.

(2) Every registered society which carries on the business of banking shall on the first Monday in February and August in each year make out, and until the next such Monday keep hung up in a conspicuous position in its registered office and in every other office or place of business belonging to the society where the business of banking is carried on, a statement in the form set out in Schedule 2 to this Act or as near thereto as the circumstances admit.

(3) The taking of deposits of not more than [four hundred pounds][25] in any one payment and not more than [four hundred pounds][26] for any one depositor, payable on not less than two clear days' notice, shall not be treated for the purposes of subsections (1) and (2) of this section as carrying on the business of banking; but no society which takes such deposits shall make any payment of withdrawable capital while any payment due on account of any such deposit is unsatisfied.

(4) Where, in the case of a society to which section 4 of this Act applies, being a society registered under the Act of 1893 before 27th April 1952—

(a) no amendment of the society's registered rules has been registered since that date; and

(b) those rules permit the taking of deposits up to, but not in excess of, ten shillings in any one payment and twenty pounds for any one depositor; and

(c) the society's committee has since that date by a resolution recorded in writing, whether passed before or after the commencement of this Act, resolved that there shall be substituted for the said limits of ten shillings and twenty pounds specified higher limits not exceeding two pounds and fifty pounds respectively,

then, subject to subsection (5) of this section, the society's registered rules shall have effect subject to that resolution.

(5) Where subsection (4) of this section applies to any society, the society's committee shall not have power to vary or revoke any resolution such as is mentioned in paragraph (c) of that subsection; but

upon the registration after the commencement of this Act under section 10 thereof of any amendment of the rules of the society—

(a) the registered rules of the society shall have effect as if any such resolution had not been passed; and

(b) if not already exercised, the power of the society's committee to pass such a resolution shall determine,

so, however, that paragraph (a) of this subsection shall not affect any sums standing deposited with the society immediately before the date of registration of the amendment.

(6) Any registered society which—

(a) carries on the business of banking in contravention of subsection (1) of this section; or

(b) fails to comply with subsection (2) of this section; or

(c) makes any payment of withdrawable capital in contravention of subsection (3) of this section,

shall be liable on summary conviction to a fine not exceeding [level 1 on the standard scale][27].

8. . . .[28]

Provisions as to rules

9 Acknowledgment of registration of rules.

Without prejudice to section 53(3) of this Act, an acknowledgment of the registration of a society issued under section 2(3) of this Act shall also constitute an acknowledgment, and be conclusive evidence, of the registration under this Act of the rules of that society in force at the date of the society's registration.

10 Amendment of registered rules.

(1) Subject to subsection (2) of this section, any amendment of a society's rules as for the time being registered under this Act shall not be valid until the amendment has been so registered, for which purpose there shall be sent to [the Authority][29] two copies of the amendment signed—

(a) in the case of a society for the time being consisting solely of registered societies, by the secretary of the society and by[30] the secretary of each [(or, if more than two, of each of any two)][31] of the constituent societies;

(b) in any other case, by three members and the secretary of the society.

(2) The foregoing subsection shall not apply to a change in the situation of a society's registered office or in the name of a society; but—

(a) notice of any change in the situation of a society's registered office shall be sent to [the Authority][32]; and

(b) where such a notice is duly sent, or where a change in the name of a registered society is made in accordance with section 5(3) of this Act, the change in the situation of the society's registered office or, as the case may be, the change in the society's name shall be registered by [the Authority][33] as an amendment of the society's rules.

(3) [The Authority][34], on being satisfied that any amendment of a society's rules is not contrary to the provisions of this Act, shall issue to the society in respect of that amendment an acknowledgment of registration [bearing the Authority's seal][35]

11 Rules as to fund for purchase of government securities.

(1) The rules of a society registered or to be registered under this Act may make provision for the setting up and administration by the society of a fund for the purchase on behalf of members contributing to the fund of defence bonds or national saving certificates or such other securities of Her Majesty's Government in the United Kingdom as may for the time being be prescribed under [section 47(1) of the Friendly Societies Act 1974][36] by the [Treasury][37]; and any such rules may make provision for enabling persons to become members of the society for the purpose only of contributing to that fund and without being entitled to any rights as members other than rights as contributors to that fund.

(2) Any rule which, immediately before the commencement of this Act, was included among the registered rules of a registered society by virtue of section 8(3) of the [Societies (Miscellaneous Provisions) Act 1940][38] shall have effect as if it had been duly passed by the society.

12 Rules of agricultural, horticultural or forestry society.

Where a society registered or to be registered under this Act consists mainly of members who are producers of agricultural or horticultural produce or persons engaged in forestry, or organisations of

such producers or persons so engaged, and the object or principal object of the society is the making to its members of advances of money for agricultural, horticultural or forestry purposes, registration under this Act of the rules of the society or any amendment thereof shall not be refused on the ground that the rules provide, or would as amended provide, for the making of such advances without security.

13 Supplementary provisions as to rules.

(1) The rules of a registered society or any schedule thereto may specify the form of any instrument necessary for carrying the purposes of the society into effect.

(2) The rules of a registered society may impose reasonable fines on persons who contravene or fail to comply with any of those rules.

(3) Any fine imposed by the rules of a registered society shall be recoverable on the summary conviction of the offender.

(4) Any provision of, or of any instrument made under, this or any other Act requiring or authorising the rules of a registered society to deal with particular matters shall be without prejudice to the power of such a society to make rules with respect to any other matter which are not inconsistent with any such provision or with any other provision of this or any other Act and which are not otherwise unlawful.

14 Rules to bind members.

(1) Subject to subsections (2) and (3) of this section, the registered rules of a registered society shall bind the society and all members thereof and all persons claiming through them respectively to the same extent as if each member had subscribed his name and affixed his seal thereto and there were contained in those rules a covenant on the part of each member and any person claiming through him to conform thereto subject to the provisions of this Act.

(2) A member of a registered society shall not, without his consent in writing having been first obtained, be bound by any amendment of the society's rules registered after he became a member, being an amendment registered after 27th March 1928, if and so far as that amendment requires him to take or subscribe for more shares than the number held by him at the date of registration of the amendment, or to pay upon the shares so held any sum exceeding the amount unpaid upon them at that date, or in any other way increases the liability of that member to contribute to the share or loan capital of the society.

(3) In the case of a society to which section 4 of this Act applies which was a registered society under the Act of 1893 on 1st January 1894, the society or the members thereof may respectively exercise any power given by this Act and not made to depend on the provisions of the society's rules notwithstanding anything in any of those rules registered before 12th September 1893.

(4) In its application to Scotland, subsection (1) of this section shall have effect as if the words "and affixed his seal" were omitted.

15 Provision of copies of rules.

(1) A copy of the registered rules of any registered society shall be delivered by the society to any person who demands it, subject to payment by that person of such sum not exceeding two shillings as the society may see fit to charge.

(2) If any person, with intent to mislead or defraud, gives to any other person—

(a) a copy of any rules other than rules for the time being registered under this Act on the pretence that they are the existing rules, or that there are no other rules, of a registered society; or

(b) a copy of the rules of a society which is not registered under this Act on the pretence that they are the rules of a registered society,

he shall be liable on summary conviction to a fine not exceeding [level 1 on the standard scale][39].

Cancellation, suspension or refusal of registration of society or rules

16 Cancellation of registration of society.

(1) Subject to the provisions of this section and sections 18(1)(c) and 59 of this Act, and without prejudice to section 52(4) thereof, [the Authority][40] may,[41], in writing, cancel the registration of any registered society—

(a) if at any time it is proved to [the Authority's][42] satisfaction—

(i) that the number of members of the society has been reduced, in the case of a society for the time being consisting solely of registered societies, to less than two or, in any other

case, to less than [three][43]; or

(ii) that an acknowledgment of registration has been obtained by fraud or mistake; or

(iii) that the society has ceased to exist;

(b) if [the Authority][44] thinks fit, at the request of the society, to be evidenced in such manner as [the Authority][45] shall from time to time direct;

(c) . .[46]

(i) on proof to [the Authority's][47] satisfaction that the society exists for an illegal purpose, or has wilfully and after notice from [the Authority][48] violated any of the provisions of this Act or any enactment repealed thereby; or

(ii) if at any time it appears to [the Authority][49] that neither of the conditions specified in section 1(2) of this Act is fulfilled in the case of that society; or

(iii) in the case of a society whose registered rules contain such a provision as is authorised by section 12 of this Act, if it appears to [the Authority][50] that the society no longer consists mainly of such members as are mentioned in that section or that the activities carried on by it do not mainly consist in making advances to its members for such purposes as are so mentioned.

(2) Subsection (1)(c)(ii) of this section shall not authorise the cancellation of the registration of any society to which section 4 of this Act applies which was registered or deemed to be registered under the Act of 1893 before 26th July 1938 if no invitation to subscribe for or to acquire or offer to acquire securities, or to lend or deposit money, has been made on or after that date by or on behalf of the society.

(3) Not less than two months previous notice in writing specifying briefly the ground of the proposed cancellation shall be given by the [the Authority][51] to a society before its registration is cancelled otherwise than—

(a) at its own request; or

(b) by virtue of section 52(4) of this Act; or

(c) after the lodging with [the Authority][52] of such a certificate as is referred to in section 59 of this Act;

and if before the expiration of the period of that notice the society duly lodges an appeal under section 18(1)(c) of this Act, then, without prejudice to section 17(2) of this Act, the society's registration shall not be cancelled before the date of the determination or abandonment of the appeal.

(4) Where the ground specified in any notice under subsection (3) of this section is that referred to in subsection (1)(c)(ii) thereof—

(a) [the Authority][53] shall consider any representations with respect to the proposed cancellation made to [the Authority][54] by the society within the period of duration of the notice and, if the society so requests, afford it an opportunity of being heard by [the Authority][55] before its registration is cancelled;

(b) if it appears to [the Authority][56] at any time after the expiration of one month from the date of the giving of the notice that there have not been taken the steps which by that time could reasonably have been taken for the purpose—

(i) of converting the society into, or amalgamating it with, or transferring its engagements to, a company in accordance with section 52 of this Act; or

(ii) of dissolving the society under section 55 of this Act,

[the Authority][57] may give such directions as [it][58] thinks fit for securing that the affairs of the society are wound up before cancellation of the registration takes effect.

(5) Any person who contravenes or fails to comply with any directions given by [and Authority][59] under subsection (4)(b) of this section shall be liable on summary conviction to a fine not exceeding [level 3 on the standard scale][60] or to imprisonment for a term not exceeding three months or to both.

(6) Notice of every cancellation under this section of a society's registration shall, as soon as practicable after it takes place, be published in the Gazette and in some local newspaper circulating in or about the locality in which the society's registered office is situated.

(7) As from the date of the publication in the Gazette under subsection (6) of this section of notice of the cancellation of a society's registration, the society shall absolutely cease to be entitled to any of the

privileges of this Act as a registered society, but without prejudice to any liability actually incurred by the society which may be enforced against it as if the cancellation had not taken place.

17 Suspension of registration of society.

(1) Where under section 16(1)(c) of this Act [the Authority][61] might . .[62] cancel the registration of a registered society, [the Authority][63] may, by [notice in writing][64]—

(a) subject to subsection (3) of this section, suspend the registration of that society for any term not exceeding three months; and

(b) . . [65] subject to section 18(1)(d) of this Act, from time to time renew any such suspension for the like period.

(2) Where before the expiration of the period of a notice under section 16(3) of this Act of the proposed cancellation of a society's registration, that society duly lodges an appeal from the proposed cancellation under section 18(1)(c) of this Act, [the Authority][66] may by [notice in writing][67] suspend the society's registration from the expiration of that period until the date of the determination or abandonment of the appeal.

(3) Not less than two months previous notice in writing specifying briefly the ground of the proposed suspension shall be given by [the Authority][68] to a society before its registration is suspended under subsection (1)(a) of this section.

(4) Notice of every suspension of a society's registration under subsection (1)(a) or (2) of this section and of any renewal of a suspension under subsection (1)(b) thereof shall, as soon as practicable after it takes place, be published in the Gazette and in some local newspaper circulating in or about the locality in which the society's registered office is situated.

(5) From the date of publication in the Gazette of a notice under subsection (4) of this section of the suspension of any society's registration under subsection (1)(a) or (2) of this section until the period of that suspension and any renewal thereof under subsection (1)(b) of this section ends (whether on the expiration of that period or on a successful appeal under section 18(1)(d) of this Act from such a renewal) the society shall not be entitled to any of the privileges of this Act as a registered society, but without prejudice to any liability actually incurred by the society which may be enforced against it as if the suspension had not taken place.

(6). . . . . [69]

18 Appeal from refusal, cancellation or suspension of registration of society or rules.

(1) A society may appeal from any decision of [the Authority][70]—

(a) to refuse registration of the society (including a refusal by reason only of anything contained in or omitted from the society's rules) on any ground other than that [the Authority][71] is not satisfied that either of the conditions specified in section 1(2) of this Act is fulfilled; or

(b) to refuse registration of any amendment of the society's rules; or

(c) to cancel the society's registration (being a cancellation of which notice is required under section 16(3), and not being a cancellation by virtue of section 16(1)(c)(ii), of this Act) if the appeal is lodged before the expiration of the period of notice of the proposed cancellation given under the said section 16(3); or

(d) to renew under section 17(1)(b) of this Act a suspension of the society's registration so far as that renewal provides for the suspension to continue more than three months from the original date of suspension.

(2) An appeal under the foregoing subsection shall lie [to the High Court or, in the case of a society whose registered office is situated in Scotland, to the Court of Session][72]

(3) If any decision such as is mentioned in subsection (1)(a) or (b) of this section is overruled on appeal, [the Authority][73] shall thereupon issue to the society an acknowledgment of registration of the society under section 2(3), or, as the case may be, of the amendment under section 10(3), of this Act.

Membership and special provisions affecting members

19 Bodies corporate as members of society.

(1) Shares in a registered society may be held by any other body corporate (if that body's regulations so permit) by its corporate name.

(2) Where a registered society is a member of another registered society, then, for the purposes of any enactment with respect to the making or signing of any application, instrument or document by

members of a registered society, any reference therein to such a member shall, in relation to the first-mentioned society as a member of the second-mentioned society, be construed as a reference to two members of the committee and the secretary of the society.

20 Members under 21.

A person under the age of [eighteen][74] but above the age of sixteen may be a member of a registered society unless provision to the contrary is made by the society's registered rules and may, subject to those rules and to the provisions of this Act, enjoy all the rights of a member and execute all instruments and give all receipts necessary to be executed or given under those rules, but shall not be a member of the committee, trustee, manager or treasurer of the society.

21 Advances to members.

Without prejudice to any provision included by virtue of section 12 of this Act, the rules of a registered society may provide for advances of money to members—

(a) on the security of real or personal property or, in Scotland, of heritable or moveable estate; or

(b) if the society is registered to carry on banking business, in any manner customary in the conduct of such business.

22 Remedy for debts from members.

(1) All moneys payable to a registered society by a member thereof shall be a debt due from that member to the society and shall be recoverable as such in the county court, or, in Scotland, before the sheriff, within whose jurisdiction the society's registered office is situate or within whose jurisdiction the member resides, at the option of the society.

(2) A registered society shall have a lien on the shares of any member for any debt due to the society by that member, and may set off any sum credited to the member on those shares in or towards the payment of that debt.

23 Nomination to property in society.

(1) Subject to subsections (2) and (3) of this section, a member of a registered society may, by a written statement signed by him and delivered at or sent to the society's registered office during his lifetime or made in any book kept at that office, nominate a person or persons to become entitled at his death to the whole, or to such part or respective parts as may be specified in the nomination, of any property in the society (whether in shares, loans or deposits or otherwise) which he may have—

(a) in the case of a nomination made before 1st January 1914, at the date of the nomination; or

(b) in any other case, at the time of his death.

(2) The nomination by a member of a society under the foregoing subsection of a person who is at the date of the nomination an officer or servant of the society shall not be valid unless that person is the husband, wife, father, mother, child, brother, sister, nephew or niece of the nominator.

(3) For the purposes of the disposal of any property which is the subject of a nomination under subsection (1) of this section—

(a) if the nomination was made before 1st January 1914 and at the date of the nomination the amount credited to the nominator in the society's books exceeded one hundred pounds, the nomination shall not be valid;

(b) if the nomination was made after 31st December 1913 and before 5th August 1954 and at the date of the nominator's death the amount of his property in the society comprised in the nomination exceeds one hundred pounds, the nomination shall be valid to the extent of one hundred pounds but not further or otherwise;

(c) if the nomination was made after 4th August 1954 and at the date of the nominator's death the amount of his property in the society comprised in the nomination exceeds [£1,500][75], the nomination shall be valid to the extent of [£1,500][76], but not further or otherwise.

(4) A nomination by a member of a society under subsection (1) of this section may be varied or revoked by a subsequent nomination by him thereunder or by any similar document in the nature of a revocation or variation signed by the nominator and delivered at or sent to the society's registered office during his lifetime, but shall not be revocable or variable by the will of the nominator or by any codicil thereto.

(5) Every registered society shall keep a book in which the names of all persons nominated under subsection (1) of this section and any revocation or variation of any nomination under that

subsection shall be recorded.

(6) The marriage of a member of a society shall operate as a revocation of any nomination made by him before the marriage and after 31st December 1913; but if any property of that member has been transferred by an officer of the society in pursuance of that nomination in ignorance of a marriage contracted by the nominator subsequent to the date of the nomination, the receipt of the nominee shall be a valid discharge to the society and the society shall be under no liability to any other person claiming the property.

24 Proceedings on death of nominator.

(1) Subject to subsections (2) and (4) of this section, where any member of a registered society has made a nomination under section 23 of this Act, the committee of the society, on receiving satisfactory proof of the death of that member, and if and to the extent that the nomination is valid under subsections (2) and (3) of that section, shall in the case of each person entitled under the nomination either transfer to him, or pay him the full value of, any property to which he is so entitled.

(2) Where any of the property comprised in such a nomination as aforesaid consists of shares in the society, the foregoing subsection shall have effect notwithstanding that the rules of the society declare the shares therein not to be transferable; but if the transfer of any shares comprised in the nomination in the manner directed by the nominator would raise the share capital of any nominee beyond the maximum for the time being permitted in the case of that society, the committee of the society shall not transfer to that nominee more of those shares than will raise his share capital to that maximum and shall pay him the value of any of those shares not transferred.

(3) Where any sum falls to be paid under the foregoing provisions of this section to a nominee who is under sixteen years of age, the society may pay that sum to either parent, or to a guardian, of the nominee or to any other person of full age who will undertake to hold it on trust for the nominee or to apply it for his benefit and whom the society may think a fit and proper person for the purpose, and the receipt of that parent, guardian or other person shall be a sufficient discharge to the society for all moneys so paid.

(4). . . . .[77] .

25 Provision for intestacy.

(1) If any member of a registered society dies . .[78] and at his death his property in the society in respect of shares, loans or deposits does not exceed in the whole [£5,000][79] and is not the subject of any nomination under section 23 of this Act, then, subject to subsection (2) of this section, the committee of the society may, without letters of administration [or probate of any will][80] or, in Scotland, without confirmation having been obtained, distribute that property among such persons as appear to the committee on such evidence as they deem satisfactory to be entitled by law to receive it.

(2) If the member aforesaid was illegitimate [and leaves no widow, widower or issue, (including any illegitimate child of the member) and mother of his parents survive him][81], the committee shall deal with his property in the society as the Treasury shall direct.

26 Payments in respect of mentally incapable persons.

(1) Subject to subsection (2) of this section, where in the case of a member of a registered society or a person claiming through such a member the society's committee are satisfied after considering medical evidence that the member or person is incapable through disorder or disability of mind of managing his own affairs and are also satisfied that no person has been duly appointed to administer his property on his behalf, and it is proved to the satisfaction of the committee that it is just and expedient so to do, the society may pay the amount of any shares, loans, and deposits belonging to that member or person to any person whom they judge proper to receive it on his behalf, whose receipt shall be a good discharge to the society for any sum so paid.

(2) The foregoing subsection shall not apply when the member or person in question is—

(a) a patient within the meaning of Part VIII of the Mental Health Act 1959; or

(b) a person as to whom powers are exercisable and have been exercised under section 104 of that Act.

27 Validity of payment to persons apparently entitled.

All payments or transfers made by the committee of a registered society under section 25 or 26(1) of this Act or any corresponding provision of any Act repealed by this Act to any person appearing to the

committee at the time of the payment or transfer to be entitled thereunder shall be valid and effectual against any demand made upon the committee or society by any other person.

Contracts, property, etc., of society

28 Promissory notes and bills of exchange.

A promissory note or bill of exchange shall be deemed to have been made, accepted or endorsed on behalf of any registered society if made, accepted or endorsed in the name of the society, or by or on behalf or account of the society, by any person acting under the authority of the society.

29 Contracts.

(1) Any contract which, if made between private persons, would be by law required to be in writing and, if made according to English law, to be under seal may be made, varied or discharged on behalf of a registered society in writing under the common seal of the society; and any contract which may be or have been made, varied or discharged in accordance with this subsection shall, so far as concerns its form, be effectual in law and binding on all parties thereto, their heirs, executors or administrators, as the case may be.

(2) A signature purporting to be made by a person holding any office in a registered society attached to a writing whereby any contract purports to be made, varied or discharged by or on behalf of the society shall, until the contrary is proved, be taken to be the signature of a person holding that office at the time when the signature was made.

(3) Subsection (1) of this section shall not apply to Scotland; and nothing in that subsection shall prejudice the operation in England and Wales of the Corporate Bodies' Contracts Act 1960.

30 Holding of land.

(1) A registered society may, unless its registered rules direct otherwise, hold, purchase or take on lease in its own name any land and may sell, exchange, mortgage or lease any such land and erect, alter or pull down buildings on it; and—

(a) no purchaser, assignee, mortgagee or tenant shall be bound to inquire as to the authority for any such dealing with the land by the society; and

(b) the receipt of the society shall be a discharge for all moneys arising from or in connection with any such dealing.

(2) In the application of the foregoing subsection to Scotland—

(a) for the word "exchange" there shall be substituted the word "excamb";

(b) for the word "mortgage" there shall be substituted the words "grant a heritable security over";

(c) for the word "mortgagee" there shall be substituted the words "creditor in a heritable security".

31 Investments.

A registered society may invest any part of its funds in or upon any security authorised by its registered rules, and also, unless those rules direct otherwise—

(a) in or upon any mortgage, bond, debenture, debenture stock, corporation stock, annuity, rentcharge, rent or other security (not being securities payable to bearer) authorised by or under any Act of ;

[[(i) a billing authority or a precepting authority, as defined in section 69 of the Local Government Finance Act 1992;

(ia)[a combined police authority or][82] a combined fire authority, as defined in section 144 of the Local Government Finance Act 1988;][83]

(ii) a levying body within the meaning of section 74 of that Act; and

(iii) a body as regards which section 75 of that Act applies][84] .

(b) in the shares or on the security of any other registered society, of any [building society within the meaning of the Building Societies Act 1986][85], or of any company registered under the Companies Acts or incorporated by Act of Parliament or by charter, being a society or company with limited liability;

(c) in or upon any other security, being a security in which trustees are for the time being authorised by law to invest, for which purpose sections 1 to 6 of the Trustee Investments Act 1961 shall apply as if the society were a trustee and its funds were trust property.

31 Investments.

A registered society may invest any part of its funds in or upon any security authorised by its registered rules, and also, unless those rules direct otherwise—

(a) in or upon any mortgage, bond, debenture, debenture stock, corporation stock, annuity, rentcharge, rent or other security (not being securities payable to bearer) authorised by or under any Act of any local authority within the meaning of the Local Loans Act 1875;

(b) in the shares or on the security of any other registered society, of any [building society within the meaning of the Building Societies Act 1986][86], or of any company registered under the Companies Acts or incorporated by Act of Parliament or by charter, being a society or company with limited liability;

(c) in or upon any other security, being a security in which trustees are for the time being authorised by law to invest, for which purpose sections 1 to 6 of the Trustee Investments Act 1961 shall apply as if the society were a trustee and its funds were trust property.

32 Proxy voting by societies.

(1) A registered society which has invested any part of its funds in the shares or on the security of any other body corporate may appoint as proxy any one of its members notwithstanding that he is not personally a shareholder of that other body corporate.

(2) Any member of the society so appointed shall during the continuance of his appointment be taken by virtue thereof as holding the number of shares held by the society for all purposes other than the transfer of any such share or the giving of a receipt for any dividend thereon.

33 Discharge of mortgages in England and Wales.

(1) Where, in the case of any mortgage or other assurance to a registered society of any property in England or Wales, a receipt in full for all moneys secured thereby on that property is endorsed on or annexed to the mortgage or other assurance, being a receipt—

(a) signed by two members of the committee and countersigned by the secretary of the society or, if the society is in liquidation, signed by the liquidator or liquidators for the time being, described as such; and

(b) in one of the forms set out in Part I of Schedule 3 to this Act, or in any other form specified in the rules of the society or any schedule thereto,

then, for the purposes of the provisions of section 115 of the Law of Property Act 1925 specified in subsection (2) of this section, that receipt shall be deemed to be a receipt which fulfils the requirements of subsection (1) of that section.

(2) The provisions of the said section 115 referred to in the foregoing subsection are—

(a) subsection (1) so far as it relates to the operation of such a receipt as is mentioned in that subsection;

(b) if, but only if, the receipt under this section states the name of the person who pays the money, subsection (2);

(c) subsections (3), (6), (8), (10) and (11);

(d) where consistent with the terms of the form authorised by subsection (1)(b) of this section which is used for the receipt, subsection (7).

34 Discharge of securities in Scotland.[87]

(1) Where land in Scotland is held in security by a registered society by virtue of a heritable security constituted by an ex facie absolute conveyance, whether qualified by a back letter or not, a receipt in or as nearly as may be in form C in Part II of Schedule 3 to this Act endorsed on or annexed to the conveyance shall, on the registration thereof in the General Register of Sasines, effectually discharge that heritable security and disburden the land comprised therein, and vest that land in the person or persons entitled thereto at the date of the granting of the receipt in the like manner and to the like effect as if a conveyance containing all usual and necessary clauses had been granted by the society to that person or persons and duly registered as aforesaid.

(2) Where land in Scotland is held in security by a registered society by virtue of a heritable security other than the one constituted by an ex facie absolute conveyance, a receipt in or as nearly as may be in form D in the said Part II endorsed on or annexed to the deed constituting that heritable security shall, on the registration thereof in the General Register of Sasines, effectually discharge that heritable security and disburden the land comprised therein in the like manner and to the like effect as if a discharge containing all usual and necessary clauses had been granted by the society and duly registered as aforesaid.

(3) Where property other than land is held in security by a registered society in Scotland, a receipt in or

as nearly as may be in form E in the said Part II shall discharge the security, and vest the property comprised therein in the person or persons entitled thereto at the date of the granting of the receipt without the necessity of any further deed:

Provided that where the original security was intimated to any person that security shall not be discharged nor the property vested as aforesaid until the receipt has been duly intimated to that person.

(4) The fees payable in respect of the registration of receipts mentioned in this section shall in no case exceed [25p][88] . .[89].

(5) In this section—

(a) the expression "a receipt", in relation to any security, means a receipt, [signed by two members of the committee and countersigned by the secretary of the society or, if the society is in liquidation, signed by the liquidator or liquidators for the time being, described as such][90], for all moneys advanced by the society on the security of the property comprised in that security;

(b) the expressions "conveyance" and "deed" have the meanings respectively assigned to them by the Conveyancing (Scotland) Act 1924.

35 Receipt on payment of moneys secured to a society.

On payment of all moneys intended to be secured to a registered society on the security of any property, the debtor or his successor or representatives shall be entitled to a receipt in the appropriate form specified in Schedule 3 to this Act.

[36 Execution of deeds in Scotland.

In Scotland, any deed or writ to which any registered society is a party shall be held to be duly executed on behalf of that society if it is sealed with the common seal of the society subscribed on behalf of the society by two members of the committee and the secretary thereof, whether that subscription is attested by witnesses or not.][91]

Accounts, etc.

37, 38. . . . [92]

39 Annual returns.

(1) Every registered society shall, [within the period of 7 months beginning immediately after the end of the period required by this section to be included in the return][93], send to [the Authority][94] a return [relating to its affairs for that period][95], together with—

[(a) where the period required to be included in the return is one at the end of which there is in force in relation to the period a disapplication under section 4A(1) of the Friendly and Industrial and Provident Societies Act 1968 (power to disapply the obligation under section 4 of that Act to have accounts audited), the documents mentioned in subsection (1A) of this section, and

(b) where it is not, the documents mentioned in subsection (1B) of this section.

(1A) The documents referred to in subsection (1)(a) of this section are—

(a) copies of the reports, if any, which the society is required, because of the disapplication, to obtain under section 9A of the Friendly and Industrial and Provident Societies Act 1968 (duty to obtain accountant's reports where section 4 of that Act disapplied); and

(b) a copy of each balance sheet made during the period included in the return.

(1B) The documents referred to in subsection (1)(b) of this section are—][96]

(a) a copy of the report of the auditor or auditors on the society's accounts for the period included in the return; and

(b) a copy of each balance sheet made during that period and of any report of the auditor or auditors on that balance sheet.

(2) The said return shall—

(a), (b). . . . . .[97]

(c) subject to subsections (3) and (4) of this section, be made up for the period beginning with the date of the society's registration under this Act or [with the date to which the society's last annual return was made up, whichever is the later, and ending—

(i) with the date of the last balance sheet published by the society before the appropriate date; or

(ii) if the date of that balance sheet is earlier than 31st August immediately preceding the appropriate date or later than 31st January of the year in which the appropriate date falls, with

31st December immediately preceding the appropriate date,][98]

[(2A) For the purposes of paragraph (c) of subsection (2) of this section "the appropriate date", in relation to an annual return of a society, is 31st March of the year in which that return is required by subsection (1) of this section to be sent to [the Authority][99]or the date on which that return is so sent, whichever is the earlier.][100]

(3) If [the Authority][101] is of opinion that special circumstances exist [it][102] may allow a society to make return under this section up to a date other than that specified in subsection (2)(c)(i) or (ii) of this section, [103]

(4) The last return under this section by a registered society which is being terminated by an instrument of dissolution under section 55(b) of this Act shall be made up to the date of the instrument of dissolution.

(5) Every registered society shall supply free of charge to every member or person interested in the funds of the society who applies for it a copy of the latest return of the society under this section.

40 Display of latest balance sheet.

Every registered society shall keep a copy of the latest balance sheet of the society,. .[104], hung up at all times in a conspicuous position at the registered office of the society.

Officers, receivers, etc.

41 Security by officers.

(1) Every officer of a registered society having receipt or charge of money shall, if the rules of the society so require, before entering upon the execution of his office give security in such sum as the society's committee may direct conditioned for his rendering a just and true account of all moneys received and paid by him on account of the society at such times as its rules appoint or as the society or its committee require him so to do and for the payment by him of all sums due from him to the society.

(2) An officer of a registered society shall give security in accordance with the foregoing subsection either—

(a) by becoming bound, either with or without a surety as the society's committee may require, in a bond in one of the forms set out in Schedule 4 to this Act or such other form as the society's committee may approve; or

(b) by giving the security of a guarantee society.

(3) In the application of this section to Scotland, for the reference in subsection (2)(a) thereof to a surety there shall be substituted a reference to a cautioner.

42 Duty of officers of society to account.

(1) Every officer of a registered society having receipt or charge of money, and every servant of such a society in receipt or charge of money who is not engaged under a special agreement to account, shall—

(a) at such times as he is required so to do by the rules of the society; or

(b) on demand; or

(c) on notice in writing requiring him so to do given or left at his last or usual place of residence,

render an account as may be required by the society or its committee to be examined and allowed or disallowed by them, and shall, on demand or on such notice as aforesaid, pay over all moneys and deliver all property for the time being in his hands or custody to such person as the society or committee may appoint.

(2) Any duty imposed by the foregoing subsection on an officer or servant of a society shall, after his death, be taken to be imposed on his personal representatives.

(3) In case of any neglect or refusal to comply with the foregoing provisions of this section, the society—

(a) may sue on any bond or security given under section 41 of this Act; or

(b) may apply to the county court (which may proceed in a summary way) or to a magistrates' court and, notwithstanding anything in [section 77 of the County Courts Act 1984][105], the order of that county court or magistrates' court shall be final and conclusive.

(4) In its application to Scotland, this section shall have effect as if for subsection (3)(b) thereof there were substituted the following:—

"(b) may apply to the sheriff, and, notwithstanding anything in section 62 of the Summary

Jurisdiction (Scotland) Act 1954, the order of the sheriff shall be final and conclusive.".

43 Duties of receiver or manager of society's property.

Every receiver or manager of the property of a registered society who has been appointed under the powers contained in any instrument shall—

(a) within one month from the date of his appointment notify [the Authority][106] of his appointment; and

(b) within one month (or such longer period as [the Authority][107] may allow) after the expiration of the period of six months from that date, and of every subsequent period of six months, deliver to [the Authority][108] a return showing his receipts and his payments during that period of six months; and

(c) within one month after he ceases to act as receiver or manager deliver to [the Authority][109] a return showing his receipts and his payments during the final period and the aggregate amount of his receipts and of his payments during all preceding periods since his appointment.

Registers, books, etc.

44 Register of members and officers.

(1) Every registered society shall keep at its registered office a register and enter therein the following particulars:—

(a) the names and addresses of the members;

(b) a statement of the number of shares held by each member and of the amount paid or agreed to be considered as paid on the shares of each member;

(c) a statement of other property in the society, whether in loans, deposits or otherwise, held by each member;

(d) the date at which each person was entered in the register as a member, and the date at which any person ceased to be a member;

(e) the names and addresses of the officers of the society, with the offices held by them respectively, and the dates on which they assumed office.

(2) The said register may be kept either by making entries in bound books or by recording the matters in question in any other manner; but, where it is not kept by making entries in a bound book but by some other means, adequate precautions shall be taken for guarding against falsification and facilitating its discovery.

(3) Every registered society shall either—

(a) keep at its registered office a duplicate register containing the particulars in the register kept under subsection (1) of this section other than those entered under paragraph (b) or (c) of that subsection; or

(b) so construct the register kept under the said subsection (1) that it is possible to open to inspection the particulars therein other than the particulars entered under the said paragraph (b) or (c) without exposing those last-mentioned particulars.

(4) [Any person authorised for the purpose by the Authority may, on producing evidence of his authority,][110] at all reasonable hours inspect any particulars in any register or duplicate register kept under this section.

(5) A registered society's register or duplicate register kept under this section, or any other register or list of members or shares kept by the society, shall be prima facie evidence of any of the following particulars entered therein, that is to say—

(a) the names, addresses and occupations of the members;

(b) the number of shares respectively held by the members, the distinguishing numbers of those shares, if they are distinguished by numbers, and the amount paid or agreed to be considered as paid on any of those shares;

(c) the date at which the name of any person, company or society was entered in that register or list as a member;

(d) the date at which any such person, company or society ceased to be a member.

45 Restriction on inspection of books.

(1) Save as provided by this Act, no member or other person shall have any right to inspect the books of a registered society.

(2) In the case of a society to which section 4 of this Act applies, the foregoing subsection shall have effect notwithstanding anything relating to such inspection in any rules of the society made before

12th September 1893.

46 Inspection of books by members, etc.

(1) Subject to any regulations as to the time and manner of inspection which may be made from time to time by the general meetings of a registered society, any member, and any person having an interest in the funds, of the society shall be allowed to inspect at all reasonable hours—

(a) his own account; and

(b) all the particulars contained in the duplicate register kept under section 44(3)(a) of this Act or, if no duplicate register is so kept, all the particulars in the register kept under section 44(1) of this Act other than those entered under paragraph (b) or (c) thereof.

(2) A registered society may by its rules (not being rules made earlier than 12th September 1893) authorise, in addition to any inspection in pursuance of the foregoing subsection, the inspection of such of the society's books upon such conditions as may be specified in the rules, but no person who is not an officer of the society or specially authorised by a resolution of the society shall be authorised by the rules to inspect the loan or deposit account of any other person without that other person's written consent.

47 Inspection of books by order of registrar.

(1) Subject to subsection (2) of this section, [the Authority][111] may, if [it][112] thinks fit, on the application of ten members of a registered society each of whom has been a member of the society for not less than twelve months immediately preceding the date of the application, appoint an accountant or actuary to inspect the books of the society and to report thereon.

(2) The members making an application under the foregoing subsection shall deposit with [the Authority][113] as security for the costs of the proposed inspection such sum as [it][114] may require; and all expenses of and incidental to the inspection shall be defrayed by the applicants, or out of the funds of the society, or by the members or officers, or former members or officers, of the society, in such proportions as [the Authority][115] may direct.

(3) A person appointed under this section shall have power to make copies of any books of the society, and to take extracts therefrom, at all reasonable hours at the society's registered office or at any other place where those books are kept.

(4) [the Authority][116] shall communicate the results of any inspection under this section to the applicants and to the society.

48 Production of documents and provision of information for certain purposes.

(1)[The Authority][117] may at any time, by notice in writing served on a registered society or on any person who is or has been an officer of such a society, require that society or person to produce to [the Authority][118] such books, accounts and other documents relating to the business of the society, and to furnish to [it][119] such other information relating to that business, as [the Authority][120] considers necessary for the exercise of any of the powers which [it][121] has by virtue of section 16(1)(c)(ii), 16(4) or 56 of this Act; and any such notice may contain a requirement that any information to be furnished in accordance with the notice shall be verified by a statutory declaration.

(2) Any society or other person failing to comply with the requirements of a notice under the foregoing subsection shall be liable on summary conviction to a fine not exceeding [level 3 on the standard scale][122] or to imprisonment for a term not exceeding three months or to both.

(3)[The Authority][123] may, if [it][124] considers it just, direct that all or any of the expenses incurred by [it][125] in exercising [its][126] powers under subsection (1) of this section in relation to any society shall, either wholly or to such extent as [it][127] may determine, be defrayed out of the funds of the society or by the officers or former officers thereof or any of them; and any sum which any society or other person is required by such a direction to pay shall be a debt due to [the Authority][128] from that society or person.

49 Appointment of inspectors and calling of special meetings.

(1) Upon the application of one-tenth of the whole number of members of a registered society or, in the case of a society with more than one thousand members, of one hundred of those members, [the Authority][129] may. .[130]

(a) appoint an inspector or inspectors to examine into and report on the affairs of the society; or

(b) call a special meeting of the society.

(2) An application under this section shall be supported by such evidence for the purpose of showing that the applicants have good reason for requiring the examination or meeting and are not actuated by malicious motives, and such notice of the application shall be given to the society, as [the Authority][131] shall direct.

(3) [the Authority][132] may, if [it][133] thinks fit, require the applicants to give security for the costs of the proposed examination or meeting before appointing any inspector or calling the meeting.

(4) All expenses of and incidental or preliminary to any such examination or meeting shall be defrayed by the members applying for it, or out of the funds of the society, or by the members or officers, or former members or officers, of the society, in such proportions as [the Authority][134] shall direct.

(5) An inspector appointed under this section may require the production of all or any of the books, accounts, securities, and documents of the society, and may examine on oath its officers, members, agents and servants in relation to its business, and may for that purpose administer oaths.

(6) [the Authority][135] may direct at what time and place a special meeting under this section is to be held, and what matters are to be discussed and determined at the meeting; and the meeting shall have all the powers of a meeting called according to the rules of the society, and shall have power to appoint its own chairman notwithstanding any rule of the society to the contrary.

(7)..... [136]

Amalgamations, transfers of engagements and conversions

50 Amalgamation of societies.

(1) Any two or more registered societies may by special resolution of each of those societies become amalgamated together as one society, with or without any dissolution or division of the funds of those societies or any of them; and the property of each of those societies shall become vested in the amalgamated society without the necessity of any form of conveyance other than that contained in the special resolution.

(2) In this section the expression "special resolution" means a resolution which is—

(a) passed by not less than two-thirds of such members of the society for the time being entitled under the society's rules to vote as may have voted in person, or by proxy where the rules allow proxies, at any general meeting of which notice, specifying the intention to propose the resolution, has been duly given according to those rules; and

(b) confirmed by a majority of such members of the society for the time being entitled as aforesaid as may have voted as aforesaid at a subsequent general meeting of which notice has been duly given held not less than fourteen days nor more than one month from the day of the meeting at which the resolution was passed in accordance with paragraph (a) of this subsection.

(3) At any such meeting as aforesaid, a declaration by the chairman that the resolution has been carried shall be deemed conclusive evidence of that fact.

(4) A copy of every special resolution for the purposes of this section signed by the chairman of the meeting at which the resolution was confirmed and countersigned by the secretary of the society shall be sent to [the Authority][137] and registered by [it][138]; and until that copy is so registered the special resolution shall not take effect.

(5) It shall be the duty of a registered society to send any special resolution for registration in accordance with the last foregoing subsection within fourteen days from the day on which the resolution is confirmed under subsection (2)(b) of this section, but this subsection shall not invalidate registration of the resolution after that time.

51 Transfer of engagements between societies.

(1) Any registered society may by special resolution transfer its engagements to any other registered society which may undertake to fulfil those engagements; and if that resolution approves the transfer of the whole or any part of the society's property to that other society, the whole or, as the case may be, that part of the society's property shall vest in that other society without any conveyance or assignment.

(2) Subsections (2) to (5) of section 50 of this Act shall have effect for the purposes of this section as they have effect for the purposes of that section.

(3) In its application to Scotland, subsection (1) of this section shall have effect as if for the word "assignment" there were substituted the word "assignation".

52 Conversion into, amalgamation with, or transfer of engagements to company.

(1) A registered society may by special resolution determine to convert itself into, or to amalgamate with or transfer its engagements to, a company under the Companies Acts.

(2) If a special resolution for converting a registered society into a company contains the particulars required by the [Companies Act 1985][139] to be contained in the memorandum of association of a company and a copy thereof has been registered by the [the Authority][140], a copy of that resolution under the seal and stamp of [the Authority][141] . . shall have the same effect as a memorandum of association duly signed and attested under the said [Act of 1985].[142]

[(3)In this section the expression "special resolution" means a resolution—

(a) which is passed at a general meeting of which notice, specifying the intention to propose the resolution, has been duly given according to the rules of the society ("the rules");

(b) which is passed by not less than three-fourths of such of the qualifying members of the society as may have voted in person or, where the rules allow proxies, by proxy;

(c) on which not less than half of the qualifying members of the society voted either in person or, where the rules allow proxies, by proxy; and

(d) which is confirmed by a majority of such of the qualifying members of the society as may have voted in person or, where the rules allow proxies, by proxy at a subsequent general meeting of which notice has been duly given held not less than fourteen days nor more than one month from the day of the meeting at which the resolution was passed in accordance with paragraphs (a) to (c) of this subsection,

and references to the qualifying members of a society are references to the members of the society who are for the time being entitled under the society's rules to vote.

(3A) At any such meeting as aforesaid, a declaration by the chairman that—

(a) all reasonably practicable steps have been taken to ascertain the number of qualifying members of the society; and

(b) the resolution has been carried,

shall be deemed conclusive evidence of those facts.

(3B) Subsections (4) and (5) of section 50 of this Act shall have effect for the purposes of this section as they have effect for the purposes of that section but as if in subsection (5) of that section for the reference to subsection (2)(b) of that section there were substituted a reference to subsection (3)(d) of this section.][143]

(4) Subject to subsection (5) of this section, if a registered society is registered as, or amalgamates with, or transfers all its engagements to, a company under the Companies Acts, the registration of that society under this Act shall thereupon become void and, subject to section 59 of this Act, shall be cancelled by [the Authority][144]. .

(5) Registration of a registered society as a company shall not affect any right or claim for the time being subsisting against the society or any penalty for the time being incurred by the society; and—

(a) for the purpose of enforcing any such right, claim or penalty, the society may be sued and proceeded against in the same manner as if it had not become registered as a company; and

(b) every such right or claim, or the liability to any such penalty, shall have priority as against the property of the company over all other rights or claims against or liabilities of the company.

53 Conversion of company into registered society.

(1) A company registered under the Companies Acts may, by a special resolution as defined by [section 378 of the Companies Act 1985][145], determine to convert itself into a registered society; and for this purpose, in any case where the nominal value of the company's shares held by any member other than a registered society exceeds [the maximum for the time being permitted by section 6(1) of this Act in the case of a member of a registered society][146], the resolution may provide for the conversion of the shares representing that excess into a transferable loan stock bearing such rate of interest as may be fixed, and repayable on such conditions only as are determined by the resolution.

(2) Any such resolution as aforesaid shall be accompanied by a copy of the rules of the society therein referred to and shall appoint [three][147] persons, being members of the company, who, together with the secretary, shall sign the rules and who may either—

(a) be authorised to accept any alterations made by [the Authority][148] therein without further consulting the company; or

(b) be required to lay any such alterations before the company in general meeting for acceptance as the resolution may direct.

(3) A copy of the resolution aforesaid shall be sent with a copy of the rules aforesaid to [the Authority][149] who, upon the registration of the society under this Act, shall give to it, in addition to an acknowledgment of registration under section 2(3) of this Act, a certificate similarly sealed or signed that the rules of the society referred to in the resolution have been registered.

(4) A copy of any such resolution as aforesaid under the seal of the company together with the certificate issued as aforesaid by [the Authority][150] shall be sent for registration to the office of the registrar of companies within the meaning of the [Companies Act 1985][151] and, upon his registering that resolution and certificate, the conversion shall take effect.

(5) The name under which any company is registered under this section as a registered society shall not include the word "company".

(6) Subject to the next following subsection, upon the conversion of a company into a registered society under this section, the registration of the company under the Companies Acts shall become void and shall be cancelled by the registrar of companies aforesaid.

(7) The registration of a company as a registered society shall not affect any right or claim for the time being subsisting against the company or any penalty for the time being incurred by the company; and—

(a) for the purpose of enforcing any such right, penalty or claim the company may be sued and proceeded against in the same manner as if it had not been registered as a society;

(b) any such right or claim and the liability to any such penalty shall have priority as against the property of the registered society over all other rights or claims against or liabilities of the society.

54 Saving for rights of creditors.

An amalgamation or transfer of engagements in pursuance of section 50, 51 or 52 of this Act shall not prejudice any right of a creditor of any registered society which is a party thereto.

Dissolution of society

55 Dissolution of registered society.

Subject to section 59 of this Act, a registered society may be dissolved—

(a) on its being wound up in pursuance of an order or resolution made as is directed in regard to companies by the [Insolvency Act 1986][152], the provisions whereof shall apply to that order or resolution as if the society were a company, but subject to the following modifications, that is to say—

(i) any reference in those provisions to the registrar within the meaning of that Act shall for the purposes of the society's winding up be construed as a reference to the [the Authority][153]. .; and

[(ia) any reference in those provisions to a company registered in Scotland shall have effect as a reference to a society registered under this Act whose registered office is situated in Scotland;][154]

(ii) if the society is wound up in Scotland, the court having jurisdiction shall be the sheriff court within whose jurisdiction the society's registered office is situated; or

(b) in accordance with section 58 of this Act, by an instrument of dissolution to which not less than three-fourths of the members of the society have given their consent testified by their signatures to the instrument.

56 Power of registrar to petition for winding up.

In the case of a society to which section 4 of this Act applies which was registered or deemed to be registered under the Act of 1893 before 26th July 1938, a petition for the winding up of the society may be presented to the court by [the Authority][155] if it appears to [the Authority][156]—

(a) that neither of the conditions specified in section 1(2) of this Act is fulfilled in the case of that society; and

(b) that it would be in the interests of persons who have invested or deposited money with the society or of any other person that the society should be wound up.

57 Liability of members in winding up.

Where a registered society is wound up by virtue of section 55(a) of this Act, the liability of a present or past member of the society to contribute for payment of the debts and liabilities of the society, the

expenses of winding up, and the adjustment of the rights of contributories amongst themselves, shall be qualified as follows, that is to say—

(a) no person who ceased to be a member not less than one year before the beginning of the winding up shall be liable to contribute;

(b) no person shall be liable to contribute in respect of any debt or liability contracted after he ceased to be a member;

(c) no person who is not a member shall be liable to contribute unless it appears to the court that the contributions of the existing members are insufficient to satisfy the just demands on the society;

(d) no contribution shall be required from any person exceeding the amount, if any, unpaid on the shares in respect of which he is liable as a past or present member;

(e) in the case of a withdrawable share which has been withdrawn, a person shall be taken to have ceased to be a member in respect of that share as from the date of the notice or application for withdrawal.

58 Instrument of dissolution.

(1) The following provisions of this section shall have effect where a society is to be dissolved by an instrument of dissolution under section 55(b) of this Act.

(2) The instrument of dissolution shall set forth—

(a) the liabilities and assets of the society in detail;

(b) the number of the members and the nature of their respective interests in the society;

(c) the claims of creditors, if any, and the provision to be made for their payment; and

(d) unless stated in the instrument of dissolution to be left to the award of [the Authority][157], the intended appropriation or division of the funds and property of the society.

(3) Alterations in the instrument of dissolution may be made by the consent of not less than three-fourths of the members of the society testified by their signatures to the alteration.

(4) The instrument of dissolution shall be sent to [the Authority][158] accompanied by a statutory declaration made by three members and the secretary of the society that all relevant provisions of this Act have been complied with; and any person knowingly making a false or fraudulent declaration in the matter shall be guilty of a misdemeanour or, in Scotland, an offence.

(5) The instrument of dissolution and any alterations thereto shall be registered in like manner as an amendment of the rules of the society and shall be binding upon all the members of the society, but shall not be so registered until [the Authority][159] has received such a final return from the society as is referred to in section 39(4) of this Act.

(6) [the Authority][160] shall cause notice of the dissolution to be advertised. .[161] in the Gazette and in some newspaper circulating in or about the locality in which the society's registered office is situated; and unless—

(a) within three months from the date of the Gazette in which that advertisement appears a member or other person interested in or having any claim on the funds of the society commences in the county court, or in Scotland before the sheriff, having jurisdiction in that locality proceedings to set aside the dissolution of the society; and

(b) that dissolution is set aside accordingly,

then, subject to subsection (7) of this section, the society shall be legally dissolved from the date of the advertisement and the requisite consents to the instrument of dissolution shall be deemed to have been duly obtained without proof of the signatures thereto.

(7) If the certificate referred to in section 59 of this Act has not been lodged with the [the Authority][162] by the date of the advertisement referred to in subsection (6) of this section, the society shall be legally dissolved only from the date when that certificate is so lodged.

(8) Notice of any proceedings to set aside the dissolution of a society shall be sent to [the Authority][163] by the person taking those proceedings not later than seven days after they are commenced or not later than the expiration of the period of three months referred to subsection (6) of this section, whichever is the earlier; and notice of any order setting the dissolution aside shall be sent by the society to [the Authority][164] within seven days after the making of the order.

(9) In the application of this section to a society which for the time being consists solely of two registered societies, the reference in subsection (4) thereof to three members shall be construed as a reference to both members.

Special restriction on dissolution, etc.

59 Restriction on dissolution or cancellation of registration of society.

Where a registered society is to be dissolved in accordance with section 55 of this Act, or where a registered society's engagements are transferred under section 51 or 52 of this Act, the society shall not be dissolved, and the registration of the society shall not be cancelled, until there has been lodged with [the Authority][165] a certificate signed by the liquidator or by the secretary or some other officer of the society approved by [the Authority][166] that all property vested in the society has been duly conveyed or transferred by the society to the persons entitled.

Disputes, offences and legal proceedings

60 Decision of disputes.

(1) Subject to subsections (2), [(2A),][167](4) and (5) of this section, every dispute between a registered society or an officer thereof and—

(a) a member of the society; or

(b) any person aggrieved who has ceased to be a member of the society not more than six months previously; or

(c) any person claiming through a member of the society or any such person aggrieved; or

(d) any person claiming under the rules of the society,

shall, if the society's rules give directions as to the manner in which such disputes are to be decided, be decided in that manner.

[(1A) Nothing in subsection (1) above or in rules of a kind mentioned in that subsection prevents any person, in accordance with the scheme for which Part XVI of the Financial Services and Markets Act 2000 provides (the ombudsman scheme), from having a complaint dealt with under such a scheme before, or instead of, determination in the manner directed in the rules.][168]

[(2)The county court or, in Scotland, the sheriff may determine a dispute in a registered society if—

(a) both parties to the dispute consent; or

(b) the rules of the society concerned contain no directions as to disputes.][169]

[(2A) If the rules contain directions by virtue of which a dispute would fall to be determined by the Authority, the dispute shall instead be referred to the county court or, in Scotland, to the sheriff for determination.][170]

(3) A decision made under subsection (1) or (2) of this section on any dispute shall be binding and conclusive on all parties without appeal; and—

(a) the decision shall not be removable into any court of law or restrainable by injunction; and

(b) application for the enforcement of the decision may be made to the county court.

(4) Subject to subsection (5) of this section, any dispute directed by the rules of a registered society to be referred to justices shall be determined by a magistrates' court.

(5) Where, whether by virtue of subsection (4) of this section or otherwise, a dispute is congnisable under the rules of a registered society by a magistrates' court, the parties to the dispute may by agreement refer the dispute to the county court, who may hear and determine it.

(6) Where the rules of a registered society contain no direction as to disputes, or where no decision is made on a dispute within forty days after application to the society for a reference under its rules, any person such as is mentioned in subsection (1)(a) to (d) of this section who is a party to the dispute may apply either to the county court or to a magistrates' court, who may hear and determine the matter in dispute.

(7) In the application of the foregoing provisions of this section to Scotland—

(a) in subsection (3), paragraph (a) shall be omitted and in paragraph (b) for the words "county court" there shall be substituted the word "sheriff";

(b) subsections (4) to (6) shall not apply, but in Scotland—

(i) any dispute directed by the rules of a registered society to be referred to justices, a justice of the peace court, or a court of summary jurisdiction, shall be determined by the sheriff;

(ii) where the rules of a registered society contain no direction as to disputes, or where no decision is made on a dispute within forty days after application to the society for a reference under its rules, any person such as is mentioned in subsection (1)(a) to (d) of this section who is a party to the dispute may apply to the sheriff, who may hear and determine the matter in

dispute.

(8) For the purposes of the hearing or determination of a dispute under this section—

[(a) a county court or, in Scotland, the sheriff shall have power to order the expenses of determining the dispute to be paid either out of the funds of the society or by such parties to the dispute as it thinks fit;][171]

(b) in England and Wales, a magistrates' court may grant to either party such discovery as to documents and otherwise, or such inspection of documents, being, in the case of discovery to be made on behalf of the society, discovery by such officer of the society as the court may determine, as [the court considers necessary for the just and expeditious disposal of the dispute][172];

(c) . . . . .[173]

[(9) The court [to which][174]any dispute is referred under subsections (2) to (7) may at the request of either party state a case on any question of law arising in the dispute for the opinion of the High Court or, as the case may be, the Court of Session.] .[175]

61 General offences by societies, etc.

If any registered society, or any officer or member thereof, or any other person—

(a) fails to give any notice, send any return or other document, do anything or allow anything to be done which that society, officer, member or other person is by this Act required to give, send, do or allow to be done, as the case may be; or

(b) wilfully neglects or refuses to do any act, or to furnish any information, required for the purposes of this Act by [the Authority][176]. or by any other person authorised under this Act, or does anything forbidden by this Act; or

(c) makes a return required by this Act, or wilfully furnishes information so required, which is in any respect false or insufficient,

that society, officer, member or other person, as the case may be, shall be liable on summary conviction to a fine not exceeding [level 3 on the standard scale][177].

62 Offences by societies to be also offences by officers, etc.

Every offence committed by a registered society under this Act shall be deemed to have been also committed by every officer of that society bound by the society's rules to fulfil the duty of which that offence is a breach or, if there is no such officer, by every member of the society's committee who is not proved to have been ignorant of, or to have attempted to prevent, the commission of that offence.

63 Continuing offences.

Every act or default under this Act constituting an offence shall constitute a new offence in every week during which it continues.

64 Punishment of fraud or misappropriation.

(1) Subject to subsection (2) of this section, any person who obtains possession by false representation or imposition of any property of a registered society, or having any such property in his possession withholds or misapplies it or wilfully applies any part of it to purposes which are not authorised by the rules of the society or which are not in accordance with this Act, shall be liable on summary conviction to a fine not exceeding [level 2 on the standard scale][178] with costs or expenses and to be ordered to deliver up that property or to repay all moneys improperly applied and, in default of such delivery or repayment or of the payment of any such fine, to be imprisoned for a term not exceeding three months; but nothing in this subsection shall prevent any such person from being proceeded against by way of indictment for any offence if he has not previously been convicted in respect of the same matters under this subsection.

(2) If on proceedings under the foregoing subsection it is not proved that the person charged acted with any fraudulent intent, he may be ordered to deliver up any property belonging to the society or to repay any money improperly applied, with costs or expenses, but shall not be liable to conviction under that subsection.

65 Penalty for falsification.

If any person, with intent to falsify it or to evade any of the provisions of this Act, wilfully makes, or orders or allows to be made, any entry or erasure in, or omission from, any balance-sheet of a registered society, or any contribution or collecting book, or any return or document required to be sent, produced

or delivered for the purposes of this Act, he shall be liable on summary conviction to a fine not exceeding [level 3 on the standard scale][179].

66 Institution of proceedings.

(1) Proceedings for the recovery of a fine which under this Act is recoverable on the summary conviction of the offender may be instituted by . .[180] the following persons, that is to say—

(a) in the case of proceedings by virtue of section 64(1) of this Act—

(i) the registered society concerned; or

(ii) any member of that society authorised by the society or its committee or by [the Authority][181]; or

[(iii) other than in Scotland, the Authority;][182]

(b) in the case of proceedings by virtue of section 13(3) of this Act, the registered society concerned;

[(c) in any other case—

(i) any person aggrieved; or

(ii) other than in Scotland, the Authority;

and (except in Scotland) no other person may institute such proceedings.][183]

(2) Notwithstanding any limitation on the time for the taking of proceedings contained in any Act, any proceedings such as are mentioned in subsection (1) of this section which are instituted by [the Authority or by the Lord Advocate][184]may be brought at any time within one year of the first discovery of the offence by [Authority (or the Lord Advocate, as the case may be)][185], but not in any case more than three years after the commission of the offence.

67 Recovery of costs, etc.

(1) Any costs or expenses ordered or directed by [the Authority][186]. . to be paid by any person under this Act shall be recoverable summarily as a civil debt.

(2) In the application of the foregoing subsection to Scotland, the word "summarily" shall be omitted.

68 Service of process.

Where proceedings are taken against a registered society for the recovery of any fine under this Act, the summons or other process shall be sufficiently served by leaving a true copy thereof at the registered office of the society or, if that office is closed, by posting that copy on the outer door of that office.

Miscellaneous and general

69 Remuneration of county court registrars.

Registrars of county courts shall be remunerated for any duties to be performed by them under this Act in such manner as the Treasury may with the consent of the Lord Chancellor from time to time direct.

70 . . . .[187]

[70A Fees for inspection or copying of documents.

Before the Authority allows any person to inspect any document held by it in connection with this Act, or provides any person with a copy of any such document (or part of such document), it may charge that person a reasonable fee.][188]

71 . . .[189]

72 Form, deposit and evidence of documents.

[Every return and other document required for the purposes of this Act shall be made in such form, shall contain such particulars and shall be deposited in such manner as the Authority may direct and the Authority shall register and record those documents with such observations thereon (if any) as it considers appropriate.][190]

[(2) Any document bearing the seal or stamp of the Authority shall be received in evidence without further proof.

(3) Any document purporting to have been signed by a person authorised to do so on behalf of the Authority, and every document purporting to be signed by any inspector under this Act, shall, in the absence of any evidence to the contrary, be received in evidence without proof of the signature.

(4) In subsections (2) and (3), "document" means any document issued, received or created by the Authority (or, as the case may be, by any inspector under this Act) for the purposes of or in connection with this Act, the Industrial and Provident Societies Act 1967 or the Friendly and Industrial and Provident Societies Act 1968.][191]

73 . . .[192]

74 Interpretation—general.

[(1)][193] In this Act, except where the context otherwise requires, the following expressions have the following meanings respectively, that is to say—

"Act of 1893", means the Industrial and Provident Societies Act 1893;

"amendment", in relation to the rules of a registered society, includes a new rule, and a resolution rescinding a rule, of the society;

["the Authority" means the Financial Services Authority;][194]

"committee", in relation to a society, means the committee of management or other directing body of the society;

"Companies Acts" includes the [Companies Act 1985][195], any earlier enactment for the like purposes which has been repealed, and any law for the like purposes which is or has been in force in Northern Ireland or any of the Channel Islands;

"Gazette", in relation to a registered society, means such one or more of the following as may be appropriate in the circumstances of the case, that is to say—

(a) the London Gazette if the society's registered office is situated, [or the society carries on business][196], in England, Wales or the Channel Islands;

(b) the Edinburgh Gazette if the society's registered office is situated, [or the society carries on business][197], in Scotland;

(c) the Belfast Gazette if the society's rules are recorded in Northern Ireland;

"heritable security" has the same meaning as in the Conveyancing (Scotland) Act 1924 except that it includes a security constituted by ex facie absolute disposition or assignation;

"land" includes hereditaments and chattels real, and in Scotland, heritable subjects of whatever description;

"meeting", in relation to a society, includes, where the rules of that society so allow, a meeting of delegates appointed by members;

"officer", in relation to a registered society, includes any treasurer, secretary, member of the committee, manager or servant of the society other than a servant appointed by the society's committee, but does not include an [auditor appointed by the society in accordance with the requirements of the Friendly and Industrial and Provident Societies Act 1968][198];

"persons claiming through a member", in relation to a registered society, includes the heirs, executors or administrators and assignees of a member and, where nomination is allowed, his nominee;

"prescribed" means prescribed by regulations under section 71 of this Act;

"property" includes all real, personal or heritable and moveable estate, including books and papers;

"registered" in relation to the name or an office of a society means for the time being registered under this Act;

"registered rules", in relation to a registered society, means the rules of the society registered or deemed to be registered under this Act as for the time being in force after any amendment thereof so registered;

"registered society" means, subject to section 76 of this Act, a society registered or deemed to be registered under this Act.

[(2) Any reference in this Act to the seal of the Authority is a reference to the seal provided for in regulations made under section 109(1)(b) of the Friendly Societies Act 1974 (and not to the Authority's common seal), and any reference to a document sealed by the Authority is a reference to a document sealed with that seal.][199]

75 Channel Islands.

(1) Subject to any express provision of this Act with respect to the Channel Islands, this Act in its application to those Islands shall have effect subject to such adaptations and modifications as Her Majesty may by Order in Council specify.

(2) Any Order in Council under the foregoing subsection may be varied or revoked by a subsequent Order in Council so made.

76 Northern Ireland societies.

(1) Where, in the case of any society for the time being registered under the law for the time being in

force in Northern Ireland for purposes corresponding to those of this Act, copies of that society's rules so registered have been sent to the [Authority to be recorded by it and have been so recorded, then, for the purposes of the operation of this Act in Great Britain and the Channel Islands][200], references to a registered society in such, but such only, of the provisions of this Act as are specified in subsection (2) of this section shall, subject to subsection (3) of this section include a reference to that society, and for the purposes of those provisions that society, those rules and any amendment of those rules registered and recorded as aforesaid shall in that area be deemed to be a society, rules or an amendment duly registered under this Act by the [Authority][201].

(2) The provisions of this Act referred to in the foregoing subsection are sections 2(2), 3, 5(4), (6) and (7), 6(1)(a), 7(1)(b), (2), (3) and (6), 10(1)(a), 13(3), 14, 15, 16(1)(a)(i), 19(2), 22, 26 to 30, 31(b), 32 to 36, 41, 42, 44(5), 45(1), 50, 51, 52(5), 54, 60 to 62, 64 to 66 and 72.

(3) Nothing in this section shall confer any power or impose any obligation or liability with respect to the taking or refraining from taking of, or a failure to take, any action outside Great Britain and the Channel Islands; and in the application of section 45(1) of this Act by virtue of this section the reference therein to this Act shall be construed as a reference to the law for the time being in force in Northern Ireland for purposes corresponding to those of this Act.

(4) In relation to any society for the time being registered as mentioned in subsection (1) of this section, Article 22 of the Government of Ireland (Companies, Societies, &c.) Order 1922 shall have effect as if the words from "a society registered in Northern Ireland" to "United Kingdom, and" and the words "both in their application to the United Kingdom exclusive of Northern Ireland and" were omitted.

77 Repeals and savings.

(1) . . . . . [202]

(2) Without prejudice to section 4 of this Act, any regulations, application or notice made or given and any other thing whatsoever done under or in pursuance of any of the enactments repealed by this Act shall be deemed for the purposes of this Act to have been made, given or done, as the case may be, under or in pursuance of the corresponding provision of this Act; and anything begun under any of the said enactments may be continued under this Act as if begun under this Act.

(3) So much of any document as refers expressly or by implication to any enactment repealed by this Act shall, if and so far as the context permits, be construed as referring to this Act or the corresponding enactment therein.

(4) Nothing in section 4 of this Act or in this section shall be taken as affecting the general application of section 38 of the Interpretation Act 1889 with regard to the effect of repeals.

78 Short title, extent and commencement.

(1) This Act may be cited as the Industrial and Provident Societies Act 1965.

(2) This Act extends to the Channel Islands but does not extend to Northern Ireland.

(3) This Act shall come into operation on such day as Her Majesty may by Order in Council appoint.

SCHEDULES

Section 1.

SCHEDULE 1 - MATTERS TO BE PROVIDED FOR IN SOCIETY'S RULES

1 The name of the society, which shall comply with the requirements of section 5 of this Act.

2 The objects of the society.

3 The place which is to be the registered office of the society to which all communications and notices to the society may be addressed.

4 The terms of admission of the members, including any society or company investing funds in the society under the provisions of this Act.

5 The mode of holding meetings, the scale and right of voting, and the mode of making, altering or rescinding rules.

6 The appointment and removal of a committee, by whatever name, and of managers or other officers and their respective powers and remuneration.

7 Determination in accordance with section 6 of this Act of the maximum amount of the interest in the shares of the society which may be held by any member otherwise than by virtue of section 6(1)(a), (b) or (c) of this Act.

8 Determination whether the society may contract loans or receive moneys on deposit subject to the

provisions of this Act from members or others; and, if so, under what conditions, under what security, and to what limits of amount.

9 Determination whether the shares or any of them shall be transferable, and provision for the form of transfer and registration of the shares, and for the consent of the committee thereto; determination whether the shares of any of them shall be withdrawable, and provision for the mode of withdrawal and for payment of the balance due thereon on withdrawing from the society.

10 Provision for the audit of accounts by one or more [auditor appointed by the society in accordance with the requirements of the Friendly and Industrial and Provident Societies Act 1968].[203]

11 Determination whether and, if so, how members may withdraw from the society, and provision for the claims of the representatives of deceased members, or the trustees of the property of bankrupt members or, in Scotland, members whose estate has been sequestrated, and for the payment of nominees.

12 The mode of application of profits of the society.

13 Provision for the custody and use of the society's seal.

14 Determination whether and, if so, by what authority, and in what manner, any part of the society's funds may be invested.

SCHEDULE 2 - FORM OF STATEMENT BY SOCIETY CARRYING ON BANKING

1 Capital of the society:—

(a) nominal amount of each share;

(b) number of shares issued;

(c) amount paid up on shares.

2 Liabilities of the society on 1st January or 1st July last previous:—.

(a) on judgments;

(b) on specialty;

(c) on notes or bills;

(d) on simple contract;

(e) on estimated liabilities.

3 Assets of the society on the same date:—.

(a) government securities (stating them);

(b) bills of exchange and promissory notes;

(c) cash at the bankers;

(d) other securities.

SCHEDULE 3 - FORM OF RECEIPT ON MORTGAGE, HERITABLE SECURITY, ETC.

Part I - Forms applicable in England and Wales

Form A

The Limited hereby acknowledges to have received all moneys intended to be secured by the [within (or above) written] [annexed] deed [and by a further charge dated, etc., or otherwise as required].

Dated this day of

Members of the Committee
Secretary

Form B

The Limited hereby acknowledges that it has this day of received the sum of pounds representing all moneys intended to be secured by the [within (or above) written] [annexed] deed [and by a further charge dated, etc.or otherwise as required], the payment having been made by C.D. of and E.F. of

Members of the Committee
Secretary

Note. If the persons paying are not entitled to the equity of redemption but are paying the money out of a fund applicable to the discharge of the mortgage or other assurance, insert a statement to that effect.

A statement may also be inserted as to whether the receipt is or is not to operate as a transfer of the benefit of the mortgage or other assurance.

Part II - Forms applicable in Scotland

Form C

The Limited acknowledges that (1) the foregoing disposition granted by A (with consent) in favour of the said society dated and recorded in the Division of the General Register of Sasines for on was granted in security only of a loan of pounds made by the said society to the said , and (2) the said society have received repayment of all moneys secured by the said disposition.

[Testing clause+

+Note—Subscription of the document by the granter of it will be sufficient for the document to be formally valid, but witnessing of it may be necessary or desirable for other purposes (see the Requirements of Writing (Scotland) Act 1995).][204]

Members of the Committee
Secretary

Form D

The Limited acknowledges to have received repayment of all moneys secured by the foregoing bond and disposition in security [bond and assignation in security] [bond and such other deed of heritable security as may have been agreed] granted by A in the said society's favour dated and recorded in the Division of the General Register of Sasines for on

[Testing clause+

+Note—Subscription of the document by the granter of it will be sufficient for the document to be formally valid, but witnessing of it may be necessary or desirable for other purposes (see the Requirements of Writing (Scotland) Act 1995).][205]

Members of the Committee
Secretary

Form E

The Limited hereby acknowledges to have received repayment of all moneys secured by the foregoing [describe deed] by A in the said society's favour.

[Testing clause+

+Note—Subscription of the document by the granter of it will be sufficient for the document to be formally valid, but witnessing of it may be necessary or desirable for other purposes (see the Requirements of Writing (Scotland) Act 1995).][206]

Members of the Committee
Secretary

SCHEDULE 4 - FORMS OF BOND FOR OFFICERS OF SOCIETY

Part I - Forms applicable in England, Wales and the Channel Islands

Form A

Know all men by these presents, that we, A. B., of , one of the officers of the Limited, herein-after referred to as "the Society," whose registered office is at in the country of , and C.D., of (as surety on behalf of the said A. B.), are jointly and severally held and firmly bound to the said society in the sum of , to be paid to the said society, or its certain attorney, for which payment well and truly to be made we jointly and severally bind ourselves, and each of us by himself, our and each of our heirs, executors, and administrators, firmly by these presents. Sealed with our seals. Dated the day of

Whereas the above-bounden A. B. has been duly appointed to the office of of the Society, and

he, together with the above-bounden C.D. as his surety, have entered into the above-written bond, subject to the condition herein-after contained: Now therefore the condition of the above-written bond is such, that if the said A. B. do render a just and true account of all moneys received and paid by him on account of the society, at such times as the rules thereof appoint, and do pay over all the moneys remaining in his hands, and assign and transfer or deliver all property (including books and papers) belonging to the society in his hands or custody to such person or persons as the society or the committee thereof appoint, according to the rules of the society, together with the proper and legal receipts or vouchers for such payments, then the above-written bond shall be void, but otherwise shall remain in full force.

Sealed and delivered in the presence of

Form B

Know all men by these presents that I , of , in the county of , am firmly bound to Limited, herein-after referred to as "the Society," whose registered office is at, in the county of, in the sum of pounds sterling to be paid to the said society or its assigns, for which payment to be truly made to the said society or its certain attorney or assigns I bind myself, my heirs, executors, and administrators, by these presents sealed with my seal.

[And know further that I [we] as surety [sureties] for the above-named principal obligor and such obligor are jointly and severally bound to the society in the sum aforesaid to be paid to the society or its assigns, for which payment to be truly made to the society or its certain attorney or assigns we firmly bind ourselves and each of us and each of our heirs, executors, and administrators by these presents sealed with our seals]

Dated the day of

The condition of the above-contained bond is that if the said faithfully execute the office of to the society during such time as he continues to hold the same in virtue either of his present appointment, or of any renewal thereof if such office is of a renewable character [without washing, embezzling, losing, misspending, misapplying, or unlawfully making away with any of the moneys, goods, chattels, wares, merchandise or effects whatsoever of the said society at any time committed to his charge, custody, or keeping by reason or means of his said office], and render a true and full account of all moneys received or paid by him on its behalf as and when he is required by the committee of the society for the time being, and pay over all the moneys remaining in his hands from time to time, and assign, transfer, and deliver up all securities, books, papers, property, and effects whatsoever of or belonging to the society in his charge, custody, or keeping, to such person or persons as the said committee may appoint, according to the rules or regulations of the society for the time being, together with the proper or legal receipts or vouchers for such payments; and in all other respects well and faithfully perform and fulfil the said office of to the society according to the rules thereof, then the above-contained bond shall be void and of no effect; but otherwise shall remain in full force.

Sealed and delivered by the above-named

[The words between brackets against which we have set out initials being first struck out][207] in the presence of us

and

Part II - Form applicable in Scotland

Form C

I,A. B., of , hereby bind and oblige myself to the extent of £ as cautioner for C.D., a person employed by the society, that he, the said C.D., shall on demand faithfully and truly account for all moneys received and paid to him for behoof of the said society, and also assign and transfer or deliver all property (including books and papers) belonging to the said society in his hands or custody, and that to such

person or persons as the said society or the committee thereof appoint, according to the rules of the said society.

[Testing clause+

+ Note—Subscription of the document by the cautioner will be sufficient for the document to be formally valid, but witnessing of it may be necessary or desirable for other purposes (see the Requirements of Writing (Scotland) Act 1995).][208]

Signature of cautioner

F., witness

G.H., witness

SCHEDULE 5[209]

---

1 Words in s. 1(1)(a) substituted (1.12.2001) by S.I. 2001/2617, arts. 2(b), 13(1), Sch. 3 Pt. III para. 215 (with art. 13(3), Sch. 5); S.I. 2001/3538, art. 2(1)

2 Words substituted by Companies Consolidation (Consequential Provisions) Act 1985 (c. 9, SIF 27), s. 30, Sch. 2

3 s. 2(1)(a)(b) word substituted (1.9.1996) by S.I. 1996/1738, arts. 1, 3(1)

4 s. 2(1)(a)(b) word substituted (1.9.1996) by S.I. 1996/1738, arts. 1, 3(1)

5 Words in s. 2(1)(b)(3) substituted (1.12.2001) by S.I. 2001/2617, arts. 2(b), 13(1), Sch. 3 Pt. III para. 215 (with art. 13(3), Sch. 5); S.I. 2001/3538, art. 2(1)

6 s. 2(2) words repealed (1.9.1996) by S.I. 1996/1738, arts. 1, 4(1)(a)(c)

7 s. 2(2) words substituted (1.9.1996) by S.I. 1996/1738, arts. 1, 4(1)(b)

8 Words in s. 2(1)(b)(3) substituted (1.12.2001) by S.I. 2001/2617, arts. 2(b), 13(1), Sch. 3 Pt. III para. 215 (with art. 13(3), Sch. 5); S.I. 2001/3538, art. 2(1)

9 Words in s. 2(3) substituted (1.12.2001) by S.I. 2001/3649, arts. 1, 181(2)

10 Words in s. 5(1)(5) substituted (1.12.2001) by S.I. 2001/2617, arts. 2(b), 13(1), Sch. 3 Pt. III para. 215 (with art. 13(3), Sch. 5); S.I. 2001/3538, art. 2(1)

11 Words in s. 5(2) substituted (21.12.1993) by 1993 c. 38, ss. 28(2), 36(1)

12 Words in s. 5(3)(b) substituted (1.12.2001) for subparagraphs (i)(ii) by S.I. 2001/2617, arts. 2(b), 13(1), Sch. 3 Pt. III para. 216(a) (with art. 13(3), Sch. 5); S.I. 2001/3538, art. 2(1)

13 Words in s. 5(1)(5) substituted (1.12.2001) by S.I. 2001/2617, arts. 2(b), 13(1), Sch. 3 Pt. III para. 215 (with art. 13(3), Sch. 5); S.I. 2001/3538, art. 2(1)

14 Word in s. 5(5) substituted (1.12.2001) by S.I. 2001/2617, arts. 2(b), 13(1), Sch. 3 Pt. III para. 216(b) (with art. 13(3), Sch. 5); S.I. 2001/3538, art. 2(1)

15 Words in s. 5(5) inserted (21.12.1993) by 1993 c. 38, ss. 28(3)(a)(c), 36(1)

16 Words in s. 5(5) substituted (21.12.1993) by 1993 c. 38, ss. 28(3)(b), 36(1)

17 Words in s. 5(1)(5) substituted (1.12.2001) by S.I. 2001/2617, arts. 2(b), 13(1), Sch. 3 Pt. III para. 215 (with art. 13(3), Sch. 5); S.I. 2001/3538, art. 2(1)

18 Word in s. 5(5) substituted (1.12.2001) by S.I. 2001/2617, arts. 2(b), 13(1), Sch. 3 Pt. III para. 216(b) (with art. 13(3), Sch. 5); S.I. 2001/3538, art. 2(1)

19 Words in s. 5(5) inserted (21.12.1993) by 1993 c. 38, ss. 28(3)(a)(c), 36(1)

20 Words substituted (E.W.S.) by virtue of Criminal Justice Act 1982 (c. 48, SIF 39:1), ss. 38, 46 and (S.) Criminal Procedure (Scotland) Act 1975 (c. 21, SIF 39:1), ss. 289F, 289G

21 s. 6(1)(b) words substituted (1.4.1997) by S.I. 1997/627, arts. 1, 2, Sch. para. 1

22 s. 6(1)(b) words inserted (1.4.1997) by S.I. 1997/627, arts. 1, 2, Sch. para. 1

23 Words substituted by Housing (Consequential Provisions) Act 1985 (c. 71, SIF 61), s. 4, Sch. 2 para. 8

24 s. 6(1) words substituted (15.3.1994) by S.I. 1994/341, arts. 1, 3

25 Words substituted by S.I. 1981/394, art. 3

26 Words substituted by S.I. 1981/394, art. 3

27 Words substituted by virtue of Criminal Justice Act 1982 (c. 48, SIF 39:1), s. 46 and (S.) Criminal Procedure (Scotland) Act 1975 (c. 21, SIF 39:1), s. 289G

28 s. 8 repealed (1.12.2001) by 2000 c. 8, ss. 338(3), 432(3) Sch. 18 Pt. IV para. 19, Sch. 22; S.I. 2001/3538, art. 2(1)

29 Words in s. 10(1)(2)(a)(b)(3)(b) substituted (1.12.2001) by S.I. 2001/2617, arts. 2(b), 13(1), Sch. 3 Pt. III para. 215 (with art. 13(3), Sch. 5); S.I. 2001/3538, art. 2(1)

30 s. 10(1)(a) words repealed (1.9.1996) by S.I. 1996/1738, arts. 1, 4(2)

31 s. 10(1)(a) words substituted (1.9.1996) by S.I. 1996/1738, arts. 1, 4(2)

32 Words in s. 10(1)(2)(a)(b)(3)(b) substituted (1.12.2001) by S.I. 2001/2617, arts. 2(b), 13(1), Sch. 3 Pt. III para. 215 (with art. 13(3), Sch. 5); S.I. 2001/3538, art. 2(1)

33 Words in s. 10(1)(2)(a)(b)(3)(b) substituted (1.12.2001) by S.I. 2001/2617, arts. 2(b), 13(1), Sch. 3 Pt. III para. 215 (with art. 13(3), Sch. 5); S.I. 2001/3538, art. 2(1)

34 Words in s. 10(1)(2)(a)(b)(3)(b) substituted (1.12.2001) by S.I. 2001/2617, arts. 2(b), 13(1), Sch. 3 Pt. III para. 215 (with

art. 13(3), Sch. 5); S.I. 2001/3538, art. 2(1)

[35] Words in s. 10(3) substituted (1.12.2001) by S.I. 2001/3649, arts. 1, 181(2)

[36] Words substituted by Friendly Societies Act 1974 (c. 46), Sch. 9 para. 18(a)

[37] Words in s. 11(1) substituted (1.12.2001) by S.I. 2001/2617, arts. 2(b), 13(1), Sch. 3 Pt. III para. 217 (with art. 13(3), Sch. 5); S.I. 2001/3538, art. 2(1)

[38] Words substituted by Friendly Societies Act 1974 (c. 46), Sch. 9 para. 18(b)

[39] Words substituted by virtue of Criminal Justice Act 1982 (c. 48, SIF 39:1), s. 46 and (S.) Criminal Procedure (Scotland) Act 1975 (c. 21, SIF 39:1), s. 289G

[40] Words in s. 16(3)(c)(4)(a)(b)(5) substituted (1.12.2001) by S.I. 2001/2617, arts. 2(b), 13(1), Sch. 3 Pt. III para. 215 (with art. 13(3), Sch. 5); S.I. 2001/3538, art. 2(1)

[41] Words in s. 16(1) repealed (1.12.2001) by S.I. 2001/3649, arts. 1, 179(1)

[42] Words in s. 16(1)(a) substituted (1.12.2001) by S.I. 2001/2617, arts. 2(b), 13(1), Sch. 3 Pt. III para. 218(b) (with art. 13(3), Sch. 5); S.I. 2001/3538, art. 2(1)

[43] s. 16(1)(a)(i) word substituted (1.9.1996) by S.I. 1996/1738, arts. 1, 3(2)(a)

[44] Words in s. 16(1)(b) substituted (1.12.2001) by S.I. 2001/2617, arts. 2(b), 13(1), Sch. 3 Pt. III para. 218(c) (with art. 13(3), Sch. 5); S.I. 2001/3538, art. 2(1)

[45] Words in s. 16(1)(b) substituted (1.12.2001) by S.I. 2001/2617, arts. 2(b), 13(1), Sch. 3 Pt. III para. 218(c) (with art. 13(3), Sch. 5); S.I. 2001/3538, art. 2(1)

[46] Words in s. 16(1)(c) repealed (1.12.2001) by S.I. 2001/2617, arts. 2(b), 13(1)(2), Sch. 3 Pt. III para. 218(d)(i), Sch. 4 (with art. 13(3), Sch. 5); S.I. 2001/3538, art. 2(1)

[47] Words in s. 16(1)(c)(i) substituted (1.12.2001) by S.I. 2001/2617, arts. 2(b), 13(1), Sch. 3 Pt. III para. 218(d)(ii)(A)(B) (with art. 13(3), Sch. 5); S.I. 2001/3538, art. 2(1)

[48] Words in s. 16(1)(c)(i) substituted (1.12.2001) by S.I. 2001/2617, arts. 2(b), 13(1), Sch. 3 Pt. III para. 218(d)(ii)(A)(B) (with art. 13(3), Sch. 5); S.I. 2001/3538, art. 2(1)

[49] Words in s. 16(1)(c)(ii)(iii) substituted (1.12.2001) by S.I. 2001/2617, arts. 2(b), 13(1), Sch. 3 Pt. III para. 218(d)(iii) (with art. 13(3), Sch. 5); S.I. 2001/3538, art. 2(1)

[50] Words in s. 16(1)(c)(ii)(iii) substituted (1.12.2001) by S.I. 2001/2617, arts. 2(b), 13(1), Sch. 3 Pt. III para. 218(d)(iii) (with art. 13(3), Sch. 5); S.I. 2001/3538, art. 2(1)

[51] Words in s. 16(3)(c)(4)(a)(b)(5) substituted (1.12.2001) by S.I. 2001/2617, arts. 2(b), 13(1), Sch. 3 Pt. III para. 215 (with art. 13(3), Sch. 5); S.I. 2001/3538, art. 2(1)

[52] Words in s. 16(3)(c)(4)(a)(b)(5) substituted (1.12.2001) by S.I. 2001/2617, arts. 2(b), 13(1), Sch. 3 Pt. III para. 215 (with art. 13(3), Sch. 5); S.I. 2001/3538, art. 2(1)

[53] Words in s. 16(3)(c)(4)(a)(b)(5) substituted (1.12.2001) by S.I. 2001/2617, arts. 2(b), 13(1), Sch. 3 Pt. III para. 215 (with art. 13(3), Sch. 5); S.I. 2001/3538, art. 2(1)

[54] Words in s. 16(4) substituted (1.12.2001) by S.I. 2001/2617, arts. 2(b), 13(1), Sch. 3 Pt. III para. 219 (with art. 13(3), Sch. 5); S.I. 2001/3538, art. 2(1)

[55] Words in s. 16(4) substituted (1.12.2001) by S.I. 2001/2617, arts. 2(b), 13(1), Sch. 3 Pt. III para. 219 (with art. 13(3), Sch. 5); S.I. 2001/3538, art. 2(1)

[56] Words in s. 16(3)(c)(4)(a)(b)(5) substituted (1.12.2001) by S.I. 2001/2617, arts. 2(b), 13(1), Sch. 3 Pt. III para. 215 (with art. 13(3), Sch. 5); S.I. 2001/3538, art. 2(1)

[57] Words in s. 16(4) substituted (1.12.2001) by S.I. 2001/2617, arts. 2(b), 13(1), Sch. 3 Pt. III para. 219 (with art. 13(3), Sch. 5); S.I. 2001/3538, art. 2(1)

[58] Words in s. 16(4) substituted (1.12.2001) by S.I. 2001/2617, arts. 2(b), 13(1), Sch. 3 Pt. III para. 219 (with art. 13(3), Sch. 5); S.I. 2001/3538, art. 2(1)

[59] Words in s. 16(3)(c)(4)(a)(b)(5) substituted (1.12.2001) by S.I. 2001/2617, arts. 2(b), 13(1), Sch. 3 Pt. III para. 215 (with art. 13(3), Sch. 5); S.I. 2001/3538, art. 2(1)

[60] Words substituted (E.W.S.) by virtue of Criminal Justice Act 1982 (c. 48, SIF 39:1), ss. 38, 46 and (S.) Criminal Procedure (Scotland) Act 1975 (c. 21, SIF 39:1), ss. 289F, 289G

[61] Words in s. 17(1)(2)(3) substituted (1.12.2001) by S.I. 2001/2617, arts. 2(b), 13(1), Sch. 3 Pt. III para. 215 (with art. 13(3), Sch. 5); S.I. 2001/3538, art. 2(1)

[62] Words in s. 17(1) repealed (1.12.2001) by S.I. 2001/2617, arts. 2(b), 13(1)(2), Sch. 3 Pt. III para. 220(a)(i), Sch. 4 (with art. 13(3), Sch. 5); S.I. 2001/3538, art. 2(1)

[63] Words in s. 17(1)(2)(3) substituted (1.12.2001) by S.I. 2001/2617, arts. 2(b), 13(1), Sch. 3 Pt. III para. 215 (with art. 13(3), Sch. 5); S.I. 2001/3538, art. 2(1)

[64] Words in s. 17(1) substituted (1.12.2001) by S.I. 2001/2617, arts. 2(b), 13(1), Sch. 3 Pt. III para. 220(a)(ii) (with art. 13(3), Sch. 5); S.I. 2001/3538, art. 2(1)

[65] Words in s. 17(1)(b) repealed (1.12.2001) by S.I. 2001/2617, arts. 2(b), 13(1)(2), Sch. 3 Pt. III para. 220(a)(iii), Sch. 4 (with art. 13(3), Sch. 5); S.I. 2001/3538, art. 2(1)

[66] Words in s. 17(1)(2)(3) substituted (1.12.2001) by S.I. 2001/2617, arts. 2(b), 13(1), Sch. 3 Pt. III para. 215 (with art. 13(3), Sch. 5); S.I. 2001/3538, art. 2(1)

[67] Words in s. 17(2) substituted (1.12.2001) by S.I. 2001/2617, arts. 2(b), 13(1), Sch. 3 Pt. III para. 220(b) (with art. 13(3),

Sch. 5); S.I. 2001/3538, art. 2(1)

[68] Words in s. 17(1)(2)(3) substituted (1.12.2001) by S.I. 2001/2617, arts. 2(b), 13(1), Sch. 3 Pt. III para. 215 (with art. 13(3), Sch. 5); S.I. 2001/3538, art. 2(1)

[69] s. 17(6) repealed (1.12.2001) by S.I. 2001/2617, arts. 2(b), 13(1)(2), Sch. 3 Pt. III para. 220(c), Sch. 4 (with art. 13(3), Sch. 5); S.I. 2001/3538, art. 2(1)

[70] Words in s. 18(1)(3) substituted (1.12.2001) by S.I. 2001/2617, arts. 2(b), 13(1), Sch. 3 Pt. III para. 215 (with art. 13(3), Sch. 5); S.I. 2001/3538, art. 2(1)

[71] Words in s. 18(1)(a) substituted (1.12.2001) by S.I. 2001/2617, arts. 2(b), 13(1), Sch. 3 Pt. III para. 221(a) (with art. 13(3), Sch. 5); S.I. 2001/3538, art. 2(1)

[72] Words in s. 18(2) substituted (1.12.2001) by S.I. 2001/2617, arts. 2(b), 13(1), Sch. 3 Pt. III para. 221(b) (with art. 13(3), Sch. 5); S.I. 2001/3538, art. 2(1)

[73] Words in s. 18(1)(3) substituted (1.12.2001) by S.I. 2001/2617, arts. 2(b), 13(1), Sch. 3 Pt. III para. 215 (with art. 13(3), Sch. 5); S.I. 2001/3538, art. 2(1)

[74] Word substituted by (S.) Age of Majority (Scotland) Act 1969 (c. 39), s. 1(3) Sch. 1 Pt. I and Family Law Reform Act 1969 (c. 46), s. 1(3), Sch. 1 Pt. I

[75] Word substituted by S.I. 1975/1137, art. 3(a)

[76] Word substituted by S.I. 1975/1137, art. 3(a)

[77] s. 24(4) repealed by Administration of Estates (Small Payments) Act 1965 (c. 32), Sch. 4

[78] Word repealed by Administration of Estates (Small Payments) Act 1965 (c. 32), Sch. 3

[79] "£5,000" substituted by virtue of Administration of Estates (Small Payments) Act 1965 (c. 32, SIF 116:1), ss. 1(1), 6, Sch. 1 Pt. I and S.I. 1984/539, art. 2(a)

[80] Words inserted by Administration of Estates (Small Payments) Act 1965 (c. 32), Sch. 3

[81] Words substituted by Family Law Reform Act 1969 (c. 46), s. 19(2)

[82] s. 31(a)(ia) words repealed (1.4.1995), by 1994 c. 29 s. 93, Sch. 9 Pt. I; S.I. 1994/3262, art. 4(1) Sch.

[83] s. 31(a)(i)(ia) substituted (2.11.1992) for s. 31(a)(i) by Local Government Finance Act 1992 (c. 14), s. 117(1), Sch. 13 para. 13 (with s. 118(1)(2)(4)); S.I. 1992/2454, art. 2.

[84] s. 31(a) paragraphs (i)–(iii) substituted for "any local authority within the meaning of the Local Loans Act 1875" by S.I.1990/776, art. 8, Sch. 3 para. 9

[85] Words substituted by Building Societies Act 1986 (c. 53, SIF 16), s. 120, Sch. 18 para. 6

[86] Words substituted by Building Societies Act 1986 (c. 53, SIF 16), s. 120, Sch. 18 para. 6

[87] This version of this provision extends to Scotland and the Channel Islands only; a separate version has been created for England and Wales only.

[88] Words substituted by virtue of Decimal Currency Act 1969 (c. 19), s. 10(1)

[89] Words repealed (1.8.1971) by Finance Act 1971 (c. 68), Sch. 14 Pt. VI

[90] Words in s. 34(5)(a) repealed (S.)(1.8.1995) by 1995 c. 7, ss. 14(2), 15(2), Sch. 5 (with ss. 9(3)(5)(7), 13, 14(3))

[91] s. 36 repealed (S.) (1.8.1995) by 1995 c. 7, ss. 14(2), 15(2) Sch. 5(with ss. 9(3)(5)(7), 13, 14(3))

[92] ss. 37, 38 repealed by Friendly and Industrial and Provident Societies Act 1968 (c. 55), Sch. 2

[93] s. 39(1) words substituted (1.9.1996) by S.I. 1996/1738, arts. 1, 5(2)(a)(b)

[94] Words in s. 39(1)(2A)(3) substituted (1.12.2001) by S.I. 2001/2617, arts. 2(b), 13(1), Sch. 3 Pt. III para. 215 (with art. 13(3), Sch. 5); S.I. 2001/3538, art. 2(1)

[95] s. 39(1) words substituted (1.9.1996) by S.I. 1996/1738, arts. 1, 5(2)(a)(b)

[96] s. 39(1) words inserted (1.9.1996) by S.I. 1996/1738, arts. 1, 9(1)

[97] s. 39(2)(a)(b) repealed by Friendly and Industrial and Provident Societies Act 1968 (c. 55), Sch. 2

[98] Words substituted by Friendly and Industrial and Provident Societies Act 1968 (c. 55), Sch. 1 para. 10

[99] Words in s. 39(1)(2A)(3) substituted (1.12.2001) by S.I. 2001/2617, arts. 2(b), 13(1), Sch. 3 Pt. III para. 215 (with art. 13(3), Sch. 5); S.I. 2001/3538, art. 2(1)

[100] s. 39(2A) inserted by Friendly and Industrial and Provident Societies Act 1968 (c. 55), Sch. 1 para. 10

[101] Words in s. 39(1)(2A)(3) substituted (1.12.2001) by S.I. 2001/2617, arts. 2(b), 13(1), Sch. 3 Pt. III para. 215 (with art. 13(3), Sch. 5); S.I. 2001/3538, art. 2(1)

[102] Word in s. 39(3) substituted (1.12.2001) by S.I. 2001/2617, arts. 2(b), 13(1), Sch. 3 Pt. III para. 222 (with art. 13(3), Sch. 5); S.I. 2001/3538, art. 2(1)

[103] s. 39(3) words repealed (1.9.1996) by S.I. 1996/1738, arts. 1, 5(3)

[104] s. 40 words repealed (1.9.1996) by S.I. 1996/1738, arts. 1, 9(2)

[105] Words substituted by County Courts Act 1984 (c. 28, SIF 34), s. 148(1), Sch. 2 para. 29

[106] Words in s. 43(a)(b)(c) substituted (1.12.2001 subject to a saving in S.I. 2001/2617, art. 13(3), Sch. 5 para. 2(d)) by S.I. 2001/2617, art. 13(1), Sch. 3 Pt. III para. 215(i)(ii) (with art. 13(3), Sch. 5 para. 2(d))

[107] Words in s. 43(a)(b)(c) substituted (1.12.2001 subject to a saving in S.I. 2001/2617, art. 13(3), Sch. 5 para. 2(d)) by S.I. 2001/2617, art. 13(1), Sch. 3 Pt. III para. 215(i)(ii) (with art. 13(3), Sch. 5 para. 2(d))

[108] Words in s. 43(a)(b)(c) substituted (1.12.2001 subject to a saving in S.I. 2001/2617, art. 13(3), Sch. 5 para. 2(d)) by S.I. 2001/2617, art. 13(1), Sch. 3 Pt. III para. 215(i)(ii) (with art. 13(3), Sch. 5 para. 2(d))

[109] Words in s. 43(a)(b)(c) substituted (1.12.2001 subject to a saving in S.I. 2001/2617, art. 13(3), Sch. 5 para. 2(d)) by S.I.

2001/2617, art. 13(1), Sch. 3 Pt. III para. 215(i)(ii) (with art. 13(3), Sch. 5 para. 2(d))

110 Words in s. 44(4) substituted (1.12.2001) by S.I. 2001/2617, arts. 2(b), 13(1), Sch. 3 Pt. III para. 223 (with art. 13(3), Sch. 5); S.I. 2001/3538, art. 2(1)

111 Words in s. 47(1)(2)(4) substituted (1.12.2001) by S.I. 2001/2617, arts. 2(b), 13(1), Sch. 3 Pt. III para. 215 (with art. 13(3), Sch. 5); S.I. 2001/3538, art. 2(1)

112 Words in s. 47(1)(2) substituted (1.12.2001) by S.I. 2001/2617, arts. 2(b), 13(1), Sch. 3 Pt. III para. 224 (with art. 13(3), Sch. 5); S.I. 2001/3538, art. 2(1)

113 Words in s. 47(1)(2)(4) substituted (1.12.2001) by S.I. 2001/2617, arts. 2(b), 13(1), Sch. 3 Pt. III para. 215 (with art. 13(3), Sch. 5); S.I. 2001/3538, art. 2(1)

114 Words in s. 47(1)(2) substituted (1.12.2001) by S.I. 2001/2617, arts. 2(b), 13(1), Sch. 3 Pt. III para. 224 (with art. 13(3), Sch. 5); S.I. 2001/3538, art. 2(1)

115 Words in s. 47(1)(2)(4) substituted (1.12.2001) by S.I. 2001/2617, arts. 2(b), 13(1), Sch. 3 Pt. III para. 215 (with art. 13(3), Sch. 5); S.I. 2001/3538, art. 2(1)

116 Words in s. 47(1)(2)(4) substituted (1.12.2001) by S.I. 2001/2617, arts. 2(b), 13(1), Sch. 3 Pt. III para. 215 (with art. 13(3), Sch. 5); S.I. 2001/3538, art. 2(1)

117 Words in s. 48(1)(3) substituted (1.12.2001) by S.I. 2001/2617, arts. 2(b), 13(1), Sch. 3 Pt. III para. 215 (with art. 13(3), Sch. 5); S.I. 2001/3538, art. 2(1)

118 Words in s. 48(1)(3) substituted (1.12.2001) by S.I. 2001/2617, arts. 2(b), 13(1), Sch. 3 Pt. III para. 215 (with art. 13(3), Sch. 5); S.I. 2001/3538, art. 2(1)

119 Words in s. 48 substituted (1.12.2001) by S.I. 2001/2617, arts. 2(b), 13(1), Sch. 3 Pt. III para. 225 (with art. 13(3), Sch. 5); S.I. 2001/3538, art. 2(1)

120 Words in s. 48(1)(3) substituted (1.12.2001) by S.I. 2001/2617, arts. 2(b), 13(1), Sch. 3 Pt. III para. 215 (with art. 13(3), Sch. 5); S.I. 2001/3538, art. 2(1)

121 Words in s. 48 substituted (1.12.2001) by S.I. 2001/2617, arts. 2(b), 13(1), Sch. 3 Pt. III para. 225 (with art. 13(3), Sch. 5); S.I. 2001/3538, art. 2(1)

122 Words substituted (E.W.S.) by virtue of Criminal Justice Act 1982 (c. 48, SIF 39:1), ss. 38, 46 and (S.) Criminal Procedure (Scotland) Act 1975 (c. 21, SIF 39:1), ss. 289F, 289G

123 Words in s. 48(1)(3) substituted (1.12.2001) by S.I. 2001/2617, arts. 2(b), 13(1), Sch. 3 Pt. III para. 215 (with art. 13(3), Sch. 5); S.I. 2001/3538, art. 2(1)

124 Words in s. 48 substituted (1.12.2001) by S.I. 2001/2617, arts. 2(b), 13(1), Sch. 3 Pt. III para. 225 (with art. 13(3), Sch. 5); S.I. 2001/3538, art. 2(1)

125 Words in s. 48 substituted (1.12.2001) by S.I. 2001/2617, arts. 2(b), 13(1), Sch. 3 Pt. III para. 225 (with art. 13(3), Sch. 5); S.I. 2001/3538, art. 2(1)

126 Words in s. 48 substituted (1.12.2001) by S.I. 2001/2617, arts. 2(b), 13(1), Sch. 3 Pt. III para. 225 (with art. 13(3), Sch. 5); S.I. 2001/3538, art. 2(1)

127 Words in s. 48 substituted (1.12.2001) by S.I. 2001/2617, arts. 2(b), 13(1), Sch. 3 Pt. III para. 225 (with art. 13(3), Sch. 5); S.I. 2001/3538, art. 2(1)

128 Words in s. 48(1)(3) substituted (1.12.2001) by S.I. 2001/2617, arts. 2(b), 13(1), Sch. 3 Pt. III para. 215 (with art. 13(3), Sch. 5); S.I. 2001/3538, art. 2(1)

129 Words in s. 49(1)(2)(3)(4)(6) substituted (1.12.2001) by S.I. 2001/2617, arts. 2(b), 13(1), Sch. 3 Pt. III para. 215 (with art. 13(3), Sch. 5); S.I. 2001/3538, art. 2(1)

130 Words in s. 49(1) repealed (1.12.2001) by S.I. 2001/2617, arts. 2(b), 13(1)(2), Sch. 3 Pt. III para. 226(a), Sch. 4 (with art. 13(3), Sch. 5); S.I. 2001/3538, art. 2(1)

131 Words in s. 49(1)(2)(3)(4)(6) substituted (1.12.2001) by S.I. 2001/2617, arts. 2(b), 13(1), Sch. 3 Pt. III para. 215 (with art. 13(3), Sch. 5); S.I. 2001/3538, art. 2(1)

132 Words in s. 49(1)(2)(3)(4)(6) substituted (1.12.2001) by S.I. 2001/2617, arts. 2(b), 13(1), Sch. 3 Pt. III para. 215 (with art. 13(3), Sch. 5); S.I. 2001/3538, art. 2(1)

133 Word in s. 49(3) substituted (1.12.2001) by S.I. 2001/2617, arts. 2(b), 13(1), Sch. 3 Pt. III para. 226(b) (with art. 13(3), Sch. 5); S.I. 2001/3538, art. 2(1)

134 Words in s. 49(1)(2)(3)(4)(6) substituted (1.12.2001) by S.I. 2001/2617, arts. 2(b), 13(1), Sch. 3 Pt. III para. 215 (with art. 13(3), Sch. 5); S.I. 2001/3538, art. 2(1)

135 Words in s. 49(1)(2)(3)(4)(6) substituted (1.12.2001) by S.I. 2001/2617, arts. 2(b), 13(1), Sch. 3 Pt. III para. 215 (with art. 13(3), Sch. 5); S.I. 2001/3538, art. 2(1)

136 s. 49(7) repealed (1.12.2001) by S.I. 2001/2617, arts. 2(b), 13(1), Sch. 3 Pt. III para. 226(c), Sch. 4 (with art. 13(3), Sch. 5); S.I. 2001/3538, art. 2(1)

137 Words in s. 50(4) substituted (1.12.2001) by S.I. 2001/2617, arts. 2(b), 13(1), Sch. 3 Pt. III para. 215 (with art. 13(3), Sch. 5); S.I. 2001/3538, art. 2(1)

138 Word in s. 50(4) substituted (1.12.2001) by S.I. 2001/2617, arts. 2(b), 13(1), Sch. 3 Pt. III para. 227 (with art. 13(3), Sch. 5); S.I. 2001/3538, art. 2(1)

139 Words substituted by Companies Consolidation (Consequential Provisions) Act 1985 (c. 9, SIF 27), s. 30, Sch. 2

140 Words in s. 52(2)(4) substituted (1.12.2001) by S.I. 2001/2617, arts. 2(b), 13(1), Sch. 3 Pt. III para. 215 (with art. 13(3),

Sch. 5); S.I. 2001/3538, art. 2(1)

[141] Words in s. 52(2)(4) substituted (1.12.2001) by S.I. 2001/2617, arts. 2(b), 13(1), Sch. 3 Pt. III para. 215 (with art. 13(3), Sch. 5); S.I. 2001/3538, art. 2(1)

[142] Words substituted by Companies Consolidation (Consequential Provisions) Act 1985 (c. 9, SIF 27), s. 30, Sch. 2

[143] s. 52(3)-(3B) substituted for s. 52(3) (8.9.2002) by 2002 c. 20, ss. 1(2), 4(2)

[144] Words in s. 52(2)(4) substituted (1.12.2001) by S.I. 2001/2617, arts. 2(b), 13(1), Sch. 3 Pt. III para. 215 (with art. 13(3), Sch. 5); S.I. 2001/3538, art. 2(1)

[145] Words substituted by Companies Consolidation (Consequential Provisions) Act 1985 (c. 9, SIF 27), s. 30, Sch. 2

[146] Words substituted by Industrial and Provident Societies Act 1975 (c. 41), s. 3(3)

[147] s. 53(2) word substituted (1.9.1996) by S.I. 1996/1738, arts. 1, 3(3)

[148] Words in s. 53(2)(a)(3)(4) substituted (1.12.2001) by S.I. 2001/2617, arts. 2(b), 13(1), Sch. 3 Pt. III para. 215 (with art. 13(3), Sch. 5); S.I. 2001/3538, art. 2(1)

[149] Words in s. 53(2)(a)(3)(4) substituted (1.12.2001) by S.I. 2001/2617, arts. 2(b), 13(1), Sch. 3 Pt. III para. 215 (with art. 13(3), Sch. 5); S.I. 2001/3538, art. 2(1)

[150] Words in s. 53(2)(a)(3)(4) substituted (1.12.2001) by S.I. 2001/2617, arts. 2(b), 13(1), Sch. 3 Pt. III para. 215 (with art. 13(3), Sch. 5); S.I. 2001/3538, art. 2(1)

[151] Words substituted by Companies Consolidation (Consequential Provisions) Act 1985 (c. 9, SIF 27), s. 30, Sch. 2

[152] Words substituted by virtue of Companies Consolidation (Consequential Provisions) Act 1985 (c. 9, SIF 27), s. 30, Sch. 2 and Insolvency Act 1986 (c. 45, SIF 66), s. 439(2), Sch. 14

[153] Words in s. 55(a)(i) substituted (1.12.2001 subject to a saving in S.I 2001/2617, art. 13(3), Sch. 5 para. 2(d)) by S.I. 2001/2617, art. 13(1), Sch. 3 Pt. III para. 215(i)

[154] S. 55(a)(ia) inserted (1.12.2001) by S.I. 2001/2617, arts. 2(b), 13(1), Sch. 3 Pt. III para. 229(b) (with art. 13(3), Sch. 5); S.I. 2001/3538, art. 2(1)

[155] Words in s. 56 substituted (1.12.2001 subject to a saving in S.I 2001/2617, art. 13(3), Sch. 5 para. 2(d)) by S.I. 2001/2617, art. 13(1), Sch. 3 Pt. III para. 215(i)(ii))

[156] Words in s. 56 substituted (1.12.2001 subject to a saving in S.I 2001/2617, art. 13(3), Sch. 5 para. 2(d)) by S.I. 2001/2617, art. 13(1), Sch. 3 Pt. III para. 215(i)(ii))

[157] Words in s. 58(2)(d) substituted (1.12.2001 subject to a saving by S.I. 2001/2617, art. 13(3), Sch. 5 para. 2(d)) by S.I. 2001/2617, art. 13(1), Sch. 3 Pt. III para. 215(iii)

[158] Words in s. 58 substituted (1.12.2001) by S.I. 2001/3617, arts. 2(b), 13(1), Sch. 3 Pt. III para. 215 (with art. 13(3), Sch. 5); S.I. 2001/3538, art. 2(1)

[159] Words in s. 58 substituted (1.12.2001) by S.I. 2001/3617, arts. 2(b), 13(1), Sch. 3 Pt. III para. 215 (with art. 13(3), Sch. 5); S.I. 2001/3538, art. 2(1)

[160] Words in s. 58 substituted (1.12.2001) by S.I. 2001/3617, arts. 2(b), 13(1), Sch. 3 Pt. III para. 215 (with art. 13(3), Sch. 5); S.I. 2001/3538, art. 2(1)

[161] Words in s. 58(6) repealed (1.12.2001) by S.I. 2001/3649, arts. 1, 180

[162] Words in s. 58 substituted (1.12.2001) by S.I. 2001/3617, arts. 2(b), 13(1), Sch. 3 Pt. III para. 215 (with art. 13(3), Sch. 5); S.I. 2001/3538, art. 2(1)

[163] Words in s. 58 substituted (1.12.2001) by S.I. 2001/3617, arts. 2(b), 13(1), Sch. 3 Pt. III para. 215 (with art. 13(3), Sch. 5); S.I. 2001/3538, art. 2(1)

[164] Words in s. 58 substituted (1.12.2001) by S.I. 2001/3617, arts. 2(b), 13(1), Sch. 3 Pt. III para. 215 (with art. 13(3), Sch. 5); S.I. 2001/3538, art. 2(1)

[165] Words in s. 59 substituted (1.12.2001 subject to a saving in S.I 2001/2617, art. 13(3), Sch. 5 para. 2(d)) by S.I. 2001/2617, art. 13(1), Sch. 3 Pt. III para. 215(i)(ii)

[166] Words in s. 59 substituted (1.12.2001 subject to a saving in S.I 2001/2617, art. 13(3), Sch. 5 para. 2(d)) by S.I. 2001/2617, art. 13(1), Sch. 3 Pt. III para. 215(i)(ii)

[167] Words in s. 60(1) inserted (1.12.2001) by S.I. 2001/2617, arts. 2(b), 13(1), Sch. 3 Pt. III para. 230(a) (with art. 13(3), Sch. 5); S.I. 2001/3538, art. 2(1)

[168] s. 60(1A) inserted (1.12.2001) by S.I. 2001/2617, arts. 2(b), 13(1), Sch. 3 Pt. III para. 230(b) (with art. 13(3), Sch. 5); S.I. 2001/3538, art. 2(1)

[169] s. 60(2) substituted (E.W.S.)(13.1.1993) by Friendly Societies Act 1992 (c. 40), s. 83 (with ss. 7(5), 93(4)); S.I. 1993/16, art. 2, Sch. 2

[170] s. 60(2A) inserted (1.12.2001) by S.I. 2001/2617, arts. 2(b), 13(1), Sch. 3 Pt. III para. 230(c) (with art. 13(3), Sch. 5); S.I. 2001/3538, art. 2(1)

[171] s. 60(8)(a) substituted (1.12.2001) by S.I. 2001/2617, arts. 2(b), 13(1), Sch. 3 Pt. III para. 230(d)(i) (with art. 13(3), Sch. 5); S.I. 2001/3538, art. 2(1)

[172] Words in s. 60(8)(b) substituted (1.12.2001) by S.I. 2001/2617, arts. 2(b), 13(1), Sch. 3 Pt. III para. 230(d)(ii) (with art. 13(3), Sch. 5); S.I. 2001/3538, art. 2(1)

[173] s. 60(8)(c) repealed (1.12.2001) by S.I. 2001/2617, arts. 2(b), 13(1)(2), Sch. 3 Pt. III para. 230(e), Sch. 4 (with art. 13(3), Sch. 5); S.I. 2001/3538, art. 2(1)

[174] Words in s. 60(9) substituted (1.12.2001) by S.I. 2001/2617, arts. 2(b), 13(1), Sch. 3 Pt. III para. 230(e) (with art. 13(3),

Sch. 5); S.I. 2001/3538, art. 2(1)

175 s. 60(9) substituted (31.1.1997) by 1996 c. 23, s. 107(1), Sch. 3 para. 20(3); S.I. 1996/3146, art. 3

176 Words in s. 61(b) substituted (1.12.2001) by S.I. 2001/2617, arts. 2(b), 13(1), Sch. 3 Pt. III para. 215 (with art. 13(3), Sch. 5); S.I. 2001/3538, art. 2(1)

177 Words substituted by virtue of Criminal Justice Act 1982 (c. 48, SIF 39:1), s. 39, Sch. 3, Sch. 6 and (S.) by Criminal Procedure (Scotland) Act 1975 (c. 21, SIF 39:1), Sch. 7D also s. 61 words substituted (S.) (1.4.1996) by vitue of 1995 c. 40 ss. 3, 7(2), Sch. 1 para. 10 Sch. 2 Pt. III

178 Words substituted by virtue of Criminal Justice Act 1982 (c. 48, SIF 39:1), s. 46 and (S.) Criminal Procedure (Scotland) Act 1975 (c. 21, SIF 39:1), s. 289G

179 Words substituted (E.W.S.) by virtue of Criminal Justice Act 1982 (c. 48, SIF 39:1), ss. 38, 46 and (S.) Criminal Procedure (Scotland) Act 1975 (c. 21, SIF 39:1), ss. 289F, 289G

180 Words in s. 66(1)(b) repealed (1.12.2001) by S.I. 2001/2617, arts. 2(b), 13(1)(2), Sch. 3 Pt. III para. 232(a)(i), Sch. 4 (with art. 13(3), Sch. 5); S.I. 2001/3538, art. 2(1)

181 Words in s. 66(1)(a)(ii) substituted (1.12.2001) by S.I. 2001/2617, arts. 2(b), 13(1), Sch. 3 Pt. III para. 215 (with art. 13(3), Sch. 5); S.I. 2001/3538, art. 2(1)

182 s. 66(a)(iii) substituted (1.12.2001) by S.I. 2001/2617, arts. 2(b), 13(1), Sch. 3 Pt. III para. 232(a)(ii) (with art. 13(3), Sch. 5); S.I. 2001/3538, art. 2(1)

183 s. 66(1)(c) substituted (1.12.2001) by S.I. 2001/2617, arts. 2(b), 13(1), Sch. 3 Pt. III para. 232(a)(iii) (with art. 13(3), Sch. 5); S.I. 2001/3538, art. 2(1)

184 Words in s. 66(2) substituted (1.12.2001) by S.I. 2001/2617, arts. 2(b), 13(1), Sch. 3 Pt. III para. 232(b)(i) (with art. 13(3), Sch. 5); S.I. 2001/3538, art. 2(1)

185 Words in s. 66(2) substituted (1.12.2001) by S.I. 2001/2617, arts. 2(b), 13(1), Sch. 3 Pt. III para. 232(b)(ii) (with art. 13(3), Sch. 5); S.I. 2001/3538, art. 2(1)

186 Words in s. 67(1) substituted (1.12.2001) by S.I. 2001/2617, arts. 2(b), 13(1), Sch. 3 Pt. III para. 215 (with art. 13(3), Sch. 5); S.I. 2001/3538, art. 2(1)

187 s. 70 repealed (1.12.2001) by 2000 c. 8, ss. 338(3), 432(3), Sch. 18 Pt. IV para. 20, Sch. 22; S.I. 2001/3538, art. 2(1)

188 s. 70A inserted (1.12.2001) by S.I. 2001/2617, arts. 2(b), 13(1), Sch. 3 Pt. III para. 234 (with art. 13(3), Sch. 5); S.I. 2001/3538, art. 2(1)

189 s. 71 repealed (1.12.2001) by S.I. 2001/3649, arts. 1, 181(1)

190 Words in s. 72 substituted (1.12.2001) for s. 72(1) by S.I. 2001/3649, arts. 1, 182

191 s. 72(2)(3)(4) (1.12.2001) by S.I. 2001/2617, arts. 2(b), 13(1), Sch. 3 Pt. III para. 235 (with art. 13(3), Sch. 5); S.I. 2001/3538, art. 2(1)

192 s. 73 repealed (1.12.2001) by S.I. 2001/2617, arts. 2(b), 13(1)(2), Sch. 3 Pt. III para. 236, Sch. 4 (with art. 13(3), Sch. 5); S.I. 2001/3538, art. 2(1)

193 s. 74 re-numbered as s. 74(1) (1.12.2001) by S.I. 2001/2617, arts. 2(b), 13(1), Sch. 3 Pt. III para. 237 (with art. 13(3), Sch. 5); S.I. 2001/3538, art. 2(1)

194 Definition in s. 74(1) inserted (1.12.2001) by S.I. 2001/2617, arts. 2(b), 13(1), Sch. 3 Pt. III para. 237(a) (with art. 13(3), Sch. 5); S.I. 2001/3538, art. 2(1)

195 Words substituted by Companies Consolidation (Consequential Provisions) Act 1985 (c. 9, SIF 27), s. 30, Sch. 2

196 Words in paragraphs (a) and (b) in definition in s. 74(1) substituted (1.12.2001) by S.I. 2001/2617, arts. 2(b), 13(1), Sch. 3 Pt. III para. 237(b) (with art. 13(3), Sch. 5); S.I. 2001/3538, art. 2(1)

197 Words in paragraphs (a) and (b) in definition in s. 74(1) substituted (1.12.2001) by S.I. 2001/2617, arts. 2(b), 13(1), Sch. 3 Pt. III para. 237(b) (with art. 13(3), Sch. 5); S.I. 2001/3538, art. 2(1)

198 Words substituted by Friendly and Industrial and Provident Societies Act 1968 (c. 55), Sch. 1 para. 11

199 s. 74(2) inserted (1.12.2001) by S.I. 2001/2617, arts. 2(b), 13(1), Sch. 3 Pt. III para. 237(c) (with art. 13(3), Sch. 5); S.I. 2001/3538, art. 2(1)

200 Words in s. 76(1) substituted (1.12.2001) by S.I. 2001/2617, arts. 2(b), 13(1), Sch. 3 Pt. III para. 238(a) (with art. 13(3), Sch. 5); S.I. 2001/3538, art. 2(1)

201 Word in s. 76(1) substituted (1.12.2001) by S.I. 2001/2617, arts. 2(b), 13(1), Sch. 3 Pt. III para. 238(b) (with art. 13(3), Sch. 5); S.I. 2001/3538, art. 2(1)

202 s. 77(1), Sch. 5 repealed by Statute Law (Repeals) Act 1974 (c. 22), Sch. 1 Pt. XI

203 Words substituted by Friendly and Industrial and Provident Societies Act 1968 (c. 55), Sch. 1 para. 12

204 Sch. 3 Forms C-E words substituted (1.8.1995) by 1995 c. 7 s. 14(1), 15(2) Sch. 4 para. 42 (with s. 9(3)(5)(7), 13, 14(3))

205 Sch. 3 Forms C-E words substituted (1.8.1995) by 1995 c. 7 s. 14(1), 15(2) Sch. 4 para. 42 (with s. 9(3)(5)(7), 13, 14(3))

206 Sch. 3 Forms C-E words substituted (1.8.1995) by 1995 c. 7 s. 14(1), 15(2) Sch. 4 para. 42 (with s. 9(3)(5)(7), 13, 14(3))

207 If no words are struck out in the bond or condition, strike out these words and let the witnesses set their initials in the margin.

208 Sch. 4 Form C words substituted (1.8.1995) by 1995 c. 7 s. 14(1), 15(2) Sch. 4 para. 43 (with s. 9(3)(5)(7), 13, 14(3))

209 s. 77(1), Sch. 5 repealed by Statute Law (Repeals) Act 1974 (c. 22), Sch. 1 Pt. XI

Local Government Act 1972

1972 CHAPTER 70

...

139 Acceptance of gifts of property.

(1) Subject to the provisions of this section a local authority may accept, hold and administer—

(a) for the purpose of discharging any of their functions, gifts of property, whether real or personal, made for that purpose; or

(b) for the benefit of the inhabitants of their area or of some part of it, gifts made for that purpose;

and may execute any work (including works of maintenance or improvement) incidental to or consequential on the exercise of the powers conferred by this section.

(2) Where any such work is executed in connection with a gift made for the benefit of the inhabitants of the area of a local authority or of some part of that area, the cost of executing the work shall be added to any expenditure under section 137 above in computing the limit imposed on that expenditure by subsection (4) of that section.

(3) This section shall not authorise the acceptance by a local authority of property which, when accepted, would be held in trust for an ecclesiastical charity or for a charity for the relief of poverty.

(4) Nothing in this section shall affect any powers exercisable by a local authority under or by virtue of [the Education Act 1996][1].

210 Charities.

(1) Where, immediately before 1st April 1974, any property is held, as sole trustee, exclusively for charitable purposes by an existing local authority for an area outside Greater London, other than the parish council, parish meeting or representative body of an existing rural parish in England (but including the corporation of a borough included in a rural district), that property shall vest (on the same trusts) in a new local authority in accordance with subsections (2) to (5) below.

(2) Subject to subsection (3) below, where the property is held by one of the existing authorities specified below, and is so held for the benefit of, or of the inhabitants of, or of any particular class or body of persons in, a specified area, the property shall vest in the new authority specified below, the area of which comprises the whole or the greater part of that specified area, and where the property is so held but is not held for such a benefit, it shall vest in the new authority specified below, the area of which comprises the whole or the greater part of the area of the existing authority, that is to say—

(a) where the existing authority is a county council, the new authority is the council of the new county;

(b) where the existing authority is the council of a borough or urban district in England, the new authority is the council of the parish constituted under Part V of Schedule 1 to this Act or, where there is no such parish, the council of the district;

(c) where the existing authority is the council of a borough or urban district in Wales, the new authority is the council of the community or, where there is no such council, the council of the district; and

(d) where the existing authority is a rural district council, then, if the rural district is coextensive with a parish, the new authority is the parish council, and in any other case the new authority is the council of the district.

(3) Where the property is held by an existing county council or county borough council for the purposes of a charity registered in the register established under section 4 of the Charities Act 1960 in any part of that register which is maintained by the Secretary of State by virtue of section 2 of that Act (educational charities) then—

(a) if the property is so held for the benefit of, or of the inhabitants of, or of any particular class or body of persons in, a specified area, the property shall vest in the new authority which is the local education authority for the whole or the greater part of that specified area, and

(b) in any other case, the property shall vest in the new authority which is the local education authority for the whole or the greater part of the area of the existing county council or county borough council by which the property is held.

(4) Where the property is held by the corporation of a borough included in a rural district, it shall vest

in the parish council for the parish consisting of the area of the existing borough.

(5) Where the property is held by the parish council, parish meeting or representative body of an existing rural parish in Wales, then—

(a) in the case of property held by an existing parish council, the property shall vest in the community council for the community or group of communities, the area or areas of which are co-extensive with the area of the parish or parishes for which the existing parish council act;

(b) in the case of property held by the parish meeting or representative body of an existing parish the area of which is comprised in a community for which there is a community council, the property shall vest in that community council; and

(c) in any other case, the property shall vest in the council of the district which comprises the area of the existing rural parish.

(6) Where, immediately before 1st April 1974, any power with respect to a charity, not being a charity incorporated under the Companies Acts or by charter, is under the trusts of the charity or by virtue of any enactment vested in, or in the holder of an office connected with, any existing local authority to which subsection (1) above applies, that power shall vest in, or in the holder of the corresponding office connected with, or (if there is no such office) the proper office of, the corresponding new authority, that is to say, the new authority in which, had the property of the charity been vested in the existing local authority, that property would have been vested under subsections (1) to (5) above.

(7) References in subsection (6) above to a power with respect to a charity do not include references to a power of any person by virtue of being a charity trustee thereof; but where under the trusts of any charity, not being a charity incorporated under the Companies Acts or by charter, the charity trustees immediately before 1st April 1974 include either an existing local authority to which subsection (1) above applies or the holder of an office connected with such an existing local authority, those trustees shall instead include the corresponding new authority as defined in subsection (6) above or, as the case may require, the holder of the corresponding office connected with, or (if there is no such office) the proper officer of, that authority.

(8)..............................[2]

(9)..............................[3]

(10) Nothing in the foregoing provisions of this section shall affect any power of Her Majesty, the court or any other person to alter the trusts of any charity and nothing in those provisions shall apply in a case to which section 211 below applies.

(11) In this section the expression "local authority", in relation to a parish, includes a parish meeting and the representative body of a parish, and the expressions "charitable purposes", "charity", "charity trustees", "court" and "trusts" have the same meanings as in the Charities Act 1960.

211 Welsh Church funds.

(1) Any property which, immediately before 1st April 1974, is vested in the council of an existing county or county borough in Wales and is required to be applied in accordance with a scheme under section 19 of the Welsh Church Act 1914 (application of Welsh Church funds for charitable or eleemosynary purposes) shall be vested, by virtue of this Act, in the council of the new county which comprises the whole or the greater part of the area of that existing county or county borough.

(2) Where, by virtue of subsection (1) above, property vested in the council of an existing county becomes vested in the council of a new county which does not comprise the whole of the area of the existing county, the new county council shall transfer an apportioned part of the property to each of the other new county councils whose areas include parts of the area of the existing county.

(3) An apportionment for the purposes of subsection (2) above shall be made by agreement between the new county councils concerned, or, in default of such an agreement, shall be determined by arbitration before a single arbitrator appointed by agreement between those councils or, in default of such an agreement, appointed by the Secretary of State.

(4) The vesting or transfer of any property by virtue of this section shall not affect the application of the property in accordance with the scheme under section 19 of the Welsh Church Act 1914 which is applicable to it immediately before 1st April 1974 or the amendment or revocation of any such scheme by a further scheme under that section.

273 Commencement.

(1) The provisions of this Act to which this subsection applies shall, except so far as brought into force

earlier by an order under subsection (2) below, come into force on 1st April 1974.

(2) The Secretary of State may by order appoint an earlier date for the coming into force of any provision to which subsection (1) above applies and different days may be appointed under this subsection for different purposes and, in particular, different days may be so appointed for the coming into force of the same provision in different areas.

(3) Subsection (1) above applies to the following provisions of this Act, that is to say—

sections 13, 16(1) and (3) and 17;
section 40;
section 48(8) and (9);
section 50(4) to (7);
sections 53 to 59 and Schedule 8;
section 62;
section 75;
section 89(6);
section 100;
Parts VI to XI, except as provided by subsections (4) and (5) below;
section 251 and Schedule 29;
section 262(3) to (7);
section 272 and Schedule 30;
paragraphs 5 to 9 and 10(2) of Schedule 6;
in Schedule 12, Parts II and III, and Part VI so far as applicable to parish councils.

(4) Subsection (1) above shall not apply to the following provisions of Parts VI to XI of this Act, that is to say—

sections 104 and 106;
section 110;
section 117;
section 138;
section 169;
section 181(3) to (9) and (11);
so much of section 183 as confers a power to make or direct the making or amendment of development plan schemes and so much of section 182 as applies to the interpretation of the provisions relating to such schemes;
section 186(6) and (7);
section 190(4);
section 192(3);
section 196(6) to (9);
section 197(2) and (3);
section 198(3) and (4);
section 200;
section 201(3) and (4);
section 202(4) to (8);
section 205;
section 207(2) to (8);
section 215(4);
section 220(4);
section 232;
section 242;
section 243;
paragraph 27(2) of Schedule 13 and so much of section 172 as relates thereto.

(5)............................... [4]
(6)...............................
(7)...............................
(8)...............................
(9)...............................

(10)...............................

274 Short title and extent.

(1) This Act may be cited as the Local Government Act 1972.

(2)...[5] this Act shall not extend to Scotland.

(3)...[6], this Act shall not extend to Northern Ireland.

---

[1] Words in s. 139(4) substituted (1.11.1996) by 1996 c. 56, ss. 582(1), 583(2), Sch. 37 Pt. I para. 24 (with s. 1(4))

[2] S. 210(8) repealed (1.9.1992) by Charities Act 1992 (c. 41), s. 78(2), Sch. 7; S.I. 1992/1900, art. 2, Sch. 1

[3] S. 210(9) repealed (1.8.1993) by 1993 c. 10, ss. 98(2), 99(1), Sch. 7.

[4] S. 273(5)-(10) repealed (22.7.2004) by Statute Law (Repeals) Act 2004 (c. 14), s. 1(1), {Sch. 1 Pt. 10 Group 1}

[5] Words in s. 274(2) repealed (22.7.2004) by Statute Law (Repeals) Act 2004 (c. 14), s. 1(1), {Sch. 1 Pt. 10 Group 1}

[6] Words repealed by House of Commons Disqualification Act 1975 (c. 24), Sch. 3 and Northern Ireland Assembly Disqualification Act 1975 (c. 25), s. 5(2), Sch. 3 Pt. I

Education Act 1973

1973 CHAPTER 16

1 General provisions as to educational trusts.

(1) There shall cease to have effect—

(a) section 2 of the Charities Act 1960 (by which, as originally enacted, the powers of the Charity Commissioners were made exercisable concurrently by the Minister of Education); and

(b) the Endowed Schools Acts 1869 to 1948 (which made provision for the modernisation of educational trusts by schemes settled and approved in accordance with those Acts).

(2) ....[1]

(3) In connection with the operation of this section there shall have effect the transitional and other consequential or supplementary provisions contained in Schedule 1 to this Act.

(4) The enactments mentioned in Schedule 2 to this Act (which includes in Part I certain enactments already spent or otherwise no longer required apart from the foregoing provisions of this section) are hereby repealed to the extent specified in column 3 of the Schedule.

(5) Subsection (1)(a) above and Part III of Schedule 2 to this Act shall not come into force until such date as may be appointed by order made by statutory instrument by the Secretary of State.

5 Citation and extent.

(1) This Act may be cited as the Education Act 1973 ...[2]

(2) Nothing in this Act extends to Scotland or to Northern Ireland.

SCHEDULE 1

1[3]

(1)................

(2) Section 210(3) of the Local Government Act 1972 (which makes special provision for certain charitable property to vest in local education authorities, if it is held for purposes of a charity registered in a part of the charities register maintained by the Secretary of State by virtue of section 2 of the Charities Act 1960) shall have effect, unless the appointed day is later than the end of March 1974, as if the reference to a charity registered in a part of the register which is maintained by the Secretary of State were a reference to a charity so registered immediately before the appointed day.

(3) ......

(4) The repeal by this Act of section 2(1) of the Charities Act 1960 shall not affect the operation of section 2(1)—

(a) in conferring on the Charity Commissioners functions belonging at the passing of that Act to the Minister of Education; or

(b) in extending to the Charity Commissioners references to the Secretary of State for Education and Science or the Secretary of State for Wales (or references having effect as if either of them were mentioned) so as to enable the Commissioners to discharge any such functions as aforesaid or to act under or for the purposes of the trusts of a charity;

but on the appointed day any functions so conferred and any reference so extended shall, subject to sub-paragraph (5) below, cease to be functions of or to extend to either Secretary of State.

[(5) Where it appears to the Secretary of State that any reference, which in accordance with sub-

paragraph (4) above ceased on the appointed day to extend to the Secretary of State for Education and Science or the Secretary of State for Wales, was not related (or not wholly related) to the functions ceasing to belong to that Minister by the repeal of section 2(1) of the Charities Act 1960, he may by order exclude the operation of that sub-paragraph in relation to the reference and make such modifications of the relevant instrument as appear to him appropriate in the circumstances.][4]

(6) The repeal of section 2(1) of the Charities Act 1960 shall not affect the validity of anything done (or having effect as if done) before the appointed day by or in relation to the Secretary of State for Education and Science or the Secretary of State for Wales, and anything so done (or having effect as if so done) in so far as it could by virtue of section 2(1) have been done by or in relation to the Charity Commissioners shall thereafter have effect as if done by or in relation to them.

(7) In this paragraph "appointed day" means the day appointed under section 1(5) of this Act.

---

[1] s. 1(2) repealed (1.11.1996) by 1996 c. 56, ss. 582(2), 583(2), Sch. 38 Pt.I (with ss. 1(4), 561, 562, Sch. 39)

[2] Words in s. 5(1) repealed (1.11.1996) by 1996 c. 56, ss. 582(2), 583(2), Sch. 38 Pt.I (with ss. 1(4), 561, 562, Sch. 39)

[3] Sch. 1 para. 1(1) and (3) repealed (1.8.1993) by 1993 c. 10, ss. 98(2), 99(1), Sch. 7

[4] Sch. 1 para. 1(5) substituted (1.1.1996) by S.I. 1995/2986, art. 11, Sch. para. 7

Consumer Credit Act 1974

1974 CHAPTER 39

16 Exempt agreements.

(1) This Act does not regulate a consumer credit agreement where the creditor is a local authority[1], or a body specified, or of a description specified, in an order made by the Secretary of State, being

[(a) an insurer;][2]

(b) a friendly society,

(c) an organisation of employers or organisation of workers,

(d) a charity,

(e) a land improvement company,[3]

(f) a body corporate named or specifically referred to in any public general Act.

[(ff) a body corporate named or specifically referred to in an order made under

section 156(4), 444(1) or 447(2)(a) of the Housing Act 1985 [section 156(4) of that Act as it has effect by virtue of section 17 of the Housing Act 1996 (the right to acquire),][4],

section [223 or 229 of the Housing (Scotland) Act 1987][5], or

Article 154(1)(a) or 156AA of the Housing (Northern Ireland) Order 1981 or Article 10(6A) of the Housing (Northern Ireland) Order 1983; or][6][, or

(g) a building society.][7][or

[(h) a deposit-taker.][8]][9]

(2) Subsection (1) applies only where the agreement is

(a) a debtor-creditor-supplier agreement financing

(i) the purchase of land, or

(ii) the provision of dwellings on any land, and secured by a land mortgage on that land; or

(b) a debtor-creditor agreement secured by any land mortgage; or

(c) a debtor-creditor-supplier agreement financing a transaction which is a linked transaction in relation to

(i) an agreement falling within paragraph (a), or

(ii) an agreement falling within paragraph (b) financing

(aa) the purchase of any land, or

(bb) the provision of dwellings on any land,

and secured by a land mortgage on the land referred to in paragraph (a) or, as the case may be, the land referred to in sub-paragraph (ii).

[(3)Before he makes, varies or revokes an order under subsection (1), the Secretary of State must undertake the necessary consultation.

(3A) The necessary consultation means consultation with the bodies mentioned in the following table in relation to the provision under which the order is to be made, varied or revoked:

TABLE

Provision of subsection (1)	***Consultee***
Paragraph (a) or (b)	The Financial Services Authority
Paragraph (d)	The [Charity Commission][10]
Paragraph (e), (f) or (ff)	Any Minister of the Crown with responsibilities in relation to the body in question
Paragraph (g) or (h)	The Treasury and the Financial Services Authority][11]

(4) An order under subsection (1) relating to a body may be limited so as to apply only to agreements by that body of a description specified in the order.

(5) The Secretary of State may by order provide that this Act shall not regulate other consumer credit agreements where—

(a) the number of payments to be made by the debtor does not exceed the number specified for that purpose in the order, or

(b) the rate of the total charge for credit does not exceed the rate so specified, or

(c) an agreement has a connection with a country outside the United Kingdom.

(6) The Secretary of State may by order provide that this Act shall not regulate consumer hire agreements of a description specified in the order where

(a) the owner is a body corporate authorised by or under any enactment to supply electricity, gas or water, and

(b) the subject of the agreement is a meter or metering equipment,

[or where the owner is a [provider of a public electronic communications service who is specified in the order][12]][13]

[(6A) This Act does not regulate a consumer credit agreement where the creditor is a housing authority and the agreement is secured by a land mortgage of a dwelling.

(6B) In subsection (6A) "housing authority" means

(a) as regards England and Wales, [the Homes and Communities Agency, the Welsh new towns residuary body,][14][the Regulator of Social Housing and][15] an authority or body within section 80(1) of the Housing Act 1985 (the landlord condition for secure tenancies), other than a housing association or a housing trust which is a charity;

(b) as regards Scotland, a development corporation established under an order made, or having effect as if made under the New Towns (Scotland) Act 1968, the Scottish Special Housing Association or the Housing Corporation;

(c) as regards Northern Ireland, the Northern Ireland Housing Executive.][16]

[(6BA) In subsection (6B)(a) "the Welsh new towns residuary body" means the Welsh Ministers so far as exercising functions in relation to anything transferred (or to be transferred) to them as mentioned in section 36(1)(a)(i) to (iii) of the New Towns Act 1981.][17]

[[(6C) This Act does not regulate a consumer credit agreement if

(a) it is secured by a land mortgage and entering into the agreement as lender is a regulated activity for the purposes of the Financial Services and Markets Act 2000; or

(b) it is or forms part of a regulated home purchase plan and entering into the agreement as home purchase provider is a regulated activity for the purposes of that Act.][18]

(6D) But section 126, and any other provision so far as it relates to section 126, applies to an agreement which would (but for [subsection (6C)(a)][19]) be a regulated agreement.

(6E) Subsection (6C) must be read with

(a) section 22 of the Financial Services and Markets Act 2000 (regulated activities: power to specify classes of activity and categories of investment);

(b) any order for the time being in force under that section; and

(c) Schedule 2 to that Act.][20]

(7) . . . . . .[21]

[(7A) Nothing in this section affects the application of sections 140A to 140C.][22]

[(8)In the application of this section to Scotland, subsection (3A) shall have effect as if the reference to the [Charity Commission][23] were a reference to the Lord Advocate.][24]

(9) In the application of this section to Northern Ireland [subsection (3A)][25] shall have effect as if any reference to a Minister of the Crown were a reference to a Northern Ireland department,[26] and any

reference to the [Charity Commission][27] were a reference to the Department of Finance for Northern Ireland.

[(10) In this section

(a) "deposit-taker" means

(i) a person who has permission under Part 4 of the Financial Services and Markets Act 2000 to accept deposits,

(ii) an EEA firm of the kind mentioned in paragraph 5(b) of Schedule 3 to that Act which has permission under paragraph 15 of that Schedule (as a result of qualifying for authorisation under paragraph 12 of that Schedule) to accept deposits,

(iii) any wholly owned subsidiary (within the meaning of [the Companies Acts (see section 1159 of the Companies Act 2006)][28]) of a person mentioned in sub-paragraph (i), or

(iv) any undertaking which, in relation to a person mentioned in sub-paragraph (ii), is a subsidiary undertaking within the meaning of any rule of law in force in the EEA State in question for purposes connected with the implementation of the European Council Seventh Company Law Directive of 13 June 1983 on consolidated accounts (No. 83/349/EEC), and which has no members other than that person;

(b) "insurer" means

(i) a person who has permission under Part 4 of the Financial Services and Markets Act 2000 to effect or carry out contracts of insurance, or

(ii) an EEA firm of the kind mentioned in paragraph 5(d) of Schedule 3 to that Act, which has permission under paragraph 15 of that Schedule (as a result of qualifying for authorisation under paragraph 12 of that Schedule) to effect or carry out contracts of insurance,

but does not include a friendly society or an organisation of workers or of employers.

(11) Subsection (10) must be read with

(a) section 22 of the Financial Services and Markets Act 2000;

(b) any relevant order under that section; and

(c) Schedule 2 to that Act.][29]

193 Short title and extent.

(1) This Act may be cited as the Consumer Credit Act 1974.

(2) This Act extends to Northern Ireland.

---

[1] Words repealed by Building Societies Act 1986 (c. 53, SIF 16), s. 120, Sch. 18 Pt. I para. 10(2), Sch. 19 Pt. I

[2] s. 16(1)(a) substituted (1.12.2001) by S.I. 2001/3649, arts. 1, 165(2)(a)

[3] Word repealed by Building Societies Act 1986 (c. 53, SIF 16), s. 120, Sch. 19 Pt. I

[4] Words in s. 16(1)(ff) inserted (E.W.S.) (1.4.1997) by S.I. 1997/627, art. 2, Sch. para. 2

[5] Words in s. 16(1)(ff) substituted (S.) by virtue of Housing (Scotland) Act 1987 (c. 26, SIF 61), s. 339, Sch. 23 para. 21

[6] s. 16(1)(ff) inserted by Housing and Planning Act 1986 (c. 63, SIF 60), s. 22(2)

[7] Words inserted by Building Societies Act 1986 (c. 53, SIF 16), s. 120, Sch. 18 para. 10(2)

[8] s. 16(1)(h) substituted (1.12.2001) by S.I. 2001/3649, arts. 1, 165(2)(b)

[9] s. 16(1)(h) and ", or " inserted by Banking Act 1987 (c. 22, SIF 10), s. 88(2)

[10] Words in s. 16(3A)(8)(9) substituted (27.2.2007) by Charities Act 2006 (c. 50), ss. 75(1), 79, Sch. 8 para. 56; S.I. 2007/309, art. 2, Sch. (subject to arts 4-13)

[11] s. 16(3)(3A) substituted for s. 16(3) (1.12.2001) by S.I. 2001/3649, arts. 1, 165(3)

[12] Words in s. 16(6) substituted (25.7.2003 for specified purposes, 29.12.2003 for further specified purposes) by Communications Act 2003 (c. 21), ss. 406, 408, 411, Sch. 17 para. 47 (with Sch. 18); S.I. 2003/1900, arts. 1(2), 2(1), 3(1), Sch. 1 (with arts. 3(2) (as amended (8.12.2003) by S.I. 2003/3142, art. 1(3))); S.I. 2003/3142, art. 3(2) (with art. 11)

[13] Words substituted by Telecommunications Act 1984 (c. 12, SIF 96), s. 109, Sch. 4 para. 60(1), Sch. 5 para. 45

[14] Words in s. 16(6B)(a) inserted (E.W.N.I.) (1.12.2008) by The Housing and Regeneration Act 2008 (Consequential Provisions) Order 2008 (S.I. 2008/3002), arts. 1(2), 3(2), 4, Sch. 1 para. 1(2) (with transitional and saving provisions in Sch. 2); S.I. 2008/3068, art. 2(1)(b) (with arts. 6-13)

[15] Words in s. 16(6B)(a) substituted (1.4.2010) by The Housing and Regeneration Act 2008 (Consequential Provisions) Order 2010 (S.I. 2010/866), art. 5, Sch. 2 para. 7 (with art. 6, Sch. 3)

[16] s. 16(6A)(6B) inserted by Housing and Planning Act 1986 (c. 63, SIF 60), s. 22(3)

[17] s. 16(6BA) inserted (E.W.N.I.) (1.12.2008) by The Housing and Regeneration Act 2008 (Consequential Provisions) Order 2008 (S.I. 2008/3002), arts. 1(2), 3(2), 4, Sch. 1 para. 1(3) (with transitional and saving provisions in Sch. 2); S.I. 2008/3068, art. 2(1)(b) (with arts. 6-13)

[18] s. 16(6C) substituted (6.11.2006 for certain purposes and 6.4.2007 otherwise) by The Financial Services and Markets Act 2000 (Regulated Activities) (Amendment) (No.2) Order 2006 (S.I. 2006/2383), arts. 1(2), 25(2)(a)

[19] Words in s. 16(6D) substituted (6.11.2006 for certain purposes and 6.4.2007 otherwise) by The Financial Services and Markets Act 2000 (Regulated Activities) (Amendment) (No.2) Order 2006 (S.I. 2006/2383), arts. 1(2), 25(2)(b)

[20] s. 16(6C)-(6E) inserted (1.9.2002) by S.I. 2001/544, arts. 2, 90(2); S.I. 2001/3538, art. 2

[21] s. 16(7) repealed (6.4.2007) by Consumer Credit Act 2006 (c. 14), ss. 70, 71, Sch. 4 (with Sch. 3 para. 15(5)); S.I. 2007/123, art. 3(2), Sch. 2 (as amended by S.I. 2007/387, art. [2(1)(3)(e)(i)])

[22] s. 16(7A) inserted (6.4.2007) by Consumer Credit Act 2006 (c. 14), ss. 22(2), 71(2); S.I. 2007/123, art. 3(2), Sch. 2

[23] Words in s. 16(3A)(8)(9) substituted (27.2.2007) by Charities Act 2006 (c. 50), ss. 75(1), 79, Sch. 8 para. 56; S.I. 2007/309, art. 2, Sch. (subject to arts 4-13)

[24] s. 16(8) substituted (1.12.2001) by S.I. 2001/3649, arts. 1, 165(4)

[25] Words in s. 16(9) substituted (1.12.2001) by S.I. 2001/3649, arts. 1, 165(5)(a)

[26] Words in s. 16(9) repealed (1.12.2001) by S.I. 2001/3649, arts. 1, 165(5)(b)

[27] Words in s. 16(3A)(8)(9) substituted (27.2.2007) by Charities Act 2006 (c. 50), ss. 75(1), 79, Sch. 8 para. 56; S.I. 2007/309, art. 2, Sch. (subject to arts 4-13)

[28] Words in s. 16(10)(a)(iii) substituted (1.10.2009) by The Companies Act 2006 (Consequential Amendments, Transitional Provisions and Savings) Order 2009 (S.I. 2009/1941), arts. 1(2), 2(1), Sch. 1 para. 28 (with art. 10)

[29] s. 16(10)(11) inserted (1.12.2001) by S.I. 2001/3649, arts. 1, 165(6)

Industrial and Provident Societies Act 1978

1978 CHAPTER 34

An Act to raise the amounts of deposits which an industrial and provident society may take without thereby carrying on the business of banking; and to authorise the further alteration of those amounts from time to time.

[20th July 1978]

1 Raising of maximum deposit.

(1) In section 7(3) of the Industrial and Provident Societies Act 1965 (hereafter in this Act referred to as "the Act of 1965") for the words "two pounds" (denoting the limit of deposits which can be taken at any one time) there shall be substituted the words "ten pounds" and for the words "fifty pounds"(denoting the maximum amount which can be taken from any one depositor) there shall be substituted the words "two hundred and fifty pounds".

Where immediately before the coming into force of this Act the registered rules of a society registered under the Act of 1965 permitted depositors under the said section 7(3) to deposit a maximum of £50 then laid down thereby, the committee may, by a resolution recorded in writing, resolve that depositors may be permitted to hold such greater amount not exceeding £250 as may be specified in the resolution, and the registered rules shall have effect accordingly.

(3) Where immediately before the coming into force of this Act the registered rules of a society registered under the Act of 1965 permitted depositors under the said section 7(3) to deposit a maximum of not more than £2 in any one payment, the committee may, by a resolution recorded in writing, resolve that depositors may be permitted to deposit a maximum of not more than £10 in any one payment as may be specified in the resolution, and the registered rules shall have effect accordingly.

(4) The powers conferred on the committees of registered societies by subsections (2) and (3) above shall not be exercisable after the expiration of the period of eighteen months beginning with the date on which this Act comes into force or after the coming into force of an order under section 2 below; and if any amendment of the rules of a society is made after the coming into force of this Act and before the expiration of the time allowed by this subsection for exercising that power the power shall cease to be exercisable by the committee of that society on the date on which the amendment is registered under section 10 of the Act of 1965.

(5) The committee of a registered society shall not have power to vary or revoke a resolution under subsections (2) or (3) above except in so far as they may be authorised to do so by an order under section 2 below.

(6) Where the committee of a registered society have exercised the power to pass a resolution under subsection (2) or (3) above and an amendment of the society's rules is subsequently registered under section 10 of the Act of 1965 the registered rules of the society shall thereupon have effect as if the resolution had not been passed, so, however, that this subsection shall not affect any interest in the funds of the society held by a depositor immediately before the date on which the amendment is

registered.

2 Further alterations of limits.

(1) The [Treasury][1] may from time to time. . . [2] by order substitute for the sums for the time being specified in section 7(3) of the Act of 1965 as the limits applicable thereunder such other sums, not being less than £10 (denoting the limit of deposits which can be taken at any one time) and £250 (denoting the maximum amount which can be taken from any one depositor), as may be specified in the order.

(2) An order under this section may make any such provision in connection with altering the limits for the time being applicable under the said section 7(3) as is made by section 1 above, and may contain such other transitional, consequential, incidental or supplementary provisions as appear to the [Treasury][3] to be necessary or appropriate in that connection.

(3) An order made under this section may vary or revoke any previous order so made.

(4) The power to make an order under this section shall be exercisable by statutory instrument, which shall be subject to annulment in pursuance of a resolution of either House of Parliament; .[4]

3 Construction, citation, commencement and extent.

(1) The Act of 1965 and this Act shall be construed as one.

(2) This Act may be cited as the Industrial and Provident Societies Act 1978, and this Act and the Industrial and Provident Societies Acts 1965 to 1975 may be cited together as the Industrial and Provident Societies Acts 1965 to 1978.

(3) This Act shall come into force on the expiration of the period of one month beginning with the date on which it is passed.

(4) This Act extends to the Channel Islands but does not extend to Northern Ireland.

---

[1] Words in s. 2(1)(2) substituted (1.12.2001) by S.I. 2001/2617, arts. 2(b), 13(1), Sch. 3 Pt. III para. 263(a)(i)(b); S.I. 2001/3538, art. 2(1)

[2] Words in s. 2(1) repealed (1.12.2001) by S.I. 2001/2617, arts. 2(b), 13(1)(2), Sch. 3 Pt. III para. 263(a)(ii); S.I. 2001/3538, art. 2(1)

[3] Words in s. 2(1)(2) substituted (1.12.2001) by S.I. 2001/2617, arts. 2(b), 13(1), Sch. 3 Pt. III para. 263(a)(i)(b); S.I. 2001/3538, art. 2(1)

[4] Words in s. 2(4) repealed (1.12.2001) by S.I. 2001/2617, arts. 2(b), 13(1)(2), Sch. 3 Pt. III para. 263(c); S.I. 2001/3538, art. 2(1)

Finance Act 1982

1982 CHAPTER 39

129 Exemption from duty on grants, transfers to charities, etc.

(1) Where any conveyance, transfer or lease is made or agreed to be made to a body of persons established for charitable purposes only or to the trustees of a trust so established or to the Trustees of the National Heritage Memorial Fund [or to the National Endowment for Science, Technology and the Arts][1], no stamp duty shall be chargeable [under Part I or II, or paragraph 16, of Schedule 13 to the Finance Act 1999][2]—

(b). . . . .[3]

on the instrument by which the conveyance, transfer or lease, or the agreement for it, is effected.

(2) An instrument in respect of which stamp duty is not chargeable by virtue only of subsection (1) above shall not be treated as duly stamped unless it is stamped in accordance with section 12 of the Stamp Act 1891 with a stamp denoting that it is not chargeable with any duty.

(3) This section applies to instruments executed on or after 22nd March 1982 and shall be deemed to have come into force on that date.

157 Short title, interpretation, construction and repeals.

(1) This Act may be cited as the Finance Act 1982.

[(2) In this Act—

(a) "the Taxes Act 1970" means the Income and Corporation Taxes Act 1970; and

(b) "the Taxes Act 1988" means the Income and Corporation Taxes Act 1988][4].

(3) Part III of this Act, so far as it relates to income tax, shall be construed as one with the Income Tax Acts, so far as it relates to corporation tax, shall be construed as one with the Corporation Tax Acts

and, so far as it relates to capital gains tax, shall be construed as one with the Capital Gains Tax Act 1979.

(4) Part IV of this Act shall be construed as one with Part III of the Finance Act 1975.

(5) Part VI of this Act shall be construed as one with Part I of the Oil Taxation Act 1975 . . . [5] and references in Part VI to the principal Act are references to that Act.

(6) The enactments and Orders mentioned in Schedule 22 to this Act (which include spent enactments) are hereby repealed to the extent specified in the third column of that Schedule, but subject to any provision at the end of any Part of that Schedule.

(7) The provisions of Part XI of Schedule 22 to this Act, except in so far as they relate to the Wellington Museum Act 1947 and the Finance (No. 2) Act 1975, shall have effect in substitution for the provisions of Section B of Part VI of Schedule 20 to the Finance Act 1980 and, accordingly, that Section shall be deemed not to have taken effect at the beginning of the year 1982-83.

---

[1] Words in s. 129(1) inserted (2.7.1998) by 1998 c. 22, ss. 24(4), 27(4)

[2] Words in s. 129(1) substituted for S. 129(1)(a) and the preceding words "by virtue of" (27.7.1999 with effect in relation to instruments executed on or after 1.10.1999) by 1999 c. 16, s. 112(4)(6), Sch. 14 para. 7

[3] s. 129(1)(b) repealed by Finance Act 1985 (c. 54, SIF 114), s. 98(6), Sch. 27 Pt. IX(1)

[4] S. 157(2) substituted by Income and Corporation Taxes Act 1988 (c. 1, SIF 63:1), Sch. 29 para. 32

[5] Words repealed by Income and Corporation Taxes 1988 (c. 1, SIF 63:1), s. 844 and Sch. 31

Inheritance Tax Act 1984

1984 CHAPTER 51

...

23 Gifts to charities.

(1) Transfers of value are exempt to the extent that the values transferred by them are attributable to property which is given to charities.

(2) Subsection (1) above shall not apply in relation to property if the testamentary or other disposition by which it is given—

(a) takes effect on the termination after the transfer of value of any interest or period, or

(b) depends on a condition which is not satisfied within twelve months after the transfer, or

(c) is defeasible;

and for this purpose any disposition which has not been defeated at a time twelve months after the transfer of value and is not defeasible after that time shall be treated as not being defeasible (whether or not it was capable of being defeated before that time).

(3) Subsection (1) above shall not apply in relation to property which is an interest in other property if—

(a) that interest is less than the donor's, or

(b) the property is given for a limited period;

and for this purpose any question whether an interest is less than the donor's shall be decided as at a time twelve months after the transfer of value.

(4) Subsection (1) above shall not apply in relation to any property if—

(a) the property is land or a building and is given subject to an interest reserved or created by the donor which entitled him, his spouse [or civil partner][1] or a person connected with him to possession of, or to occupy, the whole or any part of the land or building rent-free or at a rent less than might be expected to be obtained in a transaction at arm's length between persons not connected with each other, or

(b) the property is not land or a building and is given subject to an interest reserved or created by the donor other than—

(i) an interest created by him for full consideration in money or money's worth, or

(ii) an interest which does not substantially affect the enjoyment of the property by the person or body to whom it is given;

and for this purpose any question whether property is given subject to an interest shall be decided as at a time twelve months after the transfer of value.

(5) Subsection (1) above shall not apply in relation to property if it or any part of it may become applicable for purposes other than charitable purposes or those of a body mentioned in section 24, [or 25][2] below [or, where it is land, of a body mentioned in section 24A below][3].

(6) For the purposes of this section property is given to charities if it becomes the property of charities or is held on trust for charitable purposes only, and "donor" shall be construed accordingly.

[24A Gifts to housing associations.

(1) A transfer of value is exempt to the extent that the value transferred by it is attributable to land in the United Kingdom given to a [body falling within subsection (2) below][4].

[(2) A body falls within this subsection if it is—

(a) a registered social landlord within the meaning of Part I of the Housing Act 1996;

(b) a registered housing association within the meaning of the Housing Associations Act 1985; or

(c) a registered housing association within the meaning of Part II of the Housing (Northern Ireland) Order 1992.][5]

(3) Subsections (2) to (5) of section 23 and subsection (4) of section 24 above shall apply in relation to subsection (1) above as they apply in relation to section 24(1).][6]

25 Gifts for national purposes, etc.

(1) A transfer of value is an exempt transfer to the extent that the value transferred by it is attributable to property which becomes the property of a body within Schedule 3 to this Act.

(2) Subsections (2) to (5) of section 23 and subsection (4) of section 24 above shall apply in relation to subsection (1) above as they apply in relation to section 24(1), except that section 23(3) shall not prevent subsection (1) above from applying in relation to property consisting of the benefit of an agreement restricting the use of land.

[26A Potentially exempt transfer of property subsequently held for national purposes etc.

A potentially exempt transfer which would (apart from this section) have proved to be a chargeable transfer shall be an exempt transfer to the extent that the value transferred by it is attributable to property which has been or could be designated under section 31(1) below and which, during the period beginning with the date of the transfer and ending with the death of the transferor,—

(a) has been disposed of by sale by private treaty to a body mentioned in Schedule 3 to this Act or has been disposed of to such a body otherwise than by sale, or

(b) has been disposed of in pursuance of section 230 below.][7]

27 Maintenance funds for historic buildings, etc.

(1)[Subject to subsection (1A) below,][8] a transfer of value is an exempt transfer to the extent that the value transferred by it is attributable to property which by virtue of the transfer becomes comprised in a settlement and in respect of which—

(a) a direction under paragraph 1 of Schedule 4 to this Act has effect at the time of the transfer, or

(b) such a direction is given after the time of the transfer.

[(1A) Subsection (1) above does not apply in the case of a direction given after the time of the transfer unless the claim for the direction (if it is not made before that time) is made no more than two years after the date of that transfer, or within such longer period as the Board may allow.][9]

(2) Subsections (2) and (3) of the section 23 and subsection (4) of section 24 above shall apply in relation to subsection (1) above as they apply in relation to section 24(1).

32 Chargeable events.

(1) Where there has been a conditionally exempt transfer of any property, tax shall be charged under this section on the first occurrence after the transfer [(or, if the transfer was a potentially exempt transfer, after the death of the transferor)][10] of an event which under this section is a chargeable event with respect to the property.

(2) If the Treasury are satisfied that at any time an undertaking given with respect to the property under section 30 above or [subsection (5AA)][11] below has not been observed in a material respect, the failure to observe the undertaking is a chargeable event with respect to the property.

(3) If—

(a) the person beneficially entitled to the property dies, or

(b) the property is disposed of, whether by sale or gift or otherwise,

the death or disposal is, subject to subsections (4) and (5) below, a chargeable event with respect to the property.

(4) A death or disposal is not a chargeable event with respect to any property if the personal representatives of the deceased (or, in the case of settled property, the trustees or the person next

entitled) within three years of the death make or, as the case may be, the disposal is—

(a) a disposal of the property by sale by private treaty to a body mentioned in Schedule 3 to this Act, or a disposal of it to such a body otherwise than by sale, or

(b) a disposal in pursuance of section 230 below,

and a death or disposal of the property after such a disposal as is mentioned in paragraph (a) or (b) above is not a chargeable event with respect to the property unless there has again been a conditionally exempt transfer of it after that disposal.

(5) A death or disposal otherwise than by sale is not a chargeable event with respect to any property if—

(a) the transfer of value made on the death or the disposal is itself a conditionally exempt transfer of the property, or

[(b) the condition specified in subsection (5AA) below is satisfied with respect to the property.][12]

[(5AA) The condition referred to in subsection (5)(b) above is satisfied if—

(a) the requisite undertaking described in section 31 above is given with respect to the property by such person as the Board think appropriate in the circumstances of the case, or

(b)(where the property is an area of land within section 31(1)(d) above) the requisite undertakings described in that section are given with respect to the property by such person or persons as the Board think appropriate in the circumstances of the case.][13]

[(5A) This section does not apply where section 32A below applies.][14]

(6)(7). . . . .[15]

[32A Associated properties.

(1) For the purposes of this section the following properties are associated with each other, namely, a building falling within section 31(1)(c) above and (to the extent that any of the following exists) an area or areas of land falling within section 31(1)(d) above in relation to the building and an object or objects falling within section 31(1)(e) above in relation to the building; and this section applies where there are such properties, which are referred to as associated properties.

(2) Where there has been a conditionally exempt transfer of any property (or part), tax shall be charged under this section in respect of that property (or part) on the first occurrence after the transfer [(or, if the transfer was a potentially exempt transfer, after the death of the transferor][16] of an event which under this section is a chargeable event with respect to that property (or part).

(3) If the Treasury are satisfied that at any time an undertaking given under section 30 above or this section for the maintenance, repair, preservation, access or keeping of any of the associated properties has not been observed in a material respect, then (subject to subsection (10) below) the failure to observe the undertaking is a chargeable event with respect to the whole of each of the associated properties of which there has been a conditionally exempt transfer.

(4) If—

(a) the person beneficially entitled to property dies, or

(b) property (or part of it) is disposed of, whether by sale or gift or otherwise,

then, if the property is one of the associated properties and an undertaking for its maintenance, repair, preservation, access or keeping has been given under section 30 above or this section, the death or disposal is (subject to subsections (5) to (10) below) a chargeable event with respect to the whole of each of the associated properties of which there has been a conditionally exempt transfer.

(5) Subject to subsection (6) below, the death of a person beneficially entitled to property, or the disposal of property (or part), is not a chargeable event if the personal representatives of the deceased (or, in the case of settled property, the trustees or the person next entitled) within three years of the death make or, as the case may be, the disposal is—

(a) a disposal of the property (or part) concerned by sale by private treaty to a body mentioned in Schedule 3 to this Act, or to such a body otherwise than by sale, or

(b) a disposal of the property (or part) concerned in pursuance of section 230 below.

(6) Where a disposal mentioned in subsection (5)(a) or (b) above is a part disposal, that subsection does not make the event non-chargeable with respect to property other than that disposed of [unless—

(a) the requisite undertaking described in section 31 above is given with respect to the property (or part) not disposed of by such person as the Board think appropriate in the circumstances of the

case, or

(b)(where any of the property or part not disposed of is an area of land within section 31(1)(d) above) the requisite undertakings described in that section are given with respect to that property (or that part) by such person or persons as the Board think appropriate in the circumstances of the case;

and][17] in this subsection "part disposal" means a disposal of property which does not consist of or include the whole of each property which is one of the associated properties and of which there has been a conditionally exempt transfer.

(7) Where, after a relevant disposal (that is, a disposal mentioned in subsection (5)(a) or (b) above made in circumstances where that subsection applies), a person beneficially entitled to the property (or part) concerned dies or the property (or part) concerned is disposed of, the death or disposal is not a chargeable event with respect to the property (or part) concerned unless there has again been a conditionally exempt transfer of the property (or part) concerned after the relevant disposal.

(8) The death of a person beneficially entitled to property, or the disposal of property (or part) otherwise than by sale, is not a chargeable event if—

(a) the transfer of value made on the death or the disposal is itself a conditionally exempt transfer of the property (or part) concerned, or

[(b) the condition specified in subsection (8A) below is satisfied with respect to the property (or part) concerned.][18]

[(8A) The condition referred to in subsection (8)(b) above is satisfied if—

(a) the requisite undertaking described in section 31 above is given with respect to the property (or part) by such person as the Board think appropriate in the circumstances of the case, or

(b)(where any of the property or part is an area of land within section 31(1)(d) above) the requisite undertakings described in that section are given with respect to the property (or part) by such person or persons as the Board think appropriate in the circumstances of the case.][19]

[(9) If the whole or part of any property is disposed of by sale and—

(a) the requisite undertaking described in section 31 above is given with respect to the property (or part) by such person as the Board think appropriate in the circumstances of the case, or

(b)(where any of the property or part is an area of land within section 31(1)(d) above) the requisite undertakings described in that section are given with respect to the property (or part) by such person or persons as the Board think appropriate in the circumstances of the case,

the disposal is a chargeable event only with respect to the whole or part actually disposed of (if it is a chargeable event with respect to such whole or part apart from this subsection).][20]

(10) If—

(a) the Treasury are satisfied that there has been a failure to observe, as to one of the associated properties or part of it, an undertaking for the property's maintenance, repair, preservation, access or keeping, or

(b) there is a disposal of one of the associated properties or part of it,

and it appears to the Treasury that the entity consisting of the associated properties has not been materially affected by the failure or disposal, they may direct that it shall be a chargeable event only with respect to the property or part as to which there has been a failure or disposal (if it is a chargeable event with respect to that property or part apart from this subsection.][21]

CHAPTER III - SETTLEMENTS WITHOUT INTERESTS IN POSSESSION [, AND CERTAIN SETTLEMENTS IN WHICH INTERESTS IN POSSESSION SUBSIST][22]

58 Relevant property.

(1) In this Chapter "relevant property" means settled property in which no qualifying interest in possession subsists, other than—

(a) property held for charitable purposes only, whether for a limited time or otherwise;

(b) property to which section 71, [71A, 71D,][23] 73, 74 or 86 below applies [(but see subsection (1A) below)][24];

(c) property held on trusts which comply with the requirements mentioned in paragraph 3(1) of Schedule 4 to this Act, and in respect of which a direction given under paragraph 1 of that Schedule has effect;

[(d) property which is held for the purposes of a registered pension scheme or section 615(3)

scheme;][25]

(e) property comprised in a trade or professional compensation fund; and

(f) excluded property. . .

[(1A) Settled property to which section 86 below applies is "relevant property" for the purposes of this Chapter if—

(a) an interest in possession subsists in that property, and

(b) that interest falls within subsection (1B) or (1C) below. . .

(1B) An interest in possession falls within this subsection if—

(a) an individual is beneficially entitled to the interest in possession,

(b) the individual became beneficially entitled to the interest in possession on or after 22nd March 2006, and

(c) the interest in possession is—

(i) not an immediate post-death interest,

(ii) not a disabled person's interest, and

(iii) not a transitional serial interest.

(1C) An interest in possession falls within this subsection if—

(a) a company is beneficially entitled to the interest in possession,

(b) the business of the company consists wholly or mainly in the acquisition of interests in settled property,

(c) the company has acquired the interest in possession for full consideration in money or money's worth from an individual who was beneficially entitled to it,

(d) the individual became beneficially entitled to the interest in possession on or after 22nd March 2006, and

(e) immediately before the company acquired the interest in possession, the interest in possession was neither an immediate post-death interest nor a transitional serial interest.][26]

(2) The reference in subsection (1)(d) above to property which is...[27] held for the purposes of a ... scheme does not include a reference to a benefit which, having become payable under the ... scheme, becomes comprised in a settlement.

[(2A) For the purposes of subsection (1)(d) above—

(a) property applied to pay lump sum death benefits within section 168(1) of the Finance Act 2004 in respect of a member of a registered pension scheme is to be taken to be held for the purposes of the scheme from the time of the member's death until the payment is made, and

(b) property applied to pay lump sum death benefits in respect of a member of a section 615(3) scheme is to be taken to be so held if the benefits are paid within the period of two years beginning with the earlier of the day on which the member's death was first known to the trustees or other persons having the control of the fund and the day on which they could first reasonably be expected to have known of it.][28]

(3) In subsection (1)(e) above "trade or professional compensation fund" means a fund which is maintained or administered by a representative association of persons carrying on a trade or profession and the only or main objects of which are compensation for or relief of losses or hardship that, through the default or alleged default of persons carrying on the trade or profession or of their agents or servants, are incurred or likely to be incurred by others.

59 Qualifying interest in possession.

[(1) In this Chapter "qualifying interest in possession" means—

(a) an interest in possession—

(i) to which an individual is beneficially entitled, and

(ii) which, if the individual became beneficially entitled to the interest in possession on or after 22nd March 2006, is an immediate post-death interest, a disabled person's interest or a transitional serial interest, or

(b) an interest in possession to which, where subsection (2) below applies, a company is beneficially entitled.][29]

(2) This subsection applies where—

(a) the business of the company consists wholly or mainly in the acquisition of interests in settled property, and

(b) the company has acquired the interest for full consideration in money or money's worth from an individual who was beneficially entitled to it [, and

(c) if the individual became beneficially entitled to the interest in possession on or after 22nd March 2006, the interest is an immediate post-death interest, or a disabled person's interest within section 89B(1)(c) or (d) below or a transitional serial interest, immediately before the company acquires it.][30]

(3) Where the acquisition mentioned in paragraph (b) of subsection (2) above was before 14th March 1975—

(a) the condition set out in paragraph (a) of that subsection shall be treated as satisfied if the business of the company was at the time of the acquisition such as is described in that paragraph, and

(b) that condition need not be satisfied [if the company is an insurance company (within the meaning of Chapter I of Part XII of the Taxes Act 1988) and [has permission—

(i) under Part 4 of the Financial Services and Markets Act 2000, or

(ii) under paragraph 15 of Schedule 3 to that Act[31] (as a result of qualifying for authorisation under paragraph 12(1) of that Schedule),

to effect or carry out contracts of long-term insurance.][32],[33]

[(4) In subsection (3)(b) above "contracts of long-term insurance" means contracts which fall within Part II of Schedule 1 to the Financial Services and Markets Act 2000 (Regulated Activities) Order 2001.][34]][35]

60 Commencement of settlement.

In this Chapter references to the commencement of a settlement are references to the time when property first becomes comprised in it.

61 Ten-year anniversary.

(1) In this Chapter "ten-year anniversary" in relation to a settlement means the tenth anniversary of the date on which the settlement commenced and subsequent anniversaries at ten-yearly intervals, but subject to subsections (2) to (4) below.

(2) The ten-year anniversaries of a settlement treated as made under section 80 below shall be the dates that are (or would but for that section be) the ten-year anniversaries of the settlement first mentioned in that section.

(3) No date falling before 1st April 1983 shall be a ten-year anniversary.

(4) Where—

(a) the first ten-year anniversary of a settlement would apart from this subsection fall during the year ending with 31st March 1984, and

(b) during that year an event occurs in respect of the settlement which could not have occurred except as the result of some proceedings before a court, and

(c) the event is one on which tax was chargeable under Chapter II of Part IV of the Finance Act 1982 (or, apart from Part II of Schedule 15 to that Act, would have been so chargeable),

the first ten-year anniversary shall be taken to be 1st April 1984 (but without affecting the dates of later anniversaries).

62 Related settlements.

(1) For the purposes of this Chapter two settlements are related if and only if—

(a) the settlor is the same in each case, and

(b) they commenced on the same day,

but subject to subsection (2) below.

(2) Two settlements are not related for the purposes of this Chapter if all the property comprised in one or both of them was immediately after the settlement commenced held for charitable purposes only without limit of time (defined by a date or otherwise).

63 Minor interpretative provisions.

In this Chapter, unless the context otherwise requires—

"payment" includes a transfer of assets other than money;

"quarter" means period of three months.

Principal charge to tax

64 Charge at ten-year anniversary.

Where immediately before a ten-year anniversary all or any part of the property comprised in a settlement is relevant property, tax shall be charged at the rate applicable under sections 66 and 67 below on the value of the property or part at that time.

65 Charge at other times.

(1) There shall be a charge to tax under this section—

(a) where the property comprised in a settlement or any part of that property ceases to be relevant property (whether because it ceases to be comprised in the settlement or otherwise); and

(b) in a case in which paragraph (a) above does not apply, where the trustees of the settlement make a disposition as a result of which the value of relevant property comprised in the settlement is less than it would be but for the disposition.

(2) The amount on which tax is charged under this section shall be—

(a) the amount by which the value of relevant property comprised in the settlement is less immediately after the event in question that it would be but for the event, or

(b) where the tax payable is paid out of relevant property comprised in the settlement immediately after the event, the amount which, after deducting the tax, is equal to the amount on which tax would be charged by virtue of paragraph (a) above.

(3) The rate at which tax is charged under this section shall be the rate applicable under section 68 or 69 below.

(4) Subsection (1) above does not apply if the event in question occurs in a quarter beginning with the day on which the settlement commenced or with a ten-year anniversary.

(5) Tax shall not be charged under this section in respect of—

(a) a payment of costs or expenses (so far as they are fairly attributable to relevant property), or

(b) a payment which is (or will be) income of any person for any of the purposes of income tax or would for any of those purposes be income of a person not resident in the United Kingdom if he were so resident,

or in respect of a liability to make such a payment.

(6) Tax shall not be charged under this section by virtue of subsection (1)(b) above if the disposition is such that, were the trustees beneficially entitled to the settled property, section 10 or section 16 above would prevent the disposition from being a transfer of value.

(7) Tax shall not be charged under this section by reason only that property comprised in a settlement ceases to be situated in the United Kingdom and thereby becomes excluded property by virtue of section 48(3)(a) above.

(8) If the settlor of a settlement was not domiciled in the United Kingdom when the settlement was made, tax shall not be charged under this section by reason only that property comprised in the settlement is invested in securities issued by the Treasury subject to a condition of the kind mentioned in section 6(2) above and thereby becomes excluded property by virtue of section 48(4)(b) above.

(9) For the purposes of this section trustees shall be treated as making a disposition if they omit to exercise a right (unless it is shown that the omission was not deliberate) and the disposition shall be treated as made at the time or latest time when they could have exercised the right.

Rates of principal charge

66 Rate of ten-yearly charge.

(1) Subject to subsection (2) below, the rate at which tax is charged under section 64 above at any time shall be three tenths of the effective rate (that is to say the rate found by expressing the tax chargeable as a percentage of the amount on which it is charged) at which tax would be charged on the value transferred by a chargeable transfer of the description specified in subsection (3) below.

(2) Where the whole or part of the value mentioned in section 64 above is attributable to property which was not relevant property, or was not comprised in the settlement, throughout the period of ten years ending immediately before the ten-year anniversary concerned, the rate at which tax is charged on that value or part shall be reduced by one-fortieth for each of the successive quarters in that period which expired before the property became, or last became, relevant property comprised

in the settlement.

(3) The chargeable transfer postulated in subsection (1) above is one—

(a) the value transferred by which is equal to an amount determined in accordance with subsection (4) below;

(b) which is made immediately before the ten-year anniversary concerned by a transferor who has in the [preceding seven years][36] made chargeable transfers having an aggregate value determined in accordance with subsection (5) below; and

[(c) on which tax is charged in accordance with section 7(2) of this Act][37]

(4) The amount referred to in subsection (3)(a) above is equal to the aggregate of—

(a) the value on which is charged under section 64 above;

(b) the value immediately after it became comprised in the settlement of any property which was not then relevant property and has not subsequently become relevant property while remaining comprised in the settlement; and

(c) the value, immediately after a related settlement commenced, of the property then comprised in it;

but subject to subsection (6) below.

(5) The aggregate value referred to in subsection (3)(b) above is equal to the aggregate of—

(a) the values transferred by any chargeable transfers made by the settlor in the period of [seven][38] years ending with the day on which the settlement commenced, disregarding transfers made on that day or before 27th March 1974, and

(b) the amounts on which any charges to tax were imposed under section 65 above in respect of the settlement in the ten years before the anniversary concerned;

but subject to subsection (6) and section 67 below.

(6) In relation to a settlement which commenced before 27th March 1974—

(a) subsection (4) above shall have effect with the omission of paragraphs (b) and (c); and

(b) subsection (5) above shall have effect with the omission of paragraph (a);

and where tax is chargeable under section 64 above by reference to the first ten-year anniversary of a settlement which commenced before 9th March 1982, the aggregate mentioned in subsection (5) above shall be increased by the amounts of any distribution payments (determined in accordance with the rules applicable under paragraph 11 of Schedule 5 to the Finance Act 1975) made out of settled property before 9th March 1982 (or, where paragraph 6, 7 or 8 of Schedule 15 to the Finance Act 1982 applied, 1st April 1983, or, as the case may be, 1st April 1984) and within the period of ten years before the anniversary concerned.

67 Added property, etc.

(1) This subsection applies where, after the settlement commenced and after 8th March 1982, but before the anniversary concerned, the settlor made a chargeable transfer as a result of which the value of the property comprised in the settlement was increased.

(2) For the purposes of subsection (1) above, it is immaterial whether the amount of the property so comprised was increased as a result of the transfer, but a transfer as a result of which the value increased but the amount did not shall be disregarded if it is shown that the transfer—

(a) was not primarily intended to increase the value, and

(b) did not result in the value being greater immediately after the transfer by an amount exceeding five per cent. of the value immediately before the transfer.

(3) Where subsection (1) above applies in relation to a settlement which commenced after 26th March 1974, section 66(5)(a) above shall have effect as if it referred to the greater of—

(a) the aggregate of the values there specified, and

(b) the aggregate of the values transferred by any chargeable transfers made by the settlor in the period of [seven][39] years ending with the day on which the chargeable transfer falling within subsection (1) above was made—

(i) disregarding transfers made on that day or before 27th March 1974, and

(ii) excluding the values mentioned in subsection (5) below;

and where the settlor made two or more chargeable transfers falling within subsection (1) above, paragraph (b) above shall be taken to refer to the transfer in relation to which the aggregate there mentioned is the greatest.

(4) Where subsection (1) above applies in relation to a settlement which commenced before 27th March 1974, the aggregate mentioned in section 66(5) above shall be increased (or further increased) by the aggregate of the values transferred by any chargeable transfers made by the settlor in the period of [seven][40] years ending with the day on which the chargeable transfer falling within subsection (1) above was made—

(a) disregarding transfers made on that day or before 27th March 1974, and

(b) excluding the values mentioned in subsection (5) below; and where the settlor made two or more chargeable transfers falling within subsection (1) above, this subsection shall be taken to refer to the transfer in relation to which the aggregate to be added is the greatest.

(5) The values excluded by subsections (3)(b)(ii) and (4)(b) above are—

(a) any value attributable to property whose value is taken into account in determining the amount mentioned in section 66(4) above; and

(b) any value attributable to property in respect of which a charge to tax has been made under section 65 above and by reference to which an amount mentioned in section 66(5)(b) above is determined.

(6) Where the property comprised in a settlement immediately before the ten-year anniversary concerned, or any part of that property, had on any occasion within the preceding ten years ceased to be relevant property then, if on that occasion tax was charged in respect of the settlement under section 65 above, the aggregate mentioned in section 66(5) above shall be reduced by an amount equal to the lesser of—

(a) the amount on which tax was charged under section 65 (or so much of that amount as is attributable to the part in question), and

(b) the value on which tax is charged under section 64 above (or so much of that value as is attributable to the part in question);

and if there were two or more such occasions relating to the property or the same part of it, this subsection shall have effect in relation to each of them.

(7) References in subsection (6) above to the property comprised in a settlement immediately before an anniversary shall, if part only of the settled property was then relevant property, be construed as references to that part.

68 Rate before first ten-year anniversary.

(1) The rate at which tax is charged under section 65 above on an occasion preceding the first ten-year anniversary after the settlement's commencement shall be the appropriate fraction of the effective rate at which tax would be charged on the value transferred by a chargeable transfer of the description specified in subsection (4) below (but subject to subsection (6) below).

(2) For the purposes of this section the appropriate fraction is three tenths multiplied by so many fortieths as there are complete successive quarters in the period beginning with the day on which the settlement commenced and ending with the day before the occasion of the charge, but subject to subsection (3) below.

(3) Where the whole or part of the amount on which tax is charged is attributable to property which was not relevant property, or was not comprised in the settlement, throughout the period referred to in subsection (2) above, then in determining the appropriate fraction in relation to that amount or part—

(a) no quarter which expired before the day on which the property became, or last became, relevant property comprised in the settlement shall be counted, but

(b) if that day fell in the same quarter as that in which the period ends, that quarter shall be counted whether complete or not.

(4) The chargeable transfer postulated in subsection (1) above is one—

(a) the value transferred by which is equal to an amount determined in accordance with subsection (5) below;

(b) which is made at the time of the charge to tax under section 65 by a transferor who has in the period of [seven][41] years ending with the day of the occasion of the charge made chargeable transfers having an aggregate value equal to that of any chargeable transfers made by the settlor in the period of [seven][42] years ending with the day on which the settlement commenced, disregarding transfers made on that day or before 27th March 1974; and

[(c) on which tax is charged in accordance with section 7(2) of this Act.][43]

(5) The amount referred to in subsection (4)(a) above is equal to the aggregate of—

(a) the value, immediately after the settlement commenced, of the property then comprised in it;

(b) the value, immediately after a related settlement commenced, of the property then comprised in it; and

(c) the value, immediately after it became comprised in the settlement, of any property which became so comprised after the settlement commenced and before the occasion of the charge under section 65 (whether or not it has remained so comprised).

(6) Where the settlement commenced before 27th March 1974, subsection (1) above shall have effect with the substitution of a reference to three tenths for the reference to the appropriate fraction; and in relation to such a settlement the chargeable transfer postulated in that subsection is one—

(a) the value transferred by which is equal to the amount on which tax is charged under section 65 above;

(b) which is made at the time of that charge to tax by a transferor who has in the period of [seven][44] years ending with the day of the occasion of the charge made chargeable transfers having an aggregate value equal to the aggregate of—

(i) any amounts on which any charges to tax have been imposed under section 65 above in respect of the settlement in [the period of ten years ending with that day][45]; and

(ii) the amounts of any distribution payments (determined in accordance with the rules applicable under paragraph 11 of Schedule 5 to the Finance Act 1975) made out of the settled property before 9th March 1982 (or, where paragraph 6, 7 or 8 of Schedule 15 to the Finance Act 1982 applied, 1st April 1983, or, as the case may be, 1st April 1984) and within the said period of ten years; and

[(c) on which tax is charged in accordance with section 7(2) of this Act.][46]

69 Rate between ten-year anniversaries.

(1) Subject to subsection (2) below, the rate at which tax is charged under section 65 above on an occasion following one or more ten-year anniversaries after the settlement's commencement shall be the appropriate fraction of the rate at which it was last charged under section 64 (or would have been charged apart from section 66(2)).

(2) If at any time before the occasion of the charge under section 65 and on or after the most recent ten-year anniversary—

(a) property has become comprised in the settlement, or

(b) property which was comprised in the settlement immediately before the anniversary, but was not then relevant property, has become relevant property,

then, whether or not the property has remained comprised in the settlement or has remained relevant property, the rate at which tax is charged under section 65 shall be the appropriate fraction of the rate at which it would last have been charged under section 64 (apart from section 66(2)) if immediately before that anniversary the property had been relevant property comprised in the settlement with a value determined in accordance with subsection (3) below.

(3) In the case of property within subsection (2)(a) above which either—

(a) was relevant property immediately after it became comprised in the settlement, or

(b) was not then relevant property and has not subsequently become relevant property while remaining comprised in the settlement,

the value to be attributed to it for the purposes of subsection (2) above is its value immediately after it became comprised in the settlement; and in any other case the value to be so attributed is the value of the property when it became (or last became) relevant property.

(4) For the purposes of this section the appropriate fraction is so many fortieths as there are complete successive quarters in the period beginning with the most recent ten-year anniversary and ending with the day before the occasion of the charge; but subsection (3) of section 68 above shall have effect for the purposes of this subsection as it has effect for the purposes of subsection (2) of that section.

Special cases—charges to tax

70 Property leaving temporary charitable trusts.

(1) This section applies to settled property held for charitable purposes only until the end of a period (whether defined by a date or in some other way).

(2) Subject to subsections (3) and (4) below, there shall be a charge to tax under this section—

(a) where settled property ceases to be property to which this section applies, otherwise than by virtue of an application for charitable purposes, and

(b) in a case in which paragraph (a) above does not apply, where the trustees make a disposition (otherwise than by an application of property for charitable purposes) as a result of which the value of settled property to which this section applies is less than it would be but for the disposition.

(3) Tax shall not be charged under this section in respect of—

(a) a payment of costs or expenses (so far as they are fairly attributable to property to which this section applies), or

(b) a payment which is (or will be) income of any person for any of the purposes of income tax or would for any of those purposes be income of a person not resident in the United Kingdom if he were so resident,

or in respect of a liability to make such a payment.

(4) Tax shall not be charged under this section by virtue of subsection (2)(b) above if the disposition is such that, were the trustees beneficially entitled to the settled property, section 10 or section 16 above would prevent the disposition from being a transfer of value.

(5) The amount on which tax is charged under this section shall be—

(a) the amount by which the value of property which is comprised in the settlement and to which this section applies is less immediately after the event giving rise to the charge than it would be but for the event, or

(b) where the tax payable is paid out of settled property to which this section applies immediately after the event, the amount which, after deducting the tax, is equal to the amount on which tax would be charged by virtue of paragraph (a) above.

(6) The rate at which tax is charged under this section shall be the aggregate of the following percentages—

(a)0.25 per cent. for each of the first forty complete successive quarters in the relevant period,

(b)0.20 per cent. for each of the next forty,

(c)0.15 per cent. for each of the next forty,

(d)0.10 per cent. for each of the next forty, and

(e)0.05 per cent. for each of the next forty.

(7) Where the whole or part of the amount on which tax is charged under this section is attributable to property which was excluded property at any time during the relevant period then, in determining the rate at which tax is charged under this section in respect of that amount or part, no quarter throughout which that property was excluded property shall be counted.

(8) In subsections (6) and (7) above "the relevant period" means the period beginning with the later of—

(a) the day on which the property in respect of which tax is chargeable became (or last became) property to which this section applies, and

(b)13th March 1975,

and ending with the day before the event giving rise to the charge.

(9) Where the property in respect of which tax is chargeable—

(a) was relevant property immediately before 10th December 1981, and

(b) became (or last became) property to which this section applies on or after that day and before 9th March 1982 (or, where paragraph 6, 7 or 8 of Schedule 15 to the Finance Act 1982 applied, 1st April 1983 or, as the case may be, 1st April 1984)

subsection (8) above shall have effect as if the day referred to in paragraph (a) of that subsection were the day on which the property became (or last became) relevant property before 10th December 1981.

(10) For the purposes of this section trustees shall be treated as making a disposition if they omit to exercise a right (unless it is shown that the omission was not deliberate) and the disposition shall be treated as made at the time or latest time when they could have exercised the right.

71 Accumulation and maintenance trusts.

(1) Subject to [subsections (1A) to][47](2) below, this section applies to settled property if—

(a) one or more persons (in this section referred to as beneficiaries) will, on or before attaining a

specified age not exceeding [eighteen][48], become beneficially entitled to it ...[49] , and

(b) no interest in possession subsists in it and the income from it is to be accumulated so far as not applied for the maintenance, education or benefit of a beneficiary.

[(1A) This section does not apply to settled property at any particular time on or after 22nd March 2006 unless this section—

(a) applied to the settled property immediately before 22nd March 2006, and

(b) has applied to the settled property at all subsequent times up to the particular time.

(1B) This section does not apply to settled property at any particular time on or after 22nd March 2006 if, at that time, section 71A below applies to the settled property.][50]

(2) This section does not apply to settled property unless either—

(a) not more than twenty-five years have elapsed since the commencement of the settlement or, if it was later, since the time (or latest time) when the conditions stated in paragraphs (a) and (b) of subsection (1) above became satisfied with respect to the property, or

(b) all the persons who are or have been beneficiaries are or were either—

(i) grandchildren of a common grandparent, or

(ii) children, widows or widowers [or surviving civil partners][51] of such grandchildren who were themselves beneficiaries but died before the time when, had they survived, they would have become entitled as mentioned in subsection (1)(a) above.

(3) Subject to subsections (4) and (5) below, there shall be a charge to tax under this section—

(a) where settled property ceases to be property to which this section applies, and

(b) in a case in which paragraph (a) above does not apply, where the trustees make a disposition as a result of which the value of settled property to which this section applies is less than it would be but for the disposition.

(4) Tax shall not be charged under this section—

(a) on a beneficiary's becoming beneficially entitled to, or to an interest in possession in, settled property on or before attaining the specified age, or

(b) on the death of a beneficiary before attaining the specified age.

(5) Subsections (3) to (8) and (10) of section 70 above shall apply for the purposes of this section as they apply for the purposes of that section (with the substitution of a reference to subsection (3)(b) above for the reference in section 70(4) to section 70(2)(b)).

(6) Where the conditions stated in paragraphs (a) and (b) of subsection (1) above were satisfied on 15th April 1976 with respect to property comprised in a settlement which commenced before that day, subsection (2)(a) above shall have effect with the substitution of a reference to that day for the reference to the commencement of the settlement, and the condition stated in subsection (2)(b) above shall be treated as satisfied if—

(a) it is satisfied in respect of the period beginning with 15th April 1976, or

(b) it is satisfied in respect of the period beginning with 1st April 1977 and either there was no beneficiary living on 15th April 1976 or the beneficiaries on 1st April 1977 included a living beneficiary, or

(c) there is no power under the terms of the settlement whereby it could have become satisfied in respect of the period beginning with 1st April 1977, and the trusts of the settlement have not been varied at any time after 15th April 1976.

(7) In subsection (1) above "persons" includes unborn persons; but the conditions stated in that subsection shall be treated as not satisfied unless there is or has been a living beneficiary.

(8) For the purposes of this section a person's children shall be taken to include his illegitimate children, his adopted children and his stepchildren.

[71A Trusts for bereaved minors.

(1) This section applies to settled property (including property settled before 22nd March 2006) if—

(a) it is held on statutory trusts for the benefit of a bereaved minor under sections 46 and 47(1) of the Administration of Estates Act 1925 (succession on intestacy and statutory trusts in favour of issue of intestate), or

(b) it is held on trusts for the benefit of a bereaved minor and subsection (2) below applies to the trusts,

but this section does not apply to property in which a disabled person's interest subsists.

(2) This subsection applies to trusts—
(a) established under the will of a deceased parent of the bereaved minor, or
(b) established under the Criminal Injuries Compensation Scheme,
which secure that the conditions in subsection (3) below are met.

(3) Those conditions are—
(a) that the bereaved minor, if he has not done so before attaining the age of 18, will on attaining that age become absolutely entitled to—
(i) the settled property,
(ii) any income arising from it, and
(iii) any income that has arisen from the property held on the trusts for his benefit and been accumulated before that time,
(b) that, for so long as the bereaved minor is living and under the age of 18, if any of the settled property is applied for the benefit of a beneficiary, it is applied for the benefit of the bereaved minor, and
(c) that, for so long as the bereaved minor is living and under the age of 18, either—
(i) the bereaved minor is entitled to all of the income (if there is any) arising from any of the settled property, or
(ii) no such income may be applied for the benefit of any other person.

(4) Trusts such as are mentioned in paragraph (a) or (b) of subsection (2) above are not to be treated as failing to secure that the conditions in subsection (3) above are met by reason only of—
(a) the trustees' having the powers conferred by section 32 of the Trustee Act 1925 (powers of advancement),
(b) the trustees' having those powers but free from, or subject to a less restrictive limitation than, the limitation imposed by proviso (a) of subsection (1) of that section,
(c) the trustees' having the powers conferred by section 33 of the Trustee Act (Northern Ireland) 1958 (corresponding provision for Northern Ireland),
(d) the trustees' having those powers but free from, or subject to a less restrictive limitation than, the limitation imposed by subsection (1)(a) of that section, or
(e) the trustees' having powers to the like effect as the powers mentioned in any of paragraphs (a) to (d) above.

(5) In this section "the Criminal Injuries Compensation Scheme" means—
(a) the schemes established by arrangements made under the Criminal Injuries Compensation Act 1995,
(b) arrangements made by the Secretary of State for compensation for criminal injuries in operation before the commencement of those schemes, and
(c) the scheme established under the Criminal Injuries Compensation (Northern Ireland) Order 2002.

(6) The preceding provisions of this section apply in relation to Scotland as if, in subsection (2) above, before "which" there were inserted "the purposes of".][52]

[71B Charge to tax on property to which section 71A applies.

(1) Subject to subsections (2) and (3) below, there shall be a charge to tax under this section—
(a) where settled property ceases to be property to which section 71A above applies, and
(b) in a case where paragraph (a) above does not apply, where the trustees make a disposition as a result of which the value of settled property to which section 71A above applies is less than it would be but for the disposition.

(2) Tax is not charged under this section where settled property ceases to be property to which section 71A applies as a result of—
(a) the bereaved minor attaining the age of 18 or becoming, under that age, absolutely entitled as mentioned in section 71A(3)(a) above, or
(b) the death under that age of the bereaved minor, or
(c) being paid or applied for the advancement or benefit of the bereaved minor.

(3) Subsections (3) to (8) and (10) of section 70 above apply for the purposes of this section as they apply for the purposes of that section, but—
(a) with the substitution of a reference to subsection (1)(b) above for the reference in subsection (4) of section 70 above to subsection (2)(b) of that section,

(b) with the substitution of a reference to property to which section 71A above applies for each of the references in subsections (3), (5) and (8) of section 70 above to property to which that section applies,

(c) as if, for the purposes of section 70(8) above as applied by this subsection, property—

(i) which is property to which section 71A above applies,

(ii) which, immediately before it became property to which section 71A above applies, was property to which section 71 above applied, and

(iii) which, by the operation of section 71(1B) above, ceased on that occasion to be property to which section 71 above applied,

had become property to which section 71A above applies not on that occasion but on the occasion (or last occasion) before then when it became property to which section 71 above applied, and

(d) as if, for the purposes of section 70(8) above as applied by this subsection, property—

(i) which is property to which section 71A above applies,

(ii) which, immediately before it became property to which section 71A above applies, was property to which section 71D below applied, and

(iii) which, by the operation of section 71D(5)(a) below, ceased on that occasion ("the 71D-to-71A occasion") to be property to which section 71D below applied,

had become property to which section 71A above applies not on the 71D-to-71A occasion but on the relevant earlier occasion.

(4) In subsection (3)(d) above—

(a) "the relevant earlier occasion" means the occasion (or last occasion) before the 71D-to-71A occasion when the property became property to which section 71D below applied, but

(b) if the property, when it became property to which section 71D below applied, ceased at the same time to be property to which section 71 above applied without ceasing to be settled property, "the relevant earlier occasion" means the occasion (or last occasion) when the property became property to which section 71 above applied.]

[71C Sections 71A and 71B: meaning of "bereaved minor".

In sections 71A and 71B above "bereaved minor" means a person—

(a) who has not yet attained the age of 18, and

(b) at least one of whose parents has died.]

[71D Age 18-to-25 trusts.

(1) This section applies to settled property (including property settled before 22nd March 2006), but subject to subsection (5) below, if—

(a) the property is held on trusts for the benefit of a person who has not yet attained the age of 25,

(b) at least one of the person's parents has died, and

(c) subsection (2) below applies to the trusts.

(2) This subsection applies to trusts—

(a) established under the will of a deceased parent of the person mentioned in subsection (1)(a) above, or

(b) established under the Criminal Injuries Compensation Scheme,

which secure that the conditions in subsection (6) below are met.

(3) Subsection (4) has effect where—

(a) at any time on or after 22nd March 2006 but before 6th April 2008, or on the coming into force of paragraph 3(1) of Schedule 20 to the Finance Act 2006, any property ceases to be property to which section 71 above applies without ceasing to be settled property, and

(b) immediately after the property ceases to be property to which section 71 above applies—

(i) it is held on trusts for the benefit of a person who has not yet attained the age of 25, and

(ii) the trusts secure that the conditions in subsection (6) below are met.

(4) From the time when the property ceases to be property to which section 71 above applies, but subject to subsection (5) below, this section applies to the property (if it would not apply to the property by virtue of subsection (1) above) for so long as—

(a) the property continues to be settled property held on trusts such as are mentioned in subsection (3)(b)(i) above, and

(b) the trusts continue to secure that the conditions in subsection (6) below are met.

(5) This section does not apply—

(a) to property to which section 71A above applies,

(b) to property to which section 71 above, or section 89 below, applies, or

(c) to settled property if a person is beneficially entitled to an interest in possession in the settled property and—

(i) the person became beneficially entitled to the interest in possession before 22nd March 2006, or

(ii) the interest in possession is an immediate post-death interest, or a transitional serial interest, and the person became beneficially entitled to it on or after 22nd March 2006.

(6) Those conditions are—

(a) that the person mentioned in subsection (1)(a) or (3)(b)(i) above ("B"), if he has not done so before attaining the age of 25, will on attaining that age become absolutely entitled to—

(i) the settled property,

(ii) any income arising from it, and

(iii) any income that has arisen from the property held on the trusts for his benefit and been accumulated before that time,

(b) that, for so long as B is living and under the age of 25, if any of the settled property is applied for the benefit of a beneficiary, it is applied for the benefit of B, and

(c) that, for so long as B is living and under the age of 25, either—

(i) b is entitled to all of the income (if there is any) arising from any of the settled property, or

(ii) no such income may be applied for the benefit of any other person.

(7) For the purposes of this section, trusts are not to be treated as failing to secure that the conditions in subsection (6) above are met by reason only of—

(a) the trustees' having the powers conferred by section 32 of the Trustee Act 1925 (powers of advancement),

(b) the trustees' having those powers but free from, or subject to a less restrictive limitation than, the limitation imposed by proviso (a) of subsection (1) of that section,

(c) the trustees' having the powers conferred by section 33 of the Trustee Act (Northern Ireland) 1958 (corresponding provision for Northern Ireland),

(d) the trustees' having those powers but free from, or subject to a less restrictive limitation than, the limitation imposed by subsection (1)(a) of that section, or

(e) the trustees' having powers to the like effect as the powers mentioned in any of paragraphs (a) to (d) above.

(8) In this section "the Criminal Injuries Compensation Scheme" means—

(a) the schemes established by arrangements made under the Criminal Injuries Compensation Act 1995,

(b) arrangements made by the Secretary of State for compensation for criminal injuries in operation before the commencement of those schemes, and

(c) the scheme established under the Criminal Injuries Compensation (Northern Ireland) Order 2002.

(9) The preceding provisions of this section apply in relation to Scotland—

(a) as if, in subsection (2) above, before "which" there were inserted the purposes of, and

(b) as if, in subsections (3)(b)(ii) and (4)(b) above, before "trusts" there were inserted "purposes of the".]

[71ECharge to tax on property to which section 71D applies.

(1) Subject to subsections (2) to (4) below, there shall be a charge to tax under this section—

(a) where settled property ceases to be property to which section 71D above applies, or

(b) in a case where paragraph (a) above does not apply, where the trustees make a disposition as a result of which the value of the settled property to which section 71D above applies is less than it would be but for the disposition.

(2) Tax is not charged under this section where settled property ceases to be property to which section 71D above applies as a result of—

(a) b becoming, at or under the age of 18, absolutely entitled as mentioned in section 71D(6)(a) above,

(b) the death, under the age of 18, of B,

(c) becoming, at a time when B is living and under the age of 18, property to which section 71A above applies, or

(d) being paid or applied for the advancement or benefit of B—

(i) at a time when B is living and under the age of 18, or

(ii) on B's attaining the age of 18.

(3) Tax is not charged under this section in respect of—

(a) a payment of costs or expenses (so far as they are fairly attributable to property to which section 71D above applies), or

(b) a payment which is (or will be) income of any person for any of the purposes of income tax or would for any of those purposes be income of a person not resident in the United Kingdom if he were so resident,

or in respect of a liability to make such a payment.

(4) Tax is not charged under this section by virtue of subsection (1)(b) above if the disposition is such that, were the trustees beneficially entitled to the settled property, section 10 or section 16 above would prevent the disposition from being a transfer of value.

(5) For the purposes of this section the trustees shall be treated as making a disposition if they omit to exercise a right (unless it is shown that the omission was not deliberate) and the disposition shall be treated as made at the time or latest time when they could have exercised the right.]

[71FCalculation of tax charged under section 71E in certain cases.

(1) Where—

(a) tax is charged under section 71E above by reason of the happening of an event within subsection (2) below, and

(b) that event happens after B has attained the age of 18,

the tax is calculated in accordance with this section.

(2) Those events are—

(a) b becoming absolutely entitled as mentioned in section 71D(6)(a) above,

(b) the death of B, and

(c) property being paid or applied for the advancement or benefit of B.

(3) The amount of the tax is given by—

Chargeable amount x Relevant fraction x Settlement rate

(4) For the purposes of subsection (3) above, the "Chargeable amount" is—

(a) the amount by which the value of property which is comprised in the settlement and to which section 71D above applies is less immediately after the event giving rise to the charge than it would be but for the event, or

(b) where the tax is payable out of settled property to which section 71D above applies immediately after the event, the amount which, after deducting the tax, is equal to the amount on which tax would be charged by virtue of paragraph (a) above.

(5) For the purposes of subsection (3) above, the "Relevant fraction" is three tenths multiplied by so many fortieths as there are complete successive quarters in the period—

(a) beginning with the day on which B attained the age of 18 or, if later, the day on which the property became property to which section 71D above applies, and

(b) ending with the day before the occasion of the charge.

(6) Where the whole or part of the Chargeable amount is attributable to property that was excluded property at any time during the period mentioned in subsection (5) above then, in determining the "Relevant fraction" in relation to that amount or part, no quarter throughout which that property was excluded property shall be counted.

(7) For the purposes of subsection (3) above, the "Settlement rate" is the effective rate (that is to say, the rate found by expressing the tax chargeable as a percentage of the amount on which it is charged) at which tax would be charged on the value transferred by a chargeable transfer of the description specified in subsection (8) below.

(8) The chargeable transfer postulated in subsection (7) above is one—

(a) the value transferred by which is equal to an amount determined in accordance with subsection (9) below,

(b) which is made at the time of the charge to tax under section 71E above by a transferor who has in

the period of seven years ending with the day of the occasion of the charge made chargeable transfers having an aggregate value equal to that of any chargeable transfers made by the settlor in the period of seven years ending with the day on which the settlement commenced, disregarding transfers made on that day, and

(c) on which tax is charged in accordance with section 7(2) above.

(9) The amount referred to in subsection (8)(a) above is equal to the aggregate of—

(a) the value, immediately after the settlement commenced, of the property then comprised in it,

(b) the value, immediately after a related settlement commenced, of the property then comprised in it, and

(c) the value, immediately after it became comprised in the settlement, of any property which became so comprised after the settlement commenced and before the occasion of the charge under section 71E above (whether or not it has remained so comprised).]

[71GCalculation of tax charged under section 71E in all other cases.

(1) Where—

(a) tax is charged under section 71E above, and

(b) the tax does not fall to be calculated in accordance with section 71F above,

the tax is calculated in accordance with this section.

(2) The amount on which the tax is charged is—

(a) the amount by which the value of property which is comprised in the settlement and to which section 71D above applies is less immediately after the event giving rise to the charge than it would be but for the event, or

(b) where the tax is payable out of settled property to which section 71D above applies immediately after the event, the amount which, after deducting the tax, is equal to the amount on which tax would be charged by virtue of paragraph (a) above.

(3) The rate at which the tax is charged is the rate that would be given by subsections (6) to (8) of section 70 above—

(a) if the reference to section 70 above in subsection (8)(a) of that section were a reference to section 71D above,

(b) if the other references in those subsections to section 70 above were references to section 71E above, and

(c) if, for the purposes of section 70(8) above, property—

(i) which is property to which section 71D above applies,

(ii) which, immediately before it became property to which section 71D above applies, was property to which section 71 applied, and

(iii) which ceased on that occasion to be property to which section 71 above applied without ceasing to be settled property,

had become property to which section 71D above applies not on that occasion but on the occasion (or last occasion) before then when it became property to which section 71 above applied.]

[71HSections 71A to 71G: meaning of "parent".

(1) In sections 71A to 71G above "parent" includes step-parent.

(2) For the purposes of sections 71A to 71G above, a deceased individual ("D") shall be taken to have been a parent of another individual ("Y") if, immediately before D died, D had—

(a) parental responsibility for Y under the law of England and Wales,

(b) parental responsibilities in relation to Y under the law of Scotland, or

(c) parental responsibility for Y under the law of Northern Ireland.

(3) In subsection (2)(a) above "parental responsibility" has the same meaning as in the Children Act 1989.

(4) In subsection (2)(b) above "parental responsibilities" has the meaning given by section 1(3) of the Children (Scotland) Act 1995.

(5) In subsection (2)(c) above "parental responsibility" has the same meaning as in the Children (Northern Ireland) Order 1995.][53]

72 Property leaving employee trusts and newspaper trusts.

(1) This section applies to settled property to which section 86 below applies [if—

(a) no interest in possession subsists in it to which an individual is beneficially entitled, and

(b) no company-purchased interest in possession subsists in it.][54]

[(1A) For the purposes of subsection (1)(b) above, an interest in possession is "company-purchased" if—

(a) a company is beneficially entitled to the interest in possession,

(b) the business of the company consists wholly or mainly in the acquisition of interests in settled property, and

(c) the company has acquired the interest in possession for full consideration in money or money's worth from an individual who was beneficially entitled to it.

(1B) Section 59(3) and (4) above apply for the purposes of subsection (1A)(c) above as for those of section 59(2)(b) above, but as if the references to the condition set out in section 59(2)(a) above were to the condition set out in subsection (1A)(b) above.][55]

(2) Subject to subsections (4) [, (4A)][56] and (5) below, there shall be a charge to tax under this section—

(a) where settled property ceases to be property to which this section applies, otherwise than by virtue of a payment out of the settled property, and

(b) where a payment is made out of settled property to which this section applies for the benefit of a person within subsection (3) below, or a person connected with such a person, and

(c) in a case which paragraphs (a) and (b) above do not apply, where the trustees make a disposition (otherwise than by way of a payment out of the settled property) as a result of which the value of settled property to which this section applies is less than it would be but for the disposition.

(3) A person is within this subsection if—

(a) he has directly or indirectly provided any of the settled property otherwise than by additions not exceeding in value £1,000 in any one year; or

(b) in a case where the employment in question is employment by a close company, he is a participator in relation to that company and either—

(i) is beneficially entitled to, or to rights entitling him to acquire, not less than 5 per cent. of, or of any class of the shares comprised in, its issued share capital, or

(ii) would, on a winding-up of the company, be entitled to not less than 5 per cent. of its assets; or

(c) he has acquired an interest in the settled property for a consideration in money or money's worth.

(4) If the trusts are those of a profit sharing scheme approved in accordance with Schedule 9 to the [Taxes Act 1988][57], tax shall not be chargeable under this section by virtue of subsection (3)(b) above on an appropriation of shares in pursuance of the scheme.

[(4A) If the trusts are those of [a share incentive plan approved under Schedule 2 to the Income Tax (Earnings and Pensions) Act 2003][58] , tax shall not be chargeable under this section by virtue of subsection (3)(b) above on an appropriation of shares to, or acquisition of shares on behalf of, an individual under the plan.][59]

(5) Subsections (3) to (10) of section 70 above shall apply for the purposes of this section as they apply for the purposes of that section (with the substitution of a reference to subsection (2)(c) above for the reference in section 70(4) to section 70(2)(b)).

(6) In this section—

(a) "close company" and "participator" have the same meanings as in Part IV of this Act; and

(b) "year" means the period beginning with 26th March 1974 and ending with 5th April 1974, and any subsequent period of twelve months ending with 5th April;

and a person shall be treated for the purposes of this section as acquiring an interest for a consideration in money or money's worth if he becomes entitled to it as a result of transactions which include a disposition for such consideration (whether to him or another) of that interest or of other property.

73 Pre-1978 protective trusts.

(1) This section applies to settled property which is held on trusts to the like effect as those specified in section 33(1)(ii) of the Trustee Act 1925 and which became held on those trusts on the failure or determination before 12th April 1978 of trusts to the like effect as those specified in section 33(1)(i).

(2) Subject to subsection (3) below, there shall be a charge to tax under this section—

(a) where settled property ceases to be property to which this section applies, otherwise than by virtue of a payment out of the settled property for the benefit of the principal beneficiary within the meaning of section 33 of the Trustee Act 1925, and

(b) in a case which paragraph (a) above does not apply, where the trustees make a disposition (otherwise than by way of such a payment) as a result of which the value of settled property to which this section applies is less than it would be but for the disposition.

(3) Subsections (3) to (10) of section 70 above shall apply for the purposes of this section as they apply for the purposes of that section.

74 Pre-1981 trusts for disabled persons.

(1) This section applies to settled property transferred into settlement before 10th March 1981 and held on trusts under which, during the life of a disabled person, no interest in possession in the settled property subsists, and which secure that any of the settled property which is applied during his life is applied only or mainly for his benefit.

(2) Subject to subsection (3) below, there shall be a charge to tax under this section—

(a) where settled property ceases to be property to which this section applies, otherwise than by virtue of a payment out of the settled property for the benefit of the person mentioned in subsection (1) above, and

(b) in a case in which paragraph (a) above does not apply, where the trustees make a disposition (otherwise than by way of such a payment) as a result of which the value of settled property to which this section applies is less than it would be but for the disposition.

(3) Subsections (3) to (10) of section 70 above shall apply for the purposes of this section as they apply for the purposes of that section.

(4) In this section "disabled person" means a person who—

(a) is by reason of mental disorder (within the meaning of the Mental Health Act 1983) incapable of administering his property or managing his affairs, or

(b) is in receipt of an attendance allowance under section [64 of the Social Security Contributions and Benefits Act 1992 or][60][section 64 of the Social Security Contributions and Benefits (Northern Ireland) Act 1992] [61] [, or

(c) is in receipt of a disability living allowance under section [71 of the Social Security Contributions and Benefits Act 1992][62][or [section 71 of the Social Security Contributions and Benefits (Northern Ireland) Act 1992][63]][64] by virtue of entitlement to the care component at the highest or middle rate.][65]

Special cases—reliefs

75 Property becoming subject to employee trusts.

(1) Tax shall not be charged under section 65 above in respect of shares in or securities of a company which cease to be relevant property on becoming held on trusts of the description specified in section 86(1) below if the conditions in subsection (2) below are satisfied.

(2) The conditions referred to in subsection (1) above are—

(a) that the persons for whose benefit the trusts permit the settled property to be applied include all or most of the persons employed by or holding office with the company;

(b) that, at the date when the shares or securities cease to be relevant property or at a subsequent date not more than one year thereafter, both the conditions mentioned in subsection (2) of section 28 above (read with subsections (3) and (7)) are satisfied, without taking account of shares or securities held on other trusts; and

(c) that the trusts do not permit any of the property to be applied at any time (whether during any such period as is referred to in section 86(1) below or later) for the benefit of any of the persons mentioned in subsection (4) of section 28 above (read with subsections (5) to (7)) or for the benefit of the settlor or of any person connected with him.

(3) In its application for the purposes of subsection (2)(c) above, section 28(4) shall be construed as if—

(a) references to section 28(1) were references to subsection (2) above, and

(b) references to the time of the transfer of value were references to the time when the property ceases to be relevant property.

76 Property becoming held for charitable purposes, etc.

(1) Tax shall not be charged under this Chapter (apart from section 79 below) in respect of property which ceases to be relevant property, or ceases to be property to which section 70, 71, [71A, 71D,][66] 72, 73 or 74 above or paragraph 8 of Schedule 4 to this Act applies, on becoming—

(a) property held for charitable purposes only without limit of time (defined by a date or otherwise);

(b) the property of a political party qualifying for exemption under section 24 above; [or][67]

(c) the property of a body within Schedule 3 to this Act;

(d). . . . .[68]

(2). . . . .[69]

(3) If the amount on which tax would be charged apart from this section in respect of any property exceeds the value of the property immediately after it becomes property of a description specified in paragraphs (a) [to (c)][70] of subsection (1) above (less the amount of any consideration for its transfer received by the trustees), that subsection shall not apply but the amount on which tax is charged shall be equal to the excess.

(4) The reference in subsection (3) above to the amount on which tax would be charged is a reference to the amount on which it would be charged—

(a) assuming (if it is not in fact so) that the tax is not paid out of settled property, and

(b) apart from Chapters I and II of Part V of this Act;

and the reference in that subsection to the amount on which tax is charged is a reference to the amount on which it would be charged on that assumption and apart from those Chapters.

(5) Subsection (1) above shall not apply in relation to any property if the disposition by which it becomes property of the relevant description is defeasible; but for this purpose a disposition which has not been defeated at a time twelve months after the property concerned becomes property of the relevant description and is not defeasible after that time shall be treated as not being defeasible, whether or not it was capable of being defeated before that time.

(6) Subsection (1) above shall not apply in relation to any property if it or any part of it may become applicable for purposes other than charitable purposes or purposes of a body mentioned in subsection (1)(b), [or (c)][71] above.

(7) Subsection (1) shall not apply in relation to any property if, at or before the time when it becomes property of the relevant description, an interest under the settlement is or has been acquired for a consideration in money or money's worth by an exempt body otherwise than from a charity or a body mentioned in subsection (1)(b) or (c) above.

(8) In subsection (7) above "exempt body" means a charity or a body mentioned in subsection (1)(b), [or (c)][72] above; and for the purposes of subsection (7) above a body shall be treated as acquiring an interest for a consideration in money or money's worth if it becomes entitled to the interest as a result of transactions which include a disposition for such consideration (whether to that body or to another person) of that interest or of other property.

Works of art, historic buildings, etc.

77 Maintenance funds for historic buildings, etc.

Schedule 4 to this Act shall have effect.

78 Conditionally exempt occasions.

(1) A transfer of property or other event shall not constitute an occasion on which tax is chargeable under any provision of this Chapter other than section 64 if the property in respect of which the charge would have been made has been comprised in the settlement throughout the six years ending with the transfer or event, and—

(a) the property is, on a claim made for the purpose, designated by the Treasury under section 31 above, and

(b) the requisite undertaking described in that section is given with respect to the property by such person as the Treasury think appropriate in the circumstances of the case [or (where the property is an area of land within subsection (1)(d) of that section) the requisite undertakings described in that section are given with respect to the property by such person or persons as the Treasury think appropriate in the circumstances of the case.][73]

[(1A) a claim under subsection (1) above must be made no more than two years after the date of the transfer or other event in question or within such longer period as the Board may allow.][74]

(2) References in this Chapter to a conditionally exempt occasion are to—

(a) a transfer or event which by virtue of subsection (1) above does not constitute an occasion on which tax is chargeable under this Chapter;

(b) a transfer or event which, by virtue of section 81(1) of the Finance Act 1976, did not constitute an

occasion on which tax was chargeable under Chapter II of Part IV of the Finance Act 1982;

(c) a conditionally exempt distribution within the meaning given by section 81(2) of the Finance Act 1976 as it had effect in relation to events before 9th March 1982.

(3) Where there has been a conditionally exempt occasion in respect of any property, sections 32, [32A][75], 33(1), 33(3) to (7) and 35(2) above shall have effect (and tax shall accordingly be chargeable under section 32 [or 32A][76]) as if—

(a) references to a conditionally exempt transfer and to such a transfer of property included references respectively to a conditionally exempt occasion and to such an occasion in respect of property;

(b) references to a disposal otherwise than by sale included references to any occasion on which tax is chargeable under any provision of this Chapter other than section 64;

(c) references to an undertaking given under section 30 above included references to an undertaking given under this section;

and the references in section 33(5) above to the person who made a conditionally exempt transfer shall have effect in relation to a conditionally exempt occasion as references to the person who is the settlor of the settlement in respect of which the occasion occurred (or if there is more than one such person, whichever of them the Board may select).

(4) Where by virtue of subsection (3) above the relevant person for the purposes of section 33 above is the settlor of a settlement, the rate (or each of the rates) mentioned in section 33(1)(b)(i) or (ii)—

(a) shall, if the occasion occurred before the first ten-year anniversary to fall after the property became comprised in the settlement concerned, be 30 per cent. of what it would be apart from this subsection, and

(b) shall, if the occasion occurred after the first and before the second ten-year anniversary to fall after the property became so comprised, be 60 per cent. of what it would be apart from this subsection;

[and the appropriate provision of section 7 for the purposes of section 33(1)(b)(ii) is, if the settlement was created on his death, subsection (1) and, if not, subsection (2).][77]

(5) Where by virtue of subsection (3) above the relevant person for the purposes of section 33 above is the settlor of a settlement and that settlor died before 13th March 1975, section 33(1)(b) above shall have effect (subject to subsection (4) above) with the substitution for sub-paragraph (ii) of the following sub-paragraph:—

"(ii) the rate or rates that would have applied to that amount ("the chargeable amount") [in accordance with the appropriate provision of section 7 above][78] if the relevant person had died when the chargeable event occurred, the value transferred on his death had been equal to the amount on which estate duty was chargeable when he in fact died, and the chargeable amount had been added to that value and had formed the highest part of it."

(6) Section 34 above shall not apply to a chargeable event in respect of property if the last conditionally exempt transfer of the property has been followed by a conditionally exempt occasion in respect of it.

79 Exemption from ten-yearly charge.

(1) Where property is comprised in a settlement and there has been a conditionally exempt transfer of the property on or before the occasion on which it became comprised in the settlement, section 64 above shall not have effect in relation to the property on any ten-year anniversary falling before the first occurrence after the transfer of a chargeable event with respect to the property.

(2) Where property is comprised in a settlement and there has been, on or before the occasion on which it became comprised in the settlement, a disposal of the property in relation to which subsection (4) of section [258 of the 1992 Act][79] (capital gains tax relief for works of art etc.) had effect, section 64 above shall not have effect in relation to the property on any ten-year anniversary falling before the first occurrence after the disposal of an event on the happening of which the property is treated as sold under subsection (5) of the said section [258][80].

(3) Where property is comprised in a settlement and there has been no such transfer or disposal of the property as is mentioned in subsection (1) or (2) above on or before the occasion on which it became comprised in the settlement, then, if—

(a) the property has, on a claim made for the purpose, been designated by the Treasury under

section 31 above,

(b) the requisite undertaking described in that section has been given [with respect to the property][81] by such person as the Treasury think appropriate in the circumstances of the case, [or (where the property is an area of land within subsection (1)(d) of that section) the requisite undertakings described in that section have been given with respect to the property by such person or persons as the Treasury think appropriate in the circumstances of the case][82], and

(c) the property is relevant property,

section 64 above shall not have effect in relation to the property; but there shall be a charge to tax under this subsection on the first occurrence of an event which, if there had been a conditionally exempt transfer of the property when the claim was made and the undertaking had been given under section 30 above, would be a chargeable event with respect to the property.

(4) Tax shall not be charged under subsection (3) above in respect of property if, after the occasion and before the occurrence there mentioned, there has been a conditionally exempt occasion in respect of the property.

(5) The amount on which tax is charged under subsection (3) above shall be an amount equal to the value of the property at the time of the event.

[(5A) Where the event giving rise to a charge to tax under subsection (3) above is a disposal on sale, and the sale—

(a) was not intended to confer any gratuitous benefit on any person, and

(b) was either a transaction at arm's length between persons not connected with each other or a transaction such as might be expected to be made at arm's length between persons not connected with each other,

the value of the property at the time of that event shall be taken for the purposes of subsection (5) above to be equal to the proceeds of the sale.][83]

(6) The rate at which tax is charged under subsection (3) above shall be the aggregate of the following percentages—

(a)0·25 per cent. for each of the first forty complete successive quarters in the relevant period,

(b)0·20 per cent. for each of the next forty,

(c)0·15 per cent. for each of the next forty,

(d)0·10 per cent. for each of the next forty, and

(e)0·5 per cent. for each of the next forty.

[(7) In subsection (6) above "the relevant period" means the period given by subsection (7A) below or, if shorter, the period given by subsection (7B) below.

(7A) The period given by this subsection is the period beginning with the latest of—

(a) the day on which the settlement commenced,

(b) the date of the last ten-year anniversary of the settlement to fall before the day on which the property became comprised in the settlement,

(c) the date of the last ten-year anniversary of the settlement to fall before the day on which the property was designated under section 31 above on a claim under this section, and

(d)13th March 1975,

and ending with the day before the event giving rise to the charge.

(7B) The period given by this subsection is the period equal in length to the number of relevant-property days in the period—

(a) beginning with the day that is the latest of those referred to in paragraphs (a) to (d) of subsection (7A) above, and

(b) ending with the day before the event giving rise to the charge.

(7C) For the purposes of subsection (7B) above, a day is a "relevant-property day" if at any time on that day the property was relevant property.][84]

(8) Subsection (9) below shall have effect where—

(a) by virtue of subsection (3) above, section 64 does not have effect in relation to property on the first ten-year anniversary of the settlement to fall after the making of the claim and the giving of the undertaking,

(b) on that anniversary a charge to tax falls to be made in respect of the settlement under section 64, and

(c) the property became comprised in the settlement, and the claim was made and the undertaking was given, within the period of ten years ending with that anniversary.

[(9A) Subsection (9B) below applies where the same event gives rise—

(a) to a charge under subsection (3) above in relation to any property, and

(b) to a charge under section 32 or 32A above in relation to that property.

(9B) If the amount of each of the charges is the same, each charge shall have effect as a charge for one half of the amount that would be charged apart from this subsection; otherwise, whichever of the charges is lower in amount shall have effect as if it were a charge the amount of which is nil.][85]

(9) In calculating the rate at which tax is charged under section 64 above, the value of the consideration given for the property on its becoming comprised in the settlement shall be treated for the purposes of section 66(5)(b) above as if it were an amount on which a charge to tax was imposed in respect of the settlement under section 65 above at the time of the property becoming so comprised.

(10) In subsection (1) above, the reference to a conditionally exempt transfer of any property includes a reference to a transfer of value in relation to which the value of any property has been left out of account under the provisions of sections 31 to 34 of the Finance Act 1975 and, in relation to such property, the reference to a chargeable event includes a reference to an event on the occurrence of which tax becomes chargeable under Schedule 5 to this Act.

[79A Variation of undertakings.

(1) An undertaking given under section 78 or 79 above may be varied from time to time by agreement between the Board and the person bound by the undertaking.

(2) Where a Special Commissioner is satisfied that—

(a) the Board have made a proposal for the variation of such an undertaking to the person bound by the undertaking,

(b) that person has failed to agree to the proposed variation within six months after the date on which the proposal was made, and

(c) it is just and reasonable, in all the circumstances, to require the proposed variation to be made,

the Commissioner may direct that the undertaking is to have effect from a date specified by him as if the proposed variation had been agreed to by the person bound by the undertaking.

(3) The date specified by the Special Commissioner must not be less than sixty days after the date of his direction.

(4) A direction under this section shall not take effect if, before the date specified by the Special Commissioner, a variation different from that to which the direction relates is agreed between the Board and the person bound by the undertaking.][86]

Miscellaneous

80 Initial interest of settlor or spouse [or civil partner][87].

(1) Where a settlor or his spouse [or civil partner][88] is beneficially entitled to an interest in possession in property immediately after it becomes comprised in the settlement, the property shall for the purposes of this Chapter be treated as not having become comprised in the settlement on that occasion; but when the property or any part of it becomes held on trusts under which neither of those persons is beneficially entitled to an interest in possession, the property or part shall for those purposes be treated as becoming comprised in a separate settlement made by that one of them who ceased (or last ceased) to be beneficially entitled to an interest in possession in it.

(2) References in subsection (1) above to the spouse [or civil partner][89] of a settlor include references to the widow or widower [or surviving civil partner][90] of a settlor.

(3) This section shall not apply if the occasion first referred to in subsection (1) above occurred before 27th March 1974.

[(4) Where the occasion first referred to in subsection (1) above occurs on or after 22nd March 2006, this section applies—

(a) as though for "an interest in possession" in each place where that appears in subsection (1) above there were substituted a postponing interest, and

(b) as though, for the purposes of that subsection, each of the following were a "postponing interest"—

(i) an immediate post-death interest;

(ii) a disabled person's interest.][91]

81 Property moving between settlements.

(1) Where property which ceases to be comprised in one settlement becomes comprised in another then, unless in the meantime any person becomes beneficially entitled to the property (and not merely to an interest in possession in the property), it shall for the purposes of this Chapter be treated as remaining comprised in the first settlement.

(2) Subsection (1) above shall not apply where the property ceased to be comprised in the first settlement before 10th December 1981; but where property ceased to be comprised in one settlement before 10th December 1981 and after 26th March 1974 and, by the same disposition, became comprised in another settlement, it shall for the purposes of this Chapter be treated as remaining comprised in the first settlement.

(3) Subsection (1) above shall not apply where a reversionary interest in the property expectant on the termination of a qualifying interest in possession subsisting under the first settlement was settled on the trusts of the other settlement before 10th December 1981.

82 Excluded property.

(1) For the purposes of this Chapter (except sections 78 and 79) property to which section 80 or 81 above applies shall not be taken to be excluded property by virtue of section 48(3)(a) above unless the condition in subsection (3) below is satisfied (in addition to the conditions in section 48(3) that the property is situated outside the United Kingdom and that the settlor was not domiciled there when the settlement was made).

(2) Section 65(8) above shall not have effect in relation to property to which section 80 or 81 applies unless the condition in subsection (3) below is satisfied (in addition to the condition in section 65(8) that the settlor was not domiciled in the United Kingdom when the settlement was made).

(3) The condition referred to in subsections (1) and (2) above is—

(a) in the case of property to which section 80 above applies, that the person who is the settlor in relation to the settlement first mentioned in that section, and

(b) in the case of property to which subsection (1) or (2) of section 81 above applies, that the person who is the settlor in relation to the second of the settlements mentioned in the subsection concerned,

was not domiciled in the United Kingdom when that settlement was made.

83 Property becoming settled on a death.

Property which becomes comprised in a settlement in pursuance of a will or intestacy shall for the purposes of this Chapter be taken to have become comprised in it on the death of the testator or intestate (whether it occurred before or after the passing of this Act).

84 Income applied for charitable purposes.

For the purposes of this Chapter (except sections 78 and 79) where the trusts on which settled property is held require part of the income of the property to be applied for charitable purposes, a corresponding part of the settled property shall be regarded as held for charitable purposes.

...

230 Acceptance of property in satisfaction of tax..

(1) The Board may, if they think fit and the [Secretary of State agrees][92] , on the application of any person liable to pay tax or interest payable under section 233 below, accept in satisfaction of the whole or any part of it any property to which this section applies.

(2) This section applies to any such land as may be agreed upon between the Board and the person liable to pay tax.

(3) This section also applies to any objects which are or have been kept in any building—

(a) if the Board have determined to accept or have accepted that building in satisfaction or part satisfaction of tax or of estate duty, or

(b) if the building or any interest in it belongs to Her Majesty in right of the Crown or of the Duchy of Lancaster, or belongs to the Duchy of Cornwall or belongs to a Government department or is held for the purposes of a Government department, or

(c) if the building is one of which the Secretary of State is guardian under the Ancient Monuments and Archaeological Areas Act 1979 or of which the Department of the Environment for Northern Ireland is guardian under [the Historic Monuments and Archaeological Objects (Northern

Ireland) Order 1995][93], or

(d) if the building belongs to any body within Schedule 3 to this Act,

in any case where it appears to the [Secretary of State][94] desirable for the objects to remain associated with the building.

(4) This section also applies to—

(a) any picture, print, book, manuscript, work of art, scientific object or other thing which the [Secretary of State is][95] satisfied is pre-eminent for its national, scientific, historic or artistic interest, and

(b) any collection or group of pictures, prints, books, manuscripts, works of art, scientific objects or other things if the [Secretary of State is][96] satisfied that the collection or group, taken as a whole, is pre-eminent for its national, scientific, historic or artistic interest.

(5) In this section—

. . .[97]

"national interest" includes interest within any part of the United Kingdom;

and in determining under subsection (4) above whether an object or collection or group of objects is pre-eminent, regard shall be had to any significant association of the object, collection or group with a particular place.

[(6) The functions of the Ministers under this section in relation to the acceptance, in satisfaction of tax, of property in which there is a Scottish interest may be exercised separately.

(7) For the purposes of subsection (6) a Scottish interest in the property exists–

(a) where the property is located in Scotland; or

(b) the person liable to pay the tax has expressed a wish or imposed a condition on his offer of the property in satisfaction of tax that it be displayed in Scotland or disposed of or transferred to a body or institution in Scotland.][98]

...

Supplementary

...

274 Commencement.

(1) This Act shall come into force on 1st January 1985, but shall not apply to transfers of value made before that date or to other events before that date on which capital transfer tax is chargeable or would be chargeable but for an exemption, exception or relief.

(2) Subsection (1) above shall have effect subject to section 275 below, to Schedule 7 to this Act and to any other provision to the contrary.

275 Continuity, and construction of references to old and new law.

(1) The continuity of the operation of the law relating to capital transfer tax shall not be affected by the substitution of this Act for the repealed enactments.

(2) any reference, whether express or implied, in any enactment, instrument or document (including this Act and any enactment amended by Schedule 8 to this Act) to, or to things done or falling to be done under or for the purposes of, any provision of this Act shall, if and so far as the nature of the reference permits, be construed as including, in relation to the times, circumstances or purposes in relation to which the corresponding provision in the repealed enactments has or had effect, a reference to, or as the case may be, to things done or falling to be done under or for the purposes of, that corresponding provision.

(3) Any reference, whether express or implied, in any enactment, instrument or document (including the repealed enactments and enactments, instruments and documents passed or made after the passing of this Act) to, or to things done or falling to be done under or for the purposes of, any of the repealed enactments shall, if and so far as the nature of the reference permits, be construed as including, in relation to the times, circumstances or purposes in relation to which the corresponding provision of this Act has effect, a reference to, or as the case may be, to things done or falling to be done under or for the purposes of, that corresponding provision.

(4) Subsection (2) above shall have effect without prejudice to section 17(2) of the Interpretation Act 1978.

(5) In this section "the repealed enactments" means the enactments repealed by this Act.

...

278 Short title.

This Act may be cited as the [Inheritance Tax Act 1984].[99]

SCHEDULE 3 - GIFTS FOR NATIONAL PURPOSES, ETC.

The National Gallery.

The British Museum.

[The National Museums of Scotland.][100]

The National Museum of Wales.

The Ulster Museum.

Any other similar national institution which exists wholly or mainly for the purpose of preserving for the public benefit a collection of scientific, historic or artistic interest and which is approved for the purposes of this Schedule by the Treasury.

Any museum or art gallery in the United Kingdom which exists wholly or mainly for that purpose and is maintained by a local authority or university in the United Kingdom.

Any library the main function of which is to serve the needs of teaching and research at a university in the United Kingdom.

The Historic Buildings and Monuments Commission for England.

The National Trust for Places of Historic Interest or Natural Beauty.

The National Trust for Scotland for Places of Historic Interest or Natural Beauty.

The National Art Collections Fund.

The Trustees of the National Heritage Memorial Fund.[The National Endowment for Science, Technology and the Arts.][101]

The Friends of the National Libraries.

The Historic Churches Preservation Trust.

[Commission for Rural Communities.

Natural England.][102]

[Scottish Natural Heritage][103]

Countryside Council for Wales.

Any local authority.

Any Government department (including the National Debt Commissioners).

Any university or university college in the United Kingdom.

[A health service body, within the meaning of section 519A of the Income and Corporation Taxes Act 1988.][104]

Sections 27, 58, 77 etc.

SCHEDULE 4 MAINTENANCE FUNDS FOR HISTORIC BUILDINGS, ETC.

PART I TREASURY DIRECTIONS

Giving of directions

1 (1) If the conditions mentioned in paragraph 2(1) below are fulfilled in respect of settled property, the Treasury shall, on a claim made for the purpose, give a direction under this paragraph in respect of the property.

(2) The Treasury may give a direction under this paragraph in respect of property proposed to be comprised in a settlement or to be held on particular trusts in any case where, if the property were already so comprised or held, they would be obliged to give the direction.

(3) Property comprised in a settlement by virtue of a transfer of value made before the coming into force of section 94 of the Finance Act 1982 and exempt under section 84 of the Finance Act 1976 shall be treated as property in respect of which a direction has been given under this paragraph.

Conditions

2 (1) The conditions referred to in paragraph 1 above are—

(a) that the Treasury are satisfied—

(i) that the trusts on which the property is held comply with the requirements mentioned in paragraph 3 below, and

(ii) that the property is of a character and amount appropriate for the purposes of those trusts; and

(b) that the trustees—

(i) are approved by the Treasury,

(ii) include a trust corporation, a solicitor, an accountant

or a member of such other professional body as the Treasury may allow in the case of the property concerned, and

(iii) are, at the time the direction is given, resident in the United Kingdom.

(2) For the purposes of this paragraph trustees shall be regarded as resident in the United Kingdom if—

(a) the general administration of the trusts is ordinarily carried on in the United Kingdom, and

(b) the trustees or a majority of them (and, where there is more than one class of trustees, a majority of each class) are resident in the United Kingdom;

and where a trustee is a corporation, the question whether the trustee is resident in the United Kingdom shall, for the purposes of paragraph (b) above, be determined as for the purposes of corporation tax.

(3) In this paragraph—

"accountant" means a member of an incorporated society of accountants;

"trust corporation" means a person that is a trust corporation for the purposes of the Law of Property Act 1925 or for the purposes of Article 9 of the Administration of Estates (Northern Ireland) Order 1979.

3 (1) The requirements referred to in paragraph 2(1)(a)(i) above are (subject to paragraph 4 below)—

(a) that none of the property held on the trusts can at any time in the period of six years beginning with the date on which it became so held be applied otherwise than—

(i) for the maintenance, repair or preservation of, or making provision for public access to, property which is for the time being qualifying property, for the maintenance, repair or preservation of property held on the trusts or for such improvement of property so held as is reasonable having regard to the purposes of the trusts, or for defraying the expenses of the trustees in relation to the property so held;

(ii) as respects income not so applied and not accumulated, for the benefit of a body within Schedule 3 to this Act or of a qualifying charity; and

(b) that none of the property can, on ceasing to be held on the trusts at any time in that period or, if the settlor dies in that period, at any time before his death, devolve otherwise than on any such body or charity; and

(c) that income arising from property held on the trusts cannot at any time after the end of that period be applied except as mentioned in paragraph (a)(i) or (ii) above.

(2) Property is qualifying property for the purposes of subparagraph (1) above if—

(a) it has been designated under section 34(1) of the Finance Act 1975 or section 77(1)(b), (c), (d) or (e) of the Finance Act 1976 or section 31(1)(b), (c), (d) or (e) of this Act; and

(b) the requisite undertaking has been given with respect to it under section 34 of the Finance Act 1975 or under section 76, 78(5)(b) or 82(3) of the Finance Act 1976 or under section 30, 32(5)(b), [32A(6), (8)(b) or (9)(b)][105] or 79(3) of this Act or paragraph 5 of Schedule 5 to this Act; and

(c) tax has not (since the last occasion on which such an undertaking was given) become chargeable with respect to it under the said section 34 or under section 78 or 82(3) of the Finance Act 1976 or under section 32, [32A][106] or 79(3) of this Act or paragraph 3 of Schedule 5 to this Act.

(3) If it appears to the Treasury that provision is, or is to be, made by a settlement for the maintenance, repair or preservation of any such property as is mentioned in subsection (1)(b), (c), (d) or (e) of section 31 of this Act they may, on a claim made for the purpose—

(a) designate that property under this sub-paragraph, and

(b) accept with respect to it an undertaking such as is described in subsection (4), [or (as the case may be) undertaking such as described in subsections (4) and (4A)][107] of that section;

and, if they do so, sub-paragraph (2) above shall have effect as if the designation were under that section and the undertaking [or undertakings][108] under section 30 of this Act and as if the reference to tax becoming chargeable were a reference to the occurrence of an event on which tax would become chargeable under section 32 [or 32A][109] of this Act if there had been a conditionally exempt transfer of the property when the claim was made and the undertaking [or undertakings][110] had been given under section 30.

(4) A charity is a qualifying charity for the purposes of sub-paragraph (1) above if it exists wholly or

mainly for maintaining, repairing or preserving for the public benefit buildings of historic or architectural interest, land of scenic, historic or scientific interest or objects of national, scientific, historic or artistic interest; and in this sub-paragraph "national interest" includes interest within any part of the United Kingdom.

(5) Designations, undertakings and acceptances made under section 84(6) of the Finance Act 1976 or section 94(3) of the Finance Act 1982 shall be treated as made under sub-paragraph (3) above.

[(5A) In the case of property which, if a direction is given under paragraph 1 above, will be property to which paragraph 15A below applies, sub-paragraph (1)(b) above shall have effect as if for the reference to the settlor there were substituted a reference to either the settlor or the person referred to in paragraph 15A(2).][111]

4 (1) Paragraphs (a) and (b) of paragraph 3(1) above do not apply to property which—

(a) was previously comprised in another settlement, and

(b) ceased to be comprised in that settlement and became comprised in the current settlement in circumstances such that by virtue of paragraph 9(1) below there was no charge (or, but for paragraph 9(4), there would have been no charge) to tax in respect of it;

and in relation to any such property paragraph 3(1)(c) above shall apply with the omission of the words "at any time after the end of that period".

(2) Sub-paragraph (1) above shall not have effect if the time when the property comprised in the previous settlement devolved otherwise than on any such body or charity as is mentioned in paragraph 3(1)(a) above fell before the expiration of the period of six years there mentioned; but in such a case paragraph 3(1) above shall apply to the current settlement as if for the references to that period of six years there were substituted references to the period beginning with the date on which the property became comprised in the current settlement and ending six years after the date on which it became held on the relevant trusts of the previous settlement (or, where this sub-paragraph has already had effect in relation to the property, the date on which it became held on the relevant trusts of the first settlement in the series).

Withdrawal

5 If in the Treasury's opinion the facts concerning any property or its administration cease to warrant the continuance of the effect of a direction given under paragraph 1 above in respect of the property, they may at any time by notice in writing to the trustees withdraw the direction on such grounds, and from such date, as may be specified in the notice; and the direction shall cease to have effect accordingly.

Information

6 Where a direction under paragraph 1 above has effect in respect of property, the trustees shall from time to time furnish the Treasury with such accounts and other information relating to the property as the Treasury may reasonably require.

Enforcement of trusts

7 Where a direction under paragraph 1 above has effect in respect of property, the trusts on which the property is held shall be enforceable at the suit of the Treasury and the Treasury shall, as respects the appointment, removal and retirement of trustees, have the rights and powers of a beneficiary.

PART II PROPERTY LEAVING MAINTENANCE FUNDS

Charge to tax

8 (1) This paragraph applies to settled property which is held on trusts which comply with the requirements mentioned in paragraph 3(1) above, and in respect of which a direction given under paragraph 1 above has effect.

(2) Subject to paragraphs 9 and 10 below, there shall be a charge to tax under this paragraph—

(a) where settled property ceases to be property to which this paragraph applies, otherwise than by virtue of an application of the kind mentioned in paragraph 3(1)(a)(i) or (ii) above or by devolving on any such body or charity as is mentioned in paragraph 3(1)(a)(ii);

(b) in a case in which paragraph (a) above does not apply, where the trustees make a disposition (otherwise than by such an application) as a result of which the value of settled property to which this paragraph applies is less than it would be but for the disposition.

(3) Subsections (4), (5) and (10) of section 70 of this Act shall apply for the purposes of this

paragraph as they apply for the purposes of that section (with the substitution of a reference to sub-paragraph (2)(b) above for the reference in section 70(4) to section 70(2)(b)).

(4) The rate at which tax is charged under this paragraph shall be determined in accordance with paragraphs 11 to 15 below.

(5) The devolution of property on a body or charity shall not be free from charge by virtue of sub-paragraph (2)(a) above if, at or before the time of devolution, an interest under the settlement in which the property was comprised immediately before the devolution is or has been acquired for a consideration in money or money's worth by that or another such body or charity; but for the purposes of this sub-paragraph any acquisition from another such body or charity shall be disregarded.

(6) For the purposes of sub-paragraph (5) above a body or charity shall be treated as acquiring an interest for a consideration in money or money's worth if it becomes entitled to the interest as a result of transactions which include a disposition for such consideration (whether to that body or charity or to another person) of that interest or of other property.

Exceptions from charge

9 (1) Tax shall not be charged under paragraph 8 above in respect of property which, within the permitted period after the occasion on which tax would be chargeable under that paragraph, becomes comprised in another settlement as a result of a transfer of value which is exempt under section 27 of this Act.

(2) In sub-paragraph (1) above "the permitted period" means the period of thirty days except in a case where the occasion referred to is the death of the settlor, and in such a case means the period of two years.

(3) Sub-paragraph (1) above shall not apply to any property if the person who makes the transfer of value has acquired it for a consideration in money or money's worth; and for the purposes of this sub-paragraph a person shall be treated as acquiring any property for such consideration if he becomes entitled to it as a result of transactions which include a disposition for such consideration (whether to him or another) of that or other property.

(4) If the amount on which tax would be charged apart from sub-paragraph (1) above in respect of any property exceeds the value of the property immediately after it becomes comprised in the other settlement (less the amount of any consideration for its transfer received by the person who makes the transfer of value), that sub-paragraph shall not apply but the amount on which tax is charged shall be equal to the excess.

(5) The reference in sub-paragraph (4) above to the amount on which tax would be charged is a reference to the amount on which it would be charged apart from—

(a) section 70(5)(b) of this Act (as applied by paragraph 8(3) above), and

(b) chapters I and II of Part V of this Act;

and the reference in that sub-paragraph to the amount on which tax is charged is a reference to the amount on which it would be charged apart from section 70(5)(b) and those Chapters.

10 (1) Tax shall not be charged under paragraph 8 above in respect of property which ceases to be property to which that paragraph applies on becoming—

(a) property to which the settlor or his spouse [or civil partner][112] is beneficially entitled, or

(b) property to which the settlor's widow or widower [or surviving civil partner][113] is beneficially entitled if the settlor has died in the two years preceding the time when it becomes such property.

(2) If the amount on which tax would be charged apart from sub-paragraph (1) above in respect of any property exceeds the value of the property immediately after it becomes property of a description specified in paragraph (a) or (b) of that sub-paragraph (less the amount of any consideration for its transfer received by the trustees), that sub-paragraph shall not apply but the amount on which tax is charged shall be equal to the excess.

(3) The reference in sub-paragraph (2) above to the amount on which tax would be charged is a reference to the amount on which it would be charged apart from—

(a) section 70(5)(b) of this Act (as applied by paragraph 8(3) above), and

(b) chapters I and II of Part V of this Act;

and the reference in sub-paragraph (2) above to the amount on which tax is charged is a

reference to the amount on which it would be charged apart from section 70(5)(b) and those Chapters.

(4) Sub-paragraph (1) above shall not apply in relation to any property if, at or before the time when it becomes property of a description specified in paragraph (a) or (b) of that sub-paragraph, an interest under the settlement in which the property was comprised immediately before it ceased to be property to which paragraph 8 above applies is or has been acquired for a consideration in money or money's worth by the person who becomes beneficially entitled.

(5) For the purposes of sub-paragraph (4) above a person shall be treated as acquiring an interest for a consideration in money or money's worth if he becomes entitled to the interest as a result of transactions which include a disposition for such consideration (whether to him or to another person) of that interest or of other property.

(6) Sub-paragraph (1) above shall not apply in respect of property if it was relevant property before it became (or last became) property to which paragraph 8 above applies and, by virtue of paragraph 16(1) or 17(1) below, tax was not chargeable (or, but for paragraph 16(2) or 17(4), would not have been chargeable) under section 65 of this Act in respect of its ceasing to be relevant property before becoming (or last becoming) property to which paragraph 8 above applies.

(7) Sub-paragraph (1) above shall not apply in respect of property if—

(a) before it last became property to which paragraph 8 above applies it was comprised in another settlement in which it was property to which that paragraph applies, and

(b) it ceased to be comprised in the other settlement and last became property to which that paragraph applies in circumstances such that by virtue of paragraph 9(1) above there was no charge (or, but for paragraph 9(4), there would have been no charge) to tax in respect of it.

(8) Sub-paragraph (1) above shall not apply unless the person who becomes beneficially entitled to the property is domiciled in the United Kingdom at the time when he becomes so entitled.

Rates of charge

11(1) This paragraph applies where tax is chargeable under paragraph 8 above and—

(a) the property in respect of which the tax is chargeable was relevant property before it became (or last became) property to which that paragraph applies, and

(b) by virtue of paragraph 16(1) or 17(1) below tax was not chargeable (or, but for paragraph 16(2) or 17(4), would not have been chargeable) under section 65 of this Act in respect of its ceasing to be relevant property on or before becoming (or last becoming) property to which paragraph 8 above applies.

(2) Where this paragraph applies, the rate at which the tax is charged shall be the aggregate of the following percentages—

(a)0.25 per cent. for each of the first forty complete successive quarters in the relevant period,

(b)0.20 per cent. for each of the next forty,

(c)0.15 per cent. for each of the next forty,

(d)0.10 per cent. for each of the next forty, and

(e)0.05 per cent. for each of the next forty.

(3) In sub-paragraph (2) above "the relevant period" means the period beginning with the latest of—

(a) the date of the last ten-year anniversary of the settlement in which the property was comprised before it ceased (or last ceased) to be relevant property,

(b) the day on which the property became (or last became) relevant property before it ceased (or last ceased) to be such property, and

(c)13th March 1975,

and ending with the day before the event giving rise to the charge.

(4) Where the property in respect of which the tax is chargeable has at any time ceased to be and again become property to which paragraph 8 above applies in circumstances such that by virtue of paragraph 9(1) above there was no charge to tax in respect of it (or, but for paragraph 9(4), there would have been no charge), it shall for the purposes of this paragraph be treated as having been property to which paragraph 8 above applies throughout the period mentioned in paragraph 9(1).

12 (1) This paragraph applies where tax is chargeable under paragraph 8 above and paragraph 11 above does not apply.

(2) Where this paragraph applies, the rate at which the tax is charged shall be the higher of—

(a) the first rate (as determined in accordance with paragraph 13 below), and

(b) the second rate (as determined in accordance with paragraph 14 below).

13 (1) The first rate is the aggregate of the following percentages—

(a)0.25 per cent. for each of the first forty complete successive quarters in the relevant period,

(b)0.20 per cent. for each of the next forty,

(c)0.15 per cent. for each of the next forty,

(d)0.10 per cent. for each of the next forty, and

(e)0.05 per cent. for each of the next forty.

(2) In sub-paragraph (1) above "the relevant period" means the period beginning with the day on which the property in respect of which the tax is chargeable became (or first became) property to which paragraph 8 above applies, and ending with the day before the event giving rise to the charge.

(3) For the purposes of sub-paragraph (2) above, any occasion on which property became property to which paragraph 8 above applies, and which occurred before an occasion of charge to tax under that paragraph in respect of the property, shall be disregarded.

(4) The reference in sub-paragraph (3) above to an occasion of charge to tax under paragraph 8 does not include a reference to—

(a) the occasion by reference to which the rate is being determined in accordance with this Schedule, or

(b) an occasion which would not be an occasion of charge but for paragraph 9(4) above.

14 (1) If the settlor is alive, the second rate is the effective rate at which tax would be charged, on the amount on which it is chargeable, [in accordance with the appropriate provision of section 7 of this Act][114] if the amount were the value transferred by a chargeable transfer made by him on the occasion on which the tax becomes chargeable.

[(1A) The rate or rates of tax determined under sub-paragraph (1) above in respect of any occasion shall not be affected by the death of the settlor after that occasion.][115]

(2) If the settlor is dead, the second rate is (subject to sub-paragraph (3) below) the effective rate at which tax would have been charged, on the amount on which it is chargeable, [in accordance with the appropriate provision of section 7 of this Act][116] if the amount had been added to the value transferred on his death and had formed the highest part of it.

(3) If the settlor died before 13th March 1975, the second rate is the effective rate at which tax would have been charged, on the amount on which it is chargeable ("the chargeable amount"), [in accordance with the appropriate provision of section 7 of this Act][117] if the settlor had died when the event occasioning the charge under paragraph 8 above occurred, the value transferred on his death had been equal to the amount on which estate duty was chargeable when he in fact died, and the chargeable amount had been added to that value and had formed the highest part of it.

(4) Where, in the case of a settlement ("the current settlement"), tax is chargeable under paragraph 8 above in respect of property which—

(a) was previously comprised in another settlement, and

(b) ceased to be comprised in that settlement and became comprised in the current settlement in circumstances such that by virtue of paragraph 9(1) above was no charge (or, but for paragraph 9(4), there would have been no charge) to tax in respect of it,

then, subject to sub-paragraph (5) below, references in sub-paragraphs (1) to (3) above to the settlor shall be construed as references to the person who was the settlor in relation to the settlement mentioned in paragraph (a) above (or, if the Board so determine, the person who was the settlor in relation to the current settlement).

(5) Where, in the case of a settlement ("the current settlement"), tax is chargeable under paragraph 8 above in respect of property which—

(a) was previously comprised at different times in other settlements ("the previous settlements"), and

(b) ceased to be comprised in each of them, and became comprised in another of them or in the current settlement, in circumstances such that by virtue of paragraph 9(1) above there was no charge (or, but for paragraph 9(4), there would have been no charge) to tax in respect of it,

references in sub-paragraphs (1) to (3) above to the settlor shall be construed as references to the

person who was the settlor in relation to the previous settlement in which the property was first comprised (or, if the Board so determine, any person selected by them who was the settlor in relation to any of the other previous settlements or the current settlement).

(6) Sub-paragraph (7) below shall apply if—

(a) in the period of [seven years][118] preceding a charge under paragraph 8 above (the "current charge"), there has been another charge under that paragraph where tax was charged at the second rate, and

(b) the person who is the settlor for the purposes of the current charge is the settlor for the purposes of the other charge (whether or not the settlements are the same and, if the settlor is dead, whether or not he has died since the other charge);

and in sub-paragraph (7) below the other charge is referred to as the "previous charge".

(7) Where this sub-paragraph applies, the amount on which tax was charged on the previous charge (or, if there have been more than one, the aggregate of the amounts on which tax was charged on each)—

(a) shall, for the purposes of calculating the rate of the current charge under sub-paragraph (1) above, be taken to be the value transferred by a chargeable transfer made by the settlor immediately before the occasion of the current charge, and

(b) shall, for the purposes of calculating the rate of the current charge under sub-paragraph (2) or (3) above, be taken to increase the value there mentioned by an amount equal to that amount (or aggregate).

(8) References in sub-paragraphs (1) to (3) above to the effective rate are to the rate found by expressing the tax chargeable as a percentage of the amount on which it is charged.

[(9) For the purposes of sub-paragraph (1) above the appropriate provision of section 7 of this Act is subsection (2), and for the purposes of sub-paragraphs (2) and (3) above it is (if the settlement was made on death) subsection (1) and (if not) subsection (2).][119]

15 Where property is, by virtue of paragraph 1(3) above, treated as property in respect of which a direction has been given under paragraph 1, it shall for the purposes of paragraphs 11 to 14 above be treated as having become property to which paragraph 8 above applies when the transfer of value mentioned in paragraph 1(3) was made.

[Maintenance fund following interest in possession

15A (1) In relation to settled property to which this paragraph applies, the provisions of this Part of this Schedule shall have effect with the modifications set out in the following sub-paragraphs.

(2) This paragraph applies to property which became property to which paragraph 8 above applies on the occasion of a transfer of value which was made by a person beneficially entitled to an interest in possession in the property, and which (so far as the value transferred by it was attributable to the property)—

(a) was an exempt transfer by virtue of the combined effect of either—

(i) sections 27 and 57(5) of this Act, or

(ii) sections 27 and 57A of this Act, and

(b) would but for those sections have been a chargeable transfer;

and in the following sub-paragraphs "the person entitled to the interest in possession" means the person above referred to.

(3) Paragraph 9(2) shall have effect as if for the reference to the settlor there were substituted a reference to either the settlor or the person entitled to the interest in possession.

(4) Paragraph 10 shall not apply if the person entitled to the interest in possession had died at or before the time when the property became property to which paragraph 8 above applies; and in any other case shall have effect with the substitution in sub-paragraph (1) of the following words for the words from "on becoming" onwards—

"(a) on becoming property to which the person entitled to the interest in possession is beneficially entitled, or

(b) on becoming—

(i) property to which that person's spouse [or civil partner][120] is beneficially entitled, or

(ii) property to which that person's widow or widower [or surviving civil partner][121] is beneficially entitled if that person has died in the two years preceding the time when it

becomes such property;

but paragraph (b) above applies only where the [spouse or civil partner, or widow or widower or surviving civil partner,][122] would have become beneficially entitled to the property on the termination of the interest in possession had the property not then become property to which paragraph 8 above applies."

(5) Paragraph 11 shall not apply.

(6) Sub-paragraphs (1) to (3) of paragraph 14 shall have effect as if for the references to the settlor there were substituted references to the person entitled to the interest in possession.

(7) Sub-paragraph (4) of paragraph 14 shall have effect with the insertion after paragraph (b) of the words "and (c) was, in relation to either of those settlements, property to which paragraph 15A below applied,",

and with the substitution for the words from "settlor shall" onwards of the words "person entitled to the interest in possession shall, if the Board so determine, be construed as references to the person who was the settlor in relation to the current settlement.".

(8) Sub-paragraph (5) of paragraph 14 shall have effect with the insertion after paragraph (b) of the words "and (c) was, in relation to any of those settlements, property to which paragraph 15A below applied,",

and with the substitution for the words from "settlor shall" onwards of the words "person entitled to the interest in possession shall, if the Board so determine, be construed as references to any person selected by them who was the settlor in relation to any of the previous settlements or the current settlement."

(9) Except in a case where the Board have made a determination under sub-paragraph (4) or (5) of paragraph 14, sub-paragraphs (6) and (7) of that paragraph shall have effect as if for the references to the settlor there were substituted references to the person entitled to the interest in possession.

(10) Sub-paragraph (9) of paragraph 14 shall have effect with the substitution for the words "(if the settlement was made on death) " of the words "(if the person entitled to the interest in possession had died at or before the time when the property became property to which paragraph 8 above applies) ".][123]

PART III PROPERTY BECOMING COMPRISED IN MAINTENANCE FUNDS

16 (1) Tax shall not be charged under section 65 of this Act in respect of property which ceases to be relevant property on becoming property in respect of which a direction under paragraph 1 above then has effect.

(2) If the amount on which tax would be charged apart from sub-paragraph (1) above in respect of any property exceeds the value of the property immediately after it becomes property in respect of which the direction has effect (less the amount of any consideration for its transfer received by the trustees of the settlement in which it was comprised immediately before it ceased to be relevant property), that sub-paragraph shall not apply but the amount on which tax is charged shall be equal to the excess.

(3) Sub-paragraph (1) above shall not apply in relation to any property if, at or before the time when it becomes property in respect of which the direction has effect, an interest under the settlement in which it was comprised immediately before it ceased to be relevant property is or has been acquired for a consideration in money or money's worth by the trustees of the settlement in which it becomes comprised on ceasing to be relevant property.

(4) For the purposes of sub-paragraph (3) above trustees shall be treated as acquiring an interest for a consideration in money or money's worth if they become entitled to the interest as a result of transactions which include a disposition for such consideration (whether to them or to another person) of that interest or of other property.

17 (1) Tax shall not be charged under section 65 of this Act in respect of property which ceases to be relevant property if within the permitted period an individual makes a transfer of value—

(a) which is exempt under section 27 of this Act, and

(b) the value transferred by which is attributable to that property.

(2) In sub-paragraph (1) above "the permitted period" means the period of thirty days beginning with the day on which the property ceases to be relevant property except in a case where it does so on the death of any person, and in such a case means the period of two years beginning with that day.

(3) Sub-paragraph (1) above shall not apply if the individual has acquired the property concerned for a consideration in money or money's worth; and for the purposes of this sub-paragraph an individual shall be treated as acquiring any property for such consideration if he becomes entitled to it as a result of transactions which include a disposition for such consideration (whether to him or another) of that or other property.

(4) If the amount on which tax would be charged apart from sub-paragraph (1) above in respect of any property exceeds the value of the property immediately after the transfer there referred to (less the amount of any consideration for its transfer received by the individual), that sub-paragraph shall not apply but the amount on which tax is charged shall be equal to the excess.

18 In paragraphs 16(2) and 17(4) above the references to the amount on which tax would be charged are references to the amount on which it would be charged apart from—

(a) paragraph (b) of section 65(2) of this Act, and

(b) chapters I and II of Part V of this Act;

and the references to the amount on which tax is charged are references to the amount on which it would be charged apart from that paragraph and those Chapters.

---

1 Words in s.23(4)(a) inserted (5.12.2005) by The Tax and Civil Partnership Regulations 2005 (S.I. 2005/3229), regs.1(1), 9

2 Words in s. 23(5) substituted (31.7.1998 with effect in relation to any transfer of value made on or after 17.3.1998) by 1998 c. 36, s. 143(2)(a)

3 Finance Act 1989 s. 171(2),in relation to transfers of value made on or after 14March 1989.

4 Words in s. 24A(1) substituted (1.10.1996) by S.I. 1996/2325, art. 5(1), Sch. 2 para. 12(2)

5 S. 24A(2) substituted (1.10.1996) by S.I. 1996/2325, art. 5(1), Sch. 2 para. 12(3)

6 Finance Act 1989 s. 171(1), *with effect from* 14*March* 1989.

7 Finance Act 1986 Sch. 19, para. 6, *in relation to transfers of value made on or after 18March 1986.*

8 Words in s. 27(1) inserted (31.7.1998 with effect in relation to transfers of value made on or after 17.3.1998) by 1998 c. 36, s. 144(1)(2)

9 S. 27(1A) inserted (31.7.1998 with effect in relation to transfers of value made on or after 17.3.1998) by 1998 c. 36, s. 144(1)(2)

10 Finance Act 1986 Sch. 19, para. 9,*in relation to transfers on or after* 18*March* 1986.

11 Words in s. 32(2) substituted (31.7.1998 with effect in relation to the giving of any undertaking on or after 31.7.1998) by 1998 c. 36, s. 142, Sch. 25 para. 7(1)(9)

12 S. 32(5)(b) substituted (31.7.1998 with effect in relation to the giving of any undertaking on or after 31.7.1998) by 1998 c. 36, s. 142, Sch. 25 para. 7(2)(9)

13 S. 32(5AA) inserted (31.7.1998 with effect in relation to the giving of any undertaking on or after 31.7.1998) by 1998 c. 36, s. 142, Sch. 25 para. 7(3)(9)

14 Finance Act 1985 Sch. 26, para. 3(2),*in relation to events occurring after* 18*March* 1985.

15 Subss. (6) and (7) repealed by Finance Act 1985 s. 94; Sch. 26, para. 3(3) and Sch. 27, Part XI,*in relation to events occurring after 18March 1985.*

16 Finance Act 1986 Sch. 19, para. 10,*in relation to transfers on or after* 18*March* 1986.

17 S. 32A(6)(a)(b) and the words "unless" and "and" substituted for the words "unless" to "case; and"(31.7.1998 with effect in relation to the giving of any undertaking on or after 31.7.1998) by 1998 c. 36, s. 142, Sch. 25 para. 7(4)(9)

18 S. 32A(8)(b) substituted (31.7.1998 with effect in relation to the giving of any undertaking on or after 31.7.1998) by 1998 c. 36, s. 142, Sch. 25 para. 7(5)(9)

19 S. 32A(8A) inserted (31.7.1998 with effect in relation to the giving of any undertaking on or after 31.7.1998) by 1998 c. 36, s. 142, Sch. 25 para. 7(6)(9)

20 S. 32A(9) substituted (31.7.1998 with effect in relation to the giving of any undertaking on or after 31.7.1998) by 1998 c. 36, s. 142, Sch. 25 para. 7(7)(9)

21 Finance Act 1985 Sch. 26 para. 4,*in relation to events occurring after* 18*March* 1985.

22 Words in Pt. 3 Ch. 3 heading added (22.3.2006) by Finance Act 2006 (c. 25), s. 156, Sch. 20 para. 20(5)

23 Words in s. 58(1)(b) inserted (22.3.2006) by Finance Act 2006 (c. 25), s. 156, Sch. 20 paras. 7, 18

24 Words in s. 58(1)(b) inserted (22.3.2006) by Finance Act 2006 (c. 25), s. 156, Sch. 20 paras. 7, 19(2)

25 S. 58(1)(d) substituted (6.4.2006) by Finance Act 2004 (c. 12), ss. 203(3), 284 (with Sch. 36)

26 S. 58(1A)-(1C) inserted (22.3.2006) by Finance Act 2006 (c. 25), s. 156, Sch. 20 paras. 7, 19(3)

27 Words in s. 58(2) repealed (6.4.2006) by Finance Act 2004 (c. 12), s. 326, Sch. 42 Pt. 3 (with Sch. 36)

28 S. 58(2A) inserted (with effect in relation to lump sum death benefits paid on or after 6.4.2006) by Finance Act 2007 (c. 11), s. 70, Sch. 20 paras. 20, 24(9)

29 S. 59(1) substituted (22.3.2006) by Finance Act 2006 (c. 25), s. 156, Sch. 20 para. 20(2)

30 S. 59(2)(c) and word inserted (22.3.2006) by Finance Act 2006 (c. 25), s. 156, Sch. 20 para. 20(3)

31 Schedule 3 was amended by regulation 8 of S.I. 2000/2952.

32 S. 59(3)(b)(i)(ii) and words substituted (1.5.1995 with effect as mentioned in s. 52(5) of the amending Act) by 1995 c. 4,

s. 52(4)

[33] S. 59(3)(b)(i)(ii) and both preceding and following words substituted for s. 59(3)(b)(i)(ii) and words preceding (1.12.2001 with effect as mentioned in art. 5(4) of the amending S.I.) by S.I. 2001/3629, art. 5(1)(2)(4)

[34] S.I. 2001/544.

[35] S. 59(4) added (1.12.2001 with effect as mentioned in art. 5(4) of the amending S.I.) by S.I. 2001/3629, art. 5(1)(3)(4)

[36] Finance Act 1986 Sch. 19 para. 16(1),with effect from 18March 1986originally "preceding ten years".

[37] Finance Act 1986 Sch. 19 para. 16(2),with effect from 18March 1986. Originally "(c) for which the appropriate Table of rates is the second Table in Schedule 1 to this Act."

[38] Finance Act 1986 Sch. 19 para. 16(3),with effect from 18March 1986.Originally "ten".

[39] Finance Act 1986 Sch. 19 para. 17,with effect from 18March 1986. Originally "ten".

[40] Finance Act 1986 Sch. 19 para. 17,with effect from 18March 1986. Originally "ten".

[41] Finance Act 1986 Sch. 19 para. 18(1),with effect from 18March 1986. Originally "ten".

[42] Finance Act 1986 Sch. 19 para. 18(1),with effect from 18March 1986. Originally "ten".

[43] Finance Act 1986 Sch. 19 para. 18(2),with effect from 18March 1986.Originally "(c) for which the appropriate Table of rates is the second Table in Schedule 1 to this Act.".

[44] Finance Act 1986 Sch. 19 para. 18(3)(a),with effect from 18March 1986. Originally "ten".

[45] Finance Act 1986 Sch. 19 para. 18(3)(b),with effect from 18March 1986. Originally "that period of ten years".

[46] Finance Act 1986 Sch. 19 para. 18(2),with effect from 18March 1986. Originally "for which the appropriate Table of rates is the second Table in Schedule 1 to this Act."

[47] Words in s. 71(1) substituted (22.3.2006) by Finance Act 2006 (c. 25), s. 156, Sch. 20 para. 2(2)(6)

[48] Word in s. 71(1)(a) substituted (6.4.2008 in accordance with Sch. 20 para. 3(2) of the amending Act) by Finance Act 2006 (c. 25), s. 156, Sch. 20 para. 3(1)(a)

[49] Words in s. 71(1)(a) repealed (6.4.2008 in accordance with Sch. 20 para. 3(2) of the amending Act) by Finance Act 2006 (c. 25), s. 156, Sch. 20 para. 3(1)(b), Sch. 26 Pt. 6

[50] S. 71(1A)(1B) inserted (22.3.2006) by Finance Act 2006 (c. 25), s. 156, Sch. 20 para. 2(3)(6)

[51] Words in s. 71(2)(b)(ii) inserted (5.12.2005) by The Tax and Civil Partnership Regulations 2005 (S.I. 2005/3229), regs. 1(1), 16

[52] Ss. 71A-71H inserted (22.3.2006) by Finance Act 2006 (c. 25), s. 156, Sch. 20 para. 1(1)(2)

[53] Ss. 71A-71H inserted (22.3.2006) by Finance Act 2006 (c. 25), s. 156, Sch. 20 para. 1(1)(2)

[54] Words in s. 72(1) substituted (22.3.2006) by Finance Act 2006 (c. 25), s. 156, Sch. 20 paras. 7, 21(2)

[55] S. 71(1A)(1B) inserted (22.3.2006) by Finance Act 2006 (c. 25), s. 156, Sch. 20 paras. 7, 21(3)

[56] Word in s. 72(2) inserted (28.7.2000) by 2000 c. 17, s. 138(3)(a)

[57] Substituted by Income and Corporation Taxes Act 1988 (c. 1, SIF 63:1), Sch. 29, para. 32.Originally
"Finance Act 1978".

[58] Words in s. 72(4A) substituted (with effect as mentioned in s. 723(1)(a)(b) (subject to Sch. 7) of the amending Act) by Income Tax (Earnings and Pensions) Act 2003 (c. 1), ss. 722, 723(1), Sch. 6 para. 151(1)(b)(2)

[59] S. 72(4A) inserted (28.7.2000) by 2000 c. 17, s. 138(3)(b)

[60] Words in s. 74(4)(b)(c) substituted (1.7.1992) by Social Security (Consequential Provisions) Act 1992 (c. 6), ss. 4, 7(2), Sch. 2 para. 66(1)(2).

[61] Words in s. 74(4)(b)(c) substituted (1.7.1992) by virtue of Social Security (Consequential Provisions) (Northern Ireland) Act 1992 (c. 9), ss. 4, 7(2), Sch. 2 para. 29 (1)(2).

[62] Words in s. 74(4)(b)(c) substituted (1.7.1992) by Social Security (Consequential Provisions) Act 1992 (c. 6), ss. 4, 7(2), Sch. 2 para. 66(1)(2).

[63] Words in s. 74(4)(b)(c) substituted (1.7.1992) by virtue of Social Security (Consequential Provisions) (Northern Ireland) Act 1992 (c. 9), ss. 4, 7(2), Sch. 2 para. 29 (1)(2).

[64] Words in s. 74(4)(c) inserted (6.4.1992) by S.I. 1991/2874, art. 4(2); S.R. 1992/94, art. 2.

[65] S. 74(4)(c) and 'or' preceding it inserted (3.2.1992 for certain purposes and 6.4.1992) by Disability Living Allowance and Disability Working Allowance Act 1991 (c. 21, SIF 113:1), s. 4(2), Sch. 2 para. 14(1); S.I. 1991/2617, art. 2(c)(f).

[66] Words in s. 76(1) inserted (22.3.2006) by Finance Act 2006 (c. 25), s. 156, Sch. 20 paras. 7, 22

[67] Word in s. 76(1)(b) inserted (31.7.1998 with effect as mentioned in s. 143(5) of the amending Act) by 1998 c. 36, s. 143(4)(a)

[68] S. 76(1)(d) and word "or" immediately preceding repealed (31.7.1998 with effect as mentioned in s. 143(5) of the amending Act) by 1998 c. 36, ss. 143(4)(a), 165, Sch. 27 Pt. IV note 1

[69] S. 76(2) repealed (31.7.1998 with effect as mentioned in s. 143(5) of the amending Act) by 1998 c. 36, ss. 143(4)(a), 165, Sch. 27 Pt. IV note 1

[70] Words in s. 76(3) substituted (31.7.1998 with effect as mentioned in s. 143(5) of the amending Act) by 1998 c. 36, s. 143(4)(b)

[71] Words in s. 76(6)(8) substituted (31.7.1998 with effect as mentioned in s. 143(5) of the amending Act) by 1998 c. 36, s. 143(4)(c)

[72] Words in s. 76(6)(8) substituted (31.7.1998 with effect as mentioned in s. 143(5) of the amending Act) by 1998 c. 36, s. 143(4)(c)

[73] Finance Act 1985 Sch. 26 para. 8(a),in relation to events occurring after 18March 1985.

[74] S. 78(1A) inserted (31.7.1998 with effect in relation to transfers of property made, and other events occurring, on or after 17.3.1998) by 1998 c. 36, s. 142, Sch. 25 para. 3(1)(2)

[75] Finance Act 1985 Sch. 26 para. 8(b),in relation to events occurring after 18March 1985.

[76] Finance Act 1985 Sch. 26 para. 8(b),in relation to events occurring after 18March 1985.

[77] Finance Act 1986 Sch. 19 para. 19(1),with effect from 18March 1986. Originally "and the appropriate Table for the purposes of section 33(1)(b)(ii) is, if the settlement was created on his death, the first Table in Schedule 1 to this Act and, if not, the second Table."

[78] Finance Act 1986 Sch. 19 para. 19(2),with effect from 18March 1986.Originally "under the appropriate Table."

[79] Words in s. 79(2) substituted (6.3.1992 with effect as mentioned in s. 289(1)(2) of the substituting Act) by Taxation of Chargeable Gains Act 1992 (c. 12), ss. 289 , 290, Sch. 10 para. 8(3) (with ss. 60, 101(1), 201(3)).

[80] Words in s. 79(2) substituted (6.3.1992 with effect as mentioned in s. 289(1)(2) of the substituting Act) by Taxation of Chargeable Gains Act 1992 (c. 12), ss. 289 , 290, Sch. 10 para. 8(3) (with ss. 60, 101(1), 201(3)).

[81] Finance Act 1985 Sch. 26 para. 9,in relation to events occurring after 18March 1985.

[82] Finance Act 1985 Sch. 26 para. 9,in relation to events occurring after 18March 1985.

[83] S. 79(5A) inserted (19.7.2006) by Finance Act 2006 (c. 25), s. 156, Sch. 20 para. 34(2)

[84] S. 79(7)-(7C) substituted for s. 79(7) (19.7.2006) by Finance Act 2006 (c. 25), s. 156, Sch. 20 para. 34(3)

[85] S. 79(9A)(9B) inserted (19.7.2006) by Finance Act 2006 (c. 25), s. 156, Sch. 20 para. 34(4)

[86] S. 79A inserted (31.7.1998 with effect as mentioned in Sch. 25 para. 8(4) of the amending Act) by 1998 c. 36, s. 142, Sch. 25 para. 8(2)

[87] Words in s. 80 sidenote inserted (5.12.2005) by virtue of The Tax and Civil Partnership Regulations 2005 (S.I. 2005/3229), regs. 1(1), 17(4)

[88] Words in s. 80(1) inserted (5.12.2005) by The Tax and Civil Partnership Regulations 2005 (S.I. 2005/3229), regs. 1(1), 17(2)

[89] Words in s. 80(2) inserted (5.12.2005) by The Tax and Civil Partnership Regulations 2005 (S.I. 2005/3229), regs.1(1), 17(3)(a)

[90] Words in s. 80(2) inserted (5.12.2005) by The Tax and Civil Partnership Regulations 2005 (S.I. 2005/3229), regs. 1(1), 17(3)(b)

[91] S. 80(4) inserted (22.3.2006) by Finance Act 2006 (c. 25), s. 156, Sch. 20 paras. 7, 23

[92] Words in s. 230(1)(3)(4)(a)(b) substituted (3.7.1992) by S.I. 1992/1311, art. 12(2), Sch. 2 para. 6(2)(3)(4).

[93] Words in s. 230(3)(c) substituted (29.8.1995) by S.I. 1995/1625 (N.I. 9), art. 45(1), Sch. 3 para. 1(1)(2)(e)

[94] Words in s. 230(1)(3)(4)(a)(b) substituted (3.7.1992) by S.I. 1992/1311, art. 12(2), Sch. 2 para. 6(2)(3)(4).

[95] Words in s. 230(1)(3)(4)(a)(b) substituted (3.7.1992) by S.I. 1992/1311, art. 12(2), Sch. 2 para. 6(2)(3)(4).

[96] Words in s. 230(1)(3)(4)(a)(b) substituted (3.7.1992) by S.I. 1992/1311, art. 12(2), Sch. 2 para. 6(2)(3)(4).

[97] Definition in s. 230(5) omitted (3.7.1992) by virtue of S.I. 1992/1311, art. 12(2), Sch. 2 para. 6(5).

[98] S. 230(6)(7) inserted (1.7.1999) by S.I. 1999/1756, arts. 1(1), 2, Sch. para. 8 (with art. 8); S.I. 1998/3178, art. 3

[99] *By* Finance Act 1986 s. 100(1), *on and after* 25*July* 1986*the Capital Transfer Tax Act* 1984 *may be cited as the Inheritance Tax Act* 1984.

[100] Words substituted by the National Heritage (Scotland) Act 1985 Sch 2 para 4 with effect from 1 October 1985 by virtue of the National Heritage (Scotland) Act 1985 Commencement Order SI 1985/851 art 3 and Sch 2

[101] Words added by the National Health Service and Community Care Act 1990 s61(5) with effect from 17 September 1990 by virtue of the National Health Service and Community Care Act 1990 (commencement No 1) Order SI 1990/1329.

[102] Words substituted by the Environmental Protection Act 1990 Sch 6 para 25 with effect from 1 April 1991 by virtue of the Environmental Protection Act 1990 (Commencement No 6 and Appointed Day) Order SI 1991/685

[103] Words substituted by the National Heritage (Scotland) Act 1991 Sch 2 para 9 with effect from 1 April 1991 by virtue of the National Heritage (Scotland) Act 1991 (Commencement No2) Order SI 1991/2633

[104] Inserted by the National Lottery Act 1998 s 24 with effect from 2 July 1998

[105] Finance Act 1985 Sch. 26, para. 12,*in relation to events occurring after* 18*March* 1985.

[106] Finance Act 1985 Sch. 26, para. 12,*in relation to events occurring after* 18*March* 1985.

[107] Finance Act 1985 Sch. 26, para. 12,*in relation to events occurring after* 18*March* 1985.

[108] Finance Act 1985 Sch. 26, para. 12,*in relation to events occurring after* 18*March* 1985.

[109] Finance Act 1985 Sch. 26, para. 12,*in relation to events occurring after* 18*March* 1985.

[110] Finance Act 1985 Sch. 26, para. 12,*in relation to events occurring after* 18*March* 1985.

[111] Finance Act 1987 Sch. 9, para. 2,*in relation to directions given on or after* 17*March* 1987.

[112] Words in Sch. 4 para. 10(1)(a) inserted (5.12.2005) by The Tax and Civil Partnership Regulations 2005 (S.I. 2005/3229), regs. 1(1), 39(2)(a)

[113] Words in Sch. 4 para. 10(1)(b) inserted (5.12.2005) by The Tax and Civil Partnership Regulations 2005 (S.I. 2005/3229), regs. 1(1), 39(2)(b)

[114] Finance Act 1986 Sch. 19, para. 38(1),*with effect from* 18*March* 1986. *Originally* "under the appropriate Table".

[115] Finance Act 1986 Sch. 19, para. 38(2),*with effect from* 18*March* 1986.

[116] Finance Act 1986 Sch. 19, para. 38(1),*with effect from* 18*March* 1986. *Originally* "under the appropriate Table".
[117] Finance Act 1986 Sch. 19, para. 38(1),*with effect from* 18*March* 1986. *Originally* "under the appropriate Table".
[118] Finance Act 1986 Sch. 19, para. 38(3),*with effect from* 18*March* 1986. *Originally* "ten years".
[119] Finance Act 1986 Sch. 19, para. 38(4),*with effect from* 18*March* 1986. *Originally* "(9) For the purposes of sub-paragraph (1) above the appropriate Table is the second Table in Schedule 1 to this Act, and for the purposes of sub-paragraphs (2) and (3) above it is (if the settlement was made on death) the first Table in that Schedule and (if not) the second."
[120] Words in Sch. 4 para. 15A(4) inserted (5.12.2005) by The Tax and Civil Partnership Regulations 2005 (S.I. 2005/3229), regs. 1(1), 39(3)(a)
[121] Words in Sch. 4 para. 15A(4) inserted (5.12.2005) by The Tax and Civil Partnership Regulations 2005 (S.I. 2005/3229), regs. 1(1), 39(3)(b)
[122] Words in Sch. 4 para. 15A(4) substituted (5.12.2005) by The Tax and Civil Partnership Regulations 2005 (S.I. 2005/3229), regs. 1(1), 39(3)(c)
[123] Finance Act 1987 Sch. 9, para. 3,where the occasion of the charge or potential charge to tax under para.8 above falls on or after 17March 1987.

Housing Act 1985

1985 CHAPTER 68

Modifications of Leasehold Reform Act 1967 in relation to leases granted under this Part

172. Exclusion of leases where landlord is housing association and freeholder is a charity.

(1) Part I of the Leasehold Reform Act 1967 (enfranchisement and extension of long leaseholds) does not apply where, in the case of a tenancy or sub-tenancy to which this section applies, the landlord is a housing association and the freehold is owned by a body of persons or trust established for charitable purposes only.

(2) This section applies to a tenancy created by the grant of a lease in pursuance of this Part of a dwelling-house which is a house.

(3) Where Part I of the 1967 Act applies as if there had been a single tenancy granted for a term beginning at the same time as the term under a tenancy falling within subsection (2) and expiring at the same time as the term under a later tenancy, this section also applies to that later tenancy. .

(4) This section applies to any sub-tenancy directly or indirectly derived out of a tenancy falling within subsection (2) or (3).

...

Final provisions

625. Short title, commencement and extent.

(1) This Act may be cited as the Housing Act 1985.

(2) This Act comes into force on 1st April 1986.

(3) This Act extends to England and Wales only.

...

Section 79.

SCHEDULE 1 Tenancies which are not Secure Tenancies

...

Almshouses

[12 A licence to occupy a dwelling-house is not a secure tenancy if—

(a) the dwelling-house is an almshouse, and.

(b) the licence was granted by or on behalf of a charity which—

(i) is authorised under its trusts to maintain the dwelling-house as an almshouse, and.

(ii) has no power under its trusts to grant a tenancy of the dwelling-house;

and in this paragraph "almshouse" means any premises maintained as an almshouse, whether they are called an almshouse or not; and "trusts", in relation to a charity, means the provisions establishing it as a charity and regulating its purposes and administration, whether those provisions take effect by way of trust or not.][1]

[1] Sch. 1 para. 12 substituted (1.9.1992) by Charities Act 1992 (c. 41), s. 78(1), Sch. 6 para. 12; S.I. 1992/1900, art. 2, Sch. 1

Housing Associations Act 1985

1985 CHAPTER 69

An Act to consolidate certain provisions of the Housing Acts relating to housing associations, with amendments to give effect to recommendations of the Law Commission and of the Scottish Law Commission.

[30th October 1985]

Part I - Regulation of Housing Associations

Introductory

1 Meaning of "housing association" and related expressions.

(1) In this Act "housing association" means a society, body of trustees or company—

(a) which is established for the purpose of, or amongst whose objects or powers are included those of, providing, constructing, improving or managing, or facilitating or encouraging the construction or improvement of, housing accommodation, and

(b) which does not trade for profit or whose constitution or rules prohibit the issue of capital with interest or dividend exceeding such rate as may be prescribed by the Treasury, whether with or without differentiation as between share and loan capital [;][1]

[[but does not include Scottish Homes.][2]][3]

(2) In this Act "fully mutual", in relation to a housing association, means that the rules of the association—

(a) restrict membership to persons who are tenants or prospective tenants of the association, and

(b) preclude the granting or assignment of tenancies to persons other than members;

and "co-operative housing association" means a fully mutual housing association which is a society registered under the Industrial and Provident Societies Act 1965 [(in this part referred to as "the 1965 Act")][4].

(3) In this Act "self-build society" means a housing association whose object is to provide, for sale to, or occupation by, its members, dwellings built or improved principally with the use of its members' own labour.

2 Meaning of "housing trust".

In this Act "housing trust" means a corporation or body of persons which—

(a) is required by the terms of its constituent instrument to use the whole of its funds, including any surplus which may arise from its operations, for the purpose of providing housing accommodation, or

(b) is required by the terms of its constituent instrument to devote the whole, or substantially the whole, of its funds to charitable purposes and in fact uses the whole, or substantially the whole, of its funds for the purpose of providing housing accommodation.

2A ....[5]

[2B Meaning of "registered housing association", "registered social landlord" etc.

In this Act, unless the context otherwise requires—

"registered housing association" means a housing association registered in the register [of social landlords maintained under section 57 of the Housing (Scotland) Act 2001 (asp 10)][6],

["registered social landlord" has the same meaning as in Part I of the Housing Act 1996, and][7]

"unregistered", in relation to a housing association, means neither registered in the register [of social landlords maintained under section 57 of the Housing (Scotland) Act 2001 (asp 10)][8].][9]

Registration

3.........[10]

4........[11]

5........[12]

6........[13]

7..........[14]

Disposal of land

8..........[15]

[9 Control by [Corporation][16] of dispositions of land by housing associations.

(1) . . . .[17]

[(1A) Subject to section 10, the consent of the relevant Corporation is required for any disposition of grant-aided land (as defined in Schedule 1) by an unregistered housing association; and for this purpose "the relevant Corporation" means,—

(a) if the land is in England, the Housing Corporation;

(b) if the land is in Scotland, Scottish Homes; and

(c) if the land is in Wales, [the Secretary of State][18].][19]

(2)[Consent under this section][20] may be so given—

(a) generally to all housing associations or to a particular housing association or description of association;

(b) in relation to particular land or in relation to a particular description of land;

and may be given subject to conditions.

(3) A disposition by a housing association which requires [consent][21] under this section is valid in favour of a person claiming under the association notwithstanding that [that consent][22] has not been given; and a person dealing with the association, or with a person claiming under the association, shall not be concerned to see or inquire whether any such consent has been given.

This subsection has effect subject to section 12 (avoidance of certain dispositions of houses without consent).

(4). . . . .[23]

(5) For the purposes of this section "disposition" means sale, lease, mortgage, charge or any other disposal. .

[(6)References in this section to consent are references,—

(a) in the case of the Housing Corporation. . .[24], to consent given by order under the seal of the Corporation; and

(b) in the case of [the Secretary of State or][25] Scottish Homes, to consent in writing.][26]][27].

[Dispositions excepted from s. 9.

(1) A disposition by an unregistered housing association which is a charity is not within section 9 if by virtue of [sections 36 and 38 of the Charities Act 1993][28] it cannot be made without an order of the court or the Charity Commissioners; but [before making an order in such a case the Charity Commissioners shall consult,—

(a) in the case of dispositions of land in England, the Housing Corporation;

(b) in the case of dispositions of land in Scotland, Scottish Homes; and

(c) in the case of dispositions of land in Wales, [the Secretary of State][29].][30]

(2) A letting. . .[31] by an unregistered housing association which is a housing trust, is not within section 9 if it is—

(a) a letting of land under a secure tenancy, or

(b) a letting of land under what would be a secure tenancy but for any of paragraphs 2 to 12 of [Schedule 1 to the Housing Act 1985][32] or [paragraphs [1 to 8 of Schedule 2 to the Housing (Scotland) Act 1987][33]][34] (tenancies excepted from being secure tenancies for reasons other than that they are long leases) [or

(c) a letting of land under an assured tenancy or an assured agricultural occupancy, or

(d) a letting of land in England or Wales under what would be an assured tenancy or an assured agricultural occupancy but for any of paragraphs 4 to 8 of Schedule 1 to the Housing Act 1988, or

(e) a letting of land in Scotland under what would be an assured tenancy but for any of paragraphs 3 to 8 and 12 of Schedule 4 to the Housing (Scotland) Act 1988.][35]

(3) The grant by an unregistered housing association which does not satisfy the landlord condition in section 80 of the Housing Act 1985 (bodies which are capable of granting secure tenancies) of a lease for a term ending within the period of seven years and three months beginning on the date of the grant is not within section 9 unless—

(a) there is conferred on the lessee (by the lease or otherwise) an option for renewal for a term which, together with the original term, would expire outside that period, or

(b) the lease is granted wholly or partly in consideration of a fine.

(4) In subsection (3) the expression "lease" includes an agreement for a lease and a licence to occupy,

and the expressions "grant" and "term" shall be construed accordingly.][36]

11 .... [37]

[12Avoidance of certain disposals of houses without consent.

A disposal of a house by a housing association made without the consent required by section 9 is void unless—

(a) the disposal is to an individual (or to two or more individuals), and

(b) the disposal does not extend to any other house.][38]

Control of payments to members, etc.

13. .... [39]

14. .... [40]

15. .... [41]

15A. .... [42]

Constitution, change of rules, amalgamation and dissolution

16. .... [43]

17 .... [44]

18. .... [45]

19. .... [46]

20. .... [47]

21. .... [48]

22 .... [49]

23 .... [50]

Accounts and audit

24. .... [51]

25. .... [52]

26. .... [53]

27. .... [54]

27A. .... [55]

Inquiries into affairs of housing associations

28 .... [56]

29 .... [57]

30 .... [58]

31 .... [59]

32 .... [60]

Miscellaneous

33 .... [61]

[33 A Provision of services between the Corporations.

Any of the [following [, that is to say, the Housing Corporation, the Secretary of State][62] or Scottish Homes,][63] may enter into an agreement with the others or either of them for the provision of services of any description by the one to the other or others on such terms, as to payment or otherwise, as the parties to the agreement consider appropriate.][64]

34 Provision of land by county councils.

(1) Where a housing association wishes to erect houses [in England][65] which in the opinion of the Secretary of State are required and the local housing authority in whose district the houses are proposed to be built are unwilling to acquire land with a view to selling or leasing it to the association, the county council, on the application of the association, may acquire land for that purpose.

(2) For that purpose the county council may exercise all the powers of a local housing authority under Part II of the Housing Act 1985 (provision of housing) in regard to the acquisition and disposal of land; and the provisions of that Act as to the acquisition of land by local housing authorities for the purposes of that Part apply accordingly.

35 Housing trusts: power to transfer housing to local housing authority.

(1) A housing trust may—

(a) sell or lease to the local housing authority the houses provided by the trust, or

(b) make over to the authority the management of the houses.

(2) So far as subsection (1) confers power to dispose of land—

[(a)it does not apply to registered social landlords (on whom power to dispose of land is conferred by section 8 of the Housing Act 1996);][66]

(b) it has effect subject to section 9 (dispositions requiring consent of [Corporation][67]) where the housing trust is an unregistered housing association and the land is grant-aided land (as defined in Schedule 1); and

(c) it has effect subject to [[section 36 of the Charities Act 1993][68] (restrictions on dispositions of charity land)][69] where the housing trust is a charity.

36 Housing trusts: functions of Secretary of State with respect to legal proceedings.

(1) If it appears to the Secretary of State—

(a) that the institution of legal proceedings is requisite or desirable with respect to any property belonging to a housing trust, or

(b) that the expediting of any such legal proceedings is requisite or desirable,

he may certify the case to the Attorney-General who may institute legal proceedings or intervene in legal proceedings already instituted in such manner as he thinks proper in the circumstances.

(2) Before preparing a scheme with reference to property belonging to a housing trust, the court or body which is responsible for making the scheme shall communicate with the Secretary of State and consider any recommendations made by him with reference to the proposed scheme.

36A .... [70]

Supplementary

37 ....[71]

[38 Definitions relating to charities.

In this Part—

(a) "charity" has the same meaning as in [the Charities Act 1993][72]; and

.....................[73]][74]

[39 Minor definitions.

In this Part—

["assured tenancy" has, in England and Wales, the same meaning as in Part I of the Housing Act 1988 and, in Scotland, the same meaning as in Part II of the Housing (Scotland) Act 1988;

"assured agricultural occupancy" has the same meaning as in Part I of the Housing Act 1988.][75]

["mental disorder" has the same meaning as in [the Mental Health Act 1983 or][76] the Mental Health (Scotland) Act 1984;][77]

"secure tenancy" has the same meaning as in section 79 of the Housing Act 1985 or [44 of the Housing (Scotland) Act 1987][78];][79]

....[80]

[40 Index of defined expressions: Part I.

The following Table shows provisions defining or explaining expressions used in this Part (other than provisions defining or explaining an expression used only in the same section or paragraph):—

[appropriate registrar (in relation to a society registered under the 1965 Act)	section 37][81]
[assured agricultural occupancy	section 39][82]
[assured tenancy	section 39][83]
[bank	section 106][84]
charge (in relation to Scotland)	section 106
charity	section 38(a)
[committee (in relation to a society registered under the 1965 Act)	section 37][85]
[compulsory disposal (in Schedule 2)	paragraph 6 of that Schedule][86]
co-operative housing association	section 1(2)
[co-opted member (in relation to the committee of a society registered under the 1965 Act)	section 37][87]
[the Companies Act	section 106][88]
...[89]	...

[dissolved under the 1965 Act (in relation to a society registered under that At)	section 37][90]
district (of a local housing authority)	section 104(2)
[dwelling	section 106][91]
[eligible for registration (in relation to a housing association)	section 4][92]
[exempted disposal (in Schedule 2)	paragraph 5 of that Schedule][93]
[friendly society	section 106][94]
fully mutual (in relation to a housing association)	section 1(2)
[hostel	section 106][95]
house	section 106
[housing activities	section 106][96]
housing association	section 1(1)
. . . [97]	. . .
housing trust	section 2
[insurance company	section 106][98]
local housing authority	section 104
[member of family	section 105][99]
[mental disorder	section 39][100]
mortgage (in relation to Scotland)	section 106
[the 1965 Act	section 37][101]
[register, registered, registration and unregistered (in relation to a housing association)	section [3][102]][103]
[registered charity	section 38(b)][104]
[registered social landlord	section 2B][105]
[relevant disposal (in Schedule 2)	paragraph 4 of that Schedule][106]
. . .	. . .
secure tenancy	section 39
[shared ownership lease	section 106][107]
[shared ownership agreement (in relation to Scotland)	section 106][108]
[standard scale	section 39][109]
[trustee savings bank	section 106][110]
[unregistered (in relation to a housing association)	section 2B][111]].[112]

Part II - Housing Association Finance

41—51. . . . . [113]

52. . . . . [114]

53. . . . . [115]

Deficit grants

54. . . . .[116]

55 – 57. . . . .[117]

Arrangements with local authorities

[58Powers of local authorities to promote and assist housing associations: England and Wales.

(1) A local authority may promote the formation or extension of a housing association. .

(2) A local authority may for the assistance of a housing association subscribe for share or loan capital of the association. .

(3) A local authority may make a loan to an unregistered self-build society for the purpose of enabling it to meet the whole or part of the expenditure incurred, or to be incurred by it, in carrying out its objects. .

(4) This section does not apply where the housing association is a registered social landlord (for which corresponding provision is made by section 22 of the Housing Act 1996).][118]

[59 Powers of local authorities to promote and assist housing associations: Scotland.

(1) A local authority. . .[119] may promote the formation or extension of or, subject to section 60 (assistance restricted to registered housing associations), assist a housing association whose objects include the erection, improvement or management of housing accommodation.

(2) A local authority . . . may, with the consent of and subject to any regulations or conditions made or

imposed by the Secretary of State, for the assistance of such an association—

(a) make grants or loans to the association,

(b) subscribe for share or loan capital of the association, or

(c) guarantee or join in guaranteeing the payment of the principal of, and interest on, money borrowed by the association (including money borrowed by the issue of loan capital) or of interest on share capital issued by the association,

on such terms and conditions as to rate of interest and repayment or otherwise and on such security as the local authority . . . think fit.

(3) A term of an agreement for such a grant or loan is void if it purports to relate to the rent payable in respect of a house to which the agreement relates or the contributions payable towards the cost of maintaining such a house. .

(4) Regulations under this section shall be made by statutory instrument which shall be subject to annulment in pursuance of a resolution of either House of Parliament. .

[(5)Sections 6, 15, 320 and 329 of the Housing (Scotland) Act 1987 (general provisions with respect to housing functions of local authorities etc.) apply in relation to this section and section 61, as they apply in relation to the provisions of that Act.][120]][121]

60. . . . . [122]

[61 Power of local housing authority to supply furniture to housing association tenants.

(1) A local housing authority may sell, or supply under a hire-purchase agreement, furniture to the occupants of houses provided by a housing association under arrangements made with the authority, and may buy furniture for this purpose.

(2) In this section "hire-purchase agreement" means a hire-purchase agreement or conditional sale agreement within the meaning of the Consumer Credit Act 1974.

[(3) This section does not apply where the housing association is a registered social landlord (for which corresponding provision is made by section 22 of the Housing Act 1996).][123]][124]

62 . . . . [125]

63—66. . . . . [126]

Loans by Public Works Loan Commissioners

67. . . . . [127]

68 Loans by Public Works Loan Commissioners: Scotland.

(1) The Public Works Loan Commissioners may lend money to a [registered housing association][128]—

(a) for the purpose of constructing or improving, or facilitating or encouraging the construction or improvement of, houses,

(b) for the purchase of houses, and

(c) for the purchase and development of land.

(2) A loan for any of those purposes shall be secured with interest by a heritable security over—

(a) the land in respect of which that purpose is to be carried out, and

(b) such other land, if any, as may be offered as security for the loan;

and the money lent shall not exceed three-quarters (or, if the payment of the principal of and interest on the loan is guaranteed by a local authority, nine-tenths) of the value, to be ascertained to the satisfaction of the Public Works Loan Commissioners, of the estate or interest in the land proposed to be burdened.

(3) Loans may be made by instalments as the building of houses or other work on the land burdened under subsection (2) progresses (so, however, that the total loans do not at any time exceed the amount specified in that subsection); and the heritable security may be granted accordingly to secure such loans so to be made.

(4) If the loan exceeds two-thirds of the value referred to in subsection (2), and is not guaranteed as to principal and interest by a local authority, the Public Works Loan Commissioners shall require, in addition to such a heritable security as is mentioned in that subsection, such further security as they may think fit.

(5) Subject to subsection (6), the period for repayment of a loan under this section shall not exceed 40 years, and no money shall be lent on the security of any land unless the estate or interest proposed to be burdened is either ownership or a lease of which a period of not less than 50 years remains unexpired at the date of the loan.

(6) Where a loan under this section is made for the purposes of carrying out a scheme for the provision of houses approved by the Secretary of State, the maximum period for the repayment of the loan is 50 instead of 40 years, and money may be lent on heritable security over a lease recorded under the Registration of Leases (Scotland) Act 1857 of which a period of not less than ten years in excess of the period fixed for the repayment of the loan remains unexpired at the date of the loan.

Miscellaneous

69 Power to vary or terminate certain agreements with housing associations.

(1) This section applies to agreements of the following descriptions—

(a) an agreement for a loan to a housing association by the Housing Corporation under section 2 of the Housing Act 1964 [(including such an agreement under which rights and obligations have been transferred to Housing for Wales)][129][and then to the Secretary of State][130];

(b) an agreement which continues in force under Part I of Schedule 4 (arrangements with local authority for the provision or improvement of housing);

(c) an agreement to which Part II of Schedule 4 applies (subsidy agreements with local authorities);

(d) an agreement which continues in force under Part III of Schedule 4 (special arrangements with the Secretary of State);

[(e) an agreement for a loan or grant to a housing association under section 58(2) or 59(2) (financial assistance by local authorities);][131]

(f) a scheme which continues in force under Part V of Schedule 5 (schemes for unification of grant conditions).

[[(g) an agreement for a loan or grant to a registered housing association under section 24 of the Local Government Act 1988 (power to provide financial assistance for privately let housing accommodation).][132]][133]

(2) [If any person (other than the Secretary of State) who is a party to an agreement to which this section applies makes an application to the Secretary of State, he][134] may, if he thinks fit, direct—

(a) that the agreement shall have effect with such variations, determined by him or agreed by the parties, as may be specified in the direction, or

(b) that the agreement shall be terminated.

[and where the Secretary of State is a party to such an agreement, he may agree that it shall have effect with any variations or that it shall be terminated.][135]

[(2A) In the case of an agreement under which rights and obligations have been transferred to Housing for Wales [and then to the Secretary of State][136], the reference to a party to the agreement includes a reference to [the Secretary of State][137].][138]

(3) No variation shall be directed under subsection (2) which would have the effect of including in an agreement a term—

(a) limiting the aggregate amount of rents payable in respect of dwellings to which the agreement relates or contributions towards the cost of maintaining such dwellings, or

(b) specifying a limit which the rent of a dwelling is not to exceed.

This subsection does not extend to Scotland.

(4) No variation shall be directed under subsection (2) which would have the effect of including in an agreement a term relating to the rent payable in respect of a house to which the agreement relates or contributions towards the cost of maintaining such a house.

This subsection extends to Scotland only.

[69A Land subject to housing management agreement.

A housing association is not entitled to a [grant under section 50 (housing association grant) or section 51 (revenue deficit grant) of the Housing Act 1988][139] in respect of land comprised in—

(a) a management agreement within the meaning of the Housing Act 1985 (see sections 27(2) and 27B(4) of that Act: delegation of housing management functions by certain authorities), or

(b) an agreement to which section [22 of the Housing (Scotland) Act 1987][140] applies (agreements for exercise by housing co-operatives of certain local authority housing functions).][141]

70 Continuation of arrangements under repealed enactments.

The provisions of Schedule 4 have effect in relation to certain arrangements affecting housing associations which continue in force despite the repeal of the enactments under or by reference to

which they were made, as follows—

Part I —Arrangements with local authorities for the provision or improvement of housing.

Part II —Subsidy agreements with local authorities.

Part III —Special arrangements with the Secretary of State in Scotland.

71 Superseded contributions, subsidies and grants.

The provisions of Schedule 5 have effect with respect to superseded subsidies, contributions and grants, as follows—

Part I —Residual subsidies: England and Wales.

Part II —Residual subsidies: Scotland.

Part III—Contributions and grants under arrangements with local authorities.

Part IV—Contributions under arrangements with the Secretary of State in Scotland.

Part V —Schemes for the unification of grant conditions.

Part VI—New building subsidy and improvement subsidy.

Part VII—Payments in respect of hostels under pre-1974 enactments.

Supplementary provisions

[72 Minor definitions.

In this Part—

. . . .[142]

. . . .

. . . .

"registered charity" has the same meaning as in Part I.][143]

73 Index of defined expressions: Part II.

The following Table shows provisions defining or explaining expressions used in this Part (other than provisions defining or explaining an expression in the same section);—

. . .[144]	. . .
. . .[145]	. . .
. . .	. . .
co-operative housing association	section 1(2)
dwelling	section 106
[fully mutual (in relation to a housing association)	section 1(2)][146]
[heritable security	section 106][147]
hostel	section 106
. . .[148]	. . .
house	section 106
[housing activities	section 106][149]
housing association	section 1(1)
. . .	. . .
. . .	. . .
local authority	section 106
local housing authority	section 104
. . .[150]	. . .
. . .[151]	. . .
[registered charity	section 72][152]
[registered housing association	section 2B][153]
[registered social landlord	section 2B][154]
. . .	. . .
self-build society	section 1(3)
. . .[155]	. . .
. . .	. . .
[unregistered (in relation to a housing association)	section 2B][156]

Part III - The Housing Corporation

Constitution and other general matters

74 The Housing Corporation.[157]

(1) This Part has effect with respect to the Housing Corporation [and the Secretary of State

(1A) Each of them][158] is referred to in this part as "the [Relevant Authority][159]"

(2) The provisions of Schedule 6 have effect with respect to the constitution and proceedings of, and other matters relating to, [the Housing Corporation][160]

[(3) The functions conferred by this Part in relation to registered social landlords are exercisable by the [Relevant Authority][161] in whose register they are registered.

As to which [Relevant Authority][162] that is, see section 56 of the Housing Act 1996.][163]

[(4) In this Part,—

(a) in relation to land in Wales held by an unregistered housing association, "the Relevant Authority" means [the Secretary of State][164]; and

(b) in relation to land outside Wales held by such an association, "the [Relevant Authority][165]" means the Housing Corporation.][166]

74 The Housing Corporation.[167]

(1) This Part has effect with respect to the Housing Corporation [and the Secretary of State

(1A) Each of them][168] is referred to in this Part as "the [Relevant Authority][169]"

(2) The provisions of Schedule 6 have effect with respect to the constitution and proceedings of, and other matters relating to, [the Housing Corporation][170]

[(3)In this Part "registered housing association" in relation to the [Relevant Authority][171], means a housing association registered in the register maintained by the [Relevant Authority].[172]

(4) In this Part,—

(a) in relation to land in Wales held by an unregistered housing association, "the Relevant Authority" means [the Secretary of State][173]; and

(b) in relation to land outside Wales held by such an association, "the Relevant Authority" means the Housing Corporation.][174]

75 General functions of the [Relevant Authority][175].[176]

(1) The [Relevant Authority][177] has the following general functions—

[(a) to facilitate the proper performance of the functions of registered social landlords;

(b) to maintain a register of social landlords and to exercise supervision and control over such persons;

(c) to promote and assist the development of self-build societies (other than registered social landlords) and to facilitate the proper performance of the functions, and to publicise the aims and principles, of such societies;][178]

(d) . . . . [179]

(e) to undertake, to such extent as the [Relevant Authority][180] considers necessary, the provision (by construction, acquisition, conversion, improvement or otherwise) of dwellings for letting or for sale and of hostels, and the management of dwellings or hostels so provided.

[(f) to provide on request, to such extent as the Relevant Authority considers appropriate, advice and assistance to the Audit Commission for Local Authorities and the National Health Service in England and Wales in relation to the Commission's functions under Part I of the Local Government Act 1999 (best value).][181]

(2) The [Relevant Authority][182] shall exercise its general functions subject to and in accordance with the provisions of this Act [and Part I of the Housing Act 1996][183]

(3) Subsection (1) is without prejudice to specific functions conferred on the [Relevant Authority][184] by or under this Act [or Part I of the Housing Act 1996][185]

(4) The [Relevant Authority][186] may do such things and enter into such transactions as are incidental to or conducive to the exercise of any of its functions, general or specific, under this Act [or Part I of the Housing Act 1996][187]

(5) . . . .[188]

75 General functions of the [Relevant Authority].[189,190]

(1) The [Relevant Authority][191] has the following general functions—

(a) to promote and assist the development of registered housing associations and unregistered self-build societies;

(b) to facilitate the proper performance of the functions, and to publicise the aims and principles, of registered housing associations and unregistered self-build societies;

(c) to maintain [the register of housing associations referred to in section 3][192] and to exercise supervision and control over registered housing associations;

(d) . . . .[193]

(e) to undertake, to such extent as the [Relevant Authority][194] considers necessary, the provision (by construction, acquisition, conversion, improvement or otherwise) of dwellings for letting or for sale and of hostels, and the management of dwellings or hostels so provided.

[(f) to provide on request, to such extent as the Relevant Authority considers appropriate, advice and assistance to the Audit Commission for Local Authorities and the National Health Service in England and Wales in relation to the Commission's functions under Part I of the Local Government Act 1999 (best value).][195]

(2) The [Relevant Authority][196] shall exercise its general functions subject to and in accordance with the provisions of this Act. .

(3) Subsection (1) is without prejudice to specific functions conferred on the [Relevant Authority][197] by or under this Act. .

(4) The [Relevant Authority][198] may do such things and enter into such transactions as are incidental to or conducive to the exercise of any of its functions, general or specific, under this Act.

(5). . . . .[199]

76 Directions by the Secretary of State

(1) The Secretary of State may give directions to the [Housing Corporation][200] as to the exercise of its functions.

(2) A direction as to the terms of loans made under section 79 (lending powers of [Housing Corporation][201]) requires the consent of the Treasury.

(3) Directions may be of a general or particular character and may be varied or revoked by subsequent directions.

(4) Non-compliance with a direction does not invalidate a transaction between a person and the [Housing Corporation][202] unless the person had actual notice of the direction.

[76A Realisation of value of [Housing Corporation's][203] loans portfolio.

(1) The [Housing Corporation][204] may, and if so directed by the Secretary of State (under section 76) shall, enter into arrangements of a description approved by the Secretary of State for the purpose of realising the value of the whole or part of its loans portfolio.

(2) The arrangements may provide for—

(a) the transfer of any estate or interest of the [Housing Corporation][205], or

(b) the creation or disposal of economic interests not involving a transfer of an estate or interest,

and may extend to such incidental or ancillary matters as the [Housing Corporation][206] or the Secretary of State considers appropriate.

(3) In this section the [Housing Corporation's][207]"loans portfolio" means the [Housing Corporation's][208] rights and obligations in relation to any loans or related securities.

(4) Nothing in the terms of any loan or related transaction entered into by the [Housing Corporation][209] shall be construed as impliedly prohibiting or restricting the [Housing Corporation][210] from dealing with its loans portfolio in accordance with arrangements under this section.][211]

77 Advisory service.

(1) The [Relevant Authority][212] may provide an advisory service for the purpose of giving advice on legal, architectural and other technical matters to [registered social landlords or unregistered housing associations][213] and to persons who are forming a housing association or are interested in the possibility of doing so.

(2) The [Relevant Authority][214] may make charges for the service.

[(3) The powers conferred on the [Relevant Authority][215] by subsections (1) and (2) may be exercised by the Housing Corporation and [the Secretary of State][216] acting jointly][217]

77 *Advisory service.*[218]

(1) The [Relevant Authority][219] may provide an advisory service for the purpose of giving advice on legal, architectural and other technical matters to housing associations (whether registered or unregistered) and to persons who are forming a housing association or are interested in the possibility of doing so.

(2) The [Relevant Authority][220] may make charges for the service.

[(3) The powers conferred on the [Relevant Authority][221] by subsections (1) and (2) may be exercised by the Housing Corporation and [the Secretary of State][222] acting jointly][223]

78 Annual report.

(1) The [Housing Corporation][224] shall, as soon as possible after the end of each financial year, make a report to the Secretary of State on the exercise of its functions during the year.

(2) It shall include in the report a copy of its audited accounts and shall set out in the report any directions given to it by the Secretary of State during the year.

(3) The Secretary of State shall lay a copy of the report before each House of Parliament.

[Relevant Authority's][225] powers with respect to grants and loans

79 Lending powers.

[(1) The Relevant Authority may lend to a registered social landlord or an unregistered self-build society, and the Housing Corporation may lend to any of its subsidiaries or to any other body in which it holds an interest, for the purpose of enabling the body to meet the whole or part of expenditure incurred or to be incurred by it in carrying out its objects.

(2) The Relevant Authority may lend to an individual for the purpose of enabling him to acquire from—

(a) the Relevant Authority, or

(b) any body to which the Relevant Authority may lend under subsection (1),

a legal estate or interest in a dwelling which he intends to occupy.][226]

(3) A loan under this section may be by way of temporary loan or otherwise, and the terms of a loan made under subsection (1) may include (though the terms of a loan made under subsection (2) may not) terms for preventing repayment of the loan or part of it before a specified date without the consent of the [Relevant Authority][227].

(4) The terms of a loan under this section shall, subject to subsection (3) and [(in the case of a loan by the Housing Corporation)][228] to any direction under section 76 (general power of Secretary of State to give directions), be such as the [Relevant Authority][229] may determine, either generally or in a particular case.

80 Security for loans to unregistered self-build societies.

(1) Where the [Relevant Authority][230]—

(a) makes a loan to an unregistered self-build society under section 79(1); and

(b) under a mortgage or heritable security entered into by the society to secure the loan has an interest as mortgagee or creditor in land belonging to the society,

it may. . .[231] give the society directions with respect to the disposal of the land.

(2) The society shall comply with directions so given so long as the [Relevant Authority][232] continues to have such an interest in the land.

(3) Directions so given may be varied or revoked by subsequent directions. . . [233]

[(3A) The written consent of the Secretary of State is required for the giving, varying or revoking of directions by the Housing Corporation.][234]

(4) The Secretary of State shall not [give directions under this section requiring a society to transfer its interest in land to him or any other person, and shall not consent to the Housing Corporation's giving such directions requiring a society to transfer its interest in land to the Housing Corporation or][235] any other person, unless he is satisfied that arrangements have been made which will secure that the members of the society receive fair treatment in connection with the transfer.

81 Further advances in case of disposal on shared ownership lease.

Where—

(a) a lease of a dwelling, granted otherwise than in pursuance of the provisions of Part V of the Housing Act 1985 (the right to buy) relating to shared ownership leases, contains a provision to the like effect as that required by paragraph 1 of Schedule 8 to that Act (terms of shared ownership lease: right of tenant to acquire additional shares), and

(b) the [Relevant Authority][236] has, in exercise of any of its powers, left outstanding or advanced any amount on the security of the dwelling,

that power includes power to advance further amounts for the purpose of assisting the tenant to make payments in pursuance of that provision.

82 Loans made under s. 2 of the Housing Act 1964.

Schedule 7 (further powers of [Relevant Authority][237] with respect to land of certain housing associations) applies where a loan has been made to a housing association under section 2 of the Housing Act 1964 and the loan has not been repaid.

83 Power to guarantee loans.

[(1) The Relevant Authority may guarantee the repayment of the principal of, and the payment of interest on, sums borrowed by registered social landlords or unregistered self-build societies; and the Housing Corporation may guarantee the repayment of the principal of, and the payment of interest on, sums borrowed by other bodies in which it holds an interest.][238]

[(1A) The consent of the Secretary of State given with the approval of the Treasury is required for the giving of a guarantee by the Housing Corporation and the approval of the Treasury is required for the giving of a guarantee by the Secretary of State.][239]

(2) Where the Corporation gives such a guarantee, it may impose such terms and conditions as it thinks fit.

(3) The aggregate amount outstanding in respect of—

(a) loans for which [the Housing Corporation][240] has given a guarantee under this section, and

(b) payments made by [the Housing Corporation][241] in meeting an obligation arising by virtue of such a guarantee and not repaid to [the Housing Corporation][242],

shall not exceed £300 million or such greater sum not exceeding £500 million as the Secretary of State may specify by order made with the approval of the Treasury.

[(3A) The aggregate amount outstanding in respect of—

(a) loans for which [the Secretary of State (or Housing for Wales)][243] has given a guarantee under this section, and

(b) payments made by [the Secretary of State (or Housing for Wales)][244] in meeting an obligation arising by virtue of such a guarantee and not repaid to [the Secretary of State (or Housing for Wales)][245],

shall not exceed £30 million or such greater sum not exceeding £50 million as the Secretary of State may specify by order made with the approval of the Treasury][246]

(4) An order under subsection (3) [or subsection (3A)][247] shall be made by statutory instrument and no such order shall be made unless a draft of it has been laid before and approved by the House of Commons.

84 Agreements to indemnify certain lenders: England and Wales.

(1) The [Relevant Authority][248] may . . .[249] enter into an agreement with—

(a) a building society lending on the security of a house, or

(b) a recognised body making a relevant advance on the security of a house,

whereby, in the event of default by the mortgagor, and in circumstances and subject to conditions specified in the agreement, the [Relevant Authority][250] binds itself to indemnify the society or body in respect of the whole or part of the mortgagor's outstanding indebtedness and any loss or expense falling on the society or body in consequence of the mortgagor's default.

(2) The agreement may also, if the mortgagor is made party to it, enable or require the [Relevant Authority][251] in specified circumstances to take a transfer of the mortgage and assume rights and liabilities under it, the building society or recognised body being then discharged in respect of them.

(3) The transfer may be made to take effect—

(a) on terms provided for by the agreement (including terms involving substitution of a new mortgage agreement or modification of the existing one), and

(b) so that the [Relevant Authority][252] is treated as acquiring (for and in relation to the purposes of the mortgage) the benefit and burden of all preceding acts, omissions and events.

(4) The [Housing Corporation may not enter into an agreement without the approval of the Secretary of State who][253] may approve particular agreements or give notice that particular forms of agreement have his approval, and in either case may make his approval subject to conditions.

(5) The Secretary of State shall, before giving notice that a particular form of agreement has his approval [and before himself entering into an agreement in a form about which he has not previously consulted under this subsection][254], consult—

(a) in the case of a form of agreement with a building society, the [Financial Services Authority][255] and such organisations representative of building societies and local authorities as he thinks expedient, and

(b) in the case of a form of agreement with a recognised body, such organisations representative of such bodies and local authorities as he thinks expedient.

(6) . . . .[256]

85 Meaning of "recognised body" and "relevant advance".

(1) The expressions "recognised body" and "relevant advance" in section 84 (agreements to indemnify certain lenders) shall be construed in accordance with the following provisions.

(2) A "recognised body" means a body specified, or of a class or description specified, in an order made by statutory instrument by the Secretary of State . . . [257]

(3) Before making such an order varying or revoking an order previously made, the Secretary of State shall give an opportunity for representations to be made on behalf of a recognised body which, if the order were made, would cease to be such a body.

(4) A "relevant advance" means an advance made to a person whose interest in the dwelling is or was acquired by virtue of a conveyance of the freehold or an assignment of a long lease, or a grant of a long lease by—

a local authority,

a new town corporation,

an urban development corporation,

. . .[258]

the [Housing Corporation][259], or

a [registered social landlord][260].[or an advance made to such a person by the Secretary of State if the conveyance, assignment or grant was made under section 90.][261]

(5) In subsection (4) "long lease" has the same meaning as in Part V of the Housing Act 1985 (the right to buy).

86 Agreements to indemnify building societies: Scotland.

(1)[Scottish Homes][262] may, with the approval of the Secretary of State, enter into an agreement with a building society [or recognised body][263] under which [Scottish Homes][264] binds itself to indemnify the building society [or recognised body][265] in respect of—

(a) the whole or part of any outstanding indebtedness of a borrower; and

(b) loss or expense to the building society [or recognised body][266] resulting from the failure of the borrower duly to perform any obligation imposed on him by [a][267] heritable security.

(2) The agreement may also, where the borrower is made party to it, enable or require [Scottish Homes][268] in specified circumstances to take an assignation of the rights and liabilities of the building society [or recognised body][269] under the heritable security.

(3) Approval of the Secretary of State under subsection (1) may be given generally in relation to agreements which satisfy specified requirements, or in relation to individual agreements, and with or without conditions, as he thinks fit, and such approval may be withdrawn at any time on one month's notice.

(4) Before issuing any general approval under subsection (1) the Secretary of State shall consult with such bodies as appear to him to be representative of islands and district councils, and of building societies, and also with [Scottish Homes][270] and with the [Financial Services Authority][271].

(5). . . . .[272]

[(6) In this section, "recognised body" means a body designated, or of a class or description designated, in an order made under this subsection by statutory instrument by the Secretary of State with the consent of the Treasury.

(7) Before making an order under subsection (6) above varying or revoking an order previously so made, the Secretary of State shall give an opportunity for representations to be made on behalf of a recognised body which, if the order were made, would cease to be such a body.][273]

[87 Financial assistance with respect to formation, management, etc. of certain housing associations.

[(1) The [Relevant Authority][274] may give financial assistance to any person to facilitate the proper performance of the functions of registered social landlords or co-operative housing associations.][275]

(2) Assistance under this section may be in the form of grants, loans, guarantees or incurring expenditure for the benefit of the person assisted or in such other way as the [Relevant Authority][276] considers appropriate, except that the may not, in giving any form of financial assistance [under this section][277], purchase loan or share capital in a company.

(3) With respect to financial assistance under this section, the following—

(a) the procedure to be followed in relation to applications for assistance,

(b) the circumstances in which assistance is or is not to be given,

(c) the method for calculating, and any limitations on, the amount of assistance, and

(d) the manner in which, and the time or times at which, assistance is to be given,

shall be such as may be specified by the [Relevant Authority][278], acting in accordance with such principles as it may from time to time determine.

(4) In giving assistance under this section, the may provide that the assistance is conditional upon compliance by the person to whom the assistance is given with such conditions as it may specify.

(5) Where assistance under this section is given in the form of a grant, subsections (1), (2) and (7) to (9) of section 52 of the Housing Act 1988 (recovery, etc. of grants) shall apply as they apply in relation to a grant to which that section applies, but with the substitution, for any reference in those subsections to the [registered][279] housing association to which the grant has been given, of a reference to the person to whom assistance is given under this section.

(6) Section 53 of the Housing Act 1988 (determinations under Part II) shall apply in relation to a determination under this section as it applies to a determination under sections 50 to 52 of that Act.][280]

[87 Financial assistance with respect to formation, management, etc. of certain housing associations.[281]

(1) The [Relevant Authority][282] may give financial assistance to any person in respect of the following activities—

(a) promoting and giving advice on the formation of registered housing associations and co-operative housing associations (in this section referred to collectively as "relevant associations");

(b) managing, providing services for, and giving advice on the running of, relevant associations; and

(c) assisting tenants and licensees of a relevant association to take part in the management of the association or of some or all of the dwellings provided by the association.

(2) Assistance under this section may be in the form of grants, loans, guarantees or incurring expenditure for the benefit of the person assisted or in such other way as the [Relevant Authority][283] considers appropriate, except that the Corporation may not, in giving any form of financial assistance [under this section][284], purchase loan or share capital in a company.

(3) With respect to financial assistance under this section, the following—

(a) the procedure to be followed in relation to applications for assistance,

(b) the circumstances in which assistance is or is not to be given,

(c) the method for calculating, and any limitations on, the amount of assistance, and

(d) the manner in which, and the time or times at which, assistance is to be given,

shall be such as may be specified by the [Relevant Authority][285], acting in accordance with such principles as it may from time to time determine.

(4) In giving assistance under this section, the Corporation may provide that the assistance is conditional upon compliance by the person to whom the assistance is given with such conditions as it may specify.

(5) Where assistance under this section is given in the form of a grant, subsections (1), (2) and (7) to (9) of section 52 of the Housing Act 1988 (recovery, etc. of grants) shall apply as they apply in relation to a grant to which that section applies, but with the substitution, for any reference in those subsections to the registered housing association to which the grant has been given, of a reference to the person to whom assistance is given under this section.

(6) Section 53 of the Housing Act 1988 (determinations under Part II) shall apply in relation to a determination under this section as it applies to a determination under sections 50 to 52 of that Act.][286]

[Relevant Authority's][287] powers with respect to land and works

88 Acquisition of land.

(1) The [Relevant Authority][288] may acquire land by agreement for the purpose of—

(a) selling or leasing it to a [registered social landlord][289] or an unregistered self-build society, or

(b) providing dwellings (for letting or for sale) or hostels,

and [the Housing Corporation may be authorised by the Secretary of State to, and the Secretary of State may,][290] acquire land compulsorily for any such purpose.

(2) Land may be so acquired by the [Relevant Authority][291] notwithstanding that it is not immediately required for any such purpose.

(3) In relation to a compulsory purchase of land by the [Relevant Authority][292] under this section—

(a) in England and Wales, the Acquisition of Land Act 1981 applies;

(b) in Scotland, the Acquisition of Land (Authorisation Procedure) (Scotland) Act 1947 applies as if the [Relevant Authority][293] were a local authority and as if this section were contained in an Act in force immediately before the commencement of that Act.

(4) For the purposes of the purchase of land in Scotland by agreement by the [Relevant Authority][294]—

(a) the Lands Clauses Acts (except so much of them as relates to the acquisition of land otherwise than by agreement, the provisions relating to access to the special Act and section 120 to 125 of the Lands Clauses Consolidation (Scotland) Act 1845), and

(b) sections 6 and 70 to 78 of the Railways Clauses Consolidation (Scotland) Act 1845 (as originally enacted and not as amended by section 15 of the Mines (Working Facilities and Support) Act 1923),

are hereby incorporated with this section, and in construing those Acts for the purposes of this section this section shall be deemed to be the special Act and the [Relevant Authority] shall be deemed to be the promotors of the undertaking or company, as the case may require.

(5) In Scotland the [Relevant Authority][295] may (without prejudice to their own power to acquire land compulsorily) request the Scottish Special Housing Association to acquire land compulsorily on its behalf (as provided in section [23 of the Housing (Scotland) Act 1987][296]) for any purpose for which the [Relevant Authority][297] may purchase land compulsorily.

88 Acquisition of land.[298]

(1) The [Relevant Authority][299] may acquire land by agreement for the purpose of—

(a) selling or leasing it to a registered housing association or an unregistered self-build society, or

(b) providing dwellings (for letting or for sale) or hostels,

and [the Housing Corporation may be authorised by the Secretary of State to, and the Secretary of State may,][300] acquire land compulsorily for any such purpose.

(2) Land may be so acquired by the [Relevant Authority][301] notwithstanding that it is not immediately required for any such purpose.

(3) In relation to a compulsory purchase of land by the [Relevant Authority][302] under this section—

(a) in England and Wales, the Acquisition of Land Act 1981 applies;

(b) in Scotland, the Acquisition of Land (Authorisation Procedure) (Scotland) Act 1947 applies as if the [Relevant Authority][303] were a local authority and as if this section were contained in an Act in force immediately before the commencement of that Act.

(4) For the purposes of the purchase of land in Scotland by agreement by the [Relevant Authority][304]—

(a) the Lands Clauses Acts (except so much of them as relates to the acquisition of land otherwise than by agreement, the provisions relating to access to the special Act and section 120 to 125 of the Lands Clauses Consolidation (Scotland) Act 1845), and

(b) sections 6 and 70 to 78 of the Railways Clauses Consolidation (Scotland) Act 1845 (as originally enacted and not as amended by section 15 of the Mines (Working Facilities and Support) Act 1923),

are hereby incorporated with this section, and in construing those Acts for the purposes of this section this section shall be deemed to be the special Act and the [Relevant Authority][305] shall be deemed to be the promotors of the undertaking or company, as the case may require.

(5) In Scotland the [Relevant Authority][306] may (without prejudice to their own power to acquire land compulsorily) request the Scottish Special Housing Association to acquire land compulsorily on its behalf (as provided in section [23 of the Housing (Scotland) Act 1987][307]) for any purpose for which the [Relevant Authority][308] may purchase land compulsorily.

89 Provision of dwellings or hostels and clearance, management and development of land.

(1) The [Relevant Authority][309] may provide or improve dwellings or hostels on land belonging to it.

(2) The [Relevant Authority][310] may clear land belonging to it and carry out other work on the land to prepare it as a building site or estate, including—

(a) the laying out and construction of streets or roads and open spaces, and

(b) the provision of sewerage facilities and supplies of gas, electricity and water.

(3) The [Relevant Authority][311] may repair, maintain and insure buildings or works on land belonging to it, may generally deal in the proper course of management with such land and buildings or works on it, and may charge for the tenancy or occupation of such land, buildings or works. .

(4) The [Relevant Authority][312] may carry out such operations on, and do such other things in relation to, land belonging to it as appear to it to be conducive to facilitating the provision or improvement of dwellings or hostels on the land—

(a) by the [Relevant Authority][313] itself, or

(b) by a [registered social landlord][314] or unregistered self-build society.

(5) In the exercise of its powers under subsection (4) the [Relevant Authority][315] may carry out any development ancillary to or in connection with the provision of dwellings or hostels, including development which makes provision for buildings or land to be used for commercial, recreational or other non-domestic purposes.

89 Provision of dwellings or hostels and clearance, management and development of land.[316]

(1) The [Relevant Authority][317] may provide or improve dwellings or hostels on land belonging to it.

(2) The [Relevant Authority][318] may clear land belonging to it and carry out other work on the land to prepare it as a building site or estate, including—

(a) the laying out and construction of streets or roads and open spaces, and

(b) the provision of sewerage facilities and supplies of gas, electricity and water.

(3) The [Relevant Authority][319] may repair, maintain and insure buildings or works on land belonging to it, may generally deal in the proper course of management with such land and buildings or works on it, and may charge for the tenancy or occupation of such land, buildings or works. .

(4) The [Relevant Authority][320] may carry out such operations on, and do such other things in relation to, land belonging to it as appear to it to be conducive to facilitating the provision or improvement of dwellings or hostels on the land—

(a) by the [Relevant Authority][321] itself, or

(b) by a registered housing association or unregistered self-build society.

(5) In the exercise of its powers under subsection (4) the [Relevant Authority][322] may carry out any development ancillary to or in connection with the provision of dwellings or hostels, including development which makes provision for buildings or land to be used for commercial, recreational or other non-domestic purposes.

90 Disposal of land.[323]

(1) The [Relevant Authority][324] may dispose of land in respect of which it has not exercised its powers under section 89(1) (provision or improvement of dwellings or hostels) and on which it has not carried out any such development as is mentioned in section 89(5) [(ancillary development) to a registered social landlord or an unregistered self-build society; and the Housing Corporation may dispose of such land to any of its subsidiaries or to any other body in which it holds an interest.][325]

(2) The [Relevant Authority][326] may dispose of land on which dwellings or hostels have been provided or improved in exercise of its powers under section 89 to—

a [registered social landlord][327],

a local authority,

a new town corporation [, or

Scottish Homes;

and the Housing Corporation may dispose of any such land to any of its subsidiaries.][328]

(3) The [Relevant Authority][329] may sell or lease individual dwellings to persons for their own occupation; but where the dwelling concerned was acquired [by the Housing Corporation][330] by compulsory purchase under section 88(1), it shall not be disposed of under this subsection without the written consent of the Secretary of State.

(4) The [Relevant Authority][331] may dispose of a building or land intended for use for commercial, recreational or other non-domestic purposes in respect of which development has been carried out

by virtue of section 89; but no such building or land shall be disposed of [by the Housing Corporation][332] for less than the best consideration it commands except with the written consent of the Secretary of State.

(5) The [Relevant Authority][333] may dispose of land which is not required for the purposes for which it was acquired; but where the land—

(a) was acquired compulsorily by, or on behalf of, the [Housing Corporation][334] or by a local housing authority who transferred it to the [Housing Corporation][335], or

(b) is disposed of [by the Housing Corporation][336] (otherwise than for use as, or in connection with, a highway or street) for less than the best consideration it commands,

the [Housing Corporation][337] shall not dispose of the land except with the written consent of the Secretary of State.

(6) The [Housing Corporation][338] may not dispose of land except in accordance with the provisions of this section.

90 Disposal of land[339]

(1) The [Relevant Authority][340] may dispose of land in respect of which it has not exercised its powers under section 89(1) (provision or improvement of dwellings or hostels) and on which it has not carried out any such development as is mentioned in section 89(5) [(ancillary development) to a registered social landlord or an unregistered self-build society; and the Housing Corporation may dispose of such land to any of its subsidiaries or to any other body in which it holds an interest.][341]

(2) The [Relevant Authority][342] may dispose of land on which dwellings or hostels have been provided or improved in exercise of its powers under section 89 to—

a registered housing association,

a local authority,

a new town corporation [, or

Scottish Homes;

and the Housing Corporation may dispose of any such land to any of its subsidiaries.][343]

(3) The [Relevant Authority][344] may sell or lease individual dwellings to persons for their own occupation; but where the dwelling concerned was acquired [by the Housing Corporation][345] by compulsory purchase under section 88(1), it shall not be disposed of under this subsection without the written consent of the Secretary of State.

(4) The [Relevant Authority] may dispose of a building or land intended for use for commercial, recreational or other non-domestic purposes in respect of which development has been carried out by virtue of section 89; but no such building or land shall be disposed of [by the Housing Corporation][346] for less than the best consideration it commands except with the written consent of the Secretary of State.

(5) The [Relevant Authority][347] may dispose of land which is not required for the purposes for which it was acquired; but where the land—

(a) was acquired compulsorily by, or on behalf of, the [Housing Corporation][348] or by a local housing authority who transferred it to the [Housing Corporation][349], or

(b) is disposed of [by the Housing Corporation][350] (otherwise than for use as, or in connection with, a highway or street) for less than the best consideration it commands,

the [Housing Corporation][351] shall not dispose of the land except with the written consent of the Secretary of State.

(6) The [Housing Corporation][352] may not dispose of land except in accordance with the provisions of this section.

91 Protection of persons deriving title under transactions requiring consent.

Where the [Housing Corporation][353] purport to acquire or dispose of land—

(a) in favour of a person claiming under the [Housing Corporation][354] the transaction is not invalid by reason that any consent of the Secretary of State which is required has not been given, and

(b) a person dealing with the [Housing Corporation][355], or with a person claiming under the [Housing Corporation][356], shall not be concerned to see or inquire whether any such consent has been given.

The [Relevant Authority's][357] finances

92 Borrowing powers.

(1) The [Housing Corporation][358] may borrow from the Secretary of State, and the Secretary of State may lend to the [Housing Corporation][359], by way of temporary loan or otherwise, such sums in

sterling as the [Housing Corporation] may require.

(2) The [Housing Corporation][360] may, with the consent of the Secretary of State or in accordance with a general authorisation given by him, borrow temporarily by overdraft or otherwise such sums in sterling as the [Housing Corporation][361] may require.

(3) The [Housing Corporation][362] may, with the consent of the Secretary of State, borrow—

(a) from the European Investment Bank or the Commission of the European Communities, sums in any currency, and

(b) from any other person, sums in a currency other than sterling.

(4) A loan made to the [Housing Corporation][363] by the Secretary of State shall be repaid to him at such times and by such methods, and interest on the loan shall be paid to him at such rates and at such times, as he may from time to time determine.

(5) The Treasury may issue to the Secretary of State out of the National Loans Fund such sums as are necessary to enable him to make loans to the [Housing Corporation][364] in pursuance of this section; and sums received by the Secretary of State in pursuance of subsection (4) shall be paid into that Fund.

(6) The Secretary of State may act under this section only with the approval of the Treasury.

93 Limit on borrowing.

(1) The [Housing Corporation][365] has only the borrowing powers conferred by section 92 and those powers are exercisable subject to the following limit. .

(2) The aggregate amount outstanding by way of principal of—

(a) advances made to the [Housing Corporation][366] under section 9 of the Housing Act 1964 before 18th September 1974 (when that section was repealed),

(b) advances made to housing associations before 1st April 1975 in respect of which the rights and obligations of the Secretary of State were then transferred to the [Housing Corporation][367] by section 34 of the Housing Act 1974,

(c) money borrowed by the [Housing Corporation]368 under section 92, and

(d) money borrowed by a subsidiary of the [Housing Corporation][369] otherwise than from the [Housing Corporation][370],

[shall not exceed the limit [specified][371] under subsection (2A)][372].

[(2A) The limit referred to in subsection (2) is,—

(a) [373]. . .£2,000 million or such greater sum not exceeding £3,000 million as the Secretary of State may specify by order made with the consent of the Treasury; . . .[374]

. . . .][375]

(3) An order under subsection [(2A)][376] shall be made by statutory instrument and no such order shall be made unless a draft of it has been laid before and approved by the House of Commons.

(4) In ascertaining the limit imposed by subsection [(2A)][377], interest payable on a loan made by the Secretary of State to the [Housing Corporation][378] which, with the approval of the Treasury, is deferred and treated as part of the loan, shall, so far as outstanding, be treated as outstanding by way of principal.

(5) The power of the [Housing Corporation][379] to borrow from a subsidiary of the [Housing Corporation][380] is not affected by subsection (1) and borrowing from such a subsidiary shall be left out of account for the purposes of subsection [(2A)][381].

94 Treasury guarantees of borrowing.

(1) The Treasury may guarantee, in such manner and on such conditions as they think fit, the repayment of the principal of and the payment of interest on and the discharge of any other financial obligation in connection with sums which the [Housing Corporation][382] borrows from a person other than the Secretary of State.

(2) Immediately after a guarantee is given the Treasury shall lay a statement of the guarantee before each House of Parliament.

(3) Any sums required by the Treasury for fulfilling the guarantee shall be charged on and issued out of the Consolidated Fund.

(4) If any sums are so issued, the [Housing Corporation][383] shall make to the Treasury, at such times and in such manner as the Treasury may from time to time direct—

(a) payments of such amounts as the Treasury so direct in or towards repayment of the sums so

issued, and

(b) payments of interest, at such rate as the Treasury so direct, on what is outstanding for the time being in respect of sums so issued.

(5) Sums received by the Treasury in pursuance of subsection (4) shall be paid into the Consolidated Fund.

(6) Where a sum is issued for fulfilling a guarantee given under this section, the Treasury shall, as soon as possible after the end of each financial year, beginning with that in which the sum is issued and ending with that in which all liability in respect of the principal of the sum and in respect of interest on it is finally discharged, lay before each House of Parliament a statement relating to the sum.

95 Grants to the [Housing Corporation][384].

(1) The Secretary of State may make such grants to the [Housing Corporation][385] as appear to him to be required to enable the [Housing Corporation][386] to meet the expenses incurred by it in the exercise of its functions.

(2) A grant may be made subject to such conditions as the Secretary of State may determine.

(3) The Secretary of State may act under this section only with the consent of the Treasury.

96 General financial provisions.

(1) The [Housing Corporation][387] may turn its resources to account so far as they are not required for the exercise of its functions.

(2) If for an accounting year the revenues of the [Housing Corporation][388] exceed the total sums properly chargeable to revenue account, the [Housing Corporation][389] shall apply the excess in such manner as the Secretary of State may, after consultation with the [Housing Corporation][390], direct; and the Secretary of State may direct that the whole or part of the excess be paid to him.

(3) The Secretary of State may give directions to the [Housing Corporation][391] as to matters relating to—

(a) the establishment or management of reserves,

(b) the carrying of sums to the credit of reserves, or

(c) the application of reserves for the purposes of the [Housing Corporation's][392] functions.

(4) The Secretary of State may, after consultation with the [Housing Corporation][393], direct the [Housing Corporation][394] to pay to him the whole or part of any sums for the time being standing to the credit of reserves of the [Housing Corporation][395] or being of a capital nature and not required for the exercise of the [Housing Corporation's][396] functions.

(5) The Secretary of State may act under this section only with the approval of the Treasury.

[97 Accounts and audit.

(1) The [Housing Corporation][397] shall keep proper accounts and proper records in relation to the accounts and shall prepare in respect of each financial year annual accounts in such form as the Secretary of State may, with the approval of the Treasury, direct.

(2) The accounts of the [Housing Corporation][398] for each financial year shall be audited by a qualified accountant appointed for the purpose by the Secretary of State.

(3) As soon as the annual accounts of the [Housing Corporation][399] for a financial year have been audited, the [Housing Corporation][400] shall send to the Secretary of State a copy of the accounts prepared by it for the year in accordance with this section, together with a copy of any report made on them by the auditor.

(4) The Secretary of State shall prepare in respect of each financial year, in such form and manner as the Treasury may direct, an account of—

(a) the sums issued to him and lent to the [Housing Corporation][401], and

(b) sums received by him from the [Housing Corporation][402] and paid into the National Loans Fund in respect of the principal and interest on sums so lent, or on sums advanced to the [Housing Corporation] under section 9 of the Housing Act 1964,

and shall transmit the accounts so prepared by him to the Comptroller and Auditor General on or before 30th November in the following financial year.][403]

(5) The Comptroller and Auditor General shall examine and certify the accounts prepared by the Secretary of State and lay before each House of Parliament copies of the accounts together with his report on them.

[(6) In this section "qualified accountant" means a person who is eligible for appointment as a company auditor under section 25 of the Companies Act 1989.][404]

Acquisition of securities and control of subsidiaries

98 Acquisition of securities and promotion of body corporate.

(1) The [Housing Corporation][405] may with the consent of the Secretary of State—

(a) subscribe for or acquire securities of a body corporate, and

(b) promote or participate in the promotion of a body corporate.

(2) In the section "securities" means shares, stock, debenture stock and other securities of a like nature.

99 Control of subsidiaries.

(1) The [Housing Corporation][406] shall exercise its control over its subsidiaries so as to secure that no subsidiary—

(a) engages in an activity which the [Housing Corporation][407] is not empowered to carry on, or

(b) engages in an activity in a manner in which the [Housing Corporation][408] itself could not engage by reason of a direction given to it under section 76 (directions by Secretary of State).

(2) The [Housing Corporation][409] shall also exercise its control over its subsidiaries so as to secure that no subsidiary of its—

(a) borrows money from a person other than the [Housing Corporation][410], or

(b) raises money by the issue of shares or stock to a person other than the [Housing Corporation][411],

without the consent of the Secretary of State.

Supplementary provisions

[100 Scottish Special Housing Association may act as agents for [Relevant Authority][412] in Scotland.

The [Relevant Authority][413] may, on such terms and conditions as may be agreed between it and the Scottish Special Housing Association, authorise the Association to act in Scotland as the agents of the [Relevant Authority][414] for the purpose of carrying out any of the functions vested in the [Relevant Authority][415] under—

(a) section 77 (advisory service),

(b) sections 88 and 89 (powers with respect to land and works), or

(c) paragraph 5 of Schedule 7 (schemes for provision of housing accommodation in place of a housing association).][416]

101 Minor definitions.

In this Part—

["building society" means a building society within the meaning of the Building Societies Act 1986;][417]

"financial year" means the period of 12 months ending with the 31st March;

"highway", in relation to Scotland, includes a public right of way;

"subsidiary" has [the meaning given by section 736 of][418] the Companies Act.

102 Index of defined expressions: Part III.

The following Table shows provisions defining or explaining expressions used in this Part (other than provisions defining or explaining an expression in the same section or paragraph):—

building society	section 101
the Companies Act	section 106
dwelling	section 106
financial year	section 101
heritable security	section 106
highway (in relation to Scotland)	section 101
hostel	section 106
housing association	section 1(1)
local authority	section 106
local housing authority	section 104
new town corporation	section 106
recognised body	section 85(2)
registered (in relation to a housing association)	section 3(2)
relevant advance	section 85(4)
self-build society	section 1(3)
subsidiary	section 101
unregistered (in relation to a housing association)	section 3(2)

urban development corporation	section 106.

102 Index of defined expressions: Part III.[419]

The following Table shows provisions defining or explaining expressions used in this Part (other than provisions defining or explaining an expression in the same section or paragraph):—

building society	*section 101*
the Companies Act	*section 106*
[co-operative housing association	*section 1]*[420]
dwelling	*section 106*
financial year	*section 101*
heritable security	*section 106*
highway (in relation to Scotland)	*section 101*
hostel	*section 106*
housing association	*section 1(1)*
local authority	*section 106*
local housing authority	*section 104*
new town corporation	*section 106*
recognised body	*section 85(2)*
[registered social landlord	*section 2B]*[421]
relevant advance	*section 85(4)*
self-build society	*section 1(3)*
subsidiary	*section 101*
[unregistered (in relation to a housing association)	*section 2B]*[422]
urban development corporation	*section 106.*

102 Index of defined expressions: Part III.[423]

building society	*section 101*
the Companies Act	*section 106*
dwelling	*section 106*
financial year	*section 101*
heritable security	*section 106*
highway (in relation to Scotland)	*section 101*
hostel	*section 106*
housing association	*section 1(1)*
local authority	*section 106*
local housing authority	*section 104*
new town corporation	*section 106*
recognised body	*section 85(2)*
registered (in relation to a housing association)	*section 3(2)*
relevant advance	*section 85(4)*
self-build society	*section 1(3)*
subsidiary	*section 101*
unregistered (in relation to a housing association)	*section 3(2)*
urban development corporation	*section 106*

Part IV General Provisions

General provisions

103 Application to Isles of Scilly.

(1) This Act applies to the Isles of Scilly subject to such exceptions, adaptations and modifications as the Secretary of State may by order direct.

(2) An order shall be made by statutory instrument which shall be subject to annulment in pursuance of a resolution of either House of Parliament.

104 Local housing authorities.

(1) In this Act "local housing authority"—

(a) in relation to England and Wales, has the meaning given by section 1 of the Housing Act 1985, and

(b) in relation to Scotland, means [a council constituted under section 2 of the Local Government etc. (Scotland) Act 1994][424].

(2) References in this Act to the district of a local housing authority—

(a) in England and Wales shall be construed in accordance with section 2 of the Housing Act 1985, and

(b) in Scotland are to the [area of a council mentioned in subsection (1)(b) above][425].

105. ....[426]

106 Minor definitions — general.

(1) In the application of this Act in England and Wales—

["bank" means—

[(a) an institution authorised under the Banking Act 1987, or][427]

(b) a company as to which the Secretary of State was satisfied immediately before the repeal of the Protection of Depositors Act 1963 that it ought to be treated as a banking company or discount company for the purposes of that Act;][428]

["the Companies Act" means the Companies Act 1985;][429]

"dwelling" means a building or part of a building occupied or intended to be occupied as a separate dwelling, together with any yard, garden, outhouses and appurtenances belonging to it or usually enjoyed with it;

["friendly society" means a friendly society or branch of a friendly society registered under the Friendly Societies Act 1974 or earlier legislation;][430]

"hostel" means a building in which is provided for persons generally or for a class or classes of persons—

(a) residential accommodation otherwise than in separate and self-contained sets of premises, and

(b) either board or facilities for the preparation of food adequate to the needs of those persons, or both;

"house" includes—

(a) any part of a building which is occupied or intended to be occupied as a separate dwelling;

(b) any yard, garden, outhouses and appurtenances belonging to the house or usually enjoyed with it;

[["housing activities", in relation to a registered housing association, means all its activities in pursuance of such of its purposes, objects or powers as are of a description mentioned in section 1(1)(a) or subsections (2) to (4) of section 4.][431]][432]

["insurance company" means an insurance company to which Part II of the Insurance Companies Act 1982 applies;][433]

"local authority" means a county, [county borough,][434]district, or London borough council, the Common Council of the City of London or the Council of the Isles of Scilly and in [section 84(5)][435] includes . . . [436] a joint authority established by Part IV of the Local Government Act 1985 [and the London Fire and Emergency Planning Authority][437][and in section 85(4) includes such a joint authority [the London Fire and Planning Authority][438] and a police authority established under [section 3 of the Police Act 1996][439][and the Metropolitan Police Authority][440]][441];

"new town corporation" means the Commission for the New Towns or a development corporation within the meaning of the New Towns Act 1981;

"shared ownership lease" means a lease—

(a) granted on payment of a premium calculated by reference to a percentage of the value of the house or dwelling or of the cost of providing it, or

(b) under which the tenant (or his personal representatives) will or may be entitled to a sum calculated by reference directly or indirectly to the value of the house or dwelling;

["trustee savings bank" means a trustee savings bank registered under the Trustee Savings Bank Act 1981 or earlier legislation;][442]

"urban development corporation" means an urban development corporation established under Part XVI of the Local Government, Planning and Land Act 1980.

(2) In the application of this Act in Scotland—

["bank" has the same meaning as in subsection (1);][443]

"charge" includes a heritable security;

["the Companies Act" has the same meaning as in subsection (1);][444]

"dwelling" means a house;

["friendly society" has the same meaning as in subsection (1);][445]

["heritable security" means any security capable of being constituted over any interest in land by disposition or assignation of that interest in security of any debt and of being recorded in the Register of Sasines or, as the case may be, registered in the Land Register of Scotland and which includes a security constituted by an ex facie absolute disposition or assignation or by a standard security;][446]

"hostel" means—

(a) in relation to a building provided or converted before 3rd January 1962, a building in which is provided, for persons generally or for any class or classes of persons, residential accommodation (otherwise than in separate and self-contained dwellings) and board, and

(b) in relation to a building provided or converted on or after that date, a building in which is provided for persons generally or for any class or classes of persons, residential accommodation (otherwise than in houses) and either board or common facilities for the preparation of adequate food to the needs of those persons, or both;

"house" includes—

(a) any part of a building, being a part which is occupied or intended to be occupied as a separate dwelling, and in particular includes a flat, and

(b) includes also any yard, garden, outhouses and pertinents belonging to the house or usually enjoyed with it;

["housing activities" has the same meaning as in subsection (1);][447]

["insurance company" has the same meaning as in subsection (1);][448]

"local authority" means [a council constituted under section 2 of the Local Government etc. (Scotland) Act 1994][449];

"mortgage" means a heritable security and "mortgagee" means a creditor in such a security;

"new town corporation" means a development corporation within the meaning of the New Towns (Scotland) Act 1968;

["shared ownership lease" has the same meaning as in subsection (1);][450]

[["shared ownership agreement" means an agreement whereby—

(a) a pro indiviso right in a dwelling is sold to a person and the remaining pro indiviso rights therein are leased to him subject to his being entitled, from time to time, to purchase those remaining rights until he has purchased the entire dwelling; or

(b) pro indiviso rights in dwellings are conveyed to trustees to hold on behalf of persons each of whom, by purchasing a share in those dwellings, becomes entitled to exclusive occupancy of one of the dwellings but with any such person who wishes to sell or otherwise dispose of his share being required to do so through the agency of the trustees,

or such other agreement as may be approved whereby a person acquires a pro indiviso right in a dwelling or dwellings and thereby becomes entitled to exclusive occupancy of the dwelling or, as the case may be, one of the dwellings;][451]][452]

["trustee savings bank" has the same meaning as in subsection (1).][453]

[(3) In the definition of "shared ownership agreement" in subsection (2) above, "approved" means approved by the Secretary of State after consultation with [Scottish Homes][454].][455]

Final provisions

107 Short title, commencement and extent.

(1) This Act may be cited as the Housing Associations Act 1985.

(2) This Act comes into force on 1st April 1986.

(3) The following provisions of this Act apply to England and Wales only—

section 2,

. . . .[456]

section 8(2) and (3),

sections 11 and 12,

section [17(4)][457],

section 18,
section 20,
section 31,
sections 34 to 36,
section 38,
. . . .[458]
. . . .
section 58,
section 67,
section 69(3),
section 81,
sections 84 and 85,
section 103,
[section 105,][459]
Schedules 2 and 3,
In Schedule 4, Part I,
In Schedule 5, Part I, paragraphs 1 and 2 of Part III and paragraph 1 of Part V.

(4) The following provisions of this Act apply to Scotland only—
[. . . . .[460]
section 15A][461]
section 59,
section 66,
section 68,
section 69(4),
section 86,
In Schedule 4, Part III,
In Schedule 5, Part II, paragraphs 3 and 4 of Part III, Part IV and Part VII.

(5) This Act does not extend to Northern Ireland.

SCHEDULES

Sections 6, 9

SCHEDULE 1 Grant-Aided Land

Definition of "grant-aided land"

1 For the purposes of [section 9(1A)][462] (control . . .[463] of dispositions of land by unregistered housing associations) "grant-aided land" means land—

(a) in respect of which a payment of a description specified in paragraph 2 falls or fell to be made in respect of a period ending after 24th January 1974, or

(b) on which is, or has been, secured a loan of a description specified in paragraph 3 in respect of which a repayment (by way of principal or interest or both) falls or fell to be made after 24th January 1974.

Payments

2 The payments referred to in paragraph 1(a) are—

(a) payments by way of annual grants or exchequer contributions under—
section 31(3) of the Housing Act 1949,
section 19(3) of the Housing (Scotland) Act 1949, or
section 121(3) of the Housing (Scotland) Act 1950
(arrangements by local authorities for improvement of housing accommodation);

(b) payments by way of annual grants or exchequer contributions under—
section 12(1) or 15 of the Housing (Financial Provisions) Act 1958,
section 89(1) of the Housing (Scotland) Act 1950,
section 12 of the Housing (Scotland) Act 1962, or
section 21 of the Housing (Financial Provisions) (Scotland) Act 1968
(contributions for dwellings improved under arrangements with local authorities or grants for hostels);

(c) payments by way of annual grant or exchequer contributions under—
section 12(6) of the Housing Subsidies Act 1967,
section 121 of the Housing (Scotland) Act 1950,
section 62 of the Housing Act 1964, or
section 17 of the Housing (Financial Provisions) (Scotland) Act 1968
(subsidies for conversions or improvements by housing associations);

(d) payments by way of annual grant under—
section 21(8) of the Housing Act 1969 (contributions for dwellings provided or improved by housing associations under arrangements with local authorities);

(e) payments by way of subsidy under—
section 72, 73, 75 or 92 of the Housing Finance Act 1972,
section 52, 53, 55 or 57 of the Housing (Financial Provisions) (Scotland) Act 1972, or

Parts I, II, VI and VII of Schedule 5 to this Act (basic or special residual subsidy, new building or improvement subsidy, hostel subsidy).

Loans

3 The loans referred to in paragraph 1(b) are—

(a) loans under—
section 119 of the Housing Act 1957,
section 152 of the Housing (Scotland) Act 1966,
section 58 of this Act, or
section 59 of this Act
(powers of certain local authorities to promote and assist housing associations);

(b) loans to housing associations under—
section 47 of the Housing (Financial Provisions) Act 1958,
section 78 of the Housing (Scotland) Act 1950,
section 24 of the Housing (Financial Provisions) (Scotland) Act 1968,
section 67 of this Act, or
section 68 of this Act
(loans by Public Works Loan Commissioners to certain bodies);

(c) advances made under—
section 7 of the Housing Act 1961,
section 11 of the Housing (Scotland) Act 1962, or
section 23 of the Housing (Financial Provisions) (Scotland) Act 1968
(advances to housing associations providing housing accommodation for letting);

(d) loans under—
section 2 of the Housing Act 1964
(loans by Housing Corporation to housing associations).

SCHEDULE 2[464]

....

SCHEDULE 3[465]

....

Sections 69, 70

SCHEDULE 4 - HOUSING ASSOCIATIONS: CONTINUATION OF ARRANGEMENTS UNDER REPEALED ENACTMENTS

PART I – ARRANGEMENTS WITH LOCAL AUTHORITIES FOR PROVISION OR IMPROVEMENT OF HOUSING

(ss. 120 and 121 of the Housing Act 1957)

1 Arrangements between a local authority and a housing association under section 120 of the Housing Act 1957 (arrangements for provision of housing) which were made before 10th August 1972 and are in force immediately before the commencement of this Act remain in force under this paragraph.

2 Arrangements between a local authority and a housing association under section 121 of the Housing Act 1957 (arrangements for improvement or conversion of housing) which were made before 1st April 1975 and are in force immediately before the commencement of this Act remain in force under

this paragraph.

PART II - SUBSIDY AGREEMENTS WITH LOCAL AUTHORITIES

(s. 79 of the Housing Finance Act 1972 and s. 59 of the Housing (Financial Provisions) (Scotland) Act 1972)

1 In this Part "subsidy agreement" means an agreement made between a local authority and a housing association which provides for payments to be made under or by reference to any of the following enactments—

section 2 of the Housing (Financial Provisions) Act 1924,
section 29(1) of the Housing Act 1930,
section 27(3) of the Housing Act 1935,
section 26 of the Housing (Scotland) Act 1935,
section 94(3) of the Housing Act 1936,
section 87(1) of the Housing (Scotland) Act 1950,
section 1(2)(b) of the Housing Subsidies Act 1956,
section 2, 3 or 4 of the Housing and Town Development (Scotland) Act 1957,
section 1(2)(b) of the Housing (Financial Provisions) Act 1958,
section 1(2) of the Housing Act 1961,
section 2, 4, 5, 6 or 7 of the Housing (Scotland) Act 1962,
section 1(5) or 9(4) of the Housing Subsidies Act 1967,
section 2, 4, 6, 7, 9 or 10 of the Housing (Financial Provisions) (Scotland) Act 1968,

(being enactments with respect to which it was provided by the Housing Finance Act 1972 or the Housing (Financial Provisions) (Scotland) Act 1972 that no further payments were to be made for 1972-73 or any subsequent year).

2 Where a subsidy agreement provides for the payment of greater amounts than those which the authority would have been obliged to pay under the relevant enactment, the authority shall continue to pay to the housing association sums equal to the difference between the amounts for the payment of which the agreement provides and the amounts which they would have been obliged to pay by that enactment.

PART III SPECIAL ARRANGEMENTS WITH THE SECRETARY OF STATE IN SCOTLAND

(s.1(1)(d) of the Housing (Scotland) Act 1962; s.1(2)(d) of the Housing (Financial Provisions) (Scotland) Act 1968)

Arrangements made between the Secretary of State and a housing association under section 1(1)(d) of the Housing (Scotland) Act 1962 or section 1(2)(d) of the Housing (Financial Provisions) (Scotland) Act 1968 (special arrangements for provision of housing) which were made before 3rd August 1972 and are in force immediately before the commencement of this Act remain in force under this paragraph.

Sections 69, 71

SCHEDULE 5 - HOUSING ASSOCIATION FINANCE: SUPERSEDED SUBSIDIES, CONTRIBUTIONS AND GRANTS

PART I - RESIDUAL SUBSIDIES: ENGLAND AND WALES

(ss. 72 and 73 of the Housing Finance Act 1972) Entitlement to residual subsidies

1(1) Basic residual subsidy is payable to a housing association in accordance with the following provisions where the association received payments from the Secretary of State for the financial year 1971-72 under certain enactments under which, in accordance with the Housing Finance Act 1972, no payments were to be made for 1972-73 or any subsequent year.

(2) A housing association is entitled to basic residual subsidy for a financial year if—

(a) it was entitled to basic residual subsidy under section 72 of the Housing Finance Act 1972 for the financial year 1972-73, and

(b) it has continued to be entitled to basic residual subsidy, under that section or this Schedule, for each succeeding financial year up to and including that immediately before the year in question.

(3) The amount of basic residual subsidy payable to an association for any year is the amount (if any) by which the basic residual subsidy payable for the previous year exceeds the withdrawal factor.

(4) Subject to any direction of the Secretary of State under paragraph 4(2), the withdrawal factor is the sum produced by multiplying £20 by the number of dwellings as at 31st March 1972 in respect of

which the association's subsidies for 1971-72 (as defined in section 72(4) of the Housing Finance Act 1972) were payable.

2(1) Special residual subsidy is payable to a housing association in accordance with the following provisions in respect of dwellings which—

(a) were approved by the Secretary of State for the purposes of Part I of the Housing Subsidies Act 1967 before 10th August 1972, and

(b) were completed during the year 1972-73, 1973-74 or 1974-75

(2) A housing association is entitled to special residual subsidy for a financial year if—

(a) it was entitled by virtue of section 73 of the Housing Finance Act 1972 to special residual subsidy for any of the years 1972-73, 1973-74 or 1974-75, and

(b) it has continued to be entitled to special residual subsidy, under that section or this Schedule, for each succeeding financial year up to and including that immediately before the year in question.

(3) The amount of special residual subsidy payable to an association for any year is the amount (if any) by which the special residual subsidy payable for the previous year exceeds the reduction factor.

(4) Subject to any direction of the Secretary of State under paragraph 4(2), the reduction factor is the sum produced by multiplying £20 by the number of dwellings satisfying the description in sub-paragraph (1).

3 No basic or special residual subsidy is payable to a co-operative housing association.

Power to vary withdrawal factor or reduction factor

4(1) This paragraph applies where a housing association, by furnishing to the Secretary of State such information as to its financial position as he may require, satisfies him as regards any financial year that its income from its dwellings will be, or was, inadequate having regard to its normal sources of income to meet such expenditure (including loan charges) as in his opinion it would be, or was, reasonable for the association to incur for that financial year in the exercise of its housing functions.

(2) Where this paragraph applies, the Secretary of State may direct that the amount of basic residual subsidy or special residual subsidy payable to the association for the financial year in question shall be determined—

(a) by reference to a withdrawal factor or reduction factor calculated by reference to a smaller sum of money per dwelling than that mentioned in paragraph 1(4) or 2(4), or

(b) by reference to a withdrawal factor or reduction factor of zero.

(3) A direction under this paragraph may be varied or revoked by the Secretary of State by a further direction.

(4) In sub-paragraph (1) "housing functions" means—

(a) constructing or improving, or facilitating or encouraging the construction or improvement, of dwellings,.

(b) managing dwellings,.

(c) the provision of dwellings by conversion, and

(d) the acquisition of dwellings;

and includes functions which are supplementary or incidental to any of those functions.

(5) For the purposes of this paragraph "loan charges", in relation to money borrowed by an association, means—

(a) the sums required for the payment of interest on the money and for its repayment, either by instalments or by means of a sinking fund, and

(b) the expenses of managing the debt,.

and includes any such charges made by the association itself, whether in respect of borrowing from a capital fund kept by the association or in respect of borrowing between accounts kept by the association for different functions, or otherwise.

Administrative provisions

5(1) Payment of basic or special residual subsidy is subject to the making of a claim for the payment in such form, and containing such particulars, as the Secretary of State may from time to time determine.

(2) The amount of basic or special residual subsidy payable to a housing association for a financial year shall be calculated to the nearest pound by rounding up any odd amount of 50p or more and rounding down any lesser amount.

(3) Basic or special residual subsidy is payable . . . [466] subject to such conditions as to records, certificates, audit or otherwise as the Secretary of State may, , impose.

Powers exercisable in case of disposal of dwellings by association

6(1) The Secretary of State may reduce, suspend or discontinue the payment of basic or special residual subsidy to an association if the association leases for a term exceeding seven years or otherwise disposes of any of the dwellings in respect of which the association is entitled to the payment.

(2) If any dwellings of an association are leased for a term exceeding seven years to, or become vested in—

(a) another housing association, or trustees for another housing association, or

(b) the Housing Corporation. . .[467],

the Secretary of State may pay to them any basic or special residual subsidy which he would otherwise have paid to the former association for any financial year, beginning with that in which the dwellings are so leased or become so vested.

(3) For the purposes of this paragraph a lease shall be treated as being for a term exceeding seven years where the original term is for a lesser period but the lease confers on the lessee an option for renewal for a term which, together with the original term, exceeds seven years.

Saving for financial years beginning before the commencement of this Act

7(1) The preceding provisions apply in relation to the financial year 1986-87 and subsequent financial years.

(2) The repeal by the Housing (Consequential Provisions) Act 1985 of the provisions of the Housing Finance Act 1972 relating to basic and special residual subsidies does not affect the operation of those provisions in relation to previous financial years.

PART II - RESIDUAL SUBSIDIES: SCOTLAND

(ss. 52 and 53 of the Housing (Financial Provisions) (Scotland) Act 1972) Entitlement to residual subsidies

1(1) Basic residual subsidy is payable to a housing association in accordance with the following provisions where the association received payments from the Secretary of State for the financial year 1971-72 under certain enactments under which, in accordance with the Housing (Financial Provisions) (Scotland) Act 1972, no payments were to be made for 1972-73 or any subsequent year.

(2) A housing association is entitled to basic residual subsidy for a financial year if—

(a) it was entitled to basic residual subsidy under section 52 of the Housing (Financial Provisions) (Scotland) Act 1972 for the financial year 1972-73, and

(b) it has continued to be entitled to basic residual subsidy, under that section or this Schedule, for each succeeding financial year up to and including that immediately before the year in question.

(3) The amount of basic residual subsidy payable to an association for any year is the amount (if any) by which the basic residual subsidy payable for the previous year exceeds the withdrawal factor.

(4) Subject to any direction of the Secretary of State under paragraph 4(2), the withdrawal factor is the sum produced by multiplying £20 by the number of houses as at 31st March 1972 in respect of which the association's subsidies for 1971-72 (as defined in section 52(4) of the Housing (Financial Provisions) (Scotland) Act 1972) were payable.

2(1) Special residual subsidy is payable to a housing association in accordance with the following provisions in respect of houses—

(a) the erection of which was approved by the Secretary of State for the purposes of sections 1 to 12 of the Housing (Financial Provisions) (Scotland) Act 1968 before 3rd August 1972, and

(b) which were completed by the association during the year 1972-73, 1973-74 or 1974-75.

(2) A housing association is entitled to special residual subsidy for a financial year if—

(a) it was entitled by virtue of section 53 of the Housing (Financial Provisions) (Scotland) Act 1972 to special residual subsidy for any of the years 1972-73, 1973-74 or 1974-75, and

(b) it has continued to be entitled to special residual subsidy, under that section or this Schedule, for each succeeding financial year up to and including that immediately before the year in question.

(3) The amount of special residual subsidy payable to an association for any year is the amount (if any) by which the special residual subsidy payable for the previous year exceeds the reduction factor.

(4) Subject to any direction of the Secretary of State under paragraph 4(2), the reduction factor is the sum produced by multiplying £20 by the number of houses satisfying the description in sub-

paragraph (1).

3 No basic or special residual subsidy is payable to a co-operative housing association.

Power to vary withdrawal factor or reduction factor

4(1) This paragraph applies where a housing association, by furnishing to the Secretary of State such information as to its financial position as he may require, satisfies him as regards any financial year that its income from its houses will be, or was, inadequate having regard to its normal sources of income to meet such expenditure (including loan charges) as in his opinion it would be, or was, reasonable for the association to incur for that financial year in the exercise of its housing functions.

(2) Where this paragraph applies, the Secretary of State may direct that the amount of basic residual subsidy or special residual subsidy payable to the association for the financial year in question shall be determined—

(a) by reference to a withdrawal factor or reduction factor calculated by reference to a smaller sum of money per house than that mentioned in paragraph 1(4) or 2(4), or

(b) by reference to a withdrawal factor or reduction factor of zero.

(3) A direction under this paragraph may be varied or revoked by the Secretary of State by a further direction.

(4) In sub-paragraph (1) "housing functions" means—

(a) constructing or improving, or facilitating the construction or improvement, of houses,.

(b) managing houses,.

(c) the provision of houses by conversion, and

(d) the acquisition of houses;

and includes functions which are supplementary or incidental to any of those functions.

(5) For the purposes of this paragraph "loan charges", in relation to money borrowed by an association includes loan charges made by the association itself (including charges for debt management), whether in respect of borrowing from a capital fund kept by the association or in respect of borrowing between accounts kept by the association for different functions, or otherwise.

Administrative provisions

5(1) Payment of basic or special residual subsidy is subject to the making of a claim for the payment in such form, and containing such particulars, as the Secretary for State may from time to time determine.

(2) The amount of basic or special residual subsidy payable to a housing association for a financial year shall be calculated to the nearest pound by rounding up any odd amount of 50p or more and rounding down any lesser amount.

(3) Basic or special residual subsidy is payable . . . [468] subject to such conditions as to records, certificates, audit or otherwise as the Secretary of State may, , impose.

Powers exercisable in case of disposal of houses by association

6(1) The Secretary of State may reduce, suspend or discontinue the payment of basic or special residual subsidy to a housing association if the association leases for a term exceeding seven years or otherwise disposes of any of the houses in respect of which the association is entitled to the payment.

(2) If any houses of an association are leased for a term exceeding seven years to, or become vested in—

(a) another housing association, or trustees for another housing association, or

(b) the Housing Corporation,.

the Secretary of State may pay to that association or to the Corporation any basic or special residual subsidy which he would otherwise have paid to the former association for any financial year, beginning with that in which the houses are so leased or become so vested.

(3) For the purposes of this paragraph a lease shall be treated as being for a term exceeding seven years where the original term is for a lesser period but the lease confers on the lessee an option for renewal for a term which, together with the original term, exceeds seven years.

Saving for financial years beginning before the commencement of this Act

7(1) The preceding provisions apply in relation to the financial year 1986-87 and subsequent financial years.

(2) The repeal by the Housing (Consequential Provisions) Act 1985 of the provisions of the Housing

(Financial Provisions) (Scotland) Act 1972 relating to basic and special residual subsidies does not affect the operation of those provisions in relation to previous financial years.

PART III CONTRIBUTIONS AND GRANTS UNDER ARRANGEMENTS WITH LOCAL AUTHORITIES

(s. 12 of the Housing (Financial Provisions) Act 1958; s. 12 of the Housing Subsidies Act 1967; s. 21 of the Housing Act 1969)

1(1) Contributions by the Secretary of State in connection with arrangements made under section 121 of the Housing Act 1957 (arrangements between housing associations and local authorities for improvement of housing) remain payable—

(a) under section 12 of the Housing (Financial Provisions) Act 1958 and section 12 of the Housing Subsidies Act 1967 as regards arrangements made before 25th August 1969, and

(b) under section 21 of the Housing Act 1969 as regards arrangements made on or after that date and approved under subsection (2) of that section before 1st April 1975.

(2) The contributions are payable at such times and in such manner as the Treasury may direct, and subject to such conditions, as to records, certificates, audit or otherwise as the Secretary of State may, with the approval of the Treasury, impose.

(3) Where such a contribution is paid to a local authority, the authority shall pay to the housing association by way of annual grant an amount not less than the contribution.

2 If the Secretary of State is satisfied, in the case of contributions payable under section 12 of the Housing (Financial Provisions) Act 1958, that the housing association have made default in giving effect to the terms of the arrangements, he may, as he thinks just—

(a) reduce the amount of the contribution payable to the local authority, or

(b) suspend or discontinue the payment;

and the local authority may reduce to a proportionate or any less extent the annual grant payable by them to the association or, as the case may be, suspend the payment for a corresponding period or discontinue the payment.

(s. 17 of the Housing (Financial Provisions) (Scotland) Act 1968)

3(1) Contributions by the Secretary of State under section 17 of the Housing (Financial Provisions) (Scotland) Act 1968 remain payable in connection with arrangements made under section 121 of the Housing (Scotland) Act 1950 or section 155 of the Housing (Scotland) Act 1966 (arrangements between housing associations and local authorities for improvement of housing) and approved on or after 16th August 1964 and before 1st April 1975.

(2) The contributions are payable at such times and in such manner as the Treasury may direct, and subject to such conditions as to records, certificates, audit or otherwise as the Secretary of State may, with the approval of the Treasury, impose.

(3) Where such a contribution is paid to a local authority, the authority shall pay to the housing association by way of annual grant an amount not less than the contribution.

4(1) The Secretary of State may, in any of the circumstances mentioned in sub-paragraph (2), reduce the amount of the contributions in respect of a particular subsidised unit, or suspend or discontinue the payment of the contributions, or part of them, as he thinks just in the circumstances.

(2) The circumstances referred to in sub-paragraph (1) are—

(a) that the housing association has made default in giving effect to the terms of the arrangements with the local authority, or

(b) that the subsidised unit has been converted, demolished or destroyed, is not fit to be used or has ceased to be used for the purpose for which it was intended, has been sold or leased for a stipulated duration exceeding twelve months or has been transferred, whether by sale or otherwise.

(3) The local authority may reduce to a corresponding or less extent the annual grant payable by them to the association, or, as the case may be, suspend payment of the whole or a corresponding part of the payment for a corresponding period, or discontinue the payment or a corresponding part.

PART IV CONTRIBUTIONS UNDER ARRANGEMENTS WITH THE SECRETARY OF STATE IN SCOTLAND

(s. 16 of the Housing (Financial Provisions) (Scotland) Act 1968)

1(1) Contributions by the Secretary of State under section 16 of the Housing (Financial Provisions)

(Scotland) Act 1968 remain payable in connection with arrangements made under—

section 14 of the Housing (Scotland) Act 1962, or

section 154 of the Housing (Scotland) Act 1966,

(arrangements between Secretary of State and housing associations) and approved before 1st April 1975.

(2) The Secretary of State may, in any of the circumstances mentioned in sub-paragraph (3), reduce the amount of the contributions in respect of a particular subsidised unit, or suspend or discontinue the payment of the contributions, or part of them, as he thinks just in the circumstances.

(3) The circumstances referred to in sub-paragraph (2) are—

(a) that the housing association has made default in giving effect to the terms of the arrangements, or

(b) the subsidised unit has been converted, demolished or destroyed, is not fit to be used or has ceased to be used for the purpose for which it was intended, has been sold or leased for a stipulated duration exceeding twelve months or has been transferred, whether by sale or otherwise.

PART V SCHEMES FOR THE UNIFICATION OF GRANT CONDITIONS

(s. 123 of the Housing Act 1957; s. 157 of the Housing (Scotland) Act 1966)

1 A scheme under section 123 of the Housing Act 1957 (schemes for the unification of divergent grant conditions affecting the management of a housing association's houses) which was made before 10th August 1972 and is in force immediately before the commencement of this Act remains in force under this paragraph.

2 A scheme under section 157 of the Housing (Scotland) Act 1966 (schemes for the unification of divergent grant conditions affecting the management of a housing association's houses) which was made before 3rd August 1972 and is in force immediately before the commencement of this Act remains in force under this paragraph.

PART VI NEW BUILDING SUBSIDY AND IMPROVEMENT SUBSIDY

(s. 75 of the Housing Finance Act 1972; ss. 55 and 57 of the Housing (Financial Provisions) (Scotland) Act 1972)

1(1) The following subsidies remain payable in respect of building schemes or improvement schemes approved by the Secretary of State before 1st April 1975—

(a) new building subsidy under section 75 of the Housing Finance Act 1972 or section 55 of the Housing (Financial Provisions) (Scotland) Act 1972, and

(b) improvement subsidy under section 57 of the Housing (Financial Provisions) (Scotland) Act 1972.

(2) Payment of the subsidy is subject to the making of a claim for the payment in such form, and containing such particulars as the Secretary of State may from time to time determine.

(3) The amount of the subsidy payable for a financial year shall be calculated to the nearest pound by rounding up any odd amount of 50p or more and rounding down any lesser amount.

(4) The subsidy is payable at such times and in such manner as the Treasury may direct, and subject to such conditions as to records, certificates, audit or otherwise as the Secretary of State may, with the approval of the Treasury, impose.

2(1) The Secretary of State may make reduced payments of subsidy, or suspend or discontinue such payments, if—

(a) he made his approval of the scheme subject to conditions and is satisfied that any of the conditions has not been complied with, or

(b) he is satisfied that a dwelling comprised in the scheme has been converted, demolished or destroyed, is not fit to be used or is not being used for the purpose for which it was intended, has been sold or leased for a term exceeding seven years or has ceased for any reason whatsoever to be vested in the association or trustees for the association.

(2) If any of the dwellings comprised in the scheme become vested in, or are leased for a term exceeding seven years to—

(a) a housing association, or trustees for a housing association other than the association which received approval for the scheme, or

(b) the Housing Corporation,

the Secretary of State may, for any year beginning with that in which they come to be so vested or are so leased, pay them the whole or any part of the subsidy which he would otherwise have paid to the association which received approval for the scheme.

(3) For the purposes of this paragraph a dwelling shall be treated as leased for a term exceeding seven years if it is leased for a lesser term by a lease which confers on the lessee an option for renewal for a term which, together with the original term, exceeds seven years.

3(1) Where a housing association satisfies the Secretary of State, by furnishing him with such information as to its financial position as he may require, that the amount of new building subsidy for a year will be, or was, inadequate having regard to its normal sources of income to enable it to meet such expenditure (including loan charges) as in his opinion it would be, or was, reasonable for it to incur for that year in the exercise of its housing functions, he may direct that for that year the percentage of the initial deficit to be met by subsidy shall be greater than that otherwise applicable.

(2) The percentage shall not, however, be greater than 90 per cent. or the percentage met by subsidy for the immediately preceding year, whichever is less.

(3) This paragraph does not apply in relation to the year of completion or the second or third year for which new building subsidy is payable.

(4) In this paragraph—

"housing functions" means constructing, improving or managing, or facilitating or encouraging the construction or improvement of dwellings, the provision of dwellings by conversion and the acquisition of dwellings, and includes functions which are supplementary or incidental to any of those functions;

"loan charges" includes any loan charges made by a housing association (including charges for debt management) whether in respect of borrowing from a capital fund kept by the association or in respect of borrowing between accounts kept by the association for different functions or otherwise.

4(1) Where before 1st April 1976 a registered housing association made an application for housing association grant in respect of a housing project which was or included a building scheme or improvement scheme which had been previously approved for the purposes of any of the provisions mentioned in paragraph 1 and the Secretary of State gave his approval to that project for the purposes of housing association grant, no further payments of new building subsidy or improvement subsidy shall be made in respect of that approved scheme.

(2) A condition imposed by the Secretary of State in such a case by virtue of section 35(2)(b) of the Housing Act 1974, requiring the repayment of all or any of the payments of new building subsidy or improvement subsidy already paid, if in force immediately before the commencement of this Act, remains in force under this sub-paragraph.

(3) No account shall be taken under section 47(2)(b) (estimation of net cost of project for purposes of housing association grant: income to include subsidies) of payments of subsidy received which are required to be repaid in pursuance of such a condition.

PART VII PAYMENTS IN RESPECT OF HOSTELS UNDER PRE-1974 ENACTMENTS

(s. 21 of the Housing (Financial Provisions) (Scotland) Act 1968)

1(1) Section 21 of the Housing (Financial Provisions) (Scotland) Act 1968 (exchequer contributions for hostels) continues to have effect in relation to buildings provided or converted by a housing association which were approved by the Secretary of State for the purposes of subsection (1) of that section before 1st April 1975.

(2) A registered housing association may not make an application for housing association grant in respect of a housing project which consists of or includes the carrying out of works for the provision of hostels if before 1st April 1975 any contribution has been made under section 21 of the Housing (Financial Provisions) (Scotland) Act 1968.

(3) If in a case where sub-paragraph (2) does not prevent the making of such an application a registered housing association makes an application for housing association grant in respect of a housing project falling within that sub-paragraph and the Secretary of State gives his approval to the project for the purposes of housing association grant, section 21 of the Housing (Financial Provisions) (Scotland) Act 1968 shall cease to have effect with respect to the provision of hostels referred to in that sub-paragraph.

Status of Corporation

1(1) The Housing Corporation is a body corporate.

(2) It is a public body for the purposes of the Prevention of Corruption Acts 1889 to 1916.

(3) It shall not be regarded—

(a) as the servant or agent of the Crown, or

(b) as enjoying any status, immunity or privilege of the Crown, or

(c) as exempt from any tax, duty, rate, levy or other charge whatsoever, whether general or local;

and its property shall not be regarded as property of, or held on behalf of, the Crown.

Membership of Corporation

2(1) The members of the Housing Corporation, of whom there shall be not more than fifteen, shall be appointed by the Secretary of State.

(2) Before appointing a person to be a member of the Corporation the Secretary of State shall satisfy himself that he will have no financial or other interest likely to affect prejudicially the exercise of his functions as member; and the Secretary of State may require a person whom he proposes to appoint to give him such information as he considers necessary for that purpose.

3(1) The members of the Housing Corporation shall hold and vacate office in accordance with the terms of their appointment, subject to the following provisions.

(2) A member may resign his membership by notice in writing addressed to the Secretary of State.

(3) The Secretary of State may remove a member from office if he is satisfied that—

(a) he has been adjudged bankrupt or made an arrangement with his creditors or (in Scotland) has had his estate sequestrated or has made a trust deed for behoof of his creditors or a composition contract,.

(b). . . . .[469]

(c) he has been absent from meetings of the Corporation for a period longer than three consecutive months without the permission of the Corporation, or

(d) he is otherwise unable or unfit to discharge the functions of a member, or is unsuitable to continue as a member.

(4) The Secretary of State shall satisfy himself from time to time with respect to every member that he has no financial or other interest likely to affect prejudicially the exercise of his functions as a member; and he may require a member to give him such information as he considers necessary for that purpose.

Chairman and Deputy Chairman

4(1) The Secretary of State shall appoint one of the members to be Chairman and one to be Deputy Chairman; and the members so appointed shall hold and vacate those offices in accordance with the terms of their appointment, subject to the following provisions.

(2) The Chairman or Deputy Chairman may resign his office by notice in writing addressed to the Secretary of State.

(3) If the Chairman or Deputy Chairman ceases to be a member of the Corporation, he also ceases to be Chairman or Deputy Chairman.

Remuneration and allowances

5(1) The Secretary of State may pay the Chairman, Deputy Chairman and members such remuneration as he may, [with the consent of the Treasury][470], determine.

(2) The Housing Corporation may pay them such reasonable allowances as may be so determined in respect of expenses properly incurred by them in the performance of their duties.

Pensions

6(1) The Secretary of State may, [with the consent of the Treasury][471], determine to pay in respect of a person's office as Chairman, Deputy Chairman or member—

(a) such pension, allowance or gratuity to or in respect of that person on his retirement or death as may be so determined, or

(b) such contributions or other payments towards provision for such pension, allowance or gratuity as may be so determined.

(2) As soon as may be after the making of such a determination the Secretary of State shall lay before each House of Parliament a statement of the amount payable in pursuance of the determination.

(3) Sub-paragraph (1) does not apply in the case of a member who has been admitted in pursuance of regulations under section 7 of the Superannuation Act 1972 to participate in the benefits of a superannuation fund maintained by a local authority.

(4) In such a case the Secretary of State shall make any payments required to be made to the fund in respect of the member by the employing authority and may make such deductions from his remuneration as the employing authority might make in respect of his contributions to the fund.

Proceedings of the Corporation

7(1) The quorum of the Housing Corporation and the arrangements relating to its meetings shall, subject to any directions given by the Secretary of State, be such as the Corporation may determine.

(2) The validity of proceedings of the Corporation is not affected by any defect in the appointment of any of its members.

8(1) Where a member of the Housing Corporation is in any way directly or indirectly interested in a contract made or proposed to be made by the Corporation—

(a) he shall disclose the nature of his interest at a meeting of the Corporation, and the disclosure shall be recorded in the minutes of the Corporation, and

(b) he shall not take any part in any decision of the Corporation with respect to the contract.

(2) A general notice given by a member at a meeting of the Corporation to the effect that he is a member of a specified company or firm and is to be regarded as interested in any contract which may be made with the company or firm is a sufficient disclosure of his interest for the purposes of this paragraph in relation to a contract made after the date of the notice.

(3) A member need not attend in person at a meeting of the Corporation in order to make any disclosure which he is required to make under this paragraph provided he takes reasonable steps to secure that the disclosure is brought up and read at the meeting.

9(1) The fixing of the Housing Corporation's seal may be authenticated by the signature of the Chairman or of any other person authorised for the purpose.

(2) A document purporting to be duly executed under the seal of the Corporation shall be received in evidence and be deemed to be so executed unless the contrary is proved.

Section 82

SCHEDULE 7 POWERS EXERCISABLE WHERE LOAN OUTSTANDING UNDER SECTION 2 OF THE HOUSING ACT 1964

Introductory

1 This Schedule applies where the Housing Corporation has made a loan to a housing association under section 2 of the Housing Act 1964 before the repeal of that section by the Housing (Consequential Provisions) Act 1985 and the loan has not been repaid.

Directions as to disposal of land securing loan

2(1) The [Relevant Authority][472] may . . .[473] give the association directions with respect to the disposal of land belonging to the association in which the [Relevant Authority] has an interest as mortgagee under a mortgage, or as creditor in a heritable security, entered into by the association to secure the loan.

(2) Directions so given may be varied or revoked by subsequent directions . . .[474]

[(3) The written consent of the Secretary of State is required for the giving, varying or revoking of directions by the Housing Corporation.][475]

3 Where the [Housing Corporation][476] proposes to give a housing association directions under paragraph 2 requiring the association to transfer to the [Housing Corporation][477] the association's interest in any land, the Secretary of State shall not consent to the giving of the directions unless he at the same time approves, or has previously approved, a scheme under paragraph 5 with respect to that land [; and the Secretary of State shall not give a housing association directions under paragraph 2 unless he at the same time makes, or has previously made, such a scheme][478].

4 [(1)][479,480] Where the [Housing Corporation][481] proposes to give directions under paragraph 2 to an association whose rules restrict membership to persons entitled or prospectively entitled (whether as tenants or otherwise) to occupy a dwelling provided or managed by the association requiring the association to transfer its interest in any such land to the [Housing Corporation][482], or to any other person, the Secretary of State shall not consent to the giving of the directions unless he is satisfied that arrangements have been made which, if the directions are given, will secure that the members of the association receive fair treatment in connection with the transfer.

[(2) The Secretary of State shall not give to such an association directions under paragraph 2 requiring

the association to transfer any land to the Secretary of State, or to any other person, unless he is so satisfied.][483]

Schemes for Corporation to provide housing accommodation in place of association

5(1) If it appears to the [Housing Corporation][484]—

(a) that the association is experiencing difficulty in providing housing accommodation on any land which it has acquired or in managing housing accommodation provided by it on any land, or is in any way failing to perform its functions as a housing association in relation to any land, and that accordingly it is undesirable for the land in question to remain in the hands of the association,

(b) that there is no other housing association, whether in existence or about to be formed, to which the association's interest in the land in question can suitably be transferred, and

(c) that the land is capable of being, or continuing to be, used to provide housing accommodation for letting,

the [Housing Corporation][485] may prepare and submit to the Secretary of State a scheme.

[(1A) If it so appears to the Secretary of State, he may make a scheme.][486]

(2) The scheme shall be for the Corporation—

(a) to acquire the association's interest in the land,

(b) to undertake all such operations as may be required for the provision or continued provision on the land of housing accommodation for letting (including any operation which might have been carried out by a housing association in connection with the provision of housing accommodation), and

(c) to retain the accommodation and keep it available for letting so long as the scheme has not been terminated in any manner provided for in the scheme.

(3) Where such a scheme is submitted to the Secretary of State by the [Housing Corporation][487], the Secretary of State, on being satisfied of—

(a) the undesirability of the land remaining in the hands of the association, and

(b) the lack of any housing association to which it can suitably be transferred,

may, if he thinks fit, approve the scheme.

(4) If he does so the [Housing Corporation][488] shall have power to acquire for the purposes of the scheme the association's interest in the land and to carry through the provisions of the scheme.

(5) A scheme approved by the Secretary of State under this paragraph may be varied from time to time in accordance with proposals in that behalf made by the [Housing Corporation][489] and approved by the Secretary of State.

[(6) Where the Secretary of State makes the scheme, he shall have power to acquire for the purposes of the scheme the association's interest in the land and to carry through the provisions of the scheme.][490]

TABLE OF DERIVATIONS

1. The following abbreviations are used in this Table:—

Acts of Parliament

1957	=	The Housing Act 1957 (c.56).
1958 (c.42)	=	The Housing (Financial Provisions) Act 1958.
1959 (c.53)	=	The Town and Country Planning Act 1959.
1959 (c.70)	=	The Town and Country Planning (Scotland) Act 1959.
1960 (c.58)	=	The Charities Act 1960.
1961	=	The Housing Act 1961 (c.65).
1963 (c.33)	=	The London Government Act 1963.
1964	=	The Housing Act 1964 (c. 56).
1965 (c.12)	=	The Industrial and Provident Societies Act 1965.
1965 (c.25)	=	The Finance Act 1965.
1966 (S.)	=	The Housing (Scotland) Act 1966 (c.49).
1968 (c.13)	=	The National Loans Act 1968.
1968 (S.)	=	The Housing (Financial Provisions) (Scotland) Act 1968 (c.31).
1969	=	The Housing Act 1969 (c.33).
1970 (c.10)	=	The Income and Corporation Taxes Act 1970.

1970 (c.35)	=	The Conveyancing and Feudal Reform (Scotland) Act 1970.
1972 (S.)	=	The Housing (Financial Provisions) (Scotland) Act 1972 (c. 46).
1972	=	The Housing Finance Act 1972 (c.47).
1972 (c.70)	=	The Local Government Act 1972.
1973 (c.65)	=	The Local Government (Scotland) Act 1973.
1974	=	The Housing Act 1974 (c.44).
1975	=	The Housing Rents and Subsidies Act 1975 (c.6).
1975 (c.28)	=	The Housing Rents and Subsidies (Scotland) Act 1975.
1975 (c.55)	=	The Statutory Corporations (Financial Provisions) Act 1975.
1976 (c.75)	=	The Development of Rural Wales Act 1976.
1977 (c.42)	=	The Rent Act 1977.
1978	=	The Home Purchase Assistance and Housing Guarantee Act 1978 (c. 27).
1980 (c.43)	=	The Magistrates' Courts Act 1980.
1980	=	The Housing Act 1980 (c.51).
1980 (S.)	=	The Tenants Rights etc. (Scotland) Act 1980 (c.52)
1981 (c.64)	=	The New Towns Act 1981.
1981 (c.67)	=	The Acquisition of Land Act 1981.
1982 (c.48)	=	The Criminal Justice Act 1982.
1983 (c.29)	=	The Miscellaneous Financial Provisions Act 1983.
1984	=	The Housing and Building Control Act 1984 (c.29).
1985 (c.9)	=	The Companies Consolidation (Consequential Provisions) Act 1985.
1985 (c.51)	=	The Local Government Act 1985.

Subordinate legislation

S.I. 1972/1204	=	The Isles of Scilly (Housing) Order 1972.
S.I. 1973/886	=	The Isles of Scilly (Housing) (No. 2) Order 1973.
S.I. 1975/374	=	The Housing Act 1974 (Commencement No. 4) Order 1975.
S.I. 1975/512	=	The Isles of Scilly (Housing) Order 1975.
S.I. 1983/664	=	The Housing Corporation Advances (Increase of Limit) Order 1983.
S.I. 1984/1803	=	The Housing Association Grant (Disposal of Dwellings) Order 1984.

2. The Table does not show the effect of Transfer of Functions Orders.

3. The letter R followed by a number indicates that the provision gives effect to the Recommendation bearing that number in the Law Commission's Report on the Consolidation of the Housing Acts (Cmnd. 9515).

4. A reference followed by "passim" indicates that the provision of the consolidation derives from passages within those referred to which it is not convenient, and does not appear necessary, to itemise.

5. The entry "drafting" indicates a provision of a mechanical or editorial nature affecting the arrangement of the consolidation; for instance, a provision introducing a Schedule or introducing a definition to avoid undue repetition of the defining words.

Provision	Derivation
1(1)	1957 s. 189(1); 1964 s. 12(1); 1966 (S.) s.208(1); 1974 s. 129(1), (2), Sch. 13 para. 6.
(2)	drafting.
(3)	1974 s. 12.
2	1977 s. 2(6A); 1977 (c.42) s. 15(5); 1980 ss. 74(2), 123(7).
3	1974 s. 13(1), (7).
4(1)	1974 s. 13(1).
(2)	1974 s. 13(2).
(3)	1974 s. 13(3); 1980 s. 127(1)-(3); 1984 s. 35(4); Sch. 11 para. 27.
5(1)	1974 s. 13(1), (4), (5).
(2)	1974 s. 13(4).
(3)	1974 s. 16(1), (2).
(4)	1974 s. 13(6).
6(1)	1974 s. 15(1).

(2), (3)	1974 s. 15(2).
(4)	1974 s. 15(2A); 1980 s. 128(1)(a), (2).
(5)	1974 s. 16(1), (2).
7(1)	1974 s. 15(3).
(2)	1974 s. 15(4).
(3)	1974 s. 16(3).
8(1)-(3)	1980 s. 122(1)-(3).
9(1)	1974 s. 2(1), (6).
(2)	1974 s. 2(1A), (1B); 1980 s. 123(2).
(3)	1974 s. 2(5A); 1980 s. 123(6), 137(1).
(4)	1974 s. 15(6); 1980 s. 128.
(5)	1974 s. 2(1).
10(1)	1974 s. 2(2), (3); 1980 s. 123(3).
(2)	1974 s. 2(3A); 1980 s. 123(4).
(3)	1974 s. 2(4); 1980 s. 123(5).
(4)	1974 s. 2(3).
11	drafting.
12	1980 s. 137(1), (2); 1984 Sch. 11 para. 28.
13(1)	1974 s. 26(1).
(2)	1974 s. 26(2); 1980 Sch. 25 para. 25.
(3)	1974 s. 26(5); 1980 Sch. 11 Part II.
14(1)	1974 s. 26(3), (4), (6); 1980 Sch. 16 Part II.
(2)	1974 s. 26(5), 1980 Sch. 16 Part II.
15(1)	1974 s. 27(1)-(3); 1980 Sch. 16 Part II.
(2)	1974 s. 27(5)-(7); 1980 Sch. 16 Part II.
(3)	1974 s. 27(4); 1980 Sch. 16 Part II.
16(1)	1974 s. 20(2); 1970 (c.35) Sch. 3 para. 9(2); R.32.
(2), (3)	1974 s. 20(6).
(4)	1974 s. 20(6).
17(1), (2)	1974 s. 20(3).
(3)	1974 s. 20(4).
(4)	1980 Sch. 17 para. 8.
18(1)	1980 Sch. 17 paras. 4, 5.
(2)	1980 Sch. 17 para. 6(b).
(3)	1980 Sch. 17 para. 7.
19(1)	1974 s. 24(1).
(2)-(4)	1965 (c.12) s. 10; 1974 s. 24(5A); 1980 s. 132.
20(1)	1974 s. 25(1).
(2)	1960 (c.58) s. 46; 1974 s. 25(1)-(3).
21(1)-(6)	1974 s. 24(1)-(5), (6).
22(1), (2)	1974 s. 22(1), (2).
23(1)	1974 s. 23(1).
(2)	1974 s. 23(2).
(3)	1974 s. 23(3).
(4)	1974 s. 23(4).
(5)	1974 s. 23(3).
24(1)	1980 s. 124(1).
(2)	1980 s. 124(6).
(3)	1980 s. 124(2).
(4)	1980 s. 124(3).
(5)	1980 s. 124(7), 151(1), (3).
25	1980 s. 124(4).
26	1980 s. 124(5).
27(1)	1980 s. 125(1).

(2)	1980 s. 125(2); 1982 (c. 48) ss. 37(1), 46(2).
(3)	1980 s. 125(3).
(4)	1980 s. 125(4).
28(1)	1974 s. 19(1), (1A); 1980 Sch. 17 para. 1.
(2)	1974 s. 19(2); 1980 Sch. 17 paras. 2, 6(b).
(3)	1974 s. 19(3); 1975 (c. 21) ss. 289F, 289G; 1982 (c. 48) ss. 37, 46(1), 54.
(4)	1974 s. 19(5).
(5)	1974 s. 19(8); 1980 Sch. 17 para. 2.
(6)	1980 s. 155(2).
29(1)	1974 s. 19(4).
(2)	1974 s. 19(4); 1980 Sch. 17 para. 6(e).
(3)	1974 s. 19(5).
(4)	1974 s. 19(6).
(5)	1974 s. 19(7).
30(1)	1974 s. 20(1); 1980 Sch. 17 paras. 3(a), 6(b).
(2), (3)	1974 s. 20(6).
(4)	1974 s. 20(5); 1980 Sch. 17 para. 3(c).
(5)	1974 s. 20(1A); 1980 Sch. 17 para. 3(b).
(6)	1974 s. 20(7); 1975 (c. 21) ss. 289F, 289G; 1980 Sch. 17 para. 9; 1982 (c. 48) ss. 37, 46(1), 54.
31(1)	1974 ss. 19, 20passim; 1980 Sch. 17 paras. 4, 5, 6(a).
(2)	1980 Sch. 17 para. 7.
(3)	1980 Sch. 17 para. 6(c)(d).
32(1)	1974 s. 21(1).
(2)	1974 s. 21(2)(a).
(3)	1974 s. 21(2)(b).
(4)	1974 s. 21(3).
(5)	1974 s. 21(4).
33(1)	1957 s. 124; 1966 (S.) s. 158(1).
(2)	1957 s. 124; 1966 (S.) s. 158(2).
34(1), (2)	1957 s. 119(2).
35(1)	1957 s. 128(1); R.4(ii).
(2)	drafting.
36(1)	1957 s. 128(2); R.4(ii).
(2)	1957 s. 128(3); R.4(ii).
37	"appropriate registrar" 1974 s. 28; "committee" 1965 s. 74, 1974 s. 28; "co-opted member" 1974 s. 26(6), 1980 Sch. 16 Part II; drafting.
38	1974 ss. 28, 129(1); 1980 s. 133(1).
39	"mental disorder" 1974 s. 20(2)(a); "secure tenancy" 1974 s. 2(6A), 1980 s. 123(7).
40	drafting.
41(1)	1974 ss. 29(1), 29A(2); 1975 s. 6; 1975 (S.) s. 12; 1980 Sch. 18 para. 3.
(2)	1974 s. 29A(1); 1980 Sch. 18 Para. 3.
42(1)	1974 s. 29(2).
(2), (3)	1974 s. 29(2), (2A); 1980 Sch. 18 para. 1.
43	1980 s. 130(1).
44(1)	1984 s. 33(1).
(2)	1984 s. 33(2).
(3)	drafting.
45(1), (2)	1984 s. 35(1).
(3)	1984 s. 35(2).
(4)	1984 s. 35(3).
46	1974 s. 29(3).
47(1)	1974 s. 29(4).
(2), (3)	1974 s. 29(6).
(4)	1974 s. 29(8).

(5)	1974 s. 29(6A); 1980 Sch. 18 para. 2.
(6)	1974 s. 29(7).
48(1)	1974 s. 29(5).
(2)	1974 s. 29(8).
(3)	1980 s. 130(2); S.I. 1984/1803.
(4)	1980 s. 151(1), (3).
49(1)-(4)	1974 s. 30(1); 1980 Sch. 18 para. 4.
(5)	1974 s. 30(8).
(6)	1974 s. 15(5).
50(1), (2)	1974 s. 30(2), (2A); 1980 Sch. 18 para. 5.
51(1), (2)	1974 s. 30(4), (6).
52(1)	1974 s. 30(3); 1980 Sch. 18 para. 6; 1984 s. 34(1).
(2)	1974 s. 30(3); 1980 Sch. 18 para. 6.
(3)	1984 s. 34(2).
(4)	1984 s. 34(3).
53(1)	1980 s. 131(1).
(2)	1980 s. 131(2).
(3)	1980 s. 131(3).
(4)	1980 s. 131(3), (4).
(5)	1980 s. 131(4).
(6)	1980 s. 131(5).
(7)	1980 s. 131(6).
54(1)	1974 s. 32(1); 1975 s. 6; 1975 (S.) s. 12; 1980 Sch. 18 para. 9(a).
(2), (3)	1974 s. 32(3); 1980 Sch. 18 para. 9(c).
(4)	1976 s. 32(5); 1980 Sch. 18 para. 9(e).
(5)	1974 s. 32(3); 1980 s. 133(2), Sch. 18 para. 9(c).
55(1)	1974 s. 33(1); 1980 Sch. 18 para. 10(a).
(2)-(4)	1974 s. 33(3); 1980 Sch. 18 para. 10(c).
(5)	1974 s. 33(4); 1980 Sch. 18 para. 10(d).
(6)	1974 s. 33(5); 1980 Sch. 18 para. 10(e).
56(1)	1974 ss. 32(2), 33(2); 1980 Sch. 18 paras. 9(b)(i), 10(b).
(2)	1974 ss. 32(2)(a), (b), 33(2), (7); 1980 Sch. 18 paras. 9(b)(ii), 10(b).
(3)	1974 s. 32(2)(c); 1980 Sch. 18 para. 9(b)(iii).
57(1)-(3)	1974 ss. 32(6), 33(6); 1980 Sch. 18 paras. 9(f), 10(f).
(4)	1974 s. 15(5).
58(1)	1957 s. 119(1).
(2)	1957 s. 119(3).
(3)	1972 s. 78(1), (2)(a), (4).
59(1)	1966 (S.) s. 152(1), (3); 1973 (c.65) Sch. 12 para. 10.
(2)	1966 (S.) s. 152(2), (3); 1973 (c.65) Sch. 12 para. 10.
(3)	1972 (S.) s. 58(1), (2)(b), (3).
(4)	1966 (S.) ss. 152(2), 198.
60(1)	1974 s. 17(1)(b).
(2)	1974 s. 17(3), (5); 1975 Sch. 5 para. 13; 1975 (S.) Sch. 3 para. 13.
(3)	1974 s. 17(4).
61(1)	1957 s. 122; 1966 (S.) s. 156(1).
(2)	1957 s. 122; 1966 (S.) s. 156(2); R.33.
62(1)	1965 (c.25) s. 93(1).
(2)	1965 (c.25) s. 93(6); 1970 (c.10) Sch. 15 para. 11 Table Pt. II; 1974 s. 17(2), (3).
(3)	1965 (c.25) s. 93(4).
62(4)	1965 (c.25) s. 93(1), (2).
(5)	1965 (c.25) s. 93(2).
(6), (7)	1965 (c.25) s. 93(3).
63(1)	1964 s. 8(1); 1974 Sch. 13 para. 10(2).

(2)	1964 s. 8(2); 1974 Sch. 13 para. 10(2).
(3)	1964 s. 8(10); 1974 Sch. 13 para. 10(2).
(4)	1964 s. 8(3).
(5)	1964 s. 8(4).
(6)	1964 s. 8(3), (10).
64	1964 s. 8(8); 1975 (c.21) s. 298(1); 1977 Sch. 11; 1980 (c.44) s. 32(2); 1982 (c.48) s. 74(1).
65	1964 s. 8(5); 1974 Sch. 13 para. 10(2).
66(1)(a), (b)	1964 s. 8(12).
(c)	1964 s. 107.
(d)	drafting
(2)	1964 s. 107.
67(1)	1958 s. 47(1), (2)(b).
(2)	1958 s. 47(3), (5)(c), (6).
(3)	1958 s. 47(5)(c).
(4)	1958 s. 47(6) proviso (b).
(5)	1958 s. 47(5) (a), (b) proviso.
68(1)	1968 (S.) s. 24(1).
(2)	1968 (S.) s. 24(2), (4)(c), (5).
(3)	1968 (S.) s. 24(4)(c).
(4)	1968 (S.) s. 24(5) proviso (b).
(5), (6)	1968 (S.) s. 24(4)(a), (b) proviso.
69(1)	1972 (S.) ss. 58(2), 59(1); 1972 ss. 78(2), 79(1).
(2)	1972 (S.) ss. 58(5), 59(2); 1972 ss. 78(6), 79(2).
(3)	1972 ss. 78(1), 79(2).
(4)	1972 (S.) ss. 58(1), (5), 59(2).
70	drafting.
71	drafting.
72	"building society" 1964 s. 8(11); "Chief Registrar" 1964 s. 8(11); "officer" 1964 s. 8(11); "registered charity" drafting see 1974 s. 32(3)(1).
73	drafting.
74(1), (2)	drafting.
75(1)	1974 s. 1(2).
(2)	1974 s. 1(3).
(3)	1974 s. 1(2).
(4)	1964 Sch. 1 para. 5; 1974 Sch. 1 para. 3.
76(1)	1964 s. 1(2); R.34(i).
(2)	1974 s. 9(3).
(3)	1964 s. 1(2).
(4)	1959 (c.53) s. 29; 1959 (c.70) s. 29; 1964 s. 1(4), (9).
77	1964 s. 7; R.35.
78	1964 s. 10(6).
79(1)	1974 s. 9(1).
(2)	1974 s. 9(2).
(3)	1974 s. 9(1), (2), (4).
(4)	1974 s. 9(3).
80(1)-(3)	1974 s. 9(5).
(4)	1974 s. 9(6).
81	1984 s. 24(1).
82	drafting.
83(1), (2)	1974 s. 10(1).
(3), (4)	1974 s. 10(2); 1978 s. 5(1), (2).
84(1)	1980 s. 111(1); 1984 s. 20(1).
(2)	1980 s. 111(3); 1984 s. 20(2).
(3)	1980 s. 111(4); 1984 s. 20(3).

(4)	1980 s. 111(1), (5); 1984 s. 20(4)(a).
(5)	1980 s. 111(5), (6); 1984 s. 20(4)(b).
(6)	1980 s. 111(8); 1984 s. 20(7).
85(1)	drafting.
(2)	1984 s. 20(5); "recognised body".
(3)	1984 s. 20(6).
(4)	1984 ss. 18(3), (4), 20(5) "relevant advance".
(5)	1984 s. 18(4) "long lease".
86	1980 (S.) s. 31.
87(1)-(3)	1980 s. 121(2).
(4)	1980 s. 121(3).
88(1)	1974 ss. 1(2)(d), 3(1), (3).
(2)	1974 s. 3(6).
(3)	1974 s. 3(4); 1981 Sch. 4 para. 1.
(4)	1974 s. 3(2).
(5)	1974 s. 3(5).
89	1974 s. 4.
90(1)	1974 s. 5(2).
(2)	1974 s. 5(3); 1976 (c. 75) Sch. 7 para. 12; 1981 (c. 64) Sch. 12 para. 13(a).
(3)	1974 s. 5(3A); 1980 Sch. 25 para. 24.
(4)	1974 s. 5(4).
(5)	1974 s. 5(5)-(7).
(6)	1974 s. 5(1).
91	1959 (c.53) s. 29(1); 1959 (c.70) s. 29(1); 1964 s. 1(4), (9).
92(1)	1974 s. 7(2).
(2)	1974 s. 7(3).
(3)	1974 s. 7(4); 1975 (c.55) Sch. 4 para. 8.
(4)	1974 s. 7(6).
92(5)	1974 s. 7(8).
(6)	1974 s. 7(7).
93(1)	1974 s. 7(1).
(2)	1974 s. 7(5); 1975 Sch. 5 para. 12; S.I. 1975/374; 1980 s. 120(1); S.I. 1983/664.
(3)	1974 ss. 7(5), 128(1).
(4)	1980 s. 120(2).
(5)	1974 s. 7(9).
94(1)	1974 s. 8(1); 1983 (c.29) s. 4.
(2)	1974 s. 8(2).
(3)	1974 s. 8(3).
(4)	1974 s. 8(4).
(5)	1974 s. 8(5).
(6)	1974 s. 8(2).
95	1980 s. 121(1).
96(1)	1974 s. 10(3).
(2)	1974 s. 10(4).
(3)	1974 s. 10(5).
(4)	1974 s. 10(6).
(5)	1974 s. 10(4), (5), (6).
97(1)	1964 s. 10(1).
(2)	1964 s. 10(2).
(3)	1964 s. 10(3).
(4)	1964 s. 10(4), (5); 1968 (c.13) Sch. 1; 1974 Sch. 13 para. 10(3).
(5)	1964 s. 10(5); 1985 (c.9) Sch. 2.
(6)	1964 s. 10(7).
98(1)	1974 s. 6(1).

(2)	1974 s. 6(3).
99	1974 s. 6(2).
100	1964 s. 11; 1974 Sch. 13 para. 10(4).
101	"building society" 1980 s. 111(7); "financial year" 1964 s. 10(7); 1978 (c.30) Sch. 1; "highway" 1974 s. 12; "subsidiary" 1974 s. 12; 1985 (c.9) Sch. 2.
102	drafting.
103	1972 s. 103; 1975 Sch. 5 para. 7(1); S.I. 1972/1204; S.I. 1975/512; R.29.
104(1)	1963 (c.33) s. 21(1), (2); 1972 (c.70) s. 193(1); 1966 (S.) s. 1; 1973 (c.65) s. 130(3), Sch. 12 para. 6; S.I. 1972/1204; S.I. 1973/886; S.I. 1975/512.
(2)	drafting.
105	1957 s. 104B(4B)(c); 1984 Sch. 6 para. 1(2).
106(1), (2).	"bank" 1957 s. 104B(6), 1978 Sch. para. 7, 1984 Sch. 6 para. 1(5); "building society"passim; "dwelling" 1966 (S.) s. 208(1), 1972 s. 104(1), 1974 s. 129(1)(2); "friendly society"passim; "hostel" 1974 s. 129(1)(2), 1966 (S.) s. 208(1); "house" 1957 s. 189(1); 1966 (S.) s. 208(1), 1980 s. 130(3); "housing activities" 1980 s. 133(2), Sch. 18 para. 9, 1984 Sch. 6 para. 1(5); "insurance company" 1957 s. 104B(6), 1978 Sch. para. 8, 1984 Sch. 6 para. 1(5); "local authority" 1957 s. 1, 1974 ss. 5, 129, 1980 s. 111, 1980 (c.52) s. 31, 1984 ss. 18(3), 20(5); 1985 (c.51) Sch. 14 para. 64(a), (b); "new town corporation" 1972 (S.) s. 78(1), 1974 s. 5(3)(c)(d), 1981 (c.64) Sch. 12 para. 13(a); "shared ownership lease" drafting; "trustee savings bank" 1957 s. 104B(6), 1978 Sch. para. 6, 1984 Sch. para. 1(5); "urban development corporation" 1984 s. 18(3).
107	drafting.
Schedules	
Sch. 1	
para. 1	1974 Sch. 2 para. 1.
para. 2	1974 Sch. 2 para. 2.
para. 3	1974 Sch. 2 para. 3.
Sch. 2	1980 s. 122(4), (5), (6).
para. 1(1)	1957 s. 104B(1); 1980 s. 92.
(2)	1957 s. 104B(2), (3); 1980 s. 92; 1984 Sch. 6 para. 1(1).
para. 2(1)	1957 s. 104B(5); 1980 s. 92; 1984 Sch. 6 para. 1(3).
(2)	1957 s. 104B(5A); 1984 Sch. 6 para. 1(4).
(3)	1957 s. 104B(7); 1980 s. 92.
(4)	1957 s. 104B(6); 1978 Sch. paras. 6-9; 1984 Sch. 6 para. 1(5).
para. 3(1)	1957 s. 104C(1), (9); 1980 s. 92; 1984 Sch. 6 para. 2(1), (5).
(2)	1957 s. 104C(2); 1980 s. 92; 1984 Sch. 6 para. 2(2).
(3)	1957 s. 104C(3); 1980 s. 92.
(4)	1957 s. 104C(5); 1980 s. 92.
(5)	1957 s. 104C(6); 1980 s. 92.
(6)	1957 s. 104C(8); 1980 s. 92.
para. 4	1957 s. 104B(4), 104C(7A); 1984 Sch. 6 para. 1(2), 2(4).
para. 5(1)	1957 s. 104B(4A); 1984 Sch. 6 para. 1(2).
(2)	1957 s. 104B(4B), (8); 1984 Sch. 6 para. 1(2).
para. 6	1957 s. 104B(4A)(d); 1984 Sch. 6 para. 1(2); drafting.
para. 7	1957 ss. 104B(4C), 104C(7); 1984 Sch. 6 paras. 1(2), 2(4).
para. 8(1)	1957 ss. 104B(9), 104C(10); 1980 s. 92; 1984 Sch. 6 para. 1(6), 2(6).
(2)	1957 s. 104C(10); 1980 s. 92.
Sch. 3	
para. 1(1), (2)	1980 Sch. 16 Part I para. 1(1), (2).
para. 2(1), (2)	1980 Sch. 16 Part I para. 2(1), (2).
para. 3(1)-(4)	1980 Sch. 16 Part I para. 3(1)-(4).
para. 4(1), (2)	1980 Sch. 16 Part I para. 4(1), (2).
para. 5	1980 Sch. 16 Part I para. 5(1), (2).
para. 6	1980 Sch. 16 Part I para. 5(3), (4).

para. 7	1980 Sch. 16 Part I para. 6.
Sch. 4	
Pt. I	
para. 1	1972 s. 78(2), (3), (5).
para. 2	1974 Sch. 13 para. 5.
Pt. II	
para. 1	1972 Sch. 7 Pt. III; 1972 (S.) Sch. 1 Pts. IV, VI.
para. 2	1972 s. 79(1); 1972 (S.) s. 59(1).
Pt. III	*1972 (S.) s. 58(2)(a), (g), (4).*
Sch. 5	
Pt. I	
para. 1	1972 s. 72(1)-(7), (9).
para. 2	1972 s. 73(1)-(7).
para. 3	1972 s. 104(1) "housing association".
para. 4	1972 ss. 74(1), (5), 104(4).
para. 5	1972 ss. 15(1), (2), (5), 71(4).
para. 6	1972 s. 74(2)-(4).
para. 7	drafting.
Pt. II	
para. 1	1972 (S.) s. 52(1)-(6), 8.
para. 2	1972 (S.) s. 53(1)-(3), (8), (9).
para. 3	1972 (S.) s. 78(1) "housing association".
para. 4	1972 (S.) ss. 54(1), 68(1).
para. 5	1972 (S.) ss. 13, 51(4).
para. 6	1972 (S.) s. 54(2)-(4).
para. 7	drafting.
Pt. III	
para. 1(1)	1969 Sch. 9 para. 1; 1974 Sch. 14 para. 6.
(2)	1958 s. 28; 1967 Sch. 3 para. 6; 1969 Sch. 8 para. 17.
(3)	1958 s. 12(1); 1967 s. 12(6); 1969 s. 21(8); Sch. 9 para. 1; 1974 Sch. 14 para. 6.
para. 2	1958 s. 12(2); 1969 Sch. 9 para. 1.
para. 3(1)	1968 (S.) s. 17(3); 1974 Sch. 14 para. 6.
(2)	1968 (S.) s. 57(1).
(3)	1968 (S.) s. 17(2); 1974 Sch. 14 para. 6.
para. 4(1)	1968 (S.) s. 58(1).
(2)	1968 (S.) s. 58(3).
(3)	1968 (S.) s. 58(2).
Pt. IV	
para. 1(1)	1968 (S.) s. 16(2); 1974 Sch. 14 para. 6.
(2)	1968 (S.) s. 58(1).
(3)	1968 (S.) s. 58(3).
Pt. V	
para. 1	1972 s. 78(2)(d), (5).
para. 2	1972 (S.) s. 58(2)(f), (4).
Pt. VI	
para. 1(1)	1974 s. 35(1).
(2)-(4)	1972 ss. 15(1), (2), (5), 71(4); 1972 (S.) ss. 13(1)-(3), 51(4).
para. 2(1)	1972 (S.) ss. 56(2), 57(4); 1972 s. 76(2).
(2)	1972 (S.) ss. 56(3), 57(4); 1972 s. 76(3).
(3)	1972 (S.) ss. 56(4), 57(4); 1972 s. 76(4).
para. 3(1)-(3)	1972 (S.) s. 55(12); 1972 s. 75(12); 1974 Sch. 13 paras. 23(4), 32.
(4)	1972 (S.) s. 57(4); 1972 s. 74(5).
para. 4	1974 s. 35(2).
Pt. VII	

para. 1(1)	1974 s. 35(1).
(2)	1974 s. 35(4).
(3)	1974 s. 35(5).
Sch. 6	
para. 1(1)	1964 Sch. 1 para. 1.
(2)	1964 Sch. 1 para. 6; 1974 Sch. 1 para. 4.
(3)	1964 s. 1(3).
para. 2(1)	1964 Sch. 1 para. 2(1); 1974 Sch. 1 para. 1.
(2)	1964 Sch. 1 para. 2A(1); 1974 Sch. 1 para. 2.
para. 3(1)	1964 Sch. 1 para. 2(2).
(2)	1964 Sch. 1 para. 2(4).
(3)	1964 Sch. 1 para. 2(5).
(4)	1964 Sch. 1 para. 2A(1); 1974 Sch. 1 para. 2.
para. 4(1)	1964 Sch. 1 para. 2(1), (2).
(2)	1964 Sch. 1 para. 2(4).
(3)	1964 Sch. 1 para. 2(3).
para. 5(1), (2)	1964 Sch. 1 para. 2(7).
para. 6(1), (2)	1964 Sch. 1 para. 2(8).
(3), (4)	1964 Sch. 1 para. 2(9); 1972 (c.11) Sch. 6 para. 47.
para. 7(1)	1964 Sch. 1 para. 3(1).
(2)	1964 Sch. 1 para. 3(2).
para. 8(1)	1964 Sch. 1 para. 2A(2); 1974 Sch. 1 para. 2.
(2)	1964 Sch. 1 para. 2A(3); 1974 Sch. 1 para. 2.
(3)	1964 Sch. 1 para. 2A(4); 1974 Sch. 1 para. 2.
para. 9(1)	1964 Sch. 1 para. 4(1); 1980 Sch. 25 para. 13.
(2)	1964 Sch. 1 para. 4(2).
Sch. 7	
para. 1	R.36.
para. 2(1)	1964 s. 2(3); 1972 s. 77(2); 1974 Sch. 14 para. 1; R.36.
(2)	1964 s. 2(3).
para. 3	1964 s. 5(3); R.36.
para. 4	1964 s. 2(4); R.36.
para. 5(1), (2)	1964 s. 5(1); R.36.
(3), (4)	1964 s. 5(2); R.36.
(5)	1964 s. 5(4).

---

[1] Words added by Housing (Scotland) Act 1988 (c. 43, SIF 61), ss. 1, 3(3), Sch. 2 para. 6

[2] Words added by Housing (Scotland) Act 1988 (c. 43, SIF 61), ss. 1, 3(3), Sch. 2 para. 6

[3] Words in s. 1(1) repealed (S.) (1.11.2001) by 2001 asp 10, s. 112, Sch. 10 para. 11(2); S.S.I. 2001/336, art. 2(3) (with transitional provisions and savings in art. 3)

[4] Words in s. 1(2) repealed (1.10.1996) by S.I. 1996/2325, art. 4(1), Sch. 1 Pt. I (with art. 4(2)(3))

[5] s. 2A repealed (1.10.1996) by S.I. 1996/2325, art. 4(1), Sch. 1 Pts. I, II (with art. 4(2)(3))

[6] Words in s. 2B substituted (1.11.2001) by 2001 asp. 10, s. 112, Sch. 10 para. 11(3)(c), S.I. 2001/336, art. 2(2), Sch. Pt. II Table (with transitional provisions and savings in art. 3)

[7] Words in s. 2B repealed (1.11.2001) by 2001 asp. 10, s. 112, Sch. 10 para. 11(3)(b), S.I. 2001/336, art. 2(2), Sch. Pt. II Table (with transitional provisions and savings in art. 3)

[8] Words in s. 2B substituted (1.11.2001) by 2001 asp. 10, s. 112, Sch. 10 para. 11(3)(a), S.I. 2001/336, art. 2(2), Sch. Pt. II Table (with transitional provisions and savings in art. 3)

[9] s. 2B inserted (1.10.1996) by S.I. 1996/2325, art. 5(1), Sch. 2 para. 15(2)

[10] s. 3 repealed (1.10.1996) by 1996 c. 52, s. 227, Sch. 19 Pt. I; S.I. 1996/2402, art. 3 (subject to transitional provisions and savings in Sch.) and (1.11.2001) by 2001 asp 10, s. 112, Sch. 10 para. 11(4);

[11] s. 4 repealed (1.10.1996) by 1996 c. 52, s. 227, Sch. 19 Pt. I; S.I. 1996/2402, art. 3 (subject to transitional provisions and savings in Sch.) and (1.11.2001) by 2001 asp 10, s. 112, Sch. 10 para. 11(4); S.S.I. 2001/336, art. 2(3), Sch. Pt. II Table (subject to transitional provisions and savings in art. 3)

[12] s. 5 repealed (1.10.1996) by 1996 c. 52, s. 227, Sch. 19 Pt. I; S.I. 1996/2402, art. 3 (subject to transitional provisions and savings in Sch.) and (1.11.2001) by 2001 asp 10, s. 112, Sch. 10 para. 11(4); S.S.I. 2001/336, art. 2(3), Sch. Pt. II Table (subject to transitional provisions and savings in art. 3)

[13] s. 6 repealed (1.10.1996) by 1996 c. 52, s. 227, Sch. 19 Pt. I; S.I. 1996/2402, art. 3 (subject to transitional provisions and savings in Sch.) and (1.11.2001) by 2001 asp 10, s. 112, Sch. 10 para. 11(4); S.S.I. 2001/336, art. 2(3), Sch. Pt. II Table (subject to transitional provisions and savings in art. 3)

[14] s. 7 repealed (1.10.1996) by 1996 c. 52, s. 227, Sch. 19 Pt. I; S.I. 1996/2402, art. 3 (subject to transitional provisions and savings in Sch.) and (1.11.2001) by 2001 asp 10, s. 112, Sch. 10 para. 11(4); S.S.I. 2001/336, art. 2(3), Sch. Pt. II Table (subject to transitional provisions and savings in art. 3)

[15] s. 8 repealed (1.10.1996) by 1996 c. 52, s. 227, Sch. 19 Pt. I; S.I. 1996/2402, art. 3 (subject to transitional provisions and savings in Sch.) and (1.11.2001) by 2001 asp 10, s. 112, Sch. 10 para. 11(4); S.S.I. 2001/336, art. 2(3), Sch. Pt. II Table (subject to transitional provisions and savings in art. 3)

[16] Words substituted by Housing Act 1988 (c. 50, SIF 61), s. 59(2)(3)(4), Sch. 6 Pt. I para. 2

[17] s. 9(1) repealed (1.10.1996) by 1996 c. 52, s. 227, Sch. 19 Pt. I; S.I. 1996/2402, art. 3 (with transitional provisions and savings in Sch.)

[18] Words in s. 9(1A)(c) substituted (1.11.1998) by 1998 c. 38, s. 140, Sch. 16 para. 24(2) (with ss. 139(2), 143(2)); S.I. 1998/2244, art. 5

[19] s. 9(1A) substituted for s. 9(1) by Housing Act 1988 (c. 50, SIF 61), s. 59(2)(3)(4), Sch. 6 Pt. I para. 7(1)

[20] Words in s. 9(2) substituted (1.10.1996) by S.I. 1996/2325, art. 15(1), Sch. 2 para. 15(10)

[21] Words substituted by Housing Act 1988 (c. 50, SIF 61), s. 59(2)(3)(4), Sch. 6 Pt. I para. 7(2)(a)(b)

[22] Words substituted by Housing Act 1988 (c. 50, SIF 61), s. 59(2)(3)(4), Sch. 6 Pt. I para. 7(2)(a)(b)

[23] s. 9(4) repealed (1.10.1996) by 1996 c. 52, s. 227, Sch. 19 Pt. I; S.I. 1996/2402, art. 3 (with transitional provisions and savings in Sch.)

[24] Words in s. 9(6)(a) repealed (1.11.1998) by 1998 c. 38, ss. 140, 152, Sch. 16 para. 24(3)(a), Sch. 18 Pt. VI (with ss. 137(1), 139(2), 141(1), 143(2)); S.I. 1998/2244, art. 5

[25] Words in s. 9(6)(b) inserted (1.11.1998) by 1998 c. 38, s. 140, Sch. 16 para. 24(3)(b) (with ss. 139(2), 143(2)); S.I. 1998/2244, art. 5

[26] s. 9(6) added by Housing Act 1988 (c. 50, SIF 61), s. 59(2)(3)(4), Sch. 6 Pt. I para. 7(3)

[27] s. 9 repealed (1.11.2001) by 2001 asp 10, s. 112, Sch. 10 para. 11(4), S.S.I. 2001/336, art. 2, Sch. Pt. II (subject to transitional provisions and savings in art. 3)

[28] Words in s. 10(1) substituted (1.8.1993) by 1993 c. 10, ss. 98(1), 99(1), Sch. 6 para. 21(2).

[29] Words in s. 10(1)(c) substituted (1.11.1998) by 1998 c. 38, s. 140, Sch. 16 para. 25; S.I. 1998/2244, art. 5

[30] Words substituted by Housing Act 1988 (c. 50, SIF 61), s. 59(2)(3)(4), Sch. 6 Pt. I para. 8(1)

[31] Words in s. 10(2) repealed (1.10.1996) by S.I. 1996/2325, art. 4(1), Sch. 1 Pt. I (with art. 4(2)(3))

[32] Words beginning "Schedule 1" substituted (retrospectively1.4.1986) by Housing and Planning Act 1986 (c. 63, SIF 61), s. 24(1), Sch. 5 Pt. I para. 10(6)(9)

[33] "or" and s. 10(2)(c)–(e) inserted by Housing Act 1988 (c. 50, SIF 61), s. 59(2)(3)(4), Sch. 6 Pt. I para. 8(2)

[34] Words "1 to 8 of Schedule 2 to the Housing (Scotland) Act 1987" substituted by Housing (Scotland) Act 1988 (c. 43, SIF 61), s. 72, Sch. 9 para. 6(a) and "paragraphs 1 to 8 of Schedule 2 to the Housing (Scotland) Act 1987" substituted by Housing (Scotland) Act 1987 (c. 26, SIF 61), ss. 335, 339(2), Sch. 23 para. 31(2)

[35] "or" and s. 10(2)(c)–(e) inserted by Housing Act 1988 (c. 50, SIF 61), s. 59(2)(3)(4), Sch. 6 Pt. I para. 8(2)

[36] s. 10 repealed (1.11.2001) by 2001 asp 10, ss. 112, 113, Sch. 10 para. 11(4); S.S.I. 2001/336, art. 2(3), Sch. Pt. II Table (subject to transitional provisions and savings in art. 3)

[37] s. 11 repealed (1.10.1996) by 1996 c. 52, s. 227, Sch. 19 Pt. I; S.I. 1996/2402, art. 3 (subject to transitional provisions and savings in Sch.) and (1.11.2001) by 2001 asp 10, s. 112, Sch. 10 para. 11(4); S.S.I. 2001/336, art. 2(3), Sch. Pt. II Table (subject to transitional provisions and savings in art. 3)

[38] s. 12 repealed (1.11.2001) by 2001 asp 10, s. 112, Sch. 10 para. 11(4); S.S.I. 2001/336, art. 2(3), Sch. Pt. II Table (subject to transitional provisions and savings in art. 3)

[39] s. 13 repealed (1.10.1996) by 1996 c. 52, s. 227, Sch. 19 Pt. I; S.I. 1996/2402, art. 3 (subject to transitional provisions and savings in Sch.) and (1.11.2001) by 2001 asp 10, s. 112, Sch. 10 para. 11(4); S.S.I. 2001/336, art. 2(3), Sch. Pt. II Table (subject to transitional provisions and savings in art. 3)

[40] s. 14 repealed (1.10.1996) by 1996 c. 52, s. 227, Sch. 19 Pt. I; S.I. 1996/2402, art. 3 (subject to transitional provisions and savings in Sch.) and (1.11.2001) by 2001 asp 10, s. 112, Sch. 10 para. 11(4); S.S.I. 2001/336, art. 2(3), Sch. Pt. II Table (subject to transitional provisions and savings in art. 3)

[41] s. 15 repealed (1.10.1996) by 1996 c. 52, s. 227, Sch. 19 Pt. I; S.I. 1996/2402, art. 3 (subject to transitional provisions and savings in Sch.) and (1.11.2001) by 2001 asp 10, s. 112, Sch. 10 para. 11(4); S.S.I. 2001/336, art. 2(3), Sch. Pt. II Table (subject to transitional provisions and savings in art. 3)

[42] s. 15A repealed (1.11.2001) by 2001 asp 10, s. 112, Sch. 10 para. 11(4); S.S.I. 2001/336, art. 2(3), Sch. Pt. II Table (subject to transitional provisions and savings in art. 3)

[43] s. 16 repealed (1.10.1996) by 1996 c. 52, s. 227, Sch. 19 Pt. I; S.I. 1996/2402, art. 3 (subject to transitional provisions and savings in Sch.) and (1.11.2001) by 2001 asp 10, s. 112, Sch. 10 para. 11(4); S.S.I. 2001/336, art. 2(3), Sch. Pt. II Table (subject to transitional provisions and savings in art. 3)

[44] s. 17 repealed (1.10.1996) by 1996 c. 52, s. 227, Sch. 19 Pt. I; S.I. 1996/2402, art. 3 (subject to transitional provisions and savings in Sch.) and (1.11.2001) by 2001 asp 10, s. 112, Sch. 10 para. 11(4); S.S.I. 2001/336, art. 2(3), Sch. Pt. II Table

(subject to transitional provisions and savings in art. 3)

[45] s. 18 repealed (1.10.1996) by 1996 c. 52, s. 227, Sch. 19 Pt. I; S.I. 1996/2402, art. 3 (subject to transitional provisions and savings in Sch.) and (1.11.2001) by 2001 asp 10, s. 112, Sch. 10 para. 11(4); S.S.I. 2001/336, art. 2(3), Sch. Pt. II Table (subject to transitional provisions and savings in art. 3)

[46] s. 19 repealed (1.10.1996) by 1996 c. 52, s. 227, Sch. 19 Pt. I; S.I. 1996/2402, art. 3 (subject to transitional provisions and savings in Sch.) and (1.11.2001) by 2001 asp 10, s. 112, Sch. 10 para. 11(4); S.S.I. 2001/336, art. 2(3), Sch. Pt. II Table (subject to transitional provisions and savings in art. 3)

[47] s. 20 repealed (1.10.1996) by 1996 c. 52, s. 227, Sch. 19 Pt. I; S.I. 1996/2402, art. 3 (subject to transitional provisions and savings in Sch.) and (1.11.2001) by 2001 asp 10, s. 112, Sch. 10 para. 11(4); S.S.I. 2001/336, art. 2(3), Sch. Pt. II Table (subject to transitional provisions and savings in art. 3).

[48] s. 21 repealed (1.10.1996) by 1996 c. 52, s. 227, Sch. 19 Pt. I; S.I. 1996/2402, art. 3 (subject to transitional provisions and savings in Sch.) and (1.11.2001) by 2001 asp 10, s. 112, Sch. 10 para. 11(4); S.S.I. 2001/336, art. 2(3), Sch. Pt. II Table (subject to transitional provisions and savings in art. 3)

[49] s. 22 repealed (1.10.1996) by 1996 c. 52, s. 227, Sch. 19 Pt. I; S.I. 1996/2402, art. 3 (subject to transitional provisions and savings in Sch.) and (1.11.2001) by 2001 asp 10, s. 112, Sch. 10 para. 11(4); S.S.I. 2001/336, art. 2(3), Sch. Pt. II Table (subject to transitional provisions and savings in art. 3)

[50] s. 23 repealed (1.10.1996) by 1996 c. 52, s. 227, Sch. 19 Pt. I; S.I. 1996/2402, art. 3 (subject to transitional provisions and savings in Sch.) and (1.11.2001) by 2001 asp 10, s. 112, Sch. 10 para. 11(4); S.S.I. 2001/336, art. 2(3), Sch. Pt. II Table (subject to transitional provisions and savings in art. 3)

[51] s. 24 repealed (1.10.1996) by 1996 c. 52, s. 227, Sch. 19 Pt. I; S.I. 1996/2402, art. 3 (subject to transitional provisions and savings in Sch.) and (1.11.2001) by 2001 asp 10, s. 112, Sch. 10 para. 11(4); S.S.I. 2001/336, art. 2(3), Sch. Pt. II Table (subject to transitional provisions and savings in art. 3)

[52] s. 25 repealed (1.10.1996) by 1996 c. 52, s. 227, Sch. 19 Pt. I; S.I. 1996/2402, art. 3 (subject to transitional provisions and savings in Sch.) and (1.11.2001) by 2001 asp 10, s. 112, Sch. 10 para. 11(4); S.S.I. 2001/336, art. 2(3), Sch. Pt. II Table (subject to transitional provisions and savings in art. 3)

[53] s. 26 repealed (1.10.1996) by 1996 c. 52, s. 227, Sch. 19 Pt. I; S.I. 1996/2402, art. 3 (subject to transitional provisions and savings in Sch.) and (1.11.2001) by 2001 asp 10, s. 112, Sch. 10 para. 11(4), S.S.I. 2001/336, art. 2(3), Sch. Pt. II Table (subject to transitional provisions and savings in art. 3)

[54] s. 27 repealed (1.10.1996) by 1996 c. 52, s. 227, Sch. 19 Pt. I; S.I. 1996/2402, art. 3 (subject to transitional provisions and savings in Sch.) and (1.11.2001) by 2001 asp 10, s. 112, Sch. 10 para. 11(4); S.S.I. 2001/336, art. 2(3), Sch. Pt. II Table (subject to transitional provisions and savings in art. 3)

[55] s. 27A repealed (1.10.1996) by 1996 c. 52, s. 227, Sch. 19 Pt. I; S.I. 1996/2402, art. 3 (subject to transitional provisions and savings in Sch.) and (1.11.2001) by 2001 asp 10, s. 112, Sch. 10 para. 11(4); S.S.I. 2001/336, art. 2(3), Sch. Pt. II Table (subject to transitional provisions and savings in art. 3)

[56] s. 28 repealed (1.10.1996) by 1996 c. 52, s. 227, Sch. 19 Pt. I; S.I. 1996/2402, art. 3 (subject to transitional provisions and savings in Sch.) and (1.11.2001) by 2001 asp 10, s. 112, Sch. 10 para. 11(4); S.S.I. 2001/336, art. 2(3), Sch. Pt. II Table (subject to transitional provisions and savings in art. 3)

[57] s. 29 repealed (1.10.1996) by 1996 c. 52, s. 227, Sch. 19 Pt. I; S.I. 1996/2402, art. 3 (subject to transitional provisions and savings in Sch.) and (1.11.2001) by 2001 asp 10, s. 112, Sch. 10 para. 11(4); S.S.I. 2001/336, art. 2(3), Sch. Pt. II Table (subject to transitional provisions and savings in art. 3)

[58] s. 30 repealed (1.10.1996) by 1996 c. 52, s. 227, Sch. 19 Pt. I; S.I. 1996/2402, art. 3 (subject to transitional provisions and savings in Sch.) and (1.11.2001) by 2001 asp 10, s. 112, Sch. 10 para. 11(4); S.S.I. 2001/336, art. 2(3), Sch. Pt. II Table (subject to transitional provisions and savings in art. 3)

[59] s. 31 repealed (1.10.1996) by 1996 c. 52, s. 227, Sch. 19 Pt. I; S.I. 1996/2402, art. 3 (subject to transitional provisions and savings in Sch.) and (1.11.2001) by 2001 asp 10, s. 112, Sch. 10 para. 11(4); S.S.I. 2001/336, art. 2(3), Sch. Pt. II Table (subject to transitional provisions and savings in art. 3) S

[60] s. 32 repealed (1.10.1996) by 1996 c. 52, s. 227, Sch. 19 Pt. I; S.I. 1996/2402, art. 3 (subject to transitional provisions and savings in Sch.) and (1.11.2001) by 2001 asp 10, s. 112, Sch. 10 para. 11(4); S.S.I. 2001/336, art. 2(3), Sch. Pt. II Table (subject to transitional provisions and savings in art. 3)

[61] s. 33 repealed (1.10.1996) by 1996 c. 52, s. 227, Sch. 19 Pt. I; S.I. 1996/2402, art. 3 (subject to transitional provisions and savings in Sch.) and (1.11.2001) by 2001 asp 10, s. 112, Sch. 10 para. 11(4); S.S.I. 2001/336, art. 2(3), Sch. Pt. II Table (subject to transitional provisions and savings in art. 3)

[62] Words in s. 33A substituted (1.11.1998) by 1998 c. 38, s. 140, Sch. 16 para. 26 (with ss. 139(2), 143(2)); S.I. 1998/2244, art. 5

[63] Words in s. 33A substituted (1.10.1996) by S.I. 1996/2325, art. 5(1), Sch. 2 para. 15(19)

[64] s. 33A inserted by Housing Act 1988 (c. 50, SIF 61), s. 59(2)(3)(4), Sch. 6 Pt. I para. 24

[65] Words in s. 34(1) inserted (1.4.1996) by 1994 c. 19, s. 22(2), Sch. 8 para. 6(1) (with ss. 54(4)(7), 55(5), Sch. 17 para. 22(1), 23(2)); S.I. 1996/396, art. 3, Sch. 1

[66] s. 35(2)(a) substituted (1.10.1996) by S.I. 1996/2325, art. 5(1), Sch. 2 para. 15(20)

[67] Word substituted by Housing Act 1988 (c. 50, SIF 61), s. 59(2)(3)(4), Sch. 6 Pt. I para. 2

[68] Words in s. 35(2)(c) substituted (1.8.1993) by 1993 c. 10, ss. 98(1), 99(1), Sch. 6 para. 21(4).

[69] Words in s. 35(2)(c) substituted (1.1.1993) by Charities Act 1992 (c. 41), s. 78(2), Sch. 6 para. 13(3); S.I. 1992/1900, art. 2 Sch. 3.

[70] s. 36A repealed (1.10.1996) by 1996 c. 52, s. 227, Sch. 19 Pt. I; S.I. 1996/2402, art. 3 (subject to transitional provisions and savings in Sch.) and repealed by 2001 asp 10, s. 112, Sch. 10 para. 11(4); S.S.I. 2001/336, art. 2(3), Sch. Pt. II Table (subject to transitional provisions and savings in art. 3)

[71] s. 37 repealed (1.10.1996) by S.I. 1996/2325, art. 4(1), Sch. 1 Pt. I (with art. 4(2)(3)) and (1.11.2001) by 2001 asp 10, s. 112, Sch. 10 para. 11(4); S.S.I. 2001/336, art. 2(3), Sch. Pt. II Table (subject to transitional provisions and savings in art. 3)

[72] Words in s. 38(a)(b) substituted (1.8.1993) by 1993 c. 10, ss. 98(1), 99(1), Sch. 6 para. 21(5)(a)(b).

[73] s. 38(b) repealed (1.10.1996) by S.I. 1996/2325, art. 4(1), Sch. 1 Pt. I (with art. 4(2)(3))

[74] By 2001 asp 10, s. 112, Sch. 10 para. 11(4); S.S.I. 2001/336, art. 2(3), Sch. Pt. II Table (subject to transitional provisions and savings in art. 3), it is provided that ss. 36A-40 be repealed (1.11.2001)

[75] Definitions inserted by Housing Act 1988 (c. 50, SIF 61), s. 59(2)(3)(4), Sch. 6 Pt. I para. 25

[76] s. 39: words in definition of "mental disorder" repealed (1.10.1996) by S.I. 1996/2325, art. 4(1), Sch. 1 Pt. II (with art. 4(2)(3))

[77] s. 39: definition of "mental disorder" repealed (1.10.1996) by S.I. 1996/2325, art. 4(1), Sch. 1 Pt. I (with art. 4(2)(3))

[78] s. 39: by Housing (Scotland) Act 1987 (c. 26, SIF 61), ss. 335, 339(2), Sch. 23 para. 31(3) it is provided that in the definition of "secure tenancy" for the words "10 of the Tenants'; Rights, Etc. (Scotland) Act 1980" there shall be substituted the words "44 of the Housing (Scotland) Act 1987" and by Housing (Scotland) Act 1988 (c. 43, SIF 61), s. 72, Sch. 9 para. 8 it is provided that in s. 39, in the definition of "secure tenancy" for the words "section 10 of the Tenants'; Rights Etc. (Scotland) Act 1980" there shall be substituted the words "44 of the Housing (Scotland) Act 1987"

[79] s. 39 repealed (1.11.2001) by 2001 asp 10, s. 112, Sch. 10 para. 11(4); S.S.I. 2001/336, art. 2(3), Sch. Pt. II Table (subject to transitional provisions and savings in art. 3)

[80] s. 39: definition repealed (5.11.1993) by 1993 c. 50, s. 1(1), Sch. 1 Pt. XIV Gp. 2.

[81] s. 40: entries repealed (1.10.1996) by S.I. 1996/2325, art. 4(1), Sch. 1 Pt. I (with art. 4(2)(3))

[82] Entries inserted by Housing Act 1988 (c. 50, SIF 61), s. 59(2)(3)(4), Sch. 6 Pt. I para. 26(a)

[83] Entries inserted by Housing Act 1988 (c. 50, SIF 61), s. 59(2)(3)(4), Sch. 6 Pt. I para. 26(a)

[84] s. 40: entries repealed (1.10.1996) by S.I. 1996/2325, art. 4(1), Sch. 1 Pt. I (with art. 4(2)(3))

[85] s. 40: entries repealed (1.10.1996) by S.I. 1996/2325, art. 4(1), Sch. 1 Pt. I (with art. 4(2)(3))

[86] s. 40: entries repealed (1.10.1996) by S.I. 1996/2325, art. 4(1), Sch. 1 Pt. I (with art. 4(2)(3))

[87] s. 40: entries repealed (1.10.1996) by S.I. 1996/2325, art. 4(1), Sch. 1 Pt. I (with art. 4(2)(3))

[88] s. 40: entries repealed (1.10.1996) by S.I. 1996/2325, art. 4(1), Sch. 1 Pt. I (with art. 4(2)(3))

[89] s. 40: definition of "the Corporation" repealed (1.10.1996) by S.I. 1996/2325, art. 4(1), Sch. 1 Pts. I, II (with art. 4(2)(3))

[90] s. 40: entries repealed (1.10.1996) by S.I. 1996/2325, art. 4(1), Sch. 1 Pt. I (with art. 4(2)(3))

[91] s. 40: entries repealed (1.10.1996) by S.I. 1996/2325, art. 4(1), Sch. 1 Pt. I (with art. 4(2)(3))

[92] s. 40: entries repealed (1.10.1996) by S.I. 1996/2325, art. 4(1), Sch. 1 Pt. I (with art. 4(2)(3))

[93] s. 40: entries repealed (1.10.1996) by S.I. 1996/2325, art. 4(1), Sch. 1 Pt. I (with art. 4(2)(3))

[94] s. 40: entries repealed (1.10.1996) by S.I. 1996/2325, art. 4(1), Sch. 1 Pt. I (with art. 4(2)(3))

[95] s. 40: entries repealed (1.10.1996) by S.I. 1996/2325, art. 4(1), Sch. 1 Pt. I (with art. 4(2)(3))

[96] s. 40: entries repealed (1.10.1996) by S.I. 1996/2325, art. 4(1), Sch. 1 Pt. I (with art. 4(2)(3))

[97] Entry repealed by Housing Act 1988 (c. 50, SIF 61), s. 140(2), Sch. 18

[98] s. 40: entries repealed (1.10.1996) by S.I. 1996/2325, art. 4(1), Sch. 1 Pt. I (with art. 4(2)(3))

[99] s. 40: entries repealed (1.10.1996) by S.I. 1996/2325, art. 4(1), Sch. 1 Pt. I (with art. 4(2)(3))

[100] s. 40: entries repealed (1.10.1996) by S.I. 1996/2325, art. 4(1), Sch. 1 Pt. I (with art. 4(2)(3))

[101] s. 40: entries repealed (1.10.1996) by S.I. 1996/2325, art. 4(1), Sch. 1 Pt. I (with art. 4(2)(3))

[102] Figure substituted by Housing Act 1988 (c. 50, SIF 61), s. 59(2)(3)(4), Sch. 6 Pt. I para. 26(c)

[103] s. 40: entries repealed (1.10.1996) by S.I. 1996/2325, art. 4(1), Sch. 1 Pt. I (with art. 4(2)(3))

[104] s. 40: entries repealed (1.10.1996) by S.I. 1996/2325, art. 4(1), Sch. 1 Pt. I (with art. 4(2)(3))

[105] s. 40: entry inserted (1.10.1996) by S.I. 1996/2325, art. 5(1), Sch. 2 para. 21(a)

[106] s. 40: entries repealed (1.10.1996) by S.I. 1996/2325, art. 4(1), Sch. 1 Pt. I (with art. 4(2)(3))

[107] s. 40: entries repealed (1.10.1996) by S.I. 1996/2325, art. 4(1), Sch. 1 Pt. I (with art. 4(2)(3))

[108] Entry inserted by Housing (Scotland) Act 1986 (c. 65, SIF 61), s. 25(1), Sch. 2 para. 4(4)

[109] s. 40: entries repealed (1.10.1996) by S.I. 1996/2325, art. 4(1), Sch. 1 Pt. I (with art. 4(2)(3))

[110] s. 40: entries repealed (1.10.1996) by S.I. 1996/2325, art. 4(1), Sch. 1 Pt. I (with art. 4(2)(3))

[111] s. 40: entry inserted (1.10.1996) by S.I. 1996/2325, art. 5(1), Sch. 2 para. 21(b)

[112] s. 40 repealed (1.11.2001) by 2001 asp 10, s. 112, Sch. 10 para. 11(4); S.S.I. 2001/336, art. 2(3), Sch. Pt. II Table (subject to transitional provisions and savings in art. 3)

[113] ss. 41–51, 75(1)(d) repealed by Housing Act 1988 (c. 50, SIF 61), s. 140(2), Sch. 18

[114] s. 52 repealed (with a saving in S.I. 1989/404, art. 3(a)) by Housing Act 1988 (c. 50, SIF 61), s. 140(2), Sch. 18, and as to s. 52(3) repealed by Housing (Scotland) Act 1986 (c. 65, SIF 61), s. 25(2), Sch. 3, and s. 52(4) repealed by Land

Registration Act 1988 (c. 3, SIF 98:2), ss. 1(e), 2, Sch.

115 s. 53 repealed (with a saving in S.I. 1989/404, art. 3(b)) by Housing Act 1988 (c. 50, SIF 61), s. 140(2), Sch. 18

116 s. 54 repealed (with a saving in S.I. 1989/404, art. 3(c)) by Housing Act 1988 (c.50, SIF 61), s. 140(2), Sch. 18

117 ss. 55-57 repealed (1.4.1991) by Housing Act 1988 (c. 50, SIF 61), s. 140(2), Sch. 18; S.I. 1989/404, art. 2 and S.I. 1991/954, arts,2, 3 (by art. 3 it is provided that the repeal shall not apply in relation to hostel deficit grants payable to an association for a period which expires before 1.4.1991)

118 s. 58 substituted (1.10.1996) by S.I. 1996/2325, art. 5(1), Sch. 2 para. 15(22)

119 Words in s. 59(1)(2) repealed (1.4.1996) by 1994 c. 39, s. 180(1)(2), Sch. 13 para. 143(2), Sch. 14; S.I. 1996/323, art. 4(1)(c)(d), Sch. 2

120 s. 59(5) added by Housing (Scotland) Act 1987 (c. 26, SIF 61), ss. 335, 339(2), Sch. 23 para. 31(7)

121 s. 59 repealed (1.11.2001) by 2001 asp 10, s. 112, Sch. 10 para. 11(4), S.S.I. 2001/336, art. 2(3), Sch. Pt. II Table (subject to transitional provisions and savings in art. 3)

122 s. 60 repealed (1.10.1996) by S.I. 1996/2325, art. 4(1), Sch. 1 Pt. I (with art. 4(2)(3)) and repealed (1.11.2001) by 2001 asp 10, s. 112, Sch. 10 para. 11(4); S.S.I. 2001/336, art. 2(3), Sch. Pt. II Table (subject to transitional provisions and savings in art. 3)

123 s. 61(3) inserted (1.10.1996) by S.I. 1996/2325, art. 5(1), Sch. 2 para. 15(23)

124 s. 61 repealed (1.11.2001) by 2001 asp 10, s. 112, Sch. 10 para. 11(4); S.S.I. 2001/336, art. 2(3), Sch. Pt. II Table (subject to transitional provisions and savings in art. 3)

125 s. 62 repealed (with saving) by Housing Act 1988 (c. 50, SIF 61), s. 140(2), Sch. 18: S.I. 1989/404, art. 3(d))

126 ss. 63–66 repealed by Building Societies Act 1986 (c. 53, SIF 16), ss. 54(3)(a)(5), 119(5), 120(1)(2), Sch. 18 Pt. I para. 19(2), Sch. 19 Pt. I (and s. 64(4) is also expressed to be repealed (5.11.1993) by 1993 c. 50, s. 1(1), Sch. 1 Pt.XIV Gp. 2).

127 s. 67 repealed (1.10.1996) by 1996 c. 52, s. 227, Sch. 19 Pt. I; S.I. 1996/2402, art. 3 (subject to transitional provisions and savings in Sch.)

128 Words substituted by Housing and Planning Act 1986 (c. 63, SIF 61), s. 24(1), Sch. 5 Pt. I para. 13(b)

129 Words added by Housing Act 1988 (c. 50, SIF 61), s. 59(2)(3)(b), Sch. 6 Pt. II para. 28(1)

130 Words in s. 69(1)(a) inserted (1.11.1998) by 1998 c. 38, s. 140, Sch. 16 para. 27(2) (with ss. 139(2), 143(2)); S.I. 1998/2244, art. 5

131 s. 69(1)(e) repealed (1.10.1996) by 1996 c. 52, ss. 55(1), 227, Sch. 3 para. 4, Sch. 19 Pt. I; S.I. 1996/2402, art. 3 (subject to transitional provisions and savings in Sch.)

132 s. 69(1)(g) inserted by Local Government Act 1988 (c. 9, SIF 81:1), s. 24(5)(c)

133 s. 69(1)(g) repealed (1.10.1996) by 1996 c. 52, ss. 55(1), 227, Sch. 3 para. 4, Sch. 19 Pt. I; S.I. 1996/2402, art. 3 (subject to transitional provisions and savings in Sch.)

134 Words in s. 69(2) substituted (1.11.1998) by 1998 c. 38, s. 140, Sch. 16 para. 27(3)(a) (with ss. 139(2), 143(2)); S.I. 1998/2244, art. 5

135 Words in s. 69(2) inserted (1.11.1998) by 1998 c. 38, s. 140, Sch. 16 para. 27(3)(b) (with ss. 139(2), 143(2)); S.I. 1998/2244, art. 5

136 Words in s. 69(2A) inserted (1.11.1998) by 1998 c. 38, s. 140, Sch. 16 para. 27(4)(a) (with ss. 139(2), 143(2)); S.I. 1998/2244, art. 5

137 Words in s. 69(2A) substituted (1.11.1998) by 1998 c. 38, s. 140, Sch. 16 para. 27(4)(b) (with ss. 139(2), 143(2)); s.I. 1998/2244, art. 5

138 s. 69(2A) inserted by Housing Act 1988 (c. 50, SIF 61), s. 59(2)(3)(b), Sch. 6 Pt. II para. 28(2)

139 Words substituted by Housing Act 1988 (c. 50, SIF 61), s. 59(2)(3)(4), Sch. 6 Pt. II para. 29 (which substitution has a saving in S.I. 1989/404, arts. 3(c)(ii), 4)

140 Words "22 of the Housing (Scotland) Act 1987" substituted for "5 of the Housing Rents and Subsidies (Scotland) Act 1975" by Housing (Scotland) Act 1987 (c.26, SIF 61), ss. 335, 339(2), Sch. 23 para. 31(8)

141 s. 69A inserted by Housing and Planning Act 1986 (c. 63, SIF 61), s. 24(2), Sch. 5 Pt. II para. 42

142 Definitions repealed by Building Societies Act 1986 (c. 53, SIF 16), ss. 54(3)(a)(5), 120(1)(2), Sch. 18 Pt. I para. 19(2), Sch. 19 Pt. I

143 s. 72 repealed (1.10.1996) by S.I. 1996/2325, art. 4(1), Sch. 1 Pt. I (with art. 4(2)(3))

144 Entry repealed by Housing Act 1988 (c. 50, SIF 61), s. 140(2), Sch. 18

145 Entries repealed by Building Societies Act 1986 (c. 53, SIF 16), ss. 54(3)(a)(5), 120(1)(2), Sch. 18 Pt. I para. 19(2), Sch. 19 Pt. I

146 s. 73: definitions repealed (1.10.1996) by S.I. 1996/2325, art. 4(1), Sch. 1 Pt. I (with art. 4(2)(3))

147 s. 73: definitions repealed (1.10.1996) by S.I. 1996/2325, art. 4(1), Sch. 1 Pt. I (with art. 4(2)(3))

148 Entries repealed by Housing Act 1988 (c. 50, SIF 61), s. 140(2), Sch. 18

149 s. 73: definitions repealed (1.10.1996) by S.I. 1996/2325, art. 4(1), Sch. 1 Pt. I (with art. 4(2)(3))

150 Entry repealed by Building Societies Act 1986 (c. 53, SIF 16), ss. 54(3)(a), 120(1)(2), Sch. 18 Pt. I para. 19(2), Sch. 19 Pt.I

151 s. 73: definition repealed (1.10.1996) by S.I. 1996/2325, art. 4(1), Sch. 1 Pts. I, II (with savings in art. 4(2)(3))

152 s. 73: definitions repealed (1.10.1996) by S.I. 1996/2325, art. 4(1), Sch. 1 Pt. I (with art. 4(2)(3))

153 s. 73: definition inserted (1.10.1996) by S.I. 1996/2325, art. 5(1), Sch. 2 para. 24(a)

154 s. 73: definition inserted (1.10.1996) by S.I. 1996/2325, art. 5(1), Sch. 2 para. 24(b)

[155] By Housing and Planning Act 1986 (c. 63, SIF 61), s. 24(1), Sch. 5 Pt. I para. 8(2) an entry relating to shared ownership agreement was inserted in s. 73 at the appropriate place and by Housing Act 1988 (c. 50, SIF 61), s. 140(2), Sch. 18 that entry was repealed

[156] s. 73: definition inserted (1.10.1996) by S.I. 1996/2325, art. 5(1), Sch. 2 para. 24(c)

[157] This version of this provision extends to England and Wales only; a separate version has been created for Scotland only

[158] Words in s. 74(1) substituted (1.11.1998) by 1998 c. 38, s. 140, Sch. 16 para. 29(2) (with ss. 139(2), 143(2)); S.I. 1998/2244, art. 5

[159] Words in Pt. III (ss. 74-102) substituted (1.11.1998) by 1998 c. 38, s. 140, Sch. 16 para. 28(a) (with ss. 139(2), 143(2)); S.I. 1998/2244, art. 5

[160] Words substituted by Housing Act 1988 (c. 50, SIF 61), s. 59(2)(3)(4), Sch. 6 Pt. III para. 31(2)

[161] Words in Pt. III (ss. 74-102) substituted (1.11.1998) by 1998 c. 38, s. 140, Sch. 16 para. 28(a) (with ss. 139(2), 143(2)); S.I. 1998/2244, art. 5

[162] Words in Pt. III (ss. 74-102) substituted (1.11.1998) by 1998 c. 38, s. 140, Sch. 16 para. 28(a) (with ss. 139(2), 143(2)); S.I. 1998/2244, art. 5

[163] s. 74(3) substituted (1.10.1996) by S.I. 1996/2325, art. 5(1), Sch. 2 para. 15(25)

[164] Words in s. 74(4)(a) substituted (1.11.1998) by 1998 c. 38, s. 140, Sch. 16 para. 29(3) (with ss. 139(2), 143(2)); S.I. 1998/2244, art. 5

[165] Words in Pt. III (ss. 74-102) substituted (1.11.1998) by 1998 c. 38, s. 140, Sch. 16 para. 28(a) (with ss. 139(2), 143(2)); S.I. 1998/2244, art. 5

[166] s. 74(4) inserted by Housing Act 1988 (c. 50, SIF 61), s. 59(2)(3)(4), Sch. 6 Pt. III para. 31(3)

[167] This version of this provision extends to Scotland only; a separate version has been created for England and Wales only.

[168] Words in s. 74(1) substituted (1.11.1998) by 1998 c. 38, s. 140, Sch. 16 para. 29(2) (with ss. 139(2), 143(2)); S.I. 1998/2244, art. 5

[169] Words in Pt. III (ss. 74-102) substituted (1.11.1998) by 1998 c. 38, s. 140, Sch. 16 para. 28(a) (with ss. 139(2), 143(2)); S.I. 1998/2244, art. 5

[170] Words substituted by Housing Act 1988 (c. 50, SIF 61), s. 59(2)(3)(4), Sch. 6 Pt. III para. 31(2)

[171] Words in Pt. III (ss. 74-102) substituted (1.11.1998) by 1998 c. 38, s. 140, Sch. 16 para. 28(a) (with ss. 139(2), 143(2)); S.I. 1998/2244, art. 5

[172] Words in Pt. III (ss. 74-102) substituted (1.11.1998) by 1998 c. 38, s. 140, Sch. 16 para. 28(a) (with ss. 139(2), 143(2)); S.I. 1998/2244, art. 5

[173] Words in s. 74(4)(a) substituted (1.11.1998) by 1998 c. 38, s. 140, Sch. 16 para. 29(3) (with ss. 139(2), 143(2)); S.I. 1998/2244, art. 5

[174] s. 74(3)(4) inserted by Housing Act 1988 (c. 50, SIF 61), s. 59(2)(3)(4), Sch. 6 Pt. III para. 31(3)

[175] Words in Pt. III (ss. 74-102) substituted (1.11.1998) by 1998 c. 38, s. 140, Sch. 16 para. 28(a) (with ss. 139(2), 143(2)); S.I. 1998/2244, art. 5

[176] This version of this provision extends to England and Wales only; a separate version has been created for Scotland only

[177] Words in Pt. III (ss. 74-102) substituted (1.11.1998) by 1998 c. 38, s. 140, Sch. 16 para. 28(a) (with ss. 139(2), 143(2)); S.I. 1998/2244, art. 5

[178] s. 75(1)(a)-(c) substituted (1.10.1996) by 1996 c. 52, s. 55(1), Sch. 3 para. 5; S.I. 1996/2402, art. 3 (with transitional provisions and savings in Sch.)

[179] ss. 41–51, 75(1)(d) repealed by Housing Act 1988 (c. 50, SIF 61), s. 140(2), Sch. 18

[180] Words in Pt. III (ss. 74-102) substituted (1.11.1998) by 1998 c. 38, s. 140, Sch. 16 para. 28(a) (with ss. 139(2), 143(2)); S.I. 1998/2244, art. 5

[181] s. 75(1)(f) inserted (27.9.1999 for E. for certain purposes and 1.10.1999 for W. otherwise 27.7.2000) by 1999 c. 27, ss. 22(7), 27(2); S.I. 1999/2169, art. 3(2), Sch. 2; S.I. 1999/2815, art. 2

[182] Words in Pt. III (ss. 74-102) substituted (1.11.1998) by 1998 c. 38, s. 140, Sch. 16 para. 28(a) (with ss. 139(2), 143(2)); S.I. 1998/2244, art. 5

[183] Words in s. 75(2) inserted (1.10.1996) by S.I. 1996/2325, art. 5(1), Sch. 2 para. 15(26)(a)

[184] Words in Pt. III (ss. 74-102) substituted (1.11.1998) by 1998 c. 38, s. 140, Sch. 16 para. 28(a) (with ss. 139(2), 143(2)); S.I. 1998/2244, art. 5

[185] Words in s. 75(3)(4) inserted (1.10.1996) by S.I. 1996/2325, art. 5(1), Sch. 2 para. 15(26)(b)

[186] Words in Pt. III (ss. 74-102) substituted (1.11.1998) by 1998 c. 38, s. 140, Sch. 16 para. 28(a) (with ss. 139(2), 143(2)); S.I. 1998/2244, art. 5

[187] Words in s. 75(3)(4) inserted (1.10.1996) by S.I. 1996/2325, art. 5(1), Sch. 2 para. 15(26)(b)

[188] s. 75(5) repealed (2.4.2001) by 2000 c. 34, s. 9(2), Sch. 3 (with s. 10(5)), S.I. 2001/566, art. 2

[189] Words in Pt. III (ss. 74-102) substituted by 1998 c. 38, s. 140, Sch. 16 para. 28(a) (with ss. 139(2), 143(2)); S.I. 1998/2244, art. 5

[190] This version of this provision extends to Scotland only; a separate version has been created for England and Wales

only.

[191] Words in Pt. III (ss. 74-102) substituted by 1998 c. 38, s. 140, Sch. 16 para. 28(a) (with ss. 139(2), 143(2)); S.I. 1998/2244, art. 5

[192] Words substituted by Housing Act 1988 (c. 50, SIF 61), s. 59(2)(3)(4), Sch. 6 Pt. III para. 32

[193] Ss. 41–51, 75(1)(d) repealed by Housing Act 1988 (c. 50, SIF 61), s. 140(2), Sch. 18

[194] Words in Pt. III (ss. 74-102) substituted by 1998 c. 38, s. 140, Sch. 16 para. 28(a) (with ss. 139(2), 143(2)); S.I. 1998/2244, art. 5

[195] S. 75(1)(f) inserted (27.9.1999 for E. for certain purposes and 1.10.1999 for W. and otherwise 27.7.2000) by 1999 c. 27, ss. 22(7), 27(2); S.I. 1999/2169, art. 3(2), Sch. 2; S.I. 1999/2815, art. 2

[196] Words in Pt. III (ss. 74-102) substituted by 1998 c. 38, s. 140, Sch. 16 para. 28(a) (with ss. 139(2), 143(2)); S.I. 1998/2244, art. 5

[197] Words in Pt. III (ss. 74-102) substituted by 1998 c. 38, s. 140, Sch. 16 para. 28(a) (with ss. 139(2), 143(2)); S.I. 1998/2244, art. 5

[198] Words in Pt. III (ss. 74-102) substituted by 1998 c. 38, s. 140, Sch. 16 para. 28(a) (with ss. 139(2), 143(2)); S.I. 1998/2244, art. 5

[199] S. 75(5) repealed (2.4.2001) by 2000 c. 34, s. 9(2), Sch. 3 (with s. 10(5)), S.I. 2001/566, art. 2

[200] Words in s. 76(1)(2)(4) substituted (1.11.1998) by 1998 c. 38, s. 140, Sch. 16 para. 31 (with ss. 139(2), 143(2)); S.I. 1998/2244, art. 5

[201] Words in s. 76(1)(2)(4) substituted (1.11.1998) by 1998 c. 38, s. 140, Sch. 16 para. 31 (with ss. 139(2), 143(2)); S.I. 1998/2244, art. 5

[202] Words in s. 76(1)(2)(4) substituted (1.11.1998) by 1998 c. 38, s. 140, Sch. 16 para. 31 (with ss. 139(2), 143(2)); S.I. 1998/2244, art. 5

[203] Words in s. 76A(3) and sidenote substituted (1.11.1998) by 1998 c. 38, s. 140, Sch. 16 para. 32(3) (with ss. 139(2), 143(2)); S.I. 1998/2244, art. 5

[204] Words in s. 76A(1)(2)(4) substituted (1.11.1998) by 1998 c. 38, s. 140, Sch. 16 para. 32(2) (with ss. 139(2), 143(2)); S.I. 1998/2244, art. 5

[205] s. 76A inserted (1.10.1996) by 1996 c. 52, s. 55(1), Sch. 3 para. 6; S.I. 1996/2402, art. 3 (with transitional provisions and savings in Sch.) Words in s. 76A(1)(2)(4) substituted (1.11.1998) by 1998 c. 38, s. 140, Sch. 16 para. 32(2) (with ss. 139(2), 143(2)); S.I. 1998/2244, art. 5

[206] s. 76A inserted (1.10.1996) by 1996 c. 52, s. 55(1), Sch. 3 para. 6; S.I. 1996/2402, art. 3 (with transitional provisions and savings in Sch.)

[207] Words in s. 76A(3) and sidenote substituted (1.11.1998) by 1998 c. 38, s. 140, Sch. 16 para. 32(3) (with ss. 139(2), 143(2)); S.I. 1998/2244, art. 5

[208] Words in s. 76A(3) and sidenote substituted (1.11.1998) by 1998 c. 38, s. 140, Sch. 16 para. 32(3) (with ss. 139(2), 143(2)); S.I. 1998/2244, art. 5

[209] Words in s. 76A(1)(2)(4) substituted (1.11.1998) by 1998 c. 38, s. 140, Sch. 16 para. 32(2) (with ss. 139(2), 143(2)); S.I. 1998/2244, art. 5

[210] Words in s. 76A(1)(2)(4) substituted (1.11.1998) by 1998 c. 38, s. 140, Sch. 16 para. 32(2) (with ss. 139(2), 143(2)); S.I. 1998/2244, art. 5

[211] Words in s. 76A(1)(2)(4) substituted (1.11.1998) by 1998 c. 38, s. 140, Sch. 16 para. 32(2) (with ss. 139(2), 143(2)); S.I. 1998/2244, art. 5

[212] Words in Pt. III (ss. 74-102) substituted (1.11.1998) by 1998 c. 38, s. 140, Sch. 16 para. 28(a) (with ss. 139(2), 143(2)); S.I. 1998/2244, art. 5

[213] Words in s. 77(1) substituted (1.10.1996) by S.I. 1996/2325, art. 5(1), Sch. 2 para. 15(27)

[214] Words in Pt. III (ss. 74-102) substituted (1.11.1998) by 1998 c. 38, s. 140, Sch. 16 para. 28(a) (with ss. 139(2), 143(2)); S.I. 1998/2244, art. 5

[215] Words in Pt. III (ss. 74-102) substituted (1.11.1998) by 1998 c. 38, s. 140, Sch. 16 para. 28(a) (with ss. 139(2), 143(2)); S.I. 1998/2244, art. 5

[216] Words in s. 77(3) substituted (1.11.1998) by 1998 c. 38, s. 140, Sch. 16 para. 33 (with ss. 139(2), 143(2)); S.I. 1998/2244, art. 5

[217] S. 77(3) added by Housing Act 1988 (c. 50, SIF 61), s. 59(2)(3)(4), Sch. 6 Pt. III para. 33

[218] This version of this provision extends to Scotland only; a separate version has been created for England and Wales only.

[219] Words in Pt. III (ss. 74-102) substituted (1.11.1998) by 1998 c. 38, s. 140, Sch. 16 para. 28(a) (with ss. 139(2), 143(2)); S.I. 1998/2244, art. 5

[220] Words in Pt. III (ss. 74-102) substituted (1.11.1998) by 1998 c. 38, s. 140, Sch. 16 para. 28(a) (with ss. 139(2), 143(2)); S.I. 1998/2244, art. 5

[221] Words in Pt. III (ss. 74-102) substituted (1.11.1998) by 1998 c. 38, s. 140, Sch. 16 para. 28(a) (with ss. 139(2), 143(2)); S.I. 1998/2244, art. 5

[222] Words in s. 77(3) substituted (1.11.1998) by 1998 c. 38, s. 140, Sch. 16 para. 33 (with ss. 139(2), 143(2)); S.I. 1998/2244, art. 5

223 S. 77(3) added by Housing Act 1988 (c. 50, SIF 61), s. 59(2)(3)(4), Sch. 6 Pt. III para. 33

224 Words in s. 78(1) substituted (1.11.1998) by 1998 c. 38, s. 140, Sch. 16 para. 34 (with ss. 139(2), 143(2)); S.I. 1998/2244, art. 5

225 Words in Pt. III (ss. 74-102) substituted (1.11.1998) by 1998 c. 38, s. 140, Sch. 16 para. 28(a) (with ss. 139(2), 143(2)); S.I. 1998/2244, art. 5

226 S. 79(1)(2) substituted (1.11.1998) by 1998 c. 38, s. 140, Sch. 16 para. 35(2) (with ss. 139(2), 143(2)); S.I. 1998/2244, art. 5

227 Words in Pt. III (ss 74-102) substituted (1.11.1998) by 1998 c. 38, s. 140, Sch. 16 para. 28(a) (with ss. 139(2), 143(2)); S.I. 1998/2244, art. 5

228 Words in s. 79(4) inserted (1.11.1998) by 1998 c. 38, s. 140, Sch. 16 para. 35(3) (with ss. 139(2), 143(2)); S.I. 1998/2244, art. 5

229 Words in Pt. III (ss 74-102) substituted (1.11.1998) by 1998 c. 38, s. 140, Sch. 16 para. 28(a) (with ss. 139(2), 143(2)); S.I. 1998/2244, art. 5

230 Words in Pt. III (ss. 74-102) substituted (1.11.1998) by 1998 c. 38, s. 140, Sch. 16 para. 28(a) (with ss. 139(2), 143(2)); S.I. 1998/2244, art. 5

231 Words in s. 80(1) repealed (1.11.1998) by 1998 c. 38, ss. 140, 152, Sch. 16 para. 36(2), Sch. 18 Pt. VI (with ss. 137(1), 139(2), 141(1), 143(2)); S.I. 1998/2244, art. 5

232 Words in Pt. III (ss. 74-102) substituted (1.11.1998) by 1998 c. 38, s. 140, Sch. 16 para. 28(a) (with ss. 139(2), 143(2)); S.I. 1998/2244, art. 5

233 Words in s. 80(3) repealed (1.11.1998) by 1998 c. 38, ss. 140, 152, Sch. 16 para. 36(3), Sch. 18 Pt. VI (with ss. 137(1), 139(2), 141(1), 143(2)); S.I. 1998/2244, art. 5

234 S. 80(3A) inserted (1.11.1998) by 1998 c. 38, s. 140, Sch. 16 para. 36(4) (with ss. 139(2), 143(2)); S.I. 1998/2244, art. 5

235 Words in s. 80(5) substituted (1.11.1998) by 1998 c. 38, s. 140, Sch. 16 para. 36(5) (with ss. 139(2), 143(2)); S.I. 1998/2244, art. 5

236 Words in Pt. III (ss. 74-102) substituted (1.11.1998) by 1998 c. 38, s. 140, Sch. 16 para. 28(a) (with ss. 139(2), 143(2)); S.I. 1998/2244, art. 5

237 Words in Pt. III (ss. 74-102) substituted (1.11.1998) by 1998 c. 38, s. 140, Sch. 16 para. 28(a) (with ss. 139(2), 143(2)); S.I. 1998/2244, art. 5

238 S. 83(1) substituted (1.11.1998) by 1998 c. 38, s. 140, Sch. 16 para. 37(2) (with ss. 139(2), 143(2)); S.I. 1998/2244, art. 5

239 S. 83(1A) inserted (1.11.1998) by 1998 c. 38, s. 140, Sch. 16 para. 37(3) (with ss. 139(2), 143(2)); S.I. 1998/2244, art.

240 Words substituted by Housing Act 1988 (c. 50, SIF 61), s. 59(2)(3)(4), Sch. 6 Pt. III para. 34(1)

241 Words substituted by Housing Act 1988 (c. 50, SIF 61), s. 59(2)(3)(4), Sch. 6 Pt. III para. 34(1)

242 Words substituted by Housing Act 1988 (c. 50, SIF 61), s. 59(2)(3)(4), Sch. 6 Pt. III para. 34(1)

243 Words in s. 83(3A) substituted (1.11.1998) by 1998 c. 38, s. 140, Sch. 16 para. 37(4) (with ss. 139(2), 143(2)); S.I. 1998/2244, art. 5

244 Words in s. 83(3A) substituted (1.11.1998) by 1998 c. 38, s. 140, Sch. 16 para. 37(4) (with ss. 139(2), 143(2)); S.I. 1998/2244, art. 5

245 Words in s. 83(3A) substituted (1.11.1998) by 1998 c. 38, s. 140, Sch. 16 para. 37(4) (with ss. 139(2), 143(2)); S.I. 1998/2244, art. 5

246 S. 83(3A) inserted by Housing Act 1988 (c. 50, SIF 61), s. 59(2)(3)(4), Sch. 6 Pt. III para. 34(2)

247 Words inserted by Housing Act 1988 (c. 50, SIF 61), s. 59(2)(3)(4), Sch. 6 Pt. III para. 34(3)

248 Words in Pt. III (ss. 74-102) substituted (1.11.1998) by 1998 c. 38, s. 140, Sch. 16 para. 28(a) (with ss. 139(2), 143(2)); S.I. 1998/2244, art. 5

249 Words in s. 84(1) repealed (1.11.1998) by 1998 c. 38, ss. 140, 152, Sch. 16 para. 38(2), Sch. 18 Pt. VI (with ss. 137(1), 139(2), 141(1), 143(2)); S.I. 1998/2244, art. 5

250 Words in Pt. III (ss. 74-102) substituted (1.11.1998) by 1998 c. 38, s. 140, Sch. 16 para. 28(a) (with ss. 139(2), 143(2)); S.I. 1998/2244, art. 5

251 Words in Pt. III (ss. 74-102) substituted (1.11.1998) by 1998 c. 38, s. 140, Sch. 16 para. 28(a) (with ss. 139(2), 143(2)); S.I. 1998/2244, art. 5

252 Words in Pt. III (ss. 74-102) substituted (1.11.1998) by 1998 c. 38, s. 140, Sch. 16 para. 28(a) (with ss. 139(2), 143(2)); S.I. 1998/2244, art. 5

253 Words in s. 84(4) substituted (1.11.1998) by 1998 c. 38, s. 140, Sch. 16 para. 38(3) (with ss. 139(2), 143(2)); S.I. 1998/2244, art. 5

254 Words in s. 84(5) inserted (1.11.1998) by 1998 c. 38, s. 140, Sch. 16 para. 38(4) (with ss. 139(2), 143(2)); S.I. 1998/2244, art. 5

255 Words in s. 85(5)(a) substituted (1.12.2001) by S.I. 2001/3649, art. 301

256 S. 84(6) repealed (1.3.2000) by S.I. 2000/311, art. 16

257 Words in s. 85(2) repealed (1.10.1996) by 1996 c. 52, ss. 222, 227, Sch. 18 Pt. IV para. 22(1)(d), Sch. 19 Pt. XIII; S.I. 1996/2402, art. 3 (subject to transitional provisions and savings in Sch.)

258 Words in s. 85(4) repealed (1.11.1998) by 1998 c. 38, s. 152, Sch. 18 Pt. IV (with ss. 137(1), 139(2), 141(1), 143(2)); S.I. 1998/2244, art. 5

259 Words in s. 85(4) substituted (1.11.1998) by 1998 c. 38, s. 140, Sch. 16 para. 39(a) (with ss. 139(2), 143(2)); S.I.

1998/2244, art. 5

[260] Words in s. 85(4) substituted (1.10.1996) by S.I. 1996/2325, art. 5(1), Sch. 2 para. 15(30)

[261] Words in s. 85(4) inserted (1.11.1998) by 1998 c. 38, s. 140, Sch. 16 para. 39(b) (with ss. 139(2), 143(2)); S.I. 1998/2244, art. 5

[262] Words in s. 86(1)(2)(4) substituted (1.10.1996) by S.I. 1996/2325, art. 5(1), Sch. 2 para. 15(6)

[263] Words inserted by Housing (Scotland) Act 1986 (c. 65, SIF 61), s. 25(1), Sch. 2 para. 4(6)(a)(i)

[264] Words in s. 86(1)(2)(4) substituted (1.10.1996) by S.I. 1996/2325, art. 5(1), Sch. 2 para. 15(6)

[265] Words inserted by Housing (Scotland) Act 1986 (c. 65, SIF 61), s. 25(1), Sch. 2 para. 4(6)(a)(i)

[266] Words inserted by Housing (Scotland) Act 1986 (c. 65, SIF 61), s. 25(1), Sch. 2 para. 4(6)(a)(i)

[267] "a" substituted by Housing (Scotland) Act 1986 (c. 65, SIF 61), s. 25(1), Sch. 2 para. 4(6)(a)(ii)

[268] Words in s. 86(1)(2)(4) substituted (1.10.1996) by S.I. 1996/2325, art. 5(1), Sch. 2 para. 15(6)

[269] Words inserted by Housing (Scotland) Act 1986 (c. 65, SIF 61), s. 25(1), Sch. 2 para. 4(6)(b)

[270] Words in s. 86(1)(2)(4) substituted (1.10.1996) by S.I. 1996/2325, art. 5(1), Sch. 2 para. 15(6)

[271] Words in s. 86(4) substituted (1.12.2001) by S.I. 2001/3649, art. 302

[272] S. 86(5) repealed (1.3.2000) by S.I. 2000/311, art. 16

[273] S. 86(6)(7) added by Housing (Scotland) Act 1986 (c. 65, SIF 61), s. 25(1), Sch. 2 para. 4(6)(d)

[274] Words in Pt. III (ss. 74-102) substituted (1.11.1998) by 1998 c. 38, s. 140, Sch. 16 para. 28(a) (with ss. 139(2), 143(2)); S.I. 1998/2244, art. 5

[275] S. 87(1) substituted (1.10.1996) by 1996 c. 52, s. 55(1), Sch. 3 para. 7; S.I. 1996/2402 art. 3 (with transitional provisions and savings in Sch.)

[276] Words in Pt. III (ss. 74-102) substituted (1.11.1998) by 1998 c. 38, s. 140, Sch. 16 para. 28(a) (with ss. 139(2), 143(2)); S.I. 1998/2244, art. 5

[277] Words in s. 87(2) inserted (1.11.1998) by 1998 c. 38, s. 140, Sch. 16 para. 40 (with ss. 139(2), 143(2)); S.I. 1998/2244, art.5

[278] Words in Pt. III (ss. 74-102) substituted (1.11.1998) by 1998 c. 38, s. 140, Sch. 16 para. 28(a) (with ss. 139(2), 143(2)); S.I. 1998/2244, art. 5

[279] Word in s. 87(5) repealed (1.10.1996) by S.I. 1996/2325, art. 4(1), Sch. 1 Pt. I (with art. 4(2)(3))

[280] S. 87 beginning "The Corporation may give financial assistance" substituted for s. 87 beginning "The Corporation may make grants" by Local Government and Housing Act 1989 (c. 42 SIF 61), s.183

[281] *This version of this provision extends to Scotland only; a separate version has been created for England and Wales only*

[282] Words in Pt. III (ss. 74-102) substituted (1.11.1998) by 1998 c. 38, s. 140, Sch. 16 para. 28(a) (with ss. 139(2), 143(2)); S.I. 1998/2244, art. 5

[283] Words in Pt. III (ss. 74-102) substituted (1.11.1998) by 1998 c. 38, s. 140, Sch. 16 para. 28(a) (with ss. 139(2), 143(2)); S.I. 1998/2244, art. 5

[284] Words in s. 87(2) inserted (1.11.1998) by 1998 c. 38, s. 140, Sch. 16 para. 40 (with ss. 139(2), 143(2)); S.I. 1998/2244, art.5

[285] Words in Pt. III (ss. 74-102) substituted (1.11.1998) by 1998 c. 38, s. 140, Sch. 16 para. 28(a) (with ss. 139(2), 143(2)); S.I. 1998/2244, art. 5

[286] S. 87 beginning "The Corporation may give financial assistance" substituted for s. 87 beginning "The Corporation may make grants" by Local Government and Housing Act 1989 (c. 42 SIF 61), s.183

[287] Words in Pt. III (ss. 74-102) substituted (1.11.1998) by 1998 c. 38, s. 140, Sch. 16 para. 28(b) (with ss. 139(2), 143(2)); S.I. 1998/2244, art. 5

[288] Words in Pt. III (ss. 74-102) substituted (1.11.1998) by 1998 c. 38, s. 140, Sch. 16 para. 28(a) (with ss. 139(2), 143(2)); S.I. 1998/2244, art. 5

[289] Words in s. 88(1) substituted (1.10.1996) by S.I. 1996/2325, art. 5(1), Sch. 2 para. 15(31)

[290] Words in s. 88(1) substituted (1.11.1998) by 1998 c. 38, s. 140, Sch. 16 para. 41 (with ss. 139(2), 143(2)); S.I. 1998/2244, art. 5

[291] Words in Pt. III (ss. 74-102) substituted (1.11.1998) by 1998 c. 38, s. 140, Sch. 16 para. 28(a) (with ss. 139(2), 143(2)); S.I. 1998/2244, art. 5

[292] Words in Pt. III (ss. 74-102) substituted (1.11.1998) by 1998 c. 38, s. 140, Sch. 16 para. 28(a) (with ss. 139(2), 143(2)); S.I. 1998/2244, art. 5

[293] Words in Pt. III (ss. 74-102) substituted (1.11.1998) by 1998 c. 38, s. 140, Sch. 16 para. 28(a) (with ss. 139(2), 143(2)); S.I. 1998/2244, art. 5

[294] Words in Pt. III (ss. 74-102) substituted (1.11.1998) by 1998 c. 38, s. 140, Sch. 16 para. 28(a) (with ss. 139(2), 143(2)); S.I. 1998/2244, art. 5

[295] Words in Pt. III (ss. 74-102) substituted (1.11.1998) by 1998 c. 38, s. 140, Sch. 16 para. 28(a) (with ss. 139(2), 143(2)); S.I. 1998/2244, art. 5

[296] Words "23 of the Housing (Scotland) Act 1987" substituted for "175(2) of the Housing (Scotland) Act 1966" by Housing (Scotland) Act 1987 (c. 26, SIF 61), ss. 335, 339(2), Sch. 23 para. 31(9)

[297] Words in Pt. III (ss. 74-102) substituted (1.11.1998) by 1998 c. 38, s. 140, Sch. 16 para. 28(a) (with ss. 139(2), 143(2)); S.I. 1998/2244, art. 5

[298] *This version of this provision extends to Scotland only; a separate version has been created for England and Wales only*

[299] Words in Pt. III (ss. 74-102) substituted (1.11.1998) by 1998 c. 38, s. 140, Sch. 16 para. 28(a) (with ss. 139(2), 143(2)); S.I.

1998/2244, art. 5

300 Words in s. 88(1) substituted (1.11.1998) by 1998 c. 38, s. 140, Sch. 16 para. 41 (with ss. 139(2), 143(2)); S.I. 1998/2244, art. 5

301 Words in Pt. III (ss. 74-102) substituted (1.11.1998) by 1998 c. 38, s. 140, Sch. 16 para. 28(a) (with ss. 139(2), 143(2)); S.I. 1998/2244, art. 5

302 Words in Pt. III (ss. 74-102) substituted (1.11.1998) by 1998 c. 38, s. 140, Sch. 16 para. 28(a) (with ss. 139(2), 143(2)); S.I. 1998/2244, art. 5

303 Words in Pt. III (ss. 74-102) substituted (1.11.1998) by 1998 c. 38, s. 140, Sch. 16 para. 28(a) (with ss. 139(2), 143(2)); S.I. 1998/2244, art. 5

304 Words in Pt. III (ss. 74-102) substituted (1.11.1998) by 1998 c. 38, s. 140, Sch. 16 para. 28(a) (with ss. 139(2), 143(2)); S.I. 1998/2244, art. 5

305 Words in Pt. III (ss. 74-102) substituted (1.11.1998) by 1998 c. 38, s. 140, Sch. 16 para. 28(a) (with ss. 139(2), 143(2)); S.I. 1998/2244, art. 5

306 Words in Pt. III (ss. 74-102) substituted (1.11.1998) by 1998 c. 38, s. 140, Sch. 16 para. 28(a) (with ss. 139(2), 143(2)); S.I. 1998/2244, art. 5

307 Words "23 of the Housing (Scotland) Act 1987" substituted for "175(2) of the Housing (Scotland) Act 1966" by Housing (Scotland) Act 1987 (c. 26, SIF 61), ss. 335, 339(2), Sch. 23 para. 31(9)

308 Words in Pt. III (ss. 74-102) substituted (1.11.1998) by 1998 c. 38, s. 140, Sch. 16 para. 28(a) (with ss. 139(2), 143(2)); S.I. 1998/2244, art. 5

309 Words in Pt. III (ss. 74-102) substituted (1.11.1998) by 1998 c. 38, s. 140, Sch. 16 para. (with ss. 139(2), 143(2)); S.I. 1998/2244, art. 5

310 Words in Pt. III (ss. 74-102) substituted (1.11.1998) by 1998 c. 38, s. 140, Sch. 16 para. (with ss. 139(2), 143(2)); S.I. 1998/2244, art. 5

311 Words in Pt. III (ss. 74-102) substituted (1.11.1998) by 1998 c. 38, s. 140, Sch. 16 para. (with ss. 139(2), 143(2)); S.I. 1998/2244, art. 5

312 Words in Pt. III (ss. 74-102) substituted (1.11.1998) by 1998 c. 38, s. 140, Sch. 16 para. (with ss. 139(2), 143(2)); S.I. 1998/2244, art. 5

313 Words in Pt. III (ss. 74-102) substituted (1.11.1998) by 1998 c. 38, s. 140, Sch. 16 para. (with ss. 139(2), 143(2)); S.I. 1998/2244, art. 5

314 Words in s. 89(4)(b) substituted (1.10.1996) by S.I. 1996/2325, art. 5(1), Sch. para. 15(32)

315 Words in Pt. III (ss. 74-102) substituted (1.11.1998) by 1998 c. 38, s. 140, Sch. 16 para. (with ss. 139(2), 143(2)); S.I. 1998/2244, art. 5

316 *This version of this provision extends to Scotland only; a separate version has been created for England and Wales only*

317 Words in Pt. III (ss. 74-102) substituted (1.11.1998) by 1998 c. 38, s. 140, Sch. 16 para. (with ss. 139(2), 143(2)); S.I. 1998/2244, art. 5

318 Words in Pt. III (ss. 74-102) substituted (1.11.1998) by 1998 c. 38, s. 140, Sch. 16 para. (with ss. 139(2), 143(2)); S.I. 1998/2244, art. 5

319 Words in Pt. III (ss. 74-102) substituted (1.11.1998) by 1998 c. 38, s. 140, Sch. 16 para. (with ss. 139(2), 143(2)); S.I. 1998/2244, art. 5

320 Words in Pt. III (ss. 74-102) substituted (1.11.1998) by 1998 c. 38, s. 140, Sch. 16 para. (with ss. 139(2), 143(2)); S.I. 1998/2244, art. 5

321 Words in Pt. III (ss. 74-102) substituted (1.11.1998) by 1998 c. 38, s. 140, Sch. 16 para. (with ss. 139(2), 143(2)); S.I. 1998/2244, art. 5

322 Words in Pt. III (ss. 74-102) substituted (1.11.1998) by 1998 c. 38, s. 140, Sch. 16 para. (with ss. 139(2), 143(2)); S.I. 1998/2244, art. 5

323 *This version of this provision extends to England and Wales only; a separate version has been created for Scotland only*

324 Words in Pt. III (ss. 74-102) substituted (1.11.1998) by 1998 c. 38, s. 140, Sch. 16 para. 28(a) (with ss. 139(2), 143(2)); S.I. 1998/2244, art. 5

325 Words in s. 90(1) substituted (1.11.1998) by 1998 c. 38, s. 140, Sch. 16 para. 42(2) (with ss. 139(2), 143(2)); S.I. 1998/2244, art. 5

326 Words in Pt. III (ss. 74-102) substituted (1.11.1998) by 1998 c. 38, s. 140, Sch. 16 para. 28(a) (with ss. 139(2), 143(2)); S.I. 1998/2244, art. 5

327 Words in s. 90(2) substituted (1.10.1996) by S.I. 1996/2325, art. 5(1), Sch. 2 para. 15(33)

328 Words in s. 90(2) substituted (1.11.1998) by 1998 c. 38, s. 140, Sch. 16 para. 42(3) (with ss. 139(2), 143(2)); S.I. 1998/2244, art. 5

329 Words in Pt. III (ss. 74-102) substituted (1.11.1998) by 1998 c. 38, s. 140, Sch. 16 para. 28(a) (with ss. 139(2), 143(2)); S.I. 1998/2244, art. 5

330 Words in s. 90(3) inserted (1.11.1998) by 1998 c. 38, s. 140, Sch. 16 para. 42(4) (with ss. 139(2), 143(2)); S.I. 1998/2244, art. 5

331 Words in Pt. III (ss. 74-102) substituted (1.11.1998) by 1998 c. 38, s. 140, Sch. 16 para. 28(a) (with ss. 139(2), 143(2)); S.I. 1998/2244, art. 5

[332] Words in s. 90(4) inserted (1.11.1998) by 1998 c. 38, s. 140, Sch. 16 para. 42(5) (with ss. 139(2), 143(2)); S.I. 1998/2244, art. 5

[333] Words in Pt. III (ss. 74-102) substituted (1.11.1998) by 1998 c. 38, s. 140, Sch. 16 para. 28(a) (with ss. 139(2), 143(2)); S.I. 1998/2244, art. 5

[334] Words in s. 90(5)(a) and in the words following (b) substituted (1.11.1998) by 1998 c. 38, s. 140, Sch. 16 para. 42(6)(a) (with ss. 139(2), 143(2)); S.I. 1998/2244, art. 5

[335] Words in s. 90(5)(a) and in the words following (b) substituted (1.11.1998) by 1998 c. 38, s. 140, Sch. 16 para. 42(6)(a) (with ss. 139(2), 143(2)); S.I. 1998/2244, art. 5

[336] Words in s. 90(6)(b) inserted (1.11.1998) by 1998 c. 38, s. 140, Sch. 16 para. 42(6)(b) (with ss. 139(2), 143(2)); S.I. 1998/2244, art. 5

[337] Words in s. 90(5)(a) and in the words following (b) substituted (1.11.1998) by 1998 c. 38, s. 140, Sch. 16 para. 42(6)(a) (with ss. 139(2), 143(2)); S.I. 1998/2244, art. 5

[338] Words in s. 90(6) substituted (1.11.1998) by 1998 c. 38, s. 140, Sch. 16 para. 42(7) (with ss. 139(2), 143(2)); S.I. 1998/2244, art. 5

[339] *This version of this provision extends to Scotland only; a separate version has been created for England and Wales only*

[340] Words in Pt. III (ss. 74-102) substituted (1.11.1998) by 1998 c. 38, s. 140, Sch. 16 para. 28(a) (with ss. 139(2), 143(2)); S.I. 1998/2244, art. 5

[341] Words in s. 90(1) substituted (1.11.1998) by 1998 c. 38, s. 140, Sch. 16 para. 42(2) (with ss. 139(2), 143(2)); S.I. 1998/2244, art. 5

[342] Words in Pt. III (ss. 74-102) substituted (1.11.1998) by 1998 c. 38, s. 140, Sch. 16 para. 28(a) (with ss. 139(2), 143(2)); S.I. 1998/2244, art. 5

[343] Words in s. 90(2) substituted (1.11.1998) by 1998 c. 38, s. 140, Sch. 16 para. 42(3) (with ss. 139(2), 143(2)); S.I. 1998/2244, art. 5

[344] Words in Pt. III (ss. 74-102) substituted (1.11.1998) by 1998 c. 38, s. 140, Sch. 16 para. 28(a) (with ss. 139(2), 143(2)); S.I. 1998/2244, art. 5

[345] Words in s. 90(3) inserted (1.11.1998) by 1998 c. 38, s. 140, Sch. 16 para. 42(4) (with ss. 139(2), 143(2)); S.I. 1998/2244, art. 5

[346] Words in s. 90(4) inserted (1.11.1998) by 1998 c. 38, s. 140, Sch. 16 para. 42(5) (with ss. 139(2), 143(2)); S.I. 1998/2244, art. 5

[347] Words in Pt. III (ss. 74-102) substituted (1.11.1998) by 1998 c. 38, s. 140, Sch. 16 para. 28(a) (with ss. 139(2), 143(2)); S.I. 1998/2244, art. 5

[348] Words in s. 90(5)(a) and in the words following (b) substituted (1.11.1998) by 1998 c. 38, s. 140, Sch. 16 para. 42(6)(a) (with ss. 139(2), 143(2)); S.I. 1998/2244, art. 5

[349] Words in s. 90(5)(a) and in the words following (b) substituted (1.11.1998) by 1998 c. 38, s. 140, Sch. 16 para. 42(6)(a) (with ss. 139(2), 143(2)); S.I. 1998/2244, art. 5

[350] Words in s. 90(6)(b) inserted (1.11.1998) by 1998 c. 38, s. 140, Sch. 16 para. 42(6)(b) (with ss. 139(2), 143(2)); S.I. 1998/2244, art. 5

[351] Words in s. 90(5)(a) and in the words following (b) substituted (1.11.1998) by 1998 c. 38, s. 140, Sch. 16 para. 42(6)(a) (with ss. 139(2), 143(2)); S.I. 1998/2244, art. 5

[352] Words in s. 90(6) substituted (1.11.1998) by 1998 c. 38, s. 140, Sch. 16 para. 42(7) (with ss. 139(2), 143(2)); S.I. 1998/2244, art. 5

[353] Words in s. 91 substituted (1.11.1998) by 1998 c. 38, s. 140, Sch. 16 para. 43 (with ss. 139(2), 143(2)); S.I.1998/2244, art.5

[354] Words in s. 91 substituted (1.11.1998) by 1998 c. 38, s. 140, Sch. 16 para. 43 (with ss. 139(2), 143(2)); S.I.1998/2244, art.5

[355] Words in s. 91 substituted (1.11.1998) by 1998 c. 38, s. 140, Sch. 16 para. 43 (with ss. 139(2), 143(2)); S.I.1998/2244, art.5

[356] Words in s. 91 substituted (1.11.1998) by 1998 c. 38, s. 140, Sch. 16 para. 43 (with ss. 139(2), 143(2)); S.I.1998/2244, art.5

[357] Words in Pt. III (ss. 74-102) substituted (1.11.1998) by 1998 c. 38, s. 140, Sch. 16 para. 28(b) (with ss. 139(2), 143(2)); S.I. 1998/2244, art. 5

[358] Words in s. 92 substituted (1.11.1998) by 1998 c. 38, s. 140, Sch. 16 para. 44 (with ss. 139(2), 143(2)); S.I.1998/2244, art.5

[359] Words in s. 92 substituted (1.11.1998) by 1998 c. 38, s. 140, Sch. 16 para. 44 (with ss. 139(2), 143(2)); S.I.1998/2244, art.5

[360] Words in s. 92 substituted (1.11.1998) by 1998 c. 38, s. 140, Sch. 16 para. 44 (with ss. 139(2), 143(2)); S.I.1998/2244, art.5

[361] Words in s. 92 substituted (1.11.1998) by 1998 c. 38, s. 140, Sch. 16 para. 44 (with ss. 139(2), 143(2)); S.I.1998/2244, art.5

[362] Words in s. 92 substituted (1.11.1998) by 1998 c. 38, s. 140, Sch. 16 para. 44 (with ss. 139(2), 143(2)); S.I.1998/2244, art.5

[363] Words in s. 92 substituted (1.11.1998) by 1998 c. 38, s. 140, Sch. 16 para. 44 (with ss. 139(2), 143(2)); S.I. 998/2244, art. 5

[364] Words in s. 92 substituted (1.11.1998) by 1998 c. 38, s. 140, Sch. 16 para. 44 (with ss. 139(2), 143(2)); S.I.1998/2244, art.5

[365] Words in s. 93(1)(4)(5) substituted (1.11.1998) by 1998 c. 38, s. 140, Sch. 16 para. 45(2) (with ss. 139(2), 143(2)); S.I. 1998/2244, art. 5

[366] Words in s. 93(2) substituted (1.11.1998) by 1998 c. 38, s. 140, Sch. 16 para. 45(3)(a) (with ss. 139(2), 143(2)); S.I. 1998/2244, art. 5

[367] Words in s. 93(2) substituted (1.11.1998) by 1998 c. 38, s. 140, Sch. 16 para. 45(3)(a) (with ss. 139(2), 143(2)); S.I. 1998/2244, art. 5

[368] Words in s. 93(2) substituted (1.11.1998) by 1998 c. 38, s. 140, Sch. 16 para. 45(3)(a) (with ss. 139(2), 143(2)); S.I.

1998/2244, art. 5

369 Words in s. 93(2) substituted (1.11.1998) by 1998 c. 38, s. 140, Sch. 16 para. 45(3)(a) (with ss. 139(2), 143(2)); S.I. 1998/2244, art. 5

370 Words in s. 93(2) substituted (1.11.1998) by 1998 c. 38, s. 140, Sch. 16 para. 45(3)(a) (with ss. 139(2), 143(2)); S.I. 1998/2244, art. 5

371 Word in s. 93(2) substituted (1.11.1998) by 1998 c. 38, s. 140, Sch. 16 para. 45(3)(b) (with ss. 139(2), 143(2)); S.I. 1998/2244, art. 5

372 Words substituted by Housing Act 1988 (c. 50, SIF 61), s. 59(2)(3)(4), Sch. 6 Pt. III para. 35(1)

373 Words in s. 93(2A)(a) repealed (1.11.1998) by 1998 c. 38, ss. 140, 152, Sch. 16 para. 45(4)(a), Sch. 18 Pt. VI (with ss. 137(1), 139(2), 141(1), 143(2)); S.I. 1998/2244, art. 5

374 S. 93(2A)(b) and the word preceding it repealed (1.11.1998) by 1998 c. 38, ss. 140, 152, Sch. 16 para. 45(4)(b), Sch. 18 Pt. VI (with ss. 137(1), 139(2), 141(1), 143(2)); S.I. 1998/2244, art. 5

375 S. 93(2A) inserted by Housing Act 1988 (c. 50, SIF 61), s. 59(2)(3)(4), Sch. 6 Pt. III para. 35(2)

376 "2A" substituted by Housing Act 1988 (c. 50, SIF 61), s. 59(2)(3)(4), Sch. 6 Pt. III para. 35(3)

377 "2A" substituted by Housing Act 1988 (c. 50, SIF 61), s. 59(2)(3)(4), Sch. 6 Pt. III para. 35(3)

378 Words in s. 93(1)(4)(5) substituted (1.11.1998) by 1998 c. 38, s. 140, Sch. 16 para. 45(2) (with ss. 139(2), 143(2)); S.I. 1998/2244, art. 5

379 Words in s. 93(1)(4)(5) substituted (1.11.1998) by 1998 c. 38, s. 140, Sch. 16 para. 45(2) (with ss. 139(2), 143(2)); S.I. 1998/2244, art. 5

380 Words in s. 93(1)(4)(5) substituted (1.11.1998) by 1998 c. 38, s. 140, Sch. 16 para. 45(2) (with ss. 139(2), 143(2)); S.I. 1998/2244, art. 5

381 "2A" substituted by Housing Act 1988 (c. 50, SIF 61), s. 59(2)(3)(4), Sch. 6 Pt. III para. 35(3)

382 Words in s. 94(1)(4) substituted (1.11.1998) by 1998 c. 38, s. 140, Sch. 16 para. 46 (with ss. 139(2), 143(2)); S.I. 1998/2244, art. 5

383 Words in s. 94(1)(4) substituted (1.11.1998) by 1998 c. 38, s. 140, Sch. 16 para. 46 (with ss. 139(2), 143(2)); S.I. 1998/2244, art. 5

384 Words in s. 95(1) and sidenote substituted (1.11.1998) by 1998 c. 38, s. 140, Sch. 16 para. 47 (with ss. 139(2), 143(2)); S.I. 1998/2244, art. 5

385 Words in s. 95(1) and sidenote substituted (1.11.1998) by 1998 c. 38, s. 140, Sch. 16 para. 47 (with ss. 139(2), 143(2)); S.I. 1998/2244, art. 5

386 Words in s. 95(1) and sidenote substituted (1.11.1998) by 1998 c. 38, s. 140, Sch. 16 para. 47 (with ss. 139(2), 143(2)); S.I. 1998/2244, art. 5

387 Words in s. 96(1)-(4) substituted (1.11.1998) by 1998 c. 38, s. 140, Sch. 16 para.48(2) (with ss. 139(2), 143(2)); S.I. 1998/2244, art. 5

388 Words in s. 96(1)-(4) substituted (1.11.1998) by 1998 c. 38, s. 140, Sch. 16 para.48(2) (with ss. 139(2), 143(2)); S.I. 1998/2244, art. 5

389 Words in s. 96(1)-(4) substituted (1.11.1998) by 1998 c. 38, s. 140, Sch. 16 para.48(2) (with ss. 139(2), 143(2)); S.I. 1998/2244, art. 5

390 Words in s. 96(1)-(4) substituted (1.11.1998) by 1998 c. 38, s. 140, Sch. 16 para.48(2) (with ss. 139(2), 143(2)); S.I. 1998/2244, art. 5

391 Words in s. 96(1)-(4) substituted (1.11.1998) by 1998 c. 38, s. 140, Sch. 16 para.48(2) (with ss. 139(2), 143(2)); S.I. 1998/2244, art. 5

392 Words in s. 96(3)(4) substituted (1.11.1998) by 1998 c. 38, s. 140, Sch. 16 para. 48(3) (with ss. 139(2), 143(2)); S.I. 1998/2244, art. 5

393 Words in s. 96(1)-(4) substituted (1.11.1998) by 1998 c. 38, s. 140, Sch. 16 para.48(2) (with ss. 139(2), 143(2)); S.I. 1998/2244, art. 5

394 Words in s. 96(1)-(4) substituted (1.11.1998) by 1998 c. 38, s. 140, Sch. 16 para.48(2) (with ss. 139(2), 143(2)); S.I. 1998/2244, art. 5

395 Words in s. 96(1)-(4) substituted (1.11.1998) by 1998 c. 38, s. 140, Sch. 16 para.48(2) (with ss. 139(2), 143(2)); S.I. 1998/2244, art. 5

396 Words in s. 96(3)(4) substituted (1.11.1998) by 1998 c. 38, s. 140, Sch. 16 para. 48(3) (with ss. 139(2), 143(2)); S.I. 1998/2244, art. 5

397 Words in s. 97(1)-(4) substituted (1.11.1998) by 1998 c. 38, s. 140, Sch. 16 para. 49 (with ss. 139(2), 143(2)); S.I. 1998/2244, art. 5

398 Words in s. 97(1)-(4) substituted (1.11.1998) by 1998 c. 38, s. 140, Sch. 16 para. 49 (with ss. 139(2), 143(2)); S.I. 1998/2244, art. 5

399 Words in s. 97(1)-(4) substituted (1.11.1998) by 1998 c. 38, s. 140, Sch. 16 para. 49 (with ss. 139(2), 143(2)); S.I. 1998/2244, art. 5

400 Words in s. 97(1)-(4) substituted (1.11.1998) by 1998 c. 38, s. 140, Sch. 16 para. 49 (with ss. 139(2), 143(2)); S.I. 1998/2244, art. 5

401 Words in s. 97(1)-(4) substituted (1.11.1998) by 1998 c. 38, s. 140, Sch. 16 para. 49 (with ss. 139(2), 143(2)); S.I.

1998/2244, art. 5

402 Words in s. 97(1)-(4) substituted (1.11.1998) by 1998 c. 38, s. 140, Sch. 16 para. 49 (with ss. 139(2), 143(2)); S.I. 1998/2244, art. 5

403 Words in s. 97(1)-(4) substituted (1.11.1998) by 1998 c. 38, s. 140, Sch. 16 para. 49 (with ss. 139(2), 143(2)); S.I. 1998/2244, art. 5

404 S. 97(6) substituted (01.10.1991) by S.I. 1991/1997, reg. 2, Sch. para. 59(2) (with reg. 4).

405 Words in s. 98(1) substituted (1.11.1998) by 1998 c. 38, s. 140, Sch. 16 para. 50 (with ss. 139(2), 143(2)); S.I. 1998/2244, art. 5

406 Words in s. 99(1)(2) substituted (1.11.1998) by 1998 c. 38, s. 140, Sch. 16 para. 51 (with ss. 139(2), 143(2)); S.I. 1998/2244, art. 5

407 Words in s. 99(1)(2) substituted (1.11.1998) by 1998 c. 38, s. 140, Sch. 16 para. 51 (with ss. 139(2), 143(2)); S.I. 1998/2244, art. 5

408 Words in s. 99(1)(2) substituted (1.11.1998) by 1998 c. 38, s. 140, Sch. 16 para. 51 (with ss. 139(2), 143(2)); S.I. 1998/2244, art. 5

409 Words in s. 99(1)(2) substituted (1.11.1998) by 1998 c. 38, s. 140, Sch. 16 para. 51 (with ss. 139(2), 143(2)); S.I. 1998/2244, art. 5

410 Words in s. 99(1)(2) substituted (1.11.1998) by 1998 c. 38, s. 140, Sch. 16 para. 51 (with ss. 139(2), 143(2)); S.I. 1998/2244, art. 5

411 Words in s. 99(1)(2) substituted (1.11.1998) by 1998 c. 38, s. 140, Sch. 16 para. 51 (with ss. 139(2), 143(2)); S.I. 1998/2244, art. 5

412 Words in Pt. III (ss. 74-102) substituted (1.11.1998) by 1998 c. 38, s. 140, Sch. 16 para. 28(a) (with ss. 139(2), 143(2)); S.I. 1998/2244, art. 5

413 Words in Pt. III (ss. 74-102) substituted (1.11.1998) by 1998 c. 38, s. 140, Sch. 16 para. 28(a) (with ss. 139(2), 143(2)); S.I. 1998/2244, art. 5

414 Words in Pt. III (ss. 74-102) substituted (1.11.1998) by 1998 c. 38, s. 140, Sch. 16 para. 28(a) (with ss. 139(2), 143(2)); S.I. 1998/2244, art. 5

415 Words in Pt. III (ss. 74-102) substituted (1.11.1998) by 1998 c. 38, s. 140, Sch. 16 para. 28(a) (with ss. 139(2), 143(2)); S.I. 1998/2244, art. 5

416 S. 100 repealed by Housing (Scotland) Act 1986 (c. 65, SIF 61), s. 25(2),Sch. 3

417 Definition substituted by Building Societies Act 1986 (c. 53, SIF 16), ss. 54(3)(a)(5), 120(1), Sch. 18 Pt. I para. 19(4)

418 Words substituted by Companies Act 1989 (c. 40, SIF 27), ss. 144(4), Sch. 18 para. 41

419 *This version of this provision extends to England and Wales only; a separate version has been created for Scotland only*

420 S. 102: definition inserted (1.10.1996) by S.I. 1996/2325, art. 5(1), Sch. 2 para. 34(a)

421 S. 102: definition substituted (1.10.1996) by S.I. 1996/2325, art. 5(1), Sch. 2 para. 34(b)

422 S. 102: definition substituted (1.10.1996) by S.I. 1996/2325, art. 5(1), Sch. 2 para. 34(c)

423 *This version of this provision extends to Scotland only; a separate version has been created for England and Wales only*

424 Words in s. 104(1)(b) substituted (1.4.1996) by 1994 c. 39, s. 180(1), Sch. 13 para. 143(3)(a); S.I. 1996/323, art. 4(1)(b)(c)

425 Words in s. 104(2)(b) substituted (1.4.1996) by 1994 c. 39, s. 180(1), Sch. 13 para. 143(3)(b); S.I. 1996/323, art. 4(1)(b)(c)

426 S. 105 repealed (1.10.1996) by S.I. 1996/2325, art. 4(1), Sch. 1 Pt. I (with savings in art. 4(2)(3))

427 Words substituted by Banking Act 1987 (c. 22, SIF 10), s. 108(1), Sch. 6 para. 22

428 S. 106(1): definitions repealed (1.10.1996) by S.I. 1996/2325, art. 4(1), Sch. 1 Pt. I (with art. 4(2)(3))

429 S. 106(1): definitions repealed (1.10.1996) by S.I. 1996/2325, art. 4(1), Sch. 1 Pt. I (with art. 4(2)(3))

430 S. 106(1): definitions repealed (1.10.1996) by S.I. 1996/2325, art. 4(1), Sch. 1 Pt. I (with art. 4(2)(3))

431 Definition substituted by Housing Act 1988 (c. 50, SIF 61), s. 59(2)(3)(4), Sch. 6 Pt. III para. 36

432 S. 106(1): definition of "housing activities" repealed (1.10.1996) by S.I. 1996/2325, art. 4(1), Sch. 1 Pt. I (with art. 4(2)-(4))

433 S. 106(1): definitions repealed (1.10.1996) by S.I. 1996/2325, art. 4(1), Sch. 1 Pt. I (with art. 4(2)(3))

434 S. 106(1): words in definition of "local authority" inserted (1.4.1996) by 1994 c. 19, s. 22(2), Sch. 8 para. 6(2) (with ss. 54(4)(7), 55(5), Sch. 17 paras. 22(1), 23(2)); S.I. 1996/396, art. 3, Sch. 1

435 S. 106(1): words in definition of "local authority" substituted (1.10.1994 for specified purposes, 1.4.1995 otherwise) by 1994 c. 29, s. 43, Sch. 4 Pt. II para. 59(a); S.I. 1994/2025, art. 6(2)(e); S.I. 1994/3262, art. 4(1), Sch.

436 Words repealed by Education Reform Act 1988 (c. 40, SIF 41:1), ss. 231(7), 235(6), 237(2), Sch. 13 Pt. I

437 S. 106(1): words in definition of "local authority" inserted (3.7.2000) by 1999 c. 29, s. 328(8), Sch. 29 Pt. I para. 43 (with Sch. 12 para. 9(1)); S.I. 2000/1094, art. 4(h)

438 S. 106(1): words in definition of "local authority" inserted (3.7.2000) by 1999 c. 29, s. 328(8), Sch. 29 Pt. I para. 43 (with Sch. 12 para. 9(1)); S.I. 2000/1094, art. 4(h)

439 S. 106(1): words in definition of "local authority" substituted (22.8.1996) by 1996 c. 16, ss. 103, 104(1), Sch. 7 Pt. I para. 1(2)(w)

440 Words in s. 106(1) in the definition of "local authority" substituted (1.4.2002) by 2001 c. 16, s. 128, Sch. 6 Pt. III para. 68; S.I. 2002/344, art. 3(k) (with transitional provisions in art. 4)

441 S. 106(1): words in definition of "local authority" added (1.10.1994 for specified purposes, 1.4.1995 otherwise) by 1994

c. 29, s. 43, Sch. 4 Pt. II para. 59(b); S.I. 1994/2025, art. 6(2)(e); S.I. 1994/3262, art. 4(1), Sch.

442 S. 106(1): definitions repealed (1.10.1996) by S.I. 1996/2325, art. 4(1), Sch. 1 Pt. I (with art. 4(2)(3))

443 S. 106(1): definitions repealed (1.10.1996) by S.I. 1996/2325, art. 4(1), Sch. 1 Pt. II (with art. 4(2)(3))

444 S. 106(1): definitions repealed (1.10.1996) by S.I. 1996/2325, art. 4(1), Sch. 1 Pt. II (with art. 4(2)(3))

445 S. 106(1): definitions repealed (1.10.1996) by S.I. 1996/2325, art. 4(1), Sch. 1 Pt. II (with art. 4(2)(3))

446 Definition repealed by Housing (Scotland) Act 1986 (c. 65, SIF 61), s. 25(2), Sch. 3

447 S.106(1): definition of "housing activities" repealed (1.10.1996) by S.I. 1996/2325, art.4(1), Sch.1 Pt.II (with art. 4(2)-(4))

448 S. 106(1): definitions repealed (1.10.1996) by S.I. 1996/2325, art. 4(1), Sch. 1 Pt. II (with art. 4(2)(3))

449 S. 106(2): words in definition of "local authority" substituted (1.4.1996) by 1994 c. 39, s. 180(1), Sch. 13 para. 143(4); S.I. 1996/323, art. 4(1)(b)(c)

450 Definition beginning "shared ownership agreement" substituted for definition beginning "shared ownership lease" by virtue of Housing (Scotland) Act 1986 (c. 65, SIF 61), s. 13(2) and Housing (Scotland) Act 1988 (c. 43, SIF 61), s. 72(2), Sch. 9 para. 9

451 Words in s. 106(2) repealed (1.11.2001) by 2001 asp 10, s. 112, Sch. 10 para. 11(4), S.S.I. 2001/336, art. 2, Sch. Pt. II (subject to transitional provisions and savings in art. 3)

452 Definition beginning "shared ownership agreement" substituted for definition beginning "shared ownership lease" by virtue of Housing (Scotland) Act 1986 (c. 65, SIF 61), s. 13(2) and Housing (Scotland) Act 1988 (c. 43, SIF 61), s. 72(2), Sch. 9 para. 9

453 S. 106(1): definitions repealed (1.10.1996) by S.I. 1996/2325, art. 4(1), Sch. 1 Pt. II (with art. 4(2)(3))

454 Words in s. 106(3) substituted (1.10.1996) by S.I. 1996/2325, art. 5(1), Sch. 2 para. 15(35)

455 S. 106(3) repealed (1.11.2001) by 2001 asp. 10, s. 112, Sch. 10 para. 11(4), S.S.I. 2001/336, art. 2, Sch. Pt. II (subject to transitional provisions and savings in art. 3)

456 Entry repealed by Housing Act 1988 (c. 50, SIF 61), s. 140(1), Sch. 18

457 "17(4) " repealed by Housing (Scotland) Act 1986 (c. 65, SIF 61), s. 25(2), Sch. 3

458 Entry repealed by Housing Act 1988 (c.50, SIF 61), s. 140(2), Sch. 18

459 Words repealed by Housing (Scotland) Act 1986 (c. 65, SIF 61), s. 25(2), Sch. 3

460 Words repealed by Housing Act 1988 (c. 50, SIF 61), s. 140(2), Sch. 18

461 Words inserted by Housing (Scotland) Act 1986 (c. 65, SIF 61), s. 25(1), Sch. 2 para. 4(8)(b)

462 Words in Sch. 1 para. 1 substituted (1.10.1996) by S.I. 1996/2325, art. 5(1), Sch. 2 para. 15(35)

463 Words in Sch. 1 para. 1 repealed (1.11.1998) by 1998 c. 38, s. 152, Sch. 18 Pt. VI; S.I. 1998/2244, art. 5

464 Sch. 2 repealed (1.10.1996) by 1996 c. 52, s. 227, Sch. 19 Pt. I; S.I. 1996/2402, art. 3 (subject to transitional provisions and savings in Sch.)

465 Sch. 3 repealed (1.10.1996) by 1996 c. 52, s. 227, Sch. 19 Pt. I; S.I. 1996/2402, art. 3 (with transitional provisions and savings in Sch.); and repealed (1.10.1996) by virtue of S.I. 1996/2325, art. 4(1), Sch. 1 Pt. II (with art. 4(2)(3))

466 Words repealed by Housing Act 1988 (c. 50, SIF 61), ss. 59(2)(3)(4), 140(2), Sch. 6 Pt. II para. 30(1)(a), Sch. 18

467 Words in Sch. 5 Pt. I para. 6(2)(b) repealed (1.11.1998) by 1998 c. 38, ss. 140, 152, Sch. 16 para. 52, Sch. 18 Pt. VI; S.I. 1998/2244, art. 5

468 Words repealed by Housing Act 1988 (c. 50, SIF 61), ss. 59(2)(3)(4), 140(2), Sch. 6 Pt. II para. 30(2), Sch. 18

469 Sch. 6 para. 3(3)(b) repealed by Housing Act 1988 (c. 50, SIF 61), ss. 59(2)(3)(4), 140(2), Sch. 6 Pt. III para. 37, Sch. 18

470 Words in Sch. 6 para. 5(1) repealed (1.10.1996) by 1996 c. 52, ss. 222, 227, Sch. 18 Pt. IV para. 22(1)(d), Sch. 19 Pt. XIII; S.I. 1996/2402, art. 3 (subject to transitional provisions and savings in Sch.)

471 Words in Sch. 6 para. 6(1) repealed (1.10.1996) by 1996 c. 52, ss. 222, 227, Sch. 18 Pt. IV para. 22(1)(d), Sch. 19 Pt. XIII; S.I. 1996/2402, art. 3 (subject to transitional provisions and savings in Sch.)

472 Words in Pt. III (ss. 74-102), Sch. 7 substituted (1.11.1998) by 1998 c. 38, s. 140, Sch. 16 para. 28(a) (with ss. 139(2), 143(2)); S.I. 1998/2244, art. 5

473 Words in Sch. 7 para. 2(1) repealed (1.11.1998) by 1998 c. 38, ss. 140, 152, Sch. 16 para. 53(2)(a), Sch. 18 Pt. VI (with ss. 137(1), 139(2), 141(1), 143(2)); S.I. 1998/2244, art. 5

474 Words in Sch. 7 para. 2(2) repealed (1.11.1998) by 1998 c. 38, ss. 140, 152, Sch. 16 para. 53(2)(b), Sch. 18 Pt. VI (with ss. 137(1), 139(2), 141(1), 143(2)); S.I. 1998/2244, art. 5

475 Sch. 7 para. 2(3) inserted (1.11.1998) by 1998 c. 38, s. 140, Sch. 16 para. 53(2)(c) (with ss. 139(2), 143(2)); S.I. 1998/2244, art. 5

476 Words in Sch. 7 para. 3 substituted (1.11.1998) by 1998 c. 38, s. 140, Sch. 16 para. 53(3)(a) (with ss. 139(2), 143(2)); S.I. 1998/2244, art. 5

477 Words in Sch. 7 para. 3 substituted (1.11.1998) by 1998 c. 38, s. 140, Sch. 16 para. 53(3)(a) (with ss. 139(2), 143(2)); S.I. 1998/2244, art. 5

478 Words in Sch. 7 para. 3 inserted (1.11.1998) by 1998 c. 38, s.140, Sch.16 para.53(3)(b) (with ss.139(2), 143(2)); S.I. 1998/2244, art. 5

479 Sch. 7 para. 4(2) inserted (1.11.1998) by 1998 c. 38, s.140, Sch.16 para.53(4)(b) (with ss.139(2), 143(2)); S.I. 1998/2244, art. 5

480 Sch. 7 para. 4 renumbered as Sch. 7 para. 4(1) (1.11.1998) by 1998 c. 38, s. 140, Sch. 16 para. 53(4) (with ss. 139(2), 143(2)); S.I. 1998/2244, art. 5

[481] Words in Sch. 7 para. 4(1) substituted (1.11.1998) by 1998 c. 38, s. 140, Sch. 16 para. 53(4)(a) (with ss. 139(2), 143(2)); S.I. 1998/2244, art. 5

[482] Words in Sch. 7 para. 4(1) substituted (1.11.1998) by 1998 c. 38, s. 140, Sch. 16 para. 53(4)(a) (with ss. 139(2), 143(2)); S.I. 1998/2244, art. 5

[483] Sch. 7 para. 4(2) inserted (1.11.1998) by 1998 c. 38, s. 140, Sch. 16 para. 53(4)(b) (with ss. 139(2), 143(2)); S.I. 1998/2244, art. 5

[484] Words in Sch. 7 para. 5(1) substituted (1.11.1998) by 1998 c. 38, s. 140, Sch. 16 para. 53(5)(a) (with ss. 139(2), 143(2)); S.I. 1998/2244, art. 5

[485] Words in Sch. 7 para. 5(1) substituted (1.11.1998) by 1998 c. 38, s. 140, Sch. 16 para. 53(5)(a) (with ss. 139(2), 143(2)); S.I. 1998/2244, art. 5

[486] Sch. 7 para. 5(1A) inserted (1.11.1998) by 1998 c. 38, s. 140, Sch. 16 para. 53(5)(b) (with ss. 139(2), 143(2)); S.I. 1998/2244, art. 5

[487] Words in Sch. 7 para. 5(3)(4)(5) substituted (1.11.1998) by 1998 c. 38, s. 140, Sch. 16 para. 53(5)(c) (with ss. 139(2), 143(2)); S.I. 1998/2244, art. 5

[488] Words in Sch. 7 para. 5(3)(4)(5) substituted (1.11.1998) by 1998 c. 38, s. 140, Sch. 16 para. 53(5)(c) (with ss. 139(2), 143(2)); S.I. 1998/2244, art. 5

[489] Words in Sch. 7 para. 5(3)(4)(5) substituted (1.11.1998) by 1998 c. 38, s. 140, Sch. 16 para. 53(5)(c) (with ss. 139(2), 143(2)); S.I. 1998/2244, art. 5

[490] Sch. 7 para. 5(6) inserted (1.11.1998) by 1998 c. 38, s. 140, Sch. 16 para. 53(5)(d) (with ss. 139(2), 143(2)); S.I. 1998/2244, art. 5

Insolvency Act 1986

1986 CHAPTER 45

...

Grounds and effect of winding-up petition

122 Circumstances in which company may be wound up by the court.

(1) A company may be wound up by the court if—

(a) the company has by special resolution resolved that the company be wound up by the court,

(b) being a public company which was registered as such on its original incorporation, the company has not been issued with [a trading certificate under section 761 of the Companies Act 2006 (requirement as to minimum share capital)][1] and more than a year has expired since it was so registered,

(c) it is an old public company, within the meaning of the [Schedule 3 to the Companies Act 2006 (Consequential Amendments, Transitional Provisions and Savings) Order 2009][2],

(d) the company does not commence its business within a year from its incorporation or suspends its business for a whole year;

(e) except in the case of a private company limited by shares or by guarantee,][3] the number of members is reduced below 2,

(f) the company is unable to pay its debts,

[(fa) at the time at which a moratorium for the company under section 1A comes to an end, no voluntary arrangement approved under Part I has effect in relation to the company][4]

(g) the court is of the opinion that it is just and equitable that the company should be wound up.

(2) In Scotland, a company which the Court of Session has jurisdiction to wind up may be wound up by the Court if there is subsisting a floating charge over property comprised in the company's property and undertaking, and the court is satisfied that the security of the creditor entitled to the benefit of the floating charge is in jeopardy.

For this purpose a creditor's security is deemed to be in jeopardy if the Court is satisfied that events have occurred or are about to occur which render it unreasonable in the creditor's interests that the company should retain power to dispose of the property which is subject to the floating charge.

123 Definition of inability to pay debts.

(1) A company is deemed unable to pay its debts—

(a) if a creditor (by assignment or otherwise) to whom the company is indebted in a sum exceeding £750 then due has served on the company, by leaving it at the company's registered office, a written demand (in the prescribed form) requiring the company to pay the sum so due and the company has for 3 weeks thereafter neglected to pay the sum or to secure or compound for it to

the reasonable satisfaction of the creditor, or

(b) if, in England and Wales, execution or other process issued on a judgment, decree or order of any court in favour of a creditor of the company is returned unsatisfied in whole or in part, or

(c) if, in Scotland, the inducaie of a charge for payment on an extract decree, or an extract registered bond, or an extract registered protest, have expired without payment being made, or

(d) if, in Northern Ireland, a certificate of unenforceability has been granted in respect of a judgment against the company, or

(e) if it is proved to the satisfaction of the court that the company is unable to pay its debts as they fall due.

(2) A company is also deemed unable to pay its debts if it is proved to the satisfaction of the court that the value of the company's assets is less than the amount of its liabilities, taking into account its contingent and prospective liabilities.

(3) The money sum for the time being specified in subsection (1)(a) is subject to increase or reduction by order under section 416 in Part XV.

...

Offences of fraud, deception, etc.

206 Fraud, etc. in anticipation of winding up.

(1) When a company is ordered to be wound up by the court, or passes a resolution for voluntary winding up, any person, being a past or present officer of the company, is deemed to have committed an offence if, within the 12 months immediately preceding the commencement of the winding up, he has—

(a) concealed any part of the company's property to the value of [£500][5] or more, or concealed any debt due to or from the company, or

(b) fraudulently removed any part of the company's property to the value of [£500][6] or more, or

(c) concealed, destroyed, mutilated or falsified any book or paper affecting or relating to the company's property or affairs, or

(d) made any false entry in any book or paper affecting or relating to the company's property or affairs, or

(e) fraudulently parted with, altered or made any omission in any document affecting or relating to the company's property or affairs, or

(f) pawned, pledged or disposed of any property of the company which has been obtained on credit and has not been paid for (unless the pawning, pledging or disposal was in the ordinary way of the company's business).

(2) Such a person is deemed to have committed an offence if within the period above mentioned he has been privy to the doing by others of any of the things mentioned in paragraphs (c), (d) and (e) of subsection (1); and he commits an offence if, at any time after the commencement of the winding up, he does any of the things mentioned in paragraphs (a) to (f) of that subsection, or is privy to the doing by others of any of the things mentioned in paragraphs (c) to (e) of it.

(3) For purposes of this section, "officer" includes a shadow director.

(4) It is a defence—

(a) for a person charged under paragraph (a) or (f) of subsection (1) (or under subsection (2) in respect of the things mentioned in either of those two paragraphs) to prove that he had no intent to defraud, and

(b) for a person charged under paragraph (c) or (d) of subsection (1) (or under subsection (2) in respect of the things mentioned in either of those two paragraphs) to prove that he had no intent to conceal the state of affairs of the company or to defeat the law.

(5) Where a person pawns, pledges or disposes of any property in circumstances which amount to an offence under subsection (1)(f), every person who takes in pawn or pledge, or otherwise receives, the property knowing it to be pawned, pledged or disposed of in such circumstances, is guilty of an offence.

(6) A person guilty of an offence under this section is liable to imprisonment or a fine, or both.

(7) The money sums specified in paragraphs (a) and (b) of subsection (1) are subject to increase or reduction by order under section 416 in Part XV.

207 Transactions in fraud of creditors.

(1) When a company is ordered to be wound up by the court or passes a resolution for voluntary winding up, a person is deemed to have committed an offence if he, being at the time an officer of the company—

(a) has made or caused to be made any gift or transfer of, or charge on, or has caused or connived at the levying of any execution against, the company's property, or

(b) has concealed or removed any part of the company's property since, or within 2 months before, the date of any unsatisfied judgment or order for the payment of money obtained against the company.

(2) A person is not guilty of an offence under this section—

(a) by reason of conduct constituting an offence under subsection (1)(a) which occurred more than 5 years before the commencement of the winding up, or

(b) if he proves that, at the time of the conduct constituting the offence, he had no intent to defraud the company's creditors.

(3) A person guilty of an offence under this section is liable to imprisonment or a fine, or both.

208 Misconduct in course of winding up.

(1) When a company is being wound up, whether by the court or voluntarily, any person, being a past or present officer of the company, commits an offence if he—

(a) does not to the best of his knowledge and belief fully and truly discover to the liquidator all the company's property, and how and to whom and for what consideration and when the company disposed of any part of that property (except such part as has been disposed of in the ordinary way of the company's business), or

(b) does not deliver up to the liquidator (or as he directs) all such part of the company's property as is in his custody or under his control, and which he is required by law to deliver up, or

(c) does not deliver up to the liquidator (or as he directs) all books and papers in his custody or under his control belonging to the company and which he is required by law to deliver up, or

(d) knowing or believing that a false debt has been proved by any person in the winding up, fails to inform the liquidator as soon as practicable, or

(e) after the commencement of the winding up, prevents the production of any book or paper affecting or relating to the company's property or affairs.

(2) Such a person commits an offence if after the commencement of the winding up he attempts to account for any part of the company's property by fictitious losses or expenses; and he is deemed to have committed that offence if he has so attempted at any meeting of the company's creditors within the 12 months immediately preceding the commencement of the winding up.

(3) For purposes of this section, "officer" includes a shadow director.

(4) It is a defence—

(a) for a person charged under paragraph (a), (b) or (c) of subsection (1) to prove that he had no intent to defraud, and

(b) for a person charged under paragraph (e) of that subsection to prove that he had no intent to conceal the state of affairs of the company or to defeat the law.

(5) a person guilty of an offence under this section is liable to imprisonment or a fine, or both.

209 Falsification of company's books.

(1) When a company is being wound up, an officer or contributory of the company commits an offence if he destroys, mutilates, alters or falsifies any books, papers or securities, or makes or is privy to the making of any false or fraudulent entry in any register, book of account or document belonging to the company with intent to defraud or deceive any person.

(2) a person guilty of an offence under this section is liable to imprisonment or a fine, or both.

210 Material omissions from statement relating to company's affairs.

(1) When a company is being wound up, whether by the court or voluntarily, any person, being a past or present officer of the company, commits an offence if he makes any material omission in any statement relating to the company's affairs.

(2) When a company has been ordered to be wound up by the court, or has passed a resolution for voluntary winding up, any such person is deemed to have committed that offence if, prior to the winding up, he has made any material omission in any such statement.

(3) For purposes of this section, "officer" includes a shadow director.

(4) It is a defence for a person charged under this section to prove that he had no intent to defraud.

(5) A person guilty of an offence under this section is liable to imprisonment or a fine, or both.

211 False representations to creditors.

(1) When a company is being wound up, whether by the court or voluntarily, any person, being a past or present officer of the company—

(a) commits an offence if he makes any false representation or commits any other fraud for the purpose of obtaining the consent of the company's creditors or any of them to an agreement with reference to the company's affairs or to the winding up, and

(b) is deemed to have committed that offence if, prior to the winding up, he has made any false representation, or committed any other fraud, for that purpose.

(2) For purposes of this section, "officer" includes a shadow director.

(3) A person guilty of an offence under this section is liable to imprisonment or a fine, or both.

Penalisation of directors and officers

212 Summary remedy against delinquent directors, liquidators, etc.

(1) This section applies if in the course of the winding up of a company it appears that a person who—

(a) is or has been an officer of the company,

(b) has acted as liquidator...[7] or administrative receiver of the company, or

(c) not being a person falling within paragraph (a) or (b), is or has been concerned, or has taken part, in the promotion, formation or management of the company,

has misapplied or retained, or become accountable for, any money or other property of the company, or been guilty of any misfeasance or breach of any fiduciary or other duty in relation to the company.

(2) The reference in subsection (1) to any misfeasance or breach of any fiduciary or other duty in relation to the company includes, in the case of a person who has acted as liquidator...[8] of the company, any misfeasance or breach of any fiduciary or other duty in connection with the carrying out of his functions as liquidator.. of the company.

(3) The court may, on the application of the official receiver or the liquidator, or of any creditor or contributory, examine into the conduct of the person falling within subsection (1) and compel him—

(a) to repay, restore or account for the money or property or any part of it, with interest at such rate as the court thinks just, or

(b) to contribute such sum to the company's assets by way of compensation in respect of the misfeasance or breach of fiduciary or other duty as the court thinks just.

(4) The power to make an application under subsection (3) in relation to a person who has acted as liquidator...[9] of the company is not exercisable, except with the leave of the court, after [he][10] has had his release.

(5) The power of a contributory to make an application under subsection (3) is not exercisable except with the leave of the court, but is exercisable notwithstanding that he will not benefit from any order the court may make on the application.

213 Fraudulent trading.

(1) If in the course of the winding up of a company it appears that any business of the company has been carried on with intent to defraud creditors of the company or creditors of any other person, or for any fraudulent purpose, the following has effect.

(2) The court, on the application of the liquidator may declare that any persons who were knowingly parties to the carrying on of the business in the manner above-mentioned are to be liable to make such contributions (if any) to the company's assets as the court thinks proper.

214 Wrongful trading.

(1) Subject to subsection (3) below, if in the course of the winding up of a company it appears that subsection (2) of this section applies in relation to a person who is or has been a director of the company, the court, on the application of the liquidator, may declare that that person is to be liable to make such contribution (if any) to the company's assets as the court thinks proper.

(2) This subsection applies in relation to a person if—

(a) the company has gone into insolvent liquidation,

(b) at some time before the commencement of the winding up of the company, that person knew or ought to have concluded that there was no reasonable prospect that the company would avoid going into insolvent liquidation, and

(c) that person was a director of the company at that time;

but the court shall not make a declaration under this section in any case where the time mentioned in paragraph (b) above was before 28th April 1986.

(3) The court shall not make a declaration under this section with respect to any person if it is satisfied that after the condition specified in subsection (2)(b) was first satisfied in relation to him that person took every step with a view to minimising the potential loss to the company's creditors as (assuming him to have known that there was no reasonable prospect that the company would avoid going into solvent liquidation) he ought to have taken.

(4) For the purposes of subsections (2) and (3), the facts which a director of a company ought to know or ascertain, the conclusions which he ought to reach and the steps which he ought to take are those which would be known or ascertained, or reached or taken, by a reasonably diligent person having both—

(a) the general knowledge, skill and experience that may reasonably be expected of a person carrying out the same functions as are carried out by that director in relation to the company, and

(b) the general knowledge, skill and experience that that director has.

(5) The reference in subsection (4) to the functions carried out in relation to a company by a director of the company includes any functions which he does not carry out but which have been entrusted to him.

(6) For the purposes of this section a company goes into insolvent liquidation if it goes into liquidation at a time when its assets are insufficient for the payment of its debts and other liabilities and the expenses of the winding up.

(7) In this section "director" includes a shadow director.

(8) This section is without prejudice to section 213.

215 Proceedings under ss. 213, 214.

(1) On the hearing of an application under section 213 or 214, the liquidator may himself give evidence or call witnesses.

(2) Where under either section the court makes a declaration, it may give such further directions as it thinks proper for giving effect to the declaration; and in particular, the court may—

(a) provide for the liability of any person under the declaration to be a charge on any debt or obligation due from the company to him, or on any mortgage or charge or any interest in a mortgage or charge on assets of the company held by or vested in him, or any person on his behalf, or any person claiming as assignee from or through the person liable or any person acting on his behalf, and

(b) from time to time make such further order as may be necessary for enforcing any charge imposed under this subsection.

(3) For the purposes of subsection (2), "assignee"—

(a) includes a person to whom or in whose favour, by the directions of the person made liable, the debt, obligation, mortgage or charge was created, issued or transferred or the interest created, but

(b) does not include an assignee for valuable consideration (not including consideration by way of marriage [or the formation of a civil partnership][11]) given in good faith and without notice of any of the matters on the ground of which the declaration is made.

(4) Where the court makes a declaration under either section in relation to a person who is a creditor of the company, it may direct that the whole or any part of any debt owed by the company to that person and any interest thereon shall rank in priority after all other debts owed by the company and after any interest on those debts.

(5) Sections 213 and 214 have effect notwithstanding that the person concerned may be criminally liable in respect of matters on the ground of which the declaration under the section is to be made.

216 Restriction on re-use of company names.

(1) This section applies to a person where a company ("the liquidating company") has gone into

insolvent liquidation on or after the appointed day and he was a director or shadow director of the company at any time in the period of 12 months ending with the day before it went into liquidation.

(2) For the purposes of this section, a name is a prohibited name in relation to such a person if—

(a) it is a name by which the liquidating company was known at any time in that period of 12 months, or

(b) it is a name which is so similar to a name falling within paragraph (a) as to suggest an association with that company.

(3) Except with leave of the court or in such circumstances as may be prescribed, a person to whom this section applies shall not at any time in the period of 5 years beginning with the day on which the liquidating company went into liquidation—

(a) be a director of any other company that is known by a prohibited name, or

(b) in any way, whether directly or indirectly, be concerned or take part in the promotion, formation or management of any such company, or

(c) in any way, whether directly or indirectly, be concerned or take part in the carrying on of a business carried on (otherwise than by a company) under a prohibited name.

(4) If a person acts in contravention of this section, he is liable to imprisonment or a fine, or both.

(5) In subsection (3) "the court" means any court having jurisdiction to wind up companies; and on an application for leave under that subsection, the Secretary of State or the official receiver may appear and call the attention of the court to any matters which seem to him to be relevant.

(6) References in this section, in relation to any time, to a name by which a company is known are to the name of the company at that time or to any name under which the company carries on business at that time.

(7) For the purposes of this section a company goes into insolvent liquidation if it goes into liquidation at a time when its assets are insufficient for the payment of its debts and other liabilities and the expenses of the winding up.

(8) In this section "company" includes a company which may be wound up under Part V of this Act.

217 Personal liability for debts, following contravention of s. 216.

(1) A person is personally responsible for all the relevant debts of a company if at any time—

(a) in contravention of section 216, he is involved in the management of the company, or

(b) as a person who is involved in the management of the company, he acts or is willing to act on instructions given (without the leave of the court) by a person whom he knows at that time to be in contravention in relation to the company of section 216.

(2) Where a person is personally responsible under this section for the relevant debts of a company, he is jointly and severally liable in respect of those debts with the company and any other person who, whether under this section or otherwise, is so liable.

(3) For the purposes of this section the relevant debts of a company are—

(a) in relation to a person who is personally responsible under paragraph (a) of subsection (1), such debts and other liabilities of the company as are incurred at a time when that person was involved in the management of the company, and

(b) in relation to a person who is personally responsible under paragraph (b) of that subsection, such debts and other liabilities of the company as are incurred at a time when that person was acting or was willing to act on instructions given as mentioned in that paragraph.

(4) For the purposes of this section, a person is involved in the management of a company if he is a director of the company or if he is concerned, whether directly or indirectly, or takes part, in the management of the company.

(5) For the purposes of this section a person who, as a person involved in the management of a company, has at any time acted on instructions given (without the leave of the court) by a person whom he knew at that time to be in contravention in relation to the company of section 216 is presumed, unless the contrary is shown, to have been willing at any time thereafter to act on any instructions given by that person.

(6) In this section "company" includes a company which may be wound up under Part V.

Investigation and prosecution of malpractice

218 Prosecution of delinquent officers and members of company.

(1) If it appears to the court in the course of a winding up by the court that any past or present officer, or

any member, of the company has been guilty of any offence in relation to the company for which he is criminally liable, the court may (either on the application of a person interested in the winding up or of its own motion) direct the liquidator to refer the matter

[(a) in the case of a winding up in England and Wales, to the Secretary of State, and

(b) in the case of a winding up in Scotland, to the Lord Advocate][12]

(2). . . . .[13]

(3) If in the case of a winding up by the court in England and Wales it appears to the liquidator, not being the official receiver, that any past or present officer of the company, or any member of it, has been guilty of an offence in relation to the company for which he is criminally liable, the liquidator shall report the matter to the official receiver.

(4) If it appears to the liquidator in the course of a voluntary winding up that any past or present officer of the company, or any member of it, has been guilty of an offence in relation to the company for which he is criminally liable, he shall [forthwith report the matter—

(a) in the case of a winding up in England and Wales, to the Secretary of State, and

(b) in the case of a winding up in Scotland, to the Lord Advocate,

and shall furnish to the Secretary of State or (as the case may be) the Lord Advocate][14] such information and give to him such access to and facilities for inspecting and taking copies of documents (being information or documents in the possession or under the control of the liquidator and relating to the matter in question) as [the Secretary of State or (as the case may be) the Lord Advocate][15] requires.

[(5) Where a report is made to the Secretary of State under subsection (4) he may, for the purpose of investigating the matter reported to him and such other matters relating to the affairs of the company as appear to him to require investigation, exercise any of the powers which are exercisable by inspectors appointed under section 431 or 432 of the [the Companies Act 1985][16] to investigate a company's affairs.][17]

(6) If it appears to the court in the course of a voluntary winding up that—

(a) any past or present officer of the company, or any member of it, has been guilty as above-mentioned, and

(b) no report with respect to the matter has been made by the liquidator. . .[18] under subsection (4),

the court may (on the application of any person interested in the winding up or of its own motion) direct the liquidator to make such a report.

On a report being made accordingly, this section has effect as though the report had been made in pursuance of subsection (4).

219 Obligations arising under s. 218.

(1) For the purpose of an investigation by the Secretary of State [in consequence of a report made to him under section 218(4)][19], any obligation imposed on a person by any provision of [the Companies Act 1985][20] to produce documents or give information to, or otherwise to assist, inspectors appointed as mentioned in [section 218(5)][21] is to be regarded as an obligation similarly to assist the Secretary of State in his investigation.

(2) an answer given by a person to a question put to him in exercise of the powers conferred by section 218(5) may be used in evidence against him.

[(2A) However, in criminal proceedings in which that person is charged with an offence to which this subsection applies—

(a) no evidence relating to the answer may be adduced, and

(b) no question relating to it may be asked,

by or on behalf of the prosecution, unless evidence relating to it is adduced, or a question relating to it is asked, in the proceedings by or on behalf of that person.

(2B) Subsection (2A) applies to any offence other than—

(a) an offence under section 2 or 5 of the Perjury Act 1911 (false statements made on oath otherwise than in judicial proceedings or made otherwise than on oath), or

(b) an offence under section 44(1) or (2) of the Criminal Law (Consolidation) (Scotland) Act 1995 (false statements made on oath or otherwise than on oath).][22]

(3) Where criminal proceedings are instituted by [the Director of Public Prosecutions, the Lord Advocate][23] or the Secretary of State following any report or reference under section 218, it is the

duty of the liquidator and every officer and agent of the company past and present (other than the defendant or defender) to give to [the Director of Public Prosecutions, the Lord Advocate][24] or the Secretary of State (as the case may be) all assistance in connection with the prosecution which he is reasonably able to give.

For this purpose "agent" includes any banker or solicitor of the company and any person employed by the company as auditor, whether that person is or is not an officer of the company.

(4) If a person fails or neglects to give assistance in the manner required by subsection (3), the court may, on the application of the [Director of Public Prosecutions, the Lord Advocate][25] or the Secretary of State (as the case may be) direct the person to comply with that subsection; and if the application is made with respect to a liquidator, the court may (unless it appears that the failure or neglect to comply was due to the liquidator not having in his hands sufficient assets of the company to enable him to do so) direct that the costs shall be borne by the liquidator personally.

Adjustment of prior transactions (administration and liquidation)

238 Transactions at an undervalue (England and Wales).

(1) This section applies in the case of a company where—

[(a) the company enters administration,][26]

(b) the company goes into liquidation;

and "the office-holder" means the administrator or the liquidator, as the case may be.

(2) Where the company has at a relevant time (defined in section 240) entered into a transaction with any person at an undervalue, the office-holder may apply to the court for an order under this section.

(3) Subject as follows, the court shall, on such an application, make such order as it thinks fit for restoring the position to what it would have been if the company had not entered into that transaction.

(4) For the purposes of this section and section 241, a company enters into a transaction with a person at an undervalue if—

(a) the company makes a gift to that person or otherwise enters into a transaction with that person on terms that provide for the company to receive no consideration, or

(b) the company enters into a transaction with that person for a consideration the value of which, in money or money's worth, is significantly less than the value, in money or money's worth, of the consideration provided by the company.

(5) The court shall not make an order under this section in respect of a transaction at an undervalue if it is satisfied—

(a) that the company which entered into the transaction did so in good faith and for the purpose of carrying on its business, and

(b) that at the time it did so there were reasonable grounds for believing that the transaction would benefit the company.

239 Preferences (England and Wales).

(1) This section applies as does section 238.

(2) Where the company has at a relevant time (defined in the next section) given a preference to any person, the office-holder may apply to the court for an order under this section.

(3) Subject as follows, the court shall, on such an application, make such order as it thinks fit for restoring the position to what it would have been if the company had not given that preference.

(4) For the purposes of this section and section 241, a company gives a preference to a person if—

(a) that person is one of the company's creditors or a surety or guarantor for any of the company's debts or other liabilities, and

(b) the company does anything or suffers anything to be done which (in either case) has the effect of putting that person into a position which, in the event of the company going into insolvent liquidation, will be better than the position he would have been in if that thing had not been done.

(5) The court shall not make an order under this section in respect of a preference given to any person unless the company which gave the preference was influenced in deciding to give it by a desire to produce in relation to that person the effect mentioned in subsection (4)(b).

(6) A company which has given a preference to a person connected with the company (otherwise than

by reason only of being its employee) at the time the preference was given is presumed, unless the contrary is shown, to have been influenced in deciding to give it by such a desire as is mentioned in subsection (5).

(7) The fact that something has been done in pursuance of the order of a court does not, without more, prevent the doing or suffering of that thing from constituting the giving of a preference.

240"Relevant time" under ss. 238, 239.

(1) Subject to the next subsection, the time at which a company enters into a transaction at an undervalue or gives a preference is a relevant time if the transaction is entered into, or the preference given—

(a) in the case of a transaction at an undervalue or of a preference which is given to a person who is connected with the company (otherwise than by reason only of being its employee), at a time in the period of 2 years ending with the onset of insolvency (which expression is defined below),

(b) in the case of a preference which is not such a transaction and is not so given, at a time in the period of 6 months ending with the onset of insolvency,...[27]

[(c) in either case, at a time between the making of an administration application in respect of the company and the making of an administration order on that application, and

(d) in either case, at a time between the filing with the court of a copy of notice of intention to appoint an administrator under paragraph 14 or 22 of Schedule B1 and the making of an appointment under that paragraph.][28]

(2) Where a company enters into a transaction at an undervalue or gives a preference at a time mentioned in subsection (1)(a) or (b), that time is not a relevant time for the purposes of section 238 or 239 unless the company—

(a) is at that time unable to pay its debts within the meaning of section 123 in Chapter VI of Part IV, or

(b) becomes unable to pay its debts within the meaning of that section in consequence of the transaction or preference;

but the requirements of this subsection are presumed to be satisfied, unless the contrary is shown, in relation to any transaction at an undervalue which is entered into by a company with a person who is connected with the company.

(3) For the purposes of subsection (1), the onset of insolvency is—

[(a) in a case where section 238 or 239 applies by reason of an administrator of a company being appointed by administration order, the date on which the administration application is made,

(b) in a case where section 238 or 239 applies by reason of an administrator of a company being appointed under paragraph 14 or 22 of Schedule B1 following filing with the court of a copy of a notice of intention to appoint under that paragraph, the date on which the copy of the notice is filed,

(c) in a case where section 238 or 239 applies by reason of an administrator of a company being appointed otherwise than as mentioned in paragraph (a) or (b), the date on which the appointment takes effect,

(d) in a case where section 238 or 239 applies by reason of a company going into liquidation either following conversion of administration into winding up by virtue of Article 37 of the EC Regulation or at the time when the appointment of an administrator ceases to have effect, the date on which the company entered administration (or, if relevant, the date on which the application for the administration order was made or a copy of the notice of intention to appoint was filed), and

(e) in a case where section 238 or 239 applies by reason of a company going into liquidation at any other time, the date of the commencement of the winding up.][29]

241 Orders under ss. 238, 239.

(1) Without prejudice to the generality of sections 238(3) and 239(3), an order under either of those sections with respect to a transaction or preference entered into or given by a company may (subject to the next subsection)—

(a) require any property transferred as part of the transaction, or in connection with the giving of the preference, to be vested in the company,

(b) require any property to be so vested if it represents in any person's hands the application either

of the proceeds of sale of property so transferred or of money so transferred,

(c) release or discharge (in whole or in part) any security given by the company,

(d) require any person to pay, in respect of benefits received by him from the company, such sums to the office-holder as the court may direct,

(e) provide for any surety or guarantor whose obligations to any person were released or discharged (in whole or in part) under the transaction, or by the giving of the preference, to be under such new or revived obligations to that person as the court thinks appropriate,

(f) provide for security to be provided for the discharge of any obligation imposed by or arising under the order, for such an obligation to be charged on any property and for the security or charge to have the same priority as a security or charge released or discharged (in whole or in part) under the transaction or by the giving of the preference, and

(g) provide for the extent to which any person whose property is vested by the order in the company, or on whom obligations are imposed by the order, is to be able to prove in the winding up of the company for debts or other liabilities which arose from, or were released or discharged (in whole or in part) under or by, the transaction or the giving of the preference.

(2) An order under section 238 or 239 may affect the property of, or impose any obligation on, any person whether or not he is the person with whom the company in question entered into the transaction or (as the case may be) the person to whom the preference was given; but such an order—

(a) shall not prejudice any interest in property which was acquired from a person other than the company and was acquired [in good faith and for value][30], or prejudice any interest deriving from such an interest, and

(b) shall not require a person who received a benefit from the transaction or preference [in good faith and for value][31] to pay a sum to the office-holder, except where that person was a party to the transaction or the payment is to be in respect of a preference given to that person at a time when he was a creditor of the company.

[(2A) Where a person has acquired an interest in property from a person other than the company in question, or has received a benefit from the transaction or preference, and at the time of that acquisition or receipt—

(a) he had notice of the relevant surrounding circumstances and of the relevant proceedings, or

(b) he was connected with, or was an associate of, either the company in question or the person with whom that company entered into the transaction or to whom that company gave the preference,

then, unless the contrary is shown, it shall be presumed for the purposes of paragraph (a) or (as the case may be) paragraph (b) of subsection (2) that the interest was acquired or the benefit was received otherwise than in good faith.][32]

[(3) For the purposes of subsection (2A)(a), the relevant surrounding circumstances are (as the case may require)—

(a) the fact that the company in question entered into the transaction at an undervalue; or

(b) the circumstances which amounted to the giving of the preference by the company in question;

and subsections (3A) to (3C) have effect to determine whether, for those purposes, a person has notice of the relevant proceedings.

[(3A) Where section 238 or 239 applies by reason of a company's entering administration, a person has notice of the relevant proceedings if he has notice that—

(a) an administration application has been made,

(b) an administration order has been made,

(c) a copy of a notice of intention to appoint an administrator under paragraph 14 or 22 of Schedule B1 has been filed, or

(d) notice of the appointment of an administrator has been filed under paragraph 18 or 29 of that Schedule.][33]

[(3B) Where section 238 or 239 applies by reason of a company's going into liquidation at the time when the appointment of an administrator of the company ceases to have effect, a person has notice of the relevant proceedings if he has notice that—

(a) an administration application has been made,

(b) an administration order has been made,

(c) a copy of a notice of intention to appoint an administrator under paragraph 14 or 22 of Schedule B1 has been filed,

(d) notice of the appointment of an administrator has been filed under paragraph 18 or 29 of that Schedule, or

(e) the company has gone into liquidation.][34]

(3C) In a case where section 238 or 239 applies by reason of the company in question going into liquidation at any other time, a person has notice of the relevant proceedings if he has notice—

(a) where the company goes into liquidation on the making of a winding-up order, of the fact that the petition on which the winding-up order is made has been presented or of the fact that the company has gone into liquidation;

(b) in any other case, of the fact that the company has gone into liquidation.][35]

(4) The provisions of sections 238 to 241 apply without prejudice to the availability of any other remedy, even in relation to a transaction or preference which the company had no power to enter into or give.

...

Interpretation for First Group of Parts

247"Insolvency" and "go into liquidation".

(1) In this Group of Parts, except in so far as the context otherwise requires, "insolvency", in relation to a company, includes the approval of a voluntary arrangement under Part I, [or the appointment of an administrator or administrative receiver][36].

(2) For the purposes of any provision in this Group of Parts, a company goes into liquidation if it passes a resolution for voluntary winding up or an order for its winding up is made by the court at a time when it has not already gone into liquidation by passing such a resolution.

[(3) The reference to a resolution for voluntary winding up in subsection (2) includes a reference to a resolution which is deemed to occur by virtue of—

(a) paragraph 83(6)(b) of Schedule B1, or

(b) an order made following conversion of administration or a voluntary arrangement into winding up by virtue of Article 37 of the EC Regulation.][37]

248"Secured creditor", etc.

In this Group of Parts, except in so far as the context otherwise requires—

(a) "secured creditor", in relation to a company, means a creditor of the company who holds in respect of his debt a security over property of the company, and "unsecured creditor" is to be read accordingly; and

(b) "security" means—

(i) in relation to England and Wales, any mortgage, charge, lien or other security, and

(ii) in relation to Scotland, any security (whether heritable or moveable), any floating charge and any right of lien or preference and any right of retention (other than a right of compensation or set off).

249"Connected" with a company.

For the purposes of any provision in this Group of Parts, a person is connected with a company if—

(a) he is a director or shadow director of the company or an associate of such a director or shadow director, or

(b) he is an associate of the company,

and "associate" has the meaning given by section 435 in Part XVIII of this Act.

250"Member" of a company.

For the purposes of any provision in this Group of Parts, a person who is not a member of a company but to whom shares in the company have been transferred, or transmitted by operation of law, is to be regarded as a member of the company, and references to a member or members are to be read accordingly.

251 Expressions used generally.

In this Group of Parts, except in so far as the context otherwise requires—

"administrative receiver" means—

(a) an administrative receiver as defined by section 29(2) in Chapter I of Part III, or

(b) a receiver appointed under section 51 in Chapter II of that Part in a case where the whole (or substantially the whole) of the company's property is attached by the floating charge;

["agent" does not include a person's counsel acting as such;][38]

["books and papers" and "books or papers" includes accounts, deeds, writing and documents;][39]

"business day" means any day other than a Saturday, a Sunday, Christmas Day, Good Friday or a day which is a bank holiday in any part of Great Britain;

"chattel leasing agreement" means an agreement for the bailment or, in Scotland, the hiring of goods which is capable of subsisting for more than 3 months;

"contributory" has the meaning given by section 79;

["the court", in relation to a company, means a court having jurisdiction to wind up the company;][40]

"director" includes any person occupying the position of director, by whatever name called;

["document" includes summons, notice, order and other legal process, and registers;][41]

"floating charge" means a charge which, as created, was a floating charge an includes a floating charge within section 462 of the Companies Act (Scottish floating charges);

["the Gazette" means—

(a) as respects companies registered in England and Wales, the London Gazette;

(b) as respects companies registered in Scotland, the Edinburgh Gazette;][42]

. . . .[43]

["officer", in relation to a body corporate, includes a director, manager or secretary;][44]

"the official rate", in relation to interest, means the rate payable under section 189(4);

"prescribed" means prescribed by the rules;

"receiver", in the expression "receiver or manager", does not include a receiver appointed under section 51 in Chapter II of Part III;

"retention of title agreement" means an agreement for the sale of goods to a company, being an agreement—

(a) which does not constitute a charge on the goods, but

(b) under which, if the seller is not paid and the company is wound up, the seller will have priority over all other creditors of the company as respects the goods or any property representing the goods;

"the rules" means rules under section 411 in Part XV; and

"shadow director", in relation to a company, means a person in accordance with whose directions or instructions the directors of the company are accustomed to act (but so that a person is not deemed a shadow director by reason only that the directors act on advice given by him in a professional capacity);

. . . .[45]

...

443 Commencement.

This Act comes into force on the day appointed under section 236(2) of the Insolvency Act 1985 for the coming into force of Part III of that Act (individual insolvency and bankruptcy), immediately after that Part of that Act comes into force for England and Wales.

444 Citation.

This Act may be cited as the Insolvency Act 1986.

---

[1] Words in s. 122(1)(b) substituted (6.4.2008) by The Companies Act 2006 (Consequential Amendments etc) Order 2008 (S.I. 2008/948), art. 3(1), Sch. 1 para. 102 (with arts. 6, 11, 12)

[2] Words in s. 122(1)(c) substituted (1.10.2009) by The Companies Act 2006 (Consequential Amendments, Transitional Provisions and Savings) Order 2009, (S.I. 2009/1941) arts. 2(1), 8, {Sch. 1 para. 75(12)} (with art. 10, Sch. 1 para. 84)

[3] Words in s. 122(1)(e) inserted (15.7.1992) by S.I. 1992/1699, reg. 2, Sch. para. 8

[4] S. 122(1)(fa) inserted (1.1.2003) by 2000 c. 39, s. 1, Sch. 1 para. 6; S.I. 2002/2711, art. 2 (with transitional provisions in arts. 3-5)

[5] "£500" substituted by virtue of S.I. 1986/1996, art. 2(1), Sch. Pt. I

[6] "£500" substituted by virtue of S.I. 1986/1996, art. 2(1), Sch. Pt. I

[7] Word in s. 212(1)(b) repealed (15.9.2003) by 2002 c. 40, ss. 248(3), 278, 279, Sch. 17 para. 18(a), Sch. 26 (with s. 249(1)-(3)(6)); S.I. 2003/2093, art. 2(1), Sch. 1 (subject to arts. 3-8 (as amended by S.I. 2003/2332, art. 2))

[8] Words in s. 212(2) repealed (15.9.2003) by 2002 c. 40, ss. 248(3), 278, 279, Sch. 17 para. 18(b), Sch. 26 (with s. 249(1)-(3)(6)); S.I. 2003/2093, art. 2(1), Sch. 1 (subject to arts. 3-8 (as amended by S.I. 2003/2332, art. 2))

[9] Words in s. 212(4) repealed (15.9.2003) by 2002 c. 40, ss. 248(3), 278, 279, Sch. 17 para. 18(c)(i), Sch. 26 (with s. 249(1)-(3)(6)); S.I. 2003/2093, art. 2(1), Sch. 1 (subject to arts. 3-8 (as amended by S.I. 2003/2332, art. 2))

[10] Word in s. 212(4) substituted (15.9.2003) by 2002 c. 40, ss. 248(3), 279, Sch. 17 para. 18(c)(ii) (with s. 249(1)-(3)(6)); S.I. 2003/2093, art. 2(1), Sch. 1 (subject to arts. 3-8 (as amended by S.I. 2003/2332, art. 2))

[11] Words in s. 215(3)(b) inserted (5.12.2005) by Civil Partnership Act 2004 (c. 33), ss. 261(1), 263, Sch. 27 para. 112; S.I. 2005/3175, art. 2(2) (subject to art. 2(3)-(5))

[12] S. 218(1)(a)(b) substituted for words in s. 218(1) (2.4.2001) by 2000 c. 39, s. 10(2); S.I. 2001/766, art. 2(1)(b) (subject to art. 3)

[13] S. 218(2) repealed (2.4.2001) by 2000 c. 39, ss. 10(3), 15, Sch. 5; S.I. 2001/766, art. 2(1)(b)(c) (subject to art. 3)

[14] Words in s. 218(4)(a)(b) substituted (2.4.2001) by 2000 c. 39, s. 10(4)(a); S.I. 2001/766, art. 2(b) (subject to art. 3)

[15] Words in s. 218(4) substituted (2.4.2001) by 2000 c. 39, s. 10(4)(b); S.I. 2001/766, art. 2(b) (subject to art. 3)

[16] Words in s. 218(5) substituted (1.10.2009) by The Companies Act 2006 (Consequential Amendments, Transitional Provisions and Savings) Order 2009, (S.I. 2009/1941) arts. 2(1), 8, {Sch. 1 para. 75(24)} (with art. 10, Sch. 1 para. 84)

[17] S. 218(5) substituted (2.4.2001) by 2000 c. 39, s. 10(5); S.I. 2001/766, art. 2(b) (subject to art. 3)

[18] Words in s. 218(6)(b) repealed (2.4.2001) by 2000 c. 39, ss. 10(6), 15, Sch. 5; S.I. 2001/766, art. 2(1)(b)(c) (subject to art. 3)

[19] Words in s. 219(1) substituted (2.4.2001) by 2000 c. 39, s. 10(7)(a); S.I. 2001/766, art. 2(1)(b) (subject to art. 3)

[20] Words in s. 219(1) substituted (1.10.2009) by The Companies Act 2006 (Consequential Amendments, Transitional Provisions and Savings) Order 2009, (S.I. 2009/1941) arts. 2(1), 8, {Sch. 1 para. 75(24)} (with art. 10, Sch. 1 para. 84)

[21] Words in s. 219(1) substituted (2.4.2001) by 2000 c. 39, s. 10(7)(a); S.I. 2001/766, art. 2(1)(b) (subject to art. 3)

[22] S. 219(2A)(2B) inserted (2.4.2001) by 2000 c. 39, s. 11; S.I. 2001/766, art. 2(1)(b); (subject to art. 3)

[23] Words in s. 219(3) substituted (2.4.2001) by 2000 c. 39, s. 10(7)(b); S.I. 2001/766, art. 2(1)(b) (subject to art. 3)

[24] Words in s. 219(3) substituted (2.4.2001) by 2000 c. 39, s. 10(7)(b); S.I. 2001/766, art. 2(1)(b) (subject to art. 3)

[25] Words in s. 219(4) substituted (2.4.2001) by 2000 c. 39, s. 10(7)(c); S.I. 2001/766, art. 2(1)(b) (subject to art. 3)

[26] S. 238(1)(a) substituted (15.9.2003) by 2002 c. 40, ss. 248(3), 279, Sch. 17 para. 25 (with s. 249(1)-(3)(6)); S.I. 2003/2093, art. 2(1), Sch. 1 (subject to arts. 3-8 (as amended by S.I. 2003/2332, art. 2))

[27] Word in s. 240(1)(b) repealed (15.9.2003) by 2002 c. 40, ss. 248(3), 278, 279, Sch. 17 para. 26(3), Sch. 26 (with s. 249(1)-(3)(6)); S.I. 2003/2093, art. 2(1), Sch. 1 (subject to arts. 3-8 (as amended by S.I. 2003/2332, art. 2))

[28] S. 240(1)(c)(d) substituted (15.9.2003) for s. 240(1)(c) by 2002 c. 40, ss. 248(3), 279, Sch. 17 para. 26(2) (with s. 249(1)-(3)(6)); S.I. 2003/2093, art. 2(1), Sch. 1 (subject to arts. 3-8 (as amended by S.I. 2003/2332, art. 2))

[29] S. 240(3)(a)-(e) substituted (15.9.2003) for s. 240(3)(a)(aa)(b) by 2002 c. 40, ss. 248(3), 279, Sch. 17 para. 26(4) (with s. 249(1)-(3)(6)); S.I. 2003/2093, art. 2(1), Sch. 1 (subject to arts. 3-8 (as amended by S.I. 2003/2332, art. 2))

[30] Words in s. 241(2)(a)(b) substituted (26.7.1994) by 1994 c. 12, ss. 1(1), 5, 6(2) (with ss. 5, 6(3))

[31] Words in s. 241(2)(a)(b) substituted (26.7.1994) by 1994 c. 12, ss. 1(1), 5, 6(2) (with ss. 5, 6(3))

[32] S. 241(2A) inserted (26.7.1994) by 1994 c. 12, ss. 1(2), 5, 6(2) (with ss. 5, 6(3))

[33] S. 241(3A) substituted (15.9.2003) by 2002 c. 40, ss. 248(3), 279, Sch. 17 para. 27(2) (with s. 249(1)-(3)(6)); S.I. 2003/2093, art. 2(1), Sch. 1 (subject to arts. 3-8 (as amended by S.I. 2003/2332, art. 2))

[34] S. 241(3B) substituted (15.9.2003) by 2002 c. 40, ss. 248(3), 279, Sch. 17 para. 27(3) (with s. 249(1)-(3)(6)); S.I. 2003/2093, art. 2(1), Sch. 1 (subject to arts. 3-8 (as amended by S.I. 2003/2332, art. 2))

[35] S. 241(3)(3A)(3B)(3C) substituted (26.7.1994) for s. 241(3) by 1994 c. 12, ss. 1(3), 5, 6(2) (with ss. 5, 6(3))

[36] Words in s. 247(1) substituted (15.9.2003) by 2002 c. 40, ss. 248(3), 279, Sch. 17 para. 33(2) (with s. 249(1)-(3)(6)); S.I. 2003/2093, art. 2(1), Sch. 1 (subject to arts. 3-8 (as amended by S.I. 2003/2332, art. 2))

[37] S. 247(3) substituted (15.9.2003) by 2002 c. 40, ss. 248(3), 279, Sch. 17 para. 33(3) (with s. 249(1)-(3)(6)); S.I. 2003/2093, art. 2(1), Sch. 1 (subject to arts. 3-8 (as amended by S.I. 2003/2332, art. 2))

[38] S. 251: definition inserted (1.10.2009) by The Companies Act 2006 (Consequential Amendments, Transitional Provisions and Savings) Order 2009, (S.I. 2009/1941) arts. 2(1), 8, {Sch. 1 para. 77(2)} (with art. 10, Sch. 1 para. 84)

[39] S. 251: definition inserted (1.10.2009) by The Companies Act 2006 (Consequential Amendments, Transitional Provisions and Savings) Order 2009, (S.I. 2009/1941) arts. 2(1), 8, {Sch. 1 para. 77(2)} (with art. 10, Sch. 1 para. 84)

[40] S. 251: definition inserted (1.10.2009) by The Companies Act 2006 (Consequential Amendments, Transitional Provisions and Savings) Order 2009, (S.I. 2009/1941) arts. 2(1), 8, {Sch. 1 para. 77(2)} (with art. 10, Sch. 1 para. 84)

[41] S. 251: definition inserted (1.10.2009) by The Companies Act 2006 (Consequential Amendments, Transitional Provisions and Savings) Order 2009, (S.I. 2009/1941) arts. 2(1), 8, {Sch. 1 para. 77(2)} (with art. 10, Sch. 1 para. 84)

[42] S. 251: definition inserted (1.10.2009) by The Companies Act 2006 (Consequential Amendments, Transitional Provisions and Savings) Order 2009, (S.I. 2009/1941) arts. 2(1), 8, {Sch. 1 para. 77(2)} (with art. 10, Sch. 1 para. 84)

[43] S. 251: definition omitted (1.10.2009) by virtue of The Companies Act 2006 (Consequential Amendments, Transitional Provisions and Savings) Order 2009, (S.I. 2009/1941) arts. 2(1), 8, {Sch. 1 para. 77(3)} (with art. 10, Sch. 1 para. 84)

[44] S. 251: definition inserted (1.10.2009) by The Companies Act 2006 (Consequential Amendments, Transitional Provisions and Savings) Order 2009, (S.I. 2009/1941) arts. 2(1), 8, {Sch. 1 para. 77(2)} (with art. 10, Sch. 1 para. 84)

[45] Words in s. 251 omitted (1.10.2009) by virtue of The Companies Act 2006 (Consequential Amendments, Transitional Provisions and Savings) Order 2009, (S.I. 2009/1941) arts. 2(1), 8, {Sch. 1 para. 77(4)} (with art. 10, Sch. 1 para. 84)

Reverter of Sites Act 1987

1987 CHAPTER 15

An Act to amend the law with respect to the reverter of sites that have ceased to be used for particular purposes; and for connected purposes.

[9th April 1987]

1 Right of reverter replaced by [trust][1].

(1) Where any relevant enactment provides for land to revert to the ownership of any person at any time, being a time when the land ceases, or has ceased for a specified period, to be used for particular purposes, that enactment shall have effect, and (subject to subsection (4) below) shall be deemed always to have had effect, as if it provided (instead of for the reverter) for the land to be vested after that time, on the trust arising under this section, in the persons in whom it was vested immediately before that time.

(2) Subject to the following provisions of this Act, the trust arising under this section in relation to any land is a trust [for the persons who (but for this Act) would from time to time be entitled to the ownership of the land by virtue of its reverter with a power, without consulting them,][2] to sell the land and to stand possessed of the net proceeds of sale (after payment of costs and expenses) and of the net rents and profits until sale (after payment of rates, taxes, costs of insurance, repairs and other outgoings) [in trust for those persons; but they shall not be entitled by reason of their interest to occupy the land.][3]

(3) Where—

(a) a trust in relation to any land has arisen or is treated as having arisen under this section at such a time as is mentioned in subsection (1) above; and

(b) immediately before that time the land was vested in any persons in their capacity as the minister and churchwardens of any parish,

those persons shall be treated as having become [trustees][4] under this section in that capacity and, accordingly, their interest in the land shall pass and, if the case so requires, be treated as having passed to their successors from time to time.

(4) This section shall not confer any right on any person as a beneficiary—

(a) in relation to any property in respect of which that person's claim was statute-barred before the commencement of this Act, or in relation to any property derived from any such property; or

(b) in relation to any rents or profits received, or breach of trust committed, before the commencement of this Act;

and anything validly done before the commencement of this Act in relation to any land which by virtue of this section is deemed to have been held at the time [in trust][5] shall, if done by the beneficiaries, be deemed, so far as necessary for preserving its validity, to have been done by the trustees.

(5) Where any property is held by any persons as trustees of a trust which has arisen under this section and, in consequence of subsection (4) above, there are no beneficiaries of that trust, the trustees shall have no power to act in relation to that property except—

(a) for the purposes for which they could have acted in relation to that property if this Act had not been passed; or

(b) for the purpose of securing the establishment of a scheme under section 2 below or the making of an order under [section 554 of the Education Act 1996][6] (special powers as to trusts for religious education).

(6) In this section—

"churchwardens" includes chapel wardens;

"minister" includes a rector, vicar or perpetual curate; and

"parish" includes a parish of the Church in Wales;

and the reference to a person's claim being statute-barred is a reference to the Limitation Act 1980 providing that no proceedings shall be brought by that person to recover the property in respect of which the claim subsists.

2 Charity Commissioners' schemes.

(1) Subject to the following provisions of this section and to sections 3 and 4 below, where any persons

hold any property as trustees of a trust which has arisen under section 1 above, the Charity Commissioners may, on the application of the trustees, by order establish a scheme which—

(a) extinguishes the rights of beneficiaries under the trust; and

(b) requires the trustees to hold the property on trust for such charitable purposes as may be specified in the order.

(2) Subject to subsections (3) and (4) below, an order made under this section—

(a) may contain any such provision as may be contained in an order made by the High Court for establishing a scheme for the administration of a charity; and

(b) shall have the same effect as an order so made.

(3) The charitable purposes specified in an order made under this section on an application with respect to any trust shall be as similar in character as the Charity Commissioners think is practicable in all the circumstances to the purposes (whether charitable or not) for which the trustees held the relevant land before the cesser of use in consequence of which the trust arose; but in determining the character of the last-mentioned purposes the Commissioners, if they think it appropriate to do so, may give greater weight to the persons or locality benefited by the purposes than to the nature of the benefit.

(4) An order made under this section on an application with respect to any trust shall be so framed as to secure that if a person who—

(a) but for the making of the order would have been a beneficiary under the trust; and

(b) has not consented to the establishment of a scheme under this section,

notifies a claim to the trustees within the period of five years after the date of the making of the order, that person shall be paid an amount equal to the value of his rights at the time of their extinguishment.

(5) The Charity Commissioners shall not make any order under this section establishing a scheme unless—

(a) the requirements of section 3 below with respect to the making of the application for the order are satisfied or, by virtue of subsection (4) of that section, do not apply;

(b) one of the conditions specified in subsection (6) below is fulfilled;

(c) public notice of the Commissioners' proposals has been given inviting representations to be made to them within a period specified in the notice, being a period ending not less than one month after the date of the giving of the notice; and

(d) that period has ended and the Commissioners have taken into consideration any representations which have been made within that period and not withdrawn.

(6) The conditions mentioned in subsection (5)(b) above are—

(a) that there is no claim by any person to be a beneficiary in respect of rights proposed to be extinguished—

(i) which is outstanding; or

(ii) which has at any time been accepted as valid by the trustees or by persons whose acceptance binds the trustees; or

(iii) which has been upheld in proceedings that have been concluded;

(b) that consent to the establishment of a scheme under this section has been given by every person whose claim to be a beneficiary in respect of those rights is outstanding or has been so accepted or upheld.

(7) The Charity Commissioners shall refuse to consider an application under this section unless it is accompanied by a statutory declaration by the applicants—

(a) that the requirements of section 3 below are satisfied with respect to the making of the application or, if the declaration so declares, do not apply; and

(b) that a condition specified in subsection (6) above and identified in the declaration is fulfilled;

and the declaration shall be conclusive for the purposes of this section of the matters declared therein.

(8) A notice given for the purposes of subsection (5)(c) above shall contain such particulars of the Commissioners' proposals, or such directions for obtaining information about them, and shall be given in such manner, as they think sufficient and appropriate; and a further such notice shall not be required where the Commissioners decide, before proceeding with any proposals of which notice

has been so given, to modify them.

3 Applications for schemes.

(1) Where an application is made under section 2 above by the trustees of any trust that has arisen under section 1 above, the requirements of this section are satisfied with respect to the making of that application if, before the application is made—

(a) notices under subsection (2) below have been published in two national newspapers and in a local newspaper circulating in the locality where the relevant land is situated;

(b) each of those notices specified a period for the notification to the trustees of claims by beneficiaries, being a period ending not less than three months after the date of publication of the last of those notices to be published;

(c) that period has ended;

(d) for a period of not less than twenty-one days during the first month of that period, a copy of one of those notices was affixed to some object on the relevant land in such a position and manner as, so far as practicable, to make the notice easy for members of the public to see and read without going on to the land; and

(e) the trustees have considered what other steps could be taken to trace the persons who are or may be beneficiaries and to inform those persons of the application to be made under section 2 above and have taken such of the steps considered by them as it was reasonably practicable for them to take.

(2) A notice under this subsection shall—

(a) set out the circumstances that have resulted in a trust having arisen under section 1 above;

(b) state that an application is to be made for the establishment of a scheme with respect to the property subject to the trust; and

(c) contain a warning to every beneficiary that, if he wishes to oppose the extinguishment of his rights, he should notify his claim to the trustees in the manner, and within the period, specified in the notice.

(3) Where at the time when the trustees publish a notice for the purposes of subsection (2) above—

(a) the relevant land is not under their control; and

(b) it is not reasonably practicable for them to arrange for a copy of the notice to be affixed as required by paragraph (d) of subsection (1) above to some object on the land,

that paragraph shall be disregarded for the purposes of this section.

(4) The requirements of this section shall not apply in the case of an application made in respect of any trust if—

(a) the time when that trust is treated as having arisen was before the commencement of this Act; and

(b) more than twelve years have elapsed since that time.

4 Provisions supplemental to ss. 2 and 3.

(1) Where an order is made under section 2 above—

(a) public notice of the order shall be given in such manner as the Charity Commissioners think sufficient and appropriate; and

(b) a copy of the order shall, for not less than one month after the date of the giving of the notice, be available for public inspection at all reasonable times at the Commissioners'' office and at some convenient place in the locality where the relevant land is situated;

and a notice given for the purposes of paragraph (a) above shall contain such particulars of the order, or such directions for obtaining information about it, as the Commissioners think sufficient and appropriate.

(2) Subject to subsection (3) below, an appeal against an order made under section 2 above may be brought in the High Court by any of the following, that is to say—

(a) the Attorney General;

(b) the trustees of the trust established under the order;

(c) a beneficiary of, or the trustees of, the trust in respect of which the application for the order had been made;

(d) any person interested in the purposes for which the last-mentioned trustees or any of their predecessors held the relevant land before the cesser of use in consequence of which the trust

arose under section 1 above;

(e) any two or more inhabitants of the locality where that land is situated.

(3) An appeal shall not be brought under subsection (2) above against any order—

(a) after the end of the period of three months beginning with the day following the date on which public notice of the order is given; or

(b) without either a certificate by the Charity Commissioners that it is a proper case for an appeal or the leave of the High Court,

unless it is brought by the Attorney General.

(4) [Sections 89, 91 and 92 of the Charities Act 1993][7] (supplemental provisions with respect to orders and appeals) shall apply in relation to, and to appeals against, orders under section 2 above as they apply in relation to, and to appeals against, orders under that Act.

(5) Trustees of a trust which has arisen under section 1 above may pay or apply capital money for any of the purposes of section 2 or 3 above or of this section.

5 Orders under the Education Act 1973.

(1) An order made under [section 554 of the Education Act 1996][8] (special powers as to certain trusts for religious education) with respect to so much of any endowment as consists of—

(a) land in relation to which a trust under section 1 above has arisen or will arise after the land ceased or ceases to be used for particular purposes; or

(b) any other property subject to a trust under that section,

may extinguish any rights to which a person is or may become entitled as a beneficiary under the trust.

(2) The Secretary of State shall not by an order under [section 554 of the 1996 Act][9] extinguish any such rights unless he is satisfied that all reasonably practicable steps to trace the persons who are or may become entitled to any of those rights have been taken and either—

(a) that there is no claim by any person to be a person who is or may become so entitled—

(i) which is outstanding; or

(ii) which has at any time been accepted as valid by the trustees or by persons whose acceptance binds or will bind the trustees; or

(iii) which has been upheld in proceedings that have been concluded; or

(b) that consent to the making of an order under [section 554 of the 1996 Act][10] has been given by every person whose claim to be such a person is outstanding or has been so accepted or upheld.

(3) Where applications for the extinguishment of the rights of any beneficiaries are made with respect to the same trust property both to the Secretary of State under [section 554 of the 1996 Act][11] and to the Charity Commissioners under section 2 above, the Commissioners shall not consider, or further consider, the application made to them, unless the Secretary of State either—

(a) consents to the application made to the Charity Commissioners being considered before the application made to him; or

(b) disposes of the application made to him without extinguishing the rights of one or more of the beneficiaries.

(4) Trustees of a trust which has arisen under section 1 above may pay or apply capital money for the purposes of any provision of this section or [section 554 of the 1996 Act][12].

6 Clarification of status etc. of land before reverter.

(1) Nothing in this Act shall require any land which is or has been the subject of any grant, conveyance or other assurance under any relevant enactment to be treated as or as having been settled land.

(2) It is hereby declared—

(a) that the power conferred by section 14 of the School Sites Act 1841 (power of sale etc.) is exercisable at any time in relation to land in relation to which (but for the exercise of the power) a trust might subsequently arise under section 1 above; and

(b) that the exercise of that power in respect of any land prevents any trust from arising under section 1 above in relation to that land or any land representing the proceeds of sale of that land.

7 Construction.

(1) In this Act—

"relevant enactment" means any enactment contained in—

(a) the School Sites Acts;

(b) the Literary and Scientific Institutions Act 1854; or

(c) the Places of Worship Sites Act 1873;

"relevant land", in relation to a trust which has arisen under section 1 above, means the land which but for this Act would have reverted to the persons who are the first beneficiaries under the trust.

(2) In this Act references to land include references to—

(a) any part of any land which has been the subject of a grant, conveyance or other assurance under any relevant enactment; and

(b) any land an interest in which (including any future or contingent interest arising under any such enactment) belongs to the Crown, the Duchy of Lancaster or the Duchy of Cornwall.

(3) For the purposes of this Act a claim by any person to be a beneficiary under a trust is outstanding if—

(a) it has been notified to the trustees;

(b) it has not been withdrawn; and

(c) proceedings for determining whether it should be upheld have not been commenced or (if commenced) have not been concluded.

(4) For the purposes of this Act proceedings shall not, in relation to any person's claim, be treated as concluded where the time for appealing is unexpired or an appeal is pending unless that person has indicated his intention not to appeal or, as the case may be, not to continue with the appeal.

8 Consequential amendments, repeals and saving.

(1)................................[13]

(2) In section 3(3) of the Law of Property Act 1925 (right of certain persons to creation of legal estate), the words "of a statutory or other right of reverter, or" (which are unnecessary) shall be omitted.

(3) The enactments mentioned in the Schedule to this Act are hereby repealed to the extent specified in the third column of that Schedule.

(4) The repeals contained in the Schedule to this Act shall not affect the operation at any time after the commencement of this Act of so much of any order made before the commencement of this Act under section 2 of the Education Act 1973 as has excluded the operation of the third proviso to section 2 of the School Sites Act 1841.

9 Short title, commencement and extent.

(1) This Act may be cited as the Reverter of Sites Act 1987.

(2) This Act shall come into force on such day as the Lord Chancellor may by order made by statutory instrument appoint.

(3) This Act shall extend to England and Wales only.

Section 8.

SCHEDULE

Repeals

Chapter	Short title	Extent of repeal
15 & 16 Geo. 5. c. 20.	The Law of Property Act 1925.	In section 3(3),the words "of a statutory or other right of reverter, or". In section 7(1), the words "the School Sites Acts".
1973 c. 16.	The Education Act 1973.	In section 2(3) the words from "and in the case of" onwards.

[1] Words in s. 1 sidenote substituted (1.1.1997) by 1996 c. 47, s. 5(1), Sch. 2 para. 6(5)(6)(with ss. 24(2), 25(4)(5)); S.I. 1996/2974, art.2

[2] Words in s. 1(2) inserted (1.1.1997) by 1996 c. 47, s. 5(1), Sch. 2 para. 6(2)(a)(6)(with ss. 24(2), 25(4)(5)); S.I. 1996/2974, art.2

[3] Words in s. 1(2) substituted (1.1.1997) by 1996 c. 47, s. 5(1), Sch. 2 para. 6(2)(b)(6)(with ss. 24(2), 25(4)(5)); S.I. 1996/2974, art.2

[4] Words in s. 1(3) substituted (1.1.1997) by 1996 c. 47, s. 5(1), Sch. 2 para. 6(3)(6)(with ss. 24(2), 25(4)(5)); S.I. 1996/2974, art.2

[5] Words in s. 1(4) substituted (1.1.1997) by 1996 c. 47, s. 5(1), Sch. 2 para. 6(4)(6)(with ss. 24(2), 25(4)(5)); S.I. 1996/2974, art.2

[6] Words in s. 1(5) substituted (1.11.1996) by 1996 c. 56, ss. 582(1), 583(2), Sch. 37 Pt. I para. 67(2)(with ss. 1(4), 582(3), Sch. 39)

[7] Words in s. 4(4) substituted (1.8.1993) by 1993 c. 10, ss. 98(1), 99(1), Sch. 6 para.24.

[8] Words in s. 5(1) substituted (1.11.1996) by 1996 c. 56, ss. 582(1), 583(2), Sch. 37 Pt. I para. 67(2)(a)(with s. 1(4), 582(3), Sch. 39)

[9] Words in s. 5 substituted (1.11.1996) by 1996 c. 56, ss. 582(1), 582(2), Sch. 37 Pt. I para. 67(2)(b)(with ss. 1(4), 582(3), Sch. 39)

[10] Words in s. 5 substituted (1.11.1996) by 1996 c. 56, ss. 582(1), 582(2), Sch. 37 Pt. I para. 67(2)(b)(with ss. 1(4), 582(3), Sch. 39)

[11] Words in s. 5 substituted (1.11.1996) by 1996 c. 56, ss. 582(1), 582(2), Sch. 37 Pt. I para. 67(2)(b)(with ss. 1(4), 582(3), Sch. 39)

[12] Words in s. 5 substituted (1.11.1996) by 1996 c. 56, ss. 582(1), 582(2), Sch. 37 Pt. I para. 67(2)(b)(with ss. 1(4), 582(3), Sch. 39)

[13] S. 8(1) repealed (1.11.1996) by 1996 c. 56, ss. 582(2), 583(2), Sch. 38 Pt.I(with ss. 1(4), 582(3), Sch. 39)

Local Government and Housing Act 1989

1989 CHAPTER 42

...

Part V - Companies in which Local Authorities have interests

67 Application of, and orders under, Part V.

(1) Any reference in this Part to a company is a reference to a body corporate of one of the following descriptions—

(a) a company limited by shares;

(b) a company limited by guarantee and not having a share capital;

(c) a company limited by guarantee and having a share capital;

(d) an unlimited company; and

(e) a society registered or deemed to be registered under the Industrial and Provident Societies Act 1965 or under the Industrial and Provident Societies Act (Northern Ireland) 1969.

(2) Expressions used in paragraphs (a) to (d) of subsection (1) above have the same meaning as in Chapter I of Part I of the Companies Act 1985 or the corresponding enactment for the time being in force in Northern Ireland.

(3) Any reference in this Part to a local authority is a reference to a body of one of the following descriptions—

(a) a county council;

[(aa) a county borough council;][1]

(b) a district council;

[(bb) the Greater London Authority;

(bc) a functional body, within the meaning of the Greater London Authority Act 1999;][2]

(c) a London borough council;

(d) the Common Council of the City of London in its capacity as a local authority, police authority or port health authority;

(e) the Council of the Isles of Scilly;

(f) a parish council;

(g) a community council;

[(ga) the Greater London Magistrates' Courts Authority;.][3]

(h) a fire authority constituted by a combination scheme under the Fire Services Act 1947;

[(i) a police authority established under [section 3 of the Police Act 1996][4]...;][5]

(j) an authority established under section 10 of the Local Government Act 1985 (waste disposal authorities);

(k) a joint authority established by Part IV of that Act ([police,][6] fire services, civil defence and transport);

(l) any body established pursuant to an order under section 67 of that Act (successors to residuary bodies);

(m) the Broads Authority;

[(ma) a National Park authority;][7]

(n) any joint board the constituent members of which consist of any of the bodies specified above;

(o). . . . .[8]

[(oo) a joint planning board constituted for an area in Wales outside a National Park by an order under section 2(1B) of the Town and Country Planning Act 1990; and][9]

(p) a Passenger Transport Executive.

(4) Any power to make an order under this Part shall be exercisable by statutory instrument subject to annulment in pursuance of a resolution of either House of Parliament; and under any such power different provision maybe made for different cases and different descriptions of cases (including different provision for different areas).

68 Companies controlled by local authorities and arm's length companies.

(1) For the purposes of this Part, unless the Secretary of State otherwise directs, a company is for the time being under the control of a local authority if—

(a) by virtue of section 736 of the Companies Act 1985 the company is at that time a subsidiary of the local authority for the purposes of that Act; or

(b) paragraph (a) above does not apply but the local authority have at that time power to control a majority of the votes at a general meeting of the company as mentioned in subsection (3) below; or

(c) paragraph (a) above does not apply but the local authority have at that time power to appoint or remove a majority of the board of directors of the company; or

(d) the company is under the control of another company which, by virtue of this subsection, is itself under the control of the local authority;

and, for the purposes of paragraph (d) above, any question whether one company is under the control of another shall be determined by applying the preceding provisions of this subsection, substituting a reference to the other company for any reference to the local authority.

(2) A direction under subsection (1) above—

(a) may be limited in time and may be made conditional upon such matters as appear to the Secretary of State to be appropriate; and

(b) may be made with respect to a particular company or a description of companies specified in the direction.

(3) The reference in subsection (1)(b) above to a power to control a majority of votes at a general meeting of the company is a reference to a power which is exercisable—

(a) in the case of a company limited by shares, through the holding of equity share capital in any one or more of the following ways, namely, by the local authority, by nominees of the local authority and by persons whose shareholding is under the control of the local authority; or

(b) in the case of any company, through the holding of votes at a general meeting of the company in any one or more of the following ways, namely, by the local authority, by a group of members of the company the composition of which is controlled by the local authority and by persons who have contractually bound themselves to vote in accordance with the instructions of the local authority; or

(c) partly in one of those ways and partly in the other.

(4) Subsection (3) of section 736A of the Companies Act 1985 (right to appoint or remove a majority of a company's board of directors) and the following provisions of that section as they have effect in relation to subsection (3) apply for the purposes of subsection (1)(c) above with the substitution for the word "right", wherever it occurs, of the word "power".

(5) For the purposes of subsection (3)(a) above, a person's shareholding is under the control of a local authority if—

(a) his right to hold the shares arose because of some action which the authority took, or refrained from taking, in order to enable him to have the right; and

(b) the local authority, alone or jointly with one or more other persons can require him to transfer his shareholding (or any part of it) to another person.

(6) Notwithstanding that, by virtue of the preceding provisions of this section, a company is for the time being under the control of a local authority, the company is for the purposes of this Part an "arm's length company", in relation to any financial year if, at a time before the beginning of that year, the authority resolved that the company should be an arm's length company and, at all times from the passing of that resolution up to the end of the financial year in question, the following conditions

have applied while the company has been under the control of the local authority,—

(a) that each of the directors of the company was appointed for a fixed term of at least two years;

(b) that, subject to subsection (7) below, no director of the company has been removed by resolution under section 303 of the Companies Act 1985;

(c) that not more than one-fifth of the directors of the company have been members or officers of the authority;

(d) that the company has not occupied (as tenant or otherwise) any land in which the authority have an interest otherwise than for the best consideration reasonably obtainable;

(e) that the company has entered into an agreement with the authority that the company will use its best endeavours to produce a specified positive return on its assets;

(f) that, except for the purpose of enabling the company to acquire fixed assets or to provide it with working capital, the authority have not lent money to the company or guaranteed any sum borrowed by it or subscribed for any securities in the company;

(g) that the authority have not made any grant to the company except in pursuance of an agreement or undertaking entered into before the financial year (within the meaning of the Companies Act 1985) of the company in which the grant was made; and

(h) that the authority have not made any grant to the company the amount of which is in any way related to the financial results of the company in any period.

(7) If the Secretary of State so directs, the removal of a director shall be disregarded for the purposes of subsection (6)(b) above; but the Secretary of State shall not give such a direction if it appears to him that the director was removed with a view to influencing the management of the company for other than commercial reasons.

69 Companies subject to local authority influence.

(1) For the purposes of this Part, unless the Secretary of State otherwise directs, a company which is not at the time under the control of a local authority is for the time being subject to the influence of a local authority if it is not a banking or insurance company or a member of a banking or insurance group and at that time there is such a business relationship between the company and the authority as is referred to in subsection (3) below and either—

(a) at least 20 per cent. of the total voting rights of all the members having the right to vote at a general meeting of the company are held by persons who are associated with the authority as mentioned in subsection (5) below; or

(b) at least 20 per cent. of the directors of the company are persons who are so associated; or

(c) at least 20 per cent. of the total voting rights at a meeting of the directors of the company are held by persons who are so associated.

(2) A direction under subsection (1) above—

(a) may be limited in time and may be made conditional upon such matters as appear to the Secretary of State to be appropriate; and

(b) may be made with respect to a particular company or a description of companies specified in the direction.

(3) For the purposes of this section there is a business relationship between a company and a local authority at any time if the condition in any one or more of the following paragraphs is fulfilled—

(a) within a period of twelve months which includes that time the aggregate of the payments to the company by the authority or by another company which is under the control of the authority represents more than one-half of the company's turnover, as shown in its profit and loss account for the most recent financial year for which the company's auditors have made a report on the accounts or, if there is no such account, as estimated by the authority for the period of twelve months preceding the date of the estimate or for such part of that period as follows the formation of the company;

(b) more than one-half of the company's turnover referred to in paragraph (a) above is derived from the exploitation of assets of any description in which the local authority or a company under the control of the authority has an interest (disregarding an interest in land which is in reversion on a lease granted for more than 7 years);

(c) the aggregate of—

(i) grants made either by the authority and being expenditure for capital purposes or by a

company under the control of the authority, and

(ii) the nominal value of shares or stock in the company which is owned by the authority or by a company under the control of the authority,

exceeds one-half of the net assets of the company;

(d) the aggregate of—

(i) grants falling within paragraph (c)(i) above,

(ii) loans or other advances made or guaranteed by the authority or by a company under the control of the authority, and

(iii) the nominal value referred to in paragraph (c)(ii) above,

exceeds one-half of the fixed and current assets of the company;

(e) the company at that time occupies land by virtue of an interest which it obtained from the local authority or a company under the control of the authority and which it so obtained at less than the best consideration reasonably obtainable; and

(f) the company intends at that time to enter into (or complete) a transaction and, when that is done, there will then be a business relationship between the company and the authority by virtue of any of paragraphs (a) to (e) above.

(4) In subsection (3) above—

(a) the reference in paragraph (c) to the net assets of the company shall be construed in accordance with section 152(2) of the Companies Act 1985; and

(b) the reference in paragraph (d) to the fixed and current assets of the company shall be construed in accordance with paragraph 77 of Schedule 4 to that Act;

and in either case, the reference is a reference to those assets as shown in the most recent balance sheet of the company on which, at the time in question, the auditors have made a report or, if there is no such balance sheet, as estimated by the local authority for the time in question.

(5) For the purposes of this section, a person is at any time associated with a local authority if—

(a) he is at that time a member of the authority;

(b) he is at that time an officer of the authority;

(c) he is at that time both an employee and either a director, manager, secretary or other similar officer of a company which is under the control of the authority; or

(d) at any time within the preceding four years he has been associated with the authority by virtue of paragraph (a) above.

(6) If and to the extent that the Secretary of State by order so provides, a person is at any time associated with a local authority if—

(a) at that time he is, or is employed by or by a subsidiary of, a person who for the time being has a contractual relationship with the authority to provide—

(i) advice with regard to the authority's interest in any company (whether existing or proposed to be formed), or

(ii) advice with regard to the management of an undertaking or the development of land by a company (whether existing or proposed to be formed) with which it is proposed that the authority should enter into any lease, licence or other contract or to which it is proposed that the authority should make any grant or loan, or

(iii) services which facilitate the exercise of the authority's rights in any company (whether by acting as the authority's representative at a meeting of the company or as a director appointed by the authority or otherwise);

(b) at any time within the preceding four years, he has been associated with the authority by virtue of paragraph (b) or paragraph (c) of subsection (5) above;

(c) he is at that time the spouse of, or carries on business in partnership with, a person who is associated with the authority by virtue of subsection (5)(a) above; or

(d) he holds a relevant office in a political association or other body which, in the nomination paper of a person who is an elected member of the authority, formed part of that person's description.

(7) For the purposes of subsection (6)(d) above, an office in a political association or body is relevant to a local authority in the following circumstances—

(a) if the association or body is active only in the area of the local authority, any office in it is relevant; and

(b) in any other case, an office is relevant only if it is in a branch or other part of the association or body which is active in the area of the local authority.

(8) In relation to a company which is an industrial and provident society, any reference in this section to the directors of the company is a reference to the members of the committee of management.

(9) Subject to subsections (4) and (8) and section 67 above, expressions used in this section have the same meaning as in the Companies Act 1985.

70 Requirements for companies under control or subject to influence of local authorities.

(1) In relation to companies under the control of local authorities and companies subject to the influence of local authorities, the Secretary of State may by order make provision regulating, forbidding or requiring the taking of certain actions or courses of action; and an order under this subsection may—

(a) make provision in relation to those companies which are arm's length companies different from that applicable to companies which are not; and

(b) make provision in relation to companies under the control of local authorities different from that applicable in relation to companies under the influence of local authorities.

(2) It shall be the duty of every local authority to ensure, so far as practicable, that any company under its control complies with the provisions for the time being made by order under subsection (1) above; and if a local authority fails to perform that duty in relation to any company, any payment made by the authority to that company and any other expenditure incurred by the authority in contravention of any such provisions shall be deemed for the purposes of [the Audit Commission Act 1998][10] to be expenditure which is unlawful.

(3) In order to secure compliance, in relation to companies subject to the influence of local authorities, with provisions made by virtue of subsection (1) above, an order under that subsection may prescribe requirements to be complied with by any local authority in relation to conditions to be included in such leases, licences, contracts, gifts, grants or loans as may be so prescribed which are made with or to a company subject to the influence of the local authority.

(4) It shall be the duty of every local authority to comply with any requirements for the time being prescribed under subsection (3) above; and if a local authority fails to perform that duty, any expenditure which is incurred by the local authority under the lease, licence, contract, gift, grant or loan in question shall be deemed for the purposes of [the Audit Commission Act 1998][11] to be expenditure which is unlawful.

(5) Without prejudice to the generality of the power conferred by subsection (1) above, an order under that subsection may make provision requiring a company or local authority to obtain the consent of the Secretary of State, or of the Audit Commission for Local Authorities in England and Wales, before taking any particular action or course of action.

71 Control of minority interests etc. in certain companies.

(1) In relation to a local authority, subsection (2) below applies to any company other than—

(a) a company which is or, if the action referred to in that subsection is taken, will be under the control of the local authority; and

(b) a company of a description specified for the purposes of this section by an order made by the Secretary of State;

and in this section an "authorised company" means a company falling within paragraph (b) above.

(2) Except with the approval of the Secretary of State, in relation to acompany to which this subsection applies, a local authority may not—

(a) subscribe for, or acquire, whether in their own name or in the name of a nominee, any shares or share warrants in the company;

(b) become or remain a member of the company if it is limited by guarantee;

(c) exercise any power, however arising, to nominate any person to become a member of the company;

(d) exercise any power to appoint directors of the company;

(e) permit any officer of the authority, in the course of his employment, to make any such nomination or appointment as is referred to in paragraph (c) or paragraph (d) above; or

(f) permit an officer of the authority, in the course of his employment, to become or remain a member or director of the company.

(3) Any approval of the Secretary of State under subsection (2) above may be general or relate to any

specific matter or company.

(4) A local authority may not take any action, or refrain from exercising any right, which would have the result that a person who is disqualified from membership of the authority (otherwise than by being employed by that or any other local authority or by a company which is under the control of a local authority) becomes a member or director of an authorised company or is authorised, in accordance with section 375 of the Companies Act 1985, to act as the authority's representative at a general meeting of an authorised company (or at meetings of an authorised company which include a general meeting).

(5) In any case where,—

(a) in accordance with section 375 of the Companies Act 1985, a local authority have authorised a member or officer of the authority to act as mentioned in subsection (4) above, or

(b) a member or officer of a local authority has become a member or director of an authorised company as mentioned in subsection (7) below,

the authority shall make arrangements (whether by standing orders or otherwise) for enabling members of the authority, in the course of proceedings of the authority (or of any committee or sub-committee thereof), [or, where a local authority is operating executive arrangements under Part II of the Local Government Act 2000, for enabling members of the executive, in the course of proceedings of the executive (or of any committee of the executive),][12] to put to the member or officer concerned questions about the activities of the company.

(6) Nothing in subsection (5) above shall require the member or officer referred to in that subsection to disclose any information about the company which has been communicated to him in confidence.

(7) Any member or officer of a local authority who has become a member or director of an authorised company by virtue of—

(a) a nomination made by the authority, or

(b) election at a meeting of the company at which voting rights were exercisable (whether or not exercised) by the authority or by a person bound to vote in accordance with the instructions of the authority, or

(c) an appointment made by the directors of another company, the majority of whom became directors of that company by virtue of a nomination made by the authority or election at a meeting of the company at which voting rights were exercisable as mentioned in paragraph (b) above,

shall make a declaration to the authority, in such form as they may require, of any remuneration or re-imbursement of expenses which he receives from the company as a member or director or in respect of anything done on behalf of the company.

(8) Subject to section 67 above, expressions used in this section have the same meaning as in the Companies Act 1985.

72 Trusts influenced by local authorities.

(1) The Secretary of State may by order made by statutory instrument adapt theprovisions of section 69 above so as to make them applicable to trusts which are not charitable; and, subject to subsection (2) below, this Part shall apply in relation to trusts which are subject to local authority influence by virtue of that section as so adapted as it applies in relation to companies which are subject to local authority influence.

(2) In the exercise of the power conferred by section 70 above, as applied in relation to trusts by subsection (1) above, the Secretary of State may make different provision for trusts as compared with companies.

73 Authorities acting jointly and by committees.

(1) In any case where—

(a) apart from this section a company would not be under the control of anyone local authority, but

(b) if the actions, powers and interests of two or more local authorities were treated as those of one authority alone, the company would be under the control of that one authority,

the company shall be treated for the purposes of this Part as under the control of each of the two or more local authorities mentioned in paragraph (b) above.

(2) In any case where, apart from this section, a company would not be treated as being subject to the influence of any one local authority, it shall be treated as being subject to the influence of each of a

number of local authorities (in this section referred to as a "group") if the conditions in subsection (3) below are fulfilled with respect to the company and the group of authorities.

(3) The conditions referred to in subsection (2) above are—

(a) that at least one of the conditions in paragraphs (a) to (e) of subsection (3) of section 69 above would be fulfilled—

(i) if any reference therein to the company being under the control of a local authority were a reference to its being under the control of any one of the authorities in the group or of any two or more of them taken together; and

(ii) if any other reference therein to the local authority were a reference to any two or more of the authorities in the group taken together; and

(b) that at least one of the conditions in paragraphs (a) to (c) of subsection(1) of section 69 above would be fulfilled if any reference therein to the local authority were a reference to those local authorities who are taken into account under sub-paragraph (i) or sub-paragraph (ii) of paragraph (a) above taken together; and

(c) that if the condition (or one of the conditions) which would be fulfilled as mentioned in paragraph (b) above is that in subsection (1)(a) of section 69 above, then, so far as concerns each local authority in the group, at least one person who, in terms of subsection (5) of that section, is associated with that authority has the right to vote at a general meeting of the company; and

(d) that, if paragraph (c) above does not apply, then, so far as concerns each local authority in the group, a person who, in terms of section 69(5) above, is associated with the authority is a director of the company.

(4) For the purposes of this Part, anything done, and any power exercisable, by a committee or sub-committee of a local authority, or by any of the authority's officers [or, where a local authority is operating executive arrangements under Part II of the Local Government Act 2000, by the authority's executive, any committee of the executive, or any member of the executive][13], shall be treated as done or, as the case may be, exercisable by the authority.

(5) For the purposes of this Part, anything done, and any power exercisable, by a joint committee of two or more local authorities or by a sub-committee of such a joint committee shall be treated as done or, as the case may be, exercisable by each of the local authorities concerned.

...

195 Short title, commencement and extent.

(1) This Act may be cited as the Local Government and Housing Act 1989.

---

[1] S. 67(3)(aa) inserted (7.1.1997) by S.I. 1996/3071, art. 2, Sch. 3(6)

[2] S. 67(3)(bb)(bc) inserted (8.5.2000 for specified purposes otherwise 3.7.2000) by 1999 c. 29, s. 393(1)(2) (with Sch. 12 para. 9(1)); S.I. 2000/3434, arts. 3, 4

[3] S. 67(3)(ga) inserted (1.4.2001) by 1999 c. 22, s. 83(3), Sch. 12 paras. 4, 6 (with s. 107, Sch. 14 para. 7(2)); S.I. 2001/916, art. 2(a)(i) (with savings in Sch. 2 para. 2)

[4] S. 67(3)(i) substituted (1.10.1994 for specified purposes otherwise 1.4.1995) by 1994 c. 29, s. 43, Sch. 4 Pt. I para. 39; S.I. 1994/2025, art. 6; S.I. 1994/3262, art. 4, Sch.

[5] Words in s. 67(3)(i) substituted (22.8.1996) by 1996 c. 16, ss. 103(1), 104(1), Sch. 7 Pt. I para. 1(1)(2)(zd)

[6] Word in s. 67(3)(k) repealed (1.4.1995 (E.W.) otherwise (prosp.)) by 1994 c. 29, s. 93, Sch. 9 Pt. I; S.I. 1994/3262, art. 4, Sch.

[7] S. 67(3)(ma) inserted (19.9.1995) by 1995 c. 25, ss. 65(7), 125(2), Sch. 8 para. 10 (with ss. 7(6), 115, 117, Sch. 8 para. 7)

[8] S. 67(3)(o) repealed (1.4.1997) by 1995 c. 25, s. 120(3), Sch. 24 (with ss. 7(6), 115, 117); S.I. 1996/2560, art. 2, Sch.

[9] S. 67(3)(oo) inserted (23.11.1995) by 1995 c. 25, s. 78, Sch. 10 para. 31(3) (with ss. 7(6), 115, 117, Sch. 8 para. 7); S.I. 1995/2950, art. 2(1)

[10] Words in s. 70(2) substituted (11.9.1998) by 1998 c. 18, ss. 54(1), 55(2), Sch. 3 para. 18(3)(a)

[11] Words in s. 70(4) substituted (11.9.1998) by 1998 c. 18, ss. 54(1), 55(2), Sch. para. 18(3)(b)

[12] Words in s. 71(5) inserted (E.) (11.7.2001) and (W.) (1.4.2002) by S.I. 2001/2237, arts. 1(2), 26(1); S.I. 2002/808, arts. 1(2), 25(1)

[13] Words in s. 73(4) inserted (E.) (11.7.2001) and (W.) (1.4.2002) by S.I. 2001/2237, arts. 1(2), 26(2); S.I. 2002/808, arts. 1(2), 25(2)

Charities Act 1992

1992 CHAPTER 41

Part II - CONTROL OF FUND-RAISING FOR CHARITABLE INSTITUTIONS

Preliminary

58 Interpretation of Part II.

(1) In this Part—

"charitable contributions", in relation to any representation made by any commercial participator or other person, means—

(a) the whole or part of—

(i) the consideration given for goods or services sold or supplied by him, or

(ii) any proceeds (other than such consideration) of a promotional venture undertaken by him, or

(b) sums given by him by way of donation in connection with the sale or supply of any such goods or services (whether the amount of such sums is determined by reference to the value of any such goods or services or otherwise);

"charitable institution" means a charity or an institution (other than a charity) which is established for charitable, benevolent or philanthropic purposes;

"charity" means a charity within the meaning of [the Charities Act 1993][1];

"commercial participator", in relation to any charitable institution, means any person [(apart from a company connected with the institution)][2] who—

(a) carries on for gain a business other than a fund-raising business, but

(b) in the course of that business, engages in any promotional venture in the course of which it is represented that charitable contributions are to be given to or applied for the benefit of the institution;

"company" has the meaning given by section [97 of the Charities Act 1993][3];

"the court" means the High Court or a county court;

"credit card" means a card which is a credit-token within the meaning of the Consumer Credit Act 1974;

"debit card" means a card the use of which by its holder to make a payment results in a current account of his at a bank, or at any other institution providing banking services, being debited with the payment;

"fund-raising business" means any business carried on for gain and wholly or primarily engaged in soliciting or otherwise procuring money or other property for charitable, benevolent or philanthropic purposes;

"institution" includes any trust or undertaking;

"professional fund-raiser" means—

(a) any person (apart from a charitable institution [or a company connected with such an institution][4]) who carries on a fund-raising business, or

(b) any other person (apart from a person excluded by virtue of subsection (2) or (3)) who for reward solicits money or other property for the benefit of a charitable institution, if he does so otherwise than in the course of any fund-raising venture undertaken by a person falling within paragraph (a) above;

"promotional venture" means any advertising or sales campaign or any other venture undertaken for promotional purposes;

"radio or television programme" includes any item included in a programme service within the meaning of the Broadcasting Act 1990.

(2) In subsection (1), paragraph (b) of the definition of "professional fund-raiser" does not apply to any of the following, namely—

(a) any charitable institution or any company connected with any such institution;

(b) any officer or employee of any such institution or company, or any trustee of any such institution, acting (in each case) in his capacity as such;

(c) any person acting as a collector in respect of a public charitable collection (apart from a person

who is to be treated as a promoter of such a collection by virtue of section 65(3));

(d) any person who in the course of a relevant programme, that is to say a radio or television programme in the course of which a fund-raising venture is undertaken by—

(i) a charitable institution, or

(ii) a company connected with such an institution,

makes any solicitation at the instance of that institution or company; or

(e) any commercial participator;

and for this purpose "collector" and "public charitable collection" have the same meaning as in Part III of this Act.

(3) In addition, paragraph (b) of the definition of "professional fund-raiser" does not apply to a person if he does not receive—

(a) more than—

(i) £5 per day, or

(ii) £500 per year,

by way of remuneration in connection with soliciting money or other property for the benefit of the charitable institution referred to in that paragraph; or

(b) more than £500 by way of remuneration in connection with any fund-raising venture in the course of which he solicits money or other property for the benefit of that institution.

(4) In this Part any reference to charitable purposes, where occurring in the context of a reference to charitable, benevolent or philanthropic purposes, is a reference to charitable purposes whether or not the purposes are charitable within the meaning of any rule of law.

(5) For the purposes of this Part a company is connected with a charitable institution if—

(a) the institution, or

(b) the institution and one or more other charitable institutions, taken together,

is or are entitled (whether directly or through one or more nominees) to exercise, or control the exercise of, the whole of the voting power at any general meeting of the company.

(6) In this Part—

(a) "represent" and "solicit" mean respectively represent and solicit in any manner whatever, whether expressly or impliedly and whether done—

(i) by speaking directly to the person or persons to whom the representation or solicitation is addressed (whether when in his or their presence or not), or

(ii) by means of a statement published in any newspaper, film or radio or television programme,

or otherwise, and references to a representation or solicitation shall be construed accordingly; and

(b) any reference to soliciting or otherwise procuring money or other property is a reference to soliciting or otherwise procuring money or other property whether any consideration is, or is to be, given in return for the money or other property or not.

(7) Where—

(a) any solicitation of money or other property for the benefit of a charitable institution is made in accordance with arrangements between any person and that institution, and

(b) under those arrangements that person will be responsible for receiving on behalf of the institution money or other property given in response to the solicitation,

then (if he would not be so regarded apart from this subsection) that person shall be regarded for the purposes of this Part as soliciting money or other property for the benefit of the institution.

(8) Where any fund-raising venture is undertaken by a professional fund-raiser in the course of a radio or television programme, any solicitation which is made by a person in the course of the programme at the instance of the fund-raiser shall be regarded for the purposes of this Part as made by the fund-raiser and not by that person (and shall be so regarded whether or not the solicitation is made by that person for any reward).

(9) In this Part "services" includes facilities, and in particular—

(a) access to any premises or event;

(b) membership of any organisation;

(c) the provision of advertising space; and

(d) the provision of any financial facilities;

and references to the supply of services shall be construed accordingly.

(10) The Secretary of State may by order amend subsection (3) by substituting a different sum for any sum for the time being specified there.

Control of fund-raising

59 Prohibition on professional fund-raiser etc. raising funds for charitable institution without an agreement in prescribed form.

(1) It shall be unlawful for a professional fund-raiser to solicit money or other property for the benefit of a charitable institution unless he does so in accordance with an agreement with the institution satisfying the prescribed requirements.

(2) It shall be unlawful for a commercial participator to represent that charitable contributions are to be given to or applied for the benefit of a charitable institution unless he does so in accordance with an agreement with the institution satisfying the prescribed requirements.

(3) Where on the application of a charitable institution the court is satisfied—

(a) that any person has contravened or is contravening subsection (1) or (2) in relation to the institution, and

(b) that, unless restrained, any such contravention is likely to continue or be repeated,

the court may grant an injunction restraining the contravention; and compliance with subsection (1) or (2) shall not be enforceable otherwise than in accordance with this subsection.

(4) Where—

(a) a charitable institution makes any agreement with a professional fund-raiser or a commercial participator by virtue of which—

(i) the professional fund-raiser is authorised to solicit money or other property for the benefit of the institution, or

(ii) the commercial participator is authorised to represent that charitable contributions are to be given to or applied for the benefit of the institution,

as the case may be, but

(b) the agreement does not satisfy the prescribed requirements in any respect,

the agreement shall not be enforceable against the institution except to such extent (if any) as may be provided by an order of the court.

(5) A professional fund-raiser or commercial participator who is a party to such an agreement as is mentioned in subsection (4)(a) shall not be entitled to receive any amount by way of remuneration or expenses in respect of anything done by him in pursuance of the agreement unless—

(a) he is so entitled under any provision of the agreement, and

(b) either—

(i) the agreement satisfies the prescribed requirements, or

(ii) any such provision has effect by virtue of an order of the court under subsection (4).

(6) In this section "the prescribed requirements" means such requirements as are prescribed by regulations made by virtue of section 64(2)(a).

60 Professional fund-raisers etc. required to indicate institutions benefiting and arrangements for remuneration.

(1) Where a professional fund-raiser solicits money or other property for the benefit of one or more particular charitable institutions, the solicitation shall be accompanied by a statement clearly indicating—

(a) the name or names of the institution or institutions concerned;

(b) if there is more than one institution concerned, the proportions in which the institutions are respectively to benefit; and

(c)(in general terms) the method by which the fund-raiser's remuneration in connection with the appeal is to be determined.

(2) Where a professional fund-raiser solicits money or other property for charitable, benevolent or philanthropic purposes of any description (rather than for the benefit of one or more particular charitable institutions), the solicitation shall be accompanied by a statement clearly indicating—

(a) the fact that he is soliciting money or other property for those purposes and not for the benefit of any particular charitable institution or institutions;

(b) the method by which it is to be determined how the proceeds of the appeal are to be distributed between different charitable institutions; and

(c)(in general terms) the method by which his remuneration in connection with the appeal is to be determined.

(3) Where any representation is made by a commercial participator to the effect that charitable contributions are to be given to or applied for the benefit of one or more particular charitable institutions, the representation shall be accompanied by a statement clearly indicating—

(a) the name or names of the institution or institutions concerned;

(b) if there is more than one institution concerned, the proportions in which the institutions are respectively to benefit; and

(c)(in general terms) the method by which it is to be determined—

(i) what proportion of the consideration given for goods or services sold or supplied by him, or of any other proceeds of a promotional venture undertaken by him, is to be given to or applied for the benefit of the institution or institutions concerned, or

(ii) what sums by way of donations by him in connection with the sale or supply of any such goods or services are to be so given or applied,

as the case may require.

(4) If any such solicitation or representation as is mentioned in any of subsections (1) to (3) is made—

(a) in the course of a radio or television programme, and

(b) in association with an announcement to the effect that payment may be made, in response to the solicitation or representation, by means of a credit or debit card,

the statement required by virtue of subsection (1), (2) or (3) (as the case may be) shall include full details of the right to have refunded under section 61(1) any payment of £50 or more which is so made.

(5) If any such solicitation or representation as is mentioned in any of subsections (1) to (3) is made orally but is not made—

(a) by speaking directly to the particular person or persons to whom it is addressed and in his or their presence, or

(b) in the course of any radio or television programme,

the professional fund-raiser or commercial participator concerned shall, within seven days of any payment of £50 or more being made to him in response to the solicitation or representation, give to the person making the payment a written statement—

(i) of the matters specified in paragraphs (a) to (c) of that subsection; and

(ii) including full details of the right to cancel under section 61(2) an agreement made in response to the solicitation or representation, and the right to have refunded under section 61(2) or (3) any payment of £50 or more made in response thereto.

(6) In subsection (5) above the reference to the making of a payment is a reference to the making of a payment of whatever nature and by whatever means, including a payment made by means of a credit card or a debit card; and for the purposes of that subsection—

(a) where the person making any such payment makes it in person, it shall be regarded as made at the time when it is so made;

(b) where the person making any such payment sends it by post, it shall be regarded as made at the time when it is posted; and

(c) where the person making any such payment makes it by giving, by telephone or by means of any other telecommunication apparatus, authority for an account to be debited with the payment, it shall be regarded as made at the time when any such authority is given.

(7) Where any requirement of subsections (1) to (5) is not complied with in relation to any solicitation or representation, the professional fund-raiser or commercial participator concerned shall be guilty of an offence and liable on summary conviction to a fine not exceeding the fifth level on the standard scale.

(8) It shall be a defence for a person charged with any such offence to prove that he took all reasonable precautions and exercised all due diligence to avoid the commission of the offence.

(9) Where the commission by any person of an offence under subsection (7) is due to the act or default of some other person, that other person shall be guilty of the offence; and a person may be charged with and convicted of the offence by virtue of this subsection whether or not proceedings are taken against the first-mentioned person.

(10) In this section—

"the appeal", in relation to any solicitation by a professional fund-raiser, means the campaign or other fund-raising venture in the course of which the solicitation is made;

"telecommunication apparatus" has the same meaning as in the Telecommunications Act 1984.

61 Cancellation of payments and agreements made in response to appeals.

(1) Where—

(a) a person ("the donor"), in response to any such solicitation or representation as is mentioned in any of subsections (1) to (3) of section 60 which is made in the course of a radio or television programme, makes any payment of £50 or more to the relevant fund-raiser by means of a credit card or a debit card, but

(b) before the end of the period of seven days beginning with the date of the solicitation or representation, the donor serves on the relevant fund-raiser a notice in writing which, however expressed, indicates the donor's intention to cancel the payment,

the donor shall (subject to subsection (4) below) be entitled to have the payment refunded to him forthwith by the relevant fund-raiser.

(2) Where—

(a) a person ("the donor"), in response to any solicitation or representation falling within subsection (5) of section 60, enters into an agreement with the relevant fund-raiser under which the donor is, or may be, liable to make any payment or payments to the relevant fund-raiser, and the amount or aggregate amount which the donor is, or may be, liable to pay to him under the agreement is £50 or more, but

(b) before the end of the period of seven days beginning with the date when he is given any such written statement as is referred to in that subsection, the donor serves on the relevant fund-raiser a notice in writing which, however expressed, indicates the donor's intention to cancel the agreement,

the notice shall operate, as from the time when it is so served, to cancel the agreement and any liability of any person other than the donor in connection with the making of any such payment or payments, and the donor shall (subject to subsection (4) below) be entitled to have any payment of £50 or more made by him under the agreement refunded to him forthwith by the relevant fund-raiser.

(3) Where, in response to any solicitation or representation falling within subsection (5) of section 60, a person ("the donor")—

(a) makes any payment of £50 or more to the relevant fund-raiser, but

(b) does not enter into any such agreement as is mentioned in subsection (2) above,

then, if before the end of the period of seven days beginning with the date when the donor is given any such written statement as is referred to in subsection (5) of that section, the donor serves on the relevant fund-raiser a notice in writing which, however expressed, indicates the donor's intention to cancel the payment, the donor shall (subject to subsection (4) below) be entitled to have the payment refunded to him forthwith by the relevant fund-raiser.

(4) The right of any person to have a payment refunded to him under any of subsections (1) to (3) above—

(a) is a right to have refunded to him the amount of the payment less any administrative expenses reasonably incurred by the relevant fund-raiser in connection with—

(i) the making of the refund, or

(ii)(in the case of a refund under subsection (2)) dealing with the notice of cancellation served by that person; and

(b) shall, in the case of a payment for goods already received, be conditional upon restitution being made by him of the goods in question.

(5) Nothing in subsections (1) to (3) above has effect in relation to any payment made or to be made in respect of services which have been supplied at the time when the relevant notice is served.

(6) In this section any reference to the making of a payment is a reference to the making of a payment of whatever nature and (in the case of subsection (2) or (3)) a payment made by whatever means, including a payment made by means of a credit card or a debit card; and subsection (6) of section 60 shall have effect for determining when a payment is made for the purposes of this section as it has

effect for determining when a payment is made for the purposes of subsection (5) of that section.

(7) In this section "the relevant fund-raiser", in relation to any solicitation or representation, means the professional fund-raiser or commercial participator by whom it is made.

(8) The Secretary of State may by order—

(a) amend any provision of this section by substituting a different sum for the sum for the time being specified there; and

(b) make such consequential amendments in section 60 as he considers appropriate.

62 Right of charitable institution to prevent unauthorised fund-raising.

(1) Where on the application of any charitable institution—

(a) the court is satisfied that any person has done or is doing either of the following, namely—

(i) soliciting money or other property for the benefit of the institution, or

(ii) representing that charitable contributions are to be given to or applied for the benefit of the institution,

and that, unless restrained, he is likely to do further acts of that nature, and

(b) the court is also satisfied as to one or more of the matters specified in subsection (2),

then (subject to subsection (3)) the court may grant an injunction restraining the doing of any such acts.

(2) The matters referred to in subsection (1)(b) are—

(a) that the person in question is using methods of fund-raising to which the institution objects;

(b) that that person is not a fit and proper person to raise funds for the institution; and

(c) where the conduct complained of is the making of such representations as are mentioned in subsection (1)(a)(ii), that the institution does not wish to be associated with the particular promotional or other fund-raising venture in which that person is engaged.

(3) The power to grant an injunction under subsection (1) shall not be exercisable on the application of a charitable institution unless the institution has, not less than 28 days before making the application, served on the person in question a notice in writing—

(a) requesting him to cease forthwith—

(i) soliciting money or other property for the benefit of the institution, or

(ii) representing that charitable contributions are to be given to or applied for the benefit of the institution,

as the case may be; and

(b) stating that, if he does not comply with the notice, the institution will make an application under this section for an injunction.

(4) Where—

(a) a charitable institution has served on any person a notice under subsection (3) ("the relevant notice") and that person has complied with the notice, but

(b) that person has subsequently begun to carry on activities which are the same, or substantially the same, as those in respect of which the relevant notice was served,

the institution shall not, in connection with an application made by it under this section in respect of the activities carried on by that person, be required by virtue of that subsection to serve a further notice on him, if the application is made not more than 12 months after the date of service of the relevant notice.

(5) This section shall not have the effect of authorising a charitable institution to make an application under this section in respect of anything done by a professional fund-raiser or commercial participator in relation to the institution.

63 False statements relating to institutions which are not registered charities.

(1) Where—

(a) a person solicits money or other property for the benefit of an institution in association with a representation that the institution is a registered charity, and

(b) the institution is not such a charity,

he shall be guilty of an offence and liable on summary conviction to a fine not exceeding the fifth level on the standard scale.

[(1A) In any proceedings for an offence under subsection (1), it shall be a defence for the accused to prove that he believed on reasonable grounds that the institution was a registered charity.][5]

(2) In [this section][6] "registered charity" means a charity which is for the time being registered in the register of charities kept under [section 3 of the Charities Act 1993][7].

63 False statements relating to institutions which are not registered charities.

(1) Where—

(a) a person solicits money or other property for the benefit of an institution in association with a representation that the institution is a registered charity, and

(b) the institution is not such a charity,

he shall be guilty of an offence and liable on summary conviction to a fine not exceeding the fifth level on the standard scale.

(2) In subsection (1) "registered charity" means a charity which is for the time being registered in the register of charities kept under section 4 of the Charities Act 1960.

63 False statements relating to institutions which are not registered charities.

(1) Where—

(a) a person solicits money or other property for the benefit of an institution in association with a representation that the institution is a registered charity, and

(b) the institution is not such a charity,

he shall be guilty of an offence and liable on summary conviction to a fine not exceeding the fifth level on the standard scale.

(2) In subsection (1) "registered charity" means a charity which is for the time being registered in the register of charities kept under [section 3 of the Charities Act 1993][8].

Supplementary

64 Regulations about fund-raising.

(1) The Secretary of State may make such regulations as appear to him to be necessary or desirable for any purposes connected with any of the preceding provisions of this Part.

(2) Without prejudice to the generality of subsection (1), any such regulations may—

(a) prescribe the form and content of—

(i) agreements made for the purposes of section 59, and

(ii) notices served under section 62(3);

(b) require professional fund-raisers or commercial participators who are parties to such agreements with charitable institutions to make available to the institutions books, documents or other records (however kept) which relate to the institutions;

(c) specify the manner in which money or other property acquired by professional fund-raisers or commercial participators for the benefit of, or otherwise falling to be given to or applied by such persons for the benefit of, charitable institutions is to be transmitted to such institutions;

(d) provide for any provisions of section 60 or 61 having effect in relation to solicitations or representations made in the course of radio or television programmes to have effect, subject to any modifications specified in the regulations, in relation to solicitations or representations made in the course of such programmes—

(i) by charitable institutions, or

(ii) by companies connected with such institutions,

and, in that connection, provide for any other provisions of this Part to have effect for the purposes of the regulations subject to any modifications so specified;

(e) make other provision regulating the raising of funds for charitable, benevolent or philanthropic purposes (whether by professional fund-raisers or commercial participators or otherwise).

(3) In subsection (2)(c) the reference to such money or other property as is there mentioned includes a reference to money or other property which, in the case of a professional fund-raiser or commercial participator—

(a) has been acquired by him otherwise than in accordance with an agreement with a charitable institution, but

(b) by reason of any solicitation or representation in consequence of which it has been acquired, is held by him on trust for such an institution.

(4) Regulations under this section may provide that any failure to comply with a specified provision of the regulations shall be an offence punishable on summary conviction by a fine not exceeding the

second level on the standard scale.

Part IV - GENERAL

75 Offences by bodies corporate.

Where any offence—

(a) under this Act or any regulations made under it,

(b)...............................[9]

is committed by a body corporate and is proved to have been committed with the consent or connivance of, or to be attributable to any neglect on the part of, any director, manager, secretary or other similar officer of the body corporate, or any person who was purporting to act in any such capacity, he as well as the body corporate shall be guilty of that offence and shall be liable to be proceeded against and punished accordingly.

In relation to a body corporate whose affairs are managed by its members, "director" means a member of the body corporate.

76 Service of documents.

(1) This section applies to—

(a)...............................[10]

(b) any notice or other document required or authorised to be given or served under Part II of this Act; and

(c) any notice required to be served under Part III of this Act.

(2) A document to which this section applies may be served on or given to a person (other than a body corporate)—

(a) by delivering it to that person;

(b) by leaving it at his last known address in the United Kingdom; or

(c) by sending it by post to him at that address.

(3) A document to which this section applies may be served on or given to a body corporate by delivering it or sending it by post—

(a) to the registered or principal office of the body in the United Kingdom, or

(b) if it has no such office in the United Kingdom, to any place in the United Kingdom where it carries on business or conducts its activities (as the case may be).

(4) Any such document may also be served on or given to a person (including a body corporate) by sending it by post to that person at an address notified by that person for the purposes of this subsection to the person or persons by whom it is required or authorised to be served or given.

77 Regulations and orders.

(1) Any regulations or order of the Secretary of State under this Act—

(a) shall be made by statutory instrument; and

(b)(subject to subsection (2)) shall be subject to annulment in pursuance of a resolution of either House of Parliament.

(2) Subsection (1)(b) does not apply—

(a)...............................[11]

(b)...............................

(c)...............................

(d) to an order under section 79(2).

(3) Any regulations or order of the Secretary of State under this Act may make—

(a) different provision for different cases; and

(b) such supplemental, incidental, consequential or transitional provision or savings as the Secretary of State considers appropriate.

(4) before making any regulations under section. . .[12] 64 or 73 the Secretary of State shall consult such persons or bodies of persons as he considers appropriate.

78 Minor and consequential amendments and repeals.

(1) The enactments mentioned in Schedule 6 to this Act shall have effect subject to the amendments there specified (which are either minor amendments or amendments consequential on the provisions of this Act).

(2) The enactments mentioned in Schedule 7 to this Act (which include some that are already spent or

are no longer of practical utility) are hereby repealed to the extent specified in the third column of that Schedule.

79 Short title, commencement and extent.

(1) This Act may be cited as the Charities Act 1992.

(2) This Act shall come into force on such day as the Secretary of State may by order appoint; and different days may be so appointed for different provisions or for different purposes.

(3) Subject to subsections (4) to (6) below, this Act extends only to England and Wales.

(4)................................[13]

(5)................................

(6) The amendments in Schedule 6, and (subject to subsection (7)) the repeals in Schedule 7, have the same extent as the enactments to which they refer, and section 78 extends accordingly.

(7) The repeal in Schedule 7 of the Police, Factories, &c. (Miscellaneous Provisions) Act 1916 does not extend to Northern Ireland.

---

[1] Words in s. 58(1) substituted (1.8.1993) by 1993 c. 10, s. 98(1), Sch. 6 para. 29(5)

[2] Words in s. 58(1) inserted (3.11.1994) by 1994 c. 40, ss. 25(2), 82(2)

[3] Words in s. 58(1) substituted (1.8.1993) by 1993 c. 10, s. 98(1), Sch. 6 para. 29(5)

[4] Words in s. 58(1) inserted (3.11.1994) by 1994 c. 40, ss. 25(3), 82(2)

[5] S. 63(1)(A) inserted (3.11.1994) by 1994 c. 40, ss. 26(2), 82(2)

[6] Words in s. 63(2) substituted (3.11.1994) by 1994 c. 40, ss. 26(3), 82(2)

[7] Words in s. 63(2) substituted (1.8.1993) by 1993 c. 10, s. 98(1), Sch. 6 para. 29(6)

[8] Words in s. 63(2) substituted (1.8.1993) by 1993 c. 10, s. 98(1), Sch. 6 para. 29(6)

[9] S. 75(b) repealed (1.8.1993) by 1993 c. 10, s. 98(1), Sch.7

[10] S. 76(1)(a) repealed (1.8.1993) by 1993 c. 10, s. 98(2), Sch. 7

[11] S. 77(2)(a)-(c) repealed (1.8.1993) by 1993 c. 10, s. 98(2), Sch.7

[12] In s. 77(4) the figures 20, 22, and 23 repealed (1.8.1993) by 1993 c. 10, s. 98(2), Sch. 7

[13] S. 79(4)(5) repealed (1.8.1993) by 1993 c. 10, s. 98(2), Sch.7

Taxation of Chargeable Gains Act 1992

1992 CHAPTER 12

Charities and gifts of non-business assets etc.

256 Charities

(1) Subject to [section 505(4)][1] of the Taxes Act and [the following provisions of this section][2], a gain shall not be a chargeable gain if it accrues to a charity and is applicable and applied for charitable purposes.

(2) If property held on charitable trusts ceases to be subject to charitable trusts—

(a) the trustees shall be treated as if they had disposed of, and immediately reacquired, the property for a consideration equal to its market value, any gain on the disposal being treated as not accruing to a charity, and

(b) if and so far as any of that property represents, directly or indirectly, the consideration for the disposal of assets by the trustees, any gain accruing on that disposal shall be treated as not having accrued to a charity,

and an assessment to capital gains tax chargeable by virtue of paragraph (b) above may be made at any time not more than 3 years after the end of the year of assessment in which the property ceases to be subject to charitable trusts.

[(3) Subsection (4) below applies if a charitable trust has a non-exempt amount under section 540 of ITA 2007 for a year of assessment. .

(4) Gains accruing to the charitable trust in the year of assessment are treated as being, and always having been, chargeable gains so far as they are attributed under section 256A to the non-exempt amount. .

(5) For restrictions on exemptions under Part 10 of ITA 2007 (special rules about charitable trusts etc) see section 539 of that Act.][3]

[(6) In subsections (3) and (4) of this section, and in sections 256A and 256B, "charitable trust" has the same meaning as in Part 10 of ITA 2007 (see section 519 of that Act).][4]

[256A Attributing gains to the non-exempt amount.

(1) This section applies if a charitable trust has a non-exempt amount under section 540 of ITA 2007 for a year of assessment. .

(2) Attributable gains of the charitable trust for the year of assessment may be attributed to the non-exempt amount but only so far as the non-exempt amount has not been used up. .

(3) The non-exempt amount can be used up (in whole or in part) by—

(a) attributable gains being attributed to it under this section, or

(b) attributable income being attributed to it under section 541 of ITA 2007. .

(4) The whole of the non-exempt amount must be used up by—

(a) attributable gains being attributed to the whole of it under this section,

(b) attributable income being attributed to the whole of it under section 541 of ITA 2007, or

(c) a combination of attributable gains being attributed to some of it under this section and attributable income being attributed to the rest of it under section 541 of ITA 2007. .

(5) See section 256B for the way in which gains are to be attributed to the non-exempt amount under this section. .

(6) In this section and section 256B a charitable trust's "attributable income", and "attributable gains", for a tax year have the same meaning as in Part 10 of ITA 2007 (see section 540 of that Act). .

256B How gains are attributed to the non-exempt amount.

(1) This section is about the ways in which attributable gains can be attributed to a non-exempt amount under section 256A. .

(2) The trustees of the charitable trust may specify the attributable gains that are to be attributed to the non-exempt amount. .

(3) A specification under subsection (2) is made by notice to an officer of Revenue and Customs. .

(4) Subsection (6) applies if—

(a) an officer of Revenue and Customs requires the trustees of a charitable trust to make a specification under this section, and

(b) the trustees have not given notice under subsection (3) of the specification before the end of the required period. .

(5) The required period is 30 days beginning with the day on which the officer made the requirement. .

(6) An officer of Revenue and Customs may determine the attributable gains that are to be attributed to the non-exempt amount.][5]

257 Gifts to charities etc.

(1) Subsection (2) below shall apply where a disposal of an asset is made otherwise than under a bargain at arm's length—

(a) to a charity, or

(b) to any bodies mentioned in Schedule 3 to the [1984 c. 51.] Inheritance Tax Act 1984 (gifts for national purposes, etc).

[and the disposal is not one to which section 151A (1) has effect.][6]

(2) Sections 17(1) and 258(3) shall not apply; but if the disposal is by way of gift (including a gift in settlement) or for a consideration not exceeding the sums allowable as a deduction under section 38, then—

(a) the disposal and acquisition shall be treated for the purposes of this Act as being made for such consideration as to secure that neither a gain nor a loss accrues on the disposal, and

(b) where, after the disposal, the asset is disposed of by the person who acquired it under the disposal, its acquisition by the person making the earlier disposal shall be treated for the purposes of this Act as the acquisition of the person making the later disposal.

[(2A) Subsection (2B) applies if relief is available under Chapter 3 of Part 8 of ITA 2007 or section 587B of the Taxes Act (gifts of shares, securities and real property to charities) in relation to the disposal of a qualifying investment to a charity (whether or not a claim for relief is actually made).

(2B) The consideration for which the charity's acquisition of the qualifying investment is treated by virtue of subsection (2) above as having been made—

(a) is reduced by the relievable amount if relief in relation to the disposal is available only under Chapter 3 of Part 8 of ITA 2007,

(b) is reduced by the relevant amount if relief in relation to the disposal is available only under

section 587B of the Taxes Act,

(c) is reduced by the relievable amount if relief in relation to the disposal is available both under that Chapter and that section as a result of section 442 of ITA 2007 and section 587BA of the Taxes Act, or

(d) is reduced to nil if that consideration is less than the amount referred to in paragraph (a), (b) or (c) (as the case may be).

(2C) In subsections (2A) and (2B)—

"qualifying investment" has the same meaning as in Chapter 3 of Part 8 of ITA 2007 (see section 432 of that Act),

"relevant amount" has the same meaning as in section 587B of the Taxes Act, and

"relievable amount" has the same meaning as in Chapter 3 of Part 8 of ITA 2007 (see section 434 of that Act).][7]

(3) Where—

(a) otherwise than on the termination of a life interest (within the meaning of section 72) by the death of the person entitled thereto, any assets or parts of any assets forming part of settled property are, under section 71, deemed to be disposed of and reacquired by the trustee, and

(b) the person becoming entitled as mentioned in section 71(1) is a charity, or a body mentioned in Schedule 3 to the Inheritance Tax Act 1984 (gifts for national purposes, etc),

then, if no consideration is received by any person for or in connection with any transaction by virtue of which the charity or other body becomes so entitled, the disposal and reacquisition of the assets to which the charity or other body becomes so entitled shall, notwithstanding section 71, be treated for the purposes of this Act as made for such consideration as to secure that neither a gain nor a loss accrues on the disposal.

(4) In subsection (2)(b) above the first reference to a disposal includes a disposal to which section 146(2) of the 1979 Act applied where the person who acquired the asset on that disposal disposes of the asset after the coming into force of this section.

258 Works of art etc

(1)...[8]

(2) A gain shall not be a chargeable gain if it accrues on the disposal of an asset with respect to which an inheritance tax undertaking or an undertaking under the following provisions of this section has been given and—

(a) the disposal is by way of sale by private treaty to a body mentioned in Schedule 3 to [Inheritance Tax Act 1984 ("the 1984 Act")][9] (museums, etc.), or is to such a body otherwise than by sale, or

(b) the disposal is to the Board in pursuance of section 230 of the 1984 Act or in accordance with directions given by the Treasury under section 50 or 51 of the [1946 c. 64.] Finance Act 1946 (acceptance of property in satisfaction of tax).

(3) Subsection (4) below shall have effect in respect of the disposal of any asset which is property which has been or could be designated under section 31 of the 1984 Act, being—

(a) a disposal by way of gift, including a gift in settlement, or

(b) a disposal of settled property by the trustee on an occasion when, under section 71(1), the trustee is deemed to dispose of and immediately reacquire settled property (other than any disposal on which by virtue of section 73 no chargeable gain or allowable loss accrues to the trustee),

if the requisite undertaking described in section 31 of the 1984 Act (maintenance, preservation and access) is given by such person as the Board think appropriate in the circumstances of the case.

(4) The person making a disposal to which subsection (3) above applies and the person acquiring the asset on the disposal shall be treated for all the purposes of this Act as if the asset was acquired from the one making the disposal for a consideration of such an amount as would secure that on the disposal neither a gain nor a loss would accrue to the one making the disposal.

(5) If—

(a) there is a sale of the asset and inheritance tax is chargeable under section 32 of the 1984 Act (or would be chargeable if an inheritance tax undertaking as well as an undertaking under this section had been given), or

(b) the Board are satisfied that at any time during the period for which any such undertaking was given it has not been observed in a material respect,

the person selling that asset or, as the case may be, the owner of the asset shall be treated for the purposes of this Act as having sold the asset for a consideration equal to its market value, and, in the case of a failure to comply with the undertaking, having immediately reacquired it for a consideration equal to its market value.

(6) The period for which an undertaking under this section is given shall be until the person beneficially entitled to the asset dies or it is disposed of, whether by sale or gift or otherwise; and if the asset subject to the undertaking is disposed of—

(a) otherwise than on sale, and

(b) without a further undertaking being given under this section,

subsection (5) above shall apply as if the asset had been sold to an individual.

References in this subsection to a disposal shall be construed without regard to any provision of this Act under which an asset is deemed to be disposed of.

(7) Where under subsection (5) above a person is treated as having sold for a consideration equal to its market value any asset within section 31(1)(c), (d) or (e) of the 1984 Act, he shall also be treated as having sold and immediately reacquired for a consideration equal to its market value any asset associated with it; but the Board may direct that the preceding provisions of this subsection shall not have effect in any case in which it appears to them that the entity consisting of the asset and any assets associated with it has not been materially affected.

For the purposes of this subsection 2 or more assets are associated with each other if one of them is a building falling within section 31(1)(c) of the 1984 Act and the other or others such land or objects as, in relation to that building, fall within section 31(1)(d) or (e) of the 1984 Act.

(8) If in pursuance of subsection (5) above a person is treated as having on any occasion sold an asset and inheritance tax becomes chargeable on the same occasion, then, in determining the value of the asset for the purposes of that tax, an allowance shall be made for the capital gains tax chargeable on any chargeable gain accruing on that occasion.

(9) In this section "inheritance tax undertaking" means an undertaking under Chapter II of Part II or section 78 of, or Schedule 5 to, the 1984 Act.

289 Commencement

(1) Except where the context otherwise requires, this Act has effect in relation to tax for the year 1992-93 and subsequent years of assessment, and tax for other chargeable periods beginning on or after 6th April 1992, and references to the coming into force of this Act or any provision in this Act shall be construed accordingly.

(2) The following provisions of this Act, that is—

(a) so much of any provision of this Act as authorises the making of any order or other instrument, and

(b) except where the tax concerned is all tax for chargeable periods to which this Act does not apply, so much of any provision of this Act as confers any power or imposes any duty the exercise or performance of which operates or may operate in relation to tax for more than one chargeable period,

shall come into force for all purposes on 6th April 1992 to the exclusion of the corresponding enactments repealed by this Act.

291 Short title

This Act may be cited as the Taxation of Chargeable Gains Act 1992.

---

[1] Words in subsection (1) substituted by FA 2006 s.55(4)

[2] Words in subsection (1) inserted by paragraph 326 Schedule 1 ITA 2007

[3] subsections (3) to (5) inserted by paragraph 326 Schedule 1 ITA 2007

[4] section 256 was amended by section 55(4) of the Finance Act 2006 (c. 25) and paragraph 326 of Schedule 1 to the Income Tax Act 2007.

[5] sections 256A and 256B inserted by paragraph 327 Schedule 1 ITA 2007

[6] Inserted by FA 1995 s.72(5)

[7] subsections (2A) to (2C) inserted by paragraph 328 Schedule 1 ITA 2007

[8] Subsection (1) repealed by FA 1998 s 165, Sch 27 Part IV

[9] Words substituted by FA 1998 s 143(7)

National Lottery etc Act 1993

1993 CHAPTER 39

An Act to authorise lotteries to be promoted as part of a National Lottery; to make provision with respect to the running and regulation of that National Lottery and with respect to the distribution of its net proceeds; to increase the membership and extend the powers of the Trustees of the National Heritage Memorial Fund; to amend section 1 of the Revenue Act 1898 and the Lotteries and Amusements Act 1976; to amend the law relating to pool betting; and for connected purposes.

[21st October 1993]

Part I - AUTHORISATION AND REGULATION OF THE NATIONAL LOTTERY

Preliminary

1 The National Lottery.

(1) In this Act "the National Lottery" means all the lotteries that form part of the National Lottery, taken as a whole.

(2) A lottery forms part of the National Lottery if the following conditions are satisfied.

(3) The lottery must be promoted or proposed to be promoted—

(a) by the body licensed to run the National Lottery under section 5, or

(b) in pursuance of an agreement that has been made between that body and the lottery's promoter or proposed promoter.

(4) The promotion of the lottery must be authorised by a licence that has been granted to its promoter or proposed promoter under section 6.

2 Legality of lotteries forming part of the National Lottery.

(1) A lottery that forms part of the National Lottery shall not be unlawful.

(2) Schedule 1 contains amendments consequential on subsection (1).

................................[1]

[3A The National Lottery Commission.

(1) There shall be a body corporate known as the National Lottery Commission.

(2) Schedule 2A makes provision in relation to the Commission.][2]

4 Overriding duties of the Secretary of State and Director General.

(1) The Secretary of State and (subject to any directions he may be given by the Secretary of State under section 11) the Director General shall each exercise his functions under this Part in the manner he considers the most likely to secure—

(a) that the National Lottery is run, and every lottery that forms part of it is promoted, with all due propriety, and

(b) that the interests of every participant in a lottery that forms part of the National Lottery are protected.

(2) Subject to subsection (1), the Secretary of State and the Director General shall each in exercising those functions do his best to secure that the net proceeds of the National Lottery are as great as possible.

(3) In subsection (2) "the net proceeds of the National Lottery" means the sums that are paid to the Secretary of State by virtue of section 5(6).

The licensing system

5 Licensing of a body to run the National Lottery.

(1) The Director General may by licence authorise a body corporate to run the National Lottery.

(2) Only one body may be licensed under this section at any one time.

(3) The Director General shall not grant a licence under this section unless an application in writing, containing such information as he has specified as necessary for enabling him to determine whether to grant it, has been made to him by such date as he has specified.

(4) The Director General shall not grant such a licence unless he is satisfied that the applicant is a fit and proper body to run the National Lottery.

(5) In determining whether to grant such a licence, the Director General may consider—

(a) whether any person who appears to him to be likely to manage the business or any part of the business of running the National Lottery under the licence is a fit and proper person to do so,

and

(b) whether any person who appears to him to be likely to be a person for whose benefit that business would be carried on is a fit and proper person to benefit from it.

(6) A licence under this section shall include a condition requiring the licensee to pay to the Secretary of State at such times as may be determined by or under the licence such sums out of the proceeds of lotteries forming part of the National Lottery as may be so determined.

(7) A licence under this section may include a condition requiring the licensee to make such arrangements as may be determined by or under the licence for securing that, in circumstances specified in the licence, such sums as may be so determined are paid to the Director General for distribution to participants in lotteries forming part of the National Lottery.

6 Licensing of bodies to promote lotteries.

(1) The Director General may by licence authorise a body corporate to promote lotteries as part of the National Lottery.

(2) a licence under this section shall specify the lotteries, or descriptions of lottery, the promotion of which it authorises.

(3) The Director General shall not grant such a licence unless an application in writing, containing such information as he has specified as necessary for enabling him to determine whether to grant it, has been made to him.

(4) The Director General shall not grant such a licence unless he is satisfied that the applicant is a fit and proper body to promote lotteries under the licence.

(5) In determining whether to grant such a licence, the Director General may consider—

(a) whether any person who appears to him to be likely to manage the business or any part of the business of promoting lotteries under the licence is a fit and proper person to do so, and

(b) whether any person who appears to him to be likely to be a person for whose benefit that business would be carried on is a fit and proper person to benefit from it.

(6) A licence under this section may include a condition requiring the licensee to obtain the Director General's approval of the rules of any lottery before the lottery is promoted under the licence.

7 Licences under sections 5 and 6: further provisions.

(1) A licence granted under section 5 or 6 shall be in writing and shall specify the period for which (subject to being revoked or suspended) it is to have effect.

(2) Such a licence may include such conditions (in addition to those required or authorised by section 5 or 6) as the Director General considers appropriate and in particular may include conditions requiring the licensee—

(a) to obtain the consent of the Director General before doing anything specified, or of a description specified, in the licence;

(b) to refer matters to the Director General for approval;

(c) to ensure that such requirements as the Director General may from time to time determine or approve are complied with;

(d) to provide the Director General at times specified by him with such information as he may require (including, if the information is of a description specified in the licence, information for publication by him);

(e) to allow the Director General to inspect and take copies of any documents of the licensee, including any information kept by the licensee otherwise than in writing, relating to the National Lottery or a lottery forming part of it;

(f) where such information is kept by means of a computer, to give the Director General such assistance as he may require to enable him to inspect and take copies of the information in a visible and legible form or to inspect and check the operation of any computer, and any associated apparatus or material, that is or has been in use in connection with the keeping of the information;

(g) to do such things (and, in particular, to effect such transfers of property or rights) as the Director General may require in connection with the licence ceasing to have effect and the grant of a licence to another body.

(3) In subsection (2)(e) and (f) "the Director General" includes any representative of the Director General, as well as any member of his staff, who has been authorised by him (whether generally or

specially) to make such an inspection.

(4) Conditions in a licence granted under section 5 or 6 may impose requirements to be complied with by the licensee after the licence has ceased to have effect.

(5) On the granting of a licence under section 5 or 6, the licensee shall pay to the Director General a fee of such amount as the Secretary of State may by order prescribe.

(6) All fees received by the Director General by virtue of subsection (5) shall be paid into the Consolidated Fund.

8 Variation of conditions in licences.

(1) The Director General may vary any condition in a licence granted under section 5 or 6 if the licensee consents.

(2) Subject to subsection (3), the Director General may vary any condition in such a licence without the licensee's consent if the licensee has been given a reasonable opportunity of making representations to the Director General about the variation.

(3) Subsection (2) does not apply—

(a) where the variation would result in a condition requiring the licensee to transfer any property or rights, or

(b) in the case of a licence granted under section 5, in relation to a condition that the licence provides may only be varied with the consent of the licensee.

(4) Where the Director General varies a condition in a licence under subsection (2)—

(a) he shall serve a notice on the licensee informing the licensee of the variation, and

(b) the variation shall take effect at the end of such period as may be specified in the notice.

(5) The period specified in the notice shall be a period of at least twenty-one days beginning with the date of the notice.

(6) The Director General's power to vary a condition in a licence under subsection (1) or (2) includes power to add a condition to the licence or omit a condition from it (and references in this section to the variation of a condition are to be read accordingly).

9 Enforcement of conditions in licences.

(1) If, on an application made by the Director General, the court is satisfied—

(a) that there is a reasonable likelihood that a person will contravene a condition in a licence granted under section 5 or 6,

(b) that a person has contravened such a condition and there is a reasonable likelihood that the contravention will continue or be repeated, or

(c) that a person has contravened such a condition and there are steps that could be taken for remedying the contravention,

the court may grant an injunction restraining the contravention or, in Scotland, an interdict prohibiting the contravention or (as the case may be) make an order requiring the licensee, and any other person who appears to the court to have been party to the contravention, to take such steps as the court may direct to remedy it.

(2) In subsection (1) "the court" means the High Court or, in Scotland, the Court of Session.

(3) Any sum payable to the Secretary of State in accordance with a condition included in a licence by virtue of section 5(6) shall be recoverable by him as a debt due to him from the licensee (and the licensee's liability to pay it shall not be affected by the licence ceasing for any reason to have effect).

10 Revocation of licences..

(1) The Director General shall revoke a licence granted under section 5 if he is satisfied that the licensee no longer is, or never was, a fit and proper body to run the National Lottery.

(2) The Director General shall revoke a licence granted under section 6 if he is satisfied that the licensee no longer is, or never was, a fit and proper body to promote lotteries under the licence.

(3) The Director General may revoke a licence granted under section 5 or 6—

(a) if it appears to him that any of the grounds for revocation set out in Part I of Schedule 3 applies, or

(b) if the licensee consents.

(4) Part II of Schedule 3 shall have effect in relation to the revocation of a licence under this section, other than a revocation with the licensee's consent.

[10AFinancial penalties for breach of conditions in licences.

(1) If the Director General is satisfied that a person has contravened a condition in a licence under section 5 or 6, he may impose a financial penalty on that person in respect of the contravention.

(2) The matters to which the Director General may have regard in imposing a financial penalty include the desirability of both—

(a) deterring persons from contravening conditions in licences under section 5 or 6, and

(b) recovering any diminution in the sums paid to the Secretary of State under section 5(6) which is attributable to the contravention.

(3) If the Director General proposes to impose a financial penalty on a person, he shall serve on that person a notice—

(a) stating that the person has contravened conditions in the licence,

(b) identifying the contraventions in question,

(c) stating that the Director General proposes to impose a financial penalty,

(d) specifying the amount of the financial penalty,

(e) stating the Director General's reasons—

(i) for the imposition of a financial penalty, and

(ii) for the amount of the financial penalty,

(f) stating the person to whom the financial penalty is to be paid and the manner in which, and place at which, payment may be made, and

(g) stating the effect of subsections (5) and (12).

(4) A notice under subsection (3) must state that the person may, within the period of 21 days beginning with the date of the notice, either—

(a) make written representations about the matter to the Director General, or

(b) notify the Director General in writing of the person's intention to make oral representations,

and that the right of appeal conferred by section 10B is dependent on the person having made such written or oral representations.

(5) If, within the period mentioned in subsection (4), the Director General receives neither—

(a) written representations, nor

(b) written notification of the person's intention to make oral representations,

the financial penalty shall become payable at the end of that period.

(6) The Secretary of State may make regulations as to the procedure to be followed where a person's intention to make oral representations is notified to the Director General as mentioned in subsection (4).

(7) The regulations may in particular make provision—

(a) for the financial penalty to become payable if the person fails to comply with any requirements imposed by or under the regulations, and

(b) as to the hearing by the Director General of oral representations.

(8) If—

(a) any written representations against the imposition of the financial penalty are made as mentioned in subsection (4), or

(b) any oral representations against the imposition of the financial penalty are made in accordance with regulations under subsection (6),

subsection (9) shall apply.

(9) Where this subsection applies, the Director General shall after taking the representations into account—

(a) decide whether or not to impose a financial penalty, and

(b) serve a further notice on the person informing the person of the decision.

(10) Where the decision is to impose a financial penalty, the further notice must—

(a) identify the contraventions in question,

(b) specify the amount of the financial penalty imposed,

(c) state the Director General's reasons—

(i) for the imposition of a financial penalty, and

(ii) for the amount of the financial penalty,

(d) state the person to whom the financial penalty is to be paid and the manner in which, and place

at which, payment may be made, and

(e) state the effect of subsections (11) and (12).

(11) A financial penalty imposed by virtue of a decision under subsection (9) becomes payable on the date of the further notice.

(12) a person on whom a financial penalty is imposed is required to pay the penalty within the period of fourteen days beginning with the date on which the financial penalty becomes payable.

(13) If the whole or any part of a financial penalty is not paid within the period mentioned in subsection (12), then as from the end of that period the unpaid balance from time to time shall carry interest at the rate for the time being specified in section 17 of the Judgments Act 1838.

(14) A financial penalty imposed on any person, and any interest accrued under subsection (13) in respect of the penalty, shall be recoverable from that person as a debt due to the Secretary of State from that person (and the person's liability to pay it shall not be affected by the person's licence ceasing for any reason to have effect).][3] .

[10BAppeals against financial penalties.

(1) Where the Director General decides under subsection (9) of section 10A to impose a financial penalty on a person, the person may appeal against the decision on the grounds specified in subsection (2) or, as the case may be, subsection (3).

(2) To the extent that an appeal under this section is against a finding by the Director General that a person contravened a condition of a licence, the grounds for the appeal are—

(a) that the Director General made an error as to the facts,

(b) that there was a material procedural error, or

(c) that the Director General made some other error of law.

(3) To the extent that an appeal under this section is against the amount of a financial penalty, the grounds for the appeal are—

(a) that the amount of the penalty is unreasonable,

(b) that there was a material procedural error, or

(c) that the decision was based on a manifest material misapprehension as to the facts.

(4) Where on an appeal under this section a court reduces the amount of a financial penalty, the powers of the court shall include power to make such orders as to interest on the penalty as the court considers just and equitable in all the circumstances of the case.

(5) The power conferred by subsection (4) includes power to make orders as to—

(a) the rates of interest which are to apply, and

(b) the date from which interest is to run.

(6) An appeal under this section lies to the High Court or, in Scotland, to the Court of Session.

(7) Any appeal under this section to the Court of Session shall be heard in the Outer House.][4] .

Control by the Secretary of State

11 Directions to the Director General.

(1) The Director General shall in exercising his functions under [sections 5 to 10A][5] comply with any directions that he may be given by the Secretary of State.

(2) Such directions may deal in particular—

(a) with the matters that the Director General should take into account in deciding whether or not to grant licences;

(b) with the conditions that licences should contain.

12 Regulations as to the promotion of lotteries.

(1) The Secretary of State may by regulations make such provision in relation to the promotion of lotteries that form part of the National Lottery as he considers necessary or expedient.

(2) Such regulations may in particular impose requirements or restrictions as to—

(a) the minimum age of persons to whom or by whom tickets or chances may be sold;

(b) the places, circumstances or manner in which tickets or chances may be sold or persons may be invited to buy them;

(c) the information that must appear in an advertisement for a lottery;

(d) the places, circumstances or manner in which signs relating to a lottery may be displayed.

(3) In subsection (2) "tickets" includes any document providing evidence of a person's claim to

participate in the chances of a lottery.

(4) Regulations under this section may make different provision for different areas.

13 Contravention of regulations an offence.

(1) If any requirement or restriction imposed by regulations made under section 12 is contravened in relation to the promotion of a lottery that forms part of the National Lottery—

(a) the promoter of the lottery shall be guilty of an offence, except if the contravention occurred without the consent or connivance of the promoter and the promoter exercised all due diligence to prevent such a contravention,

(b) any director, manager, secretary or other similar officer of the promoter, or any person purporting to act in such a capacity, shall be guilty of an offence if he consented to or connived at the contravention or if the contravention was attributable to any neglect on his part, and

(c) any other person who was party to the contravention shall be guilty of an offence.

(2) A person guilty of an offence under this section shall be liable—

(a) on summary conviction, to a fine not exceeding the statutory maximum;

(b) on conviction on indictment, to imprisonment for a term not exceeding two years, to a fine or to both.

(3) Summary proceedings in Scotland for an offence under this section may be commenced within a period of six months from the date on which evidence sufficient in the opinion of the procurator fiscal to warrant proceedings came to his knowledge; but no proceedings in Scotland shall be commenced by virtue of this section more than three years after the commission of the offence.

(4) For the purposes of this section, a certificate signed by or on behalf of the procurator fiscal and stating the date on which evidence sufficient in his opinion to warrant the proceedings came to his knowledge shall be conclusive evidence of that fact; and a certificate stating that matter and purporting to be so signed shall be taken to be so signed unless the contrary is proved.

Provision of information by the Director General

14 Annual report.

(1) as soon as possible after the end of every financial year, the Director General shall make a report on the exercise of his functions during that year to the Secretary of State.

(2) In subsection (1) "financial year" means—

(a). . . . .[6]

[(aa) the period beginning with the date on which section 3A comes into force and ending with the next 31st March, and][7] .

(b) each successive period of twelve months ending with 31st March.

(3) The Secretary of State shall lay a copy of every report received by him under this section before Parliament.

[(4) Where a report is made by the National Lottery Commission under sub-section (1) to the Scottish Ministers (by virtue of provision made under section 63 of the Scotland Act 1998), the Scottish Ministers shall lay a copy of the report before the Scottish Parliament.][8] .

15 Power of the Secretary of State to require information.

The Director General shall provide the Secretary of State with such information relating to the National Lottery or a lottery forming part of it as the Secretary of State may direct.

Miscellaneous and supplementary

16 False representations as to the National Lottery.

(1) If a person advertising, or offering the opportunity to participate in, a lottery, competition or game of another description gives, by whatever means, a false indication that it is a lottery forming part of, or is otherwise connected with, the National Lottery, he shall be guilty of an offence.

(2) A person guilty of an offence under this section shall be liable—

(a) on summary conviction, to a fine not exceeding the statutory maximum;

(b) on conviction on indictment, to imprisonment for a term not exceeding two years, to a fine or to both.

...

19 Restriction of enactments relating to the rehabilitation of offenders.

(1) Neither section 4(1) of the Rehabilitation of Offenders Act 1974 nor Article 5(1) of the Rehabilitation of Offenders (Northern Ireland) Order 1978 (exclusion of evidence and questions relating to an individual's previous convictions) shall apply in relation to any proceedings—

(a) before the Director General in respect of the grant or revocation of a licence, or

(b) by way of appeal to the Secretary of State against the revocation of a licence by the Director General.

(2) A conviction shall not be regarded as spent for the purposes of section 4(2) of that Act or Article 5(2) of that Order (restrictions in respect of such questions put otherwise than in proceedings) if the question is put by the Director General and the following conditions are satisfied.

(3) The question must be put for the purpose of determining whether to grant or revoke a licence.

(4) The question must relate to an individual—

(a) who manages the business or any part of the business carried on under the licence (or who is likely to do so if the licence is granted), or

(b) for whose benefit that business is carried on (or is likely to be carried on if the licence is granted).

(5) When the question is asked, the person questioned must be informed that by virtue of this section all the individual's previous convictions are to be disclosed.

20 Interpretation of Part I.

In this Part—

["the Commission" means the National Lottery Commission;][9]

"contravention", in relation to a condition or requirement, includes a failure to comply with that condition or requirement (and "contravened" is to be read accordingly);

. . .[10]

"participant", in relation to a lottery, means a person who has bought a ticket or chance in the lottery;

"promote" includes conduct (and "promotion" is to be read accordingly);

and any reference to a lottery forming part of the National Lottery is to be read in accordance with section 1.

Part II - DISTRIBUTION OF THE NET PROCEEDS OF THE NATIONAL LOTTERY

The distribution system

21 The National Lottery Distribution Fund.

(1) There shall be a fund maintained under the control and management of the Secretary of State and known as the National Lottery Distribution Fund.

(2) The Secretary of State shall pay into the Distribution Fund all the sums that are paid to him by virtue of section 5(6) [or 10A][11].

22 Apportionment of money in Distribution Fund.

(1) Every sum that is paid into the Distribution Fund under section 21(2) shall be apportioned as follows.

(2) So much of the sum as the Secretary of State considers appropriate shall be allocated for making payments under section 31 and held in the Distribution Fund for that purpose.

(3) Of the balance—

(a)[162/3 per cent.][12]shall be allocated for expenditure on or connected with the arts,

(b)[162/3 per cent.][13]shall be allocated for expenditure on or connected with sport,

(c)[162/3 per cent.][14]shall be allocated for expenditure on or connected with the national heritage,

(d)[162/3 per cent.]shall be allocated for charitable expenditure,. . .[15]

(e)20 per cent. shall be allocated for expenditure on projects to mark the year 2000 and the beginning of the third millennium [and

(f)[331/3 per cent.][16] shall be allocated for expenditure on or connected with health, education or the environment.][17].

[(4) This section has effect subject to section 19 of the National Lottery Act 1998.][18] .

23 The distributing bodies.

(1) So much of any sum paid into the Distribution Fund as is allocated for expenditure on or connected with the arts shall be held in the Distribution Fund—

[(a) as to [71.1 per cent.][19], for distribution by the Arts Council of England,
(b) as to [7.74 per cent.][20], for distribution by the Scottish Arts Council,
(c) as to 5 per cent., for distribution by the Arts Council of Wales,. . . .[21]
(d) as to 2.8 per cent., for distribution by [the Arts Council of Northern Ireland][22][. . . .[23]
(e) as to 12.2 per cent., for distribution by the Film Council][24][, and
(f) as to 1.16 per cent, for distribution by Scottish Screen.][25][26] .

(2) So much of any sum paid into the Distribution Fund as is allocated for expenditure on or connected with sport shall be held in the Distribution Fund—
(a) as to [75.6 per cent.][27], for distribution by [the English Sports Council][28],
(b) as to [8.1 per cent.][29], for distribution by the Scottish Sports Council,
(c) as to [4.5 per cent.][30], for distribution by the Sports Council for Wales, and
(d) as to [2.6 per cent.][31], for distribution by the Sports Council for Northern Ireland[and
(e) as to 9.2 per cent., for distribution by the United Kingdom Sports Council.][32] .

(3) So much of any sum paid into the Distribution Fund as is allocated for expenditure on or connected with the national heritage shall be held in the Distribution Fund for distribution by the Trustees of the National Heritage Memorial Fund.

(4) So much of any sum paid into the Distribution Fund as is allocated for charitable expenditure shall be held in the Distribution Fund for distribution by the National Lottery Charities Board (established under section 37).

(5) So much of any sum paid into the Distribution Fund as is allocated for expenditure on projects to mark the year 2000 and the beginning of the third millennium shall be held in the Distribution Fund for distribution by the Millennium Commission (established under section 40).

[(6) So much of any sum paid into the Distribution Fund as is allocated for expenditure on or connected with health, education or the environment shall be held in the Distribution Fund for distribution by the New Opportunities Fund (established under section 43A).][33]

24 Payments from Distribution Fund to distributing bodies.

At such times as the Secretary of State thinks appropriate, payments of such amounts as he thinks appropriate may be made to a body specified in section 23 out of so much of any money in the Distribution Fund as is held for distribution by that body.

25 Application of money by distributing bodies.

(1) Subject to the provisions of this Part, a body shall distribute any money paid to it under section 24 for meeting expenditure of the relevant description mentioned in section 22(3).

[(1A) The manner in which a body may distribute any money paid to it under section 24 includes making or entering into arrangements for or in connection with meeting expenditure (including arrangements with respect to vouchers); and this subsection shall apply notwithstanding anything to the contrary in any enactment or instrument relating to the functions of the body.][34] .

(2) a body shall not under subsection (1) distribute money for any purpose or in any manner if it does not have power to distribute money for that purpose or in that manner apart from subsection (1).

[(2A) a body which distributes money under subsection (1) shall have power to solicit applications from other bodies or persons for any of the money which the body so distributes, notwithstanding anything to the contrary in any enactment or instrument relating to the functions of the body.

(2B) In determining whether a decision of a body concerning its distribution of money under subsection (1) was unlawful, it shall be immaterial whether or not the body, or any person acting on behalf of the body, solicited an application from a body or person for such money.][35] .

(3) a body may defray out of any money paid to it under section 24 any expenses incurred by the body in consequence of this Act.

(4) The Trustees of the National Heritage Memorial Fund may apply any money paid to them under section 24 for any purpose for which they have power to apply money under section 4 of the National Heritage Act 1980 [(other expenditure out of the fund)][36].

[25A Delegation by distributing bodies of their powers of distribution.

(1) a body which distributes money under subsection (1) of section 25 may appoint any other body or person to exercise on its behalf any of its functions relating to, or connected with, the distribution of money under that subsection (including its function of making decisions as to the persons to whom such distributions are to be made)—

(a) in any particular case, or

(b) in cases of any particular description.

(2) The persons who may be appointed by a body under subsection (1) include a member, employee or committee of the body itself.

(3) a body which makes an appointment under subsection (1) may defray out of any money paid to it under section 24 any expenses incurred by the appointee in consequence of the appointment.

(4) Power to accept any such appointment as is mentioned in subsection (1) is conferred by this subsection on the following bodies—

(a) any body which distributes money under section 25(1),

(b) any charity or any charitable, benevolent or philanthropic institution,

(c) any body established by or under an enactment, and

(d) any body established by Royal Charter.

(5) a body appointed by virtue of subsection (1) to exercise a function on behalf of another may itself appoint any of its members or employees, or a committee, to exercise the function in its stead, but only if—

(a) the terms of the body's appointment by virtue of subsection (1) so permit, and

(b) the body has power apart from this section to appoint a member or, as the case may be, an employee or committee of the body to exercise some or all of its functions.

(6) Subject to the following provisions of this section—

(a) a body which distributes money under section 25(1) may establish a committee for the purpose of exercising on behalf of the body any such function as is mentioned in subsection (1), and

(b) a body falling within any paragraph of subsection (4) may establish a committee for the purpose of exercising on behalf of any body which distributes money under section 25(1) any such function as is mentioned in subsection (1).

(7) a committee established under subsection (6)—

(a) must consist of or include one or more members, or one or more employees, of the body establishing the committee, but

(b) may include persons who are neither members nor employees of that body.

(8) any power conferred on a body by subsections (1) to (7) is so conferred—

(a) to the extent that the body would not have the power apart from this section, and

(b) notwithstanding anything to the contrary in any enactment or instrument relating to the functions of the body.

(9) In this section—

"charity" means a body, or the trustees of a trust, established for charitable purposes only;

"charitable, benevolent or philanthropic institution" means a body, or the trustees of a trust, which is established for charitable purposes (whether or not those purposes are charitable within the meaning of any rule of law), benevolent purposes or philanthropic purposes, and which is not a charity.

(10) For the purposes of this section—

(a) the trustees of a trust shall be regarded as a body, and

(b) any reference to a member of a body shall, in the case of a body of trustees, be taken as a reference to any of the trustees,

and references to a committee shall be construed accordingly.

(11) any reference in this section to a member of a body includes a reference to the chairman or deputy chairman of (or the holder of any corresponding office in relation to) the body.][37] .

[25BJoint schemes for distribution of money by distributing bodies..

(1) a body which distributes money under subsection (1) of section 25 may, in accordance with the following provisions of this section, participate with one or more other such bodies in a joint scheme for the distribution of money under that subsection.

(2) a body may participate in a joint scheme if the principal purposes of the joint scheme include purposes for which the body has power to distribute money under subsection (1) of section 25, notwithstanding that the body would not, apart from this section, have power to distribute money under that subsection for meeting expenditure on some of the particular projects for which money may be distributed under the scheme.

(3) Money shall not, under a joint scheme, be distributed for meeting expenditure on any particular project unless the expenditure is such that—

(a) at least one of the bodies participating in the joint scheme has power, acting alone, to distribute money under section 25(1) for meeting the expenditure, or

(b) two or more of the bodies participating in the joint scheme, taken together, have power between them to distribute money under section 25(1) for meeting the expenditure.

(4) Nothing in subsection (3) affects the liability of each body participating in a scheme in relation to the distribution of any money under section 25(1) under the scheme.

(5) Schedule 3A contains supplementary provision in relation to joint schemes.][38] .

---

[1] S. 3 repealed (1.4.1999) by 1998 c. 22, ss. 1(2), 26, Sch. 5 Pt. I; S.I. 1999/650, art. 2.

[2] S. 3A inserted (1.4.1999) by 1998 c. 22, s. 1(3); S.I. 1999/650, art. 2

[3] S. 10A inserted (2.9.1998) by 1998 c. 22, ss. 2(1)(5), 27(5)

[4] S. 10B inserted (2.9.1998) by 1998 c. 22, ss. 3, 27(5).

[5] Words in s. 11(1) substituted (2.9.1998) by 1998 c. 22, ss. 2(2), 27(5).

[6] S. 14(2)(a) repealed (1.4.1999) by 1998 c. 22, ss. 1(5), 26, Sch. 1 Pt. I para. 6(5) Pt. III para. 13(a), Sch. 5 Pt. I; S.I. 1999/650, art. 2

[7] S. 14(2)(aa) inserted (1.4.1999) by 1998 c. 22, s. 1(5), Sch. 1 Pt. I para. 6(5) Pt. III para. 13(b); S.I. 1999/650, art. 2

[8] S. 14(4) inserted (1.7.1999) by S.I. 1999/1750, arts. 1(1), 6(1), Sch. 5 para. 12(2); S.I. 1999/1378, art. 3

[9] Definition inserted (1.4.1999) by 1998 c. 22, s. 1(5), Sch. 1 Pt. III para. 14(a); S.I. 1999/650, art. 2.

[10] Definition repealed (1.4.1999) by 1998 c. 22, ss. 1(5), 26, Sch. 1 Pt. III para. 14(b), Sch. 5 Pt. I; S.I. 1999/650, art. 2.

[11] Words in s. 21(2) inserted (2.9.1998) by 1998 c. 22, ss. 2(3), 27(5).

[12] Words in s. 22(3)(a)-(d) substituted (17.5.1999) by S.I. 1999/344, art. 3(1)-(5)

[13] Words in s. 22(3)(a)-(d) substituted (17.5.1999) by S.I. 1999/344, art. 3(1)-(5)

[14] Words in s. 22(3)(a)-(d) substituted (17.5.1999) by S.I. 1999/344, art. 3(1)-(5)

[15] Word at the end of s. 22(3)(d) repealed (2.7.1998) by 1998 c. 22, ss. 26, 27(4), Sch. 5 Pt. II.

[16] Words in s. 22(3)(f) substituted (22.12.2000 with effect as mentioned in art. 2 of the amending S.I.) by S.I. 2000/3356, art. 2

[17] S. 22(3)(f) and word preceding it inserted (2.7.1998) by 1998 c. 22, ss. 6(2)(9), 27(4)

[18] S. 22(4) inserted (2.7.1998) by 1998 c. 22, ss. 19(7), 27(4).

[19] Words in s. 23(1)(a) substituted (1.10.1999) by S.I. 1999/2090, art. 2(1)(2)

[20] Words in s. 23(1)(b) substituted (7.4.2000) by S.S.I. 2000/78, art. 2

[21] Word in s. 23(1)(c) omitted (1.10.1999) by S.I. 1999/2090, art. 2(1)(3)

[22] Words in s. 23(1) substituted (1.9.1995) by S.I. 1995/2088, art. 2.

[23] Word in s. 23(1)(d) omitted (7.4.2000) by S.S.I. 2000/78, art. 2

[24] S. 23(1)(e) and the preceding "and"inserted (1.10.1999) by S.I. 1999/2090, art. 2(1)(3)

[25] S. 23(1)(f) and the preceding "and"inserted (7.4.2000) by S.S.I. 2000/78, art. 2

[26] S. 23(1)(a)-(d) substituted (13.6.1994) by S.I. 1994/1342, art. 2.

[27] Words in s. 23(2)(a) substituted (1.7.1999) by S.I. 1999/1563, art. 2(1)(2)

[28] Words in s. 23(2)(a) substituted (1.1.1997) by S.I. 1996/3095, art. 2.

[29] Words in s. 23(2)(b) substituted (1.7.1999) by S.I. 1999/1563, art. 2(1)(3)

[30] Words in s. 23(2)(c) substituted (1.7.1999) by S.I. 1999/1563, art. 2(1)(4)

[31] Words in s. 23(2)(d) substituted (1.7.1999) by S.I. 1999/1563, art. 2(1)(5)

[32] S. 23(2)(e) and the preceding "and" inserted (1.7.1999) by S.I. 1999/1563, art. 2(6)

[33] S. 23(6) inserted (2.7.1998) by 1998 c. 22, ss. 7(1), 27(4).

[34] S. 25(1A) inserted (2.7.1998) by 1998 c. 22, ss. 9(1), 27(4).

[35] S. 25(2A)-(2B) inserted (2.7.1998) by 1998 c. 22, ss. 10, 27(4).

[36] Words in s. 25(4) substituted (4.3.1998) by 1997 c. 14, s. 3, Sch. para. 4; S.I. 1998/292, art. 2

[37] S. 25A inserted (2.7.1998) by 1998 c. 22, ss. 11(1), 27(4)

[38] S. 25B inserted (2.7.1998) by 1998 c. 22, ss. 12(1), 27(4).

Local Government (Wales) Act 1994

1994 CHAPTER 19

49 Charities.

(1) Where, immediately before the commencement of this section, any property is held exclusively for charitable purposes by any of the old authorities, as sole trustee, that property shall vest on the same trusts in the appropriate council.

(2) Where, immediately before the commencement of this section, any power with respect to a charity was vested in the proper officer of an old authority or in the holder of any other office of an old

authority that power shall vest in the corresponding officer of the appropriate council.

(3) Where, immediately before the commencement of this section, an old authority or any officer of an old authority is included among the charity trustees of a charity, those trustees shall include instead the appropriate council or (as the case may be) the corresponding officer of that council.

(4) Where subsection (1) applies and the property in question is held for the benefit of—

(a) a specified area,

(b) the inhabitants of a specified area, or

(c) any particular class or body of persons in a specified area,

the appropriate council is the new principal council whose area comprises the whole, or the greater part, of the specified area.

(5) In any other case falling within this section, the appropriate council is the new principal council whose area comprises the whole, or the greater part, of the area of the old authority in question.

(6) The Secretary of State may by order make provision with respect to any of the matters dealt with by this section, either in substitution for the provision made by this section or by way of supplementing or modifying that provision, and either generally or in relation to prescribed cases or classes of case.

(7) Nothing in this section—

(a) affects any power of Her Majesty, the court or any other person to alter the trusts of any charity; or

(b) applies in a case to which section 50 applies.

(8) In this section "charity", "charitable purposes", "charity trustees", "court" and "trusts" have the same meaning as in the Charities Act 1993.

...

64 Interpretation.

(1) In this Act—

"the 1972 Act" means the Local Government Act 1972;

"the Commission" means the Staff Commission for Wales or Comisiwn Staff Cymru;

"decentralisation scheme" has the meaning given in section 27;

"financial year" means the period of twelve months beginning with 1st April;

"new", in relation to any area or authority, means an area or authority established by or under this Act;

"old authority" means an authority which ceases to exist as a result of this Act;

"the planning Act" means the Town and Country Planning Act 1990;

"prescribed" means prescribed by an order or by regulations made by the Secretary of State;

"preserved county" means any county created by the 1972 Act as a county in Wales, as that county stood immediately before the passing of this Act but subject to any provision of this Act, or made under the 1972 Act, redrawing its boundaries;

"the Residuary Body" means the Residuary Body for Wales or Corff Gweddilliol Cymru.

(2) a county borough established by this Act shall not be treated as a borough for the purposes of any Act passed before 1st April 1974.

(3) Subject to the provisions of this section, this Act and the 1972 Act shall be construed as one.

(4) Subject to any provision to the contrary, in any amendment of an enactment made by or under this Act "Wales" has the same meaning as in section 269 of the 1972 Act.

...

66 Short title, commencement, extent etc.

(1) This Act may be cited as the Local Government (Wales) Act 1994.

(2) The following provisions of this Act—

(a) sections 1(1), (2) and (7), 3, 6, 7, 39, 40, 43, 46, 47, 48, 54, 55, 63 and 64,

(b) Schedules 1, 3, 13 and 14 and paragraphs 1, 4, 6 and 9 of Schedule 17, and

(c) subsections (1) to (4) and (9) of this section,

shall come into force on the passing of this Act.

(3) The other provisions of this Act shall come into force on such day as the Secretary of State may by order appoint.

(4) Different days may be appointed by an order under subsection (3) for different purposes and different provisions.

(5) Schedule 15 makes minor and consequential amendments of the 1972 Act.

(6) Schedule 16 makes certain miscellaneous consequential amendments.

(7) Schedule 17 contains transitional provisions and savings.

(8) The repeals set out in Schedule 18, which include repeals of certain enactments which are spent, shall have effect.

(9) This Act does not extend to Scotland or Northern Ireland except that any amendment or repeal of another enactment by this Act has the same extent as the enactment amended or repealed.

Value Added Tax Act 1994

1994 CHAPTER 23

Part II - Reliefs, exemptions and repayments

Reliefs etc. generally available

[29A Reduced rate

(1) VAT charged on—

(a) any supply that is of a description for the time being specified in Schedule 7A, or

(b) any equivalent acquisition or importation,

shall be charged at the rate of 5 per cent.

(2) The reference in subsection (1) above to an equivalent acquisition or importation, in relation to any supply that is of a description for the time being specified in Schedule 7A, is a reference (as the case may be) to—

(a) any acquisition from another member State of goods the supply of which would be such a supply; or

(b) any importation from a place outside the member States of any such goods.

(3) The Treasury may by order vary Schedule 7A by adding to or deleting from it any description of supply or by varying any description of supply for the time being specified in it.

(4) The power to vary Schedule 7A conferred by subsection (3) above may be exercised so as to describe a supply of goods or services by reference to matters unrelated to the characteristics of the goods or services themselves. In the case of a supply of goods, those matters include, in particular, the use that has been made of the goods.][1]

30 Zero-rating.

(1) Where a taxable person supplies goods or services and the supply is zero-rated, then, whether or not VAT would be chargeable on the supply apart from this section—

(a) no VAT shall be charged on the supply; but

(b) it shall in all other respects be treated as a taxable supply;

and accordingly the rate at which VAT is treated as charged on the supply shall be nil.

(2) A supply of goods or services is zero-rated by virtue of this subsection if the goods or services are of a description for the time being specified in Schedule 8 or the supply is of a description for the time being so specified.

[(2A) A supply by a person of services which consist of applying a treatment or process to another person's goods is zero-rated by virtue of this subsection if by doing so he produces goods, and either—

(a) those goods are of a description for the time being specified in Schedule 8; or

(b) a supply by him of those goods to the person to whom he supplies the services would be of a description so specified.][2]

(3) Where goods of a description for the time being specified in that Schedule, or of a description forming part of a description of supply for the time being so specified, are acquired in the United Kingdom from another member State or imported from a place outside the member States, no VAT shall be chargeable on their acquisition or importation, except as otherwise provided in that Schedule.

(4) The Treasury may by order vary Schedule 8 by adding to or deleting from it any description or by varying any description for the time being specified in it.

[(5) The export of any goods by a charity to a place outside the member States shall for the purposes of this Act be treated as a supply made by the charity—

(a) in the United Kingdom, and

(b) in the course or furtherance of a business carried on by the charity.][3]

(6) A supply of goods is zero-rated by virtue of this subsection if the Commissioners are satisfied that the person supplying the goods—

(a) has exported them to a place outside the member States; or

(b) has shipped them for use as stores on a voyage or flight to an eventual destination outside the United Kingdom, or as merchandise for sale by retail to persons carried on such a voyage or flight in a ship or aircraft,

and in either case if such other conditions, if any, as may be specified in regulations or the Commissioners may impose are fulfilled.

(7) Subsection (6)(b) above shall not apply in the case of goods shipped for use as stores on a voyage or flight to be made by the person to whom the goods were supplied and to be made for a purpose which is private.

(8) Regulations may provide for the zero-rating of supplies of goods, or of such goods as may be specified in the regulations, in cases where—

(a) the Commissioners are satisfied that the goods have been or are to be exported to a place outside the member States or that the supply in question involves both—

(i) the removal of the goods from the United Kingdom; and

(ii) their acquisition in another member State by a person who is liable for VAT on the acquisition in accordance with provisions of the law of that member State corresponding, in relation to that member State, to the provisions of section 10; and

(b) such other conditions, if any, as may be specified in the regulations or the Commissioners may impose are fulfilled.

[(8A) Regulations may provide for the zero-rating of supplies of goods, or of such goods as may be specified in regulations, in cases where—

(a) the Commissioners are satisfied that the supply in question involves both—

(i) the removal of the goods from a fiscal warehousing regime within the meaning of section 18F(2); and

(ii) their being placed in a warehousing regime in another member State, or in such member State or States as may be prescribed, where that regime is established by provisions of the law of that member State corresponding, in relation to that member State, to the provisions of sections 18A and 18B; and

(b) such other conditions, if any, as may be specified in the regulations or the Commissioners may impose are fulfilled.][4]

(9) Regulations may provide for the zero-rating of a supply of services which is made where goods are let on hire and the Commissioners are satisfied that the goods have been or are to be removed from the United Kingdom during the period of the letting, and such other conditions, if any, as may be specified in the regulations or the Commissioners may impose are fulfilled.

(10) Where the supply of any goods has been zero-rated by virtue of subsection (6) above or in pursuance of regulations made under [subsection (8), (8A) or (9)][5] above and—

(a) the goods are found in the United Kingdom after the date on which they were alleged to have been or were to be exported or shipped or otherwise removed from the United Kingdom; or

(b) any condition specified in the relevant regulations under [subsection (6), (8), (8A) or (9)][6] above or imposed by the Commissioners is not complied with,

and the presence of the goods in the United Kingdom after that date or the non-observance of the condition has not been authorised for the purposes of this subsection by the Commissioners, the goods shall be liable to forfeiture under the Management Act and the VAT that would have been chargeable on the supply but for the zero-rating shall become payable forthwith by the person to whom the goods were supplied or by any person in whose possession the goods are found in the United Kingdom; but the Commissioners may, if they think fit, waive payment of the whole or part of that VAT.

31 Exempt supplies and acquisitions.

(1) A supply of goods or services is an exempt supply if it is of a description for the time being specified in Schedule 9 and an acquisition of goods from another member State is an exempt acquisition if the

goods are acquired in pursuance of an exempt supply.

(2) The Treasury may by order vary that Schedule by adding to or deleting from it any description of supply or by varying any description of supply for the time being specified in it, and the Schedule may be varied so as to describe a supply of goods by reference to the use which has been made of them or to other matters unrelated to the characteristics of the goods themselves.

32. . . . .[7]

33 Refunds of VAT in certain cases.

(1) Subject to the following provisions of this section, where—

(a) VAT is chargeable on the supply of goods or services to a body to which this section applies, on the acquisition of any goods by such a body from another member State or on the importation of any goods by such a body from a place outside the member States, and

(b) the supply, acquisition or importation is not for the purpose of any business carried on by the body,

the Commissioners shall, on a claim made by the body at such time and in such form and manner as the Commissioners may determine, refund to it the amount of the VAT so chargeable.

(2) Where goods or services so supplied to or acquired or imported by the body cannot be conveniently distinguished from goods or services supplied to or acquired or imported by it for the purpose of a business carried on by it, the amount to be refunded under this section shall be such amount as remains after deducting from the whole of the VAT chargeable on any supply to or acquisition or importation by the body such proportion thereof as appears to the Commissioners to be attributable to the carrying on of the business; but where—

(a) the VAT so attributable is or includes VAT attributable, in accordance with regulations under section 26, to exempt supplies by the body, and

(b) the VAT attributable to the exempt supplies is in the opinion of the Commissioners an insignificant proportion of the VAT so chargeable,

they may include it in the VAT refunded under this section.

(3) The bodies to which this section applies are—

(a) a local authority;

(b) a river purification board established under section 135 of the Local Government (Scotland) Act 1973, and a water development board within the meaning of section 109 of the Water (Scotland) Act 1980;

(c) an internal drainage board;

(d) a passenger transport authority or executive within the meaning of Part II of the Transport Act 1968;

(e) a port health authority within the meaning of the Public Health (Control of Disease) Act 1984, and a port local authority and joint port local authority constituted under Part X of the Public Health (Scotland) Act 1897;

(f) a police authority and the Receiver for the Metropolitan Police District;

(g) a development corporation within the meaning of the New Towns Act 1981 or the New Towns (Scotland) Act 1968, a new town commission within the meaning of the New Towns Act (Northern Ireland) 1965 and the Commission for the New Towns;

(h) a general lighthouse authority within the meaning of [Part VIII of the Merchant Shipping Act 1995][8];

(i) the British Broadcasting Corporation;

(j) a nominated news provider, as defined by section 31(3) of the Broadcasting Act 1990; and

(k) any body specified for the purposes of this section by an order made by the Treasury.

(4) No VAT shall be refunded under this section to a general lighthouse authority which in the opinion of the Commissioners is attributable to activities other than those concerned with the provision, maintenance or management of lights or other navigational aids.

(5) No VAT shall be refunded under this section to a nominated news provider which in the opinion of the Commissioners is attributable to activities other than the provision of news programmes for broadcasting by holders of regional Channel 3 licences (within the meaning of Part I of the Broadcasting Act 1990).

(6) References in this section to VAT chargeable do not include any VAT which, by virtue of any order

under section 25(7), is excluded from credit under that section.

33A[9] Refunds of VAT to museums and galleries

(1) Subsections (2) to (5) below apply where—

(a) VAT is chargeable on—

(i) the supply of goods or services to a body to which this section applies,

(ii) the acquisition of any goods by such a body from another member State, or

(iii) the importation of any goods by such a body from a place outside the member States,

(b) the supply, acquisition or importation is attributable to the provision by the body of free rights of admission to a relevant museum or gallery, and

(c) the supply is made, or the acquisition or importation takes place, on or after 1st April 2001.

(2) The Commissioners shall, on a claim made by the body in such form and manner as the Commissioners may determine, refund to the body the amount of VAT so chargeable.

(3) The claim must be made before the end of the claim period.

(4) Subject to subsection (5) below, "the claim period" is the period of 3 years beginning with the day on which the supply is made or the acquisition or importation takes place.

(5) If the Commissioners so determine, the claim period is such shorter period beginning with that day as the Commissioners may determine.

(6) Subsection (7) below applies where goods or services supplied to, or acquired or imported by, a body to which this section applies that are attributable to free admissions cannot conveniently be distinguished from goods or services supplied to, or acquired or imported by, the body that are not attributable to free admissions.

(7) The amount to be refunded on a claim by the body under this section shall be such amount as remains after deducting from the VAT related to the claim such proportion of that VAT as appears to the Commissioners to be attributable otherwise than to free admissions.

(8) For the purposes of subsections (6) and (7) above—

(a) goods or services are, and VAT is, attributable to free admissions if they are, or it is, attributable to the provision by the body of free rights of admission to a relevant museum or gallery;

(b) the VAT related to a claim is the whole of the VAT chargeable on—

(i) the supplies to the body, and

(ii) the acquisitions and importations by the body,

to which the claim relates.

(9) The Treasury may by order—

(a) specify a body as being a body to which this section applies;

(b) when specifying a body under paragraph (a), specify any museum or gallery that, for the purposes of this section, is a "relevant" museum or gallery in relation to the body;

(c) specify an additional museum or gallery as being, for the purposes of this section, a "relevant" museum or gallery in relation to a body to which this section applies;

(d) when specifying a museum or gallery under paragraph (b) or (c), provide that this section shall have effect in the case of the museum or gallery as if in subsection (1)(c) there were substituted for 1st April 2001 a later date specified in the order.

(10) References in this section to VAT do not include any VAT which, by virtue of any order under section 25(7), is excluded from credit under that section.

34 Capital goods.

(1) The Treasury may by order make provision for the giving of relief, in such cases, to such extent and subject to such exceptions as may be specified in the order, from VAT paid on the supply, acquisition or importation for the purpose of a business carried on by any person of machinery or plant or any specified description of machinery or plant in cases where that VAT or part of that VAT cannot be credited under section 25 and such other conditions are satisfied as may be specified in the order.

(2) Without prejudice to the generality of subsection (1) above, an order under this section may provide for relief to be given by deduction or refunding of VAT and for aggregating or excluding the aggregation of value where goods of the same description are supplied, acquired or imported together.

35 Refund of VAT to persons constructing certain buildings.

[(1) Where—

(a) a person carries out works to which this section applies,

(b) his carrying out of the works is lawful and otherwise than in the course or furtherance of any business, and

(c) VAT is chargeable on the supply, acquisition or importation of any goods used by him for the purposes of the works,

the Commissioners shall, on a claim made in that behalf, refund to that person the amount of VAT so chargeable.

(1A) The works to which this section applies are—

(a) the construction of a building designed as a dwelling or number of dwellings;

(b) the construction of a building for use solely for a relevant residential purpose or relevant charitable purpose; and

(c) a residential conversion.

(1B) For the purposes of this section goods shall be treated as used for the purposes of works to which this section applies by the person carrying out the works in so far only as they are building materials which, in the course of the works, are incorporated in the building in question or its site.

(1C) Where—

(a) a person ("the relevant person") carries out a residential conversion by arranging for any of the work of the conversion to be done by another ("a contractor"),

(b) the relevant person's carrying out of the conversion is lawful and otherwise than in the course or furtherance of any business,

(c) the contractor is not acting as an architect, surveyor or consultant or in a supervisory capacity, and

(d) VAT is chargeable on services consisting in the work done by the contractor,

the Commissioners shall, on a claim made in that behalf, refund to the relevant person the amount of VAT so chargeable.

(1D) For the purposes of this section works constitute a residential conversion to the extent that they consist in the conversion of a non-residential building, or a non-residential part of a building, into—

(a) a building designed as a dwelling or a number of dwellings;

(b) a building intended for use solely for a relevant residential purpose; or

(c) anything which would fall within paragraph (a) or (b) above if different parts of a building were treated as separate buildings.][10]

(2) The Commissioners shall not be required to entertain a claim for a refund of VAT under this section unless the claim—

(a) is made within such time and in such form and manner, and

(b) contains such information, and

(c) is accompanied by such documents, whether by way of evidence or otherwise, as the Commissioners may by regulations prescribe [or, in the case of documents, as the Commissioners may determine in accordance with the regulations][11].

(3) This section shall have effect—

(a) as if the reference in subsection (1) above to the VAT chargeable on the supply of any goods included a reference to VAT chargeable on the supply in accordance with the law of another member State; and

(b) in relation to VAT chargeable in accordance with the law of another member State, as if references to refunding VAT to any person were references to paying that person an amount equal to the VAT chargeable in accordance with the law of that member State;

and the provisions of this Act and of any other enactment or subordinate legislation (whenever passed or made) so far as they relate to a refund under this section shall be construed accordingly.

[(4) The notes to Group 5 of Schedule 8 shall apply for construing this section as they apply for construing that Group.

(5) The power of the Treasury by order under section 30 to vary Schedule 8 shall include—

(a) power to apply any variation made by the order for the purposes of this section; and

(b) power to make such consequential modifications of this section as they may think fit [but this is

subject to subsection (4A) below.][12].][13]

[(4A) The meaning of "non-residential" given by Note (7A) of Group 5 of Schedule 8 (and not that given by Note (7) of that Group) applies for the purposes of this section but as if—

(a) references in that Note to item 3 of that Group were references to this section, and

(b) paragraph (b)(iii) of that Note were omitted.][14]

36 Bad debts.

(1) Subsection (2) below applies where—

(a) a person has supplied goods or services. . .[15] and has accounted for and paid VAT on the supply,

(b) the whole or any part of the consideration for the supply has been written off in his accounts as a bad debt, and

(c) a period of 6 months (beginning with the date of the supply) has elapsed.

(2) Subject to the following provisions of this section and to regulations under it the person shall be entitled, on making a claim to the Commissioners, to a refund of the amount of VAT chargeable by reference to the outstanding amount.

[(3) In subsection (2) above "the outstanding amount" means—

(a) if at the time of the claim no part of the consideration written off in the claimant's accounts as a bad debt has been received, an amount equal to the amount of the consideration so written off;

(b) if at that time any part of the consideration so written off has been received, an amount by which that part is exceeded by the amount of the consideration written off;

and in this subsection "received" means received either by the claimant or by a person to whom has been assigned a right to receive the whole or any part of the consideration written off.][16]

[(3A) For the purposes of this section, where the whole or any part of the consideration for the supply does not consist of money, the amount in money that shall be taken to represent any non-monetary part of the consideration shall be so much of the amount made up of—

(a) the value of the supply, and

(b) the VAT charged on the supply,

as is attributable to the non-monetary consideration in question.][17]

(4) a person shall not be entitled to a refund under subsection (2) above unless—

(a) the value of the supply is equal to or less than its open market value,. . .[18]

(b). . . . .

(4A). . . . .[19]

(5) Regulations under this section may—

(a) require a claim to be made at such time and in such form and manner as may be specified by or under the regulations;

(b) require a claim to be evidenced and quantified by reference to such records and other documents as may be so specified;

(c) require the claimant to keep, for such period and in such form and manner as may be so specified, those records and documents and a record of such information relating to the claim and to [anything subsequently received][20] by way of consideration as may be so specified;

(d) require the repayment of a refund allowed under this section where any requirement of the regulations is not complied with;

(e) require the repayment of the whole or, as the case may be, an appropriate part of a refund allowed under this section [where any part (or further part) of the consideration written off in the claimant's accounts as a bad debt is subsequently received either by the claimant or, except in such circumstances as may be prescribed, by a person to whom has been assigned a right to receive the whole or any part of that consideration;][21]

(ea). . . . .[22]

(f) include such supplementary, incidental, consequential or transitional provisions as appear to the Commissioners to be necessary or expedient for the purposes of this section;

(g) make different provision for different circumstances.

(6) The provisions which may be included in regulations by virtue of subsection (5)(f) above may include rules for ascertaining—

(a) whether, when and to what extent consideration is to be taken to have been written off in accounts as a bad debt;

(b) whether [anything received][23] is to be taken as received by way of consideration for a particular supply;

(c) whether, and to what extent, [anything received][24] is to be taken as received by way of consideration written off in accounts as a bad debt.

(7) The provisions which may be included in regulations by virtue of subsection (5)(f) above may include rules dealing with particular cases, such as those involving [receipt of part of the consideration][25] or mutual debts; and in particular such rules may vary the way in which the following amounts are to be calculated—

(a) the outstanding amount mentioned in subsection (2) above, and

(b) the amount of any repayment where a refund has been allowed under this section.

(8) Section 6 shall apply for determining the time when a supply is to be treated as taking place for the purposes of construing this section.

...

51 Buildings and land.

(1) Schedule 10 shall have effect with respect to buildings and land.

(2) The Treasury may by order amend Schedule 10.

...

101 Commencement and extent.

(1) This Act shall come into force on 1st September 1994 and Part I shall have effect in relation to the charge to VAT on supplies, acquisitions and importations in prescribed accounting periods ending on or after that date.

(2) Without prejudice to section 16 of the Interpretation Act 1978 (continuation of proceedings under repealed enactments) except in so far as it enables proceedings to be continued under repealed enactments, section 72 shall have effect on the commencement of this Act to the exclusion of section 39 of the 1983 Act.

(3) This Act extends to Northern Ireland.

(4) Paragraph 23 of Schedule 13 and paragraph 7 of Schedule 14 shall extend to the Isle of Man but no other provision of this Act shall extend there.

SCHEDULE 7A[26] - CHARGE AT REDUCED RATE

Part 1 INDEX TO REDUCED-RATE SUPPLIES OF GOODS AND SERVICES

Children's car seats....................	Group 5
Domestic fuel or power....................	Group 1
Energy-saving materials: installation....................	Group 2
Heating equipment, security goods and gas supplies: grant-funded installation or connection....................	Group 3
Renovation and alteration of dwellings....................	Group 7
Residential conversions....................	Group 6
Women's sanitary products....................	Group 4

Part 2 THE GROUPS

Group 1 — Supplies of domestic fuel or power

ITEM NO.

1 Supplies for qualifying use of—

(a) coal, coke or other solid substances held out for sale solely as fuel;

(b) coal gas, water gas, producer gases or similar gases;

(c) petroleum gases, or other gaseous hydrocarbons, whether in a gaseous or liquid state;

(d) fuel oil, gas oil or kerosene; or

(e) electricity, heat or air-conditioning.

NOTES:

Matters included or not included in the supplies

1(1) Item 1(a) shall be deemed to include combustible materials put up for sale for kindling fires but shall not include matches.

(2) Item 1(b) and (c) shall not include any road fuel gas (within the meaning of the Hydrocarbon Oil Duties Act 1979 (c. 5)) on which a duty of excise has been charged or is chargeable.

(3) Item 1(d) shall not include hydrocarbon oil on which a duty of excise has been or is to be charged without relief from, or rebate of, such duty by virtue of the provisions of the Hydrocarbon Oil Duties Act 1979.

Meaning of "fuel oil", "gas oil" and "kerosene"

2(1) In this Group "fuel oil" means heavy oil which contains in solution an amount of asphaltenes of not less than 0.5 per cent. or which contains less than 0.5 per cent. but not less than 0.1 per cent. of asphaltenes and has a closed flash point not exceeding 150°C.

(2) In this Group "gas oil" means heavy oil of which not more than 50 per cent. by volume distils at a temperature not exceeding 240°C and of which more than 50 per cent. by volume distils at a temperature not exceeding 340°C.

(3) In this Group "kerosene" means heavy oil of which more than 50 per cent. by volume distils at a temperature not exceeding 240°C.

(4) In this paragraph "heavy oil" has the same meaning as in the Hydrocarbon Oil Duties Act 1979.

Meaning of "qualifying use"

3In this Group "qualifying use" means—

(a) domestic use; or

(b) use by a charity otherwise than in the course or furtherance of a business.

Supplies only partly for qualifying use

4 For the purposes of this Group, where there is a supply of goods partly for qualifying use and partly not—

(a) if at least 60 per cent. of the goods are supplied for qualifying use, the whole supply shall be treated as a supply for qualifying use; and

(b) in any other case, an apportionment shall be made to determine the extent to which the supply is a supply for qualifying use.

Supplies deemed to be for domestic use

5 For the purposes of this Group the following supplies are always for domestic use—

(a) a supply of not more than one tonne of coal or coke held out for sale as domestic fuel;

(b) a supply of wood, peat or charcoal not intended for sale by the recipient;

(c) a supply to a person at any premises of piped gas (that is, gas within item 1(b), or petroleum gas in a gaseous state, provided through pipes) where the gas (together with any other piped gas provided to him at the premises by the same supplier) was not provided at a rate exceeding 150 therms a month or, if the supplier charges for the gas by reference to the number of kilowatt hours supplied, 4397 kilowatt hours a month;

(d) a supply of petroleum gas in a liquid state where the gas is supplied in cylinders the net weight of each of which is less than 50 kilogrammes and either the number of cylinders supplied is 20 or fewer or the gas is not intended for sale by the recipient;

(e) a supply of petroleum gas in a liquid state, otherwise than in cylinders, to a person at any premises at which he is not able to store more than two tonnes of such gas;

(f) a supply of not more than 2,300 litres of fuel oil, gas oil or kerosene;

(g) a supply of electricity to a person at any premises where the electricity (together with any other electricity provided to him at the premises by the same supplier) was not provided at a rate exceeding 1000 kilowatt hours a month.

Other supplies that are for domestic use

6 For the purposes of this Group supplies not within paragraph 5 are for domestic use if and only if the goods supplied are for use in—

(a) a building, or part of a building, that consists of a dwelling or number of dwellings;

(b) a building, or part of a building, used for a relevant residential purpose;

(c) self-catering holiday accommodation;

(d) a caravan; or

(e) a houseboat.

Interpretation of paragraph 6

7(1) For the purposes of this Group, "use for a relevant residential purpose" means use as—

(a) a home or other institution providing residential accommodation for children,

(b) a home or other institution providing residential accommodation with personal care for persons

in need of personal care by reason of old age, disablement, past or present dependence on alcohol or drugs or past or present mental disorder,

(c) a hospice,

(d) residential accommodation for students or school pupils,

(e) residential accommodation for members of any of the armed forces,

(f) a monastery, nunnery or similar establishment, or

(g) an institution which is the sole or main residence of at least 90 per cent. of its residents,

except use as a hospital, a prison or similar institution or an hotel or inn or similar establishment.

(2) For the purposes of this Group "self-catering holiday accommodation" includes any accommodation advertised or held out as such.

(3) In paragraph 6 "houseboat" means a boat or other floating decked structure designed or adapted for use solely as a place of permanent habitation and not having means of, or capable of being readily adapted for, self-propulsion.

Group 2 — Installation of energy-saving materials

NOTES:

1Supplies of services of installing energy-saving materials in—

(a) residential accommodation, or

(b) a building intended for use solely for a relevant charitable purpose.

2Supplies of energy-saving materials by a person who installs those materials in—

(a) residential accommodation, or

(b) a building intended for use solely for a relevant charitable purpose.

NOTES:

Meaning of "energy-saving materials"

1 For the purposes of this Group "energy-saving materials" means any of the following—

(a) insulation for walls, floors, ceilings, roofs or lofts or for water tanks, pipes or other plumbing fittings;

(b) draught stripping for windows and doors;

(c) central heating system controls (including thermostatic radiator valves);

(d) hot water system controls;

(e) solar panels;

(f) wind turbines;

(g) water turbines.

Meaning of "residential accommodation"

2(1) For the purposes of this Group "residential accommodation" means—

(a) a building, or part of a building, that consists of a dwelling or a number of dwellings;

(b) a building, or part of a building, used for a relevant residential purpose;

(c) a caravan used as a place of permanent habitation; or

(d) a houseboat.

(2) For the purposes of this Group "use for a relevant residential purpose" has the same meaning as it has for the purposes of Group 1 (see paragraph 7(1) of the Notes to that Group).

(3) In sub-paragraph (1)(d) "houseboat" has the meaning given by paragraph 7(3) of the Notes to Group 1.

Meaning of "use for a relevant charitable purpose"

3For the purposes of this Group "use for a relevant charitable purpose" means use by a charity in either or both of the following ways, namely—

(a) otherwise than in the course or furtherance of a business;

(b) as a village hall or similarly in providing social or recreational facilities for a local community.

Group 3 — Grant-funded installation of heating equipment or security goods or connection of gas supply

ITEM NO.

1 Supplies to a qualifying person of any services of installing heating appliances in the qualifying person's sole or main residence.

2 Supplies of heating appliances made to a qualifying person by a person who installs those

appliances in the qualifying person's sole or main residence.

3 Supplies to a qualifying person of services of connecting, or reconnecting, a mains gas supply to the qualifying person's sole or main residence.

4 Supplies of goods made to a qualifying person by a person connecting, or reconnecting, a mains gas supply to the qualifying person's sole or main residence, being goods whose installation is necessary for the connection, or reconnection, of the mains gas supply.

5 Supplies to a qualifying person of services of installing, maintaining or repairing a central heating system in the qualifying person's sole or main residence.

6 Supplies of goods made to a qualifying person by a person installing, maintaining or repairing a central heating system in the qualifying person's sole or main residence, being goods whose installation is necessary for the installation, maintenance or repair of the central heating system.

7 Supplies consisting in the leasing of goods that form the whole or part of a central heating system installed in the sole or main residence of a qualifying person.

8 Supplies of goods that form the whole or part of a central heating system installed in a qualifying person's sole or main residence and that, immediately before being supplied, were goods leased under arrangements such that the consideration for the supplies consisting in the leasing of the goods was, in whole or in part, funded by a grant made under a relevant scheme.

[8A Supplies to a qualifying person of services of installing, maintaining or repairing a renewable source heating system in the qualifying person's sole or main residence.

8B Supplies of goods made to a qualifying person by a person installing, maintaining or repairing a renewable source heating system in the qualifying person's sole or main residence, being goods whose installation is necessary for the installation, maintenance or repair of the system.][27]

9 Supplies to a qualifying person of services of installing qualifying security goods in the qualifying person's sole or main residence.

10 Supplies of qualifying security goods made to a qualifying person by a person who installs those goods in the qualifying person's sole or main residence.

NOTES:

Supply only included so far as grant-funded

1(1) Each of [items 1 to 7 and 8A to 10][28] applies to a supply only to the extent that the consideration for the supply is, or is to be, funded by a grant made under a relevant scheme.

(2) Item 8 applies to a supply only to the extent that the consideration for the supply—

(a) is, or is to be, funded by a grant made under a relevant scheme; or

(b) is a payment becoming due only by reason of the termination (whether by the passage of time or otherwise) of the leasing of the goods in question.

Meaning of "relevant scheme"

2(1) For the purposes of this Group a scheme is a "relevant scheme" if it is one which satisfies the conditions specified in this paragraph.

(2) The first condition is that the scheme has as one of its objectives the funding of the installation of energy-saving materials in the homes of any persons who are qualifying persons.

(3) The second condition is that the scheme disburses, whether directly or indirectly, its grants in whole or in part out of funds made available to it in order to achieve that objective—

(a) by the Secretary of State,

(b) by the Scottish Ministers,

(c) by the National Assembly for Wales,

(d) by a Minister (within the meaning given by section 7(3) of the Northern Ireland Act 1998 (c. 47)) or a Northern Ireland department,

(e) by the European Community,

(f) under an arrangement approved by the Gas and Electricity Markets Authority,

(g) under an arrangement approved by the Director General of Electricity Supply for Northern Ireland, or

(h) by a local authority.

(4) The reference in sub-paragraph (3)(f) to an arrangement approved by the Gas and Electricity Markets Authority includes a reference to an arrangement approved by the Director General of Electricity Supply, or the Director General of Gas Supply, before the transfer (under the Utilities Act

2000 (c. 27)) of his functions to the Authority.

Apportionment of grants that also cover other supplies

3 Where a grant is made under a relevant scheme in order—

(a) to fund a supply of a description to which any of items 1 to 10 applies ("the relevant supply"), and

(b) also to fund a supply to which none of those items applies ("the non-relevant supply"),

the proportion of the grant that is to be attributed, for the purposes of paragraph 1, to the relevant supply shall be the same proportion as the consideration reasonably attributable to that supply bears to the consideration for that supply and for the non-relevant supply.

Meaning of "heating appliances"

4 For the purposes of items 1 and 2 "heating appliances" means any of the following—

(a) gas-fired room heaters that are fitted with thermostatic controls;

(b) electric storage heaters;

(c) closed solid fuel fire cassettes;

(d) electric dual immersion water heaters with [factory-insulated][29] hot water tanks;

(e) gas-fired boilers;

(f) oil-fired boilers;

(g) radiators.

Meaning of "central heating system"

[4A For the purposes of items 5 to 8 "central heating system" includes a system which generates electricity.

Meaning of "renewable source heating system"

4B For the purposes of items 8A and 8B "renewable source heating system" means a space or water heating system which uses energy from—

(a) renewable sources, including solar, wind and hydroelectric power, or

(b) near renewable resources, including ground and air heat.][30]

Meaning of "qualifying security goods"

5 For the purposes of items 9 and 10 "qualifying security goods" means any of the following—

(a) locks or bolts for windows;

(b) locks, bolts or security chains for doors;

(c) spy holes;

(d) smoke alarms.

Meaning of "qualifying person"

6(1) For the purposes of this Group, a person to whom a supply is made is "a qualifying person" if at the time of the supply he—

(a) is aged 60 or over; or

(b) is in receipt of one or more of the benefits mentioned in sub-paragraph (2).

(2) Those benefits are—

(a) council tax benefit under Part 7 of the Contributions and Benefits Act;

(b) disability living allowance under Part 3 of the Contributions and Benefits Act or Part 3 of the Northern Ireland Act;

(c) disabled person's tax credit, working families' tax credit, housing benefit or income support under Part 7 of the Contributions and Benefits Act or Part 7 of the Northern Ireland Act;

(d) an income-based jobseeker's allowance within the meaning of section 1(4) of the Jobseekers Act 1995 (c. 18) or Article 3(4) of the Jobseekers (Northern Ireland) Order 1995 (S.I. 1995/275 (N.I. 15));

(e) disablement pension under Part 5 of the Contributions and Benefits Act, or Part 5 of the Northern Ireland Act, that is payable at the increased rate provided for under section 104 (constant attendance allowance) of the Act concerned;

(f) war disablement pension under the Naval, Military and Air Forces Etc. (Disablement and Death) Service Pensions Order 1983 (S.I. 1983/883) that is payable at the increased rate provided for under article 14 (constant attendance allowance) or article 26A (mobility supplement) of that Order.

(3) In sub-paragraph (2)—

(a) "the Contributions and Benefits Act" means the Social Security Contributions and Benefits Act

1992 (c. 4); and

(b) "the Northern Ireland Act" means the Social Security Contributions and Benefits (Northern Ireland) Act 1992 (c. 7).

Group 4 — Women's sanitary products

ITEM NO.

1 Supplies of women's sanitary products.

NOTES:

Meaning of "women's sanitary products"

1(1) In this Group "women's sanitary products" means women's sanitary products of any of the following descriptions—

(a) subject to sub-paragraph (2), products that are designed, and marketed, as being solely for use for absorbing, or otherwise collecting, lochia or menstrual flow;

(b) panty liners, other than panty liners that are designed as being primarily for use as incontinence products;

(c) sanitary belts.

(2) Sub-paragraph (1)(a) does not include protective briefs or any other form of clothing.

Group 5 — Children's car seats

ITEM NO.

1 Supplies of children's car seats.

NOTES:

Meaning of "children's car seats"

1(1) For the purposes of this Group, the following are "children's car seats"—

(a) a safety seat;

(b) the combination of a safety seat and a related wheeled framework;

(c) a booster seat;

(d) a booster cushion.

(2) In this Group "child" means a person aged under 14 years.

Meaning of "safety seat"

2 In this Group "safety seat" means a seat—

(a) designed to be sat in by a child in a road vehicle,

(b) designed so that, when in use in a road vehicle, it can be restrained—

(i) by a seat belt fitted in the vehicle, or

(ii) by belts, or anchorages, that form part of the seat being attached to the vehicle, or

(iii) in either of those ways, and

(c) incorporating an integral harness, or integral impact shield, for restraining a child seated in it.

Meaning of "related wheeled framework"

3 For the purposes of this Group, a wheeled framework is "related" to a safety seat if the framework and the seat are each designed so that—

(a) when the seat is not in use in a road vehicle it can be attached to the framework, and

(b) when the seat is so attached, the combination of the seat and the framework can be used as a child's pushchair.

Meaning of "booster seat"

4 In this Group "booster seat" means a seat designed—

(a) to be sat in by a child in a road vehicle, and

(b) so that, when in use in a road vehicle, it and a child seated in it can be restrained by a seat belt fitted in the vehicle.

Meaning of "booster cushion"

5 In this Group "booster cushion" means a cushion designed—

(a) to be sat on by a child in a road vehicle, and

(b) so that a child seated on it can be restrained by a seat belt fitted in the vehicle

Group 6 — Residential conversions

ITEM NO.

1 The supply, in the course of a qualifying conversion, of qualifying services related to the conversion.

2 The supply of building materials if—

(a) the materials are supplied by a person who, in the course of a qualifying conversion, is supplying qualifying services related to the conversion, and

(b) those services include the incorporation of the materials in the building concerned or its immediate site.

NOTES:

Supplies only partly within item 1

1(1) Sub-paragraph (2) applies where a supply of services is only in part a supply to which item 1 applies.

(2) The supply, to the extent that it is one to which item 1 applies, is to be taken to be a supply to which item 1 applies.

(3) An apportionment may be made to determine that extent.

Meaning of "qualifying conversion"

2(1) A "qualifying conversion" means—

(a) a changed number of dwellings conversion (see paragraph 3);

(b) a house in multiple occupation conversion (see paragraph 5); or

(c) a special residential conversion (see paragraph 7).

(2) Sub-paragraph (1) is subject to paragraphs 9 and 10.

Meaning of "changed number of dwellings conversion"

3(1) A "changed number of dwellings conversion" is—

(a) a conversion of premises consisting of a building where the conditions specified in this paragraph are satisfied, or

(b) a conversion of premises consisting of a part of a building where those conditions are satisfied.

(2) The first condition is that after the conversion the premises being converted contain a number of single household dwellings that is—

(a) different from the number (if any) that the premises contain before the conversion, and

(b) greater than, or equal to, one.

(3) The second condition is that there is no part of the premises being converted that is a part that after the conversion contains the same number of single household dwellings (whether zero, one or two or more) as before the conversion.

Meaning of "single household dwelling" and "multiple occupancy dwelling"

4(1) For the purposes of this Group "single household dwelling" means a dwelling—

(a) that is designed for occupation by a single household, and

(b) in relation to which the conditions set out in sub-paragraph (3) are satisfied.

(2) For the purposes of this Group "multiple occupancy dwelling" means a dwelling—

(a) that is designed for occupation by persons not forming a single household,...[31]

[(aa) that is not to any extent used for a relevant residential purpose, and][32]

(b) in relation to which the conditions set out in sub-paragraph (3) are satisfied.

(3) The conditions are—

(a) that the dwelling consists of self-contained living accommodation,

(b) that there is no provision for direct internal access from the dwelling to any other dwelling or part of a dwelling,

(c) that the separate use of the dwelling is not prohibited by the terms of any covenant, statutory planning consent or similar provision, and

(d) that the separate disposal of the dwelling is not prohibited by any such terms.

(4) For the purposes of this paragraph, a dwelling "is designed" for occupation of a particular kind if it is so designed—

(a) as a result of having been originally constructed for occupation of that kind and not having been subsequently adapted for occupation of any other kind, or

(b) as a result of adaptation.

Meaning of "house in multiple occupation conversion"

5(1) A "house in multiple occupation conversion" is—

(a) a conversion of premises consisting of a building where the condition specified in sub-paragraph (2) below is satisfied, or

(b) a conversion of premises consisting of a part of a building where that condition is satisfied.

(2) The condition is that—

[(a) before the conversion the premises being converted do not contain any multiple occupancy dwellings,][33]

(b) after the conversion those premises contain only a multiple occupancy dwelling or two or more such dwellings, and

(c) the use to which those premises are intended to be put after the conversion is not to any extent use for a relevant residential purpose.

Meaning of "use for a relevant residential purpose"

6 For the purposes of this Group "use for a relevant residential purpose" means use as—

(a) a home or other institution providing residential accommodation for children,

(b) a home or other institution providing residential accommodation with personal care for persons in need of personal care by reason of old age, disablement, past or present dependence on alcohol or drugs or past or present mental disorder,

(c) a hospice,

(d) residential accommodation for students or school pupils,

(e) residential accommodation for members of any of the armed forces,

(f) a monastery, nunnery or similar establishment, or

(g) an institution which is the sole or main residence of at least 90 per cent. of its residents,

except use as a hospital, prison or similar institution or an hotel, inn or similar establishment.

Meaning of "special residential conversion"

7(1) A "special residential conversion" is a conversion of premises consisting of—

(a) a building or two or more buildings,

(b) a part of a building or two or more parts of buildings, or

(c) a combination of—

(i) a building or two or more buildings, and

(ii) a part of a building or two or more parts of buildings,

where the conditions specified in this paragraph are satisfied.

[(2) The first condition is that—

(a) the use to which the premises being converted were last put before the conversion was not to any extent use for a relevant residential purpose, and

(b) those premises are intended to be used solely for a relevant residential purpose after the conversion.][34]

(3)................................[35]

(4)................................[36]

(5)................................[37]

(6) The [second][38] condition is that, where the relevant residential purpose [for which the premises are intended to be used][39] is an institutional purpose, the premises being converted must be intended to form after the conversion the entirety of an institution used for that purpose.

(7) In sub-paragraph (6) "institutional purpose" means a purpose within paragraph 6(a) to (c), (f) or (g).

Special residential conversions: reduced rate only for supplies made to intended user of converted accommodation

8(1) This paragraph applies where the qualifying conversion concerned is a special residential conversion.

(2) Item 1 or 2 does not apply to a supply unless—

(a) it is made to a person who intends to use the premises being converted for the relevant residential purpose, and

(b) before it is made, the person to whom it is made has given to the person making it a certificate that satisfies the requirements in sub-paragraph (3).

(3) Those requirements are that the certificate—

(a) is in such form as may be specified in a notice published by the Commissioners, and

(b) states that the conversion is a special residential conversion.

(4) In sub-paragraph (2)(a) "the relevant residential purpose" means the purpose within paragraph 6 for which the premises being converted are intended to be used after the conversion.

"Qualifying conversion" includes related garage works

9(1) A qualifying conversion includes any garage works related to the—

(a) changed number of dwellings conversion,

(b) house in multiple occupation conversion, or

(c) special residential conversion,

concerned.

(2) In this paragraph "garage works" means—

(a) the construction of a garage, or

(b) a conversion of a non-residential building, or of a non-residential part of a building, that results in a garage.

(3) For the purposes of sub-paragraph (1), garage works are "related" to a conversion if—

(a) they are carried out at the same time as the conversion, and

(b) the resulting garage is intended to be occupied with—

(i) where the conversion concerned is a changed number of dwellings conversion, a single household dwelling that will after the conversion be contained in the building, or part of a building, being converted,

(ii) where the conversion concerned is a house in multiple occupation conversion, a multiple occupancy dwelling that will after the conversion be contained in the building, or part of a building, being converted, or

(iii) where the conversion concerned is a special residential conversion, the institution or other accommodation resulting from the conversion.

(4) In sub-paragraph (2) "non-residential" means neither designed, nor adapted, for use—

(a) as a dwelling or two or more dwellings, or

(b) for a relevant residential purpose.

Conversion not "qualifying" if planning consent and building control approval not obtained

10(1) A conversion is not a qualifying conversion if any statutory planning consent needed for the conversion has not been granted.

(2) a conversion is not a qualifying conversion if any statutory building control approval needed for the conversion has not been granted.

Meaning of "supply of qualifying services"

11(1) In the case of a conversion of a building, "supply of qualifying services" means a supply of services that consists in—

(a) the carrying out of works to the fabric of the building, or

(b) the carrying out of works within the immediate site of the building that are in connection with—

(i) the means of providing water, power, heat or access to the building,

(ii) the means of providing drainage or security for the building, or

(iii) the provision of means of waste disposal for the building.

(2) In the case of a conversion of part of a building, "supply of qualifying services" means a supply of services that consists in—

(a) the carrying out of works to the fabric of the part, or

(b) the carrying out of works to the fabric of the building, or within the immediate site of the building, that are in connection with—

(i) the means of providing water, power, heat or access to the part,

(ii) the means of providing drainage or security for the part, or

(iii) the provision of means of waste disposal for the part.

(3) In this paragraph—

(a) references to the carrying out of works to the fabric of a building do not include the incorporation, or installation as fittings, in the building of any goods that are not building materials;

(b) references to the carrying out of works to the fabric of a part of a building do not include the incorporation, or installation as fittings, in the part of any goods that are not building materials.

Meaning of "building materials"

12 In this Group "building materials" has the meaning given by Notes (22) and (23) of Group 5 to Schedule 8 (zero-rating of construction and conversion of buildings).

Group 7 – [RESIDENTIAL RENOVATIONS AND ALTERATIONS][40]

ITEM NO.

1 The supply, in the course of the renovation or alteration of [qualifying residential premises][41] , of qualifying services related to the renovation or alteration.

2 The supply of building materials if—

(a) the materials are supplied by a person who, in the course of the renovation or alteration of [qualifying residential premises][42], is supplying qualifying services related to the renovation or alteration, and

(b) those services include the incorporation of the materials in [the premises concerned or their immediate site][43].

NOTES:

Supplies only partly within item 1

1(1) Sub-paragraph (2) applies where a supply of services is only in part a supply to which item 1 applies.

(2) The supply, to the extent that it is one to which item 1 applies, is to be taken to be a supply to which item 1 applies.

(3) An apportionment may be made to determine that extent.

Meaning of "alteration" and "qualifying residential premises"

[2(1) For the purposes of this Group—

"alteration" includes extension;

"qualifying residential premises" means—

(a) a single household dwelling,

(b) a multiple occupancy dwelling, or

(c) a building, or part of a building, which, when it was last lived in, was used for a relevant residential purpose.

(2) Where a building, when it was last lived in, formed part of a relevant residential unit then, to the extent that it would not be so regarded otherwise, the building shall be treated as having been used for a relevant residential purpose.

(3) a building forms part of a relevant residential unit at any time when—

(a) it is one of a number of buildings on the same site, and

(b) the buildings are used together as a unit for a relevant residential purpose.

(4) The following expressions have the same meaning in this Group as they have in Group 6—

"multiple occupancy dwelling"(paragraph 4(2) of the Notes to that Group);

"single household dwelling"(paragraph 4(1) of the Notes);

"use for a relevant residential purpose"(paragraph 6 of the Notes).][44]

Items 1 and 2 only apply where [premises have][45] been empty for at least 3 years

3[(1) Item 1 or 2 does not apply to a supply unless—

(a) the first empty home condition is satisfied, or

(b) if the premises are a single household dwelling, either of the empty home conditions is satisfied.][46]

[(2) The first "empty home condition" is that neither—

(a) the premises concerned, nor

(b) where those premises are a building, or part of a building, which, when it was last lived in, formed part of a relevant residential unit, any of the other buildings that formed part of the unit,

have been lived in during the period of 3 years ending with the commencement of the relevant works.][47]

(3) The second "empty home condition" is that—

(a) the dwelling was not lived in during a period of at least 3 years;

(b) the person, or one of the persons, whose beginning to live in the dwelling brought that period to an end was a person who (whether alone or jointly with another or others) acquired the dwelling at a time—

(i) no later than the end of that period, and

(ii) when the dwelling had been not lived in for at least 3 years;

(c) no works by way of renovation or alteration were carried out to the dwelling during the period of

3 years ending with the acquisition;

(d) the supply is made to a person who is—

(i) the person, or one of the persons, whose beginning to live in the property brought to an end the period mentioned in paragraph (a), and

(ii) the person, or one of the persons, who acquired the dwelling as mentioned in paragraph (b); and

(e) the relevant works are carried out during the period of one year beginning with the day of the acquisition.

(4) In this paragraph "the relevant works" means—

(a) where the supply is of the description set out in item 1, the works that constitute the services supplied;

(b) where the supply is of the description set out in item 2, the works by which the materials concerned are incorporated in [the premises concerned or their immediate site][48].

(5) In sub-paragraph (3), references to a person acquiring a dwelling are to that person having a major interest in the dwelling granted, or assigned, to him for a consideration.

Items 1 and 2 apply to related garage works

[3A(1) For the purposes of this Group a renovation or alteration of any premises includes any garage works related to the renovation or alteration.

(2) In this paragraph "garage works" means—

(a) the construction of a garage,

(b) the conversion of a building, or of a part of a building, that results in a garage, or

(c) the renovation or alteration of a garage.

(3) For the purposes of sub-paragraph (1), garage works are "related" to a renovation or alteration if—

(a) they are carried out at the same time as the renovation or alteration of the premises concerned, and

(b) the garage is intended to be occupied with the premises.][49]

Items 1 and 2 only apply if planning consent and building control approval obtained

4(1) Item 1 or 2 does not apply to a supply unless any statutory planning consent needed for the renovation or alteration has been granted.

(2) Item 1 or 2 does not apply to a supply unless any statutory building control approval needed for the renovation or alteration has been granted.

Items 1 and 2 only apply if building used for relevant residential purpose is subsequently used solely for that purpose

[4A(1) Item 1 or 2 does not apply to a supply if the premises in question are a building, or part of a building, which, when it was last lived in, was used for a relevant residential purpose unless—

(a) the building or part is intended to be used solely for such a purpose after the renovation or alteration, and

(b) before the supply is made the person to whom it is made has given to the person making it a certificate stating that intention.

(2) Where a number of buildings on the same site are—

(a) renovated or altered at the same time, and

(b) intended to be used together as a unit solely for a relevant residential purpose,

then each of those buildings, to the extent that it would not be so regarded otherwise, shall be treated as intended for use solely for a relevant residential purpose.][50]

Meaning of "supply of qualifying services"

5(1) "Supply of qualifying services" means a supply of services that consists in—

(a) the carrying out of works to the fabric of the [premises][51] , or

(b) the carrying out of works within the immediate site of the [premises][52] that are in connection with—

(i) the means of providing water, power, heat or access to the [premises][53] ,

(ii) the means of providing drainage or security for the [premises][54] , or

(iii) the provision of means of waste disposal for the [premises][55] .

(2) In sub-paragraph (1)(a), the reference to the carrying out of works to the fabric of the [premises][56] does not include the incorporation, or installation as fittings, in the [premises][57] of any goods that are

not building materials.

Meaning of "building materials"

6 In this Group "building materials" has the meaning given by Notes (22) and (23) of Group 5 to Schedule 8 (zero-rating of construction and conversion of buildings).

SCHEDULE 8

Part I Index to zero-rated supplies of goods and services

Subject matter	**Group Number**	**1983 Group Number**
Bank notes	Group 11	*Group 13*
Books etc.	Group 3	*Group 3*
Caravans and houseboats	Group 9	*Group 11*
Charities etc.	Group 15	*Group 16*
Clothing and footwear	Group 16	*Group 17*
Construction of buildings etc.	Group 5	*Group 8*
Drugs, medicines, aids for the handicapped etc.	Group 12	*Group 14*
Food	Group 1	*Group 1*
Gold	Group 10	*Group 12*
Imports, exports etc.	Group 13	*Group 15*
International services	Group 7	*Group 9*
Protected buildings	Group 6	*Group 8A*
Sewerage services and water	Group 2	*Group 2*
Talking books for the blind and handicapped and wireless sets for the blind	Group 4	*Group 4*
. . .[58]	. . .	. . .
Transport	Group 8	*Group 10*

Part II The Groups

Group 1— Food

The supply of anything comprised in the general items set out below, except—

(a) a supply in the course of catering; and

(b) a supply of anything comprised in any of the excepted items set out below, unless it is also comprised in any of the items overriding the exceptions set out below which relates to that excepted item.

General items

Item No.

1 Food of a kind used for human consumption.

2 Animal feeding stuffs.

3 Seeds or other means of propagation of plants comprised in item 1 or 2.

4 Live animals of a kind generally used as, or yielding or producing, food for human consumption.

Excepted items

Item No.

1 Ice cream, ice lollies, frozen yogurt, water ices and similar frozen products, and prepared mixes and powders for making such products.

2 Confectionery, not including cakes or biscuits other than biscuits wholly or partly covered with chocolate or some product similar in taste and appearance.

3 Beverages chargeable with any duty of excise specifically charged on spirits, beer, wine or made-wine and preparations thereof.

4 Other beverages (including fruit juices and bottled waters) and syrups, concentrates, essences, powders, crystals or other products for the preparation of beverages.

5 Any of the following when packaged for human consumption without further preparation, namely, potato crisps, potato sticks, potato puffs, and similar products made from the potato, or from potato flour, or from potato starch, and savoury food products obtained by the swelling of cereals or cereal products; and salted or roasted nuts other than nuts in shell.

6 Pet foods, canned, packaged or prepared; packaged foods (not being pet foods) for birds other than

poultry or game; and biscuits and meal for cats and dogs.

7 Goods described in items 1, 2 and 3 of the general items which are canned, bottled, packaged or prepared for use—

(a) in the domestic brewing of any beer;

(b) in the domestic making of any cider or perry;

(c) in the domestic production of any wine or made-wine.

Items overriding the exceptions

Item No.

1 Yoghurt unsuitable for immediate consumption when frozen.

2 Drained cherries.

3 Candied peels.

4 Tea, mateg, herbal teas and similar products, and preparations and extracts thereof.

5 Cocoa, coffee and chicory and other roasted coffee substitutes, and preparations and extracts thereof.

6 Milk and preparations and extracts thereof.

7 Preparations and extracts of meat, yeast or egg.

Notes:

(1) "Food" includes drink.

(2) "Animal" includes bird, fish, crustacean and mollusc.

(3) a supply of anything in the course of catering includes—

(a) any supply of it for consumption on the premises on which it is supplied; and

(b) any supply of hot food for consumption off those premises;

and for the purposes of paragraph (b) above "hot food" means food which, or any part of which—

(i) has been heated for the purposes of enabling it to be consumed at a temperature above the ambient air temperature; and

(ii) is at the time of the supply above that temperature.

(4) Item 1 of the items overriding the exceptions relates to item 1 of the excepted items.

(5) Items 2 and 3 of the items overriding the exceptions relate to item 2 of the excepted items; and for the purposes of item 2 of the excepted items "confectionery" includes chocolates, sweets and biscuits; drained, glaceg or crystallised fruits; and any item of sweetened prepared food which is normally eaten with the fingers.

(6)[Items 4 to 7][59] of the items overriding the exceptions relate to item 4 of the excepted items.

(7) any supply described in this Group shall include a supply of services described in paragraph 1(1) of Schedule 4.

Notes:

(1) "Food" includes drink.

(2) "Animal" includes bird, fish, crustacean and mollusc.

(3) A supply of anything in the course of catering includes—

(a) any supply of it for consumption on the premises on which it is supplied; and

(b) any supply of hot food for consumption off those premises;

and for the purposes of paragraph (b) above "hot food" means food which, or any part of which—

(i) has been heated for the purposes of enabling it to be consumed at a temperature above the ambient air temperature; and

(ii) is at the time of the supply above that temperature.

(4) Item 1 of the items overriding the exceptions relates to item 1 of the excepted items.

(5) Items 2 and 3 of the items overriding the exceptions relate to item 2 of the excepted items; and for the purposes of item 2 of the excepted items "confectionery" includes chocolates, sweets and biscuits; drained, glaceg or crystallised fruits; and any item of sweetened prepared food which is normally eaten with the fingers.

(6) Items 4 to 6 of the items overriding the exceptions relate to item 4 of the excepted items.

(7) Any supply described in this Group shall include a supply of services described in paragraph 1(1) of Schedule 4.

...

Group 3— Books, etc.

Item No.

1 Books, booklets, brochures, pamphlets and leaflets.

2 Newspapers, journals and periodicals.

3 Children's picture books and painting books.

4 Music (printed, duplicated or manuscript).

5 Maps, charts and topographical plans.

6 Covers, cases and other articles supplied with items 1 to 5 and not separately accounted for.

Note:

Items 1 to 6—

(a) do not include plans or drawings for industrial, architectural, engineering, commercial or similar purposes; but

(b) include the supply of the services described in paragraph 1(1) of Schedule 4 in respect of goods comprised in the items.

Group 4— Talking books for the blind and handicapped and wireless sets for the blind

Item No.

1 The supply to the Royal National Institute for the Blind, the National Listening Library or other similar charities of—

(a) magnetic tape specially adapted for the recording and reproduction of speech for the blind or severely handicapped;

(b) apparatus designed or specially adapted for the making on a magnetic tape, by way of the transfer of recorded speech from another magnetic tape, of a recording described in paragraph (f) below;

(c) apparatus designed or specially adapted for transfer to magnetic tapes of a recording made by apparatus described in paragraph (b) above;

(d) apparatus for re-winding magnetic tape described in paragraph (f) below;

(e) apparatus designed or specially adapted for the reproduction from recorded magnetic tape of speech for the blind or severely handicapped which is not available for use otherwise than by the blind or severely handicapped;

(f) magnetic tape upon which has been recorded speech for the blind or severely handicapped, such recording being suitable for reproduction only in the apparatus mentioned in paragraph (e) above;

(g) apparatus solely for the making on a magnetic tape of a sound recording which is for use by the blind or severely handicapped;

(h) parts and accessories (other than a magnetic tape for use with apparatus described in paragraph (g) above) for goods comprised in paragraphs (a) to (g) above;

(i) the supply of a service of repair or maintenance of any goods comprised in paragraphs (a) to (h) above.

2 The supply to a charity of—

(a) wireless receiving sets; or

(b) apparatus solely for the making and reproduction of a sound recording on a magnetic tape permanently contained in a cassette,

being goods solely for gratuitous loan to the blind.

Note: The supply mentioned in items 1 and 2 includes the letting on hire of goods comprised in the items.

[GROUP 5-CONSTRUCTION OF BUILDINGS, ETC.][60]

Item No.

[1 The first grant by a person—

(a) constructing a building—

(i) designed as a dwelling or number of dwellings; or

(ii) intended for use solely for a relevant residential or a relevant charitable purpose; or

(b) converting a non-residential building or a non-residential part of a building into a building designed as a dwelling or number of dwellings or a building intended for use solely for a relevant residential purpose,

of a major interest in, or in any part of, the building, dwelling or its site.][61]

[2 The supply in the course of the construction of—

(a) a building designed as a dwelling or number of dwellings or intended for use solely for a relevant residential purpose or a relevant charitable purpose; or

(b) any civil engineering work necessary for the development of a permanent park for residential caravans,

of any services related to the construction other than the services of an architect, surveyor or any person acting as a consultant or in a supervisory capacity.][62]

[3 The supply to a [relevant housing association][63] in the course of conversion of a non-residential building or a non-residential part of a building into—

(a) a building or part of a building designed as a dwelling or number of dwellings; or

(b) a building or part of a building intended for use solely for a relevant residential purpose,

of any services related to the conversion other than the services of an architect, surveyor or any person acting as a consultant or in a supervisory capacity.][64]

[4 The supply of building materials to a person to whom the supplier is supplying services within item 2 or 3 of this Group which include the incorporation of the materials into the building (or its site) in question.][65]

[Notes:

(1) "Grant" includes an assignment or surrender.

(2) A building is designed as a dwelling or a number of dwellings where in relation to each dwelling the following conditions are satisfied—

(a) the dwelling consists of self-contained living accommodation;

(b) there is no provision for direct internal access from the dwelling to any other dwelling or part of a dwelling;

(c) the separate use, or disposal of the dwelling is not prohibited by the term of any covenant, statutory planning consent or similar provision; and

(d) statutory planning consent has been granted in respect of that dwelling and its construction or conversion has been carried out in accordance with that consent.

(3) The construction of, or conversion of a non-residential building to, a building designed as a dwelling or a number of dwellings includes the construction of, or conversion of a non-residential building to, a garage provided that—

(a) the dwelling and the garage are constructed or converted at the same time; and

(b) the garage is intended to be occupied with the dwelling or one of the dwellings.

(4) Use for a relevant residential purpose means use as—

(a) a home or other institution providing residential accommodation for children;

(b) a home or other institution providing residential accommodation with personal care for persons in need of personal care by reason of old age, disablement, past or present dependence on alcohol or drugs or past or present mental disorder;

(c) a hospice;

(d) residential accommodation for students or school pupils;

(e) residential accommodation for members of any of the armed forces;

(f) a monastery, nunnery or similar establishment; or

(g) an institution which is the sole or main residence of at least 90 per cent. of its residents,

except use as a hospital, prison or similar institution or an hotel, inn or similar establishment.

(5) Where a number of buildings are—

(a) constructed at the same time and on the same site; and

(b) are intended to be used together as a unit solely for a relevant residential purpose;

then each of those buildings, to the extent that they would not be so regarded but for this Note, are to be treated as intended for use solely for a relevant residential purpose.

(6) Use for a relevant charitable purpose means use by a charity in either or both the following ways, namely—

(a) otherwise than in the course or furtherance of a business;

(b) as a village hall or similarly in providing social or recreational facilities for a local community.

[(7) For the purposes of item 1(b), and for the purposes of these Notes so far as having effect for the

purposes of item 1(b), a building or part of a building is "non-residential" if—

(a) it is neither designed, nor adapted, for use—

(i) as a dwelling or number of dwellings, or

(ii) for a relevant residential purpose; or

(b) it is designed, or adapted, for such use but—

(i) it was constructed more than 10 years before the grant of the major interest; and

(ii) no part of it has, in the period of 10 years immediately preceding the grant, been used as a dwelling or for a relevant residential purpose.

(7A) For the purposes of item 3, and for the purposes of these Notes so far as having effect for the purposes of item 3, a building or part of a building is "non-residential" if—

(a) it is neither designed, nor adapted, for use—

(i) as a dwelling or number of dwellings, or

(ii) for a relevant residential purpose; or

(b) it is designed, or adapted, for such use but—

(i) it was constructed more than 10 years before the commencement of the works of conversion, and

(ii) no part of it has, in the period of 10 years immediately preceding the commencement of those works, been used as a dwelling or for a relevant residential purpose, and

(iii) no part of it is being so used.][66]

(8) References to a non-residential building or a non-residential part of a building do not include a reference to a garage occupied together with a dwelling.

(9) The conversion, other than to a building designed for a relevant residential purpose, of a non-residential part of a building which already contains a residential part is not included within items 1(b) or 3 unless the result of that conversion is to create an additional dwelling or dwellings.

(10) Where—

(a) part of a building that is constructed is designed as a dwelling or number of dwellings or is intended for use solely for a relevant residential purpose or relevant charitable purpose (and part is not); or

(b) part of a building that is converted is designed as a dwelling or number of dwellings or is used solely for a relevant residential purpose (and part is not)—

then in the case of—

(i) a grant or other supply relating only to the part so designed or intended for that use (or its site) shall be treated as relating to a building so designed or intended for such use;

(ii) a grant or other supply relating only to the part neither so designed nor intended for such use (or its site) shall not be so treated; and

(iii) any other grant or other supply relating to, or to any part of, the building (or its site), an apportionment shall be made to determine the extent to which it is to be so treated.

(11) Where, a service falling within the description in items 2 or 3 is supplied in part in relation to the construction or conversion of a building and in part for other purposes, an apportionment may be made to determine the extent to which the supply is to be treated as falling within items 2 or 3.

(12) Where all or part of a building is intended for use solely for a relevant residential purpose or a relevant charitable purpose—

(a) a supply relating to the building (or any part of it) shall not be taken for the purposes of items 2 and 4 as relating to a building intended for such use unless it is made to a person who intends to use the building (or part) for such a purpose; and

(b) a grant or other supply relating to the building (or any part of it) shall not be taken as relating to a building intended for such use unless before it is made the person to whom it is made has given to the person making it a certificate in such form as may be specified in a notice published by the Commissioners stating that the grant or other supply (or a specified part of it) so relates.

(13) The grant of an interest in, or in any part of—

(a) a building designed as a dwelling or number of dwellings; or

(b) the site of such a building,

is not within item 1 if—

(i) the interest granted is such that the grantee is not entitled to reside in the building or part, throughout the year; or

(ii) residence there throughout the year, or the use of the building or part as the grantee's principal private residence, is prevented by the terms of a covenant, statutory planning consent or similar permission.

(14) Where the major interest referred to in item 1 is a tenancy or lease—

(a) if a premium is payable, the grant falls within that item only to the extent that it is made for consideration in the form of the premium; and

(b) if a premium is not payable, the grant falls within that item only to the extent that it is made for consideration in the form of the first payment of rent due under the tenancy or lease.

(15) The reference in item 2(b) of this Group to the construction of a civil engineering work does not include a reference to the conversion, reconstruction, alteration or enlargement of a work.

(16) For the purpose of this Group, the construction of a building does not include—

(a) the conversion, reconstruction or alteration of an existing building; or

(b) any enlargement of, or extension to, an existing building except to the extent the enlargement or extension creates an additional dwelling or dwellings; or

(c) subject to Note (17) below, the construction of an annexe to an existing building.

(17) Note 16(c) above shall not apply [where the whole or a part of an annexe is intended for use solely for a relevant charitable purpose and][67]—

(a)[the annexe][68] is capable of functioning independently from the existing building; and

(b) the only access or where there is more than one means of access, the main access to:

(i) the annexe is not via the existing building; and

(ii) the existing building is not via the annexe.

(18) A building only ceases to be an existing building when:

(a) demolished completely to ground level; or

(b) the part remaining above ground level consists of no more than a single facade or where a corner site, a double facade, the retention of which is a condition or requirement of statutory planning consent or similar permission.

(19) A caravan is not a residential caravan if residence in it throughout the year is prevented by the terms of a covenant, statutory planning consent or similar permission.

(20) Item 2 and Item 3 do not include the supply of services described in paragraph 1(1) or 5(4) of Schedule 4.

[(21) In item 3 "relevant housing association" means–

(a) a registered social landlord within the meaning of Part I of the Housing Act 1996[69],

(b) a registered housing association within the meaning of the Housing Associations Act 1985[70] (Scottish registered housing associations), or

(c) a registered housing association within the meaning of Part II of the Housing (Northern Ireland) Order 1992[71] (Northern Irish registered housing associations).][72]

(22) "Building materials", in relation to any description of building, means goods of a description ordinarily incorporated by builders in a building of that description, (or its site), but does not include—

(a) finished or prefabricated furniture, other than furniture designed to be fitted in kitchens;

(b) materials for the construction of fitted furniture, other than kitchen furniture;

(c) electrical or gas appliances, unless the appliance is an appliance which is—

(i) designed to heat space or water (or both) or to provide ventilation, air cooling, air purification, or dust extraction; or

(ii) intended for use in a building designed as a number of dwellings and is a door-entry system, a waste disposal unit or a machine for compacting waste; or

(iii) a burglar alarm, a fire alarm, or fire safety equipment or designed solely for the purpose of enabling aid to be summoned in an emergency; or

(iv) a lift or hoist;

(d) carpets or carpeting material.

(23) For the purposes of Note (22) above the incorporation of goods in a building includes their installation as fittings.

(24) Section 30(3) does not apply to goods forming part of a description of supply in this Group.][73]

[GROUP 6—PROTECTED BUILDINGS][74]

Item No.

[1 The first grant by a person substantially reconstructing a protected building, of a major interest in, or in any part of, the building or its site.][75]

[2 The supply, in the course of an approved alteration of a protected building, of any services other than the services of an architect, surveyor or][76]

[3 The supply of building materials to a person to whom the supplier is supplying services within item 2 of this Group which include the incorporation of the materials into the building (or its site) in question.][77]

[Notes:

(1) "Protected building" means a building which is designed to remain as or become a dwelling or number of dwellings (as defined in Note (2) below) or is intended for use solely for a relevant residential purpose or a relevant charitable purpose after the reconstruction or alteration and which, in either case, is—

(a) a listed building within the meaning of—

(i) the Planning (Listed Buildings and Conservation Areas) Act 1990[78]; or

(ii) [the Planning (Listed Buildings and Conservation Areas) (Scotland) Act 1997][79]; or

(iii) the Planning (Northern Ireland) Order 1991[80]; or

(b) a scheduled monument, within the meaning of—

(i) the Ancient Monuments and Archaeological Areas Act 1979; or

(ii) [the Historic Monuments and Archaeological Objects (Northern Ireland) Order 1995][81].

(2) A building is designed to remain as or become a dwelling or number of dwellings where in relation to each dwelling the following conditions are satisfied—

(a) the dwelling consists of self-contained living accommodation;

(b) there is no provision for direct internal access from the dwelling to any other dwelling or part of a dwelling;

(c) the separate use, or disposal of the dwelling is not prohibited by the terms of any covenants, statutory planning consent or similar provision,

and includes a garage (occupied together with a dwelling) either constructed at the same time as the building or where the building has been substantially reconstructed at the same time as that reconstruction.

(3) Notes (1), (4), (6), (12) to (14) and (22) to (24) of Group 5 apply in relation to this Group as they apply in relation to that Group but subject to any appropriate modifications.

(4)[82]For the purposes of item 1, a protected building shall not be regarded as substantially reconstructed unless the reconstruction is such that at least one of the following conditions is fulfilled when the reconstruction is completed—

(a) that, of the works carried out to effect the reconstruction, at least three-fifths, measured by reference to cost, are of such a nature that the supply of services (other than excluded services), materials and other items to carry out the works, would, if supplied by a taxable person, be within either item 2 or item 3 of this Group; and

[(b) that the reconstructed building incorporates no more of the original building (that is to say, the building as it was before the reconstruction began) than the external walls, together with other external features of architectural or historic interest;][83]

and in paragraph (a) above "excluded services" means the services of an architect, surveyor or other person acting as consultant or in a supervisory capacity.

(5) Where part of a protected building that is substantially reconstructed is designed to remain as or become a dwelling or a number of dwellings or is intended for use solely for a relevant residential or relevant charitable purpose (and part is not)—

(a) a grant or other supply relating only to the part so designed or intended for such use (or its site) shall be treated as relating to a building so designed or intended for such use;

(b) a grant or other supply relating only to the part neither so designed nor intended for such use (or its site) shall not be so treated; and

(c) in the case of any other grant or other supply relating to, or to any part of, the building (or its

site), an apportionment shall be made to determine the extent to which it is to be so treated.

(6) "Approved alteration" means—

(a) in the case of a protected building which is an ecclesiastical building to which section 60 of the Planning (Listed Buildings and Conservation Areas) Act 1990 applies, any works of alteration; and

(b) in the case of a protected building which is a scheduled monument within the meaning of the Historic Monuments Act (Northern Ireland) 1971 and in respect of which a protection order, within the meaning of that Act, is in force, works of alteration for which consent has been given under section 10 of that Act; and

(c) in any other case, works of alteration which may not, or but for the existence of a Crown interest or Duchy interest could not, be carried out unless authorised under, or under any provision of—

(i) Part I of the Planning (Listed Buildings and Conservation Areas) Act 1990,

(ii) Part IV of the Town and Country Planning (Scotland) Act 1972,

(iii) Part V of the Planning (Northern Ireland) Order 1991,

(iv) Part I of the Ancient Monuments and Archaeological Areas Act 1979,

and for which, except in the case of a Crown interest or Duchy interest, consent has been obtained under any provision of that Part,

but does not include any works of repair or maintenance, or any incidental alteration to the fabric of a building which results from the carrying out of repairs, or maintenance work.

(7) For the purposes of paragraph (a) of Note (6), a building used or available for use by a minister of religion wholly or mainly as a residence from which to perform the duties of his office shall be treated as not being an ecclesiastical building.

(8) For the purposes of paragraph (c) of Note (6) "Crown interest" and "Duchy interest" have the same meaning as in section 50 of the Ancient Monuments and Archaeological Areas Act 1979.

(9) Where a service is supplied in part in relation to an approved alteration of a building, and in part for other purposes, an apportionment may be made to determine the extent to which the supply is to be treated as falling within item 2.

(10) For the purposes of item 2 the construction of a building separate from, but in the curtilage of, a protected building does not constitute an alteration of the protected building.

(11) Item 2 does not include the supply of services described in paragraph 1(1) or 5(4) of Schedule 4.][84]

Group 12— Drugs, medicines, aids for the handicapped, etc.

Item No.

1 The [supply of any qualifying goods dispensed to an individual for his personal use where the dispensing is][85] by a person registered in the register of pharmaceutical chemists kept under the Pharmacy Act 1954 or the Pharmacy (Northern Ireland) Order 1976, on the prescription of a person registered in the register of medical practitioners, the register of medical practitioners with limited registration or the dentists' register.

[1A The supply of any [qualifying][86] goods in accordance with a requirement or authorisation under—

(a) regulation 20 of the National Health Service (Pharmaceutical Services) Regulations 1992[87];

(b) regulation 34 of the National Health Service (General Medical Services) (Scotland) Regulations 1995[88]; or

(c) [regulation 12 of the Pharmaceutical Services Regulations (Northern Ireland) 1997][89],

by a person registered in the register of medical practitioners or the register of medical practitioners with limited registration.][90]

2 The supply to a handicapped person for domestic or his personal use, or to a charity for making available to handicapped persons by sale or otherwise, for domestic or their personal use, of—

(a) medical or surgical appliances designed solely for the relief of a severe abnormality or severe injury;

(b) electrically or mechanically adjustable beds designed for invalids;

(c) commode chairs, commode stools, devices incorporating a bidet jet and warm air drier and frames or other devices for sitting over or rising from a sanitary appliance;

(d) chair lifts or stair lifts designed for use in connection with invalid wheelchairs;

(e) hoists and lifters designed for use by invalids;

(f) motor vehicles designed or substantially and permanently adapted for the carriage of a person in

a wheelchair or on a stretcher and of no more than [11][91] other persons;

(g) equipment and appliances not included in paragraphs (a) to (f) above designed solely for use by a handicapped person;

(h) parts and accessories designed solely for use in or with goods described in paragraphs (a) to (g) above;

(i) boats designed or substantially and permanently adapted for use by handicapped persons.

[2A The supply of a qualifying motor vehicle—

(a) to a handicapped person—

(i) who usually uses a wheelchair, or

(ii) who is usually carried on a stretcher,

for domestic or his personal use; or

(b) to a charity for making available to such a handicapped person by sale or otherwise, for domestic or his personal use.][92]

3 The supply to a handicapped person of services of adapting goods to suit his condition.

4 The supply to a charity of services of adapting goods to suit the condition of a handicapped person to whom the goods are to be made available, by sale or otherwise, by the charity.

5 The supply to a handicapped person or to a charity of a service of repair or maintenance of any goods specified in item 2, [2A,][93] 6, 18 or 19 and supplied as described in that item.

6 The supply of goods in connection with a supply described in item 3, 4 or 5.

7 The supply to a handicapped person or to a charity of services necessarily performed in the installation of equipment or appliances (including parts and accessories therefor) specified in item 2 and supplied as described in that item.

8 The supply to a handicapped person of a service of constructing ramps or widening doorways or passages for the purpose of facilitating his entry to or movement within his private residence.

9 The supply to a charity of a service described in item 8 for the purpose of facilitating a handicapped person's entry to or movement within any building.

10 The supply to a handicapped person of a service of providing, extending or adapting a bathroom, washroom or lavatory in his private residence where such provision, extension or adaptation is necessary by reason of his condition.

[11 The supply to a charity of a service of providing, extending or adapting a bathroom, washroom or lavatory for use by handicapped persons—

(a) in residential accommodation, or

(b) in a day-centre where at least 20 per cent. of the individuals using the centre are handicapped persons,

where such provision, extension or adaptation is necessary by reason of the condition of the handicapped persons.][94]

12 The supply to a charity of a service of providing, extending or adapting a washroom or lavatory for use by handicapped persons in a building, or any part of a building, used principally by a charity for charitable purposes where such provision, extension or adaptation is necessary to facilitate the use of the washroom or lavatory by handicapped persons.

13 The supply of goods in connection with a supply described in items 8, 9, 10 or 11.

14 The letting on hire of a motor vehicle for a period of not less than 3 years to a handicapped person in receipt of a disability living allowance by virtue of entitlement to the mobility component or of mobility supplement where the lessor's business consists predominantly of the provision of motor vehicles to such persons.

15 The sale of a motor vehicle which had been let on hire in the circumstances described in item 14, where such sale constitutes the first supply of the vehicle after the end of the period of such letting.

16 The supply to a handicapped person of services necessarily performed in the installation of a lift for the purpose of facilitating his movement between floors within his private residence.

17 The supply to a charity providing a permanent or temporary residence or day-centre for handicapped persons of services necessarily performed in the installation of a lift for the purpose of facilitating the movement of handicapped persons between floors within that building.

18 The supply of goods in connection with a supply described in item 16 or 17.

19 The supply to a handicapped person for domestic or his personal use, or to a charity for making

available to handicapped persons by sale or otherwise for domestic or their personal use, of an alarm system designed to be capable of operation by a handicapped person, and to enable him to alert directly a specified person or a control centre.

20 The supply of services necessarily performed by a control centre in receiving and responding to calls from an alarm system specified in item 19.

Notes:

(1) Section 30(3) does not apply to goods forming part of a description of supply in item 1 [or item 1A][95], nor to other goods forming part of a description of supply in this Group, except where those other goods are acquired from another member State or imported from a place outside the member States by a handicapped person for domestic or his personal use, or by a charity for making available to handicapped persons, by sale or otherwise, for domestic or their personal use.

(2) For the purposes of item 1 a person who is not registered in the visiting EEC practitioners list in the register of medical practitioners at the time he performs services in an urgent case as mentioned in subsection (3) of section 18 of the Medical Act 1983 is to be treated as being registered in that list where he is entitled to be registered in accordance with that section.

[(2A) In items 1 and 1A, "qualifying goods" means any goods designed or adapted for use in connection with any medical or surgical treatment except—

(a) hearing aids;

(b) dentures; and

(c) spectacles and contact lenses.][96]

(3) "Handicapped" means chronically sick or disabled.

(4) Item 2 shall not include hearing aids (except hearing aids designed for the auditory training of deaf children), dentures, spectacles and contact lenses but shall be deemed to include—

(a) clothing, footwear and wigs;

(b) invalid wheelchairs, and invalid carriages.. . [97].; and

(c) renal haemodialysis units, oxygen concentrators, artificial respirators and other similar apparatus.

(5) The supplies described in items 1 [,1A][98] and [, 2 and 2A][99] include supplies of services of letting on hire of the goods respectively comprised in those items.

[(5A) In item 1 the reference to personal use does not include any use which is, or involves, a use by or in relation to an individual while that individual, for the purposes of being provided (whether or not by the person making the supply) with medical or surgical treatment, or with any form of care—

(a) is an in-patient or resident in a relevant institution which is a hospital or nursing home; or

(b) is attending at the premises of a relevant institution which is a hospital or nursing home.

(5B) Subject to Notes (5C) and (5D), in item 2 the reference to domestic or personal use does not include any use which is, or involves, a use by or in relation to a handicapped person while that person, for the purposes of being provided (whether or not by the person making the supply) with medical or surgical treatment, or with any form of care—

(a) is an in-patient or resident in a relevant institution; or

(b) is attending at the premises of a relevant institution.

(5C) Note (5B) does not apply for the purpose of determining whether any of the following supplies falls within item 2, that is to say—

(a) a supply to a charity;

(b) a supply by a person mentioned in any of paragraphs (a) to (g) of Note (5H) of an invalid wheelchair or invalid carriage;

(c) a supply by a person so mentioned of any parts or accessories designed solely for use in or with an invalid wheelchair or invalid carriage.

(5D) Note (5B) applies for the purpose of determining whether a supply of goods by a person not mentioned in any of paragraphs (a) to (g) of Note (5H) falls within item 2 only if those goods are—

(a) goods falling within paragraph (a) of that item;

(b) incontinence products and wound dressings; or

(c) parts and accessories designed solely for use in or with goods falling within paragraph (a) of this Note.

(5E) Subject to Note (5F), item 2 does not include—

(a) a supply made in accordance with any agreement, arrangement or understanding (whether or not legally enforceable) to which any of the persons mentioned in paragraphs (a) to (g) of Note (5H) is or has been a party otherwise than as the supplier; or

(b) any supply the whole or any part of the consideration for which is provided (whether directly or indirectly) by a person so mentioned.

(5F) A supply to a handicapped person of an invalid wheelchair or invalid carriage is excluded from item 2 by Note (5E) only if—

(a) that Note applies in relation to that supply by reference to a person falling within paragraph (g) of Note (5H); or

(b) the whole of the consideration for the supply is provided (whether directly or indirectly) by a person falling within any of paragraphs (a) to (f) of Note (5H).

(5G) In Notes (4), (5C) and (5F), the references to an invalid wheelchair and to an invalid carriage do not include references to any mechanically propelled vehicle which is intended or adapted for use on roads.

(5H) The persons referred to in Notes (5C) to (5F) are—

[(a) a Strategic Health Authority or Special Health Authority in England;

(aa) a Health Authority, Special Health Authority or Local Health Board in Wales;][100]

(b) a Health Board or Special Health Board in Scotland;

(c) a Health and Social Services Board in Northern Ireland;

(d) the Common Services Agency for the Scottish Health Service, the Northern Ireland Central Services Agency for Health and Social Services and the Isle of Man Health Services Board;

(e) a National Health Service trust established under Part I of the National Health Service and Community Care Act 1990[101] or the National Health Service (Scotland) Act 1978[102];

[(ea) a Primary Care Trust established under section 16A of the National Health Service Act 1977[103];][104]

(f) a Health and Social Services trust established under Article 10 of the Health and Personal Social Services (Northern Ireland) Order 1991[105]; or

(g) any person not falling within any of paragraphs (a) to (f) above who is engaged in the carrying on of any activity in respect of which a relevant institution is required to be approved, licensed or registered or as the case may be, would be so required if not exempt.

(5I) In Notes (5A), (5B) and (5H), "relevant institution" means any institution (whether a hospital, nursing home or other institution) which provides care or medical or surgical treatment and is either—

(a) approved, licensed or registered in accordance with the provisions of any enactment or Northern Ireland legislation; or

(b) exempted by or under the provisions of any enactment or Northern Ireland legislation from any requirement to be approved, licensed or registered;,

and in this Note the references to the provisions of any enactment or Northern Ireland legislation include references only to provisions which, so far as relating to England, Wales, Scotland or Northern Ireland, have the same effect in every locality within that part of the United Kingdom.][106]

[(5J) For the purposes of item 11 "residential accommodation" means—

(a) a residential home, or

(b) self-contained living accommodation,

provided as a residence (whether on a permanent or temporary basis or both) for handicapped persons, but does not include an inn, hotel, boarding house or similar establishment or accommodation in any such type of establishment.

(5K) In this Group "washroom" means a room that contains a lavatory or washbasin (or both) but does not contain a bath or a shower or cooking, sleeping or laundry facilities.][107]

[(5L) A "qualifying motor vehicle" for the purposes of item 2A is a motor vehicle (other than a motor vehicle capable of carrying more than 12 persons including the driver)—

(a) that is designed or substantially and permanently adapted to enable a handicapped person—

(i) who usually uses a wheelchair, or

(ii) who is usually carried on a stretcher,

to enter, and drive or be otherwise carried in, the motor vehicle; or

(b) that by reason of its design, or being substantially and permanently adapted, includes features whose design is such that their sole purpose is to allow a wheelchair used by a handicapped person to be carried in or on the motor vehicle.][108]

(6) Item 14 applies only—

(a) where the vehicle is unused at the commencement of the period of letting; and

(b) where the consideration for the letting consists wholly or partly of sums paid to the lessor by [the Department for Work and Pensions][109] or the Ministry of Defence on behalf of the lessee in respect of the mobility component of the disability living allowance or mobility supplement to which he is entitled.

(7) In item 14—

(a) "disability living allowance" is a disability living allowance within the meaning of section 71 of the Social Security Contributions and Benefits Act 1992, or section 71 of the Social Security Contributions and Benefits (Northern Ireland) Act 1992; and

(b) "mobility supplement" is a mobility supplement within the meaning of Article 26A of the Naval, Military and Air Forces etc. (Disablement and Death Service Pensions Order 1983, Article 25A of the Personal Injuries (Civilians) Scheme 1983, Article 3 of the Motor Vehicles (Exemption from Vehicles Excise Duty) Order 1985 or Article 3 of the Motor Vehicles (Exemption from Vehicles Excise Duty) (Northern Ireland) Order 1985.

(8) Where in item 3 or 4 the goods are adapted in accordance with that item prior to their supply to the handicapped person or the charity, an apportionment shall be made to determine the supply of services which falls within item 3 or 4.

(9) In item 19 or 20, a specified person or control centre is a person or centre who or which—

(a) is appointed to receive directly calls activated by an alarm system described in that item, and

(b) retains information about the handicapped person to assist him in the event of illness, injury or similar emergency.

Group 15— Charities etc.

[[1 The sale, or letting on hire, by a charity of any goods donated to it for—

(a) sale,

(b) letting,

(c) sale or letting,

(d) sale or export,

(e) letting or export, or

(f) sale, letting or export.][110]

1A The sale, or letting on hire, by a taxable person of any goods donated to him for—

(a) sale,

(b) letting,

(c) sale or letting,

(d) sale or export,

(e) letting or export, or

(f) sale, letting or export,

if he is a profits-to-charity person in respect of the goods.

[2 The donation of any goods for any one or more of the following purposes—

(a) sale by a charity or a taxable person who is a profits-to-charity person in respect of the goods;

(b) export by a charity or such a taxable person;

(c) letting by a charity or such a taxable person.][111]][112]

3 The export of any goods by a charity to a place outside the member States.

4 The supply of any relevant goods for donation to a nominated eligible body where the goods are purchased with funds provided by a charity or from voluntary contributions.

5 The supply of any relevant goods to an eligible body which pays for them with funds provided by a charity or from voluntary contributions or to an eligible body which is a charitable institution providing care or medical or surgical treatment for handicapped persons.

6 Repair and maintenance of relevant goods owned by an eligible body.

7 The supply of goods in connection with the supply described in item 6.

[8 The supply to a charity of a right to promulgate an advertisement by means of a medium of communication with the public.

8A A supply to a charity that consists in the promulgation of an advertisement by means of such a medium.

8B The supply to a charity of services of design or production of an advertisement that is, or was intended to be, promulgated by means of such a medium.] [113]

9 The supply to a charity, providing care or medical or surgical treatment for human beings or animals, or engaging in medical or veterinary research, of a medicinal product where the supply is solely for use by the charity in such care, treatment or research.

10 The supply to a charity of a substance directly used for synthesis or testing in the course of medical or veterinary research.

Notes:

[(1) Item 1 or 1A does not apply unless the sale or letting—

(a) takes place as a result of the goods having been made available—

(i) to two or more specified persons, or

(ii) to the general public,

for purchase or hire (whether so made available in a shop or elsewhere), and

(b) does not take place as a result of any arrangements (whether legally binding or not) relating to the goods and entered into, before the goods were made so available, by—

(i) each of the parties to the sale or letting, or

(ii) the donor of the goods and either or both of those parties.

(1A) For the purposes of items 1, 1A and 2, goods are donated for letting only if they are donated for—

(a) letting, and

(b) re-letting after the end of any first or subsequent letting, and

(c) all or any of—

(i) sale,

(ii) export, or

(iii) disposal as waste,

if not, or when no longer, used for letting.

(1B) Items 1 and 1A do not include (and shall be treated as having not included) any sale, or letting on hire, of particular donated goods if the goods, at any time after they are donated but before they are sold, exported or disposed of as waste, are whilst unlet used for any purpose other than, or in addition to, that of being available for purchase, hire or export.

(1C) In Note (1) "specified person" means a person who—

(a) is handicapped, or

(b) is entitled to any one or more of the specified benefits, or

(c) is both handicapped and so entitled.

(1D) For the purposes of Note (1C) the specified benefits are—

(a) income support under Part VII of the Social Security Contributions and Benefits Act 1992[114] or Part VII of the Social Security Contributions and Benefits (Northern Ireland) Act 1992[115];

(b) housing benefit under Part VII of the Social Security Contributions and Benefits Act 1992 or Part VII of the Social Security Contributions and Benefits (Northern Ireland) Act 1992;

(c) council tax benefit under Part VII of the Social Security Contributions and Benefits Act 1992;

(d) an income-based jobseeker's allowance within the meaning of section 1(4) of the Jobseekers Act 1995[116] or article 3(4) of the Jobseekers (Northern Ireland) Order 1995[117];

(e) working families' tax credit under Part VII of the Social Security Contributions and Benefits Act 1992[118] or Part VII of the Social Security Contributions and Benefits (Northern Ireland) Act 1992; and

(f) disabled person's tax credit under Part VII of the Social Security Contributions and Benefits Act 1992[119] or Part VII of the Social Security Contributions and Benefits (Northern Ireland) Act 1992.

(1E) For the purposes of items 1A and 2 a taxable person is a "profits-to-charity" person in respect of any goods if—

(a) he has agreed in writing (whether or not contained in a deed) to transfer to a charity his profits from supplies and lettings of the goods, or

(b) his profits from supplies and lettings of the goods are otherwise payable to a charity.

(1F) In items 1, 1A and 2, and any Notes relating to any of those items, "goods" means goods (and, in particular, does not include anything that is not goods even though provision made by or under an enactment provides for a supply of that thing to be, or be treated as, a supply of goods).][120]

(2) "Animals" includes any species of the animal kingdom.

(3) "Relevant goods" means—

(a) medical, scientific, computer, video, sterilising, laboratory or refrigeration equipment for use in medical or veterinary research, training, diagnosis or treatment;

(b) ambulances;

(c) parts or accessories for use in or with goods described in paragraph (a) or (b) above;

(d) goods of a kind described in item 2 of Group 12 of this Schedule;

(e) motor vehicles (other than vehicles with more than 50 seats) designed or substantially and permanently adapted for the safe carriage of a handicapped person in a wheelchair provided that—

(i) in the case of vehicles with more than 16 but fewer than 27 seats, the number of persons for which such provision shall exist shall be at least 2;

(ii) in the case of vehicles with more than 26 but fewer than 37 seats, the number of persons for which such provision shall exist shall be at least 3;

(iii) in the case of vehicles with more than 36 but fewer than 47 seats, the number of persons for which such provision shall exist shall be at least 4;

(iv) in the case of vehicles with more than 46 seats, the number of persons for which such provision shall exist shall be at least 5;

(v) there is either a fitted electrically or hydraulically operated lift or, in the case of vehicles with fewer than 17 seats, a fitted ramp to provide access for a passenger in a wheelchair;

(f) motor vehicles (with more than 6 but fewer than 51 seats) for use by an eligible body providing care for blind, deaf, mentally handicapped or terminally sick persons mainly to transport such persons;

(g) telecommunication, aural, visual, light enhancing or heat detecting equipment (not being equipment ordinarily supplied for private or recreational use) solely for use for the purpose of rescue or first aid services undertaken by a charitable institution providing such services.

(4) "Eligible body" means—

[(a) a Strategic Health Authority or Special Health Authority in England;

(aa) a Health Authority, Special Health Authority or Local Health Board in Wales;][121]

(b) a Health Board in Scotland;

(c) a Health and Social Services Board in Northern Ireland;

(d) a hospital whose activities are not carried on for profit;

(e) a research institution whose activities are not carried on for profit;

(f) a charitable institution providing care or medical or surgical treatment for handicapped persons;

(g) the Common Services Agency for the Scottish Health Service, the Northern Ireland Central Services Agency for Health and Social Services or the Isle of Man Health Services Board;

(h) a charitable institution providing rescue or first-aid services;

(i) a National Health Service trust established under Part I of the National Health Service and Community Care Act 1990 or the National Health Service (Scotland) Act 1978.

[(j) a Primary Care Trust established under section 16A of the National Health Service Act 1977][122]

[(4A) Subject to Note (5B), a charitable institution shall not be regarded as providing care or medical or surgical treatment for handicapped persons unless—

(a) it provides care or medical or surgical treatment in a relevant establishment; and

(b) the majority of the persons who receive care or medical or surgical treatment in that establishment are handicapped persons.

(4B) "Relevant establishment" means—

(a) a day-centre, other than a day-centre which exists primarily as a place for activities that are social or recreational or both; or

(b) an institution which is—

(i) approved, licensed or registered in accordance with the provisions of any enactment or

Northern Ireland legislation; or

(ii) exempted by or under the provisions of any enactment or Northern Ireland legislation from any requirement to be approved, licensed or registered;

and in paragraph (b) above the references to the provisions of any enactment or Northern Ireland legislation are references only to provisions which, so far as relating to England, Wales, Scotland or Northern Ireland, have the same effect in every locality within that part of the United Kingdom.][123]

(5) "Handicapped" means chronically sick or disabled.

[(5A) Subject to Note (5B), items 4 to 7 do not apply where the eligible body falls within Note (4)(f) unless the relevant goods are or are to be used in a relevant establishment in which that body provides care or medical or surgical treatment to persons the majority of whom are handicapped.

(5B) Nothing in Note (4A) or (5A) shall prevent a supply from falling within items 4 to 7 where—

(a) the eligible body provides medical care to handicapped persons in their own homes;

(b) the relevant goods fall within Note (3)(a) or are parts or accessories for use in or with goods described in Note (3)(a); and

(c) those goods are or are to be used in or in connection with the provision of that care.][124]

(6) Item 4 does not apply where the donee of the goods is not a charity and has contributed in whole or in part to the funds for the purchase of the goods.

(7) Item 5 does not apply where the body to whom the goods are supplied is not a charity and has contributed in whole or in part to the funds for the purchase of the goods.

(8) Items 6 and 7 do not apply unless—

(a) the supply is paid for with funds which have been provided by a charity or from voluntary contributions, and

(b) in a case where the owner of the goods repaired or maintained is not a charity, it has not contributed in whole or in part to those funds.

(9) Items 4 and 5 include the letting on hire of relevant goods; accordingly in items 4, 5 and 6 and the notes relating thereto, references to the purchase or ownership of goods shall be deemed to include references respectively to their hiring and possession.

(10) Item 5 includes computer services by way of the provision of computer software solely for use in medical research, diagnosis or treatment.

[(10A) Neither of items 8 and 8A includes a supply where any of the members of the public (whether individuals or other persons) who are reached through the medium are selected by or on behalf of the charity.

For this purpose "selected" includes selected by address (whether postal address or telephone number, e-mail address or other address for electronic communications purposes) or at random.

(10B) None of items 8 to 8C includes a supply used to create, or contribute to, a website that is the charity's own.

For this purpose a website is a charity's own even though hosted by another person.

(10C) Neither of items 8B and 8C includes a supply to a charity that is used directly by the charity to design or produce an advertisement.][125]

(11) In item 9—

(a) a "medicinal product" means any substance or article (not being an instrument, apparatus or appliance) which is for use wholly or mainly in either or both of the following ways—

(i) by being administered to one or more human beings or animals for a medicinal purpose;

(ii) as an ingredient in the preparation of a substance or article which is to be administered to one or more human beings or animals for a medicinal purpose;

(b) a "medicinal purpose" has the meaning assigned to it by section 130(2) of the Medicines Act 1968;

(c) "administer" has the meaning assigned to it by section 130(9) of the Medicines Act 1968;

(12) In items 9 and 10 "substance" and "ingredient" have the meanings assigned to them by section 132 of the Medicines Act 1968.

Sections 8 and 31.

SCHEDULE 9

Exemptions

Part I Index to exempt supplies of goods and services

Betting, gaming and lotteries	Group 4
Burial and cremation	Group 8
[Cultural services etc	Group 13][126]
Education	Group 6
Finance	Group 5
Fund raising events by charities and other qualifying bodies	Group 12
Health and welfare	Group 7
Insurance	Group 2
[Investment gold	Group 15][127]
Land	Group 1
Postal services	Group 3
Sport, sports competitions and physical education	Group 10
[Supplies of goods where input tax cannot be recovered	Group 14][128]
[Subscriptions to trade unions, professional and other public interest bodies	Group 9][129]
Works of art etc	Group 11

Part II The Groups

Group 1— Land

Item No.

1 The grant of any interest in or right over land or of any licence to occupy land, or, in relation to land in Scotland, any personal right to call for or be granted any such interest or right, other than—

(a) the grant of the fee simple in—

(i) a building which has not been completed and which is neither designed as a dwelling or number of dwellings nor intended for use solely for a relevant residential purpose or a relevant charitable purpose;

(ii) a new building which is neither designed as a dwelling or number of dwellings nor intended for use solely for a relevant residential purpose or a relevant charitable purpose after the grant;

(iii) a civil engineering work which has not been completed;

(iv) a new civil engineering work;

(b) a supply made pursuant to a developmental tenancy, developmental lease or developmental licence;

(c) the grant of any interest, right or licence consisting of a right to take game or fish unless at the time of the grant the grantor grants to the grantee the fee simple of the land over which the right to take game or fish is exercisable;

(d) the provision in an hotel, inn, boarding house or similar establishment of sleeping accommodation or of accommodation in rooms which are provided in conjunction with sleeping accommodation or for the purpose of a supply of catering;

(e) the grant of any interest in, right over or licence to occupy holiday accommodation;

(f) the provision of seasonal pitches for caravans, and the grant of facilities at caravan parks to persons for whom such pitches are provided;

(g) the provision of pitches for tents or of camping facilities;

(h) the grant of facilities for parking a vehicle;

(j) the grant of any right to fell and remove standing timber;

(k) the grant of facilities for housing, or storage of, an aircraft or for mooring, or storage of, a ship, boat or other vessel;

(l) the grant of any right to occupy a box, seat or other accommodation at a sports ground, theatre, concert hall or other place of entertainment;

(m) the grant of facilities for playing any sport or participating in any physical recreation; and

(n) the grant of any right, including—

(i) an equitable right,

(ii) a right under an option or right of pre-emption, or

(iii) in relation to land in Scotland, a personal right,

to call for or be granted an interest or right which would fall within any of paragraphs (a) or (c) to (m) above.

Notes:

[(1) "Grant" includes an assignment or surrender and the supply made by the person to whom an interest is surrendered when there is a reverse surrender.][130]

[(1A) A "reverse surrender" is one in which the person to whom the interest is surrendered is paid by the person by whom the interest is being surrendered to accept the surrender.][131]

(2) A building shall be taken to be completed when an architect issues a certificate of practical completion in relation to it or it is first fully occupied, whichever happens first; and a civil engineering work shall be taken to be completed when an engineer issues a certificate of completion in relation to it or it is first fully used, whichever happens first.

(3) [Notes (2) to (10) and (12)][132] to Group 5 of Schedule 8 apply in relation to this Group as they apply in relation to that Group.

(4) A building or civil engineering work is new if it was completed less than three years before the grant.

(5) Subject to Note (6), the grant of the fee simple in a building or work completed before 1st April 1989 is not excluded from this Group by paragraph (a)(ii) or (iv).

(6) Note (5) does not apply where the grant is the first grant of the fee simple made on or after 1st April 1989 and the building was not fully occupied, or the work not fully used, before that date.

(7) A tenancy of, lease of or licence to occupy a building or work is treated as becoming a developmental tenancy, developmental lease or developmental licence (as the case may be) when a tenancy of, lease of or licence to occupy a building or work, whose construction, reconstruction, enlargement or extension commenced on or after 1st January 1992, is treated as being supplied to and by the developer under paragraph 6(1) of Schedule 10 [(except where that paragraph applies by virtue of paragraph 5(1)(b) of that Schedule)][133].

(8) Where a grant of an interest in, right over or licence to occupy land includes a valuable right to take game or fish, an apportionment shall be made to determine the supply falling outside this Group by virtue of paragraph (c).

(9) "Similar establishment" includes premises in which there is provided furnished sleeping accommodation, whether with or without the provision of board or facilities for the preparation of food, which are used by or held out as being suitable for use by visitors or travellers.

(10) "Houseboat" includes a houseboat within the meaning of Group 9 of Schedule 8.

(11) Paragraph (e) includes—

(a) any grant excluded from item 1 of Group 5 of Schedule 8 by [Note (13)][134] in that Group;

(b) any supply made pursuant to a tenancy, lease or licence under which the grantee is or has been permitted to erect and occupy holiday accommodation.

(12) Paragraph (e) does not include a grant in respect of a building or part which is not a new building of—

(a) the fee simple, or

(b) a tenancy, lease or licence to the extent that the grant is made for a consideration in the form of a premium.

(13) "Holiday accommodation" includes any accommodation in a building, hut (including a beach hut or chalet), caravan, houseboat or tent which is advertised or held out as holiday accommodation or as suitable for holiday or leisure use, but excludes any accommodation within paragraph (d).

(14) A seasonal pitch is a pitch—

(a) which is provided for a period of less than a year, or

(b) which is provided for a year or a period longer than a year but which the person to whom it is provided is prevented by the terms of any covenant, statutory planning consent or similar permission from occupying by living in a caravan at all times throughout the period for which the pitch is provided.

(15) "Mooring" includes anchoring or berthing.

(16) Paragraph (m) shall not apply where the grant of the facilities is for—
(a) a continuous period of use exceeding 24 hours; or
(b) a series of 10 or more periods, whether or not exceeding 24 hours in total, where the following conditions are satisfied—
(i) each period is in respect of the same activity carried on at the same place;
(ii) the interval between each period is not less than one day and not more than 14 days;
(iii) consideration is payable by reference to the whole series and is evidenced by written agreement;
(iv) the grantee has exclusive use of the facilities; and
(v) the grantee is a school, a club, an association or an organisation representing affiliated clubs or constituent associations.

Group 6— Education

Item No.

1 The provision by an eligible body of—
(a) education;
(b) research, where supplied to an eligible body; or
(c) vocational training.

2 The supply of private tuition, in a subject ordinarily taught in a school or university, by an individual teacher acting independently of an employer.

3 The provision of examination services—
(a) by or to an eligible body; or
(b) to a person receiving education or vocational training which is—
(i) exempt by virtue of items 1, 2 [, 5 or 5A][135]; or
(ii) provided otherwise than in the course or furtherance of a business.

4 The supply of any goods or services (other than examination services) which are closely related to a supply of a description falling within item 1 (the principal supply) by or to the eligible body making the principal supply provided—
(a) the goods or services are for the direct use of the pupil, student or trainee (as the case may be) receiving the principal supply; and
(b) where the supply is to the eligible body making the principal supply, it is made by another eligible body.

5 The provision of vocational training, and the supply of any goods or services essential thereto by the person providing the vocational training, to the extent that the consideration payable is ultimately a charge to funds provided pursuant to arrangements made under section 2 of the Employment and Training Act 1973, section 1A of the Employment and Training Act (Northern Ireland) 1950 or section 2 of the Enterprise and New Towns (Scotland) Act 1990.

[5A The provision of education or vocational training and the supply, by the person providing that education or training, of any goods or services essential to that provision, to the extent that the consideration payable is ultimately a charge to funds provided by the Learning and Skills Council for England or the National Council for Education and Training for Wales under Part I or Part II of the Learning and Skills Act 2000.][136]

6 The provision of facilities by—
(a) a youth club or an association of youth clubs to its members; or
(b) an association of youth clubs to members of a youth club which is a member of that association.

Notes:

(1) For the purposes of this Group an "eligible body" is—
(a) a school within the meaning of [the Education Act 1996][137], the Education (Scotland) Act 1980, the Education and Libraries (Northern Ireland) Order 1986 or the Education Reform (Northern Ireland) Order 1989, which is—
(i) provisionally or finally registered or deemed to be registered as a school within the meaning of the aforesaid legislation in a register of independent schools; or
(ii) a school in respect of which of which grants are made by the Secretary of State to the proprietor or managers; or
(iii)[a community, foundation or voluntary school within the meaning of the school Standards

and Framework Act 1998, a special school within the meaning of section 337 of the Education Act 1996][138][or a maintained school within the meaning of][139] the Education and Libraries (Northern Ireland) Order 1986; or

(iv) a public school within the meaning of section 135(1) of the Education (Scotland) Act 1980; or

(v)...............................[140]

(vi) a self-governing school within the meaning of section 1(3) of the Self-Governing Schools (Scotland) Act 1989; or

(vii)...............................[141]

(viii) a grant-maintained integrated school within the meaning of Article 65 of the Education Reform (Northern Ireland) Order 1989;

(b) a United Kingdom university, and any college, institution, school or hall of such a university;

(c) an institution—

(i) falling within section 91(3)(a) or (b) or section 91(5)(b) or (c) of the Further and Higher Education Act 1992; or

(ii) which is a designated institution as defined in section 44(2) of the Further and Higher Education (Scotland) Act 1992; or

(iii) managed by a board of management as defined in section 36(1) of the Further and Higher Education (Scotland) Act 1992; or

(iv) to which grants are paid by the Department of Education for Northern Ireland under Article 66(2) of the Education and Libraries (Northern Ireland) Order 1986; [or

(v) managed by a governing body established under the Further Education (Northern Ireland) Order 1997;][142]

(d) a public body of a description in Note (5) to Group 7 below;

[(e) a body which—

(i) is precluded from distributing and does not distribute any profit it makes; and

(ii) applies any profits made from supplies of a description within this Group to the continuance or improvement of such supplies;][143]

[(f) a body not falling within paragraphs (a) to (e) above which provides the teaching of English as a foreign language.][144]

(2) A supply by a body, which is an eligible body only by virtue of falling within Note [1(f)][145], shall not fall within this Group insofar as it consists of the provision of anything other than the teaching of English as a foreign language.

[(3) "Vocational training" means—

training, re-training or the provision of work experience for—

(a) any trade, profession or employment; or

(b) any voluntary work connected with—

(i) education, health, safety, or welfare; or

(ii) the carrying out of activities of a charitable nature.][146]

(4) "Examination services" include the setting and marking of examinations, the setting of educational or training standards, the making of assessments and other services provided with a view to ensuring educational and training standards are maintained.

(5) For the purposes of item 5 a supply of any goods or services shall not be taken to be essential to the provision of vocational training unless the goods or services in question are provided directly to the trainee.

[(5A) For the purposes of item 5A a supply of any goods or services shall not be taken to be essential to the provision of education or vocational training unless—

(a) in the case of the provision of education, the goods or services are provided directly to the person receiving the education;

(b) in the case of the provision of vocational training, the goods or services are provided directly to the person receiving the training.][147]

(6) For the purposes of item 6 a club is a "youth club" if—

(a) it is established to promote the social, physical, educational or spiritual development of its members;

(b) its members are mainly under 21 years of age; and

(c) it satisfies the requirements of Note (l)(f)(i) and (ii).

Group 7— Health and welfare

Item No.

1 The supply of services by a person registered or enrolled in any of the following—

(a) the register of medical practitioners or the register of medical practitioners with limited registration;

(b) either of the registers of ophthalmic opticians or the register of dispensing opticians kept under the Opticians Act 1989 or either of the lists kept under section 9 of that Act of bodies corporate carrying on business as ophthalmic opticians or as dispensing opticians;

(c)[the register kept under the Health Professions Order 2001][148] ;

[(ca) the register of osteopaths maintained in accordance with the provisions of the Osteopaths Act 1993[149]][150]

[(cb) the register of chiropractors maintained in accordance with the provisions of the Chiropractors Act 1994;][151]

(d)[the register of qualified nurses and midwives maintained under article 5 of the Nursing and Midwifery Order 2001][152];

(e) the register of dispensers of hearing aids or the register of persons employing such dispensers maintained under section 2 of the Hearing Aid Council Act 1968.

2 The supply of any services or dental prostheses by—

(a) a person registered in the dentists' register;

(b) a person enrolled in any roll of dental auxiliaries having effect under section 45 of the Dentists Act 1984; or

(c) a dental technician.

3 The supply of any services by a person registered in the register of pharmaceutical chemists kept under the Pharmacy Act 1954 or the Pharmacy (Northern Ireland) Order 1976.

4 The provision of care or medical or surgical treatment and, in connection with it, the supply of any goods, in any hospital [or state-regulated institution][153] .

5 The provision of a deputy for a person registered in the register of medical practitioners or the register of medical practitioners with limited registration.

6 Human blood.

7 Products for therapeutic purposes, derived from human blood.

8 Human (including foetal) organs or tissue for diagnostic or therapeutic purposes or medical research.

[9 The supply by—

(a) a charity,

(b) a state-regulated private welfare institution, or

(c) a public body,

of welfare services and of goods supplied in connection with those welfare services.][154]

10 The supply, otherwise than for profit, of goods and services incidental to the provision of spiritual welfare by a religious community to a resident member of that community in return for a subscription or other consideration paid as a condition of membership.

11 The supply of transport services for sick or injured persons in vehicles specially designed for that purpose.

Notes:

(1) Item 1 does not include the letting on hire of goods except where the letting is in connection with a supply of other services comprised in the item.

(2) Paragraphs (a) to (d) of item 1 and paragraphs (a) and (b) of item 2 include supplies of services made by a person who is not registered or enrolled in any of the registers or rolls specified in those paragraphs where the services are wholly performed or directly supervised by a person who is so registered or enrolled.

[(2A) Item 3 includes supplies of services made by a person who is not registered in either of the registers specified in that item where the services are wholly performed by a person who is so registered.][155]

(3) Item 3 does not include the letting on hire of goods.

(4) For the purposes of this Group a person who is not registered in the visiting EEC practitioners list in the register of medical practitioners at the time he performs services in an urgent case as mentioned in subsection (3) of section 18 of the Medical Act 1983 is to be treated as being registered in that list where he is entitled to be registered in accordance with that section.

(5) In item 9 "public body" means—

(a) a Government department within the meaning of section 41(6);

(b) a local authority;

(c) a body which acts under any enactment or instrument for public purposes and not for its own profit and which performs functions similar to those of a Government department or local authority.

[(6) In item 9 "welfare services" means services which are directly connected with—

(a) the provision of care, treatment or instruction designed to promote the physical or mental welfare of elderly, sick, distressed or disabled persons,

(b) the care or protection of children and young persons, or

(c) the provision of spiritual welfare by a religious institution as part of a course of instruction or a retreat, not being a course or a retreat designed primarily to provide recreation or a holiday,

and, in the case of services supplied by a state-regulated private welfare institution, includes only those services in respect of which the institution is so regulated.][156]

(7) Item 9 does not include the supply of accommodation or catering except where it is ancillary to the provision of care, treatment or instruction.

[(8) In this Group "state-regulated" means approved, licensed, registered or exempted from registration by any Minister or other authority pursuant to a provision of a public general Act, other than a provision that is capable of being brought into effect at different times in relation to different local authority areas.

Here "Act" means—

(a) an Act of Parliament;

(b) an Act of the Scottish Parliament;

(c) an Act of the Northern Ireland Assembly;

(d) an Order in Council under Schedule 1 to the Northern Ireland Act 1974[157];

(e) a Measure of the Northern Ireland Assembly established under section 1 of the Northern Ireland Assembly Act 1973[158];

(f) an Order in Council under section 1(3) of the Northern Ireland (Temporary Provisions) Act 1972[159];

(g) an Act of the Parliament of Northern Ireland.][160]

Group 8— Burial and cremation

Item No.

1 The disposal of the remains of the dead.

2 The making of arrangements for or in connection with the disposal of the remains of the dead.

[Group 9— SUBSCRIPTIONS TO TRADE UNIONS, PROFESSIONAL AND OTHER PUBLIC INTEREST BODIES][161]

Item No.

1 The supply to its members of such services and, in connection with those services, of such goods as are both referable only to its aims and available without payment other than a membership subscription by any of the following non-profit-making organisations—

(a) a trade union or other organisation of persons having as its main object the negotiation on behalf of its members of the terms and conditions of their employment;

(b) a professional association, membership of which is wholly or mainly restricted to individuals who have or are seeking a qualification appropriate to the practice of the profession concerned;

(c) an association, the primary purpose of which is the advancement of a particular branch of knowledge, or the fostering of professional expertise, connected with the past or present professions or employments of its members;

(d) an association, the primary purpose of which is to make representations to the Government on legislation and other public matters which affect the business or professional interests of its members.

[(e) a body which has objects which are in the public domain and are of a political, religious, patriotic, philosophical, philanthropic or civic nature.][162]

Note:

(1) Item 1 does not include any right of admission to any premises, event or performance, to which non-members are admitted for a consideration.

(2) "Trade union" has the meaning assigned to it by section 1 of the Trade Union and Labour Relations (Consolidation) Act 1992.

(3) Item 1 shall include organisations and associations the membership of which consists wholly or mainly of constituent or affiliated associations which as individual associations would be comprised in the item; and "member" shall be construed as including such an association and "membership subscription" shall include an affiliation fee or similar levy.

(4) Paragraph (c) does not apply unless the association restricts its membership wholly or mainly to individuals whose present or previous professions or employments are directly connected with the purposes of the association.

(5) Paragraph (d) does not apply unless the association restricts its membership wholly or mainly to individuals or corporate bodies whose business or professional interests are directly connected with the purposes of the association.

Group 10— Sport, sports competitions and physical education

Item No.

1 The grant of a right to enter a competition in sport or physical recreation where the consideration for the grant consists in money which is to be allocated wholly towards the provision of a prize or prizes awarded in that competition.

2 The grant, by [an eligible body][163] established for the purposes of sport or physical recreation, of a right to enter a competition in such an activity.

3 The supply by [an eligible body][164] to an individual, except, where the body operates a membership scheme, an individual who is not a member, of services closely linked with and essential to sport or physical education in which the individual is taking part.

Notes:

(1) Item 3 does not include the supply of any services by [an eligible body][165] of residential accommodation, catering or transport.

(2) An individual shall only be considered to be a member of [an eligible body][166] for the purpose of Item 3 where he is granted membership for a period of three months or more.

[(2A) Subject to Notes (2C) and (3), in this Group "eligible body" means [an eligible body][167] which–

(a) is precluded from distributing any profit it makes, or is allowed to distribute any such profit by means only of distributions to a non-profit making body;

(b) applies in accordance with Note (2B) any profits it makes from supplies of a description within Item 2 or 3; and

(c) is not subject to commercial influence.

(2B) For the purposes of Note (2A)(b) the application of profits made by any body from supplies of a description within Item 2 or 3 is in accordance with this Note only if those profits are applied for one or more of the following purposes, namely–

(a) the continuance or improvement of any facilities made available in or in connection with the making of the supplies of those descriptions made by that body;

(b) the purposes of a non-profit making body.

(2C) In determining whether the requirements of Note (2A) for being an eligible body are satisfied in the case of any body, there shall be disregarded any distribution of amounts representing unapplied or undistributed profits that falls to be made to the body's members on its winding-up or dissolution.][168]

(3) In Item 3 a "non-profit making body" does not include—

(a) a local authority;

(b) a Government department within the meaning of section 41(6); or

(c) a non-departmental public body which is listed in the 1993 edition of the publication prepared by the Office of Public Service and Science and known as Public Bodies.

[(4) For the purposes of this Group a body shall be taken, in relation to a sports supply, to be subject to

commercial influence if, and only if, there is a time in the relevant period when–

(a) a relevant supply was made to that body by a person associated with it at that time;

(b) an emolument was paid by that body to such a person;

(c) an agreement existed for either or both of the following to take place after the end of that period, namely–

(i) the making of a relevant supply to that body by such a person; or

(ii) the payment by that body to such a person of any emoluments.

(5) In this Group "the relevant period", in relation to a sports supply, means–

(a) where that supply is one made before 1st January 2003, the period beginning with 14th January 1999 and ending with the making of that sports supply; and

(b) where that supply is one made on or after 1st January 2003, the period of three years ending with the making of that sports supply.

(6) Subject to Note (7), in this Group "relevant supply", in relation to any body, means a supply falling within any of the following paragraphs–

(a) the grant of any interest in or right over land which at any time in the relevant period was or was expected to become sports land;

(b) the grant of any licence to occupy any land which at any such time was or was expected to become sports land;

(c) the grant, in the case of land in Scotland, of any personal right to call for or be granted any such interest or right as is mentioned in paragraph (a) above;

(d) a supply arising from a grant falling within paragraph (a), (b) or (c) above, other than a grant made before 1st April 1996;

(e) the supply of any services consisting in the management or administration of any facilities provided by that body;

(f) the supply of any goods or services for a consideration in excess of what would have been agreed between parties entering into a commercial transaction at arm's length.

(7) A supply which has been, or is to be or may be, made by any person shall not be taken, in relation to a sports supply made by any body, to be a relevant supply for the purposes of this Group if–

(a) the principal purpose of that body is confined, at the time when the sports supply is made, to the provision for employees of that person of facilities for use for or in connection with sport or physical recreation, or both;

(b) the supply in question is one made by a charity or local authority or one which (if it is made) will be made by a person who is a charity or local authority at the time when the sports supply is made;

(c) the supply in question is a grant falling within Note (6)(a) to (c) which has been made, or (if it is made) will be made, for a nominal consideration;

(d) the supply in question is one arising from such a grant as is mentioned in paragraph (c) above and is not itself a supply the consideration for which was, or will or may be, more than a nominal consideration; or

(e) the supply in question–

(i) is a grant falling within Note (6)(a) to (c) which is made for no consideration; but

(ii) falls to be treated as a supply of goods or services, or (if it is made) will fall to be so treated, by reason only of the application, in accordance with paragraph 9 of Schedule 4, of paragraph 5 of that Schedule.

(8) Subject to Note (10), a person shall be taken, for the purposes of this Group, to have been associated with a body at any of the following times, that is to say–

(a) the time when a supply was made to that body by that person;

(b) the time when an emolument was paid by that body to that person; or

(c) the time when an agreement was in existence for the making of a relevant supply or the payment of emoluments,

if, at that time, or at another time (whether before or after that time) in the relevant period, that person was an officer or shadow officer of that body or an intermediary for supplies to that body.

(9) Subject to Note (10), a person shall also be taken, for the purposes of this Group, to have been associated with a body at a time mentioned in paragraph (a), (b) or (c) of Note (8) if, at that time, he

was connected with another person who in accordance with that Note–

(a) is to be taken to have been so associated at that time; or

(b) would be taken to have been so associated were that time the time of a supply by the other person to that body.

(10) Subject to Note (11), a person shall not be taken for the purposes of this Group to have been associated with a body at a time mentioned in paragraph (a), (b) or (c) of Note (8) if the only times in the relevant period when that person or the person connected with him was an officer or shadow officer of the body are times before 1st January 2000.

(11) Note (10) does not apply where (but for that Note) the body would be treated as subject to commercial influence at any time in the relevant period by virtue of–

(a) the existence of any agreement entered into on or after 14th January 1999 and before 1st January 2000; or

(b) anything done in pursuance of any such agreement.

(12) For the purposes of this Group a person shall be taken, in relation to a sports supply, to have been at all times in the relevant period an intermediary for supplies to the body making that supply if–

(a) at any time in that period either a supply was made to him by another person or an agreement for the making of a supply to him by another was in existence; and

(b) the circumstances were such that, if–

(i) that body had been the person to whom the supply was made or (in the case of an agreement) the person to whom it was to be or might be made; and

(ii) Note (7) above were to be disregarded to the extent (if at all) that it would prevent the supply from being a relevant supply, the body would have fallen to be regarded in relation to the sports supply as subject to commercial influence.

(13) In determining for the purposes of Note (12) or this Note whether there are such circumstances as are mentioned in paragraph (b) of that Note in the case of any supply, that Note and this Note shall be applied first for determining whether the person by whom the supply was made, or was to be or might be made, was himself an intermediary for supplies to the body in question, and so on through any number of other supplies or agreements.

(14) In determining for the purposes of this Group whether a supply made by any person was made by an intermediary for supplies to a body, it shall be immaterial that the supply by that person was made before the making of the supply or agreement by reference to which that person falls to be regarded as such an intermediary.

(15) Without prejudice to the generality of subsection (1AA) of section 43, for the purpose of determining–

(a) whether a relevant supply has at any time been made to any person;

(b) whether there has at any time been an agreement for the making of a relevant supply to any person; and

(c) whether a person falls to be treated as an intermediary for the supplies to any body by reference to supplies that have been, were to be or might have been made to him,

references in the preceding Notes to a supply shall be deemed to include references to a supply falling for other purposes to be disregarded in accordance with section 43(1)(a).

(16) In this Group–

"agreement" includes any arrangement or understanding (whether or not legally enforceable);

"emolument" means any emolument (within the meaning of the Income Tax Acts) the amount of which falls or may fall, in accordance with the agreement under which it is payable, to be determined or varied wholly or partly by reference–

(i) to the profits from some or all of the activities of the body paying the emolument; or

(ii) to the level of that body's gross income from some or all of its activities;

"employees", in relation to a person, includes retired employees of that person;

"grant" includes an assignment or surrender;

"officer", in relation to a body, includes–

(i) a director of a body corporate; and

(ii) any committee member or trustee concerned in the general control and management of the administration of the body;

"shadow officer", in relation to a body, means a person in accordance with whose directions or instructions the members or officers of the body are accustomed to act;

"sports land", in relation to any body, means any land used or held for use for or in connection with the provision by that body of facilities for use for or in connection with sport or physical recreation, or both;

"sports supply" means a supply which, if made by an eligible body, would fall within Item 2 or 3.

(17) For the purposes of this Group any question whether a person is connected with another shall be determined in accordance with section 839 of the Taxes Act (connected persons)[169].][170]

Group 11— Works of art etc

Item No.

1 The disposal of an object with respect to which estate duty is not chargeable by virtue of section 30(3) of the Finance Act 1953, section 34(1) of the Finance Act 1956 or the proviso to section 40(2) of the Finance Act 1930.

[GROUP 12—FUND-RAISING EVENTS BY CHARITIES AND OTHER QUALIFYING BODIES][171]

Item No.

1 The supply of goods and services by a charity in connection with an event—

(a) that is organised for charitable purposes by a charity or jointly by more than one charity,

(b) whose primary purpose is the raising of money, and

(c) that is promoted as being primarily for the raising of money.

2 The supply of goods and services by a qualifying body in connection with an event—

(a) that is organised exclusively for the body's own benefit,

(b) whose primary purpose is the raising of money, and

(c) that is promoted as being primarily for the raising of money.

3 The supply of goods and services by a charity or a qualifying body in connection with an event—

(a) that is organised jointly by a charity, or two or more charities, and the qualifying body,

(b) that is so organised exclusively for charitable purposes or exclusively for the body's own benefit or exclusively for a combination of those purposes and that benefit,

(c) whose primary purpose is the raising of money, and

(d) that is promoted as being primarily for the raising of money.

Notes:

(1) For the purposes of this Group "event" includes an event accessed (wholly or partly) by means of electronic communications.

For this purpose "electronic communications" includes any communications by means of a telecommunications system (within the meaning of the Telecommunications Act 1984).

(2) For the purposes of this Group "charity" includes a body corporate that is wholly owned by a charity if—

(a) the body has agreed in writing (whether or not contained in a deed) to transfer its profits (from whatever source) to a charity, or

(b) the body's profits (from whatever source) are otherwise payable to a charity.

(3) For the purposes of this Group "qualifying body" means—

(a) any non-profit making organisation mentioned in item 1 of Group 9;

(b) any body that is an eligible body for the purposes of Group 10 and whose principal purpose is the provision of facilities for persons to take part in sport or physical education; or

(c) any body that is an eligible body for the purposes of item 2 of Group 13.

(4) Where in a financial year of a charity or qualifying body there are held at the same location more than 15 events involving the charity or body that are of the same kind, items 1 to 3 do not apply (or shall be treated as having not applied) to a supply in connection with any event involving the charity or body that is of that kind and is held in that financial year at that location.

(5) In determining whether the limit of 15 events mentioned in Note (4) has been exceeded in the case of events of any one kind held at the same location, disregard any event of that kind held at that location in a week during which the aggregate gross takings from events involving the charity or body that are of that kind and are held in that location do not exceed £1,000.

(6) In the case of a financial year that is longer or shorter than a year, Notes (4) and (5) have effect as if for "15" there were substituted the whole number nearest to the number obtained by—

(a) first multiplying the number of days in the financial year by 15, and

(b) then dividing the result by 365.

(7) For the purposes of Notes (4) and (5)—

(a) an event involves a charity if the event is organised by the charity or a connected charity;

(b) an event involves a qualifying body if the event is organised by the body.

[GROUP 13— CULTURAL SERVICES ETC

Item No.

1The supply by a public body of a right of admission to—

(a) a museum, gallery, art exhibition or zoo; or

(b) a theatrical, musical or choreographic performance of a cultural nature.

2 The supply by an eligible body of a right of admission to—

(a) a museum, gallery, art exhibition or zoo; or

(b) a theatrical, musical or choreographic performance of a cultural nature.

Notes:

(1) For the purposes of this Group "public body" means—

(a) a local authority;

(b) a government department within the meaning of section 41(6); or

(c) a non-departmental public body which is listed in the 1995 edition of the publication prepared by the Office of Public Service and known as "Public Bodies".

(2) For the purposes of item 2 "eligible body" means any body (other than a public body) which—

(a) is precluded from distributing, and does not distribute, any profit it makes;

(b) applies any profits made from supplies of a description falling within item 2 to the continuance or improvement of the facilities made available by means of the supplies; and

(c) is managed and administered on a voluntary basis by persons who have no direct or indirect financial interest in its activities.

(3) Item 1 does not include any supply the exemption of which would be likely to create distortions of competition such as to place a commercial enterprise carried on by a taxable person at a disadvantage.

(4) Item 1(b) includes the supply of a right of admission to a performance only if the performance is provided exclusively by one or more public bodies, one or more eligible bodies or any combination of public bodies and eligible bodies.][172]

Section 51.

SCHEDULE 10 - Buildings and land

Residential and charitable buildings: change of use etc

1(1) In this paragraph "relevant zero-rated supply" means a grant or other supply taking place on or after 1st April 1989 which—

(a) relates to a building intended for use solely for a relevant residential purpose or a relevant charitable purpose or part of such a building; and

(b) is zero-rated, in whole or in part, by virtue of Group 5 of Schedule 8.

(2) Sub-paragraph (3) below applies where—

(a) one or more relevant zero-rated supplies relating to a building (or part of a building) have been made to any person,

(b) within the period of 10 years beginning with the day on which the building is completed, the person grants an interest in, right over or licence to occupy the building or any part of it (or the building or any part of it including, consisting of or forming part of the part to which the relevant zero-rated supply or supplies related), and

(c) after the grant the whole or any part of the building, or of the part to which the grant relates, (or the whole of the building or of the part to which the grant relates, or any part of it including, consisting of or forming part of the part to which the relevant zero-rated supply or supplies related) is not intended for use solely for a relevant residential purpose or a relevant charitable purpose.

(3) Where this sub-paragraph applies, to the extent that the grant relates to so much of the building as—

(a) by reason of its intended use gave rise to the relevant zero-rated supply or supplies; and

(b) is not intended for use solely for a relevant residential purpose or a relevant charitable purpose

after the grant,

it shall be taken to be a taxable supply in the course or furtherance of a business which is not zero-rated by virtue of Group 5 of Schedule 8 (if it would not otherwise be such a supply).

(4) Sub-paragraph (5) below applies where—

(a) one or more relevant zero-rated supplies relating to a building (or part of a building) have been made to any person; and

(b) within the period of 10 years beginning with the day on which the building is completed, the person uses the building or any part of it (or the building or any part of it including, consisting of or forming part of the part to which the relevant zero-rated supply or supplies related) for a purpose which is neither a relevant residential purpose nor a relevant charitable purpose.

(5) Where this sub-paragraph applies, his interest in, right over or licence to occupy so much of the building as—

(a) by reason of its intended use gave rise to the relevant zero-rated supply or supplies, and

(b) is used otherwise than for a relevant residential purpose or a relevant charitable purpose,

shall be treated for the purposes of this Act as supplied to him for the purpose of a business carried on by him and supplied by him in the course or furtherance of the business when he first uses it for a purpose which is neither a relevant residential purpose nor a relevant charitable purpose.

(6) Where sub-paragraph (5) applies—

(a) the supply shall be taken to be a taxable supply which is not zero-rated by virtue of Group 5 of Schedule 8 (if it would not otherwise be such a supply); and

[(b) the value of the supply shall be taken to be such amount as is obtained by using the formula—

$$A = \frac{(10 - B)}{10}$$

where—

A is the amount that yields an amount of VAT chargeable on it equal to the VAT which would have been chargeable on the relevant zero-rated supply (or, where there was more than one supply, the aggregate amount which would have been chargeable on them) had so much of the building as is mentioned in sub-paragraph (5) above not been intended for use solely for a relevant residential purpose or a relevant charitable purpose; and

B is the number of whole years since the day the building was completed for which the building or part concerned has been used for a relevant residential purpose or a relevant charitable purpose.][173]

Election to waive exemption

2(1) Subject to sub-paragraphs [(2), (3) and (3A)][174] and paragraph 3 below, where an election under this paragraph has effect in relation to any land, if and to the extent that any grant made in relation to it at a time when the election has effect by the person who made the election, or where that person is a body corporate by that person or a relevant associate, would (apart from this sub-paragraph) fall within Group 1 of Schedule 9, the grant shall not fall within that Group.

(2) Sub-paragraph (1) above shall not apply in relation to a grant if the grant is made in relation to—

(a) a building or part of a building intended for use as a dwelling or number of dwellings or solely for a relevant residential purpose; or

(b) a building or part of a building intended for use solely for a relevant charitable purpose, other than as an office.

[(c) a pitch for a residential caravan;

(d) facilities for the mooring of a residential houseboat.][175]

[(2A) Subject to the following provisions of this paragraph, where—

(a) an election has been made for the purposes of this paragraph in relation to any land, and

(b) a supply is made that would fall, but for sub-paragraph (2)(a) above, to be treated as excluded by virtue of that election from Group 1 of Schedule 9,

then, notwithstanding sub-paragraph (2)(a) above, that supply shall be treated as so excluded if the conditions in sub-paragraph (2B) below are satisfied.

(2B) The conditions mentioned in sub-paragraph (2A) above are—

(a) that an agreement in writing made, at or before the time of the grant, between—

(i) the person making the grant, and

(ii) the person to whom it is made,

declares that the election is to apply in relation to the grant; and

(b) that the person to whom the supply is made intends, at the time when it is made, to use the land for the purpose only of making a supply which is zero-rated by virtue of paragraph (b) of item 1 of Group 5 of Schedule 8.][176]

(3) Sub-paragraph (1) above shall not apply in relation to a grant if—

(a) the grant is made to a [relevant housing association][177] and the association has given to the grantor a certificate stating that the land is to be used (after any necessary demolition work) for the construction of a building or buildings intended for use as a dwelling or number of dwellings or solely for a relevant residential purpose; or

(b) the grant is made to an individual and the land is to be used for the construction, otherwise than in the course or furtherance of a business carried on by him, of a building intended for use by him as a dwelling.

[(3AA) Where an election has been made under this paragraph in relation to any land, a supply shall not be taken by virtue of that election to be a taxable supply if—

(a) the grant giving rise to the supply was made by a person ("the grantor") who was a developer of the land; and

(b) at the time of the grant [or at the time it was treated as made by virtue of sub-paragraph (3AAA) below][178], it was the intention or expectation of—

(i) the grantor, or

(ii) a person responsible for financing the grantor's development of the land for exempt use,

that the land would become exempt land (whether immediately or eventually and whether or not by virtue of the grant) or, as the case may be, would continue, for a period at least, to be such land.][179]

[(3AAA) For the purposes of sub-paragraph (3AA) above a grant (the original grant) in relation to land made on or after 19th March 1997 and before 10th March 1999 shall be treated as being made on 10th March 1999 if at the time of the original grant—

(a) the grantor or a person responsible for financing the grantor's development of the land for exempt use, intended or expected that the land or a building or part of a building on, or to be constructed on, that land would become an asset falling in relation to—

(i) the grantor, or

(ii) any person to whom that land, building or part of a building was to be transferred either in the course of a supply or in the course of a transfer of a business or part of a business as a going concern,

to be treated as a capital item for the purposes of any regulations made under section 26(3) and (4) providing for adjustments relating to the deduction of input tax to be made as respects that item, and

(b) the land or a building or part of a building on, or to be constructed on, that land had not become such an asset.][180]

(3A). . . . .

(4) Subject to the following provisions of this paragraph, no input tax on any supply or importation which, apart from this sub-paragraph, would be allowable by virtue of the operation of this paragraph shall be allowed if the supply or importation took place before the first day for which the election in question has effect.

(5) Subject to sub-paragraph (6) below, sub-paragraph (4) above shall not apply where the person by whom the election was made—

(a) has not, before the first day for which the election has effect, made in relation to the land in relation to which the election has effect any grant falling within Group 1 of Schedule 9; or

(b) has before that day made in relation to that land a grant or grants so falling but the grant, or all the grants—

(i) were made in the period beginning with 1st April 1989 and ending with 31st July 1989; and

(ii) would have been taxable supplies but for the amendments made by Schedule 3 to the Finance Act 1989.

(6) Sub-paragraph (5) above does not make allowable any input tax on supplies or importations taking place before 1st August 1989 unless—

(a) it is attributable by or under regulations to grants made by the person on or after 1st April 1989 which would have been taxable supplies but for the amendments made by Schedule 3 to the Finance Act 1989, and

(b) the election has effect from 1st August 1989.

(7) Sub-paragraph (4) above shall not apply in relation to input tax on grants or other supplies which are made in the period beginning with 1st April 1989 and ending with 31st July 1989 [if][181]—

(a) they would have been zero-rated by virtue of item 1 or 2 of Group 5 of Schedule 8 or exempt by virtue of item 1 of Group 1 of Schedule 9 but for the amendments made by Schedule 3 to the Finance Act 1989; and

(b) the election has effect from 1st August 1989.

(8) Sub-paragraph (4) above shall not apply in relation to any election having effect from any day on or after 1st January 1992, except in respect of the input tax on a supply or importation which took place before 1st August 1989.

(9) Where a person has made an exempt grant in relation to any land and has made an election in relation to that land which has effect from any day before 1st January 1992, he may apply to the Commissioners for sub-paragraph (4) above to be disapplied in respect of any input tax on a supply or importation which took place on or after 1st August 1989, but the Commissioners shall only permit the disapplication of that sub-paragraph if they are satisfied, having regard to all the circumstances of the case, and in particular to—

(a) the total value of—

(i) exempt grants made;

(ii) taxable grants made or expected to be made, in relation to the land; and

(b) the total amount of input tax in relation to the land which had been incurred before the day from which the election had effect,

that a fair and reasonable attribution of the input tax mentioned in paragraph (b) above will be secured.

Developers of certain non-residential buildings etc.

5[(1) Paragraph 6 below shall apply—

(a) on the first occasion during the period beginning with the day when the construction of a building or work within sub-paragraph (2) below is first planned and ending 10 years after the completion of the building or work on which a person who is a developer in relation to the building or work—

(i) grants an interest in, right over or licence to occupy the building or work (or any part of it) which is an exempt supply; or

(ii) is in occupation of the building, or uses the work (or any part of it) when not a fully taxable person (or, if a person treated under section 43 as a member of a group when the representative member is not a fully taxable person); or

(b) if construction commenced before 1st March 1995 and the period referred to in paragraph (a) above has not then expired, on 1st March 1997;

whichever is the earlier.][182]

(2) Subject to sub-paragraph (3) [and (3A)][183] below, the buildings and works within this sub-paragraph are—

(a) any building neither designed as a dwelling or number of dwellings nor intended for use solely for a relevant residential purpose or a relevant charitable purpose; and

(b) any civil engineering work, other than a work necessary for the development of a permanent park for residential caravans.

(3) A building or work is not within sub-paragraph (2) above if—

(a) construction of it was commenced before 1st August 1989 [or after 28th February 1995][184]; or

(b) a grant of the fee simple in it which falls within paragraph (a)(ii) or (iv) of item 1 of Group 1 of Schedule 9 has been made before the occasion concerned.

[(3A) A building or work which would, apart from this sub-paragraph, fall within sub-paragraph (2) above is not within that sub-paragraph if—

(a) construction of it was commenced before 1st March 1995 but had not been completed by that date; and

(b) the developer—

(i) makes no claim after that date to credit for input tax, entitlement to which is dependent upon his being treated in due course as having made a supply by virtue of paragraph 6 below; and

(ii) has made no such claim prior to that date; or

(iii) accounts to the Commissioners for a sum equal to any such credit that has previously been claimed.][185]

(4) For the purposes of this paragraph a taxable person is, in relation to any building or work, a fully taxable person throughout a prescribed accounting period if—

(a) at the end of that period he is entitled to credit for input tax on all supplies to, and [acquisitions and][186] importations by, him in the period (apart from any on which input tax is excluded from credit by virtue of section 25(7); or

(b) the building or work is not used by him at any time during the period in, or in connection with, making any exempt supplies of goods or services.

(5) Subject to sub-paragraph (6) below, in this paragraph and paragraph 6 below "developer", in relation to a building or work, means any person who—

(a) constructs it;

(b) order it to be constructed; or

(c) finances its construction,

with a view to granting an interest in, right over or licence to occupy it (or any part of it) or to occupying or using it (or any part of it) for his own purposes.

(6) Where—

(a) a body corporate treated under section 43 as a member of a group is a developer in relation to a building or work; and

(b) it grants an interest in, right over or licence to occupy the building or work (or any part of it) to another body corporate which is treated under that section as a member of the group,

then, for the purposes of this paragraph and paragraph 6 below, as from the time of the grant any body corporate such as is mentioned in sub-paragraph (7) below shall be treated as also being a developer in relation to the building or work.

(7) The bodies corporate referred to in sub-paragraph (6) above are any which under section 43—

(a) was treated as a member of the same group as the body corporate making the grant at the time of the grant; or

(b) has been so treated at any later time when the body corporate by which the grant was made had an interest in, right over or licence to occupy the building or work (or any part of it); or

(c) has been treated as a member of the same group as a body corporate within paragraph (a) or (b) above or this paragraph at a time when that body corporate had an interest in, right over or licence to occupy the building or work (or any part of it).

(8) Subject to sub-paragraph (10) below, [sub-paragraphs (1), (2) and (3A) to (7)][187] above shall apply in relation to any of the following reconstructions, enlargements or extensions—

(a) a reconstruction, enlargement or extension of an existing building which is commenced on or after 1st January 1992 [and before 1st March 1995][188] and—

(i) which is carried out wholly or partly on land (hereafter referred to as new building land) adjoining the curtilage of the existing building, or

(ii) as a result of which the gross external floor area of the reconstructed, enlarged or extended building (excluding any floor area on new building land) exceeds the gross external floor area of the existing building by not less than 20 per cent. of the gross external floor area of the existing building;

(b) a reconstruction of an existing building which is commenced on or after 1st January 1992 [and before 1st March 1995][189] and in the course of which at least 80 per cent. of the area of the floor structures of the existing building are removed;

(c) a reconstruction, enlargement or extension of a civil engineering work which is commenced on or after 1st January 1992 [and before 1st March 1995][190] and which is carried out wholly or partly on land (hereafter referred to as new land) adjoining the land on or in which the existing work is situated,

as if references to the building or work were references to the reconstructed, enlarged or extended building or work and as if references to construction were references to reconstruction,

enlargement or extension.

(9) For the purposes of sub-paragraph (8)(a) above, extensions to an existing building shall include the provision of any annex having internal access to the existing building.

(10) Sub-paragraphs (1) and (2) and [sub-paragraphs (3A) to (7)][191] above shall not apply to a reconstruction, enlargement or extension—

(a) falling within sub-paragraph (8)(a)(i) or (ii) or (c) above where the developer has held an interest in at least 75 per cent. of all of the land on which the reconstructed, enlarged or extended building or work stands, or is constructed, throughout the period of 10 years ending with the last day of the prescribed accounting period during which the reconstructed, enlarged or extended building or work becomes substantially ready for occupation or use; or

(b) to the extent that it falls within sub-paragraph (8)(a)(ii) above or falling within sub-paragraph (8)(b) above, where the interest in, right over or licence to occupy the building concerned (or any part of it) has already been treated as supplied to and by the developer under paragraph 6(1) below.

6(1) Where this paragraph applies the interest in, right over or licence to occupy the buildings or work (or any part of it) held by the developer shall be treated for the purposes of this Act as supplied to the developer for the purpose of a business carried on by him and supplied by him in the course or furtherance of the business on the last day of the prescribed accounting period during which it applies, or, if later, of the prescribed accounting period during which the building or work becomes substantially ready for occupation or use.

(2) The supply treated as made by sub-paragraph (1) above shall be taken to be a taxable supply and the value of the supply shall be the aggregate of—

(a) the value of grants relating to the land on which the building or work is constructed made or to be made to the developer, but excluding, in a case where construction of the building or work in question commenced before 1st January 1992, the value of any grants to be made for consideration in the form of rent the amount of which cannot be ascertained by the developer when the supply is treated as made, and in any other case excluding the value of any—

(i) grants made before the relevant day to the extent that consideration for such grants was in the form of rent, and to the extent that such rent was properly attributable to a building which has been demolished,

(ii) grants made before the relevant day in respect of a building which has been reconstructed, enlarged or extended so that the reconstruction, enlargement or extension falls within paragraph 5(8)(a)(ii) above, and does not fall also within paragraph 5(8)(b) above, to the extent that consideration for such grants was in the form of rent, and to the extent that such rent was properly attributable to the building as it existed before the commencement of the reconstruction, enlargement or extension,

(iii) grants made before the relevant day in respect of a building which has been so reconstructed that the reconstruction falls within paragraph 5(8)(b) above, to the extent that consideration for such grants was in the form of rent, and to the extent that such rent was properly attributable to the building before the reconstruction commenced,

(iv) grants falling within paragraph (b) of item 1 of Group 1 of Schedule 9, and

(b) the value of all the taxable supplies of goods and services, other than any that are zero-rated, made or to be made for or in connection with the construction of the building or work.

(3) Where the rate of VAT (the lower rate) chargeable on a supply (the construction supply) falling within sub-paragraph (2)(b) above, the value of which is included in the value of a supply (the self-supply) treated as made by sub-paragraph (1) above, is lower than the rate of VAT (the current rate) chargeable on that self-supply, then VAT on the self-supply shall be charged—

(a) on so much of its value as is comprised of the relevant part of the value of the construction supply, at the lower rate; and

(b) on the remainder of its value at the current rate.

(4) For the purposes of sub-paragraph (3)(a) above, the relevant part of the value of the construction supply means—

(a) where the construction supply is a supply of goods, the value of such of those goods as have actually been delivered by the supplier;

(b) where the construction supply is a supply of services, the value of such of those services as have actually been performed by the supplier,

on or before the last day upon which the lower rate is in force.

(5) Where the value of a supply which, apart from this sub-paragraph, would be treated as made by sub-paragraph (1) above would be less than £100,000, no supply shall be treated as made by that sub-paragraph.

(6) For the purposes of sub-paragraph (2)(a)(i) above, the relevant day is the day on which the demolition of the building in question commenced and, for the purposes of sub-paragraph (2)(a)(ii) and (iii) above, the relevant day is the day on which the reconstruction, enlargement or extension in question commenced.

(7) In the application of sub-paragraphs (1) to (6) above to a reconstruction, enlargement or extension to which sub-paragraphs (1) and (2) and [sub-paragraphs (3A) to (7)][192] of paragraph 5 above apply by virtue of paragraph 5(8) above—

(a) references to the building or work shall be construed as references to the reconstructed enlarged or extended building or work, and references to construction shall be construed as references to reconstruction, enlargement or extension;

(b) the reference in paragraph (a) of sub-paragraph (2) to the value of grants relating to the land on which the building or work is constructed shall be construed as a reference—

(i) in relation to a reconstruction, enlargement or extension of an existing building to the extent that it falls within paragraph 5(8)(a)(i) above and does not fall also within paragraph 5(8)(b) above, to the value of grants relating to the new building land;

(ii) in relation to a reconstruction, enlargement or extension of an existing building, to the extent that it falls within paragraph 5(8)(a)(ii) above and does not fall also within paragraph 5(8)(b) above, to the value of grants relating to the land on which the existing building stands multiplied by the appropriate fraction;

(iii) in relation to a reconstruction, enlargement or extension to a work falling within paragraph 5(8)(c) above, to the value of grants relating to the new land.

(8) For the purposes of sub-paragraph (7)(b)(ii) above the appropriate fraction shall be calculated by dividing the additional gross external floor area resulting from the reconstruction, enlargement or extension (excluding any floor area on new building land) by the gross external floor area of the reconstructed, enlarged or extended building (excluding any floor area on new building land).

[(9) Where this paragraph applies by virtue of paragraph 5(1)(b) above it shall have effect as if—

(a) in sub-paragraph (1)—

(i) the words "(or any part of it) " were omitted; and

(ii) for the words "the last day" to "ready for occupation or use" there were substituted " 1st March 1997 "][193]

7(1) Where a developer is a tenant, lessee or licensee and becomes liable to a charge to VAT under paragraph 6(1) above [(except where that paragraph applies by virtue of paragraph 5(1)(b))][194] in respect of his tenancy, lease or licence he shall notify forthwith in writing his landlord, lessor or licensor (as the case may be)—

(a) of the date from which the tenancy, lease or licence becomes a developmental tenancy, developmental lease or developmental licence for the purposes of paragraph (b) of item 1 of Group 1 of Schedule 9;

(b) in a case falling within paragraph 5(8)(a)(ii) above, of the appropriate fraction determined in accordance with paragraph 6(8) above.

(2) Where the appropriate fraction has been notified in accordance with sub-paragraph (1)(b) above, any supply made pursuant to the tenancy, lease or licence in question shall be treated as made pursuant to a developmental tenancy, developmental lease or developmental licence (a developmental supply) as if, and only to the extent that, the consideration for the developmental supply is for an amount equal to the whole of the consideration for the supply made pursuant to the tenancy, lease or licence, multiplied by the appropriate fraction.

[Part 2 Residential and Charitable Buildings: Change of Use etc

[Introductory

35(1) This Part of this Schedule applies where one or more relevant zero-rated supplies relating to a

building (or part of a building) have been made to a person ("P").

(2) In this Part of this Schedule--

"relevant zero-rated supply" means a grant or other supply which relates to a building (or part of a building) intended for use solely for--

(a) a relevant residential purpose, or

(b) a relevant charitable purpose,

and which, as a result of Group 5 of Schedule 8, is zero-rated (in whole or in part);

"relevant premises" means the building (or part of a building) in relation to which a relevant zero-rated supply has been made to P;

"relevant period", in relation to relevant premises, means 10 years beginning with the day on which the relevant premises are completed.

(3) Where P is a body corporate treated as a member of a group under sections 43A to 43D, any reference in this Part of this Schedule to P includes a reference to any member of that group.][195]

[Disposal of interest or change of use following relevant zero-rated supply

36 (1) Paragraph 37 applies on each occasion during the relevant period when--

(a) there is an increase in the proportion of the relevant premises falling within sub-paragraph (2) or (3), and

(b) as a result, the proportion of the relevant premises so falling ("R2") exceeds the maximum proportion of those premises so falling at any earlier time in the relevant period ("R1").

(2) The relevant premises fall (or part of the relevant premises falls) within this sub-paragraph if P has, since the beginning of the relevant period, disposed of P's entire interest in the relevant premises (or part).

(3) The relevant premises fall (or a part of the relevant premises falls) within this sub-paragraph if--

(a) those premises do not (or that part does not) fall within sub-paragraph (2), and

(b) those premises are (or that part is) being used for a purpose that is neither a relevant residential purpose nor a relevant charitable purpose.

(4) Sub-paragraph (5) applies where--

(a) only a proportion of the use of the relevant premises (or the use of a part of those premises) is for a relevant residential purpose or a relevant charitable purpose, and

(b) that use is not confined to a part of those premises (or of that part) which is used solely for a relevant residential purpose or a relevant charitable purpose.

(5) Where this sub-paragraph applies, sub-paragraph (3) applies as if--

(a) the same proportion of the relevant premises (or part) were being used for a relevant residential purpose or a relevant charitable purpose, and

(b) the remainder of the relevant premises (or part) were being used for a purpose that is neither a relevant residential purpose nor a relevant charitable purpose.

(6) Where P is a charity using the relevant premises (or a part of the relevant premises) as a village hall or similarly in providing social or recreational facilities for a local community the premises are (or the part is) treated as being used for a relevant charitable purpose whether or not any person in occupation is using the premises (or part) for a relevant charitable purpose.][196]

[Charge to VAT

37(1) Where this paragraph applies, P's interest, right or licence in the relevant premises held immediately prior to the time when the increase referred to in paragraph 36(1) occurs is treated for the purposes of this Part of this Schedule as--

(a) supplied to P for the purposes of a business which P carries on, and

(b) supplied by P in the course or furtherance of that business

immediately prior to the time of that increase.

(2) The supply is taken to be a taxable supply which is not zero-rated as a result of Group 5 of Schedule 8.

(3) The value of the supply is taken to be--

(*a*) in the case of the first deemed supply under this paragraph, the amount obtained by the formula-

$R2 \times Y \times ((120 - Z) / 120)$, and

(*b*) in the case of any subsequent deemed supply under this paragraph, the amount obtained by the formula-

(*R*2 - *R*1) × *Y* × ((120 - *Z*) / 120)

(4) For the purpose of sub-paragraph (3)--

(a) R1 and R2 have the meaning given by paragraph 36(1)(*b*),

(b) Y is the amount that yields an amount of VAT chargeable on it equal to--

(i) the VAT which would have been chargeable on the relevant zero-rated supply, or

(ii) if there was more than one supply, the aggregate amount of the VAT which would have been chargeable on the supplies,

had the relevant premises not been intended for use solely for a relevant residential purpose or a relevant charitable purpose, and

(c) Z is the number of whole months since the day on which the relevant premises were completed.][197]

[Supplies in relation to a building where part designed for residential or charitable use and part designed for other uses

38 Note (10) of Group 5 of Schedule 8 applies for the purposes of this Part of this Schedule.][198]

[Definitions

39 In this Part of this Schedule, references to the expressions listed in the first column are to be read in accordance with the provisions listed in the second column

Expression	*Provision*
completion of a building	Note (2) to Group 1 of Schedule 9
Grant	Note (1) to Group 5 of Schedule 8/ Notes (1) and (1A) to Group 1 of Schedule 9
use for a relevant charitable purpose	Notes (6) and (12) to Group 5 of Schedule 8
use for a relevant residential purpose	Notes (4), (5) and (12) to Group 5 of Schedule 8][199]

---

[1]S. 29A inserted (11.5.2001 with effect as mentioned in s. 99(7)(c) of the amending Act) by 2001 c. 9, s. 99(4)

[2] S. 30(2A) inserted (29.4.1996 with effect as mentioned in s. 29(5) of the amending Act) by 1996 c. 8, s. 29(2)(5)

[3] S. 30(5) substituted (1.5.1995 with effect as mentioned in s. 28(2) of the amending Act) by 1995 c. 4, s. 28(1)

[4] S. 30(8A) inserted (29.4.1996 for specified purposes and otherwise 1.6.1996 with application to any acquisition of goods from another member State and any supply taking place on or after 1.6.1996) by 1996 c. 8, ss. 25, 26, Sch. 3 para. 7; S.I. 1996/1249, art. 2

[5] Words in s. 30(10) substituted (1.6.1996 with application to any acquisition of goods from another member State and any su pply taking place on or after that day) by 1996 c. 8, ss. 25, 26, Sch. 3 para. 7; S.I. 1996/1249, art. 2

[6] Words in s. 30(10) substituted (1.6.1996 with application to any acquisition of goods from another member State and any su pply taking place on or after that day) by 1996 c. 8, ss. 25, 26, Sch. 3 para. 7; S.I. 1996/1249, art. 2

[7] S. 32 repealed (1.6.1995) by 1995 c. 4, ss. 24(2), 162, Sch. 29 Pt. VI(3) Note; S.I. 1995/1374, art. 2

[8] Words in s. 33(3)(h) substituted (1.1.1996) by 1995 c. 21, ss. 314(2), 316(2), Sch. 13 para. 95 (with s. 312(1))

[9] S. 33A inserted (11.5.2001 for specified purposes otherwise 1.9.2001) by 2001 c. 9, s. 98(2)(10)(11)

[10] S. 35(1)(1A)-(1D) substituted (29.4.1996 with application as mentioned in s. 30(4) of the amending Act) for s. 35(1) by 1996 c. 8, s. 30(1)

[11] Words in s. 35(2) inserted (29.4.1996 with application as mentioned in s. 30(4) of the amending Act) by 1996 c. 8, s. 30(2)

[12] Words in s. 35(4) inserted (1.8.2001) by S.I. 2001/2305, art. 4(a)

[13] S. 35(4)(5) inserted (29.4.1996 with application as mentioned in s. 30(4) of the amending Act) by 1996 c. 8, s. 30(3)

[14] S. 35(4A) inserted (1.8.2001) by S.I. 2001/2305, art. 4(b)

[15] Words in s. 36(1)(a) repealed (31.7.1998 with effect as mentioned in s. 23(7) of the amending Act) by 1998 c. 36, ss. 23(1)(7), 165, Sch. 27 Pt. II Note

[16] S. 36(3) substituted (27.7.1999 with effect as mentioned in s. 15(5) of the amending Act) by S.I. 1999 c. 16, s. 15(1)

[17] S. 36(3A) inserted (31.7.1998 with effect as mentioned in s. 23(7) of the amending Act) by 1998 c. 36, s. 23(3)(7)

[18] S. 36(4)(b) and word "and" immediately preceding it repealed (19.3.1997 with effect as mentioned in s. 39 of the amending Act) by 1997 c. 16, ss. 39, 113, Sch. 18 Pt. IV(3) Note

[19] S. 36(4A) repealed (with effect as mentioned in s. 22(3) of the amending Act) by Finance Act 2002 (c. 23), s. 22(2), Sch. 40 Pt. 2(1); S.I. 2002/3028, art. 2

[20] Words in s. 36(5)(c) substituted (31.7.1998) by 1998 c. 36, s. 23(4)(a)

[21] Words in s. 36(5)(e) substituted (27.7.1999 with effect as mentioned in s. 15(5) of the amending Act) by 1999 c. 16, s. 15(2)

[22] S. 36(5)(ea) repealed (with effect as mentioned in s. 22(3) of the amending Act) by Finance Act 2002 (c. 23), s. 22(2),

Sch. 40 Pt. 2(1); S.I. 2002/3028, art. 2

23 Words in s. 36(6)(b)(c) substituted (31.7.1998) by 1998 c. 36, s. 23(5)

24 Words in s. 36(6)(b)(c) substituted (31.7.1998) by 1998 c. 36, s. 23(5)

25 Words in s. 36(7) substituted (31.7.1998) by 1998 c. 36, s. 23(6)

26 Sch. 7A inserted (11.5.2001 with effect as mentioned in s. 99(7)(a) of the amending Act) by 2001 c. 9, s. 99(5)(7)(a), Sch. 31 Pt. 1 para. 1

27 Sch. 7A Pt. 2 Group 3 Item 8A, 8B inserted (1.6.2002) by The Value Added Tax (Reduced Rate) Order 2002 (S.I. 2002/1100), art. 3(a)

28 Words in Sch. 7A Pt. 2 Group 3 Note 1(1) substituted (1.6.2002) by The Value Added Tax (Reduced Rate) Order 2002 (S.I. 2002/1100), art. 3(b)

29 Words in Sch. 7A Pt. 2 Group 3 Note 4(d) substituted (1.6.2002) by The Value Added Tax (Reduced Rate) Order 2002 (S.I. 2002/1100), art. 3(c)

30 Sch. 7A Pt. 2 Group 3 Note 4A, 4B substituted (1.6.2002) by The Value Added Tax (Reduced Rate) Order 2002 (S.I. 2002/1100), art. 3(d)

31 Word in Sch. 7A Pt. 2 Group 6 Note 4(2)(a) omitted (1.6.2002) by virtue of The Value Added Tax (Reduced Rate) Order 2002 (S.I. 2002/1100), art. 4(a)(i)

32 Sch. 7A Pt. 2 Group 6 Note 4(2)(aa) inserted (1.6.2002) by The Value Added Tax (Reduced Rate) Order 2002 (S.I. 2002/1100), art. 4(a)(ii)

33 Sch. 7A Pt. 2 Group 6 Note 5(2)(a) substituted (1.6.2002) by The Value Added Tax (Reduced Rate) Order 2002 (S.I. 2002/1100), art. 4(b)

34 Sch. 7A Pt. 2 Group 6 Note 7(2) substituted (1.6.2002) by The Value Added Tax (Reduced Rate) Order 2002 (S.I. 2002/1100), art. 4(c)(i)

35 Sch. 7A Pt. 2 Group 6 Note 7(3) omitted (1.6.2002) by virtue of The Value Added Tax (Reduced Rate) Order 2002 (S.I. 2002/1100), art. 4(c)(ii)

36 Sch. 7A Pt. 2 Group 6 Note 7(4) omitted (1.6.2002) by virtue of The Value Added Tax (Reduced Rate) Order 2002 (S.I. 2002/1100), art. 4(c)(ii)

37 Sch. 7A Pt. 2 Group 6 Note 7(5) omitted (1.6.2002) by virtue of The Value Added Tax (Reduced Rate) Order 2002 (S.I. 2002/1100), art. 4(c)(ii)

38 Word in Sch. 7A Pt. 2 Group 6 Note 7(6) substituted (1.6.2002) by The Value Added Tax (Reduced Rate) Order 2002 (S.I. 2002/1100), art. 4(c)(iii)(a)

39 Words in Sch. 7A Pt. 2 Group 6 Note 7(6) inserted (1.6.2002) by The Value Added Tax (Reduced Rate) Order 2002 (S.I. 2002/1100), art. 4(c)(iii)(b)

40 Sch. 7A Pt. 2 Group 7 Title substituted (1.6.2002) by virtue of The Value Added Tax (Reduced Rate) Order 2002 (S.I. 2002/1100), art. 5(a)

41 Words in Sch. 7A Pt. 2 Group 7 Item 1 substituted (1.6.2002) by The Value Added Tax (Reduced Rate) Order 2002 (S.I. 2002/1100), art. 5(b)

42 Words in Sch. 7A Pt. 2 Group 7 Item 2 substituted (1.6.2002) by The Value Added Tax (Reduced Rate) Order 2002 (S.I. 2002/1100), art. 5(b)

43 Words in Sch. 7A Pt. 2 Group 7 Item 2(b) substituted (1.6.2002) by The Value Added Tax (Reduced Rate) Order 2002 (S.I. 2002/1100), art. 5(c)

44 Sch. 7A Pt. 2 Group 7 Note 2 substituted (1.6.2002) by The Value Added Tax (Reduced Rate) Order 2002 (S.I. 2002/1100), art. 5(d)

45 Words in Sch. 7A Pt. 2 Group 7 Note 3 heading substituted (1.6.2002) by The Value Added Tax (Reduced Rate) Order 2002 (S.I. 2002/1100), art. 5(e)(i)

46 Sch. 7A Pt. 2 Group 7 Note 3(1) substituted (1.6.2002) by The Value Added Tax (Reduced Rate) Order 2002 (S.I. 2002/1100), art. 5(e)(ii)

47 Sch. 7A Pt. 2 Group 7 Note 3(2) substituted (1.6.2002) by The Value Added Tax (Reduced Rate) Order 2002 (S.I. 2002/1100), art. 5(e)(iii)

48 Words in Sch. 7A Pt. 2 Group 7 Note 3(4)(b) substituted (1.6.2002) by The Value Added Tax (Reduced Rate) Order 2002 (S.I. 2002/1100), art. 5(e)(iv)

49 Sch 7A Pt. 2 Group 7 Note 3A inserted (1.6.2002) by The Value Added Tax (Reduced Rate) Order 2002 (S.I. 2002/1100), art. 5(f)

50 Sch. 7A Pt. 2 Group 7 Note 4A inserted (1.6.2002) by The Value Added Tax (Reduced Rate) Order 2002 (S.I. 2002/1100), art. 5(g)

51 Word in Sch. 7A Pt. 2 Group 7 Note 5 substituted (1.6.2002) by The Value Added Tax (Reduced Rate) Order 2002 (S.I. 2002/1100), art. 5(h)

52 Word in Sch. 7A Pt. 2 Group 7 Note 5 substituted (1.6.2002) by The Value Added Tax (Reduced Rate) Order 2002 (S.I. 2002/1100), art. 5(h)

53 Word in Sch. 7A Pt. 2 Group 7 Note 5 substituted (1.6.2002) by The Value Added Tax (Reduced Rate) Order 2002 (S.I. 2002/1100), art. 5(h)

54 Word in Sch. 7A Pt. 2 Group 7 Note 5 substituted (1.6.2002) by The Value Added Tax (Reduced Rate) Order 2002 (S.I.

2002/1100), art. 5(h)

[55] Word in Sch. 7A Pt. 2 Group 7 Note 5 substituted (1.6.2002) by The Value Added Tax (Reduced Rate) Order 2002 (S.I. 2002/1100), art. 5(h)

[56] Word in Sch. 7A Pt. 2 Group 7 Note 5 substituted (1.6.2002) by The Value Added Tax (Reduced Rate) Order 2002 (S.I. 2002/1100), art. 5(h)

[57] Word in Sch. 7A Pt. 2 Group 7 Note 5 substituted (1.6.2002) by The Value Added Tax (Reduced Rate) Order 2002 (S.I. 2002/1100), art. 5(h)

[58] Sch. 8 Pt. I: entry relating to "tax-free shops" deleted (1.7.1999) by S.I. 1999/1642, art. 2(a)

[59] Words in Sch. 8 Group 1(food) Note 6 substituted (retrospectively) by 1999 c. 16, s. 14

[60] Sch. 8 Group 5 substituted (1.3.1995) by S.I. 1995/280, arts. 1, 2

[61] Sch. 8 Group 5 substituted (1.3.1995) by S.I. 1995/280, arts. 1, 2

[62] Sch. 8 Group 5 substituted (1.3.1995) by S.I. 1995/280, arts. 1, 2

[63] Words in Sch. 8 Group 5 item 3 substituted (1.3.1997) by S.I. 1997/50, arts. 1, 2

[64] Sch. 8 Group 5 substituted (1.3.1995) by S.I. 1995/280, arts. 1, 2

[65] Sch. 8 Group 5 substituted (1.3.1995) by S.I. 1995/280, arts. 1, 2

[66] Sch. 8 Group 5 Notes (7)(7A) substituted for Sch. 8 Group 5 Note (7) (1.8.2001) by S.I. 2001/2305, arts. 2, 3

[67] Words in Sch. 8 Pt. 2 Group 5 Note (17) substituted (1.6.2002) by The Value Added Tax (Construction of Buildings) Order 2002 (S.I. 2002/1101), art. 2(a)

[68] Words in Sch. 8 Pt. 2 Group 5 Note (17)(a) substituted (1.6.2002) by The Value Added Tax (Construction of Buildings) Order 2002 (S.I. 2002/1101), art. 2(b)

[69] 1996 c.52.

[70] 1985 c.69.

[71] S.I. 1992/1725 (N.I.15)

[72] Sch. 8 Group 5 Note (21) substituted (1.3.1997) by S.I. 1997/50, arts. 1, 2

[73] Sch. 8 Group 5 substituted (1.3.1995) by S.I. 1995/280, arts. 1, 2

[74] Sch. 8 Group 6 substituted (1.3.1995) by S.I. 1995/283, arts. 1, 2

[75] Sch. 8 Group 6 substituted (1.3.1995) by S.I. 1995/283, arts. 1, 2

[76] Sch. 8 Group 6 substituted (1.3.1995) by S.I. 1995/283, arts. 1, 2

[77] Sch. 8 Group 6 substituted (1.3.1995) by S.I. 1995/283, arts. 1, 2

[78] 1990 c. 9

[79] Words in Sch. 8 Group 6 Note (1)(a)(ii) substituted (27.5.1997) by 1997 c. 11, ss. 4, 6(2), Sch. 2 para. 57(a)

[80] S.I. 1991/1220 (N.I.11).

[81] Words in Sch. 8 Group 6 Note (1)(b)(ii) substituted (N.I.) (29.8.1995) by S.I. 1995/1625 (N.I. 9), arts. 1(2), 45(1), Sch. 3 para. 4(1)

[82] Sch. 8 Group 6 Note (4)(c): by S.I. 1995/1625 (N.I. 9), arts. 1(2), 45(1), Sch. 3 para. 4(2)(b) it is provided that Sch. 8 Group 6 Note (4)(c)(v) and the word preceding it shall be inserted (N.I.) (29.8.1995)

Sch. 8 Group 6 Note (4)(c): by S.I. 1995/1625 (N.I. 9), arts. 1(2), 45(2), Sch. 4 it is provided that the word "or" at the end of Sch. 8 Group 6 Note (4)(c)(iii) shall be repealed (N.I.) (29.8.1995)

Words in Sch. 8 group 6 Note (4)(c)(ii): by 1997 c. 11, Sch. 2 para. 57(b) it is provided that for "Part IV of the Town and Country Planning (Scotland) Act 1972" there be substituted "Part I of the Planning (Listed Buildings and Conservation Areas) (Scotland) Act 1997"

[83] Sch. 8 Group 6 Note (4)(b) repealed (N.I.) (29.8.1995) by S.I. 1995/1625 (N.I. 9), arts. 1(2), 45(1)(2), Sch. 3 para. 4(2)(a), Sch. 4

[84] Sch. 8 Group 6 substituted (1.3.1995) by S.I. 1995/283, arts. 1, 2

[85] Words in Sch. 8 group 12 item 1 substituted (1.1.1998) by S.I. 1997/2744, art. 3

[86] Word in Sch. 8 group 12 item 1A inserted (1.1.1998) by S.I. 1998/2744, art. 4

[87] S.I. 1992/662.

[88] S.I. 1995/416.

[89] Words in Sch. 8 group 12 item 1A substituted (1.1.1998) by S.I. 1998/2744, art. 4

[90] Sch. 8 group 12 item 1A inserted (1.5.1995) by S.I. 1995/652, art. 3

[91] Word in Sch. 8 Group 12 item 2(f) substituted (1.4.2001 with effect as mentioned in art. 1 of the amending S.I.) by S.I. 2001/754, art. 2

[92] Sch. 8 Group 12 item 2A inserted (1.4.2001 with effect as mentioned in art. 1 of the amending S.I.) by S.I. 2001/754, art.3

[93] Word in Sch. 8 Group 12 item 5 inserted (1.4.2001 with effect as mentioned in art. 1 of the amending S.I.) by S.I. 2001/754, art. 4

[94] Sch. 8 Group 12 item 11 substituted (1.4.2000) by S.I. 2000/805, art. 3

[95] Words in Sch. 8 Group 12 Note (1) inserted (1.4.1995) by S.I. 1995/652, art. 4

[96] Sch. 8 Group 12 Note (2A) inserted (1.1.1998) by S.I. 1998/2744, art. 5

[97] Words in Sch. 8 Group 12 Note (4)(b) deleted (1.1.1998) by S.I. 1997/2744, arts. 1, 6

[98] Words in Sch. 8 Group 12 Note (5) inserted (1.4.1995) by S.I. 1995/652, art. 5

[99] Sch. 8 Group 12 Note (5): Words "and 2" deleted and words ", 2 and 2A" inserted (1.4.2001 with effect as mentioned in art. 1 of the amending S.I.) by S.I. 2001/754, art. 5

[100] Sch. 8 Pt. 2 Group 12 Note (5H)(a)(aa) substituted for Sch. 8 Pt. 2 Group 12 Note (5H)(a) (5.12.2002) by The Value Added Tax (Drugs, Medicines, Aids for the Handicapped and Charities Etc) Order 2002 (S.I. 2002/2813), art. 3

[101] 1990 c.19.

[102] 1978 c.29.

[103] 1977 c. 49; section 16A of the National Health Service Act 1977 was inserted by section 2(1) of the Health Act 1999 (c. 8).

[104] Sch. 8 Group 12 Note (5H)(ea) inserted (1.4.2000) by S.I. 2000/503, art. 3

[105] S.I. 1991/194 (N.I.1).

[106] Sch. 8 Group 12 Notes (5A)-(5I) inserted (1.1.1998) by S.I. 1997/2744, arts. 1, 7

[107] Sch. 8 Group 12 Notes (5J)(5K) inserted (1.4.2000) by S.I. 2000/805, art. 4

[108] Sch. 8 Group 12 Note (5L) inserted (1.4.2001 with effect as mentioned in art. 1 of the amending S.I.) by S.I. 2001/754, art. 6

[109] Words in Sch. 8 Pt. 2 Group 12 Note (6)(b) substituted (27.6.2002) by The Secretaries of State for Education and Skills and for Work and Pensions Order 2002 (S.I. 2002/1397), art. 12, Sch. para. 11

[110] Sch. 8 Group 15 items 1, 1A, 2 substituted for items 1, 2 (1.4.2000) by S.I. 2000/805, art. 6

[111] Sch. 8 Group 15 items 1, 1A, 2 substituted for items 1, 2 (1.4.2000) by S.I. 2000/805, art. 6

[112] Sch. 8 Group 15 items 1, 1A, 2 substituted for items 1, 2 (1.4.2000) by S.I. 2000/805, art. 6

[113] Sch. 8 Group 15 items 8-8C substituted for item 8 (1.4.2000) by S.I. 2000/805, art. 7

[114] 1992 c. 4.

[115] 1992 c. 7.

[116] 1995 c. 18; definition amended by paragraph 2(4)(a) of Schedule 7 to the Welfare Reform and Pensions Act 1999 (c. 30).

[117] S.I. 1995/2705 (N.I. 15); definition amended by the Welfare Reform and Pensions (Northern Ireland) Order 1999 (S.I. 1999/3147 (N.I. 11)).

[118] "working families' tax credit" substituted by section 1 of and Schedule 1 to the Tax Credits Act 1999 (c. 10).

[119] disabled person's tax credit" substituted by section 1 of and Schedule 1 to the Tax Credits Act 1999 (c. 10).

[120] Sch. 8 Group 15 Notes (1)-(1F) substituted for Note (1) (1.4.2000) by S.I. 2000/805, art. 8

[121] Sch. 8 Pt. 2 Group 15 Notes (4)(a)(aa) substituted (5.12.2002) for Note (4)(a) by The Value Added Tax (Drugs, Medicines, Aids for the Handicapped and Charities Etc) Order 2002 (S.I.2002/2813), art. 4

[122] Sch. 8 Group 15 Note (4)(j) added (1.4.2000) by S.I. 2000/503, art. 4

[123] Sch. 8 Group 15 Notes (4A)(4B) inserted (19.3.1997 with effect as mentioned in s. 34(3) of the amending Act) by S.I. 1997 c. 16, s. 34(1)(3)

[124] Sch. 8 Group 15 Note (5A)(5B) inserted (19.3.1997 with effect as mentioned in s. 34(3) of the amending Act) by S.I. 1997 c. 16, s. 34(2)(3)

[125] Sch. 8 Group 15 Notes (10A)-(10C) inserted (1.4.2000) by S.I. 2000/805, art. 9

[126] Sch. 9 Pt. I: entry inserted (1.12.1999) by S.I. 1999/2834, art. 3(b)

[127] Sch. 9 Pt. I: entry inserted (1.1.2000) by S.I. 1999/3116, art. 2(2)

[128] Sch. 9 Pt. I: entry inserted (1.3.2000) by S.I. 1999/2833, art. 2(2)

[129] Sch. 9 Pt. I: entry substituted (1.12.1999) by S.I. 1999/2834, art. 3(a)

[130] Sch. 9 Pt. II Group 1 Note (1) substituted (1.3.1995) by S.I. 1995/282, arts. 1, 3

[131] Sch. 9 Pt. II Group 1 Note (1A) inserted (1.3.1995) by S.I. 1995/282, arts. 1, 4

[132] Words in Sch. 9 Pt. II Group 1 Note (3) substituted (1.3.1995) by S.I. 1995/282, arts. 1, 5

[133] Words in Sch. 9 Pt. II Group 1 Note (7) inserted (1.3.1995) by S.I. 1995/282, arts. 1, 6

[134] Words in Sch. 9 Pt. II Group 1 Note (11)(a) substituted (1.3.1995) by S.I. 1995/282, arts. 1, 7

[135] Words in Sch. 9 Group 6 item 3(b)(i) substituted (28.7.2000 for certain purposes otherwise 1.4.2001) by 2000 c. 21, s. 149, Sch. 9 para. 47(2); S.I. 2001/654, art. 2(2), Sch. Pt. II (with art. 3)

[136] Sch. 9 Group 6 item 5A inserted (28.7.2000 for certain purposes otherwise 1.4.2001) by 2000 c. 21, s. 149, Sch. 9 para. 47(3); S.I. 2001/654, art. 2(2), Sch. Pt. II (with art. 3)

[137] Words in Sch. 9 Group 6 Note (1)(a) substituted (1.11.1996) by 1996 c. 56, ss. 582(1), 583(2), Sch. 37 Pt. I para. 125(a)

[138] Words in Sch. 9 Group 6 Note (1)(a)(iii) substituted (1.9.1999) by 1998 c. 31, s. 140(1), Sch. 30 para. 51(a) (with ss. 138(9), 144(6)); S.I. 1999/2323, art. 2(1), Sch.

[139] Words in Sch. 9 Group 6 Note (1)(a)(iii) substituted (1.11.1996) by 1996 c. 56, ss. 582(1), 583(2), Sch. 37 Pt. I para. 125(b)

[140] Sch. 9 Group 6 Note (1)(a)(v) repealed (1.9.1999) by 1998 c. 31, s. 140(1)(3), Sch. 30 para. 51(b), Sch. 31 (with ss. 138(9), 144(6)); S.I. 1999/2323, art. 2(1), Sch.

[141] Sch. 9 Group 6 Note (1)(a)(vii) repealed (1.9.1999) by 1998 c. 31, s. 140(1)(3), Sch. 30 para. 51(b), Sch. 31 (with ss. 138(9), 144(6)); S.I. 1999/2323, art. 2(1), Sch.

[142] Sch. 9 Group 6 Note 1(c)(v) and preceding word inserted (1.4.1998) by S.I. 1997/ 1772 (N.I. 15), art. 25, Sch. 4; S.R. 1998/82, art. 2

[143] Sch. 9 Group 6 Note (1)(e) substituted (1.1.1995) by S.I. 1994/2969, arts. 1, 3

[144] Sch. 9 Group 6 Note (1)(f) substituted (1.1.1995) by S.I. 1994/2969, arts. 1, 4

[145] Words in Sch. 9 Group 6 Note (2) substituted (1.1.1995) by S.I. 1994/2969, arts. 1, 5

[146] Words in Sch. 9 Group 6 Note (3) substituted (1.1.1995) by S.I. 1994/2969, arts. 1, 6

[147] Sch. 9 Group 6 Note (5A) inserted (28.7.2000 for certain purposes otherwise 1.4.2001) by 2000 c. 21, s. 149, Sch. 9 para. 47(4); S.I. 2001/654, art. 2(2), Sch. Pt. II (with art. 3)

[148] Words in Sch. 9 Pt. II Group 7 item 1(c) substituted (coming into force in accordance with art. 1(2)(3) of the amending S.I.) by The Health Professions Order 2001 (S.I. 2002/254), art. 48, Sch. 4 para. 6 (with art. 3(19))

[149] 1993 c.21; this Act was amended by Schedule 2 to the Chiropractors Act 1994 (c.17).

[150] Sch. 9 Group 7 item 1(ca) inserted (12.6.1998) by S.I. 1998/1294, arts. 1, 2

[151] Sch. 9 Pt. II Group 7 item 1 (cb) inserted (29.6.1999) by S.I. 1999/1575, art. 2

[152] Sch. 9 Pt. II Group 7 item 1: words "the register of qualified nurses and midwives maintained under article 5 of the Nursing and Midwifery Order 2001" substituted for Sch. 9 Pt. II Group 7 item 1(d) (coming into force in accordance with art. 1(2)(3) of the amending S.I.) by virtue of The Nursing and Midwifery Order 2001 (S.I. 2002/253), art. 54, Sch. 5 para. 12 (with art. 3(18))

[153] Words in Sch. 9 Pt. 2 Group 7 Item 4 substituted (21.3.2002) by The Value Added Tax (Health and Welfare) Order 2002 (S.I. 2002/762), art. 3

[154] Sch. 9 Pt. 2 Group 7 Item 9 substituted (21.3.2002) by The Value Added Tax (Health and Welfare) Order 2002 (S.I. 2002/762), art. 4

[155] Sch. 9 group 7 Note (2A) inserted (1.1.1997) by S.I. 1996/2949, arts. 1, 2

[156] Sch. 9 Pt. 2 Group 7 Note (8) inserted (21.3.2002) by The Value Added Tax (Health and Welfare) Order 2002 (S.I. 2002/762), art. 6

[157] 1974 c. 28, repealed by section 100 of and Schedule 15 to the Northern Ireland Act 1998 (c. 47).

[158] 1973 c. 17, repealed by section 100 of and Schedule 15 to the Northern Ireland Act 1998 (c. 47).

[159] 1972 c. 22, repealed by section 100 of and Schedule 15 to the Northern Ireland Act 1998 (c. 47).

[160] Sch. 9 Pt. 2 Group 7 Note (6) substituted (21.3.2002) by The Value Added Tax (Health and Welfare) Order 2002 (S.I. 2002/762), art. 5

[161] Sch. 9 Pt. II Group 9: heading substituted (1.12.1999) by S.I. 1999/2834, art. 4(a)

[162] Sch. 9 Pt. II Group 9 Item 1(e) added (1.12.1999) by S.I. 1999/2834, art. 4(b)

[163] Words in Sch. 9 Pt. II Group 10 Item 2 substituted (1.1.2000) by S.I. 1999/1994, art. 3

[164] Words in Sch. 9 Pt. II Group 10 Item 3 substituted (1.1.2000) by S.I. 1999/1994, art. 3

[165] Words in Sch. 9 Group 10 Notes (1)-(3) substituted (1.1.2000) by S.I. 1999/1994, art. 3

[166] Words in Sch. 9 Group 10 Notes (1)-(3) substituted (1.1.2000) by S.I. 1999/1994, art. 3

[167] Words in Sch. 9 Group 10 Notes (1)-(3) substituted (1.1.2000) by S.I. 1999/1994, art. 3

[168] Sch. 9 Group 10 Notes (2A)(2B)(2C) inserted (1.1.2000) by S.I. 1999/1994, art. 4

[169] Section 96(1) of the Value Added Tax Act 1994 defines "the Taxes Act" to mean the Income and Corporation Taxes Act 1988 (c. 1).

[170] Sch. 9 Group 10 Notes (4)-(17) inserted (1.1.2000) by S.I. 1999/1994, art. 5

[171] Sch. 9 Group 12 items 1-3, Notes (1)-(11) substituted for Sch. 9 Group 12 items 1-2, Notes (1)-(3) (1.4.2000) by S.I. 2000/802, art. 3

[172] Sch. 9 Pt. II Group 13 inserted (1.6.1996) by S.I. 1996/1256, arts. 1, 2(b)

[173] Sch. 10 para. 1(6)(b) substituted (1.6.2002) by The Value Added Tax (Buildings and Land) Order 2002 (S.I. 2002/1102), art. 2

[174] Words in Sch. 10 para. 2(1) substituted (30.11.1994) by S.I. 1994/3013, arts. 1, 2(a)(i)

[175] Sch. 10 para. 2(c)(d) inserted (1.3.1995) by S.I. 1995/279, arts. 1, 3(a)

[176] Sch. 10 para. 2(2A)(2B) inserted (19.3.1997 with effect as mentioned in s. 36(2) of the amending Act) by 1997 c. 16, s. 36(1)(2)

[177] Words in Sch. 10 para. 2(3)(a) substituted (1.3.1997) by S.I. 1997/51, arts. 1, 2(a)

[178] Words in Sch. 10 para. 2(3AA)(b) inserted (10.3.1999) by S.I. 1999/593, art. 3

[179] Sch. 10 para. 2(3AA) inserted (19.3.1997 with effect as mentioned in s. 37(4)-(6) of the amending Act) by 1997 c. 16, s. 37(2)(4)(6)

[180] Sch. 10 para. 2(3AAA) inserted (10.3.1999) by S.I. 1999/593, art. 4

[181] Word in Sch. 10 para. 2(7) inserted (1.3.1995) by S.I. 1995/279, arts. 1, 3(b)

[182] Sch. 10 para. 5(1) substituted (1.3.1995) by S.I. 1995/279, arts. 1, 6(a)

[183] Words in Sch. 10 para. 5(2) inserted (1.3.1995) by S.I. 1995/279, arts. 1, 6(b)

[184] Words in Sch. 10 para. 5(3)(a) inserted (1.3.1995) by S.I. 1995/279, arts. 1, 6(c)

[185] Sch. 10 para. 5(3A) inserted (1.3.1995) by S.I. 1995/279, arts. 1, 6(d)

[186] Sch. 10 para. 5(4)(a) inserted (1.3.1995) by S.I. 1995/279, arts. 1, 6(e)

[187] Words in Sch. 10 para. 5(8) substituted (1.3.1995) by S.I. 1995/279, arts. 1, 6(f)(i)

[188] Words in Sch. 10 para. 5(8) inserted (1.3.1995) by S.I. 1995/279, arts. 1, 6(f)(ii)

[189] Words in Sch. 10 para. 5(8) inserted (1.3.1995) by S.I. 1995/279, arts. 1, 6(f)(ii)

[190] Words in Sch. 10 para. 5(8) inserted (1.3.1995) by S.I. 1995/279, arts. 1, 6(f)(ii)

[191] Words in Sch. 10 para. 5(10) substituted (1.3.1995) by S.I. 1995/279, arts. 1, 6(g)

[192] Words in Sch. 10 para. 6(7) substituted (1.3.1995) by S.I. 1995/279, arts. 1, 7(a)

[193] Sch. 10 para. 6(9) added (1.3.1995) by S.I. 1995/279, arts. 1, 7(b)

[194] Words in Sch. 10 para. 7 inserted (1.3.1995) by S.I. 1995/279, arts. 1, 8

[195] Paras 35-37 substituted by the VAT (Buildings and Land) Order, SI 2011/86 arts 4, 8 with effect in relation to buildings that are completed on or after 1 March 2011. Para 35 previously read as follows--

*"**Meaning of "relevant zero-rated supply"***

35 For the purposes of this Part of this Schedule a "relevant zero-rated supply" means a grant or other supply which—

(a) relates to a building (or part of a building) intended for use solely for a relevant residential purpose, or

(b) relates to a building (or part of a building) intended for use solely for a relevant charitable purpose,

and which, as a result of Group 5 of Schedule 8, is zero-rated (in whole or in part)."

[196] Paras 35-37 substituted by the VAT (Buildings and Land) Order, SI 2011/86 arts 4, 8 with effect in relation to buildings that are completed on or after 1 March 2011. Para 36 previously read as follows-

"Person to whom supply made grants interest etc in building and building not intended solely for relevant residential or charitable purpose

36(1) This paragraph applies if-

(a) one or more relevant zero-rated supplies relating to a building (or part of a building) have been made to a person, and

(b) conditions A and B are met.

(2) Condition A is that, within the period of 10 years beginning with the day on which the building is completed, the person grants an interest in, right over or licence to occupy-

(a) the building or any part of it, or

(b) the building or any part of it including, consisting of or forming part of the part to which the relevant zero-rated supply or supplies related.

(3) Condition B is that after the grant-

(a) the whole or any part of the building or of the part to which the grant relates, or

(b) the whole of the building or of the part to which the grant relates, or any part of it including, consisting of or forming part of the part to which the relevant zero-rated supply or supplies related,

is not intended for use solely for a relevant residential purpose or a relevant charitable purpose.

(4) So far as the grant relates to so much of the building as-

(a) by reason of its intended use gave rise to the relevant zero-rated supply or supplies, and

(b) is not intended for use solely for a relevant residential purpose or a relevant charitable purpose after the grant,

it is taken to be a taxable supply in the course or furtherance of a business which is not zero-rated as a result of Group 5 of Schedule 8."

[197] Paras 35-37 substituted by the VAT (Buildings and Land) Order, SI 2011/86 arts 4, 8 with effect in relation to buildings that are completed on or after 1 March 2011. Para 37 previously read as follows-

"Person to whom supply made uses building otherwise than for relevant residential or charitable purpose

37*(1) This paragraph applies if one or more relevant zero-rated supplies relating to a building (or part of a building) have been made to a person and, within the period of 10 years beginning with the day on which the building is completed, the person uses--*

(a) the building or any part of it, or

(b) the building or any part of it including, consisting of or forming part of the part to which the relevant zero-rated supply or supplies related,

for a purpose which is neither a relevant residential purpose nor a relevant charitable purpose.

(2) The person's interest in, right over or licence to occupy so much of the building as-

(a) by reason of its intended use gave rise to the relevant zero-rated supply or supplies, and

(b) is used otherwise than for a relevant residential purpose or a relevant charitable purpose,

is treated as follows.

(3) The interest, right or licence is treated for the purposes of this Act as-

(a) supplied to the person for the purposes of a business which the person carries on, and

(b) supplied by the person in the course or furtherance of the business when the person first uses it for a purpose which is neither a relevant residential purpose nor a relevant charitable purpose.

(4) The supply is taken to be a taxable supply which is not zero-rated as a result of Group 5 of Schedule 8.

(5) The value of the supply is taken to be the amount obtained by the formula--

$$A \times \left(\frac{10 - B}{10}\right)$$

(6) For the purposes of the formula, A is the amount that yields an amount of VAT chargeable on it equal to-

(a) the VAT which would have been chargeable on the relevant zero-rated supply, or

(b) if there was more than one supply, the aggregate amount of the VAT which would have been chargeable on the supplies,

had so much of the building not been intended for use solely for a relevant residential purpose or a relevant charitable

purpose.

(7) *For the purposes of the formula, B is the number of whole years since the day the building was completed for which the building or part concerned has been used for-*

(a) *a relevant residential purpose, or*

(b) *a relevant charitable purpose.".*

198 Schedule 10 substituted by the Value Added Tax (Buildings and Land) Order, SI 2008/1146, art 2 with effect in relation to supplies made on or after 1 June 2008, subject to savings in Sch 2 of the Order.

199 Schedule 10 substituted by the Value Added Tax (Buildings and Land) Order, SI 2008/1146, art 2 with effect in relation to supplies made on or after 1 June 2008, subject to savings in Sch 2 of the Order.

Education Act 1996

1996 CHAPTER 56

An Act to consolidate the Education Act 1944 and certain other enactments relating to education, with amendments to give effect to recommendations of the Law Commission.

[24th July 1996]

Part I General

Chapter I The statutory system of education

General

1 The stages of education.

(1) The statutory system of public education consists of three progressive stages: primary education, secondary education and further education.

(2) This Part—

(a) confers functions on the Secretary of State and local education authorities with respect to primary, secondary and further education;. . .[1]

(b). . . . .

(3) Part I of the Further and Higher Education Act 1992 [makes provision with respect to further education.][2].

(4) Apart from section 10 (general duty of Secretary of State), nothing in this Act confers any functions with respect to higher education.

2 Definition of primary, secondary and further education.

[(1) In this Act "primary education" means—

(a) full-time or part-time education suitable to the requirements of children who have attained the age of two but are under compulsory school age;

(b) full-time education suitable to the requirements of junior pupils of compulsory school age who have not attained the age of 10 years and six months; and

(c) full-time education suitable to the requirements of junior pupils who have attained the age of 10 years and six months and whom it is expedient to educate together with junior pupils within paragraph (b).][3]

(2) In this Act "secondary education" means—

(a) full-time education suitable to the requirements of pupils of compulsory school age who are either—

(i) senior pupils, or

(ii) junior pupils who have attained the age of 10 years and six months and whom it is expedient to educate together with senior pupils of compulsory school age; and

(b)(subject to subsection (5)) full-time education suitable to the requirements of pupils who are over compulsory school age but under the age of 19 which is provided at a school at which education within paragraph (a) is also provided.

[(2A) Education is also secondary education for the purposes of this Act (subject to subsection (5)) if it is provided by an institution which—

(a) is maintained by a local education authority [or is an Academy][4], and

(b) is principally concerned with the provision of full-time education suitable to the requirements of pupils who are over compulsory school age but under the age of 19.

(2B) Where—

(a) a person is in full-time education,

(b) he receives his education partly at a school and, by virtue of arrangements made by the school, partly at another institution [or any other establishment][5], and

(c) the education which he receives at the school would be secondary education if it was full-time education at the school,

the person's education, both at the school and at the other institution [or establishment][6], is secondary education for the purposes of this Act (subject to subsection (5)).][7]

(3) Subject to subsection (5), in this Act "further education" means—

(a) full-time and part-time education suitable to the requirements of persons who are over compulsory school age [...(including vocational, social, physical and recreational training)][8]..., and

(b) organised leisure-time occupation provided in connection with the provision of such education,

except that it does not include secondary education or (in accordance with subsection (7)) higher education.

(4) Accordingly, unless it is education within subsection (2)(b) [or (2A)][9], full-time education suitable to the requirements of persons over compulsory school age who have not attained the age of 19 is further education for the purposes of this Act and not secondary education.

(5) For the purposes of this Act education provided for persons who have attained the age of 19 is further education not secondary education; but where a person—

(a) has begun a particular course of secondary education before attaining the age of 18, and

(b) continues to attend that course,

the education does not cease to be secondary education by reason of his having attained the age of 19.

(6) In subsection (3)(b) "organised leisure-time occupation" means leisure-time occupation, in such organised cultural training and recreative activities as are suited to their requirements, for any persons over compulsory school age who are able and willing to profit by facilities provided for that purpose.

[(6A) In the context of the definitions of secondary education and further education, references in this section to education include vocational, social, physical and recreational training.][10]

(7) References in this section to education do not include references to higher education.

3 Definition of pupil etc.

(1) In this Act "pupil" means a person for whom education is being provided at a school, other than—

(a) a person who has attained the age of 19 for whom further education is being provided, or

(b) a person for whom part-time education suitable to the requirements of persons of any age over compulsory school age is being provided.

[and references to pupils in the context of the admission of pupils to, or the exclusion of pupils from, a school are references to persons who following their admission will be, or (as the case may be) before their exclusion were, pupils as defined by this subsection.][11]

[(1A) A person is not for the purposes of this Act to be treated as a pupil at a school merely because any education is provided for him at the school in the exercise of the powers conferred by section 27 of the Education Act 2002 (power of governing body of maintained school to provide community facilities etc.).][12]

(2) In this Act—

"junior pupil" means a child who has not attained the age of 12; and

"senior pupil" means a person who has attained the age of 12 but not the age of 19.

(3) The definition of "pupil" in [Subsections (1) and (1A) also apply][13](unless the context otherwise requires) for the purposes of any instrument made or having effect as if made under the Education Acts.

Educational institutions

4 Schools: general.

[(1) In this Act "school" means an educational institution which is outside the further education sector and the higher education sector and is an institution for providing—

(a) primary education,

(b) secondary education, or

(c) both primary and secondary education,

whether or not the institution also provides [...part-time education suitable to the requirements of junior pupils or][14] ... further education.][15]

(2) [Nothing in subsection (1) shall be taken to preclude the making of arrangements under section 19(1) (exceptional educational provision) under which part-time education is to be provided at a school; and for][16] the purposes of this Act an educational institution that would fall within subsection (1) but for the fact that it provides part-time rather than full-time education shall nevertheless be treated as a school if that part-time education is provided under arrangements made under section 19(1). . . .[17]

(3) For the purposes of this Act an institution is outside the further education sector if it is not—

(a) an institution conducted by a further education corporation established under section 15 or 16 of the Further and Higher Education Act 1992, or

(b) a designated institution for the purposes of Part I of that Act (defined in section 28(4) of that Act);

and references to institutions within that sector shall be construed accordingly.

(4) For the purposes of this Act an institution is outside the higher education sector if it is not—

(a) a university receiving financial support under section 65 of that Act,

(b) an institution conducted by a higher education corporation within the meaning of that Act, or

(c) a designated institution for the purposes of Part II of that Act (defined in section 72(3) of that Act);

and references to institutions within that sector shall be construed accordingly.

5 Primary schools, secondary schools and middle schools.

(1) In this Act "primary school" means (subject to regulations under subsection (4)) a school for providing primary education, whether or not it also provides [...part-time education suitable to the requirements of junior pupils or][18]... further education.

(2) In this Act "secondary school" means (subject to regulations under subsection (4)) a school for providing secondary education, whether or not it also provides further education.

(3) In this Act "middle school" means a school in respect of which proposals authorised by [section 28(4) of the School Standards and Framework Act 1998][19] are implemented (that is, a school providing full-time education suitable to the requirements of pupils who have attained a specified age below 10 years and six months and are under a specified age above 12 years).

(4) The Secretary of State shall make regulations for determining, or enabling him to determine, whether a middle school is to be treated for the purposes of this Act and the other enactments relating to education as a primary school or as a secondary school.

(5) The powers conferred by [section 28(4) of the School Standards and Framework Act 1998][20] and subsection (4) above are exercisable—

(a) notwithstanding anything in this Act (and in particular section 1); but

(b) without prejudice to the exercise of any other power conferred by this Act.

6 Nursery schools and special schools.

(1) A primary school is a nursery school if it is used [wholly or][21] mainly for the purpose of providing education for children who have attained the age of two but are under [compulsory school age][22].

(2) A school is a special school if it is specially organised, [and (in the case of a school which is not maintained by a local education authority) is for the time being approved, as mentioned in section 337.][23].

Compulsory education

7 Duty of parents to secure education of children of compulsory school age.

The parent of every child of compulsory school age shall cause him to receive efficient full-time education suitable—

(a) to his age, ability and aptitude, and

(b) to any special educational needs he may have,

either by regular attendance at school or otherwise.

8 Compulsory school age.

(1) Subsections (2) and (3) apply to determine for the purposes of any enactment whether a person is of compulsory school age.

[(2) A person begins to be of compulsory school age—

(a) when he attains the age of five, if he attains that age on a prescribed day, and

(b) otherwise at the beginning of the prescribed day next following his attaining that age.][24]

(3) A person ceases to be of compulsory school age at the end of the day which is the school leaving date for any calendar year—

(a) if he attains the age of 16 after that day but before the beginning of the school year next following,

(b) if he attains that age on that day, or

(c)(unless paragraph (a) applies) if that day is the school leaving date next following his attaining that age.

[(4) The Secretary of State may by order—

(a) provide that such days in the year as are specified in the order shall be, for each calendar year, prescribed days for the purposes of subsection (2);

(b) determine the day in any calendar year which is to be the school leaving date for that year.][25]

Education in accordance with parental wishes

9 Pupils to be educated in accordance with parents' wishes.

In exercising or performing all their respective powers and duties under the Education Acts, the Secretary of [State and local education authorities][26] shall have regard to the general principle that pupils are to be educated in accordance with the wishes of their parents, so far as that is compatible with the provision of efficient instruction and training and the avoidance of unreasonable public expenditure.

Chapter II Functions of the Secretary of State

10 General duty of Secretary of State.

The Secretary of State shall promote the education of the people of England and Wales.

11 Duty in the case of primary, secondary and further education.

(1) The Secretary of State shall exercise his powers in respect of those bodies in receipt of public funds which—

(a) carry responsibility for securing that the required provision for primary, secondary or further education is made—

(i) in schools, or

(ii) in institutions within the further education sector,

in or in any area of England or Wales, or

(b) conduct schools or institutions within the further education sector in England and Wales,

for the purpose of promoting primary, secondary and further education in England and Wales.

(2) The Secretary of State shall, in the case of his powers to regulate the provision made in schools and institutions within the further education sector in England and Wales, exercise his powers with a view to (among other things) improving standards, encouraging diversity and increasing opportunities for choice.

Chapter III Local education authorities

The authorities

12 Local education authorities and their areas.

(1) The local education authority for a county in England having a county council is the county council.

(2) The local education authority for a district in England which is not in a county having a county council is the district council.

(3) The local education authority for a London borough is the borough council.

(4) The local education authority for the City of London (which for the purposes of this Act shall be treated as including the Inner Temple and the Middle Temple) is the Common Council of the City of London (in their capacity as a local authority).

(5) As respects Wales—

(a) the local education authority for a county is the county council; and

(b) the local education authority for a county borough is the county borough council.

(6) Any reference in this Act to the area of a local education authority shall be construed in accordance with the preceding provisions of this section.

General functions

13 General responsibility for education.

(1) A local education authority shall (so far as their powers enable them to do so) contribute towards the spiritual, moral, mental and physical development of the community by securing that efficient primary education, [and secondary education][27] are available to meet the needs of the population of their area.

(2) The duty imposed by subsection (1) does not extend to matters in respect of which any duty is imposed on—

[(a) the Learning and Skills Council for England or the National Council for Education and Training for Wales, or

(b) the higher education funding councils established under section 62 of the Further and Higher Education Act 1992.][28]

[13A Duty to promote high standards in primary and secondary education.

(1) A local education authority shall ensure that their functions relating to the provision of education to which this section applies are (so far as they are capable of being so exercised) exercised by the authority with a view to promoting high standards.

(2) This section applies to education for—

(a) persons of compulsory school age (whether at school or otherwise); and

(b) persons of any age above or below that age who are registered as pupils at schools maintained by the authority;

and in subsection (1) "functions" means functions of whatever nature.][29]

14 Functions in respect of provision of primary and secondary schools.

(1) A local education authority shall secure that sufficient schools for providing—

(a) primary education, and

(b) education that is secondary education by virtue of section 2(2)(a),

are available for their area.

(2) The schools available for an area shall not be regarded as sufficient for the purposes of subsection (1) unless they are sufficient in number, character and equipment to provide for all pupils the opportunity of appropriate education.

(3) In subsection (2) "appropriate education" means education which offers such variety of instruction and training as may be desirable in view of—

(a) the pupils' different ages, abilities and aptitudes, and

(b) the different periods for which they may be expected to remain at school,

including practical instruction and training appropriate to their different needs.

(4) A local education authority is not by virtue of subsection (1)(a) under any duty in respect of children under [compulsory school age][30].

[(4A) A local education authority for an area in Wales may secure that regional schools for providing—

(a) primary education, and

(b) education that is secondary education by virtue of section 2(2)(a),

are available for Wales or any part of Wales that includes the area of the authority.

(4B) For this purpose a "regional school", in relation to a local education authority, is a school maintained by that authority which provides education to meet both—

(a) the needs of pupils with particular special educational needs in their area, and

(b) the needs of such pupils in the rest, or any other part, of Wales,

whether or not the institution also provides education suitable to the requirements of other pupils.][31]

(5)..............................[32]

(6) In exercising their functions under this section, a local education authority shall in particular have regard to—

(a) the need for securing that primary and secondary education are provided in separate schools;

(b) the need for securing that special educational provision is made for pupils who have special educational needs; and

(c) the expediency of securing the provision of boarding accommodation (in boarding schools or otherwise) for pupils for whom education as boarders is considered by their parents and the

authority to be desirable.

(7) The duty imposed by subsection (6)(a) does not apply in relation to middle schools or special schools.

15 Functions in respect of provision of further education.

................................[33]

[15A Functions in respect of full-time education for 16 to 18 year olds.

(1) A local education authority may secure the provision for their area of full-time [or part-time][34] education suitable to the requirements of persons over compulsory school age who have not attained the age of 19, including provision for persons from other areas.

[(1A) The power under subsection (1) to secure the provision of education includes power to secure the provision—

(a) of training, including vocational, social, physical and recreational training, and

(b) of organised leisure time occupation (within the meaning of section 2(6)) which is provided in connection with the provision of education or of training within paragraph (a).][35]

(2) Subsections (6) and (7) of section 14 shall apply in relation to functions under this section [in respect of secondary education] as they apply in relation to functions under that section.][36]

[(3) In exercising their functions under this section in respect of further education a local education authority shall in particular have regard to the needs of persons with learning difficulties (within the meaning of section 13(5) and (6) of the Learning and Skills Act 2000).

(4) A local education authority may do anything which appears to them to be necessary or expedient for the purposes of or in connection with the exercise of their functions under this section.][37]

[15B Functions in respect of education for persons over 19.

(1) A local education authority may secure the provision for their area of full-time or part-time education suitable to the requirements of persons who have attained the age of 19, including provision for persons from other areas.

(2) The power under subsection (1) to secure the provision of education includes power to secure the provision—

(a) of training, including vocational, social, physical and recreational training, and

(b) of organised leisure time occupation (within the meaning of section 2(6)) which is provided in connection with the provision of education or of training within paragraph (a).

(3) In exercising their functions under this section a local education authority shall in particular have regard to the needs of persons with learning difficulties (within the meaning of section 13(5) and (6) of the Learning and Skills Act 2000).

(4) A local education authority may do anything which appears to them to be necessary or expedient for the purposes of or in connection with the exercise of their functions under this section.

(5) This section does not apply to higher education.][38]

Establishment etc. of schools

16 Power to establish, maintain and assist primary and secondary schools.

(1) For the purpose of fulfilling their functions under this Act, a local education authority may—

(a) establish primary schools and secondary schools;

(b) maintain primary and secondary schools, whether established by them or not; and

(c) assist any primary or secondary school which is not maintained by them.

(2) A local education authority may under subsection (1) establish, maintain and assist schools outside as well as inside their area.

(3) A local education authority may not under subsection (1) establish a school to provide—

(a) part-time education suitable to the requirements of persons of any age over compulsory school age; or

(b) full-time education suitable to the requirements of persons who have attained the age of 19.

17 Powers in respect of nursery education.

(1) A local education authority may—

(a) establish nursery schools;

(b) maintain nursery schools established by them or by an authority which was a local education authority within the meaning of any enactment repealed by the Education Act 1944 or an earlier

Act; and

(c) assist any nursery school not so established.

(2) Section 14(4) does not affect a local education authority's power under section 16(1) to establish, maintain and assist schools at which education is provided both for children under [compulsory school age][39] and for older pupils (including schools at which there are nursery classes for children under [compulsory school age][40]).

Other arrangements for provision of education

18 Power to arrange provision of education at non-maintained schools.

A local education authority may make arrangements for the provision of primary and secondary education for pupils at schools not maintained by them or another local education authority.

19 Exceptional provision of education in pupil referral units or elsewhere.

(1) Each local education authority shall make arrangements for the provision of suitable. . . [41] education at school or otherwise than at school for those children of compulsory school age who, by reason of illness, exclusion from school or otherwise, may not for any period receive suitable education unless such arrangements are made for them.

(2) Any school established (whether before or after the commencement of this Act) and maintained by a local education authority which—

(a) is specially organised to provide education for such children, and

(b) is not a county school or a special school,

shall be known as a "pupil referral unit".

(3) A local education authority may secure the provision of boarding accommodation at any pupil referral unit.

(4) A local education authority may make arrangements for the provision of suitable . . . education otherwise than at school for those young persons who, by reason of illness, exclusion from school or otherwise, may not for any period receive suitable education unless such arrangements are made for them.

[(4A) In determining what arrangements to make under subsection (1) or (4) in the case of any child or young person a local education authority shall have regard to any guidance given from time to time by the Secretary of State.][42]

(5) Any child for whom education is provided otherwise than at school in pursuance of this section, and any young person for whom full-time education is so provided in pursuance of this section, shall be treated for the purposes of this Act as a pupil.

(6) In this section "suitable education", in relation to a child or young person, means efficient education suitable to his age, ability and aptitude and to any special educational needs he may have.

(7) Schedule 1 has effect in relation to pupil referral units.

Chapter IV The Funding Authorities

The Authorities

20. . . . .[43]

21. . . . .[44]

Functions

22. . . . .[45]

23. . . . .[46]

24. . . . .[47]

Supplemental

25. . . . .[48]

26. . . . .[49]

Chapter V Allocation of responsibility for education at school between LEA and funding authority

27. . . . .[50]

Chapter VI Supplemental

Allocation of functions

28. . . . .[51]

Provision of information

29 Provision of information by local education authorities.

(1) A local education authority shall—

(a) make such reports and returns to the Secretary of State, and

(b) give to the Secretary of State such information,

as he may require for the purpose of the exercise of his functions under this Act.

(2). . . . .[52]

(3) A local education authority shall—

(a) compile such information, and

(b) make such provision for conducting, or assisting the conduct of, research,

as may be required for the purpose of providing the Secretary of State. . .[53] , in such form and at such times as may be prescribed, with such information relating to the provision of primary or secondary education in the area of the local education authority as may be prescribed.

(4) The Secretary of State shall exercise his powers under subsection (3) so as to secure, in particular, the provision of information relating to the provision of education for children with special educational needs.

(5) A local education authority shall, at such time or times and in such manner as may be required by regulations, publish such information as may be so required with respect to their policy and arrangements in respect of any matter relating to primary or secondary education.

(6) Nothing in subsection (5) applies in relation to—

(a) nursery schools, or

(b) children who will be under [compulsory school age][54] at the time of their proposed admission.

30. . . . .[55]

Part II Schools maintained by local education authorities[56]

Chapter I Preliminary

31. . . . .[57]

32. . . . .[58]

33. . . . .[59]

34. . . . .[60]

Chapter II Establishment, alteration etc. of county and voluntary schools

County schools: establishment, alteration or change of site

35. . . . .[61]

36. . . . .[62]

37. . . . .[63]

38. . . . .[64]

39. . . . .[65]

40. . . . .[66]

Voluntary schools: establishment, alteration or change of site

41. . . . .[67]

42. . . . .[68]

43. . . . .[69]

44. . . . .[70]

45. . . . .[71]

46. . . . .[72]

47. . . . .[73]

Status of new voluntary school

48. . . . .[74]

Proposals for a middle school

49...............................[75]

Division of a single school into two or more schools

50...............................[76]

51...............................[77]

Change of status from controlled school to aided school

52...............................[78]

53...............................[79]

54...............................[80]

55...............................[81]

56...............................[82]

Change of status from aided or special agreement school to controlled or aided school

57...............................[83]

58...............................[84]

Chapter III Funding of voluntary schools

Obligations of governing bodies

59...............................[85]

Obligations of LEAs as regards new sites and buildings

60...............................[86]

61...............................[87]

62...............................[88]

Financial assistance for controlled schools

63...............................[89]

64...............................[90]

Financial assistance by Secretary of State for aided and special agreement schools

65...............................[91]

66...............................[92]

67...............................[93]

Assistance by LEAs for governing bodies of aided and special agreement schools

68...............................[94]

Assistance by LEAs for promoters of new voluntary schools

69...............................[95]

Miscellaneous and supplemental

70...............................[96]

71...............................[97]

72...............................[98]

73...............................[99]

74...............................[100]

75...............................[101]

Chapter IV Government of county, voluntary and maintained special schools

Instruments of government

76...............................[102]

77...............................[103]

Categories of governor

78...............................[104]

Governing bodies of county, controlled and maintained special schools

79...............................[105]

80...............................[106]

81...............................[107]

Chapter IV Establishing new grant-maintained schools

Proposals for establishment of new grant-maintained school

Approval and implementation of proposals

Supplementary

Chapter V Government, conduct etc. of grant-maintained schools

The governing instruments

Governors

Powers

Schools acquiring grant-maintained status: determination etc. of initial governors

New grant-maintained schools: determination etc. of initial governors

General and supplementary

Chapter VI Funding of grant-maintained schools

Grants: general

[245 Special purpose grants.

(1) Grant regulations may provide for the payment by the funding authority to the governing bodies of grant-maintained schools of grants (known as special purpose grants) in respect of expenditure, of any class or description specified in the regulations, incurred or to be incurred by the governing

bodies—

(a) for or in connection with educational purposes of any class or description so specified,

(b) in making any provision (whether of educational services or facilities or otherwise) of any class or description so specified which appears to the funding authority to be required for meeting any special needs of the population of the area served by the schools in question, or

(c) in respect of expenses of any class or description so specified, being expenses which it appears to the funding authority the governing bodies of such schools cannot reasonably be expected to meet from maintenance grant.

(2) Grant regulations may provide for special purpose grants to be payable—

(a) on a regular basis in respect of expenditure of a recurrent kind, or

(b) by reference to expenditure incurred or to be incurred on particular occasions or during any particular period.][247]

[246 Capital grants.

(1) Grant regulations may provide for the payment by the funding authority to the governing bodies of grant-maintained schools of grants (known as capital grants) in respect of expenditure of a capital nature, of any class or description specified in the regulations, incurred or to be incurred by the governing bodies.

(2) The descriptions of expenditure which are to be regarded for the purposes of capital grant as expenditure of a capital nature shall be such as may be determined by or in accordance with the regulations.

(3) Where the governing body of a grant-maintained school include sponsor governors, the funding authority shall, if directed to do so by the Secretary of State, pay capital grant of such amount as may be specified in the directions in respect of such expenditure falling within subsection (1) as is incurred, or to be incurred, by the governing body for such purposes as may be specified in the directions.

(4) Before giving a direction under subsection (3), the Secretary of State shall consult the funding authority.

(5) A direction under subsection (3) may not be given after the end of the period of twelve months beginning—

(a)(in the case of a governing body incorporated in pursuance of proposals for acquisition of grant-maintained status which include sponsor governors on the incorporation date) with that date,

(b)(in the case of a governing body incorporated in pursuance of proposals for the establishment of a new grant-maintained school which include sponsor governors on the date of implementation of the proposals) with that date, and

(c)(in any other case) with the date when the instrument of government naming a person as the sponsor of the school came into effect.][248]

[247 Imposition of requirements on governing body in receipt of grant.

(1) A governing body to whom any payments in respect of maintenance grant, capital grant or special purpose grant are made shall comply with such requirements of a kind mentioned in subsection (2) as the funding authority may from time to time impose.

(2) The kinds of requirements which may be imposed under subsection (1) are—

(a) requirements specified in grant regulations as requirements which may be imposed by the funding authority on governing bodies to whom such payments are made, and

(b) requirements determined in accordance with grant regulations by the funding authority.

(3) Requirements imposed under subsection (1)—

(a) may be imposed on or at any time after the making of any payment by reference to which they are imposed, and

(b) subject to subsection (4), may at any time be varied by the funding authority.

(4) The power of the funding authority to vary such a requirement—

(a) does not apply to a requirement of the kind mentioned in subsection (2)(a), or a requirement required to be imposed by the regulations (by virtue of subsection (9)) or by directions under section 24, unless the Secretary of State has consented to the variation, and

(b) is subject, in the case of a requirement of the kind mentioned in subsection (2)(b), to the provisions of the regulations relating to the determination of the requirements that may be

imposed in the case of payments in respect of the grant in question.

(5) Requirements imposed under subsection (1) may at any time be waived or removed by the funding authority with the consent of the Secretary of State.

(6) The requirements which may be specified in or authorised by grant regulations as requirements which may be imposed on governing bodies to whom payments are made in respect of special purpose grant or capital grant may, in particular, if any conditions specified in the requirements are satisfied, require the payment to the funding authority of the whole or any part of the following amount.

(7) That amount is—

(a) the amount of the payments made in respect of the grant, or

(b) so much of the value of any premises or equipment in respect of which the grant was paid as is determined in accordance with the requirements to be properly attributable to the payment of such grant,

whichever is the greater.

(8) No such requirement as is referred to in subsection (6) may be imposed where any payment is made in respect of capital grant if—

(a) the grant is made in respect of the provision, alteration or repair of premises for a school, and

(b) any freehold interest in the premises in respect of which the grant is made is, or is to be, held on trust for the purposes of the school.

(9) Grant regulations may require the funding authority to impose any such requirements as may be imposed under the preceding provisions of this section.][249]

[248 Grants: further provisions.

(1) The times at which, and the manner in which, payments are made in respect of—

(a) maintenance grant for a grant-maintained school in respect of any financial year,

(b) special purpose grant, and

(c) capital grant,

shall be such as may be determined from time to time by the funding authority.

(2) Payments in respect of maintenance grant for a school in respect of any financial year may be made, before any amount has been determined in accordance with grant regulations as the amount of such grant payable for that year in respect of the school, by reference to an estimate of the amount which will be so payable made by the funding authority.

(3) Where in respect of any financial year an over-payment of maintenance grant is made to the governing body of a school, a sum equal to the amount of that over-payment shall be recoverable from the governing body by the funding authority.

(4) Where a sum is payable by the governing body of a school to the funding authority—

(a) in respect of an over-payment of maintenance grant in respect of a financial year, or

(b) by way of repayment of special purpose grant or capital grant (whether by virtue of a requirement such as is mentioned in section 247(6) or otherwise),

the funding authority may (without prejudice to any other mode of recovery) recover the whole or any part of that sum by deducting it from any grant payable by them to the governing body.

(5) In this section references to an over-payment of maintenance grant in respect of a financial year are to any amount by which the aggregate amount of any payments in respect of maintenance grant made to the governing body of the school in question in respect of the year exceeds the amount finally determined in accordance with grant regulations as the amount of maintenance grant payable for that year in respect of the school.

(6) The funding authority shall exercise any power conferred on them by this section, by any of sections 216 and 244 to 247, or by paragraph 6 of Schedule 21 in such manner (if any) as may be specified in or determined in accordance with grant regulations.][250]

Grants: Wales (until establishment of the SFCW)

[249 Application of sections 250 to 254.

Before the Schools Funding Council for Wales begin to exercise their functions, sections 250 to 254 shall have effect in relation to grant-maintained schools in Wales in place of sections 244(1) and (3), 245(1), 246(1), 247 and 248.][251]

250. . . . .[252]

251. . . . .[253]

252. . . . .[254]

[253 Imposition of requirements on governing body in receipt of grant.

(1) A governing body to whom any payments in respect of maintenance grant or special purpose grants are made shall comply with such requirements of a kind mentioned in subsection (2) as the Secretary of State may from time to time impose.

(2) The kinds of requirements which may be imposed under subsection (1) are—

(a) requirements specified in grant regulations as requirements which may be imposed by the Secretary of State on governing bodies to whom such payments are made, and

(b) requirements determined in accordance with grant regulations by the Secretary of State.

(3) A governing body to whom any payments in respect of capital grant are made shall comply with such requirements determined by the Secretary of State as he may from time to time impose.

(4) Requirements imposed under subsection (1) or (3)—

(a) may be imposed on or at any time after the making of any payment by reference to which they are imposed, and

(b) may at any time be waived or removed or, subject to subsection (5), varied by the Secretary of State.

(5) The power of the Secretary of State to vary such a requirement—

(a) does not apply to a requirement of the kind mentioned in subsection (2)(a), and

(b) is subject, in the case of a requirement of the kind mentioned in subsection (2)(b), to the provisions of the regulations relating to the determination of the requirements that may be imposed in the case of payments in respect of the grants in question.

(6) The requirements—

(a) which may be specified in or authorised by grant regulations as requirements which may be imposed on governing bodies to whom payments are made in respect of special purpose grant, or

(b) which may be imposed by the Secretary of State on a governing body to whom payments in respect of capital grant are made,

may, in particular, if any conditions specified in the requirements are satisfied, require the payment to the Secretary of State of the whole or any part of the following amount.

(7) That amount is—

(a) the amount of the payments made in respect of the grant, or

(b) so much of the value of any premises or equipment in respect of which the grant was paid as is determined in accordance with the requirements to be properly attributable to the payment of such grant,

whichever is the greater.

(8) No such requirement as is referred to in subsection (6) may be imposed where any payment is made in respect of capital grant if—

(a) the grant is made in respect of the provision, alteration or repair of premises for a school, and

(b) any freehold interest in the premises in respect of which the grant is made is, or is to be, held on trust for the purposes of the school.][255]

[254 Grants: further provisions.

(1) The times at which, and the manner in which, payments are made in respect of—

(a) maintenance grant for a grant-maintained school in respect of any financial year,

(b) special purpose grants, and

(c) capital grants,

shall be such as may be determined from time to time by the Secretary of State.

(2) Payments in respect of maintenance grant for a school in respect of any financial year may be made, before any amount has been determined in accordance with grant regulations as the amount of such grant payable for that year in respect of the school, by reference to an estimate of the amount which will be so payable made by the Secretary of State.

(3) Where in respect of any financial year an over-payment of maintenance grant is made to the governing body of a school, a sum equal to the amount of that over-payment shall be recoverable from the governing body by the Secretary of State.

(4) Where a sum is payable by the governing body of a school to the Secretary of State—

(a) in respect of an over-payment of maintenance grant in respect of a financial year, or

(b) by way of repayment of special purpose grant or capital grant (whether by virtue of a requirement such as is mentioned in section 253(6) or otherwise),

the Secretary of State may (without prejudice to any other mode of recovery) recover the whole or any part of that sum by deducting it from any grant payable by him to the governing body.

(5) In this section references to an over-payment of maintenance grant in respect of a financial year are to any amount by which the aggregate amount of any payments in respect of maintenance grant made to the governing body of the school in question in respect of the year exceeds the amount finally determined in accordance with grant regulations as the amount of maintenance grant payable for that year in respect of the school.][256]

Loans

255. . . . .[257]

Recovery from local funds

256. . . . .[258]

257. . . . .[259]

258. . . . .[260]

Chapter VII Alteration etc. of grant-maintained schools

259. . . . .[261]

260. . . . .[262]

261. . . . .[263]

262. . . . .[264]

263. . . . .[265]

264. . . . .[266]

265. . . . .[267]

266. . . . .[268]

Chapter VIII Discontinuance of grant-maintained schools

Proposals for discontinuance

267. . . . .[269]

268. . . . .[270]

269. . . . .[271]

270. . . . .[272]

271. . . . .[273]

Withdrawal of grant

272. . . . .[274]

273. . . . .[275]

Winding up and disposal of property

274. . . . .[276]

275. . . . .[277]

276. . . . .[278]

277. . . . .[279]

278. . . . .[280]

279. . . . .[281]

Chapter IX Groups of grant-maintained schools

280. . . . .[282]

281. . . . .[283]

282. . . . .[284]

283. . . . .[285]

284. . . . .[286]

285. . . . .[287]

286. . . . .[288]

Chapter X General and Miscellaneous

Part IV Special educational needs

Chapter I Children with special educational needs

Introductory

312 Meaning of "special educational needs" and "special educational provision" etc.

(1) A child has "special educational needs" for the purposes of this Act if he has a learning difficulty which calls for special educational provision to be made for him.

(2) Subject to subsection (3) (and except for the purposes of [section 15A or 15B][317]) a child has a "learning difficulty" for the purposes of this Act if—

(a) he has a significantly greater difficulty in learning than the majority of children of his age,

(b) he has a disability which either prevents or hinders him from making use of educational facilities of a kind generally provided for children of his age in schools within the area of the local education authority, or

(c) he is under [compulsory school age][318] and is, or would be if special educational provision were not made for him, likely to fall within paragraph (a) or (b) when of. . .[319] that age.

(3) A child is not to be taken as having a learning difficulty solely because the language (or form of the language) in which he is, or will be, taught is different from a language (or form of a language) which has at any time been spoken in his home.

(4) In this Act "special educational provision" means—

(a) in relation to a child who has attained the age of two, educational provision which is additional to, or otherwise different from, the educational provision made generally for children of his age in schools maintained by the local education authority (other than special schools). . .[320], and

(b) in relation to a child under that age, educational provision of any kind.

(5) In this Part—

"child" includes any person who has not attained the age of 19 and is a registered pupil at a school;

["maintained school" means any community, foundation or voluntary school or any community or foundation special school not established in a hospital.][321]

Code of Practice

313 Code of Practice.

(1) The Secretary of State shall issue, and may from time to time revise, a code of practice giving practical guidance in respect of the discharge by local education authorities and the governing bodies of [maintained schools][322] of their functions under this Part.

(2) It shall be the duty of—

(a) local education authorities, and such governing bodies, exercising functions under this Part, and

(b) any other person exercising any function for the purpose of the discharge by local education authorities, and such governing bodies, of functions under this Part,

to have regard to the provisions of the code.

(3) On any appeal under this Part to the Tribunal, the Tribunal shall have regard to any provision of the code which appears to the Tribunal to be relevant to any question arising on the appeal.

(4) The Secretary of State shall publish the code as for the time being in force.

[(5) In this Part (except sections 333 to 336), "the Tribunal", in relation to an appeal, means—

(a) where the local education authority concerned is in England, the Special Educational Needs and Disability Tribunal,

(b) where the local education authority concerned is in Wales, the Special Educational Needs Tribunal for Wales.][323]

314 Making and approval of code.

(1) Where the Secretary of State proposes to issue or revise a code of practice, he shall prepare a draft of the code (or revised code).

(2) The Secretary of State shall consult such persons about the draft as he thinks fit and shall consider any representations made by them.

(3) If he determines to proceed with the draft (either in its original form or with such modifications as he thinks fit) he shall lay it before both Houses of Parliament.

(4) If the draft is approved by resolution of each House, the Secretary of State shall issue the code in the form of the draft, and the code shall come into effect on such day as the Secretary of State may by order appoint.

Special educational provision: general

315 Review of arrangements.

(1) A local education authority shall keep under review the arrangements made by them for special educational provision.

(2) In doing so the authority shall, to the extent that it appears necessary or desirable for the purpose of co-ordinating provision for children with special educational needs, consult [the governing bodies of community, foundation and voluntary and community and foundation special schools [and maintained nursery schools][324] in their area.][325].

[316 Duty to educate children with special educational needs in mainstream schools

(1) This section applies to a child with special educational needs who should be educated in a school.

(2) If no statement is maintained under section 324 for the child, he must be educated in a mainstream school.

(3) If a statement is maintained under section 324 for the child, he must be educated in a mainstream school unless that is incompatible with—

(a) the wishes of his parent, or

(b) the provision of efficient education for other children.

(4) In this section and section 316A "mainstream school" means any school other than—

(a) a special school, or

(b) an independent school which is not—

(i) a city technology college,

(ii) a city college for the technology of the arts, or

(iii)[an Academy][326].][327]

[316A Education otherwise than in mainstream schools

(1) Section 316 does not prevent a child from being educated in—

(a) an independent school which is not a mainstream school, or

(b) a school approved under section 342,

if the cost is met otherwise than by a local education authority.

(2) Section 316(2) does not require a child to be educated in a mainstream school during any period in which—

(a) he is admitted to a special school for the purposes of an assessment under section 323 of his educational needs and his admission to that school is with the agreement of—

(i) the local education authority,

(ii) the head teacher of the school or, if the school is in Wales, its governing body,

(iii) his parent, and

(iv) any person whose advice is to be sought in accordance with regulations made under paragraph 2 of Schedule 26;

(b) he remains admitted to a special school, in prescribed circumstances, following an assessment under section 323 at that school;

(c) he is admitted to a special school, following a change in his circumstances, with the agreement of—

(i) the local education authority,

(ii) the head teacher of the school or, if the school is in Wales, its governing body, and

(iii) his parent;

(d) he is admitted to a community or foundation special school which is established in a hospital.

(3) Section 316 does not affect the operation of—

(a) section 348, or

(b) paragraph 3 of Schedule 27.

(4) If a local education authority decide—

(a) to make a statement for a child under section 324, but

(b) not to name in the statement the school for which a parent has expressed a preference under paragraph 3 of Schedule 27,

they shall, in making the statement, comply with section 316(3).

(5) A local education authority may, in relation to their mainstream schools taken as a whole, rely on the exception in section 316(3)(b) only if they show that there are no reasonable steps that they could take to prevent the incompatibility.

(6) An authority in relation to a particular mainstream school may rely on the exception in section 316(3)(b) only if it shows that there are no reasonable steps that it or another authority in relation to the school could take to prevent the incompatibility.

(7) The exception in section 316(3)(b) does not permit a governing body to fail to comply with the duty imposed by section 324(5)(b).

(8) An authority must have regard to guidance about section 316 and this section issued—

(a) for England, by the Secretary of State,

(b) for Wales, by the National Assembly for Wales.

(9) That guidance shall, in particular, relate to steps which may, or may not, be regarded as reasonable for the purposes of subsections (5) and (6).

(10) "Prescribed", in relation to Wales, means prescribed in regulations made by the National Assembly for Wales.

(11) "Authority"—

(a) in relation to a maintained school, means each of the following—

(i) the local education authority,

(ii) the school's governing body, and][328]

317 Duties of governing body or LEA in relation to pupils with special educational needs.

(1) The governing body, in the case of [a community, foundation or voluntary school,][329] and the local education authority, in the case of a maintained nursery school, shall—

(a) use their best endeavours, in exercising their functions in relation to the school, to secure that, if any registered pupil has special educational needs, the special educational provision which his learning difficulty calls for is made,

(b) secure that, where the responsible person has been informed by the local education authority that a registered pupil has special educational needs, those needs are made known to all who are likely to teach him, and

(c) secure that the teachers in the school are aware of the importance of identifying, and providing for, those registered pupils who have special educational needs.

(2) In subsection (1)(b) "the responsible person" means—

(a) in the case of [a community, foundation or voluntary school,][330] the head teacher or the appropriate governor (that is, the chairman of the governing body or, where the governing body have designated another governor for the purposes of this paragraph, that other governor), and

(b) in the case of a nursery school, the head teacher.

(3) To the extent that it appears necessary or desirable for the purpose of co-ordinating provision for children with special educational needs—

(a) the governing bodies of [community, foundation and voluntary schools][331] shall, in exercising functions relating to the provision for such children, consult the local education authority . . .[332] and the governing bodies of other such schools, and

(b) in relation to maintained nursery schools, the local education authority shall, in exercising those functions, consult [the governing bodies of community, foundation and voluntary schools.][333]

(4) Where a child who has special educational needs is being educated in [a community, foundation or voluntary school][334] or a maintained nursery school, those concerned with making special educational provision for the child shall secure, so far as is reasonably practicable and is compatible with—

(a) the child receiving the special educational provision which his learning difficulty calls for,

(b) the provision of efficient education for the children with whom he will be educated, and

(c) the efficient use of resources,

that the child engages in the activities of the school together with children who do not have special educational needs.

(5)[Each governors' report][335] shall include a report containing such information as may be prescribed about the implementation of the governing body's policy for pupils with special educational needs.

[(6) Each governors' report shall also include information as to—

(a) the arrangements for the admission of disabled persons as pupils at the school,

(b) the steps taken to prevent disabled pupils from being treated less favourably than other pupils,

(c) the facilities provided to assist access to the school by disabled pupils, and

(d) the plan prepared by the governing body under section 28D of the Disability Discrimination Act 1995 ("the 1995 Act").

(7) "Governors' report" means the report prepared under [section 30(1) of the Education Act 2002][336].

(7A) "Disabled person" means a person who is a disabled person for the purposes of the 1995 Act; and section 28Q of the 1995 Act (interpretation) applies for the purposes of subsection (6) as it applies for the purposes of Chapter 1 of Part 4 of that Act.][337]

[317A Duty to inform parent where special educational provision made

(1) This section applies if—

(a) a child for whom no statement is maintained under section 324 is a registered pupil at—

(i) a community, foundation or voluntary school, or

(ii) a pupil referral unit,

(b) special educational provision is made for him at the school because it is considered that he has special educational needs, and

(c) his parent has not previously been informed under this section of special educational provision made for him at the school.

(2) If the school is a pupil referral unit, the local education authority must secure that the head teacher informs the child's parent that special educational provision is being made for him at the school because it is considered that he has special educational needs.

(3) In any other case, the governing body must inform the child's parent that special educational provision is being made for him there because it is considered that he has special educational needs.][338]

318 Provision of goods and services in connection with special educational needs.

(1) A local education authority may, for the purpose only of assisting—

(a) the governing bodies of [community, foundation or voluntary schools][339] (in their or any other area) in the performance of the governing bodies' duties under section 317(1)(a), or

(b) the governing bodies of [community or foundation special schools][340] (in their or any other area) in the performance of the governing bodies' duties,

supply goods or services to those bodies.

(2) The terms on which goods or services are supplied by local education authorities under [this section to the governing bodies of community, foundation or voluntary schools or community or foundation special schools in any other area][341] may, in such circumstances as may be prescribed, include such terms as to payment as may be prescribed.

[(3) A local education authority [in England][342] may supply goods and services to any authority [in England][343] or other person (other than a governing body within subsection (1)) for the purpose only of assisting them in making for any child to whom subsection (3A) applies any special educational provision which any learning difficulty of the child calls for.

(3A) This subsection applies to any child—

(a) who is receiving relevant nursery education within the meaning of section 123 of the School Standards and Framework Act 1998, or

(b) in respect of whose education grants are (or are to be) made under section 1 of the Nursery Education and Grant-Maintained Schools Act 1996.][344]

[(3B) A local education authority in Wales may supply goods and services to any authority in Wales or other person (other than a governing body within subsection(1)) for the purpose of assisting them in making for a child any special educational provision which any learning difficulty of the child calls for.][345]

(4) This section is without prejudice to the generality of any other power of local education authorities to supply goods or services.

319 Special educational provision otherwise than in schools.

(1) Where a local education authority are satisfied that it would be inappropriate for—

(a) the special educational provision which a learning difficulty of a child in their area calls for, or

(b) any part of any such provision,

to be made in a school, they may arrange for the provision (or, as the case may be, for that part of it) to be made otherwise than in a school.

(2) Before making an arrangement under this section, a local education authority shall consult the child's parent.

320 Provision outside England and Wales for certain children.

(1) A local education authority may make such arrangements as they think fit to enable a child for whom they maintain a statement under section 324 to attend an institution outside England and Wales which specialises in providing for children with special needs.

(2) In subsection (1) "children with special needs" means children who have particular needs which

would be special educational needs if those children were in England and Wales.

(3) Where a local education authority make arrangements under this section in respect of a child, those arrangements may in particular include contributing to or paying—

(a) fees charged by the institution,

(b) expenses reasonably incurred in maintaining him while he is at the institution or travelling to or from it,

(c) his travelling expenses, and

(d) expenses reasonably incurred by any person accompanying him while he is travelling or staying at the institution.

(4) This section is without prejudice to any other powers of a local education authority.

Identification and assessment of children with special educational needs

321 General duty of local education authority towards children for whom they are responsible.

(1) A local education authority shall exercise their powers with a view to securing that, of the children for whom they are responsible, they identify those to whom subsection (2) below applies.

(2) This subsection applies to a child if—

(a) he has special educational needs, and

(b) it is necessary for the authority to determine the special educational provision which any learning difficulty he may have calls for.

(3) For the purposes of this Part a local education authority are responsible for a child if he is in their area and—

(a) he is a registered pupil at a [maintained school][346],

[(b) education is provided for him at a school which is not a maintained school but is so provided at the expense of the authority,][347]

(c) he does not come within paragraph (a) or (b) above but is a registered pupil at a school and has been brought to the authority's attention as having (or probably having) special educational needs, or

(d) he is not a registered pupil at a school but is not under the age of two or over compulsory school age and has been brought to their attention as having (or probably having) special educational needs.

322 Duty of Health Authority or local authority to help local education authority.

(1) Where it appears to a local education authority that any Health Authority [Primary Care Trust][348] or local authority could, by taking any specified action, help in the exercise of any of their functions under this Part, they may request the help of the authority [or trust][349], specifying the action in question.

(2) An authority [or a trust][350] whose help is so requested shall comply with the request unless—

(a) they consider that the help requested is not necessary for the purpose of the exercise by the local education authority of those functions, or

(b) subsection (3) applies.

(3) This subsection applies—

(a) in the case of a Health Authority [or Primary Care Trust][351], if that authority [or trust][352] consider that, having regard to the resources available to them for the purpose of the exercise of their functions under the National Health Service Act 1977, it is not reasonable for them to comply with the request, or

(b) in the case of a local authority, if that authority consider that the request is not compatible with their own statutory or other duties and obligations or unduly prejudices the discharge of any of their functions.

(4) Regulations may provide that, where an authority [or a trust][353] are under a duty by virtue of subsection (2) to comply with a request to help a local education authority in the making of an assessment under section 323 or a statement under section 324 of this Act, they must, subject to prescribed exceptions, comply with the request within the prescribed period.

(5) In this section "local authority" means a county council, a county borough council, a district council (other than one for an area for which there is a county council), a London borough council or the Common Council of the City of London.

323 Assessment of educational needs.

(1) Where a local education authority are of the opinion that a child for whom they are responsible falls, or probably falls, within subsection (2), they shall serve a notice on the child's parent informing him—

(a) that they [are considering whether][354] to make an assessment of the child's educational needs,

(b) of the procedure to be followed in making the assessment,

(c) of the name of the officer of the authority from whom further information may be obtained, and

(d) of the parent's right to make representations, and submit written evidence, to the authority within such period (which must not be less than 29 days beginning with the date on which the notice is served) as may be specified in the notice.

(2) A child falls within this subsection if—

(a) he has special educational needs, and

(b) it is necessary for the authority to determine the special educational provision which any learning difficulty he may have calls for.

(3) Where—

(a) a local education authority have served a notice under subsection (1) and the period specified in the notice in accordance with subsection (1)(d) has expired, and

(b) the authority remain of the opinion, after taking into account any representations made and any evidence submitted to them in response to the notice, that the child falls, or probably falls, within subsection (2),

they shall make an assessment of his educational needs.

(4) Where a local education authority decide to make an assessment under this section, they shall give notice in writing to the child's parent of that decision and of their reasons for making it.

(5) Schedule 26 has effect in relation to the making of assessments under this section.

(6) Where, at any time after serving a notice under subsection (1), a local education authority decide not to assess the educational needs of the child concerned they shall give notice in writing to the child's parent of their decision.

324 Statement of special educational needs.

(1) If, in the light of an assessment under section 323 of any child's educational needs and of any representations made by the child's parent in pursuance of Schedule 27, it is necessary for the local education authority to determine the special educational provision which any learning difficulty he may have calls for, the authority shall make and maintain a statement of his special educational needs.

(2) The statement shall be in such form and contain such information as may be prescribed.

(3) In particular, the statement shall—

(a) give details of the authority's assessment of the child's special educational needs, and

(b) specify the special educational provision to be made for the purpose of meeting those needs, including the particulars required by subsection (4).

(4) The statement shall—

(a) specify the type of school or other institution which the local education authority consider would be appropriate for the child,

(b) if they are not required under Schedule 27 to specify the name of any school in the statement, specify the name of any school or institution (whether in the United Kingdom or elsewhere) which they consider would be appropriate for the child and should be specified in the statement, and

(c) specify any provision for the child for which they make arrangements under section 319 and which they consider should be specified in the statement.

[(4A) Subsection (4)(b) does not require the name of a school or institution to be specified if the child's parent has made suitable arrangements for the special educational provision specified in the statement to be made for the child.][355]

(5) Where a local education authority maintain a statement under this section, then—

(a) unless the child's parent has made suitable arrangements, the authority—

(i) shall arrange that the special educational provision specified in the statement is made for the child, and

(ii) may arrange that any non-educational provision specified in the statement is made for him in such manner as they consider appropriate, and

(b) if the name of a [maintained school][356] is specified in the statement, the governing body of the school shall admit the child to the school.

[(5A) Subsection (5)(b) has effect regardless of any duty imposed on the governing body of a school by section 1(6) of the School Standards and Framework Act 1998.][357]

(6) Subsection (5)(b) does not affect any power to exclude from a school a pupil who is already a registered pupil there.

(7) Schedule 27 has effect in relation to the making and maintenance of statements under this section.

325 Appeal against decision not to make statement.

(1) If, after making an assessment under section 323 of the educational needs of any child for whom no statement is maintained under section 324, the local education authority do not propose to make such a statement, they shall give notice in writing of their decision,. . .[358] to the child's parent.

(2) In such a case, the child's parent may appeal to the Tribunal against the decision.

[(2A) A notice under subsection (1) must inform the parent of the right of appeal under subsection (2) and contain such other information as may be prescribed.

(2B) Regulations may provide that where a local education authority are under a duty under this section to serve any notice, the duty must be performed within the prescribed period.][359]

(3) On an appeal under this section, the Tribunal may—

(a) dismiss the appeal,

(b) order the local education authority to make and maintain such a statement, or

(c) remit the case to the authority for them to reconsider whether, having regard to any observations made by the Tribunal, it is necessary for the authority to determine the special educational provision which any learning difficulty the child may have calls for.

326 Appeal against contents of statement.

[(1) The parent of a child for whom a local education authority maintain a statement under section 324 may appeal to the Tribunal—

(a) when the statement is first made,

(b) if an amendment is made to the statement, or

(c) if, after conducting an assessment under section 323, the local education authority determine not to amend the statement.

(1A) An appeal under this section may be against any of the following—

(a) the description in the statement of the local education authority's assessment of the child's special educational needs,

(b) the special educational provision specified in the statement (including the name of a school so specified),

(c) if no school is specified in the statement, that fact.][360]

(2) Subsection (1)(b) does not apply where the amendment is made in pursuance of—

(a) paragraph 8 (change of named school) or 11(3)(b) (amendment ordered by Tribunal) of Schedule 27, or

(b) directions under section 442 (revocation of school attendance order);

and subsection (1)(c) does not apply to a determination made following the service of notice under [paragraph 2A][361] (amendment by LEA) of Schedule 27 of a proposal to amend the statement.

(3) On an appeal under this section, the Tribunal may—

(a) dismiss the appeal,

(b) order the authority to amend the statement, so far as it describes the authority's assessment of the child's special educational needs or specifies the special educational provision, and make such other consequential amendments to the statement as the Tribunal think fit, or

(c) order the authority to cease to maintain the statement.

(4) On an appeal under this section the Tribunal shall not order the local education authority to specify the name of any school in the statement (either in substitution for an existing name or in a case where no school is named) unless—

(a) the parent has expressed a preference for the school in pursuance of arrangements under paragraph 3 (choice of school) of Schedule 27, or

(b) in the proceedings the parent, the local education authority, or both have proposed the school.

(5) Before determining any appeal under this section the Tribunal may, with the agreement of the parties, correct any deficiency in the statement.

[326A Unopposed appeals

(1) This section applies if—

(a) the parent of a child has appealed to the Tribunal under section 325, 328, 329 or 329A or paragraph 8(3) of Schedule 27 against a decision of a local education authority, and

(b) the authority notifies the Tribunal that they have determined that they will not, or will no longer, oppose the appeal.

(2) The appeal is to be treated as having been determined in favour of the appellant.

(3) If an appeal is treated as determined in favour of the appellant as a result of subsection (2), the Tribunal is not required to make any order.

(4) before the end of the prescribed period, the authority must—

(a) in the case of an appeal under section 325, make a statement under section 324 of the child's educational needs,

(b) in the case of an appeal under section 328, 329 or 329A, make an assessment of the child's educational needs,

(c) in the case of an appeal under paragraph 8(3) of Schedule 27 against a determination of the authority not to comply with the parent's request, comply with the request.

(5) An authority required by subsection (4)(a) to make a statement under section 324 must maintain the statement under that section.

[(6) In this section, "prescribed" means prescribed by regulations made—

(a) in relation to an appeal to the Special Educational Needs and Disability Tribunal, by the Secretary of State,

(b) in relation to an appeal to the Special Educational Needs Tribunal for Wales, by the National Assembly for Wales.][362]][363]

327 Access for local education authority to certain schools.

(1) This section applies where—

(a) a local education authority maintain a statement for a child under section 324, and

[(b) in pursuance of the statement education is provided for the child at a school maintained by another local education authority.][364]

(2) Any person authorised by the local education authority shall be entitled to have access at any reasonable time to the premises of any such school for the purpose of monitoring the special educational provision made in pursuance of the statement for the child at the school.

328 Reviews of educational needs.

(1) Regulations may prescribe the frequency with which assessments under section 323 are to be repeated in respect of children for whom statements are maintained under section 324.

(2) Where—

(a) the parent of a child for whom a statement is maintained under section 324 asks the local education authority to arrange for an assessment to be made in respect of the child under section 323,

(b) no such assessment has been made within the period of six months ending with the date on which the request is made, and

(c) it is necessary for the authority to make a further assessment under section 323,

the authority shall comply with the request.

(3) If in any case where subsection (2)(a) and (b) applies the authority determine not to comply with the request—

(a) they shall give [notice in writing of that fact][365] to the child's parent, and

(b) the parent may appeal to the Tribunal against the determination.

[(3A) A notice under subsection (3)(a) must inform the parent of the right of appeal under subsection (3)(b) and contain such other information as may be prescribed.

(3B) Regulations may provide that where a local education authority are under a duty under this section to serve any notice, the duty must be performed within the prescribed period.][366]

(4) On an appeal under subsection (3) the Tribunal may—

(a) dismiss the appeal, or

(b) order the authority to arrange for an assessment to be made in respect of the child under section 323.

(5) A statement under section 324 shall be reviewed by the local education authority—

(a) on the making of an assessment in respect of the child concerned under section 323, and

(b) in any event, within the period of 12 months beginning with the making of the statement or, as the case may be, with the previous review.

(6) Regulations may make provision—

(a) as to the manner in which reviews of such statements are to be conducted,

(b) as to the participation in such reviews of such persons as may be prescribed, and

(c) in connection with such other matters relating to such reviews as the Secretary of State considers appropriate.

329 Assessment of educational needs at request of child's parent.

(1) Where—

(a) the parent of a child for whom a local education authority are responsible but for whom no statement is maintained under section 324 asks the authority to arrange for an assessment to be made in respect of the child under section 323,

(b) no such assessment has been made within the period of six months ending with the date on which the request is made, and

(c) it is necessary for the authority to make an assessment under that section,

the authority shall comply with the request.

(2) If in any case where subsection (1)(a) and (b) applies the authority determine not to comply with the request—

(a) they shall give [notice in writing of that fact][367] to the child's parent, and

(b) the parent may appeal to the Tribunal against the determination.

[(2A) a notice under subsection (2)(a) must inform the parent of the right of appeal under subsection (2)(b) and contain such other information as may be prescribed.][368]

(3) On an appeal under subsection (2) the Tribunal may—

(a) dismiss the appeal, or

(b) order the authority to arrange for an assessment to be made in respect of the child under section 323.

[329A Review or assessment of educational needs at request of responsible body

(1) This section applies if—

(a) a child is a registered pupil at a relevant school (whether or not he is a child in respect of whom a statement is maintained under section 324),

(b) the responsible body asks the local education authority to arrange for an assessment to be made in respect of him under section 323, and

(c) no such assessment has been made within the period of six months ending with the date on which the request is made.

(2) If it is necessary for the authority to make an assessment or further assessment under section 323, they must comply with the request.

(3) Before deciding whether to comply with the request, the authority must serve on the child's parent a notice informing him—

(a) that they are considering whether to make an assessment of the child's educational needs,

(b) of the procedure to be followed in making the assessment,

(c) of the name of their officer from whom further information may be obtained, and

(d) of the parent's right to make representations, and submit written evidence, to them before the end of the period specified in the notice ("the specified period").

(4) The specified period must not be less than 29 days beginning with the date on which the notice is served.

(5) The authority may not decide whether to comply with the request until the specified period has expired.

(6) The authority must take into account any representations made, and any evidence submitted, to them in response to the notice.

(7) If, as a result of this section, a local education authority decide to make an assessment under section 323, they must give written notice to the child's parent and to the responsible body which made the request, of the decision and of their reasons for making it.

(8) If, after serving a notice under subsection (3), the authority decide not to assess the educational needs of the child—

(a) they must give written notice of the decision and of their reasons for making it to his parent and to the responsible body which made the request, and

(b) the parent may appeal to the Tribunal against the decision.

(9) A notice given under subsection (8)(a) to the child's parent must—

(a) inform the parent of his right to appeal, and

(b) contain such other information (if any) as may be prescribed.

(10) On an appeal under subsection (8) the Tribunal may—

(a) dismiss it, or

(b) order the authority to arrange for an assessment to be made in respect of the child under section 323.

(11) This section applies to a child for whom relevant nursery education is provided as it applies to a child who is a registered pupil at a relevant school.

(12) "Relevant school" means—

(a) a maintained school,

(b) a maintained nursery school,

(c) a pupil referral unit,

(d) an independent school,

(e) a school approved under section 342.

(13) "The responsible body" means—

(a) in relation to a maintained nursery school or a pupil referral unit, the head teacher,

(b) in relation to any other relevant school, the proprietor or head teacher, and

(c) in relation to a provider of relevant nursery education, the person or body of persons responsible for the management of the provision of that nursery education.

(14) "Relevant nursery education" has the same meaning as in section 123 of the School Standards and Framework Act 1998, except that it does not include nursery education provided by a local education authority at a maintained nursery school.

(15) "Prescribed", in relation to Wales, means prescribed in regulations made by the National Assembly for Wales.][369]

330. . . . .

331 Assessment of educational needs of children under two.

(1) Where a local education authority are of the opinion that a child in their area who is under the age of two falls, or probably falls, within subsection (2)—

(a) they may, with the consent of his parent, make an assessment of the child's educational needs, and

(b) they shall make such an assessment if requested to do so by his parent.

(2) A child falls within this subsection if—

(a) he has special educational needs, and

(b) it is necessary for the authority to determine the special educational provision which any learning difficulty he may have calls for.

(3) An assessment under this section shall be made in such manner as the authority consider appropriate.

(4) After making an assessment under this section, the authority—

(a) may make a statement of the child's special educational needs, and

(b) may maintain that statement,

in such manner as they consider appropriate.

332 Duty of Health Authority or National Health Service trust to notify parent etc.

(1) This section applies where a Health Authority [, a Primary Care Trust][370] or a National Health Service trust, in the course of exercising any of their functions in relation to a child who is under [compulsory school age][371], form the opinion that he has (or probably has) special educational needs.

(2) The Authority or trust—

(a) shall inform the child's parent of their opinion and of their duty under paragraph (b), and

(b) after giving the parent an opportunity to discuss that opinion with an officer of the Authority or trust, shall bring it to the attention of the appropriate local education authority.

(3) If the Authority or trust are of the opinion that a particular voluntary organisation is likely to be able to give the parent advice or assistance in connection with any special educational needs that the child may have, they shall inform the parent accordingly.

[General duties of local education authorities

332A Advice and information for parents

(1) A local education authority must arrange for the parent of any child in their area with special educational needs to be provided with advice and information about matters relating to those needs.

(2) In making the arrangements, the authority must have regard to any guidance given—

(a) for England, by the Secretary of State,

(b) for Wales, by the National Assembly for Wales.

(3) The authority must take such steps as they consider appropriate for making the services provided under subsection (1) known to—

(a) the parents of children in their area,

(b) the head teachers and proprietors of schools in their area, and

(c) such other persons as they consider appropriate.

332B Resolution of disputes

(1) A local education authority must make arrangements with a view to avoiding or resolving disagreements between authorities (on the one hand) and parents of children in their area (on the other) about the exercise by authorities of functions under this Part.

(2) A local education authority must also make arrangements with a view to avoiding or resolving, in each relevant school, disagreements between the parents of a relevant child and the proprietor of the school about the special educational provision made for that child.

(3) The arrangements must provide for the appointment of independent persons with the function of facilitating the avoidance or resolution of such disagreements.

(4) In making the arrangements, the authority must have regard to any guidance given—

(a) for England, by the Secretary of State,

(b) for Wales, by the National Assembly for Wales.

(5) The authority must take such steps as they consider appropriate for making the arrangements made under subsections (1) and (2) known to—

(a) the parents of children in their area,

(b) the head teachers and proprietors of schools in their area, and

(c) such other persons as they consider appropriate.

(6) The arrangements cannot affect the entitlement of a parent to appeal to the Tribunal.

(7) In this section—

"authorities" means the governing bodies of maintained schools and the local education authority,

"relevant child" means a child who has special educational needs and is a registered pupil at a relevant school.

(8) For the purposes of this section a school is a relevant school in relation to a child if it is—

(a) a maintained school or a maintained nursery school,

(b) a pupil referral unit,

(c) a city technology college, a city college for the technology of the arts or a city academy,

(d) an independent school named in the statement maintained for the child under section 324, or

(e) a school approved under section 342.][372]][373]

Special Educational Needs Tribunal

333 Constitution of Tribunal.

[(1Z) In this section and sections 334 to 336, "the Tribunal" means the Special Educational Needs and Disability Tribunal.][374]

[(1) The Tribunal shall exercise the jurisdiction conferred on it by this Part.][375]

(2) There shall be appointed—

(a) a President of the Tribunal (referred to in this Part as "the President"),

(b) a panel of persons (referred to in this Part as "the chairmen's panel") who may serve as chairman of the Tribunal, and

(c) a panel of persons (referred to in this Part as "the lay panel") who may serve as the other two members of the Tribunal apart from the chairman.

(3) The President and the members of the chairmen's panel shall each be appointed by the Lord Chancellor.

(4) The members of the lay panel shall each be appointed by the Secretary of State.

(5) Regulations may—

(a) provide for the jurisdiction of the Tribunal to be exercised by such number of tribunals as may be determined from time to time by the President, and

(b) make such other provision in connection with the establishment and continuation of the Tribunal as the Secretary of State considers necessary or desirable.

(6) The Secretary of State may, with the consent of the Treasury, provide such staff and accommodation as the Tribunal may require.

334 The President and members of the panels.

(1) No person may be appointed President or member of the chairmen's panel unless he has a seven year general qualification (within the meaning of section 71 of the Courts and Legal Services Act 1990).

(2) No person may be appointed member of the lay panel unless he satisfies such requirements as may be prescribed.

(3) If, in the opinion of the Lord Chancellor, the President is unfit to continue in office or is incapable of performing his duties, the Lord Chancellor may revoke his appointment.

(4) Each member of the chairmen's panel or lay panel shall hold and vacate office under the terms of the instrument under which he is appointed.

(5) The President or a member of the chairmen's panel or lay panel—

(a) may resign office by notice in writing to the Lord Chancellor or (as the case may be) the Secretary of State, and

(b) is eligible for re-appointment if he ceases to hold office.

335 Remuneration and expenses.

(1) The Secretary of State may pay to the President, and to any other person in respect of his service as a member of the Tribunal, such remuneration and allowances as the Secretary of State may, with the consent of the Treasury, determine.

(2) The Secretary of State may defray the expenses of the Tribunal to such amount as he may, with the consent of the Treasury, determine.

336 Tribunal procedure.

(1) Regulations may make provision about the proceedings of the Tribunal on an appeal under this Part and the initiation of such an appeal.

(2) The regulations may, in particular, include provision—

(a) as to the period within which, and the manner in which, appeals are to be instituted,

(b) where the jurisdiction of the Tribunal is being exercised by more than one tribunal—

(i) for determining by which tribunal any appeal is to be heard, and

(ii) for the transfer of proceedings from one tribunal to another,

(c) for enabling any functions which relate to matters preliminary or incidental to an appeal to be performed by the President, or by the chairman,

(d). . . . .[376]

(e) for hearings to be conducted in the absence of any member other than the chairman,

(f) as to the persons who may appear on behalf of the parties,

(g) for granting any person such [disclosure][377] or inspection of documents or right to further particulars as might be granted by a county court,

(h) requiring persons to attend to give evidence and produce documents,

(i) for authorising the administration of oaths to witnesses,

(j) for the determination of appeals without a hearing in prescribed circumstances,

(k) as to the withdrawal of appeals,

(l) for the award of costs or expenses,

(m) for taxing or otherwise settling any such costs or expenses (and, in particular, for enabling such costs to be taxed in the county court),

(n) for the registration and proof of decisions and orders, and

(o) for enabling the Tribunal to review its decisions, or revoke or vary its orders, in such circumstances as may be determined in accordance with the regulations.

[(2A) Proceeding before the Tribunal shall be held in private, except in prescribed circumstances.][378]

(3) The Secretary of State may pay such allowances for the purpose of or in connection with the attendance of persons at the Tribunal as he may, with the consent of the Treasury, determine.

(4) Part I of the Arbitration Act 1996 shall not apply to any proceedings before the Tribunal but regulations may make provision corresponding to any provision of [that Part][379].

[(4A) The regulations may make provision for an appeal under this Part to be heard, in prescribed circumstances, with a claim under Chapter 1 of Part 4 of the Disability Discrimination Act 1995.][380]

(5) Any person who without reasonable excuse fails to comply with—

(a) any requirement in respect of the discovery or inspection of documents imposed by the regulations by virtue of subsection (2)(g), or

(b) any requirement imposed by the regulations by virtue of subsection (2)(h),

is guilty of an offence.

(6) A person guilty of an offence under subsection (5) is liable on summary conviction to a fine not exceeding level 3 on the standard scale.

[336ZA Special Educational Needs Tribunal for Wales

(1) There shall be a tribunal to be known as Tribiwnlys Anghenion Addysgol Arbennig Cymru or the Special Educational Needs Tribunal for Wales.

(2) Sections 333 to 336 shall apply in relation to that tribunal as they apply in relation to the Special Educational Needs and Disability Tribunal, but as if—

(a) functions of the Secretary of State were functions of the National Assembly for Wales,

(b) references to the Secretary of State were references to the National Assembly for Wales,

(c) requirements for the Treasury's consent were omitted.

(3) The powers of the National Assembly for Wales under sections 333(4) and (5) and 334(2) are exercisable only with the agreement of the Secretary of State.][381]

[336A Compliance with orders

(1) If the Tribunal makes an order, the local education authority concerned must comply with the order before the end of the prescribed period beginning with the date on which it is made.

[(2) In subsection (1), "prescribed" means prescribed by regulations made—

(a) as to orders of the Special Educational Needs and Disability Tribunal, by the Secretary of State,

(b) as to orders of the Special Educational Needs Tribunal for Wales, by the National Assembly for Wales with the agreement of the Secretary of State.][382]][383]

Chapter II Schools providing for special educational needs

Special schools

[337 Special schools.

(1) A school is a special school if it is specially organised to make special educational provision for pupils with special educational needs.

(2) There are the following categories of special school—

(a) special schools maintained by local education authorities, comprising—

(i) community special schools, and

(ii) foundation special schools; and

(b) special schools which are not so maintained but are for the time being approved by the Secretary of State under section 342.][384]

Establishment etc. of special schools

338. . . . .[385]

339. . . . .[386]

340. . . . .[387]

341. . . . .[388]

[Approval of non-maintained special schools][389]

[342 Approval of non-maintained special schools.

(1) The Secretary of State may approve under this section any school which—

(a) is specially organised to make special educational provision for pupils with special educational needs, and

(b) is not a community or foundation special school,

and may give his approval before or after the school is established.

(2) Regulations may make provision as to the requirements which are to be complied with as a condition of approval under subsection (1) above.

(3) Any school which was a special school immediately before 1st April 1994 shall be treated, subject to subsection (4) below, as approved under this section.

(4) Regulations may make provision as to—

(a) the requirements which are to be complied with by a school while approved under this section, and

(b) the withdrawal of approval from a school (including approval treated as given under subsection (3)) at the request of the proprietor or on the ground that there has been a failure to comply with any prescribed requirement.

(5) Without prejudice to the generality of subsections (2) and (4), the requirements which may be imposed by the regulations include requirements—

(a) which call for arrangements to be approved by the Secretary of State, or

(b) as to the organisation of any special school as a primary school or as a secondary school.

(6) Regulations shall make provision for securing that, so far as practicable, every pupil attending a special school approved under this section—

(a) receives religious education and attends religious worship, or

(b) is withdrawn from receiving such education or from attendance at such worship in accordance with the wishes of his parent.][390]

343. . . . .[391]

Government etc. of special schools

344. . . . .[392]

Maintained special school becoming grant-maintained

345. . . . .[393]

Grouping of grant-maintained special schools

346. . . . .[394]

Independent schools providing special education

347 Approval of independent schools.

(1) The Secretary of State may approve an independent school as suitable for the admission of children for whom statements are maintained under section 324.

(2) Regulations may make provision as to—

(a) the requirements which are to be complied with by a school as a condition of its approval under this section,

(b) the requirements which are to be complied with by a school while an approval under this section is in force in respect of it, and

(c) the withdrawal of approval from a school at the request of the proprietor or on the ground that there has been a failure to comply with any prescribed requirement.

(3) An approval under this section may be given subject to such conditions (in addition to those prescribed) as the Secretary of State sees fit to impose.

(4) In any case where there is a failure to comply with such a condition imposed under subsection (3), the Secretary of State may withdraw his approval.

(5) No person shall so exercise his functions under this Part that a child with special educational needs is educated in an independent school unless—

(a) the school is for the time being approved by the Secretary of State as suitable for the admission of children for whom statements are maintained under section 324, or

(b) the Secretary of State consents to the child being educated there.

[(5A) But that does not apply to a local education authority deciding, for the purposes of section 324(5), whether a parent has made suitable arrangements.][395]

348 Provision of special education at non-maintained schools.

(1) This section applies where—

(a) special educational provision in respect of a child with special educational needs is made at a school which is not a maintained school, and

(b) either the name of the school is specified in a statement in respect of the child under section 324 or the local education authority are satisfied—

(i) that his interests require the necessary special educational provision to be made for him at a school which is not a maintained school, and

(ii) that it is appropriate for the child to be provided with education at the particular school.

(2) Where this section applies, the local education authority shall pay the whole of the fees payable in respect of the education provided for the child at the school, and if—

(a) board and lodging are provided for him at the school, and

(b) the authority are satisfied that the necessary special educational provision cannot be provided for him at the school unless the board and lodging are also provided,

the authority shall pay the whole of the fees payable in respect of the board and lodging.

[(3) In this section "maintained school" means a school maintained by a local education authority.][396]

Variation of deeds

349 Variation of trust deeds etc. by order.

(1) The Secretary of State may by order make such modifications of any trust deed or other instrument relating to a school as, after consultation with the governing body or other proprietor of the school, appear to him to be necessary to enable the governing body or proprietor to meet any requirement imposed by regulations under section 342 or 347.

(2) Any modification made by an order under this section may be made to have permanent effect or to have effect for such period as may be specified in the order.

Part V The Curriculum

Chapter I Preliminary

350 Meaning of "maintained school" etc. in Part V.

. . . .[397]

351 General duties in respect of the curriculum.

. . . .[398]

352 Basic curriculum for every maintained school.

. . . .[399]

Chapter II Secular education

The National Curriculum: general

353 The National Curriculum.

. . . .[400]

354 The core subjects and other foundation subjects.

. . . .[401]

354 The core subjects and other foundation subjects.

[[(1) The following are the core subjects–

(a) mathematics;

(b) English;

(c) science; and

(d) in relation to schools in Wales which are Welsh-speaking schools, Welsh.

(2) In relation to schools in England, the following are the other foundation subjects–

(a) technology;

(b) physical education;

(c) in relation to the first, second and third key stages–

(i) history;
(ii) geography;
(iii) art and design;
(iv) music;
(d) in relation to the third and fourth key stages–
(i) citizenship;
(ii) a modern foreign language.

(3) In relation to schools in Wales, the following are the other foundation subjects–
(a) physical education;
(b) Welsh, if the school is not a Welsh-speaking school;
(c) in relation to the first, second and third key stages–
(i) history;
(ii) geography;
(iii) art;
(iv) music;
(v) technology;
(d) in relation to the third key stage, a modern foreign language.

(4) "Modern foreign language"–
(a) in relation to schools in England, means a modern foreign language specified in an order of the Secretary of State, or, if the order so provides, any modern foreign language; and
[(b) in relation to schools in Wales, means a modern foreign language specified in an order of the National Assembly for Wales, or if the order so provides, any modern foreign language][402].

(5) An order under subsection (4)(a) [or (b)][403] may–
(a) specify circumstances in which a language is not to be treated as a foundation subject;
(b) provide for the determination under the order of any question arising as to whether a particular language is a modern foreign language.][404]

(6) The Secretary of State may by order amend subsections (1) to (5).

(7) In this section "school" includes part of a school.

(8) For the purposes of this section a school is Welsh-speaking if more than one half of the following subjects are taught (wholly or partly) in Welsh—
(a) religious education, and
(b) the subjects other than English and Welsh which are foundation subjects in relation to pupils at the school.][405]

355 The key stages.

. . . .[406]

355 The key stages.

[(1) The key stages in relation to a pupil are—
(a) the period beginning with his becoming of compulsory school age and ending at the same time as the school year in which the majority of pupils in his class attain the age of seven ("the first key stage"),
(b) the period beginning at the same time as the school year in which the majority of pupils in his class attain the age of eight and ending at the same time as the school year in which the majority of pupils in his class attain the age of 11 ("the second key stage"),
(c) the period beginning at the same time as the school year in which the majority of pupils in his class attain the age of 12 and ending at the same time as the school year in which the majority of pupils in his class attain the age of 14 ("the third key stage"), and
(d) the period beginning at the same time as the school year in which the majority of pupils in his class attain the age of 15 and ending with the expiry of the school year in which the majority of pupils in his class cease to be of compulsory school age ("the fourth key stage").

(2) The Secretary of State may by order—
(a) amend subsection (1), or
(b) provide that, in relation to any subject specified in the order, subsection (1) shall have effect as if for the ages of seven and eight there mentioned there were substituted such other ages (less than 11 and 12 respectively) as may be specified in the order.

(3) The head teacher of a school may elect, in relation to a particular pupil and a particular subject, that subsection (1) shall have effect as if any reference to the school year in which the majority of pupils in that pupil's class attain a particular age were a reference to the school year in which that pupil attains that age.

(4) If at any time, in the case of a pupil of compulsory school age, subsection (1) does not, apart from this subsection, apply to determine the period within which that time falls, that subsection shall have effect as if—

(a) in the case of paragraphs (a) to (c), any reference to the school year in which the majority of pupils in that pupil's class attain a particular age were a reference to the school year in which that pupil attains that age, and

(b) in the case of paragraph (d), the period were a period beginning at the same time as the school year in which he attains the age of 15 and ending when he ceases to be of compulsory school age.

(5) In this section—

"class", in relation to a particular pupil and a particular subject, means—

(a) the teaching group in which he is regularly taught that subject, or

(b) where there are two or more such groups, such one of them as may be designated by the head teacher of the school;. . .[407]

. . .][408]

356 Establishment of the National Curriculum by order.

. . . .[409]

357 Implementation of the National Curriculum in schools.

. . . .[410]

The School Curriculum and Assessment Authority

358. . . . .[411]

359. . . . .[412]

The Curriculum and Assessment Authority for Wales

360. . . . .[413]

361. . . . .[414]

The National Curriculum: special cases

362 Development work and experiments.

. . . .[415]

363 Exceptions by regulations.

. . . .[416]

364 Pupils with statements of special educational needs.

. . . .[417]

365 Temporary exceptions for individual pupils.

. . . .[418]

366 Information concerning directions under section 365.

. . . .[419]

367 Appeals against directions under section 365 etc.

. . . .[420]

The National Curriculum: supplementary provisions

368 Procedure for making certain orders and regulations.

. . . .[421]

369 Programmes of research etc. in relation to Wales.

. . . .[422]

General functions of LEA, governing body and head teacher in relation to curriculum

370. . . . .[423]

371. . . . .[424]

372. . . . .[425]

373. . . . .[426]

374. . . . .[427]

Chapter III Religious education and worship

Agreed syllabuses

375 Agreed syllabuses of religious education.

(1) Subject to the provisions of Schedule 31, any agreed syllabus in force immediately before the commencement of this Act shall continue to have effect.

(2) In this Act "agreed syllabus" means a syllabus of religious education—

(a) prepared before the commencement of this Act in accordance with Schedule 5 to the Education Act 1944 or after commencement in accordance with Schedule 31, and

(b) adopted by a local education authority under that Schedule,

whether it is for use in all the schools maintained by them or for use in particular such schools or in relation to any particular class or description of pupils in such schools.

(3) Every agreed syllabus shall reflect the fact that the religious traditions in Great Britain are in the main Christian whilst taking account of the teaching and practices of the other principal religions represented in Great Britain.

(4) Any reference in this Act to an agreed syllabus adopted by a local education authority includes a reference to an agreed syllabus deemed to be adopted by such an authority by virtue of paragraph 11 of Schedule 5 to the Education Act 1944 or paragraph 14 of Schedule 31; and accordingly, in relation to an agreed syllabus deemed to be so adopted, any reference to the date on which an agreed syllabus was adopted is a reference to the date of deemed adoption specified by the Secretary of State in a direction under that paragraph.

(5) Subsection (3) does not apply to any agreed syllabus adopted before 29th September 1988.

Required provision for religious education

376. . . . .[428]

377. . . . .[429]

378. . . . .[430]

379. . . . .[431]

380. . . . .[432]

381. . . . .[433]

382. . . . .[434]

383. . . . .[435]

384. . . . .[436]

Religious worship

385. . . . .[437]

386. . . . .[438]

387. . . . .[439]

388. . . . .[440]

Exceptions and special arrangements

389. . . . .[441]

Constitution of standing advisory councils on religious education

390 Constitution of advisory councils.

(1) A local education authority shall constitute a standing advisory council on religious education for the purposes mentioned in section 391(1).

[(2) The council shall consist of such groups of persons appointed by the authority as representative members ("representative groups") as are required by subsection (4).][442]

(3) The council may also include co-opted members (that is, persons co-opted as members of the council by members of the council who have not themselves been so co-opted).

(4) The representative groups required by this subsection are—

(a) a group of persons to represent such Christian denominations and other religions and denominations of such religions as, in the opinion of the authority, will appropriately reflect the principal religious traditions in the area;

(b) except in the case of an area in Wales, a group of persons to represent the Church of England;

(c) a group of persons to represent such associations representing teachers as, in the opinion of the authority, ought to be represented, having regard to the circumstances of the area; and

(d) a group of persons to represent the authority.

(5) Where a representative group is required by subsection (4)(b), the representative group required by subsection (4)(a) shall not include persons appointed to represent the Church of England.

(6) The number of representative members appointed to any representative group under subsection (4)(a) to represent each denomination or religion required to be represented shall, so far as consistent with the efficient discharge of the group's functions, reflect broadly the proportionate strength of that denomination or religion in the area.

(7) On any question to be decided by the council only the representative groups on the council shall be entitled to vote, and each representative group shall have a single vote.

391 Functions of advisory councils.

(1) The purposes referred to in section 390(1) are—

[(a) to advise the local education authority on such matters connected with—

(i) religious worship in community schools or in foundation schools which (within the meaning of Part II of the School Standards and Framework Act 1998) do not have a religious character, and

(ii) the religious education to be given in accordance with an agreed or other syllabus in accordance with Schedule 19 to that Act,

as the authority may refer to the council or as the council may see fit, and][443]

(b) to carry out the functions conferred on them by section 394.

(2) The matters referred to in subsection (1)(a) include, in particular, methods of teaching, the choice of materials and the provision of training for teachers.

(3) The representative groups on the council required by section 390(4), other than the group consisting of persons appointed to represent the authority, may at any time require a review of any agreed syllabus for the time being adopted by the authority.

(4) Each representative group concerned shall have a single vote on the question of whether to require such a review.

(5) Paragraph 3 of Schedule 31 has effect to require the authority, on receiving written notification of any such requirement, to cause a conference constituted in accordance with that Schedule to be convened for the purpose of reconsidering any agreed syllabus to which the requirement relates.

(6) The council shall in each year publish a report as to the exercise of their functions and any action taken by representative groups on the council under subsection (3) during the last preceding year.

(7) The council's report shall in particular—

(a) specify any matters in respect of which the council have given advice to the authority,

(b) broadly describe the nature of the advice given, and

(c) where any such matter was not referred to the council by the authority, give the council's reasons for offering advice on that matter.

(8)...............................[444]

(9)...............................

(10) The council shall send a copy of each report published by them under subsection (6)—

(a) in the case of a council for an area in England, to [the Qualifications and Curriculum Authority][445], and

(b) in the case of a council for an area in Wales, to [the Qualifications, Curriculum and Assessment Authority for Wales][446].

392 Advisory councils: supplementary provisions.

(1) In this section "the council" means the standing advisory council on religious education constituted by a local education authority under section 390.

(2) Before appointing a person to represent any religion, denomination or associations as a member of the council, the authority shall take all reasonable steps to assure themselves that he is representative of the religion, denomination or associations in question.

(3) A member of the council who was appointed by the authority may be removed from membership by the authority if, in their opinion, he ceases to be representative of the religion, denomination or

associations which he was appointed to represent or (as the case may be) he ceases to be representative of the authority.

(4). . . . .[447]

(5) A person co-opted as a member of the council shall hold office on such terms as may be determined by the members co-opting him.

(6) A member of the council may at any time resign his office.

(7) Subject to section 390(7), the council and, in relation to any question falling to be decided by members of the council of any particular category, the members of that category, may regulate their own proceedings.

(8) The validity of proceedings of the council or of the members of the council of any particular category shall not be affected—

(a) by a vacancy in the office of any member of the council required by section 390(2), or

(b) on the ground that a member of the council appointed to represent any religion, denomination or associations does not at the time of the proceedings represent the religion, denomination or associations in question.

393. . . . .[448]

Determinations by standing advisory councils

394 Determination of cases in which requirement for Christian collective worship is not to apply.

(1) The council constituted by a local education authority under section 390 shall, on an application made by the head teacher of—

(a) any [community school][449] maintained by the authority, or

[(b) any foundation school which has not been designated under section 69(3) of the School Standards and Framework Act 1998 by the Secretary of State as having a religious character,][450]

consider whether it is appropriate for the requirement imposed by [paragraph 3(2) of Schedule 20 to the School Standards and Framework Act 1998 (requirement for Christian collective worship)][451] to apply in the case of the school or in the case of any class or description of pupils at the school.

(2) In determining whether it is appropriate for that requirement to apply as mentioned in subsection (1), the council shall have regard to any circumstances relating to the family backgrounds of the pupils at the school, or of the pupils of the particular class or description in question, which are relevant for determining the character of the collective worship appropriate in their case.

(3) The council shall give the head teacher written notification of their decision on the application.

(4) Where the council determine that it is not appropriate for the requirement to apply as mentioned in subsection (1), the determination shall take effect for the purposes of [paragraph 4 of Schedule 20 to the School Standards and Framework Act 1998 (disapplication of requirement for Christian collective worship)][452] on such date as may be specified in the notification of the council's decision under subsection (3).

(5) Before making an application under subsection (1), the head teacher of a school shall consult the governing body.

(6) On being consulted by the head teacher, the governing body may if they think fit take such steps as they consider appropriate for consulting all persons appearing to them to be parents of registered pupils at the school.

(7) An application under subsection (1) shall be made in such manner and form as the council may require.

(8) Where an application is made under subsection (1)(a) in respect of [a community school which becomes a foundation school (by virtue of section 35 of, and Schedule 8 to, the School Standards and Framework Act 1998)][453] before the application is determined, it shall, unless withdrawn by the head teacher, continue as if made under subsection (1)(b).

395 Review of determinations under section 394.

(1) Any determination by a council under section 394 by virtue of which the requirement imposed by [paragraph 3(2) of Schedule 20 to the School Standards and Framework Act 1998][454] does not for the time being apply in the case of a school or a class or description of pupils at a school shall be reviewed by the council—

(a) at any time on an application made by the head teacher, and

(b) in any event not later than the end of the period of five years beginning with the date on which

the determination first took effect or (where it has since been reviewed under this section) with the effective date of the decision on the last review.

(2) On any review under subsection (1)(b) the council shall give the head teacher an opportunity of making representations as to the determination under review.

(3) On a review under this section, the council may—

(a) confirm the determination, with or without variation, or

(b) revoke it (without prejudice to any further determination under section 394).

(4) The council shall give the head teacher written notification of their decision, specifying the effective date of that decision for the purposes of subsection (1)(b).

(5) Any determination which is required to be reviewed under subsection (1)(b) shall cease to have effect, if not confirmed on such a review, at the end of the period there mentioned.

(6) The head teacher of a school shall consult the governing body before making an application under subsection (1)(a) or any representations under subsection (2).

(7) On being consulted by the head teacher, the governing body may if they think fit take such steps as they consider appropriate for consulting all persons appearing to them to be parents of registered pupils at the school.

(8) An application under subsection (1)(a) shall be made in such manner and form as the council may require.

396 Power of Secretary of State to direct advisory council to revoke determination or discharge duty.

(1) Where the Secretary of State is satisfied, either on complaint by any person or otherwise, that any standing advisory council on religious education constituted by a local education authority under section 390—

(a) have acted, or are proposing to act, unreasonably in determining for the purposes of section 394 or 395 whether it is appropriate for the requirement imposed by [paragraph 3(2) of Schedule 20 to the School Standards and Framework Act 1998][455] to apply in the case of any school or any class or description of pupils at a school, or

(b) have failed to discharge any duty imposed under section 394 or 395,

he may give the council such directions as to the revocation of the determination, or the withdrawal of the proposed determination or (as the case may be) the discharge of the duty as appear to him to be expedient; and the council shall comply with the directions.

(2) Directions under subsection (1) may provide for the making by the council of a new determination to take effect in place of the determination or proposed determination to be revoked or withdrawn by them.

Access to meetings and documents

397 Religious education: access to meetings and documents.

(1) This section applies to—

(a) any conference convened under any of paragraphs 1 to 3 of Schedule 31, and

(b) any standing advisory council on religious education constituted under section 390.

(2) Regulations may make provision—

(a) for meetings of conferences or councils to be, subject to prescribed exceptions, open to members of the public,

(b) requiring conferences or councils to give notice, in such manner as may be prescribed, of the time and place of such meetings, and

(c) requiring conferences or councils, at such time or times as may be prescribed—

(i) to make available for inspection, or

(ii) to provide on payment of such fee as they think fit (not exceeding the cost of supply),

copies of the agendas and reports for such meetings to members of the public.

(3) Regulations made under subsection (2) may apply to—

(a) committees appointed by local education authorities under paragraph 4 of Schedule 31,

(b) sub-committees appointed by conferences under that Schedule, and

(c) representative groups on councils appointed under section 390(4),

as they apply to conferences and councils.

Miscellaneous

398 No requirement of attendance at Sunday school etc.

It shall not be required, as a condition of—

(a) a pupil attending a maintained school, or

(b) a person attending such a school to receive further education or teacher training,

that he must attend or abstain from attending a Sunday school or a place of religious worship.

399 Determination of question whether religious education in accordance with trust deed.

Where any trust deed relating to [a foundation or voluntary school][456] makes provision whereby a bishop or any other ecclesiastical or denominational authority has power to decide whether the religious education given in the school which purports to be in accordance with the provisions of the trust deed does or does not accord with those provisions, that question shall be determined in accordance with the provisions of the trust deed.

Chapter IV Miscellaneous and supplementary provisions

Courses leading to external qualifications

400. . . . .[457]

401. . . . .[458]

Obligation to enter pupils for public examinations

402 Obligation to enter pupils for public examinations.

(1) Subject to subsections (2) and (3), the governing body of a maintained school shall secure that each registered pupil at the school is entered, at such time as they consider appropriate, for each prescribed public examination for which he is being prepared at the school at the time in question in each syllabus for that examination for which he is being so prepared.

(2) The governing body are not required to secure that a pupil is entered for any examination, or for an examination in any syllabus for that examination, if either—

(a) they consider that there are educational reasons in the case of that particular pupil for not entering him for that examination or (as the case may be) for not entering him for that examination in that syllabus, or

(b) the parent of the pupil requests in writing that the pupil should not be entered for that examination or (as the case may be) for that examination in that syllabus;

but this subsection does not apply to an examination which is part of the assessment arrangements for the fourth key stage and applies in the case of that pupil.

(3) The governing body are not required to secure that a pupil is entered for any examination in any syllabus for that examination if they have secured his entry for another prescribed public examination in a corresponding syllabus.

(4) For the purposes of subsection (3) a syllabus for a prescribed public examination shall be regarded as corresponding to a syllabus for another prescribed public examination if the same course of study is provided at the school in preparation for both syllabuses.

(5) As soon as practicable after determining whether or not to secure the entry of any pupil for a prescribed public examination in any syllabus for which he is being prepared at the school, the governing body shall notify the pupil's parent in writing of their determination in relation to each such syllabus.

(6) In this section—

(a) "maintained school" includes [a community or foundation special school][459] established in a hospital;

[(aa) "assessment arrangements" and "fourth key stage"—

(i) in relation to a school maintained by a local education authority in England, have the same meaning as in Part 6 of the Education Act 2002 (the curriculum in England), and

(ii) in relation to a school maintained by a local education authority in Wales, have the same meaning as in Part 7 of that Act (the curriculum in Wales); and][460]

(b) references to a prescribed public examination shall be construed in accordance with section 462.

Sex education

403 Sex education: manner of provision.

(1) The. . .[461], governing body and head teacher shall take such steps as are reasonably practicable to secure that where sex education is given to any registered pupils at a maintained school, it is given in such a manner as to encourage those pupils to have due regard to moral considerations and the value of family life.

[(1A) The Secretary of State must issue guidance designed to secure that when sex education is given to registered pupils at maintained schools—

(a) they learn the nature of marriage and its importance for family life and the bringing up of children, and

(b) they are protected from teaching and materials which are inappropriate having regard to the age and the religious and cultural background of the pupils concerned.

(1B) In discharging their functions under subsection (1) governing bodies and head teachers must have regard to the Secretary of State's guidance.

(1C) Guidance under subsection (1A) must include guidance about any material which may be produced by NHS bodies for use for the purposes of sex education in schools.

(1D) The Secretary of State may at any time revise his guidance under subsection (1A).][462]

(2) In [this section][463]"maintained school" includes [a community or foundation special school][464] established in a hospital [and "NHS body" has the same meaning as in section 22 of the National Health Service Act 1977.][465]

404 Sex education: statements of policy.

(1) The governing body of a maintained school shall—

(a) make, and keep up to date, a separate written statement of their policy with regard to the provision of sex education, and

(b) make copies of the statement available for inspection (at all reasonable times) by parents of registered pupils at the school and provide a copy of the statement free of charge to any such parent who asks for one.

[(1A) A statement under subsection (1) must include a statement of the effect of section 405.][466]

(2) In subsection (1) "maintained school" includes, in relation to pupils who are provided with secondary education, [a community or foundation special school][467] established in a hospital.

(3). . . . .[468]

405 Exemption from sex education.

If the parent of any pupil in attendance at a maintained school requests that he may be wholly or partly excused from receiving sex education at the school, the pupil shall, except so far as such education is comprised in the National Curriculum, be so excused accordingly until the request is withdrawn.

Politics

406 Political indoctrination.

(1) The local education authority, governing body and head teacher shall forbid—

(a) the pursuit of partisan political activities by any of those registered pupils at a maintained school who are junior pupils, and

(b) the promotion of partisan political views in the teaching of any subject in the school.

(2) In the case of activities which take place otherwise than on the school premises, subsection (1)(a) applies only where arrangements for junior pupils to take part in the activities are made by—

(a) any member of the school's staff (in his capacity as such), or

(b) anyone acting on behalf of the school or of a member of the school's staff (in his capacity as such).

(3) In this section "maintained school" includes [a community or foundation special school][469] established in a hospital.

407 Duty to secure balanced treatment of political issues.

(1) The local education authority, governing body and head teacher shall take such steps as are reasonably practicable to secure that where political issues are brought to the attention of pupils while they are—

(a) in attendance at a maintained school, or

(b) taking part in extra-curricular activities which are provided or organised for registered pupils at

the school by or on behalf of the school,

they are offered a balanced presentation of opposing views.

(2) In this section "maintained school" includes [a community or foundation special school][470] established in a hospital.

Information

408 Provision of information.

(1) Regulations may require, in relation to every maintained school, the local education authority, the governing body or the head teacher to make available either generally or to prescribed persons, in such form and manner and at such times as may be prescribed—

(a) such information (including information as to the matters mentioned in subsection (2)) relevant for the purposes of any of the relevant provisions of this Part [or Part V of the Education Act 1997][471][or section 96 of the Learning and Skills Act 2000][472][or the relevant provisions of the Education Act 2002][473], and

[(b) such copies of the documents mentioned in subsection (3),

as may be prescribed.][474]

(2) The matters referred to in subsection (1)(a) are—

(a) the curriculum for maintained schools,

(b) the educational provision made by the school for pupils at the school and any syllabuses to be followed by those pupils,

(c) the educational achievements of pupils at the school (including the results of any assessments of those pupils, whether under this Part or otherwise, for the purpose of ascertaining those achievements), and

(d) the educational achievements of [such classes or descriptions of pupils][475] as may be prescribed (including results of the kind mentioned in paragraph (c)). [, and

(e) arrangements relating to external qualifications (within the meaning given by section 96(5) of the Learning and Skills Act 2000) and to courses leading to such qualifications.][476]

[(3) The documents referred to in subsection (1)(b) are—

(a) any written statement made by the local education authority under section 370,

(b) any written statement made by the governing body in pursuance of provision made under section 371,

(c) any written statement made by the governing body of their policy as to the curriculum for the school, and

(d) any report prepared by the governing body under section 161 or paragraph 7 of Schedule 23 (governors' annual reports).][477]

(4) For the purposes of subsection (1) the relevant provisions of this Part are—

(a). . . . .[478]

[(b) sections 375(3) and 384;

(c) sections 385 and 388 and, so far as relating to county schools, sections 386 and 387;] [479]

(d) sections [390][480] to 392;

(e) sections 394 to 396;

(f) sections 398. . .[481] and 405; and

(g) section 409.

[(4A) For the purposes of subsection (1) the relevant provisions of the Education Act 2002 are—

(a) Part 6 (the curriculum in England), and

(b) sections 97 to 117 (the curriculum in Wales).][482]

(5) Before making any regulations under this section, the Secretary of State shall consult any persons with whom consultation appears to him to be desirable.

(6) Regulations under this section shall not require information as to the results of an individual pupil's assessment (whether under [Part 6 or 7 of the Education Act 2002][483] or otherwise) to be made available to any persons other than—

(a) the parents of the pupil concerned,

(b) the pupil concerned,

(c) in the case of a pupil who has transferred to a different school, the head teacher of that school,

(d) the governing body of the school, or

(e) the local education authority;

and shall not require such information to be made available to the governing body, the head teacher or the local education authority except where relevant for the purposes of the performance of any of their functions.

(7) Regulations under this section may authorise local education authorities, governing bodies and head teachers to make a charge (not exceeding the cost of supply) for any documents supplied by them in pursuance of the regulations.

(8) In relation to any maintained school, the local education authority and the governing body shall exercise their functions with a view to securing that the head teacher complies with any regulations made under this section.

Complaints and enforcement

409[Complaints and enforcement: maintained schools.][484]

(1) A local education authority shall,...[485] after consultation with governing bodies [of foundation and voluntary aided schools,][486] make arrangements for the consideration and disposal of any complaint to which subsection (2) applies.

(2) This subsection applies to any complaint which is to the effect that the authority, or the governing body of [any community, foundation or voluntary school maintained by the authority or any community or foundation special school][487] so maintained which is not established in a hospital—

(a) have acted or are proposing to act unreasonably in relation to the exercise of a power conferred on them by or under a relevant enactment, or

(b) have acted or are proposing to act unreasonably in relation to the performance of, or have failed to discharge, a duty imposed on them by or under a relevant enactment.

(3) In subsection (2) "relevant enactment" means—

(a) any provision which by virtue of section 408(4) is a relevant provision of this Part for the purposes of section 408(1),

[(aa) any provision which by virtue of section 408(4A) is a relevant provision of the Education Act 2002 for the purposes of section 408(1),][488] and

(b) any other enactment (whether contained in this Part or otherwise) so far as relating to the curriculum for, or religious worship in, maintained schools. . ..[489]

(4) The Secretary of State shall not entertain under section 496 (power to prevent unreasonable exercise of functions) or 497 (powers where a local education authority or governing body fail to discharge their duties) any complaint to which subsection (2) applies, unless a complaint concerning the same matter has been made and disposed of in accordance with arrangements made under subsection (1).

Nursery education

410 Application of Part V in relation to nursery education.

[Nothing in this Part applies in relation to a nursery school or in relation to a nursery class in a primary school.][490]

Part VI School admissions, attendance and charges

Chapter I[Admission, registration and withdrawal of pupils][491]

Parental preferences

411 Parental preferences.

. . . .[492]

411A. . . . .[493]

Admission arrangements for county and voluntary schools

412. . . . .[494]

413. . . . .[495]

413A. . . . .[496]

413B. . . . .[497]

414. . . . .[498]

Admission numbers for county and voluntary schools

415. . . . .[499]

416. . . . .[500]

417. ....[501]
418. ....[502]
419. ....[503]
420. ....[504]
421. ....[505]
421A. ....[506]

New county and voluntary schools

422. ....[507]

Admissions appeals relating to county and voluntary schools

423. ....[508]
423A. ....[509]

Nursery and special schools, etc.

424. ....[510]

Admission arrangements for grant-maintained schools

425. ....[511]
425A. ....[512]
425B. ....[513]

Admission numbers for grant-maintained schools

426. ....[514]
426A. ....[515]
427. ....[516]
428. ....[517]

Admissions appeals relating to grant-maintained schools

429. ....[518]

Co-ordinated arrangements for admissions

430. ....[519]

Power to direct admission of child to school

431. ....[520]
432. ....[521]

Time for admission of pupils

433 Time for admission of pupils.

(1) Section 14 (which requires a local education authority to secure that sufficient schools for providing primary and secondary education are available for their area) shall not be construed as imposing any obligation on the proprietor of a school to admit children as pupils otherwise than at the beginning of a school term.

(2) Where, however, a child was prevented from entering a school at the beginning of a term—

(a) by his being ill or by other circumstances beyond his parent's control, or

(b) by his parent's having been then resident at a place from which the school was not accessible with reasonable facility,

the school's proprietor is not entitled by virtue of subsection (1) to refuse to admit him as a pupil during the currency of the term.

(3) In cases where subsection (2) does not apply, the governing body of a school maintained by a local education authority shall comply with any general directions given by the authority as to the time of admission of children as pupils.

(4). ....[522]

(5) Despite section 7 (duty of parent of child of compulsory school age to cause him to receive full-time education), a parent is not under a duty to cause a child to receive full-time education during any period during which, having regard to subsections (1) and (2), it is not practicable for the parent to arrange for him to be admitted as a pupil at a school.

Registration of pupils

434 Registration of pupils.

(1) The proprietor of a school shall cause to be kept, in accordance with regulations, a register containing the prescribed particulars in respect of all persons who are pupils at the school.

(2) Without prejudice to the generality of subsection (1), the prescribed particulars shall include particulars of the name and address of every person known to the proprietor to be a parent of a pupil at the school.

(3) The regulations shall prescribe the grounds on which names are to be deleted from a register kept under this section; and the name of a person entered in such a register as a pupil at a school—

(a) shall, when any of the prescribed grounds is applicable, be deleted from the register on that ground; and

(b) shall not be deleted from the register otherwise than on any such ground.

(4) The regulations may make provision—

(a) for enabling registers kept under this section to be inspected;

(b) for enabling extracts from such registers to be taken for the purposes of this Act by persons authorised to do so under the regulations; and

(c) for requiring the person by whom any such register is required to be kept to make to—

(i) the Secretary of State, [and][523]

(ii). . . . .[524]

(iii) local education authorities,

such periodical or other returns as to the contents of the register as may be prescribed.

(5) In this Act—

"registered pupil", in relation to a school, means a person registered as a pupil at the school in the register kept under this section; and

"registered", in relation to the parents of pupils at a school or in relation to the names or addresses of such parents or pupils, means shown in that register.

(6) A person who contravenes or fails to comply with any requirement imposed on him by regulations under this section is guilty of an offence and liable on summary conviction to a fine not exceeding level 1 on the standard scale.

Withdrawal of pupils from primary school for secondary education

435 Withdrawal of pupils from a primary school for secondary education.

A local education authority may make arrangements in respect of a primary school maintained by them (other than one that is for the time being organised for the provision of both primary and secondary education) under which any registered pupils who are under the age of 12 but have attained the age of 10 years and six months may be required to be withdrawn from the school for the purpose of receiving secondary education.

Supplementary

436. . . . .[525]

Chapter II School attendance

School attendance orders

437 School attendance orders.

(1) If it appears to a local education authority that a child of compulsory school age in their area is not receiving suitable education, either by regular attendance at school or otherwise, they shall serve a notice in writing on the parent requiring him to satisfy them within the period specified in the notice that the child is receiving such education.

(2) That period shall not be less than 15 days beginning with the day on which the notice is served.

(3) If—

(a) a parent on whom a notice has been served under subsection (1) fails to satisfy the local education authority, within the period specified in the notice, that the child is receiving suitable education, and

(b) in the opinion of the authority it is expedient that the child should attend school,

the authority shall serve on the parent an order (referred to in this Act as a "school attendance

order"), in such form as may be prescribed, requiring him to cause the child to become a registered pupil at a school named in the order.

(4) A school attendance order shall (subject to any amendment made by the local education authority) continue in force for so long as the child is of compulsory school age, unless—

(a) it is revoked by the authority, or

(b) a direction is made in respect of it under section 443(2) or 447(5).

(5) Where a maintained. . .[526] school is named in a school attendance order, the local education authority shall inform the governing body and the head teacher.

(6) Where a maintained . . . school is named in a school attendance order, the governing body (and, in the case of a maintained school, the local education authority) shall admit the child to the school.

(7) Subsection (6) does not affect any power to exclude from a school a pupil who is already a registered pupil there.

(8) In this Chapter—

["maintained school" means any community, foundation or voluntary school or any community or foundation special school not established in a hospital; and][527]

"suitable education", in relation to a child, means efficient full-time education suitable to his age, ability and aptitude and to any special educational needs he may have.

438 Choice of school: child without statement of special educational needs.

(1) This section applies where a local education authority are required by virtue of section 437(3) to serve a school attendance order in respect of a child, other than a child for whom they maintain a statement under section 324.

(2) before serving the order, the authority shall serve on the parent a notice in writing—

(a) informing him of their intention to serve the order,

(b) specifying the school which the authority intend to name in the order and, if they think fit, one or more other schools which they regard as suitable alternatives, and

(c) stating the effect of subsections (3) to (6).

(3) If the notice specifies one or more alternative schools and the parent selects one of them within the period of 15 days beginning with the day on which the notice is served, the school selected by him shall be named in the order.

(4) If—

[(a) within the period mentioned in subsection (3) the parent applies for the child to be admitted to a school maintained by a local education authority and, where that authority are not the authority by whom the notice was served, notifies the latter authority of the application, and][528]

(b) the child is offered a place at the school as a result of the application,

that school shall be named in the order.

[(5) If—

(a) within the period mentioned in subsection (3), the parent applies to the local education authority by whom the notice was served for education to be provided at a school which is not a school maintained by a local education authority, and

(b) the child is offered a place at the school and the authority are required by virtue of regulations under section 18(3) to pay the fees payable in respect of the education provided for him at the school,

that school shall be named in the order.][529]

(6) If, within the period mentioned in subsection (3)—

(a) the parent—

(i) applies for the child to be admitted to a school which is not maintained by a local education authority. . .[530], and in respect of which no application is made under subsection (5), and

(ii) notifies the local education authority by whom the notice was served of the application,

(b) the child is offered a place at the school as a result of the application, and

(c) the school is suitable to his age, ability and aptitude and to any special educational needs he may have,

that school shall be named in the order.

439 Specification of schools in notices under section 438(2).

(1) Subject to subsection (3), a local education authority shall not, if it appears to them that subsection

(2) applies in relation to any school, specify the school in a notice under section 438(2) unless they are responsible for determining the arrangements for the admission of pupils to the school.

(2) This subsection applies where, if the child concerned were admitted to the school in accordance with a school attendance order resulting from the notice, the number of pupils at the school in the child's age group would exceed the number [[determined in accordance with section 89 of the School Standards and Framework Act 1998 (determination of admission numbers)][531]) as the number][532] of pupils in that age group which it is intended to admit to the school in the school year in which he would be admitted.

(3) Subsection (1) does not prevent a local education authority specifying in a notice under section 438(2) any maintained. . .[533] school if—

(a) there is no maintained . . . school in their area which—

(i) the authority are not (apart from this subsection) prevented by subsection (1) from specifying, and

(ii) is, in the opinion of the authority, a reasonable distance from the home of the child concerned, and

(b) in the opinion of the authority, the school in question is a reasonable distance from the home of the child concerned.

(4) A local education authority shall not specify in a notice under section 438(2) a school from which the child concerned is permanently excluded.

[(4A) A local education authority shall not specify a school in a notice under section 438(2) if the admission of the child concerned would result in prejudice of the kind referred to in section 86(3)(a) of the School Standards and Framework Act 1998 (parental preferences) by reason of measures required to be taken as mentioned in subsection (4) of that section.][534]

(5) Before deciding to specify a particular maintained . . . school in a notice under section 438(2) a local education authority shall consult—

(a) the governing body, and

(b) if another local education authority are responsible for determining the arrangements for the admission of pupils to the school, that authority.

(6) Where a local education authority decide to specify a particular maintained . . .school in a notice under section 438(2) they shall, before serving the notice, serve notice in writing of their decision on—

(a) the governing body and head teacher of the school, and

(b) if another local education authority are responsible for determining the arrangements for the admission of pupils to the school, that authority.

(7) A governing body or local education authority on whom notice is served under subsection (6) may, within the period of 15 days beginning with the day on which the notice was received, apply to the Secretary of State for a direction under this section and, if they do so, shall inform the local education authority which served the notice.

(8) Where the Secretary of State gives a direction under this section, the school or schools to be specified in the notice under section 438(2) shall be determined in accordance with the direction.

440 Amendment of order at request of parent: child without statement of special educational needs.

(1) This section applies where a school attendance order is in force in respect of a child, other than a child for whom the local education authority maintain a statement under section 324.

(2) If at any time—

(a) the parent applies for the child to be admitted to a school maintained by a local education authority. . .[535] which is different from the school named in the order,

(b) the child is offered a place at the school as a result of the application, and

(c) the parent requests the local education authority by whom the order was served to amend it by substituting that school for the one currently named,

the authority shall comply with the request.

(3) If at any time—

[(a) the parent applies to the authority for education to be provided for the child at a school which is not a school maintained by a local education authority and which is different from the school named in the order,

(b) the child is offered a place at the school and the authority are required by virtue of regulations under section 18(3) to pay the fees payable in respect of the education provided for him at the school, and][536]

(c) the parent requests the authority to amend the order by substituting that school for the one currently named,

the authority shall comply with the request.

(4) If at any time –

(a) the parent applies for the child to be admitted to a school which is not maintained by a local education authority. . .[537], which is different from the school named in the order and in respect of which no application is made under subsection (3),

(b) as a result of the application, the child is offered a place at the school, being a school which is suitable to his age, ability and aptitude and to any special educational needs he may have, and

(c) the parent requests the authority to amend the order by substituting that school for the one currently named,

the authority shall comply with the request.

441 Choice of school: child with statement of special educational needs.

(1) Subsections (2) and (3) apply where a local education authority are required by virtue of section 437(3) to serve a school attendance order in respect of a child for whom they maintain a statement under section 324.

(2) Where the statement specifies the name of a school, that school shall be named in the order.

(3) Where the statement does not specify the name of a school—

(a) the authority shall,. . .[538], amend the statement so that it specifies the name of a school, and

[(3A) an amendment to a statement required to be made under subsection (3)(a) shall be treated for the purposes of Schedule 27 as if it were an amendment proposed following a periodic review (within the meaning of that Schedule).][539]

(b) that school shall then be named in the order.

(4) Where—

(a) a school attendance order is in force in respect of a child for whom the local education authority maintain a statement under section 324, and

(b) the name of the school specified in the statement is changed,

the local education authority shall amend the order accordingly.

442 Revocation of order at request of parent.

(1) This section applies where a school attendance order is in force in respect of a child.

(2) If at any time the parent applies to the local education authority requesting that the order be revoked on the ground that arrangements have been made for the child to receive suitable education otherwise than at school, the authority shall comply with the request, unless they are of the opinion that no satisfactory arrangements have been made for the education of the child otherwise than at school.

(3) If a parent is aggrieved by a refusal of the local education authority to comply with a request under subsection (2), he may refer the question to the Secretary of State.

(4) Where a question is referred to the Secretary of State under subsection (3), he shall give such direction determining the question as he thinks fit.

(5) Where the child in question is one for whom the authority maintain a statement under section 324—

(a) subsections (2) to (4) do not apply if the name of a school or other institution is specified in the statement, and

(b) in any other case a direction under subsection (4) may require the authority to make such amendments in the statement as the Secretary of State considers necessary or expedient in consequence of his determination.

School attendance: offences and education supervision orders

443 Offence: failure to comply with school attendance order.

(1) If a parent on whom a school attendance order is served fails to comply with the requirements of the order, he is guilty of an offence, unless he proves that he is causing the child to receive suitable education otherwise than at school.

(2) If, in proceedings for an offence under this section, the parent is acquitted, the court may direct that the school attendance order shall cease to be in force.

(3) A direction under subsection (2) does not affect the duty of the local education authority to take further action under section 437 if at any time the authority are of the opinion that, having regard to any change of circumstances, it is expedient to do so.

(4) A person guilty of an offence under this section is liable on summary conviction to a fine not exceeding level 3 on the standard scale.

444 Offence: failure to secure regular attendance at school of registered pupil.

(1) If a child of compulsory school age who is a registered pupil at a school fails to attend regularly at the school, his parent is guilty of an offence.

[(1A) If in the circumstances mentioned in subsection (1) the parent knows that his child is failing to attend regularly at the school and fails without reasonable justification to cause him to do so, he is guilty of an offence.][540]

(2) Subsections (3) to (6) below apply in proceedings for an offence under this section in respect of a child who is not a boarder at the school at which he is a registered pupil.

(3) The child shall not be taken to have failed to attend regularly at the school by reason of his absence from the school—

(a) with leave,

(b) at any time when he was prevented from attending by reason of sickness or any unavoidable cause, or

(c) on any day exclusively set apart for religious observance by the religious body to which his parent belongs.

(4) The child shall not be taken to have failed to attend regularly at the school if the parent proves—

(a) that the school at which the child is a registered pupil is not within walking distance of the child's home, and

(b) that no suitable arrangements have been made by the local education authority. . .[541] for any of the following—

(i) his transport to and from the school,

(ii) boarding accommodation for him at or near the school, or

(iii) enabling him to become a registered pupil at a school nearer to his home.

(5) In subsection (4) "walking distance"—

(a) in relation to a child who is under the age of eight, means 3.218688 kilometres (two miles), and

(b) in relation to a child who has attained the age of eight, means 4.828032 kilometres (three miles),

in each case measured by the nearest available route.

(6) If it is proved that the child has no fixed abode, subsection (4) shall not apply, but the parent shall be acquitted if he proves—

(a) that he is engaged in a trade or business of such a nature as to require him to travel from place to place,

(b) that the child has attended at a school as a registered pupil as regularly as the nature of that trade or business permits, and

(c) if the child has attained the age of six, that he has made at least 200 attendances during the period of 12 months ending with the date on which the proceedings were instituted.

(7) In proceedings for an offence under this section in respect of a child who is a boarder at the school at which he is a registered pupil, the child shall be taken to have failed to attend regularly at the school if he is absent from it without leave during any part of the school term at a time when he was not prevented from being present by reason of sickness or any unavoidable cause.

(8) A person guilty of an offence under [subsection (1)][542] is liable on summary conviction to a fine not exceeding level 3 on the standard scale.

[(8A) A person guilty of an offence under subsection (1A) is liable on summary conviction—

(a) to a fine not exceeding level 4 on the standard scale, or

(b) to imprisonment for a term not exceeding three months,

or both.

(8B) If, on the trial of an offence under subsection (1A), the court finds the defendant not guilty of that offence but is satisfied that he is guilty of an offence under subsection (1), the court may find him

guilty of that offence.][543]

(9) In this section "leave", in relation to a school, means leave granted by any person authorised to do so by the governing body or proprietor of the school.

445 Presumption of age.

(1) This section applies for the purposes of any proceedings for an offence under section 443 or 444.

(2) In so far as it is material, the child in question shall be presumed to have been of compulsory school age at any time unless the parent proves the contrary.

(3) Where a court is obliged by virtue of subsection (2) to presume a child to have been of compulsory school age, section 565(1) (provisions as to evidence) does not apply.

446 Institution of proceedings.

Proceedings for an offence under section 443 or 444 shall not be instituted except by a local education authority.

447 Education supervision orders.

(1) Before instituting proceedings for an offence under section 443 or 444, a local education authority shall consider whether it would be appropriate (instead of or as well as instituting the proceedings) to apply for an education supervision order with respect to the child.

(2) The court—

(a) by which a person is convicted of an offence under section 443, or

(b) before which a person is charged with an offence under section 444,

may direct the local education authority instituting the proceedings to apply for an education supervision order with respect to the child unless the authority, having consulted the appropriate local authority, decide that the child's welfare will be satisfactorily safeguarded even though no education supervision order is made.

(3) Where, following such a direction, a local education authority decide not to apply for an education supervision order, they shall inform the court of the reasons for their decision.

(4) Unless the court has directed otherwise, the information required under subsection (3) shall be given to the court before the end of the period of eight weeks beginning with the date on which the direction was given.

(5) Where—

(a) a local education authority apply for an education supervision order with respect to a child who is the subject of a school attendance order, and

(b) the court decides that section 36(3) of the Children Act 1989 (education supervision orders) prevents it from making the order,

the court may direct that the school attendance order shall cease to be in force.

(6) In this section—

"the appropriate local authority" has the same meaning as in section 36(9) of the Children Act 1989, and

"education supervision order" means an education supervision order under that Act.

Exemption

448. . . . .[544]

[Chapter III Charges in connection with education at maintained schools][545]

[Preliminary][546]

[449 Meaning of "maintained school" in Chapter III.

In this Chapter "maintained school" means any school maintained by a local education authority.][547]

Prohibition of charges

450 Prohibition of charges for admission.

(1) No charge shall be made in respect of admission to a maintained school.

(2) Subsection (1) does not apply to the admission of any person to any maintained school for the purpose of—

(a) part-time education suitable to the requirements of persons of any age over compulsory school age;

(b) full-time education suitable to the requirements of persons who have attained the age of 19; or

(c) teacher training.

451 Prohibition of charges for provision of education.

(1). . .[548], this section applies in relation to education provided at any maintained school for a registered pupil at the school.

(2) Where the education is provided for the pupil during school hours no charge shall be made in respect of it.

(3) Subsection (2) does not apply in relation to tuition in playing a musical instrument where the tuition is provided either individually or to a group of not more than four pupils, unless the tuition is—

(a) required as part of a syllabus for a prescribed public examination which is a syllabus for which the pupil is being prepared at the school, or

(b) provided in pursuance of a duty imposed by [section 88 or 109 of the Education Act 2002 (implementation of National Curriculum for England or National Curriculum for Wales)][549] or section 69 of the School Standards and Framework Act 1998 (duty to secure due provision of religious education)..

(4) Where the education is provided for the pupil outside school hours no charge shall be made in respect of it if it is—

(a) required as part of a syllabus for a prescribed public examination which is a syllabus for which the pupil is being prepared at the school, or

(b) provided in pursuance of a duty imposed by [section 88 or 109 of the Education Act 2002][550] or [section 69 of the School Standards and Framework Act 1998][551].

(5). . . . .[552]

452 Application of section 451 where education is provided partly during and partly outside school hours etc.

(1) Where a period allowed for any educational activity at a maintained school falls partly during school hours and partly outside school hours, then—

(a) if 50 per cent. or more of the time occupied by that period together with any connected school travelling time falls during school hours, so much of the education provided during that period as is provided outside school hours shall be treated for the purposes of section 451 as provided during school hours, and

(b) in any other case, so much of the education provided during that period as is provided during school hours shall be treated for those purposes as provided outside school hours.

(2) In subsection (1) "connected school travelling time" means time spent during school hours by the pupils taking part in the educational activity concerned in getting to or from the place where the activity takes place.

(3) Where any education provided at a maintained school is provided on a residential trip, then—

(a) if the number of school sessions taken up by the trip is equal to or greater than 50 per cent. of the number of half days spent on the trip, any education provided on the trip which is provided outside school hours shall be treated for the purposes of section 451 as provided during school hours, and

(b) in any other case, any education provided on the trip which is provided during school hours shall be treated for those purposes as provided outside school hours.

(4) In this section "half day" means any period of 12 hours ending with noon or midnight on any day.

(5) For the purposes of subsection (3)—

(a) where 50 per cent. or more of a half day is spent on a residential trip, the whole of that half day shall be treated as spent on the trip, and

(b) a school session on any day on which such a session takes place at the school concerned shall be treated as taken up by a residential trip if the time spent on the trip occupies 50 per cent. or more of the time allowed for that session at the school.

(6) Nothing in section 451 shall be read as prohibiting the making of a charge in respect of board and lodging provided for a registered pupil at a maintained school on a residential trip.

453 Examinations: prohibition of charges and recovery of wasted fees.

(1) No charge shall be made in respect of the entry of a registered pupil at a maintained school for a prescribed public examination in any syllabus for that examination for which the pupil has been prepared at the school.

(2) Despite subsection (1), where—

(a) the governing body of a maintained school or the local education authority have paid or are liable to pay a fee in respect of the entry of a registered pupil at the school for a public examination in any syllabus for that examination, and

(b) the pupil fails without good reason to meet any examination requirement for that syllabus,

that body or authority may recover the amount of the fee from the pupil's parent.

(3) It shall be for the body or authority who have paid or are liable to pay the fee in question to determine for the purposes of this section any question whether a pupil who has failed to meet an examination requirement had good reason for the failure.

454 Prohibition of incidental charges.

(1) Neither the parent of a registered pupil at a maintained school nor the pupil himself shall be required to pay for or supply any materials, books, instruments or other equipment for use for the purposes of or in connection with—

(a) education provided for the pupil at the school in respect of which, by virtue of section 451, no charge may be made, or

(b) a syllabus for a prescribed public examination which is a syllabus for which the pupil has been prepared at the school.

(2) Nothing in subsection (1) shall prevent the parent of a pupil from being required to pay for or supply any materials for use for the purposes of the production, in the course of the provision of education for the pupil at the school, of any article incorporating those materials, where the parent has indicated before that requirement is made that he wishes the article to be owned by him or by the pupil.

(3) No charge shall be made in respect of transport provided for a registered pupil at a maintained school where the transport is either—

(a) incidental to education provided for the pupil at the school in respect of which, by virtue of section 451, no charge may be made, or

(b) provided for the purpose of enabling him to meet any examination requirement for any syllabus for a prescribed public examination which is a syllabus for which he has been prepared at the school.

(4) For the purposes of subsection (3)(a) transport is incidental to education provided for registered pupils at a school if it is provided for the purpose of carrying such pupils—

(a) to or from any part of the school premises in which education is provided for those pupils, from or to any other part of those premises, or

(b) to or from any place outside the school premises in which education is provided for those pupils under arrangements made by or on behalf of the governing body or the local education authority, from or to the school premises or any other such place.

Permitted charges

455 Permitted charges.

(1) Subject to subsection (2), a charge may be made in respect of—

(a) education provided for a registered pupil at a maintained school other than education in respect of which, by virtue of section 451, no charge may be made,

(b) the entry of a registered pupil at a maintained school for a public examination in any syllabus for that examination otherwise than in circumstances in which, by virtue of section 453(1), no charge may be made,

(c) transport provided for a registered pupil at a maintained school other than transport in respect of which, by virtue of section 454(3) or 509(2), no charge may be made, and

(d) board and lodging provided for a registered pupil at a maintained school on a residential trip.

(2) A charge may not be made—

(a) by virtue of subsection (1)(a) in respect of the provision for a pupil of education,

(b) by virtue of subsection (1)(b) in respect of the entry of a pupil for an examination in any syllabus for that examination, or

(c) by virtue of subsection (1)(c) in respect of the provision for a pupil of transport,

unless the education is provided, the pupil is entered for the examination in that syllabus, or the transport is provided, by agreement with the pupil's parent.

(3) Any education, examination entry or transport in respect of which a charge may be made by virtue of subsection (1) is referred to in this Chapter as an "optional extra".

456 Regulation of permitted charges.

(1) This section applies in relation to any charge permitted under section 455. . .[553]; and a charge to which this section applies is referred to in this section as a "regulated charge".

(2) The amount of any regulated charge shall be payable by the parent of the pupil concerned.

(3) A regulated charge shall not exceed the cost of the provision of the optional extra or the board and lodging in question.

(4) Without prejudice to the generality of subsection (3), the cost of the provision of an optional extra includes costs, or an appropriate proportion of the costs—

(a) incurred in respect of the provision of any materials, books, instruments or other equipment used for the purposes of or in connection with the provision of the optional extra, or

(b) attributable to the provision of non-teaching staff for any purpose connected with the provision of the optional extra, or

(c) attributable to the provision of teaching staff engaged under contracts for services for the purpose of providing it.

(5) Subject to subsection (6), the cost of the provision of an optional extra shall not be taken to include any costs attributable to the provision of teaching staff other than staff engaged as mentioned in subsection (4)(c).

(6) Where the optional extra in question consists of tuition in playing a musical instrument, the cost of its provision shall include costs, or an appropriate proportion of the costs, attributable to the provision of teaching staff employed for the purpose of providing the tuition.

(7) Where charging is permitted under section 455 and the charge would be a regulated charge, the question whether any charge should be made, and the amount of any charge to be made, shall be determined—

(a) in a case where the cost of the provision of the optional extra or board and lodging in question is met by or from funds at the disposal of the governing body, by the governing body, and

(b) in any other case, by the local education authority.

(8) The whole or any part of the amount of any charge which the local education authority determine under subsection (7)(b) to make—

(a) shall, if the governing body so determine, be met by or from funds at the disposal of the governing body, and

(b) to the extent that it is so met, shall not be payable by the parent of the pupil concerned.

457 Charges and remissions policies.

(1) Every governing body of a maintained school and every local education authority shall determine and keep under review a policy with respect to—

(a) the provision of, and

(b) the classes or descriptions of case in which they propose to make charges for,

any optional extra or board and lodging in respect of which charges are permitted by section 455. . . .[554]

(2) No such body or authority shall make such a charge unless they have both—

(a) determined a policy under subsection (1)(b) (their "charging policy"), and

(b) determined a policy (their "remissions policy") setting out any circumstances in which they propose to remit (in whole or in part) any charge which would otherwise be payable to them in accordance with their charging policy.

(3) A remissions policy determined by the governing body of a school. . .[555] shall set out any circumstances in which the governing body propose to meet (in whole or in part) any charge payable to the local education authority, in accordance with the authority's charging policy, for an optional extra or board and lodging provided for a registered pupil at the school.

(4) A remissions policy shall provide for complete remission of any charges otherwise payable in respect of board and lodging provided for a pupil on a residential trip if—

(a) the education provided on the trip is education in respect of which, by virtue of section 451, no charge may be made, and

[(b) the pupil's parent is—

(i) in receipt of income support,

(ii) in receipt of an income-based jobseeker's allowance (payable under the Jobseekers Act 1995), or

(iii) in receipt of any other benefit or allowance, or entitled to any tax credit under the Tax Credits Act 2002 or element of such a tax credit, prescribed for the purposes of this paragraph, in such circumstances as may be so prescribed,

in respect of any period wholly or partly comprised in the time spent on the trip.][556]

(5) A remissions policy shall be kept under review by the governing body or local education authority by whom it was determined.

458 Charges for board and lodging at boarding schools.

(1) Subject to subsections (2) to (5), where a registered pupil at a maintained school is provided at the school with board and lodging, there shall be payable in respect of the board and lodging by the parent of the [pupil concerned, to the local education authority, charges][557] not exceeding the cost to the authority. . .[558] of providing the board and lodging.

(2) Where—

(a). . . . .[559]

(b) the local education authority [for that pupil's area][560] are of the opinion that education suitable to his age, ability and aptitude and to any special educational needs he may have cannot otherwise be provided for him,

then, where the school is maintained by the local education authority for his area, that authority shall remit the whole of the charges payable under this section and, in any other case, that authority shall pay the whole of the charges payable under this section to the authority which maintain the school.

(3). . . . .[561]

(4) Where the local education authority for the pupil's area are satisfied that payment of the full charges payable under this section would involve financial hardship to the parent of the pupil concerned, the authority—

(a) in the case of charges payable to the authority, shall remit so much of those charges as falls in accordance with subsection (5) to be so remitted, and

(b) in the case of charges payable to another local education authority. . .[562] in respect of board and lodging, shall pay so much of those charges as falls in accordance with subsection (5) to be so paid.

(5) The amount that falls to be remitted or paid by a local education authority by virtue of subsection (4)(a) or (b) is—

(a) such part of the charges in question as the authority consider ought not to be paid by the pupil's parent in order to avoid such hardship as is mentioned in subsection (4), or

(b) the whole of those charges if, in their opinion, such hardship cannot otherwise be avoided.

Supplementary

459 Provision of information.

Regulations may require, in relation to every maintained school, the local education authority, the governing body or the head teacher to make available either generally or to prescribed persons, in such form and manner and at such times as may be prescribed—

(a) such information relevant for the purposes of this Chapter as to the school hours at the school, and

(b) such information as to the policies determined under section 457 which apply in relation to the school,

as may be prescribed.

460 Contributions and charges unaffected by Chapter III.

(1) Nothing in this Chapter shall be read as prohibiting or in any way restricting or regulating any request or invitation by or on behalf of the governing body of a maintained school or a local education authority for voluntary contributions for the benefit of the school or any school activities.

(2) Any request or invitation made by or on behalf of such a body or authority for contributions for the benefit of a school or school activities shall not be regarded for the purposes of subsection (1) as a request or invitation for voluntary contributions unless it is clear from the terms in which it is

made—

(a) that there is no obligation to make any contribution, and

(b) that registered pupils at the school will not be treated differently according to whether or not their parents have made any contribution in response to the request or invitation.

(3) Nothing in this Chapter relating to charges in respect of a registered pupil at a maintained school shall be read as relating to—

(a) charges made by persons other than the governing body or the local education authority, or

(b) charges to be paid by persons other than the parent of the pupil or the pupil himself.

461 Recovery of sums as civil debt.

Any sum payable under section 453(2), 455 or 458 by the parent of a registered pupil at a maintained school shall be recoverable summarily as a civil debt.

462 Interpretation of Chapter III.

(1) In this Chapter—

"equipment" does not include clothing;

"examination requirement", in relation to a syllabus for an examination, means a requirement which a pupil must meet in order to qualify for assessment for the purposes of determining his achievements in that examination in that syllabus.

(2) In this Chapter "residential trip" means any trip—

(a) which is arranged for registered pupils at a maintained school by or on behalf of the governing body or the local education authority, and

(b) which requires the pupils taking part to spend one or more nights away from their usual overnight accommodation.

(3) For the purposes of this Chapter, a pupil shall be regarded as having been prepared at a school for a syllabus for a prescribed public examination if any part of the education provided with a view to preparing him for that examination in that syllabus has been provided for him at that school.

(4) In this Chapter references to a public examination (or a prescribed public examination) are references to such an examination as it applies in relation to persons who are entered for a syllabus for that examination with a view to meeting the examination requirements for that syllabus so as to qualify for assessment for the purposes of determining their achievements in that examination on any particular occasion in any year when an assessment takes place.

(5) For the purposes of subsection (4)—

(a) "an assessment" means an assessment for the purposes of determining the achievements of persons entered for the examination in question; and

(b) such an assessment is to be regarded as taking place on any occasion on which it is determined in relation to each person entered for any syllabus in that examination who has met the examination requirements for that syllabus—

(i) whether he has passed or failed, and

(ii) if grades are assigned for the purposes of the examination, the grade to be assigned in his case.

Part VII Independent Schools

Chapter I Preliminary

463 Meaning of "independent school".

In this Act "independent school" means any school at which full-time education is provided for five or more pupils of compulsory school age (whether or not such education is also provided at it for pupils under or over that age) and which is not—

(a) a school maintained by a local education authority, [or][563]

(b) a special school not so maintained,. . .[564]

(c). . . . .[565]

Chapter II Registration of independent schools

Registration

464 Separate registration for England and for Wales.

(1) A register of all independent schools in England shall be kept by an officer of the Secretary of State

who is appointed by the Secretary of State to be Registrar of Independent Schools for England.

(2) A register of all independent schools in Wales shall be kept by an officer of the Secretary of State who is appointed by the Secretary of State to be Registrar of Independent Schools for Wales.

(3) Each register shall be open to public inspection at all reasonable times.

(4) In this Part "the Registrar of Independent Schools" (or "the Registrar") means—

(a) in relation to a school in England, the Registrar of Independent Schools for England, and

(b) in relation to a school in Wales, the Registrar of Independent Schools for Wales,

and references, in relation to a school, to the register or to registration are to the register kept by the relevant Registrar or to registration in that register.

465 Provisional and final registration of a school.

(1) Subject to subsection (2), the Registrar of Independent Schools shall enter in the register the name of any independent school whose proprietor—

(a) makes an application for registration in such manner as may be prescribed, and

(b) provides such particulars as may be prescribed.

(2) a school shall not be registered if—

(a) by virtue of an order made under section 470 or 471, the proprietor is disqualified from being the proprietor of an independent school or the school premises are disqualified from being used as a school, or

(b) the school premises are used or proposed to be used for any purpose for which they are disqualified by virtue of such an order.

(3) The registration of a school shall initially be provisional only, and shall remain so until such time as the Secretary of State, after the school has been inspected on his behalf under Part I of the School Inspections Act 1996, gives notice to the proprietor that the registration is final.

(4) In this Part—

"provisionally registered school" means an independent school whose registration is provisional only, and

"registered school" means an independent school whose registration is final.

(5) In this section "proprietor", in relation to a school, includes any person or body of persons proposing to be the proprietor.

466 Enforcement of registration: offences.

(1) Subject to subsection (2), a person is guilty of an offence if he conducts an independent school which is not a registered school or a provisionally registered school.

(2) A person is not guilty of an offence under subsection (1) by reason of conducting a school at any time within the period of one month from the date on which it was first conducted (whether by that person or another) if an application for the registration of the school has been duly made under section 465 within that period.

(3) The proprietor of an independent school is guilty of an offence if, while it is a provisionally registered school, he does any act calculated to lead to the belief that it is a registered school.

467 Provision of information about registered and provisionally registered schools.

(1) Regulations may make provision for requiring the proprietor of a registered or provisionally registered school to provide the Registrar of Independent Schools from time to time with such particulars relating to the school as may be prescribed.

(2) Regulations made under this section may in particular require the proprietor of a school to furnish the Registrar with such information as is required by the local authority for the purpose of determining whether the school is a children's home (within the meaning of the [Care Standards Act 2000][566].

(3) Regulations may make provision for enabling the Secretary of State to order the deletion from the register of the name of any school in respect of which any requirement imposed by or under regulations made under this section is not complied with.

(4) Subsection (9) of section 537 (general power of Secretary of State to require information from governing bodies etc.) confers power on the Secretary of State to make similar provision in relation to non-compliance with any requirement imposed by or under regulations under that section.

468 School may be struck off for contravention of regulations about employment of teachers.

Where the Secretary of State is satisfied that a person whose employment is prohibited or restricted by virtue of regulations under section 218(6) of the Education Reform Act 1988 (employment prohibited or restricted on medical grounds or for misconduct etc.)—

(a) is employed in a registered or provisionally registered school in contravention of those regulations, or

(b) is the proprietor of such a school,

he may order that the school be struck off the register or (as the case may be) that the Registrar is not to register the school.

[(2) Where the Secretary of State is satisfied that a person who is included (otherwise than provisionally) in the list kept under section 1 of the Protection of Children Act 1999 (individuals considered unsuitable to work with children) or is subject to an order under section 28 or 29 of the Criminal Justice and Court Services Act 2000 (disqualification from working with children)—

(a) is employed in a registered or provisionally registered school, or

(b) is the proprietor of such a school,

he may order that the school be struck off the register or (as the case may be) that the Registrar is not to register the school.][567]

Complaints about registered and provisionally registered schools

469 Notice of complaint by Secretary of State.

(1) This section applies where the Secretary of State is satisfied that one or more of the following grounds of complaint apply in relation to a registered or provisionally registered school—

(a) the school premises or any parts of them are unsuitable for a school;

(b) the accommodation provided at the school premises is inadequate or unsuitable having regard to the number, ages, and sex of the pupils attending the school;

(c) efficient and suitable instruction is not being provided at the school having regard to the ages and sex of the pupils attending it;

[(d) the proprietor of the school or any teacher or other employee employed in the school—

(i) is unsuitable to work with children; or

(ii) is for any other reason not a proper person to be the proprietor of an independent school or (as the case may be) to be a teacher or other employee in any school;][568]

(e) there has been a failure, in relation to a child provided with accommodation by the school, to comply with the duty imposed by section 87 of the Children Act 1989 (welfare of children accommodated in independent schools).

(2) The Secretary of State shall serve on the proprietor of the school a notice of complaint stating the grounds of complaint which apply together with full particulars of the matters complained of.

(3) Unless any of those matters are stated in the notice to be in the opinion of the Secretary of State irremediable, the notice shall specify—

(a) the measures necessary in the opinion of the Secretary of State to remedy those matters, and

(b) the time, not being less than six months after the service of the notice, within which those measures are required to be taken.

(4) If it is alleged by the notice that a person employed as a teacher or other employee at the school is [unsuitable to work with children or is for any other reason][569] not a proper person to be a teacher or other employee in any school—

(a) that person shall be named in the notice,

(b) the particulars given in the notice shall specify the grounds of the allegation, and

(c) a copy of the notice shall be served on him.

(5) Any notice of complaint, or copy of a notice of complaint, served under this section shall limit the time, not being less than one month after the service of the notice or copy, within which the complaint may be referred to an Independent Schools Tribunal under section 470.

(6) In this section and sections 470 to 473 "employee" means a person employed in work which brings him regularly into contact with persons who have not attained the age of 19.

470 Determination of complaint by an Independent Schools Tribunal.

(1) Any person on whom a notice of complaint or copy of a notice of complaint is served under section 469 may, within the time limited by the notice or copy, appeal against the notice by referring the

complaint to an Independent Schools Tribunal.

(2) On the complaint being so referred, the tribunal, after giving all parties concerned an opportunity of being heard and after considering such evidence as may be tendered by them or on their behalf, may—

(a) order that the complaint be annulled;

(b) order that the school to which the complaint relates be struck off the register;

(c) order that the school be so struck off unless the requirements of the notice (subject to such modifications, if any, as may be specified in the order) are complied with to the satisfaction of the Secretary of State before the expiry of such time as may be specified in the order;

(d) if satisfied—

(i) that any premises alleged by the notice to be unsuitable for use as a school are in fact unsuitable for such use, or

(ii) that any part of such premises is in fact unsuitable for such use,

by order disqualify the premises, or that part, from being so used;

(e) if satisfied that the accommodation provided at the school premises is inadequate or unsuitable having regard to the number, ages and sex of the pupils attending the school, by order disqualify the premises from being used as a school for pupils exceeding such number or of such age or sex as may be specified in the order;

[(f) if satisfied that any person alleged by the notice of complaint to be a person who—

(i) is unsuitable to work with children; or

(ii) is for any other reason not a proper person to be the proprietor of an independent school or to be a teacher or other employee in any school,

is in fact such a person, by order disqualify that person from being the proprietor of any independent school or (as the case may be) from being a teacher or other employee in any school.][570]

471 Determination of complaint by Secretary of State.

(1) Where—

(a) a notice of complaint has been served on the proprietor of a school under section 469, and

(b) the complaint is not referred by him to an Independent Schools Tribunal under section 470 within the time limited by the notice,

the Secretary of State may (subject to subsection (2)) make any order which such a tribunal would have had power to make if the complaint had been so referred.

(2) If—

(a) it is alleged by the notice that a person employed as a teacher or other employee at the school is [unsuitable to work with children or is for any other reason][571] not a proper person to be a teacher or other employee in any school, and

(b) that person has, within the time limited by the copy of the notice served on him, referred the complaint to an Independent Schools Tribunal under section 470,

the Secretary of State may not make an order disqualifying him from being a teacher or other employee in any school.

472 Effect of personal disqualification.

Where, by virtue of an order made—

(a) by an Independent Schools Tribunal under section 470, or

(b) by the Secretary of State under section 471,

a person is disqualified either from being the proprietor of an independent school or from being a teacher or other employee in any school, then (unless the order otherwise directs) he shall by virtue of the order be disqualified both from being the proprietor of an independent school and from being a teacher or other employee in any school.

473 Enforcement of disqualification.

(1) A person is guilty of an offence if he uses any premises for purposes for which they are disqualified by virtue of an order made under section 470 or 471.

(2) A person is guilty of an offence if he—

(a) acts as the proprietor of an independent school, or

(b) accepts or endeavours to obtain employment as a teacher or other employee in any school,

while he is disqualified from so acting or from being so employed by virtue of an order made under

section 470 or 471.

[473A Removal of disqualification: persons no longer unsuitable to work with children.

(1) Subject to section 473B, a person to whom this section applies may make an application under this section to the Tribunal.

(2) This section applies to any person who is disqualified, by an order made under section 470 or 471 on the grounds that he is unsuitable to work with children—

(a) from being the proprietor of any independent school; or

(b) from being a teacher or other employee in any school.

(3) On an application under this section the Tribunal shall determine whether or not the individual shall continue to be subject to the order.

(4) If the Tribunal is satisfied that the individual is no longer unsuitable to work with children, it shall direct that the order shall cease to have effect; otherwise it shall dismiss the application.

(5) In this section and section 473B, "the Tribunal" means the tribunal established by section 9 of the Protection of Children Act 1999.

473B Conditions for application under section 473A.

(1) A person may only make an application under section 473A with the leave of the Tribunal.

(2) An application for leave under this section may not be made unless the appropriate conditions are satisfied in the person's case.

(3) In the case of a person who was a child when the order was made, the appropriate conditions are satisfied if—

(a) at least five years have elapsed since the order was made; and

(b) in the period of five years ending with the time when he makes the application under this section, he has made no other such application.

(4) In the case of any other person, the appropriate conditions are satisfied if—

(a) at least ten years have elapsed since the order was made; and

(b) in the period of ten years ending with the time when he makes the application under this section, he has made no other such application.

(5) The Tribunal shall not grant an application under this section unless it considers—

(a) that the person's circumstances have changed since the order was made, or, as the case may be, since he last made an application under this section; and

(b) that the change is such that leave should be granted.][572]

474[Removal of disqualification: other cases][573].

(1) If on the application of any person the Secretary of State is satisfied that any disqualification imposed by an order made under section 470 or 471 is, by reason of any change of circumstances, no longer necessary, he may by order remove the disqualification .

[But this subsection does not apply in relation to the disqualification of a person to whom section 473A applies.][574]

(2) Any person who is aggrieved by the refusal of the Secretary of State to remove any such disqualification may appeal to an Independent Schools Tribunal within such time after the refusal has been communicated to him as may be limited by rules made under section 476.

475 Duty of Registrar to comply with order for the deletion of a school from the register.

Where an order directing that a school be struck off the register is made—

(a) by the Secretary of State under section 468 or 471, or

(b) by an Independent Schools Tribunal under section 470,

the Registrar of Independent Schools shall strike the school off the register as from the date on which the direction takes effect.

Independent Schools Tribunals

476 Constitution and proceedings of Independent Schools Tribunals.

(1) Schedule 34 has effect in relation to the constitution of Independent Schools Tribunals and the remuneration of their members.

(2) The Lord Chancellor may, with the concurrence of the Lord President of the Council, make rules as to—

(a) the practice and procedure to be followed with respect to the constitution of Independent Schools

Tribunals;

(b) the manner of making appeals to such tribunals; and

(c) proceedings before such tribunals and matters incidental to or consequential on such proceedings.

(3) The rules may, in particular, make provision—

(a) requiring such a tribunal to sit at such places as may be directed in accordance with the rules; and

(b) as to appearance before such tribunals by counsel or a solicitor.

(4) Part I of the Arbitration Act 1996 shall not apply to any proceedings before an Independent Schools Tribunal, except so far as any provisions of that Act may be applied, with or without modifications, to such proceedings by the rules.

(5) Every order of an Independent Schools Tribunal shall be registered by the Registrar of Independent Schools and shall be open to public inspection at all reasonable times.

Supplementary

477 Disqualification in Scotland.

For the purposes of this Part, except section 474, a person who is disqualified by an order made (or having effect as if made) under section 100 of the Education (Scotland) Act 1980—

(a) from being the proprietor of an independent school within the meaning of that Act, or

(b) from being a teacher in any school,

shall be taken to be disqualified from being the proprietor of an independent school within the meaning of this Act, or (as the case may be) from being a teacher in any school, by virtue of an order made under section 470 or 471.

478 Offences: institution of proceedings and punishment.

(1) No proceedings shall be instituted for an offence under section 466 or 473 except by or on behalf of the Secretary of State.

(2) A person guilty of an offence under section 466 or 473 is liable on summary conviction—

(a) to a fine not exceeding level 4 on the standard scale, or

(b) to imprisonment for a term not exceeding three months,

or both.

Chapter III Assisted places at independent schools

479. . . . .[575]

480. . . . .[576]

481. . . . .[577]

Chapter IV City colleges

[482 Academies

(1) The Secretary of State may enter into an agreement with any person under which—

(a) that person undertakes to establish and maintain, and to carry on or provide for the carrying on of, an independent school in England with the characteristics mentioned in subsection (2) and such other characteristics as are specified in the agreement, and

(b) the Secretary of State agrees to make payments to that person in consideration of those undertakings.

(2) The characteristics mentioned above are that the school—

(a) has a curriculum satisfying the requirements of section 78 of the Education Act 2002, but with an emphasis on a particular subject area, or particular subject areas, specified in the agreement, and

(b) provides education for pupils of different abilities who are wholly or mainly drawn from the area in which the school is situated.

(3) Before entering into an agreement under this section, the Secretary of State must consult the following about the establishment of the school—

(a) the local education authority in whose area the school is to be situated; and

(b) if the Secretary of State thinks a significant proportion of the pupils at the school is likely to be resident within the area of another local education authority, that authority.

(4) An agreement under this section shall make any payments by the Secretary of State dependent on the fulfilment of—

(a) conditions and requirements imposed for the purpose of securing that no charge is made in respect of admission to (or attendance at) the school or, subject to such exceptions as may be specified in the agreement, in respect of education provided at the school, and

(b) such other conditions and requirements in relation to the school as are specified in the agreement.

(5) A school to which an agreement under this section relates shall be known as an Academy.

(6) Schedule 35A (which makes provision about land in relation to Academies) has effect.][578]

483 City colleges: financial provisions.

(1) Payments under an agreement under section 482 may be in respect of capital or current expenditure.

(2) In so far as such payments relate to current expenditure, the agreement shall provide for their continuance (subject to the fulfilment of the conditions and requirements falling within section 482(4))—

(a) for a period of not less than seven years, or

(b) for an indefinite period terminable by the Secretary of State by not less than seven years' written notice.

(3) Where such payments relate to capital expenditure, the agreement [may][579] provide for the repayment to the Secretary of State, in the event of the school at any time discontinuing or ceasing to have the characteristics specified in the agreement and in section 482(2), of sums determined by reference to—

(a) the value at that time of the school premises and other assets held for the purposes of the school, and

(b) the extent to which expenditure incurred in providing those assets was met by payments under the agreement.

[(3A) [If the school is a city academy, subsection (3) shall apply with such modifications (if any) as may be specified by the Secretary of State by order.][580]][581]

(4) Without prejudice to subsection (1), an agreement under section 482 may provide for indemnifying a person, in the event of the agreement being terminated by the Secretary of State, for expenditure—

(a) incurred by that person in carrying out the undertakings mentioned in section 482(1), or

(b) incurred by that person (otherwise than by virtue of subsection (3)) in consequence of the termination of the agreement.

[483A City colleges and academies: special educational needs.

(1) This section applies in relation to any child falling within subsection (2) if the condition in subsection (3) is satisfied.

(2) A child falls within this subsection if—

(a) he is a child for whom a statement is maintained under section 324, and

(b) he attends (or proposes to attend) a school which is a city technology college, a city college for the technology of the arts or [an Academy][582] .

(3) The condition in this subsection is satisfied if—

(a) the school is approved by the Secretary of State under section 347(1), or

(b) the Secretary of State consents to the child being educated at the school.

(4) The Secretary of State may by regulations make provision for securing that arrangements are made—

(a) for making the special educational provision specified in the statement;

(b) for making any non-educational provision specified in the statement.

(5) Regulations under subsection (4) may require or authorise a local education authority—

(a) to make payments to the school in respect of the child, or

(b) to provide any other assistance to the school in respect of the child.

(6) No condition or requirement imposed by virtue of section 482(4)(a) is to prevent a local education authority making payments or providing assistance by virtue of subsection (5).

(7) [This section does not apply to schools in Wales.][583]][584]

Part VIII Grants and other financial matters

Grants

484[Education standards grants.][585]

(1) The [National Assembly for Wales][586] may pay grants, known as [education standards grants,][587] to local education authorities [in Wales][588] in respect of eligible expenditure incurred or to be incurred by them.

(2) In this section "eligible expenditure" means expenditure of any class or description for the time being specified in regulations, being expenditure for or in connection with educational purposes which it appears to the [National Assembly for Wales][589] that local education authorities should be encouraged to incur in the interests of education in [...England and][590]... Wales.

(3) The regulations shall provide that [any education standards grant][591] payable in pursuance of the regulations—

(a) shall only be payable in respect of eligible expenditure incurred or to be incurred by a local education authority in a financial year to the extent to which that expenditure is approved for that year by the [National Assembly for Wales][592] for the purposes of the regulations, and

(b) shall be payable at such rate as may be specified in the regulations.

(4) The regulations may provide for the time and manner of payment of [any education standards grant][593].

(5) The regulations may provide for expenditure incurred or to be incurred by any local education authority in making payments, whether by way of maintenance, assistance or otherwise, to any body or persons who incur expenditure for or in connection with educational purposes (including another local education authority) to be treated, in such circumstances as may be specified in the regulations, as eligible expenditure.

(6) [The [National Assembly for Wales][594] may exercise his power under subsection (1) separately and differently in relation to local education authorities in England and local education authorities in Wales, and "education in England and Wales" in subsection (2) shall be construed accordingly.][595]

(7) Nothing in section 29(1) or 507 applies in relation to any function of the [National Assembly for Wales][596] under this section or under section 489 so far as it relates to regulations under this section; and nothing in sections 495 to 497 applies in relation to any function arising by virtue of section 489 so far as it relates to such regulations.

485 Grants in aid of educational services or research.

Regulations shall make provision for the payment by the Secretary of State to persons other than local education authorities of grants in respect of expenditure incurred or to be incurred by them—

(a) for the purposes of, or in connection with, the provision (or proposed provision) of educational services, or

(b) for the purposes of educational research.

486 Grants to bodies whose objects are promotion of learning or research.

Regulations may provide for the payment of grants to bodies other than local education authorities whose object or main object is, in the opinion of the Secretary of State, the promotion of learning or research.

487 Grants for education in Welsh.

Regulations shall make provision for the payment by the Secretary of State to local education authorities and other persons of grants in respect of expenditure incurred or to be incurred in, or in connection with, the teaching of the Welsh language or the teaching in that language of other subjects.

488 Grants for education of travellers and displaced persons.

(1) Regulations may make provision for the payment to local education authorities of grants in respect of expenditure incurred or to be incurred by them in making provision the purpose (or main purpose) of which is to promote and facilitate the education of persons to whom this section applies.

(2) This section applies to a person if—

(a) by reason of his way of life (or, in the case of a child, his parent's way of life) he either has no fixed abode or leaves his main abode to live elsewhere for significant periods in each year;

(b) he fell within paragraph (a) within a prescribed period immediately preceding the making of the provision in question; or

(c) he is for the time being resident in a camp or other accommodation or establishment provided for refugees or for displaced or similar persons.

(3) The regulations may—

(a) prescribe classes or descriptions of expenditure in respect of which grants are payable under the regulations, and

(b) provide for the determination of the amount of any grant so payable.

489 Conditions as to payment of grants under sections 484 to 488.

(1) Regulations made under any of sections 484 to 488 may provide—

(a) for the payment of grant under the regulations to be dependent on the fulfilment of such conditions as may be determined by or in accordance with the regulations, and

(b) for requiring persons to whom payments have been made under the regulations to comply with such requirements as may be so determined.

(2) Conditions and requirements determined under subsection (1)(a) and (b) by or in accordance with regulations made under section 484 may include conditions and requirements obliging the local education authority in question to delegate decisions about the spending of—

(a)[education standards grant,][597] and

(b) amounts allocated by the authority to meet eligible expenditure (within the meaning of that section) which is approved by the Secretary of State,

to such persons as may be determined by or in accordance with the regulations.

(3) The Secretary of State may by order make such modifications of any trust deed or other instrument relating to or regulating any institution that—

(a) provides or is concerned in the provision of educational services, or

(b) is concerned in educational research,

as, after consultation with the persons responsible for the management of the institution, appear to him to be requisite to enable them to fulfil any condition or meet any requirement imposed by regulations under section 485.

(4) Any modification made by an order under subsection (3) may be made to have permanent effect or to have effect for such period as may be specified in the order.

490 Grants in respect of special provision for ethnic minorities.

(1) Where subsection (2) applies, the power conferred by section 11 of the Local Government Act 1966 (grants in respect of ethnic minority population) shall apply in relation to the payment of grants by the Secretary of State to—

(a). . . . .[598]

(b) a person who in pursuance of undertakings under an agreement under section 482 maintains and carries on, or provides for the carrying on of, a city technology college [, a city college for the technology of the arts or a city academy][599] of the arts,

as it applies in relation to the payment of grants to a local authority who in his opinion are required to make special provision in exercise of any of their functions in consequence of the presence within their area of such persons as are referred to in section 11 of that Act.

(2) This subsection applies if, in the Secretary of State's opinion, special provision is made by the governing body or person in question in consequence of the presence within the locality of the school [, college or academy][600] of such persons as are referred to in section 11 of that Act.

Payment of fees etc.

491 Payment of school fees and expenses.

(1) Regulations shall make provision for the payment by the Secretary of State, for the purpose of enabling pupils to take advantage without hardship to themselves or their parents of any educational facilities available to them, of the whole or any part of the fees and expenses payable in respect of children attending schools at which fees are payable.

(2) Regulations under this section may provide—

(a) for the making of payments under the regulations to be dependent on the fulfilment of such conditions as may be determined by or in accordance with the regulations, and

(b) for requiring persons to whom payments have been made under the regulations to comply with such requirements as may be so determined.

Recoupment

492 Recoupment: adjustment between local education authorities.

(1) Regulations may provide, in relation to cases where any provision for education to which this section applies is made by a local education authority in respect of a person who belongs to the area of another local education authority, for requiring or authorising the other authority to pay to the providing authority—

(a) such amount as the authorities may agree, or

(b) failing agreement, such amount as may be determined by or under the regulations.

(2) This section applies to primary education, secondary education and further education and to part-time education for those who have not attained [compulsory school age][601].

(3) The regulations may provide for the amounts payable by one authority to another—

(a) to reflect the whole or any part of the average costs incurred by local education authorities in the provision of education (whether in England and Wales as a whole or in any particular area or areas); and

(b) to be based on figures for average costs determined by such body or bodies representing local education authorities, or on such other figures relating to costs so incurred, as the Secretary of State considers appropriate.

(4) The regulations may provide for the amounts so payable, in such cases as may be specified in or determined in accordance with the regulations, to be such amounts as may be determined by the Secretary of State.

(5) Any dispute between local education authorities as to whether one of them is entitled to be paid any amount by another under the regulations shall be determined by the Secretary of State.

(6) In this section—

(a) references to provision for education include provision of any benefits or services for which provision is made by or under this Act or any other enactment relating to education; and

(b) "further education" does not include further education of a kind such that expenditure on its provision would fall within paragraph 6 of Schedule 10 to the Local Government, Planning and Land Act 1980.

493 Recoupment: cross-border provisions.

(1) Regulations may make provision requiring or authorising payments of amounts determined by or under the regulations to be made by one authority to another where—

(a) the authority receiving the payment makes, in such cases or circumstances as may be specified in the regulations, provision for education in respect of a person having such connection with the area of the paying authority as may be so specified, and

(b) one of the authorities is a local education authority and the other an education authority in Scotland.

(2) Subsections (3) and (4) of section 492 shall apply for the purposes of this section as they apply for the purposes of that section.

(3) Any question concerning the connection of any person with the area of a particular local education authority or education authority shall be decided in accordance with the regulations.

(4) In subsection (1) "provision for education" includes provision of any benefits or services for which provision is made by or under this Act or any other enactment relating to education.

[494 Recoupment: excluded pupils.

(1) Subsection (2) applies where a pupil is permanently excluded from any school maintained by a local education authority ("the old authority") and, in the financial year in which the exclusion first takes effect, he is subsequently provided with education by another local education authority ("the new authority"), whether at a school maintained by that authority or otherwise than at school.

(2) The old authority shall pay to the new authority, in connection with the provision of education for that pupil in that financial year, such amount, if any, as is payable in accordance with regulations.

(3) Where a pupil is permanently excluded from any school maintained by a local education authority and, in the financial year in which the exclusion first takes effect, the following events subsequently occur—

(a) he is first provided by another local education authority ("the intermediate authority") with

education in a pupil referral unit or otherwise than at school, and

(b) at any time afterwards he is provided with education by a local education authority other than the intermediate authority ("the last authority"), whether at a school maintained by that authority or otherwise than at school,

then, in connection with the provision of the education mentioned in paragraph (b), subsection (2) shall apply to the intermediate authority and the last authority as if they were an old authority and a new authority respectively.

(4) Any dispute as to whether any local education authority are entitled to be paid any amount under this section by any other such authority shall be determined by the Secretary of State.

(5) Regulations may prescribe the time when the permanent exclusion of a pupil is to be regarded as taking effect for the purposes of this section.][602]

Part IX Ancillary functions

Chapter I Ancillary functions of Secretary of State

General functions

495 Determination of disputes.

(1) Except where this Act expressly provides otherwise, any dispute between a local education authority and the governing body of a school as to the exercise of any power conferred or the performance of any duty imposed by or under this Act may be referred to the Secretary of State (despite any enactment which makes the exercise of the power or the performance of the duty contingent upon the opinion of the authority or of the governing body).

(2) The Secretary of State shall determine any dispute referred to him under subsection (1).

(3) Any dispute between two or more local education authorities as to which of them is responsible for the provision of education for any pupil shall be determined by the Secretary of State.

496 Power to prevent unreasonable exercise of functions.

(1) If the Secretary of State is satisfied (either on a complaint by any person or otherwise) that a body to which this section applies have acted or are proposing to act unreasonably with respect to the exercise of any power conferred or the performance of any duty imposed by or under this Act, he may give such directions as to the exercise of the power or the performance of the duty as appear to him to be expedient (and may do so despite any enactment which makes the exercise of the power or the performance of the duty contingent upon the opinion of the body).

(2) The bodies to which this section applies are—

(a) any local education authority, [and][603]

[(b) the governing body of any community, foundation or voluntary school or any community or foundation special school.][604]

497 General default powers.

(1) If the Secretary of State is satisfied (either on a complaint by any person interested or otherwise) that a body to which this section applies have failed to discharge any duty imposed on them by or for the purposes of this Act, he may make an order—

(a) declaring the body to be in default in respect of that duty, and

(b) giving such directions for the purpose of enforcing the performance of the duty as appear to him to be expedient.

(2) The bodies to which this section applies are—

(a) any local education authority, [and][605]

[(b) the governing body of any community, foundation or voluntary school or any community or foundation special school.][606]

(3) Any directions given under subsection (1)(b) shall be enforceable, on an application made on behalf of the Secretary of State, by an order of mandamus.

[497A Power to secure proper performance of LEA's functions.

[(1) This section applies to a local education authority's functions under this Act and to other functions (of whatever nature) which are conferred on them in their capacity as a local education authority.][607]

(2) If the Secretary of State is satisfied (either on a complaint by any person interested or otherwise) that a local education authority are failing in any respect to perform any function to which this section

applies to an adequate standard (or at all), he may exercise his powers under subsection ([(4), (4A) or (4B)][608]).

[(2A) The Secretary of State may also exercise his powers under subsection (4), (4A) or (4B) where—

(a) he has given a previous direction under subsection (4), (4A) or (4B) in relation to a local education authority in respect of any function towhich this section applies, and

(b) he is satisfied that it is likely that if no further direction were given under subsection (4), (4A) or (4B) on the expiry or revocation of theprevious direction the authority would fail in any respect to perform that function to an adequate standard (or at all).][609]

(3). . . . .[610]

[(4) The Secretary of State may under this subsection give the authority or an officer of the authority such directions as the Secretary of State thinks expedient for the purpose of securing that the function is performed on behalf of the authority by such person as is specified in the direction; and such directions may require that any contract or other arrangement made by the authority with that person contains such terms and conditions as may be so specified.][611]

[(4A) The Secretary of State may under this subsection direct that the function shall be exercised by the Secretary of State or a person nominated by him and that the authorityshall comply with any instructions of the Secretary of State or his nominee in relation to the exercise of the function.

(4B) The Secretary of State may under this subsection (whether or not he exercises the power conferred by subsection (4) or (4A) in relation to any function) give the authority or an officer of the authority such other directions as the Secretary of State thinks expedient for the purpose of securing that the function is performed to an adequate standard.][612]

[(5) Where the Secretary of State considers it expedient that—

(a) in the case of directions given under subsection (4), the person specified in the directions, or

(b) in the case of directions given under subsection (4A), the Secretary of State or a person nominated by him,

should perform other functions to which this section applies in addition to the function to which subsection (2) or (2A) applies, the directions under subsection (4) or (4A) may relate to the performance of those other functions as well; and in considering whether it is expedient that that person should perform any such additional functions, the Secretary of State may have regard to financial considerations.][613]

(6) Any direction under this section may either—

(a) have effect for an indefinite period until revoked by the Secretary of State, or

[(b) have effect for a period specified in the direction unless revoked earlier by the Secretary of State.][614]

(7) Any direction given under subsection [(4), (4A) or (4B)][615] shall be enforceable, on an application made on behalf of the Secretary of State, by an order of mandamus.][616]

[497AA Power to secure proper performance: duty of authority where directions contemplated

Where, in relation to any function to which section 497A applies, the Secretary of State—

(a) is satisfied as mentioned in subsection (2) or (2A)(b) of that section, and

(b) has notified the local education authority that he is so satisfied and that he is contemplating the giving of directions under subsection (4) or (4A) of that section,

the authority shall give the Secretary of State, and any person authorised by him for the purposes of this section, all such assistance, in connection with the proposed exercise of the function by the Secretary of State or another person in pursuance of directions, as they are reasonably able to give.][617]

[497B Power to secure proper performance: further provisions.

(1) Where the Secretary of State gives directions under [section 497A(4) or (4A) to a local education authority or to an officer of such an authority, the specified person][618] shall, in the performance of the function or functions specified in the directions, be entitled to exercise the powers conferred by this section.

[(1A) In this section "the specified person" means—

(a) in relation to directions under section 497A(4), the person specified in the directions, and

(b) in relation to directions under section 497A(4A), the Secretary of State or the person nominated by him.][619]

(2) The specified person shall have at all reasonable times—

(a) a right of entry to the premises of the authority, and

(b) a right to inspect, and take copies of, any records or other documents kept by the authority, and any other documents containing information relating to the authority, which he considers relevant to the performance of the specified function or functions.

(3) In exercising the right to inspect records or other documents under subsection (2), the specified person—

(a) shall be entitled at any reasonable time to have access to, and inspect and check the operation of, any computer and any associated apparatus or material which is or has been in use in connection with the records or other documents in question, and

(b) may require—

(i) the person by whom or on whose behalf the computer is or has been so used, or

(ii) any person having charge of, or otherwise concerned with the operation of, the computer, apparatus or material,

to afford him such assistance as he may reasonably require (including, in particular, the making of information available for inspection or copying in a legible form).

(4) Without prejudice to subsection (2), the authority shall give the specified person all assistance in connection with the performance of the specified function or functions which they are reasonably able to give.

(5) Subsection (2) shall apply in relation to any school maintained by the authority as it applies in relation to the authority; and without prejudice to that subsection (as it so applies)—

(a) the governing body of any such school shall give the specified person all assistance in connection with the exercise of his functions which they are reasonably able to give; and

(b) the governing body of any such school and the authority shall secure that all such assistance is also given by persons who work at the school.

(6) Any reference in this section to the specified person includes a reference to any person assisting him in the performance of the specified function or functions.

(7) In this section "document" and "records" each include information recorded in any form.][620]

Appointment of governors, etc.

498 Powers where no properly constituted governing body.

(1) Where it appears to the Secretary of State that, by reason of the default of any person, there is no properly constituted governing body of a school to which this section applies, the Secretary of State—

(a) may make such appointments and give such directions as he thinks desirable for the purpose of securing that there is a properly constituted governing body of that school, and

(b) may give directions rendering valid any acts or proceedings which in his opinion are invalid or otherwise defective by reason of the default.

[(2) This section applies to any community, foundation or voluntary school or any community or foundation special school.][621]

Membership of education committees

499 Power to direct appointment of members of education committees.

(1) Subsection (2) applies to any local authorities which in accordance with section 102(1) of the Local Government Act 1972 have appointed any committees wholly or partly for the purpose of discharging any functions with respect to education which are conferred on them in their capacity as local education authorities.

(2) The Secretary of State may by directions to any local authorities to which this subsection applies require—

(a) every such committee, or

(b) any such committee of a description specified in the direction,

to include persons appointed, in accordance with the directions, for securing the representation on the committee of persons who appoint foundation governors for voluntary schools in the area for which the committee acts.

(3) Subsection (4) applies to any two or more local authorities which in accordance with section 102(1) of the Local Government Act 1972 have appointed any committees wholly or partly for the purpose of

discharging any functions with respect to education which are conferred on them in their capacity as local education authorities.

(4) The Secretary of State may by directions to any local authorities to which this subsection applies require—

(a) every such committee, or

(b) any such committee of a description specified in the direction,

to include persons appointed, in accordance with the directions, for securing the representation on the committee of persons who appoint foundation governors for voluntary schools in the area for which the committee acts or in such area as may be specified in the direction.

(5) The power of the Secretary of State to give directions under subsection (2) or (4) shall be exercisable in relation to any sub-committees which—

(a) are appointed by the authorities concerned or any such committee as is mentioned in that subsection, and

(b) are so appointed wholly or partly for the purpose of discharging the authorities' functions as mentioned in subsection (1) or (3) or the committee's functions with respect to education,

as it is exercisable in relation to the committees themselves.

[(6) Regulations may require—

(a) any such committee as is mentioned in subsection (1) or (3), and

(b) any sub-committee appointed by any authorities within subsection (1) or (3), or by any committee within paragraph (a) of this subsection, for the purpose mentioned in subsection (5)(b),

to include one or more persons elected, in accordance with the regulations, as representatives of parent governors at maintained schools in relation to which the committee or sub-committee acts.

(7) Regulations may make provision for—

(a) the number of persons who are to be elected for the purposes of subsection (6) in the case of any local education authority;

(b) the procedure to be followed in connection with the election of such persons and the persons who are entitled to vote at such an election;

(c) the circumstances in which persons are qualified or disqualified for being so elected or for holding office once elected;

(d) the term of office of persons so elected and their voting rights;

(e) the application to any such committee or sub-committee, with or without any modification, of any provision made by or under any other enactment and relating to committees or (as the case may be) sub-committees of a local authority;

(f) such other matters connected with such elections or persons so elected as the Secretary of State considers appropriate.

(8) Regulations may also make provision—

(a) enabling the Secretary of State to determine, where he considers it expedient to do so in view of the small number of maintained schools in relation to which a committee or sub-committee acts, that the requirement imposed on the committee or sub-committee by virtue of subsection (6) is to have effect as if it referred to representatives of parents of registered pupils (rather than representatives of parent governors) at those schools;

(b) for any regulations under subsection (7) to have effect, where the Secretary of State makes any such determination, with such modifications as may be prescribed.

(9) In subsections (6) and (8) "maintained school" and "parent governor" have the same meaning as in the School Standards and Framework Act 1998.][622]

Rationalisation of school places

500. . . . .[623]

501. . . . .[624]

502. . . . .[625]

503. . . . .[626]

504. . . . .[627]

505. . . . .[628]

Medical examinations

506 Power to require medical examination of pupils.

(1) Where—

(a) a question is referred to the Secretary of State under section 442(3) or 495, and

(b) in his opinion the examination of any pupil by a registered medical practitioner appointed by him for the purpose would assist in determining the question,

he may serve a notice on the parent of that pupil requiring the parent to present the pupil for examination by such a practitioner.

(2) Any parent who without reasonable excuse fails to comply with any requirements of a notice served on him under subsection (1) is guilty of an offence.

(3) A person guilty of an offence under this section is liable on summary conviction to a fine not exceeding level 1 on the standard scale.

Local inquiries

507 Power to direct local inquiries.

(1) The Secretary of State may cause a local inquiry to be held for the purpose of the exercise of any of his functions under this Act.

(2) Subsections (2) to (5) of section 250 of the Local Government Act 1972 (giving evidence at and defraying costs of local inquiries) shall have effect with respect to any such inquiry as they have effect with respect to an inquiry held under that section.

Chapter II Ancillary functions of local education authorities

Provision of services

508 Functions in respect of facilities for recreation and social and physical training.

(1) A local education authority shall secure that the facilities for primary, [and secondary education][629] provided for their area include adequate facilities for recreation and social and physical training.

[(1A) a local education authority may provide facilities for recreation and social and physical training as part of the facilities for further education provided (whether or not by them) for their area.][630]

(2)[For the purpose of subsection (1) or (1A)][631] a local education authority—

(a) may establish, maintain and manage, or assist the establishment, maintenance and management of,—

(i) camps, holiday classes, playing fields, play centres, and

(ii) other places, including playgrounds, gymnasiums and swimming baths not appropriated to any school or other educational institution,

at which facilities for recreation and social and physical training are available for persons receiving primary, secondary or further education;

(b) may organise games, expeditions and other activities for such persons; and

(c) may defray, or contribute towards, the expenses of such games, expeditions and other activities.

(3) When making arrangements for the provision of facilities or the organisation of activities in the exercise of their powers under subsection (2), a local education authority shall, in particular, have regard to the expediency of co-operating with any voluntary societies or bodies whose objects include the provision of facilities or the organisation of activities of a similar character.

509 Provision of transport etc.

(1) A local education authority shall make such arrangements for the provision of transport and otherwise as they consider necessary, or as the Secretary of State may direct, for the purpose of facilitating the attendance of persons [not of sixth form age][632] receiving education—

(a) at schools,

(b) at any institution maintained or assisted by the authority which provides further education or higher education (or both),[or;][633]

(c) at any institution within the further education sector,. . .[634]

(d). . . . .

[(1A) A local education authority shall make such arrangements for the provision of transport and otherwise as they consider necessary, or as the Secretary of State may direct, for the purpose of facilitating the attendance of persons [not of sixth form age][635] receiving education or training at an

institution outside both the further education and higher education sectors.

(1B) Arrangements under subsection (1A) may be made in relation to a person only if the Learning and Skills Council for England or the National Council for Education and Training for Wales has secured for him—

(a) the provision of education or training at the institution, and

(b) the provision of boarding accommodation under section 13 or 41 of the Learning and Skills Act 2000.][636]

(2) Any transport provided in pursuance of arrangements under subsection (1) [or (1A)][637] shall be provided free of charge.

(3) A local education [or training][638] authority may pay the whole or any part, as they think fit, of the reasonable travelling expenses of any person [not of sixth form age][639] receiving education—

(a) at a school, or

(b) at any such institution as is mentioned in subsection (1) [or (1A)][640],

for whose transport no arrangements are made under [either of those subsections][641].

(4) In considering whether or not they are required by subsection (1) [or (1A)][642] to make arrangements in relation to a particular person, a local education authority shall have regard (amongst other things)—

(a) to the age of the person and the nature of the route, or alternative routes, which he could reasonably be expected to take; and

(b) to any wish of his parent for him to be provided with education [or training][643] at a school or institution in which the religious education provided is that of the religion or denomination to which his parent adheres.

(5) Arrangements made by a local education authority under subsection (1) [or (1A)][644] shall—

(a). . . . .[645]

(b) make provision for persons receiving full-time education at any institution within the further education sector which is no less favourable than the provision made in pursuance of the arrangements for pupils of the same age at schools maintained by a local education authority; and

[(c) make provision for persons receiving full-time education or training at institutions mentioned in subsection (1A) which is no less favourable than the provision made in pursuance of the arrangements for persons of the same age with learning difficulties (within the meaning of section 13 of the Learning and Skills Act 2000) for whom the authority secures the provision of education at any other institution.][646]

[(6) [Regulations may require a local education authority to publish, at such times and in such manner as may be prescribed, such information as may be prescribed with respect to the authority's policy and arrangements relating to the making of—

(a) provision under this section for persons attending institutions mentioned in subsection (1)(c) [or (1A)][647] who are over compulsory school age and have not attained the age of 19; or

(b) provision under section 509A (travel arrangements for children receiving nursery education otherwise than at school).][648]][649]

[(7) References in this section to persons not of sixth form age shall be construed in accordance with subsection (1) of section 509AC.][650]

[509AA Provision of transport etc. for persons of sixth form age

(1) A local education authority shall prepare for each academic year a transport policy statement complying with the requirements of this section.

(2) The statement shall specify the arrangements for the provision of transport or otherwise that the authority consider it necessary to make for facilitating the attendance of persons of sixth form age receiving education or training—

(a) at schools,

(b) at any institution maintained or assisted by the authority which provides further education or higher education (or both),

(c) at any institution within the further education sector, or

(d) at any establishment (not falling within paragraph (b) or (c)) which is supported by the Learning and Skills Council for England or the National Council for Education and Training for Wales.

(3) The statement shall specify the arrangements that the authority consider it necessary to make for the provision of financial assistance in respect of the reasonable travelling expenses of persons of sixth form age receiving education or training at any establishment such as is mentioned in subsection (2).

(4) The statement shall specify the arrangements proposed to be made by the governing bodies of—

(a) schools maintained by the authority at which education suitable to the requirements of persons over compulsory school age is provided, and

(b) institutions within the further education sector in the authority's area,

for the provision of transport for facilitating the attendance of persons of sixth form age receiving education or training at the schools and institutions and for the provision of financial assistance in respect of the travelling expenses of such persons.

(5) Those governing bodies shall co-operate in giving the local education authority any information and other assistance that is reasonably required by the authority for the performance of their functions under this section and section 509AB.

(6) The statement shall specify any travel concessions (within the meaning of Part 5 of the Transport Act 1985 (c. 67)) which are to be provided under any scheme established under section 93 of that Act to persons of sixth form age receiving education at any establishment such as is mentioned in subsection (2) above in the authority's area.

(7) The authority shall—

(a) publish the statement, in a manner which they consider appropriate, on or before 31st May in the year in which the academic year in question begins, and

(b) make, and secure that effect is given to, any arrangements specified under subsections (2) and (3).

(8) Nothing in this section prevents a local education authority from making, at any time in an academic year, arrangements—

(a) which are not specified in the transport policy statement published by the authority for that year, but

(b) which they have come to consider necessary for the purposes mentioned in subsections (2) and (3).

(9) The Secretary of State may, if he considers it expedient to do so, direct a local education authority to make for any academic year—

(a) arrangements for the provision of transport or otherwise for facilitating the attendance of persons of sixth form age receiving education or training at establishments such as are mentioned in subsection (2), or

(b) arrangements for providing financial assistance in respect of the reasonable travelling expenses of such persons,

which have not been specified in the transport policy statement published by the authority for that academic year.

(10) The Secretary of State may by order amend subsection (7)(a) by substituting a different date for 31st May.][651]

[509AB Further provision about transport policy statements

(1) A statement prepared under section 509AA shall state to what extent arrangements specified in accordance with subsection (2) of that section include arrangements for facilitating the attendance at establishments such as are mentioned in that subsection of disabled persons and persons with learning difficulties.

(2) A statement prepared under that section shall—

(a) specify arrangements for persons receiving full-time education or training at establishments other than schools maintained by the local education authority which are no less favourable than the arrangements specified for pupils of the same age attending such schools, and

(b) specify arrangements for persons with learning difficulties receiving education or training at establishments other than schools maintained by the authority which are no less favourable than the arrangements specified for pupils of the same age with learning difficulties attending such schools.

(3) In considering what arrangements it is necessary to make for the purposes mentioned in subsections (2) and (3) of section 509AA the local education authority shall have regard (amongst other things)

to—

(a) the needs of those for whom it would not be reasonably practicable to attend a particular establishment to receive education or training if no arrangements were made,

(b) the need to secure that persons in their area have reasonable opportunities to choose between different establishments at which education or training is provided,

(c) the distance from the homes of persons of sixth form age in their area of establishments such as are mentioned in section 509AA(2) at which education or training suitable to their needs is provided, and

(d) the cost of transport to the establishments in question and of any alternative means of facilitating the attendance of persons receiving education or training there.

(4) In considering whether or not it is necessary to make arrangements for those purposes in relation to a particular person, a local education authority shall have regard (amongst other things)—

(a) to the nature of the route, or alternative routes, which he could reasonably be expected to take; and

(b) to any wish of his parent for him to be provided with education or training at a school, institution or other establishment in which the religious education provided is that of the religion or denomination to which his parent adheres.

(5) In preparing a statement under section 509AA a local education authority shall have regard to any guidance issued by the Secretary of State under this section.

(6) In preparing a statement under that section a local education authority shall consult—

(a) any other local education authority that they consider it appropriate to consult,

(b) the governing bodies mentioned in subsection (4) of that section,

(c) the Learning and Skills Council for England (in the case of a local education authority in England) or the National Council for Education and Training for Wales (in the case of a local education authority in Wales), and

(d) any other person specified by the Secretary of State for the purposes of this section.

(7) In preparing a statement under that section a local education authority shall also consult—

(a) where they are the local education authority for a district in a metropolitan county, the Passenger Transport Authority for that county, and

(b) where they are the local education authority for a London borough or the City of London, Transport for London.][652]

[509AC Interpretation of sections 509AA and 509AB

(1) For the purposes of sections 509AA and 509AB a person receiving education or training at an establishment is of sixth form age if he is over compulsory school age but—

(a) is under the age of 19, or

(b) has begun a particular course of education or training at the establishment before attaining the age of 19 and continues to attend that course.

(2) References in section 509AA to an establishment supported by the Learning and Skills Council for England are to any establishment at which education or training is provided by a person to whom that Council secures the provision of financial resources in any of the ways mentioned in section 5(2) of the Learning and Skills Act 2000.

(3) References in section 509AA to an establishment supported by the National Council for Education and Training for Wales are to any establishment at which education or training is provided by a person to whom that Council secures the provision of financial resources in any of the ways mentioned in section 34(2) of the Learning and Skills Act 2000.

(4) References in section 509AB to persons with learning difficulties are to be construed in accordance with section 13(5) and (6) of the Learning and Skills Act 2000.

(5) In sections 509AA and 509AB and this section—

"academic year" means any period commencing with 1st August and ending with the next 31st July;

"disabled person" has the same meaning as in the Disability Discrimination Act 1995;

"establishment" means an establishment of any kind, including a school or institution;

"governing body", in relation to an institution within the further education sector, has the same meaning as in the Further and Higher Education Act 1992.

(6) The Secretary of State may by order amend the definition of "academic year" in subsection (5).][653]

[509A Travel arrangements for children receiving nursery education otherwise than at school.

(1) A local education authority may provide a child with assistance under this section if they are satisfied that, without such assistance, he would be prevented from attending at any premises—

(a) which are not a school or part of a school, but

(b) at which relevant nursery education is provided,

for the purpose of receiving such education there.

(2) The assistance which may be provided for a child under this section consists of either—

(a) making arrangements (whether for the provision of transport or otherwise) for the purpose of facilitating the child's attendance at the premises concerned, or

(b) paying the whole or any part of his reasonable travel expenses.

(3) When considering whether to provide a child with assistance under this section in connection with his attendance at any premises, a local education authority may have regard (among other things) to whether it would be reasonable to expect alternative arrangements to be made for him to receive relevant nursery education at any other premises (whether nearer to his home or otherwise).

(4) Where the assistance to be provided for a child under this section consists of making arrangements for the provision of transport, the authority may, if they consider it appropriate to do so, determine that the assistance shall not be so provided unless—

(a) the child's parent, or

(b) the person providing the relevant nursery education concerned,

agrees to make to the authority such payments in respect of the provision of the transport (not exceeding the cost to the authority of its provision) as they may determine.

[(4A) Regulations may require a local education authority to publish, at such times and in such manner as may be prescribed, such information as may be prescribed with respect to the authority's policy and arrangements relating to the making of provision under this section.][654]

(5) In this section "relevant nursery education" means nursery education which is provided—

(a) by a local education authority, or

(b) by any other person—

(i) who is in receipt of financial assistance given by such an authority and whose provision of nursery education is taken into account by the authority in formulating proposals for the purposes of section 120(2)(a) of the School Standards and Framework Act 1998, or

(ii) who is in receipt of grants under section 1 of the Nursery Education and Grant-Maintained Schools Act 1996.][655]

510 Provision of clothing.

(1) A local education authority may provide clothing for—

(a) any pupil who is a boarder at an educational institution maintained by the authority [or at a grant-maintained school][656],

(b) any pupil at a nursery school maintained by the authority, and

(c) any pupil in a nursery class at a school maintained by the authority [or at a grant-maintained school].

(2) A local education authority may also provide clothing for any pupil—

(a) for whom they are providing board and lodging elsewhere than at an educational institution maintained by them, and

(b) for whom special educational provision is made in pursuance of arrangements made by them.

(3) Where it appears to a local education authority, in a case where neither subsection (1) nor subsection (2) applies, that a pupil at—

(a) a school maintained by them [or a grant-maintained school][657], or

(b) a special school (whether maintained by them or not),

is unable by reason of the inadequacy or unsuitability of his clothing to take full advantage of the education provided at the school, the authority may provide him with such clothing as in their opinion is necessary for the purpose of ensuring that he is sufficiently and suitably clad while he remains a pupil at the school.

(4) A local education authority may provide—

(a) for pupils at a school maintained by them [, at a grant-maintained school][658] or at an institution maintained by them which provides further education or higher education (or both),

(b) for persons who have not attained the age of 19 and who are receiving education at an institution within the further education sector, and

(c) for persons who make use of facilities for physical training made available for them by the authority under section 508(2),

such articles of clothing as the authority may determine suitable for the physical training provided at that school or institution or under those facilities.

(5) A local education authority may—

(a) with the consent of the proprietor of a school not maintained by the authority, other than a [grant-maintained school or][659] special school, and

(b) on such financial and other terms, if any, as may be determined by agreement between the authority and the proprietor,

make arrangements, in the case of any pupil at the school who is unable by reason of the inadequacy or unsuitability of his clothing to take full advantage of the education provided at the school, for securing for the pupil the provision of such clothing as is necessary for the purpose of ensuring that he is sufficiently and suitably clad while he remains a pupil at the school.

(6) Any arrangements made under subsection (5) shall be such as to secure, so far as is practicable, that the expense incurred by the authority in connection with the provision of any article under the arrangements does not exceed the expense which would have been incurred by them in the provision of it if the pupil had been a pupil at a school maintained by them.

511 Provisions supplementary to section 510.

(1) Provision of clothing under section 510 may be made in such way as to confer either a right of property in the clothing or a right of user only (at the option of the providing authority), except in any circumstances for which the adoption of one or other of those ways of making such provision is prescribed.

(2) Where a local education authority have provided a person with clothing under section 510, then, in such circumstances respectively as may be prescribed—

(a) the authority shall require his parent to pay to them in respect of its provision such sum (if any) as in their opinion he is able to pay without financial hardship, not exceeding the cost to the authority of its provision;

(b) the authority may require his parent to pay to them in respect of its provision such sum as is mentioned in paragraph (a) or any lesser sum; or

(c) his parent shall not be required to pay any sum in respect of its provision.

(3) Any sum which a parent is duly required to pay by virtue of subsection (2)(a) or (b) may be recovered summarily as a civil debt.

(4) Where a person who has attained the age of 18 (other than a registered pupil at a school) is provided with clothing under section 510, any reference in subsection (2) or (3) to his parent shall be read as a reference to him.

[512 LEA functions concerning provision of meals, etc.

(1) A local education authority may provide—

(a) registered pupils at any school maintained by the authority,

(b) other persons who receive education at such a school, and

(c) children who receive relevant funded nursery education,

with milk, meals and other refreshments.

(2) Where provision is made under subsection (1), it shall be made—

(a) in a case within paragraph (a) or (b) of that subsection, either on the school premises or at any other place where education is being provided, and

(b) in a case within paragraph (c) of that subsection, at any place where education is being provided.

(3) A local education authority shall exercise their power under subsection (1) to provide school lunches for any person within paragraph (a) or (c) of that subsection if—

(a) any prescribed requirements are met,

(b) a request for the provision of school lunches has been made by or on behalf of that person to the authority, and

(c) either—

(i) that person is eligible for free lunches (within the meaning of section 512ZB(2)), or

(ii) in the case of a person within subsection (1)(a), it would not be unreasonable for the authority to provide the lunches.

(4) Subject to section 114(2) of the School Standards and Framework Act 1998 (c. 31) (lunches provided by LEAs to meet nutritional standards), any school lunches provided by a local education authority pursuant to subsection (3) may take such form as the authority think fit.

(5) A local education authority shall provide at any school maintained by them such facilities as they consider appropriate for the consumption of any meals or other refreshment brought to the school by registered pupils.

(6) In this section—

"prescribed" means prescribed by the Secretary of State by order;

"relevant funded nursery education", in relation to a local education authority, means education provided by a person other than the governing body of a maintained school (within the meaning of section 20(7) of the School Standards and Framework Act 1998) or a maintained nursery school—

(a) under arrangements made with that person by the authority in pursuance of the duty imposed on the authority by section 118 of that Act (duty of LEA to secure sufficient nursery education), and

(b) in consideration of financial assistance provided by the authority under those arrangements;

"school lunch"—

(a) in relation to a pupil, means food made available for consumption by the pupil as his midday meal on a school day, and

(b) in relation to a child receiving relevant funded nursery education at an establishment other than a school, means food made available for consumption by the child as his midday meal on a day on which he receives that education,

whether involving a set meal or the selection of items by him or otherwise;

and references, in relation to a local education authority, to a school maintained by the authority are to a community, foundation or voluntary school, a community or foundation special school, a maintained nursery school or a pupil referral unit maintained by the authority.][660]

[512ZA Duty to charge for meals etc.

(1) A local education authority shall charge for anything provided by them under subsection (1) or (3) of section 512.

(2) A local education authority shall charge every person the same price for the same quantity of the same item.

(3) This section is subject to section 512ZB.

512ZB Provision of free school lunches and milk

(1) Where the local education authority provide a school lunch in accordance with section 512(3) to a person who is eligible for free lunches, the authority shall provide the meal free of charge.

(2) For this purpose a person is eligible for free lunches if—

(a) he is within subsection (4), and

(b) a request that the school lunches be provided free of charge has been made by him or on his behalf to the authority.

(3) Where a local education authority exercise their power under subsection (1) of section 512 to provide a person within paragraph (a) or (c) of that subsection with milk, the authority shall provide the milk free of charge if—

(a) the person is within subsection (4), and

(b) a request that the milk be provided free of charge has been made by him or on his behalf to the authority.

(4) A person is within this subsection if—

(a) his parent is—

(i) in receipt of income support,

(ii) in receipt of an income-based jobseeker's allowance (payable under the Jobseekers Act 1995 (c. 18)),

(iii) in receipt of support provided under Part 6 of the Immigration and Asylum Act 1999 (c. 33), or

(iv) in receipt of any other benefit or allowance, or entitled to any tax credit under the Tax Credits Act 2002 (c. 21) or element of such a tax credit, prescribed for the purposes of this paragraph, in such circumstances as may be so prescribed, or

(b) he, himself, is—

(i) in receipt of income support,

(ii) in receipt of an income-based jobseeker's allowance, or

(iii) in receipt of any other benefit or allowance, or entitled to any tax credit under the Tax Credits Act 2002 (c. 21) or element of such a tax credit, prescribed for the purposes of this paragraph, in such circumstances as may be so prescribed.

(5) In this section "prescribed" and "school lunch" have the same meaning as in section 512.][661]

[512A Transfer of functions under section 512 to governing bodies.

(1) The Secretary of State may by order make provision for imposing on the governing body of any school to which the order applies a duty or duties corresponding to one or more of the duties of the local education authority which are mentioned in subsection (2).

(2) Those duties are—

(a) the duty to provide school lunches in accordance with [section 512(3) and (4)][662];

(b) the duty to provide school lunches free of charge in accordance with [section 512ZB(1)][663]; and

(c) the duty to provide milk free of charge in accordance with [section 512ZB(3)][664].

(3) An order under this section may (subject to subsection (6)) apply to—

(a) all maintained schools; or

(b) any specified class of such schools; or

(c) all such schools, or any specified class of such schools, maintained by specified local education authorities.

(4) Where any duty falls to be performed by the governing body of a school by virtue of an order under this section—

(a) the corresponding duty mentioned in subsection (2) shall no longer fall to be performed by the local education authority in relation to the school; and

(b) if the duty corresponds to the one mentioned in subsection (2)(b) or (c), section 533(3) shall not apply to any school lunches or milk provided by the governing body in pursuance of the order.

(5) An order under this section may provide for section 513(2) not to apply—

(a) to local education authorities generally, or

(b) to any specified local education authority,

either in relation to all pupils for whom provision is made by the authority under section 513 or in relation to all such pupils who are of such ages as may be specified.

(6) An order under this section shall not operate to—

(a) impose any duty on the governing body of a school, or

(b) relieve a local education authority of any duty in relation to a school,

at any time when the school does not have a delegated budget; and such an order may provide for [section 512ZA(2)][665] above to have effect, in relation to any provision made at any such time by the local education authority for pupils at the school, with such modifications as may be specified.

(7) In this section—

"delegated budget" and "maintained school" have the same meaning as in the School Standards and Framework Act 1998;

"school lunch" has the same meaning as in section 512 above;

"specified" means specified in an order under this section.][666]

513 Provision of meals etc. at schools not maintained by local education authorities.

(1) A local education authority may, with the consent of the proprietor of a school in their area which is not maintained by them, make arrangements for securing the provision of milk, meals and other refreshment for pupils in attendance at the school.

(2) Any arrangements under this section—

(a) shall be on such financial and other terms, if any, as may be determined by agreement between the authority and the proprietor of the school; and

(b) shall be such as to secure, so far as is practicable, that the expense incurred by the authority in

connection with the provision of any service or item under the arrangements shall not exceed the expense which would have been incurred by them in providing it if the pupil had been a pupil at a school maintained by them.

514 Provision of board and lodging otherwise than at school.

(1) Where a local education authority are satisfied with respect to any pupil—

(a) that primary or secondary education suitable to his age, ability and aptitude and to any special educational needs he may have can best be provided for him at a [particular community, foundation or voluntary or community or foundation special school, but][667]

(b) that such education cannot be so provided unless boarding accommodation is provided for him otherwise than at the school,

they may provide such board and lodging for him under such arrangements as they think fit.

(2) Where a local education authority are satisfied with respect to a pupil with special educational needs that provision of board and lodging for him is necessary for enabling him to receive the required special educational provision, they may provide such board and lodging for him under such arrangements as they think fit.

(3) In making any arrangements under this section, a local education authority shall, so far as practicable, give effect to the wishes of the pupil's parent as to the religion or religious denomination of the person with whom the pupil will reside.

(4) Subject to subsection (5), where a local education authority have provided a pupil with board and lodging under arrangements under this section, they shall require the pupil's parent to pay them such sums, if any, in respect of the board and lodging as in their opinion he is able to pay without financial hardship.

(5) No sum is recoverable under subsection (4) if the arrangements were made by the authority on the ground that in their opinion education suitable to the pupil's age, ability and aptitude or special educational needs could not otherwise be provided for him.

(6) The sums recoverable under subsection (4) shall not exceed the cost to the authority of providing the board and lodging.

(7) Any sum payable under subsection (4) may be recovered summarily as a civil debt.

515 Provision of teaching services for day nurseries.

(1) Subject to subsection (2), a local education authority may, in accordance with arrangements made by them for that purpose, make available to a day nursery the services of any teacher who—

(a) is employed by them in a nursery school or in a primary school having one or more nursery classes, and

(b) has agreed to provide his services for the purposes of the arrangements.

(2) Arrangements under subsection (1) in respect of a teacher in a [foundation or voluntary school][668] require the concurrence of the governing body of the school.

(3) Arrangements under this section may make provision—

(a) for the supply of equipment for use in connection with the teaching services made available under the arrangements;

(b) for regulating the respective functions of any teacher whose services are made available under the arrangements, the head teacher of his school and the person in charge of the day nursery; and

(c) for any supplementary or incidental matters connected with the arrangements, including, where the teacher's school and the day nursery are in the areas of different local education authorities, financial adjustments between those authorities.

(4) In this section "day nursery" means a day nursery provided under section 18 of the Children Act 1989 (provision by local authorities of day care for pre-school and other children).

(5) A teacher shall not be regarded as ceasing to be a member of the teaching staff of his school and subject to the general directions of his head teacher by reason only of his services being made available in pursuance of arrangements under this section.

516. . . . .[669]

Payment of fees

517 Payment of fees at schools not maintained by a local education authority.

(1) Where, in pursuance of arrangements made under section 18 or Part IV (special educational needs),

primary or secondary education is provided for a pupil at a school not maintained by them or another local education authority, the local education authority by whom the arrangements are made shall—

(a) if subsection (2), (3) or (4) applies, pay the whole of the fees payable in respect of the education provided in pursuance of the arrangements; and

(b) if board and lodging are provided for the pupil at the school and subsection (5) applies, pay the whole of the fees payable in respect of the board and lodging.

(2) This subsection applies where—

(a) the pupil fills a place in the school which the proprietor of the school has put at the disposal of the authority; and

(b) the school is one in respect of which grants are made by the Secretary of State under section 485.

(3) This subsection applies where the authority are satisfied that, by reason of a shortage of places in every school maintained by them or another local education authority to which the pupil could be sent with reasonable convenience, education suitable—

(a) to his age, ability and aptitude, and

(b) to any special educational needs he may have,

cannot be provided by them for him except at a school not maintained by them or another local education authority.

(4) This subsection applies where (in a case in which neither subsection (2) nor subsection (3) applies) the authority are satisfied—

(a) that the pupil has special educational needs, and

(b) that it is expedient in his interests that the required special educational provision should be made for him at a school not maintained by them or another local education authority.

(5) This subsection applies where the authority are satisfied that education suitable—

(a) to the pupil's age, ability and aptitude, and

(b) to any special educational needs he may have,

cannot be provided by them for him at any school unless board and lodging are also provided for him (either at school or elsewhere)

(6) As from such day as the Secretary of State may by order appoint this section shall have effect with the following modifications—

(a) in subsections (1) and (3), for "not maintained by them or another local education authority" substitute "which is neither a maintained nor a grant-maintained school";

(b) in subsection (3), for "every school maintained by them or another local education authority" substitute "every maintained or grant-maintained school";

(c) in subsections (3) and (5), for "provided by them" substitute "provided";

(d) omit subsection (4) and the reference to it in subsection (1); and

(e) at the end add—

"(7) In this section "grant-maintained school" includes a grant-maintained special school, and subsection (5) does not apply where section 348(2) applies."

(7) An order under subsection (6) may appoint different days for different provisions and for different purposes.

Subordinate Legislation Made

[518 Payment of school expenses; grant of scholarships, etc.

(1) A local education authority, for the purpose of enabling persons to take advantage of any educational facilities available to them, may in such circumstances as may be specified in or determined in accordance with regulations—

(a) pay such expenses of children attending community, foundation, voluntary or special schools as may be necessary to enable them to take part in any school activities,

(b) grant scholarships, exhibitions, bursaries and other allowances in respect of persons over compulsory school age.

(2) Regulations may make provision—

(a) for requiring a local education authority to make, in relation to each financial year, a determination relating to the extent to which they propose to exercise their power under subsection (1)(b) in that year; and

(b) for authorising an authority to determine not to exercise that power in a financial year—
(i) generally,
(ii) in such cases as may be prescribed, or
(iii) in such cases as may be determined by the authority.][670]

Allowances for governors

519 Travelling and subsistence allowances for governors of schools and further or higher education institutions.

(1) A local education authority may, in accordance with the provisions of a scheme made by them for the purposes of this section, pay [such allowances as may be prescribed to governors of—
(a) any community, foundation or voluntary school or community or foundation special school which does not have a delegated budget (within the meaning of Part II of the School Standards and Framework Act 1998);][671] and
(b) any institution providing higher education or further education (or both) which is maintained by a local education authority.

(2) Such a scheme may make different provision in relation to schools or other institutions of different categories (including provision for allowances not to be paid in respect of certain categories) but shall not make different provision in relation to different categories of governor of the same school or institution.

(3) Subject to subsections (4) and (5), a local education authority may pay [such allowances as may be prescribed][672] to any person appointed to represent them on the governing body of—
(a) any institution providing higher education or further education (or both) which is not maintained by them; or
(b) any independent school or special school which is not maintained by them.

(4) A local education authority shall not pay any allowance under subsection (3) for expenses in respect of which the person incurring them is entitled to reimbursement by any person other than the authority.

(5) A local education authority shall not pay any allowance under subsection (3) if they have not made any scheme under subsection (1) or if the arrangements under which the allowance would otherwise be payable—
(a) provide for allowances which are to any extent more generous than the most generous payable by the authority under any such scheme; or
(b) contain any provision which the authority would not have power to include in any such scheme.

(6) No allowance may be paid to any governor of a school or institution of a kind mentioned in subsection (1), in respect of the discharge of his functions as such a governor, otherwise than under this section.

[(7) Regulations may impose a limit on the amount which may be paid by way of any allowance under this section.][673]

Medical arrangements

520 Medical inspection and treatment of pupils.

(1) A local education authority shall make arrangements for encouraging and assisting pupils to take advantage of the provision for medical and dental inspection and treatment made for them in pursuance of section 5(1) or (1A) of the National Health Service Act 1977 or paragraph 1(a)(i) of Schedule 1 to that Act.

(2) If the parent of a pupil gives notice to the authority that he objects to the pupil availing himself of any of the provision so made, the pupil shall not be encouraged or assisted to do so.

(3). . . . .[674]

Cleanliness of pupils

521 Examination of pupils for cleanliness.

(1) A local education authority may by directions in writing authorise a medical officer of theirs to have the persons and clothing of pupils in attendance at relevant schools examined whenever in his opinion such examinations are necessary in the interests of cleanliness.

(2) Directions under subsection (1) may be given with respect to—
(a) all relevant schools, or

(b) any relevant schools named in the directions.

(3) An examination under this section shall be made by a person authorised by the authority to make such examinations; and, if the examination is of a girl, it shall not be made by a man unless he is a registered medical practitioner.

(4) For the purposes of this section "relevant schools" are—

(a) schools maintained by the authority; . . .[675]

(b). . . . .[676]

522 Compulsory cleansing of a pupil.

(1) If, on an examination under section 521, the person or clothing of a pupil is found to be infested with vermin or in a foul condition, any officer of the local education authority may serve a notice on the pupil's parent requiring him to cause the pupil's person and clothing to be cleansed.

(2) The notice shall inform the parent that, unless within the period specified in the notice the pupil's person and clothing are cleansed to the satisfaction of such person as is specified in the notice, the cleansing will be carried out under arrangements made by the authority.

(3) The period so specified shall not be less than 24 hours from the service of the notice.

(4) If, on a report being made to him by the specified person at the end of the specified period, a medical officer of the authority is not satisfied that the pupil's person and clothing have been properly cleansed, he may by order direct that they shall be cleansed under arrangements made by the authority under section 523.

(5) An order made under subsection (4) shall be sufficient to authorise any officer of the authority—

(a) to cause the pupil's person and clothing to be cleansed in accordance with arrangements made by the authority under section 523, and

(b) for that purpose to convey the pupil to, and detain him at, any premises provided in accordance with such arrangements.

523 Arrangements for cleansing of pupils.

(1) A local education authority shall make arrangements for securing that the person or clothing of any pupil required to be cleansed under section 522 may be cleansed (whether at the request of a parent or in pursuance of an order under section 522(4)) at suitable premises, by suitable persons and with suitable appliances.

(2) Where the council of a district in the area of the authority are entitled to the use of any premises or appliances for cleansing the person or clothing of persons infested with vermin, the authority may require the council to permit the authority to use those premises or appliances for such purposes upon such terms as may be determined—

(a) by agreement between the authority and the council, or

(b) in default of such agreement, by the Secretary of State.

(3) Subsection (2) does not apply in relation to Wales.

(4) A girl may be cleansed under arrangements under this section only by a registered medical practitioner or by a woman authorised for the purpose by the authority.

524[Suspension of a pupil pending examination or cleansing.][677]

(1) Where—

(a) a medical officer of a local education authority suspects that the person or clothing of a pupil in attendance at a relevant school is infested with vermin or in a foul condition, but

(b) action for the examination or cleansing of the pupil's person and clothing cannot be taken immediately,

the medical officer may direct that the pupil is to be [suspended][678] from the school until such action has been taken, if he considers it necessary to do so in the interests either of the pupil or of other pupils in attendance at the school.

(2) A direction under subsection (1) is a defence to any proceedings under Chapter II of Part VI in respect of the failure of the pupil to attend school on any day on which he is excluded in pursuance of the direction, unless it is proved that the giving of the direction was necessitated by the wilful default of the pupil or his parent.

(3) For the purposes of this section a "relevant school" is—

(a) a school maintained by the local education authority, . . .[679]

(b). . .

525 Offence of neglecting the cleanliness of a pupil.

(1) If, after the person or clothing of a pupil has been cleansed under section 522—

(a) his person or clothing is again infested with vermin, or in a foul condition, at any time while he is in attendance at a relevant school, and

(b) the condition of his person or clothing is due to neglect on the part of his parent,

the parent is guilty of an offence.

(2) A person guilty of an offence under this section is liable on summary conviction to a fine not exceeding level 1 on the standard scale.

(3) For the purposes of this section a "relevant school" is a school maintained by a local education authority. . ..[680]

Educational research and conferences

526 Powers as to educational research.

A local education authority may make such provision for conducting, or assisting the conduct of, research as appears to them to be desirable for the purpose of improving the educational facilities provided for their area.

527 Powers as to educational conferences.

A local education authority may—

(a) organise, or participate in the organisation of, conferences for the discussion of questions relating to education, and

(b) expend such sums as may be reasonable in paying, or contributing towards, any expenditure incurred in connection with conferences for the discussion of such questions, including the expenses of any person authorised by them to attend such a conference.

[Plans relating to children with behavioural difficulties][681]

[527A Duty of LEA to prepare plan relating to children with behavioural difficulties.

(1) Every local education authority shall prepare, and from time to time review, a statement setting out the arrangements made or proposed to be made by the authority in connection with the education of children with behavioural difficulties.

(2) The arrangements to be covered by the statement include in particular—

(a) the arrangements made or to be made by the authority for the provision of advice and resources to relevant schools, and other arrangements made or to be made by them, with a view to—

(i) meeting requests by such schools for support and assistance in connection with the promotion of good behaviour and discipline on the part of their pupils, and

(ii) assisting such schools to deal with general behavioural problems and the behavioural difficulties of individual pupils;

(b) the arrangements made or to be made by the authority in pursuance of section 19(1) (exceptional provision of education for children not receiving education by reason of being excluded or otherwise); and

(c) any other arrangements made or to be made by them for assisting children with behavioural difficulties to find places at suitable schools.

(3) The statement shall also deal with the interaction between the arrangements referred to in subsection (2) and those made by the authority in relation to pupils with behavioural difficulties who have special educational needs.

(4) In the course of preparing the statement required by this section or any revision of it the authority shall carry out such consultation as may be prescribed.

(5) The authority shall—

(a) publish the statement in such manner and by such date, and

(b) publish revised statements in such manner and at such intervals,

as may be prescribed, and shall provide such persons as may be prescribed with copies of the statement or any revised statement.

(6) In discharging their functions under this section a local education authority shall have regard to any guidance given from time to time by the Secretary of State.

[(7) In this section "relevant school", in relation to a local education authority, means a school maintained by the authority (whether situated in their area or not).][682]][683]

Disability statements relating to further education

528. . . . .[684]

Acquisition and holding of property

529 Power to accept gifts on trust for educational purposes.

(1) A local education authority may accept, hold and administer any property on trust for purposes connected with education.

(2) Any intention on the part of a local education authority that a school (other than a nursery school or a special school) should be vested in the authority as trustees shall be treated for the purposes of [section 28 of the School Standards and Framework Act 1998 as an intention to establish a new community school (so that proposals for that purpose shall be published as required by that section); and Schedule 6 to that Act (statutory proposals: procedure and implementation) shall apply accordingly.] [685]

(3) Any school which in accordance with subsection (2) is vested in a local education authority as trustees shall be [a community school][686].

530 Compulsory purchase of land.

(1) The Secretary of State may authorise a local education authority to purchase compulsorily any land (whether within or outside their area) which—

(a) is required for the purposes of any school or institution which is, or is to be, maintained by them or which they have power to assist, or

(b) is otherwise required for the purposes of their functions under this Act.

(2) The Secretary of State shall not authorise the compulsory purchase of any land required for the purposes of a [foundation, voluntary or foundation special school][687] unless he is satisfied that the arrangements made—

(a) as to the vesting of the land to be purchased, and

(b) as to the appropriation of that land for the purposes of the school,

are such as to secure that the expenditure ultimately borne by the local education authority will not include any expenditure which, if the land had been purchased by the governing body of the school, would have fallen to be borne by the governing body.

(3) Subsection (2) shall not, however, apply where the local education authority propose that expenditure to be incurred in connection with the purchase should ultimately be borne by them [under paragraph 18 of Schedule 6 to the School Standards and Framework Act 1998 (power to give assistance to governing body of voluntary aided school in carrying out statutory proposals)][688][(including that provision as applied by any enactment)][689].

(4) In this section "land" includes buildings and other structures and land covered with water.

531 Acquisition of land by agreement.

(1) For the removal of doubt, it is declared that making land available for the purposes of a school or institution—

(a) which is, or is to be, maintained by a local education authority, or

(b) which such an authority have power to assist,

is a function of the authority within the meaning of section 120 of the Local Government Act 1972 (which relates to the acquisition by a local authority by agreement of land for the purpose of any of their functions), even though the land will not be held by the authority.

(2) A local education authority shall not acquire by agreement any land required for the purposes of [foundation, voluntary or foundation special school][690] unless they are satisfied that the arrangements made—

(a) as to the vesting of the land to be acquired, and

(b) as to the appropriation of that land for the purposes of the school,

are such as to secure that the expenditure ultimately borne by them will not include any expenditure which, if the land had been acquired by the governing body of the school, would have fallen to be borne by the governing body.

Appointment of chief education officer

532 Appointment of chief education officer.

A local education authority's duties under the Local Government Act 1972 with respect to the

appointment of officers shall (without prejudice to the generality of the provisions of that Act) include the duty of appointing a fit person to be the chief education officer of the authority.

Chapter III Ancillary functions of governing bodies

Provision of services

533 Duties of governing bodies of maintained schools with respect to provision of school meals etc.

(1) The governing body of any school maintained by a local education authority shall—

(a) afford the authority such facilities as they require to enable them to perform their functions under section 512, and

(b) allow the authority to make such use of the premises and equipment of the school, and such alterations to the school buildings, as the authority consider necessary for that purpose.

(2) Nothing in subsection (1) shall require the governing body of [any such][691] school to incur any expenditure.

(3) Where the governing body of a school which has a delegated budget (within the meaning of Part II [of the School Standards and Framework Act 1998][692]) provide pupils or other persons who receive education at the school with milk, meals or other refreshment, they shall—

(a) charge for everything so provided,[and

(b) charge every person the same price for the same quantity of the same item.][693]

534. . . . .[694]

535 Provision of teaching services for day nurseries.

(1) Subject to subsection (2), the governing body of [a community, foundation or voluntary primary school][695] having one or more nursery classes may, in accordance with arrangements made by them for that purpose, make available to a day nursery the services of any teacher who is employed by them in the school and has agreed to provide his services for the purposes of the arrangements.

(2) No arrangements shall be made under subsection (1) except at the request of the local education authority and on terms approved by them.

(3) Arrangements under this section may make provision—

(a) for the supply of equipment for use in connection with the teaching services made available under the arrangements,

(b) for regulating the respective functions of any teacher whose services are made available under the arrangements, the head teacher of his school and the person in charge of the day nursery, and

(c) for any supplementary or incidental matters connected with the arrangements, including, where the teacher's school and the day nursery are in the areas of different local education authorities, financial adjustments between those authorities.

(4) In this section "day nursery" means a day nursery provided under section 18 of the Children Act 1989 (provision by local authorities of day care for pre-school and other children).

(5) A teacher shall not be regarded as ceasing to be a member of the teaching staff of his school and subject to the general directions of his head teacher by reason only of his services being made available in pursuance of arrangements under this section.

Medical arrangements

536. . . . .[696]

Chapter IV Provision of information by governing bodies etc.

537 Power of Secretary of State to require information from governing bodies etc.

[(1) The Secretary of State may by regulations make provision requiring—

(a) the governing body of every school which is—

(i) maintained by a local education authority, or

(ii) a special school which is not maintained by such an authority, and

(b) the proprietor of every independent school,

to provide such information about the school as may be prescribed.][697]

(2) For the purposes of this section information about the continuing education of pupils leaving a school, or the employment or training taken up by such pupils on leaving, is to be treated as information about the school.

(3) Where the Secretary of State exercises his power to make regulations under this section he shall do

so with a view to making available information which is likely to—

(a) assist parents in choosing schools for their children;

(b) increase public awareness of the quality of the education provided by the schools concerned and of the educational standards achieved in those schools; or

(c) assist in assessing the degree of efficiency with which the financial resources of those schools are managed.

(4) Information which is required by virtue of regulations under this section shall be provided—

(a) in such form and manner,

(b) on such occasions, and

(c) to such person or persons, in addition to or in place of the Secretary of State,

as may be prescribed [; and regulations under this section may provide that, in such circumstances as may be prescribed, the provision of information to a person other than the Secretary of State is to be treated, for the purposes of any provision of such regulations or this section, as compliance with any requirement of such regulations relating to the provision of information to the Secretary of State.][698].

(5) No information provided in accordance with regulations under this section shall name any pupil to whom it relates.

(6) The Secretary of State may—

(a) publish information provided in accordance with regulations under this section in such form and manner as he considers appropriate;

(b) make arrangements for such information to be published in such form and manner, and by such persons, as he may specify for the purposes of this section;

(c) make regulations requiring local education authorities to publish prescribed categories of such information, together with such supplementary information as may be prescribed, in such form and manner as may be prescribed.

(7) The Secretary of State may make regulations requiring—

(a) the governing body of any school which is maintained by a local education authority. . .[699],

(b) the proprietor of any city technology college [, city college for the technology of the arts or [Academy][700]][701], or

(c) any local education authority,

to provide prescribed persons with prescribed categories of information published under subsection (6).

(8) Information provided under subsection (7) shall be provided in such form and manner as may be prescribed.

(9) Regulations under this section may make provision enabling the Secretary of State, in such circumstances as may be prescribed, to order the deletion from the register of independent schools of the name of any independent school the proprietor of which fails to comply with any requirement imposed by or under the regulations.

(10) In subsection (9) "the register of independent schools" means—

(a) in relation to any school in England, the register of independent schools kept under section 464 by the Registrar of Independent Schools for England; and

(b) in relation to any school in Wales, the equivalent register kept by the Registrar of Independent Schools for Wales.

(11) Without prejudice to the generality of section 569(4), regulations under this section may make provision for the designation by the Secretary of State, in accordance with the regulations, of particular schools or classes of schools for the purposes of the application of particular provisions of the regulations in relation to such schools.

(12) This section is not to be taken as restricting, or otherwise affecting, any other powers that the Secretary of State may have to make regulations with respect to, or otherwise to require, the provision of information by any person.

(13) This section does not apply to nursery schools.

[537A Provision of information about individual pupils.

(1) Regulations may make provision requiring—

(a) the governing body of every school which is—

(i) maintained by a local education authority, or

(ii) a special school which is not maintained by such an authority, and

(b) the proprietor of every independent school,

to provide to the relevant person such individual pupil information as may be prescribed.

(2) In subsection (1) "the relevant person" means one or more of the following—

(a) the Secretary of State, and

(b) any prescribed person.

(3) Where any person within paragraph (b) of subsection (2) receives information by virtue of subsection (1), the Secretary of State may require that person to provide any such information—

(a) to him, or

(b) to any prescribed person.

(4) The Secretary of State may provide any individual pupil information—

(a) to any information collator,

(b) to any prescribed person, or

(c) to any person falling within a prescribed category.

(5) Any information collator—

(a) may provide any individual pupil information—

(i) to the Secretary of State,

(ii) to any other information collator, or

(iii) to the governing body or proprietor of the school attended by the pupil or pupils to whom the information relates; and

(b) may, at such times as the Secretary of State may determine, provide such individual pupil information as may be prescribed—

(i) to any prescribed person, or

(ii) to any person falling within a prescribed category.

(6) Any person holding any individual pupil information (other than the Secretary of State or an information collator) may provide that information to—

(a) the Secretary of State,

(b) any information collator, or

(c) any prescribed person.

(7) No information received under or by virtue of this section shall be published in any form which includes the name of the pupil or pupils to whom it relates.

(8) Regulations under this section may provide that, in such circumstances as may be prescribed, the provision of information to a person other than the Secretary of State is to be treated, for the purposes of any provision of such regulations or this section, as compliance with any requirement imposed by or by virtue of any such provision and relating to the provision of information to the Secretary of State.

(9) In this section—

"individual pupil information" means information relating to and identifying individual pupils or former pupils at any school within subsection (1), whether obtained under subsection (1) or otherwise;

"information collator" means any body which, for the purposes of or in connection with the functions of the Secretary of State relating to education, is responsible for collating or checking information relating to pupils.][702]

538 Provision of information to Secretary of State by governing bodies of maintained schools.

The governing body or temporary governing body of [a community, foundation or voluntary school or a community or foundation special school][703] shall make such reports and returns, and give such information, to the Secretary of State as he may require for the purpose of the exercise of his functions in relation to education.

539. . . . .[704]

540 Distribution of information about schools providing secondary education.

(1) Where the governing body of any school providing primary education receive a request which—

(a) is made by the governing body of any school providing secondary education, and

(b) relates to the distribution of information about the school providing secondary education to

parents of pupils at the school providing primary education without charge to those parents, the governing body of that school shall secure that the request is treated no less favourably (whether as to services provided or as to the terms on which they are provided) than any such request made by the governing body of any other school providing secondary education.

[(2) In this section "school" means—

(a) any community, foundation or voluntary school, or

(b) any community or foundation special school (which is not established in a hospital).][705]

541 Distribution of information about further education institutions.

(1) The Secretary of State may by regulations require—

(a) the governing body of any school providing secondary education, and

(b) the proprietor of any city technology college [, city college for the technology of the arts or [Academy][706]][707],

to provide such persons as may be prescribed with such categories of information falling within subsection (2) as may be prescribed.

(2) Information falls within this subsection if it is—

(a) published under section 50 of the Further and Higher Education Act 1992 (information with respect to institutions within the further education sector), and

(b) made available to governing bodies and proprietors for distribution.

(3) Information provided under subsection (1) shall be provided in such form and manner as may be prescribed.

[(4) In this section "school" means—

(a) any community, foundation or voluntary school, or

(b) any community or foundation special school (which is not established in a hospital).][708]

Part X Miscellaneous and general

Chapter I Educational premises

Required standards for educational premises

542 Prescribed standards for school premises.

(1) Regulations shall prescribe the standards to which the premises of schools maintained by local education authorities . . .[709] are to conform; and without prejudice to the generality of section 569(4) different standards may be prescribed for such descriptions of schools as are specified in the regulations.

(2) Where a school is maintained by a local education authority, the authority shall secure that the school premises conform to the prescribed standards.

(3). . . . .[710]

(4)[subsection (2) has][711] effect subject to section 543.

543 Relaxation of prescribed standards in special cases.

(1) Where subsection (2), (3) [, (4) or (4A)][712] applies in relation to a school, the Secretary of State may direct that, despite the fact that the prescribed requirement referred to in that subsection is not satisfied, the school premises shall be taken, as respects the matters specified in the direction, to conform to the standards prescribed under section 542 so long as—

(a) the direction remains in force, and

(b) any conditions specified in the direction as respects those matters are observed.

(2) This subsection applies if the Secretary of State is satisfied, having regard—

(a) to the nature of the school's existing site,

(b) to any existing buildings on the site, or

(c) to other special circumstances affecting the school premises,

that it would be unreasonable to require conformity with any prescribed requirement as to any matter.

(3) This subsection applies if—

(a) the school is to have an additional or new site, and

(b) the Secretary of State is satisfied, having regard to the shortage of suitable sites, that it would be unreasonable to require conformity with any prescribed requirement relating to sites.

(4) This subsection applies if—

(a) the school is to have additional buildings, or is to be transferred to a new site,

(b) existing buildings not previously part of the school premises, or temporary buildings, are to be used for that purpose, and

(c) the Secretary of State is satisfied, having regard to the need to control public expenditure in the interests of the national economy, that it would be unreasonable to require conformity with any prescribed requirement relating to buildings.

[(4A) This subsection applies, in relation to any playing fields used by the school for the purposes of the school, if the Secretary of State is satisfied that, having regard to other facilities for physical education available to the school, it would be unreasonable to require conformity with any prescribed requirement relating to playing fields.

In this subsection "playing fields" has the same meaning as in section 77 of the School Standards and Framework Act 1998 (control of disposals or changing use of school playing fields).][713]

(5) In this section "prescribed requirement" means a requirement of regulations under section 542.

544 Approval etc. of school premises and boarding hostels.

(1) Regulations may make provision requiring the Secretary of State's approval. . .[714] to be obtained for the provision of new premises for, or the alteration of the premises of—

(a) any school to which this section applies, or

(b) any boarding hostel provided by a local education authority for persons receiving education at any such school.

(2) Regulations may make provision for the inspection of any such hostel.

(3) The schools to which this section applies are—

(a) any school maintained by a local education authority, [and][715]

(b). . . . .[716]

(c) any special school not maintained by a local education authority.

545 Exemption from building byelaws of approved buildings.

(1) Where plans for, or particulars in respect of, a building required for the purposes of any school or other educational institution are approved by the Secretary of State, he may by order direct that any provision of a local Act or of a byelaw made under such an Act—

(a) shall not apply in relation to the building, or

(b) shall apply in relation to it with such modifications as may be specified in the order.

(2) The reference in subsection (1) to plans or particulars approved by the Secretary of State includes a reference to—

(a) particulars submitted to and approved by him under regulations under section 544 or section 218(7) of the Education Reform Act 1988,. . .[717]

(b). . . . .

Control of potentially harmful materials and apparatus

546 Control of potentially harmful materials and apparatus in schools.

(1) Regulations may make provision for requiring the Secretary of State's approval to be obtained for the use in schools to which this section applies of such materials or apparatus as may be specified in the regulations, being materials or apparatus which could or might involve a serious risk to health.

(2) The schools to which this section applies are—

(a) any school maintained by a local education authority, [and][718]

(b). . . . .[719]

(c) any special school not maintained by a local education authority.

Nuisance or disturbance on school premises

547 Nuisance or disturbance on school premises.

(1) Any person who without lawful authority is present on premises to which this section applies and causes or permits nuisance or disturbance to the annoyance of persons who lawfully use those premises (whether or not any such persons are present at the time) is guilty of an offence and liable on summary conviction to a fine not exceeding level 2 on the standard scale.

(2) This section applies to premises, including playgrounds, playing fields and other premises for outdoor recreation, of—

(a) any school maintained by a local education authority,. . .

[(aa) any special school not so maintained, and

(ab) any independent school.] [720]

(b)................................[721]

[(2A) This section also applies to any premises which are—

(a) provided by a local education authority under section 508, and

(b) used wholly or mainly in connection with the provision of instruction or leadership in sporting, recreational or outdoor activities.][722]

(3) If—

(a) a police constable, or

(b)(subject to subsection (5)) a person whom [the appropriate authority has][723] authorised to exercise the power conferred by this subsection,

has reasonable cause to suspect that any person is committing or has committed an offence under this section, he may remove him from the premises in question.

[(4) In subsection (3) "the appropriate authority" means—

(a) in relation to premises of a foundation, voluntary aided or foundation special school, a local education authority or the governing body,

(b) in relation to—

(i) premises of any other school maintained by a local education authority, and

(ii) premises provided by a local education authority as mentioned in subsection (2A),

a local education authority, and

(c) in relation to premises of a special school which is not so maintained or of an independent school, the proprietor of the school.][724]

(5) A local education authority may not authorise a person to exercise the power conferred by subsection (3) in relation to premises of [a foundation, voluntary or foundation special school][725] without first obtaining the consent of the governing body.

[(6) No proceedings for an offence under this section shall be brought by any person other than—

(a) a police constable, or

(b) an authorised person.

(7) In subsection (6) "authorised person" means—

(a) in relation to an offence committed on premises of a foundation, voluntary aided or foundation special school, a local education authority or a person whom the governing body have authorised to bring such proceedings,

(b) in relation to an offence committed—

(i) on premises of any other school maintained by a local education authority, or

(ii) on premises provided by a local education authority as mentioned in subsection (2A),

a local education authority, and

(c) in relation to an offence committed on premises of a special school which is not so maintained or of an independent school, a person whom the proprietor of the school has authorised to bring such proceedings.][726]

(8) A local education authority may not bring proceedings for an offence under this section committed on premises of [a foundation, voluntary or foundation special school][727] without first obtaining the consent of the governing body.

Chapter II [PUNISHMENT AND RESTRAINT OF PUPILS][728]

[Corporal punishment][729]

[548 No right to give corporal punishment.

(1) Corporal punishment given by, or on the authority of, a member of staff to a child—

(a) for whom education is provided at any school, or

(b) for whom education is provided, otherwise than at school, under any arrangements made by a local education authority, or

(c) for whom specified nursery education is provided otherwise than at school,

cannot be justified in any proceedings on the ground that it was given in pursuance of a right exercisable by the member of staff by virtue of his position as such.

(2) Subsection (1) applies to corporal punishment so given to a child at any time, whether at the school or other place at which education is provided for the child, or elsewhere.

(3) The following provisions have effect for the purposes of this section.

(4) Any reference to giving corporal punishment to a child is to doing anything for the purpose of punishing that child (whether or not there are other reasons for doing it) which, apart from any justification, would constitute battery.

(5) However, corporal punishment shall not be taken to be given to a child by virtue of anything done for reasons that include averting—

(a) an immediate danger of personal injury to, or

(b) an immediate danger to the property of,

any person (including the child himself).

(6) "Member of staff", in relation to the child concerned, means—

(a) any person who works as a teacher at the school or other place at which education is provided for the child, or

(b) any other person who (whether in connection with the provision of education for the child or otherwise)—

(i) works at that school or place, or

(ii) otherwise provides his services there (whether or not for payment),

and has lawful control or charge of the child.

(7) "Child" (except in subsection (8)) means a person under the age of 18.

(8) "Specified nursery education" means full-time or part-time education suitable for children who have not attained compulsory school age which is provided—

(a) by a local education authority; or

(b) by any other person—

(i) who is (or is to be) in receipt of financial assistance given by such an authority and whose provision of nursery education is taken into account by the authority in formulating proposals for the purposes of section 120(2)(a) of the School Standards and Framework Act 1998, or

(ii) who is (or is to be) in receipt of grants under section 1 of the Nursery Education and Grant-Maintained Schools Act 1996; or

(c) [(otherwise than as mentioned in paragraph (a) or (b)) in any educational institution which would fall within section 4(1) above (definition of "school") but for the fact that it provides part-time, rather than full-time, primary education.][730]][731]

549. . . . .[732]

550. . . . .[733]

[Power to restrain pupils][734]

[550A Power of members of staff to restrain pupils.

(1) A member of the staff of a school may use, in relation to any pupil at the school, such force as is reasonable in the circumstances for the purpose of preventing the pupil from doing (or continuing to do) any of the following, namely—

(a) committing any offence,

(b) causing personal injury to, or damage to the property of, any person (including the pupil himself), or

(c) engaging in any behaviour prejudicial to the maintenance of good order and discipline at the school or among any of its pupils, whether that behaviour occurs during a teaching session or otherwise.

(2) Subsection (1) applies where a member of the staff of a school is—

(a) on the premises of the school, or

(b) elsewhere at a time when, as a member of its staff, he has lawful control or charge of the pupil concerned;

but it does not authorise anything to be done in relation to a pupil which constitutes the giving of corporal punishment within the meaning of section 548.

(3) Subsection (1) shall not be taken to prevent any person from relying on any defence available to him otherwise than by virtue of this section.

(4) In this section—

"member of the staff", in relation to a school, means any teacher who works at the school and any

other person who, with the authority of the head teacher, has lawful control or charge of pupils at the school;

"offence" includes anything that would be an offence but for the operation of any presumption that a person under a particular age is incapable of committing an offence.][735]

[Detention][736]

[550B Detention outside school hours lawful despite absence of parental consent.

(1) Where a pupil to whom this section applies is required on disciplinary grounds to spend a period of time in detention at his school after the end of any school session, his detention shall not be rendered unlawful by virtue of the absence of his parent's consent to it if the conditions set out in subsection (3) are satisfied.

(2) This section applies to any pupil who has not attained the age of 18 and is attending—

(a) a school maintained by a local education authority;

. . .[737] or

(c) a city technology college [, city college for the technology of the arts or [Academy][738]][739].

(3) The conditions referred to in subsection (1) are as follows—

(a) the head teacher of the school must have previously determined, and have—

(i) made generally known within the school, and

(ii) taken steps to bring to the attention of the parent of every person who is for the time being a registered pupil there,

that the detention of pupils after the end of a school session is one of the measures that may be taken with a view to regulating the conduct of pupils;

(b) the detention must be imposed by the head teacher or by another teacher at the school specifically or generally authorised by him for the purpose;

(c) the detention must be reasonable in all the circumstances; and

(d) the pupil's parent must have been given at least 24 hours' notice in writing that the detention was due to take place.

(4) In determining for the purposes of subsection (3)(c) whether a pupil's detention is reasonable, the following matters in particular shall be taken into account—

(a) whether the detention constitutes a proportionate punishment in the circumstances of the case; and

(b) any special circumstances relevant to its imposition on the pupil which are known to the person imposing it (or of which he ought reasonably to be aware) including in particular—

(i) the pupil's age,

(ii) any special educational needs he may have,

(iii) any religious requirements affecting him, and

(iv) where arrangements have to be made for him to travel from the school to his home, whether suitable alternative arrangements can reasonably be made by his parent.

(5) Section 572, which provides for the methods by which notices may be served under this Act, does not preclude a notice from being given to a pupil's parent under this section by any other effective method.][740]

Chapter III Other provisions about schools

Duration of school day etc.

551 Regulations as to duration of school day etc.

(1) Regulations may make provision with respect to the duration of the school day and school year at, and the granting of leave of absence from, any schools to which this section applies.

[(1A) In subsection (1) the reference to the duration of the school year at any such schools is a reference to the number of school sessions that must be held during any such year.][741]

(2) The schools to which this section applies are—

(a) any school maintained by a local education authority; [and][742]

(b). . .[743]

(c) any special school not maintained by a local education authority.

Single-sex schools

552. . . . .

Educational trusts

553 Schemes under the Endowed Schools Acts.

(1) Where under any provision (however expressed) of a scheme made under the Endowed Schools Acts 1869 to 1948 the power of the trustees under the scheme to apply any property to which the scheme relates for purposes authorised by the scheme is subject to the approval or order of any other person, the scheme shall have effect as if no such approval or order was required.

(2) The Secretary of State may, on the application of any person whose approval or order would apart from this section be required under such a scheme, direct that the requirement shall continue to have effect despite subsection (1); but no liability shall be taken to have been incurred in respect of any failure before the making of such a direction to obtain any such approval or order.

Religious educational trusts

554 Power to make new provision as to use of endowments.

[(1) This section applies where—

(a) in relation to any time before the appointed day, the premises of a voluntary or grant-maintained school (within the meaning of this Act) have ceased to be used for such a voluntary or (as the case may be) grant-maintained school; or

(b) in relation to any time on or after the appointed day—

(i) the premises of a foundation or voluntary school (within the meaning of the School Standards and Framework Act 1998) have ceased to be used for such a foundation or (as the case may be) voluntary school; or

(ii) in the opinion of the Secretary of State it is likely such premises will cease to be so used;

and in this subsection "the appointed day" has the meaning given by section 20(7) of the School Standards and Framework Act 1998.][744]

(2) In such a case the Secretary of State may (subject to sections 555 and 556(1) and (2)) by order make new provision as to the use of any endowment if it is shown either—

(a) that the endowment is or has been held wholly or partly for or in connection with the provision at the school of religious education in accordance with the tenets of a particular religion or religious denomination; or

(b) that the endowment is or has been used wholly or partly for or in connection with the provision at the school of such religious education and that (subject to subsection (4)) the requirements of subsection (3) are fulfilled.

(3) The requirements of this subsection are—

[(a) that the school was or has been maintained as a voluntary or grant-maintained school (within the meaning of this Act) or as a foundation or voluntary school (within the meaning of the School Standards and Framework Act 1998) since 1st April 1945 (the date when Part II of the Education Act 1944 came into force); and][745]

(b) that religious education in accordance with the tenets of the religion or denomination concerned—

(i) is, and has been from that date, provided at the school, or

(ii) where the premises have ceased to be used for the purposes of the school, was provided at the school from that date until immediately before the premises ceased to be so used,

in pursuance of section 377 or 378 or section 380 or 381 [of this Act (or any corresponding earlier enactment) or paragraph 3 or 4 of Schedule 19 to the School Standards and Framework Act 1998][746].

(4) For the purposes of this section—

(a) where in the case of any school falling within subsection (3)(a) it is shown—

(i) that religious education in accordance with the tenets of a particular religion or denomination is provided at the school, or

(ii) if the premises have ceased to be used for the purposes of the school, such religious education was so provided immediately before the premises ceased to be so used,

such religious education shall be taken to have been provided at the school from 1st April 1945, unless the contrary is shown; and

[(b) where religious education in accordance with such tenets is shown to have been given to any

pupils at—

(i) a controlled school (within the meaning of this Act),

(ii) a grant-maintained school (within the meaning of this Act) which was a controlled school immediately before it became a grant-maintained school, or

(iii) a foundation or voluntary controlled school with a religious character (within the meaning of Part II of the School Standards and Framework Act 1998),

the religious education shall be taken to have been given to them at the request of their parents, unless the contrary is shown.][747]

(5) For the purposes of this section—

"endowment" includes property not subject to any restriction on the expenditure of capital; and

"shown" means shown to the satisfaction of the Secretary of State.

(6) This section applies where the premises of a non-provided public elementary school ceased before 1st April 1945 to be used for such a school as it applies where the premises of a voluntary school have ceased to be used for such a school.

555 Procedure applicable to orders under section 554.

(1) No order shall be made under section 554 except on the application of the persons appearing to the Secretary of State to be the appropriate authority of the religion or denomination concerned.

(2) The Secretary of State shall, not less than one month before making an order under section 554, give notice of the proposed order and of the right of persons interested to make representations on it.

(3) Such notice shall be given—

(a) by giving to any persons appearing to the Secretary of State to be trustees of an endowment affected by the proposed order a notice of the proposal to make it, together with a draft or summary of the provisions proposed to be included; and

(b) by publishing, in such manner as the Secretary of State thinks sufficient for informing any other persons interested, a notice of the proposal to make the order and of the place where any person interested may (during a period of not less than a month) inspect such a draft or summary, and by keeping a draft or summary available for inspection in accordance with the notice.

(4) The Secretary of State shall take into account any representations made to him by any person interested before the order is made.

(5) In this section "endowment" has the same meaning as in section 554.

556 Content of orders under section 554.

(1) An order under section 554—

(a) may require or authorise the disposal by sale or otherwise of any land or other property forming part of an endowment affected by the order, including the premises of the school and any teacher's dwelling-house; and

(b) may consolidate any endowments to be dealt with by the scheme.

(2) Subject to subsection (1), and to any provision affecting the endowments which is a provision of a public general Act of Parliament, an order under section 554 shall establish and give effect, with a view to enabling the religion or denomination concerned to participate more effectively in the administration of the statutory system of public education, to a scheme or schemes for the endowments dealt with by the order to be used for appropriate educational purposes either—

(a) in connection with schools which are [foundation schools or voluntary schools][748]; or

(b) partly in connection with such schools (or either description of such schools) and partly in other ways related to the locality served by the [school at the premises referred to in section 554(1).][749].

(3) In subsection (2) "use for appropriate educational purposes" means use for educational purposes in connection with the provision of religious education in accordance with the tenets of the religion or denomination concerned (including in particular, but without prejudice to the generality of the foregoing, use for any purpose specified in Schedule 36).

(4) A scheme given effect under section 554—

(a) may provide for the retention of the capital of any endowment and application of the accruing income; or

(b) may authorise the application or expenditure of capital to such extent and subject to such conditions as may be determined by or in accordance with the scheme;

and any such scheme may provide for the endowments dealt with by the scheme or any part of

them to be added to any existing endowment applicable for any such purpose as is authorised for the scheme by subsection (2).

(5) Where a scheme given effect under section 554 provides for the endowments dealt with by the order or any part of them to be used for the purposes specified in Schedule 36, any such scheme may provide for the endowments thereby dealt with or any part of them to be added to any existing endowment applicable for those purposes (whether it is so applicable by virtue of a scheme given effect to under that section or otherwise).

(6) Section 568(5) does not apply to an order under section 554, but such an order may include such incidental or supplementary provisions as appear to the Secretary of State to be necessary or expedient either for the bringing into force or for the operation of any scheme established by it, including in particular provisions—

(a) for the appointment and powers of trustees of the property comprised in the scheme or, if the property is not all applicable for the same purposes, of any part of that property; and

(b) for the property or any part of it to vest by virtue of the scheme in the first trustees under the scheme or trustees of any endowment to which it is to be added or, if not so vested, to be transferred to them.

(7) Any order under section 554 shall have effect despite any Act of Parliament (other than a public general Act), letters patent or other instrument relating to, or trust affecting, the endowments dealt with by the order.

(8) In this section "endowment" has the same meaning as in section 554.

557 Adoption of statutory trusts.

(1) This section applies to endowments which are—

(a) regulated by a qualifying scheme under the Endowed Schools Acts 1869 to 1948 as applied by section 86(1) of the Education Act 1944 or by an order under section 554 of this Act or section 2 of the Education Act 1973; and

(b) held under any such scheme or order on trusts which provide for capital or income or both to be applicable for or in connection with—

(i) the provision of religious education at relevant schools, or relevant schools of any description (but not only at a particular school or schools) in a diocese or other geographical area; or

(ii) the provision of premises for relevant schools, or relevant schools of any description (but not only at a particular school or schools) at which religious education is or is to be provided in a diocese or other geographical area;

but this section does not apply to an endowment if or in so far as it constitutes a religious education fund.

(2) The trustees of any endowments to which this section applies may, by resolution complying with subsection (6), adopt the uniform statutory trusts as the trusts on which those endowments are to be held.

(3) The uniform statutory trusts are those set out in Schedule 36.

(4) On the adoption by trustees of the uniform statutory trusts in respect of any endowments the scheme or order which regulates the endowments shall have effect as if the uniform statutory trusts are incorporated in the scheme or order to the exclusion of the corresponding provisions of the scheme or order.

(5) The trustees of two or more endowments which are held on the uniform statutory trusts may, by resolution complying with subsection (6), consolidate all or any of those endowments and, where they do so, the endowments shall be treated, for all purposes, as held for the purposes of a single charity.

(6) For a resolution to comply with this subsection—

(a) it must be passed by a simple majority of the trustees or, if the trustees are a body corporate or a company, by a simple majority of the members of the body corporate or an ordinary resolution of the company; and

(b) it must be recorded in the records of the decisions of the trustees affecting the endowments of the trust.

(7) Where trustees pass a resolution under subsection (2), it shall be their duty to send a copy of the resolution to the Secretary of State.

(8) The uniform statutory trusts applicable to endowments to which this section applies shall not affect—

(a) the rights of any person under the third proviso to section 2 of the School Sites Act 1841, under section 86(3) of the Education Act 1944 or under section 1 of the Reverter of Sites Act 1987 (rights replacing certain reversionary interests in land), or

(b) the rights of any local education authority which have arisen under paragraph 7 or 8 of the First Schedule to the Education Act 1946 (rights in relation to school sites provided by such authorities) or which may arise under section 60(4) or 62(2),

except in so far as any right falling within paragraph (a) above is or has been extinguished by an order under section 554 of this Act or section 2 of the Education Act 1973 made by virtue of section 5 of the Reverter of Sites Act 1987.

(9) In this section—

"company" means a company formed under the Companies Acts;

"the Companies Acts" means the Companies Act 1985, the Companies Act 1948 or any Act repealed by that Act of 1948;

"endowment" has the same meaning as in section 554;

"provision", in relation to premises, means provision by the purchase of a site, the erection of premises or the maintenance, improvement or enlargement of premises;

"qualifying scheme" means a scheme in force on 1st January 1994 (the date when section 287 of the Education Act 1993 came into force);

"relevant school" means [a foundation or voluntary school][750];

"religious education" means religious education in accordance with the tenets of a particular religion or religious denomination; and

"religious education fund" includes a Sunday school fund.

(10) In Schedule 36 as incorporated in any scheme or order—

"the area" means the diocese or other geographical area within which the trust assets may be applied under the scheme or order, as the case may be;

"relevant school" means a relevant school [, Academy, city technology college or city college for the technology of the arts,][751] at which the religious education provided for in the scheme or order, as the case may be, is or is to be provided; and

"the relevant trust assets" means the endowments in respect of which the trustees have adopted the uniform statutory trusts, including the income derived therefrom.

Chapter IV Employment of children and young persons

558 Meaning of "child" for purposes of enactments relating to employment of children or young persons.

For the purposes of any enactment relating to the prohibition or regulation of the employment of children or young persons, any person who is not over compulsory school age shall be deemed to be a child within the meaning of that enactment.

559 Power of local education authorities to prohibit or restrict employment of children.

(1) If it appears to a local education authority that a child who is a registered pupil at a [community, foundation][752], voluntary or special school is being employed in such a manner as to be prejudicial to his health, or otherwise to render him unfit to obtain the full benefit of the education provided for him, the authority may serve a notice in writing on the employer—

(a) prohibiting him from employing the child, or

(b) imposing such restrictions upon his employment of the child as appear to them to be expedient in the interests of the child.

(2) A local education authority may serve a notice in writing on the parent or employer of a child who is a registered pupil at a [community, foundation][753], voluntary or special school requiring the parent or employer to provide the authority, within such period as may be specified in the notice, with such information as appears to the authority to be necessary for the purpose of enabling them to ascertain whether the child is being employed in such a manner as to render him unfit to obtain the full benefit of the education provided for him.

(3) A person who—

(a) employs a child in contravention of any prohibition or restriction imposed under subsection (1),

or

(b) fails to comply with the requirements of a notice served under subsection (2),

shall be guilty of an offence.

(4) A person guilty of an offence under this section shall be liable on summary conviction—

(a) to a fine not exceeding level 1 on the standard scale, or

(b) to imprisonment for a term not exceeding one month,

or both.

(5) Section 28(1) and (3) of the Children and Young Persons Act 1933 (powers of entry for the enforcement of the provisions of Part II of that Act as to the employment of children) shall apply with respect to the provisions of any notice served under this section as they apply with respect to the provisions of Part II of that Act.

(6) This section shall cease to have effect on the coming into force of section 2 of the Employment of Children Act 1973.

560 Work experience in last year of compulsory schooling.

[(1) The enactments relating to the prohibition or regulation of the employment of children shall not apply to the employment of a child in his last two years of compulsory schooling if the employment is in pursuance of arrangements made—

(a) by a local education authority, or

(b) by the governing body of a school on behalf of such an authority,

with a view to providing him with work experience as a part of his education.

(2) For the purposes of subsection (1) a child shall be taken to be in his last two years of compulsory schooling as from the beginning of the last two school years at his school during the whole or part of which he is of compulsory school age.][754]

(3) Subsection (1) shall not be taken to permit the employment of a person in any way contrary to—

(a) an enactment which in terms applies to persons of less than, or not over, a specified age expressed as a number of years, or

(b) section 1(2) of the Employment of Women, Young Persons and Children Act 1920 or section 55(1) of the Merchant Shipping Act 1995 (which prohibit the employment of children in ships).

(4) No arrangements shall be made under subsection (1) for a child to be employed in any way which would be contrary to an enactment prohibiting or regulating the employment of young persons if he were a young person (within the meaning of the enactment) and not a child.

(5) Where a child is employed in pursuance of arrangements made under subsection (1), so much of any enactment as—

(a) regulates the employment of young persons (whether by excluding them from any description of work, prescribing the conditions under which they may be permitted to do it or in any other way), and

(b) would apply in relation to him if he were of an age to be treated as a young person for the purposes of that enactment,

shall apply in relation to him, in and in respect of the employment arranged for him, in all respects as if he were of an age to be so treated.

(6) Nothing in section 495 or 496 applies in relation to any power conferred on a local education authority. . .[755] by subsection (1).

(7) In this section "enactment" includes any byelaw, regulation or other provision having effect under an enactment.

Chapter V Persons not covered by Act

561 Act not to apply to persons in service of the Crown.

No power or duty conferred or imposed by this Act on—

(a) the Secretary of State,

(b) local education authorities, or

(c) parents,

shall be construed as relating to any person who is employed by or under the Crown in any service or capacity with respect to which the Secretary of State certifies that, by reason of the arrangements made for the education of children and young persons so employed, the exercise and performance of those powers and duties with respect to such children and young persons is unnecessary.

562 Act not to apply to persons detained under order of a court.

(1) No power or duty conferred or imposed by or under this Act on—

(a) the Secretary of State,

(b) local education authorities, or

(c) parents,

shall be construed as relating to any person who is detained in pursuance of an order made by a court or of an order of recall made by the Secretary of State, but a local education authority may make arrangements for a person who is detained in pursuance of such an order to receive the benefit of educational facilities provided by the authority.

(2) A child or young person who is being educated as a boarder at a school shall not be regarded for the purposes of subsection (1) as detained in pursuance of an order made by a court by reason of the fact that he is required to be at the school—

(a) by virtue of an order made by a court under the Children and Young Persons Act 1933 or by virtue of anything done under such an order; or

(b) by virtue of a requirement of a probation order or by virtue of anything done under such a requirement.

Chapter VI General

Documents and evidence

563 Educational records.

(1) Regulations may make provision as to—

(a) the keeping, disclosure and transfer of educational records about persons receiving education at schools to which this section applies; and

(b) the supply of copies of such records to such persons, and in such circumstances, as may be determined by or under the regulations.

(2) The regulations may authorise persons who supply copies of such records in pursuance of the regulations to charge such fee as they think fit (not exceeding the cost of supply) in respect of each copy so supplied.

(3) The schools to which this section applies are—

(a) any school maintained by a local education authority; [and][756]

(b)................................[757]

(c) any special school not maintained by a local education authority.

564 Certificates of birth and registrars' returns.

(1) Where the age of any person is required to be proved for the purposes of this Act or of any enactment relating to the employment of children or young persons, the registrar having the custody of the register of birth and deaths containing the entry relating to the birth of that person shall—

(a) on being presented by any person ("the applicant") with a written requisition in such form and containing such particulars as may be determined by regulations, and

(b) on payment of a fee of [£3.50][758][£7.00][759],

supply the applicant with a copy of the entry certified under his hand.

(2) A registrar shall, on being requested so to do, supply free of charge a form of requisition for the purposes of subsection (1).

(3) A registrar shall supply to a local education authority such particulars of the entries contained in any register of births and deaths in his custody, and in such form, as (subject to regulations) the authority may from time to time require.

(4) In this section—

"register of births and deaths" means a register of births and deaths kept under the Births and Deaths Registration Act 1953, and

"registrar" includes a registrar of births and deaths and a superintendent registrar.

565 Evidence: presumption as to age.

(1) Where in any proceedings under this Act the person by whom the proceedings are brought—

(a) alleges that any person whose age is material to the proceedings is under, of, or over, any age, and

(b) satisfies the court that, having used all reasonable diligence to obtain evidence as to the age of that person, he has been unable to do so,

the court may, unless the contrary is proved, presume that person to be under, of, or (as the case may be) over, the age alleged.

(2) This section has effect subject to section 445(3).

566 Evidence: documents.

(1) In any legal proceedings, any of the following documents, namely—

(a) a document purporting to be a document issued by a local education authority, and to be signed by the clerk of that authority or by the chief education officer of that authority or by any other officer of the authority authorised to sign it,

(b) a document purporting to be an extract from the minutes of the proceedings of the governing body of [a maintained school][760], and to be signed by the chairman of the governing body or by their clerk,

(c) a document purporting to be a certificate giving particulars of the attendance of a child or young person at a school, and to be signed by the head teacher of the school, and

(d) a document purporting to be a certificate issued by a medical officer of a local education authority, and to be signed by such an officer,

shall be received in evidence and shall be treated, without further proof, as the document which it purports to be and as having been signed by the person by whom it purports to have been signed, unless the contrary is proved.

(2) In any legal proceedings, any such extract or certificate as is mentioned in subsection (1)(b), (c) or (d) shall be evidence of the matters stated in it.

Stamp duty

567. . . . .[761]

Orders, regulations and directions

568 Orders.

(1) Any power of the Secretary of State to make orders under this Act (other than an order under any of the excepted provisions) shall be exercised by statutory instrument.

[(2) For the purposes of subsection (1) "the excepted provisions" are—

section 349;

sections 468, 471(1) and 474;

section 489(3);

section 497; and

section 545.][762]

(3) A statutory instrument containing any order made by the Secretary of State under this Act, other than an order under—

[...section 354(6), 355(2)(a), 356(2)(c) or 401,][763]...

. . .[764]

section 554,

section 583(3) or (4), or

Schedule 40,

shall be subject to annulment in pursuance of a resolution of either House of Parliament.

(4) [No order shall be made under section 354(6), 355(2)(a) or 401 unless a draft of the instrument containing the order has been laid before, and approved by a resolution of, each House of Parliament.][765]

(5) Any order made—

(a) by the Secretary of State under this Act by statutory instrument,. . .[766]

(b). . . . .

may make different provision for different cases, circumstances or areas and may contain such incidental, supplemental, saving or transitional provisions as the Secretary of State thinks fit.

(6) Without prejudice to the generality of subsection (5), an order made by the Secretary of State under this Act by statutory instrument may make in relation to Wales provision different from that made in relation to England.

569 Regulations.

(1) Any power of the Secretary of State to make regulations under this Act shall be exercised by statutory instrument.

(2) A statutory instrument containing regulations under this Act, other than regulations under [section 492,][767] shall be subject to annulment in pursuance of a resolution of either House of Parliament.

(3) No regulations shall be made under [section 492][768] unless a draft of the instrument containing the regulations has been laid before, and approved by a resolution of, each House of Parliament.

(4) Regulations under this Act may make different provision for different cases, circumstances or areas and may contain such incidental, supplemental, saving or transitional provisions as the Secretary of State thinks fit.

(5) Without prejudice to the generality of subsection (4), regulations under this Act may make in relation to Wales provision different from that made in relation to England.

(6) Subsection (5) does not apply to regulations under section 579(4).

570 Revocation and variation of certain orders and directions.

(1) This section applies to any order or directions made or given under this Act by—

(a) the Secretary of State, [or][769]

(b). . . . .[770]

(c) a local education authority,

other than an order to which section 568(1) applies.

(2) Subject to subsection (3), any such order or directions may be varied or revoked by a further order or directions made or given by the Secretary of State,. . .[771] or the local education authority, as the case may be.

(3) Where the power to make or give any such order or directions is only exercisable—

(a) on the application or with the consent of any person or body of persons, or

(b) after consultation with any person or body of persons, or

(c) subject to any other conditions,

no order or directions made or given under that power may be varied or revoked under subsection (2) unless the same conditions are complied with.

Guidance

571 Publication of guidance.

(1) The Secretary of State shall publish any guidance given by him for the purposes of any [provision of this Act][772] in such manner as he thinks fit.

(2). . . . .[773]

Service of documents

572 Service of notices and other documents.

Any order, notice or other document required or authorised by this Act to be served on any person may be served—

(a) by delivering it to that person, or

(b) by leaving it at his usual or last known place of residence, or

(c) by sending it in a prepaid letter addressed to him at that place.

Construction

573 Meaning of expressions relating to alteration etc. of premises or character of schools.

(1) The following provisions apply for the purposes of this Act except where the context otherwise requires.

(2) References to the alteration of school premises include making improvements, extensions or additions to the premises;. . ..[774]

(3) References to the enlargement of any school premises include any modification of the school's existing premises which has the effect of increasing the number of pupils for whom accommodation can be provided.

(4). . . . .[775]

(5). . . . .

(6). . . . .

574 Changes to school not amounting to discontinuance etc.

(1) For the purposes of this Act and any other enactment relating to the duties of a local education authority neither—

(a) references in whatever terms to discontinuing a school (including those to a local authority ceasing to maintain a school), nor

(b) references in whatever terms to establishing a new school,

shall be read as applying by reason only of a change such as is mentioned in subsection (2) being made to an existing school (so that, where such a change is made to an existing school, the school shall be regarded as continuing despite the change and as being the same school before and after it, unless for other reasons it is to be regarded as discontinued).

(2) The changes are—

(a) education beginning or ceasing to be provided for pupils above or below a particular age, for boys as well as girls or for girls as well as boys;

(b) an enlargement or alteration of the school premises; and

(c) the transfer of the school to a new site.

575. . . . .

576 Meaning of "parent".

(1) In this Act, unless the context otherwise requires, "parent", in relation to a child or young person, includes any person—

(a) who is not a parent of his but who has parental responsibility for him, or

(b) who has care of him,

except that in [section 499(8)][776] it only includes such a person if he is an individual.

(2). . . . .[777]

(3) In subsection (1) "parental responsibility" has the same meaning as in the Children Act 1989.

(4) In determining for the purposes of subsection (1) whether an individual has care of a child or young person, any absence of the child or young person at a hospital or boarding school and any other temporary absence shall be disregarded.

577. . . . .[778]

578 Meaning of "the Education Acts".

In this Act "the Education Acts" means this Act together with the following Acts—

. . .[779]

the Education Act 1967;

the Education Act 1973;

the Education Act 1980;

the Education (Fees and Awards) Act 1983;

the Further Education Act 1985 (except sections 4 and 5);

the Education Act 1986;

the Education (No. 2) Act 1986;

the Education Reform Act 1988;

. . .

the School Teachers' Pay and Conditions Act 1991;

the Further and Higher Education Act 1992;

the Education Act 1994;

. . .

the Nursery Education and Grant-Maintained Schools Act 1996;

the School Inspections Act 1996;

[the Education Act 1997;][780]

[the Education (Schools) Act 1997;][781]

. . .[782]

[the Teaching and Higher Education Act 1998;][783]

[the School Standards and Framework Act 1998 (c. 31);][784]

[the Education Act 2002 (c. 32)][785].

579 General interpretation.

(1) In this Act, unless the context otherwise requires—

. . . .[786]

["assist", in relation to any school, institution or university, shall be construed in accordance with subsections (5) to (7) below;][787]

"boarder" includes a pupil who boards during the week but not at weekends;

"child" means a person who is not over compulsory school age;

"clothing" includes footwear;

. . . .

"financial year" means a period of twelve months ending with 31st March;

"functions" includes powers and duties;

. . . .

"head teacher" includes acting head teacher;

"higher education" means education provided by means of a course of any description mentioned in Schedule 6 to the Education Reform Act 1988;

"land" includes buildings and other structures, land covered with water, and any interest in land;

"liability" includes obligation;

"local authority" means a county council, a county borough council, a district council, a London borough council or the Common Council of the City of London;

. . . .

"local government elector" has the meaning given by section 270(1) of the Local Government Act 1972;

"medical officer", in relation to a local education authority, means a registered medical practitioner who is employed or engaged (whether regularly or for the purposes of any particular case) by the authority or whose services are made available to the authority by the Secretary of State;

"modifications" includes additions, alterations and omissions and "modify" shall be construed accordingly;

["the National Curriculum"(without more) means—

(a) in relation to England, the National Curriculum for England, and

(b) in relation to Wales, the National Curriculum for Wales;][788]

"premises", in relation to a school, includes any detached playing fields but, except where otherwise expressly provided, does not include a teacher's dwelling-house;

"prescribed" means prescribed by regulations;

"proprietor", in relation to a school, means the person or body of persons responsible for the management of the school (so that, in relation to [a community, foundation or voluntary or community or foundation special school,][789] it means the governing body);

. . . .

"regulations" means regulations made by the Secretary of State;

. . . .

["sex education" includes education about—

(a) Acquired Immune Deficiency Syndrome and Human Immunodeficiency Virus, and

(b) any other sexually transmitted disease;][790]

"school buildings", in relation to a school, means any building or part of a building forming part of the school premises, other than a building or part required only—

(a) as a caretaker's dwelling,

(b) for use in connection with playing fields,

(c) to afford facilities for enabling the Secretary of State facilities to carry out his functions under section 5(1) or (1A) of, and Schedule 1 to, the National Health Service Act 1977 (which relate to the provision of medical and dental services for pupils), or

(d) to afford facilities for providing milk, meals or other refreshment for pupils in attendance at the school;

"school day", in relation to a school, means any day on which at that school there is a school session;

["school year", in relation to a school, means the period beginning with the first school term to begin after July and ending with the beginning of the first such term to begin after the following July;][791]

["trust deed" includes any instrument (other than an instrument of government) regulating the

constitution of the school's governing body or the maintenance, management or conduct of the school;][792]

"young person" means a person over compulsory school age but under the age of 18.

(2) References in this Act to an interest in land include any easement, right or charge in, to or over land.

(3)..............................[793]

(4) For the purposes of this Act a person shall be treated as belonging, or as not belonging, to the area of a particular local education authority in accordance with regulations; and any question under the regulations shall, in the case of a dispute, be determined by the Secretary of State.

(5) For the purposes of this Act a school shall be regarded as "assisted" by a local education authority who do not maintain it if the authority make to its proprietor any grant in respect of the school or any payment in consideration of the provision of educational facilities there.

(6) Subject to subsection (7), an institution other than a school shall be regarded for the purposes of this Act as "assisted" by a local education authority if the authority make to the persons responsible for its maintenance any grant in respect of the institution or any payment in consideration of the provision of educational facilities there.

(7) Neither—

(a) a university, nor

(b) any institution within the further education sector or within the higher education sector other than a university,

shall be regarded for the purposes of this Act as "assisted" by a local education authority by virtue of the making by the authority to the persons responsible for the maintenance of the university or institution of any grant or payment such as is mentioned in subsection (6).

580 Index.

The expressions listed in the left-hand column below are defined by, or (as the case may be) are to be interpreted in accordance with, the provisions of this Act listed in the right-hand column in relation to those expressions.

Expression	Relevant provision
[Academy	section 482][794]
admission authority (in Chapter I of Part VI)	section 415
admitted to a school for nursery education	section 579(3)
aggregated budget (in Part II)	sections 101(3) and 105
agreed syllabus	section 375(2) and (4)
aided school	section 32(1) and (3)
allocation formula (in Part II)	section 106(2)
alteration (of school premises) and alterations (in relation to such premises)	section 573(2)
annual parents' meeting (in Chapter VI of Part II)	section 162(1)
appropriate diocesan authority (in Part III in relation to a Church of England, Church in Wales or Roman Catholic Church school)	section 311(1)
appropriate further education funding council	section 579(1)
area (of a local education authority)	section 12(6)
articles of government	
(in relation to a county, voluntary or maintained special school)	section 127(1)
(in relation to a grant-maintained school)	section 218(1)
(in relation to a grant-maintained special school)	paragraph 1 of Schedule 28
(in relation to a group of grant-maintained schools)	section 280(2)
assess (in Part V)	section 350(2)
assessment arrangements (in Part V)	section 353
assisted (in relation to a school or other institution)	section 579(5) to (7)
. . .	. . .[795]
attainment targets (in Part V)	section 353
authority responsible for election arrangements (in Chapter V of Part III)	section 243(2)

belonging to the area of a local education authority (in relation to a person)	section 579(4)
boarder	section 579(1)
budget share (in Part II)	section 101(3) and (6)
capital grant (in relation to grant-maintained schools)	section 246(1) (or section 252)
cease to maintain (in relation to a school)	section 574
the chairmen's panel (in Part IV)	section 333(2)
change in character (in relation to a school)	section 573(4)
character (of a school) (in Part III)	section 311(4)
child	
(generally)	section 579(1)
(in Part IV)	section 312(5)
[(in Chapter I of Part VI except sections 431 to 433)	section 411(8)][796]
child for whom a local education authority are responsible (in Part IV)	section 321(3)
Church in Wales school	section 311(1)
Church of England school	section 311(1)
[[... city academy...[797]	...section 482][798]...]
[...city college for the technology of the arts...	...section 482(3)][799]...
[...city technology college...	...section 482(3)][800]...
clothing	section 579(1)
commencement of this Act	section 583(2)
compulsory school age	section 8 (or paragraph 1 of Schedule 40)
contract of employment (in relation to provisions specified in section 575(2))	section 575(1)
controlled school	section 32(1) and (2)
co-opted governor (in relation to a county, voluntary or maintained special school)	section 78(1)
core governor	section 285 and Schedule 25
county school	section 31(1)
date of implementation	
(in Part III in relation to proposals for acquisition of grant-maintained status)	section 200(2)
(in Part III in relation to a new grant-maintained school)	section 217
date of publication of proposals (in Part III in relation to proposals under that Part)	section 311(6)
delegation requirement (in Part II)	section 107(2)
discontinue (in relation to a school)	section 574
disposal of premises (in sections 297 to 300)	section 301(3)
dissolution date (in sections 274 to 279)	section 274(6)
the Education Acts	section 578
eligible for grant-maintained status (in Part III)	section 184
eligible governor (in Part III)	paragraph 4 of Schedule 24
eligible to vote in a ballot held in accordance with section 189 (in Chapter II of Part III)	section 190(1)
employed, employee, employer (in relation to provisions specified in section 575(2))	section 575(1)
employed to work, or to work solely, at a school (in relation to provisions specified in section 575(2))	section 575(3)
employee (in sections 469 to 473)	section 469(6)
enlargement (in relation to school premises)	section 573(3)

establish (in relation to a new school)	section 574
examination requirement (in Chapter III of Part VI)	section 462(1)
exclude, exclusion (except in section 524)	section 579(1)
financial year	section 579(1)
first governor (in relation to a grant-maintained school)	paragraphs 7 and 12 of Schedule 24
foundation governor	
(in relation to a voluntary school)	section 78(2)
(in relation to a grant-maintained school)	paragraphs 8 and 13 of Schedule 24
foundation subjects	section 354. . .[801]
functions	section 579(1)
funding authority	section 26
further education	section 2(3) to (5)
general schools budget (in Part II)	section 101(3)
governing body, governor	
(in Chapters IV to VI of Part II)	section 182
(in relation to a school grouped for purposes of Chapter IV of Part II)	section 89(6)
(in relation to a voluntary school and functions of foundation governors)	section 579(1)
governing body in liquidation (in sections 274 to 279)	section 274(3)
governor of an elected category (in Part III)	paragraph 3 of Schedule 24
governors' report (in Chapter VI of Part II)	section 161(1)
grant-maintained school	
(generally)	section 183(1)
(in sections 500 to 504)	section 505(8)
grant-maintained school formerly conducted by a governing body in liquidation (in sections 274 to 279)	section 274(5)
grant-maintained special school	sections 337(4) and 346(3)
grant regulations (in Chapter VI of Part III)	section 244(2)
grants for education support and training	section 484(1)
group (of schools)	
(in Part II)	section 89(5)
(in Chapter IX of Part III)	section 280(7)
head teacher	
(generally)	section 579(1)
(in relation to a county, voluntary or maintained special school organised into separate departments)	section 132
higher education	section 579(1)
incorporation date	
(in Chapter II of Part III)	section 200(5)
(in Chapter IV of Part III)	section 217
(in Part IV)	section 345(3)
independent school	section 463
initial governor (in Part III)	paragraph 2 of Schedule 24
institution outside (or within) the further education sector	section 4(3)
institution outside (or within) the higher education sector	section 4(4)
instrument of government	
(in relation to a county, voluntary or maintained special school)	section 76(1)
(in relation to a grant-maintained school)	section 218(1)
(in relation to a grant-maintained special school)	paragraph 1 of Schedule 28

(in relation to a group of grant-maintained schools)	section 280(2)
interest in land	section 579(2)
junior pupil	section 3(2)
key stage	section 355(1)
land	section 579(1)
the lay panel (in Part IV)	section 333(2)
learning difficulty	section 312(2) and (3)
liability	section 579(1)
local authority	section 579(1)
local education authority	section 12(1) to (5)
the local education authority	
(generally)	section 579(1)
(in relation to a scheme under Part II)	section 101(2)
local government elector	
(generally)	section 579(1)
(in Part III in relation to an area)	section 311(7)
maintain (in relation to a school maintained by a local education authority)	section 34
maintained school	
(in Part IV)	section 312(5)
(in Part V)	section 350(1)
(in Chapter II of Part VI)	section 437(8)
(in Chapter III of Part VI)	section 449
(in sections 500 to 504)	section 505(8)
maintained nursery school	sections 6(1) and 33(1)
maintained special school	sections 6(2), 33(1) and 337(3)
maintenance grant (in relation to grant-maintained schools)	section 244(1) (or section 250(1))
medical officer (in relation to a local education authority)	section 579(1)
minor authority	section 577
middle school	section 5(3)
modifications, modify	section 579(1)
the National Curriculum	sections 352(1) and 353
new governing body (in Part III)	section 195(2)
new school (in Part II)	section 181(1)
nursery school	section 6(1)
optional extra (in Chapter III of Part VI)	section 455(3)
parent	section 576
parent governor	
(in relation to a county, voluntary or maintained special school)	section 78(3)
(in relation to a grant-maintained school)	paragraphs 5 and 10 of Schedule 24
. . .	. . .
. . .	. . .
pending	
(in Part III in relation to proposals published under section 193)	section 193(4)
(in Chapter III of Part III in relation to the procedure for acquisition of grant-maintained status)	section 203(1)
powers to make proposals for the alteration of their school (in sections 500 to 504 in relation to the governing body of a voluntary school)	section 505(7)
powers to make proposals for the establishment, alteration or discontinuance of schools (in sections 500 to 504)	section 505(8)
premises	

(in relation to a school)	section 579(1)
(in Part III)	section 311(1)
prescribed	section 579(1)
the President (in Part IV)	section 333(2)
primary education	section 2(1)
primary school	section 5(1)
programmes of study (in Part V)	section 353
proceeds of disposal (in sections 297 to 300)	section 301(3)
procedure applicable under Chapter IV of Part II (in Chapter V of Part III)	section 243(3)
promoters (in Part III)	section 212(1)
proposals (in Chapter VII of Part III)	section 266(2)
proposals for acquisition of grant-maintained status (in Part III)	section 183(2)
proposals for the establishment of a new grant-maintained school (in Part III)	section 183(2)
proprietor (in relation to a school)	section 579(1)
prospectively disqualified (in Chapter V of Part III)	section 243(4)
provisionally registered school (in Part VII)	section 465(4)
pupil	sections 3(1) and 19(5)
reception class	section 579(1)
register, registration (in Part VII in relation to independent schools)	section 464(4)
registered (in relation to parents or pupils)	section 434(5)
registered school (in Part VII)	section 465(4)
Registrar of Independent Schools (or the Registrar in Part VII)	section 464(4)
regulations	section 579(1)
relevant age group	section 579(1)
relevant education (in relation to an order under section 27(1))	section 27(7)
relevant particulars (in relation to a proposed initial governor of a grant-maintained school)	section 200(4)
relevant proposals (in Part II)	section 181(2)
relevant standard number (in Chapter I of Part VI)	section 411(7)
required to be covered by a scheme (in Part II in relation to a school)	section 102
reserved teacher (in Chapter VI of Part II in relation to a controlled school)	section 143(2)
reserved teacher (in Chapter VI of Part II in relation to a special agreement school)	section 144(1)
residential trip (in Chapter III of Part VI)	section 462(2)
responsible for a child (in Part IV in relation to a local education authority)	section 321(3)
right to a delegated budget (in Part II)	section 115(a)
Roman Catholic Church school	section 311(1)
scheme (in Part II)	section 101(1)
school	section 4(1) and (2)
school in respect of which financial delegation is required (in Part II)	section 115
school which has a delegated budget (in Part II)	section 115
school attendance order	section 437(3)
school buildings	section 579(1)
school day	section 579(1)
school property (in sections 274 to 279)	section 274(4)
[school year	section 579(1)][802]
secondary education	section 2(2) and (5)
secondary school	section 5(2)
section 67 loan liabilities (in sections 274 to 279)	section 274(7)
senior pupil	section 3(2)

sex education	section 352(3)
significant (in relation to a change in character or enlargement of premises of a school)	section 573(5)
special agreement	section 32(5)
special agreement school	section 32(1) and (4)
special educational needs	section 312(1)
special educational provision	section 312(4)
special purpose grant (in relation to grant-maintained schools)	section 245(1) (or section 251)
special school	sections 6(2) and 337
sponsor governor (in Part III)	paragraphs 9 and 14 of Schedule 24
suitable education (in Chapter II of Part VI)	section 437(8)
teacher governor	
(in relation to a county, voluntary or maintained special school)	section 78(4)
(in relation to a grant-maintained school)	paragraphs 6 and 11 of Schedule 24
temporary governing body, temporary governor (in Part II)	section 181(3)
time of publication of proposals (in Part III in relation to proposals under that Part)	section 311(6)
the Tribunal (in Part IV)	section 313(5)
trust deed (in relation to a voluntary school)	section 579(1)
trustees of the school (in sections 296 to 300)	section 301(2)
voluntary school	sections 31(2) and 32
[wholly based on selection by reference to ability or aptitude (in Chapter I of Part VI)	section 411(9)][803]
young person	section 579(1)

Final provisions

581 Application to Isles of Scilly.

This Act shall apply to the Isles of Scilly—

(a) as if the Isles were a separate non-metropolitan county (and the Council of the Isles of Scilly were accordingly a county council), and

(b) subject to such other modifications as are specified in an order made by the Secretary of State.

582 Consequential amendments, repeals, transitional provisions etc.

(1) The enactments specified in Schedule 37 are amended in accordance with that Schedule, the amendments being consequential on the provisions of this Act.

(2) The enactments and instruments specified in Schedule 38 are repealed or revoked to the extent specified.

(3) The transitional and saving provisions contained in Schedule 39 shall have effect.

(4) The transitory provisions contained in Schedule 40 shall have effect.

583 Short title, commencement and extent.

(1) This Act may be cited as the Education Act 1996.

(2) Subject to subsection (3), this Act shall come into force on 1st November 1996 (and references to the commencement of this Act are to its coming into force on that date).

(3) The following provisions—

section 8,

section 317(6),

section 348,

section 528,

Part II of Schedule 37 and section 582(1) so far as relating thereto, and

Part II of Schedule 38 and section 582(2) so far as relating thereto,

shall come into force on such day as the Secretary of State may by order appoint; and different days may be appointed for different provisions and for different purposes.

(4) The Secretary of State may by order make such incidental, supplemental, saving or transitional provision as he thinks fit in connection with the coming into force in accordance with subsection (2) of any provision of this Act reproducing the effect of a provision of the Education Act 1993 which has not previously been brought into force by an order under section 308(3) of that Act (commencement).

(5) Where an order under subsection (3) brings into force any provision of section 317(6) or 528, then in relation to the coming into force of that provision—

(a) section 568(5) and (6) shall not apply to the order, but

(b) the order may make such provision as is authorised to be made, by virtue of section 67(2) and (3) of the Disability Discrimination Act 1995 (regulations and orders), by an order under section 70(3) of that Act (commencement).

(6) Subject to subsections (7) and (8), this Act extends to England and Wales only.

(7) This section, section 493 and section 569 so far as relating to regulations under section 493 extend also to Scotland; and this section extends also to Northern Ireland.

(8) Section 582 and Schedules 37 to 40 have the same extent as the enactments to which they relate.

SCHEDULES

Section 19.

SCHEDULE 1 Pupil referral units

General adaptations of enactments

1 References in any enactment to the proprietor or governing body of a school shall be read, in relation to a pupil referral unit, as references to the local education authority.

2 References in any enactment to the head teacher of a school shall be read, in relation to a pupil referral unit, as references to the teacher in charge of the unit (whether known as the head teacher or not).

Modifications of enactments by regulations

3 Regulations may provide for any enactments relating to schools maintained by local education authorities (or schools including such schools)—

(a) to apply in relation to pupil referral units,

(b) to apply in relation to such units with such modifications as may be prescribed, or

(c) not to apply in relation to such units.

Registration

4(1) A person who is registered as a pupil at a school other than a pupil referral unit shall not, by reason only of being registered also as a pupil at such a unit, cease for the purposes of the Education Acts to be treated as a registered pupil at that school.

(2) In this Schedule "registered" means shown in the register kept under section 434.

Application of Local Government Act 1986

5 A pupil referral unit is a maintained school for the purposes of section 2A(1)(b) of the Local Government Act 1986 (prohibition on promoting homosexuality).

Curriculum

6[(1) In relation to every pupil referral unit, the local education authority, the management committee (where applicable) and the teacher in charge shall exercise their functions with a view to securing that the curriculum for the unit satisfies the requirements of [section 78(1) or 99(1) of the Education Act 2002][804] (1) (balanced and broadly based curriculum).

(2) Regulations may make provision for the determination and organisation of the curriculum in relation to every pupil referral unit, including provision as to making, and keeping up to date, a written statement of the policy in relation to that curriculum for the unit; and such regulations may require—

(a) the local education authority, the management committee (where applicable), or the teacher in charge to exercise, or

(b) such of them as may be prescribed to collaborate with each other in exercising,

such functions in relation to the curriculum as may be prescribed.][805]

(3) Each local education authority shall, with the approval of the Secretary of State, make arrangements

for the consideration and disposal of any complaint to the effect that the authority, or the teacher in charge of any pupil referral unit—

(a) have acted or are proposing to act unreasonably with respect to the exercise of any power conferred, or the performance of any duty imposed, on them by [sub-paragraph (1) or (2)][806] above, or

(b) have failed to discharge any such duty.

(4) The Secretary of State shall not entertain under section 496 or 497 (power to prevent unreasonable exercise of functions; general default powers) any complaint in respect of any local education authority if it is a complaint—

(a) for which arrangements are required to be made under sub-paragraph (3) above, or

(b) that a local education authority have failed to exercise their powers to secure compliance by the teacher in charge of a pupil referral unit with any such duty as is referred to in that sub-paragraph,

unless a complaint in respect of the local education authority or, as the case may be, the teacher in charge of the unit has been made in respect of the same matter and disposed of in accordance with arrangements under that sub-paragraph.

Discipline

7. . . . .[807]

Sex education, political indoctrination and political issues

8 Sections 403, 406 and 407 (sex education, political indoctrination, and treatment of political issues) apply in relation to pupil referral units as they apply in relation to [community schools][808].

Charges

9(1) Chapter III of Part VI applies in relation to pupil referral units as if the references to governing bodies were omitted.

(2) Section 458(2)(b) (charges for board and lodging) shall have effect in relation to a pupil provided with board and lodging at a unit as if after "that" there were inserted "for the time being".

Application of Environmental Protection Act 1990

10 A pupil referral unit is an educational institution for the purposes of Part IV of the Environmental Protection Act 1990 (litter).

Information

11 Each local education authority shall—

(a) on such occasions, and

(b) in such form and manner,

as may be prescribed, make available to registered parents of registered pupils at any pupil referral unit such information about the unit as may be prescribed.

Disapplication of Schedule 4

12. . . . .[809]

Children with special educational needs

13. . . . .[810]

School attendance orders

14(1) Where a pupil referral unit is named in a school attendance order—

(a) the local education authority shall inform the teacher in charge of the unit, and

(b) if another local education authority are responsible for determining the arrangements for the admission of pupils to the unit, that authority shall admit the child to the unit;

but paragraph (b) above does not affect any power to exclude from a unit a pupil who is already a registered pupil there.

(2) Section 438(4) does not apply in relation to a pupil referral unit.

(3) A local education authority—

(a) shall, before deciding to specify a particular pupil referral unit in a notice under section 438(2) where another local education authority are responsible for determining the arrangements for the admission of pupils to the unit, consult that authority; and

(b) if they decide to specify the unit in the notice, shall serve notice in writing of their decision on

that authority.

(4) Section 439(7) and (8) apply where a notice is served on a local education authority under sub-paragraph (3) above as they apply where notice is served under section 439(6).

(5) The parent of a child in respect of whom a school attendance order is in force may not under section 440 request the local education authority to amend the order by substituting a pupil referral unit for the school named in the order.

(6) Where a child is a registered pupil at both a pupil referral unit and at a school other than a unit, the references in section 444 to the school at which he is a registered pupil shall be read as references to the unit.

[Management committees[811]

15(1) Regulations may make provision—

(a) for requiring any local education authority who maintain a pupil referral unit to establish a committee to act as the management committee for the unit; and

(b) for that committee to discharge on behalf of the authority such of their functions in connection with the unit as are delegated by them to the committee in accordance with the regulations.

(2) Regulations under this paragraph may in particular make provision—

(a) for enabling a local education authority to establish a joint committee to act as the management committee for two or more pupil referral units maintained by the authority;

(b) for requiring the approval of the Secretary of State to be obtained before any such joint committee is established;

(c) as to the composition of a management committee established under the regulations and—

(i) the appointment and removal of its members, and

(ii) their terms of office,

and in particular for requiring such a committee to include persons representing schools. . . [812] situated in the area from which the unit or units in question may be expected to draw pupils;

[(d) for requiring or (as the case may be) prohibiting the delegation by—

(i) a local education authority; or

(ii) in the case of a local education authority which are operating executive arrangements, the executive of that authority or any person on behalf of that executive,

to a management committee of such functions in connection with pupil referral units as are specified in the regulations.][813]

(e) for authorising a management committee to establish sub-committees;

(f) for enabling (subject to any provisions of the regulations) a local education authority [, and in the case of a local education authority which are operating executive arrangements the executive of that authority or any person acting on behalf of that executive,][814] or a management committee to determine to any extent the committee's procedure and that of any sub-committee;

(g) for limiting the personal liability of members of any such committee or sub-committee in respect of their acts or omissions as such members;

(h) for applying to any such committee or sub-committee, with or without modification—

(i) any provision of the Education Acts, or

(ii) any provision made by or under any other enactment and relating to committees or (as the case may be) sub-committees of a local authority.][815]

[(3) In sub-paragraph (2), "executive" and "executive arrangements" have the same meaning as in the Local Government Act 2000.][816]

SCHEDULE 2[817]

. . . .

SCHEDULE 3[818]

. . . .

SCHEDULE 4[819]

. . . .

SCHEDULE 5[820]

. . . .

SCHEDULE 6[821]

....

SCHEDULE 7[822]

....

SCHEDULE 8[823]

....

SCHEDULE 9[824]

....

SCHEDULE 10[825]

....

Sections 122 and 124.

SCHEDULE 11 Contents of statements under section 122(2) and section 124(1)

Part I Statements under section 122(2)

1(1) This Part of this Schedule applies to any statement prepared by a local education authority under section 122(2).

(2) In this Part of this Schedule "the scheme" means the scheme referred to in section 122(1).

2 The statement shall contain the following particulars in respect of the financial year to which it relates—

(a) the amount of the authority's general schools budget for the year (as initially determined for the purposes of the scheme),

(b) the amount of the authority's aggregated budget for the year under the scheme (as so determined),

(c) such particulars as may be prescribed of amounts deducted in respect of excepted heads or items of expenditure (as defined in section 105(3)) in arriving at the amount specified in the statement by virtue of sub-paragraph (b),

(d) such particulars as may be prescribed of amounts deducted by virtue of section 105(1)(b) in arriving at the amount so specified, and

(e) such particulars of the allocation formula under the scheme as may be prescribed.

3(1) The statement shall also contain, with respect to each school required to be covered by the scheme in the year in question, particulars in relation to that year of the planned expenditure per pupil arising from the division of the school's budget share (as initially determined for the purposes of the scheme) by the initial pupil number.

(2) In sub-paragraph (1) "the initial pupil number" means the number of registered pupils at the school in question which is required under the scheme to be used in applying the allocation formula under the scheme for initial determination of the school's budget share for the year.

4 The statement shall contain such further information in respect of the financial provision the authority plan to make in the year in question for county and voluntary schools maintained by them as may be prescribed.

Part II Statements under section 124(1)

5(1) A statement prepared by a local education authority under section 124(1) shall give the following particulars in respect of the financial year to which it relates—

(a) the initial amount appropriated for meeting expenditure in the year in respect of all the schools required to be covered by the statement,

(b) the amount remaining after deducting from that initial amount the aggregate of the amounts referred to in sub-paragraph (2), and

(c) such particulars as may be prescribed of the amounts referred to in sub-paragraph (2).

(2) Those amounts are the initial amounts appropriated for meeting the following descriptions of expenditure in the year in respect of all the schools required to be covered by the statement—

(a) expenditure treated by the authority as expenditure of a capital nature,

(b) expenditure in respect of the repayment of the principal of, the payment of interest on and the discharge of any other financial obligation in connection with any loan used to meet expenditure falling within paragraph (a), and

(c) expenditure of such other descriptions as may be prescribed.

6(1) The statement shall also give, in relation to each school required to be covered by it, the following particulars in respect of the year—

(a) the share of the general expenditure amount which is appropriated by the authority for meeting expenditure for the purposes of the school,

(b) the share which is so appropriated of such of the amounts referred to in paragraph 5(2)(c) as may be prescribed,

(c) the amount of any expenditure initially planned for the purposes of the school and treated by the authority as expenditure of a capital nature, and

(d) such particulars as may be prescribed of the basis on which the authority determine the shares specified in the statement by virtue of paragraphs (a) and (b).

(2) In sub-paragraph (1) "the general expenditure amount" means the amount of which particulars are required to be given by paragraph 5(1)(b).

7 The statement shall contain such further information in respect of the financial provision initially planned by the authority for the schools required to be covered by the statement as may be prescribed.

8 Where only one school is required to be covered by the statement, the references in paragraph 5 to all the schools are references to that school and paragraph 6 does not apply.

Section 126.

SCHEDULE 12 Financial delegation and new schools

Preliminary

1 In this Schedule "temporary governing body" does not include a temporary governing body who by virtue of paragraph 2 of Schedule 10 fall to be treated as a governing body.

New county and voluntary schools

2(1) For the purposes of applying (in accordance with this Schedule) sections 101 to 122 and Part I of Schedule 11 in relation to new schools which will be county or voluntary schools—

(a) references to a school conducted by a governing body shall be read as including a new school which has a temporary governing body, and

(b) other references to the governing body of a school shall be read as including the temporary governing body of a new school.

(2) For those purposes—

(b) references to a county or voluntary school maintained by a local education authority, and

(b) references, in a context referring to a local education authority, to county and voluntary schools,

shall be read as including a new school which on implementation of the relevant proposals will be a county or voluntary school maintained by the authority.

3(1) A new school which will be a county or voluntary school is required to be covered by a scheme in any financial year if it has a temporary governing body during the whole or any part of that year.

(2) In the case of such a school, sections 101 to 122 and Part I of Schedule 11 apply subject to the modifications set out in paragraphs 4 to 7.

4(1) Where a school required to be covered by a scheme in a financial year is a new school during the whole or any part of that year, the provision required by section 106(4)(a) shall not apply in relation to the determination of the school's budget share for the year, so far as that share falls in accordance with the scheme to be treated as referable to planned expenditure by the local education authority for the purposes of the school in respect of any period before the implementation of the relevant proposals.

(2) Accordingly—

(a) paragraph 3(1) of Schedule 11 shall apply in relation to the school as if it referred to such part (if any) of the school's budget share for the year as falls to be determined in accordance with the provision required by section 106(4)(a); and

(b) the statement under section 122(2) shall include in relation to the school the additional particulars mentioned in sub-paragraph (3).

(3) Those particulars are the amount of such part (if any) of the school's budget share for the year (as initially determined for the purposes of the scheme) as falls in accordance with the scheme to be treated as referable to planned expenditure such as is mentioned in sub-paragraph (1).

(4) Sub-paragraph (1) shall not be taken as prejudicing the inclusion in the allocation formula under a scheme, by virtue of section 106(4)(b), of provision taking into account in relation to a new school any forecast made in accordance with the scheme of the number of pupils it will have on implementation of the relevant proposals.

5 The delegation requirement under a scheme shall not apply in relation to a new school (where it is not a school to which section 110 applies) until such date as may be determined by or under the scheme.

6 Section 110 shall have effect, in relation to a new school to which it applies, with the omission of subsection (3)(a).

7 Section 122(7) shall not apply in relation to the temporary governing body of a new school.

New special schools

8(1) Any reference—

(a) in section 120, to maintained special schools or to a maintained special school, or

(b) in section 124, to special schools or to a special school,

shall be read as including a new school proposed to be established by a local education authority which will be a maintained special school and which has a temporary governing body.

(2) Any reference in section 120 or 124 to a school's governing body shall be read, in relation to such a new school, as a reference to its temporary governing body.

(3) The reference in section 124(1) to a local education authority maintaining a special school or special schools shall be read, in relation to such a new school, as a reference to the authority being under a duty by virtue of paragraph 20 of Schedule 9 to defray expenses in relation to its temporary governing body.

9 Section 124(8) shall not apply in relation to the temporary governing body of a new school.

Financial delegation apart from schemes

10 Section 125 shall not apply in relation to a new school.

Section 133.

SCHEDULE 13 *Staffing of county, controlled, special agreement and maintained special schools*

The selection panel

1(1) The articles of government for a county, controlled, special agreement or maintained special school shall provide—

(a) for the constitution of a selection panel whenever such a panel is required by virtue of this Schedule in relation to the appointment of a head teacher or deputy head teacher, and

(b) for a selection panel to consist of a specified number of persons appointed to it by the local education authority and a specified number of governors appointed to it by the governing body.

(2) Neither of the numbers specified by virtue of sub-paragraph (1)(b) shall be less than three; and the number specified in relation to appointments made by the governing body shall not be less than the number specified in relation to appointments made by the authority.

(3) The articles shall provide for the governing body and the authority to have power to replace, at any time, any member of a selection panel whom they have appointed.

2 Regulations may make provision as to the meetings and proceedings of selection panels.

Appointment of head teacher

3(1) The articles of government for a county, controlled, special agreement or maintained special school shall, in relation to the appointment of a head teacher for the school, make provision for the matters set out in sub-paragraphs (2) to (11).

(2) If the post of head teacher is vacant, the local education authority shall appoint an acting head teacher after consulting the governing body.

(3) before appointing a head teacher, the local education authority shall advertise the vacancy in such publications circulating throughout England and Wales as they consider appropriate.

(4) The local education authority shall not appoint a person to be head teacher unless his appointment has been recommended by a selection panel constituted in accordance with the articles.

(5) The selection panel shall interview such applicants for the post as they think fit.

(6) If the panel fail to agree on the applicants whom they wish to interview—

(a) the members of the panel appointed by the governing body are to have the right to nominate not

more than two applicants to be interviewed by the panel, and

(b) the other members of the panel are to have the right to nominate not more than two other applicants to be interviewed.

(7) Where the panel consider it appropriate to do so, they shall recommend to the authority for appointment as head teacher one of the applicants interviewed by them.

(8) If the panel are unable to agree on a person to recommend to the authority, they shall—

(a) repeat (with a view to reaching agreement) such of the steps mentioned in sub-paragraphs (5) to (7) as they think fit,

(b) where—

(i) they have repeated any of those steps in pursuance of paragraph (a) and remain unable to agree, or

(ii) they have decided that it is not appropriate to repeat any of those steps,

require the authority to re-advertise the vacancy, and

(c) where the vacancy is re-advertised, repeat all of the steps mentioned in sub-paragraphs (5) to (7).

(9) If the authority decline to appoint a person recommended by the panel, the panel shall—

(a) where there are applicants for the post whom they have not interviewed, interview such of those applicants (if any) as they think fit,

(b) recommend another of the applicants interviewed by them, if they think fit,

(c) ask the authority to re-advertise the vacancy, if they consider that it should be re-advertised, and

(d) where the vacancy is re-advertised, repeat the steps mentioned in sub-paragraphs (5) to (7).

(10) The authority shall re-advertise the vacancy where they are required to do so by the panel, and may do so where—

(a) it has been duly advertised,

(b) the panel have failed either to make a recommendation which is acceptable to the authority or to request that the vacancy be re-advertised, and

(c) the authority are of the opinion that the panel have had sufficient time in which to carry out their functions.

(11) The chief education officer of the authority, or a member of his department nominated by him, shall have the right to attend all proceedings of the panel (including interviews) for the purpose of giving advice to members of the panel.

(12) In this paragraph "head teacher" does not include an acting head teacher.

Appointment of deputy head teacher

4(1) The articles of government for a county, controlled, special agreement or maintained special school shall, in relation to the appointment of a deputy head teacher for the school, make either—

(a) the same provision, modified as mentioned in sub-paragraphs (2) and (3), as that made (in accordance with paragraph 3) in relation to the appointment of a head teacher for the school, or

(b) the same provision as that made (in accordance with paragraph 5) in relation to the appointment of other teachers at the school.

(2) If the articles (in accordance with sub-paragraph (1)(a)) provide for the appointment of a deputy head teacher to be on the recommendation of a selection panel, they shall provide that where the head teacher is not a member of the panel—

(a) he may be present, for the purpose of giving advice, at any proceedings of the panel (including interviews), and

(b) whether or not he attends any such proceedings, he shall be consulted by the panel before they make any recommendation to the local education authority.

(3) No provision similar to that set out in paragraph 3(2) is required in the articles in relation to the appointment of a deputy head teacher.

Appointment of other staff: general

5(1) The articles of government for a county, controlled, special agreement or maintained special school shall make provision for the matters set out in sub-paragraphs (2) and (3).

(2) Where there is a vacancy in a post (other than that of head teacher or deputy head teacher) which is part of the complement of the school, the local education authority shall decide whether, if the post is not a new one, it should be retained.

(3) If the authority decide that the post should be retained or it is a new post, they shall—

(a) advertise the vacancy and fill it in accordance with the procedure laid down by virtue of paragraph 6, unless they have the intention mentioned in paragraph (b) below;

(b) fill the vacancy in accordance with the procedure laid down by virtue of paragraph 7, if they intend to appoint a person who, at the time when they form that intention, is an employee of theirs or has been appointed to take up employment with them at a future date.

(4) Nothing in this paragraph (or in any of paragraphs 6 to 9) applies in relation to any temporary appointment pending—

(a) the return to work of the holder of the post in question, or

(b) the taking of any steps required by the articles in relation to the vacancy in question.

Appointment of other staff: vacancy advertised

6(1) The articles of government for any school to which paragraph 5(1) applies shall make provision for the matters set out in sub-paragraphs (2) to (7).

(2) Where the local education authority decide to advertise the vacancy, they shall do so in a manner likely in their opinion to bring it to the notice of persons (including employees of theirs) who are qualified to fill the post.

(3) Where the vacancy is advertised, the governing body shall—

(a) interview such applicants for the post as they think fit, and

(b) where they consider it appropriate to do so, recommend to the authority for appointment to the post one of the applicants interviewed by them.

(4) If the governing body are unable to agree on a person to recommend to the authority, they shall—

(a) repeat the steps mentioned in sub-paragraph (3), if they consider that to do so might lead to their reaching agreement,

(b) where they have repeated those steps and remain unable to agree, or decide that it is not appropriate to repeat them, ask the authority to re-advertise the vacancy, and

(c) where the vacancy is re-advertised, repeat those steps.

(5) If the authority decline to appoint a person recommended by the governing body, the governing body shall—

(a) where there are applicants for the post whom they have not interviewed, interview such of those applicants (if any) as they think fit,

(b) recommend another of the applicants interviewed by them, if they think fit,

(c) ask the authority to re-advertise the vacancy, if they consider that it should be re-advertised, and

(d) where the vacancy is re-advertised, repeat the steps mentioned in sub-paragraph (3).

(6) Where the authority are asked to re-advertise the vacancy by the governing body, they shall do so unless—

(a) they decide that the post is to be removed from the complement of the school, or

(b) they decide to appoint a person who, at the time when that decision is made, is an employee of theirs or has been appointed to take up employment with them at a future date.

(7) Whenever governors meet to discuss the appointment or an applicant is interviewed—

(a) the head teacher (if he would not otherwise be entitled to be present), and

(b) such person (if any) as the authority appoint to represent them,

shall be entitled to be present for the purpose of giving advice.

Appointment of other staff: vacancy not advertised

7(1) The articles of government for any school to which paragraph 5(1) applies shall make provision for the matters set out in sub-paragraphs (2) and (3).

(2) Where the vacancy is not advertised, the governing body—

(a) shall be entitled to determine a specification for the post in consultation with the head teacher, and

(b) if they do so, shall send a copy of it to the local education authority.

(3) When considering whom to appoint to the post, the authority shall—

(a) have regard to any such specification, and

(b) consult the governing body and the head teacher.

Delegation of functions under paragraph 6 or 7

8(1) The articles of government for any school to which paragraph 5(1) applies shall make provision for the matters set out in sub-paragraphs (2) and (3).

(2) The governing body shall have power, in relation to the filling of a particular vacancy or a vacancy of a kind specified by them, to delegate any of the functions which are theirs by virtue of paragraph 6 or 7—

(a) to one or more governors,

(b) to the head teacher, or

(c) to one or more governors and the head teacher acting together.

(3) In such a case, the provision made by virtue of paragraph 6(6) shall apply with the substitution of references to the person or persons to whom the functions are delegated for references to the governing body.

Restriction on making appointment where vacancy advertised

9 Where a local education authority have advertised a vacancy in accordance with the provision made by the articles of government for a school by virtue of paragraph 6(2), they shall not appoint a person to the post unless—

(a) his appointment has been recommended in accordance with the provision made by the articles by virtue of paragraph 6(3) to (5), or

(b) they decide to appoint a person who, at the time when that decision is made, is an employee of theirs or has been appointed to take up employment with them at a future date.

Consultation by LEA before appointing certain non-teaching staff

10 The articles of government for a county, controlled, special agreement or maintained special school shall require the local education authority to consult the governing body and the head teacher before appointing any person to work solely at the school otherwise than—

(a) in a teaching post,

(b) in a non-teaching post which is part of the complement of the school, or

(c) solely in connection with either or both of the following—

(i) the provision of meals;

(ii) the supervision of pupils at midday.

Dismissal etc. of staff

11(1) The articles of government for a county, controlled, special agreement or maintained special school shall make provision for the matters set out in sub-paragraphs (2) to (7).

(2) The local education authority shall consult the governing body and (except where he is the person concerned) the head teacher before—

(a) dismissing a person to whom sub-paragraph (3) applies, or

(b) otherwise requiring such a person to cease to work at the school, or

(c) permitting such a person to retire in circumstances in which he would be entitled to compensation for premature retirement.

(3) This sub-paragraph applies to any person who is—

(a) employed in a post which is part of the complement of the school, or

(b) employed to work solely at the school in any other post, otherwise than solely in connection with either or both of the following—

(i) the provision of meals;

(ii) the supervision of pupils at midday.

(4) Where a teacher at the school is required to complete an initial period of probation, the local education authority shall consult the governing body and the head teacher before—

(a) extending his period of probation, or

(b) deciding whether he has completed it successfully.

(5) Where the governing body recommend to the local education authority that a person should cease to work at the school, the authority shall consider their recommendation.

(6) Both the governing body and the head teacher shall have power to suspend a person employed to work at the school where, in the opinion of the governing body or (as the case may be) the head teacher, his exclusion from the school is required.

(7) The governing body or head teacher shall—

(a) when exercising that power, immediately inform the local education authority and the head teacher or (as the case may be) governing body, and

(b) end the suspension if directed to do so by the authority.

(8) In this paragraph "suspend" means suspend without loss of emoluments; and in sub-paragraph (2) the reference to dismissing a person does not include a dismissal under section 143(6) or 144(3) (dismissal of teachers of religious education).

SCHEDULE 14[826]

....

SCHEDULE 15[827]

....

SCHEDULE 16[828]

....

Section 161.

SCHEDULE 17 Governors' annual reports

General

1(1) The articles of government for a county, voluntary or maintained special school shall impose the requirements set out in paragraphs 2 to [9F][829].

(2) In those paragraphs "the report" means a governors' report prepared under section 161.

2 The report shall be as brief as is reasonably consistent with the requirements as to its contents.

Requirements as to contents

3 Where there is an obligation on the governing body (by virtue of section 162) to hold an annual parents' meeting, the report shall—

(a) give details of the date, time and place for the next annual parents' meeting and its agenda;

(b) indicate that the purpose of that meeting will be to discuss both the governors' report and the discharge by the governing body, the head teacher and the local education authority of their functions in relation to the school; and

(c) report on the consideration which has been given to any resolutions passed at the previous annual parents' meeting.

4 The report shall—

(a) give the name of each governor and indicate whether he—

(i) is a parent, teacher or foundation governor,

(ii) was co-opted or otherwise appointed as a governor, or

(iii) is an ex officio governor;

(b) in the case of an appointed governor, say by whom he was appointed;

(c) in relation to each governor who is not an ex officio governor, give the date on which his term of office comes to an end; and

(d) name, and give the address of, the chairman of the governing body and their clerk.

5 The report shall give such information as is available to the governing body about arrangements for the next election of parent governors.

6 The report shall contain a financial statement—

(a) reproducing or summarising any financial statement of which a copy has been provided to the governing body by the local education authority under section 122 or 124 since the last governors' report was prepared under section 161;

(b) indicating, in general terms, how any sum made available to the governing body by the authority—

(i) in respect of the school's budget share, or

(ii) under section 125,

in the period covered by the report was used;

(c) giving details of the application of any gifts made to the school in that period; and

(d) stating the total amount of any travelling and subsistence allowances paid to members of the governing body in that period.

7 The report shall give such information about—

(a) public examinations and other assessments of pupils' achievements,

(b) pupils' absences from the school,

(c) the continuing education of pupils leaving the school, and

(d) the employment or training taken up by such pupils,

as is required to be published by virtue of section 414(6) and (7).

[7A The report shall give the information about public examinations and other assessments of pupils' achievements—

(a) at schools in England (where the school is in England), or

(b) at schools in Wales (where the school is in Wales),

which has most recently been made available to the governing body by the Secretary of State.][830]

8 The report shall describe what steps have been taken by the governing body to develop or strengthen the school's links with the community (including links with the police).

9 The report shall draw attention to the information made available by the governing body in accordance with regulations made under section 408 so far as relating to the matters mentioned in subsection (2)(b) of that section (information as to educational provision made for pupils at the school and syllabuses followed by them).

[[9A The report shall summarise, where the school is in England, the nature, amount and purpose of training and professional development undertaken by the school's teaching staff in the period since the last governors' report was prepared under section 161, identifying in particular the nature, amount and purpose of any training and professional development so undertaken on any day when the staff were required to be available for work but were not required to teach pupils.][831]

9B The report shall give, where the school is in Wales, such information about any targets for improvement set by the governing body in respect of the performance of pupils at the school as is required to be published by virtue of regulations made under section 414(6).

9C The report shall describe in general terms—

(a) the arrangements made for the security of the pupils and staff at the school and the school premises, and

(b) any changes to those arrangements since the last governors' report was prepared under section 161.

9D The report shall indicate in relation to the period since the last governors' report was prepared under section 161—

(a) to what extent the aims of the governing body with respect to sport at the school have been attained; and

(b) any notable sporting achievements of the school's teams during that period.

9E The report shall give the dates of the beginning and end of each school term, and of half-term holidays, for the next school year.

9F The report shall summarise any changes to information contained in the school prospectus since it was last published pursuant to regulations made under section 414(6).][832]

Power of Secretary of State to make amendments

10 The Secretary of State may by order amend the preceding provisions of this Schedule.

SCHEDULE 18 Annual parents' meetings

Proceedings at an annual parents' meeting

1 The articles of government for a county, voluntary or maintained special school shall provide for the proceedings at an annual parents' meeting to be under the control of the governing body.

2(1) The articles of government for a county, voluntary or maintained special school shall provide for any annual parents' meeting at which the required number of parents of registered pupils at the school are present to be entitled to pass (by a simple majority) resolutions on any matters which may properly be discussed at the meeting.

(2) In sub-paragraph (1) "the required number", in relation to a school, means any number equal to or greater than 20 per cent. of the number of registered pupils at the school.

3 No person who is not a parent of a registered pupil at the school may vote on any question put to an annual parents' meeting.

Consideration of resolutions passed at an annual parents' meeting

4(1) The articles of government for a county, voluntary or maintained special school shall require the governing body—

(a) to consider any resolution which is duly passed at an annual parents' meeting and which they

consider is a matter for them;

(b) to send to the head teacher a copy of any resolution which is so passed and which they consider is a matter for him; and

(c) to send to the local education authority a copy of any resolution which is so passed and which they consider is a matter for the authority.

(2) The articles of government shall in addition—

(a) require the head teacher to consider any resolution a copy of which has been sent to him by virtue of sub-paragraph (1)(b) and to provide the governing body with a brief comment on it (in writing) for inclusion in their next governors' report; and

(b) require the local education authority to do likewise in relation to any resolution a copy of which has been sent to them by virtue of sub-paragraph (1)(c).

Determination of question whether person is to be treated as pupil's parent

5(1) The articles of government for a county, controlled or maintained special school shall provide for any question whether any person is to be treated, for the purposes of any provision of the articles relating to the annual parents' meeting, as the parent of a registered pupil at the school to be determined by the local education authority.

(2) The articles of government for an aided or a special agreement school shall provide for any such question to be determined by the governing body.

Section 166.

SCHEDULE 19 Conduct and staffing of new county, voluntary and maintained special schools

Part I General

Articles of government for new schools

1(1) The requirement for there to be articles of government for a school (imposed by section 127) shall not apply in relation to a new school until the requirement for there to be an instrument of government for the school takes effect under section 99.

(2) Before making an order under section 127 as to the articles of government for a new school, the local education authority shall consult the temporary governing body and the head teacher.

(3) Before making such an order in respect of a new school which will be a voluntary school, the authority shall—

(a) secure the agreement of the temporary governing body to the terms of the proposed order, and

(b) secure the agreement of the temporary foundation governors to any provisions which are of particular concern to those governors.

(4) Where a local education authority propose to make an order under section 127 in respect of a new school but cannot secure any agreement required by this paragraph, they or (as the case may be) the temporary governing body or temporary foundation governors may refer the matter to the Secretary of State.

(5) On a reference to him under this paragraph, the Secretary of State shall give such direction as he thinks fit.

2 Section 129(2) (amendment of articles) shall not apply in relation to a new school; but if the articles of government for a new county or voluntary school contain any provisions to which section 129(1) would apply during any period when the school had a delegated budget ("inconsistent provisions") they shall also include in relation to each inconsistent provision the statement required by section 129(3).

Conduct of new schools: general

3 The determination of those matters relating to the conduct of a new school which require to be determined before a governing body is constituted for the school under an instrument of government shall be under the direction of the temporary governing body, but subject to any provision made by or under this Act (including, in particular, this Schedule) or any other enactment.

4 Regulations may make in relation to consultation with temporary governing bodies provision similar to the provision that may be made in relation to consultation with governing bodies by regulations under section 131 (consultation not required in urgent cases).

Part II Staffing of new schools: financial delegation not proposed

Staffing of new county, controlled or maintained special schools

5 Subject to paragraph 19(4), paragraphs 6 to 11 apply in relation to any new school for which a temporary governing body have been constituted and which will be a county, controlled or maintained special school.

6(1) The complement of teaching and non-teaching posts for the school shall be determined by the local education authority.

(2) Section 133(2) and (3) (staff complements) shall apply in relation to a complement determined under this paragraph.

7(1) Whenever a selection panel is required by virtue of paragraph 8 or 9, it shall be constituted in accordance with this paragraph.

(2) A selection panel shall consist of—

(a) such number of persons appointed to it by the local education authority, and

(b) such number of temporary governors appointed to it by the temporary governing body,

as the authority shall determine.

(3) Neither of the numbers so determined shall be less than three; and the number determined in relation to appointments made by the temporary governing body shall not be less than the number determined in relation to appointments made by the authority.

(4) The temporary governing body and the authority may replace, at any time, any member of a selection panel whom they have appointed.

(5) Regulations may make provision, for the purposes of this paragraph, as to the meetings and proceedings of selection panels.

8(1) Subject to sub-paragraph (2) below, sub-paragraphs (3) to (11) of paragraph 3 of Schedule 13 (appointment of head teacher) shall apply in relation to the appointment of a head teacher for the school—

(a) as if they had effect as independent enactments (rather than for the purposes of the provision to be made by articles of government); and

(b) subject to any necessary modifications.

(2) Where—

(a) two or more schools are to be discontinued ("the discontinued schools"), and

(b) the registered pupils at those schools, or a substantial number of those pupils, are expected to transfer to the new school,

the local education authority may, in consultation with the temporary governing body, appoint one of the head teachers of the discontinued schools as the first head teacher for the new school, instead of following the procedure set out in sub-paragraphs (3) to (11) of paragraph 3 of Schedule 13 (as applied by sub-paragraph (1) above).

(3) If the post of head teacher is vacant, the authority may, if they think fit, appoint an acting head teacher after consulting the temporary governing body.

9(1) Subject to sub-paragraph (2) below, sub-paragraphs (3) to (11) of paragraph 3 of Schedule 13 shall apply in relation to the appointment of a deputy head teacher for the school—

(a) as if they had effect as independent enactments (rather than for the purposes of the provision to be made by articles of government); and

(b) subject to any necessary modifications.

(2) If the local education authority so decide, those provisions of Schedule 13 shall not so apply and instead the general staff appointment provisions shall apply in relation to the appointment of a deputy head teacher for the school—

(a) as if they had effect as independent enactments (rather than for the purposes of the provision to be made by articles of government); and

(b) subject to any necessary modifications.

(3) Where (in accordance with sub-paragraph (1)) the appointment of a deputy head teacher is on the recommendation of a selection panel and the head teacher is not a member of the panel, the head teacher—

(a) shall be entitled to be present, for the purpose of giving advice, at any proceedings of the panel (including interviews), and

(b) whether or not he attends any such proceedings, shall be consulted by the panel before they make any recommendation to the local education authority.

(4) In this paragraph and paragraph 10 "the general staff appointment provisions" means the following provisions of Schedule 13—

(a) paragraph 5(3);

(b) paragraph 6(2) to (7);

(c) paragraph 7(2) and (3); and

(d) paragraph 8(2) and (3).

10(1) The general staff appointment provisions shall apply in relation to the appointment of a person to a post (other than that of head teacher or deputy head teacher) which is part of the complement of the school as if they had effect as independent enactments (rather than for the purposes of the provision to be made by articles of government).

(2) The local education authority shall consult the temporary governing body and the head teacher before appointing any person to work solely at the school otherwise than—

(a) in a teaching post,

(b) in a non-teaching post which is part of the complement of the school, or

(c) solely in connection with either or both of the following—

(i) the provision of meals;

(ii) the supervision of pupils at midday.

(3) This paragraph does not apply in relation to a temporary appointment pending—

(a) the return to work of the holder of the post in question, or

(b) the taking of any steps required by virtue of this Schedule in relation to the vacancy in question.

(4) Paragraph 9(4) applies for the purposes of this paragraph.

11(1) The clerk to the temporary governing body shall be appointed by the local education authority.

(2) When the arrangement for the constitution of the temporary governing body comes to an end under section 96 or 97, the person who was the clerk to that body shall act as clerk to the governing body who succeed them, pending the appointment of a clerk under section 135.

12 Subject to paragraph 19(4), a local education authority shall, in discharging their duty under paragraph 21 of Schedule 9 (temporary governing bodies) to provide information to the temporary governing body of a new school which will be a county, controlled or maintained special school, inform the temporary governing body, in particular—

(a) of the number of members of any selection panel required by virtue of paragraph 8 or 9 above who are to be appointed by the authority and the number who are to be appointed by the temporary governing body;

(b) where the authority intend to exercise the power conferred on them by paragraph 8(2) above, of their intention to do so;

(c) of the provision which is to apply in relation to the appointment of the deputy head teacher of the school;

(d) of the complement of staff for the school; and

(e) of the authority's proposals with regard to the appointment of staff for the school and the timing of appointments.

Staffing of new aided schools

13 Subject to paragraph 19(5), paragraphs 14 to 16 apply in relation to a new school which will be an aided school.

14 Subject to paragraph 15(1), the local education authority and the temporary governing body shall have the same powers, and be under the same duties, for the purposes of the appointment and dismissal of staff at the school as would the authority and the governing body for an aided school whose articles of government provided for—

(a) staff employed solely in connection with the provision of school meals to be appointed by the authority, and

(b) other staff employed at the school to be appointed by the governing body.

15(1) The first appointment of a clerk to the temporary governing body shall be made by the promoters of the school (that is, the persons making the relevant proposals).

(2) When the arrangement for the constitution of the temporary governing body comes to an end under

section 97, the person who was the clerk to that body shall act as clerk to the governing body who succeed them, pending the appointment of their clerk.

16(1) The local education authority shall, with a view to enabling staff to be appointed in good time, notify the temporary governing body of any determination, prohibition or direction they intend to make or give pursuant to subsection (2)(b), (4)(a) or (b) or (5) of section 134 (staffing of aided schools).

(2) The authority shall, in discharging their duty under paragraph 21 of Schedule 9 to provide information to the temporary governing body of a new school which will be an aided school, inform the temporary governing body, in particular, of the authority's proposals with regard to the appointment of staff for the school and the timing of appointments.

Expenditure on staff for new schools

17 Where a temporary governing body are constituted for a new school, the local education authority shall be under the same duty to defray the expenses incurred in relation to the staff appointed in accordance with paragraphs 6 to 11 or (as the case may be) 14 and 15, as they would be if the relevant proposals had been implemented and the temporary governing body were the governing body of the school.

Part III Staffing of new schools: financial delegation proposed

Adaptation of references

18 For the purposes of the application (in accordance with paragraphs 19 to 24) of sections 136 to 141 and Schedule 14 in relation to new schools which will be county or voluntary schools—

(a) references to the governing body of a school shall be read as including the temporary governing body of a new school;

(b) references to a county school shall be read as including a new school which on implementation of the relevant proposals will be a county school; and

(c) references to a voluntary school of a particular category, or maintained by a particular local education authority, shall be read as including a new school which on implementation of the relevant proposals will be a voluntary school of that category, or maintained by that authority.

Application or otherwise of provisions about staffing

19(1) Subject to paragraphs 20 to 24, section 136 or (as the case may be) section 137 (staffing of county or voluntary schools with delegated budgets) shall apply to a new school which on implementation of the relevant proposals will be a school of a category to which that section applies not only at any time when (by virtue of Schedule 12) the new school has a delegated budget but also at any time when it has a temporary governing body and sub-paragraph (2) or (3) is satisfied.

(2) This sub-paragraph is satisfied if the delegation requirement under the scheme will apply to the school on or before the implementation of the relevant proposals.

(3) This sub-paragraph is satisfied if the local education authority propose to exercise any power under the scheme to delegate the management of the school's budget share for a financial year by making such a delegation—

(a) to the temporary governing body before the implementation of the relevant proposals, or

(b) to the governing body of the school on implementation of those proposals.

(4) Paragraphs 6 to 12 of this Schedule shall not apply in relation to a new school to which section 136 for the time being applies.

(5) Paragraphs 14 to 16 of this Schedule shall not apply in relation to a new school to which section 137 for the time being applies.

20 Sections 136, 137 and 138 and Schedule 14 (staffing of schools with delegated budgets) shall apply, in the case of a new school, for the purposes only of—

(a) the appointment of staff at the school, and

(b) the taking of such steps with respect to any other matters referred to in those provisions as may be appropriate in preparation for the conduct of the school following implementation of the relevant proposals.

21 In the case of a new school which is a proposed county, controlled, aided or special school, no appointments of staff for the school shall be made by the local education authority before the constitution of a temporary governing body for the school.

22 Section 139(2) and (5) (payments in respect of dismissal) shall not apply in relation to a new school.

23 Any provision included in a scheme by virtue of subsection (3) of section 140 (community schools), so far as it relates to the appointment of staff at a school to which that section applies, shall apply in relation to a new school which on implementation of the relevant proposals will be a school to which that section applies.

24(1) Section 141 (amendment of articles) shall not apply in relation to a new school.

(2) The local education authority shall, however, incorporate—

(a) the statement mentioned in section 141(2) in the articles of government for a new school which will be a county or controlled school and to which section 136 applies, or

(b) the statement mentioned in section 141(3) in the articles of government for a new school which will be an aided school and to which section 137 applies.

Part IV Other matters relating to conduct etc. of new schools

Preparation of curriculum

25(1) The head teacher of a new school for which a temporary governing body have been constituted shall, in preparing to discharge his functions under Part V in relation to the curriculum for the school, consult that body and the local education authority.

(2) any authority who have been consulted under this paragraph shall inform the head teacher of the resources which are likely to be made available to the school; and the head teacher shall have regard to any information so given to him.

School terms, holidays and sessions

26(1) Pending the coming into force of the articles of government for a new school which will be a county or controlled school—

(a) the dates when the school terms and holidays are to begin and end shall be determined by the local education authority, and

(b) the times of the school sessions shall be determined by the temporary governing body after consultation with the authority.

(2) Pending the coming into force of the articles of government for a new school which will be an aided school—

(a) the dates and times when the school terms and holidays are to begin and end, and

(b) the times of the school sessions,

shall be determined by the temporary governing body.

(3) In this paragraph "the times of the school sessions" means the times at which each of the school sessions (or, if there is only one, the school session) is to begin and end on any day.

Discipline

27 Pending the coming into force of the articles of government for a new school, section 154(2) to (6) (responsibility for discipline) shall apply—

(a) in relation to the head teacher, and

(b) subject to any necessary modifications, in relation to the temporary governing body,

as if they had effect as independent enactments (rather than for the purposes of the provision to be made by articles of government).

Reports and information

28(1) A temporary governing body shall provide the local education authority with such reports in connection with the discharge of their functions as the authority may require (either on a regular basis or from time to time).

(2) The head teacher of a new school for which a temporary governing body have been constituted shall provide that body or (as the case may be) the local education authority with such reports in connection with the discharge of his functions as that body or the authority may require (either on a regular basis or from time to time).

(3) In the case of a new school which will be an aided school—

(a) the local education authority shall notify the temporary governing body of any requirement imposed by them on the head teacher under sub-paragraph (2), and

(b) the head teacher shall provide the temporary governing body with a copy of any report which he makes in complying with any such requirement.

Consultation on expenditure by local education authority

29(1) Where a temporary governing body have been constituted for a new school, the local education authority shall consult that body and the head teacher on their proposed expenditure on books, equipment and stationery for the school.

(2) Sub-paragraph (1) does not apply in relation to a new school which has a delegated budget.

SCHEDULE 20[833]

....

SCHEDULE 21[834]

....

Section 218(4).

[SCHEDULE 22 Governing bodies of grant-maintained schools

Introductory

1 In this Schedule—

"school" means a grant-maintained school, and

"instrument", in relation to a school, means the instrument of government for the school.

Election of governors

2 The instrument for a school may make provision—

(a) as to the procedure for the election of members of the governing body, and

(b) for the determination of any questions arising in connection with, or matters relating to, such elections.

Disqualification for, tenure of and removal from office

3 A person who is a member of the teaching or other staff at a school which is required to have first governors shall be disqualified for holding office as such a governor on the governing body.

4 The instrument for a school may make provision as to the circumstances in which persons are to be disqualified for holding office as members of the governing body.

5 Subject to paragraph 10, the instrument for a school must provide for each governor of an elected category to hold office for a term of four years.

6(1) Subject to paragraph 10, the instrument for a school must make the following provision for the term of office of—

(a) first or, as the case may be, foundation governors, other than a foundation governor who is a governor ex officio, and

(b) where there are sponsor governors, those governors.

(2) Except where sub-paragraph (3), (4) or (5) applies, such a governor is to hold office for such term (not being less than five nor more than seven years) as may be specified in the instrument.

(3) The initial instrument must provide, except where sub-paragraph (4) or (5) applies—

(a) subject to paragraph (b), for such a governor to hold office for such term as was specified in the proposals for acquisition of grant-maintained status or, as the case may be, the proposals for the establishment of a new grant-maintained school as the proposed term of office for initial governors of the category in question, and

(b) in the case of a governing body incorporated in pursuance of proposals for the establishment of a new grant-maintained school which name a person as a sponsor of the school, for any sponsor governor to hold office for such term as was specified as the proposed term of office for such governors in those proposals.

(4) Any additional first or foundation governor appointed in pursuance of provision made in the instrument by virtue of section 230(2) is to hold office for such term (not being more than five years) as may be specified in the terms of that governor's appointment.

(5) Any first governor appointed in pursuance of provision made in the instrument by virtue of section 227 is to hold office for such term (not being less than five nor more than seven years) as may be specified in the terms of his appointment.

7 No provision made in the instrument by virtue of paragraph 5, 6 or 10 shall be taken to prevent a governor—

(a) from being elected or appointed for a further term, or

(b) from being disqualified, by virtue of paragraph 3 or any provision made by virtue of paragraph

4, for continuing to hold office.

8 The instrument for a school must provide that any member of the governing body may at any time resign his office.

9(1) The instrument for a school must provide that any foundation governor (other than one holding office ex officio) and any sponsor governor may be removed from office by the person or persons who appointed him.

(2) For the purposes of this paragraph, an initial foundation governor shall be treated as having been appointed by the person or persons entitled to appoint foundation governors under provision included in the instrument in accordance with section 228(7)(b).

Initial appointments: terms of office

10(1) The instrument for a school must, until every initial governor has ceased to hold office, make the provision required by sub-paragraphs (2) and (3).

(2) In the case of a governing body incorporated under Chapter II of Part III—

(a) an initial governor of an elected category who was a governor of that category on the governing body of the school immediately before the incorporation date shall hold office for the remainder of his term of office on the former governing body, and

(b) an initial governor of an elected category who was elected under section 234, or elected or nominated under section 237 to hold office as such, shall hold office for a term of four years.

(3) An initial first governor, initial foundation governor (other than a foundation governor who is a governor ex officio) or initial sponsor governor shall hold office for such term (not being less than five nor more than seven years) beginning with the incorporation date as may be specified as his proposed term of office in the proposals for acquisition of grant-maintained status or, as the case may be, the proposals for the establishment of a new grant-maintained school.

(4) In the case of a governing body incorporated under Chapter IV of Part III, the instrument for a school must, until every governor of an elected category appointed before the date of implementation of the proposals has ceased to hold office, provide for any such governor to hold office for the prescribed term.

Meetings and proceedings

11 The proceedings of the governing body of a school shall not be invalidated by—

(a) any vacancy among their number, or

(b) any defect in the election or appointment of any governor.

12 Subject to the provisions of Chapter V of Part III and any instrument of government or articles of government made under that Chapter, the governing body of a school may regulate their own procedure.

13(1) The instrument for a school may make provision as to the meetings and proceedings of the governing body.

(2) The provision that may be made in pursuance of this paragraph includes, in particular, provision—

(a) as to the election of a chairman and vice-chairman,

(b) as to the establishment, constitution, meetings and proceedings of committees,

(c) for the delegation of the governing body's functions, in such circumstances as may be specified in the instrument, to committees established by that body or to any member of that body, and

(d) as to the procedure (including any quorum) when business is transacted by members of the governing body of a particular category.

(3) The provision mentioned in sub-paragraph (2)(b) may provide for a committee to include persons who are not members of the governing body.

(4) The instrument shall make provision for an appeal committee for the purposes of paragraph 6(1) of Schedule 23 to include among its members (with full voting powers) a person nominated by the governing body from among persons who are eligible to be lay members.

(5) A person is eligible to be a lay member for the purposes of sub-paragraph (4) if—

(a) he is a person without personal experience in the management of any school or the provision of education in any school (disregarding any such experience as a governor or in any other voluntary capacity), and

(b) he does not have, and has not at any time had, any connection with—

(i) the school, or

(ii) any person who is a member of, or employed by, the governing body of the school,

of a kind which might reasonably be taken to raise doubts about his ability to act impartially in relation to the school.

Information as to meetings and proceedings

14(1) Regulations may require the governing body of a school to make available, to such persons or classes of person as may be prescribed, such documents and information relating to the meetings and proceedings of the governing body as may be prescribed.

(2) Documents and information required by the regulations to be made available shall be made available in such form and manner, and at such times, as may be prescribed.

Allowances for governors

15. . . . .[835]

Seal etc.

16(1) The application of the seal of the governing body of a school must be authenticated by the signature—

(a) of the chairman of the governing body, or

(b) of some other member authorised either generally or specially by the governing body to act for that purpose,

together with the signature of any other member.

(2) Every document purporting to be an instrument made or issued by or on behalf of the governing body of a school and—

(a) to be duly executed under the seal of the governing body, or

(b) to be signed or executed by a person authorised by the governing body to act in that behalf,

shall be received in evidence and be treated, without further proof, as being so made or issued unless the contrary is shown.][836]

Section 218(5).

SCHEDULE 23

Content of articles of government for grant-maintained schools

Introductory

1 In this Schedule—

"school" means a grant-maintained school, and

"articles", in relation to a school, means the articles of government for the school.

Performance and delegation of functions

2(1) The articles must make provision as to the functions to be exercised in relation to the school by—

(a) the Secretary of State,

(b) the funding authority,

(c) the governing body,

(d) any committee or other body established by the governing body,

(e) the head teacher, and

(f) any other persons specified in or determined under the articles.

(2) The articles must also include provision as to the delegation of such functions by those on whom they are imposed or conferred by or under the articles.

(3) The articles may include provision as to the establishment by the governing body of committees or other bodies of persons for the purposes of or in connection with the performance in relation to the school of such functions as may be determined by or under the articles.

Staff

3(1) The articles must include provision as to—

(a) disciplinary rules and procedures applicable to members of the staff of the school, and

(b) procedures for giving them opportunities for seeking redress of any grievances relating to their employment.

(2) The articles must also include provision as to arrangements—

(a) for giving any member of the staff an opportunity of making representations as to any proposal to dismiss him by the governing body or any persons authorised under the articles to dismiss

him, including (if he so wishes) oral representations to such person or persons as may be appointed for the purpose,

(b) for requiring the governing body or any persons authorised under the articles to dismiss him to have regard to any representations made by him before taking any decision to dismiss him, and

(c) for giving any member of staff whom it has been decided to dismiss an opportunity of appealing against that decision before any action is taken to implement it.

Curriculum

4(1) The articles must include provision for securing the discharge by the governing body and the head teacher of duties imposed on them under Chapters I and II of Part V and sections 384, 388, 389, 400 and 408.

(2) The articles must include provision as to arrangements for the consideration and disposal of complaints relating to any matter concerning the curriculum followed within the school including, in particular, the discharge by the governing body of those duties.

(3) The articles must require the governing body, when considering the content of the secular curriculum for the school, to have regard to any representations with regard to that curriculum—

(a) which are made to them by any persons connected with the community served by the school, or

(b) which are made to them by the chief officer of police and are connected with his responsibilities.

Admission arrangements

5(1) The articles must—

(a) provide for the governing body to be responsible for determining the arrangements for admitting pupils to the school; and

(b) include provision as to the policy to be followed in deciding admissions.

(2) The articles must also require the governing body to publish, for each school year, particulars of—

(a) the arrangements for admission of pupils to the school; and

(b) the procedures applicable under the articles in relation to the admission of pupils to the school.

Appeals relating to admission and exclusion of pupils

6(1) The articles must include provision as to the arrangements for appeals (in such circumstances as may be provided by the articles) to an appeal committee constituted in accordance with the instrument of government against any decision or action taken—

(a) by the governing body, or

(b) by any persons authorised under the articles to take any decision or action of the kind in question,

in relation to admissions of pupils to the school or the permanent exclusion of a pupil from the school.

(2) The articles must enable the governing body to make such arrangements jointly with the governing body of one or more other grant-maintained schools.

[(2A) Sub-paragraphs (1) and (2), so far as they apply in relation to arrangements in respect of appeals—

(a) do not require the articles to provide for any matter for which provision is made by Schedule 25A (exclusion appeals); and

(b) have effect subject to paragraph 4(2) of Schedule 33B (refusal of admission in case of children permanently excluded from two or more schools).][837]

(3) The articles must require the governing body to publish, for each school year, particulars of any arrangements made by them in respect of appeals by parents against any such decision or action in relation to admissions of pupils to the school as is mentioned in sub-paragraph (1) above.

Annual reports

7(1) The articles must require the governing body to prepare once in every school year a report in such form and containing such information as the articles may require.

(2) The articles must require the governing body to take such steps as are reasonably practicable to secure that—

(a) the registered parents of all registered pupils at the school and all persons employed at the school are given (free of charge) a copy of the report, and

(b) copies of the report are available for inspection (at all reasonable times and free of charge) at the school.

Annual parents' meetings

8(1) The articles must require the governing body, subject to any exceptions provided for in the articles, to hold a meeting once in every school year which is open to—

(a) all parents of registered pupils at the school, and

(b) such other persons as the governing body may invite.

(2) The articles must include provision as to—

(a) the procedure to be followed and the matters to be considered at such a meeting,

(b) the determination of any questions arising in connection with such a meeting, and

(c) the taking by the governing body or any other persons of such action as may be required by the articles for the purposes of, or in connection with, such a meeting or any resolutions passed at it.

Section 222.

SCHEDULE 24 Categories of governors

Part I Introductory

Application

1(1) This Schedule applies, in relation to the governing body of a grant-maintained school, for the purposes of Part III.

(2) Part II of this Schedule applies for the purpose of determining who are to be the initial governors of a grant-maintained school.

(3) Part III of this Schedule applies for the purpose of determining who are to be the governors of a grant-maintained school on and after the incorporation date.

General interpretation

2 References to an initial governor are to any person who becomes a member of the governing body on the incorporation date.

3 References to a governor of an elected category are to a person who is a parent or teacher governor as defined by section 78(3) or (4) or is such a governor within the meaning of this Schedule.

4 In relation to any proposals for acquisition of grant-maintained status in respect of a school, a person who is a governor of an elected category on the existing governing body of the school is an eligible governor of that category if—

(a) his term of office as a governor is due to end after the date of implementation of the proposals, and

(b) he has notified the existing governing body that he is willing to serve on the proposed governing body and has not withdrawn that notification.

Part II Initial governors

Parent governors

5(1) In relation to a governing body to be incorporated under Chapter II of Part III, "parent governor" means—

(a) a person who, immediately before the incorporation date in relation to the school, is a parent governor (as defined by section 78(3)) in relation to the school, or

(b) a person elected or appointed under section 234, or elected, appointed or nominated under section 237, to hold office as an initial parent governor on the governing body.

(2) A person elected under section 234 to hold office as an initial parent governor must be elected by registered parents of registered pupils at the school and a person elected or appointed under that section to hold such office must when he is elected or appointed be such a parent.

(3) A person elected, appointed or nominated under section 237 to hold office as an initial parent governor—

(a) in the case of an election, must be elected by registered parents of registered pupils at the school and must when he is elected be such a parent, and

(b) in the case of an appointment or nomination, must be a registered parent of a registered pupil at the school at the time of his appointment or nomination.

Teacher governors

6(1) In relation to a governing body to be incorporated under Chapter II of Part III, "teacher governor" means—

(a) a person who, immediately before the incorporation date in relation to the school, is a teacher governor (as defined by section 78(4)) in relation to the school, or

(b) a person elected under section 234, or elected or nominated under section 237, to hold office as an initial teacher governor on the governing body.

(2) A person elected under section 234 to hold office as an initial teacher governor must be elected by teachers at the school and must when he is elected be such a teacher.

(3) A person elected or nominated under section 237 to hold office as an initial teacher governor—

(a) in the case of an election, must be elected by teachers at the school and must when he is elected be such a teacher, and

(b) in the case of a nomination, must be a teacher at the school at the time of his nomination.

First governors

7(1) In relation to a governing body to be incorporated under Chapter II of Part III, "first governor" means a person who is selected under section 236(1), or nominated under section 238(1), and appears to the persons selecting or nominating him to be committed to the good government and continuing viability of the school.

(2) In relation to a governing body to be incorporated under Chapter IV of Part III, "first governor" means a person appointed by the funding authority who appears to them to be committed to the good government and continuing viability of the proposed school.

Foundation governors

8(1) In relation to a governing body to be incorporated under Chapter II of Part III, "foundation governor" means—

(a) a person who is selected under section 236(2) or nominated under section 238(2),

(b) where the statement annexed (under paragraph 2 of Schedule 20) to the proposals for acquisition of grant-maintained status describes the religious character of the school, a person who is appointed for the purpose of securing that (subject to the approval or adoption under section 261 of any proposals) the religious character of the school is such as is indicated in the statement, and

(c) where there is a trust deed relating to the school, a person who is appointed for the purpose of securing that the school is conducted in accordance with the deed.

(2) In relation to a governing body to be incorporated under Chapter IV of Part III, "foundation governor" means—

(a) a person who is appointed by the promoters,

(b) where the statement annexed under paragraph 8 of Schedule 20 to the proposals for the establishment of a new grant-maintained school describes the religious character of the school, a person who is appointed for the purpose of securing that (subject to the approval or adoption under section 261 of any proposals) the religious character of the proposed school is such as is indicated in the statement, and

(c) where there is a trust deed relating to the proposed school, a person who is appointed for the purpose of securing that the proposed school is conducted in accordance with that deed.

Sponsor governors

9 In relation to a governing body to be incorporated under Chapter II of Part III, "sponsor governor" means a person appointed by a person named as a sponsor of the school in the proposals for acquisition of grant-maintained status.

Part III Governors other than initial governors

Parent governors

10(1) "Parent governor" means a person who—

(a) is elected by registered parents of registered pupils at the school,

(b) is appointed under a provision of the instrument of government made by virtue of section 223(3),

(c) is appointed by virtue of section 223(6), or

(d) is an initial parent governor.

(2) To qualify for such election, the person must when he is elected be a registered parent of a registered pupil at the school.

Teacher governors

11(1) "Teacher governor" means a person who—

(a) is elected by teachers at the school,

(b) is appointed by virtue of section 224(4), or

(c) is an initial teacher governor.

(2) To qualify for such election, the person must when he is elected be a teacher at the school.

First governors

12 "First governor" means—

(a) a person appointed by the governing body who appears to them to be committed to the good government and continuing viability of the school,

(b) a person appointed under a provision of the instrument of government made by virtue of section 227 who appears to the person appointing him to be committed to the good government and continuing viability of the school, or

(c) an initial first governor.

Foundation governors

13 "Foundation governor" means a person who—

(a) is appointed otherwise than by a local education authority or the funding authority,

(b) where paragraph 8(1)(b) or (2)(b) applies, is appointed for the purpose there referred to, and

(c) where there is a trust deed relating to the school, is appointed for the purpose of securing that the school is conducted in accordance with that deed.

Sponsor governors

14 "Sponsor governor" means—

(a) a person appointed by a person named in the instrument of government as a sponsor of the school,

(b) while the instrument of government is the initial instrument, a person appointed by a person named as a sponsor of the school in the proposals for acquisition of grant-maintained status or, as the case may be, the proposals for the establishment of a new grant-maintained school, or

(c) an initial sponsor governor.

Section 285.

SCHEDULE 25 Core governors for groups

Introductory

1 The provision made for core governors in the instrument of government for the governing body of a group must be in accordance with this Schedule.

Kinds of core governor

2(1) Core governors may be either—

(a) appointed by the governing body, or

(b) externally appointed.

(2) Externally appointed core governors may be either—

(a) appointed in respect of a particular school in the group, being a school—

(i) which was a voluntary school immediately before it became grant-maintained, or

(ii) which was established in pursuance of proposals published under section 212, or

(b) where the group consists only of such schools, appointed in respect of the group otherwise than by the governing body.

(3) A person appointed as mentioned in sub-paragraph (2)(a) must be appointed by the persons named in the instrument of government for the group as being entitled to appoint externally appointed core governors in respect of the school.

(4) A person appointed as mentioned in sub-paragraph (2)(a) must be appointed—

(a)(where any statement annexed to the proposals in pursuance of which the school became a grant-maintained school described the religious character of the school) for the purpose of securing that, subject to any change in the character of the school which may be authorised by or under Part III, the religious character of the school is such as was indicated in the statement, and

(b)(where there is a trust deed relating to the school) for the purpose of securing that the school is conducted in accordance with the deed.

(5) Core governors, other than externally appointed core governors appointed in respect of particular schools in the group, must be appointed from among persons who appear to the person making the

appointment to be committed to the good government and continuing viability of all the schools in the group.

(6) A person who is a member of the teaching or other staff at any of the schools in the group is disqualified from holding office as a core governor, other than an externally appointed core governor.

Groups consisting only of former voluntary schools or section 212 schools

3(1) This paragraph applies in the case of such a group as is mentioned in paragraph 2(2)(b).

(2) The minimum number of externally appointed core governors (referred to in this paragraph as "MN") is one greater than the number of governors other than externally appointed core governors.

(3) Any head teacher of a school in the group who has chosen not to be a governor shall be counted as one for the purposes of sub-paragraph (2).

(4) In respect of each school in the group there must be the same number of externally appointed core governors.

(5) The total number of externally appointed core governors in respect of schools in the group must not be less than the highest number, not exceeding MN, that is consistent with sub-paragraph (4).

Other groups

4(1) This paragraph applies in the case of a group other than such a group as is mentioned in paragraph 2(2)(b).

(2) If any school in the group falls within paragraph 2(2)(a), one externally appointed governor must be appointed in respect of that school.

(3) The appropriate number of the core governors must (on the date or dates on which they respectively take office) be parents of registered pupils at schools in the group, and the appropriate number of the core governors must (on the date or dates on which they respectively take office) be members of the local community; but one person may satisfy both requirements.

(4) In sub-paragraph (3) "the appropriate number" means not less than two or, if all but one of the schools in the group fall within paragraph 2(2)(a), at least one.

(5) In appointing core governors, the governing body must secure that those governors include persons appearing to the governing body to be members of the local business community (and such persons may also satisfy one or both of the requirements of sub-paragraph (3)).

(6) The number of core governors must be such number, not being—

(a) less than five, or

(b)(subject to paragraph (a)) more than the number of schools in the group,

as will secure that they and the parent governors outnumber the other governors.

(7) Any head teacher of a school in the group who has chosen not to be a governor shall be counted as one for the purposes of sub-paragraph (6).

[SCHEDULE 25A Appeals against exclusion of pupils from grant-maintained schools[838]

Introductory[839]

1 In this Schedule—

"appeal" means an appeal mentioned in section 307A;

"appeal committee" means an appeal committee constituted for the purposes of an appeal in accordance with the instrument of government of the school;

"the relevant person" means—

(a) in relation to a pupil under the age of 18, a parent of his;

(b) in relation to a pupil who has attained that age, the pupil himself.

Procedure on appeal

2 An appeal shall be by notice in writing setting out the grounds on which it is made.

3(1) Subject to sub-paragraph (2), the appeal committee shall meet to consider an appeal—

(a) within the period ending with the 15th school day after the day on which the appeal is lodged, or

(b) if the governing body have determined a shorter period, within that period.

(2) The governing body may extend the period within which the appeal committee are to consider an appeal where—

(a) the relevant person requests them to do so; and

(b) they are satisfied that the circumstances are exceptional and justify the period under sub-

paragraph (1) being extended.

4(1) For the purpose of fixing the time (falling within the period mentioned in paragraph 3) at which the hearing of an appeal is to take place, the governing body shall take reasonable steps to ascertain any times falling within that period when—

(a) the relevant person, or

(b) any other person who wishes, and would be entitled, to appear and make oral representations in accordance with paragraph 5,

would be able to attend.

(2) Where in accordance with sub-paragraph (1) the governing body have ascertained any such times in the case of any such person, they shall, when fixing the time at which the hearing is to take place, take those times into account with a view to ensuring, so far as it is reasonably practicable to do so, that that person is able to appear and make such representations at the hearing.

5(1) The appeal committee shall give the relevant person an opportunity of appearing and making oral representations, and shall allow him to be represented or to be accompanied by a friend.

(2) The appeal committee shall allow—

(a) the head teacher and a member of the governing body to make written representations;

(b) the head teacher and a member of the governing body to appear and make oral representations; and

(c) the governing body to be represented.

6 An appeal shall be held in private except when otherwise directed by the governing body, but any member of the Council on Tribunals may attend as an observer any meeting of the appeal committee at which an appeal is considered.

7 Two or more appeals may be combined and dealt with in the same proceedings if the appeal committee consider that it is expedient to do so because the issues raised by the appeals are the same or connected.

8(1) In deciding whether the pupil in question should be reinstated (and, if so, the time when this should take place), the appeal committee shall have regard to both the interests of that pupil and the interests of other pupils at his school and members of its staff.

(2) In making its decision on an appeal, the appeal committee shall also have regard to the measures publicised by the head teacher under section 306A(7).

(3) Sub-paragraphs (1) and (2) do not apply where the appeal committee decides that the pupil in question was not guilty of the conduct which the head teacher relied on as grounds for his permanent exclusion.

(4) Sub-paragraphs (1) and (2) shall not be read as precluding an appeal committee from having regard to any other relevant matters.

9 In the event of a disagreement between the members of the appeal committee the appeal under consideration shall be decided by a simple majority of the votes cast and, in the case of an equality of votes, the chairman of the committee shall have a second or casting vote.

10 Subject to paragraph 11, the decision of the appeal committee and the grounds on which it is made shall be communicated by the committee in writing to the relevant person, the governing body, the head teacher and the local education authority to whose area the pupil belongs within—

(a) the period ending with the 17th school day after the day on which the appeal is lodged; or

(b) if the governing body have determined a shorter period, that period.

11 Where the governing body extend the period for the consideration of an appeal in accordance with paragraph 3(2), they shall (to the extent it appears to them to be necessary as a result of the extension of that period) extend the period within which the appeal committee are to communicate their decision.

12 Subject to paragraphs 2 to 11, all matters relating to the procedure on appeals shall be determined by the governing body.

13(1) Subject to sub-paragraph (2), where joint arrangements for appeals have been made in accordance with paragraph 6(2) of Schedule 23 (content of articles of government), paragraphs 2 to 12 shall have effect in respect of appeals to committees established in accordance with the joint arrangements.

(2) In the case of any appeal made in pursuance of the joint arrangements—

(a) paragraphs 3, 4, 6, 10(b), 11 and 12 shall have effect as if for "the governing body" there were

substituted "the governing body and the governing body of every other school which is a party to the arrangements, acting jointly"; and

(b) paragraphs 5(2) and 10 (except paragraph 10(b)) shall have effect as if for "the governing body" there were substituted "the governing body against whose decision the appeal is made".

Power of Secretary of State to make amendments

14 The Secretary of State may by order amend the preceding provisions of this Schedule.][840]

Section 323.

SCHEDULE 26 Making of assessments under section 323

Introductory

1 In this Schedule "assessment" means an assessment of a child's educational needs under section 323.

Medical and other advice

2(1) Regulations shall make provision as to the advice which a local education authority are to seek in making assessments.

(2) Without prejudice to the generality of sub-paragraph (1), the regulations shall require the authority, except in such circumstances as may be prescribed, to seek medical, psychological and educational advice and such other advice as may be prescribed.

Manner, and timing, of assessments, etc.

3(1) Regulations may make provision—

(a) as to the manner in which assessments are to be conducted,

(b) requiring the local education authority, where, after conducting an assessment under section 323 of the educational needs of a child for whom a statement is maintained under section 324, they determine not to amend the statement, to serve on the parent of the child a notice giving the prescribed information, and

(c) in connection with such other matters relating to the making of assessments as the Secretary of State considers appropriate.

(2) Sub-paragraph (1)(b) does not apply to a determination made following the service of notice under [paragraph 2A][841] of Schedule 27 (amendment of statement by LEA) of a proposal to amend the statement.

[(3) Regulations may provide—

(a) that where a local education authority are under a duty under section 323, 329 or 329A to serve any notice, the duty must be performed within the prescribed period,

(b) that where a local education authority have served a notice under section 323(1) or 329A(3) on a child's parent, they must decide within the prescribed period whether or not to make an assessment of the child's educational needs,

(c) that where a request has been made to a local education authority under section 329(1), they must decide within the prescribed period whether or not to comply with the request, and

(d) that where a local education authority are under a duty to make an assessment, the duty must be performed within the prescribed period.

(4) Provision made under sub-paragraph (3)—

(a) may be subject to prescribed exceptions, and

(b) does not relieve the authority of the duty to serve a notice, or make a decision or assessment, which has not been served or made within the prescribed period.][842]

Attendance at examinations

4(1) Where a local education authority [are considering whether][843] to make an assessment, they may serve a notice on the parent of the child concerned requiring the child's attendance for examination in accordance with the provisions of the notice.

(2) The parent of a child examined under this paragraph may be present at the examination if he so desires.

(3) A notice under this paragraph shall—

(a) state the purpose of the examination,

(b) state the time and place at which the examination will be held,

(c) name an officer of the authority from whom further information may be obtained,

(d) inform the parent that he may submit such information to the authority as he may wish, and

(e) inform the parent of his right to be present at the examination.

Offence

5(1) Any parent who fails without reasonable excuse to comply with any requirements of a notice served on him under paragraph 4 commits an offence if the notice relates to a child who is not over compulsory school age at the time stated in it as the time for holding the examination.

(2) A person guilty of an offence under this paragraph is liable on summary conviction to a fine not exceeding level 2 on the standard scale.

Section 324.

SCHEDULE 27 Making and maintenance of statements under section 324

Introductory

[1In this Schedule—

"amendment notice" has the meaning given in paragraph 2A,

"statement" means a statement under section 324,

"periodic review" means a review conducted in accordance with section 328(5)(b), and

"re-assessment review" means a review conducted in accordance with section 328(5)(a).][844]

Copy of proposed statement

[2(1) before making a statement, a local education authority shall serve on the parent of the child concerned a copy of the proposed statement.

(2) But that is subject to sub-paragraphs (3) and (4).

(3) The copy of the proposed statement shall not specify any prescribed matter.

(4) The copy of the proposed statement shall not specify any matter in pursuance of section 324(4).][845]

Amendments to a statement

[2A(1) a local education authority shall not amend a statement except—

(a) in compliance with an order of the Tribunal,

(b) as directed by the Secretary of State under section 442(4), or

(c) in accordance with the procedure laid down in this Schedule.

(2) If, following a re-assessment review, a local education authority propose to amend a statement, they shall serve on the parent of the child concerned a copy of the proposed amended statement.

(3) Sub-paragraphs (3) and (4) of paragraph 2 apply to a copy of a proposed amended statement served under sub-paragraph (2) as they apply to a copy of a proposed statement served under paragraph 2(1).

(4) If, following a periodic review, a local education authority propose to amend a statement, they shall serve on the parent of the child concerned—

(a) a copy of the existing statement, and

(b) an amendment notice.

(5) If, at any other time, a local education authority propose to amend a statement, they shall proceed as if the proposed amendment were an amendment proposed after a periodic review.

(6) An amendment notice is a notice in writing giving details of the amendments to the statement proposed by the authority.][846]

[Provision of additional information

2B(1) Sub-paragraph (2) applies when a local education authority serve on a parent—

(a) a copy of a proposed statement under paragraph 2,

(b) a copy of a proposed amended statement under paragraph 2A, or

(c) an amendment notice under paragraph 2A.

(2) The local education authority shall also serve on the parent a written notice explaining (to the extent that they are applicable)—

(a) the arrangements under paragraph 3,

(b) the effect of paragraph 4, and

(c) the right to appeal under section 326.

(3) A notice under sub-paragraph (2) must contain such other information as may be prescribed.][847]

Choice of school

3(1) Every local education authority shall make arrangements for enabling [a parent—

(a) on whom a copy of a proposed statement has been served under paragraph 2,

(b) on whom a copy of a proposed amended statement has been served under paragraph 2A, or

(c) on whom an amendment notice has been served under paragraph 2A which contains a proposed amendment about —

(i) the type or name of a school or institution, or

(ii) the provision made for the child concerned under arrangements made under section 319,

to be specified in the statement,][848] to express a preference as to [the maintained school][849] at which he wishes education to be provided for his child and to give reasons for his preference.

(2) Any such preference must be expressed or made within the period of 15 days beginning—

(a) with the date on which the written notice mentioned in [paragraph 2B][850] was served on the parent, or

(b) if a meeting has (or meetings have) been arranged under paragraph 4(1)(b) or (2), with the date fixed for that meeting (or the last of those meetings).

(3) Where a local education authority make a statement in a case where the parent of the child concerned has expressed a preference in pursuance of such arrangements as to the school at which he wishes education to be provided for his child, they shall specify the name of that school in the statement unless—

(a) the school is unsuitable to the child's age, ability or aptitude or to his special educational needs, or

(b) the attendance of the child at the school would be incompatible with the provision of efficient education for the children with whom he would be educated or the efficient use of resources.

[(4) A local education authority shall, before specifying the name of [any maintained school][851] in a statement, consult the governing body of the school and, if the school is maintained by another local education authority, that authority.][852]

3(1) Every local education authority shall make arrangements for enabling [a parent—

(a) on whom a copy of a proposed statement has been served under paragraph 2,

(b) on whom a copy of a proposed amended statement has been served under paragraph 2A, or

(c) on whom an amendment notice has been served under paragraph 2A which contains a proposed amendment about —

(i) the type or name of a school or institution, or

(ii) the provision made for the child concerned under arrangements made under section 319,

to be specified in the statement,][853] to express a preference as to [the maintained school][854] at which he wishes education to be provided for his child and to give reasons for his preference.

(2) Any such preference must be expressed or made within the period of 15 days beginning—

(a) with the date on which the written notice mentioned in [paragraph 2B][855] was served on the parent, or

(b) if a meeting has (or meetings have) been arranged under paragraph 4(1)(b) or (2), with the date fixed for that meeting (or the last of those meetings).

(3) Where a local education authority make a statement in a case where the parent of the child concerned has expressed a preference in pursuance of such arrangements as to the school at which he wishes education to be provided for his child, they shall specify the name of that school in the statement unless—

(a) the school is unsuitable to the child's age, ability or aptitude or to his special educational needs, or

(b) the attendance of the child at the school would be incompatible with the provision of efficient education for the children with whom he would be educated or the efficient use of resources.

(4)...............................[856]

Consultation on specifying name of school in statement

[3A(1) Sub-paragraph (2) applies if a local education authority are considering—

(a) specifying the name of a maintained school in a statement, or

(b) amending a statement—

(i) if no school was specified in the statement before the amendment, so that a maintained school will be specified in it,

(ii) if a school was specified in the statement before the amendment, so that a different school,

which is a maintained school, will be specified in it.

(2) The local education authority shall—

(a) serve a copy of the proposed statement or amended statement, or of the existing statement and of the amendment notice, on each affected body, and

(b) consult each affected body.

(3) "Affected body" means—

(a) the governing body of any school which the local education authority are considering specifying; and

(b) if a school which the local education authority are considering specifying is maintained by another local education authority, that authority.][857]

Representations

4(1) A parent on whom a copy of a proposed statement has been served under paragraph 2 [, or on whom a proposed amended statement or an amendment notice has been served under paragraph 2A,][858] may—

(a) make representations (or further representations) to the local education authority about the content of the [proposed statement or the statement as it will have effect if amended in the way proposed by the authority][859], and

(b) require the authority to arrange a meeting between him and an officer of the authority at which the [proposed statement or the statement as it will have effect if amended in the way proposed by the authority][860] can be discussed.

(2) Where a parent, having attended a meeting arranged by a local education authority under sub-paragraph (1)(b) [in relation to—,

(c) a proposed statement, or

(d) an amendment proposed following a re-assessment review,][861]

disagrees with any part of the assessment in question, he may require the authority to arrange such meeting or meetings as they consider will enable him to discuss the relevant advice with the appropriate person or persons.

(3) In this paragraph—

"relevant advice" means such of the advice given to the authority in connection with the assessment as they consider to be relevant to that part of the assessment with which the parent disagrees, and

"appropriate person" means the person who gave the relevant advice or any other person who, in the opinion of the authority, is the appropriate person to discuss it with the parent.

(4) Any representations under sub-paragraph (1)(a) must be made within the period of 15 days beginning—

(a) with the date on which the written notice mentioned in [paragraph 2B][862] was served on the parent, or

(b) if a meeting has (or meetings have) been arranged under sub-paragraph (1)(b) or (2), with the date fixed for that meeting (or the last of those meetings).

(5) A requirement under sub-paragraph (1)(b) must be made within the period of 15 days beginning with the date on which the written notice mentioned in [paragraph 2B][863] was served on the parent.

(6) A requirement under sub-paragraph (2) must be made within the period of 15 days beginning with the date fixed for the meeting arranged under sub-paragraph (1)(b).

Making the statement

5(1) Where representations are made to a local education authority under paragraph 4(1)(a), the authority shall not make [or amend][864] the statement until they have considered the representations and the period or the last of the periods allowed by paragraph 4 for making requirements or further representations has expired.

(2) [If a local education authority make a statement, it][865] may be in the form originally proposed (except as to the matters required to be excluded from the copy of the proposed statement) or in a form modified in the light of the representations.

[(2A) If a local education authority amend a statement following service of a proposed amended statement under paragraph 2A, the amended statement made may be in the form proposed or in a form modified in the light of the representations.

(2B) If a local education authority amend a statement following service of an amendment notice, the amendments may be those proposed in the notice or amendments modified in the light of the representations.][866]

(3) Regulations may provide that, where a local education authority are under a duty (subject to compliance with the preceding requirements of this Schedule) to make a statement, the duty, or any step required to be taken for performance of the duty, must, subject to prescribed exceptions, be performed within the prescribed period.

(4) Such provision shall not relieve the authority of the duty to make a statement, or take any step, which has not been performed or taken within that period.

Service of statement

[6(1) Where a local education authority make or amend a statement they shall serve a copy of the statement, or the amended statement, on the parent of the child concerned.

(2) They shall, at the same time, give the parent written notice of his right to appeal under section 326(1) against—

(a) the description in the statement of the authority's assessment of the child's special educational needs,

(b) the special educational provision specified in the statement (including the name of a school specified in the statement), or

(c) if no school is named in the statement, that fact.

(3) A notice under sub-paragraph (2) must contain such other information as may be prescribed.][867]

Keeping, disclosure and transfer of statements

7(1) Regulations may make provision as to the keeping and disclosure of statements.

(2) Regulations may make provision, where a local education authority become responsible for a child for whom a statement is maintained by another authority, for the transfer of the statement to them and for Part IV to have effect as if the duty to maintain the transferred statement were their duty.

Change of named school

8(1) Sub-paragraph (2) applies where—

(a) the parent of a child for whom a statement is maintained which specifies the name of a school or institution asks the local education authority to substitute for that name the name of a maintained, grant-maintained or grant-maintained special school specified by the parent, and

(b) the request is not made less than 12 months after—

(i) an earlier request under this paragraph,

(ii) the service of a copy of the statement under paragraph 6,

(iii)[if the statement has been amended, the date when notice of the amendment is given under paragraph 10(3)(b), or][868]

(iv) if the parent has appealed to the Tribunal under section 326 or this paragraph, the date when the appeal is concluded,

whichever is the later.

(2) The local education authority shall comply with the request unless—

(a) the school is unsuitable to the child's age, ability or aptitude or to his special educational needs, or

(b) the attendance of the child at the school would be incompatible with the provision of efficient education for the children with whom he would be educated or the efficient use of resources.

(3) Where the local education authority determine not to comply with the request—

(a) they shall give [notice in writing of that fact][869] to the parent of the child, and

(b) the parent of the child may appeal to the Tribunal against the determination.

[(3A) A notice under sub-paragraph (3)(a) must inform the parent of the right of appeal under sub-paragraph (3)(b) and contain such other information as may be prescribed.][870]

(4) On the appeal the Tribunal may—

(a) dismiss the appeal, or

(b) order the local education authority to substitute for the name of the school or other institution specified in the statement the name of the school specified by the parent.

(5) Regulations may provide that, where a local education authority are under a duty to comply with a request under this paragraph, the duty must, subject to prescribed exceptions, be performed within

the prescribed period.

(6) Such provision shall not relieve the authority of the duty to comply with such a request which has not been complied with within that period.

Procedure for amending or ceasing to maintain a statement

9(1) A local education authority may not [amend, or][871] cease to maintain, a statement except in accordance with paragraph [10 or][872] 11.

(2) Sub-paragraph (1) does not apply where the local education authority—

(a) cease to maintain a statement for a child who has ceased to be a child for whom they are responsible, [or][873]

[(b) amend a statement in pursuance of paragraph 8,][874]

(c) are ordered to cease to maintain a statement under section 326(3)(c), [or][875]

[(d) amend a statement in pursuance of directions under section 442 (revocation of school attendance order).][876]

9(1) A local education authority may not. . .[877] cease to maintain, a statement except in accordance with paragraph . . . 11.

(2) Sub-paragraph (1) does not apply where the local education authority—

(a) cease to maintain a statement for a child who has ceased to be a child for whom they are responsible, [or][878]

(b). . . . .[879]

(c) are ordered to cease to maintain a statement under section 326(3)(c),. . .[880]

(d). . . . .[881]

10. . . . .[882]

11(1) A local education authority may cease to maintain a statement only if it is no longer necessary to maintain it.

(2) Where the local education authority determine to cease to maintain a statement—

(a) they shall give [notice in writing of that fact][883] to the parent of the child, and

(b) the parent of the child may appeal to the Tribunal against the determination.

[(2A) a notice under sub-paragraph (2)(a) must inform the parent of the right of appeal under sub-paragraph (2)(b) and contain such other information as may be prescribed.][884]

(3) On an appeal under this paragraph the Tribunal may—

(a) dismiss the appeal, or

(b) order the local education authority to continue to maintain the statement in its existing form or with such amendments of—

(i) the description in the statement of the authority's assessment of the child's special educational needs, or

(ii) the special educational provision specified in the statement,

and such other consequential amendments, as the Tribunal may determine.

(4) Except where the parent of the child appeals to the Tribunal under this paragraph, a local education authority may only cease to maintain a statement under this paragraph within the prescribed period beginning with the service of the notice under sub-paragraph (2).

[(5) A local education authority may not, under this paragraph, cease to maintain a statement if—

(a) the parent of the child has appealed under this paragraph against the authority's determination to cease to maintain the statement, and

(b) the appeal has not been determined by the Tribunal or withdrawn.][885]

SCHEDULE 28[886]

. . . .

SCHEDULE 29[887]

. . . .

SCHEDULE 30[888]

. . . .

Section 375.

SCHEDULE 31 Agreed syllabuses of religious education

Duty to convene conference to reconsider agreed syllabus

1(1) Where the agreed syllabus for the time being adopted by a local education authority was adopted by them on or after 29th September 1988 but before 1st April 1994, they shall, within the period of five years beginning with the date on which they adopted the syllabus, convene a conference for the purpose of reconsidering the syllabus.

(2) Sub-paragraph (1) does not apply where the authority have already convened such a conference on or after 1st April 1994 in pursuance of paragraph 12(3) of Schedule 5 to the Education Act 1944.

2(1) A local education authority shall from time to time cause further conferences to be convened for the purpose of reconsidering any agreed syllabus for the time being adopted by them (whether adopted before, on or after 1st April 1994).

(2) No such conference shall be convened later than the end of the period of five years beginning with the date (falling after 31st March 1994) on which—

(a) the authority adopted the syllabus, or

(b) the authority gave effect to a recommendation under paragraph 10(2) below (or under paragraph 13 of Schedule 5 to the Education Act 1944) that the syllabus should continue to be the agreed syllabus.

3 On receipt by a local education authority of written notification of any such requirement as is mentioned in section 391(3), the authority shall cause a conference to be convened for the purpose of reconsidering any agreed syllabus to which the requirement relates.

Constitution of conference

4(1) A conference convened under this Schedule shall consist of such groups of persons ("committees") appointed by the local education authority which convenes the conference as are required by sub-paragraph (2).

(2) Those committees are—

(a) a committee of persons representing such Christian denominations and other religions and denominations of such religions as, in the opinion of the authority, will appropriately reflect the principal religious traditions in the area;

(b) except in the case of an area in Wales, a committee of persons representing the Church of England;

(c) a committee of persons representing such associations representing teachers as, in the opinion of the authority, ought to be represented, having regard to the circumstances of the area; and

(d) a committee of persons representing the authority.

(3) Where a committee is required to be appointed by virtue of sub-paragraph (2)(b), the committee required to be appointed by virtue of sub-paragraph (2)(a) shall not include persons appointed to represent the Church of England.

(4) The number of persons appointed under sub-paragraph (2)(a) to represent each denomination or religion required to be represented shall, so far as is consistent with the efficient discharge of the committee's functions, reflect broadly the proportionate strength of that denomination or religion in the area.

5 Any sub-committees appointed by the conference shall each include at least one member of each of the committees constituting the conference.

6 On any question to be decided by the conference or by any sub-committee of the conference, a single vote shall be given for each of the committees constituting the conference.

7(1) Before appointing a person to represent any religion, denomination or associations as a member of a committee, the local education authority shall take all reasonable steps to assure themselves that he is representative of the religion, denomination or associations in question.

(2) No proceedings under this Schedule shall be invalidated on the ground that a member of a committee did not represent the religion, denomination or associations which he was appointed to represent, unless it is shown that the authority failed to take the steps required by sub-paragraph (1).

8 A person appointed as a member of a committee—

(a) may resign his membership, or

(b) may be withdrawn from membership by the local education authority if, in their opinion, he ceases to be representative of the religion, denomination or associations which he was

appointed to represent or (as the case may be) of the authority.

9 Where a person resigns or is withdrawn from a committee, the local education authority shall appoint someone in his place in the same manner as that in which they made the original appointment.

Reconsideration of agreed syllabus

10(1) This paragraph applies where a local education authority cause a conference to be convened for the purpose of reconsidering any agreed syllabus under any of paragraphs 1 to 3.

(2) If—

(a) the conference—

(i) unanimously recommend that the existing syllabus should continue to be the agreed syllabus, or

(ii) unanimously recommend a new syllabus to be adopted in substitution for the existing syllabus, and

(b) it appears to the local education authority that the syllabus or, as the case may be, the new syllabus, reflects the fact that the religious traditions in Great Britain are in the main Christian while taking account of the teaching and practices of the other principal religions represented in Great Britain,

the authority may give effect to the recommendation.

(3) If—

(a) the authority report to the Secretary of State that the conference are unable to reach unanimous agreement, or

(b) the conference unanimously recommend that the existing syllabus should continue to be the agreed syllabus but the local education authority consider that sub-paragraph (2)(b) prevents them from giving effect to the recommendation, or

(c) it appears to the Secretary of State that the authority have failed to exercise their power under sub-paragraph (2) to give effect to the unanimous recommendation of the conference,

the Secretary of State shall proceed in accordance with paragraph 12.

11. . . . .[889]

Preparation of new syllabus by appointed body

12(1) Where required by paragraph 10 to proceed in accordance with this paragraph, the Secretary of State shall appoint a body of persons having experience in religious education to prepare a syllabus of religious education.

(2) The appointed body shall, so far as is practicable, be of a representative character which is the same as that required by paragraph 4 in the case of a conference.

13(1) The appointed body shall—

(a) give the local education authority, the conference and every committee constituting the conference an opportunity of making representations to it;

(b) after considering any such representations made to it, prepare a syllabus of religious education; and

(c) transmit a copy of that syllabus to the authority and to the Secretary of State.

(2) Subject to sub-paragraph (1)(a), the appointed body may conduct its proceedings in such manner as it thinks fit.

14 The syllabus prepared by the appointed body shall be deemed to be the agreed syllabus adopted for use in the schools for which, or for the class or description of pupils for which, it was prepared—

(a) as from such date as the Secretary of State may direct, and

(b) until a new syllabus is adopted for use in those schools, or for pupils of that class or description, in accordance with this Schedule.

Special provisions applicable where order under section 27(1)(b) applies

15. . . . .[890]

SCHEDULE 32[891]

. . . .

SCHEDULE 33[892]

. . . .

SCHEDULE 33A[893]

....

Schedule 33B[894]

....

Section 476.

SCHEDULE 34 Independent Schools Tribunals

Appointment of legal and educational panels

1(1) For the purpose of enabling Independent Schools Tribunals to be constituted as occasion may require there shall be two panels.

(2) One of the panels (the "legal panel") shall consist of persons who will be available to act when required as chairmen of such tribunals and shall be appointed by the Lord Chancellor.

(3) The other panel (the "educational panel") shall consist of persons who will be available to act when required as members of such tribunals and shall be appointed by the Lord President of the Council.

Qualifications for appointment

2(1) A person is not qualified to be appointed to the legal panel unless he possesses such legal qualifications as the Lord Chancellor considers suitable.

(2) A person is not qualified to be appointed to the educational panel unless he has had such experience in teaching or in the conduct, management or administration of schools as the Lord President of the Council considers suitable.

(3) A person who is—

(a) an officer of a government department, or

(b) employed by a local education authority otherwise than as a teacher,

is disqualified from being appointed to either panel.

Terms and conditions of appointment

3(1) Subject (in the case of a member of the legal panel) to sub-paragraph (2), a person appointed to be a member of a panel shall hold office as such subject to such conditions as to the period of his membership and otherwise as may be determined by the Lord Chancellor or the Lord President of the Council, as the case may be.

(2) No appointment of a person to be a member of the legal panel shall be such as to extend beyond the day on which he attains the age of 70; but this sub-paragraph has effect subject to section 26(4) to (6) of the Judicial Pensions and Retirement Act 1993 (power to authorise continuance in office up to the age of 75).

Constitution of tribunal

4(1) Where an appeal is required to be determined by an Independent Schools Tribunal, the tribunal shall consist of—

(a) a chairman who is a member of the legal panel, and

(b) two other members who are members of the educational panel.

(2) The chairman and other members of the tribunal shall be impartial persons appointed from those panels by the Lord Chancellor and the Lord President of the Council respectively.

Remuneration

5 The Secretary of State may pay to the members of an Independent Schools Tribunal such remuneration and allowances as he may determine with the consent of the Treasury.

SCHEDULE 35[895]

....

[SCHEDULE 35AAcademies: land

Transfer schemes

1(1) The Secretary of State may make a scheme in relation to land if these requirements are met—

(a) a local education authority holds a freehold or leasehold interest in the land when the scheme is made;

(b) at any time in the period of eight years ending with the day on which the scheme is made the land was used wholly or mainly for the purposes of a county school or community school;

(c) at the time the scheme is made the land is no longer used as mentioned in paragraph (b) or the Secretary of State thinks it is about to be no longer so used;

(d) before making the scheme the Secretary of State consulted the authority.

(2) The Secretary of State may also make a scheme in relation to land if these requirements are met—

(a) a local education authority holds a freehold or leasehold interest in the land when the scheme is made;

(b) the land forms the whole or part of a site specified in a notice published under section 70 of the Education Act 2002 (new schools to meet increased demand for secondary education) as a possible site for a new school;

(c) before making the scheme, the Secretary of State consulted the authority.

(3) These requirements must be met as regards a scheme under sub-paragraph (1) or (2)—

(a) the scheme must provide for a transfer of the authority's interest in the land or in such part of it as is specified in the scheme;

(b) the transfer must be to a person (the transferee) who is specified in the scheme and is concerned with the running of an Academy;

(c) the transfer must be made to the transferee for the purposes of the Academy;

(d) in the case of a scheme under sub-paragraph (2), the Academy must have been the subject of proposals published under section 70 of the Education Act 2002;

(e) the scheme must provide for the transfer to the transferee of any right or liability held by the authority as holder of the interest in the land or specified part concerned.

(4) In sub-paragraph (3) the reference to a right or liability—

(a) includes a reference to a right or liability as a trustee, but

(b) excludes a reference to a liability in respect of the principal of or interest on a loan.

(5) A scheme may include such supplementary, incidental, consequential or transitional provisions as the Secretary of State thinks are appropriate.

(6) A scheme must be so expressed that it does not come into force while the land concerned is used as mentioned in sub-paragraph (1)(b).

(7) A scheme comes into force—

(a) on the day it specifies for it to come into force, or

(b) on the day it otherwise identifies as the day for it to come into force.

(8) When a scheme comes into force it has effect to transfer (in accordance with its provisions) the interests, rights and liabilities to which it applies.

(9) A transfer made by virtue of a scheme is binding on all persons (as well as on the authority and the transferee) even if, apart from this sub-paragraph, it would have required the consent or concurrence of any person.

Restriction on disposal

2(1) Sub-paragraph (2) applies if—

(a) a freehold or leasehold interest in land is held by a local education authority,

(b) the authority proposes to make a disposal in respect of the interest, or to enter into a contract to make a disposal in respect of it, or to grant an option to make an acquisition in respect of it, and

(c) at any time in the period of eight years ending with the day on which the disposal, contract or option is proposed to be made, entered into or granted, the land was used wholly or mainly for the purposes of a county school or community school.

(2) Unless the Secretary of State consents, the authority must not make the disposal or enter into the contract or grant the option.

(3) Sub-paragraph (2) does not apply to a disposal made in pursuance of a contract made, or option granted, before the coming into force of this paragraph.

(4) Sub-paragraph (2) does not apply to—

(a) a disposal in favour of a person for the purposes of an Academy and for no consideration;

(b) a contract to make such a disposal;

(c) a grant of an option for a person to make an acquisition for the purposes of an Academy and for no consideration.

(5) A disposal or contract or grant is not invalid by reason only that it is made in contravention of sub-paragraph (2).

(6) A person acquiring an interest in land or entering into a contract to acquire it is not to be concerned to enquire whether consent required by sub-paragraph (2) has been given.

3(1) This paragraph applies if an authority makes a disposal or enters into a contract or grants an option in contravention of paragraph 2(2).

(2) In the case of a grant of an option, the Secretary of State may by notice served on the option holder repudiate the option at any time before it is exercised.

(3) In the case of a contract to make a disposal in respect of an interest, the Secretary of State may by notice served on the other party to the contract repudiate it at any time before a conveyance of the interest is executed.

(4) A repudiation under sub-paragraph (2) or (3) has effect—

(a) when the notice is served, and

(b) as if the repudiation were made by the authority.

(5) In the case of a disposal in respect of an interest (whether or not in pursuance of an option or contract falling within sub-paragraph (2) or (3)) the Secretary of State may purchase the interest concerned compulsorily.

(6) The Acquisition of Land Act 1981 (c. 67) is to apply in relation to the compulsory purchase of an interest under sub-paragraph (5).

(7) On completion of a compulsory purchase of an interest under sub-paragraph (5) the Secretary of State must transfer it to a person concerned with the running of an Academy.

(8) If the Secretary of State acquires an interest by compulsory purchase under sub-paragraph (5) he is entitled to recover from the authority an amount equal to the aggregate of—

(a) the compensation agreed or awarded in respect of the purchase,

(b) any interest payable by him in respect of the compensation, and

(c) the costs and expenses incurred by him in connection with the making of the compulsory purchase order.

(9) The authority must provide the Secretary of State with such information as he may require it to provide in connection with a compulsory purchase under sub-paragraph (5).

4(1) For the purposes of paragraphs 2 and 3—

(a) references to a disposal in respect of an interest are to a disposal of the whole interest or of a lesser interest;

(b) references to an acquisition in respect of an interest are to an acquisition of the whole interest or of a lesser interest.

(2) If the disposal referred to in paragraph 3(3) or (5) is a disposal of a lesser interest, the reference there to the interest concerned is to the lesser interest.

Restriction on appropriation

5(1) Sub-paragraph (2) applies if—

(a) a freehold or leasehold interest in land is held by a local education authority,

(b) the authority proposes to make an appropriation of the land under section 122 of the Local Government Act 1972 (c. 70), and

(c) at any time in the period of eight years ending with the day on which the appropriation is proposed to be made the land was used wholly or mainly for the purposes of a county school or community school.

(2) Unless the Secretary of State consents, the authority must not make the appropriation.

6(1) This paragraph applies if an authority makes an appropriation in contravention of paragraph 5(2).

(2) The Secretary of State may purchase the interest concerned compulsorily.

(3) Paragraph 3(6) to (9) apply to a compulsory purchase of an interest under sub-paragraph (2) above as they apply to a compulsory purchase of an interest under paragraph 3(5).

Duty to inform

7(1) Sub-paragraph (2) applies if—

(a) a freehold or leasehold interest in land is held by a local education authority,

(b) the authority proposes to change the use of the land in such a way that (were the change made) the land would cease to be capable of use wholly or mainly for the purposes of a school, and

(c) at any time in the period of eight years ending with the date of the proposed change of use the land was used wholly or mainly for the purposes of a county school or community school.

(2) The authority must inform the Secretary of State of the proposal.

Former Academies

8(1) This paragraph applies if—

(a) a freehold or leasehold interest in land is transferred from a local education authority on or after 28th July 2000,

(b) the transfer is made to a person for the purposes of an Academy, and

(c) the first or the second condition set out below is satisfied.

(2) The first condition is that—

(a) the school concerned ceases to be an Academy, and

(b) immediately before the school ceases to be an Academy the interest is held by a person for the purposes of the Academy.

(3) The second condition is that, although the school concerned continues to be an Academy, the interest ceases to be held for the purposes of the Academy.

(4) This paragraph applies whether or not the transfer is made by virtue of a scheme under paragraph 1.

(5) Sub-paragraph (2) applies whether or not, on the school ceasing to be an Academy, it simultaneously ceases to function as a school.

(6) The Secretary of State may make a scheme providing for the transfer of the interest—

(a) from the person holding it;

(b) to the authority from which the transfer mentioned in sub-paragraph (1)(a) was made.

(7) A scheme may include such supplementary, incidental, consequential or transitional provisions as the Secretary of State thinks are appropriate.

(8) A scheme comes into force on the day it specifies for it to come into force.

(9) When a scheme comes into force it has effect to transfer (in accordance with its provisions) the interest to which it applies.

(10) A transfer made by virtue of a scheme is binding on all persons (as well as on the authority and the transferee) even if, apart from this sub-paragraph, it would have required the consent or concurrence of any person.

Disapplication of rule against perpetuities

9 Where—

(a) a freehold or leasehold interest in land is transferred for no consideration from a local authority to a person for the purposes of an Academy (whether or not by virtue of a scheme under paragraph 1), and

(b) at any time on or after the day on which this Schedule comes into force the authority is granted an option to make a re-acquisition of the interest (subject to whatever conditions),

the rule against perpetuities does not apply to the option.

Other Acts

10(1) Where a lease is granted by or transferred from a local authority to a person for the purposes of an Academy on or after the day on which this Schedule comes into force, section 153 of the Law of Property Act 1925 (c.20) (enlargement of leases granted for no rent etc) does not apply to permit that person to enlarge the term under the lease.

(2) Section 123(2) of the Local Government Act 1972 (c. 70) (disposal for consideration less than the best reasonably obtainable) does not apply to a disposal to a person for the purposes of an Academy.

(3) Section 123(2A) of that Act (disposal of open space requires certain procedures) does not apply to a disposal which is made—

(a) to a person for the purposes of an Academy, and

(b) for no consideration.

(4) Section 77(1) of the School Standards and Framework Act 1998 (c. 31) (restriction on disposal of playing fields) does not apply to a disposal which is made—

(a) by a local authority (within the meaning of that section) to a person for the purposes of an Academy, and

(b) for no consideration.

Regulations

11 Regulations under this Schedule may in particular include—

(a) provision requiring a person to be appointed by the Secretary of State in connection with the proposed making of a scheme under paragraph 1;

(b) provision requiring the appointed person to identify the interests, rights and liabilities to be the subject of a scheme under paragraph 1;

(c) provision requiring the authority concerned to provide the appointed person with such documents as he may require in order to identify the interests, rights and liabilities to be the subject of a scheme under paragraph 1;

(d) provision requiring an authority whose interest is (or is to be) transferred by virtue of a scheme under paragraph 1 to execute instruments and deliver certificates for the purposes of the enactments relating to registered land;

(e) provision treating such an authority as having given acknowledgement in writing of the right to production of documents;

(f) provision that consent under paragraph 2 is to be sought in a specified way;

(g) provision that information is to be given under paragraph 7 in a specified way.

Class consents

12 For the purposes of paragraphs 2(2) and 5(2), the consent of the Secretary of State—

(a) may be given in relation to a particular case or class of case, and

(b) may be given subject to conditions.

Interpretation

13 A dwelling-house used by an authority for occupation by a person employed to work at a school is to be treated for the purposes of this Schedule as used for the purposes of the school.][896]

Section 557.

SCHEDULE 36 Uniform statutory trusts for educational endowments

1 The trustees may, after payment of any expenses incurred in connection with the administration of the trust, apply the capital and income of the relevant trust assets for any of the following purposes—

(a) in or towards the purchase of a site for, or the erection, improvement or enlargement of, the premises of any relevant school in the area,

(b) for the maintenance of any relevant school in the area;

(c) in or towards the purchase of a site for, or the erection, improvement or enlargement of, the premises of a teacher's house for use in connection with any relevant school in the area; and

(d) for the maintenance of a teacher's house for use in connection with any relevant school in the area.

2 The trustees may also, after payment of any expenses incurred in connection with the administration of the trust, apply the income of the relevant trust assets for any of the following purposes—

(a) in or towards the provision of advice, guidance and resources (including materials) in connection with any matter related to the management of, or education provided at, any relevant school in the area;

(b) the provision of services for the carrying out of any inspection of any relevant school in the area required by Part I of the School Inspections Act 1996; and

(c) to defray the cost of employing or engaging staff in connection with—

(i) the application of income of the relevant trust assets for either of the purposes referred to in sub-paragraphs (a) and (b) above, or

(ii) the application of capital or income of the relevant trust assets for any of the purposes referred to in paragraph 1 above.

Section 582(1).

SCHEDULE 37 Consequential amendments

Part I Amendments coming into force on 1st November 1996

Children and Young Persons Act 1933 (c. 12)

1 Section 96 of the Children and Young Persons Act 1933 (provisions as to local authorities) shall continue to have effect with the following amendments (originally made by Schedule 8 to the Education Act 1944)—

(a) in subsection (3), for the words from "for elementary education" onwards there is substituted "

shall be defrayed as expenses under the enactments relating to education "; and

(b) in subsection (4), for the second "under" there is substituted "in accordance with".

Public Records Act 1958 (c. 51)

2 In Schedule 1 to the Public Records Act 1958 (definition of public records) Part II of the Table at the end of paragraph 3 (organisations whose records are public records) shall continue to include the following entries (originally inserted by Schedule 19 to the Education Act 1993, taken with Schedule 15 to that Act)—

"Curriculum and Assessment Authority for Wales",

"Funding Agency for Schools",

"School Curriculum and Assessment Authority", and

"Schools Funding Council for Wales".

Church Schools (Assistance by Church Commissioners) Measure 1958 (1958 No. 2)

3 In section 2(1) of the Church Schools (Assistance by Church Commissioners) Measure 1958 (interpretation) for "the Education Acts, 1944 to 1993" there is substituted "the Education Act 1996" .

Education Act 1962 (c. 12)

4(1) Section 1 of the Education Act 1962 (local education authority awards for designated courses) shall continue to have effect with the following amendment (originally made by section 4 of the Education (Grants and Awards) Act 1984).

(2) In subsection (3)(d), for the words from "for the higher diploma" onwards there is substituted " or for the higher national diploma of the body corporate known at the passing of the Education (Grants and Awards) Act 1984 as the Business & Technician Education Council. "

5 In section 3(c)(i) of that Act (awards by Secretary of State) for "section 100 of the Education Act 1944" there is substituted " section 485 of the Education Act 1996 ".

6 For section 14(4) of that Act there is substituted—

"(4) This Act shall be construed as one with the Education Act 1996."

7 In paragraph 2 of Schedule 1 to that Act (ordinary residence) for "section 31(3) of the Education Act 1980" there is substituted " the Education Act 1996 in accordance with regulations made under section 579(4) of that Act. "

London Government Act 1963 (c. 33)

8 In section 30(1) of the London Government Act 1963 (local education authorities) for "the Education Acts 1944 to 1962 or in any other Act" there is substituted " any Act ".

9. . . . .[897]

Children and Young Persons Act 1963 (c. 37)

10 In section 37(3) of the Children and Young Persons Act 1963 (exceptions to restriction on persons under 16 taking part in public performances etc.) for "the Education Act 1944" there is substituted " the Education Act 1996 ".

11 In section 38 of that Act (restriction on licences for performances by children under 13)—

(a) in subsection (1) for "thirteen" there is substituted " fourteen ";

(b) subsection (2) is omitted; and

(c) in the sidenote, for "13" there is substituted "14".

Veterinary Surgeons Act 1966 (c. 36)

12 In Schedule 3 to the Veterinary Surgeons Act 1966 (exemptions from restrictions on practice of veterinary surgery), in the definition of "recognised institution" following paragraph 5, for "the Education Act 1944" there is substituted "the Education Act 1996".

Education Act 1967 (c. 3)

13 In section 6(2) of the Education Act 1967 (construction as one) for "the Education Acts 1944 to 1965" there is substituted "the Education Act 1996."

Public Expenditure and Receipts Act 1968 (c. 14)

14 In Schedule 3 to the Public Expenditure and Receipts Act 1968 (variation of fees, etc.) for "The Education Act 1944 (c.31) section 94" there is substituted "The Education Act 1996 (c.56) section 564".

Children and Young Persons Act 1969 (c. 54)

15. . . . .[898]

16. . . . .[899]

Local Authorities (Goods and Services) Act 1970 (c. 39)

17. . . . .[900]

Local Authority Social Services Act 1970 (c. 42)

18 In Schedule 1 to the Local Authority Social Services Act 1970 (enactments conferring functions assigned to social services committee) the entry relating to the Education Act 1993 is omitted and at the end there is added—

"Education Act 1996.

Section 322....................	Help for local education authority in exercising functions under Part IV of the Act."

Chronically Sick and Disabled Persons Act 1970 (c. 44)

19 In section 8(2) of the Chronically Sick and Disabled Persons Act 1970 (access to and facilities at university and school buildings) for the words from "and expressions used" onwards there is substituted " and expressions used in paragraph (b) above and in the Education Act 1996 have the same meanings as in that Act. "

Pensions (Increase) Act 1971 (c. 56)

20 In Part II of Schedule 2 to the Pensions (Increase) Act 1971 (official pensions payable out of local funds), in paragraph 57, for "the Education Act 1944" there is substituted " the Education Act 1996. "

Superannuation Act 1972 (c. 11)

21(1) Schedule 1 to the Superannuation Act 1972 shall continue—

(a) to include. . .[901] and the entries relating to the Funding Agency for Schools and the Schools Funding Council for Wales (originally inserted by Schedule 19 to that Act);. . .[902]

(b). . . . .

(2). . . . .[903]

Local Government Act 1972 (c. 70)

22(1) Section 104(2)(a) of the Local Government Act 1972 (teachers not disqualified for being members of committees) shall continue to have effect with the following amendment (originally made by Schedule 19 to the Education Act 1993).

(2) For "for the purposes of the enactments relating to education" there is substituted " wholly or partly for the purpose of discharging any functions with respect to education conferred on them in their capacity as local education authorities ".

23 In section 112(4)(b) of that Act (appointment of staff) for "section 88 of the Education Act 1944" there is substituted " section 532 of the Education Act 1996 ".

24 In section 139(4) of that Act (acceptance of gifts of property) for "the Education Acts 1944 to 1971" there is substituted " the Education Act 1996 ".

25 In section 177(1) of that Act (supplementary provisions as to allowances) for "paragraph 4 of Schedule 2 to the Education Act 1980" there is substituted " paragraph 4 of Schedule 33 to the Education Act 1996 ".

Fair Trading Act 1973 (c. 41)

26 In Schedule 4 to the Fair Trading Act 1973 (services excluded from sections 14 and 109), in paragraph 14, for "the Education Act 1944," there is substituted " the Education Act 1996, ".

Local Government Act 1974 (c. 7)

27. . . . .[904]

28 In section 31A(2) of that Act (consideration of adverse reports) for "paragraph 1 of Schedule 2 to the Education Act 1980" there is substituted " paragraph 1 of Schedule 33 to the Education Act 1996 ".

29 In paragraph 5(1) of Schedule 5 to that Act (matters not subject to investigation) for the words from "section 23" to "1986" there is substituted " section 370 of the Education Act 1996 or section 17 of the Education (No.2) Act 1986 ".

House of Commons Disqualification Act 1975 (c. 24)

30(1) Part III of Schedule 1 to the House of Commons Disqualification Act 1975 (disqualifying offices)—

(a) shall be amended as provided in sub-paragraphs (2) and (3); and

(b) shall continue to include the entries set out in sub-paragraph (4) (originally inserted by Schedule 19 to the Education Act 1993).

(2) For the entry relating to the Curriculum and Assessment Authority for Wales there is substituted—

"Any member of the Curriculum and Assessment Authority for Wales constituted under section 360 of the Education Act 1996 in receipt of remuneration".

(3) For the entry relating to the School Curriculum and Assessment Authority there is substituted—

"Any member of the School Curriculum and Assessment Authority constituted under section 358 of the Education Act 1996 in receipt of remuneration".

(4) The entries referred to in sub-paragraph (1)(b) are—

"Any member of an education association in receipt of remuneration",

"Any member of the Funding Agency for Schools in receipt of remuneration", and

"Any member of the Schools Funding Council for Wales in receipt of remuneration".

Sex Discrimination Act 1975 (c. 65)

31 In section 23(1) of the Sex Discrimination Act 1975 (other discrimination by local education authorities) for "the Education Acts 1944 to 1996" there is substituted "the Education Acts".

32 In section 23A of that Act (discrimination by Further Education and Higher Education Funding Councils) for "the Education Acts 1944 to 1994" there is substituted "the Education Acts".

33. . . . .[905]

34 In section 24(2)(c) of that Act (designated establishments) for "the Education Act 1944" there is substituted "the Education Act 1996".

35(1) Section 25 of that Act (general duty in public sector of education)—

(a) shall be amended in accordance with sub-paragraphs (2)(a) to (c), (3)(b), and (4)(a); and

(b) shall continue to have effect with the amendments set out in sub-paragraphs (2)(d), (3)(a) and (4)(b) (originally made by Schedule 19 to the Education Act 1993 and subsequently amended by the Education Act 1994).

(2) In subsection (2)—

(a) for "the Education Act 1944" there is substituted " the Education Act 1996 ";

(b) in paragraph (a), for "section 68" there is substituted " section 496 ";

(c) in paragraph (b), for "section 99" there is substituted " section 497 "; and

(d) for "and 23" there is substituted " 23, 23A, 23C and 23D ".

(3) In subsection (4)—

(a) for "and 23" there is substituted "23, 23A, 23C and 23D"; and

(b) for "either" there is substituted "any".

(4) In subsection (6)—

(a) in paragraph (c)(iii), for "section 100 of the Education Act 1944" there is substituted " section 485 of the Education Act 1996 "; and

(b) after paragraph (d) there is added—

"(e) the Funding Agency for Schools and the Schools Funding Council for Wales."

36 In section 82 of that Act (general interpretation), in subsection (1)—

(a) after the definition of "education" there is inserted—

""the Education Acts" has the meaning given by section 578 of the Education Act 1996;";

(b) in the definition of "further education", for "section 41(3) of the Education Act 1944 as read with section 14 of the Further and Higher Education Act 1992" there is substituted "section 2 of the Education Act 1996";

(c) in the definition of "independent school", for "section 114(1) of the Education Act 1944" there is substituted " section 463 of the Education Act 1996 ";

(d) in the definition of "proprietor", for "section 114(1) of the Education Act 1944" there is substituted "section 579 of the Education Act 1996"; and

(e) in the definition of "school", for "section 114(1) of the Education Act 1944" there is substituted " section 4 of the Education Act 1996 ".

37 In Schedule 2 to that Act (transitional exemption orders for educational admissions)—

(a). . . . .[906]

(b) in paragraph 3—

(i) for "section 100 of the Education Act 1944" there is substituted "section 485 of the Education Act 1996"; and

(ii) for "subsection (1)(b) of the said section 100" there is substituted "the said section 485".

Restrictive Trade Practices Act 1976 (c. 34)

38 In Schedule 1 to the Restrictive Trade Practices Act 1976 (services excluded from section 13), in paragraph 14, for "the Education Act 1944," there is substituted "the Education Act 1996,".

Race Relations Act 1976 (c. 74)

39 In section 18(1) of the Race Relations Act 1976 (other discrimination by local education authorities) for "the Education Acts 1944 to 1996" there is substituted "the Education Acts".

40 In section 18A of that Act (discrimination by Further Education and Higher Education Funding Councils) for "the Education Acts 1944 to 1994" there is substituted "the Education Acts".

41. . . . .[907]

42. . . . .[908]

43 In section 78 of that Act (general interpretation), in subsection (1)—

(a) after the definition of "education" there is inserted—

""the Education Acts" has the meaning given by section 578 of the Education Act 1996;";

(b) in the definition of "independent school", for "section 114(1) of the Education Act 1944" there is substituted " section 463 of the Education Act 1996 ";

(c) in the definition of "proprietor", for "section 114(1) of the Education Act 1944" there is substituted " section 579 of the Education Act 1996 "; and

(d) in the definition of "school", for "section 114(1) of the Education Act 1944" there is substituted "section 4 of the Education Act 1996".

National Health Service Act 1977 (c. 49)

44 In section 28A(2)(c) of the National Health Service Act 1977 (power to make payments to local education authority)—

(a) for "the Education Acts 1944 to 1996" there is substituted "the Education Act 1996"; and

(b) for "those Acts" there is substituted "the Education Acts (within the meaning of that Act) ".

45 In section 128(1) of that Act (interpretation), in the definition of "local education authority", for "the Education Act 1944" there is substituted "the Education Act 1996".

46 In Schedule 1 to that Act (medical and dental inspection and treatment of pupils etc.)—

(a) in paragraph 1(a)(ii), for "section 163 or 298 of the Education Act 1993" there is substituted " section 19 or 319 of the Education Act 1996 "; and

(b) in paragraph 4, for "by section 114(1) of the Education Act 1944" there is substituted " for the purposes of the Education Act 1996 ".

Education Act 1980 (c.20)

47(1) Section 38 of the Education Act 1980 (citation etc.) shall be amended as follows.

(2) Subsections (2) and (4) to (6) are omitted.

(3) For subsection (3) there is substituted—

"(3) This Act shall, in its application to England and Wales, be construed as one with the Education Act 1996."

(4) In subsection (7), for the words from the beginning to "Northern Ireland;" there is substituted "In this Act section 20 and this section extend to Northern Ireland,".

Education (Scotland) Act 1980 (c. 44)

48(1) Section 48A of the Education (Scotland) Act 1980 (corporal punishment) shall continue to have effect with the following amendments (originally made by section 294 of the Education Act 1993).

(2) In subsection (1), after "pupil" there is inserted "to whom this subsection applies", and after that subsection there is inserted—

"(1A) Where, in any proceedings, it is shown that corporal punishment has been given to a pupil by or on the authority of a member of the staff, giving the punishment cannot be justified if the punishment was inhuman or degrading.

(1B) In determining whether punishment is inhuman or degrading regard shall be had to all the circumstances of the case, including the reason for giving it, how soon after the event it is given,

its nature, the manner and circumstances in which it is given, the persons involved and its mental and physical effects."

(3) In subsection (5) for the words preceding paragraph (a) there is substituted "In this section "pupil" means a person for whom education is provided at a school or for whom school education is provided by an education authority otherwise than at a school.

(5A) Subsection (1) above applies to a pupil".

(4) In subsection (8)(a) for "(5)(a)(iii) " there is substituted "(5A)(a)(iii) ".

Local Government, Planning and Land Act 1980 (c.65)

49 In paragraph 10 of Schedule 10 to the Local Government, Planning and Land Act 1980 (adjustment of block grant in connection with education etc.: interpretation) for "Section 38(5) of the Education Act 1980" there is substituted " Section 579(4) of the Education Act 1996 ".

Acquisition of Land Act 1981 (c. 67)

50 In section 1(2) of the Acquisition of Land Act 1981 (application of Act) for "section 90(1) of the Education Act 1944" there is substituted " section 530(1) of the Education Act 1996 ".

51(1) Section 17(4) of that Act (statutory undertakers) shall have effect with the following amendment instead of that made by section 11 of the Education Act 1993.

(2) After paragraph (aa) of the definition of "statutory undertakers" there is inserted—

"the Funding Agency for Schools,

the Schools Funding Council for Wales,".

Greater London Council (General Powers) Act 1981 (c. xvii)

52 In section 16 of the Greater London Council (General Powers) Act 1981 (exemptions from Part IV)—

(a) in paragraph (b) for "the Education Act 1944" there is substituted "the Education Act 1996"; and

(b) in paragraph (k) for "section 100(1)(b) of the said Act of 1944" there is substituted "section 485 of the Education Act 1996".

Agricultural Training Board Act 1982 (c. 9)

53 In section 4(5) of the Agricultural Training Board Act 1982 (meaning of "post-school education"), for paragraph (a) there is substituted—

"(a) in England and Wales, "higher education" as defined by section 120(1) of the Education Reform Act 1988 or "further education" as defined by section 2(3) to (5) of the Education Act 1996; and".

Industrial Training Act 1982 (c. 10)

54 In section 5 of the Industrial Training Act 1982 (functions of boards) for the subsection (7) inserted by the Education Reform Act 1988 there is substituted—

"(8) In this section "post-school education" means—

(a) in England and Wales, "higher education" as defined by section 120(1) of the Education Reform Act 1988 or "further education" as defined by section 2(3) to (5) of the Education Act 1996; and

(b) in Scotland, "further education" within the meaning of the Education (Scotland) Act 1980."

Local Government (Miscellaneous Provisions) Act 1982 (c. 30)

55 [In section 40 of the Local Government (Miscellaneous Provisions) Act 1982 (nuisance and disturbance on educational premises) for subsections (2) to (10) there is substituted—

"(2) This section applies to premises, including playing fields and other premises for outdoor recreation, of an institution (other than a school) which—

(a) is maintained by a local education authority; and

(b) provides further education or higher education (or both).

(3) If—

(a) a police constable; or

(b) a person whom a local education authority have authorised to exercise the power conferred by this subsection,

has reasonable cause to suspect that any person is committing or has committed an offence under this section, he may remove him from the premises in question.

(4) No proceedings under this section shall be brought by any person other than—

(a) a police constable; or

(b) a local education authority.

(5) Expressions used in this section and in the Education Act 1996 have the same meaning as in that Act."][909]

Representation of the People Act 1983 (c. 2)

56(1) Paragraph 22 of Schedule 1 to the Representation of the People Act 1983 (use of schools for the purpose of taking a poll) shall continue to have effect with the following amendment (originally made by Schedule 19 to the Education Act 1993).

(2) In sub-paragraph (1)(i), after "authority" there is inserted " a grant-maintained school ".

Education (Fees and Awards) Act 1983 (c. 40)

57 In section 1(4) of the Education (Fees and Awards) Act 1983 (fees at universities and further education establishments)—

(a) for "section 100(1)(b) of the Education Act 1944" there is substituted " section 485 of the Education Act 1996 "; and

(b) for "the Education Act 1944" there is substituted " the 1996 Act ".

Registered Homes Act 1984 (c. 23)

58. . . . .[910]

Building Act 1984 (c. 55)

59 In section 4(1)(a) of the Building Act 1984 (exemption of educational buildings etc) for sub-paragraphs (i) to (iv) substitute—

"(i) plans that have been approved by the Secretary of State,

(ii) particulars submitted and approved under section 39 or 44 of the Education Act 1996 or under regulations made under section 544 of that Act or section 218(7) of the Education Reform Act 1988,

(iii) particulars approved or adopted under section 214, 262 or 341 of the Education Act 1996, or

(iv) particulars given in a direction under section 428 of that Act."

Greater London Council (General Powers) Act 1984 (c. xxvii)

60 In section 10(2)(g) of the Greater London Council (General Powers) Act 1984 (buildings excepted from Part IV) for "section 100(1)(b) of the Education Act 1944" there is substituted " section 485 of the Education Act 1996 ".

Further Education Act 1985 (c. 47)

61 In section 8(3) (short title etc.) for "the Education Act 1944" there is substituted " the Education Act 1996. "

Housing Act 1985 (c. 68)

62 In Schedule 1 (tenancies which are not secure tenancies), in paragraph 10(4), for "the Education Act 1944" there is substituted " the Education Act 1996 ".

Local Government Act 1986 (c. 10)

63. . . . .[911]

Disabled Persons (Services, Consultation and Representation) Act 1986 (c. 33)

64(1) Section 5 of the Disabled Persons (Services, Consultation and Representation) Act 1986 (disabled persons leaving special education) shall be amended as follows.

(2) In subsection (1)(a) for "or 168 of the Education Act 1993" there is substituted " section 168 of the Education Act 1993 or section 324 of the Education Act 1996 ".

(3) In subsection (8)—

(a) for "paragraph 7 of Schedule 10 to the Education Act 1993" there is substituted " paragraph 7 of Schedule 27chedul to the Education Act 1996 ", and

(b) for "maintained under section 168" there is substituted " maintained under section 324 ".

(4) In subsection (9)—

(a) for "Part III of the Education Act 1993" there is substituted " Part IV of the Education Act 1996 "; and

(b) for "the Education Act 1944" there is substituted " the Education Act 1996 ".

Education (No. 2) Act 1986 (c. 61)

65(1) Section 50 of the Education (No. 2) Act 1986 (grants for teacher training etc.) shall continue to have effect with the following amendments (originally made by section 278 of and Schedule 19 to the

Education Act 1993).

(2) In subsection (1)—

(a) for "local authorities and other persons" there is substituted "persons other than local education authorities"; and

(b) for the words from the end of paragraph (a) onwards there is substituted— "and

(b) such other classes of persons as may be prescribed."

(3) In subsection (2)(b), for "capacity as an employee of the kind in question" there is substituted "employment ".

66(1) Section 67 of that Act (short title etc.) shall be amended as follows.

(2) Subsections (2), (5) and (6) are omitted.

(3) In subsection (3), for "the 1944 Act" there is substituted "the Education Act 1996. "

(4) In subsection (7), for the words from the beginning to "Northern Ireland;" there is substituted "In this Act section 48 and this section extend to Scotland, ".

Reverter of Sites Act 1987 (c. 15)

67(1) The Reverter of Sites Act 1987 shall be amended as follows.

(2) In section 1(5) (right of reverter replaced by trust for sale) for "section 2 of the Education Act 1973" there is substituted " section 554 of the Education Act 1996 ".

(2) In section 5 (orders under Education Act 1973)—

(a) in subsection (1), for "section 2 of the Education Act 1973" there is substituted "section 554 of the Education Act 1996 "; and

(b) for "section 2 of the said Act of 1973", wherever occurring, there is substituted "section 554 of the 1996 Act ".

Local Government Act 1988 (c. 9)

68 In paragraph 8(3)(a) of Schedule 1 to the Local Government Act 1988 (competition) for "section 53 of the Education Act 1944 (whether or not also provided under section 41 of that Act) " there is substituted "section 508 of the Education Act 1996 (whether or not also provided under section 15 of that Act) ".

Criminal Justice Act 1988 (c. 33)

69 In section 139A(6) and (7) of the Criminal Justice Act 1988 (as amended by the Offensive Weapons Act 1996), for "section 14(5) of the Further and Higher Education Act 1992" there is substituted "section 4 of the Education Act 1996".

Education Reform Act 1988 (c. 40)

70. . . . .[912]

71 In section 161(1)(b)(i) of that Act (interpretation of Part II) for "section 41 of the 1944 Act" there is substituted " section 15 of the Education Act 1996 ".

72 In section 163(1) of that Act (new education authorities for London) for "the Education Acts 1944 to 1996" there is substituted " the Education Act 1996 ".

73 In section 166(5) of that Act (responsibility for schools) for "the Education Acts 1944 to 1993" there is substituted " the Education Act 1996 ".

74 (1) Section 197 of that Act ([Education Transfer Council][913]) shall be amended as follows.

(2) In subsection (6), for "the Education Acts 1944 to 1993" there is substituted " the Education Acts ".

(3) Subsection (7) shall continue to have effect with the insertion of the words "and any governing body of a maintained or grant-maintained school" (originally inserted by section 47(5) of the Education Act 1993); and in that subsection for "the Education Acts 1944 to 1993" there is substituted " the Education Acts ".

(4) In subsection (7B), for "the Education Acts 1944 to 1992" there is substituted " the Education Acts ".

(5) At the end of the section there is added—

"(10) In this section "the Education Acts" has the meaning given by section 578 of the Education Act 1996."

75. . . . .[914]

76(1) Section 218 of that Act (school and further and higher regulations)—

(a) shall be amended as provided in sub-paragraphs (2) to (5); and

(b) shall continue to have effect with the amendments set out in sub-paragraph (6) (originally made

by section 290 of the Education Act 1993).

(2) In subsection (1) the following are omitted—

(a) in paragraphs (e) and (f), the words "schools and"; and

(b) paragraph (g).

(3) For subsection (2B) (renumbered by paragraph 8(4) of Schedule 2 to the Education Act 1994) there is substituted—

"(2B) Regulations under subsection (2) above may impose requirements on persons carrying on city technology colleges or city colleges for the technology of the arts as to the training and teaching experience of persons employed as teachers at such colleges who seek to become (in relation to schools) qualified teachers."

(4) In subsection (7), the following are omitted—

(a) the words from "or, in such cases" to "the funding authority"; and

(b) the words "school or" (where first occurring) and "any school or".

(5) Subsections (8) and (13) are omitted.

(6) The amendments referred to in sub-paragraph (1)(b) are—

(a) after subsection (6)(c) there is added "or

(d) by the proprietors of independent schools or at such schools as teachers or in any such work,"; and

(b) in subsection (12) after "section" there is inserted "other than in subsection (6)(d) above".

77 For section 219 of that Act there is substituted—

"219 Powers of the Secretary of State in relation to certain educational institutions.

(1) This section applies to any institution which is maintained by a local education authority and provides higher education or further education (or both).

(2) Section 495(1) of the Education Act 1996 (determination of disputes by the Secretary of State) shall apply in relation to the governing body of an institution to which this section applies as it applies in relation to the governing body of a school.

(3) Each of sections 496 and 497 of that Act (power of Secretary of State to prevent unreasonable exercise of functions and Secretary of State's general default powers) shall have effect as if any reference to a body to which that section applies included a reference to the governing body of an institution to which this section applies.

(4) Section 498 of that Act (powers of Secretary of State where there is no properly constituted governing body) shall have effect as if any reference to a school to which that section applies included a reference to an institution to which this section applies."

78. . . . .[915]

79 In section 228 of that Act (transfer of property to grant-aided institutions in Wales), in subsection (2)(a), for "section 100(1)(b) of the 1944 Act" there is substituted " section 485 of the Education Act 1996 ".

80 In section 232 of that Act (orders and regulations)—

(a) in subsection (2), for the words from "sections" to "Schedule 5" there is substituted " section 157 ";

(b) subsection (3) is omitted; and

(c) in subsection (4), "3(4)(a), 4(2)(c), 24," is omitted.

81(1) Section 235 of that Act (general interpretation) shall be amended as follows.

(2) In subsection (1) the definition of "the 1980 Act" is omitted.

(3) In subsection (2)(c), after "1944 Act" there is inserted " or section 485 of the Education Act 1996".

(4) In subsections (7) and (8), for "the 1944 Act" in each place there is substituted "the Education Act 1996".

82(1) Schedule 10 to that Act (supplementary provisions with respect to transfers)—

(a) shall continue to have effect with the amendments set out in sub-paragraph (2) (originally made by section 47 of the Education Act 1993);. . .[916]

(b). . . . .

(2) The amendments mentioned in sub-paragraph (1)(a) are as follows—

(a). . . . .[917]

(b) in paragraph 4(1) of the Schedule, for "by virtue of section 126 or 130" there is substituted " to

which this Schedule applies ";. . .[918]

(c). . . . .

(3). . . . .[919]

Copyright, Designs and Patents Act 1988 (c. 48)

83 In section 174(3) of the Copyright, Patents and Designs Act 1988 (meaning of "school") for "the Education Act 1944" there is substituted "the Education Act 1996".

Children Act 1989 (c. 41)

84 In section 28(4) of the Children Act 1989 (local authority support for children and families: consultation with local education authorities) for "Part III of the Education Act 1993" there is substituted "Part IV of the Education Act 1996".

85 In section 36(5) of that Act (education supervision orders: presumption that child is not being properly educated)—

(a) for "section 37 of the Education Act 1944" there is substituted "section 437 of the Education Act 1996 "; and

(b) for "section 39" there is substituted " section 444".

86. . . . .[920]

87 In section 87(10) of that Act (welfare of children accommodated in independent schools) for "the Education Act 1944" there is substituted " the Education Act 1996 ".

88. . . . .[921]

89. . . . .[922]

90 In section 91(5) of that Act (effect and duration of orders: school attendance orders) for "section 37 of the Education Act 1944" there is substituted " section 437 of the Education Act 1996 ".

91 In section 105(1) of that Act (interpretation) for "the Education Act 1944" in each place where it occurs, and for "the Education Act 1993", there is substituted " the Education Act 1996 ".

92 In paragraph 3(b) of Schedule 2 to that Act (local authority support for children and families: assessment of children's needs) for "Part III of the Education Act 1993" there is substituted " Part IV of the Education Act 1996 ".

93(1) Part III of Schedule 3 to that Act (education supervision orders) shall be amended as follows.

(2) In paragraph 13—

(a) in sub-paragraph (1) for "section 36 of the Education Act 1944 (duty to secure education of children) and section 199 of the Education Act 1993 (duty" there is substituted "sections 7 and 444 of the Education Act 1996 (duties to secure education of children and"; and

(b) in sub-paragraph (2)—

(i) in paragraph (a)(i) for "section 192 of that Act" there is substituted "section 437 of the Education Act 1996",

(ii) in paragraph (b)(i) for "section 192" there is substituted "section 437",

(iii) in paragraph (b)(ii) for "section 76 of the Education Act 1944" there is substituted "section 9 of that Act", and

(iv) in paragraph (b)(iii) for "sections 6 and 7 of the Education Act 1980" there is substituted "sections 411 and 423 of that Act ".

(3) In paragraph 21 for "the Education Act 1944 (as amended by Schedule 13) " there is substituted "the Education Act 1996."

94(1) Paragraph 3 of Schedule 9 to that Act (child minding and day care: exemption of certain schools) shall be amended as follows.

(2) In sub-paragraph (1)—

(a) for "section 100 of the Education Act 1944" there is substituted "section 485 of the Education Act 1996", and

(b) for "section 53 of the Act of 1944" there is substituted "section 508 of that Act".

(3) In sub-paragraph (3)—

(a) for "the Education Act 1944" there is substituted "the Education Act 1996", and

(b) for "the Education Act 1993" there is substituted "that Act".

Local Government and Housing Act 1989 (c. 42)

95 In section 2(6)(a) of the Local Government and Housing Act 1989 (politically restricted posts) for "section 88 of the Education Act 1944" there is substituted "section 532 of the Education Act 1996".

96(1) Section 13 of that Act (voting rights of members of committees)—

(a) shall be amended as provided in sub-paragraphs (2), (3) and (5); and

(b) shall continue to have effect with the amendment set out in sub-paragraph (4) (originally made by Schedule 19 to the Education Act 1993).

(2). . . . .[923]

(3) For subsection (5) there is substituted—

"(5) Nothing in this section shall prevent the appointment of a person who is not a member of a local education authority as a voting member of—

(a) any committee or sub-committee appointed by the local authority wholly or partly for the purpose of discharging any functions with respect to education conferred on them in their capacity as a local education authority,

(b) any joint committee appointed by two or more local authorities wholly or partly for the purpose of discharging any functions with respect to education conferred on them in their capacity as local education authorities, or

(c) any sub-committee appointed by any such committee or joint committee wholly or partly for the purpose of discharging any of that committee's functions with respect to education,

where that appointment is required by directions given by the Secretary of State under section 499 of the Education Act 1996 (power of Secretary of State to direct appointment of members of committees)."

(4) In subsection (7) for "education committee or sub-committee of an education committee" there is substituted "committee, joint committee or sub-committee appointed for the purpose mentioned in that subsection".

(5) In subsection (9) the definition of "foundation governors" and the "and" immediately following it are omitted.

97. . . . .[924]

Education (Student Loans) Act 1990 (c. 6)

98 In section 1(3)(a) of the Education (Student Loans) Act 1990 (meaning of "institutions receiving support from public funds") for "section 100(1)(b) of the Education Act 1944" there is substituted " section 485 of the Education Act 1996 ".

Town and Country Planning Act 1990 (c. 8)

99 In section 76 of the Town and Country Planning Act 1990 (duty to draw attention to certain provisions for benefit of disabled) for subsection (3) there is substituted—

"(3) Expressions used in subsection (1)(e) and in the Education Act 1996 have the same meanings as in that Act."

Environmental Protection Act 1990 (c. 43)

100 In section 98(2) of the Environmental Protection Act 1990 (definitions)—

(a) in paragraph (c)(i) for "section 100(1)(b) of the Education Act 1944" there is substituted " section 485 of the Education Act 1996 "; and

(b) in paragraph (e) for "section 105 of the Education Reform Act 1988) " there is substituted "section 482 of the Education Act 1996) ".

School Teachers' Pay and Conditions Act 1991 (c. 49)

101(1) The School Teachers' Pay and Conditions Act 1991—

(a) shall continue to have effect with the amendment set out in sub-paragraph (2) (originally made by Schedule 19 to the Education Act 1993); and

(b) shall be amended as provided in sub-paragraphs (3) and (4).

(2) In section 2 (orders relating to statutory conditions of employment), in subsections (6) and (7) for "section 3" there is substituted " sections 3 and 3A ".

(3) For the section 3A inserted by section 289 of the Education Act 1993 there is substituted—

"3A Special provisions for teachers on transfer of employment.

(1) This section applies where a school teacher employed to teach at an independent school—

(a) which becomes a county or voluntary school in pursuance of proposals published under section 35(1)(b) or, as the case may be, 41(1) of the Education Act 1996, or

(b) in place of which a grant-maintained school is established in pursuance of proposals

published under section 212 of that Act,

becomes employed (in the case of a county or voluntary school) by the local education authority or the governing body or (in the case of a grant-maintained school) by the governing body in accordance with the Transfer of Undertakings (Protection of Employment) Regulations 1981.

(2) A pay and conditions order shall not apply to the statutory conditions of employment of such a teacher unless he gives notice in writing to the new employer that the order is to so apply.

(3) Where the governing body of an aided school receive notice given under subsection (2) above, they shall inform the local education authority."

(4) In section 5 (interpretation etc.)—

(a) in subsection (1)—

(i) in the definition of "school which has a delegated budget" for "Chapter III of Part I of the Education Reform Act 1988" there is substituted "Part II of the Education Act 1996", and

(ii) for "the Education Act 1944" there is substituted " that Act "; and

(b) in subsection (5), for "sections 68 and 99(1) of the Education Act 1944" there is substituted "sections 496 and 497 of the Education Act 1996".

Diocesan Boards of Education Measure 1991 (1991 No. 2)

102. . . . .[925]

103. . . . .[926]

104(1) Section 6 of that Measure (Board to be consulted in certain cases) shall be amended as follows.

(2) In subsection (1)—

(a) for "section 13(1) of the 1988 Act" there is substituted " section 392(2) of the Education Act 1996 "; and

(b) for "section 11" there is substituted " section 390 ".

(3). . . . .[927]

105. . . . .[928]

106. . . . .[929]

107. . . . .[930]

Further and Higher Education Act 1992 (c. 13)

108. . . . .[931]

109 In section 28(3)(a) of that Act (institutions which are grant-aided or eligible to receive aid by way of grant) for "section 100(1)(b) of the Education Act 1944" there is substituted "section 485 of the Education Act 1996".

110(1) Section 37 of that Act (attribution of surpluses and deficits) shall be amended as follows.

(2). . . . .[932]

(3) In subsection (7)—

(a). . . . .

(b) in the definition of "financial year", for "the Education Reform Act 1988" there is substituted "the Education Act 1996".

111 In section 54(2) of that Act (duty to give information) for the words from "section 51" to "section 52 of that Act" there is substituted "regulations under section 492 or 493 of the Education Act 1996".

112. . . . .[933]

113. . . . .[934]

114 In section 89(5) of that Act (orders, regulations and directions) for "Section 111 of the Education Act 1944" there is substituted " Section 570 of the Education Act 1996 ".

115(1) Section 90 of that Act (interpretation) shall be amended as follows.

(2) In subsection (1)—

(a) in the definition of "the Education Acts", for "means the Education Acts 1944 to 1996" there is substituted " has the meaning given by section 578 of the Education Act 1996 "; and

(b) after that definition there is inserted—

""further education" has the meaning given by section 2(3) to (5) of that Act;".

(3) In subsection (5), for "the Education Act 1944" there is substituted " the Education Act 1996 ".

116 In section 92 of that Act (Index)—

(a) in the entry for "further education", for "section 14(1) to (4) " there is substituted " section 90(1) ";

and

(b) the entries for "pupil", "secondary education" and "school" are omitted.

117(1) Schedule 8 to that Act—

(a) shall continue to have effect with the amendment set out in sub-paragraph (2) (originally made by section 47(6) of the Education Act 1993); and

(b) shall be amended as provided in sub-paragraphs (3) and (4).

(2) In paragraph 61, for "by virtue of section 126 or 130 and in such a case" there is substituted " and ".

(3) In paragraph 62(3), for "or (as the case may be) the Education Act 1993" there is substituted " or (as the case may be) the Education Act 1996 ".

(4) In—

(a) paragraph 79(2) (which provides that, in relation to a further education corporation or a Further Education Funding Council, the reference in section 25(2) of the Sex Discrimination Act 1975 to section 99 of the Education Act 1944 is to be read as a reference to section 57(3) of the 1992 Act),. . .[935]

(b). . . . .

for "section 99 of the Education Act 1944" there is substituted "section 497 of the Education Act 1996".

Tribunals and Inquiries Act 1992 (c. 53)

118(1) The Tribunals and Inquiries Act 1992 shall be amended as follows.

(2) Section 11(1) (appeals from certain tribunals) shall continue to have effect with the substitution for "15(a) or (d) " of "15(a), (d) or (e) " (originally made by section 181 of the Education Act 1993).

(3) In paragraph 15 of Schedule 1 (tribunals under general supervision of Council on Tribunals)—

(a) in sub-paragraph (a), for "section 72 of, and Schedule 6 to, the Education Act 1944 (c. 31) " there is substituted "section 476 of, and Schedule 34 to, the Education Act 1996 (c. 56) ";

(b) in sub-paragraph (b), for "Part I of Schedule 2 to the Education Act 1980 (c. 20) " there is substituted "Part I of Schedule 33 to that Act";

(c) in sub-paragraph (c), for "paragraph 5(1) of Schedule 6 to the Education Act 1993" there is substituted "paragraph 6(1) of Schedule 23 to that Act"; and

(d). . . . .[936]

Charities Act 1993 (c. 10)

119 For section 79(9) of the Charities Act 1993 (parochial charities) there is substituted—

"(9) This section shall not affect the trusteeship, control or management of any voluntary or grant-maintained school within the meaning of the Education Act 1996."

120(1) Schedule 2 to that Act (exempt charities) shall continue to have effect with the following amendments (originally made by Schedules 15 and 19 to the Education Act 1993).

(2) After paragraph (d) there is inserted—

"(da) the School Curriculum and Assessment Authority;".

(3) For paragraph (f) there is substituted—

"(f) the Curriculum and Assessment Authority for Wales;".

121 At the end of paragraph 1(b) of Schedule 4 to that Act (charities over which the court has jurisdiction) there is added "or section 554 of the Education Act 1996".

Welsh Language Act 1993 (c. 38)

122. . . . .[937]

Local Government (Wales) Act 1994 (c. 19)

123(1) Section 30 of the Local Government (Wales) Act 1994 (area committees) shall be amended as follows.

(2) In subsection (7) for "section 297 of the Education Act 1993" there is substituted " section 499 of the Education Act 1996 ".

(3) In subsections (9) and (14) for "section 297 of the Act of 1993" there is substituted " section 499 of the Act of 1996 ".

124(1) Section 31 of that Act (sub-committees of area committees) shall be amended as follows.

(2) In subsection (6) for "section 297 of the Education Act 1993" there is substituted " section 499 of the Education Act 1996 ".

(3) In subsections (8) and (12) for "section 297 of the Act of 1993" there is substituted " section 499 of the

Act of 1996 ".

Value Added Tax Act 1994 (c. 23)

125 In Schedule 9 to the Value Added Tax Act 1994 (exemptions), in paragraph (a) of Note (1) to Group 6 (education)—

(a) for "the Education Acts 1944 to 1996" there is substituted " the Education Act 1996 ";

(b) in sub-paragraph (iii), for "a maintained school within the meaning of the Education Act 1993 or" there is substituted " a county school, voluntary school or maintained special school (other than one established in a hospital) within the meaning of the Education Act 1996 or a maintained school within the meaning of ";

(c)...............................[938]

(d)...............................

Education Act 1994 (c. 30)

126 After section 11 of the Education Act 1994 there is inserted—

" General duty of Secretary of State

11A General duty of Secretary of State with respect to teacher training.

In carrying out his duties under sections 10 and 11 of the Education Act 1996 the Secretary of State shall, in particular, make such arrangements as he considers expedient for securing that sufficient facilities are available for the training of teachers to serve in schools maintained by local education authorities, grant-maintained schools, institutions within the further education sector and institutions which are maintained by such authorities and provide higher education or further education (or both)."

127(1) Section 12 of that Act (power of schools to provide courses of initial teacher training) shall be amended as follows.

(2) In subsection (5), for "section 12 or 13 of the Education Act 1980 or section 96 of the Education Act 1993" there is substituted " section 35, 41 or 259 of the Education Act 1996 ".

(3) In subsection (6)—

(a) for "sections 33 to 43 of the Education Reform Act 1988" there is substituted " sections 101 to 123 of the Education Act 1996 ", and

(b) for "Chapter VI of Part II of the Education Act 1993" there is substituted " Chapter VI of Part III of that Act ".

128 In section 19 of that Act (interpretation)—

(a) in subsection (3), for "section 156 of the Education Act 1993" there is substituted " section 312 of the Education Act 1996 "; and

(b) in subsection (5), for "the Education Act 1944" there is substituted " the Education Act 1996 ".

Disability Discrimination Act 1995 (c. 50)

129...............................[939]

Employment Rights Act 1996 (c. 18)

130 In section 134(1) of the Employment Rights Act 1996 (dismissal of teachers in aided schools) for "paragraph (a) of the proviso to section 24(2) of the Education Act 1944" there is substituted " section 134(3) of the Education Act 1996 ".

Nursery Education and Grant-Maintained Schools Act 1996 (c. 57)

131(1) Section 4 of the Nursery Education and Grant-Maintained Schools Act 1996 (children with special educational needs) shall be amended as follows.

(2) In subsection (1)—

(a) for "section 157 of the Education Act 1993) " there is substituted " section 313 of the Education Act 1996) "; and

(b) for "Part III" there is substituted " Part IV ".

(3) In each of subsections (2) and (3), for "Part III of the Education Act 1993" there is substituted " Part IV of the Education Act 1996 ".

132 In section 11 of that Act (citation etc.) for subsection (2) there is substituted—

"(2) This Act shall be construed as one with the Education Act 1996."

Part II Amendments coming into force on appointed day

Children and Young Persons Act 1933 (c. 12)

133 In section 30(1)(a) of the Children and Young Persons Act 1933 (interpretation) for the words from "for the purposes" to the end of paragraph (a) there is substituted " over compulsory school age (construed in accordance with section 8 of the Education Act 1996) ".

Agriculture (Safety, Health and Welfare Provisions) Act 1956 (c. 49)

134 In section 24(1) of the Agriculture (Safety, Health and Welfare Provisions) Act 1956 (interpretation) in the definition of "young person", for "for the purposes of the Education Act 1944" there is substituted " (construed in accordance with section 8 of the Education Act 1996) ".

Factories Act 1961 (c. 34)

135 In section 176(1) of the Factories Act 1961 (general interpretation) for the definition of "child" there is substituted—

""child" means any person who is not over—

(a) compulsory school age (construed in accordance with section 8 of the Education Act 1996), or

(b) school age (construed in accordance with section 31 of the Education (Scotland) Act 1980);".

Matrimonial Causes Act 1973 (c. 18)

136 In section 29(2)(a) of the Matrimonial Causes Act 1973 (age limit on making certain orders in favour of children) for the words from "(that is to say" to "that section) " there is substituted " (construed in accordance with section 8 of the Education Act 1996) ".

Sex Discrimination Act 1975 (c. 65)

137 In section 24(2)(d) of the Sex Discrimination Act 1975 (designated establishments) after "school age" there is inserted " (construed in accordance with section 8 of the Education Act 1996) ".

Domestic Proceedings and Magistrates' Courts Act 1978 (c. 22)

138 In section 5(2)(a) of the Domestic Proceedings and Magistrates' Courts Act 1978 (age limit on making certain orders in favour of children) for the words from "(that is to say" to "that section) " there is substituted " (construed in accordance with section 8 of the Education Act 1996) ".

Employment Act 1989 (c. 38)

139 In section 10 of the Employment Act 1989 (removal of restrictions relating to employment of young persons), in subsection (6), for "for the purposes of the Education Act 1944" there is substituted " (construed in accordance with section 8 of the Education Act 1996) ".

Section 582(2).

SCHEDULE 38 Repeals and revocations

Part I Repeals coming into force on 1st November 1996

Chapter	Short title	Extent of repeal
1944 c.31.	Education Act 1944.	The whole Act.
1946 c.49.	Acquisition of Land (Authorisation Procedure) Act 1946.	In Schedule 4, the entry relating to the Education Act 1944.
1946 c.50.	Education Act 1946.	The whole Act.
1948 c.40.	Education (Miscellaneous Provisions) Act 1948.	The whole Act.
1953 c.33.	Education (Miscellaneous Provisions) Act 1953.	The whole Act.
1959 c.53.	Town and Country Planning Act 1959.	In Schedule 4, paragraph 4.
1959 c.60.	Education Act 1959.	The whole Act.
1961 c.45.	Rating and Valuation Act 1961.	The whole Act.
1962 c.12.	Education Act 1962.	Section 9.
		Section 13(4).
		Section 14(2).
1963 c.37.	Children and Young Persons	Section 38(2).

	Act 1963.	
1964 c.82.	Education Act 1964.	The whole Act.
1967 c.3.	Education Act 1967.	Section 2.
		In section 6(1), the words from "and this Act" onwards.
1967 c.80.	Criminal Justice Act 1967.	In Part I of Schedule 3, the entry relating to the Education Act 1944.
1968 c.17.	Education Act 1968.	The whole Act.
1968 c.xxxix	Greater London Council (General Powers) Act 1968.	Section 56.
1970 c.42.	Local Authority Social Services Act 1970.	In Schedule 1, the entry relating to the Education Act 1993.
1970 c.52.	Education (Handicapped Children) Act 1970.	The whole Act.
1972 c.70.	Local Government Act 1972.	Section 192.
1973 c.16.	Education Act 1973.	Section 1(2).
		Section 2.
		In section 5(1), the words from ", and the Education Acts" onwards.
		In Schedule 1, paragraph 3.
1973 c.23.	Education (Work Experience) Act 1973.	The whole Act.
1975 c.2.	Education Act 1975.	The whole Act.
1976 c.5.	Education (School-leaving Dates) Act 1976.	The whole Act.
1976 c.81.	Education Act 1976.	The whole Act.
1977 c.49.	National Health Service Act 1977.	In Schedule 14, in paragraph 13(1)(b) "7 to 9".
		In Schedule 15, paragraphs 2 and 3.
1979 c.49.	Education Act 1979.	The whole Act.
1980 c.20.	Education Act 1980.	Sections 1 to 18.
		Sections 21 and 22.
		Section 24.
		Section 26.
		Sections 28 to 30.
		Section 33(3).
		Sections 34 and 35.
		Section 37.
		In section 38, subsections (2) and (4) to (6).
		Schedules 1 to 4.
		Schedule 7.
1980 c.65.	Local Government, Planning and Land Act 1980.	Section 2(3).
1981 c.60.	Education Act 1981.	The whole Act.
1982 c.48.	Criminal Justice Act 1982.	In Schedule 3, the entries relating to the Education Act 1944.
1984 c.11.	Education (Grants and Awards) Act 1984.	The whole Act.
1985 c.47.	Further Education Act 1985.	Section 8(2).
1986 c.50.	Social Security Act 1986.	Section 77 so far as relating to section 22 of the Education Act 1980.

1986 c.61.	Education (No.2) Act 1986.	Sections 1 to 42.
		Sections 44 to 47.
		Sections 51 to 60.
		In section 62(1), paragraph (a) and the "(b) " immediately following it.
		In section 63, in subsection (1) the words "(other than under section 2(7), 9(6) or 54) ", in subsection (2) "51 or", and subsection (2A).
		In section 65(1), all the definitions except that of "establishment of higher or further education".
		In section 66, in subsection (1) "60 and" and "to (3) ", and in subsection (2) "and 59".
		In section 67, subsections (2), (5) and (6).
		Schedules 1 to 3.
		In Schedule 4, paragraphs 1, 2 and 5.
		Schedules 5 and 6.
1987 c.15.	Reverter of Sites Act 1987.	Section 8(1).
1988 c.40.	Education Reform Act 1988.	Part I.
		Section 120(5) and (9).
		In section 210, in each of subsections (1) and (3)(d) the words "local education authorities or".
		In section 211, paragraphs (a) and (b) and the words "the school or".
		Sections 212 and 213.
		In section 218, in subsection (1) in each of paragraphs (e) and (f) the words "schools and" and paragraph (g), in subsection (7) the words from "or, in such cases" to "the funding authority" and the words "school or" (where first occurring) and "any school or", and subsections (8) and (13).
		Section 222.
		Sections 225 and 227.
		Section 229(1).
		In section 230(1), "section 15(2) ".
		In section 232, subsection (3) and, in subsection (4)(b), "3(4)(a), 4(2)(c), 24".
		Section 234.
		In section 235, in subsection (1) the definition of "the 1980 Act".
		In section 236, in subsection (1) the words from "section 1" to "section 119" and "sections 212 and 213", and subsections (2) and (3).
		Section 238(2).
		Schedules 1 to 4.
		In Schedule 12, paragraphs 1 to 8, 14, 17, 24, 25, 34, 35, 37, 54 to 62, 69(4), 76, 77, 81, 82, 87(3), 99, 102, 103 and 106.
1989 c.41.	Children Act 1989.	In Schedule 13, paragraphs 9 and 10.
1989 c.42.	Local Government and Housing Act 1989.	In section 13(9), the definition of "foundation governors" and the "and" immediately following it.

		Section 188.
1990 c.6.	Education (Student Loans) Act 1990.	Section 4(2).
1990 c.19.	National Health Service and Community Care Act 1990.	In Schedule 9, paragraph 31.
1990 c.38.	Employment Act 1990.	Section 14.
		In section 18(2), the words from "section 14" to "experience) ".
1991 c.21.	Disability Living Allowance and Disability Working Allowance Act 1991.	In Schedule 3, paragraph 12.
1991 c.49.	School Teachers' Pay and Conditions Act 1991.	Section 6(2).
1991 No.2.	Diocesan Boards of Education Measure 1991.	In section 10(1), the definition of "the 1988 Act".
1992 c.13.	Further and Higher Education Act 1992.	Sections 10 to 14.
		Section 59.
		In section 92, the entries for "pupil", "secondary education" and "school".
		Section 94(2).
		In Schedule 8, paragraphs 1 to 17, 24 to 26, 28, 43(b), 50, 53, 54, 56, 57 and 82.
1992 c.38.	Education (Schools) Act 1992.	Section 16.
		In Schedule 4, paragraphs 1 and 4 to 6.
1993 c.8.	Judicial Pensions and Retirement Act 1993.	In Schedule 6, paragraph 51.
1993 c.10.	Charities Act 1993.	In Schedule 2, paragraphs (e) and (g).
1993 c.35.	Education Act 1993.	The whole Act.
1994 c.19.	Local Government (Wales) Act 1994.	Section 21.
		In Schedule 16, paragraphs 8 and 105.
1994 c.30.	Education Act 1994.	Section 27(2).
		In Schedule 2, paragraphs 5(2) and (4)(a), 6(2) and (4)(a) and 8(2) to (4).
1995 c.17.	Health Authorities Act 1995.	In Schedule 1, paragraphs 112 and 124.
1995 c.18.	Jobseekers Act 1995.	In Schedule 2, paragraphs 3 and 17.
1995 c.21.	Merchant Shipping Act 1995.	In Schedule 13, paragraph 48.
1995 c.50.	Disability Discrimination Act 1995.	Section 29(1) and (2).
		Section 30(7) to (9).
1996 c.9.	Education (Student Loans) Act 1996.	Section 4(2).
1996 c.18.	Employment Rights Act 1996.	In Schedule 1, paragraph 59.
1996 c.23.	Arbitration Act 1996.	In Schedule 3, paragraphs 4 and 59.
1996 c.50.	Nursery Education and Grant-Maintained Schools Act 1996.	Section 7.
		In Schedule 3, paragraphs 1 to 8 and 10 to 15.

Part II Repeals coming into force on appointed day

Chapter	Short title	Extent of repeal
1975 c.65.	Sex Discrimination Act 1975.	In section 82(1), the definition of "upper limit of compulsory school age".

1976 c.74.	Race Relations Act 1976.	In section 78(1), the definition of "upper limit of compulsory school age".
1995 c.36.	Children (Scotland) Act 1995.	In Schedule 4, paragraph 10(a).

Part III Revocations

S.I. Number	Title	Extent of revocation
S.I. 1977/293.	Local Authorities etc. (Miscellaneous Provision) Order 1977.	Article 4(1) and (5).
S.I. 1991/1890.	Education (Financial Delegation for Primary Schools) Regulations 1991.	The whole Regulations.
S.I. 1992/110.	Education (Financial Delegation for Primary Schools) (Amendment) Regulations 1992.	The whole Regulations.
S.I. 1992/1548.	Education (National Curriculum) (Foundation Subjects at Key Stage 4) Order 1992.	The whole Order.
S.I. 1993/2709.	Education (No. 2) Act 1986 (Amendment) Order 1993.	The whole Order.
S.I. 1993/2827.	Education (No. 2) Act 1986 (Amendment) (No. 2) Order 1993.	The whole Order.
S.I. 1994/692.	Education (No. 2) Act 1986 (Amendment) Order 1994.	The whole Order.
S.I. 1994/1814.	Education (National Curriculum) (Foundation Subjects at Key Stage 4) Order 1994.	The whole Order.
S.I. 1994/2092.	Education (No. 2) Act 1986 (Amendment) (No. 2) Order 1994.	The whole Order.
S.I. 1994/2732.	Education (No. 2) Act 1986 (Amendment) (No. 3) Order 1994.	The whole Order.
S.I. 1996/710.	Local Government Changes for England (Education) (Miscellaneous Provisions) Regulations 1996.	Regulation 19.
S.I. 1996/951.	Deregulation (Length of the School Day) Order 1996.	The whole Order.

Section 582(3).

SCHEDULE 39 Transitional provisions and savings

Part I General

General transitional provisions

1(1) The repeal and re-enactment of provisions by this Act does not affect the continuity of the law.

(2) Any subordinate legislation made or other thing done, or having effect as if made or done, under or for the purposes of any provision repealed and re-enacted by this Act shall, if in force or effective immediately before the commencement of the corresponding provision of this Act, have effect thereafter as if made or done under or for the purposes of that corresponding provision.

(3) Any reference (express or implied) in this Act or any other enactment or in any instrument or document—

(a) to any provision of this Act, or

(b) to things done or falling to be done under or for the purposes of any provision of this Act,

shall (so far as the context permits) be construed as including, in relation to times, circumstances or purposes in relation to which the corresponding provision repealed by this Act had effect, a reference—

(i) to that corresponding provision, or

(ii) to things done or falling to be done under or for the purposes of that corresponding provision,

as the case may be.

(4) Any reference (express or implied) in any enactment or in any instrument or document—

(a) to any provision repealed and re-enacted by this Act, or

(b) to things done or falling to be done under or for the purposes of any such provision,

shall (so far as the context permits) be construed as including, in relation to times, circumstances or purposes in relation to which the corresponding provision of this Act has effect, a reference—

(i) to that corresponding provision, or

(ii) to things done or falling to be done under or for the purposes of that corresponding provision,

as the case may be.

(5) Without prejudice to the generality of sub-paragraph (4), where a power conferred by an Act is expressed to be exercisable in relation to enactments contained in Acts passed before or in the same

Session as the Act conferring the power, the power is also exercisable in relation to provisions of this Act which reproduce such enactments.

(6) Sub-paragraphs (1) to (5) have effect instead of section 17(2) of the Interpretation Act 1978 (but are without prejudice to any other provision of that Act); and sub-paragraph (1) has effect subject to any amendments of the law which give effect to recommendations of the Law Commission.

(7) Sub-paragraph (2) does not apply to any subordinate legislation in so far as it is reproduced in this Act.

Extension of references to provisions repealed by Education Act 1993

2(1) Paragraph 1(3) above shall have effect, for the purpose of extending references so as to include references to (or to things done or falling to be done under) the pre-1993 Act enactments, as if any reference in paragraph 1(3) to the corresponding provision repealed by this Act were a reference to the corresponding provision of those enactments.

(2) Paragraph 1(4) above shall have effect, for the purpose of extending references to (or to things done or falling to be done under) the pre-1993 Act enactments, as if any reference in paragraph 1(4) to any provision repealed and re-enacted by this Act were a reference to a provision of those enactments.

(3)...............................[940]

(4) In this paragraph "the pre-1993 Act enactments" means the enactments specified in Part I of Schedule 21 to the Education Act 1993 (repeals).

Construction of pre-1944 Act references

3 Where immediately before the commencement of this Act any reference in any enactment, instrument or document had effect as if it were a reference to the Secretary of State or the Department for Education and Employment by virtue of the operation of section 2(1) of the Education Act 1944 and any order made under the Ministers of the Crown Act 1975, it shall continue to do so despite the repeal of that provision by this Act.

4(1) This paragraph applies to enactments passed before 1st April 1945.

(2) Unless the context otherwise requires any such enactment shall be construed as if—

(a) any reference to an elementary school or to a public elementary school (whether or not any reference is made there to the payment of parliamentary grants in respect of the school) were a reference to a county school or voluntary school, as the context may require;

(b) any reference to a school certified by the Board of Education, in accordance with the provisions of Part V of the Education Act 1921, as suitable for providing education for blind, deaf, defective or epileptic children were a reference to a special school;

(c) any reference to the managers of a school, in relation to a county school or voluntary school, were a reference to the governors (or, if the context so requires, the governing body) of the school;

(d) any reference to elementary education or to higher education were a reference to such education as may be provided by a local education authority in the exercise of their functions under sections 13 to 15 of this Act; and

(e) any reference to a local education authority, to a local education authority for elementary education or to a local education authority for higher education were a reference to a local education authority within the meaning of this Act.

Effect of old transitional provisions and savings

5 The repeals made by this Act shall not affect the operation of any transitional provision or saving relating to the coming into force of a provision reproduced in this Act in so far as the transitional provision or saving is not specifically reproduced in this Act but remains capable of having effect in relation to the corresponding provision of this Act or otherwise.

6(1) The repeal by this Act of an enactment previously repealed subject to savings does not affect the continued operation of those savings.

(2) The repeal by this Act of a saving on the previous repeal of an enactment does not affect the saving so far as it is not specifically reproduced in this Act but remains capable of having effect.

Use of existing forms etc.

7 Any reference to an enactment repealed by this Act which is contained in a document made, served or issued after the commencement of that repeal shall be construed, except so far as a contrary intention appears, as a reference or (as the context may require) including a reference to the

corresponding provision of this Act.

Pre-commencement offences

8 Nothing in this Act affects the enactments repealed by this Act in their operation in relation to offences committed before the commencement of this Act.

Part II Specific provisions

Governing bodies of LEA-maintained schools

9(1) Any governing body which immediately before the commencement of this Act was incorporated by virtue of section 238 of the Education Act 1993 (incorporation of governing bodies of county, voluntary and maintained special schools) shall continue in existence as a body corporate despite the repeal of that section by this Act.

(2) In Schedule 7 to this Act any reference to a governing body incorporated under section 88(1) of this Act includes a reference to a governing body falling within sub-paragraph (1).

(3) Despite the repeal by this Act of Schedule 13 to the Education Act 1993 (incorporated governing bodies for county, voluntary and maintained special schools)—

(a) paragraph 3 of that Schedule (contracts of employment) shall continue to apply to, or in relation to, any contract of employment to which it applied immediately before the commencement of this Act; and

(b) to the extent that any provision of paragraphs 13 to 15 (general provisions about transfers) applied in relation to any transfer immediately before the commencement of this Act, it shall continue so to apply.

10(1) The reproduction by this Act of any reference, in an enactment repealed by this Act, to the governors of a school of any description as a reference to the governing body of a school of that description shall not be taken to affect the construction or operation of that enactment in relation to any times, circumstances or purposes in relation to which it had effect.

(2) Where by virtue of section 1(4) of the Education Act 1980 any enactment or document referred immediately before the commencement of this Act to the governors, foundation governors, instrument of government or articles of government of a primary school to which section 1(2) and (3) of that Act applied, it shall continue to do so despite the repeal of section 1(4) by this Act.

11 Where any instrument under which the governing body of an aided or special agreement school is constituted was in force immediately before the commencement of this Act by virtue of paragraph 1 of Schedule 5 to the Education (No. 2) Act 1986, the instrument shall have effect thereafter as if made by order under section 76 of this Act; but this paragraph shall cease to apply to any such school if it is grouped with any other school or schools under section 89 of this Act.

Special agreement schools

12(1) Any order under section 15(2) of the Education Act 1944 directing that a school is to be a special agreement school shall, if in force immediately before the commencement of this Act, continue in force despite the repeal by this Act of section 15(2) of that Act.

(2) Sub-paragraph (1) does not prejudice the operation of paragraph 1(2) above in relation to other orders in force under section 15(2) of that Act immediately before the commencement of this Act.

Proposals to establish etc. maintained or grant-maintained schools

13(1) Nothing in sections 35 to 45 or in sections 259 to 263 of this Act applies in relation to any proposals published before the commencement of this Act; and the corresponding provisions of the Education Act 1980 and the Education Act 1993 shall continue to apply in relation to any proposals duly published under section 12(1)(a) to (d) or 13 of the 1980 Act or section 96 or 97 of the 1993 Act as if this Act had not been passed.

(2) Sub-paragraph (1) does not prevent references in other provisions of this Act to proposals published or implemented under any of those sections of this Act from applying, by virtue of paragraph 1(3) above, to any proposals falling within sub-paragraph (1).

Review of constitution of governing bodies

14(1) Subject to sub-paragraph (2), nothing in section 82 of this Act applies in relation to the implementation of any proposal made before the commencement of this Act, and section 11 of the Education (No. 2) Act 1986 shall continue to apply in relation to the implementation of any such proposal falling within subsection (2)(a) of that section as if this Act had not been passed.

(2) In section 82(2) of this Act—

(a) in paragraph (b), the reference to proposals falling within subsection (3) of that section includes a reference to proposals falling within section 11(2) of the 1986 Act; and

(b) in paragraph (c) the reference to a relevant event for the purposes of section 82 includes a reference to a relevant event for the purposes of section 11 of the 1986 Act;

and any date determined by the local authority under section 11(6) of the 1986 Act shall be taken, for the purposes of section 82(2) of this Act, to be the date on which the proposals in question were implemented.

Confirmation of certain decisions of governing body

15. . . . .[941]

Review of grouping

16 The reference in section 94(2)(c) of this Act to an order under section 50 or 51 or 58(1) of this Act does not, by virtue of paragraph 1(3) above, include a reference to an order made before the commencement of this Act under section 2 of the Education Act 1946 or section 15(5) of the Education Act 1944.

Financial delegation

17(1) Without prejudice to paragraph 1(3) above—

(a) the reference in section 101(1) of this Act to a scheme made by a local education authority under section 103 of this Act includes a reference to a scheme in force immediately before the commencement of this Act which was made under section 33 of the Education Reform Act 1988 (including one made by way of variation or replacement of such a scheme under section 35 of that Act); and

(b) the reference in section 104(6) of this Act to section 104(5) includes a reference to section 34(6) of that Act.

(2) In relation to any such scheme made (or treated as if made) under section 33 of that Act, the reference in section 110(2) of this Act to the date of the coming into force of the scheme is (subject to sub-paragraph (3) below) a reference to the date of its coming into force as first made under section 33 (or 34(6)) of that Act.

(3) Where the initial period of any such scheme made before 1st January 1994 (the date on which section 274 of the Education Act 1993 came into force) was before 1st January 1994 determined by reference to a date later than that referred to in sub-paragraph (2) above, section 110(2) of this Act shall have effect in relation to the scheme as if it instead referred to that later date.

18 Nothing in section 141 of this Act requires a local education authority to amend the articles of government of a school if, before the commencement of this Act, they have already amended those articles in accordance with section 44(4) of the Education Reform Act 1988.

School sessions

19 For the purposes of section 147(1)(b) of this Act as it applies to a county, controlled or maintained special school, any determination as to the times of the school sessions (within the meaning of section 147) which had effect immediately before the commencement of this Act, whether made—

(a) by the governing body, or

(b) by the local education authority before 1st May 1989 (the date on which section 115 of the Education Reform Act 1988 came into force),

shall continue to have effect, as if made for those purposes, subject to any new determination under section 148 of this Act.

Exclusion of pupils

20 Nothing in section 157 of this Act applies in relation to any pupil excluded from a school before the commencement of this Act, and section 23 of the Education (No. 2) Act 1986 shall continue to apply to any such pupil as if this Act had not been passed.

School premises: pre-1993 Act transfer of control agreements

21(1) This paragraph applies to any agreement to which paragraph 6 or 7 of Schedule 13 to the Education Act 1993 (pre-existing transfer of control agreements) applied immediately before the commencement of this Act.

(2) The provisions of paragraph 6 or (as the case may be) paragraph 7 shall continue to apply in relation

to any such agreement as if this Act had not been passed.

Variation of trust deeds etc.

22 In section 179(1) of this Act—

(a) paragraph (b) does not apply to a transfer made before the commencement of this Act unless it was made in pursuance of proposals that fell to be implemented under section 12 or 13 of the Education Act 1980; but

(b) in paragraph (d) the reference to any order made by the Secretary of State under section 47 of this Act includes a reference to any order made under section 16(1) of the Education Act 1944 (whether made in relation to a county school or a voluntary school).

Ballots relating to acquisition of grant-maintained status

23 Section 190(2)(b) of this Act applies where after the commencement of this Act the Secretary of State has given his consent for the purposes of section 186(3) or section 187(5) of this Act.

Instruments and articles for grant-maintained schools incorporated under pre-1993 Act law

24(1) This paragraph applies in relation to a grant-maintained school where—

(a) the governing body of the school were incorporated under Chapter IV of Part I of the Education Reform Act 1988;

(b) an instrument and articles of government were made for the school under that Chapter before 1st January 1994; and

(c) immediately before the commencement of this Act those instruments had effect (in accordance with paragraph 1(2) of Schedule 20 to the Education Act 1993 (transitional provisions and savings)) subject to the modifications specified in either or both of paragraphs 8 and 9 of the Education Act 1993 (Commencement No. 2 and Transitional Provisions) Order 1993.

(2) The instrument and articles of government for the school shall continue to have effect, subject to those modifications, as if made under section 220 of this Act and in accordance with Part III of this Act.

25(1) This paragraph applies in relation to a grant-maintained school where—

(a) the governing body of the school were incorporated under Chapter IV of Part I of the Education Reform Act 1988;

(b) paragraph 24(1)(b) above does not apply; and

(c) immediately before the commencement of this Act the instrument and articles of government prescribed by virtue of section 56 of the Education Act 1993 had effect in relation to the school (in accordance with paragraph 1(3) of Schedule 20 to that Act).

(2) The instrument and articles of government for the school shall continue to have effect as if made under section 219 of this Act; and while they remain in force Schedule 24 to this Act shall apply in relation to the school with the following modifications.

(3) In paragraph 10(1) there shall be inserted at the end of paragraph (d) "or

(e) in the case of a governing body incorporated under Chapter IV of Part I of the Education Reform Act 1988, became a member of the governing body on the incorporation date in relation to the school (as defined by section 104(3) of that Act) and—

(i) immediately before that date, was a parent governor (within the meaning of the Education (No. 2) Act 1986) in relation to the school, or

(ii) was elected under section 66, or elected or nominated under section 68, of the Education Reform Act 1988 to hold office as a parent governor on the governing body."

(4) In paragraph 11(1) there shall be inserted at the end of paragraph (c) "or

(d) in the case of a governing body incorporated under Chapter IV of Part I of the Education Reform Act 1988, became a member of the governing body on the incorporation date in relation to the school (as defined by section 104(3) of that Act) and—

(i) immediately before that date, was a teacher governor (within the meaning of the Education (No. 2) Act 1986) in relation to the school, or

(ii) was elected under section 66, or elected or nominated under section 68, of the Education Reform Act 1988 to hold office as a teacher governor on the governing body."

(5) In paragraph 12(1) there shall be inserted at the end of paragraph (c) "or

(d) in the case of a governing body incorporated under Chapter IV of Part I of the Education Reform Act 1988—

(i) became a member of the governing body on the incorporation date in relation to the school (as defined by section 104(3) of that Act), and

(ii) was selected under section 66, or nominated under section 68, of that Act as being a person appearing to be a member of the local community committed to the good government and continuing viability of the school."

26(1) This paragraph applies in relation to a grant-maintained school where—

(a) the governing body of the school were incorporated under Chapter IV of Part I of the Education Reform Act 1988; and

(b) the school was a voluntary school before it became grant-maintained.

(2) Schedule 24 to this Act shall apply in relation to the school with the substitution of the following paragraph for paragraph 13—

"13"Foundation governor" means—

(a) a person appointed otherwise than by a local education authority for the purpose of securing, so far as is practicable, that the established character of the school at the time when it became grant-maintained is preserved and developed and, in particular, that the school is conducted in accordance with the provisions of any trust deed relating to it; or

(b) a person selected under section 66, or nominated under section 68, of the Education Reform Act 1988 for the purpose referred to in sub-paragraph (a) above."

Appeal committees

27 Nothing in—

(a) section 308(3) of this Act, or

(b) paragraph 7 of Schedule 33 to this Act,

applies in relation to any decision or action taken by the members of an appeal committee before 1st January 1994.

28 Paragraph 13(4) of Schedule 22 to this Act does not apply to any appeal committee constituted before 1st January 1994 in accordance with the instrument of government for any grant-maintained school for the purposes referred to in section 58(5)(d) of the Education Reform Act 1988 (articles of government admission appeal committees) while all the members of the committee are persons who were nominated before that date.

29 Where immediately before the commencement of this Act an appeal committee was constituted in accordance with the provisions of Part I of Schedule 2 to the Education (No. 2) Act 1986 as they had effect by virtue of paragraph 6 of Schedule 20 to the Education Act 1993 (namely without the amendments made by Schedule 16 to that Act), those provisions shall continue to apply to the committee (in place of the corresponding provisions of Part I of Schedule 33 to this Act) while all the members of the committee are persons nominated before 1st January 1994.

30 Nothing in this Act affects the restriction imposed by paragraph 4(2) of Schedule 2 to the Education Act 1993 (Commencement No.1 and Transitional Provisions) Order 1993 on the jurisdiction exercisable by a Local Commissioner, by virtue of section 25(5) of the Local Government Act 1974, in relation to cases where notice of appeal was served before 1st October 1993.

Maintenance etc. grants

31(1) The former grants code shall continue to have effect in relation to—

(a) any payments of maintenance grant under section 79(1) of the Education Reform Act 1988 in respect of any financial year ending before 1st April 1994; and

(b) any payments of capital and special purpose grants under section 79(3) of that Act made before that date.

(2) The functions conferred on the Secretary of State by or under the former grants code (as it has effect by virtue of sub-paragraph (1) above) shall, so far as relating to any amounts which—

(a) fall or may fall to be paid in any financial year beginning on or after 1st April 1994 in respect of any grant under that code, or

(b) have been paid by the Secretary of State before that date in respect of any such grant,

be exercisable by the funding authority.

(3) In this paragraph "the former grants code" means sections 79 and 80 of the Education Reform Act 1988 (maintenance, special purpose and capital grants) in their application to England.

32 Section 81 of the Education Reform Act 1988 (recovery from local funds of sums in respect of

maintenance grant) shall continue to have effect in relation to any sums recoverable by the Secretary of State under section 81(1) of that Act for any financial year ending before 1st April 1994.

33 The Education (Grant-maintained Schools) (Finance) Regulations 1990, so far as in force immediately before the commencement of this Act, shall continue in force despite the repeals made by this Act.

Assessments and statements of special educational needs

34 Any assessment or statement of special educational needs which—

(a) was made pursuant to a notice or copy of a proposed statement served before 1st September 1994, and

(b) immediately before the commencement of this Act was treated, by virtue of paragraph 2(7) or 4(3) of Schedule 4 to the Education Act 1993 (Commencement No.5 and Transitional Provisions) Order 1994, as if it had been made under section 167 or 168 of the Education Act 1993,

shall have effect as if made under section 323 or 324 of this Act (as the case may be).

Applications relating to special schools

35 Any application which—

(a) was made to the Secretary of State before 1st April 1994, and

(b) immediately before the commencement of this Act was treated, by virtue of paragraph 5 of Schedule 3 to the Education Act 1993 (Commencement No. 3 and Transitional Provisions) Order 1994, as if it had been made in accordance with—

(i) paragraph (a) or paragraph (b) of subsection (2), and subsection (6), of section 183 of the Education Act 1993, and

(ii) section 184(1) to (3) of that Act,

shall have effect as if made in accordance with paragraph (a) or (as the case may be) paragraph (b) of subsection (1), and subsection (5), of section 339 of this Act and section 340(1) to (3) of this Act.

Contracts of staff transferred to School Curriculum and Assessment Authority or Curriculum and Assessment Authority for Wales

36(1) The repeal by this Act of—

(a) section 15 of the Education Reform Act 1988 (transfer of staff of School Curriculum Development Committee or Secondary Examinations Council), or

(b) section 248 of the Education Act 1993 (transfer of staff of National Curriculum Council and School Examinations and Assessment Council),

shall not affect the continued operation of section 15(3) to (5) or (as the case may be) section 248(2) and (3) in relation to any contract of employment in relation to which those provisions applied immediately before the commencement of this Act.

(2) Nothing in this Act shall affect the continued operation of Article 4 of the Education (School Curriculum and Assessment Authority) (Transfer of Functions) Order 1995 in relation to the person mentioned in that Article.

Information about directions under section 365

37 Nothing in section 366 of this Act applies, by virtue of paragraph 1 above, to any direction given before the commencement of this Act under regulations made under section 19 of the Education Reform Act 1988, and that section shall continue to apply in relation to any such direction as if this Act had not been passed.

Review of conclusions about policy relating to curriculum

38 Any articles of government of a county, controlled or maintained special school made under section 18(7) of the Education (No. 2) Act 1986 shall, in their operation after the commencement of this Act in accordance with paragraph 1 above, have effect as if the events requiring the governing body to review their conclusions about the matters mentioned in section 371(2) and (3) of this Act included the implementation of any proposals made after that time which—

(a) would fall to be published by virtue of section 35 of this Act but for subsection (2)(b) of that section, and

(b) materially affect the school.

Agreed syllabuses of religious education

39(1) Nothing in this Act affects the constitution of, or the operation of Schedule 5 to the Education Act

1944 in relation to, any conference convened (or reconvened) before the commencement of this Act.

(2) Any regulations made under section 258(2) of the Education Act 1993 and having effect immediately before the commencement of this Act in relation to any conference or other body falling within section 258(1) or (3) shall continue to have effect in relation to any such conference or body, subject to the provisions of any regulations made under section 397(2) of this Act.

Arrangements for collective worship

40 In section 385 of this Act—

(a) subsection (4)(b) does not affect any arrangements for collective worship in the case of a grant-maintained school that was formerly a voluntary school which were made before the commencement of this Act for the purposes of section 6 of the Education Reform Act 1988; and

(b) subsection (6) does not affect any arrangements made for the purposes of section 6(5) of that Act before the commencement of this Act.

Disqualification for purposes of Part VII

41 Sections 472 and 473 of this Act shall apply to a person who is disqualified—

(a) from being the proprietor of an independent school, or

(b) from being a teacher in any school,

by virtue of an order under Part III of the Education Act 1944 made before 1st January 1994 as if the words "or other employee" were omitted, wherever occurring.

Chairmen of Independent Schools Tribunals

42 In its application to a person who, immediately before 31st March 1995, was a member of the legal panel appointed under paragraph 1 of Schedule 6 to the Education Act 1944, paragraph 3(2) of Schedule 34 to this Act has effect subject to Schedule 7 to the Judicial Pensions and Retirement Act 1993 (transitional provisions), as well as to section 26(4) to (6) of that Act.

Training grants

43 The Education (Training Grants) Regulations 1993 shall continue to have effect in so far as they relate to the payment of grant on and after 1st April 1994, or to grant paid before that date, in respect of expenditure incurred before that date.

Education committees etc. and members of those committees

44(1) Sub-paragraph (2) below applies to—

(a) any education committee established in accordance with paragraph 1 of Part II of Schedule 1 to the Education Act 1944, and

(b) any sub-committee of any such committee appointed in accordance with paragraph 10 of that Part,

which was in existence immediately before 1st April 1994.

(2) Any committee or sub-committee to which this sub-paragraph applies shall, for the purposes of any enactment, be treated as if it had been—

(a) appointed on that date—

(i) in the case of a committee, by the local authority, or

(ii) in the case of a sub-committee, by the committee appointed by the authority,

in accordance with section 102(1) of the Local Government Act 1972, and

(b) so appointed wholly or partly for the purpose of discharging any functions with respect to education conferred on them in their capacity as a local education authority or, as the case may be, the committee's functions with respect to education.

(3) Sub-paragraph (4) below applies to any person who was immediately before 1st April 1994 a member of an education committee or sub-committee of such a committee appointed for a term of office.

(4) Any person to whom this sub-paragraph applies shall, for the purposes of any enactment, be treated—

(a) as if he had been appointed on that date as a member of a committee or sub-committee appointed as mentioned in sub-paragraph (2) above for the residue of that term, and

(b) if he was a member of an education committee or sub-committee by virtue of directions given by the Secretary of State under paragraph 5A of Part II of Schedule 1 to the Education Act 1944, as if he had been appointed on that date as a member of a committee or sub-committee appointed as

mentioned in sub-paragraph (2) above by virtue of directions given by the Secretary of State under section 297 of the Education Act 1993 or, in relation to any time after the commencement of this Act, under section 499 of this Act.

Documents issued by divisional executives

45 Section 566(1) of this Act applies to a document purporting—

(a) to be a document issued by a divisional executive (within the meaning of Part III of Schedule 1 to the Education Act 1944), and

(b) to be signed by the person authorised by the executive to sign it,

as it applies to a document falling within paragraph (a) of that provision.

Part III Miscellaneous savings etc.

Handicapped children

46 The repeal by this Act of the Education (Handicapped Children) Act 1970 shall not affect the operation of any order made under section 1 of that Act so far as in force immediately before the commencement of this Act or of any statement of terms and conditions of employment given in connection with any such order.

Byelaws under Children and Young Persons Act 1933

47 Despite the repeal by this Act of section 120(5) of the Education Act 1944—

(a) references to a "child" in any byelaws made under Part II of the Children and Young Persons Act 1933 (employment of children) shall continue to be construed as references to a child within the meaning of that Part of that Act; and

(b) any such byelaws made before 1st April 1945 which were continued in force by section 120(5) shall, if in force immediately before the commencement of this Act, continue in force as if made by the local education authority for the area in question and may be varied or revoked accordingly.

Disputes as to property transferred by virtue of 1944 Act

48 Any question which, if it had arisen before the commencement of this Act, would have fallen to be determined by the Secretary of State in accordance with section 96(2) of the Education Act 1944 (questions relating to property etc. transferred to LEAs) shall be determined by him despite the repeal of that provision by this Act.

Modifications of deeds made prior to Education Act 1973

49 Without prejudice to the generality of paragraph 6(2) above, any order to which paragraph 3 of Schedule 1 to the Education Act 1973 (saving on repeals made by that Act) applied immediately before the commencement of this Act shall continue in force despite the repeal by this Act of that paragraph; and section 570 of this Act shall apply to any such order as if it had been made under this Act.

Instruments made prior to Local Government Act 1972

50 The repeal by this Act of section 192(5) and (6) of the Local Government Act 1972 (transitional provisions about instruments made by old LEAs) shall not affect the continued operation of those provisions in relation to any instrument in relation to which they applied or were applicable immediately before the commencement of this Act.

Part IV Interpretation

51 In this Schedule "repeal" includes (so far as the context permits) revoke or revocation.

SCHEDULE 40[942]

....

TABLE OF DERIVATIONS

Notes:

1This Table shows the derivation of the provisions of the Bill.

2The following abbreviations are used in the Table:—

Acts of Parliament

1944	= Education Act 1944 (c.31)
1946	= Education Act 1946 (c.50)
1948	= Education (Miscellaneous Provisions) Act 1948 (c.40)

1953	= Education (Miscellaneous Provisions) Act 1953 (c.33)
1962	= Education Act 1962 (c.12)
1964	= Education Act 1964 (c.82)
1967	= Education Act 1967 (c.3)
1968	= Education Act 1968 (c.17)
1972LG	= Local Government Act 1972 (c.70)
1973EWE	= Education (Work Experience) Act 1973 (c.23)
1973NHSR	= National Health Service Reorganisation Act 1973 (c.32)
1976	= Education Act 1976 (c.81)
1978IA	= Interpretation Act 1978 (c.30)
1980	= Education Act 1980 (c.20)
1981	= Education Act 1981 (c.60)
1982LG(MP)	= Local Government (Miscellaneous Provisions) Act 1982 (c.30)
1984	= Education (Grants and Awards) Act 1984 (c.11)
1986	= Education (No.2) Act 1986 (c.61)
1988	= Education Reform Act 1988 (c.40)
1992FHE	= Further and Higher Education Act 1992 (c.13)
1992(S)	= Education (Schools) Act 1992 (c.38)
1993	= Education Act 1993 (c.35)
1994LG(W)	= Local Government (Wales) Act 1994 (c. 19)
1994	= Education Act 1994 (c.30)
1995HA	= Health Authorities Act 1995 (c.17)
1996ER	= Employment Rights Act 1996 (c.18)
1996N	= Nursery Education and Grant-Maintained Schools Act 1996 (c.50)

Subordinate legislation

S.I. 1968/1699	= Secretary of State for Social Services Order 1968
S.I. 1977/293	= Local Authorities etc. (Miscellaneous Provision) Order 1977
S.I. 1991/1890	= Education (Financial Delegation for Primary Schools) Regulations 1991
S.I. 1992/110	= Education (Financial Delegation for Primary Schools) (Amendment) Regulations 1992
S.I. 1992/1548	= Education (National Curriculum) (Foundation Subjects at Key Stage 4) Order 1992
S.I. 1993/1975	= Education Act 1993 (Commencement No. 1 and Transitional Provisions) Order 1993
S.I. 1993/3106	= Education Act 1993 (Commencement No. 2 and Transitional Provisions) 1993
S.I. 1994/507	= Education Act 1993 (Commencement No. 3 and Transitional Provisions) Order 1994
S.I. 1994/1814	= Education (National Curriculum) (Foundation Subjects at Key Stage 4) Order 1994
S.I. 1994/2038	= Education Act 1993 (Commencement No. 5 and Transitional Provisions) Order 1994
S.I. 1994/2092	= Education (No.2) Act 1986 (Amendment) (No.2) Order 1994
S.I. 1996/951	= Deregulation (Length of the School Day) Order 1996

3 The abbreviation "Law Com. Rec. No." followed by a number refers to a recommendation set out in the paragraph of that number in Appendix 1 to the Report of the Law Commission (Cm.3251).

4 By virtue of the Secretary of State for Education and Science Order 1964 (S.I. 1964/490) all the functions of the Minister of Education were transferred to the Secretary of State for Education and Science. By virtue of further Transfer of Functions Orders (S.Is.1970/1536, 1978/274 and 1995/2986) all the functions so transferred are now exercisable by the Secretary of State at large. The effect of these Orders is not separately acknowledged in the Table against each of the provisions affected.

5 The Table also does not separately acknowledge the provisions of general effect contained in the Criminal Law Act 1977 and the Criminal Justice Act 1982 which secure that, where the maximum fine that may be imposed on the commission of a summary offence was originally expressed as a particular amount (or one particular amount on a first conviction and another on subsequent convictions), the amount of the maximum fine is now a particular level on the standard scale.

Provision	Derivation
1(1)	1944 s.7.
(2) to (4)	Drafting.
2(1)	1944 ss.8(1)(a), 114(1) ("primary education"); 1948 s.3(2).

(2)	1944 ss.8(1)(b), 114(1) ("secondary education"); 1992FHE ss.10(1), 14(2), Sch.8 para.13(2).
(3)	1944 ss.41(3), (4), 114(1) ("further education"); 1992FHE s.11, Sch.8 para.13(2).
(4)	1992FHE s.14(1).
(5)	1992FHE s.14(3).
(6)	1944 s.41(5); 1992FHE s.11.
(7)	1992FHE s.14(4).
3(1)	1944 s.114(1) ("pupil"); 1992FHE s.14(6), Sch.8 para.13(2).
(2)	1944 s.114(1) ("junior pupil"; "senior pupil").
(3)	1992FHE s.14(6).
4(1)	1944 s.114(1) ("school"); 1992FHE s.14(5); 1993 s.304(1).
(2)	Law Com. Rec. No. 2.
(3)	1992FHE s.91(3).
(4)	1992FHE s.91(5).
5(1)	1944 s.114(1) ("primary school"); 1992FHE Sch.8 para.13(2); 1993 s.304(2).
(2)	1944 s.114(1) ("secondary school"); 1992FHE Sch.8 para.13(2); 1993 Sch.19 para.24(1).
(3)	Drafting.
(4)	1964 s.1(2); 1980 Sch.3 para.12.
(5)	1964 s.1(3); 1993 Sch.19 para.38(3).
6(1)	1944 s.9(4).
(2)	1993 s.182(1).
7	1944 s.36; 1981 s.17.
8	1993 s.277.
9	1944 s.76; 1993 Sch.19 para.20; 1996N Sch.3 para.1.
10	1993 s.1.
11	1993 s.2.
12(1)	1944 ss.6(1), 114(1) ("county"; "local education authority"); 1972LG ss.179(2), 192(1); S.I. 1977/293; 1994LG(W) s.21(2).
(2)	1944 s.114(1) ("local education authority"); 1972LG s.192(1); S.I. 1977/293 art.4; Local Government Changes for England Regulations 1994 (S.I. 1994/867) reg.5(6); Local Government Changes for England (Amendment) Regulations 1996 (S.I. 1996/611) reg.2.
(3)	London Government Act 1963 (c.33) s.30(1)(a); 1988 s.163.
(4)	1988 ss.163, 235(4).
(5)	1944 ss.6(1), 114(1) ("local education authority"); 1972LG s.192(1); S.I. 1977/293; 1994LG(W) s.21(1), (2).
(6)	Drafting.
13(1)	1944 s.7.
(2)	1992FHE s.91(2), (4), Sch.8 para.2.
14(1)	1944 s.8(1); 1992FHE s.10(1).
(2), (3)	1944 s.8(1).
(4)	1980 s.24(2).
(5)	1944 s.8(1A); 1992FHE s.10(2).
(6)	1944 s.8(2); 1981 s.2(1); 1992FHE s.10(3).
(7)	1944 s.8(2) proviso; 1964 s.1(3).
15(1) to (3)	1944 s.41(1), (2); 1992FHE s.11.
(4)	1944 s.41(6); 1992FHE s.11.
(5)	1944 s.41(7), (8); 1992FHE s.11.
(6), (7)	1944 s.41(9), (10); 1992FHE s.11.
(8)	1944 s.41(2), (11); 1992FHE s.11.
16(1)	1944 s.9(1); 1992FHE Sch.8 para.4.
(2)	1944 s.9(6).
(3)	1944 s.9(7); 1992FHE s.12(1).
17(1)	1980 s.24(1).
(2)	1980 s.24(2).
18	1953 s.6(1).

19(1) to (4)	1993 s.298(1) to (4).
(5) to (7)	1993 s.298(6) to (8).
20	1993 s.3.
21	1993 s.4.
22	Drafting.
23	1993 s.8.
24	1993 s.9.
25	1993 s.6.
26	1993 s.5.
27	1993 s.12.
28	1993 s.20.
29(1)	1944 s.92.
(2)	1993 s.7(3).
(3), (4)	1993 s.21(2), (3).
(5)	1980 s.8(5B), (7); 1992(S) Sch.4 para.4.
(6)	1980 s.9(1).
30(1), (2)	1993 s.7(1), (2).
(3)	1993 s.7(4).
(4)	1993 s.21(1).
(5)	1993 s.21(3).
31(1), (2)	1944 s.9(2).
(3)	1944 s.9(2); 1993 s.298(5).
32(1)	1944 s.15(1).
(2)	1944 s.15(2); 1986 Sch.4 para.1.
(3), (4)	Drafting.
(5)	1944 s.114(1), Sch.3 para.11.
(6)	Drafting.
33	Drafting.
34(1)	1944 s.114(1) ("maintain"), (2); 1993 s.305(1) ("local education authority"); drafting.
(2)	1944 s.114(2).
(3)	1944 s.114(2); 1946 Sch.1 para.1.
(4)	1944 s.114(2); 1946 Sch.1 para.1.
(5)	Rating and Valuation Act 1961 (c.45) s.12(6).
35(1)	1980 s.12(1); 1993 s.229(1).
(2)	1980 s.16(1A); 1993 Sch.19 para.78; Law Com. Rec. No. 3.
(3)	1980 s.12(2).
(4)	1980 s.12(2A); 1988 s.31(4).
(5)	1980 s.12(1A); 1993 s.229(1).
(6)	1992FHE s.59(3), (4).
(7)	1993 ss.272(6), 273(1).
(8)	1993 s.273(2).
36(1)	1980 s.12(3); 1993 s.229(2).
(2)	1980 s.12(3).
(3)	1993 s.229(3).
(4)	1980 s.12(3).
(5), (6)	1980 s.16(3A), (3B); 1988 Sch.12 para.81.
37(1)	1980 s.12(4), (5); 1993 s.273(4).
(2)	1980 s.12(4).
(3)	1980 s.12(5).
(4)	1993 s.273(3).
(5)	1980 s.12(6).
(6)	1980 s.12(4).
(7)	1993 s.273(4).
(8)	1993 s.273(5).

(9)	1993 s.273(6).
38(1), (2)	1980 s.12(7).
(3)	1980 s.12(8).
39(1), (2)	1980 s.14(1).
(3)	Drafting.
40(1)	1980 s.12(9).
(2)	1980 s.14(3).
(3)	1980 s.12(9).
(4), (5)	1980 s.16(1).
41(1)	1980 s.13(1).
(2)	1980 s.13(1); 1993 s.230(1).
(3)	1980 s.16(1A); 1993 Sch.19 para.78; Law Com. Rec. No. 3.
(4)	1980 s.13(1A); 1992FHE s.12(2).
(5), (6)	1980 s.13(2); 1988 s.31(5).
(7)	1980 s.13(1B); 1993 s.230(1).
(8)	1992FHE s.59(3), (4).
(9)	1993 s.273(2).
42(1)	1980 s.13(3); 1993 s.230(2).
(2)	1980 s.13(3).
(3)	1980 s.13(3A); 1993 s.230(3).
(4)	1993 s.230(6).
(5), (6)	1980 s.16(3A), (3B); 1988 Sch.12 para.81.
43(1), (2)	1980 s.13(4).
(3) to (6)	1993 s.273(3) to (6).
(7)	Law Com. Rec. No. 4.
44(1)	1980 s.14(1); 1993 Sch.19 para.77.
(2)	1980 s.14(1).
(3), (4)	1980 s.14(2); Law Com. Rec. No. 4.
45(1)	1980 s.13(5); Law Com. Rec. No. 4.
(2)	1980 s.13(6); 1993 s.230(4).
(3)	1980 s.14(3).
(4)	1980 s.13(7).
(5), (6)	1980 s.16(1).
(7)	1980 s.13(8); 1993 s.230(5).
46(1)	1944 s.16(2); 1980 Sch.3 para.1.
(2)	1944 s.16(2).
(3)	1944 s.16(2).
(4)	1944 s.16(3).
(5)	1944 s.16(3).
47(1)	1944 s.16(1).
(2)	1946 Sch.1 para.2(1); Law Com. Rec. No. 5.
(3), (4)	1944 s.16(3).
48(1)	1944 s.15(2); 1986 Sch.4 para.1.
(2)	1944 s.15(2); 1993 Sch.19 para.7.
(3)	1944 s.105(3).
(4)	1944 s.105(3); 1993 Sch.19 para.23(b).
49	1964 s.1(1); 1968 s.2; 1980 Sch.3 para.11.
50(1)	1946 s.2(1).
(2)	1946 s.2(1), (7).
(3)	1946 s.2(7).
(4)	1946 s.2(2); 1980 Sch.3 para.7.
(5)	1946 s.16(1) ("department").
51(1)	1946 ss.2(1).
(2), (3)	1946 s.2(3), (4).

(4)	1946 s.2(1), (7).
(5)	1946 s.2(7).
(6)	1946 s.2(2); 1980 Sch.3 para.7.
(7)	1946 s.2(8).
(8)	1946 s.16(1) ("department").
52(1)	1986 s.54(3).
(2)	1986 s.54(4).
(3)	1986 s.54(3).
53(1), (2)	1986 s.54(5).
(3), (4)	1986 s.54(13), (14); 1988 Sch.12 para.102.
54(1)	1986 s.54(1).
(2)	1986 s.54(2); Law Com. Rec. No. 6.
(3)	1986 s.54(7).
(4)	1986 s.54(6).
(5), (6)	1986 s.54(12).
55	1986 s.54(8) to (11).
56(1)	1986 s.55(1), (2).
(2)	1986 s.55(2).
(3)	1986 s.55(1).
(4), (5)	1986 s.55(3), (4).
57(1)	1944 s.15(4); 1946 s.2(5), Sch.1 para.2(1).
(2)	1944 s.15(4); 1946 Sch.1 para.2(1).
(3)	1944 s.15(4A); 1946 Sch.1 para.2(2); 1993 s.282(2), (4).
(4)	1944 s.15(4); 1946 s.2(5), Sch.1 para.2(1); drafting.
58(1)	1944 s.15(5).
(2)	1944 s.15(5); 1993 Sch.19 para.7.
(3)	Drafting.
59(1)	1944 s.15(3).
(2)	1944 s.15(3); 1946 Sch.2 Pt.II.
(3)	1944 s.15(3); 1946 Sch.2 Pt.II.
(4)	1944 s.15(3); 1946 Sch.2 Pt.II.
(5)	1946 Sch.1 para.2(1).
60(1)	1946 Sch.1 para.1; 1980 Sch.3 para.8.
(2), (3)	1946 Sch.1 para.6.
(4) to (6)	1946 Sch.1 para.7.
(7)	Reverter of Sites Act 1987 (c.15) s.8(1).
61(1)	1946 Sch.1 para.1; 1980 Sch.3 para.8.
(2), (3)	1946 Sch.1 para.6.
(4)	1946 Sch.1 para.3.
(5)	1946 Sch.1 para.4.
(6)	1946 Sch.1 para.5.
62(1)	1946 s.16(1) ("site").
(2), (3)	1946 Sch.1 para.8.
(4)	1946 Sch.1 para.9; 1992FHE Sch.8 para.14.
63(1)	1953 s.2; 1980 Sch.3 para.9.
(2)	1953 s.2.
(3)	1953 s.2; 1988 s.114, Sch.12 para.8.
64(1)	1946 s.1(1); 1953 s.3; 1968 Sch.1 para.6; 1980 Sch.3 para.6.
(2)	1946 s.1(1).
(3)	1946 s.1(1); 1953 s.3; 1967 s.2.
65	1993 s.281.
66	1988 s.212.
67(1), (2)	1944 s.105(1).
(3)	1944 s.105(2); 1968 Sch.1 para.4(2); 1993 Sch.19 para.23(a).

(4)	1944 s.105(2); 1993 Sch.19 para.23(a).
68	1993 s.282(1).
69	1993 s.283.
70	1993 s.284.
71	1944 s.99(3).
72	1944 s.65.
73	1946 s.4(1).
74	1946 s.6.
75	1993 s.285.
76(1)	1986 s.1(1).
(2)	1986 s.1(2).
(3), (4)	1986 s.1(3), (5).
(5)	1986 s.1(6).
77(1) to (7)	1986 s.2.
(8)	Drafting.
78(1)	1986 s.65(1) ("co-opted governor").
(2)	1944 s.114(1) ("foundation governors"); 1980 Sch.1 para.13(a).
(3)	1986 s.65(1) ("parent governor").
(4)	1986 s.65(1) ("teacher governor").
(5)	1986 s.65(1) ("parent governor"; "teacher governor").
79(1), (2)	1986 s.3(1) to (5).
(3), (4)	1986 s.3(6), (7).
80(1)	1986 s.7(1).
(2)	1986 s.7(2); National Health Service and Community Care Act 1990 (c.19) Sch.9 para.31; 1995HA Sch.1 para.112.
(3) to (5)	1986 s.7(3) to (5).
(6)	1986 s.7(6).
(7)	1986 s.7(6).
(8)	1986 s.7(6).
(9)	1986 s.7(7).
81(1)	1986 s.5(1).
(2)	1986 s.5(3).
(3)	1986 s.5(2).
(4), (5)	1986 s.5(4).
82(1)	1986 s.11(1).
(2)	1986 s.11(2).
(3)	1986 s.11(2); 1993 Sch.19 para.91(a); Law Com. Rec. No. 3.
(4)	1986 s.11(3); 1993 Sch.19 para.91(d); Law Com. Rec. No. 7.
(5), (6)	1986 s.11(4), (5).
(7)	1986 s.11(6); 1993 Sch.19 para.91(d); Law Com. Rec. No. 7.
83	1986 s.14.
84(1)	1986 s.4(1), (2).
(2)	1986 s.4(3).
(3)	1986 s.4(2).
(4) to (6)	1986 s.4(4) to (6).
85	1986 s.4A; 1993 s.271(1).
86	1986 s.13(1) to (3).
87(1)	1986 s.13(4).
(2)	1986 s.13(7), (9).
(3)	1986 s.13(8).
(4)	1986 s.13(5).
(5)	1986 s.13(6), (9).
88(1)	1993 s.238(1), (8); drafting.
(2)	Drafting.

89(1)	1986 s.9(1).
(2)	1986 s.9(1A); 1993 s.271(3)(a).
(3)	1986 s.9(2).
(4)	1986 s.9(3).
(5), (6)	1986 Sch.1 para.1(1), (2).
90(1), (2)	1986 s.10(1).
(3)	1986 s.10(3).
(4)	1986 s.10(2).
(5)	1986 s.10(4).
(6)	1986 s.10(7).
91(1)	1986 s.10(5).
(2)	1986 s.10(6).
92(1)	1986 Sch.1 para.2(1).
(2)	1986 Sch.1 para.2(1).
(3)	1986 Sch.1 para.2(2).
(4)	1986 Sch.1 para.2(3).
93	1986 Sch.1 para.3.
94(1)	1986 s.9(4).
(2)	1986 s.9(5); 1993 Sch.19 para.90; Law Com. Rec. No. 8.
(3)	1986 s.9(4).
95(1)	1986 s.9(6).
(2)	1986 s.9(7).
(3)	1986 s.9(7); 1993 s.271(3)(b).
(4)	1986 s.9(8).
96(1)	1986 s.12(1); 1993 Sch.19 para.92(a).
(2)	1986 s.12(2); 1993 Sch.19 para.92(b).
(3)	1986 s.12(4); 1993 Sch.19 para.92(d).
(4)	1986 Sch.2 para.5(2); 1993 Sch.19 para.109(c).
(5)	1986 Sch.2 para.5(1).
97(1)	1986 s.12(1), (2), (9).
(2)	1986 s.12(4).
(3)	1986 ss.12(5), (9), 65(1) ("promoters"); Law Com. Rec. No. 9.
(4)	1986 ss.12(6), (9), 65(1) ("promoters"); Law Com. Rec. No. 9.
(5)	1986 ss.12(7), 65(1) ("promoters"); Law Com. Rec. No. 9.
(6)	1986 s.12(8).
(7)	1986 Sch.2 para.5(2).
(8)	1986 Sch.2 para.5(1).
98	Drafting.
99(1)	1986 Sch.2 para.3(1).
(2)	1986 Sch.2 para.3(7).
(3)	Drafting.
100(1), (2)	Law Com. Rec. No. 10.
(3)	1986 Sch.2 para.3(6).
(4)	1986 Sch.2 para.3(6); drafting.
101(1)	1988 s.51(2)(a)(i); 1993 s.274(4).
(2)	1988 s.51(2)(a)(ii).
(3)	1988 s.33(2), (4); 1992FHE s.12(5).
(4)	1988 s.33(4); 1992FHE s.12(5).
(5)	1988 s.33(5).
(6)	1988 s.51(2)(b).
102	1988 s.33(3).
103	1988 s.33(1), (2).
104(1), (2)	1988 s.34(1), (2).
(3)	1988 s.34(4); 1993 s.274(1).

(4) to (6)	1988 s.34(5) to (7)
105(1)	1988 s.33(4).
(2)	1988 s.33(5).
(3)	1988 ss.33(4), 38(4), 51(1) ("expenditure of a capital nature").
106(1)	1988 s.38(1).
(2)	1988 s.38(1), (2).
(3)	1988 s.38(2).
(4)	1988 s.38(3).
(5)	1988 s.38(3A); 1992FHE s.12(7).
(6)	1988 s.33(5).
107(1)	1988 s.39(1); S.I. 1991/1890; S.I. 1992/110.
(2)	1988 s.39(4); S.I. 1991/1890; S.I. 1992/110.
108	1988 s.39(10).
109(1)	1988 s.39(11).
(2)	1988 s.39(12).
(3)	1988 s.39(11).
110(1)	1988 s.40(1).
(2)	1988 s.40(2); 1993 s.274(3).
(3) to (5)	1988 s.40(3) to (5).
111	1988 s.35(1), (2); 1993 s.274(2).
112(1) to (3)	1988 s.35(3); 1993 s.274(2).
(4)	1988 s.35(4); 1993 s.274(2).
113(1), (2)	1988 s.35(5); 1993 s.274(2).
(3), (4)	1988 s.35(6); 1993 s.274(2).
(5)	1988 s.35(4); 1993 s.274(2).
114	1988 s.35(7), (8); 1993 s.274(2).
115	1988 s.33(6)(a), (b).
116(1) to (3)	1988 s.36(1) to (3).
(4)	1988 s.36(4); 1993 Sch.19 para.125(a).
(5)	1988 s.36(5).
(6)	1988 s.36(5A); 1992FHE s.12(6).
(7)	1988 s.36(5B); 1993 Sch.19 para.125(b).
(8)	1988 s.36(6).
117(1)	1988 s.37(1).
(2), (3)	1988 s.37(2).
(4), (5)	1988 s.37(3).
(6)	1988 s.37(4).
118(1) to (3)	1988 s.37(5).
(4), (5)	1988 s.37(6), (7).
119	1988 s.37(8), (9).
120	1988 s.43; 1993 s.276.
121	1988 s.42(1).
122(1), (2)	1988 s.42(2), (3).
(3)	Drafting.
(4)	1988 s.42(4); 1993 s.275(1)(c).
(5)	1988 s.42(7).
(6)	1988 s.42(8); 1993 s.275(1)(d).
(7)	1988 s.42(9).
123	1988 s.42A; 1993 s.275(2).
124(1)	1988 s.50(2), (5).
(2)	1988 s.50(3)
(3)	Drafting.
(4)	1988 s.50(6).
(5)	1988 s.50(10).

(6) to (8)	1988 s.50(7) to (9).
125(1)	1988 s.49(1).
(2), (3)	1988 s.49(2).
(4)	1988 s.49(3).
126	Drafting.
127(1), (2)	1986 s.1(1), (2).
(3), (4)	1986 s.1(4), (5).
128(1) to (3)	1986 s.2(1) to (3).
(4) to (6)	1986 s.2(5) to (7).
(7)	Drafting.
129(1)	1988 s.51(3).
(2), (3)	1988 s.51(4), (5).
(4)	1988 s.51(4).
(5)	1988 s.51(6).
130	1986 s.16(1).
131	1986 s.16(2).
132	1986 s.16(3); Law Com. Rec. No. 11.
133(1) to (3)	1986 s.34.
(4)	Drafting.
(5)	1986 s.35(1).
(6)	Drafting.
134(1)	1944 s.24(2).
(2), (3)	1944 s.24(2), proviso (a).
(4)	1944 s.24(2), proviso (b).
(5)	1944 s.22(4); 1986 Sch.4 para.2; 1993 Sch.13 para.4(6).
(6)	1944 s.22(5); 1993 Sch.13 para.4(4).
(7)	Drafting.
135(1) to (4)	1986 s.40(1) to (4).
(5), (6)	1986 s.40(6), (7).
(7)	Drafting.
(8)	1986 s.40(5).
136(1), (2)	1988 s.44(1), (2); Law Com. Rec. No. 12.
(3)	1988 s.44(3), (5).
137(1), (2)	1988 s.45(1), (2).
(3), (4)	1988 s.45(3).
(5)	1988 s.45(9).
(6)	1988 s.45(10).
138(1)	1988 s.45(1), (4).
(2)	1988 s.45(6).
(3)	1988 s.45(5).
(4)	1988 s.45(7).
(5)	1988 s.45(8).
139(1), (2)	1988 s.46(2).
(3) to (6)	1988 s.46(3) to (6).
(7)	1988 s.235(2)(f); 1996ER Sch.1 para.37(5).
140	1988 s.47.
141(1)	1988 ss.44(4), 45(11).
(2)	1988 s.44(4); Law Com. Rec. No. 12.
(3)	1988 s.45(11).
(4)	1988 s.51(6).
142	Drafting.
143(1), (2)	1944 s.27(2).
(3)	1944 s.27(2) proviso.
(4) to (6)	1944 s.27(3) to (5); 1988 Sch.1 para.2(1).

(7)	Drafting.
144(1), (2)	1944 s.28(3), Sch.3 para.7; 1988 Sch.1 para.3(2).
(3)	1944 s.28(4); 1988 Sch.1 para.3(2).
(4)	Drafting.
145	1944 s.28(2); 1988 Sch.1 para.3(2).
146(1)	1944 s.30.
(2) to (4)	1944 s.30; 1988 Sch.1 para.4(b).
147(1)	1986 s.21(1); 1988 s.115; S.I. 1996/951 art.3(1).
(2)	1986 s.21(4); 1988 s.115.
(3)	1986 s.21(4); 1988 s.115; S.I. 1996/951 art.3(1).
148(1) to (4)	S.I. 1996/951 art.3(2) to (5).
(5)	Drafting.
149(1), (2)	1986 s.42(1), (2); 1993 Sch.13 para.5.
(3), (4)	1986 s.42(3); 1993 Sch.13 para.5.
(5)	1986 s.42(4); 1993 Sch.13 para.5; S.I. 1996/951 art.5.
150(1)	1944 s.22(3); 1993 Sch.13 para.4(2), (6).
(2)	1944 s.22(1).
(3)	1944 s.22(5); 1993 Sch.13 para.4(4).
151(1) to (3)	1944 s.22(3A) to (3C); 1993 Sch.13 para.4(3).
(4), (5)	1944 s.22(3D); 1993 Sch.13 para.4(3).
(6)	1944 s.22(3E); 1993 Sch.13 para.4(3).
(7)	1944 s.22(6); 1978IA s.17(2)(a); 1993 Sch.13 para.4(5).
(8)	Drafting.
152(1), (2)	1944 s.22(1); 1993 Sch.13 para.4(6).
(3), (4)	1944 s.22(2); 1993 Sch.13 para.4(6).
(5)	Drafting.
153	1986 s.21(5); 1988 s.115.
154(1)	1986 s.22.
(2)	1986 s.22(d).
(3)	1986 s.22(a); 1993 Sch.19 para.95.
(4)	1986 s.22(b).
(5)	1986 s.22(c).
(6)	1986 s.22(e).
155	1986 s.28.
156(1)	1986 s.22(f).
(2), (3)	1993 s.261(1), (2).
157(1)	Law Com. Rec. No. 13.
(2)	1986 s.23(a); Law Com. Rec. No. 13.
(3)	1986 s.23(b).
(4)	1986 s.23(a), (b); Law Com. Rec. No. 13.
(5)	1986 s.23(a); Law Com. Rec. No. 13.
158	Drafting.
159(1) to (4)	1986 s.26(1) to (4).
(5), (6)	1986 s.26(5).
(7)	1986 s.26(1), (2).
160	1986 s.27.
161(1)	1986 s.30(1).
(2)	Drafting.
(3)	1986 s.30(3).
(4)	1986 s.30(4).
162(1), (2)	1986 s.31(1), (2).
(3)	Drafting.
163	1986 s.31(7), (8).
164(1)	1986 Sch.1 paras.4, 5.

(2)	1986 Sch.1 para.4(1).
(3)	1986 Sch.1 para.4(2).
(4) to (7)	1986 Sch.1 para.5.
165	1986 s.32.
166	Drafting.
167(1)	1980 s.12(1).
(2)	1980 s.12(2).
(3)	1993 s.273(1).
(4)	1980 s.12(1A); 1993 s.229(1).
(5)	1992FHE s.59(3), (4).
(6)	1993 s.273(2).
168(1)	1980 s.12(3); 1993 s.229(2).
(2)	1980 s.12(3).
(3)	1993 s.229(3).
(4)	1980 s.12(3).
(5), (6)	1980 s.16(3A), (3B); 1988 Sch.12 para.81.
169(1)	1980 s.12(4), (5); 1993 s.273(4).
(2)	1980 s.12(4).
(3)	1980 s.12(5).
(4)	1993 s.273(3).
(5)	1980 s.12(6).
(6)	1993 s.273(4), (5)(a).
170(1), (2)	1980 s.12(7).
(3)	1980 s.12(8).
171	1980 s.12(9).
172	1980 s.16(1).
173(1)	1944 s.14(1).
(2)	1944 s.14(1), 114(1) ("former authority"); 1946 Sch.2 Pt.II.
(3)	1944 s.14(1); 1946 Sch.2 Pt.II.
(4)	1992FHE s.59(3), (4).
(5)	1993 s.273(2).
(6)	1944 s.14(2).
(7)	1944 s.14(5).
(8)	Drafting.
174(1)	1944 s.14(3).
(2), (3)	1944 s.14(4).
175	1992FHE s.59(1), (2).
176	1986 s.16A; FHE 1992 s.12(3).
177	Drafting.
178	1988 s.222.
179(1)	1973 s.1(2); 1980 Sch.3 para.17; Law Com. Rec. No. 3.
(2)	1973 s.1(2).
180	1980 s.5.
181(1)	1986 Sch.2 para.1 ("new school"); 1988 s.48(2).
(2)	1986 Sch.2 para.1 ("relevant proposal"); 1988 s.48(2).
(3)	1988 s.48(2) ("temporary governing body"); drafting.
182	1986 s.65(2).
183	1993 s.22.
184	1993 s.23.
185	1993 s.24.
186	1993 s.25.
187	1993 s.26.
188	1993 s.27.
189	1993 s.28.

190(1)	1993 s.29(1).
(2)	1993 s.29(2); Law Com. Rec. No. 14.
(3)	1993 s.29(3).
191	1993 s.30.
192	1993 s.31.
193	1993 s.32.
194	1993 s.33.
195	1993 s.34.
196	1993 s.35.
197	1993 s.36.
198(1) to (5)	1993 s.272(1) to (5).
(6)	1964 s.1(1); 1993 Sch.19 para.38.
199(1) to (3)	1993 s.273(3) to (5).
(4)	1993 s.273(7).
200	1993 s.37.
201(1) to (8)	1993 s.38(1) to (8).
(9)	1993 s.155(8).
(10)	1993 s.38(9).
202	1993 s.39.
203	1993 s.40.
204	1993 s.41.
205	1993 s.42.
206	1993 s.43.
207	1993 s.44.
208	1993 s.45.
209	1993 s.46.
210	1993 s.47(1) to (4).
211	1993 s.48.
212	1993 s.49(1) to (3).
213	1993 s.50.
214	1993 s.51.
215	1993 s.52.
216	1993 s.53.
217	1993 s.54.
218	1993 s.55.
219(1) to (3)	1993 s.56.
(4)	1993 s.301(5).
220	1993 s.57.
221	1993 s.58.
222	1993 s.59.
223	1993 s.60.
224	1993 s.61.
225	1993 s.62.
226	1993 s.63.
227	1993 s.64.
228	1993 s.65.
229	1993 s.66.
230	1993 s.67.
231(1) to (4)	1993 s.68(1) to (4)
(5) to (7)	1993 s.68(5) to (7); 1996N s.7(2) to (4).
(8)	1993 s.68(8).
232	1993 s.69.
233	1993 s.70.
234	1993 s.71.

235	1993 s.72.
236	1993 s.73.
237	1993 s.74.
238	1993 s.75.
239	1993 s.76.
240	1993 s.77.
241	1993 s.78.
242	1993 s.79.
243	1993 s.80.
244	1993 s.81.
245	1993 s.82.
246	1993 s.83.
247	1993 s.84.
248	1993 s.85.
249	1993 s.86.
250	1993 s.87.
251	1993 s.88.
252	1993 s.89.
253	1993 s.90.
254	1993 s.91.
255	1993 s.92.
256	1993 s.93(1) to (6).
257	1993 s.94.
258	1993 s.95.
259	1993 s.96; Law Com. Rec. No. 3.
260	1993 s.97; Law Com. Rec. No. 3.
261	1993 s.98.
262	1993 s.99.
263	1993 s.100; Law Com. Rec. No. 3.
264	1993 s.101.
265	1993 s.102.
266	1993 s.103(2), (3).
267	1993 s.104.
268	1993 s.105.
269	1993 s.106.
270	1993 s.107.
271	1993 s.108.
272	1993 s.109.
273	1993 s.110.
274	1993 s.111.
275	1993 s.112.
276	1993 s.113.
277	1993 s.114.
278	1993 s.115.
279	1993 s.116.
280	1993 s.117.
281	1993 s.118.
282	1993 s.119.
283	1993 s.120.
284	1993 s.121.
285	1993 s.122.
286	1993 s.123.
287	1993 s.124.
288	1993 s.125.

289	1993 s.126.
290(1) to (7)	1993 s.127(1) to (7).
(8), (9)	1993 s.127(8).
(10), (11)	1993 s.127(9), (10).
(12)	1993 s.305(1).
(13)	1993 s.127(11).
291	1964 s.1(1); 1993 Sch.19 para.38.
292(1)	1993 s.231(1); drafting.
(2)	1993 s.232(2).
293	1993 s.128.
294	Drafting.
295	1993 s.129.
296(1)	1993 s.130(1).
(2)	1993 s.130(2); 1996N Sch.3 para.11.
297	1993 s.131.
298	1993 s.132.
299	1993 s.133.
300	1993 s.134.
301	1993 s.135.
302	1993 s.136.
303	1993 s.137.
304	1993 s.143.
305	1993 s.144.
306	1993 s.145.
307(1), (2)	1993 s.261(1), (2).
308(1)	1993 ss.267(1), 268(1).
(2)	1993 s.267(2).
(3)	1993 s.268(2).
309	1993 s.152.
310	1993 s.154.
311(1)	1993 ss.155(1) ("premises"), 305(1) ("Church in Wales school"; "Church of England school"; "Roman Catholic Church school").
(2)	1993 s.305(4).
(3)	1993 s.155(2).
(4)	1993 s.155(3).
(5)	1993 s.155(6).
(6)	1993 s.155(7)
(7)	Drafting.
(8)	1993 s.155(11).
312(1) to (4)	1993 s.156(1) to (4).
(5)	1993 ss.156(5), 305(1) ("maintained school").
313(1) to (4)	1993 s.157.
(5)	Drafting.
314	1993 s.158.
315	1993 s.159.
316	1993 s.160.
317(1) to (5)	1993 s.161(1) to (5).
(6), (7)	1993 s.161(6), (7); Disability Discrimination Act 1995 (c.50) s.29(2).
318(1), (2)	1993 s.162(1), (2)
(3)	1993 s.162(2A); 1996N Sch.3 para.12.
(4)	1993 s.162(3).
319	1993 s.163.
320	1993 s.164.
321	1993 s.165.

322(1)	1993 s.166(1); 1995HA Sch.1 para.124(2).
(2)	1993 s.166(2)
(3)	1993 s.166(3); 1995HA Sch.1 para.124(2).
(4)	1993 s.166(4).
(5)	1993 s.166(5); 1994LG(W) Sch.16 para.105(1); Local Government Changes for England Regulations 1994 (S.I. 1994/867) reg.5(6); Local Government Changes for England (Amendment) Regulations 1996 (S.I. 1996/611) reg.2.
323	1993 s.167.
324	1993 s.168.
325	1993 s.169.
326	1993 s.170.
327	1993 s.171.
328	1993 s.172.
329	1993 s.173.
330	1993 s.174.
331	1993 s.175.
332	1993 s.176; 1995HA Sch.1 para.124(3).
333	1993 s.177.
334	1993 s.178.
335	1993 s.179.
336	1993 s.180; Arbitration Act 1996 (c.23) Sch.3 para.59.
337(1)	1993 s.182(1).
(2)	Drafting.
(3), (4)	1993 s.182(2), (3).
338(1)	1993 s.183(1).
(2)	Drafting.
339	1993 s.183(2) to (10).
340	1993 s.184.
341	1993 s.185.
342	1993 s.188.
343	1993 s.231.
344(1)	Drafting.
(2)	1993 s.182(4).
345	1993 s.186.
346	1993 s.187.
347	1993 s.189.
348	1993 s.190
349	1993 s.191.
350(1)	1988 s.25(1) ("maintained school"); 1993 s.245(5).
(2)	1988 s.25(1) ("assess").
351(1)	1988 s.1(2).
(2) to (5)	1988 s.1(1).
352(1)	1988 ss.2(1), 8(2); 1993 s.241(1), Sch.19 para.114.
(2)	1988 s.2(3).
(3)	1944 s.114(1) ("sex education"); 1993 s.241(2).
353	1988 s.2(2); 1993 ss.240(1), 245(5).
354(1)	1988 s.3(1).
(2)	1988 s.3(2); S.I. 1992/1548 art.2; S.I. 1994/1814 art.2(2) to (4).
(3) to (5)	1988 s.3(2A), (2B); S.I. 1994/1814 art.2(5).
(6)	1988 s.3(4).
(7)	1988 s.3(6) ("school").
(8)	1988 s.3(7).
355(1)	1988 s.3(3); 1993 Sch.19 para.113.
(2)	1988 s.3(4).

(3)	1988 s.3(5).
(4)	1988 s.3(5A); 1993 s.240(2).
(5)	1988 s.3(6) ("class"; "school year"); 1993 s.240(3).
356(1) to (4)	1988 s.4(1) to (4).
(5) to (8)	1988 s.4(5) to (8); 1993 s.240(4).
(9)	1993 s.241(4).
357(1)	1988 s.10(2).
(2)	1988 s.10(3).
358	1993 s.244.
359(1)	1993 s.245(1).
(2)	1993 s.245(4).
(3)	1993 s.245(3).
(4)	1993 s.245(2).
(5)	1993 s.245(5).
360(1)	1988 s.14(1); 1993 s.253(1).
(2) to (4)	1988 s.14(2); 1993 Sch.15 para.4(3), Sch.19 para.118(a).
(5)	1988 s.14(7).
361(1)	1988 s.14(3); 1993 Sch.15 para.4(3), Sch.19 para.118(b); Education (School Curriculum and Assessment Authority) (Transfer of Functions) Order 1994 (S.I. 1994/645); Education (School Curriculum and Assessment Authority) (Transfer of Functions) Order 1995 (S.I. 1995/903).
(2)	1988 s.14(5); 1993 Sch.15 para.4(3), Sch.19 para.118(c).
(3), (4)	1988 s.14(6); 1993 Sch.15 para.4(3), Sch.19 para.118(d).
(5)	Drafting.
362(1), (2)	1988 s.16(1), (2).
(3), (4)	1988 s.16(3); 1993 Sch.19 para.119(a).
(5), (6)	1988 s.16(4), (5).
(7)	1988 s.16(6); 1993 Sch.15 para.4(4), Sch.19 para.119(b).
363	1988 s.17.
364	1988 s.18; 1993 Sch.19 para.120.
365(1)	1988 s.19(1).
(2) to (4)	1988 s.19(2).
(5)	1988 s.19(1).
(6)	1988 s.19(10).
366(1)	1988 s.19(3).
(2)	1988 s.19(4).
(3)	1988 s.19(4); 1993 Sch.19 para.121(a); Law Com. Rec. No. 15.
(4)	Law Com. Rec. No. 15.
(5)	1988 s.19(5); Law Com. Rec. No. 15.
(6)	1988 s.19(6); 1993 Sch.19 para.121(b); Law Com. Rec. No. 15.
(7)	Law Com. Rec. No. 15.
367(1)	1988 s.19(7).
(2), (3)	1988 s.19(8).
(4)	1988 s.19(9).
368(1)	1988 ss.20(1), 21(1).
(2)	1988 ss.20(2), 21(2); 1993 s.243.
(3)	1988 ss.20(3), 21(3); 1993 s.243.
(4), (5)	1988 ss.20(4), 21(3A); 1993 s.243.
(6), (7)	1988 ss.20(5), 21(3B); 1993 s.243.
(8)	1988 ss.20(6), 21(4).
(9)	1993 s.242(1), (3).
(10)	1988 ss.20(2), 21(2); 1993 Sch.15 para.4(5), Sch.19 para.122; drafting.
369	1988 s.227(1).
370(1)	1986 s.17(1)

(2), (3)	1986 s.17(2), (3).
371(1), (2)	1986 s.18(1).
(3)	1986 s.18(2).
(4)	1986 s.18(3).
(5)	1986 s.18(7); 1993 Sch.19 para.94.
(6)	1986 s.18(8).
(7)	1986 s.18(7); Law Com. Rec. No. 3.
(8)	Drafting.
372(1)	1986 s.18(5).
(2) to (4)	1986 s.18(6).
(5)	Drafting.
373(1), (2)	1986 s.19.
374	Drafting.
375(1)	Drafting.
(2)	1944 s.114(1) ("agreed syllabus"); 1988 Sch.1 para.6.
(3)	1988 s.8(3).
(4)	1944 s.114(1) ("agreed syllabus"), Sch.5 para.11; 1988 Sch.1 para.6.
(5)	1988 s.8(3).
376(1)	1944 s.26(1); 1988 Sch.1 para.1.
(2)	1944 s.26(2); 1988 Sch.1 para.1.
(3)	1944 s.26(3), (4); 1988 Sch.1 para.1; 1993 Sch.19 para.9.
377(1)	1944 s.27(6); 1988 Sch.1 para.2(2).
(2)	1944 s.27(1); 1988 Sch.1 para.2(1).
378(1)	1944 s.28(1); 1988 Sch.1 para.3(1).
(2), (3)	1944 s.28(1B); 1988 Sch.1 para.3(1).
(4)	1944 s.28(1C); 1988 Sch.1 para.3(1).
(5)	1944 s.28(1A); 1988 Sch.1 para.3(1).
379(1)	1993 s.138(1).
(2) to (4)	1993 s.138(9) to (11).
380	1993 s.139.
381	1993 s.140.
382	1993 s.142.
383	1993 s.141.
384	1988 s.10(1).
385(1)	1988 s.6(1), (7).
(2)	1988 s.6(2).
(3)	1988 s.6(7).
(4)	1988 s.6(3); 1993 s.138(8); Law Com. Rec. No. 16.
(5)	1988 s.6(4).
(6)	1988 s.6(5); Law Com. Rec. No. 16.
(7)	1988 s.6(6).
386(1)	1988 s.7(1); 1993 s.138(1).
(2)	1988 s.7(1); 1993 s.138(2).
(3)	1988 s.7(2); 1993 s.138(3).
(4)	1988 s.7(3); 1993 s.138(4).
(5)	1988 s.7(4); 1993 s.138(5).
(6)	1988 s.7(5); 1993 s.138(6).
(7)	1993 s.138(12).
387	1988 s.7(6); 1993 s.138(7).
388	1988 s.10(1).
389(1)	1988 s.9(3).
(2)	1988 s.9(9).
(3)	1988 s.9(4).
(4)	1988 s.9(6).

(5)	1988 s.9(7); 1993 Sch.19 para.115.
(6)	1988 s.9(8).
(7)	1988 s.9(2), (5).
390(1)	1988 s.11(1).
(2)	1988 s.11(3), (4); 1993 s.147(1).
(3)	1988 ss.11(3), 13(4).
(4)	1988 s.11(4); 1993 Sch.19 para.116(a).
(5)	1988 s.11(5).
(6)	1988 s.11(5); 1993 s.255(2).
(7)	1988 s.11(6).
391(1)	1988 s.11(1).
(2)	1988 s.11(2).
(3)	1988 s.11(7).
(4)	1988 s.11(7).
(5)	1988 s.11(8).
(6)	1988 s.11(9).
(7)	1988 s.11(10).
(8), (9)	1988 s.11(11), (12); 1993 s.147(2).
(10)	1988 s.11(13); 1993 Sch.15 para.4(2), Sch.19 para.116(b).
392(1)	1988 s.11(1).
(2)	1988 s.13(1); 1993 Sch.19 para.117.
(3)	1988 s.13(2); 1993 Sch.19 para.117.
(4)	1988 s.13(3).
(5)	1988 s.13(4).
(6)	1988 s.13(5).
(7)	1988 s.13(6).
(8)	1988 s.13(7); 1993 Sch.19 para.117.
393	1993 s.16.
394(1)	1988 ss.11(1), 12(1); 1993 s.148(a).
(2), (3)	1988 s.12(2), (3).
(4)	1988 s.12(4); 1993 s.148(b).
(5)	1988 s.12(1).
(6)	1988 s.12(9); 1993 s.148(c).
(7)	1988 s.12(10).
(8)	1988 s.12(11); 1993 s.148(d).
395(1)	1988 s.12(5).
(2)	1988 s.12(6).
(3), (4)	1988 s.12(7).
(5)	1988 s.12(8).
(6)	1988 s.12(5), (6).
(7)	1988 s.12(9); 1993 s.148(c).
(8)	1988 s.12(10).
396(1)	1988 s.12A(1), (3); 1993 s.257.
(2)	1988 s.12A(2); 1993 s.257.
397	1993 s.258.
398	1988 s.9(1), 9(1A); 1992FHE s.12(4); 1994 Sch.2 para.8(2).
399	1944 s.67(3); 1988 Sch.1 para.4, Sch.12 para.4.
400(1), (2)	1988 s.5(1).
(3)	1988 s.5(2).
(4)	1988 s.10(2).
(5)	1988 s.5(3).
401(1)	1988 s.24(1); 1992FHE Sch.8 para.28.
(2)	1988 s.24(2); 1993 Sch.19 para.124.
(3), (4)	1988 s.24(3), (4).

(5)	1988 s.235(2)(c).
402(1)	1988 s.117(1).
(2)	1988 s.117(2); 1993 s.240(5).
(3) to (5)	1988 s.117(3) to (5).
(6)	1988 s.118(7), (8).
403(1)	1986 ss.46, 46A; 1988 Sch.12 para.34.
(2)	1986 s.46.
404(1), (2)	1993 s.241(5)
(3)	1993 s.241(6)
405	1988 s.17A; 1993 s.241(3).
406(1), (2)	1986 ss.44(1), (2), 46A; 1988 Sch.12 para.34.
(3)	1986 s.44(1).
407(1)	1986 ss.45, 46A; 1988 Sch.12 para.34.
(2)	1986 s.45.
408(1)	1988 s.22(1).
(2)	1988 s.22(2); 1992(S) Sch.4 para.6(2).
(3)	1988 s.22(3); 1993 Sch.19 para.123.
(4)	1988 s.22(1); Law Com. Rec. No. 17.
(5)	1988 s.22(4).
(6)	1988 s.22(5); 1992(S) Sch.4 para.6(3), (4).
(7), (8)	1988 s.22(6), (7).
409(1) to (3)	1988 s.23(1).
(4)	1988 s.23(2).
410	1988 s.25(2); Law Com. Rec. No. 17.
411(1), (2)	1980 s.6(1), (2).
(3)	1980 s.6(3); 1988 s.30(2).
(4)	1980 s.6(4).
(5)	1980 s.6(5); 1978IA s.17(2)(a).
(6)	1988 s.26(9).
(7)	1988 s.26(10).
(8)	1980 s.38(4).
412	1986 s.33.
413(1)	1980 s.6(6); 1988 s.30(3).
(2) to (4)	1980 s.6(7) to (9); 1993 s.270.
414(1), (2)	1980 s.8(1), (2).
(3), (4)	1980 s.8(3); 1988 s.31(2).
(5)	1980 s.8(4).
(6) to (8)	1980 s.8(5), (5A), (6); 1992(S) Sch.4 para.4(1).
(9)	1980 s.8(7).
415	Drafting.
416(1)	1988 s.26(1).
(2) to (7)	1988 s.26(3) to (8).
(8)	1988 s.26(1), (3), (4).
417(1)	1988 ss.27(1), (2), 32(4).
(2), (3)	1988 s.27(3).
(4), (5)	1988 s.27(9).
418(1)	1988 ss.27(1), (2), 32(4); Education Reform Act 1988 (Commencement No.9) Order 1991 (S.I. 1991/409).
(2)	1988 s.27(3).
(3)	1988 s.27(3), (9).
419(1)	1988 s.29(7).
(2) to (5)	1988 s.29(1) to (4).
420(1) to (3)	1988 s.27(4) to (6).
(4), (5)	1988 s.27(7).

421(1)	1988 s.27(8).
(2)	1988 s.32(1).
422(1) to (6)	1986 Sch.2 para.19.
(7)	1986 s.65(1) ("promoters"), Sch.2 para.1; drafting; Law Com. Rec. No. 9.
423(1)	1980 s.7(1); 1993 Sch.19 para.73.
(2), (3)	1980 s.7(2), (3).
(4)	1980 s.7(4).
(5)	1980 s.7(5).
(6)	1980 s.38(4).
424(1)	1980 s.9(1); 1988 s.31(3).
(2)	1980 s.9(1A); 1988 s.31(3).
(3)	1980 s.9(2); 1981 Sch.3 para.14; 1992(S) Sch.4 para.4(2); 1993 Sch.19 para.74.
425	Drafting.
426	1993 s.149(1) to (4).
427	1993 s.150.
428	1993 s.151.
429	Drafting.
430(1) to (8)	1993 s.260.
(9)	1993 s.305(1) ("maintained school").
431(1) to (6)	1993 s.13(1) to (6).
(7), (8)	1993 ss.13(7), (8), 305(1) ("maintained school").
432	1993 s.14.
433(1), (2)	1948 s.4(2).
(3)	1948 s.4(3).
(4)	1948 s.4(3A); 1996N Sch.3 para.2.
(5)	1948 s.4(2).
434(1)	1944 s.80(1).
(2)	1944 s.80(1A); 1988 Sch.12 para.58.
(3)	1948 s.4(6).
(4)	1944 s.80(1); 1993 Sch.19 para.21.
(5)	1944 s.114(1); 1993 s.155(1), Sch.19 para.24(a)(ii).
(6)	1944 s.80(2).
435	1948 s.4(1).
436(1)	1980 s.9(1A); 1988 ss.29(5), 31(3); 1993 s.155(6).
(2)	1988 s.29(5), (6); 1993 s.149(5).
437(1) to (7)	1993 s.192(1) to (7).
(8)	1993 ss.192(8), 197(6), 198(4), 305(1) ("maintained school").
438	1993 s.193.
439	1993 s.194.
440	1993 s.195.
441	1993 s.196.
442	1993 s.197(1) to (5).
443(1) to (3)	1993 s.198(1) to (3).
(4)	1993 s.201(2).
444(1) to (4)	1993 s.199(1) to (4).
(5)	1993 s.199(5); Units of Measurement Regulations 1995 (S.I. 1995/1804) Reg.3.
(6), (7)	1993 s.199(6), (7).
(8)	1993 s.201(2).
(9)	1993 s.199(8).
445	1993 s.200.
446	1993 s.201(1).
447	1993 s.202.
448	1993 s.203.
449	1988 s.118(7).

450(1)	1988 s.106(1).
(2)	1988 s.106(1A); 1992FHE s.12(9); 1994 Sch.2 para.8(3).
451(1), (2)	1988 s.106(2).
(3)	1988 s.106(3), (4); 1993 s.280.
(4)	1988 s.106(4).
(5)	1988 s.106(3), (4); 1993 Sch.19 para.127.
452(1) to (4)	1988 s.107(1) to (4).
(5)	1988 s.107(5), (6).
(6)	1988 s.106(9).
453(1)	1988 s.106(5).
(2), (3)	1988 s.108.
454(1)	1988 s.106(6).
(2)	1988 s.118(3).
(3), (4)	1988 s.106(7), (8).
455(1)	1988 s.109(1).
(2)	1988 s.109(2).
(3)	1988 ss.109(2), 110(5).
456(1)	1988 s.109(3); 1978IA s.17(2)(a).
(2) to (8)	1988 s.109(4) to (10).
457(1)	1988 s.110(1); 1993 Sch.19 para.128.
(2), (3)	1988 s.110(2).
(4)	1988 s.110(3); Disability Living Allowance and Disability Working Allowance Act 1991 (c.21) Sch.3 para.12; Jobseekers Act 1995 (c.18) Sch.2 para.17.
(5)	1988 s.110(4).
458(1) to (4)	1988 s.111(1) to (3) and (5); 1993 Sch.19 para.129.
(5)	1988 s.111(6).
459	1988 s.118(5).
460(1), (2)	1988 s.118(1), (2).
(3)	1988 s.118(4).
461	1988 s.118(6).
462(1)	1988 s.118(7)(a), (e).
(2)	1988 s.106(10).
(3)	1988 s.106(11).
(4)	1988 s.118(7)(d).
(5)	1988 s.118(7)(d), (8).
463	1944 s.114(1) ("independent school"); 1980 s.34(1); 1988 Sch.12 para.7.
464(1) to (3)	1944 s.70(1); Transfer of Functions (Education and Employment) Order 1995 (S.I 1995/2986) art.11(2).
(4)	Drafting.
465(1)	1944 s.70(1).
(2)	1944 s.70(1) proviso (a).
(3)	1944 s.70(1) proviso (b).
(4)	1944 s.114(1) ("provisionally registered school"; "registered school").
466(1)	1944 s.70(3).
(2)	1944 s.70(3A); 1980 s.34(6).
(3)	1944 s.70(3).
467(1)	1944 s.70(4); 1980 s.34(7).
(2)	1944 s.70(4A); 1993 s.292(2).
(3)	1944 s.70(4); 1980 s.34 (7).
(4)	Drafting.
468	1944 s.71(4); 1993 s.290(1).
469(1)	1944 s.71(1); Children Act 1989 (c.41) Sch.13 para.9; 1993 s.290(2).
(2), (3)	1944 s.71(1).
(4)	1944 s.71(2); 1993 s.290(2).

(5)	1944 s.71(3).
(6)	1944 s.71(5); 1993 s.290(1).
470(1)	1944 s.72(1).
(2)	1944 s.72(2); 1993 s.290(2).
471(1)	1944 s.72(3).
(2)	1944 s.72(3) proviso; 1993 s.290(2).
472	1944 s.72(4); 1993 s.290(2).
473(1)	1944 s.73(2).
(2)	1944 s.73(3); 1993 s.290(2).
474	1944 s.74.
475	1944 s.73(1).
476(1)	Drafting.
(2), (3)	1944 s.75(1).
(4)	1944 s.75(2); Arbitration Act 1996 (c.23) Sch.3 para.4.
(5)	1944 s.75(3).
477	1944 s.73(5); 1946 Sch.2 Pt.I; 1978IA s.17(2)(a).
478(1)	1944 s.73(4).
(2)	1944 ss.70(3), 73(2), (3); Criminal Justice Act 1982 (c.48) Sch.3.
479(1) to (3)	1980 s.17(1) to (3).
(4)	1980 s.17(2).
(5)	1980 s.17(4), (5).
(6), (7)	1980 s.17(10).
480(1), (2)	1980 s.17(6), (7).
(3)	1980 s.17(9).
(4)	1980 s.17(8), (9).
481	1980 s.18.
482(1)	1988 s.105(1).
(2)	1988 s.105(2).
(3)	1988 s.105(1), (2).
(4)	1988 s.105(3).
(5)	1988 s.218(2B); 1993 s.291; 1994 Sch.2 para.8(4).
483(1), (2)	1988 s.105(4).
(3), (4)	1988 s.105(5), (6).
484(1)	1984 s.1(1), (2); 1993 s.278(2).
(2)	1984 s.1(2), (6).
(3), (4)	1984 s.1(3), (4); 1993 s.278(2).
(5)	1984 s.1(5).
(6)	1984 s.1(7).
(7)	Drafting.
485	1944 s.100(1)(b); 1988 s.213(3).
486	1988 s.213(1); Transfer of Functions (Science) Order 1995 (S.I. 1995/2985) Sch. para.5.
487	1980 s.21(1).
488	1988 s.210.
489(1)	1944 s.100(3); 1980 s.21(2); 1984 s.1(4); 1988 ss.210(3), 213(2).
(2)	1984 s.1(4A); 1993 s.278(4).
(3), (4)	1973 s.1(2).
490	1988 s.211; 1978IA s.17(2)(a).
491(1)	1944 s.100(1)(c).
(2)	1944 s.100(3).
492(1) to (4)	1986 s.51(1) to (4); 1993 s.279(1).
(5)	1986 s.51(11); 1993 Sch.19 para.103(d).
(6)	1986 s.51(7), (8); 1993 Sch.19 para.103(a).
493(1)	1986 s.52(1); 1992FHE Sch.8 para.25.
(2)	1986 s.52(2); 1993 Sch.19 para.104.

(3)	1986 s.52(3); 1992FHE Sch.8 para.25.
(4)	1986 s.52(4).
494	1993 s.262.
495(1), (2)	1944 s.67(1).
(3)	1944 s.67(2).
496(1)	1944 s.68.
(2)	1944 s.68; 1988 s.219(2).
497(1)	1944 s.99(1).
(2)	1944 s.99(1); 1988 s.219(3).
(3)	1944 s.99(1).
498(1)	1944 s.99(2).
(2)	1944 s.99(2); 1988 s.219(3).
499	1993 s.297.
500	1993 s.232.
501	1993 s.233.
502	1993 s.234.
503(1) to (6)	1993 s.235(1) to (6).
(7)	1993 s.235(8).
504	1993 s.236.
505(1) to (7)	1993 s.237(1) to (7).
(8)	1993 ss.237(8), 305(1) ("maintained school")
506	1944 s.69(2); Criminal Justice Act 1967 (c.80) Sch.3; 1978IA s.17(2)(a); Medical Act 1983 (c.54) Sch. 6 para.11.
507(1)	1944 s.93.
(2)	1944 s.93; 1972LG s.272(2); 1993 s.235(7).
508(1)	1944 s.53(1).
(2)	1944 s.53(1); 1948 Sch.1 Pt.I; 1988 Sch.12 para.54.
(3)	1944 s.53(2).
509(1), (2)	1944 s.55(1); 1992FHE Sch.8 para.5.
(3)	1944 s.55(2); 1948 Sch.1 Pt.I; 1988 Sch.12 para.55; 1992FHE Sch.8 para.5.
(4)	1944 s.55(3); 1986 s.53; 1992FHE Sch.8 para.5; 1993 Sch.19 para.15.
(5)	1944 s.55(4); 1992FHE Sch.8 para.5.
(6)	1944 s.55(5); 1992FHE Sch.8 para.5.
510(1)	1948 s.5(1); 1988 s.100(4).
(2)	1948 s.5(1); 1953 Sch.1; 1981 Sch.3 para.7.
(3)	1948 s.5(2); 1988 s.100(4).
(4)	1948 s.5(3); 1980 s.29(1); 1988 s.100(4), Sch.12 para.61; 1992FHE Sch.8 para.16.
(5)	1948 s.5(4); 1988 s.100(4).
(6)	1948 s.5(4).
511(1)	1948 s.5(5).
(2), (3)	1948 s.5(6).
(4)	1948 s.5(6A); 1980 s.29(2).
512(1)	1980 s.22(1); Social Security Act 1986 (c.50) s.77(1).
(2)	1980 s.22(2); Social Security Act 1986 (c.50) s.77(2).
(3)	1980 s.22(3); Social Security Act 1986 (c.50) s.77(2); Jobseekers Act 1995 (c.18) Sch.2 para.3.
(4)	1980 s.22(1).
(5)	1980 s.22(3B); 1992FHE Sch.8 para.17.
513	1944 s.78(2).
514(1)	1944 s.50(1); 1946 Sch.2 Pt.I; 1981 Sch.3 para.3; 1988 s.100(2).
(2)	1944 s.50(1); 1948 Sch.1 Pt.I; 1981 Sch.3 para.3.
(3)	1944 s.50(2); 1946 Sch.2 Pt.I; 1993 Sch.19 para.12.
(4)	1944 s.52(1).
(5)	1944 s.52(1) proviso; 1981 Sch.3 para.4.

(6)	1944 s.52(2).
(7)	1944 s.52(3).
515(1)	1980 s.26(1).
(2)	1980 s.26(3).
(3)	1980 s.26(4).
(4)	1980 s.26(5); 1978IA s.17(2)(a).
(5)	1980 s.26(6).
516	1993 s.295.
517(1)	1953 s.6(2); 1993 Sch.19 para.31(a).
(2)	1953 s.6(2)(a)(i).
(3)	1953 s.6(2)(a)(ii); 1981 Sch.3 para.8.
(4)	1953 s.6(2)(a)(iii).
(5)	1953 s.6(2)(b); 1981 Sch.3 para.8.
(6)	1993 Sch.19 para.31(b) to (f).
(7)	1993 s.308(3).
518	1944 s.81; 1988 Sch.12 para.6; 1992FHE Sch.8 para.11.
519(1)	1986 s.58(1); 1988 Sch.12 para.103; 1993 Sch.19 para.106.
(2)	1986 s.58(2).
(3)	1986 s.58(5); 1988 Sch.12 para.103.
(4), (5)	1986 s.58(6).
(6)	1986 s.58(7).
520(1), (2)	1944 s.48(4); 1973NHSR Sch.4 para.7; National Health Service Act 1977 (c.49) Sch.15 para.2; 1978IA s.17(2)(a).
(3)	Drafting.
521(1), (2)	1944 s.54(1).
(3)	1944 s.54(2), (8); Medical Act 1983 (c.54) Sch.6 para.11.
(4)	1944 s.54(1); 1993 Sch.19 para.14(a).
522(1)	1944 s.54(2).
(2) to (4)	1944 s.54(3).
(5)	1944 s.54(5).
523(1), (2)	1944 s.54(4); S.I. 1968/1699 art.5; 1972LG s.179(3).
(3)	1944 s.54(9); 1994LG(W) Sch.16 para.8.
(4)	1944 s.54(8); Medical Act 1983 (c.54) Sch.6 para.11.
524(1), (2)	1944 s.54(7).
(3)	1944 s.54(7); 1993 Sch.19 para.14(c).
525(1)	1944 s.54(6).
(2)	1944 s.54(6).
(3)	1944 s.54(6); 1993 Sch.19 para.14(b).
526	1944 s.82.
527	1944 s.83.
528	1944 s.41(2A), (2B); Disability Discrimination Act 1995 (c.50) s.30(8).
529(1)	1944 s.85(1).
(2), (3)	1944 s.85(2), (3); 1980 Sch.3 para.3.
530(1)	1944 s.90(1); Acquisition of Land (Authorisation Procedure) Act 1946 (c.49) Sch.4; 1948 s.10(1); 1988 Sch.12 para.59.
(2)	1944 s.90(1) proviso; Acquisition of Land (Authorisation Procedure) Act 1946 (c.49) Sch.4.
(3)	1944 s.90(1A); 1993 s.282(3).
531(1)	1948 s.10(2); 1972LG s.272(2); 1988 Sch.12 para.62.
(2)	1948 s.10(3).
532	1944 s.88; 1978IA s.17(2)(a).
533(1), (2)	1980 s.22(4).
(3)	1980 s.22(4A); 1993 Sch.19 para.79.
534(1) to (4)	1980 s.22(3A); 1988 Sch.12 para.24.

(5)	1980 s.22(3B); 1992FHE Sch.8 para.17.
535(1)	1980 s.26(2).
(2)	1980 s.26(3).
(3)	1980 s.26(4).
(4)	1980 s.26(5); 1978IA s.17(2)(a).
(5)	1980 s.26(6).
536(1), (2)	1944 s.48(4); 1973NHSR Sch.4 para.7; National Health Service Act 1977 (c.49) Sch.15 para.2; 1978IA s.17(2)(a); 1988 Sch.12 para.2.
537(1) to (6)	1992(S) s.16(1) to (6).
(7)	1992(S) s.16(7); 1993 s.263.
(8) to (10)	1992(S) s.16(8) to (10).
(11)	1992(S) s.19(2)
(12), (13)	1992(S) s.16(11), (12).
538	1986 s.56, Sch.2 para.13(2).
539	1993 s.153.
540(1)	1993 s.264(1).
(2)	1993 ss.264(2), 305(1) ("maintained school").
541(1) to (3)	1993 s.265.
(4)	1993 ss. 265(1), 305(1) ("maintained school").
542(1)	1944 s.10(1); 1988 Sch.12 para.1.
(2) to (4)	1944 s.10(2); 1988 Sch.12 para.1.
543	1944 s.10(2) proviso; 1948 s.7(1); 1968 s.3(3).
544(1)	1988 s.218(7); 1992FHE Sch.8 para.49; 1993 Sch.19 para.136.
(2)	1988 s.218(7).
(3)	1988 s.218(12).
545(1)	1944 s.63(2); 1993 Sch.19 para.18.
(2)	1988 s.218(8); 1993 Sch.19 para.19.
546(1)	1988 s.218(1)(e).
(2)	1988 s.218(12).
547(1)	1982LG(MP) s.40(1).
(2)	1982LG(MP) s.40(2); 1988 Sch.12 para.29.
(3)	1982LG(MP) s.40(3).
(4), (5)	1982LG(MP) s.40(4), (5); 1988 Sch.12 para.29.
(6)	1982LG(MP) s.40(6).
(7), (8)	1982LG(MP) s.40(7), (8); 1988 Sch.12 para.29.
548(1)	1986 s.47(1); 1993 s.293(2).
(2)	1986 s.47(1A); 1993 s.293(2).
(3)	1986 s.47(5); 1988 Sch.12 para.35; 1993 s.293(3), Sch.19 para.101(a).
(4)	1986 s.47(6); 1993 Sch.19 para.101(b).
(5)	1986 s.47(7).
(6)	1986 s.47(4).
549(1), (2)	1986 s.47(2), (3).
(3)	1986 s.47(1B); 1993 s.293(2).
(4)	1986 s.47(10).
(5)	1986 s.47(5); 1993 s.293(3).
550	1986 s.47(8).
551(1).	1988 s.218(1)(g).
(2)	1988 s.218(12).
552(1)	1993 Sch.19 para.62(5).
(2), (3)	1993 Sch.19 para.62(2), (3).
(4)	1993 Sch.19 para.62(1).
(5)	1993 Sch.19 para.62(4)
(6)	1993 Sch.19 para.62(6).
553	1988 s.113.

554(1)	1973 s.2(1); 1988 s.112(2).
(2)	1973 s.2(1); 1988 s.112(2); 1993 Sch.19 para.52(a).
(3)	1973 s.2(1A); 1988 s.112(2); 1993 Sch.19 para.52(b).
(4)	1973 s.2(1C); 1988 s.112(2); 1993 Sch.19 para.52(c).
(5)	1973 s.2(1B); 1988 s.112(2).
(6)	1973 s.2(8).
555(1)	1973 s.2(2); 1993 Sch.19 para.52(c).
(2) to (4)	1973 s.2(2).
(5)	1973 s.2(1B); 1988 s.112(2).
556(1)	1973 s.2(3); 1993 s.288(3)
(2)	1973 s.2(4); 1988 s.112(3); 1993 Sch.19 para.52(c).
(3)	1973 s.2(4); 1993 s.288(2), Sch.19 para.52(c).
(4)	1973 s.2(5).
(5)	1973 s.2(5A); 1993 s.288(4).
(6), (7)	1973 s.2(6), (7).
(8)	1973 s.2(1B); 1988 s.112(2).
557	1993 s.287.
558	1944 s.58.
559(1), (2)	1944 s.59(1), (2).
(3), (4)	1944 s.59(3).
(5)	1944 s.59(4).
(6)	Employment of Children Act 1973 (c.24) s.3(4).
560(1)	1973EWE s.1(1); 1988 Sch.12 para.14.
(2)	1973EWE s.1(4); Employment Act 1990 (c.38) s.14.
(3)	1973EWE s.1(2); Merchant Shipping Act 1995 (c.21) Sch.13 para.48.
(4), (5)	1973EWE s.1(3).
(6)	Drafting.
(7)	1973EWE s.1(4).
561	1944 s.115.
562	1944 s.116; 1948 Sch.1 Pt.I; 1993 Sch.19 para.25.
563(1)	1988 s.218(1)(f); 1992FHE Sch.8 para.49.
(2)	1988 s.218(4).
(3)	1988 s.218(12).
564(1)	1944 s.94(1); S.I. 1968/1699 art.5; Registration of Births, Deaths and Marriages (Fees) Order 1995 (S.I. 1995/3162) Sch.
(2)	1944 s.94(1).
(3)	1944 s.94(2); S.I. 1968/1699 art.5.
(4)	1944 s.94(3); 1978IA s.17(2)(a).
565(1)	1944 s.95(1).
(2)	1993 s.200(3).
566	1944 s.95(2).
567(1), (2)	1993 s.299(1), (2).
(3)	1993 ss.299(3), 305(1) ("maintained school")
(4), (5)	1993 s.299(4), (5).
568(1)	1973 s.2(1); 1986 s.63(1); 1988 s.232(1); 1993 s.301(1); Law Com. Rec. No. 19.
(2)	1986 ss.4A(8), 63(1); 1988 s.232(2); 1993 ss.271(1), 301(2).
(3)	1986 s.63(2); 1988 s.232(4); 1993 s.301(3).
(4)	1988 s.232(3).
(5)	1986 s.63(3); 1988 s.232(5); 1993 s.301(6); Law Com. Rec. No. 18.
(6)	1988 s.232(6); Law Com. Rec. No. 18.
569(1)	Statutory Instruments Act 1946 (c.36) s.1(2); 1948 s.12; 1980 s.35(1); 1984 s.3(1); 1986 s.63(1); 1988 s.232(1); 1992(S) s.19(1); 1993 s.301(1); Law Com. Rec. No. 18.
(2)	1944 s.112; Statutory Instruments Act 1946 (c.36) s.5(2); 1948 s.12; 1980 s.35(3); 1984 s.3(3); 1986 s.63(2); 1988 s.232(4); 1992(S) s.19(2); 1993 ss.279(2)(a), 301(3).

(3)	1980 s.35(2); 1986 s.63(2A); 1993 ss.279(2)(b), 301(4).
(4)	1980 s.35(4); 1984 s.3(4); 1986 s.63(3); 1988 s.232(5); 1992(S) s.19(3); 1993 s.301(6), Sch.19 para.107(a); Law Com. Rec. No. 18.
(5)	1944 s.111A; 1980 s.35(5); 1988 ss.229(1), 232(6); Law Com. Rec. No. 18.
(6)	1980 s.35(5).
570(1), (2)	1944 s.111; S.I. 1968/1699 art.5; 1993 s.301(7).
(3)	1944 s.111 proviso.
571	1980 ss.12(1B), 13(1C); 1988 s.34(3); 1993 ss.229(1), 230(1), 300.
572	1944 s.113; 1946 Sch.2 Pt.I.
573(1)	Drafting.
(2)	1944 s.114(1) ("alterations"); 1968 Sch.1 para.5(a); 1993 s.305(1).
(3)	1944 s.114(1) ("enlargement"); 1968 Sch.1 para.5(b).
(4)	1980 s.16(2); 1993 s.103(1).
(5)	1944 s.114(1) ("significant"); 1968 Sch.1 para.5(c).
(6)	1944 s.67(4); 1968 Sch.1 para.3; 1988 Sch.12 para.4.
574	1968 s.1(1); 1980 Sch.3 para.15; 1993 Sch.19 para.41.
575(1), (2)	1988 s.235(1); 1993 s.305(1); 1996ER Sch.1 paras.37(5), 59.
(3)	1988 s.235(3); 1933 s.155(9), (10).
(4)	1988 s.235(1); 1993 s.305(1) 1996ER Sch.1 paras.37(5), 59.
576(1)	1944 s.114(1D); Children Act 1989 (c.41) Sch.13 para.10.
(2)	1944 s.114(1E); Children Act 1989 (c.41) Sch.13 para.10; 1993 Sch.19 para.24(b).
(3), (4)	1944 s.114(1F); Children Act 1989 (c.41) Sch.13 para.10.
577	1944 s.114 ("minor authority"); 1972LG s.192(4); Local Government Changes for England (Education) (Miscellaneous Provisions) Regulations 1996 (S.I. 1996/710) reg.19.
578	1992FHE s.90(1) ("the Education Acts"); 1993 s.305(1)("the Education Acts"); 1996N Sch.3 para.8.
579(1)	"boarder": 1986 s.65(1). "child": 1944 s.114(1). "clothing": 1944 s.114(1). "exclude": 1986 s.65(1). "financial year": 1984 s.1(6); 1988 s.235(1), Sch.2 para.18; 1993 s.305(1), Sch.14 para.20. "functions": 1988 s.235(1); 1993 s.305(1). "governing body"; "governor": 1944 s.114(1); 1980 Sch.1 para.13. "higher education": 1944 s.114(1); 1988 s.120(9). "land": 1988 s.235(1); 1993 s.306(1). "liability": 1988 s.235(1); 1993 s.305(1). "local authority": 1988 s.235; 1993 s.305(1); 1994LG(W) Sch.16 paras.83, 105(2). "the local education authority": 1944 s.114(1); 1988 s.118(7)(b); 1993 s.305(1). "local government elector": 1944 s.114(1); 1972LG s.272(2). "medical officer": 1944 s.114(1); 1973NHSR Sch.4 para.8; Medical Act 1983 (c.54) Sch.6 para.11. "modifications": 1988 s.235(1); 1993 s.305(1). "premises": 1944 s.114(1). "prescribed": 1944 s.114(1); 1993 s.305(1). "proprietor": 1944 ss.80(1), 114(1); 1988 Sch.12 para.5. "reception class": 1980 s.38(5A)(b); 1988 ss.31(6), 119(1)(b); 1993 s.155(1). "relevant age group": 1980 s.16(3); 1988 s.32(2); 1993 s.155(4). "school buildings": 1946 s.4(2); 1973NHSR Sch.4 para.9; National Health Service Act 1977 (c.49) Sch.15 para.3; 1978IA s.17(2)(a). "school day": 1986 s.65(1). "trust deed": 1944 s.114(1). "young person": 1944 s.114(1).
(2)	1988 s.235(3)(g); 1993 s.305(2).
(3)	1980 s.38(5A); 1988 ss.31(6), 119(1)(a); 1993 s.155(5).
(4)	1980 s.38(5); 1986 s.51(10); 1993 Sch.19 para.103.
(5)	1944 s.114(2)(b).
(6)	1944 s.114(2)(b); 1988 s.234(2)(a), (3)(a).
(7)	1944 s.114(2A); 1988 s.234(2)(b); 1992FHE Sch.8 para.13(4).
580	
581	1944 s.118; S.I. 1977/293 art.4; Law Com. Rec. No. 19.
582	
583	
Sch. 1	1993 Sch.18.
Sch. 2	
para.1	1993 Sch.1 para.16

paras.2 to 8	1993 Sch.1 paras.1 to 7.
para.9	1993 Sch.19 paras.46 to 48.
paras.10 to 14	1993 Sch.1 paras.8 to 12.
para.15	1993 Sch.1 para.15.
paras.16, 17	1993 Sch.1 paras.13, 14.
Sch. 3	
para.1	1993 s.17; 1996N Sch.3 para.10.
para.2	1993 s.18.
para.3	1993 s.19.
Sch. 4	
para.1	1993 Sch.2 para.1, s.305(1) ("maintained school")
paras.2 to 23	1993 Sch.2 paras.2 to 23.
Sch. 5	
para.1	
para.2	1944 Sch.3 para.8.
para.3	1944 Sch.3 paras.4, 5; 1948 Sch.1,Pt.I; 1980 Sch.3 para.5.
para.4	1944 Sch.3 para.7; drafting.
para.5	1944 Sch.3 para.9.
para.6	1944 Sch.3 para.10.
Sch. 6	1944 Sch.2.
Sch. 7	
para.1	1993 s.238(5) to (7).
para.2	1993 s.239.
para.3	1993 Sch.13 para.2
para.4	1993 Sch.13 para.1
para.5	1993 Sch.13 para.3
paras.6 to 10	1993 Sch.3 paras.8 to 12.
paras.11, 12	1993 Sch.13 paras.14, 15
Sch. 8	
para.1	Drafting.
para.2	1986 ss.6, 15(12), (13); drafting.
para.3	1986 s.15(11).
para.4	1986 s.15(7).
para.5	1986 s.15(1).
para.6	1986 s.15(8).
para.7	Drafting; 1986 s.15(2) to (6), (15).
para.8	1986 s.15(14).
para.9	1986 s.15(10).
para.10	1986 ss.8(6), (9), 15(9).
para.11	1986 s.8(2), (3); 1993 s.271(2).
para.12	1986 s.8(4).
para.13	1986 s.8(5).
para.14	1986 s.8(1).
para.15	1986 s.8(6), (7), (9); 1988 s.116; drafting.
para.16	1986 s.8(11), (12); Law Com. Rec. Nos. 3, 20.
para.17	1986 s.8(8).
para.18	1986 s.62.
para.19	Drafting.
para.20	1986 s.57.
para.21	1986 s.8(10).
Sch. 9	
para.1	1986 s.65(1) ("promoters"), Sch.2 para.1; Law Com. Rec. No. 9.
para.2	1986 Sch.2 para.2(1), (2); 1993 Sch.19 para.109(a), (b)(i).
para.3	1986 Sch.2 para.6.

para.4	1986 Sch.2 para.7(1).
para.5	1986 Sch.2 para.8(1).
para.6	1986 Sch.2 para.7(2) to (5).
para.7	1986 Sch.2 paras.7(6), (7), 8(2).
para.8	1986 Sch.2 para.9(1), (2); 1993 Sch.19 para.109(e).
para.9	1986 Sch.2 paras.2(3), 11(4), (5).
para.10	1986 Sch.2 para.11(3).
para.11	1986 Sch.2 para.11(6).
para.12	1986 Sch.2 para.11(1), (2).
para.13	1986 Sch.2 para.10(4).
para.14	1986 Sch.2 para.10(2).
para.15	1986 Sch.2 paras.10(1), 26(3).
para.16	1986 Sch.2 para.10(4).
para.17	1986 Sch.2 para.2(4).
para.18	1986 Sch.2 para.10(3).
para.19	1986 Sch.2 para.27.
para.20	1986 Sch.2 para.28.
para.21	1986 Sch.2 para.30(1).
para.22	1986 Sch.2 para.29.
Sch. 10	
para.1	1986 Sch.2 para.3(4).
para.2	1986 Sch.2 para.3(5).
para.3	1986 Sch.2 para.4.
para.4	1986 Sch.2 para.13(3), (4).
para.5	1986 Sch.2 paras.2(2), 3(2), (3); 1993 Sch.19 para.109(b)(i).
para.6	1986 Sch.2 para.13(3), (5).
Sch. 11	
para.1	Drafting.
para.2	1988 ss.33(6), 42(4)(a) to (d).
para.3	1988 s.42(4)(e), (5)(a).
para.4	1988 s.42(4)(j).
paras.5 to 7	1988 s.50(5); 51(1) ("expenditure of a capital nature").
para.8	1988 s.50(10).
Sch. 12	
para.1	1988 s.48(2) ("temporary governing body").
para.2	1988 Sch.4 para.1(2)(a), (b).
para.3	1988 Sch.4 paras.1(1), 2(1).
para.4	1988 Sch.4 para.2(2) to (5).
para.5	1988 Sch.4 para.2(6); S.I. 1991/1890; S.I. 1992/110.
para.6	1988 Sch.4 para.2(8).
para.7	1988 Sch.4 para.2(9).
para.8	1988 Sch.4 para.3.
para.9	1988 Sch.4 para.6.
para.10	1988 Sch.4 para.5.
Sch. 13	
para.1	1986 s.36(1).
para.2	1986 s.36(2).
para.3	1986 s.37.
para.4	1986 s.39.
para.5	1986 s.38(1), (2).
para.6	1986 s.38(3).
para.7	1986 s.38(4).
para.8	1986 s.38(6).
para.9	1986 s.38(5).

para.10	1986 s.35(2).
para.11(1), (2)	1986 s.41(1)(a).
(3)	1986 s.41(3).
(4) to (7)	1986 s.41(1)(b) to (e).
(8)	1986 s.41(3).
Sch. 14	
para.1	1988 Sch.3 paras.1(1), (2), (6), 2(1), 4(1), 5(1), 6(1), 7(1), 8(1), 10(1), 11(3); 1978IA s.17(2)(a).
para.2	1988 Sch.3 para.1(1).
para.3	1988 Sch.3 para.1(3).
para.4	1988 Sch.3 para.1(4), (5), (12).
para.5	1988 Sch.3 para.1(7).
para.6	1988 Sch.3 para.1(8) to (10).
para.7	1988 Sch.3 para.1(11), (13).
para.8	1988 Sch.3 para.2(1).
para.9	1988 Sch.3 para.2(2), (3).
para.10	1988 Sch.3 para.2(4).
para.11	1988 Sch.3 para.2(5).
para.12	1988 Sch.3 para.2(6), (7).
para.13	1988 Sch.3 para.2(8), (9).
para.14	1988 Sch.3 para.2(10), (11).
para.15	1988 Sch.3 para.2(12).
para.16	1988 Sch.3 para.3(1) to (3).
para.17	1988 Sch.3 para.3(4).
para.18	1988 Sch.3 para.4(1) to (3), (5).
para.19	1988 Sch.3 para.4(4).
para.20	1988 Sch.3 para.5.
para.21	1988 Sch.3 para.6.
para.22	1988 Sch.3 para.7.
para.23	1988 Sch.3 para.8(1) to (3), (6).
para.24	1988 Sch.3 para.8(4), (5).
para.25	1988 Sch.3 para.8(7), (8).
para.26	1988 Sch.3 para.8(9).
para.27	1988 Sch.3 para.9; 1978IA s.17(2)(a).
para.28	1988 Sch.3 para.10; 1993 Sch.19 para.142.
Sch. 15	
para.1	1986 s.24.
para.2	1986 s.24(a), (h); 1993 Sch.13 para.97.
para.3	1986 s.24(b), (f), (g).
para.4	1986 s.24(h).
para.5	1986 s.24(b), (g).
para.6	1986 s.24(d), (h).
para.7	1986 s.24(h).
para.8	1986 s.25.
para.9	1986 s.25(a), (h).
para.10	1986 s.25(b).
para.11	1986 s.25(b), (g).
para.12	1986 s.25(c), (h); 1993 Sch.19 para.98.
para.13	1986 s.25(h).
para.14	1993 Sch.19 para.99.
para.15	Drafting.
Sch. 16	
para.1	1986 Sch.3 paras.1, 2; S.I. 1994/2092.
para.2	1986 Sch.3 para.3; S.I. 1994/2092.

para.3	1986 Sch.3 para.3A; S.I. 1994/2092.
para.4	1986 Sch.3 para.4; drafting.
para.5	1986 Sch.3 para.16.
para.6	1986 Sch.3 para.6.
para.7	1986 Sch.3 para.6A; S.I. 1994/2092.
para.8	1986 Sch.3 para.7; Education (No.2) Act 1986 (Amendment) (No.2) Order 1993 (S.I. 1993/2827) art.2.
para.9	1986 Sch.3 para.8; Education (No.2) Act 1986 (Amendment) Order 1993 (S.I. 1993/2709) art.2.
para.10	1986 Sch.3 para.9; S.I. 1994/2092 art.8.
para.11	1986 Sch.3 para.13.
para.12	1986 Sch.3 para.14.
para.13	1986 Sch.3 para.11.
para.14	1986 Sch.3 para.12; S.I. 1994/2092 art.9.
para.15	1986 Sch.3 para.15.
para.16	1986 Sch.3 para.17; S.I. 1994/2092 art.10.
para.17	Drafting.
para.18	1986 Sch.3 para.5.
Sch. 17	
para.1	1986 s.30(2).
para.2	1986 s.30(2)(a).
para.3	1986 s.30(2)(b).
para.4	1986 s.30(2)(c) to (e).
para.5	1986 s.30(2)(g).
para.6	1986 s.30(2)(h); 1988 s.51(9); Education (No.2) Act 1986 (Amendment) Order 1994 (S.I. 1994/692) art.2.
para.7	1986 s.30(2)(i); Education (No.2) Act 1986 (Amendment) (No.3) Order 1994 (S.I. 1994/2732).
para.8	1986 s.30(2)(j).
para.9	1986 s.30(2)(k); 1978IA s.17(2)(a).
para.10	1986 s.30(5); 1992(S) Sch.4 para.5.
Sch. 18	
para.1	1986 s.31(4)(a).
para.2	1986 s.31(4)(b), (9).
para.3	1986 s.31(3).
para.4	1986 s.31(4)(c), (d).
para.5	1986 s.31(5), (6).
Sch. 19	
para.1	1986 Sch.2 paras.4, 12(1).
para.2	1988 Sch.4 para.7.
para.3	1986 Sch.2 para.12(2).
para.4	1986 Sch.2 para.12(3).
para.5	1986 Sch.2 para.20(5).
para.6	1986 Sch.2 para.21.
para.7	1986 Sch.2 para.22.
para.8	1986 Sch.2 para.23.
para.9	1986 Sch.2 para.25.
para.10	1986 Sch.2 para.24.
para.11	1986 Sch.2 para.26(1), (2).
para.12	1986 Sch.2 para.30(2).
para.13	Drafting.
para.14	1986 Sch.2 para.20(1).
para.15	1986 Sch.2 para.20(2), (3); Law Com. Rec. No. 9.
para.16	1986 Sch.2 paras.20(4), 30(3).

para.17	1986 Sch.2 para.28.
para.18	1988 Sch.4 para.1.
para.19	1988 Sch.4 para.4(1), (4), (5).
para.20	1988 Sch.4 para.4(2).
para.21	1988 Sch.4 para.4(3); Education (Application of Financing Schemes to Special Schools) Regulations 1992 (S.I. 1992/164).
para.22	1988 Sch.4 para.4(7).
para.23	1988 Sch.4 para.4(8).
para.24	1988 Sch.4 para.4(6).
para.25	1986 Sch.2 para.15.
para.26	1986 Sch.2 para.16; 1988 Sch.12 para.106.
para.27	1986 Sch.2 para.17.
para.28	1986 Sch.2 paras.13(1), 14.
para.29	1986 Sch.2 para.18; 1988 Sch.4 para.2(10).
Sch. 20	
para.1	1993 Sch.3 para.1(1) to (4); drafting.
paras.2 to 12	1993 Sch.3 paras.2 to 12.
Sch. 21	1993 Sch.4.
Sch. 22	
paras.1 to 13	1993 Sch.5 paras.1 to 13.
para.14	1986 s.62; 1988 Sch.12 para.37.
paras.15, 16	1993 Sch.5 paras.14, 15.
Sch. 23	
paras.1 to 3	1993 Sch.6 paras.1 to 3.
para.4	1993 Sch.6 para.7
para.5	1993 Sch.6 paras.4, 6.
para.6	1993 Sch.6 paras.5, 6.
paras.7, 8	1993 Sch.6 paras.8, 9.
Sch. 24	1993 Sch.7.
Sch. 25	1993 Sch.8.
Sch. 26	1993 Sch.9.
Sch. 27	1993 Sch.10.
Sch. 28	
paras.1 to 14	1993 Sch.11, paras.1 to 14.
para.15	1993 s.261(1), (2), (5).
Sch. 29	
paras.1 to 16	1993 Sch.14 paras.1 to 16.
para.17	1993 Sch.14 para.17; 1993 Sch.15 para.6(2).
paras.18 to 22	1993 Sch.14 paras.18 to 22.
Sch. 30	
paras.1 to 5	1988 Sch.2 paras.2 to 6; 1993 Sch.15 para.4(6).
paras.6, 7	1988 Sch.2 para.7; 1993 Sch.15 para.4(6).
para.8	1988 Sch.2 para.8; 1993 Sch.15 para.4(6), Sch.19 para.141.
paras.9, 10	1988 Sch.2 para.10; 1993 Sch.15 para.4(6).
para.11	1988 Sch.2 para.11; 1993 s.249, Sch.15 para.4(6).
paras.12, 13	1988 Sch.2 paras.12, 13; 1993 Sch.15 para.4(6).
para.14	1988 Sch.2 para.13A; 1993 s.250, Sch.15 para.4(6).
paras.15, 16	1988 Sch.2 paras.14, 15; 1993 Sch.15 para.4(6).
para.17	1988 Sch.2 para.18; 1993 s.251(3), Sch.15 para.4(6).
paras.18, 19	1988 Sch.2 paras.16, 17; 1993 Sch.15 para.4(6).
Sch. 31	
para.1	1944 Sch.5 para.12(1), (3); 1993 s.256(1).
para.2	1944 Sch.5 para.12(4); 1993 s.256(1).
para.3	1988 s.11(8).

para.4	1944 Sch.5 paras.2, 5; 1988 Sch.1 para.7; 1993 s.254(3), Sch.19 para.27.
paras.5, 6	1944 Sch.5 paras.7, 8.
para.7	1944 Sch.5 para.3; 1988 Sch.1 para.7; 1993 Sch.19 para.27.
paras.8, 9	1944 Sch.5 para.4; 1993 Sch.19 para.27.
para.10	1944 Sch.5 para.13; 1988 Sch.1 para.7; 1993 s.256(2).
para.11	1993 s.146.
para.12	1944 Sch.5 paras.10, 13(4); 1988 Sch.1 para.7.
para.13	1944 Sch.5 para.11; 1988 Sch.1 para.7.
para.14	1944 Sch.5 para.11.
para.15	1993 s.15.
Sch. 32	
para.1	1988 s.28(1).
para.2	1988 s.28(2).
para.3	1988 s.28(3), (4).
para.4	1988 s.28(5).
para.5	1988 ss.28(6), (7), 32(1).
para.6	1988 s.28(8).
para.7	1988 s.119(2), (3).
Sch. 33	
para.1	1980 Sch.2 para.1; 1993 Sch.16 para.2.
para.2	1980 Sch.2 para.2; 1993 Sch.16 para.3.
para.3	1980 Sch.2 para.3.
para.4	1980 Sch.2 para.4; Local Government and Housing Act 1989 (Commencement No.11 and Savings) Order 1991 (S.I. 1991/344) Sch. para.1.
para.5	1980 Sch.2 para.4A; 1993 Sch.16 para.4.
para.6	1993 s.267.
para.7	1993 s.268.
para.8	Drafting.
paras.9 to 11	1980 Sch.2 paras.5 to 7.
para.12	1980 Sch.2 para.10.
para.13	1980 Sch.2 para.8.
para.14	1980 Sch.2 para.9
para.15	1980 Sch.2 para.11.
Sch. 34	
para.1	1944 Sch.6 para.1.
para.2	1944 Sch.6 para.2.
para.3	1944 Sch.6 paras.3, 3A; Judicial Pensions and Retirement Act 1993 (c.8) Sch.6 para.51.
para.4	1944 Sch.6 para.4.
para.5	1976 s.6(1).
Sch. 35	
paras.1 to 3	1980 Sch.4 paras.1 to 3.
para.4	1980 Sch.4 para.4; 1986 s.47(9).
paras.5, 6	1980 Sch.4 paras.5, 6.
Sch. 36	1993 Sch.17.
Schs. 37, 38	
Sch. 39	
para.1	
para.2	1993 s.303.
para.3	1944 s.2(1).
para.4	1944 s.120(1).
paras.5 to 9	
para.10(1)	
(2)	1980 s.1(4).

para.11	1986 Sch.5 para.1.
paras.12 to 16	
para.17(1)	
(2)	1993 s.274(3).
(3)	1993 s.274(5).
para.18	Law Com. Rec. No.12.
para.19	S.I. 1996/951 art.4.
paras.20 to 23	
para.24	1993 Sch.20 para.1; S.I. 1993/3106 Sch.2 paras.8, 9.
para.25	1993 Sch.20 para.1; S.I. 1993/3106 Sch.2 para.10.
para.26	S.I. 1993/3106 para.11.
para.27	S.I. 1993/3106 Sch.2 para.14.
para.28	1993 Sch.20 para.5.
para.29	1993 Sch.20 para.6.
para.30	S.I. 1993/1975 Sch.2 para.4(2).
para.31	1993 Sch.20 para.2; S.I. 1994/507 Sch.3 para.10.
para.32	S.I. 1994/507 Sch.3 para.11.
para.33	S.I. 1994/507 Sch.3 para.12.
para.34	S.I. 1994/2038 Sch.4 paras.2(7), 4(3).
para.35	S.I. 1994/507 Sch.3 para.5.
paras.36 to 42	
para.43	S.I. 1993/507 Sch.3 para.7.
para.44	1993 Sch.20 para.4.
para.45	1946 s.13(1).
para.46	
para.47	1944 s.120(5).
para.48	
para.49	1973 Sch.1 para.3.
para.50	
Sch. 40	
(5)	1986 Sch.2 para.5(1).
97(1)	1986 s.12(1), (2), (9).
(2)	1986 s.12(4).
(3)	1986 ss.12(5), (9), 65(1) ("promoters"); Law Com. Rec. No. 9.
(4)	1986 ss.12(6), (9), 65(1) ("promoters"); Law Com. Rec. No. 9.
(5)	1986 ss.12(7), 65(1) ("promoters"); Law Com. Rec. No. 9.
(6)	1986 s.12(8).
(7)	1986 Sch.2 para.5(2).
(8)	1986 Sch.2 para.5(1).
98	Drafting.
99(1)	1986 Sch.2 para.3(1).
(2)	1986 Sch.2 para.3(7).
(3)	Drafting.
100(1), (2)	Law Com. Rec. No. 10.
(3)	1986 Sch.2 para.3(6).
(4)	1986 Sch.2 para.3(6); drafting.
101(1)	1988 s.51(2)(a)(i); 1993 s.274(4).
(2)	1988 s.51(2)(a)(ii).
(3)	1988 s.33(2), (4); 1992FHE s.12(5).
(4)	1988 s.33(4); 1992FHE s.12(5).
(5)	1988 s.33(5).
(6)	1988 s.51(2)(b).
102	1988 s.33(3).
103	1988 s.33(1), (2).

104(1), (2)	1988 s.34(1), (2).
(3)	1988 s.34(4); 1993 s.274(1).
(4) to (6)	1988 s.34(5) to (7)
105(1)	1988 s.33(4).
(2)	1988 s.33(5).
(3)	1988 ss.33(4), 38(4), 51(1) ("expenditure of a capital nature").
106(1)	1988 s.38(1).
(2)	1988 s.38(1), (2).
(3)	1988 s.38(2).
(4)	1988 s.38(3).
(5)	1988 s.38(3A); 1992FHE s.12(7).
(6)	1988 s.33(5).
107(1)	1988 s.39(1); S.I. 1991/1890; S.I. 1992/110.
(2)	1988 s.39(4); S.I. 1991/1890; S.I. 1992/110.
108	1988 s.39(10).
109(1)	1988 s.39(11).
(2)	1988 s.39(12).
(3)	1988 s.39(11).
110(1)	1988 s.40(1).
(2)	1988 s.40(2); 1993 s.274(3).
(3) to (5)	1988 s.40(3) to (5).
111	1988 s.35(1), (2); 1993 s.274(2).
112(1) to (3)	1988 s.35(3); 1993 s.274(2).
(4)	1988 s.35(4); 1993 s.274(2).
113(1), (2)	1988 s.35(5); 1993 s.274(2).
(3), (4)	1988 s.35(6); 1993 s.274(2).
(5)	1988 s.35(4); 1993 s.274(2).
114	1988 s.35(7), (8); 1993 s.274(2).
115	1988 s.33(6)(a), (b).
116(1) to (3)	1988 s.36(1) to (3).
(4)	1988 s.36(4); 1993 Sch.19 para.125(a).
(5)	1988 s.36(5).
(6)	1988 s.36(5A); 1992FHE s.12(6).
(7)	1988 s.36(5B); 1993 Sch.19 para.125(b).
(8)	1988 s.36(6).
117(1)	1988 s.37(1).
(2), (3)	1988 s.37(2).
(4), (5)	1988 s.37(3).
(6)	1988 s.37(4).
118(1) to (3)	1988 s.37(5).
(4), (5)	1988 s.37(6), (7).
119	1988 s.37(8), (9).
120	1988 s.43; 1993 s.276.
121	1988 s.42(1).
122(1), (2)	1988 s.42(2), (3).
(3)	Drafting.
(4)	1988 s.42(4); 1993 s.275(1)(c).
(5)	1988 s.42(7).
(6)	1988 s.42(8); 1993 s.275(1)(d).
(7)	1988 s.42(9).
123	1988 s.42A; 1993 s.275(2).
124(1)	1988 s.50(2), (5).
(2)	1988 s.50(3)
(3)	Drafting.

(4)	1988 s.50(6).
(5)	1988 s.50(10).
(6) to (8)	1988 s.50(7) to (9).
125(1)	1988 s.49(1).
(2), (3)	1988 s.49(2).
(4)	1988 s.49(3).
126	Drafting.
127(1), (2)	1986 s.1(1), (2).
(3), (4)	1986 s.1(4), (5).
128(1) to (3)	1986 s.2(1) to (3).
(4) to (6)	1986 s.2(5) to (7).
(7)	Drafting.
129(1)	1988 s.51(3).
(2), (3)	1988 s.51(4), (5).
(4)	1988 s.51(4).
(5)	1988 s.51(6).
130	1986 s.16(1).
131	1986 s.16(2).
132	1986 s.16(3); Law Com. Rec. No. 11.
133(1) to (3)	1986 s.34.
(4)	Drafting.
(5)	1986 s.35(1).
(6)	Drafting.
134(1)	1944 s.24(2).
(2), (3)	1944 s.24(2), proviso (a).
(4)	1944 s.24(2), proviso (b).
(5)	1944 s.22(4); 1986 Sch.4 para.2; 1993 Sch.13 para.4(6).
(6)	1944 s.22(5); 1993 Sch.13 para.4(4).
(7)	Drafting.
135(1) to (4)	1986 s.40(1) to (4).
(5), (6)	1986 s.40(6), (7).
(7)	Drafting.
(8)	1986 s.40(5).
136(1), (2)	1988 s.44(1), (2); Law Com. Rec. No. 12.
(3)	1988 s.44(3), (5).
137(1), (2)	1988 s.45(1), (2).
(3), (4)	1988 s.45(3).
(5)	1988 s.45(9).
(6)	1988 s.45(10).
138(1)	1988 s.45(1), (4).
(2)	1988 s.45(6).
(3)	1988 s.45(5).
(4)	1988 s.45(7).
(5)	1988 s.45(8).
139(1), (2)	1988 s.46(2).
(3) to (6)	1988 s.46(3) to (6).
(7)	1988 s.235(2)(f); 1996ER Sch.1 para.37(5).
140	1988 s.47.
141(1)	1988 ss.44(4), 45(11).
(2)	1988 s.44(4); Law Com. Rec. No. 12.
(3)	1988 s.45(11).
(4)	1988 s.51(6).
142	Drafting.
143(1), (2)	1944 s.27(2).

(3)	1944 s.27(2) proviso.
(4) to (6)	1944 s.27(3) to (5); 1988 Sch.1 para.2(1).
(7)	Drafting.
144(1), (2)	1944 s.28(3), Sch.3 para.7; 1988 Sch.1 para.3(2).
(3)	1944 s.28(4); 1988 Sch.1 para.3(2).
(4)	Drafting.
145	1944 s.28(2); 1988 Sch.1 para.3(2).
146(1)	1944 s.30.
(2) to (4)	1944 s.30; 1988 Sch.1 para.4(b).
147(1)	1986 s.21(1); 1988 s.115; S.I. 1996/951 art.3(1).
(2)	1986 s.21(4); 1988 s.115.
(3)	1986 s.21(4); 1988 s.115; S.I. 1996/951 art.3(1).
148(1) to (4)	S.I. 1996/951 art.3(2) to (5).
(5)	Drafting.
149(1), (2)	1986 s.42(1), (2); 1993 Sch.13 para.5.
(3), (4)	1986 s.42(3); 1993 Sch.13 para.5.
(5)	1986 s.42(4); 1993 Sch.13 para.5; S.I. 1996/951 art.5.
150(1)	1944 s.22(3); 1993 Sch.13 para.4(2), (6).
(2)	1944 s.22(1).
(3)	1944 s.22(5); 1993 Sch.13 para.4(4).
151(1) to (3)	1944 s.22(3A) to (3C); 1993 Sch.13 para.4(3).
(4), (5)	1944 s.22(3D); 1993 Sch.13 para.4(3).
(6)	1944 s.22(3E); 1993 Sch.13 para.4(3).
(7)	1944 s.22(6); 1978IA s.17(2)(a); 1993 Sch.13 para.4(5).
(8)	Drafting.
152(1), (2)	1944 s.22(1); 1993 Sch.13 para.4(6).
(3), (4)	1944 s.22(2); 1993 Sch.13 para.4(6).
(5)	Drafting.
153	1986 s.21(5); 1988 s.115.
154(1)	1986 s.22.
(2)	1986 s.22(d).
(3)	1986 s.22(a); 1993 Sch.19 para.95.
(4)	1986 s.22(b).
(5)	1986 s.22(c).
(6)	1986 s.22(e).
155	1986 s.28.
156(1)	1986 s.22(f).
(2), (3)	1993 s.261(1), (2).
157(1)	Law Com. Rec. No. 13.
(2)	1986 s.23(a); Law Com. Rec. No. 13.
(3)	1986 s.23(b).
(4)	1986 s.23(a), (b); Law Com. Rec. No. 13.
(5)	1986 s.23(a); Law Com. Rec. No. 13.
158	Drafting.
159(1) to (4)	1986 s.26(1) to (4).
(5), (6)	1986 s.26(5).
(7)	1986 s.26(1), (2).
160	1986 s.27.
161(1)	1986 s.30(1).
(2)	Drafting.
(3)	1986 s.30(3).
(4)	1986 s.30(4).
162(1), (2)	1986 s.31(1), (2).
(3)	Drafting.

163	1986 s.31(7), (8).
164(1)	1986 Sch.1 paras.4, 5.
(2)	1986 Sch.1 para.4(1).
(3)	1986 Sch.1 para.4(2).
(4) to (7)	1986 Sch.1 para.5.
165	1986 s.32.
166	Drafting.
167(1)	1980 s.12(1).
(2)	1980 s.12(2).
(3)	1993 s.273(1).
(4)	1980 s.12(1A); 1993 s.229(1).
(5)	1992FHE s.59(3), (4).
(6)	1993 s.273(2).
168(1)	1980 s.12(3); 1993 s.229(2).
(2)	1980 s.12(3).
(3)	1993 s.229(3).
(4)	1980 s.12(3).
(5), (6)	1980 s.16(3A), (3B); 1988 Sch.12 para.81.
169(1)	1980 s.12(4), (5); 1993 s.273(4).
(2)	1980 s.12(4).
(3)	1980 s.12(5).
(4)	1993 s.273(3).
(5)	1980 s.12(6).
(6)	1993 s.273(4), (5)(a).
170(1), (2)	1980 s.12(7).
(3)	1980 s.12(8).
171	1980 s.12(9).
172	1980 s.16(1).
173(1)	1944 s.14(1).
(2)	1944 s.14(1), 114(1) ("former authority"); 1946 Sch.2 Pt.II.
(3)	1944 s.14(1); 1946 Sch.2 Pt.II.
(4)	1992FHE s.59(3), (4).
(5)	1993 s.273(2).
(6)	1944 s.14(2).
(7)	1944 s.14(5).
(8)	Drafting.
174(1)	1944 s.14(3).
(2), (3)	1944 s.14(4).
175	1992FHE s.59(1), (2).
176	1986 s.16A; FHE 1992 s.12(3).
177	Drafting.
178	1988 s.222.
179(1)	1973 s.1(2); 1980 Sch.3 para.17; Law Com. Rec. No. 3.
(2)	1973 s.1(2).
180	1980 s.5.
181(1)	1986 Sch.2 para.1 ("new school"); 1988 s.48(2).
(2)	1986 Sch.2 para.1 ("relevant proposal"); 1988 s.48(2).
(3)	1988 s.48(2) ("temporary governing body"); drafting.
182	1986 s.65(2).
183	1993 s.22.
184	1993 s.23.
185	1993 s.24.
186	1993 s.25.
187	1993 s.26.

188	1993 s.27.
189	1993 s.28.
190(1)	1993 s.29(1).
(2)	1993 s.29(2); Law Com. Rec. No. 14.
(3)	1993 s.29(3).
191	1993 s.30.
192	1993 s.31.
193	1993 s.32.
194	1993 s.33.
195	1993 s.34.
196	1993 s.35.
197	1993 s.36.
198(1) to (5)	1993 s.272(1) to (5).
(6)	1964 s.1(1); 1993 Sch.19 para.38.
199(1) to (3)	1993 s.273(3) to (5).
(4)	1993 s.273(7).
200	1993 s.37.
201(1) to (8)	1993 s.38(1) to (8).
(9)	1993 s.155(8).
(10)	1993 s.38(9).
202	1993 s.39.
203	1993 s.40.
204	1993 s.41.
205	1993 s.42.
206	1993 s.43.
207	1993 s.44.
208	1993 s.45.
209	1993 s.46.
210	1993 s.47(1) to (4).
211	1993 s.48.
212	1993 s.49(1) to (3).
213	1993 s.50.
214	1993 s.51.
215	1993 s.52.
216	1993 s.53.
217	1993 s.54.
218	1993 s.55.
219(1) to (3)	1993 s.56.
(4)	1993 s.301(5).
220	1993 s.57.
221	1993 s.58.
222	1993 s.59.
223	1993 s.60.
224	1993 s.61.
225	1993 s.62.
226	1993 s.63.
227	1993 s.64.
228	1993 s.65.
229	1993 s.66.
230	1993 s.67.
231(1) to (4)	1993 s.68(1) to (4)
(5) to (7)	1993 s.68(5) to (7); 1996N s.7(2) to (4).
(8)	1993 s.68(8).
232	1993 s.69.

233	1993 s.70.
234	1993 s.71.
235	1993 s.72.
236	1993 s.73.
237	1993 s.74.
238	1993 s.75.
239	1993 s.76.
240	1993 s.77.
241	1993 s.78.
242	1993 s.79.
243	1993 s.80.
244	1993 s.81.
245	1993 s.82.
246	1993 s.83.
247	1993 s.84.
248	1993 s.85.
249	1993 s.86.
250	1993 s.87.
251	1993 s.88.
252	1993 s.89.
253	1993 s.90.
254	1993 s.91.
255	1993 s.92.
256	1993 s.93(1) to (6).
257	1993 s.94.
258	1993 s.95.
259	1993 s.96; Law Com. Rec. No. 3.
260	1993 s.97; Law Com. Rec. No. 3.
261	1993 s.98.
262	1993 s.99.
263	1993 s.100; Law Com. Rec. No. 3.
264	1993 s.101.
265	1993 s.102.
266	1993 s.103(2), (3).
267	1993 s.104.
268	1993 s.105.
269	1993 s.106.
270	1993 s.107.
271	1993 s.108.
272	1993 s.109.
273	1993 s.110.
274	1993 s.111.
275	1993 s.112.
276	1993 s.113.
277	1993 s.114.
278	1993 s.115.
279	1993 s.116.
280	1993 s.117.
281	1993 s.118.
282	1993 s.119.
283	1993 s.120.
284	1993 s.121.
285	1993 s.122.
286	1993 s.123.

287	1993 s.124.
288	1993 s.125.
289	1993 s.126.
290(1) to (7)	1993 s.127(1) to (7).
(8), (9)	1993 s.127(8).
(10), (11)	1993 s.127(9), (10).
(12)	1993 s.305(1).
(13)	1993 s.127(11).
291	1964 s.1(1); 1993 Sch.19 para.38.
292(1)	1993 s.231(1); drafting.
(2)	1993 s.232(2).
293	1993 s.128.
294	Drafting.
295	1993 s.129.
296(1)	1993 s.130(1).
(2)	1993 s.130(2); 1996N Sch.3 para.11.
297	1993 s.131.
298	1993 s.132.
299	1993 s.133.
300	1993 s.134.
301	1993 s.135.
302	1993 s.136.
303	1993 s.137.
304	1993 s.143.
305	1993 s.144.
306	1993 s.145.
307(1), (2)	1993 s.261(1), (2).
308(1)	1993 ss.267(1), 268(1).
(2)	1993 s.267(2).
(3)	1993 s.268(2).
309	1993 s.152.
310	1993 s.154.
311(1)	1993 ss.155(1) ("premises"), 305(1) ("Church in Wales school"; "Church of England school"; "Roman Catholic Church school").
(2)	1993 s.305(4).
(3)	1993 s.155(2).
(4)	1993 s.155(3).
(5)	1993 s.155(6).
(6)	1993 s.155(7)
(7)	Drafting.
(8)	1993 s.155(11).
312(1) to (4)	1993 s.156(1) to (4).
(5)	1993 ss.156(5), 305(1) ("maintained school").
313(1) to (4)	1993 s.157.
(5)	Drafting.
314	1993 s.158.
315	1993 s.159.
316	1993 s.160.
317(1) to (5)	1993 s.161(1) to (5).
(6), (7)	1993 s.161(6), (7); Disability Discrimination Act 1995 (c.50) s.29(2).
318(1), (2)	1993 s.162(1), (2)
(3)	1993 s.162(2A); 1996N Sch.3 para.12.
(4)	1993 s.162(3).
319	1993 s.163.

320	1993 s.164.
321	1993 s.165.
322(1)	1993 s.166(1); 1995HA Sch.1 para.124(2).
(2)	1993 s.166(2)
(3)	1993 s.166(3); 1995HA Sch.1 para.124(2).
(4)	1993 s.166(4).
(5)	1993 s.166(5); 1994LG(W) Sch.16 para.105(1); Local Government Changes for England Regulations 1994 (S.I. 1994/867) reg.5(6); Local Government Changes for England (Amendment) Regulations 1996 (S.I. 1996/611) reg.2.
323	1993 s.167.
324	1993 s.168.
325	1993 s.169.
326	1993 s.170.
327	1993 s.171.
328	1993 s.172.
329	1993 s.173.
330	1993 s.174.
331	1993 s.175.
332	1993 s.176; 1995HA Sch.1 para.124(3).
333	1993 s.177.
334	1993 s.178.
335	1993 s.179.
336	1993 s.180; Arbitration Act 1996 (c.23) Sch.3 para.59.
337(1)	1993 s.182(1).
(2)	Drafting.
(3), (4)	1993 s.182(2), (3).
338(1)	1993 s.183(1).
(2)	Drafting.
339	1993 s.183(2) to (10).
340	1993 s.184.
341	1993 s.185.
342	1993 s.188.
343	1993 s.231.
344(1)	Drafting.
(2)	1993 s.182(4).
345	1993 s.186.
346	1993 s.187.
347	1993 s.189.
348	1993 s.190
349	1993 s.191.
350(1)	1988 s.25(1) ("maintained school"); 1993 s.245(5).
(2)	1988 s.25(1) ("assess").
351(1)	1988 s.1(2).
(2) to (5)	1988 s.1(1).
352(1)	1988 ss.2(1), 8(2); 1993 s.241(1), Sch.19 para.114.
(2)	1988 s.2(3).
(3)	1944 s.114(1) ("sex education"); 1993 s.241(2).
353	1988 s.2(2); 1993 ss.240(1), 245(5).
354(1)	1988 s.3(1).
(2)	1988 s.3(2); S.I. 1992/1548 art.2; S.I. 1994/1814 art.2(2) to (4).
(3) to (5)	1988 s.3(2A), (2B); S.I. 1994/1814 art.2(5).
(6)	1988 s.3(4).
(7)	1988 s.3(6) ("school").
(8)	1988 s.3(7).

355(1)	1988 s.3(3); 1993 Sch.19 para.113.
(2)	1988 s.3(4).
(3)	1988 s.3(5).
(4)	1988 s.3(5A); 1993 s.240(2).
(5)	1988 s.3(6) ("class"; "school year"); 1993 s.240(3).
356(1) to (4)	1988 s.4(1) to (4).
(5) to (8)	1988 s.4(5) to (8); 1993 s.240(4).
(9)	1993 s.241(4).
357(1)	1988 s.10(2).
(2)	1988 s.10(3).
358	1993 s.244.
359(1)	1993 s.245(1).
(2)	1993 s.245(4).
(3)	1993 s.245(3).
(4)	1993 s.245(2).
(5)	1993 s.245(5).
360(1)	1988 s.14(1); 1993 s.253(1).
(2) to (4)	1988 s.14(2); 1993 Sch.15 para.4(3), Sch.19 para.118(a).
(5)	1988 s.14(7).
361(1)	1988 s.14(3); 1993 Sch.15 para.4(3), Sch.19 para.118(b); Education (School Curriculum and Assessment Authority) (Transfer of Functions) Order 1994 (S.I. 1994/645); Education (School Curriculum and Assessment Authority) (Transfer of Functions) Order 1995 (S.I. 1995/903).
(2)	1988 s.14(5); 1993 Sch.15 para.4(3), Sch.19 para.118(c).
(3), (4)	1988 s.14(6); 1993 Sch.15 para.4(3), Sch.19 para.118(d).
(5)	Drafting.
362(1), (2)	1988 s.16(1), (2).
(3), (4)	1988 s.16(3); 1993 Sch.19 para.119(a).
(5), (6)	1988 s.16(4), (5).
(7)	1988 s.16(6); 1993 Sch.15 para.4(4), Sch.19 para.119(b).
363	1988 s.17.
364	1988 s.18; 1993 Sch.19 para.120.
365(1)	1988 s.19(1).
(2) to (4)	1988 s.19(2).
(5)	1988 s.19(1).
(6)	1988 s.19(10).
366(1)	1988 s.19(3).
(2)	1988 s.19(4).
(3)	1988 s.19(4); 1993 Sch.19 para.121(a); Law Com. Rec. No. 15.
(4)	Law Com. Rec. No. 15.
(5)	1988 s.19(5); Law Com. Rec. No. 15.
(6)	1988 s.19(6); 1993 Sch.19 para.121(b); Law Com. Rec. No. 15.
(7)	Law Com. Rec. No. 15.
367(1)	1988 s.19(7).
(2), (3)	1988 s.19(8).
(4)	1988 s.19(9).
368(1)	1988 ss.20(1), 21(1).
(2)	1988 ss.20(2), 21(2); 1993 s.243.
(3)	1988 ss.20(3), 21(3); 1993 s.243.
(4), (5)	1988 ss.20(4), 21(3A); 1993 s.243.
(6), (7)	1988 ss.20(5), 21(3B); 1993 s.243.
(8)	1988 ss.20(6), 21(4).
(9)	1993 s.242(1), (3).
(10)	1988 ss.20(2), 21(2); 1993 Sch.15 para.4(5), Sch.19 para.122; drafting.

369	1988 s.227(1).
370(1)	1986 s.17(1)
(2), (3)	1986 s.17(2), (3).
371(1), (2)	1986 s.18(1).
(3)	1986 s.18(2).
(4)	1986 s.18(3).
(5)	1986 s.18(7); 1993 Sch.19 para.94.
(6)	1986 s.18(8).
(7)	1986 s.18(7); Law Com. Rec. No. 3.
(8)	Drafting.
372(1)	1986 s.18(5).
(2) to (4)	1986 s.18(6).
(5)	Drafting.
373(1), (2)	1986 s.19.
374	Drafting.
375(1)	Drafting.
(2)	1944 s.114(1) ("agreed syllabus"); 1988 Sch.1 para.6.
(3)	1988 s.8(3).
(4)	1944 s.114(1) ("agreed syllabus"), Sch.5 para.11; 1988 Sch.1 para.6.
(5)	1988 s.8(3).
376(1)	1944 s.26(1); 1988 Sch.1 para.1.
(2)	1944 s.26(2); 1988 Sch.1 para.1.
(3)	1944 s.26(3), (4); 1988 Sch.1 para.1; 1993 Sch.19 para.9.
377(1)	1944 s.27(6); 1988 Sch.1 para.2(2).
(2)	1944 s.27(1); 1988 Sch.1 para.2(1).
378(1)	1944 s.28(1); 1988 Sch.1 para.3(1).
(2), (3)	1944 s.28(1B); 1988 Sch.1 para.3(1).
(4)	1944 s.28(1C); 1988 Sch.1 para.3(1).
(5)	1944 s.28(1A); 1988 Sch.1 para.3(1).
379(1)	1993 s.138(1).
(2) to (4)	1993 s.138(9) to (11).
380	1993 s.139.
381	1993 s.140.
382	1993 s.142.
383	1993 s.141.
384	1988 s.10(1).
385(1)	1988 s.6(1), (7).
(2)	1988 s.6(2).
(3)	1988 s.6(7).
(4)	1988 s.6(3); 1993 s.138(8); Law Com. Rec. No. 16.
(5)	1988 s.6(4).
(6)	1988 s.6(5); Law Com. Rec. No. 16.
(7)	1988 s.6(6).
386(1)	1988 s.7(1); 1993 s.138(1).
(2)	1988 s.7(1); 1993 s.138(2).
(3)	1988 s.7(2); 1993 s.138(3).
(4)	1988 s.7(3); 1993 s.138(4).
(5)	1988 s.7(4); 1993 s.138(5).
(6)	1988 s.7(5); 1993 s.138(6).
(7)	1993 s.138(12).
387	1988 s.7(6); 1993 s.138(7).
388	1988 s.10(1).
389(1)	1988 s.9(3).
(2)	1988 s.9(9).

(3)	1988 s.9(4).
(4)	1988 s.9(6).
(5)	1988 s.9(7); 1993 Sch.19 para.115.
(6)	1988 s.9(8).
(7)	1988 s.9(2), (5).
390(1)	1988 s.11(1).
(2)	1988 s.11(3), (4); 1993 s.147(1).
(3)	1988 ss.11(3), 13(4).
(4)	1988 s.11(4); 1993 Sch.19 para.116(a).
(5)	1988 s.11(5).
(6)	1988 s.11(5); 1993 s.255(2).
(7)	1988 s.11(6).
391(1)	1988 s.11(1).
(2)	1988 s.11(2).
(3)	1988 s.11(7).
(4)	1988 s.11(7).
(5)	1988 s.11(8).
(6)	1988 s.11(9).
(7)	1988 s.11(10).
(8), (9)	1988 s.11(11), (12); 1993 s.147(2).
(10)	1988 s.11(13); 1993 Sch.15 para.4(2), Sch.19 para.116(b).
392(1)	1988 s.11(1).
(2)	1988 s.13(1); 1993 Sch.19 para.117.
(3)	1988 s.13(2); 1993 Sch.19 para.117.
(4)	1988 s.13(3).
(5)	1988 s.13(4).
(6)	1988 s.13(5).
(7)	1988 s.13(6).
(8)	1988 s.13(7); 1993 Sch.19 para.117.
393	1993 s.16.
394(1)	1988 ss.11(1), 12(1); 1993 s.148(a).
(2), (3)	1988 s.12(2), (3).
(4)	1988 s.12(4); 1993 s.148(b).
(5)	1988 s.12(1).
(6)	1988 s.12(9); 1993 s.148(c).
(7)	1988 s.12(10).
(8)	1988 s.12(11); 1993 s.148(d).
395(1)	1988 s.12(5).
(2)	1988 s.12(6).
(3), (4)	1988 s.12(7).
(5)	1988 s.12(8).
(6)	1988 s.12(5), (6).
(7)	1988 s.12(9); 1993 s.148(c).
(8)	1988 s.12(10).
396(1)	1988 s.12A(1), (3); 1993 s.257.
(2)	1988 s.12A(2); 1993 s.257.
397	1993 s.258.
398	1988 s.9(1), 9(1A); 1992FHE s.12(4); 1994 Sch.2 para.8(2).
399	1944 s.67(3); 1988 Sch.1 para.4, Sch.12 para.4.
400(1), (2)	1988 s.5(1).
(3)	1988 s.5(2).
(4)	1988 s.10(2).
(5)	1988 s.5(3).
401(1)	1988 s.24(1); 1992FHE Sch.8 para.28.

(2)	1988 s.24(2); 1993 Sch.19 para.124.
(3), (4)	1988 s.24(3), (4).
(5)	1988 s.235(2)(c).
402(1)	1988 s.117(1).
(2)	1988 s.117(2); 1993 s.240(5).
(3) to (5)	1988 s.117(3) to (5).
(6)	1988 s.118(7), (8).
403(1)	1986 ss.46, 46A; 1988 Sch.12 para.34.
(2)	1986 s.46.
404(1), (2)	1993 s.241(5)
(3)	1993 s.241(6)
405	1988 s.17A; 1993 s.241(3).
406(1), (2)	1986 ss.44(1), (2), 46A; 1988 Sch.12 para.34.
(3)	1986 s.44(1).
407(1)	1986 ss.45, 46A; 1988 Sch.12 para.34.
(2)	1986 s.45.
408(1)	1988 s.22(1).
(2)	1988 s.22(2); 1992(S) Sch.4 para.6(2).
(3)	1988 s.22(3); 1993 Sch.19 para.123.
(4)	1988 s.22(1); Law Com. Rec. No. 17.
(5)	1988 s.22(4).
(6)	1988 s.22(5); 1992(S) Sch.4 para.6(3), (4).
(7), (8)	1988 s.22(6), (7).
409(1) to (3)	1988 s.23(1).
(4)	1988 s.23(2).
410	1988 s.25(2); Law Com. Rec. No. 17.
411(1), (2)	1980 s.6(1), (2).
(3)	1980 s.6(3); 1988 s.30(2).
(4)	1980 s.6(4).
(5)	1980 s.6(5); 1978IA s.17(2)(a).
(6)	1988 s.26(9).
(7)	1988 s.26(10).
(8)	1980 s.38(4).
412	1986 s.33.
413(1)	1980 s.6(6); 1988 s.30(3).
(2) to (4)	1980 s.6(7) to (9); 1993 s.270.
414(1), (2)	1980 s.8(1), (2).
(3), (4)	1980 s.8(3); 1988 s.31(2).
(5)	1980 s.8(4).
(6) to (8)	1980 s.8(5), (5A), (6); 1992(S) Sch.4 para.4(1).
(9)	1980 s.8(7).
415	Drafting.
416(1)	1988 s.26(1).
(2) to (7)	1988 s.26(3) to (8).
(8)	1988 s.26(1), (3), (4).
417(1)	1988 ss.27(1), (2), 32(4).
(2), (3)	1988 s.27(3).
(4), (5)	1988 s.27(9).
418(1)	1988 ss.27(1), (2), 32(4); Education Reform Act 1988 (Commencement No.9) Order 1991 (S.I. 1991/409).
(2)	1988 s.27(3).
(3)	1988 s.27(3), (9).
419(1)	1988 s.29(7).
(2) to (5)	1988 s.29(1) to (4).

420(1) to (3)	1988 s.27(4) to (6).
(4), (5)	1988 s.27(7).
421(1)	1988 s.27(8).
(2)	1988 s.32(1).
422(1) to (6)	1986 Sch.2 para.19.
(7)	1986 s.65(1) ("promoters"), Sch.2 para.1; drafting; Law Com. Rec. No. 9.
423(1)	1980 s.7(1); 1993 Sch.19 para.73.
(2), (3)	1980 s.7(2), (3).
(4)	1980 s.7(4).
(5)	1980 s.7(5).
(6)	1980 s.38(4).
424(1)	1980 s.9(1); 1988 s.31(3).
(2)	1980 s.9(1A); 1988 s.31(3).
(3)	1980 s.9(2); 1981 Sch.3 para.14; 1992(S) Sch.4 para.4(2); 1993 Sch.19 para.74.
425	Drafting.
426	1993 s.149(1) to (4).
427	1993 s.150.
428	1993 s.151.
429	Drafting.
430(1) to (8)	1993 s.260.
(9)	1993 s.305(1) ("maintained school").
431(1) to (6)	1993 s.13(1) to (6).
(7), (8)	1993 ss.13(7), (8), 305(1) ("maintained school").
432	1993 s.14.
433(1), (2)	1948 s.4(2).
(3)	1948 s.4(3).
(4)	1948 s.4(3A); 1996N Sch.3 para.2.
(5)	1948 s.4(2).
434(1)	1944 s.80(1).
(2)	1944 s.80(1A); 1988 Sch.12 para.58.
(3)	1948 s.4(6).
(4)	1944 s.80(1); 1993 Sch.19 para.21.
(5)	1944 s.114(1); 1993 s.155(1), Sch.19 para.24(a)(ii).
(6)	1944 s.80(2).
435	1948 s.4(1).
436(1)	1980 s.9(1A); 1988 ss.29(5), 31(3); 1993 s.155(6).
(2)	1988 s.29(5), (6); 1993 s.149(5).
437(1) to (7)	1993 s.192(1) to (7).
(8)	1993 ss.192(8), 197(6), 198(4), 305(1) ("maintained school").
438	1993 s.193.
439	1993 s.194.
440	1993 s.195.
441	1993 s.196.
442	1993 s.197(1) to (5).
443(1) to (3)	1993 s.198(1) to (3).
(4)	1993 s.201(2).
444(1) to (4)	1993 s.199(1) to (4).
(5)	1993 s.199(5); Units of Measurement Regulations 1995 (S.I. 1995/1804) Reg.3.
(6), (7)	1993 s.199(6), (7).
(8)	1993 s.201(2).
(9)	1993 s.199(8).
445	1993 s.200.
446	1993 s.201(1).
447	1993 s.202.

448	1993 s.203.
449	1988 s.118(7).
450(1)	1988 s.106(1).
(2)	1988 s.106(1A); 1992FHE s.12(9); 1994 Sch.2 para.8(3).
451(1), (2)	1988 s.106(2).
(3)	1988 s.106(3), (4); 1993 s.280.
(4)	1988 s.106(4).
(5)	1988 s.106(3), (4); 1993 Sch.19 para.127.
452(1) to (4)	1988 s.107(1) to (4).
(5)	1988 s.107(5), (6).
(6)	1988 s.106(9).
453(1)	1988 s.106(5).
(2), (3)	1988 s.108.
454(1)	1988 s.106(6).
(2)	1988 s.118(3).
(3), (4)	1988 s.106(7), (8).
455(1)	1988 s.109(1).
(2)	1988 s.109(2).
(3)	1988 ss.109(2), 110(5).
456(1)	1988 s.109(3); 1978IA s.17(2)(a).
(2) to (8)	1988 s.109(4) to (10).
457(1)	1988 s.110(1); 1993 Sch.19 para.128.
(2), (3)	1988 s.110(2).
(4)	1988 s.110(3); Disability Living Allowance and Disability Working Allowance Act 1991 (c.21) Sch.3 para.12; Jobseekers Act 1995 (c.18) Sch.2 para.17.
(5)	1988 s.110(4).
458(1) to (4)	1988 s.111(1) to (3) and (5); 1993 Sch.19 para.129.
(5)	1988 s.111(6).
459	1988 s.118(5).
460(1), (2)	1988 s.118(1), (2).
(3)	1988 s.118(4).
461	1988 s.118(6).
462(1)	1988 s.118(7)(a), (e).
(2)	1988 s.106(10).
(3)	1988 s.106(11).
(4)	1988 s.118(7)(d).
(5)	1988 s.118(7)(d), (8).
463	1944 s.114(1) ("independent school"); 1980 s.34(1); 1988 Sch.12 para.7.
464(1) to (3)	1944 s.70(1); Transfer of Functions (Education and Employment) Order 1995 (S.I 1995/2986) art.11(2).
(4)	Drafting.
465(1)	1944 s.70(1).
(2)	1944 s.70(1) proviso (a).
(3)	1944 s.70(1) proviso (b).
(4)	1944 s.114(1) ("provisionally registered school"; "registered school").
466(1)	1944 s.70(3).
(2)	1944 s.70(3A); 1980 s.34(6).
(3)	1944 s.70(3).
467(1)	1944 s.70(4); 1980 s.34(7).
(2)	1944 s.70(4A); 1993 s.292(2).
(3)	1944 s.70(4); 1980 s.34 (7).
(4)	Drafting.
468	1944 s.71(4); 1993 s.290(1).
469(1)	1944 s.71(1); Children Act 1989 (c.41) Sch.13 para.9; 1993 s.290(2).

(2), (3)	1944 s.71(1).
(4)	1944 s.71(2); 1993 s.290(2).
(5)	1944 s.71(3).
(6)	1944 s.71(5); 1993 s.290(1).
470(1)	1944 s.72(1).
(2)	1944 s.72(2); 1993 s.290(2).
471(1)	1944 s.72(3).
(2)	1944 s.72(3) proviso; 1993 s.290(2).
472	1944 s.72(4); 1993 s.290(2).
473(1)	1944 s.73(2).
(2)	1944 s.73(3); 1993 s.290(2).
474	1944 s.74.
475	1944 s.73(1).
476(1)	Drafting.
(2), (3)	1944 s.75(1).
(4)	1944 s.75(2); Arbitration Act 1996 (c.23) Sch.3 para.4.
(5)	1944 s.75(3).
477	1944 s.73(5); 1946 Sch.2 Pt.I; 1978IA s.17(2)(a).
478(1)	1944 s.73(4).
(2)	1944 ss.70(3), 73(2), (3); Criminal Justice Act 1982 (c.48) Sch.3.
479(1) to (3)	1980 s.17(1) to (3).
(4)	1980 s.17(2).
(5)	1980 s.17(4), (5).
(6), (7)	1980 s.17(10).
480(1), (2)	1980 s.17(6), (7).
(3)	1980 s.17(9).
(4)	1980 s.17(8), (9).
481	1980 s.18.
482(1)	1988 s.105(1).
(2)	1988 s.105(2).
(3)	1988 s.105(1), (2).
(4)	1988 s.105(3).
(5)	1988 s.218(2B); 1993 s.291; 1994 Sch.2 para.8(4).
483(1), (2)	1988 s.105(4).
(3), (4)	1988 s.105(5), (6).
484(1)	1984 s.1(1), (2); 1993 s.278(2).
(2)	1984 s.1(2), (6).
(3), (4)	1984 s.1(3), (4); 1993 s.278(2).
(5)	1984 s.1(5).
(6)	1984 s.1(7).
(7)	Drafting.
485	1944 s.100(1)(b); 1988 s.213(3).
486	1988 s.213(1); Transfer of Functions (Science) Order 1995 (S.I. 1995/2985) Sch. para.5.
487	1980 s.21(1).
488	1988 s.210.
489(1)	1944 s.100(3); 1980 s.21(2); 1984 s.1(4); 1988 ss.210(3), 213(2).
(2)	1984 s.1(4A); 1993 s.278(4).
(3), (4)	1973 s.1(2).
490	1988 s.211; 1978IA s.17(2)(a).
491(1)	1944 s.100(1)(c).
(2)	1944 s.100(3).
492(1) to (4)	1986 s.51(1) to (4); 1993 s.279(1).
(5)	1986 s.51(11); 1993 Sch.19 para.103(d).

(6)	1986 s.51(7), (8); 1993 Sch.19 para.103(a).
493(1)	1986 s.52(1); 1992FHE Sch.8 para.25.
(2)	1986 s.52(2); 1993 Sch.19 para.104.
(3)	1986 s.52(3); 1992FHE Sch.8 para.25.
(4)	1986 s.52(4).
494	1993 s.262.
495(1), (2)	1944 s.67(1).
(3)	1944 s.67(2).
496(1)	1944 s.68.
(2)	1944 s.68; 1988 s.219(2).
497(1)	1944 s.99(1).
(2)	1944 s.99(1); 1988 s.219(3).
(3)	1944 s.99(1).
498(1)	1944 s.99(2).
(2)	1944 s.99(2); 1988 s.219(3).
499	1993 s.297.
500	1993 s.232.
501	1993 s.233.
502	1993 s.234.
503(1) to (6)	1993 s.235(1) to (6).
(7)	1993 s.235(8).
504	1993 s.236.
505(1) to (7)	1993 s.237(1) to (7).
(8)	1993 ss.237(8), 305(1) ("maintained school")
506	1944 s.69(2); Criminal Justice Act 1967 (c.80) Sch.3; 1978IA s.17(2)(a); Medical Act 1983 (c.54) Sch. 6 para.11.
507(1)	1944 s.93.
(2)	1944 s.93; 1972LG s.272(2); 1993 s.235(7).
508(1)	1944 s.53(1).
(2)	1944 s.53(1); 1948 Sch.1 Pt.I; 1988 Sch.12 para.54.
(3)	1944 s.53(2).
509(1), (2)	1944 s.55(1); 1992FHE Sch.8 para.5.
(3)	1944 s.55(2); 1948 Sch.1 Pt.I; 1988 Sch.12 para.55; 1992FHE Sch.8 para.5.
(4)	1944 s.55(3); 1986 s.53; 1992FHE Sch.8 para.5; 1993 Sch.19 para.15.
(5)	1944 s.55(4); 1992FHE Sch.8 para.5.
(6)	1944 s.55(5); 1992FHE Sch.8 para.5.
510(1)	1948 s.5(1); 1988 s.100(4).
(2)	1948 s.5(1); 1953 Sch.1; 1981 Sch.3 para.7.
(3)	1948 s.5(2); 1988 s.100(4).
(4)	1948 s.5(3); 1980 s.29(1); 1988 s.100(4), Sch.12 para.61; 1992FHE Sch.8 para.16.
(5)	1948 s.5(4); 1988 s.100(4).
(6)	1948 s.5(4).
511(1)	1948 s.5(5).
(2), (3)	1948 s.5(6).
(4)	1948 s.5(6A); 1980 s.29(2).
512(1)	1980 s.22(1); Social Security Act 1986 (c.50) s.77(1).
(2)	1980 s.22(2); Social Security Act 1986 (c.50) s.77(2).
(3)	1980 s.22(3); Social Security Act 1986 (c.50) s.77(2); Jobseekers Act 1995 (c.18) Sch.2 para.3.
(4)	1980 s.22(1).
(5)	1980 s.22(3B); 1992FHE Sch.8 para.17.
513	1944 s.78(2).
514(1)	1944 s.50(1); 1946 Sch.2 Pt.I; 1981 Sch.3 para.3; 1988 s.100(2).
(2)	1944 s.50(1); 1948 Sch.1 Pt.I; 1981 Sch.3 para.3.

(3)	1944 s.50(2); 1946 Sch.2 Pt.I; 1993 Sch.19 para.12.
(4)	1944 s.52(1).
(5)	1944 s.52(1) proviso; 1981 Sch.3 para.4.
(6)	1944 s.52(2).
(7)	1944 s.52(3).
515(1)	1980 s.26(1).
(2)	1980 s.26(3).
(3)	1980 s.26(4).
(4)	1980 s.26(5); 1978IA s.17(2)(a).
(5)	1980 s.26(6).
516	1993 s.295.
517(1)	1953 s.6(2); 1993 Sch.19 para.31(a).
(2)	1953 s.6(2)(a)(i).
(3)	1953 s.6(2)(a)(ii); 1981 Sch.3 para.8.
(4)	1953 s.6(2)(a)(iii).
(5)	1953 s.6(2)(b); 1981 Sch.3 para.8.
(6)	1993 Sch.19 para.31(b) to (f).
(7)	1993 s.308(3).
518	1944 s.81; 1988 Sch.12 para.6; 1992FHE Sch.8 para.11.
519(1)	1986 s.58(1); 1988 Sch.12 para.103; 1993 Sch.19 para.106.
(2)	1986 s.58(2).
(3)	1986 s.58(5); 1988 Sch.12 para.103.
(4), (5)	1986 s.58(6).
(6)	1986 s.58(7).
520(1), (2)	1944 s.48(4); 1973NHSR Sch.4 para.7; National Health Service Act 1977 (c.49) Sch.15 para.2; 1978IA s.17(2)(a).
(3)	Drafting.
521(1), (2)	1944 s.54(1).
(3)	1944 s.54(2), (8); Medical Act 1983 (c.54) Sch.6 para.11.
(4)	1944 s.54(1); 1993 Sch.19 para.14(a).
522(1)	1944 s.54(2).
(2) to (4)	1944 s.54(3).
(5)	1944 s.54(5).
523(1), (2)	1944 s.54(4); S.I. 1968/1699 art.5; 1972LG s.179(3).
(3)	1944 s.54(9); 1994LG(W) Sch.16 para.8.
(4)	1944 s.54(8); Medical Act 1983 (c.54) Sch.6 para.11.
524(1), (2)	1944 s.54(7).
(3)	1944 s.54(7); 1993 Sch.19 para.14(c).
525(1)	1944 s.54(6).
(2)	1944 s.54(6).
(3)	1944 s.54(6); 1993 Sch.19 para.14(b).
526	1944 s.82.
527	1944 s.83.
528	1944 s.41(2A), (2B); Disability Discrimination Act 1995 (c.50) s.30(8).
529(1)	1944 s.85(1).
(2), (3)	1944 s.85(2), (3); 1980 Sch.3 para.3.
530(1)	1944 s.90(1); Acquisition of Land (Authorisation Procedure) Act 1946 (c.49) Sch.4; 1948 s.10(1); 1988 Sch.12 para.59.
(2)	1944 s.90(1) proviso; Acquisition of Land (Authorisation Procedure) Act 1946 (c.49) Sch.4.
(3)	1944 s.90(1A); 1993 s.282(3).
531(1)	1948 s.10(2); 1972LG s.272(2); 1988 Sch.12 para.62.
(2)	1948 s.10(3).
532	1944 s.88; 1978IA s.17(2)(a).

533(1), (2)	1980 s.22(4).
(3)	1980 s.22(4A); 1993 Sch.19 para.79.
534(1) to (4)	1980 s.22(3A); 1988 Sch.12 para.24.
(5)	1980 s.22(3B); 1992FHE Sch.8 para.17.
535(1)	1980 s.26(2).
(2)	1980 s.26(3).
(3)	1980 s.26(4).
(4)	1980 s.26(5); 1978IA s.17(2)(a).
(5)	1980 s.26(6).
536(1), (2)	1944 s.48(4); 1973NHSR Sch.4 para.7; National Health Service Act 1977 (c.49) Sch.15 para.2; 1978IA s.17(2)(a); 1988 Sch.12 para.2.
537(1) to (6)	1992(S) s.16(1) to (6).
(7)	1992(S) s.16(7); 1993 s.263.
(8) to (10)	1992(S) s.16(8) to (10).
(11)	1992(S) s.19(2)
(12), (13)	1992(S) s.16(11), (12).
538	1986 s.56, Sch.2 para.13(2).
539	1993 s.153.
540(1)	1993 s.264(1).
(2)	1993 ss.264(2), 305(1) ("maintained school").
541(1) to (3)	1993 s.265.
(4)	1993 ss. 265(1), 305(1) ("maintained school").
542(1)	1944 s.10(1); 1988 Sch.12 para.1.
(2) to (4)	1944 s.10(2); 1988 Sch.12 para.1.
543	1944 s.10(2) proviso; 1948 s.7(1); 1968 s.3(3).
544(1)	1988 s.218(7); 1992FHE Sch.8 para.49; 1993 Sch.19 para.136.
(2)	1988 s.218(7).
(3)	1988 s.218(12).
545(1)	1944 s.63(2); 1993 Sch.19 para.18.
(2)	1988 s.218(8); 1993 Sch.19 para.19.
546(1)	1988 s.218(1)(e).
(2)	1988 s.218(12).
547(1)	1982LG(MP) s.40(1).
(2)	1982LG(MP) s.40(2); 1988 Sch.12 para.29.
(3)	1982LG(MP) s.40(3).
(4), (5)	1982LG(MP) s.40(4), (5); 1988 Sch.12 para.29.
(6)	1982LG(MP) s.40(6).
(7), (8)	1982LG(MP) s.40(7), (8); 1988 Sch.12 para.29.
548(1)	1986 s.47(1); 1993 s.293(2).
(2)	1986 s.47(1A); 1993 s.293(2).
(3)	1986 s.47(5); 1988 Sch.12 para.35; 1993 s.293(3), Sch.19 para.101(a).
(4)	1986 s.47(6); 1993 Sch.19 para.101(b).
(5)	1986 s.47(7).
(6)	1986 s.47(4).
549(1), (2)	1986 s.47(2), (3).
(3)	1986 s.47(1B); 1993 s.293(2).
(4)	1986 s.47(10).
(5)	1986 s.47(5); 1993 s.293(3).
550	1986 s.47(8).
551(1).	1988 s.218(1)(g).
(2)	1988 s.218(12).
552(1)	1993 Sch.19 para.62(5).
(2), (3)	1993 Sch.19 para.62(2), (3).
(4)	1993 Sch.19 para.62(1).

(5)	1993 Sch.19 para.62(4)
(6)	1993 Sch.19 para.62(6).
553	1988 s.113.
554(1)	1973 s.2(1); 1988 s.112(2).
(2)	1973 s.2(1); 1988 s.112(2); 1993 Sch.19 para.52(a).
(3)	1973 s.2(1A); 1988 s.112(2); 1993 Sch.19 para.52(b).
(4)	1973 s.2(1C); 1988 s.112(2); 1993 Sch.19 para.52(c).
(5)	1973 s.2(1B); 1988 s.112(2).
(6)	1973 s.2(8).
555(1)	1973 s.2(2); 1993 Sch.19 para.52(c).
(2) to (4)	1973 s.2(2).
(5)	1973 s.2(1B); 1988 s.112(2).
556(1)	1973 s.2(3); 1993 s.288(3)
(2)	1973 s.2(4); 1988 s.112(3); 1993 Sch.19 para.52(c).
(3)	1973 s.2(4); 1993 s.288(2), Sch.19 para.52(c).
(4)	1973 s.2(5).
(5)	1973 s.2(5A); 1993 s.288(4).
(6), (7)	1973 s.2(6), (7).
(8)	1973 s.2(1B); 1988 s.112(2).
557	1993 s.287.
558	1944 s.58.
559(1), (2)	1944 s.59(1), (2).
(3), (4)	1944 s.59(3).
(5)	1944 s.59(4).
(6)	Employment of Children Act 1973 (c.24) s.3(4).
560(1)	1973EWE s.1(1); 1988 Sch.12 para.14.
(2)	1973EWE s.1(4); Employment Act 1990 (c.38) s.14.
(3)	1973EWE s.1(2); Merchant Shipping Act 1995 (c.21) Sch.13 para.48.
(4), (5)	1973EWE s.1(3).
(6)	Drafting.
(7)	1973EWE s.1(4).
561	1944 s.115.
562	1944 s.116; 1948 Sch.1 Pt.I; 1993 Sch.19 para.25.
563(1)	1988 s.218(1)(f); 1992FHE Sch.8 para.49.
(2)	1988 s.218(4).
(3)	1988 s.218(12).
564(1)	1944 s.94(1); S.I. 1968/1699 art.5; Registration of Births, Deaths and Marriages (Fees) Order 1995 (S.I. 1995/3162) Sch.
(2)	1944 s.94(1).
(3)	1944 s.94(2); S.I. 1968/1699 art.5.
(4)	1944 s.94(3); 1978IA s.17(2)(a).
565(1)	1944 s.95(1).
(2)	1993 s.200(3).
566	1944 s.95(2).
567(1), (2)	1993 s.299(1), (2).
(3)	1993 ss.299(3), 305(1) ("maintained school")
(4), (5)	1993 s.299(4), (5).
568(1)	1973 s.2(1); 1986 s.63(1); 1988 s.232(1); 1993 s.301(1); Law Com. Rec. No. 19.
(2)	1986 ss.4A(8), 63(1); 1988 s.232(2); 1993 ss.271(1), 301(2).
(3)	1986 s.63(2); 1988 s.232(4); 1993 s.301(3).
(4)	1988 s.232(3).
(5)	1986 s.63(3); 1988 s.232(5); 1993 s.301(6); Law Com. Rec. No. 18.
(6)	1988 s.232(6); Law Com. Rec. No. 18.
569(1)	Statutory Instruments Act 1946 (c.36) s.1(2); 1948 s.12; 1980 s.35(1); 1984 s.3(1); 1986

	s.63(1); 1988 s.232(1); 1992(S) s.19(1); 1993 s.301(1); Law Com. Rec. No. 18.
(2)	1944 s.112; Statutory Instruments Act 1946 (c.36) s.5(2); 1948 s.12; 1980 s.35(3); 1984 s.3(3); 1986 s.63(2); 1988 s.232(4); 1992(S) s.19(2); 1993 ss.279(2)(a), 301(3).
(3)	1980 s.35(2); 1986 s.63(2A); 1993 ss.279(2)(b), 301(4).
(4)	1980 s.35(4); 1984 s.3(4); 1986 s.63(3); 1988 s.232(5); 1992(S) s.19(3); 1993 s.301(6), Sch.19 para.107(a); Law Com. Rec. No. 18.
(5)	1944 s.111A; 1980 s.35(5); 1988 ss.229(1), 232(6); Law Com. Rec. No. 18.
(6)	1980 s.35(5).
570(1), (2)	1944 s.111; S.I. 1968/1699 art.5; 1993 s.301(7).
(3)	1944 s.111 proviso.
571	1980 ss.12(1B), 13(1C); 1988 s.34(3); 1993 ss.229(1), 230(1), 300.
572	1944 s.113; 1946 Sch.2 Pt.I.
573(1)	Drafting.
(2)	1944 s.114(1) ("alterations"); 1968 Sch.1 para.5(a); 1993 s.305(1).
(3)	1944 s.114(1) ("enlargement"); 1968 Sch.1 para.5(b).
(4)	1980 s.16(2); 1993 s.103(1).
(5)	1944 s.114(1) ("significant"); 1968 Sch.1 para.5(c).
(6)	1944 s.67(4); 1968 Sch.1 para.3; 1988 Sch.12 para.4.
574	1968 s.1(1); 1980 Sch.3 para.15; 1993 Sch.19 para.41.
575(1), (2)	1988 s.235(1); 1993 s.305(1); 1996ER Sch.1 paras.37(5), 59.
(3)	1988 s.235(3); 1933 s.155(9), (10).
(4)	1988 s.235(1); 1993 s.305(1) 1996ER Sch.1 paras.37(5), 59.
576(1)	1944 s.114(1D); Children Act 1989 (c.41) Sch.13 para.10.
(2)	1944 s.114(1E); Children Act 1989 (c.41) Sch.13 para.10; 1993 Sch.19 para.24(b).
(3), (4)	1944 s.114(1F); Children Act 1989 (c.41) Sch.13 para.10.
577	1944 s.114 ("minor authority"); 1972LG s.192(4); Local Government Changes for England (Education) (Miscellaneous Provisions) Regulations 1996 (S.I. 1996/710) reg.19.
578	1992FHE s.90(1) ("the Education Acts"); 1993 s.305(1)("the Education Acts"); 1996N Sch.3 para.8.
579(1)	"boarder": 1986 s.65(1). "child": 1944 s.114(1). "clothing": 1944 s.114(1). "exclude": 1986 s.65(1). "financial year": 1984 s.1(6); 1988 s.235(1), Sch.2 para.18; 1993 s.305(1), Sch.14 para.20. "functions": 1988 s.235(1); 1993 s.305(1). "governing body"; "governor": 1944 s.114(1); 1980 Sch.1 para.13. "higher education": 1944 s.114(1); 1988 s.120(9). "land": 1988 s.235(1); 1993 s.306(1). "liability": 1988 s.235(1); 1993 s.305(1). "local authority": 1988 s.235; 1993 s.305(1); 1994LG(W) Sch.16 paras.83, 105(2). "the local education authority": 1944 s.114(1); 1988 s.118(7)(b); 1993 s.305(1). "local government elector": 1944 s.114(1); 1972LG s.272(2). "medical officer": 1944 s.114(1); 1973NHSR Sch.4 para.8; Medical Act 1983 (c.54) Sch.6 para.11. "modifications": 1988 s.235(1); 1993 s.305(1). "premises": 1944 s.114(1). "prescribed": 1944 s.114(1); 1993 s.305(1). "proprietor": 1944 ss.80(1), 114(1); 1988 Sch.12 para.5. "reception class": 1980 s.38(5A)(b); 1988 ss.31(6), 119(1)(b); 1993 s.155(1). "relevant age group": 1980 s.16(3); 1988 s.32(2); 1993 s.155(4). "school buildings": 1946 s.4(2); 1973NHSR Sch.4 para.9; National Health Service Act 1977 (c.49) Sch.15 para.3; 1978IA s.17(2)(a). "school day": 1986 s.65(1). "trust deed": 1944 s.114(1). "young person": 1944 s.114(1).
(2)	1988 s.235(3)(g); 1993 s.305(2).
(3)	1980 s.38(5A); 1988 ss.31(6), 119(1)(a); 1993 s.155(5).
(4)	1980 s.38(5); 1986 s.51(10); 1993 Sch.19 para.103.
(5)	1944 s.114(2)(b).
(6)	1944 s.114(2)(b); 1988 s.234(2)(a), (3)(a).
(7)	1944 s.114(2A); 1988 s.234(2)(b); 1992FHE Sch.8 para.13(4).
580	
581	1944 s.118; S.I. 1977/293 art.4; Law Com. Rec. No. 19.

582	
583	
Sch. 1	1993 Sch.18.
Sch. 2	
para.1	1993 Sch.1 para.16
paras.2 to 8	1993 Sch.1 paras.1 to 7.
para.9	1993 Sch.19 paras.46 to 48.
paras.10 to 14	1993 Sch.1 paras.8 to 12.
para.15	1993 Sch.1 para.15.
paras.16, 17	1993 Sch.1 paras.13, 14.
Sch. 3	
para.1	1993 s.17; 1996N Sch.3 para.10.
para.2	1993 s.18.
para.3	1993 s.19.
Sch. 4	
para.1	1993 Sch.2 para.1, s.305(1) ("maintained school")
paras.2 to 23	1993 Sch.2 paras.2 to 23.
Sch. 5	
para.1	
para.2	1944 Sch.3 para.8.
para.3	1944 Sch.3 paras.4, 5; 1948 Sch.1,Pt.I; 1980 Sch.3 para.5.
para.4	1944 Sch.3 para.7; drafting.
para.5	1944 Sch.3 para.9.
para.6	1944 Sch.3 para.10.
Sch. 6	1944 Sch.2.
Sch. 7	
para.1	1993 s.238(5) to (7).
para.2	1993 s.239.
para.3	1993 Sch.13 para.2
para.4	1993 Sch.13 para.1
para.5	1993 Sch.13 para.3
paras.6 to 10	1993 Sch.3 paras.8 to 12.
paras.11, 12	1993 Sch.13 paras.14, 15
Sch. 8	
para.1	Drafting.
para.2	1986 ss.6, 15(12), (13); drafting.
para.3	1986 s.15(11).
para.4	1986 s.15(7).
para.5	1986 s.15(1).
para.6	1986 s.15(8).
para.7	Drafting; 1986 s.15(2) to (6), (15).
para.8	1986 s.15(14).
para.9	1986 s.15(10).
para.10	1986 ss.8(6), (9), 15(9).
para.11	1986 s.8(2), (3); 1993 s.271(2).
para.12	1986 s.8(4).
para.13	1986 s.8(5).
para.14	1986 s.8(1).
para.15	1986 s.8(6), (7), (9); 1988 s.116; drafting.
para.16	1986 s.8(11), (12); Law Com. Rec. Nos. 3, 20.
para.17	1986 s.8(8).
para.18	1986 s.62.
para.19	Drafting.
para.20	1986 s.57.

para.21	1986 s.8(10).
Sch. 9	
para.1	1986 s.65(1) ("promoters"), Sch.2 para.1; Law Com. Rec. No. 9.
para.2	1986 Sch.2 para.2(1), (2); 1993 Sch.19 para.109(a), (b)(i).
para.3	1986 Sch.2 para.6.
para.4	1986 Sch.2 para.7(1).
para.5	1986 Sch.2 para.8(1).
para.6	1986 Sch.2 para.7(2) to (5).
para.7	1986 Sch.2 paras.7(6), (7), 8(2).
para.8	1986 Sch.2 para.9(1), (2); 1993 Sch.19 para.109(e).
para.9	1986 Sch.2 paras.2(3), 11(4), (5).
para.10	1986 Sch.2 para.11(3).
para.11	1986 Sch.2 para.11(6).
para.12	1986 Sch.2 para.11(1), (2).
para.13	1986 Sch.2 para.10(4).
para.14	1986 Sch.2 para.10(2).
para.15	1986 Sch.2 paras.10(1), 26(3).
para.16	1986 Sch.2 para.10(4).
para.17	1986 Sch.2 para.2(4).
para.18	1986 Sch.2 para.10(3).
para.19	1986 Sch.2 para.27.
para.20	1986 Sch.2 para.28.
para.21	1986 Sch.2 para.30(1).
para.22	1986 Sch.2 para.29.
Sch. 10	
para.1	1986 Sch.2 para.3(4).
para.2	1986 Sch.2 para.3(5).
para.3	1986 Sch.2 para.4.
para.4	1986 Sch.2 para.13(3), (4).
para.5	1986 Sch.2 paras.2(2), 3(2), (3); 1993 Sch.19 para.109(b)(i).
para.6	1986 Sch.2 para.13(3), (5).
Sch. 11	
para.1	Drafting.
para.2	1988 ss.33(6), 42(4)(a) to (d).
para.3	1988 s.42(4)(e), (5)(a).
para.4	1988 s.42(4)(j).
paras.5 to 7	1988 s.50(5); 51(1) ("expenditure of a capital nature").
para.8	1988 s.50(10).
Sch. 12	
para.1	1988 s.48(2) ("temporary governing body").
para.2	1988 Sch.4 para.1(2)(a), (b).
para.3	1988 Sch.4 paras.1(1), 2(1).
para.4	1988 Sch.4 para.2(2) to (5).
para.5	1988 Sch.4 para.2(6); S.I. 1991/1890; S.I. 1992/110.
para.6	1988 Sch.4 para.2(8).
para.7	1988 Sch.4 para.2(9).
para.8	1988 Sch.4 para.3.
para.9	1988 Sch.4 para.6.
para.10	1988 Sch.4 para.5.
Sch. 13	
para.1	1986 s.36(1).
para.2	1986 s.36(2).
para.3	1986 s.37.
para.4	1986 s.39.

para.5	1986 s.38(1), (2).
para.6	1986 s.38(3).
para.7	1986 s.38(4).
para.8	1986 s.38(6).
para.9	1986 s.38(5).
para.10	1986 s.35(2).
para.11(1), (2)	1986 s.41(1)(a).
(3)	1986 s.41(3).
(4) to (7)	1986 s.41(1)(b) to (e).
(8)	1986 s.41(3).
Sch. 14	
para.1	1988 Sch.3 paras.1(1), (2), (6), 2(1), 4(1), 5(1), 6(1), 7(1), 8(1), 10(1), 11(3); 1978IA s.17(2)(a).
para.2	1988 Sch.3 para.1(1).
para.3	1988 Sch.3 para.1(3).
para.4	1988 Sch.3 para.1(4), (5), (12).
para.5	1988 Sch.3 para.1(7).
para.6	1988 Sch.3 para.1(8) to (10).
para.7	1988 Sch.3 para.1(11), (13).
para.8	1988 Sch.3 para.2(1).
para.9	1988 Sch.3 para.2(2), (3).
para.10	1988 Sch.3 para.2(4).
para.11	1988 Sch.3 para.2(5).
para.12	1988 Sch.3 para.2(6), (7).
para.13	1988 Sch.3 para.2(8), (9).
para.14	1988 Sch.3 para.2(10), (11).
para.15	1988 Sch.3 para.2(12).
para.16	1988 Sch.3 para.3(1) to (3).
para.17	1988 Sch.3 para.3(4).
para.18	1988 Sch.3 para.4(1) to (3), (5).
para.19	1988 Sch.3 para.4(4).
para.20	1988 Sch.3 para.5.
para.21	1988 Sch.3 para.6.
para.22	1988 Sch.3 para.7.
para.23	1988 Sch.3 para.8(1) to (3), (6).
para.24	1988 Sch.3 para.8(4), (5).
para.25	1988 Sch.3 para.8(7), (8).
para.26	1988 Sch.3 para.8(9).
para.27	1988 Sch.3 para.9; 1978IA s.17(2)(a).
para.28	1988 Sch.3 para.10; 1993 Sch.19 para.142.
Sch. 15	
para.1	1986 s.24.
para.2	1986 s.24(a), (h); 1993 Sch.13 para.97.
para.3	1986 s.24(b), (f), (g).
para.4	1986 s.24(h).
para.5	1986 s.24(b), (g).
para.6	1986 s.24(d), (h).
para.7	1986 s.24(h).
para.8	1986 s.25.
para.9	1986 s.25(a), (h).
para.10	1986 s.25(b).
para.11	1986 s.25(b), (g).
para.12	1986 s.25(c), (h); 1993 Sch.19 para.98.
para.13	1986 s.25(h).

para.14	1993 Sch.19 para.99.
para.15	Drafting.
Sch. 16	
para.1	1986 Sch.3 paras.1, 2; S.I. 1994/2092.
para.2	1986 Sch.3 para.3; S.I. 1994/2092.
para.3	1986 Sch.3 para.3A; S.I. 1994/2092.
para.4	1986 Sch.3 para.4; drafting.
para.5	1986 Sch.3 para.16.
para.6	1986 Sch.3 para.6.
para.7	1986 Sch.3 para.6A; S.I. 1994/2092.
para.8	1986 Sch.3 para.7; Education (No.2) Act 1986 (Amendment) (No.2) Order 1993 (S.I. 1993/2827) art.2.
para.9	1986 Sch.3 para.8; Education (No.2) Act 1986 (Amendment) Order 1993 (S.I. 1993/2709) art.2.
para.10	1986 Sch.3 para.9; S.I. 1994/2092 art.8.
para.11	1986 Sch.3 para.13.
para.12	1986 Sch.3 para.14.
para.13	1986 Sch.3 para.11.
para.14	1986 Sch.3 para.12; S.I. 1994/2092 art.9.
para.15	1986 Sch.3 para.15.
para.16	1986 Sch.3 para.17; S.I. 1994/2092 art.10.
para.17	Drafting.
para.18	1986 Sch.3 para.5.
Sch. 17	
para.1	1986 s.30(2).
para.2	1986 s.30(2)(a).
para.3	1986 s.30(2)(b).
para.4	1986 s.30(2)(c) to (e).
para.5	1986 s.30(2)(g).
para.6	1986 s.30(2)(h); 1988 s.51(9); Education (No.2) Act 1986 (Amendment) Order 1994 (S.I. 1994/692) art.2.
para.7	1986 s.30(2)(i); Education (No.2) Act 1986 (Amendment) (No.3) Order 1994 (S.I. 1994/2732).
para.8	1986 s.30(2)(j).
para.9	1986 s.30(2)(k); 1978IA s.17(2)(a).
para.10	1986 s.30(5); 1992(S) Sch.4 para.5.
Sch. 18	
para.1	1986 s.31(4)(a).
para.2	1986 s.31(4)(b), (9).
para.3	1986 s.31(3).
para.4	1986 s.31(4)(c), (d).
para.5	1986 s.31(5), (6).
Sch. 19	
para.1	1986 Sch.2 paras.4, 12(1).
para.2	1988 Sch.4 para.7.
para.3	1986 Sch.2 para.12(2).
para.4	1986 Sch.2 para.12(3).
para.5	1986 Sch.2 para.20(5).
para.6	1986 Sch.2 para.21.
para.7	1986 Sch.2 para.22.
para.8	1986 Sch.2 para.23.
para.9	1986 Sch.2 para.25.
para.10	1986 Sch.2 para.24.
para.11	1986 Sch.2 para.26(1), (2).

para.12	1986 Sch.2 para.30(2).
para.13	Drafting.
para.14	1986 Sch.2 para.20(1).
para.15	1986 Sch.2 para.20(2), (3); Law Com. Rec. No. 9.
para.16	1986 Sch.2 paras.20(4), 30(3).
para.17	1986 Sch.2 para.28.
para.18	1988 Sch.4 para.1.
para.19	1988 Sch.4 para.4(1), (4), (5).
para.20	1988 Sch.4 para.4(2).
para.21	1988 Sch.4 para.4(3); Education (Application of Financing Schemes to Special Schools) Regulations 1992 (S.I. 1992/164).
para.22	1988 Sch.4 para.4(7).
para.23	1988 Sch.4 para.4(8).
para.24	1988 Sch.4 para.4(6).
para.25	1986 Sch.2 para.15.
para.26	1986 Sch.2 para.16; 1988 Sch.12 para.106.
para.27	1986 Sch.2 para.17.
para.28	1986 Sch.2 paras.13(1), 14.
para.29	1986 Sch.2 para.18; 1988 Sch.4 para.2(10).
Sch. 20	
para.1	1993 Sch.3 para.1(1) to (4); drafting.
paras.2 to 12	1993 Sch.3 paras.2 to 12.
Sch. 21	1993 Sch.4.
Sch. 22	
paras.1 to 13	1993 Sch.5 paras.1 to 13.
para.14	1986 s.62; 1988 Sch.12 para.37.
paras.15, 16	1993 Sch.5 paras.14, 15.
Sch. 23	
paras.1 to 3	1993 Sch.6 paras.1 to 3.
para.4	1993 Sch.6 para.7
para.5	1993 Sch.6 paras.4, 6.
para.6	1993 Sch.6 paras.5, 6.
paras.7, 8	1993 Sch.6 paras.8, 9.
Sch. 24	1993 Sch.7.
Sch. 25	1993 Sch.8.
Sch. 26	1993 Sch.9.
Sch. 27	1993 Sch.10.
Sch. 28	
paras.1 to 14	1993 Sch.11, paras.1 to 14.
para.15	1993 s.261(1), (2), (5).
Sch. 29	
paras.1 to 16	1993 Sch.14 paras.1 to 16.
para.17	1993 Sch.14 para.17; 1993 Sch.15 para.6(2).
paras.18 to 22	1993 Sch.14 paras.18 to 22.
Sch. 30	
paras.1 to 5	1988 Sch.2 paras.2 to 6; 1993 Sch.15 para.4(6).
paras.6, 7	1988 Sch.2 para.7; 1993 Sch.15 para.4(6).
para.8	1988 Sch.2 para.8; 1993 Sch.15 para.4(6), Sch.19 para.141.
paras.9, 10	1988 Sch.2 para.10; 1993 Sch.15 para.4(6).
para.11	1988 Sch.2 para.11; 1993 s.249, Sch.15 para.4(6).
paras.12, 13	1988 Sch.2 paras.12, 13; 1993 Sch.15 para.4(6).
para.14	1988 Sch.2 para.13A; 1993 s.250, Sch.15 para.4(6).
paras.15, 16	1988 Sch.2 paras.14, 15; 1993 Sch.15 para.4(6).
para.17	1988 Sch.2 para.18; 1993 s.251(3), Sch.15 para.4(6).

paras.18, 19	1988 Sch.2 paras.16, 17; 1993 Sch.15 para.4(6).
Sch. 31	
para.1	1944 Sch.5 para.12(1), (3); 1993 s.256(1).
para.2	1944 Sch.5 para.12(4); 1993 s.256(1).
para.3	1988 s.11(8).
para.4	1944 Sch.5 paras.2, 5; 1988 Sch.1 para.7; 1993 s.254(3), Sch.19 para.27.
paras.5, 6	1944 Sch.5 paras.7, 8.
para.7	1944 Sch.5 para.3; 1988 Sch.1 para.7; 1993 Sch.19 para.27.
paras.8, 9	1944 Sch.5 para.4; 1993 Sch.19 para.27.
para.10	1944 Sch.5 para.13; 1988 Sch.1 para.7; 1993 s.256(2).
para.11	1993 s.146.
para.12	1944 Sch.5 paras.10, 13(4); 1988 Sch.1 para.7.
para.13	1944 Sch.5 para.11; 1988 Sch.1 para.7.
para.14	1944 Sch.5 para.11.
para.15	1993 s.15.
Sch. 32	
para.1	1988 s.28(1).
para.2	1988 s.28(2).
para.3	1988 s.28(3), (4).
para.4	1988 s.28(5).
para.5	1988 ss.28(6), (7), 32(1).
para.6	1988 s.28(8).
para.7	1988 s.119(2), (3).
Sch. 33	
para.1	1980 Sch.2 para.1; 1993 Sch.16 para.2.
para.2	1980 Sch.2 para.2; 1993 Sch.16 para.3.
para.3	1980 Sch.2 para.3.
para.4	1980 Sch.2 para.4; Local Government and Housing Act 1989 (Commencement No.11 and Savings) Order 1991 (S.I. 1991/344) Sch. para.1.
para.5	1980 Sch.2 para.4A; 1993 Sch.16 para.4.
para.6	1993 s.267.
para.7	1993 s.268.
para.8	Drafting.
paras.9 to 11	1980 Sch.2 paras.5 to 7.
para.12	1980 Sch.2 para.10.
para.13	1980 Sch.2 para.8.
para.14	1980 Sch.2 para.9
para.15	1980 Sch.2 para.11.
Sch. 34	
para.1	1944 Sch.6 para.1.
para.2	1944 Sch.6 para.2.
para.3	1944 Sch.6 paras.3, 3A; Judicial Pensions and Retirement Act 1993 (c.8) Sch.6 para.51.
para.4	1944 Sch.6 para.4.
para.5	1976 s.6(1).
Sch. 35	
paras.1 to 3	1980 Sch.4 paras.1 to 3.
para.4	1980 Sch.4 para.4; 1986 s.47(9).
paras.5, 6	1980 Sch.4 paras.5, 6.
Sch. 36	1993 Sch.17.
Schs. 37, 38	
Sch. 39	
para.1	
para.2	1993 s.303.
para.3	1944 s.2(1).

para.4	1944 s.120(1).
paras.5 to 9	
para.10(1)	
(2)	1980 s.1(4).
para.11	1986 Sch.5 para.1.
paras.12 to 16	
para.17(1)	
(2)	1993 s.274(3).
(3)	1993 s.274(5).
para.18	Law Com. Rec. No.12.
para.19	S.I. 1996/951 art.4.
paras.20 to 23	
para.24	1993 Sch.20 para.1; S.I. 1993/3106 Sch.2 paras.8, 9.
para.25	1993 Sch.20 para.1; S.I. 1993/3106 Sch.2 para.10.
para.26	S.I. 1993/3106 para.11.
para.27	S.I. 1993/3106 Sch.2 para.14.
para.28	1993 Sch.20 para.5.
para.29	1993 Sch.20 para.6.
para.30	S.I. 1993/1975 Sch.2 para.4(2).
para.31	1993 Sch.20 para.2; S.I. 1994/507 Sch.3 para.10.
para.32	S.I. 1994/507 Sch.3 para.11.
para.33	S.I. 1994/507 Sch.3 para.12.
para.34	S.I. 1994/2038 Sch.4 paras.2(7), 4(3).
para.35	S.I. 1994/507 Sch.3 para.5.
paras.36 to 42	
para.43	S.I. 1993/507 Sch.3 para.7.
para.44	1993 Sch.20 para.4.
para.45	1946 s.13(1).
para.46	
para.47	1944 s.120(5).
para.48	
para.49	1973 Sch.1 para.3.
para.50	
Sch. 40	

---

[1] S. 1(2)(b) and preceding word repealed (1.9.1999) by 1998 c. 31, s. 140(1)(3), Sch. 30 para. 58, Sch. 31 (with ss. 138(9), 144(6)); S.I. 1999/2323, art. 2(1), Sch. 1 (with savings in Sch. 7 paras. 2-4, 6, 7, 10, 12)

[2] Words in s. 1(3) substituted (28.7.2000 for certain purposes otherwise 1.4.2001) by 2000 c. 21, ss. 149, 154(5), Sch. 9 para. 51 (with s. 150); S.I. 2001/654, art. 2(2), Sch. Pt. II (with art. 3); S.I. 2001/1274, art. 2(1), Sch. Pt. I

[3] S. 2(1) substituted (1.10.2002 for E., otherwise prosp.) by Education Act 2002 (c. 32), ss. 156(2), 216(4) (with ss. 210(8), 214(4)); S.I. 2002/2439, art. 3

[4] Words in s. 2(2A)(a) inserted (26.7.2002) by Education Act 2002 (c. 32), ss. 65(3), 216(2), Sch. 7 para. 6(2) (with ss. 210(8), 214(4)); S.I. 2002/2002, art. 2

[5] Words in s. 2(2B)(b) inserted (1.10.2002 for E., otherwise prosp.) by Education Act 2002 (c. 32), ss. 177(2)(a), 216(4) (with ss. 210(8), 214(4)); S.I. 2002/2439, art. 3

[6] Words in s. 2(2B) inserted (1.10.2002 for E., otherwise prosp.) by Education Act 2002 (c. 32), ss. 177(2)(b), 216(4) (with ss. 210(8), 214(4)); S.I. 2002/2439, art. 3

[7] S. 2(2A)(2B) inserted (1.9.2000 for E. for certain purposes and 1.4.2001 otherwise for E.W.) by 2000 c. 21, s. 110(1) (with s. 150); S.I. 2000/2114, art. 2(3), Sch. Pt. III; S.I. 2001/654, art. 2(2), Sch. Pt. II (with art. 3); S.I. 2001/1274, art. 2(1), Sch. Pt. I (with art. 3)

[8] Words in s. 2(3)(a) repealed (1.10.2002 for E., otherwise prosp.) by Education Act 2002 (c. 32), ss. 215(2), 216(4), Sch. 22 Pt. 3 (with ss. 210(8), 214(4)); S.I. 2002/2439, art. 3

[9] S. 2(6A) inserted (1.10.2002 for E., otherwise prosp.) by Education Act 2002 (c. 32), ss. 177(3), 216(4) (with ss. 210(8), 214(4)); S.I. 2002/2439, art. 3

[10] Words in s. 2(4) inserted (1.10.2002 for E., 19.12.2002 for W.) by Education Act 2002 (c. 32), ss. 215(1), 216(4), Sch. 21 para. 33 (with ss. 210(8), 214(4)); S.I. 2002/2439, art. 3; S.I. 2002/3185, art. 4, Sch. Pt. 1

[11] Words in s. 3(1) inserted (1.9.1997) by 1997 c. 44, s. 57(1), Sch. 7 para. 9(2); S.I. 1997/1468, art. 2, Sch. 1 Pt. II

[12] S. 3(1A) inserted (2.9.2002 for E., otherwise prosp.) by Education Act 2002 (c. 32), ss. 215(1), 216(4), Sch. 21 para. 34(2) (with ss. 210(8), 214(4)); S.I. 2002/2002, art. 4

[13] Words in s. 3(3) substituted (2.9.2002 for E., otherwise prosp.) by Education Act 2002 (c. 32), ss. 215(1), 216(4), Sch. 21 para. 34(3) (with ss. 210(8), 214(4)); S.I. 2002/2002, art. 4

[14] Words in s. 4(1) repealed (1.10.2002 for E., otherwise prosp.) by Education Act 2002 (c. 32), ss. 215(2), 216(4), Sch. 22 Pt. 3 (with ss. 210(8), 214(4)); S.I. 2002/2439, art. 3

[15] S. 4(1) substituted (1.9.1997) by 1997 c. 44, s. 51; S.I. 1997/1468, art. 2, Sch. 1 Pt. II

[16] Words in s. 4(2) substituted (1.9.1998) by 1997 c. 44, s. 57(1), Sch. 7 para. 10(a); S.I. 1998/386, art.2, Sch. 1 Pt. IV

[17] Words in s. 4(2) repealed (1.9.1998) by 1997 c. 44, s. 57(1)(4), Sch. 7 para. 10(b), Sch. 8; S.I. 1998/386, art. 2, Sch. 1 Pt. IV

[18] Words in s. 5(1) repealed (1.10.2002 for E., otherwise prosp.) by Education Act 2002 (c. 32), ss. 215(2), 216(4), Sch. 22 Pt. 3 (with ss. 210(8), 214(4)); S.I. 2002/2439, art. 3

[19] Words in s. 5(3) and (5) substituted (1.9.1999) by 1998 c. 31, s. 140(1), Sch. 30 para. 59(a)(b) (with ss. 138(9), 144(6)); S.I. 1999/2323, art. 2(1), Sch. 1 (with savings in art. 18, Sch. 7 paras. 2-4, 6, 7, 10, 12)

[20] Words in s. 5(3) and (5) substituted (1.9.1999) by 1998 c. 31, s. 140(1), Sch. 30 para. 59(a)(b) (with ss. 138(9), 144(6)); S.I. 1999/2323, art. 2(1), Sch. 1 (with savings in art. 18, Sch. 7 paras. 2-4, 6, 7, 10, 12)

[21] Words in s. 6(1) inserted (1.10.2002 for E., otherwise prosp.) by Education Act 2002 (c. 32), ss. 156(1), 216(4) (with ss. 210(8), 214(4)); S.I. 2002/2439, art. 3

[22] Words in s. 6(1) substituted (1.8.1998) by 1997 c. 44, s. 51(1), Sch. 7 para. 11; S.I. 1998/386, art. 2, Sch. 1 Pt. III

[23] Words in s. 6(2) substituted (1.9.1999) by 1998 c. 31, s. 141(1), Sch. 30 para.60 (with ss. 138(9), 144(6)); S.I. 1999/2323, art. 2(1), Sch. 1 (with savings in Sch. 7 paras. 2-4, 6, 7, 10, 12)

[24] S. 8(2) substituted (1.8.1998) by 1997 c. 44, s. 52(2); S.I. 1998/386, art. 2, Sch. 1 Pt.III

[25] S. 8(4) substituted (1.8.1998) by 1997 c. 44, s. 52(3); S.I. 1998/386, art. 2, Sch. 1 Pt. III

[26] Words in s. 9 substituted (1.4.1999) by 1998 c. 31, s. 140(1), Sch. 30 para. 61 (with ss. 138(9), 144(6)); S.I. 1999/1016, art. 2(1), Sch. 1

[27] Words in s. 13(1) substituted (28.7.2000 for certain purposes, otherwise 1.4.2001) by 2000 c. 21, ss. 149, 154, Sch. 9 para. 52(2) (with s. 150); S.I. 2001/654, art. 2(2), Sch. Pt. II (with art. 3); S.I. 2001/1274, art. 2(1), Sch. Pt. I

[28] S. 13(2)(a)(b) substituted (28.7.2000 for certain purposes, otherwise 1.4.2001) by 2000 c. 21, ss. 149, 154, Sch. 9 para. 52(3) (with s. 150); S.I. 2001/654, art. 2(2), Sch. Pt. II (with art. 3)

[29] S. 13A inserted (1.10.1998) by 1998 c. 31, s. 5 (with ss. 138(9), 144(6)); S.I. 1998/2212, art. 2, Sch. 1 Pt. I.

[30] Words in s. 14(4) substituted (1.8.1998) by 1997 c. 44, s. 57(1), Sch. 7 para. 12; S.I. 1998/386, art. 2, Sch. 1 Pt. III

[31] S. 14(4A)(4B) inserted (19.12.2002) by Education Act 2002 (c. 32), ss. 194(1), 216(3) (with ss. 210(8), 214(4)); S.I. 2002/3185, arts. 2, 4, Sch. Pt. 1

[32] S. 14(5) repealed (1.9.1999) by 1998 c. 31, s. 140(1)(3), Sch. 30 para. 62, Sch.31 (with 138(9), 144(6)); S.I. 1999/2323, art. 2(1), Sch. 1 (with savings in Sch. 7 paras. 2-4, 6, 7, 10, 12)

[33] S. 15 repealed (28.7.2000 for certain purposes otherwise 1.4.2001) by 2000 c. 21, ss. 149, 153, 154, Sch. 9 para. 53, Sch. 11 (with s. 150); S.I. 2001/654, art. 2(2), Sch. Pt. II (with art. 3); S.I. 2001/1274, art. 2(1), Sch. Pt. I

[34] Words in s. 15A(1) inserted (28.7.2000 for certain purposes otherwise 1.4.2001) by 2000 c. 21, ss. 149, 154(5), Sch. 9 para. 54(2) (with s. 150); S.I. 2001/654, art. 2(2), Sch. Pt. II (with art. 3); S.I. 2001/1274, art. 2(1), Sch. Pt. I

[35] S. 15A(1A) inserted (28.7.2000 for certain purposes otherwise 1.4.2001) by 2000 c. 21, ss. 149, 154(5), Sch. 9 para. 54(3) (with s. 150) S.I. 2001/654, art. 2(2), Sch. Pt. II (with art. 3); S.I. 2001/1274, art. 2(1), Sch. Pt. I

[36] S. 15A inserted (1.9.1999) by 1998 c. 31, s. 140(1), Sch. 30 para. 63 (with ss. 138(9), 144(6)); S.I. 1999/2323, art. 2(1), Sch. 1 (with savings in Sch. 7 paras. 2-4, 6, 7, 10, 12)

[37] S. 15A(3)(4) inserted (28.7.2000 for certain purposes otherwise 1.4.2001) by 2000 c. 21, ss. 149, 154(5), Sch. 9 para. 54(5) (with s. 150) S.I. 2001/654, art. 2(2), Sch. Pt. II (with art. 3); S.I. 2001/1274, art. 2(1), Sch. Pt. I

[38] S. 15B inserted (28.7.2000 for certain purposes otherwise 1.4.2001) by 2000 c. 21, ss. 149, 154(5), Sch. 9 para. 55 (with s. 150); S.I. 2001/654, art. 2(2), Sch. Pt. II (with art. 3); S.I. 2001/1274, art. 2(1), Sch. Pt. I

[39] Words in s. 17(2) substituted (1.8.1998) by 1997 c. 44, s. 57(1), Sch. 7 para.13; S.I. 1998/386, art. 2, Sch. 1 Pt.III

[40] Words in s. 17(2) substituted (1.8.1998) by 1997 c. 44, s. 57(1), Sch. 7 para.13; S.I. 1998/386, art. 2, Sch. 1 Pt.III

[41] Words in s. 19(1) and (4) repealed (1.9.1998) by 1997 c. 44, ss. 47(2)(3), 57(4), Sch.8; S.I. 1998/386, art. 2, Sch. 1 Pt. IV

[42] S. 19(4A) inserted (1.9.1998) by 1997 c. 44, s. 47(4); S.I. 1998/386, art. 2, Sch. 1 Pt.IV

[43] S. 20 repealed (1.11.1999) by 1998 c. 31, s. 140(1)(3), Sch. 30 para. 66, Sch.31 (with ss. 138(9), 144(6)); S.I. 1999/2323, art. 2(2), Sch. 2 (with savings in Sch. 7 paras. 2-4, 6, 7, 10, 12)

[44] S. 21 repealed (1.4.1999) by 1998 c. 31, ss. 133, 140(1)(3), Sch. 30 para. 66, Sch.31; S.I. 1999/1016, art. 2(1), Sch. 1

[45] S. 22 repealed (1.4.1999 in relation to s. 22 except s. 22(1)(a) and otherwise 1.11.1999) by 1998 c. 31, s. 140(1)(3), Sch. 30 para. 66, Sch. 31 (with ss. 138(9), 144(6)); S.I. 1999/1016, art. 2(1), Sch. 1; S.I. 1999/2323, art. 2(2), Sch. 2 (with savings in Sch. 7 paras. 2-4, 6, 7, 10, 12)

[46] S. 23 repealed (1.11.1999) by 1998 c. 31, s. 140(1)(3), Sch. 30 para. 66, Sch.31 (with ss. 138(9), 144(6)); S.I. 1999/2323, art. 2(2), Sch. 2 (with savings in Sch. 7 paras. 2-4, 6, 7, 10, 12)

47 S. 24 repealed (1.11.1999) by 1998 c. 31, s. 140(1)(3), Sch. 30 para. 66, Sch.31 (with ss. 138(9), 144(6)); S.I. 1999/2323, art. 2(2), Sch. 2 (with savings in Sch. 7 paras. 2-4, 6, 7, 10, 12)

48 S. 25 repealed (1.11.1999) by 1998 c. 31, s. 140(1)(3), Sch. 30 para. 66, Sch.31 (with ss. 138(9), 144(6)); S.I. 1999/2323, art. 2(2), Sch. 2 (with savings in Sch. 7 paras. 2-4, 6, 7, 10, 12)

49 S. 26 repealed (1.11.1999) by 1998 c. 31, s. 140(1)(3), Sch. 30 para. 66, Sch. 31 (with ss. 138(9), 144(6)); S.I. 1999/2323, art. 2(2), Sch. 2 (with savings in Sch. 7 paras. 2-4, 6, 7, 10, 12)

50 S. 27 repealed (1.4.1999) by 1998 c. 31, ss. 140(1)(3), Sch. 30 para. 66, Sch.31 (with ss. 138(9), 144(6)); S.I. 1999/1016, art. 2(1), Sch. 1

51 S. 28 repealed (1.11.1999) by 1998 c. 31, s. 140(1)(3), Sch. 30 para. 66, Sch.31 (with ss. 138(9), 144(6)); S.I. 1999/2323, art. 2(2), Sch. 2 (with savings in Sch. 7 paras. 2-4, 6, 7, 10, 12)

52 . 29(2) repealed (1.11.1999) by 1998 c. 31, s. 140(1)(3), Sch. 30 para. 67(a), Sch.31 (with ss. 138(9), 144(6)); S.I. 1999/2323, art. 2(2), Sch. 2 (with savings in Sch. 7 paras. 2-4, 6, 7, 10, 12)

53 Words in s. 29(3) repealed (1.11.1999) by 1998 c. 31, s. 140(1)(3), Sch. 30 para. 67(b), Sch.31; S.I. 1999/2323, art. 2(2), Sch. 2 (with savings in Sch. 7 paras. 2-4, 6, 7, 10, 12)

54 Words in s. 29(6)(b) substituted (1.8.1998) by 1997 c. 44, s. 57(1), Sch. 7 para. 14; S.I. 1998/386, art. 2, Pt. III

55 S. 30 repealed (1.11.1999) by 1998 c. 31, ss. 140(1)(3), Sch. 30 para. 68, Sch.31; S.I. 1999/2323, art. 2(2), Sch. 2 (with savings in Sch. 7 paras. 2-4, 6, 7, 10, 12)

56 Pt. II (ss. 31-182) repealed (1.10.1998, 10.3.1999, 1.4.1999 respectively in relation to specified provisions and otherwise 1.9.1999) by 1998 c. 31, s. 140(1)(3), Sch. 30 para. 69, Sch.31 (with ss. 138(9), 144(6)); S.I. 1998/2212, art. 2, Sch. 1 Pts. I, IV; S.I. 1999/120, art. 2(2), Sch. 2 ; S.I. 1999/1016, art. 2(1), Sch. 1; S.I. 1999/2323, art. 2(1), Sch. 1 (with savings as specified in those S.I.s and subject to savings in S.I. 1999/704 , S.I. 1999/711, S.I. 1999/2243 and S.I. 1999/2262)

57 S. 31 repealed (1.9.1999) by 1998 c. 31, s. 140(1)(3), Sch. 30 para. 69, Sch. 31 (with ss. 138(9), 144(6)); S.I. 1999/2323, art. 2(1), Sch. 1 (with savings in Sch. 7 paras. 2-4, 6, 7, 10, 12)

58 S. 32 repealed (1.9.1999) by 1998 c. 31, s. 140(1)(3), Sch. 30 para. 69, Sch. 31 (with ss. 138(9), 144(6)); S.I. 1999/2323, art. 2(1), Sch. 1 (with savings in Sch. 7 paras. 2-4, 6, 7, 10, 12)

59 S. 33 repealed (1.9.1999) by 1998 c. 31, s. 140(1)(3), Sch. 30 para. 69, Sch. 31 (with ss. 138(9), 144(6)); S.I. 1999/2323, art. 2(1), Sch. 1 (with savings in Sch. 7 paras. 2-4, 6, 7, 10, 12)

60 S. 34 repealed (1.9.1999) by 1998 c. 31, s. 140(1)(3), Sch. 30 para. 69, Sch. 31 (with ss. 138(9), 144(6)); S.I. 1999/2323, art. 2(1), Sch. 1 (with savings in Sch. 7 paras. 2-4, 6, 7, 10, 12)

61 S. 35 repealed (1.4.1999 in respect of s. 35(8) and otherwise 1.9.1999) by 1998 c. 31, s. 140(1)(3), Sch. 30 para. 69, Sch. 31 (with ss. 138(9), 144(6)); S.I. 1999/1016, art. 2(1), Sch. 1; S.I. 1999/2323, art. 2(1), Sch. 1 (with savings in Sch. 7 paras. 2-4, 6, 7, 10, 12)

62 S. 36 repealed (1.4.1999 in respect of s. 36(3) and otherwise 1.9.1999) by 1998 c. 31, s. 140(1)(3), Sch. 30 para. 69, Sch. 31 (with ss. 138(9), 144(6)); S.I. 1999/1016, art. 2(1), Sch. 1 ; S.I. 1999/2323, art. 2(1), Sch. 1 (with savings in Sch. 7 paras. 2-4, 6, 7, 10, 12 and subject to savings in S.I. 1999/704, regs. 8(2)(a), 14(2)(a))

63 S. 37 repealed (1.4.1999 in respect of s. 37(4)(7)-(9) and otherwise 1.9.1999) by 1998 c. 31, s. 140(1)(3), Sch. 30 para. 69, Sch. 31 (with ss. 138(9), 144(6)); S.I. 1999/1016, art. 2(1), Sch. 1 ; S.I. 1999/2323, art. 2(1), Sch. 1 (with savings in Sch. 7 paras. 2-4, 6, 7, 10, 12 and subject to savings in S.I. 1999/704, regs. 8(2)(a), 14(2)(a))

64 S. 38 repealed (1.9.1999) by 1998 c. 31, s. 140(1)(3), Sch. 30 para. 69, Sch. 31 (with ss. 138(9), 144(6)); S.I. 1999/2323, art. 2(1), Sch. 1 (with savings in Sch. 7 paras. 2-4, 6, 7, 10, 12 and subject to savings in S.I. 1999/704, regs. 8(2)(a), 14(2)(a))

65 S. 39 repealed (1.9.1999) by 1998 c. 31, s. 140(1)(3), Sch. 30 para. 69, Sch. 31 (with ss. 138(9), 144(6)); S.I. 1999/2323, art. 2(1), Sch. 1 ((with savings in Sch. 7 paras. 2-4, 6, 7, 10, 12) and subject to savings in S.I. 1999/704, regs. 8(2)(a), 14(2)(a))

66 S. 40 repealed (1.9.1999) by 1998 c. 31, s. 140(1)(3), Sch. 30 para. 69, Sch. 31 (with ss. 138(9), 144(6)) ;S.I. 1999/2323, art. 2(1), Sch. 1 (with savings in Sch. 7 paras. 2-4, 6, 7, 10, 12)

67 S. 41 repealed (1.9.1999) by 1998 c. 31, s. 140(1)(3), Sch. 30 para. 69, Sch. 31 (with ss. 138(9), 144(6)) ;S.I. 1999/2323, art. 2(1), Sch. 1 (with savings in Sch. 7 paras. 2-4, 6, 7, 10, 12)

68 S. 42 repealed (1.4.1999 in respect of s. 42(4) and otherwise 1.9.1999) by 1998 c. 31, s. 140(1)(3), Sch. 30 para. 69, Sch. 31 (with ss. 138(9), 144(6)) ;S.I. 1999/1016, art. 2(1), Sch. 1 ; S.I. 1999/2323, art. 2(1), Sch. 1 (with savings in Sch. 7 paras. 2-4, 6, 7, 10, 12 and subject to savings in S.I. 1999/704, regs. 8(2)(b), 14(2)(b))

69 S. 43 repealed (1.4.1999 in respect of s. 43(3)-(6) and words in s. 43(2) and otherwise 1.9.1999) by 1998 c. 31, s. 140(1)(3), Sch. 30 para. 69, Sch. 31 (with ss. 138(9), 144(6)); S.I. 1999/1016, art. 2(1), Sch. 1; S.I. 1999/2323, art. 2(1), Sch. 1 (with savings in Sch. 7 paras. 2-4, 6, 7, 10, 12 and subject to savings in S.I. 1999/704, regs. 8(2)(b), 14(2)(b))

70 S. 44 repealed (1.9.1999) by 1998 c. 31, s. 140(1)(3), Sch. 30 para. 69, Sch. 31 (with ss. 138(9), 144(6)); S.I. 1999/2323, art. 2(1), Sch. 1 (with savings in Sch. 7 paras. 2-4, 6, 7, 10, 12 and subject to savings in S.I. 1999/704, regs. 8(2)(b), 14(2)(b))

71 S. 45 repealed (1.9.1999) by 1998 c. 31, s. 140(1)(3), Sch. 30 para. 69, Sch. 31 (with ss. 138(9), 144(6)); S.I. 1999/2323, art. 2(1), Sch. 1 (with savings in Sch. 7 paras. 2-4, 6, 7, 10, 12)

72 S. 46 repealed (1.9.1999) by 1998 c. 31, s. 140(1)(3), Sch. 30 para. 69, Sch. 31 (with ss. 138(9), 144(6)); S.I. 1999/2323, art. 2(1), Sch. 1 (with savings in Sch. 7 paras. 2-4, 6, 7, 10, 12)

[73] S. 47 repealed (1.9.1999) by 1998 c. 31, s. 140(1)(3), Sch. 30 para. 69, Sch. 31 (with ss. 138(9), 144(6)); S.I. 1999/2323, art. 2(1), Sch. 1 (with savings in Sch. 7 paras. 2-4, 6, 7, 10, 12)

[74] S. 48 repealed (1.9.1999) by 1998 c. 31, s. 140(1)(3), Sch. 30 para. 69, Sch. 31 (with ss. 138(9), 144(6)); S.I. 1999/2323, art. 2(1), Sch. 1 (with savings in Sch. 7 paras. 2-4, 6, 7, 10, 12)

[75] S. 49 repealed (1.9.1999) by 1998 c. 31, s. 140(1)(3), Sch. 30 para. 69, Sch. 31 (with ss. 138(9), 144(6)); S.I. 1999/2323, art. 2(1), Sch. 1 (with savings in Sch. 7 paras. 2-4, 6, 7, 10, 12)

[76] S. 50 repealed (1.9.1999) by 1998 c. 31, s. 140(1)(3), Sch. 30 para. 69, Sch. 31 (with ss. 138(9), 144(6)); S.I. 1999/2323, art. 2(1), Sch. 1 (with savings in Sch. 7 paras. 2-4, 6, 7, 10, 12)

[77] S. 51 repealed (1.9.1999) by 1998 c. 31, s. 140(1)(3), Sch. 30 para. 69, Sch. 31 (with ss. 138(9), 144(6)) ; S.I. 1999/2323, art. 2(1), Sch. 1 (with savings in Sch. 7 paras. 2-4, 6, 7, 10, 12)

[78] S. 52 repealed (1.9.1999) by 1998 c. 31, s. 140(1)(3), Sch. 30 para. 69, Sch. 31 (with ss. 138(9), 144(6)) ; S.I. 1999/2323, art. 2(1), Sch. 1 (with savings in Sch. 7 paras. 2-4, 6, 7, 10, 12)

[79] S. 53 repealed (1.9.1999) by 1998 c. 31, s. 140(1)(3), Sch. 30 para. 69, Sch. 31 (with ss. 138(9), 144(6)) ; S.I. 1999/2323, art. 2(1), Sch. 1 (with savings in Sch. 7 paras. 2-4, 6, 7, 10, 12)

[80] S. 54 repealed (10.3.1999 in respect of s. 54(6)(c) and otherwise 1.9.1999) by 1998 c. 31, s. 140(1)(3), Sch. 30 para. 69, Sch. 31 (with ss. 138(9), 144(6)); S.I. 1999/120, art. 2(1), Sch. 1; S.I. 1999/2323, art. 2(2), Sch. 2 (with savings in Sch. 7 paras. 2-4, 6, 7, 10, 12)

[81] S. 55 repealed (1.9.1999) by 1998 c. 31, s. 140(1)(3), Sch. 30 para. 69, Sch. 31 (with ss. 138(9), 144(6)) ; S.I. 1999/2323, art. 2(1), Sch. 1 (with savings in Sch. 7 paras. 2-4, 6, 7, 10, 12)

[82] S. 56 repealed (1.9.1999) by 1998 c. 31, s. 140(1)(3), Sch. 30 para. 69, Sch. 31 (with ss. 138(9), 144(6)) ; S.I. 1999/2323, art. 2(1), Sch. 1 (with savings in Sch. 7 paras. 2-4, 6, 7, 10, 12)

[83] S. 57 repealed (1.9.1999) by 1998 c. 31, s. 140(1)(3), Sch. 30 para. 69, Sch. 31 (with ss. 138(9), 144(6)) ; S.I. 1999/2323, art. 2(1), Sch. 1 (with savings in Sch. 7 paras. 2-4, 6, 7, 10, 12)

[84] S. 58 repealed (1.9.1999) by 1998 c. 31, s. 140(1)(3), Sch. 30 para. 69, Sch. 31 (with ss. 138(9), 144(6)) ; S.I. 1999/2323, art. 2(1), Sch. 1 (with savings in Sch. 7 paras. 2-4, 6, 7, 10, 12)

[85] S. 59 repealed (1.9.1999) by 1998 c. 31, s. 140(1)(3), Sch. 30 para. 69, Sch. 31 (with ss. 138(9), 144(6)); S.I. 1999/2323, art. 2(1), Sch. 1 (with savings in Sch. 7 paras. 2-4, 6, 7, 10, 12)

[86] S. 60 repealed (1.9.1999) by 1998 c. 31, s. 140(1)(3), Sch. 30 para. 69, Sch. 31 (with ss. 138(9), 144(6)); S.I. 1999/2323, art. 2(1), Sch. 1 (with savings in art. 14, Sch. 7 paras. 2-4, 6, 7, 10, 12)

[87] S. 61 repealed (1.9.1999) by 1998 c. 31, s. 140(1)(3), Sch. 30 para. 69, Sch. 31 (with ss. 138(9), 144(6)) ; S.I. 1999/2323, art. 2(1), Sch. 1 (with savings in art. 15, Sch. 7 paras. 2-4, 6, 7, 10, 12) and subject to an amendment (1.9.1999) by S.I. 1999/2243, reg. 59

[88] S. 62 repealed (1.9.1999) by 1998 c. 31, s. 140(1)(3), Sch. 30 para. 69, Sch. 31 (with ss. 138(9), 144(6)); S.I. 1999/2323, art. 2(1), Sch. 1 (with savings in Sch. 7 paras. 2-4, 6, 7, 10, 12)

[89] S. 63 repealed (1.9.1999) by 1998 c. 31, s. 140(1)(3), Sch. 30 para. 69, Sch. 31 (with ss. 138(9), 144(6)); S.I. 1999/2323, art. 2(1), Sch. 1 ((with savings in Sch. 7 paras. 2-4, 6, 7, 10, 12 and subject to savings in S.I. 1999/704, regs. 8, 10)

[90] S. 64 repealed (1.9.1999) by 1998 c. 31, s. 140(1)(3), Sch. 30 para. 69, Sch. 31 (with ss. 138(9), 144(6)); S.I. 1999/2323, art. 2(1), Sch. 1 ((with savings in Sch. 7 paras. 2-4, 6, 7, 10, 12 and subject to savings in S.I. 1999/704, regs. 14, 15)

[91] S. 65 repealed (1.9.1999) by 1998 c. 31, s. 140(1)(3), Sch. 30 para. 69, Sch. 31 (with ss. 138(9), 144(6)); S.I. 1999/2323, art. 2(1), Sch. 1 (with savings in Sch. 7 paras. 2-4, 6, 7, 10, 12)

[92] S. 66 repealed (1.9.1999) by 1998 c. 31, s. 140(1)(3), Sch. 30 para. 69, Sch. 31 (with ss. 138(9), 144(6)); S.I. 1999/2323, art. 2(1), Sch. 1 (with savings in Sch. 7 paras. 2-4, 6, 7, 10, 12)

[93] S. 67 repealed (1.9.1999) by 1998 c. 31, s. 140(1)(3), Sch. 30 para. 69, Sch. 31 (with ss. 138(9), 144(6)); S.I. 1999/2323, art. 2(1), Sch. 1 (with savings in Sch. 7 paras. 2-4, 6, 7, 10, 12)

[94] S. 68 repealed (1.9.1999) by 1998 c. 31, s. 140(1)(3), Sch. 30 para. 69, Sch. 31 (with ss. 138(9), 144(6)); S.I. 1999/2323, art. 2(1), Sch. 1 (with savings in Sch. 7 paras. 2-4, 6, 7, 10, 12)

[95] S. 69 repealed (1.9.1999) by 1998 c. 31, s. 140(1)(3), Sch. 30 para. 69, Sch. 31 (with ss. 138(9), 144(6)); S.I. 1999/2323, art. 2(1), Sch. 1 (with savings in Sch. 7 paras. 2-4, 6, 7, 10, 12)

[96] S. 70 repealed (1.9.1999) by 1998 c. 31, s. 140(1)(3), Sch. 30 para. 69, Sch. 31 (with ss. 138(9), 144(6)); S.I. 1999/2323, art. 2(1), Sch. 1 (with savings in Sch. 7 paras. 2-4, 6, 7, 10, 12)

[97] S. 71 repealed (1.9.1999) by 1998 c. 31, s. 140(1)(3), Sch. 30 para. 69, Sch. 31 (with ss. 138(9), 144(6)); S.I. 1999/2323, art. 2(1), Sch. 1 (with savings in Sch. 7 paras. 2-4, 6, 7, 10, 12)

[98] S. 72 repealed (1.9.1999) by 1998 c. 31, s. 140(1)(3), Sch. 30 para. 69, Sch. 31 (with ss. 138(9), 144(6)); S.I. 1999/2323, art. 2(1), Sch. 1 (with savings in Sch. 7 paras. 2-4, 6, 7, 10, 12)

[99] S. 73 repealed (1.9.1999) by 1998 c. 31, s. 140(1)(3), Sch. 30 para. 69, Sch. 31 (with ss. 138(9), 144(6)); S.I. 1999/2323, art. 2(1), Sch. 1 (with savings in Sch. 7 paras. 2-4, 6, 7, 10, 12)

[100] S. 74 repealed (1.9.1999) by 1998 c. 31, s. 140(1)(3), Sch. 30 para. 69, Sch. 31 (with ss. 138(9), 144(6)); S.I. 1999/2323, art. 2(1), Sch. 1 (with savings in Sch. 7 paras. 2-4, 6, 7, 10, 12)

[101] S. 75 repealed (1.9.1999) by 1998 c. 31, s. 140(1)(3), Sch. 30 para. 69, Sch. 31 (with ss. 138(9), 144(6)); S.I. 1999/2323, art. 2(1), Sch. 1 (with savings in Sch. 7 paras. 2-4, 6, 7, 10, 12)

[102] S. 76 repealed (1.9.1999) by 1998 c. 31, s. 140(1)(3), Sch. 30 para. 69, Sch. 31 (with ss. 138(9), 144(6)); S.I. 1999/2323, art.

2(1), Sch. 1 (with savings in Sch. 7 paras. 2-4, 6, 7, 10, 12)

[103] S. 77 repealed (1.9.1999) by 1998 c. 31, s. 140(1)(3), Sch. 30 para. 69, Sch. 31 (with ss. 138(9), 144(6)); S.I. 1999/2323, art. 2(1), Sch. 1 (with savings in Sch. 7 paras. 2-4, 6, 7, 10, 12)

[104] S. 78 repealed (1.9.1999) by 1998 c. 31, s. 140(1)(3), Sch. 30 para. 69, Sch. 31 (with ss. 138(9), 144(6)); S.I. 1999/2323, art. 2(1), Sch. 1 (with savings in Sch. 7 paras. 2-4, 6, 7, 10, 12)

[105] S. 79 repealed (1.9.1999) by 1998 c. 31, s. 140(1)(3), Sch. 30 para. 69, Sch. 31 (with ss. 138(9), 144(6)); S.I. 1999/2323, art. 2(1), Sch. 1 (with savings in Sch. 7 paras. 2-4, 6, 7, 10, 12)

[106] S. 80 repealed (1.9.1999) by 1998 c. 31, s. 140(1)(3), Sch. 30 para. 69, Sch. 31 (with ss. 138(9), 144(6)); S.I. 1999/2323, art. 2(1), Sch. 1 (with savings in Sch. 7 paras. 2-4, 6, 7, 10, 12)

[107] S. 81 repealed (1.9.1999) by 1998 c. 31, s. 140(1)(3), Sch. 30 para. 69, Sch. 31 (with ss. 138(9), 144(6)); S.I. 1999/2323, art. 2(1), Sch. 1 (with savings in Sch. 7 paras. 2-4, 6, 7, 10, 12)

[108] S. 82 repealed (1.9.1999) by 1998 c. 31, s. 140(1)(3), Sch. 30 para. 69, Sch. 31 (with ss. 138(9), 144(6)); S.I. 1999/2323, art. 2(1), Sch. 1 (with savings in Sch. 7 paras. 2-4, 6, 7, 10, 12)

[109] S. 83 repealed (1.9.1999) by 1998 c. 31, s. 140(1)(3), Sch. 30 para. 69, Sch. 31 (with ss. 138(9), 144(6)); S.I. 1999/2323, art. 2(1), Sch. 1 (with savings in Sch. 7 paras. 2-4, 6, 7, 10, 12)

[110] S. 84 repealed (1.9.1999) by 1998 c. 31, s. 140(1)(3), Sch. 30 para. 69, Sch. 31 (with ss. 138(9), 144(6)); S.I. 1999/2323, art. 2(1), Sch. 1 (with savings in Sch. 7 paras. 2-4, 6, 7, 10, 12)

[111] S. 85 repealed (1.9.1999) by 1998 c. 31, s. 140(1)(3), Sch. 30 para. 69, Sch. 31 (with ss. 138(9), 144(6)); S.I. 1999/2323, art. 2(1), Sch. 1 (with savings in Sch. 7 paras. 2-4, 6, 7, 10, 12)

[112] S. 86 repealed (1.9.1999) by 1998 c. 31, s. 140(1)(3), Sch. 30 para. 69, Sch. 31 (with ss. 138(9), 144(6)); S.I. 1999/2323, art. 2(1), Sch. 1 (with savings in Sch. 7 paras. 2-4, 6, 7, 10, 12)

[113] S. 87 repealed (1.9.1999) by 1998 c. 31, s. 140(1)(3), Sch. 30 para. 69, Sch. 31 (with ss. 138(9), 144(6)); S.I. 1999/2323, art. 2(1), Sch. 1 (with savings in Sch. 7 paras. 2-4, 6, 7, 10, 12)

[114] S. 88 repealed (1.9.1999) by 1998 c. 31, s. 140(1)(3), Sch. 30 para. 69, Sch. 31 (with ss. 138(9), 144(6)); S.I. 1999/2323, art. 2(1), Sch. 1 (with savings in Sch. 7 paras. 2-4, 6, 7, 10, 12)

[115] S. 89 repealed (10.3.1999 in respect of s. 89(1)(2) and otherwise 1.9.1999) by 1998 c. 31, s. 140(1)(3), Sch. 30 para. 69, Sch. 31 (with ss. 138(9), 144(6)); S.I. 1999/120, art. 2(2), Sch. 2; S.I. 1999/2323, art. 2(1), Sch. 1 (with savings in Sch. 7 paras. 2-4, 6, 7, 10, 12)

[116] S. 90 repealed (10.3.1999) by 1998 c. 31, s. 140(1)(3), Sch. 30 para. 69, Sch. 31 (with ss. 138(9), 144(6)); S.I. 1999/120, art. 2(2), Sch. 2 (with art. 5(1)(3) and subject to savings in S.I. 1999/2323, Sch. 7 paras. 2-4, 6, 7, 10, 12)

[117] S. 91 repealed (10.3.1999) by 1998 c. 31, s. 140(1)(3), Sch. 30 para. 69, Sch. 31 (with ss. 138(9), 144(6)); S.I. 1999/120, art. 2(2), Sch. 2 (subject to savings in S.I. 1999/2323, Sch. 7 paras. 2-4, 6, 7, 10, 12)

[118] S. 92 repealed (10.3.1999 in respect of s. 92(1)(2)(4) and otherwise 1.9.1999) by 1998 c. 31, s. 140(1)(3), Sch. 30 para. 69, Sch. 31 (with ss. 138(9), 144(6)); S.I. 1999/120, art. 2(2), Sch. 2 (with art. 5(2)); S.I. 1999/2323, art. 2(1), Sch. 1 (with savings in Sch. 7 paras. 2-4, 6, 7, 10, 12)

[119] S. 93 repealed (1.9.1999) by 1998 c. 31, s. 140(1)(3), Sch. 30 para. 69, Sch. 31 (with ss. 138(9), 144(6)); S.I. 1999/2323, art. 2(1), Sch. 1 (with savings in Sch. 7 paras. 2-4, 6, 7, 10, 12)

[120] S. 94 repealed (10.3.1999) by 1998 c. 31, s. 140(1)(3), Sch. 30 para. 69, Sch. 31 (with ss. 138(9), 144(6)); S.I. 1999/120, art. 2(2), Sch. 2 (subject to savings in S.I. 1999/2323, Sch. 7 paras. 2-4, 6, 7, 10, 12)

[121] S. 95 repealed (10.3.1999) by 1998 c. 31, s. 140(1)(3), Sch. 30 para. 69, Sch. 31 (with ss. 138(9), 144(6)); S.I. 1999/120, art. 2(2), Sch. 2 (with art. 5(3) and subject to savings in S.I. 1999/2323, Sch. 7 paras. 2-4, 6, 7, 10, 12)

[122] S. 96 repealed (1.9.1999) by 1998 c. 31, s. 140(1)(3), Sch. 30 para. 69, Sch. 31 (with ss. 138(9), 144(6)); S.I. 1999/2323, art. 2(1), Sch. 1 (with savings in Sch. 7 paras. 2-4, 6, 7, 10, 12 and subject to savings in S.I. 1999/2243, reg. 8(2) and S.I. 1999/2262, reg. 8(2))

[123] S. 97 repealed (1.9.1999) by 1998 c. 31, s. 140(1)(3), Sch. 30 para. 69, Sch. 31 (with ss. 138(9), 144(6));S.I. 1999/2323, art. 2(1), Sch. 1 (with savings in Sch. 7 paras. 2-4, 6, 7, 10, 12 and subject to savings in S.I. 1999/2243, reg. 8(2) and S.I. 1999/2262, reg. 8(2))

[124] S. 98 repealed (1.9.1999) by 1998 c. 31, s. 140(1)(3), Sch. 30 para. 69, Sch. 31 (with ss. 138(9), 144(6)); S.I. 1999/2323, art. 2(1), Sch. 1 (with savings in Sch. 7 paras. 2-4, 6, 7, 10, 12)

[125] S. 99 repealed (1.9.1999) by 1998 c. 31, s. 140(1)(3), Sch. 30 para. 69, Sch. 31 (with ss. 138(9), 144(6)); S.I. 1999/2323, art. 2(1), Sch. 1 (with savings in Sch. 7 paras. 2-4, 6, 7, 10, 12)

[126] S. 100 repealed (1.9.1999) by 1998 c. 31, s. 140(1)(3), Sch. 30 para. 69, Sch. 31 (with ss. 138(9), 144(6)); S.I. 1999/2323, art. 2(1), Sch. 1 (with savings in Sch. 7 paras. 2-4, 6, 7, 10, 12)

[127] Part II Chapter V (ss. 101-126) repealed (1.4.1999 subject to savings) by 1998 c. 31, s. 140(1)(3), Sch. 30 para. 69, Sch.31 (with ss. 138(9), 144(6)); S.I. 1998/2212, arts. 2, 4, Sch. 1 Pt.IV, Sch. 2 Pt. II para. 8 (subject to savings in S.I. 1999/711, reg. 5 and S.I. 1999/2323, Sch. 7 paras. 2-4, 6, 7, 10, 12))

[128] S. 127 repealed (1.9.1999) by 1998 c. 31, s. 140(1)(3), Sch. 30 para. 69, Sch. 31 (with ss. 138(9), 144(6)); S.I. 1999/2323, art. 2(1), Sch. 1 (with savings in Sch. 7 paras. 2-4, 6, 7, 10, 12)

[129] S. 128 repealed (1.9.1999) by 1998 c. 31, s. 140(1)(3), Sch. 30 para. 69, Sch. 31 (with ss. 138(9), 144(6)); S.I. 1999/2323, art. 2(1), Sch. 1 (with savings in Sch. 7 paras. 2-4, 6, 7, 10, 12)

[130] S. 129 repealed (1.9.1999) by 1998 c. 31, s. 140(1)(3), Sch. 30 para. 69, Sch. 31 (with ss. 138(9), 144(6)); S.I. 1999/2323,

art. 2(1), Sch. 1 (with savings in Sch. 7 paras. 2-4, 6, 7, 10, 12)

131 S. 130 repealed (1.9.1999) by 1998 c. 31, s. 140(1)(3), Sch. 30 para. 69, Sch. 31 (with ss. 138(9), 144(6)); S.I. 1999/2323, art. 2(1), Sch. 1 (with savings in Sch. 7 paras. 2-4, 6, 7, 10, 12)

132 S. 131 repealed (1.9.1999) by 1998 c. 31, s. 140(1)(3), Sch. 30 para. 69, Sch. 31 (with ss. 138(9), 144(6)); S.I. 1999/2323, art. 2(1), Sch. 1 (with savings in Sch. 7 paras. 2-4, 6, 7, 10, 12)

133 S. 132 repealed (1.9.1999) by 1998 c. 31, s. 140(1)(3), Sch. 30 para. 69, Sch. 31 (with ss. 138(9), 144(6)); S.I. 1999/2323, art. 2(1), Sch. 1 (with savings in Sch. 7 paras. 2-4, 6, 7, 10, 12)

134 S. 133 repealed (1.9.1999) by 1998 c. 31, s. 140(1)(3), Sch. 30 para. 69, Sch. 31 (with ss. 138(9), 144(6)); S.I. 1999/2323, art. 2(1), Sch. 1 (with savings in Sch. 7 paras. 2-4, 6, 7, 10, 12)

135 S. 134 repealed (1.9.1999) by 1998 c. 31, s. 140(1)(3), Sch. 30 para. 69, Sch. 31 (with ss. 138(9), 144(6)); S.I. 1999/2323, art. 2(1), Sch. 1 (with savings in Sch. 7 paras. 2-4, 6, 7, 10, 12)

136 S. 135 repealed (1.9.1999) by 1998 c. 31, s. 140(1)(3), Sch. 30 para. 69, Sch. 31 (with ss. 138(9), 144(6)); S.I. 1999/2323, art. 2(1), Sch. 1 (with savings in Sch. 7 paras. 2-4, 6, 7, 10, 12)

137 S. 136 repealed (1.9.1999) by 1998 c. 31, s. 140(1)(3), Sch. 30 para. 69, Sch. 31 (with ss. 138(9), 144); S.I. 1999/2323, art. 2(1), Sch. 1 (with savings in Sch. 7 paras. 2, 5, 6, 10, 12)

138 S. 137 repealed (1.9.1999) by 1998 c. 31, s. 140(1)(3), Sch. 30 para. 69, Sch. 31 (with ss. 138(9), 144(6)); S.I. 1999/2323, art. 2(1), Sch. 1 (with savings in Sch. 7 paras. 2-4, 6, 7, 10, 12)

139 S. 138 repealed (1.9.1999) by 1998 c. 31, s. 140(1)(3), Sch. 30 para. 69, Sch. 31 (with ss. 138(9), 144(6)); S.I. 1999/2323, art. 2(1), Sch. 1 (with savings in art. 6, Sch. 7 paras. 2-4, 6, 7, 10, 12)

140 S. 139 repealed (1.4.1999) by 1998 c. 31, s. 140(1)(3), Sch. 30 para. 69, Sch. 31 (with ss. 138(9), 144(6)); S.I. 1999/1016, art. 2(1), Sch. 1 (subject to savings in S.I. 1999/2323, Sch. 7 paras. 2-4, 6, 7, 10, 12)

141 S. 140 repealed (1.9.1999) by 1998 c. 31, s. 140(1)(3), Sch. 30 para. 69, Sch. 31 (with ss. 138(9), 144(6)); S.I. 1999/2323, art. 2(1), Sch. 1 (with savings in Sch. 7 paras. 2-4, 6, 7, 10, 12)

142 S. 141 repealed (1.9.1999) by 1998 c. 31, s. 140(1)(3), Sch. 30 para. 69, Sch. 31 (with ss. 138(9), 144(6)); S.I. 1999/2323, art. 2(1), Sch. 1 (with savings in Sch. 7 paras. 2-4, 6, 7, 10, 12)

143 S. 142 repealed (1.9.1999) by 1998 c. 31, s. 140(1)(3), Sch. 30 para. 69, Sch. 31 (with ss. 138(9), 144(6)); S.I. 1999/2323, art. 2(1), Sch. 1 (with savings in Sch. 7 paras. 2-4, 6, 7, 10, 12)

144 S. 143 repealed (1.9.1999) by 1998 c. 31, s. 140(1)(3), Sch. 30 para. 69, Sch. 31 (with ss. 138(9), 144(6)); S.I. 1999/2323, art. 2(1), Sch. 1 (with savings in Sch. 7 paras. 2-4, 6, 7, 10, 12)

145 S. 144 repealed (1.9.1999) by 1998 c. 31, s. 140(1)(3), Sch. 30 para. 69, Sch. 31 (with ss. 138(9), 144(6)); S.I. 1999/2323, art. 2(1), Sch. 1 (with savings in Sch. 7 paras. 2-4, 6, 7, 10, 12)

146 S. 145 repealed (1.9.1999) by 1998 c. 31, s. 140(1)(3), Sch. 30 para. 69, Sch. 31 (with ss. 138(9), 144(6)); S.I. 1999/2323, art. 2(1), Sch. 1 (with savings in Sch. 7 paras. 2-4, 6, 7, 10, 12)

147 S. 146 repealed (1.9.1999) by 1998 c. 31, s. 140(1)(3), Sch. 30 para. 69, Sch. 31 (with ss. 138(9), 144(6)); S.I. 1999/2323, art. 2(1), Sch. 1 (with savings in Sch. 7 paras. 2-4, 6, 7, 10, 12)

148 S. 147 repealed (1.9.1999) by 1998 c. 31, s. 140(1)(3), Sch. 30 para. 69, Sch. 31 (with ss. 138(9), 144(6)); S.I. 1999/2323, art. 2(1), Sch. 1 (with savings in Sch. 7 paras. 2-4, 6, 7, 10, 12)

149 S. 148 repealed (1.9.1999) by 1998 c. 31, s. 140(1)(3), Sch. 30 para. 69, Sch. 31 (with ss. 138(9), 144(6)); S.I. 1999/2323, art. 2(1), Sch. 1 (with savings in Sch. 7 paras. 2-4, 6, 7, 10, 12)

150 S. 149 repealed (1.9.1999) by 1998 c. 31, s. 140(1)(3), Sch. 30 para. 69, Sch. 31 (with ss. 138(9), 144(6)); S.I. 1999/2323, art. 2(1), Sch. 1 (with savings in Sch. 7 paras. 2-4, 6, 7, 10, 12)

151 S. 150 repealed (1.9.1999) by 1998 c. 31, s. 140(1)(3), Sch. 30 para. 69, Sch. 31 (with ss. 138(9), 144(6)); S.I. 1999/2323, art. 2(1), Sch. 1 (with savings in Sch. 7 paras. 2-4, 6, 7, 10, 12)

152 S. 151 repealed (1.9.1999) by 1998 c. 31, s. 140(1)(3), Sch. 30 para. 69, Sch. 31 (with ss. 138(9), 144(6)); S.I. 1999/2323, art. 2(1), Sch. 1 (with savings in Sch. 7 paras. 2-4, 6, 7, 10, 12)

153 S. 152 repealed (1.9.1999) by 1998 c. 31, s. 140(1)(3), Sch. 30 para. 69, Sch. 31 (with ss. 138(9), 144(6)); S.I. 1999/2323, art. 2(1), Sch. 1 (with savings in Sch. 7 paras. 2-4, 6, 7, 10, 12)

154 S. 153 repealed (1.9.1999) by 1998 c. 31, s. 140(1)(3), Sch. 30 para. 69, Sch. 31 (with ss. 138(9), 144(6)); S.I. 1999/2323, art. 2(1), Sch. 1 (with savings in Sch. 7 paras. 2-4, 6, 7, 10, 12)

155 S. 154 repealed (1.9.1999) by 1998 c. 31, s. 140(1)(3), Sch. 30 para. 69, Sch. 31 (with ss. 138(9), 144(6)); S.I. 1999/2323, art. 2(1), Sch. 1 (with savings in Sch. 7 paras. 2-4, 6, 7, 10, 12)

156 S. 155 repealed (1.10.1998 in respect of s. 155(1)(4) and otherwise 1.4.1999) by 1998 c. 31, s. 140(1)(3), Sch. 30 para. 69, Sch. 31 (with ss. 138(9), 144(6)); S.I. 1998/2212, art. 2, Sch. 1 Pt. I; S.I. 1999/1016, art. 2(1), Sch. 1 (subject to savings in S.I. 1999/2323, Sch. 7 paras. 2-4, 6, 7, 10, 12)

157 S. 156 repealed (1.9.1999) by 1998 c. 31, s. 140(1)(3), Sch. 30 para. 69, Sch. 31 (with ss. 138(9), 144(6)); S.I. 1999/2323, art. 2(1), Sch. 1 (with savings in Sch. 6 paras. 2-6, Sch. 7 paras. 2-4, 6, 7, 10, 12)

158 S. 157 repealed (1.9.1999) by 1998 c. 31, s. 140(1)(3), Sch. 30 para. 69, Sch. 31 (with ss. 138(9), 144(6)); S.I. 1999/2323, art. 2(1), Sch. 1 (with savings in Sch. 6 paras. 2-6, Sch. 7 paras. 2-4, 6, 7, 10, 12)

159 S. 158 repealed (1.9.1999) by 1998 c. 31, s. 140(1)(3), Sch. 30 para. 69, Sch. 31 (with ss. 138(9), 144(6)); S.I. 1999/2323, art. 2(1), Sch. 1 (with savings in Sch. 6 paras. 2-6, Sch. 7 paras. 2-4, 6, 7, 10, 12)

160 S. 159 repealed (1.9.1999) by 1998 c. 31, s. 140(1)(3), Sch. 30 para. 69, Sch. 31 (with ss. 138(9), 144(6)); S.I. 1999/2323,

art. 2(1), Sch. 1 (with savings in Sch. 6 paras. 2-6, Sch. 7 paras. 2-4, 6, 7, 10, 12)

[161] S. 160 repealed (1.9.1999) by 1998 c. 31, s. 140(1)(3), Sch. 30 para. 69, Sch. 31 (with ss. 138(9), 144(6)); S.I. 1999/2323, art. 2(1), Sch. 1 (with savings in Sch. 6 paras. 2-6, Sch. 7 paras. 2-4, 6, 7, 10, 12)

[162] S. 161 repealed (1.9.1999) by 1998 c. 31, s. 140(1)(3), Sch. 30 para. 69, Sch. 31 (with ss. 138(9), 144(6)); S.I. 1999/2323, art. 2(1), Sch. 1 (with savings in Sch. 6 paras. 2-6, Sch. 7 paras. 2-4, 6, 7, 10, 12)

[163] S. 162 repealed (1.9.1999) by 1998 c. 31, s. 140(1)(3), Sch. 30 para. 69, Sch. 31 (with ss. 138(9), 144(6)); S.I. 1999/2323, art. 2(1), Sch. 1 (with savings in Sch. 6 paras. 2-6, Sch. 7 paras. 2-4, 6, 7, 10, 12)

[164] S. 163 repealed (1.9.1999) by 1998 c. 31, s. 140(1)(3), Sch. 30 para. 69, Sch. 31 (with ss. 138(9), 144(6)); S.I. 1999/2323, art. 2(1), Sch. 1 (with savings in Sch. 6 paras. 2-6, Sch. 7 paras. 2-4, 6, 7, 10, 12)

[165] S. 164 repealed (1.9.1999) by 1998 c. 31, s. 140(1)(3), Sch. 30 para. 69, Sch. 31 (with ss. 138(9), 144(6)); S.I. 1999/2323, art. 2(1), Sch. 1 (with savings in Sch. 6 paras. 2-6, Sch. 7 paras. 2-4, 6, 7, 10, 12)

[166] S. 165 repealed (1.9.1999) by 1998 c. 31, s. 140(1)(3), Sch. 30 para. 69, Sch. 31 (with ss. 138(9), 144(6)); S.I. 1999/2323, art. 2(1), Sch. 1 (with savings in Sch. 6 paras. 2-6, Sch. 7 paras. 2-4, 6, 7, 10, 12)

[167] S. 166 repealed (1.9.1999) by 1998 c. 31, s. 140(1)(3), Sch. 30 para. 69, Sch. 31 (with ss. 138(9), 144(6)); S.I. 1999/2323, art. 2(1), Sch. 1 (with savings in Sch. 6 paras. 2-6, Sch. 7 paras. 2-4, 6, 7, 10, 12)

[168] S. 167 repealed (1.4.1999 in respect of s. 167(6) and words in s. 167(1) and otherwise 1.9.1999) by 1998 c. 31, s. 140(1)(3), Sch. 30 para. 69, Sch. 31 (with ss. 138(9), 144(6)); S.I. 1999/1016, art. 2(1), Sch. 1; S.I. 1999/2323, art. 2(1), Sch. 1 (with savings in Sch. 6 paras. 2-6, Sch. 7 paras. 2-4, 6, 7, 10, 12)

[169] S. 168 repealed (1.4.1999 in respect of s. 168(3) and otherwise 1.9.1999) by 1998 c. 31, s. 140(1)(3), Sch. 30 para. 69, Sch. 31 (with ss. 138(9), 144(6)); S.I. 1999/1016, art. 2(1), Sch. 1; S.I. 1999/2323, art. 2(1), Sch. 1 (with savings in Sch. 7 paras. 2-4, 6, 7, 10, 12 and subject to savings in S.I. 1999/704, reg. 14(2)(c))

[170] S. 169 repealed (1.4.1999 in respect of s. 169(4)(6) and words in s. 169(5) and otherwise 1.9.1999) by 1998 c. 31, s. 140(1)(3), Sch. 30 para. 69, Sch. 31 (with ss. 138(9), 144(6)); S.I. 1999/1016, art. 2(1), Sch. 1; S.I. 1999/2323, art. 2(1), Sch. 1 (with savings in Sch. 7 paras. 2-4, 6, 7, 10, 12 and subject to savings in S.I. 1999/704, reg. 14(2)(c))

[171] S. 170 repealed (1.9.1999) by 1998 c. 31, s. 140(1)(3), Sch. 30 para. 69, Sch. 31 (with ss. 138(9), 144(6)); S.I. 1999/2323, art. 2(1), Sch. 1 (with savings in Sch. 7 paras. 2-4, 6, 7, 10, 12 and subject to savings in S.I. 1999/704, reg. 14(2)(c))

[172] S. 171 repealed (1.9.1999) by 1998 c. 31, s. 140(1)(3), Sch. 30 para. 69, Sch. 31 (with ss. 138(9), 144(6)); S.I. 1999/2323, art. 2(1), Sch. 1 (with savings in Sch. 7 paras. 2-4, 6, 7, 10, 12)

[173] S. 172 repealed (1.9.1999) by 1998 c. 31, s. 140(1)(3), Sch. 30 para. 69, Sch. 31 (with ss. 138(9), 144(6)); S.I. 1999/2323, art. 2(1), Sch. 1 (with savings in Sch. 7 paras. 2-4, 6, 7, 10, 12)

[174] S. 173 repealed (1.9.1999) by 1998 c. 31, s. 140(1)(3), Sch. 30 para. 69, Sch. 31 (with ss. 138(9), 144(6)); S.I. 1999/2323, art. 2(1), Sch. 1 (with savings in Sch. 7 paras. 2-4, 6, 7, 10, 12)

[175] S. 174 repealed (1.9.1999) by 1998 c. 31, s. 140(1)(3), Sch. 30 para. 69, Sch. 31 (with ss. 138(9), 144(6)); S.I. 1999/2323, art. 2(1), Sch. 1 (with savings in Sch. 7 paras. 2-4, 6, 7, 10, 12)

[176] S. 175 repealed (1.9.1999) by 1998 c. 31, s. 140(1)(3), Sch. 30 para. 69, Sch. 31 (with ss. 138(9), 144(6)); S.I. 1999/2323, art. 2(1), Sch. 1 (with savings in Sch. 7 paras. 2-4, 6, 7, 10, 12)

[177] S. 176 repealed (1.9.1999) by 1998 c. 31, s. 140(1)(3), Sch. 30 para. 69, Sch. 31 (with ss. 138(9), 144(6)); S.I. 1999/2323, art. 2(1), Sch. 1 (with savings in Sch. 7 paras. 2-4, 6, 7, 10, 12)

[178] S. 177 repealed (1.9.1999) by 1998 c. 31, s. 140(1)(3), Sch. 30 para. 69, Sch. 31 (with ss. 138(9), 144(6)); S.I. 1999/2323, art. 2(1), Sch. 1 (with savings in Sch. 7 paras. 2-4, 6, 7, 10, 12)

[179] S. 178 repealed (1.9.1999) by 1998 c. 31, s. 140(1)(3), Sch. 30 para. 69, Sch. 31 (with ss. 138(9), 144(6)); S.I. 1999/2323, art. 2(1), Sch. 1 (with savings in Sch. 7 paras. 2-4, 6, 7, 10, 12)

[180] S. 179 repealed (1.9.1999) by 1998 c. 31, s. 140(1)(3), Sch. 30 para. 69, Sch. 31 (with ss. 138(9), 144(6)); S.I. 1999/2323, art. 2(1), Sch. 1 (with savings in art. 23(1), Sch. 7 paras. 2-4, 6, 7, 10, 12)

[181] S. 180 repealed (1.9.1999) by 1998 c. 31, s. 140(1)(3), Sch. 30 para. 69, Sch. 31 (with ss. 138(9), 144(6)); S.I. 1999/2323, art. 2(1), Sch. 1 (with savings in Sch. 7 paras. 2-4, 6, 7, 10, 11, 12)

[182] S. 181 repealed (1.9.1999) by 1998 c. 31, s. 140(1)(3), Sch. 30 para. 69, Sch. 31 (with ss. 138(9), 144(6)); S.I. 1999/2323, art. 2(1), Sch. 1 (with savings in Sch. 7 paras. 2-4, 6, 7, 10, 12)

[183] S. 182 repealed (1.9.1999) by 1998 c. 31, s. 140(1)(3), Sch. 30 para. 69, Sch. 31 (with ss. 138(9), 144(6)); S.I. 1999/2323, art. 2(1), Sch. 1 (with savings in Sch. 7 paras. 2-4, 6, 7, 10, 12) and subject to an amendment (1.9.1999) by S.I. 1999/2001, reg. 24, Sch. 8 para. 5

[184] Pt. III (ss. 183-311) repealed (1.10.1998, 1.4.1999 and otherwise 1.9.1999) by 1998 c. 31, s. 140(1)(3), Sch. 30 para. 70, Sch.31 (with ss. 138(9), 144(6)); S.I. 1998/2212, art. 2, Sch. 1 Pt.I; S.I. 1999/120, art. 2(2), Sch. 2; S.I. 1999/1016, art. 2(1), Sch. 1; S.I. 1999/2323, art. 2(1), Sch. 1 (with savings as specified in those S.I.s and subject to savings in S.I. 1999/704)

[185] S. 183 repealed (1.4.1999 in respect of s. 183(4) and otherwise 1.9.1999) by 1998 c. 31, s. 140(1)(3), Sch. 30 para. 69, Sch. 31 (with ss. 138(9), 144(6)); S.I. 1999/1016, art. 2(1), Sch. 1; S.I. 1999/2323, art. 2(1), Sch. 1 (with savings in Sch. 7 paras. 2, 5, 6, 10, 12)

[186] Ss. 184-199 repealed (1.10.1998) by 1998 c. 31, s. 140(1)(3), Sch. 30, para. 70, Sch. 31 (with ss. 138(9), 144(6)); S.I. 1998/2212, art. 2(1), Sch. 1, Pt. I (subject to savings in S.I. 1999/2323, Sch. 7 paras. 2, 5, 6, 10, 12)

[187] Ss. 184-199 repealed (1.10.1998) by 1998 c. 31, s. 140(1)(3), Sch. 30, para. 70, Sch. 31 (with ss. 138(9), 144(6)); S.I. 1998/2212, art. 2(1), Sch. 1, Pt. I (subject to savings in S.I. 1999/2323, Sch. 7 paras. 2, 5, 6, 10, 12)

[188] Ss. 184-199 repealed (1.10.1998) by 1998 c. 31, s. 140(1)(3), Sch. 30, para. 70, Sch. 31 (with ss. 138(9), 144(6)); S.I. 1998/2212, art. 2(1), Sch. 1, Pt. I (subject to savings in S.I. 1999/2323, Sch. 7 paras. 2, 5, 6, 10, 12)

[189] Ss. 184-199 repealed (1.10.1998) by 1998 c. 31, s. 140(1)(3), Sch. 30, para. 70, Sch. 31 (with ss. 138(9), 144(6)); S.I. 1998/2212, art. 2(1), Sch. 1, Pt. I (subject to savings in S.I. 1999/2323, Sch. 7 paras. 2, 5, 6, 10, 12)

[190] Ss. 184-199 repealed (1.10.1998) by 1998 c. 31, s. 140(1)(3), Sch. 30, para. 70, Sch. 31 (with ss. 138(9), 144(6)); S.I. 1998/2212, art. 2(1), Sch. 1, Pt. I (subject to savings in S.I. 1999/2323, Sch. 7 paras. 2, 5, 6, 10, 12)

[191] Ss. 184-199 repealed (1.10.1998) by 1998 c. 31, s. 140(1)(3), Sch. 30, para. 70, Sch. 31 (with ss. 138(9), 144(6)); S.I. 1998/2212, art. 2(1), Sch. 1, Pt. I (subject to savings in S.I. 1999/2323, Sch. 7 paras. 2, 5, 6, 10, 12)

[192] Ss. 184-199 repealed (1.10.1998) by 1998 c. 31, s. 140(1)(3), Sch. 30, para. 70, Sch. 31 (with ss. 138(9), 144(6)); S.I. 1998/2212, art. 2(1), Sch. 1, Pt. I (subject to savings in S.I. 1999/2323, Sch. 7 paras. 2, 5, 6, 10, 12)

[193] Ss. 184-199 repealed (1.10.1998) by 1998 c. 31, s. 140(1)(3), Sch. 30, para. 70, Sch. 31 (with ss. 138(9), 144(6)); S.I. 1998/2212, art. 2(1), Sch. 1, Pt. I (subject to savings in S.I. 1999/2323, Sch. 7 paras. 2, 5, 6, 10, 12)

[194] Ss. 184-199 repealed (1.10.1998) by 1998 c. 31, s. 140(1)(3), Sch. 30, para. 70, Sch. 31 (with ss. 138(9), 144(6)); S.I. 1998/2212, art. 2(1), Sch. 1, Pt. I (subject to savings in S.I. 1999/2323, Sch. 7 paras. 2, 5, 6, 10, 12)

[195] Ss. 184-199 repealed (1.10.1998) by 1998 c. 31, s. 140(1)(3), Sch. 30, para. 70, Sch. 31 (with ss. 138(9), 144(6)); S.I. 1998/2212, art. 2(1), Sch. 1, Pt. I (subject to savings in S.I. 1999/2323, Sch. 7 paras. 2, 5, 6, 10, 12)

[196] Ss. 184-199 repealed (1.10.1998) by 1998 c. 31, s. 140(1)(3), Sch. 30, para. 70, Sch. 31 (with ss. 138(9), 144(6)); S.I. 1998/2212, art. 2(1), Sch. 1, Pt. I (subject to savings in S.I. 1999/2323, Sch. 7 paras. 2, 5, 6, 10, 12)

[197] Ss. 184-199 repealed (1.10.1998) by 1998 c. 31, s. 140(1)(3), Sch. 30, para. 70, Sch. 31 (with ss. 138(9), 144(6)); S.I. 1998/2212, art. 2(1), Sch. 1, Pt. I (subject to savings in S.I. 1999/2323, Sch. 7 paras. 2, 5, 6, 10, 12)

[198] Ss. 184-199 repealed (1.10.1998) by 1998 c. 31, s. 140(1)(3), Sch. 30, para. 70, Sch. 31 (with ss. 138(9), 144(6)); S.I. 1998/2212, art. 2(1), Sch. 1, Pt. I (subject to savings in S.I. 1999/2323, Sch. 7 paras. 2, 5, 6, 10, 12)

[199] Ss. 184-199 repealed (1.10.1998) by 1998 c. 31, s. 140(1)(3), Sch. 30, para. 70, Sch. 31 (with ss. 138(9), 144(6)); S.I. 1998/2212, art. 2(1), Sch. 1, Pt. I (subject to savings in S.I. 1999/2323, Sch. 7 paras. 2, 5, 6, 10, 12)

[200] Ss. 184-199 repealed (1.10.1998) by 1998 c. 31, s. 140(1)(3), Sch. 30, para. 70, Sch. 31 (with ss. 138(9), 144(6)); S.I. 1998/2212, art. 2(1), Sch. 1, Pt. I (subject to savings in S.I. 1999/2323, Sch. 7 paras. 2, 5, 6, 10, 12)

[201] Ss. 184-199 repealed (1.10.1998) by 1998 c. 31, s. 140(1)(3), Sch. 30, para. 70, Sch. 31 (with ss. 138(9), 144(6)); S.I. 1998/2212, art. 2(1), Sch. 1, Pt. I (subject to savings in S.I. 1999/2323, Sch. 7 paras. 2, 5, 6, 10, 12)

[202] S. 200 repealed (1.10.1998 in respect of s. 200(4) and otherwise 1.9.1999) by 1998 c. 31, s. 140(1)(3), Sch. 30, para. 70, Sch. 31 (with ss. 138(9), 144(6)); S.I. 1998/2212, art. 2(1), Sch. 1, Pt. I; S.I. 1999/2323, art 2(1), Sch. 1 (with savings in Sch. 7 paras. 2, 5, 6, 10, 12)

[203] S. 201 repealed (1.9.1999) by 1998 c. 31, s. 140(1)(3), Sch. 30 para. 70, Sch. 31 (with ss. 138(9), 144); S.I. 1999/2323, art. 2(1), Sch. 1 (with savings in art. 8, Sch. 7 paras. 2, 5, 6, 10, ,12)

[204] S. 202 repealed (1.10.1998) by 1998 c. 31, s. 140(1)(3), Sch. 30, para. 70, Sch. 31 (with ss. 138(9), 144(6)); S.I. 1998/2212, art. 2(1), Sch. 1, Pt. I (subject to savings in S.I. 1999/2323, Sch. 7 paras. 2, 5, 6, 10, 12)

[205] S. 203 repealed (1.10.1998) by 1998 c. 31, s. 140(1)(3), Sch. 30, para. 70, Sch. 31 (with ss. 138(9), 144(6)); S.I. 1998/2212, art. 2(1), Sch. 1, Pt. I (subject to savings in S.I. 1999/2323, Sch. 7 paras. 2, 5, 6, 10, 12)

[206] S. 204 repealed (1.9.1999) by 1998 c. 31, s. 140(1)(3), Sch. 30 para. 70, Sch. 31 (with ss. 138(9), 144); S.I. 1999/2323, art. 2(1), Sch. 1 (with savings in art. 9, Sch. 7 paras. 2, 5, 6, 10, 12)

[207] S. 205 repealed (1.9.1999) by 1998 c. 31, s. 140(1)(3), Sch. 30 para. 70, Sch. 31 (with ss. 138(9), 144); S.I. 1999/2323, art. 2(1), Sch. 1 (with savings in art. 10, Sch. 7 paras. 2, 5, 6, 10, 12)

[208] S. 206 repealed (1.9.1999) by 1998 c. 31, s. 140(1)(3), Sch. 30 para. 70, Sch. 31 (with ss. 138(9), 144); S.I. 1999/2323, art. 2(1), Sch. 1 (with savings in Sch. 7 paras. 2, 5, 6, 10, 12)

[209] S. 207 repealed (1.9.1999) by 1998 c. 31, s. 140(1)(3), Sch. 30 para. 70, Sch. 31 (with ss. 138(9), 144); S.I. 1999/2323, art. 2(1), Sch. 1 (with savings in art. 11, Sch. 7 paras. 2, 5, 6, 10, 12)

[210] S. 208 repealed (1.9.1999) by 1998 c. 31, s. 140(1)(3), Sch. 30 para. 70, Sch. 31 (with ss. 138(9), 144); S.I. 1999/2323, art. 2(1), Sch. 1 (with savings in art. 12, Sch. 7 paras. 2, 5, 6, 10, 12)

[211] S. 209 repealed (1.10.1998) by 1998 c. 31, s. 140(1)(3), Sch. 30, para. 70, Sch. 31 (with ss. 138(9), 144(6)); S.I. 1998/2212, art. 2(1), Sch. 1, Pt. I (subject to savings in S.I. 1999/2323, Sch. 7 paras. 2, 5, 6, 10, 12)

[212] S. 210 repealed (1.9.1999) by 1998 c. 31, s. 140(1)(3), Sch. 30 para. 70, Sch. 31 (with ss. 138(9), 144); S.I. 1999/2323, art. 2(1), Sch. 1 (with savings in Sch. 7 paras. 2, 5, 6, 10, 12)

[213] S. 211 repealed (1.4.1999) by 1998 c. 31, s. 140(1)(3), Sch. 30 para. 70, Sch. 31 (with ss. 138(9), 144); S.I. 1999/1016, art. 2(1), Sch. 1 (subject to savings in S.I 1999/2323, Sch. 7 paras. 2, 5, 6, 10, 12)

[214] S. 212 repealed (1.10.1998) by 1998 c. 31, s. 140(1)(3), Sch. 30, para. 70, Sch. 31 (with ss. 138(9), 144(6)); S.I. 1998/2212, art. 2(1), Sch. 1, Pt. I (with Sch. 2 para. 4 and subject to savings in S.I. 1999/2323, Sch. 7 paras. 2, 5, 6, 10, 12)

[215] S. 213 repealed (1.10.1998 in respect of s. 213(2)(3) and otherwise 1.4.1999) by 1998 c. 31, s. 140(1)(3), Sch. 30, para. 70, Sch. 31 (with ss. 138(9), 144(6)); S.I. 1998/2212, art. 2(1), Sch. 1, Pt. I; S.I. 1999/1016, art. 2(1), Sch. 1 (subject to savings in S.I. 1999/2323, Sch. 7 paras. 2, 5, 6, 10, 12)

[216] S. 214 repealed (1.4.1999) by 1998 c. 31, s. 140(1)(3), Sch. 30 para. 70, Sch. 31 (with ss. 138(9), 144); S.I. 1999/1016, art. 2(1), Sch. 1 (subject to savings in S.I. 1999/2323, Sch. 7 paras. 2, 5, 6, 10, 12)

[217] S. 215 repealed (1.4.1999) by 1998 c. 31, s. 140(1)(3), Sch. 30 para. 70, Sch. 31 (with ss. 138(9), 144); S.I. 1999/1016, art.

2(1), Sch. 1 (subject to savings in S.I. 1998/2323, Sch. 7 paras. 2, 5, 6, 10, 12 and in S.I. 1999/704, reg. 3)

218 S. 216 repealed (1.4.1999 in respect of s. 216(2)-(9) and otherwise 1.9.1999) by 1998 c. 31, s. 140(1)(3), Sch. 30 para. 70, Sch. 31 (with ss. 138(9), 144); S.I. 1999/1016, art. 2(1), Sch. 1; S.I. 1999/2323, art. 2(1), Sch. 1 (with savings in S.I. 1998/2323, Sch. 7 paras. 2, 5, 6, 10, 12 and in S.I. 1999/704, reg. 3)

219 S. 217 repealed (1.4.1999) by 1998 c. 31, s. 140(1)(3), Sch. 30 para. 70, Sch. 31 (with ss. 138(9), 144); S.I. 1999/1016, art. 2(1), Sch. 1 (subject to savings in S.I. 1998/2323, Sch. 7 paras. 2, 5, 6, 10, 12 and in S.I. 1999/704, reg. 3)

220 S. 218 repealed (1.9.1999) by 1998 c. 31, s. 140(1)(3), Sch. 30 para. 70, Sch. 31 (with ss. 138(9), 144); S.I. 1999/2323, art. 2(1), Sch. 1 (with savings in Sch. 7 paras. 2, 5, 6, 10, 12)

221 S. 219 repealed (1.9.1999) by 1998 c. 31, s. 140(1)(3), Sch. 30 para. 70, Sch. 31 (with ss. 138(9), 144); S.I. 1999/2323, art. 2(1), Sch. 1 (with savings in Sch. 7 paras. 2, 5, 6, 10, 12)

222 S. 220 repealed (1.9.1999) by 1998 c. 31, s. 140(1)(3), Sch. 30 para. 70, Sch. 31 (with ss. 138(9), 144); S.I. 1999/2323, art. 2(1), Sch. 1 (with savings in Sch. 7 paras. 2, 5, 6, 10, 12)

223 S. 221 repealed (1.9.1999) by 1998 c. 31, s. 140(1)(3), Sch. 30 para. 70, Sch. 31 (with ss. 138(9), 144); S.I. 1999/2323, art. 2(1), Sch. 1 (with savings in Sch. 7 paras. 2, 5, 6, 10, 12)

224 S. 222 repealed (1.9.1999) by 1998 c. 31, s. 140(1)(3), Sch. 30 para. 70, Sch. 31 (with ss. 138(9), 144); S.I. 1999/2323, art. 2(1), Sch. 1 (with savings in Sch. 7 paras. 2, 5, 6, 10, 12)

225 S. 223 repealed (1.9.1999) by 1998 c. 31, s. 140(1)(3), Sch. 30 para. 70, Sch. 31 (with ss. 138(9), 144); S.I. 1999/2323, art. 2(1), Sch. 1 (with savings in Sch. 7 paras. 2, 5, 6, 10, 12)

226 S. 224 repealed (1.9.1999) by 1998 c. 31, s. 140(1)(3), Sch. 30 para. 70, Sch. 31 (with ss. 138(9), 144); S.I. 1999/2323, art. 2(1), Sch. 1 (with savings in Sch. 7 paras. 2, 5, 6, 10, 12)

227 S. 225 repealed (1.9.1999) by 1998 c. 31, s. 140(1)(3), Sch. 30 para. 70, Sch. 31 (with ss. 138(9), 144); S.I. 1999/2323, art. 2(1), Sch. 1 (with savings in Sch. 7 paras. 2, 5, 6, 10, 12)

228 S. 226 repealed (1.9.1999) by 1998 c. 31, s. 140(1)(3), Sch. 30 para. 70, Sch. 31 (with ss. 138(9), 144); S.I. 1999/2323, art. 2(1), Sch. 1 (with savings in Sch. 7 paras. 2, 5, 6, 10, 12)

229 S. 227 repealed (1.9.1999) by 1998 c. 31, s. 140(1)(3), Sch. 30 para. 70, Sch. 31 (with ss. 138(9), 144); S.I. 1999/2323, art. 2(1), Sch. 1 (with savings in Sch. 7 paras. 2, 5, 6, 10, 12)

230 S. 228 repealed (1.9.1999) by 1998 c. 31, s. 140(1)(3), Sch. 30 para. 70, Sch. 31 (with ss. 138(9), 144); S.I. 1999/2323, art. 2(1), Sch. 1 (with savings in Sch. 7 paras. 2, 5, 6, 10, 12)

231 S. 229 repealed (1.9.1999) by 1998 c. 31, s. 140(1)(3), Sch. 30 para. 70, Sch. 31 (with ss. 138(9), 144); S.I. 1999/2323, art. 2(1), Sch. 1 (with savings in Sch. 7 paras. 2, 5, 6, 10, 12)

232 S. 230 repealed (1.9.1999) by 1998 c. 31, s. 140(1)(3), Sch. 30 para. 70, Sch. 31 (with ss. 138(9), 144); S.I. 1999/2323, art. 2(1), Sch. 1 (with savings in Sch. 7 paras. 2, 5, 6, 10, 12)

233 S. 231 repealed (1.9.1999) by 1998 c. 31, s. 140(1)(3), Sch. 30 para. 70, Sch. 31 (with ss. 138(9), 144); S.I. 1999/2323, art. 2(1), Sch. 1 (with savings in Sch. 7 paras. 2, 5, 6, 10, 12)

234 Ss. 232-240 repealed (1.10.1998) by 1998 c. 31, s. 140(1)(3), Sch. 30, para. 70, Sch. 31 (with ss. 138(9), 144(6)); S.I. 1998/2212, art. 2(1), Sch. 1, Pt. I (subject to savings in S.I. 1999/2323, Sch. 7 paras. 2, 5, 6, 10, 12)

235 Ss. 232-240 repealed (1.10.1998) by 1998 c. 31, s. 140(1)(3), Sch. 30, para. 70, Sch. 31 (with ss. 138(9), 144(6)); S.I. 1998/2212, art. 2(1), Sch. 1, Pt. I (subject to savings in S.I. 1999/2323, Sch. 7 paras. 2, 5, 6, 10, 12)

236 Ss. 232-240 repealed (1.10.1998) by 1998 c. 31, s. 140(1)(3), Sch. 30, para. 70, Sch. 31 (with ss. 138(9), 144(6)); S.I. 1998/2212, art. 2(1), Sch. 1, Pt. I (subject to savings in S.I. 1999/2323, Sch. 7 paras. 2, 5, 6, 10, 12)

237 Ss. 232-240 repealed (1.10.1998) by 1998 c. 31, s. 140(1)(3), Sch. 30, para. 70, Sch. 31 (with ss. 138(9), 144(6)); S.I. 1998/2212, art. 2(1), Sch. 1, Pt. I (subject to savings in S.I. 1999/2323, Sch. 7 paras. 2, 5, 6, 10, 12)

238 Ss. 232-240 repealed (1.10.1998) by 1998 c. 31, s. 140(1)(3), Sch. 30, para. 70, Sch. 31 (with ss. 138(9), 144(6)); S.I. 1998/2212, art. 2(1), Sch. 1, Pt. I (subject to savings in S.I. 1999/2323, Sch. 7 paras. 2, 5, 6, 10, 12)

239 Ss. 232-240 repealed (1.10.1998) by 1998 c. 31, s. 140(1)(3), Sch. 30, para. 70, Sch. 31 (with ss. 138(9), 144(6)); S.I. 1998/2212, art. 2(1), Sch. 1, Pt. I (subject to savings in S.I. 1999/2323, Sch. 7 paras. 2, 5, 6, 10, 12)

240 Ss. 232-240 repealed (1.10.1998) by 1998 c. 31, s. 140(1)(3), Sch. 30, para. 70, Sch. 31 (with ss. 138(9), 144(6)); S.I. 1998/2212, art. 2(1), Sch. 1, Pt. I (subject to savings in S.I. 1999/2323, Sch. 7 paras. 2, 5, 6, 10, 12)

241 Ss. 232-240 repealed (1.10.1998) by 1998 c. 31, s. 140(1)(3), Sch. 30, para. 70, Sch. 31 (with ss. 138(9), 144(6)); S.I. 1998/2212, art. 2(1), Sch. 1, Pt. I (subject to savings in S.I. 1999/2323, Sch. 7 paras. 2, 5, 6, 10, 12)

242 Ss. 232-240 repealed (1.10.1998) by 1998 c. 31, s. 140(1)(3), Sch. 30, para. 70, Sch. 31 (with ss. 138(9), 144(6)); S.I. 1998/2212, art. 2(1), Sch. 1, Pt. I (subject to savings in S.I. 1999/2323, Sch. 7 paras. 2, 5, 6, 10, 12)

243 S. 241 repealed (1.9.1999) by 1998 c. 31, s. 140(1)(3), Sch. 30, para. 70, Sch. 31 (with ss. 138(9), 144(6)); S.I. 1998/2323, art. 2(1), Sch. 1 (with savings in Sch. 7 paras. 2, 5, 6, 10, 12)

244 S. 242 repealed (1.9.1999) by 1998 c. 31, s. 140(1)(3), Sch. 30 para. 70, Sch. 31 (with ss. 138(9), 144(6)); S.I. 1999/2323, art. 2(1), Sch. 1 (with savings in Sch. 7 paras. 2, 5, 6, 10, 12)

245 S. 243 repealed (1.9.1999) by 1998 c. 31, s. 140(1)(3), Sch. 30 para. 70, Sch. 31 (with ss. 138(9), 144); S.I. 1999/2323, art. 2(1), Sch. 1 (with savings in Sch. 7 paras. 2, 5, 6, 10, 12)

246 S. 244 repealed (1.4.1999) by 1998 c. 31, s. 140(1)(3),Sch. 30, para. 70, Sch. 31 (with ss. 138(9), 144(6)); S.I. 1999/1016, art. 2(1), Sch. 1 (subject to savings in S.I. 1999/2323, Sch. 7 paras. 2, 5, 6, 10, 12)

247 S. 245 repealed (1.4.1999 for specified purposes and otherwise prosp.) by 1998 c. 31, ss. 140(1)(3), 145(3), Sch. 30,

para. 70, Sch. 31 (with ss. 138(9), 144(6)); S.I. 1999/1016, art. 2(1), Sch. 1 (subject to savings in S.I. 1999/2323, Sch. 7 paras. 2, 5, 6, 10, 12)

248 S. 246 repealed (1.4.1999 for specified purposes and otherwise prosp.) by 1998 c. 31, ss. 140(1)(3), 145(3), Sch. 30, para. 70, Sch. 31 (with ss. 138(9), 144(6)); S.I. 1999/1016, art. 2(1), Sch. 1 (subject to savings in S.I. 1999/2323, Sch. 7 paras. 2, 5, 6, 10, 12)

249 S. 247 repealed (1.4.1999 for specified purposes and otherwise prosp.) by 1998 c. 31, ss. 140(1)(3), 145(3), Sch. 30, para. 70, Sch. 31 (with ss. 138(9), 144(6)); S.I. 1999/1016, art. 2(1), Sch. 1 (subject to savings in S.I. 1999/2323, Sch. 7 paras. 2, 5, 6, 10, 12)

250 S. 248 repealed (1.4.1999 for specified purposes and otherwise prosp.) by 1998 c. 31, ss. 140(1)(3), 145(3), Sch. 30, para. 70, Sch. 31 (with ss. 138(9), 144(6)); S.I. 1999/1016, art. 2(1), Sch. 1 (subject to savings in S.I. 1999/2323, Sch. 7 paras. 2, 5, 6, 10, 12)

251 S. 249 repealed (1.4.1999 for specified purposes and otherwise prosp.) by 1998 c. 31, ss. 140(1)(3), 145(3), Sch. 30, para. 70, Sch. 31 (with ss. 138(9), 144(6)); S.I. 1999/1016, art. 2(1), Sch. 1 (subject to savings in S.I. 1999/2323, Sch. 7 paras. 2, 5, 6, 10, 12)

252 S. 250 repealed (1.4.1999) by 1998 c. 31, s. 140(1)(3), Sch. 30, para. 70, Sch. 31 (with ss. 138(9), 144(6)); S.I. 1999/1016, art. 2(1), Sch. 1 (subject to savings in S.I. 1999/2323, Sch. 7 paras. 2, 5, 6, 10, 12)

253 S. 251 repealed (1.4.1999) by 1998 c. 31, s. 140(1)(3), Sch. 30, para. 70, Sch. 31 (with ss. 138(9), 144(6)); S.I. 1999/1016, art. 2(1), Sch. 1 (subject to savings in S.I. 1999/2323, Sch. 7 paras. 2, 5, 6, 10, 12)

254 S. 252 repealed (1.9.1999) by 1998 c. 31, s. 140(1)(3), Sch. 30 para. 70, Sch. 31 (with ss. 138(9), 144); S.I. 1999/2323, art. 2(1), Sch. 1 (with savings in Sch. 7 paras. 2, 5, 6, 10, 12)

255 S. 253 repealed (1.4.1999 for specified purposes and otherwise prosp.) by 1998 c. 31, ss. 140(1)(3), 145(3), Sch. 30, para. 70, Sch. 31 (with ss. 138(9), 144(6)); S.I. 1999/1016, art. 2(1), Sch. 1 (subject to savings in S.I. 1999/2323, Sch. 7 paras. 2, 5, 6, 10, 12)

256 S. 254 repealed (1.4.1999 for specified purposes and otherwise prosp.) by 1998 c. 31, ss. 140(1)(3), 145(3), Sch. 30, para. 70, Sch. 31 (with ss. 138(9), 144(6)); S.I. 1999/1016, art. 2(1), Sch. 1 (subject to savings in S.I. 1999/2323, Sch. 7 paras. 2, 5, 6, 10, 12)

257 S. 255-258 repealed (1.4.1999) by 1998 c. 31, s. 140(1)(3), Sch. 30, para. 70, Sch. 31 (with ss. 138(9), 144(6)); S.I. 1999/1016, art. 2(1), Sch. 1 (subject to savings in S.I. 1999/2323, Sch. 7 paras. 2, 5, 6, 10, 12)

258 S. 255-258 repealed (1.4.1999) by 1998 c. 31, s. 140(1)(3), Sch. 30, para. 70, Sch. 31 (with ss. 138(9), 144(6)); S.I. 1999/1016, art. 2(1), Sch. 1 (subject to savings in S.I. 1999/2323, Sch. 7 paras. 2, 5, 6, 10, 12)

259 S. 255-258 repealed (1.4.1999) by 1998 c. 31, s. 140(1)(3), Sch. 30, para. 70, Sch. 31 (with ss. 138(9), 144(6)); S.I. 1999/1016, art. 2(1), Sch. 1 (subject to savings in S.I. 1999/2323, Sch. 7 paras. 2, 5, 6, 10, 12)

260 S. 255-258 repealed (1.4.1999) by 1998 c. 31, s. 140(1)(3), Sch. 30, para. 70, Sch. 31 (with ss. 138(9), 144(6)); S.I. 1999/1016, art. 2(1), Sch. 1 (subject to savings in S.I. 1999/2323, Sch. 7 paras. 2, 5, 6, 10, 12)

261 S. 259 repealed (1.9.1999) by 1998 c. 31, s. 140(1)(3), Sch. 30 para. 70, Sch. 31 (with ss. 138(9), 144); S.I. 1999/2323, art. 2(1), Sch. 1 (with savings in Sch. 7 paras. 2, 5, 6, 10, 12 and subject to savings by S.I. 1999/704, reg. 14(2)(d))

262 S. 260 repealed (1.4.1999) by 1998 c. 31, s. 140(1)(3), Sch. 30, para. 70, Sch. 31 (with ss. 138(9), 144(6)); S.I. 1999/1016, art. 2(1), Sch. 1 (subject to savings in S.I. 1999/2323, Sch. 7 paras. 2, 5, 6, 10, 12 and in S.I. 1999/704, reg. 4(1))

263 S. 261 repealed (1.4.1999 in respect of s. 261(2)(4)(5) and in respect of words in s. 261(3) and otherwise 1.9.1999) by 1998 c. 31, s. 140(1)(3), Sch. 30, para. 70, Sch. 31 (with ss. 138(9), 144(6)); S.I. 1999/1016, art. 2(1), Sch. 1; S.I. 1999/2323, art. 2(1), Sch. 1 (with Sch. 7 paras. 2, 5, 6, 10, 12 and subject to savings in S.I. 1999/704, regs. 4(1), 14(2)(d))

264 S. 262 repealed (1.9.1999) by 1998 c. 31, s. 140(1)(3), Sch. 30 para. 70, Sch. 31 (with ss. 138(9), 144); S.I. 1999/2323, art. 2(1), Sch. 1 (with savings in Sch. 7 paras. 2, 5, 6, 10, 12 and subject to savings in S.I. 1999/704, reg. 14(2)(d)(e))

265 S. 263 repealed (1.4.1999 in respect of s. 263(4)(b) and otherwise 1.9.1999) by 1998 c. 31, s. 140(1)(3), Sch. 30 para. 70, Sch. 31 (with ss. 138(9), 144);S.I. 1999/1016, art. 2(1), Sch. 1; S.I. 1999/2323, art. 2(1), Sch. 1 (with savings in Sch. 7 paras. 2, 5, 6, 10, 12)

266 S. 264 repealed (1.4.1999) by 1998 c. 31, s. 140(1)(3), Sch. 30, para. 70, Sch. 31 (with ss. 138(9), 144(6)); S.I. 1999/1016, art. 2(1), Sch. 1 (subject to savings in S.I. 1999/2323, Sch. 7 paras. 2, 5, 6, 10, 12)

267 S. 265 repealed (1.4.1999) by 1998 c. 31, s. 140(1)(3), Sch. 30, para. 70, Sch. 31 (with ss. 138(9), 144(6)); S.I. 1999/1016, art. 2(1), Sch. 1 (subject to savings in S.I. 1999/2323, Sch. 7 paras. 2, 5, 6, 10, 12)

268 S. 266 repealed (1.9.1999) by 1998 c. 31, s. 140(1)(3), Sch. 30 para. 70, Sch. 31 (with ss. 138(9), 144); S.I. 1999/2323, art. 2(1), Sch. 1 (with savings in Sch. 7 paras. 2, 5, 6, 10, 12)

269 S. 267 repealed (1.9.1999) by 1998 c. 31, s. 140(1)(3), Sch. 30 para. 70, Sch. 31 (with ss. 138(9), 144); S.I. 1999/2323, art. 2(1), Sch. 1 (with savings in Sch. 7 paras. 2, 5, 6, 10, 12 and subject to savings in S.I. 1999/704, reg. 14(2)(f))

270 S. 268 repealed (1.4.1999) by 1998 c. 31, s. 140(1)(3), Sch. 30, para. 70, Sch. 31 (with ss. 138(9), 144(6)); S.I. 1999/1016, art. 2(1), Sch. 1 (subject to savings in S.I. 1999/2323, Sch. 7 paras. 2, 5, 6, 10, 12 and in S.I. 1999/704, reg. 6)

271 S. 269 repealed (1.4.1999 in respect of s. 269(2)(5)(6) and in respect of words in s. 269(3) and otherwise 1.9.1999) by 1998 c. 31, s. 140(1)(3), Sch. 30 para. 70, Sch. 31 (with ss. 138(9), 144); S.I. 1999/1016, art. 2(1), Sch. 1; S.I. 1999/2323, art. 2(1), Sch. 1 (with savings in Sch. 7 paras. 2, 5, 6, 10, 12 and subject to savings in S.I. 1999/704, reg. 14(2)(f))

272 S. 270 repealed (1.4.1999 in respect of s. 270(2)(b)(ii) and otherwise 1.9.1999) by 1998 c. 31, s. 140(1)(3), Sch. 30 para. 70, Sch. 31 (with ss. 138(9), 144); S.I. 1999/1016, art. 2(1), Sch. 1; S.I. 1999/2323, art. 2(1), Sch. 1 (with savings in Sch. 7

paras. 2, 5, 6, 10, 12)

[273] S. 271 repealed (1.4.1999) by 1998 c. 31, s. 140(1)(3), Sch. 30, para. 70, Sch. 31 (with ss. 138(9), 144(6)); S.I. 1999/1016, art. 2(1), Sch. 1 (subject to savings in S.I. 1999/2323, Sch. 7 paras. 2, 5, 6, 10, 12)

[274] S. 272 repealed (1.4.1999) by 1998 c. 31, s. 140(1)(3), Sch. 30, para. 70, Sch. 31 (with ss. 138(9), 144(6)); S.I. 1999/1016, art. 2(1), Sch. 1 (subject to savings in S.I. 1999/2323, Sch. 7 paras. 2, 5, 6, 10, 12)

[275] S. 273 repealed (1.4.1999) by 1998 c. 31, s. 140(1)(3), Sch. 30, para. 70, Sch. 31 (with ss. 138(9), 144(6)); S.I. 1999/1016, art. 2(1), Sch. 1 (subject to savings in S.I. 1999/2323, Sch. 7 paras. 2, 5, 6, 10, 12)

[276] S. 274 repealed (1.9.1999) by 1998 c. 31, s. 140(1)(3), Sch. 30 para. 70, Sch. 31 (with ss. 138(9), 144); S.I. 1999/2323, art. 2(1), Sch. 1 (with savings in art. 16, Sch. 7 paras. 2, 5, 6, 10, 12)

[277] S. 275 repealed (1.9.1999) by 1998 c. 31, s. 140(1)(3), Sch. 30 para. 70, Sch. 31 (with ss. 138(9), 144); S.I. 1999/2323, art. 2(1), Sch. 1 (with savings in art. 16, Sch. 7 paras. 2, 5, 6, 10, 12)

[278] S. 276 repealed (1.9.1999) by 1998 c. 31, s. 140(1)(3), Sch. 30 para. 70, Sch. 31 (with ss. 138(9), 144); S.I. 1999/2323, art. 2(1), Sch. 1 (with savings in art. 16, Sch. 7 paras. 2, 5, 6, 10, 12)

[279] S. 277 repealed (1.9.1999) by 1998 c. 31, s. 140(1)(3), Sch. 30 para. 70, Sch. 31 (with ss. 138(9), 144); S.I. 1999/2323, art. 2(1), Sch. 1 (with savings in art. 16, Sch. 7 paras. 2, 5, 6, 10, 12)

[280] S. 278 repealed (1.9.1999) by 1998 c. 31, s. 140(1)(3), Sch. 30 para. 70, Sch. 31 (with ss. 138(9), 144); S.I. 1999/2323, art. 2(1), Sch. 1 (with savings in art. 16, Sch. 7 paras. 2, 5, 6, 10, 12)

[281] S. 279 repealed (1.9.1999) by 1998 c. 31, s. 140(1)(3), Sch. 30 para. 70, Sch. 31 (with ss. 138(9), 144); S.I. 1999/2323, art. 2(1), Sch. 1 (with savings in art. 16, Sch. 7 paras. 2, 5, 6, 10, 12)

[282] S. 280 repealed (1.9.1999) by 1998 c. 31, s. 140(1)(3), Sch. 30 para. 70, Sch. 31 (with ss. 138(9), 144); S.I. 1999/2323, art. 2(1), Sch. 1 (with savings in Sch. 7 paras. 2, 5, 6, 10, 12)

[283] S. 281 repealed (1.9.1999) by 1998 c. 31, s. 140(1)(3), Sch. 30 para. 70, Sch. 31 (with ss. 138(9), 144); S.I. 1999/2323, art. 2(1), Sch. 1 (with savings in Sch. 7 paras. 2, 5, 6, 10, 12)

[284] S. 282 repealed (1.9.1999) by 1998 c. 31, s. 140(1)(3), Sch. 30 para. 70, Sch. 31 (with ss. 138(9), 144); S.I. 1999/2323, art. 2(1), Sch. 1 (with savings in Sch. 7 paras. 2, 5, 6, 10, 12)

[285] S. 283 repealed (1.9.1999) by 1998 c. 31, s. 140(1)(3), Sch. 30 para. 70, Sch. 31 (with ss. 138(9), 144); S.I. 1999/2323, art. 2(1), Sch. 1 (with savings in Sch. 7 paras. 2, 5, 6, 10, 12)

[286] S. 284 repealed (1.9.1999) by 1998 c. 31, s. 140(1)(3), Sch. 30 para. 70, Sch. 31 (with ss. 138(9), 144); S.I. 1999/2323, art. 2(1), Sch. 1 (with savings in Sch. 7 paras. 2, 5, 6, 10, 12)

[287] S. 285 repealed (1.9.1999) by 1998 c. 31, s. 140(1)(3), Sch. 30 para. 70, Sch. 31 (with ss. 138(9), 144); S.I. 1999/2323, art. 2(1), Sch. 1 (with savings in Sch. 7 paras. 2, 5, 6, 10, 12)

[288] S. 286 repealed (1.9.1999) by 1998 c. 31, s. 140(1)(3), Sch. 30 para. 70, Sch. 31 (with ss. 138(9), 144); S.I. 1999/2323, art. 2(1), Sch. 1 (with savings in Sch. 7 paras. 2, 5, 6, 10, 12)

[289] S. 287 repealed (1.9.1999) by 1998 c. 31, s. 140(1)(3), Sch. 30 para. 70, Sch. 31 (with ss. 138(9), 144); S.I. 1999/2323, art. 2(1), Sch. 1 (with savings in Sch. 7 paras. 2, 5, 6, 10, 12)

[290] S. 288 repealed (1.9.1999) by 1998 c. 31, s. 140(1)(3), Sch. 30 para. 70, Sch. 31 (with ss. 138(9), 144); S.I. 1999/2323, art. 2(1), Sch. 1 (with savings in Sch. 7 paras. 2, 5, 6, 10, 12)

[291] S. 289 repealed (1.9.1999) by 1998 c. 31, s. 140(1)(3), Sch. 30 para. 70, Sch. 31 (with ss. 138(9), 144); S.I. 1999/2323, art. 2(1), Sch. 1 (with savings in Sch. 7 paras. 2, 5, 6, 10, 12)

[292] S. 290 repealed (1.10.1998) by 1998 c. 31, s. 140(1)(3), Sch. 30, para. 70, Sch. 31 (with ss. 138(9), 144(6)); S.I. 1998/2212, art. 2(1), Sch. 1, Pt. I (subject to savings in S.I. 1999/2323, Sch. 7 paras. 2, 5, 6, 10, 12)

[293] S. 291 repealed (1.9.1999) by 1998 c. 31, s. 140(1)(3), Sch. 30 para. 70, Sch. 31 (with ss. 138(9), 144); S.I. 1999/2323, art. 2(1), Sch. 1 (with savings in Sch. 7 paras. 2, 5, 6, 10, 12)

[294] S. 292 repealed (1.9.1999) by 1998 c. 31, s. 140(1)(3), Sch. 30 para. 70, Sch. 31 (with ss. 138(9), 144); S.I. 1999/2323, art. 2(1), Sch. 1 (with savings in Sch. 7 paras. 2, 5, 6, 10, 12)

[295] S. 293 repealed (1.9.1999) by 1998 c. 31, s. 140(1)(3), Sch. 30 para. 70, Sch. 31 (with ss. 138(9), 144); S.I. 1999/2323, art. 2(1), Sch. 1 (with savings in Sch. 7 paras. 2, 5, 6, 10, 12)

[296] S. 294 repealed (1.9.1999) by 1998 c. 31, s. 140(1)(3), Sch. 30 para. 70, Sch. 31 (with ss. 138(9), 144); S.I. 1999/2323, art. 2(1), Sch. 1 (with savings in Sch. 7 paras. 2, 5, 6, 10, 12)

[297] S. 295 repealed (1.9.1999) by 1998 c. 31, s. 140(1)(3), Sch. 30 para. 70, Sch. 31 (with ss. 138(9), 144); S.I. 1999/2323, art. 2(1), Sch. 1 (with savings in Sch. 7 paras. 2, 5, 6, 10, 12)

[298] S. 296 repealed (1.9.1999) by 1998 c. 31, s. 140(1)(3), Sch. 30 para. 70, Sch. 31 (with ss. 138(9), 144); S.I. 1999/2323, art. 2(1), Sch. 1 (with savings in Sch. 7 paras. 2, 5, 6, 10, 12)

[299] S. 297 repealed (1.9.1999) by 1998 c. 31, s. 140(1)(3), Sch. 30 para. 70, Sch. 31 (with ss. 138(9), 144); S.I. 1999/2323, art. 2(1), Sch. 1 (with savings in Sch. 7 paras. 2, 5, 6, 10, 12)

[300] S. 298 repealed (1.9.1999) by 1998 c. 31, s. 140(1)(3), Sch. 30 para. 70, Sch. 31 (with ss. 138(9), 144); S.I. 1999/2323, art. 2(1), Sch. 1 (with savings in Sch. 7 paras. 2, 5, 6, 10, 12)

[301] S. 299 repealed (1.9.1999) by 1998 c. 31, s. 140(1)(3), Sch. 30 para. 70, Sch. 31 (with ss. 138(9), 144); S.I. 1999/2323, art. 2(1), Sch. 1 (with savings in Sch. 7 paras. 2, 5, 6, 10, 12)

[302] S. 300 repealed (1.9.1999) by 1998 c. 31, s. 140(1)(3), Sch. 30 para. 70, Sch. 31 (with ss. 138(9), 144); S.I. 1999/2323, art. 2(1), Sch. 1 (with savings in Sch. 7 paras. 2, 5, 6, 10, 12)

[303] S. 301 repealed (1.9.1999) by 1998 c. 31, s. 140(1)(3), Sch. 30 para. 70, Sch. 31 (with ss. 138(9), 144); S.I. 1999/2323, art. 2(1), Sch. 1 (with savings in Sch. 7 paras. 2, 5, 6, 10, 12)

[304] S. 302 repealed (1.9.1999) by 1998 c. 31, s. 140(1)(3), Sch. 30 para. 70, Sch. 31 (with ss. 138(9), 144); S.I. 1999/2323, art. 2(1), Sch. 1 (with savings in Sch. 7 art. 23(2), paras. 2, 5, 6, 10, 12)

[305] S. 303 repealed (1.9.1999) by 1998 c. 31, s. 140(1)(3), Sch. 30 para. 70, Sch. 31 (with ss. 138(9), 144); S.I. 1999/2323, art. 2(1), Sch. 1 (with savings in Sch. 7 paras. 2, 5, 6, 10, 12)

[306] S. 304 repealed (1.9.1999) by 1998 c. 31, s. 140(1)(3), Sch. 30 para. 70, Sch. 31 (with ss. 138(9), 144); S.I. 1999/2323, art. 2(1), Sch. 1 (with savings in Sch. 7 paras. 2, 5, 6, 10, 12)

[307] S. 305 repealed (1.9.1999) by 1998 c. 31, s. 140(1)(3), Sch. 30 para. 70, Sch. 31 (with ss. 138(9), 144); S.I. 1999/2323, art. 2(1), Sch. 1 (with savings in Sch. 7 paras. 2, 5, 6, 10, 12)

[308] S. 306 repealed (1.9.1999) by 1998 c. 31, s. 140(1)(3), Sch. 30 para. 70, Sch. 31 (with ss. 138(9), 144); S.I. 1999/2323, art. 2(1), Sch. 1 (with savings in Sch. 7 paras. 2, 5, 6, 10, 12)

[309] S. 306A (and the heading immediately preceding it) inserted (1.4.1998) by 1997 c. 44, s. 3(1) (with s. 57(3)); S.I. 1998/386, art. 2, Sch. 1 Pt.II

[310] S. 306A (and the heading immediately preceding it) inserted (1.4.1998) by 1997 c. 44, s. 3(1) (with s. 57(3)); S.I. 1998/386, art. 2, Sch. 1 Pt. II and repealed (1.9.1999) by 1998 c. 31, s. 140(1)(3), Sch. 30 para. 70, Sch. 31 (with ss. 138(9), 144); S.I. 1999/2323, art. 2(1), Sch. 1 (with savings in Sch. 7 paras. 2, 5, 6, 10, 12)

[311] S. 307 repealed (1.9.1999) by 1998 c. 31, s. 140(1)(3), Sch. 30 para. 70, Sch. 31 (with ss. 138(9), 144); S.I. 1999/2323, art. 2(1), Sch. 1 (with savings in Sch. 7 paras. 2, 5, 6, 10, 12)

[312] S. 307A inserted (1.9.1998) by 1997 c. 44, s. 8(1) (with s. 57(3)); S.I. 1998/386, art. 2, Sch. 1 Pt. IV and repealed (1.9.1999) by 1998 c. 31, s. 140(1)(3), Sch. 30 para. 70, Sch. 31 (with ss. 138(9), 144); S.I. 1999/2323, art. 2(1), Sch. 1 (with savings in Sch. 7 paras. 2, 5, 6, 10, 12)

[313] S. 308 repealed (1.9.1999) by 1998 c. 31, s. 140(1)(3), Sch. 30 para. 70, Sch. 31 (with ss. 138(9), 144); S.I. 1999/2323, art. 2(1), Sch. 1 (with savings in Sch. 7 paras. 2, 5, 6, 10, 12)

[314] S. 309 repealed (1.9.1999) by 1998 c. 31, s. 140(1)(3), Sch. 30 para. 70, Sch. 31 (with ss. 138(9), 144); S.I. 1999/2323, art. 2(1), Sch. 1 (with savings in Sch. 7 paras. 2, 5, 6, 10, 12)

[315] S. 310 repealed (1.4.1999) by 1998 c. 31, s. 140(1)(3), Sch. 30, para. 70, Sch. 31 (with ss. 138(9), 144(6)); S.I. 1999/1016, art. 2(1), Sch. 1 (with art. 5 and subject to savings in S.I. 1999/2323, art. 20, Sch. 7 paras. 2, 5, 6, 10, 12)

[316] S. 311 repealed (1.9.1999) by 1998 c. 31, s. 140(1)(3), Sch. 30 para. 70, Sch. 31 (with ss. 138(9), 144); S.I. 1999/2323, art. 2(1), Sch. 1 (with savings in Sch. 7 paras. 2, 5, 6, 10, 12)

[317] Words in s. 312(2) substituted (28.7.2000 for certain purposes otherwise 1.4.2001) by 2000 c. 21, ss. 149, 154, Sch. 9 para. 56 (with s. 150); S.I. 2001/654, art. 2(2), Sch. Pt. II (with art. 3); S.I. 2001/1274, art. 2(1), Sch. Pt. I

[318] Words in s. 312(2)(c) substituted (1.8.1998) by 1997 c. 44, s. 57(1), Sch. 7 para. 23(a); S.I. 1998/386, art. 2, Sch. 1 Pt. III

[319] Words in s. 312(2)(c) repealed (1.8.1998) by 1997 c. 44, s. 57(1)(4), Sch. 7 para. 23(b), Sch. 8; S.I. 1998/386, art. 2, Sch. 1 Pt. III

[320] Words in s. 312(4)(a) repealed (1.9.1999) by 1998 c. 31, s. 140(1)(3), Sch. 30 para. 71(a), Sch. 31 (with ss. 138(9), 144(6)); S.I. 1999/2323, art. 2(1), Sch. 1

[321] Words in s. 312(5) substituted (1.9.1999) by 1998 c. 31, s. 140(1), Sch. 30 para. 71(b) (with ss. 138(9), 144(6)); S.I. 1999/2323, art. 2(1), Sch. 1

[322] Words in s. 313(1) substituted (1.9.1999) by 1998 c. 31, s. 140(1), Sch. 30 para. 72 (with ss. 138(9), 144(6)); S.I. 1999/2323, art. 2(1), Sch.1

[323] S. 313(5) substituted (1.9.2003) by Education Act 2002 (c. 32), ss. 195, 216(3), Sch. 18 para. 2 (with ss. 210(8), 214(4), Sch. 18 para. 17); S.I. 2002/3185, art. 6, Sch. Pt. III

[324] Words in s. 315(2) inserted (1.9.2003 for E. and otherwise prosp.) by Education Act 2002 (c. 32), ss. 215(1), 216(4), Sch. 21 para. 37 (with savings in ss. 210(8), 214(4)); S.I. 2003/1667, art. 4

[325] Words in s. 315(2) substituted (1.9.1999) by 1998 c. 31, s. 140(1), Sch. 30 para.73 (with ss. 138(9), 144(6)); S.I. 1999/2323, art. 2(1), Sch. 1

[326] Words s. 316(4)(b)(iii) substituted (26.7.2002) by Education Act 2002 (c. 32), ss. 65(3), 216(2), Sch. 7 para. 6(3) (with ss. 210(8), 214(4)); S.I. 2002/2002, art. 2

[327] Ss. 316, 316A substituted (15.6.2001 for certain purposes and otherwise 1.1.2002 for E., 21.1.2002 for certain purposes and otherwise 1.4.2002 for W.) for s. 316 by 2001 c. 10, s. 1 (with s. 43(13)); S.I. 2001/2217, arts. 4, 5, Sch. Pts. I, II (as amended by S.I. 2001/2614, art. 4); S.I. 2002/74, arts. 4, 5, Sch. Pts. I, II

[328] Ss. 316, 316A substituted (15.6.2001 for certain purposes and otherwise 1.1.2002 for E., 21.1.2002 for certain purposes and otherwise 1.4.2002 for W.) for s. 316 by 2001 c. 10, s. 1 (with s. 43(13)); S.I. 2001/2217, arts. 4, 5, Sch. Pts. I, II (as amended by S.I. 2001/2614, art. 4); S.I. 2002/74, arts. 4, 5, Sch. Pts. I, II

[329] Words in s. 317(1)(2)(a) substituted (1.9.1999) by 1998 c. 31, s. 140(1), Sch. 30 para. 74(2)(3) (with ss. 138(9), 144(6))

[330] Words in s. 317(1)(2)(a) substituted (1.9.1999) by 1998 c. 31, s. 140(1), Sch. 30 para. 74(2)(3) (with ss. 138(9), 144(6))

[331] Words in s. 317(3)(a) substituted (1.9.1999) by 1998 c. 31, s. 140(1), Sch. 30 para. 74(4)(a)(i) (with ss. 138(9), 144(6)) S.I. 1999/2323, art. 2(1), Sch. 1

[332] Words in s. 317(3)(a) repealed (1.9.1999) by 1998 c. 31, s. 140(1)(3), Sch. 30 para. 74(4)(a)(ii), Sch. 31 (with ss. 138(9), 144(6)); S.I. 1999/2323, art. 2(1), Sch. 1

[333] Words in s. 317(3)(b) substituted (1.9.1999) by 1998 c. 31, s. 140(1), Sch. 30 para. 74(4)(b) (with ss. 138(9), 144(6)); S.I. 1999/2323, art. 2(1), Sch. 1

[334] Words in s. 317(4) substituted (1.9.1999) by 1998 c. 31, s. 140(1), Sch. 30 para. 74(5) (with ss. 138(9), 144(6)); S.I. 1999/2323, art. 2(1), Sch. 1

[335] Words in s. 317(5) substituted (1.1.2002 (E.) and 1.4.2002 (W.)) by 2001 c. 10, s. 42(1), Sch. 8 para. 5 (with s. 43(13)); S.I. 2001/2217, art. 5, Sch. Pt. II (as amended by S.I. 2001/2614, art. 4; S.I. 2002/74, art. 5, Sch. Pt. II

[336] Words in s. 317(7) substituted (1.10.2002 for E., otherwise prosp.) by Education Act 2002 (c. 32), ss. 215(1), 216(4)(5), Sch. 21 para. 39(5) (with ss. 210(8), 214(4)); S.I. 2002/2439, art. 3

[337] S. 317(6)-(7A) substituted (1.9.2002 for E., otherwise prosp.) for s. 317(6)(7) by 2001 (c. 10), ss. 14(2), 43(3) (with s. 43(13); S.I. 2002/2217, art. 4, Sch. 1 Pt. 2

[338] S. 317A inserted (1.1.2002 (E.) and 1.4.2002 (W.)) by 2001 c. 10, s. 7(1) (with s. 43(13)); S.I. 2001/2217, art. 5, Sch. Pt. II (as amended by S.I. 2001/2614, art. 4); S.I. 2002/74, art. 5, Sch. Pt. II

[339] Words in s. 318(1)(a)(b) substituted (1.9.1999) by 1998 c. 31, s. 140(1), Sch. 30 para. 75(2)(a)(b) (with ss. 138(9), 144(6)); S.I. 1999/2323, art. 2(1), Sch. 1

[340] Words in s. 318(1)(a)(b) substituted (1.9.1999) by 1998 c. 31, s. 140(1), Sch. 30 para. 75(2)(a)(b) (with ss. 138(9), 144(6)); S.I. 1999/2323, art. 2(1), Sch. 1

[341] Words in s. 318(2) substituted (1.9.1999) by 1998 c. 31, s. 140(1), Sch. 30 para. 75(3) (with ss. 138(9), 144(6)); S.I. 1999/2323, art. 2(1), Sch. 1

[342] S. 318(3): words inserted (19.12.2002) after the word "authority" by virtue of Education Act 2002 (c. 32), ss. 194(2)(a), 216(3) (with ss. 210(8), 214(4)); S.I. 2002/3185, art. 4, Sch. Pt. 1

[343] S. 318(3): words inserted (19.12.2002) after the word "authority" by virtue of Education Act 2002 (c. 32), ss. 194(2)(a), 216(3) (with ss. 210(8), 214(4)); S.I. 2002/3185, art. 4, Sch. Pt. 1

[344] S. 318(3)(3A) substituted (1.10.1998) for s. 318(3) by 1998 c. 31, ss. 140(1), Sch. 30 para. 75(4) (with ss. 138(9), 144(6)); S.I. 1998/2212, art. 2, Sch. 1 Pt. I

[345] S. 318(3B) inserted (19.12.2002) by Education Act 2002 (c. 32), ss. 194(2)(b), 216(3) (with ss. 210(8), 214(4)); S.I. 2002/3185, art. 4, Sch. Pt. 1

[346] Words in s. 321(3)(a) substituted (1.9.1999) by 1998 c. 31, s. 140(1), Sch. 30 para. 76(a) (with ss. 138(9), 144(6)); S.I. 1999/2323, art. 2(1), SCh. 1

[347] S. 321(3)(b) substituted (1.9.1999) by 1998 c. 31, s. 140(1), Sch. 30 para. 76(b) (with ss. 138(9), 144(6)); S.I. 1999/2323, art. 2(1), Sch. 1

[348] Words in s. 322(1) inserted (8.2.2000) by S.I. 2000/90, art. 3(1), Sch. 1 para. 32(2)(a)(i)(ii) (with s. 2(5))

[349] Words in s. 322(1) inserted (8.2.2000) by S.I. 2000/90, art. 3(1), Sch. 1 para. 32(2)(a)(i)(ii) (with s. 2(5))

[350] Words in s. 322(2) inserted (8.2.2000) by S.I. 2000/90, art. 3(1), Sch. 1 para. 32(2)(b) (with s. 2(5))

[351] Words in s. 322(3)(a) inserted (8.2.2000) by S.I. 2000/90, art. 3(1), Sch. 1 para. 32(2)(c)(i)(ii) (with s. 2(5))

[352] Words in s. 322(3)(a) inserted (8.2.2000) by S.I. 2000/90, art. 3(1), Sch. 1 para. 32(2)(c)(i)(ii) (with s. 2(5))

[353] Words in s. 322(4) inserted (8.2.2000) by S.I. 2000/90, art. 3(1), Sch. 1 para. 32(2)(d) (with 2(5))

[354] Words in s. 323(1)(a) substituted (1.1.2002 (E.) and 1.4.2002 (W.)) by 2001 c. 10, s. 42(1), Sch. 8 para. 11(1) (with s. 43(13)); S.I. 2001/2217, art. 5, Sch. Pt. II (as amended by S.I. 2001/2614, art. 4); S.I. 2002/74, art. 5, Sch. Pt. II

[355] S. 324(4A) inserted (11.5.2001 for certain purposes, 1.1.2002 otherwise for E., 1.4.2002 otherwise for W.) by 2001 c. 10, ss. 9, 43(4)(c) (with s. 43(13)); S.I. 2001/2217, art. 5, Sch. Pt. II (as amended by S.I. 2001/2614, art. 4); S.I. 2002/74, art. 5, Sch. Pt. II

[356] Words in s. 324(5)(b) substituted (1.9.1999) by 1998 c. 31, s. 140(1), Sch. 30 para. 77(a) (with ss. 138(9), 144(6)); S.I. 1999/2323, art. 2(1), Sch. 1

[357] S. 324(5A) inserted (1.10.1998) by 1998 c. 31, ss. 140(1), 145(3), Sch. 30 para. 77(b) (with ss. 138(9), 144(6))

[358] Words in s. 325(1) repealed (11.5.2001 for certain purposes, 1.1.2002 otherwise for E. and 1.4.2002 otherwise for W.) by 2001 c. 10, ss. 42(1)(6), 43(4)(e), Sch. 8 para. 6(1), Sch. 9 (with s. 43(13)); S.I. 2001/2217, art. 5, Sch. Pt. II (as amended by S.I. 2001/2614 art. 4); S.I. 2002/74, art. 5, Sch. Pt. II

[359] Ss. 325(2A)(2B) inserted (11.5.2001 for certain purposes, 1.1.2002 otherwise for E. and 1.4.2002 otherwise for W.) by 2001 c. 10, s. 42(1), 43(4)(e), Sch. 8 para. 6(2) (with s. 43(13)); S.I. 2001/2217, art. 5, Sch. Pt II (as amended by 2001/2614 art. 4); S.I. 2002/74, art. 5, Sch. Pt. II

[360] S. 326(1)(1A) substituted (1.1.2002 (E.), 1.4.2002 (W.)) by 2001 c. 10, s. 10, Sch. 1 para. 19 (with s. 43(13)); S.I. 2001/2217, art. 5, Sch. Pt. II (as amended by S.I. 2001/2614, art. 4); S.I. 2001/3992, art. 5, Sch. Pt. II

[361] Words in s. 326(2) substituted (1.1.2002 (E.), 1.4.2002 (W.)) by 2001 c. 10, s. 10, Sch. 1 para. 20 (with s. 43(13)); S.I. 2001/2217, art. 5, Sch. Pt. II (as amended by 2001/2614, art. 4); S.I. 2001/3992, art. 5, Sch. Pt. II

[362] S. 326A(6) substituted (1.9.2003) by Education Act 2002 (c. 32), s. 195, 216(4)(5), Sch. 18 para. 3 (with ss. 210(8), 214(4), Sch. 18 para. 17); S.I. 2002/3185, art. 6, Sch. Pt. III

[363] S. 326A inserted (11.5.2001 for certain purposes, 1.1.2002 otherwise for E. and 1.4.2002 otherwise for W.) by 2001 c. 10, ss. 5, 43(4)(b) (with s. 43(13)); S.I. 2001/2217, art. 5, Sch. Pt. II (as amended by S.I. 2001/2614, art. 4); S.I. 2001/3992, art. 5, Sch. Pt. II

[364] S. 327(1)(b) substituted (1.9.1999) for s. 327(1)(b)(i)-(iii) by 1998 c. 31, s. 140(1), Sch. 30 para.78 (with ss. 138(9), 144(6)); S.I. 1999/2323, art. 2(1), Sch. 1

365 Words in s. 328(3)(a) substituted (11.5.2001 for certain purposes, 1.1.2002 otherwise for E. and 1.4.2002 otherwise for W.) by 2001 c. 10, ss. 42(1), 43(4)(e), Sch. 8 para 7(1) (with s. 43(13)); S.I. 2001/2217, art. 5, Sch. Pt. II (as amended by S.I. 2001/2614, art. 4); S.I. 2002/74, art. 5, Sch. Pt. II

366 S. 328(3A)(3B) inserted (11.5.2001 for certain purposes, 1.1.2002 otherwise for E. and 1.4.2002 otherwise for W.) by 2001 c. 10, ss. 42(1), 43(4)(e), Sch. 8 para. 7(2) (with s. 43(13)); S.I. 2001/2217, art. 5, Sch. Pt. II (as amended by S.I. 2001/2614, art. 4); S.I. 2002/74, art. 5, Sch. Pt. II

367 Words in s. 329(2)(a) inserted (11.5.2001 for certain purposes, 1.1.2002 otherwise for E. and 1.4.2002 otherwise for W.) by 2001 c. 10, ss. 42(1), 43(4)(e), Sch. 8 para. 8(1) (with s. 43(13)); S.I. 2001/2217, art. 5, Sch. Pt. II (as amended by S.I. 2001/2614, art. 4); S.I. 2002/74, art. 5, Sch. Pt. II

368 S. 329(2A) inserted (11.5.2001 for certain purposes, 1.1.2002 otherwise for E. and 1.4.2002 otherwise for W.) by 2001 c. 10, ss. 42(1), 43(4)(e), Sch. 8 para. 8(2) (with s. 43(13)); S.I. 2001/2217, art. 5, Sch. Pt. II (as amended by S.I. 2001/2614, art. 4); S.I. 2002/74, art. 5, Sch. Pt. II

369 S. 329A inserted (15.6.2001 for certain purposes and 1.1.2002 otherwise for E., 21.1.2002 for certain purposes and 1.4.2002 otherwise for W.) by 2001 c. 10, s. 8 (with s. 43(13)); S.I. 2001/2217, arts, 4, 5, Sch. Pts. I, II (as amended by S.I. 2001/2614, art. 4); S.I. 2002/74, arts. 4, 5, Sch. Pts. I, II

370 Words in s. 332(1) inserted (8.2.2000) by S.I. 2000/90, art. 3(1), Sch. 1 para. 32(3) (with s. 2(5))

371 Words in s. 332(1) substituted (1.8.1998) by 1997 c. 44, s. 57(1), Sch. 7 para. 24; S.I. 1998/386, art. 2, Sch. 1 Pt. III

372 S. 332B inserted (1.1.2002 (E.) and 1.4.2002 (W.)) by 2001 c. 10, s. 3 (with s. 43(13)); S.I. 2001/2217, art. 5, Sch. Pt. II (as amended by S.I. 2001/2614, art. 4); S.I. 2002/74, art. 5, Sch. Pt. II

373 S. 332A and preceding cross-heading inserted (1.1.2002 (E.) and 1.4.2002 (W.)) by 2001 c. 10, s. 2 (with s. 43(13)); S.I. 2001/2217, art. 5, Sch. Pt. II (as amended by S.I. 2001/2614, art. 4); S.I. 2002/74, art. 5, Sch. Pt. II

374 S. 333(1Z) inserted (31.3.2003) by Education Act 2002 (c. 32), ss. 195, 216(3), Sch. 18 para 4 (with ss. 210(8), 214(4), Sch. 18 para. 17); S.I. 2002/3185, art. 5, Sch. Pt. II

375 S. 333(1) substituted (1.9.2002) by 2001 c. 10, ss. 42(1), 43(3), Sch. 8 para. 3 (with s. 43(13)); S.I. 2002/2217, art. 3, Sch. 1 Pt. 1

376 Section 336(2)(d) repealed (11.5.2001 for certain purposes, 1.1.2002 otherwise for E. and 1.4.2002 otherwise for W.) by 2001 c. 10, ss. 42(1)(6), 43(4)(e), Sch. 8 para. 13(2)(a), Sch. 9 (with s. 43(13)); S.I. 2001/2217, art. 5, Sch. Pt II (as amended by S.I. 2001/2614, art. 4); S.I. 2001/3992, art. 5, Sch. Pt. II

377 Word in s. 336(2)(g) substituted (11.5.2001 for certain purposes, 1.1.2002 otherwise for E. and 1.4.2002 otherwise for W.) by 2001 c. 10, ss. 42(1), 43(4)(e), Sch. 8 para. 13(2)(b) (with s. 43(13)); S.I. 2001/2217, art. 5, Sch. Pt. II (as amended by S.I. 2001/2614, art. 4); S.I. 2001/3992, art. 5, Sch. Pt. II

378 S. 336(2A) inserted (11.5.2001 for certain purposes, 1.1.2002 otherwise for E. and 1.4.2002 otherwise for W.) by 2001 c. 10, ss. 42(1), 43(4)(e), Sch. 8 para. 13(3) (with s. 43(13)); S.I. 2001/2217, art. 5, Sch. Pt. II (as amended by S.I. 2001/2614, art. 4); S.I. 2001/3992, art. 5, Sch. Pt. II

379 Words in s. 336(4) substituted (11.5.2001 for certain purposes, 1.1.2002 otherwise for E. and 1.4.2002 otherwise for W.) by 2001 c. 10, ss. 42(1), 43(4)(e), Sch. 8 para. 13(4) (with s. 43(13)); S.I. 2001/2217, art. 5, Sch. Pt. II (as amended by S.I. 2001/2614, art. 4); S.I. 2001/3992, art. 5, Sch. Pt. II

380 S. 336(4A) inserted (1.7.2002) by 2001 c. 10, s. 42(1), Sch. 8 para. 13(5) (with s. 43(13)); S.I. 2002/1721, art. 4, Sch. Pt. I

381 S. 336ZA inserted (31.3.2003) by Education Act 2002 (c. 32), ss. 195, 216(3), Sch. 18 para. 5 (with ss. 210(8), 214(4), Sch. 18 para. 17); S.I. 2002/3185, art. 5, Sch. Pt. II

382 S. 336A(2) substituted (1.9.2003) by Education Act 2002 (c. 32), ss. 195, 216(3), Sch. 18 para 6 (with ss. 210(8), 214(4), Sch. 18 para. 17); S.I. 2002/3185, art. 6, Sch. Pt. III

383 S. 336A inserted (11.5.2001 for certain purposes, 1.1.2002 otherwise for E. and 1.4.2002 otherwise for W.) by 2001 c. 10, ss. 4, 43(4)(a) (with s. 43(13)); S.I. 2001/2217, art. 5, Sch. Pt. II (as amended by S.I. 2001/2614, art. 4); S.I. 2001/3992, art. 5, Sch. Pt. II

384 S. 337 substituted (1.9.1999) by 1998 c. 31, s. 140(1), Sch. 30 para.80 (with ss. 138(9), 144(6)); S.I. 1999/2323, art. 2(1), Sch.1

385 S. 338 omitted (1.4.1999) by virtue of 1998 c. 31, s. 140(1), Sch. 30 para. 81 (with ss. 138(9), 144(6)); S.I. 1999/1016, art. 2(1), Sch. 1; ss. 338-341 repealed (1.9.1999) by 1998 c. 31, s. 140(1)(3), Sch. 30 para. 81, Sch. 31 (with ss. 138(9), 144(6)); S.I. 1999/2323, art. 2(1), Sch. 1

386 S. 339 repealed (1.4.1999 so far as relating to the omission of s. 339(2) and certain words in s. 339(4)(a) and 1.9.1999 otherwise) by 1998 c. 31, s. 140(1)(3), Sch. 30 para. 81, Sch. 31 (with ss. 138(9), 144(6)); S.I. 1999/1016, art. 2(1), Sch. 1; S.I. 1999/2323, art. 2(1), Sch. 1

387 S. 340 repealed (1.9.1999) by 1998 c. 31, s. 140(1)(3), Sch. 30 para.81, Sch. 31 (with ss. 138(9), 144(6) and subject to savings in S.I. 1999/704, regs. 7, 8, 14(2)(g)); S.I. 1999/2323, art. 2(1), Sch. 1

388 S. 341 repealed (1.9.1999) by 1998 c. 31, s. 140(1)(3), Sch. 30 para. 81, Sch.31 (with ss. 138(9), 144(6) and subject to savings in S.I. 1999/704, regs. 8, 14(2)(g) and S.I. 1999/2323, art. 17(b)); S.I. 1999/2323, art. 2(1), Sch. 1

389 S. 342 and crossheading substituted for s. 342 (1.9.1999) by 1998 c. 31, s. 140(1), Sch. 30 para. 82 (with ss. 138(9), 144(6)); S.I. 1999/2323, art. 2(1), Sch. 1

390 S. 342 and crossheading substituted for s. 342 (1.9.1999) by 1998 c. 31, s. 140(1), Sch. 30 para. 82 (with ss. 138(9), 144(6)); S.I. 1999/2323, art. 2(1), Sch. 1

[391] S. 343 repealed (1.9.1999) by 1998 c. 31, s. 140(1)(3), Sch. 30 para. 83, Sch. 31 (with ss. 138(9), 144(6)); S.I. 1999/2323, art. 2(1), Sch. 1

[392] S. 344 repealed (1.9.1999) by 1998 c. 31, s. 140(1)(3), Sch. 30 para. 83, Sch. 31 (with ss. 138(9), 144(6) and subject to savings in S.I. 1999/2323, art. 5, Sch. 7 paras. 2, 10); S.I. 1999/2323, art, 2(1), Sch. 1

[393] S. 345 repealed (1.4.1999) by 1998 c. 31, s. 140(1)(3), Sch. 30 para. 83, Sch.31 (with ss. 138(9), 144(6)); S.I. 1999/1016, art. 2(1), Sch. 1

[394] S. 346 repealed (1.10.1998) by 1998 c. 31, s. 140(1)(3), Sch. 30 para. 83, Sch.31 (with ss. 138(9), 144(6)); S.I. 1998/2212, art. 2, Sch. 1 Pt.I

[395] S. 347(5A) inserted (1.1.2002 (E.) and 1.4.2002 (W.)) by 2001 c. 10, s. 42(1), Sch. 8 para. 12 (with s. 43(13)); S.I. 2001/2217, art. 5, Sch. Pt. II (as amended by S.I. 2001/2614, art. 4); S.I. 2002/74, art. 5, Sch. Pt. II

[396] S. 348(3) substituted (1.9.1999) for s. 348(3)(a)-(c) by 1998 c. 31, s. 140(1), Sch. 30 para.84 (with ss. 138(9), 144(6))

[397] Ss. 350-369 repealed (1.10.2002 for E., 19.12.2002 for W.) by Education Act 2002 (c. 32), ss. 215(2), 216(4), Sch. 22 Pt. 3 (with ss. 210(8), 214(4)); S.I. 2002/2439, art. 3; S.I. 2002/3185, art. 4, Sch. Pt. 1

[398] Ss. 350-369 repealed (1.10.2002 for E., 19.12.2002 for W.) by Education Act 2002 (c. 32), ss. 215(2), 216(4), Sch. 22 Pt. 3 (with ss. 210(8), 214(4)); S.I. 2002/2439, art. 3; S.I. 2002/3185, art. 4, Sch. Pt. 1

[399] Ss. 350-369 repealed (1.10.2002 for E., 19.12.2002 for W.) by Education Act 2002 (c. 32), ss. 215(2), 216(4), Sch. 22 Pt. 3 (with ss. 210(8), 214(4)); S.I. 2002/2439, art. 3; S.I. 2002/3185, art. 4, Sch. Pt. 1

[400] Ss. 350-369 repealed (1.10.2002 for E., 19.12.2002 for W.) by Education Act 2002 (c. 32), ss. 215(2), 216(4), Sch. 22 Pt. 3 (with ss. 210(8), 214(4)); S.I. 2002/2439, art. 3; S.I. 2002/3185, art. 4, Sch. Pt. 1

[401] Ss. 350-369 repealed (1.10.2002 for E., 19.12.2002 for W.) by Education Act 2002 (c. 32), ss. 215(2), 216(4), Sch. 22 Pt. 3 (with ss. 210(8), 214(4)); S.I. 2002/2439, art. 3; S.I. 2002/3185, art. 4, Sch. Pt. 1

[402] S. 354(1)-(5) substituted (E.) (2.5.2000 in accordance with article 1 of S.I. 2000/1146) by S.I. 2000/1146, arts. 1, 2 and by S.I. 2000/1882, arts. 2-4, Sch. 2 it is provided (20.7.2000) that the said substitution shall have effect in Wales subject to the further amendments set out in art. 3 therein (and duly reflected in the text of this version of s. 354)

[403] S. 354(1)-(5) substituted (E.) (2.5.2000 in accordance with article 1 of S.I. 2000/1146) by S.I. 2000/1146, arts. 1, 2 and by S.I. 2000/1882, arts. 2-4, Sch. 2 it is provided (20.7.2000) that the said substitution shall have effect in Wales subject to the further amendments set out in art. 3 therein (and duly reflected in the text of this version of s. 354)

[404] S. 354(1)-(5) substituted (E.) (2.5.2000 in accordance with article 1 of S.I. 2000/1146) by S.I. 2000/1146, arts. 1, 2

[405] Ss. 350-369 repealed (1.10.2002 for E., 19.12.2002 for W.) by Education Act 2002 (c. 32), ss. 215(2), 216(4), Sch. 22 Pt. 3 (with ss. 210(8), 214(4)); S.I. 2002/2439, art. 3; S.I. 2002/3185, art. 4, Sch. Pt. 1

[406] Ss. 350-369 repealed (1.10.2002 for E., 19.12.2002 for W.) by Education Act 2002 (c. 32), ss. 215(2), 216(4), Sch. 22 Pt. 3 (with ss. 210(8), 214(4)); S.I. 2002/2439, art. 3; S.I. 2002/3185, art. 4, Sch. Pt. 1

[407] S. 355(5); definition of "school year" and the word immediately preceeding it repealed (14.6.1997) by 1997 c. 44, s. 57(4), Sch.8; S.I. 1997/1468, art. 2, Sch. 1 Pt.I

[408] Ss. 350-369 repealed (1.10.2002 for E., 19.12.2002 for W.) by Education Act 2002 (c. 32), ss. 215(2), 216(4), Sch. 22 Pt. 3 (with ss. 210(8), 214(4)); S.I. 2002/2439, art. 3; S.I. 2002/3185, art. 4, Sch. Pt. 1

[409] Ss. 350-369 repealed (1.10.2002 for E., 19.12.2002 for W.) by Education Act 2002 (c. 32), ss. 215(2), 216(4), Sch. 22 Pt. 3 (with ss. 210(8), 214(4)); S.I. 2002/2439, art. 3; S.I. 2002/3185, art. 4, Sch. Pt. 1

[410] Ss. 350-369 repealed (1.10.2002 for E., 19.12.2002 for W.) by Education Act 2002 (c. 32), ss. 215(2), 216(4), Sch. 22 Pt. 3 (with ss. 210(8), 214(4)); S.I. 2002/2439, art. 3; S.I. 2002/3185, art. 4, Sch. Pt. 1

[411] S. 358 repealed (1.3.1998) by 1997 c. 44, s. 57(1)(4), Sch. 7 para. 26, Sch. 8; S.I. 1998/386, art. 2(1), Sch. 1 Pt. I

[412] S. 359 repealed (1.3.1998) by 1997 c. 44, s. 57(1)(4), Sch. 7 para. 26, Sch. 8; S.I. 1998/386, art. 2(1), Sch. 1 Pt. I

[413] S. 360 repealed (1.10.1997) by 1997 c. 44, s. 57(1)(4), Sch. 7 para. 26, Sch. 8; S.I. 1997/1468, art. 2, Sch. 1 Pt. I

[414] S. 361 repealed (1.10.1997) by 1997 c. 44, s. 57(1)(4), Sch. 7 para. 26, Sch. 8; S.I. 1997/1468, art. 2, Sch. 1 Pt. I

[415] Ss. 350-369 repealed (1.10.2002 for E., 19.12.2002 for W.) by Education Act 2002 (c. 32), ss. 215(2), 216(4), Sch. 22 Pt. 3 (with ss. 210(8), 214(4)); S.I. 2002/2439, art. 3; S.I. 2002/3185, art. 4, Sch. Pt. 1

[416] Ss. 350-369 repealed (1.10.2002 for E., 19.12.2002 for W.) by Education Act 2002 (c. 32), ss. 215(2), 216(4), Sch. 22 Pt. 3 (with ss. 210(8), 214(4)); S.I. 2002/2439, art. 3; S.I. 2002/3185, art. 4, Sch. Pt. 1

[417] Ss. 350-369 repealed (1.10.2002 for E., 19.12.2002 for W.) by Education Act 2002 (c. 32), ss. 215(2), 216(4), Sch. 22 Pt. 3 (with ss. 210(8), 214(4)); S.I. 2002/2439, art. 3; S.I. 2002/3185, art. 4, Sch. Pt. 1

[418] Ss. 350-369 repealed (1.10.2002 for E., 19.12.2002 for W.) by Education Act 2002 (c. 32), ss. 215(2), 216(4), Sch. 22 Pt. 3 (with ss. 210(8), 214(4)); S.I. 2002/2439, art. 3; S.I. 2002/3185, art. 4, Sch. Pt. 1

[419] Ss. 350-369 repealed (1.10.2002 for E., 19.12.2002 for W.) by Education Act 2002 (c. 32), ss. 215(2), 216(4), Sch. 22 Pt. 3 (with ss. 210(8), 214(4)); S.I. 2002/2439, art. 3; S.I. 2002/3185, art. 4, Sch. Pt. 1

[420] Ss. 350-369 repealed (1.10.2002 for E., 19.12.2002 for W.) by Education Act 2002 (c. 32), ss. 215(2), 216(4), Sch. 22 Pt. 3 (with ss. 210(8), 214(4)); S.I. 2002/2439, art. 3; S.I. 2002/3185, art. 4, Sch. Pt. 1

[421] Ss. 350-369 repealed (1.10.2002 for E., 19.12.2002 for W.) by Education Act 2002 (c. 32), ss. 215(2), 216(4), Sch. 22 Pt. 3 (with ss. 210(8), 214(4)); S.I. 2002/2439, art. 3; S.I. 2002/3185, art. 4, Sch. Pt. 1

[422] Ss. 350-369 repealed (1.10.2002 for E., 19.12.2002 for W.) by Education Act 2002 (c. 32), ss. 215(2), 216(4), Sch. 22 Pt. 3 (with ss. 210(8), 214(4)); S.I. 2002/2439, art. 3; S.I. 2002/3185, art. 4, Sch. Pt. 1

[423] S. 370 repealed (1.10.1998) by 1998 c. 31, s. 140(1)(3), Sch. 30 para. 91, Sch.31 (with ss. 138(9), 144(6)); S.I. 1998/2212,

art. 2, Sch. 1 Pt.I

424 S. 371 repealed (1.10.1998) by 1998 c. 31, s. 140(1)(3), Sch. 30 para. 91, Sch.31 (with ss. 138(9), 144(6)); S.I. 1998/2212, art. 2, Sch. 1 Pt.I

425 S. 372 repealed (1.10.1998) by 1998 c. 31, s. 140(1)(3), Sch. 30 para. 91, Sch.31 (with ss. 138(9), 144(6)); S.I. 1998/2212, art. 2, Sch. 1 Pt.I

426 S. 373 repealed (1.10.1998) by 1998 c. 31, s. 140(1)(3), Sch. 30 para. 91, Sch.31 (with ss. 138(9), 144(6)); S.I. 1998/2212, art. 2, Sch. 1 Pt.I

427 S. 374 repealed (1.9.1999) by 1998 c. 31, s. 140(1)(3), Sch. 30 para. 91, Sch.31 (with ss. 138(9), 144(6)); S.I. 1999/2323, art. 2(1), Sch. 1

428 S. 376 repealed (1.9.1999) by 1998 c. 31, s. 140(1)(3), Sch. 30 para. 92, Sch.31 (with ss. 138(9), 144(6)); S.I. 1999/2323, art. 2(1), Sch. 1

429 S. 377 repealed (1.9.1999) by 1998 c. 31, s. 140(1)(3), Sch. 30 para. 92, Sch.31 (with ss. 138(9), 144(6)); S.I. 1999/2323, art. 2(1), Sch. 1

430 S. 378 repealed (1.9.1999) by 1998 c. 31, s. 140(1)(3), Sch. 30 para. 92, Sch.31 (with ss. 138(9), 144(6)); S.I. 1999/2323, art. 2(1), Sch. 1

431 S. 379 repealed (1.9.1999) by 1998 c. 31, s. 140(1)(3), Sch. 30 para. 92, Sch.31 (with ss. 138(9), 144(6)); S.I. 1999/2323, art. 2(1), Sch. 1

432 S. 380 repealed (1.9.1999) by 1998 c. 31, s. 140(1)(3), Sch. 30 para. 92, Sch.31 (with ss. 138(9), 144(6)); S.I. 1999/2323, art. 2(1), Sch. 1

433 S. 381 repealed (1.9.1999) by 1998 c. 31, s. 140(1)(3), Sch. 30 para. 92, Sch.31 (with ss. 138(9), 144(6)); S.I. 1999/2323, art. 2(1), Sch. 1

434 S. 382 repealed (1.9.1999) by 1998 c. 31, s. 140(1)(3), Sch. 30 para. 92, Sch.31 (with ss. 138(9), 144(6)); S.I. 1999/2323, art. 2(1), Sch. 1

435 S. 383 repealed (1.9.1999) by 1998 c. 31, s. 140(1)(3), Sch. 30 para. 92, Sch.31 (with ss. 138(9), 144(6)); S.I. 1999/2323, art. 2(1), Sch. 1

436 S. 384 repealed (1.9.1999) by 1998 c. 31, s. 140(1)(3), Sch. 30 para. 92, Sch.31 (with ss. 138(9), 144(6)); S.I. 1999/2323, art. 2(1), Sch. 1

437 S. 385 repealed (1.9.1999) by 1998 c. 31, s. 140(1)(3), Sch. 30 para. 92, Sch.31 (with ss. 138(9), 144(6)); S.I. 1999/2323, art. 2(1), Sch. 1

438 S. 386 repealed (1.9.1999) by 1998 c. 31, s. 140(1)(3), Sch. 30 para. 92, Sch.31 (with ss. 138(9), 144(6)); S.I. 1999/2323, art. 2(1), Sch. 1

439 S. 387 repealed (1.9.1999) by 1998 c. 31, s. 140(1)(3), Sch. 30 para. 92, Sch.31 (with ss. 138(9), 144(6)); S.I. 1999/2323, art. 2(1), Sch. 1

440 S. 388 repealed (1.9.1999) by 1998 c. 31, s. 140(1)(3), Sch. 30 para. 92, Sch.31 (with ss. 138(9), 144(6)); S.I. 1999/2323, art. 2(1), Sch. 1

441 S. 389 repealed (1.9.1999) by 1998 c. 31, s. 140(1)(3), Sch. 30 para. 92, Sch.31 (with ss. 138(9), 144(6)); S.I. 1999/2323, art. 2(1), Sch. 1; S.I. 1999/2323, art. 2(1), Sch. 1

442 S. 390(2) substituted (1.9.1999) by 1998 c. 31, s. 140(1), Sch. 30 para.93 (with ss. 138(9), 144(6)); S.I. 1999/2323, art. 2(1), Sch. 1

443 S. 391(1)(a)(i)(ii) substituted (1.9.1999) for s. 391(1)(a) by 1998 c. 31, s. 140(1), Sch. 30 para. 94(2) (with ss. 138(9), 144(6)); S.I. 1999/2323, art. 2(1), Sch. 1

444 S. 391(8)(9) repealed (1.9.1999) by 1998 c. 31, s. 140(1)(3), Sch. 30 para. 94(3), Sch.31 (with ss. 138(9), 144(6)); S.I. 1999/2323, art. 2(1), Sch. 1

445 Words in s. 391(10) substituted (1.10.1997) by 1997 c. 44, s. 57(1), Sch. 7 para. 29(a); S.I. 1997/1468, art. 2, Sch. 1 Pt. III

446 Words in s. 391(10) substituted (1.10.1997) by 1997 c. 44, s. 57(1), Sch. 7 para 29(b); S.I. 1997/1468, art. 2, Sch. 1 Pt. III

447 S. 392(4) repealed (1.9.1999) by 1998 c. 31, s. 140(1)(3), Sch. 30 para. 95, Sch.31 (with ss. 138(9), 144(6)); S.I. 1999/2323, art. 2(1), Sch. 1

448 S. 393 repealed (1.4.1999) by 1998 c. 31, s. 140(1)(3), Sch. 30 para. 96, Sch.31 (with ss. 138(9), 144(6)); S.I. 1999/1016, art. 2(1), Sch. 1

449 Words in s. 394(1)(a) substituted (1.9.1999) by 1998 c. 31, s. 140(1), Sch. 30 para. 97(2)(a) (with ss. 138(9), 144(6)); S.I. 1999/2323, art. 2(1), Sch. 1

450 S. 394(1)(b) substituted (1.9.1999) by 1998 c. 31, s. 140(1), Sch. 30 para. 97(2)(b) (with ss. 138(9), 144(6)); S.I. 1999/2323, art. 2(1), Sch. 1

451 Words in s. 394(1) substituted (1.9.1999) by 1998 c. 31, s. 140(1), Sch. 30 para. 97(2)(c) (with ss. 138(9), 144(6)); S.I. 1999/2323, art. 2(1), Sch. 1

452 Words in s. 394(4) substituted (1.9.1999) by 1998 c. 31, s. 140(1), Sch. 30 para. 97(3) (with ss. 138(9), 144(6)); S.I. 1999/2323, art. 2(1), Sch. 1

453 Words in s. 394(8) substituted (1.9.1999) by 1998 c. 31, s. 140(1), Sch. 30 para. 97(4) (with ss. 138(9), 144(6)); S.I. 1999/2323, art. 2(1), Sch. 1

454 Words in s. 395(1) substituted (1.9.1999) by 1998 c. 31, s. 140(1), Sch. 30 para.98 (with ss. 138(9), 144(6)); S.I. 1999/2323, art. 2(1), Sch. 1

455 Words in s. 396(1)(a) substituted (1.9.1999) by 1998 c. 31, s. 140(1), Sch. 30 para.99 (with ss. 138(9), 144(6)); S.I. 1999/2323, art. 2(1), Sch. 1

456 Words in s. 399 substituted (1.9.1999) by 1998 c. 31, s. 140(1), Sch. 30 para.100 (with ss. 138(9), 144(6)); S.I. 1999/2323, art. 2(1), Sch. 1

457 S. 400 repealed (1.9.2001) by 1997 c. 44, ss. 57(1)(4), Sch.8; S.I. 2001/1215, art. 2

458 S. 401 repealed (1.9.2001) by 1997 c. 44, ss. 57(1)(4), 58(3), Sch.8; S.I. 2001/1215, art. 2

459 Words in s. 402(6) substituted (1.9.1999) by 1998 c. 31, s. 140(1), Sch. 30 para.101 (with ss. 138(9), 144(6)); S.I. 1999/2323, art. 2(1), Sch. 1

460 S. 402(6)(aa) substituted (1.10.2002 for E. for certain purposes, 19.12.2002 for W. and otherwise prosp.) for word at the end of s. 402(6)(a) by Education Act 2002 (c. 32), ss. 215(1), 216(4), Sch. 21 para. 45 (with ss. 210(8), 214(4)); S.I. 2002/2439, art. 3; S.I. 2002/3185, art. 4, Sch. Pt. 1

461 Words in s. 403(1) repealed (1.11.2000 (E.) 1.9.2001 (W.)) by 2000 c. 21, ss. 148(3), 153, Sch. 11 (with s. 150); S.I. 2000/2559, art. 2(2), Sch. Pt. II; S.I. 2001/1274, art. 2(2), Sch. Pt. II

462 S. 403(1A)-(1D) inserted (1.11.2000 (E.) 1.9.2001 (W.)) by 2000 c. 21, s. 148(4) (with s. 150); S.I. 2000/2559, art. 2(2), Sch. Pt. II; S.I. 2001/1274, art. 2(2), Sch. Pt. II

463 Words in s. 403(2) substituted (1.11.2000 (E.) 1.9.2001 (W.)) by 2000 c. 21, s. 148(5)(a) (with s. 150); S.I. 2000/2559, art. 2(2), Sch. Pt. II; S.I. 2001/1274, art. 2(2), Sch. Pt. II

464 Words in s. 403(2) substituted (1.9.1999) by 1998 c. 31, s. 140(1), Sch. 30 para. 102 (with ss. 138(9), 144(6)); S.I. 1999/2323, art. 2(1), Sch. 1

465 Words in s. 403(2) inserted (1.11.2000 (E.) 1.9.2001 (W.)) by 2000 c. 21, s. 148(5)(b) (with s. 150); S.I. 2000/2559, art. 2(2), Sch. Pt. II; S.I. 2001/1274, art. 2(2), Sch. Pt. II

466 S. 404(1A) inserted (1.11.2000 (E.), 1.9.2001 (W.)) by 2000 c. 21, ss. 148(6), 154 (with s. 150)); S.I. 2000/2559, art. 2(2), Sch. Pt. II; S.I. 2001/1274 art. 2(2) Sch. Pt. II

467 Words in s. 404(2) substituted (1.9.1999) by 1998 c. 31, s. 140(1), Sch. 30 para. 103(a) (with ss. 138(9), 144(6)); S.I. 1999/2323, art. 2(1), Sch. 1

468 S. 404(3) repealed (1.10.1998) by 1998 c. 31, s. 140(1)(3), Sch. 30 para. 103(b), Sch. 31 (with ss. 138(9), 144(6)); S.I. 1998/2212, art. 2, Sch. 1 Pt. I

469 Words in s. 406(3) substituted (1.9.1999) by 1998 c. 31, s. 140(1), Sch. 30 para.104 (with ss. 138(9), 144(6)); S.I. 1999/2323, art. 2(1), Sch. 1

470 Words in s. 407(2) substituted (1.9.1999) by 1998 c. 31, s. 140(1), Sch. 30 para.105 (with ss. 138(9), 144(6)); S.I. 1999/2323, art. 2(1), Sch. 1

471 Words in s. 408(1)(a) inserted (1.10.1997) by 1997 c. 44, s. 57(1), Sch. 7 para. 30(a); S.I. 1997/1468, art. 2, Sch. 1 Pt. III

472 Words in s. 408(1)(a) inserted (28.7.2000 for certain purposes otherwise 1.9.2001) by 2000 c. 21, ss. 149, 154, Sch. 9 para. 57(2) (with s.150); S.I. 2001/654, art. 2(3), Sch. Pt. III (with art. 3); S.I. 2001/1274, art. 2(2), Sch. Pt. II

473 Words in s. 408(1)(a) inserted (1.10.2002 for E., 19.12.2002 for W.) by Education Act 2002 (c. 32), ss. 215(1), 216(4), Sch. 21 para. 46(2) (with ss. 210(8), 214(4)); S.I. 2002/2439, art. 3; S.I. 2002/3185, art. 4; Sch. Pt. I

474 S. 408(1)(b) repealed (1.9.1999) by 1998 c. 31, s. 140(1)(3), Sch. 30 para. 106(a), Sch. 31 (with ss. 138(9), 144(6)); S.I. 1999/2323, art. 2(1), Sch. 1

475 Words in s. 408(2)(d) substituted (1.10.1998) by 1998 c. 31, s. 140(1), Sch. 30 para. 106(b) (with ss. 138(9), 144(6)); S.I. 1998/2212, art. 2, Sch. 1 Pt. I

476 S. 408(2)(e) and preceding ", and" inserted (28.7.2000 for certain purposes, otherwise 1.9.2001) by 2000 c. 21, ss. 149, 154, Sch. 9 para. 57(3) (with 150); S.I. 2001/654, art. 2(3), Sch. Pt. III (with art. 3); S.I. 2001/1274, art. 2(2), Sch. Pt. II

477 S. 408(3) repealed (1.9.1999) by 1998 c. 31, s. 140(1)(3), Sch. 30 para. 106(c), Sch. 31 (with ss. 138(9), 144(6)); S.I. 1999/2323, art. 2(1), Sch. 1

478 S. 408(4)(a) repealed (1.10.2002 for E., 19.12.2002 for W.) by Education Act 2002 (c. 32), ss. 215, 216(4), Sch. 21 para. 46(3), Sch. 22 Pt. 3 (with ss. 210(8), 214(4)); S.I. 2002/2439, art. 3; S.I. 2002/3185, art. 4, Sch. Pt. I

479 S. 408(4)(b)(c) repealed (1.9.1999) by 1998 c. 31, s. 140(1)(3), Sch. 30 para. 106(d)(i), Sch. 31 (with ss. 138(9), 144(6)); S.I. 1999/2323, art. 2(1), Sch. 1

480 Word in s. 408(4)(d) substituted (1.9.1999) by 1998 c. 31, s. 140(1), Sch. 30 para. 106(d)(ii) (with ss. 138(9), 144(6))

481 Words in s. 408(4)(f) repealed (1.9.2001) by 1997 c. 44, ss. 57(1)(4), Sch. 7 para. 30(b), Sch. 8; S.I. 2001/1215, art. 2

482 S. 408(4A) inserted (1.10.2002 for E. for certain purposes, 19.12.2002 for W. and otherwise prosp.) by Education Act 2002 (c. 32), ss. 215, 216(4), Sch. 21 para. 46(4) (with ss. 210(8), 214(4)); S.I. 2002/2439, art. 3; S.I. 2002/3185, art. 4, Sch. Pt. I

483 Words in s. 408(6) substituted (1.10.2002 for E. for certain purposes, 19.12.2002 for W. and otherwise prosp.) by Education Act 2002 (c. 32), ss. 215, 216(4), Sch. 21 para. 46(5) (with ss. 210(8), 214(4)); S.I. 2002/2439, art. 3; S.I. 2002/3185, art. 4, Sch. Pt. I

484 S. 409 sidenote substituted (1.9.1999) by 1998 c. 31, s. 140(1), Sch. 30 para. 107(d) (with ss. 138(9), 144(6)); S.I. 1999/2323, art. 2(1), Sch. 1

485 Words in s. 409(1) repealed (1.10.2002 for E., 19.12.2002 for W.) by Education Act 2002 (c. 32), ss. 215, 216(4), Sch. 21 para. 47(2), Sch. 22 Pt. 3 (with ss. 210(8), 214(4)); S.I. 2002/2439, art. 3; S.I. 2002/3185, art. 4, Sch. Pt. I

486 Words in s. 409(1) substituted (1.9.1999) by 1998 c. 31, s. 140(1), Sch. 30 para. 107(a) (with ss. 138(9), 144(6)); S.I.

1999/2323, art. 2(1), Sch. 1

[487] Words in s. 409(2) substituted (1.9.1999) by 1998 c. 31, s. 140(1), Sch. 30 para. 107(b) (with ss. 138(9), 144(6)); S.I. 1999/2323, art. 2(1), Sch. 1

[488] S. 409(3)(aa) inserted (1.10.2002 for E., 19.12.2002 for W.) by Education Act 2002 (c. 32), ss. 215(1), 216(4), Sch. 21 para. 47(4) (with ss. 210(8), 214(4)); S.I. 2002/2439, art. 3; S.I. 2002/3185, art. 4, Sch. Pt. I

[489] Words in s. 409(3)(b) repealed (1.9.1999) by 1998 c. 31, s. 140(1)(3), Sch. 30 para. 107(c), Sch.31 (with ss. 138(9), 144(6)); S.I. 1999/2323, art. 2(1), Sch. 1

[490] S. 410 repealed (1.10.2002 for E., otherwise prosp.) by Education Act 2002 (c. 32), ss. 205, 215(2), 216(4), Sch. 22 Pt. 3 (with ss. 210(8), 214(4)); S.I. 2002/2439, art. 3

[491] Words in cross-heading substituted (1.9.1999) by 1998 c. 31, s. 140(1), Sch. 30 para.108 (with ss. 138(9), 144(6)); S.I. 1999/1016, art. 2(3), Sch. 2

[492] S. 411 repealed (1.9.1999) by 1998 c. 31, s. 140(1)(3), Sch. 30 para. 109, Sch. 31 (with ss. 138(9), 144(6) and subject to savings in S.I. 1999/1016, Sch. 4 paras. 2, 12 (as added (31.8.1999) by S.I. 1999/2484, art. 2(4)) and in S.I. 1999/2800, reg. 8(3)(4)); S.I. 1999/1016, art. 2(3), Sch. 3

[493] S. 411A repealed (1.9.1999) by 1998 c. 31, s. 140(1)(3), Sch. 30 para. 109, Sch.31 (with ss. 138(9), 144(6) and subject to savings in S.I. 1999/1016, Sch. 4 paras. 2, 12 (as added (31.8.1999) by S.I. 1999/2484, art. 2(4)), and in S.I. 1999/2800, reg. 8(3)); S.I. 1999/1016, art. 2(3), Sch. 3

[494] S. 412 repealed (1.9.1999) by 1998 c. 31, s. 140(1)(3), Sch. 30 para. 109, Sch.31 (with ss. 138(9), 144(6)); S.I. 1999/1016, art. 2(3), Sch. 3

[495] S. 413 repealed (1.9.1999) by 1998 c. 31, s. 140(1)(3), Sch. 30 para. 109, Sch. 31 (with ss. 138(9), 144(6) and subject to savings in S.I. 1999/1016, Sch. 4 paras. 11, 12 (as added (31.8.1999) by S.I. 1999/2484, art. 2(4)) and in S.I. 1999/2800, reg. 8(3)); S.I. 1999/1016, art. 2(3), Sch. 3

[496] S. 413A repealed (1.9.1999) by 1998 c. 31, s. 140(1)(3), Sch. 30 para. 109, Sch. 31 (with ss. 138(9), 144(6) subject to savings in S.I. 1999/1016, Sch. 4 para. 12 (as added (31.8.1999) by S.I. 1999/2484, art. 2(4)) and in S.I. 1999/2800, reg. 8(3)); S.I. 1999/1016, art. 2(3), Sch. 3

[497] S. 413B repealed (1.9.1999) by 1998 c. 31, s. 140(1)(3), Sch. 30 para. 109, Sch. 31 (with ss. 138(9), 144(6) and subject to savings in S.I. 1999/1016, Sch. 4 para. 12 (as added (31.8.1999) by S.I. 1999/2484, art. 2(4)) and in S.I. 1999/2800, reg. 8(3)); S.I. 1999/1016, art. 2(3), Sch. 3

[498] S. 414 repealed (1.9.1999) by 1998 c. 31, s. 140(1)(3), Sch. 30 para. 109, Sch. 31 (with ss. 138(9), 144(6) and subject to savings in S.I. 1999/1016, Sch. 4 para. 12 (as added (31.8.1999) by S.I. 1999/2484, art. 2(4)) and in S.I. 1999/2800, reg. 8(3)); S.I. 1999/1016, art. 2(3), Sch. 3

[499] S. 415 repealed (1.9.1999) by 1998 c. 31, s. 140(1)(3), Sch. 30 para. 109, Sch.31 (with ss. 138(9), 144(6) and subject to savings in S.I. 1999/1016, Sch. 4 para. 11); S.,I. 1999/1016, art. 2(3), Sch. 3.

[500] S. 416 repealed (1.9.1999) by 1998 c. 31, s. 140(1)(3), Sch. 30 para. 109, Sch.31 (with ss. 138(9), 144(6)); S.I. 1999/1016, art. 2(3), Sch. 3.

[501] S. 417 repealed (1.9.1999) by 1998 c. 31, s. 140(1)(3), Sch. 30 para. 109, Sch.31 (with ss. 138(9), 144(6)); S.I. 1999/1016, art. 2(3), Sch. 3.

[502] S. 418 repealed (1.9.1999) by 1998 c. 31, s. 140(1)(3), Sch. 30 para. 109, Sch.31 (with ss. 138(9), 144(6)); S.I. 1999/1016, art. 2(3), Sch. 3

[503] S. 419 repealed (1.9.1999) by 1998 c. 31, s. 140(1)(3), Sch. 30 para. 109, Sch. 31 (with ss. 138(9), 144(6)); S.I. 1999/1016, art. 2(3), Sch. 3.

[504] S. 420 repealed (1.9.1999) by 1998 c. 31, s. 140(1)(3), Sch. 30 para. 109, Sch.31 (with ss. 138(9), 144(6) and subject to savings in S.I. 1999/1016, Sch. 4 para. 6); S.I. 1999/1016, art. 2(3), Sch. 3.

[505] S. 421 repealed (1.9.1999) by 1998 c. 31, s. 140(1)(3), Sch. 30 para. 109, Sch.31 (with ss. 138(9), 144(6)); S.I. 1999/1016, art. 2(3), Sch. 3.

[506] S. 421A repealed (1.9.1999) by 1998 c. 31, s. 140(1)(3), Sch. 30 para. 109, Sch. 31 (with ss. 138(9), 144(6)); S.I. 1999/1016, art. 2(3), Sch. 3

[507] S. 422 repealed (1.9.1999) by 1998 c. 31, s. 140(1)(3), Sch. 30 para. 109, Sch.31 (with ss. 138(9), 144(6) and subject to savings in S.I. 1999/1016, Sch. 4 paras. 11, 12 (as added (31.8.1999) by S.I. 1999/2484, art. 2(4)), and savings in S.I. 1999/2800, reg. 8(3)); S.I. 1999/1016, art. 2(3), Sch. 3.

[508] S. 423 repealed (1.9.1999) by 1998 c. 31, s. 140(1)(3), Sch. 30 para. 109, Sch. 31 (with ss. 138(9), 144(6) and subject to savings in S.I. 1999/1016, Sch. 4 paras. 8, 12 (as added (31.8.1999) by S.I. 1999/2484, art. 2(4)) and in S.I. 1999/2800, reg. 8(3)); S.I. 1999/1016, art. 2(3), Sch. 3

[509] S. 423A repealed (1.9.1999) by 1998 c. 31, s. 140(1)(3), Sch. 30 para. 109, Sch. 31 (with ss. 138(9), 144(6) and subject to savings in S.I. 1999/1016, Sch. 4 paras. 8, 12 (as added (31.8.1999) by S.I. 1999/2484, art. 2(4)) and in S.I. 1999/2800, reg. 8(3)); S.I. 1999/1016, art. 2(3), Sch. 3

[510] S. 424 repealed (1.9.1999) by 1998 c. 31, s. 140(1)(3), Sch. 30 para. 109, Sch.31 (with ss. 138(9), 144(6) and subject to savings in S.I. 1999/1016, Sch. 4 para. 11); S.I. 1999/1016, art. 2(3), Sch. 3.

[511] S. 425 repealed (1.9.1999) by 1998 c. 31, s. 140(1)(3), Sch. 30 para. 109, Sch.31 (with ss. 138(9), 144(6)); S.I. 1999/1016, art. 2(3), Sch. 3.

[512] S. 425A repealed (1.9.1999) by 1998 c. 31, s. 140(1)(3), Sch. 30 para. 109, Sch.31 (with ss. 138(9), 144(6) and subject to

savings in S.I. 1999/1016, Sch. 4 paras. 8, 11); S.I. 1999/1016, art. 2(3), Sch. 3.

[513] S. 425B repealed (1.9.1999) by 1998 c. 31, s. 140(1)(3), Sch. 30 para. 109, Sch. 31 (with ss. 138(9), 144(6) and subject to savings in S.I. 1999/1016, Sch. 4 para. 2); S.I. 1999/1016, art. 2(3), Sch. 3

[514] S. 426 repealed (1.4.1999 to the extent of the repeal of s. 426(6) and 1.9.1999 to the extent of the repeal of s. 426(1)-(5)) by 1998 c. 31, s. 140(1)(3), Sch. 30 para. 109, Sch. 31 (with ss. 138(9), 144(6) and subject to savings in S.I. 1999/1016, Sch. 4 para. 7); S.I. 1999/1016, art. 2(1)(3), Sch. 1, Sch. 3

[515] S. 426A repealed (1.9.1999) by 1998 c. 31, s. 140(1)(3), Sch. 30 para. 109, Sch. 31 (with ss. 138(9),144(6); S.I. 1999/1016, art. 2(3), Sch. 3

[516] S. 427 repealed (1.9.1999) by 1998 c. 31, s. 140(1)(3), Sch. 30 para. 109, Sch.31 (with ss. 138(9), 144(6)); S.I. 1999/1016, art. 2(3), Sch. 3.

[517] S. 428 repealed (1.4.1999) by 1998 c. 31, s. 140(1)(3), Sch. 30 para. 109, Sch.31 (with ss. 138(9), 144(6)); S.I. 1999/1016, art. 2(1), Sch. 1.

[518] S. 429 repealed (1.9.1999) by 1998 c. 31, s. 140(1)(3), Sch. 30 para. 109, Sch.31 (with ss. 138(9), 144(6) and subject to savings in S.I. 1999/1016, Sch. 4 paras. 8, 11);,S.I. 1999/1016, art. 2(3), Sch. 3.

[519] S. 430 repealed (1.9.1999) by 1998 c. 31, s. 140(1)(3), Sch. 30 para. 109, Sch.31 (with ss. 138(9), 144(6) and subject to savings in S.I. 1999/1016, Sch. 4 paras. 2, 11); S.I. 1999/1016, art. 2(3), Sch. 3.

[520] S. 431 repealed (1.4.1999) by 1998 c. 31, s. 140(1)(3), Sch. 30 para. 109, Sch.31 (with ss. 138(9), 144(6) and subject to savings in S.I. 1999/1016, Sch. 4 paras. 10, 11); S.I. 1999/1016, art. 2(1), Sch. 1.

[521] S. 432 repealed (1.4.1999) by 1998 c. 31, s. 140(1)(3), Sch. 30 para. 109, Sch.31 (with ss. 138(9), 144(6) and subject to savings in S.I. 1999/1016, Sch. 4 para. 10); S.I. 1999/1016, art. 2(1), Sch. 1.

[522] S. 433(4) repealed (1.10.1998) by 1998 c. 31, s. 140(1), Sch. 30 para. 110, Sch.31 (with ss. 138(9), 144(6)); S.I. 1998/2212, art. 2(1), Sch.1 Pt. I.

[523] Word in s. 434(4)(c)(i) inserted (1.9.1999) by 1998 c. 31, s. 140(1), Sch. 30 para. 111(a) (with ss. 138(9), 144(6)); S.I. 1999/2323, art. 2(1), Sch. 1.

[524] S. 434(4)(c)(ii) repealed (1.9.1999) by 1998 c. 31, s. 140(1)(3), Sch. 30 para. 111(b), Sch.31 (with ss. 138(9), 144(6)); S.I. 1999/2323, art. 2(1), Sch. 1.

[525] S. 436 repealed (1.9.1999) by 1998 c. 31, s. 140(1)(3), Sch. 30 para. 112, Sch.31 (with ss. 138(9), 144(6) and subject to savings in S.I. 1999/1016, Sch. 4 para. 11); S.I. 1999/2323, art. 2(1), Sch. 1.

[526] Words in s. 437(5)(6) repealed (1.9.1999) by 1998 c. 31, s. 140(1)(3), Sch. 30 para. 113(a), Sch.31 (with ss. 138(9), 144(6)); S.I. 1999/2323, art. 2(1), Sch. 1

[527] Definition substituted (1.9.1999) by 1998 c. 31, s. 140(1), Sch. 30 para. 113(b) (with ss. 138(9), 144(6)); S.I. 1999/2323, art. 2(1), Sch. 1

[528] S. 438(4)(a) substituted (1.9.1999) by 1998 c. 31, s. 140(1), Sch. 30 para. 114(a) (with ss. 138(9), 144(6)); S.I. 1999/2323, art. 2(1), Sch. 1.

[529] S. 438(5) substituted (1.9.1999 for certain purposes, otherwise prosp.) by 1998 c. 31, ss. 140(1), 145(3), Sch. 30 para. 114(b) (with ss. 138(9), 144(6)); S.I. 1999/2323, art. 2(1), Sch. 1

[530] Words in s. 438(6)(a)(i) repealed (1.9.1999) by 1998 c. 31, s. 140(1)(3), Sch. 30 para. 114(c), Sch.31 (with ss. 138(9), 144(6)); S.I. 1999/2323, art. 2(1), Sch. 1

[531] Words in s. 439(2) substituted (1.10.2002 for E., otherwise prosp.) by Education Act 2002 (c. 32), ss. 51, 216(4), Sch. 4 para. 14 (with ss. 210(8), 214(4)); S.I. 2002/2439, art. 3 (with art. 4, Sch. para. 10)

[532] Words in s. 439(2) substituted (1.9.1999) by 1998 c. 31, s. 140(1), Sch. 30 para. 115(2) (with ss. 138(9), 144(6)); S.I. 1999/2323, ar. 2(1), Sch. 1

[533] Words in s. 439(3)(5)(6) repealed (1.9.1999) by 1998 c. 31, s. 140(1)(3), Sch. 30 para. 115(3), Sch.31 (with ss. 138(9), 144(6)); S.I. 1999/2323, art. 2(1), Sch. 1.

[534] S. 439(4A) inserted (1.9.1999) by 1998 c. 31, s. 140(1), Sch. 30 para. 115(4) (with ss. 138(9), 144(6)); S.I. 1999/2323, art. 2(1), Sch. 1

[535] Words in S. 440(2)(a) repealed (1.9.1999) by 1998 c. 31, s. 140(1)(3), Sch. 30 para. 116(a), Sch.31 (with ss. 138(9), 144(6)); S.I. 1999/2323, art. 2(1), Sch. 1.

[536] S. 440(3)(a)(b) substituted (1.9.1999 for certain purposes, otherwise prosp.) by 1998 c. 31, ss. 140(1), 145(3), Sch. 30 para. 116(b) (with ss. 138(9), 144(6)); S.I. 1999/2323, art. 2(1), Sch. 1

[537] Words in S. 440(4)(a) repealed (1.9.1999) by 1998 c. 31, s. 140(1)(3), Sch. 30 para. 116(c), Sch.31 (with ss. 138(9), 144(6)); S.I. 1999/2323, art. 2(1), Sch. 1

[538] Words in s. 441(3)(a) repealed (1.1.2002 (E.) and 1.4.2002 (W.)) by 2001 c. 10, s. 42(1)(6), Sch. 8 para. 15(2), Sch. 9 (with s. 43(13)); S.I. 2001/2217, art. 5, Sch. Pt. II (as amended by S.I. 2001/2614, art. 4); S.I. 2001/3992, art. 5, Sch. Pt. II

[539] S. 441(3A) inserted (1.1.2002 (E.) and 1.4.2002 (W.)) by 2001 c. 10, s. 42(1), Sch. 8 para. 15(3) (with s. 43(13)); S.I. 2001/2217, art. 5, Sch. Pt. II (as amended by S.I. 2001/2614, art. 4); S.I. 2001/3992, art. 5, Sch. Pt. II

[540] S. 444(1A) inserted (1.3.2001) by 2000 c. 43, s. 72(1)(a)(2); S.I. 2001/562, art. 2

[541] Words in S. 444(4)(b) repealed (1.9.1999) by 1998 c. 31, s. 140(1)(3), Sch. 30 para. 117, Sch. 31 (with ss. 138(9), 144(6)); S.I. 1999/2323, art. 2(1), Sch. 1.

[542] Words in s. 444(8) substituted (1.3.2001) by 2000 c. 43, s. 72(1)(b)(2); S.I. 2001/562, art. 2

[543] S. 444(8A)(8B) inserted (1.3.2001) by 2000 c. 43, s. 72(1)(c)(2); S.I. 2001/562, art. 2

[544] S. 448 repealed (1.9.1999) by 1998 c. 31, s. 140(1)(3), Sch. 30 para. 118, Sch.31 (with ss. 138(9), 144(6)); S.I. 1999/2323, art. 2(1), Sch. 1.

[545] Crossheading substituted (1.9.1999) by 1998 c. 31, s. 140(1), Sch. 30 para.119 (with ss. 138(9), 144(6)); S.I. 1999/2323, art. 2(1), Sch. 1.

[546] S. 449 and cross-heading substituted (1.9.1999) by 1998 c. 31, s. 140(1), Sch. 30 para. 119 (with ss. 138(9), 144(6)); S.I. 1999/2323, art. 2(1), Sch. 1

[547] S. 449 substituted (1.9.1999) by 1998 c. 31, s. 140(1), Sch. 30 para. 119 (with ss. 138(9), 144(6)); S.I. 1999/2323, art. 2(1), Sch. 1.

[548] Words in s. 451(1) repealed (1.9.1999) by 1998 c. 31, s. 140(1)(3), Sch. 30 para. 120(a), Sch.31 (with ss. 138(9), 144(6)); S.I. 1999/2323, art. 2(1), Sch. 1

[549] Words in s. 451(3)(b) substituted (1.10.2002 for E. for certain purposes, 19.12.2002 for W. and otherwise prosp.) by Education Act 2002 (c. 32), ss. 215(1), 216(4), Sch. 21 para. 48(2) (with ss. 210(8), 214(4)); S.I. 2002/2439, art. 3; S.I. 2002/3185, art. 4, Sch. Pt. I

[550] Words in s. 451(4)(b) substituted (1.10.2002 for E. for certain purposes, 19.12.2002 for W. and otherwise prosp.) by Education Act 2002 (c. 32), ss. 215(1), 216(4), Sch. 21 para. 48(3) (with ss. 210(8), 214(4)); S.I. 2002/2439, art. 3; S.I. 2002/3185, art. 4, Sch. Pt. I

[551] Words in s. 451(4)(b) substituted (1.9.1999) by 1998 c. 31, s. 140(1), Sch. 30 para. 120(c) (with ss. 138(9), 144(6)); S.I. 1999/2323, art. 2(1), Sch. 1

[552] S. 451(5) repealed (1.9.1999) by 1998 c. 31, s. 140(1)(3), Sch. 30 para. 120(d), Sch.31 (with ss. 138(9), 144(6)); S.I. 1999/2323, art. 2(1), Sch. 1

[553] Words in s. 456(1) repealed (1.9.1999) by 1998 c. 31, s. 140(1)(3), Sch. 30 para. 121, Sch.31 (with ss. 138(9), 144(6)); S.I. 1999/2323, art. 2(1), Sch. 1

[554] Words in s. 457(1) repealed (1.9.1999) by 1998 c. 31, s. 140(1)(3), Sch. 30 para. 122(a), Sch. 31 (with ss. 138(9), 144(6)); S.I. 1999/2323, art. 2(1), Sch. 1.

[555] Words in s. 457(3) repealed (1.9.1999) by 1998 c. 31, s. 140(1)(3), Sch. 30 para. 122(b), Sch. 31 (with ss. 138(9), 144(6)); S.I. 1999/2323, art. 2(1), Sch. 1.

[556] S. 457(4)(b) substituted (31.3.2003 for W., otherwise prosp.) by Education Act 2002 (c. 32), ss. 200, 216(4), (with ss. 210(8), 214(4)); S.I. 2002/3185, art. 5, Sch. Pt. II

[557] Words in s. 458(1) substituted (1.9.1999) by 1998 c. 31, s. 140(1), Sch. 30 para. 123(a)(i) (with ss. 138(9), 144(6)); S.I. 1999/2323, art. 2(1), Sch. 1

[558] Words in s. 458(1) repealed (1.9.1999) by 1998 c. 31, s. 140(1)(3), Sch. 30 para. 123(a)(ii), Sch.31 (with ss. 138(9), 144(6)); S.I. 1999/2323, art. 2(1), Sch. 1.

[559] S. 458(2)(a) repealed (1.9.1999) by 1998 c. 31, s. 140(1)(3), Sch. 30 para. 123(b)(i), Sch.31 (with ss. 138(9), 144(6)); S.I. 1999/2323, art. 2(1), Sch. 1

[560] Words in s. 458(2)(b) substituted (1.9.1999) by 1998 c. 31, s. 140(1), Sch. 30 para. 123(b)(ii) (with ss. 138(9), 144(6)); S.I. 1999/2323, art. 2(1), Sch. 1

[561] S. 458(3) repealed (1.9.1999) by 1998 c. 31, s. 140(1)(3), Sch. 30 para. 123(c), Sch.31 (with ss. 138(9), 144(6)); S.I. 1999/2323, art. 2(1), Sch. 1

[562] Words in s. 458(4)(b) repealed (1.9.1999) by 1998 c. 31, s. 140(1)(3), Sch. 30 para. 123(d), Sch.31 (with ss. 138(9), 144(6)); S.I. 1999/2323, art. 2(1), Sch. 1

[563] Word in s. 463(a) inserted (1.9.1999) by 1998 c. 31, s. 140(1), Sch. 30 para. 124(a) (with ss. 1 38(9), 144(6)); S.I. 1999/2323, art. 2(1), Sch. 1.

[564] Word in s. 463(b) repealed (1.9.1999) by virtue of 1998 c. 31, s. 140(1)(3), Sch. 30 para. 124(b), Sch.31 (with ss. 138(9), 144(6)); S.I. 1999/2323, art. 2(1), Sch. 1.

[565] S. 463(c) repealed (1.9.1999) by virtue of 1998 c. 31, s. 140(1)(3), Sch. 30 para. 124(b), Sch.31 (with ss. 138(9), 144(6)); S.I. 1999/2323, art. 2(1), Sch. 1.

[566] Words in s. 467(2) substituted (1.4.2002) by 2000 c. 14, ss. 116, 122, Sch. 4 para. 24(2); S.I. 2001/4150, art. 3(3)(a) (subject to art. 4); S.I. 2002/920, art. 3(3)(d) (subject to art. 3(2), Schs. 1-3 and with art. 3(4)-(10))

[567] S. 468(2) inserted (11.1.2001) by 2000 c. 43, s. 74, Sch. 7 Pt. II para. 128; S.I. 2000/3302, art. 2(b)

[568] S. 469(1)(d) substituted (2.10.2000) by 2000 c. 14, s. 100(1); S.I. 2000/2544, art. 2(2)(d)

[569] Words in s. 469(4) inserted (1. 4.2002) by 2000 c. 14, ss. 116, 122, Sch. 4 para. 24(3); S. I. 2002/920,
(subject to savings and transitional provisions in Schs. 1-3)

[570] S. 470(2)(f) substituted (2.10.2000) by 2000 c. 14, s. 100(2); S.I. 2000/2544, art. 2(2)(d)

[571] Words in s. 471(2)(a) inserted (1.4.2002) by 2000 c. 14, ss. 116, 122, Sch. 4 para. 24(4); S. I. 2002/920, {arts. 2, 3(3)(d)} (subject to savings and transitional provisions in Schs. 1-3)

[572] Ss. 473A, 473B inserted (11.1.2001) by 2000 c. 43, s. 74, Sch. 7 Pt. II para. 129; S.I. 2000/3302, art. 2(b)

[573] S. 474: sidenote substituted (11.1.2001) by 2000 c. 43, s. 74, Sch. 7 Pt. II para. 130(b); S.I. 2000/3302, art. 2(b)

[574] Words inserted (11.1.2001) at the end of s. 474(1) by 2000 c. 43, s. 74, Sch. 7 Pt. II para. 130(a); S.I. 2000/3302, art. 2(b)

[575] S. 479 repealed (1.9.1997) by 1997 c. 59, ss. 1(1)(a)(b)(3), 6(3), 7(3)(a), Sch., Pt.I.

[576] S. 480 repealed (1.9.1997) by 1997 c. 59, ss. 1(1)(a)(b)(3), 6(3), 7(3), Sch. Pt.I.

[577] S. 481 repealed (1.9.1997) by 1997 c. 59, ss. 1(1)(a)(b)(3), 6(3), 7(3), Sch. Pt.I.

[578] S. 482 substituted (26.7.2002) by Education Act 2002 (c. 32), ss. 65(1), 216(2) (with ss. 210(8), 214(4)); S.I. 2002/2002, art. 2

[579] Word in s. 483(3) substituted (26.7.2002) by Education Act 2002 (c. 32), ss. 65(2), 216(2) (with ss. 210(8), 214(4)); S.I. 2002/2002, art. 2

[580] S. 483(3A) repealed (1.10.2002 for E., otherwise prosp.) by Education Act 2002 (c. 32), ss. 215(2), 216(4), Sch. 22 Pt. 3 (with ss. 210(8), 214(4)); S.I. 2002/2439, art. 3

[581] S. 483(3A) inserted (1.10.2000) by 2000 c. 21, s. 132 (with s. 150); S.I. 2000/2559, art. 2(1), Sch. Pt. I

[582] Words in s. 483A(2)(b) substituted (26.7.2002) by Education Act 2002 (c. 32), ss. 65, 216; Sch. 7 Pt. 2 para. 6(4)(a); (with savings in ss. 210(8), 214(4)) S.I. 2002/2002, art. 2

[583] S. 483A(7) ceased to have effect (26.7.2002) and repealed (1.10.2002 for E., otherwise prosp.) by Education Act 2002 (c. 32), ss. 65(3), 215, 216(4), Sch. 7 para. 6(4)(b), Sch. 22 Pt. 3 (with ss. 210(8), 214(4)); S.I. 2002/2002, art. 2; S.I. 2002/2439, art. 3

[584] S. 483A inserted (1.10.2000) by 2000 c. 21, s. 133 (with s. 150); S.I. 2000/2559, art. 2(1), Sch. Pt. I

[585] S. 484 sidenote substituted (1.2.1999) by 1998 c. 31, s. 140(1), Sch. 30 para. 125(c) (with ss. 138(9), 144(6)); S.I. 1999/120, art. 2, Sch. 1

[586] Words in s. 484 substituted (31.3.2003 for W., otherwise prosp.) by Education Act 2002 (c. 32), ss. 215(1), 216(4), Sch. 21 para. 49(2) (with ss. 210(8), 214(4)); S.I. 2002/3185, art. 5, Sch. Pt. II

[587] Words in s. 484(1) substituted (1.2.1999) by 1998 c. 31, s. 140(1), Sch. 30 para. 125(a) (with ss. 138(9), 144(6)); S.I. 1999/120, art. 2, Sch. 1

[588] Words in s. 484(1) inserted (31.3.2003 for W., otherwise prosp.) by Education Act 2002 (c. 32), ss. 215(1), 216(4), Sch. 21 para. 49(3) (with ss. 210(8), 214(4)); S.I. 2002/3185, art. 5, Sch. Pt. II

[589] Words in s. 484 substituted (31.3.2003 for W., otherwise prosp.) by Education Act 2002 (c. 32), ss. 215(1), 216(4), Sch. 21 para. 49(2) (with ss. 210(8), 214(4)); S.I. 2002/3185, art. 5, Sch. Pt. II

[590] Words in s. 484 repealed (31.3.2003 for W., otherwise prosp.) by Education Act 2002 (c. 32), ss. 215(1), 216(4), Sch. 21 para. 49(4), Sch. 22 Pt. 3 (with ss. 210(8), 214(4)); S.I. 2002/3185, art. 5, Sch. Pt. II

[591] Words in s. 484 substituted (31.3.2003 for W., otherwise prosp.) by Education Act 2002 (c. 32), ss. 215(1), 216(4), Sch. 21 para. 49(2) (with ss. 210(8), 214(4)); S.I. 2002/3185, art. 5, Sch. Pt. II

[592] Words in s. 484 substituted (31.3.2003 for W., otherwise prosp.) by Education Act 2002 (c. 32), ss. 215(1), 216(4), Sch. 21 para. 49(2) (with ss. 210(8), 214(4)); S.I. 2002/3185, art. 5, Sch. Pt. II

[593] Words in s. 484(3)(4) substituted (1.2.1999) by 1998 c. 31, s. 140(1), Sch. 30 para. 125(b) (with ss. 138(9), 144(6)); S.I. 1999/120, art. 2, Sch. 1

[594] Words in s. 484 substituted (31.3.2003 for W., otherwise prosp.) by Education Act 2002 (c. 32), ss. 215(1), 216(4), Sch. 21 para. 49(2) (with ss. 210(8), 214(4)); S.I. 2002/3185, art. 5, Sch. Pt. II

[595] S. 484(6) repealed (31.3.2003 for W., otherwise prosp.) by Education Act 2002 (c. 32), ss. 215(1), 216(4), Sch. 21 para. 49(5), Sch. 22 Pt. 3 (with ss. 210(8), 214(4)); S.I. 2002/3185, art. 5, Sch. Pt. II

[596] Words in s. 484 substituted (31.3.2003 for W., otherwise prosp.) by Education Act 2002 (c. 32), ss. 215(1), 216(4), Sch. 21 para. 49(2) (with ss. 210(8), 214(4)); S.I. 2002/3185, art. 5, Sch. Pt. II

[597] Words in s. 489(2)(a) substituted (1.2.1999) by 1998 c. 31, s. 140(1), Sch. 30 para.126 (with ss. 138(9), 144(6)); S.I. 1999/120, art. 2, Sch. 1.

[598] S. 490(1)(a) repealed (1.9.1999) by 1998 c. 31, s. 140(1)(3), Sch. 30 para. 127, Sch. 31 (with ss. 138(9), 144(6)); S.I. 1999/2323, art. 2(1), Sch. 1

[599] Words in s. 490(1)(b) substituted (28.7.2000 for certain purposes, otherwise prosp.) by 2000 c. 21, ss. 149, 154, Sch. 9 para. 58(2) (with s. 150)

[600] Words in s. 490(2) substituted (28.7.2000 for certain purposes, otherwise prosp.) by 2000 c. 21, ss. 149, 154, Sch. 9 para. 58(3) (with s. 150)

[601] Words in s. 492(2) substituted (1.8.1998) by 1997 c. 44, s. 57(1), Sch. 7 para.36; S.I. 1998/386, art. 2(3), Sch. 1 Pt.III.

[602] S. 494 substituted (1.4.1999) by 1998 c. 31, s. 140(1), Sch. 30 para.128 (with ss. 138(9), 144(6)); S.I. 1998/2212, art. 2(4), Sch.1 Pt. IV.

[603] Word in s. 496(2)(a) inserted (1.9.1999) by 1998 c. 31, s. 140(1), Sch. 30 para. 129(a) (with ss. 138(9), 144(6)); S.I. 1999/2323, art. 2(1), Sch. 1

[604] S. 496(2)(b) substituted (1.9.1999) for s. 496(2)(b)(c) by 1998 c. 31, ss. 140(1), 145(3), Sch. 30 para. 129(b) (with ss. 138(9), 144(6)); S.I. 1999/2323, art. 2(1), Sch. 1

[605] Word in s. 497(2)(a) inserted (1.9.1999) by 1998 c. 31, s. 140(1), Sch. 30 para. 130(a) (with ss. 138(9), 144(6)); S.I. 1999/2323, art. 2(1), Sch. 1

[606] S. 497(2)(b)(c) substituted (1.9.1999) by 1998 c. 31, s. 140(1), Sch. 30 para. 130(b) (with ss. 138(9), 144(6)); S.I. 1999/2323, art. 2(1), Sch. 1.

[607] S. 497A inserted (1.10.1998) by 1998 c. 31, s. 8 (with ss. 138(9), 144(6)); S.I. 1998/2212, art. 2(1), Sch.1 Pt. I.

[608] S. 497A(1) substituted (26.7.2002 for E., otherwise prosp.) by Education Act 2002 (c. 32), ss. 60(2), 216(4) (with ss. 210(8), 214(4)); S.I. 2002/2002, art. 3

[609] Words in s. 497A(2) substituted (26.7.2002 for E., otherwise prosp.) by Education Act 2002 (c. 32), ss. 60(3), 216(4) (with ss. 210(8), 214(4)); S.I. 2002/2002, art. 3

610 S. 497A(2A) inserted (26.7.2002 for E., otherwise prosp.) by Education Act 2002 (c. 32), ss. 60(4), 216(4) (with ss. 210(8), 214(4)); S.I. 2002/2002, art. 3

611 S. 497A(3) omitted (26.7.2002 for E., otherwise prosp.) and repealed (1.10.2002 for E., otherwise prosp.) by virtue of Education Act 2002 (c. 32), ss. 60(5), 215(2), 216(4), Sch. 22 Pt. 3 (with ss. 210(8), 214(4)); S.I. 2002/2002, art. 3; S.I. 2002/2439, art. 3

612 S. 497A(4) substituted (26.7.2002 for E., otherwise prosp.) by Education Act 2002 (c. 32), ss. 60(6), 216(4) (with ss. 210(8), 214(4)); S.I. 2002/2002, art. 3

613 S. 497A(5) substituted (26.7.2002 for E., otherwise prosp.) by Education Act 2002 (c. 32), ss. 60(8), 216(4) (with ss. 210(8), 214(4)); S.I. 2002/2002, art. 3

614 S. 497A(6)(b) substituted (26.7.2002 for E., otherwise prosp.) by Education Act 2002 (c. 32), ss. 60(9), 216(4) (with ss. 210(8), 214(4)); S.I. 2002/2002, art. 3

615 Words in s. 497A(7) substituted (26.7.2002 for E., otherwise prosp.) by Education Act 2002 (c. 32), ss. 60(10), 216(4) (with ss. 210(8), 214(4)); S.I. 2002/2002, art. 3

616 S. 497A(4A)(4B) inserted (26.7.2002 for E., otherwise prosp.) by Education Act 2002 (c. 32), ss. 60(7), 216(4) (with ss. 210(8), 214(4)); S.I. 2002/2002, art. 3

617 S. 497AA inserted (26.7.2002 for E., otherwise prosp.) by Education Act 2002 (c. 32), ss. 61, 216(4) (with ss. 210(8), 214(4)); S.I. 2002/2002, art. 3

618 Words in s. 497B(1) substituted (1.10.2002 for E., otherwise prosp.) by Education Act 2002 (c. 32), ss. 62(2), 216(4) (with ss. 210(8), 214(4)); S.I. 2002/2439, art. 3

619 S. 497B(1A) substituted (1.10.2002 for E., otherwise prosp.) by Education Act 2002 (c. 32), ss. 62(3), 216(4) (with ss. 210(8), 214(4)); S.I. 2002/2439, art. 3

620 S. 497B inserted (1.10.1998) by 1998 c. 31, s. 8 (with ss. 138(9), 144(6)); S.I. 1998/2212, art. 2(1), Sch. 1 Pt. I

621 S. 498(2) substituted (1.9.1999) by 1998 c. 31, s. 140(1), Sch. 30 para.131 (with ss. 138(9), 144(6)); S.I. 1999/2323, art. 2(1), Sch. 1.

622 S. 499(6)-(9) added (1.10.1998) by 1998 c. 31, s.9 (with ss. 138(9), 144(6)); S.I. 1998/2212, art. 2, Sch. 1 Pt.I

623 S. 500 repealed (1.4.1999 to the extent that it relates to s. 500(2) and words in s. 502(3)(4) and 1.9.1999 otherwise) by 1998 c. 31, s. 140(1)(3), Sch. 30 para. 132, Sch.31 (with ss. 138(9), 144(6)); S.I. 1999/1016, art. 2(1), Sch. 1; S.I. 1999/2323, art. 2(1), Sch. 1

624 S. 501 repealed (1.4.1999 to the extent that it relates to s. 501(1)(a) and 1.9.1999 otherwise) by 1998 c. 31, s. 140(1)(3), Sch. 30 para. 132, Sch.31 (with ss. 138(9), 144(6)); S.I. 1999/1016, art. 2(1), Sch. 1; S.I. 1999/2323, art. 2(1), Sch. 1

625 S. 502 repealed (1.4.1999 to the extent that it relates to s. 502(6) and 1.9.1999 otherwise) by 1998 c. 31, s. 140(1)(3), Sch. 30 para. 132, Sch.31 (with ss. 138(9), 144(6)); S.I. 1999/1016, Art. 2(1), Sch. 1; S.I. 1999/2323, art. 2(1), Sch. 1

626 S. 503 repealed (1.9.1999) by 1998 c. 31, s. 140(1)(3), Sch. 30 para. 132, Sch.31 (with ss. 138(9), 144(6)); S.I. 1999/2323, art. 2(1), Sch. 1

627 S. 504 repealed (1.9.1999) by 1998 c. 31, s. 140(1)(3), Sch. 30 para. 132, Sch.31 (with ss. 138(9), 144(6)); S.I. 1999/2323, art. 2(1), Sch. 1

628 S. 505 repealed (1.9.1999) by 1998 c. 31, s. 140(1)(3) Sch. 30 para. 132, Sch.31 (with ss. 138(9), 144(6)); S.I. 1999/2323, art. 2(1), Sch. 1

629 Words in s. 508(1) substituted (1.4.2001) by 2000 c. 21, s. 137(2), (with s. 150); S.I. 2001/654, art. 2(2), Sch. Pt. II; S.I. 2001/1274, art. 2(1), Sch. Pt. I

630 S. 508(1A) inserted (1.4.2001) by 2000 c. 21, s. 137(3) (with s. 150); S.I. 2001/654, art. 2(2), Sch. Pt. II; S.I. 2001/1274, art. 2(1), Sch. Pt. I

631 Words in s. 508(2) substituted (1.4.2001) by 2000 c. 21, s. 137(4), (with s. 150); S.I. 2001/654, art. 2(2), Sch. Pt. II; S.I. 2001/1274, art. 2(1), Sch. Pt. I

632 Words in s. 509(1)(1A) inserted (20.1.2003 for E., otherwise prosp.) by Education Act 2002 (c. 32), ss. 199, 216(4), Sch. 19 para 2(a) (with ss. 210(8), 214(4)); S.I. 2002/2952, art. 2

633 Word in s. 509(1)(b) inserted (28.7.2000 for certain purposes, otherwise 1.4.2001) by 2000 c. 21, s. 149, Sch. 9 para. 59(2)(a) (with s. 150); S.I. 2001/654, art. 2(2), Sch. Pt. II (with art. 3); S.I. 2001/1274, art. 2(1), Sch. Pt. I

634 S. 509(1)(d) and preceding word repealed (28.7.2000 for certain purposes, otherwise 1.4.2001) by 2000 c. 21, ss. 149, 153, Sch. 9 para. 59(2)(b), Sch. 11 (with s. 150); S.I. 2001/654, art. 2(2), Sch. Pt. II (with art. 3); S.I. 2001/1274, art. 2(1), Sch. Pt. I

635 Words in s. 509(1)(1A) inserted (20.1.2003 for E., otherwise prosp.) by Education Act 2002 (c. 32), ss. 199, 216(4), Sch. 19 para 2(a) (with ss. 210(8), 214(4)); S.I. 2002/2952, art. 2

636 S. 509(1A)(1B) inserted (28.7.2000 for certain purposes, otherwise 1.4.2001) by 2000 c. 21, s. 149, Sch. 9 para. 59(3) (with s. 150); S.I. 2001/654, art. 2(2), Sch. Pt. II (with art. 3); S.I. 2001/1274, art. 2(1), Sch. Pt. I

637 Words in s. 509(2) inserted (28.7.2000 for certain purposes, otherwise 1.4.2001) by 2000 c. 21, s. 149, Sch. 9 para. 59(4) (with s. 150); S.I. 2001/654, art. 2(2), Sch. Pt. II (with art. 3); S.I. 2001/1274, art. 2(1), Sch. Pt. I

638 Words in s. 509(3) inserted (28.7.2000 for certain purposes, otherwise 1.4.2001) by 2000 c. 21, s. 149, Sch. 9 para. 59(5)(a) (with s. 150); S.I. 2001/654, art. 2(2), Sch. Pt. II (with art. 3); S.I. 2001/1274, art. 2(1), Sch. Pt. I

639 Words in s. 509(3) inserted (20.1.2003 for E., otherwise prosp.) by Education Act 2002 (c. 32), ss. 199, 216(4), Sch. 19 para 2(b) (with ss. 210(8), 214(4)); S.I. 2002/2952, art. 2

[640] Words in s. 509(3)(b) inserted (28.7.2000 for certain purposes, otherwise 1.4.2001) by 2000 c. 21, s. 149, Sch. 9 para. 59(5)(b) (with s. 150); S.I. 2001/654, art. 2(2), Sch. Pt. II (with art. 3); S.I. 2001/1274, art. 2(1), Sch. Pt. I

[641] Words in s. 509(3) substituted (28.7.2000 for certain purposes, otherwise 1.4.2001) by 2000 c. 21, s. 149, Sch. 9 para. 59(5)(c) (with s. 150); S.I. 2001/654, art. 2(2), Sch. Pt. II (with art. 3); S.I. 2001/1274, art. 2(1), Sch. Pt. I

[642] Words in s. 509(4) inserted (28.7.2000 for certain purposes, otherwise 1.4.2001) by 2000 c. 21, s. 149, Sch. 9 para. 59(6)(a) (with s. 150); S.I. 2001/654, art. 2(2), Sch. Pt. II (with art. 3); S.I. 2001/1274, art. 2(1), Sch. Pt. I

[643] Words in s. 509(4) inserted (28.7.2000 for certain purposes, otherwise 1.4.2001) by 2000 c. 21, s. 149, Sch. 9 para. 59(6)(b) (with s. 150); S.I. 2001/654, art. 2(2), Sch. Pt. II (with art. 3); S.I. 2001/1274, art. 2(1), Sch. Pt. I

[644] Words in s. 509(5) inserted (28.7.2000 for certain purposes, otherwise 1.4.2001) by 2000 c. 21, s. 149, Sch. 9 para. 59(7)(a) (with s. 150); S.I. 2001/654, art. 2(2), Sch. Pt. II (with art. 3); S.I. 2001/1274, art. 2(1), Sch. Pt. I

[645] S. 509(5)(a) repealed (1.9.1999) by 1998 c. 31, s. 140(1)(3), Sch. 30 para. 133(a), Sch. 31 (with ss. 138(9), 144(6)); S.I. 1999/2323, art. 2(1), Sch. 1

[646] S. 509(5)(c) substituted (20.1.2003 for E., otherwise prosp.) by Education Act 2002 (c. 32), ss. 199, 215(1), 216(4), Sch. 19 para. 2(c) (with ss. 210(8), 214(4)); S.I. 2002/2952, art. 2

[647] Words in s. 509(6)(a) substituted (28.7.2000 for certain purposes, otherwise 1.4.2001) by 2000 c. 21, s. 149, Sch. 9 para. 59(8) (with s. 150); S.I. 2001/654, art. 2(2), Sch. Pt. II (with art. 3); S.I. 2001/1274, art. 2(1), Sch. Pt. I

[648] S. 509(6) repealed (20.1.2003 for E., otherwise prosp.) by Education Act 2002 (c. 32), ss. 215(2), 216(4), Sch. 22 Pt. 3 (with ss. 210(8), 214(4)); S.I. 2002/2952, art. 2

[649] S. 509(6) substituted (1.4.1999) by 1998 c. 31, s. 140(1), Sch. 30 para. 133(b) (with ss. 138(9), 144(6)); S.I. 1998/2212, art. 2(4), Sch. 1 Pt. IV

[650] S. 509(7) inserted (20.1.2003 for E., otherwise prosp.) by Education Act 2002 (c. 32), ss. 199, 216(4), Sch. 19 para 2(d) (with ss. 210(8), 214(4)); S.I. 2002/2952, art. 2

[651] S. 509AA inserted (20.1.2003 for E., otherwise prosp.) by Education Act 2002 (c. 32), ss. 199, 216(4), Sch. 19 para 3 (with ss. 210(8), 214(4)); S.I. 2002/2952, art. 2

[652] S. 509AB inserted (20.1.2003 for E., otherwise prosp.) by Education Act 2002 (c. 32), ss. 199, 216(4), Sch. 19 para 4 (with ss. 210(8), 214(4)); S.I. 2002/2952, art. 2

[653] S. 509AC inserted (20.1.2003 for E., otherwise prosp.) by Education Act 2002 (c. 32), ss. 199, 216(4), Sch. 19 para 5 (with ss. 210(8), 214(4)); S.I. 2002/2952, art. 2

[654] S. 509A inserted (1.4.1999) by 1998 c. 31, s. 124 (with ss. 138(9), 144(6)); S.I. 1998/2212, art. 2(4), Sch. 1 Pt. IV

[655] S. 509A(4A) inserted (20.1.2003 for E., otherwise prosp.) by Education Act 2002 (c. 32), ss. 199, 216(4), Sch. 19 para 6 (with ss. 210(8), 214(4)); S.I. 2002/2952, art. 2

[656] Words in s. 510(1)(a)(c) repealed (1.9.1999) by 1998 c. 31, s. 140(1)(3), Sch. 30 para. 134(a), Sch.31 (with ss. 138(9), 144(6)); S.I. 1999/2323, art. 2(1), Sch. 1.

[657] Words in s. 510(3)(a) repealed (1.9.1999) by 1998 c. 31, s. 140(1)(3), Sch. 30 para. 134(b), Sch.31 (with ss. 138(9), 144(6)); S.I. 1999/2323, art. 2(1), Sch. 1.

[658] Words in s. 510(4)(a) repealed (1.9.1999) by 1998 c. 31, s. 140(1)(3), Sch. 30 para. 134(c), Sch.31 (with ss. 138(9), 144(6)); S.I. 1999/2323, art. 2(1), Sch. 1.

[659] Words in s. 510(5)(a) repealed (1.9.1999) by 1998 c. 31, s. 140(1)(3), Sch. 30 para. 134(d), Sch.31 (with ss. 138(9), 144(6)); S.I. 1999/2323, art. 2(1), Sch. 1.

[660] Ss. 512-512ZB substituted (31.3.2003 for W. for certain purposes, otherwise prosp.) for s. 512 by Education Act 2002 (c. 32), ss. 201(1), 216(4) (with ss. 210(8), 214(4)); S.I. 2002/3185, art. 5, Sch. Pt. II

[661] Ss. 512-512ZB substituted (31.3.2003 for W. for certain purposes, otherwise prosp.) for s. 512 by Education Act 2002 (c. 32), ss. 201(1), 216(4) (with ss. 210(8), 214(4)); S.I. 2002/3185, art. 5, Sch. Pt. II

[662] Words in s. 512A(2)(a) substituted (31.3.2003 for W., otherwise prosp.) by Education Act 2002 (c. 32), ss. 201(2)(a)(i), 216(4) (with ss. 210(8), 214(4)); S.I. 2002/3185, art. 5, Sch. Pt. II

[663] Words in s. 512A(2)(b) substituted (31.3.2003 for W., otherwise prosp.) by Education Act 2002 (c. 32), ss. 201(2)(a)(ii), 216(4) (with ss. 210(8), 214(4)); S.I. 2002/3185, art. 5, Sch. Pt. II

[664] Words in s. 512A(2)(c) substituted (31.3.2003 for W., otherwise prosp.) by Education Act 2002 (c. 32), ss. 201(2)(a)(iii), 216(4) (with ss. 210(8), 214(4)); S.I. 2002/3185, art. 5, Sch. Pt. II

[665] Words in s. 512A(6) substituted (31.3.2003 for W., otherwise prosp.) by Education Act 2002 (c. 32), ss. 201(2)(b), 216(4) (with ss. 210(8), 214(4)); S.I. 2002/3185, art. 5, Sch. Pt. II

[666] S. 512A inserted (1.2.1999) by 1998 c. 31, s. 116 (with ss. 138(9), 144(6)); S.I. 1998/3198, art. 2(2), Sch.

[667] Words in s. 514(1)(a) substituted (1.9.1999) by 1998 c. 31, s. 140(1), Sch. 30 para.135 (with ss. 138(9), 144(6)); S.I. 1999/2323, art. 2(1), Sch. 1.

[668] Words in s. 515(2) substituted (1.9.1999) by 1998 c. 31, s. 140(1), Sch. 30 para.136 (with ss. 138(9), 144(6)); S.I. 1999/2323, art. 2(1), Sch. 1.

[669] S. 516 repealed (1.4.1999) by 1998 c. 31, s. 140(1)(3), Sch. 30 para. 137, Sch.31 (with ss. 138(9), 144(6)); S.I. 1998/2212, art. 2(4), Sch.1 Pt. IV.

[670] S. 518 substituted (1.2.1999) by 1998. c. 31, s. 129 (with ss. 138(9), 144(6)) (subject to savings indicated in S.I. 1999/120, art. 3(2)); S.I. 1999/120, art. 2, Sch. 1

[671] Words in s. 519(1) substituted (20.11.1998 for the purposes of making schemes and regulations and 1.4.1999 for all

other purposes) by 1998 c. 31, s. 140(1), Sch. 30 para. 139(2) (with ss. 138(9), 144(6)); S.I. 1998/2791, art. 2(a)(b).

672 Words in s. 519(3) substituted (20.11.1998 for the purposes of making schemes and regulations and 1.4.1999 for all other purposes) by 1998 c. 31, s. 140(1), Sch. 30 para. 139(3) (with ss. 138(9), 144(6)); S.I. 1998/2791, art. 2(a)(b).

673 S. 519(7) added (20.11.1998 for the purposes of making schemes and regulations and 1.4.1999 for all other purposes) by 1998 c. 31, s. 140(1), Sch. 30 para. 139(4) (with ss. 138(9), 144(6)); S.I. 1998/2791, art. 2(a)(b).

674 S. 520(3) repealed (1.9.1999) by 1998 c. 31, s. 140(1)(3), Sch. 30 para. 140, Sch.31 (with ss. 138(9), 144(6)); S.I. 1999/2323, art. 2(1), Sch. 1

675 Word in s. 521(4)(a) repealed (1.9.1999) by 1998 c. 31, s. 140(1)(3), Sch. 30 para. 141, Sch.31 (with ss. 138(9), 144(6)); S.I. 1999/2323, art. 2(1), Sch. 1.

676 S. 521(4)(b) repealed (1.9.1999) by 1998 c. 31, s. 140(1)(3), Sch. 30 para. 141, Sch.31 (with ss. 138(9), 144(6)); S.I. 1999/2323, art. 2(1), Sch. 1.

677 Sidenote substituted (1.9.1999) by 1998 c. 31, ss. 140(1), Sch. 30 para. 142(c) (with ss. 138(9), 144(6)); S.I. 1999/2323, art. 2(1), Sch. 1.

678 Word in s. 524(1) substituted (1.9.1999) by 1998 c. 31, ss. 140(1), 145(3), Sch. 30 para. 142(a) (with ss. 138(9), 144(6)); S.I. 1999/2323, art. 2(1), Sch. 1.

679 S. 524(3)(b) and the word "or" preceding it repealed (1.9.1999) by 1998 c. 31, s. 140(1)(3), Sch. 30 para. 142(b), Sch.31 (with ss. 138(9), 144(6)); S.I. 1999/2323, art. 2(1), Sch. 1.

680 Words in s. 525(3) repealed (1.9.1999) by 1998 c. 31, s. 140(1)(3), Sch. 30 para.143, Sch. 31 (with ss. 138(9), 144(6)); S.I. 1999/2323, art. 2(1), Sch. 1.

681 S. 527A and cross-heading inserted (1.4.1998) by 1997 c. 44, s.9 (with s. 57(3)); S.I. 1998/386, art. 2(2), Sch. 1 Pt. II

682 S. 527A(7) substituted (1.9.1999) by 1998 c. 31, s. 140(1), Sch. 30 para.144 (with ss. 138(9), 144(6)); S.I. 1999/2323, art. 2(1), Sch. 1.

683 S. 527A inserted (1.4.1998) by 1997 c. 44, s. 9 (with s. 57(3)); S.I. 1998/386, art. 2(2), Sch. 1 Pt. II.

684 S. 528 repealed (1.9.2002) by 2001 c.10, ss. 34(3), 42(6), Sch. 9 (with s. 43(13)); S.I. 2002/2217, art. 3, Sch. 1 Pt. 1

685 Words in s. 529(2) substituted (1.9.1999) by 1998 c. 31, s. 140(1), Sch. 30 para. 145(a) (with ss. 138(9), 144(6)); S.I. 1999/2323, art. 2(1), Sch. 1.

686 Words in s. 529(3) substituted (1.9.1999) by 1998 c. 31, s. 140(1), Sch. 30 para. 145(b) (with ss. 138(9), 144(6)); S.I. 1999/2323, art. 2(1), Sch. 1.

687 Words in s. 530(2) substituted (1.9.1999) by 1998 c. 31, s. 140(1), Sch. 30 para. 146(a) (with ss. 138(9), 144(6)); S.I. 1999/2323, art. 2(1), Sch. 1.

688 Words in s. 530(3) substituted (1.9.1999) by 1998 c. 31, s. 140(1), Sch. 30 para. 146(b) (with ss. 138(9), 144(6)); S.I. 1999/2323, art. 2(1), Sch. 1.

689 Words in s. 530(3) inserted (19.12.2002 for W., otherwise prosp.) by Education Act 2002 (c. 32), ss. 215(1), 216(4), Sch. 21 para. 53 (with ss. 210(8), 214(4)); S.I. 2002/3185, art. 4, Sch. Pt. I

690 Words in s. 531(2) substituted (1.9.1999) by 1998 c. 31, s. 140(1), Sch. 30 para.147 (with ss. 138(9), 144(6)); S.I. 1999/2323, art. 2(1), Sch. 1.

691 Words in s. 533(2) substituted (1.4.1999) by 1998 c. 31, s. 140(1), Sch. 30 para. 148(a) (with ss. 138(9), 144(6)); S.I. 1999/1016, art. 2(1), Sch. 1.

692 Words in s. 533(3) inserted (1.4.1999) by 1998 c. 31, s. 140(1), Sch. 30 para. 148(b) (with ss. 138(9), 144(6)); S.I. 1999/1016, art. 2(1), Sch. 1

693 S. 533(3)(b) and preceding word substituted (31.3.2003 for W., otherwise prosp.) for s. 533(b)(c) by Education Act 2002 (c. 32), ss. 215(1), 216(4), Sch. 21 para. 54 (with ss. 210(8), 214(4)); S.I. 2002/3185, art. 5, Sch. Pt. II

694 S. 534 repealed (1.9.1999) by 1998 c. 31, s. 140(1)(3), Sch. 30 para. 149, Sch.31 (with ss. 138(9), 144(6)); S.I. 1999/2323, art. 2(1), Sch. 1.

695 Words in s. 535(1) substituted (1.9.1999) by 1998 c. 31, s. 140(1), Sch. 30 para.150 (with ss. 138(9), 144(6)); S.I. 1999/2323, art. 2(1), Sch. 1.

696 S. 536 repealed (1.9.1999) by 1998 c. 31, s. 140(1)(3), Sch. 30 para. 151, Sch. 31 (with ss. 138(9), 144(6)); S.I. 1999/2323, art. 2(1), Sch. 1.

697 S. 537(1) substituted (1.9.1999) by 1998 c. 31, s. 140(1), Sch. 30 para. 152(a) (with ss. 138(9), 144(6)); S.I. 1999/2323, art. 2(1), Sch. 1

698 Words in s. 537(4) added (14.6.1997) by 1997 c. 44, s. 57(1), Sch. 7 para. 37; S.I. 1997/1468, art. 2(1), Sch. 1 Pt. I

699 Words in s. 537(7)(a) repealed (1.9.1999) by 1998 c. 31, s. 140(1)(3), Sch. 30 para. 152(b), Sch. 31 (with ss. 138(9), 144(6)); S.I. 1999/2323, art. 2(1), Sch. 1

700 Words in s. 537(7)(b) substituted (26.7.2002) by Education Act 2002 (c. 32), ss. 65(3), 216(2), Sch. 7 para. 6(5) (with ss. 210(8), 214(4)); S.I. 2002/2002, art. 2

701 Words in s. 537(7)(b) substituted (28.7.2000 for certain purposes, otherwise prosp.) by 2000 c. 21, ss. 149, 154, Sch. 9 para. 60 (with s. 150)

702 S. 537A substituted (20.11.1998 with savings as mentioned in art. 5 of the S.I. 1998/2791) by 1998 c. 31, s. 140(1), Sch. 30 para.153 (with ss. 138(9), 144(6)); S.I. 1998/2791, arts.3, 5

703 Words in s. 538 substituted (1.9.1999) by 1998 c. 31, s. 140(1), Sch. 30 para.154 (with ss. 138(9), 144(6)); S.I. 1999/2323, art. 2(1), Sch. 1.

704 S. 539 repealed (1.11.1999) by 1998 c. 31, s. 140(1)(3), Sch. 30 para. 155, Sch.31 (with ss. 138(9), 144(6) and subject to savings by S.I. 1999/2323, art. 21); S.I. 1999/2323, art. 2(2), Sch. 2.

705 S. 540(2) substituted (1.9.1999) by 1998 c. 31, s. 140(1), Sch. 30 para.156 (with ss. 138(9), 144(6)); S.I. 1999/2323, art. 2(1), Sch. 1

706 Words in s. 541(1)(b) substituted (26.7.2002) by Education Act 2002 (c. 32), ss. 65(3), 216(2), Sch. 7 para. 6(6) (with ss. 210(8), 214(4)); S.I. 2002/2002, art. 2

707 Words in s. 541(1)(b) substituted (28.7.2000 for certain purposes, otherwise prosp.) by 2000 c. 21, ss. 149, 154, Sch. 9 para. 61 (with s. 150)

708 S. 541(4) substituted (1.9.1999) by 1998 c. 31, s. 140(1), Sch. 30 para. 157 (with ss. 138(9), 144(6)); S.I. 1999/2323, art. 2(1), Sch. 1.

709 Words in s. 542(1) repealed (1.9.1999) by 1998 c. 31, s. 140(1)(3), Sch. 30 para. 158(a), Sch.31 (with ss. 138(9), 144(6)); S.I. 1999/2323, art. 2(1), Sch. 1

710 S. 542(3) repealed (1.9.1999) by 1998 c. 31, s. 140(1)(3), Sch. 30 para. 158(b), Sch.31 (with ss. 138(9), 144(6)); S.I. 1999/2323, art. 2(1), Sch. 1

711 Words in s. 542(4) substituted (1.9.1999) by 1998 c. 31, s. 140(1), Sch. 30 para. 158(c) (with ss. 138(9), 144(6)); S.I. 1999/2323, art. 2(1), Sch. 1

712 Words in s. 543(1) substituted (1.2.1999) by 1998 c. 31, s. 140(1), Sch. 30 para. 159(a) (with ss. 138(9), 144(6)); S.I. 1998/2212, art. 2(3), Sch. 1 Pt.III

713 S. 543(4A) inserted (1.2.1999) by 1998 c. 31, s. 140(1), Sch. 30 para. 159(b) (with ss. 138(9), 144(6)); S.I. 1998/2212, art. 2(3), Sch. 1 Pt.III

714 Words in s. 544(1) repealed (1.4.1999) by 1998 c. 31, s. 140(1), Sch. 30 para. 160(a), Sch. 31 (with ss. 138(9), 144(6)); S.I. 1999/1016, art. 2(1), Sch. 1

715 Word at the end of s. 544(3)(a) inserted (1.9.1999) by 1998 c. 31, s. 140(1), Sch. 30 para. 160(b)(i) (with ss. 138(9), 144(6)); S.I. 1999/2323, art. 2(1), Sch. 1

716 S. 544(3)(b) repealed (1.9.1999) by 1998 c. 31, s. 140(1)(3), Sch. 30 para. 160(b)(ii), Sch. 31 (with ss. 138(9), 144(6)); S.I. 1999/2323, art. 2(1), Sch. 1

717 S. 545(2)(b) and preceding word repealed (1.9.1999) by 1998 c. 31, s. 140(1)(3), Sch. 30 para. 161, Sch. 31 (with ss. 138(9), 144(6)); S.I. 1999/2323, art. 2(1), Sch. 1

718 Word at the end of s. 546(2)(a) inserted (1.9.1999) by 1998 c. 31, s. 140(1), Sch. 30 para. 162(a) (with ss. 138(9), 144(6)); S.I. 1999/2323, art. 2(1), Sch. 1

719 s. 546(2)(b) repealed (1.9.1999) by 1998 c. 31, s. 140(1)(3), Sch. 30 para. 162(b), Sch.31 (with ss. 138(9), 144(6)); S.I. 1999/2323, art. 2(1), Sch. 1

720 S. 547(2)(aa)(ab) inserted (1.10.2002 for E., otherwise prosp.) by Education Act 2002 (c. 32), ss. 206, 216(4), Sch. 20 para. 1(2) (with ss. 210(8), 214(4)); S.I. 2002/2439, art. 3

721 S. 547(2)(b) and preceding word repealed (1.9.1999) by 1998 c. 13, s. 140(1)(3), Sch. 30 para. 163(a), Sch. 31 (with ss. 138(9), 144(6)); S.I. 1999/2323, art. 2(1), Sch. 1

722 S. 547(2A) inserted (1.10.2002 for E., otherwise prosp.) by Education Act 2002 (c. 32), ss. 206, 216(4), Sch. 20 para. 1(3) (with ss. 210(8), 214(4)); S.I. 2002/2439, art. 3

723 Words in s. 547(3)(b) substituted (1.10.2002 for E., otherwise prosp.) by Education Act 2002 (c. 32), ss. 206, 216(4), Sch. 20 para. 1(4) (with ss. 210(8), 214(4)); S.I. 2002/2439, art. 3

724 S. 547(4) substituted (1.10.2002 for E., otherwise prosp.) by Education Act 2002 (c. 32), ss. 206, 216(4), Sch. 20 para. 1(5) (with ss. 210(8), 214(4)); S.I. 2002/2439, art. 3

725 S. 547(6)(7) substituted (1.9.1999) by 1998 c. 31, s. 140(1), Sch. 30 para. 163(c) (with ss. 138(9), 144(6)); S.I. 1999/2323, art. 2(1), Sch. 1

726 S. 547(6)(7) substituted (1.10.2002 for E., otherwise prosp.) by Education Act 2002 (c. 32), ss. 206, 216(4), Sch. 20 para. 1(6) (with ss. 210(8), 214(4)); S.I. 2002/2439, art. 3

727 S. 547(6)(7) substituted (1.9.1999) by 1998 c. 31, s. 140(1), Sch. 30 para. 163(c) (with ss. 138(9), 144(6)); S.I. 1999/2323, art. 2(1), Sch. 1

728 Pt. X Ch. II: Chapter heading and cross-heading substituted for Chapter heading (1.9.1998) by virtue of 1997 c. 44, s. 57(1), Sch. 7 para. 38; S.I. 1998/386, art. 2(4), Sch. 1 Pt. IV

729 Pt. X Ch. II: Chapter heading and cross-heading substituted for Chapter heading (1.9.1998) by virtue of 1997 c. 44, s. 57(1), Sch. 7 para. 38; S.I. 1998/386, art. 2(4), Sch. 1 Pt. IV

730 S. 548(8)(c) repealed (1.10.2002 for E., otherwise prosp.) by Education Act 2002 (c. 32), ss. 215, 216(4), Sch. 22 Pt. 3 (with ss. 210(8), 214(4)); S.I. 2002/2439, art. 3

731 S. 548 substituted (1.9.1999) by 1998 c. 31, ss. 131(1) (with ss. 138(9), 144(6)); S.I. 1999/2323, art. 2(1), Sch. 1

732 S. 549 repealed (1.9.1999) by 1998 c. 31, ss. 131(2), 140(1)(3), Sch. 30 para. 164, Sch.31 (with ss. 138(9), 144(6)); S.I. 1999/2323, art. 2(1), Sch. 1

733 S. 550 repealed (1.9.1999) by 1998 c. 31, ss. 131(2), 140(1)(3), Sch. 30 para. 164, Sch.31 (with ss. 138(9), 144(6)); S.I. 1999/2323, art. 2(1), Sch. 1

734 S. 550A and cross-heading inserted (1.9.1998) by 1997 c. 44, s. 4 (with s. 57(3)); S.I. 1998/386, art. 2(4), Sch. 1 Pt. IV

735 S. 550A and cross-heading inserted (1.9.1998) by 1997 c. 44, s. 4 (with s. 57(3)); S.I. 1998/386, art. 2(4), Sch. 1 Pt. IV

736 S. 550B and cross-heading inserted (1.9.1998) by 1997 c. 44, s. 5 (with s. 57(3)); S.I. 1998/386, art. 2(4), Sch. 1 Pt. IV

737 S. 550B(2): the words "(b) a grant-maintained or grant-maintained special school;" repealed (1.9.1999) by 1998 c. 31, s. 140(1)(3), Sch. 30 para. 165, Sch. 31 (with ss. 138(9), 144(6)); S.I. 1999/2323, art. 2(1), Sch. 1

738 Words in s. 550B(2)(c) substituted (26.7.2002) by Education Act 2002 (c. 32), ss. 65(3), 216(2), Sch. 7 para. 6(7) (with ss. 210(8), 214(4)); S.I. 2002/2002, art. 2

739 Words in s. 550B(2)(c) substituted (28.7.2000) by 2000 c. 21, s. 149, Sch. 9 para. 62

740 S. 550B and cross-heading inserted (1.9.1998) by 1997 c. 44, s. 5 (with s. 57(3)); S.I. 1998/386, art. 2(4), Sch. 1 Pt. IV

741 S. 551(1A) inserted (14.6.1997) by 1997 c. 44, s. 57(1), Sch. 7 para. 39; S.I. 1997/1468, art. 2(1), Sch. 1 Pt. I

742 Word at the end of s. 551(2)(a) inserted (1.9.1999) by 1998 c. 31, s. 140(1), Sch. 30 para.166 (with ss. 138(9), 144(6)); S.I. 1999/2323, art. 2(1), Sch. 1

743 S. 551(2)(b) repealed (1.9.1999) by 1998 c. 31, s. 140(1)(3), Sch. 30 para. 166(b), Sch.31 (with ss. 138(9), 144(6)); S.I. 1999/2323, art. 2(1), Sch. 1

744 S. 554(1) substituted (1.9.1999) by 1998 c. 31, s. 140(1), Sch. 30 para. 168(2) (with ss. 138(9), 144(6)); S.I. 1999/2323, art. 2(1), Sch. 1

745 S. 554(3)(a) substituted (1.9.1999) by 1998 c. 31, s. 140(1), Sch. 30 para. 168(3)(a) (with ss. 138(9), 144(6)); S.I. 1999/2323, art. 2(1), Sch. 1

746 Words in s. 554(3)(b) substituted (1.9.1999) by 1998 c. 31, s. 140(1), Sch. 30 para. 168(3)(b) (with ss. 138(9), 144(6)); S.I. 1999/2323, art. 2(1), Sch. 1

747 S. 554(4)(b) substituted (1.9.1999) by 1998 c. 31, s. 140(1), Sch. 30 para. 168(4) (with ss. 138(9), 144(6)); S.I. 1999/2323, art. 2(1), Sch. 1

748 Words in s. 556(2)(a) substituted (1.9.1999) by 1998 c. 31, s. 140(1), Sch. 30 para. 169(a) (with ss. 138(9), 144(6))

749 Words in s. 556(2)(b) substituted (1.9.1999) by 1998 c. 31, s. 140(1), Sch. 30 para. 169(b) (with s. 138(9), 144(6))

750 Words in s. 557(9) substituted (1.9.1999) by 1998 c. 31, s. 140(1), Sch. 30 para.170 (with ss. 138(9), 144(6)); S.I. 1999/2323, art. 2(1), Sch. 1

751 S. 557(10): words in definition of "relevant school" inserted (26.7.2002) by Education Act 2002 (c. 32), ss. 69, 216(2) (with ss. 210(8), 214(4)); S.I. 2002/2002, art. 2

752 Words in s. 559(1) substituted (1.9.1999) by 1998 c. 31, s. 140(1), Sch. 30 para. 171(a) (with ss. 138(9), 144(6)); S.I. 1999/2323, art. 2(1), Sch. 1

753 Words in s. 559(2) substituted (1.9.1999) by 1998 c. 31, s. 140(1), Sch. 30 para. 171(b) (with ss. 138(9), 144(6)); S.I. 1999/2323, art. 2(1), Sch. 1

754 S. 560(1)(2) substituted (1.10.1998) by 1998 c. 31, s. 112(2) (with ss. 138(9), 144(6)); S.I. 1998/2212, art. 2(1) Sch. 1 Pt. I

755 Words in s. 560(6) repealed (1.9.1999) by 1998 c. 31, ss. 112(3), 140(3), Sch.31 (with ss. 138(9), 144(6)); S.I. 1999/2323, art. 2(1), Sch. 1

756 Word at the end of s. 563(3)(a) inserted (1.9.1999) by 1998 c. 31, s. 140(1), Sch. 30 para. 172(a) (with ss. 138(9), 144(6)); S.I. 1999/2323, art. 2(1), Sch. 1

757 S. 563(3)(b) repealed (1.9.1999) by 1998 c. 31, s. 140(1)(3), Sch 30 para. 172(b), Sch.31 (with ss. 138(9), 144(6)); S.I. 1999/2323, art. 2(1), Sch. 1

758 S. 564(1)(b): fee of £3.50 made payable (1.4.1999) in respect of copies issued by a registrar by virtue of S.I. 1998/3171, art. 2, Sch. (which S.I. was revoked (1.4.2000) by S.I. 1999/3311, art. 3); and that same fee payable (1.4.2000) by virtue of S.I. 1999/3311, art. 2, Sch. (which S.I. was revoked (1.4.2003) by S.I. 2002/3076, art. 3); and that same fee payable (1.4.2003) by virtue of S.I. 2002/3076, art. 2, Sch.

759 S. 564(1)(b): fee of £7.00 made payable (1.4.2003) in respect of copies issued by a superintendent registrar by virtue of The Registration of Births, Deaths and Marriages (Fees) Order 2002 (S.I. 2002/3076), art. 2, Sch.

760 Words in s. 566(1)(b) substituted (1.9.1999) by 1998 c. 31, ss. 140(1), 145(3), Sch. 30 para.173 (with ss. 138(9), 144(6)); S.I. 1999/2323, art. 2(1), Sch. 1

761 S. 567 repealed (1.9.1999) by 1998 c. 31, s. 140(1), Sch. 30 para. 174, Sch.31 (with ss. 138(9), 144(6) and subject to savings in S.I. 1999/2323, art. 13); S.I. 1999/2323, art. 2(1), Sch. 1

762 S. 568(2) substituted (1.9.1999) by 1998 c. 31, s. 140(1), Sch. 30 para. 175(a), (with ss. 138(9), 144(6)); S.I. 1999/2323, art. 2(1), Sch. 1 (subject to savings in S.I. 1999/2323, art. 16(3) as amended (31.8.1999) by S.I. 1999/2484, reg. 3

763 Words in s. 568(3) repealed (1.10.2002 for E., otherwise prosp.) by Education Act 2002 (c. 32), ss. 215(2), 216(4), Sch. 22 Pt. 3 (with ss. 210(8), 214(4)); S.I. 2002/2439, art. 3

764 Words in s. 568(3) repealed (1.9.1999) by 1998 c. 31, s. 140(1)(3), Sch. 30 para. 175(b), Sch. 31 (with ss. 138(9), 144(6)); S.I. 1999/2323, art. 2(1), Sch.1 (subject to savings in S.I. 1999/2323, art. 16(3) (as amended (31.8.1999) by S.I. 1999/2484, art. 3))

765 S. 568(4) repealed (1.10.2002 for E., otherwise prosp.) by Education Act 2002 (c. 32), ss. 215(2), 216(4), Sch. 22 Pt. 3 (with ss. 210(8), 214(4)); S.I. 2002/2439, art. 3

766 S. 568(5)(b) and preceding word repealed (1.9.1999) by 1998 c. 31, s. 140(1)(3), Sch. 30 para. 175(c), Sch. 31 (with ss. 138(9), 144(6)); S.I. 1999/2323, art. 2(1), Sch. 1 (subject to savings in S.I. 1999/2323, art. 16(3) (as amended (31.8.1999) by S.I. 1999/2484, art. 3))

767 Words in s. 569(2) substituted (1.9.1999) by 1998 c. 31, s. 140(1), Sch. 30 para. 176(a) (with ss. 138(9), 144(6)); S.I. 1999/2323, art. 2(1), Sch. 1

768 Words in s. 569(3) substituted (1.9.1999) by 1998 c. 31, s. 140(1), Sch. 30 para. 176(b) (with ss. 138(9), 144(6)); S.I. 1999/2323, art. 2(1), Sch. 1

769 Word at the end of s. 570(1)(a) inserted (1.4.1999) by 1998 c. 31, s. 140(1), Sch. 30 para. 177(a)(i) (with ss. 138(9), 144(6)); S.I. 1999/1016, art. 2(1), Sch. 1

770 S. 570(1)(b) repealed (1.4.1999) by 1998 c. 31, s. 140(1)(3), Sch. 30 para. 177(a)(ii), Sch.31 (with ss. 138(9), 144(6)); S.I. 1999/1016, art. 2(1), Sch. 1

771 Words in s. 570(2) repealed (1.4.1999) by 1998 c. 31, s. 140(1)(3), Sch. 30 para. 177(b), Sch.31 (with ss. 138(9), 144(6)); S.I. 1999/1016, art. 2(1), Sch. 1

772 Words in s. 571(1) substituted (14.6.1997) by 1997 c. 44, s. 57(1), Sch. 7 para. 41(a); S.I. 1997/1468, art. 2(1), Sch. 1 Pt.I

773 S. 571(2) repealed (14.6.1997) by 1997 c. 44, s. 57(1)(4), Sch. 7 para. 41(b), Sch.8; S.I. 1997/1468, art. 2(1), Sch. 1 Pt.I

774 Words in s. 573(2) repealed (1.9.1999) by 1998 c. 31, s. 140(1)(3), Sch. 30 para. 178(a), Sch.31 (with ss. 138(9), 144(6)); S.I. 1999/2323, art. 2(1), Sch. 1

775 S. 573(4)-(6) repealed (1.9.1999) by 1998 c. 31, s. 140(1)(3), Sch. 30 para. 178(b), Sch.31 (with ss. 138(9), 144(6) and subject to savings for s. 573(4)-(6) in S.I. 1999/2323, art. 19); S.I. 1999/2323, art. 2(1), Sch. 1

776 Words in s. 576(1) substituted (1.9.1999) by 1998 c. 31, s. 140(1), Sch. 30 para. 180(a) (with ss. 138(9), 144(6)); S.I. 1999/2323, art. 2(1), Sch. 1

777 S. 576(2) repealed (1.9.1999) by 1998 c. 31, s. 140(1)(3), Sch. 30 para. 180(b), Sch.31 (with ss. 138(9), 144(6)); S.I. 1999/2323, art. 2(1), Sch. 1

778 S. 577 repealed (1.9.1999) by 1998 c. 31, s. 140(1)(3), Sch. 30 para. 181, Sch.31 (with ss. 138(9), 144(6)); S.I. 1999/2323, art. 2(1), Sch. 1

779 Entries in s. 578 repealed (1.1.1999) by 1998 c. 30, s. 44(2), Sch. 4 (with s. 42(8)); S.I. 1998/3237, art. 2(1) (subject to arts. 3, 4)

780 Entry in s. 578 added (14.6.1997) by virtue of 1997 c. 44, ss. 57(1), 58(2), Sch. 7 para. 42; S.I. 1997/1468, art. 2(1), Sch. 1 Pt. I

781 Entry in s. 578 inserted (31.7.1997) by 1997 c. 59, ss. 6(2), 7(2)(3)

782 Entry in s. 578 (as inserted (27.1.1998) by 1998 c. 1, ss. 6(1), 7(2)) repealed (1.1.1999) by 1998 c. 30, s. 44(2), Sch. 4 (with s. 42(8)); S.I. 1998/3237, art. 2(1) (subject to arts. 3, 4)

783 Entry in s. 578 inserted (1.10.1998) by 1998 c. 30, ss. 44(1), 46(2), Sch. 3 para. 15 (with s. 42(8)); S.I. 1998/2215, art. 2

784 Entry in s. 578 inserted (1.2.1999) by 1998 c. 31, s. 140(1), Sch. 30 para.182 (with ss. 138(9), 144(6)); S.I. 1999/120, art. 2(1), Sch. 1

785 Entry in s. 578 inserted (24.7.2002) by virtue of Education Act 2002 (c. 32), ss. 216(1), 217(2) (with ss. 210(8), 214(4))

786 S. 579(1): definitions of "the appropriate further education funding council", "exclude", "governing body" (and "governors"), "the local education authority", "reception class" and "relevant age group" repealed (1.9.1999) by 1998 c. 31, s. 140(1)(3), Sch. 30 para. 183(a)(ii), Sch. 31 (with ss. 138(9), 144(6)); S.I. 1999/2323, art. 2(1), Sch. 1

787 Definition in s. 579(1) inserted (1.9.1999) by 1998 c. 31, s. 140(1), Sch. 30 para. 183(a)(i) (with ss. 138(9), 144(6)); S.I. 1999/2323, art. 2(1), Sch. 1

788 S. 579(1): definition of "the National Curriculum" inserted (1.10.2002 for E., 19.12.2002 for W.) by Education Act 2002 (c. 32), ss. 215(1), 216(4), Sch. 21 para. 57(b) (with ss. 210(8), 214(4)); S.I. 2002/2439, art. 3; S.I. 2002/3185, art. 4, Sch. Pt. I

789 Words in s. 579(1) substituted (1.9.1999) by 1998 c. 31, s. 140(1), Sch. 30 para. 183(a)(iii) (with ss. 138(9), 144(6)); S.I. 1999/2323, art. 2(1), Sch. 1

790 S. 579(1): definition of "sex education" inserted (1.10.2002 for E., 19.12.2002 for W.) by Education Act 2002 (c. 32), ss. 215(1), 216(4), Sch. 21 para. 57(c) (with ss. 210(8), 214(4)); S.I. 2002/2439, art. 3; S.I. 2002/3185, art. 4, Sch. Pt. I

791 Definition in s. 579(1) inserted (14.6.1997) by 1997 c. 44, s. 57(1), Sch. 7 para. 43; S.I. 1997/1468, art. 2(1), Sch. 1 Pt. I

792 Definition in s. 579(1) substituted (1.9.1999) by 1998 c. 31, s. 140(1), Sch. 30 para. 183(a)(iv) (with ss. 138(9), 144(6)); S.I. 1999/2323, art. 2(1), Sch. 1

793 S. 579(3) repealed (1.9.1999) by 1998 c. 31, s. 140(1)(3), Sch. 30 para. 183(b), Sch.31 (with ss. 138(9), 144(6)); S.I. 1999/2323, art. 2(1), Sch. 1

794 S. 580 table: entry inserted (26.7.2002) by Education Act 2002 (c. 32), ss. 215(1), 216(4), Sch. 7 para. 6(8) (with ss. 210(8), 214(4)); S.I. 2002/2002, art. 2

795 S. 580 table: entry repealed (1.9.1997) by 1997 c. 59, ss. 6(3), 7(3)(a), Sch. Pt. I

796 S. 580 table: entry inserted (1.9.1997) by 1997 c. 44, s. 57(1), Sch. 7 para. 44; S.I. 1997/1468, art. 2(2), Sch. 1 Pt. II

797 S. 580 table: entry inserted (28.7.2000 for certain purposes, otherwise prosp.) by 2000 c. 21, ss. 149, 154, Sch. 9 para. 63 (with s. 150)

798 S. 580 table: entries relating to "city academy", "city college for the technology of the arts" and "city technology college" repealed (26.7.2002 for E., otherwise prosp.) by Education Act 2002 (c. 32), ss. 215(2), 216(4), Sch. 22 Pt. 3 (with ss. 210(8), 214(4)); S.I. 2002/2002, art. 3

799 S. 580 table: entries relating to "city academy", "city college for the technology of the arts" and "city technology college" repealed (26.7.2002 for E., otherwise prosp.) by Education Act 2002 (c. 32), ss. 215(2), 216(4), Sch. 22 Pt. 3 (with ss. 210(8), 214(4)); S.I. 2002/2002, art. 3

800 S. 580 table: entries relating to "city academy", "city college for the technology of the arts" and "city technology

college" repealed (26.7.2002 for E., otherwise prosp.) by Education Act 2002 (c. 32), ss. 215(2), 216(4), Sch. 22 Pt. 3 (with ss. 210(8), 214(4)); S.I. 2002/2002, art. 3

[801] S. 580 table: words in the entry relating to "foundation subjects" omitted (2.5.2000 for E. and 20.7.2000 for W.) by virtue of S.I. 2000/1146, art. 3 and S.I. 2000/1882, art. 2

[802] S. 580 table: entry inserted (14.6.1997) by 1997 c. 44, s. 57(1), Sch. 7 para. 44; S.I. 1997/1468, art. 2(1), Sch. 1 Pt. I

[803] S. 580 table: entry inserted (1.9.1997) by 1997 c. 44, s. 57(1), Sch. 7 para. 44; S.I. 1997/1468, art. 2(2), Sch. 1 Pt. II

[804] Words in Sch. 1 para. 6(1) substituted (20.1.2003) by The Education Act 2002 (Modification of Provisions) (No. 2) (England) Regulations 2002 (S.I. 2002/2953), reg. 2(1)

[805] Sch. 1 para. 6(1)(2) substituted (1.10.1998) by 1998 c. 31, s. 140(1), Sch. 30 para. 184(a)(i) (with ss. 138(9), 144(6)); S.I. 1998/2212, art. 2(1), Sch. 1 Pt.I

[806] Words in Sch. 1 para. 6(3) substituted (1.10.1998) by 1998 c. 31, s. 140(1), Sch. 30 para. 184(a)(ii) (with ss. 138(9), 144(6)); S.I. 1998/2212, art. 2(1), Sch. 1 Pt.I

[807] Sch. 1 para. 7 repealed (20.1.2003) by The Education Act 2002 (Modification of Provisions) (No. 2) (England) Regulations 2002 (S.I. 2002/2953), reg. 2(2)

[808] Words in Sch. 1 para. 8 substituted (1.10.2000 for E. and 1.1.2001 for W.) by 2000 c. 21, s. 149, Sch. 9 para. 64 (with s. 150); S.I. 2000/2559, art. 2(1), Sch. Pt. I; S.I. 2000/3230, art. 2, Sch.

[809] Sch. 1 para. 12 repealed (1.9.1999) by 1998 c. 31, s. 140(1)(3), Sch. 30, para. 184(b), Sch.31 (with ss. 138(9), 144(6)); S.I. 1999/2323, art. 2(1), Sch. 1

[810] Sch. 1 para. 13 repealed (1.9.1999) by 1998 c. 31, s. 140(1)(3), Sch. 30 para. 184(b), Sch.31 (with ss. 138(9), 144(6)); S.I. 1999/2323, art. 2(1), Sch. 1

[811] Sch. 1 para. 15 and cross heading added (1.12.1997) by virtue of 1997 c. 44, s.48; S.I. 1997/1468, art. 2(5), Sch. 1 Pt.V

[812] Words in Sch. 1 para. 15 repealed (1.9.1999) by 1998 c. 31, s. 140(1)(3), Sch. 30 para. 184(c), Sch. 31 (with ss. 138(9), 144(6)); S.I. 1999/2323, art. 2(1), Sch. 1

[813] Sch. 1 para. 15(2)(d) substituted (E.) (11.7.2001) and (W.) (1.4.2002) by S.I. 2001/2237, art. 32(a)(i) and S.I. 2002/808, art. 31(a)(i)

[814] Words in Sch. 1 para. 15(2)(f) inserted (E.) (11.7.2001) and (W.) (1.4.2002) by S.I. 2001/2237, art. 32(a)(ii) and S.I. 2002/808, art. 31(a)(ii)

[815] Sch. 1 para. 15 and cross heading added (1.12.1997) by virtue of 1997 c. 44, s. 48; S.I. 1997/1468, art. 2(5), Sch. 1 Pt. V

[816] Sch. 1 para. 15(3) inserted (E.) (11.7.2001) and (W.) (1.4.2002) by S.I. 2001/2237, art. 32(b) and S.I. 2002/808, art. 31(b)

[817] Sch. 2 repealed (1.11.1999) by 1998 c. 31, s. 140(1)(3), Sch. 30 para. 185, Sch. 31 (with ss. 138(9), 144(6)); S.I. 1999/2323, art. 2(2), Sch. 2

[818] Sch. 3 repealed (1.4.1999) by 1998 c. 31, s. 140(1)(3), Sch. 30 para. 185, Sch. 31 (with ss. 138(9), 144(6)); S.I. 1999/1016, art. 2(1), Sch. 1

[819] Sch. 4 repealed (1.10.1998 so far as relating to the repeal of paras. 7 and 8 and otherwise 1.4.1999) by 1998 c. 31, s. 140(1)(3), Sch. 30 para. 185, Sch. 31 (with ss. 138(9), 144(6)); S.I. 1998/2212, art. 2(1), Sch. 1 Pt. I and S.I. 1999/1016, art. 2(1), Sch. 1

[820] Sch. 5 repealed (1.9.1999) by 1998 c. 31, s. 140(1)(3), Sch. 30 para. 185, Sch. 31 (with ss. 138(9), 144(6)); S.I. 1999/2323, art. 2(1), Sch. 1

[821] Sch. 6 repealed (1.9.1999) by 1998 c. 31, s. 140(1)(3), Sch. 30 para. 185, Sch. 31 (with ss. 138(9), 144(6)); S.I. 1999/2323, art. 2(1), Sch. 1

[822] Sch. 7 repealed (1.9.1999) by 1998 c. 31, s. 140(1)(3), Sch. 30 para. 185, Sch. 31 (with ss. 138(9), 144(6)); S.I. 1999/2323, art. 2(1), Sch. 1

[823] Sch. 8 repealed (1.9.1999) by 1998 c. 31, s. 140(1)(3), Sch. 30 para. 185, Sch. 31 (with ss. 138(9), 144(6)); S.I. 1999/2323, art. 2(1), Sch. 1

[824] Sch. 9 repealed (1.9.1999) by 1998 c. 31, s. 140(1)(3), Sch. 30 para. 185, Sch. 31 (with ss. 138(9), 144(6)); S.I. 1999/2323, art. 2(1), Sch. 1

[825] Sch. 10 repealed (1.9.1999) by 1998 c. 31, s. 140(1)(3), Sch. 30 para. 185, Sch. 31 (with ss. 138(9), 144(6)); S.I. 1999/2323, art. 2(1), Sch. 1

[826] Sch. 14 repealed (1.9.1999) by 1998 c. 31, s. 140(1)(3), Sch. 30 para. 185, Sch.31 (with ss. 138(9), 144(6) and with savings in S.I. 1999/711, reg. 5); S.I. 1999/2323, reg. 2(1), Sch. 1

[827] Sch. 15 repealed (1.9.1999) by 1998 c. 31, s. 140(1)(3), Sch. 30 para. 185, Sch.31 (with ss. 138(9), 144(6)); S.I. 1999/2323, art. 2(1), Sch. 1

[828] Sch. 16 repealed (1.9.1999) by 1998 c. 31, s. 140(1)(3), Sch. 30 para. 185, Sch.31 (with ss. 138(9), 144(6)); S.I. 1999/2323, art. 2(1), Sch. 1

[829] Word in Sch. 17 para. 1(1) substituted (10.1.1997) by S.I. 1996/3210, art. 2(2)

[830]Sch. 17 para. 7A added (10.1.1997) by S.I. 1996/3210, art. 2(3)

[831] Sch. 17 paras. 9A-9F added (10.1.1997) by S.I. 1996/3210, art. 2(4)

[832] Sch. 17 paras. 9A-9F added (10.1.1997) by S.I. 1996/3210, art. 2(4)

[833] Sch. 20 repealed (1.10.1998 so far as relating to the repeal of Pt. I and otherwise 1.4.1999) by 1998 c. 31, ss. 140(1)(3), 145(3), Sch. 30 para. 185, Sch. 31 (with ss. 138(9), 144(6)); S.I. 1998/2212, art. 2(1), Sch. 1 Pt. I; S.I. 1999/1016, art. 2(1), Sch. 1

[834] Sch. 21 repealed (1.10.1998) by 1998 c. 31, ss. 140(1)(3), 145(1), Sch. 30 para. 185, Sch.31 (with ss. 138(9), 144(6)); S.I. 1998/2212, art. 2(1), Sch. 1 Pt.I

[835] Sch. 22 para. 15 repealed (1.4.1999) by 1998 c. 31, s. 140(1)(3), Sch. 30 para. 185, Sch.31 (with ss. 138(9), 144(6)); S.I. 1998/2212, art. 2(4), Sch. 1 Pt.IV

[836] Sch. 22 repealed (1.4.1999 so far as relating to the repeal of para. 15 and otherwise prosp.) by 1998 c. 31, ss. 140(1)(3), 145(1), Sch. 30 para. 185, Sch. 31 (with ss. 138(9), 144(6)); S.I. 1998/2212, art. 2(4), Sch. 1 Pt. IV

[837] Sch. 23 para. 6(2A) inserted (1.9.1997 except in relation to the insertion of para. 6(2A)(a), as to which the insertion came into force on 1.9.1998) by 1997 c. 44, s. 57(1), Sch. 7 para. 49(3); S.I. 1997/1468, art. 2(2), Sch. 1 Pt. II (with transitional provisions); S.I. 1998/386, art. 2(4), Sch. 1 Pt. IV (with transitional provisions); and Sch. 7 para. 49 of the amending Act is repealed (1.9.1999) by 1998 c. 31, s. 140(1)(3), Sch. 30 para. 223, Sch.31 (with ss. 138(9), 144(6)); S.I. 1999/2323, art. 2(1), Sch. 1.

[838] Sch. 25A inserted (1.9.1998) by 1997 c. 44, s. 8(2), Sch.1; S.I. 1998/386, art. 2(4), Sch. 1 Pt.IV (with transitional provisions)

[839] Sch. 25A inserted (1.9.1998) by 1997 c. 44, s. 8(2), Sch.1; S.I. 1998/386, art. 2(4), Sch. 1 Pt.IV (subject to transitional provisions in Sch. 2 Pt. II); and Sch. 1 of the amending Act is repealed (1.9.1999) by 1998 c. 31, s. 140(1)(3), Sch. 30 para. 222(a), Sch.31 (with ss. 138(9), 144(6)); S.I. 1999/2323, art. 2(1), Sch. 1

[840] Sch. 25A inserted (1.9.1998) by 1997 c. 44, s. 8(2), Sch.1; S.I. 1998/386, art. 2(4), Sch. 1 Pt.IV (subject to transitional provisions in Sch. 2 Pt. II); and Sch. 1 of the amending Act is repealed (1.9.1999) by 1998 c. 31, s. 140(1)(3), Sch. 30 para. 222(a), Sch.31 (with ss. 138(9), 144(6)); S.I. 1999/2323, art. 2(1), Sch. 1

[841] Words in Sch. 26. para. 3(2) substituted (1.1.2002 (E.) and 1.4.2002 (W.)) by 2001 c. 10, s. 42(1), Sch. 8 para. 14(2) (with s. 43(13)); S.I. 2001/2217, art. 5, Sch. Pt. II (as amended by S.I. 2001/2614, art. 4); S.I. 2002/74, art. 5, Sch. Pt. II

[842] Sch. 26 para. 3(3)(4) substituted (11.5.2001 for certain purposes, 1.1.2002 otherwise for E. and 1.4.2002 otherwise for W.) by 2001 c. 10, ss. 42(1), 43(4)(e), Sch. 8 para. 14(3) (with s. 43(13)); S.I. 2001/2217, art. 5, Sch. Pt. II (as amended by S.I. 2001/2614, art. 4); S.I. 2002/74, art. 5, Sch. Pt. II

[843] Words in Sch. 26 para. 4(1) substituted (1.1.2002 (E.) and 1.4.2002 (W.)) by 2001 c. 10, s. 42(1), Sch. 8 para. 11(2) (with s. 43(13)); S.I. 2001/2217, art. 5, Sch. Pt. II (as amended by S.I. 2001/2614, art. 4); S.I. 2002/74, art. 5, Sch. Pt. II

[844] Sch. 27 para. 1 substituted (1.1.2002 (E.), 1.4.2002 (W.)) by 2001 c. 10, s. 10, Sch. 1 para. 2 (with s. 43(13)); S.I. 2001/2217, art. 5, Sch. Pt. II (as amended by S.I. 2001/2614, art. 4; S.I. 2001/3992, art. 5, Sch. Pt. II

[845] Sch. 27 paras. 2-2B substituted for Sch. 27 para. 2 (15.6.2001 for E. for certain purposes and otherwise 1.1.2002 and 8.12.2001 for W. for certain purposes and otherwise 1.4.2002) by 2001 c. 10, s. 10, Sch. 1 para. 3 (with s. 43(13)); S.I. 2001/2217, arts. 4, 5, Sch. Pts. I, II (as amended by S.I. 2001/2614, art. 4); S.I. 2001/3992, arts. 4, 5, Sch. Pts. I, II

[846] Sch. 27 paras. 2-2B substituted for Sch. 27 para. 2 (15.6.2001 for E. for certain purposes and otherwise 1.1.2002 and 8.12.2001 for W. for certain purposes and otherwise 1.4.2002) by 2001 c. 10, s. 10, Sch. 1 para. 3 (with s. 43(13)); S.I. 2001/2217, arts. 4, 5, Sch. Pts. I, II (as amended by S.I. 2001/2614, art. 4); S.I. 2001/3992, arts. 4, 5, Sch. Pts. I, II

[847] Sch. 27 paras. 2-2B substituted for Sch. 27 para. 2 (15.6.2001 for E. for certain purposes and otherwise 1.1.2002 and 8.12.2001 for W. for certain purposes and otherwise 1.4.2002) by 2001 c. 10, s. 10, Sch. 1 para. 3 (with s. 43(13)); S.I. 2001/2217, arts. 4, 5, Sch. Pts. I, II (as amended by S.I. 2001/2614, art. 4); S.I. 2001/3992, arts. 4, 5, Sch. Pts. I, II

[848] Words in Sch. 27 para. 3(1) substituted (1.1.2002 for E., otherwise prosp.) by 2001 c. 10, ss. 10, 43(3), Sch. 1 para. 4 (with s. 43(13)); S.I. 2001/2217, art. 5, Sch. Pt II (as amended by S.I. 2001/2614, art. 4)

[849] Words in Sch. 27 para 3(1) substituted (1.9.1999) by 1998 c. 31, s. 140(1), Sch. 30 para. 186(2)(a)(with ss. 138(9), 144(6)); S.I. 1999/2323, art. 2(1), Sch. 1

[850] Words in Sch. 27 para 3(2) substituted (1.1.2002 for E., otherwise prosp.) by 2001 c. 10, ss. 10, 43(3), Sch. 1 para. 5 (with s. 43(13)); S.I. 2001/2217, art. 5, Sch. Pt II (as amended by S.I. 2001/2614, art. 4)

[851] Words in Sch. 27 para. 3(4) substituted (1.9.1999) by 1998 c, 31, s. 140(1), Sch. 30 para. 186(2)(b) (with ss. 138(9), 144(6)); S.I. 1999/2323, art. 2(1), Sch. 1

[852] Sch. 27 para. 3(4) repealed (1.1.2002 for E., otherwise prosp.) by 2001 c. 10, ss. 10, 42(6), 43(3), Sch. 1 para. 6, Sch. 9 (with s. 43(13)); S.I. 2001/2217, art. 5, Sch. Pt. II (as amended by S.I. 2001/2614, art. 4)

[853] Words in Sch. 27 para. 3(1) substituted (1.1.2002 (E.) and 1.4.2002 (W.)) by 2001 c. 10, s. 10, Sch. 1 para. 4 (with s. 43(13)); S.I. 2001/2217, art. 5, Sch. Pt II (as amended by S.I. 2001/2614, art. 4); S.I. 2001/3992, art. 5, Sch. Pt. II

[854] Words in Sch. 27 para 3(1) substituted (1.9.1999) by 1998 c. 31, s. 140(1), Sch. 30 para. 186(2)(a)(with ss. 138(9), 144(6)); S.I. 1999/2323, art. 2(1), Sch. 1

[855] Words in Sch. 27 para 3(2) substituted (1.1.2002 (E.) and 1.4.2002 (W.)) by 2001 c. 10, s. 10, Sch. 1 para. 5 (with s. 43(13)); S.I. 2001/2217, art. 5, Sch. Pt II (as amended by S.I. 2001/2614, art. 4); S.I. 2001/3992, art. 5, Sch. Pt. II

[856] Sch. 27 para. 3(4) repealed (1.1.2002 (E.) and 1.4.2002 (W.)) by 2001 c. 10, ss. 10, 42(6), Sch. 1 para. 6, Sch. 9 (with s. 43(13)); S.I. 2001/2217, art. 5, Sch. Pt. II (as amended by S.I. 2001/2614, art. 4); S.I. 2002/74, art. 5, Sch. Pt. II

[857] Sch. 27 para. 3A inserted (1.1.2002 (E.) 1.4.2002 (W.)) by 2001 c. 10, s. 10 Sch. 1 para. 7 (with s. 43(13)); S.I. 2001/2217, art. 5, Sch. Pt. II (as amended by S.I. 2001/2614 art. 4); S.I. 2001/3992, art. 5, Sch. Pt. II

[858] Words in Sch. 27 para. 4(1) inserted (1.1.2002 (E.), 1.4.2002 (W.)) by 2001 c. 10, s. 10, Sch. 1 para. 8(a) (with s. 43(13)); S.I. 2001/2217, art. 5, Sch. Pt. II (as amended by S.I. 2001/2614, art. 4); S.I. 2001/3992, art. 5, Sch. Pt. II

[859] Words in Sch. 27 para. 4(1)(a)(b) substituted (1.1.2002 (E.), 1.4.2002 (W.)) by 2001 c. 10, s. 10, Sch. 1 para. 8(b) (with s. 43(13)); S.I. 2001/2217, art. 5, Sch. Pt. II (as amended by S.I. 2001/2614 art. 4); S.I. 2001/3992, art. 5, Sch. Pt. II

860 Words in Sch. 27 para. 4(1)(a)(b) substituted (1.1.2002 (E.), 1.4.2002 (W.)) by 2001 c. 10, s. 10, Sch. 1 para. 8(b) (with s. 43(13)); S.I. 2001/2217, art. 5, Sch. Pt. II (as amended by S.I. 2001/2614 art. 4); S.I. 2001/3992, art. 5, Sch. Pt. II

861 Sch. 27 para. 4(2)(c)(d) inserted (1.1.2002 (E.), 1.4.2002 (W.)) by virtue of 2001 c. 10, s. 10, Sch. 1 para 9 (with s. 43(13)); S.I. 2001/2217, art. 5, Sch. Pt. II (as amended by S.I. 2001/2614 art. 4); S.I. 2001/3992, art. 5, Sch. Pt. II

862 Words in Sch. 27 para. 4(4)(a) substituted (1.1.2002 (E.), 1.4.2002 (W.)) by 2001 c. 10, s. 10, Sch. 1 para. 10 (with s. 43(13)); S.I. 2001/2217, art. 5, Sch. Pt. II (as amended by S.I. 2001/2614, art. 4); S.I. 2001/3992, art. 5, Sch. Pt. II

863 Words in Sch. 27 para. 4(5) substituted (1.1.2002 (E.), 1.4.2002 (W.)) by 2001 c. 10, s. 10, Sch. 1 para. 10 (with s. 43(13)); S.I. 2001/2217, art. 5, Sch. Pt. II (as amended by S.I. 2001/2614, art. 4); S.I. 2001/3992, art. 5, Sch. Pt. II

864 Words in Sch. 27 para. 5(1) inserted (1.1.2002 (E.), 1.4.2002 (W.)) by 2001 c. 10, s. 10, Sch. 1 para. 11 (with s. 43(13)); S.I. 2001/2217, art. 5, Sch. Pt. II (as amended by S.I. 2001/2614, art. 4); S.I. 2001/3992, art. 5, Sch. Pt. II

865 Words in Sch. 27 para. 5(2) inserted (1.1.2002 (E.), 1.4.2002 (W.)) by 2001 c. 10, s. 10, Sch. 1 para. 12 (with s. 43(13)); S.I. 2001/2217, art. 5, Sch. Pt. II (as amended by S.I. 2001/2614, art. 4); S.I. 2001/3992, art. 5, Sch. Pt. II

866 Sch. 27 para. 5(2A)(2B) inserted (1.1.2002 (E.), 1.4.2002 (W.)) by 2001 c. 10, s. 10, Sch. 1 para. 13 (with s. 43(13)); S.I. 2001/2217, art. 5, Sch. Pt. II (as amended by S.I. 2001/2614, art. 4); S.I. 2001/3992, art. 5, Sch. Pt. II

867 Sch. 27 para. 6 substituted (15.6.2001 for E. for certain purposes and otherwise 1.1.2002 and 8.12.2001 for W. for certain purposes and otherwise 1.4.2002) by 2001 c. 10, s. 10, Sch. 1 para. 14 (with s. 43(13)); S.I. 2001/2217, arts. 4, 5, Sch. Pts. I, II (as amended by S.I. 2001/2614, art. 4); S.I. 2001/3992, arts. 4, 5, Sch. Pts. I, II

868 Sch. 27 para. 8(1)(b)(iii) repealed (1.4.2002 for W., otherwise prosp.) by 2001 c. 10, ss. 10, 42(6), 43, Sch. 1 para. 15(f), Sch. 9 (with s. 43(13)); S.I. 2002/74, art. 5, Sch. Pt. II

869 Words in Sch. 27 para. 8(3)(a) substituted (1.4.2002 for W., otherwise prosp.) by 2001 c. 10, ss. 42(1), 43, Sch. 8 para. 9(1) (with s. 43(13)); S.I. 2002/74, art. 5, Sch. Pt. II

870 Sch. 27 para. 8(3A) inserted (1.4.2002 for W., otherwise prosp.) by 2001 c. 10, ss. 42(1), 43, Sch. 8 para. 9(2) (with s. 43(13)); S.I. 2002/74, art. 5, Sch. Pt. II

871 Words in Sch. 27 para. 9(1) repealed (1.1.2002 for E., otherwise prosp.) by 2001 c. 10, ss. 10, 42(6), 43(3), Sch. 1 para. 16(g), Sch. 9 (with s. 43(13)); S.I. 2001/2217, art. 5, Sch. Pt. II (as amended by S.I. 2001/2614, art. 4)

872 Words in Sch. 27 para. 9(1) repealed (1.1.2002 for E., otherwise prosp.) by 2001 c. 10, ss. 10, 42(6), 43(3), Sch. 1 para. 16(g), Sch. 9 (with s. 43(13)); S.I. 2001/2217, art. 5, Sch. Pt. II (as amended by S.I. 2001/2614, art. 4)

873 Word in Sch. 27 para. 9(2)(a) inserted (1.1.2002 for E., otherwise prosp.) by 2001 c. 10, ss. 10, 43(3) Sch. 1 para. 16(h)(i) (with s. 43(13)); S.I. 2001/2217, art. 5, Sch. Pt. II (as amended by S.I. 2001/2614, art. 4)

874 Sch. 27 para. 9(2)(b) omitted (1.1.2002 for E., otherwise prosp.) by virtue of 2001 c. 10, ss. 10, 43(3), Sch. 1 para. 16(h)(ii) (with s. 43(13)); S.I. 2001/2217, art. 5, Sch. Pt. II (as amended by S.I. 2001/2614, art. 4)

875 Word in Sch 27 para. 9(2)(c) omitted (1.1.2002 for E., otherwise prosp.) by virtue of 2001 c. 10, ss. 10, 43(3), Sch. 1 para. 16(h)(ii) (with s. 42(13)); S.I. 2001/2217, art. 5, Sch. Pt. II (as amended by S.I. 2001/2614, art. 4)

876 Sch. 27 para. 9(2)(d) omitted (1.1.2002 for E., otherwise prosp.) by virtue of 2001 c. 10, ss. 10, 43(3), Sch. 1 para. 16(h)(ii) (with s. 42(13)); S.I. 2001/2217, art. 5, Sch. Pt. II (as amended by S.I. 2001/2614, art. 4)

877 Words in Sch. 27 para. 9(1) repealed (1.1.2002 (E.) and 1.4.2002 (W.)) by 2001 c. 10, ss. 10, 42(6), Sch. 1 para. 16(g), Sch. 9 (with s. 43(13)); S.I. 2001/2217, art. 5, Sch. Pt. II (as amended by S.I. 2001/2614, art. 4); S.I. 2002/74, art. 5, Sch. Pt. II

878 Word in Sch. 27 para. 9(2)(a) inserted (1.1.2002 (E.) and 1.4.2002 (W.)) by 2001 c. 10, s. 10, Sch. 1 para. 16(h)(i) (with s. 43(13)); S.I. 2001/2217, art. 5, Sch. Pt. II (as amended by S.I. 2001/2614, art. 4); S.I. 2001/3992, art. 5, Sch. Pt. II

879 Sch. 27 para. 9(2)(b) omitted (1.1.2002 (E.) and 1.4.2002 (W.)) by virtue of 2001 c. 10, s. 10, Sch. 1 para. 16(h)(ii) (with s. 43(13)); S.I. 2001/2217, art. 5, Sch. Pt. II, (as amended by 2001/2614, art. 4); S.I. 2001/3992, art. 5, Sch. Pt. II

880 Word in Sch 27 para. 9(2)(c) omitted (1.1.2002 (E.) and 1.4.2002 (W.)) by virtue of 2001 c. 10, s. 10, Sch. 1 para. 16(h)(ii) (with s. 42(13)); S.I. 2001/2217, art. 5, Sch. Pt. II (as amended by S.I. 2001/2614, art. 4); S.I. 2001/3992, art. 5, Sch. Pt. II

881 Sch. 27 para 9(2)(d) omitted (1.1.2002 (E.) and 1.4.2002 (W.)) by virtue of 2001 c. 10, s. 10, Sch. 1 para. 16(h)(ii) (with s. 42(13)); S.I. 2001/2217, art. 5, Sch. Pt. II (as amended by S.I. 2001/2614, art. 4); S.I. 2001/3992, art. 5, Sch. Pt. II

882 Sch. 27 para. 10 repealed (1.1.2002 (E.), 1.4.2002 (W.)) by 2001 c. 10, ss. 10, 42(6), Sch. 1 para. 17, Sch. 9 (with s. 42(13)); S.I 2001/2217, art. 5, Sch. Pt. II (as amended by S.I. 2001/2614, art. 4); S.I. 2002/74, art. 5, Sch. Pt. II

883 Words in Sch. 27 para. 11(2)(a) substituted (11.5.2001 for certain purposes, 1.1.2002 otherwise for E. and 1.4.2002 otherwise for W.) by 2001 c. 10, ss. 42(1), 43(4)(e), Sch. 8 para. 10(1) (with s. 43(13)); S.I. 2001/2217, art. 5, Sch. Pt. II (as amended by S.I. 2001/2614, art. 4); S.I. 2002/74, art. 5, Sch. Pt. II

884 Sch. 27 para. 11(2A) inserted (11.5.2001 for certain purposes, 1.1.2002 otherwise for E. and 1.4.2002 otherwise for W.) by 2001 c. 10, ss. 42(1), 43(4)(e), Sch. 8 para. 10(2) (with s. 43(13)); S.I. 2001/2217, art. 5, Sch. Pt. II (as amended by S.I. 2001/2614, art. 4); S.I. 2002/74, art. 5, Sch. Pt. II

885 Sch. 27 para. 11(5) inserted (1.1.2002 (E.), 1.4.2002 (W.)) by 2001 c. 10, s. 6 (with s. 42(13)); S.I. 2001/2217, art. 5, Sch. Pt. II (as amended by S.I. 2001/2614, art. 4); S.I. 2001/3992, art. 5, Sch. Pt. II

886 Sch. 28 repealed (1.9.1999) by 1998 c. 31, s. 140(1)(3), Sch. 30 para. 187, Sch. 31 (with ss. 138(9), 144(6) and subject to savings in S.I. 1999/2323, Sch. 6 para. 2, Sch. 7 paras. 2, 10); S.I. 1999/2323, art. 2(1), Sch. 1

887 Sch. 29 repealed (1.3.1998) by 1997 c. 44, s. 57(4), Sch.8; S.I. 1998/386, art. 2(1), Sch. 1 Pt.I

888 Sch. 30 repealed and replaced (1.10.1997) by 1997 c. 44, ss. 27(5), 57(4), Schs. 5,8; S.I. 1997/1468, art. 2(3), Sch. 1 Pt. III

[889] Sch. 31 para. 11 repealed (1.9.1999) by 1998 c. 31, s. 140(1)(3), Sch. 30 para. 188, Sch.31 (with ss. 138(9), 144(6)); S.I. 1999/2323, art. 2(1), Sch. 1

[890] Sch. 31 para. 15 repealed (1.9.1999) by 1998 c. 31, s. 140(1)(3), Sch. 30 para. 188, Sch.31 (with ss. 138(9), 144(6)); S.I. 1999/2323, art. 2(1), Sch. 1

[891] Sch. 32 repealed (1.9.1999) by 1998 c. 31, s. 140(1)(3), Sch. 30 para. 189(a), Sch.31 (with ss. 138(9), 144(6) and with savings in S.I. 1999/1016, art. 6, Sch. 4 para. 6); S.I. 1999/1016, art. 2(3), Sch. 3

[892] Sch. 33 repealed (1.9.1999) by 1998 c. 31, s. 140(1)(3), Sch. 30 para. 189(b), Sch. 31 (with ss. 138(9), 144(6) and subject to savings in S.I. 1999/1016, art. 6, Sch. 4 para. 8 and S.I. 1999/2323, Sch. 6 paras. 2, 5); S.I. 1999/1016, art. 2(3), Sch. 3

[893] Sch. 33A repealed (1.9.1999) by 1998 c. 31, s. 140(1)(3), Sch. 30 para. 189(c), Sch. 31 (with ss. 138(9), 144(6) and with savings in S.I. 1999/1016, art. 6, Sch. 4 para. 8); S.I. 1999/1016, art. 2(3), Sch. 3

[894] Sch. 33B repealed (1.9.1999) by 1998 c. 31, s. 140(1)(3), Sch. 30 para. 189(d), Sch. 31 (with ss. 138(9), 144(6) and with savings in S.I. 1999/1016, art. 6, Sch. 4 paras. 2, 8); S.I. 1999/1016, art. 2(3), Sch. 3

[895] Sch. 35 repealed (1.9.1997) by 1997 c. 59, ss. 1(1)(c), 6(3), 7(3)(a), Sch. Pt. I (with s. 1(3))

[896] Sch. 35A inserted (26.7.2002) by Education Act 2002 (c. 32), ss. 65(3), 216(2), Sch. 7 para. 1 (with ss. 210(8), 214(4)); S.I. 2002/2002, art. 2

[897] Sch. 37 para. 9 repealed (1.9.1999) by 1998 c. 31, s. 140(1)(3), Sch. 30 para. 189(e), Sch.31 (with ss. 138(9), 144(6)); S.I. 1999/2323, art. 2(1), Sch. 1

[898] Sch. 37 paras. 15, 16 repealed (25.8.2000) by 2000 c. 6, ss. 165(4), 168, Sch. 12 Pt. I (with Sch. 11 paras. 1, 2)

[899] Sch. 37 paras. 15, 16 repealed (25.8.2000) by 2000 c. 6, ss. 165(4), 168, Sch. 12 Pt. I (with Sch. 11 paras. 1, 2)

[900] Sch. 37 para. 17 repealed (1.3.1998 in so far as Sch. 37 relates to School Curriculum and Assessment Authority and otherwise 1.10.1997) by 1997 c. 44, ss. 57(4), 58(3), Sch.8; S.I. 1997/1468, art. 2(3), Sch. 1 Pt. III; S.I. 1998/386, art. 2(1), Sch. 1 Pt.I

[901] Words in Sch. 37 para. 21(1)(a) repealed (1.3.1998 in so far as relating to School Curriculum and Assessment Authority and otherwise 1.10.1997) by 1997 c. 44, ss. 57(4), 58(3), Sch.8; S.I. 1997/1468, art. 2(3), Sch. 1 Pt. III; S.I. 1998/386, art. 2(1), Sch. 1 Pt.I

[902] Sch. 37 para. 21(1)(b) and the word immediately preceding it repealed (1.3.1998 in so far as relating to the School Curriculum and Assessment Authority and otherwise 1.10.1997) by 1997 c. 44, ss. 57(4), 58(3), Sch.8; S.I. 1997/1468, art. 2(3), Sch. 1 Pt. III; S.I. 1998/386, art. 2(1), Sch. 1 Pt.I

[903] Sch. 37 para. 21(2) repealed (1.3.1998 in so far as relating to the School Curriculum and Assessment Authority and otherwise 1.10.1997) by 1997 c. 44, ss. 57(4), 58(3), Sch. 8; S.I. 1997/1468, art. 2(3), Sch. 1 Pt. III; S.I. 1998/386, art. 2(1), Sch. 1 Pt.I

[904] Sch. 37 para. 27 repealed (1.9.1999) by 1998 c. 31, s. 140(1)(3), Sch. 30 para. 189(e), Sch.31 (with ss. 138(9), 144(6)); S.I. 1999/2323, art. 2(1), Sch. 1

[905] Sch. 37 para. 33 repealed (1.9.1999) by 1998 c. 31, s. 140(1)(3), Sch. 30 para. 189(e), Sch.31 (with ss. 138(9), 144(6)); S.I. 1999/2323, art. 2(1), Sch. 1

[906] Sch. 37 para. 37(a) repealed (1.9.1999) by 1998 c. 31, s. 140(1)(3), Sch. 30 para. 189(e), Sch.31 (with ss. 138(9), 144(6)); S.I. 1999/2323, art. 2(1), Sch. 1

[907] Sch. 37 para. 41 repealed (1.9.1999) by 1998 c. 31, s. 140(1)(3), Sch. 30 para. 189(e), Sch.31 (with ss. 138(9), 144(6)); S.I. 1999/2323, art. 2(1), Sch. 1

[908] Sch. 37 para. 42 repealed (2.4.2001) by 2000 c. 34, s. 9(2), Sch. 3 (with s. 10(5)); S.I. 2001/566, art. 2(1)

[909] Sch. 37 para. 55 repealed (1.10.2002 for E., otherwise prosp.) by Education Act 2002 (c. 32), ss. 215(2), 216(4), Sch. 22 Pt. 3 (with ss. 210(8), 214(4)); S.I. 2002/2439, art. 3

[910] Sch. 37 para. 58 repealed (1.4.2002) by 2000 c. 14, s. 117(2), Sch. 6; S.I. 2001/4150, art. 3(c)(xii) (subject to art. 4); S.I. 2002/920, art. 3(3)(g)(x) (subject to art. 3(2), Schs. 1-3 and with art. 3(5)-(10))

[911] Sch. 37 para. 63 repealed (28.9.2000) by 2000 c. 22, ss. 107(2), 108(2)(c), Sch. 6

[912] Sch. 37 para. 70 repealed (1.4.2001) by 2000 c. 21, s. 153, Sch. 11 (with s. 150); S.I. 2001/654, art. 2(2), Sch. Pt. II (with art. 3); S.I. 2001/1274, art. 2(2), Sch. Pt. I (with art. 3)

[913] Words in Sch. 37 para. 74 substituted (1.10.1998) by 1998 c. 31, s. 136 (with ss. 138(9), 144(6)); S.I. 1998/2212, art. 2, Sch. 1 Pt. I

[914] Sch. 37 para. 75 repealed (1.9.1999) by 1998 c. 31, s. 140(1)(3), Sch. 30 para. 189(e), Sch. 31 (with ss. 138(9), 144(6)); S.I. 1999/2323, art. 2(1), Sch. 1

[915] Sch. 37 para. 78 repealed (11.9.1998) by 1998 c. 18, ss. 54(3), 55(2), Sch.5

[916] Sch. 37 para. 82(1)(b) and the word immediately preceding it repealed (1.9.1999) by 1998 c. 31, s. 140(1)(3), Sch. 30 para. 189(e), Sch.31 (with ss. 138(9), 144(6)); S.I. 1999/2323, art. 2(1), Sch. 1

[917] Sch. 37 para. 82(2)(a) repealed (1.9.1999) by 1998 c. 31, s. 140(1)(3), Sch. 30 para. 189(e), Sch.31 (with ss. 138(9), 144(6)); S.I. 1999/2323, art. 2(1), Sch. 1

[918] Sch. 37 para. 82(2)(c) and the word immediately preceding it repealed (1.9.1999) by 1998 c. 31, s. 140(1)(3), Sch. 31 para. 189(e), Sch.31 (with ss. 138(9), 144(6)); S.I. 1999/2323, art. 2(1), Sch. 1

[919] Sch. 37 para. 82(3) repealed (1.9.1999) by 1998 c. 31, s. 140(1)(3), Sch. 30 para. 189(e), Sch.31 (with ss. 138(9), 144(6)); S.I 1999/2323, art. 2(1), Sch. 1

[920] Sch. 37 para. 86 repealed (1.4.2002) by 2000 c. 14, s. 117(2), Sch. 6; S.I. 2001/4150, arts. 3(3)(c)(xii) (subject to art. 4); S.I.

2002/920, art. 3(3)(g)(x) (subject to art. 3(2), Schs. 1-3 and with art. 3(5)-(10))

921 Sch. 37 para. 88 repealed (1.4.2002) by 2000 c. 14, ss. 117(2), Sch. 6; S.I. 2001/4150, arts. 3(3)(c)(xii) (subject to art. 4); S.I. 2002/920, art. 3(3)(g)(x) (subject to art. 3(2), Schs. 1-3 and with art. 3(5)-(10))

922 Sch. 37 para. 89 repealed (1.4.2002) by 2000 c. 14, s. 117(2), Sch. 6; S.I. 2001/4150, arts. 3(3)(c)(xii) (subject to art. 4); S.I. 2002/920, art. 3(3)(g)(x) (subject to art. 3(2), Schs. 1-3 and with art. 3(5)-(10))

923 Sch. 37 para. 96(2) repealed (1.9.1999) by 1998 c. 31, s. 140(1)(3), Sch. 30 para. 189(e), Sch.31 (with ss. 138(9), 144(6)); S.I. 1999/2323, art. 2(1), Sch. 1

924 Sch. 37 para. 97 repealed (1.9.1999) by 1998 c. 31, s. 140(1)(3), Sch. 30 para. 189(e), Sch.31 (with ss. 138(9), 144(6)); S.I. 1999/2323, art. 2(1), Sch. 1

925 Sch. 37 para. 102 repealed (1.9.1999) by 1998 c. 31, s. 140(1)(3), Sch. 30 para. 189(e), Sch.31 (with ss. 138(9), 144(6)); S.I. 1999/2323, art. 2(1), Sch. 1

926 Sch. 37 para. 103 repealed (1.9.1999) by 1998 c. 31, s. 140(1)(3), Sch. 30 para. 189(e), Sch.31 (with ss. 138(9), 144(6)); S.I. 1999/2323, art. 2(1), Sch. 1

927 Sch. 37 para. 104(3) repealed (1.9.1999) by 1998 c. 31, s. 140(1)(3), Sch. 30 para. 189(e), Sch.31 (with ss. 138(9), 144(6)); S.I. 1999/2323, art. 2(1), Sch. 1

928 Sch. 37 para. 105 repealed (1.9.1999) by 1998 c. 31, s. 140(1)(3), Sch. 30 para. 189(e), Sch.31 (with ss. 138(9), 144(6)); S.I. 1999/2323, art. 2(1), Sch. 1

929 Sch. 37 para. 106 repealed (1.9.1999) by 1998 c. 31, s. 140(1)(3), Sch. 30 para. 189(e), Sch.31 (with ss. 138(9), 144(6)); S.I. 1999/2323, art. 2(1), Sch. 1

930 Sch. 37 para. 107 repealed (1.9.1999) by 1998 c. 31, s. 140(1)(3), Sch. 30 para. 107, Sch.31 (with ss. 138(9), 144(6)); S.I. 1999/2323, art. 2(1), Sch. 1

931 Sch. 37 para. 108 repealed (1.9.1999) by 1998 c. 31, s. 140(1)(3), Sch. 30 para. 189(e), Sch.31 (with ss. 138(9), 144(6)); S.I. 1999/2323, art. 2(1), Sch. 1

932 Sch. 37 para. 110(2)(3)(a) repealed (1.9.1999) by 1998 c. 31, s. 140(1)(3), Sch. 30 para. 189(e), Sch.31 (with ss. 138(9), 144(6)); S.I. 1999/2323, art. 2(1), Sch. 1

933 Sch. 37 para. 112 repealed (1.4.2001) by 2000 c. 21, s. 153, Sch. 11 (with s. 150); S.I. 2001/654, art. 2(2), Sch. Pt. II (with art. 3); S.I. 2001/1274, art. 2(2), Sch. Pt. I (with art. 3)

934 Sch. 37 para. 113 repealed (1.1.2001 (W.) 1.4.2001 (E.)) by 2000 c. 21, s. 153, Sch. 11 (with s. 150); S.I. 2000/3230, art. 2, Sch.; S.I. 2001/654, art. 2(2), Sch. Pt. II

935 Sch. 37 para. 117(4)(b) and preceding word repealed (2.4.2001) by 2000 c. 34, s. 9(2), Sch. 3 (with s. 10(5)); S.I. 2001/566, art. 2(1) (with art. 2(2))

936 Sch. 37 para. 118(3)(d) repealed (1.9.2002) by 2001 c. 10, s. 42(1)(6), Sch. 8 para. 4, Sch. 9 (with s. 43(13)); S.I. 2002/2217, art. 3, Sch. 1 Pt. 1

937 Sch. 37 para. 122 repealed (1.9.1999) by 1998 c. 31, s. 140(1)(3), Sch. 30 para. 189(e), Sch.31 (with ss. 138(9), 144(6)); S.I. 1999/2323, art. 2(1), Sch. 1

938 Sch. 37 para. 125(c)(d) repealed (1.9.1999) by 1998 c. 31, s. 140(1)(3), Sch. 30 para. 189(e), Sch.31 (with ss. 138(9), 144(6)); S.I. 1999/2323, art. 2(1), Sch. 1

939 Sch. 37 para. 129 repealed (1.9.2002) by 2001 c. 10, ss. 38(14), 42(6), Sch. 9 (with s. 43(13)); S.I. 2002/2217, art. 3, Sch. 1 Pt. 1

940 Sch. 39 Pt. I para. 2(3) repealed (1.9.1999) by 1998 c. 31, s. 140(1)(3), Sch. 30 para. 189(f) (with ss. 138(9), 144(6)); S.I. 1999/2323, art. 2, Sch. 1

941 Sch. 39 para. 15 repealed (1.9.1999) by 1998 c. 31, s. 140(1)(3), Sch. 30 para. 189(f), Sch.31 (with ss. 138(9), 144(6)); S.I. 1999/2323, art. 2(1), Sch. 1

942 Sch. 40 repealed (1.10.1998) by 1998 c. 31, s. 140(1)(3), Sch. 30 para. 189(g), Sch. 31 (with ss. 138(9), 144(6)); S. I. 1998/2212, art. 2, Sch. 1 Pt.I

Housing Act 1996

1996 CHAPTER 52

PART I SOCIAL RENTED SECTOR

Chapter I Registered social landlords

Registration

1 The register of social landlords.

(1) The [Relevant Authority][1] shall maintain a register of social landlords which shall be open to inspection at all reasonable times. . ..[2]

[(1A) In this Part "the Relevant Authority" means the Housing Corporation or the Secretary of State, as provided by section 56.

(1B) The register maintained by the Housing Corporation shall be maintained at its head office.][3]

(2). . . . .[4]

2 Eligibility for registration.

(1) A body is eligible for registration as a social landlord if it is—

(a) a registered charity which is a housing association,

(b) a society registered under the Industrial and Provident Societies Act 1965 which satisfies the conditions in subsection (2), or

(c) a company registered under the Companies Act 1985 which satisfies those conditions.

(2) The conditions are that the body is non-profit-making and is established for the purpose of, or has among its objects or powers, the provision, construction, improvement or management of—

(a) houses to be kept available for letting,

(b) houses for occupation by members of the body, where the rules of the body restrict membership to persons entitled or prospectively entitled (as tenants or otherwise) to occupy a house provided or managed by the body, or

(c) hostels,

and that any additional purposes or objects are among those specified in subsection (4).

(3) For the purposes of this section a body is non-profit-making if—

(a) it does not trade for profit, or

(b) its constitution or rules prohibit the issue of capital with interest or dividend exceeding the rate prescribed by the Treasury for the purposes of section 1(1)(b) of the Housing Associations Act 1985.

(4) The permissible additional purposes or objects are—

(a) providing land, amenities or services, or providing, constructing, repairing or improving buildings, for its residents, either exclusively or together with other persons;

(b) acquiring, or repairing and improving, or creating by the conversion of houses or other property, houses to be disposed of on sale, on lease or on shared ownership terms;

(c) constructing houses to be disposed of on shared ownership terms;

(d) managing houses held on leases or other lettings (not being houses within subsection (2)(a) or (b)) or blocks of flats;

(e) providing services of any description for owners or occupiers of houses in arranging or carrying out works of maintenance, repair or improvement, or encouraging or facilitating the carrying out of such works;

(f) encouraging and giving advice on the forming of housing associations or providing services for, and giving advice on the running of, such associations and other voluntary organisations concerned with housing, or matters connected with housing.

(5) A body is not ineligible for registration as a social landlord by reason only that its powers include power—

(a) to acquire commercial premises or businesses as an incidental part of a project or series of projects undertaken for purposes or objects falling within subsection (2) or (4);

(b) to repair, improve or convert commercial premises acquired as mentioned in paragraph (a) or to carry on for a limited period any business so acquired;

(c) to repair or improve houses, or buildings in which houses are situated, after a disposal of the houses by the body by way of sale or lease or on shared ownership terms.

(6) In this section—

"block of flats" means a building containing two or more flats which are held on leases or other lettings and which are occupied or intended to be occupied wholly or mainly for residential purposes;

"disposed of on shared ownership terms" means disposed of on a lease—

(a) granted on a payment of a premium calculated by reference to a percentage of the value of the house or of the cost of providing it, or

(b) under which the tenant (or his personal representatives) will or may be entitled to a sum calculated by reference directly or indirectly to the value of the house;

"letting" includes the grant of a licence to occupy;

"residents", in relation to a body, means persons occupying a house or hostel provided or managed by the body; and

"voluntary organisation" means an organisation whose activities are not carried on for profit.

(7) The Secretary of State may by order specify permissible purposes, objects or powers additional to those specified in subsections (4) and (5).

The order may (without prejudice to the inclusion of other incidental or supplementary provisions) contain such provision as the Secretary of State thinks fit with respect to the priority of mortgages entered into in pursuance of any additional purposes, objects or powers.

(8) An order under subsection (7) shall be made by statutory instrument which shall be subject to annulment in pursuance of a resolution of either House of Parliament.

3 Registration.

(1) The [Relevant Authority][5] may register as a social landlord any body which is eligible for such registration.

(2) An application for registration shall be made in such manner, and shall be accompanied by such fee (if any), as the [Relevant Authority][6] may determine.

(3) As soon as may be after registering a body as a social landlord the [Relevant Authority][7] shall give notice of the registration—

(a) in the case of a registered charity, to the Charity Commissioners,

(b) in the case of an industrial and provident society, to the [Financial Services Authority][8], and

(c) in the case of a company registered under the Companies Act 1985 (including such a company which is also a registered charity), to the registrar of companies,

who shall record the registration.

(4) A body which at any time is, or was, registered as a social landlord shall, for all purposes other than rectification of the register, be conclusively presumed to be, or to have been, at that time a body eligible for registration as a social landlord.

4 Removal from the register.

(1) A body which has been registered as a social landlord shall not be removed from the register except in accordance with this section.

(2) If it appears to the [Relevant Authority][9] that a body which is on the register of social landlords—

(a) is no longer a body eligible for such registration, or

(b) has ceased to exist or does not operate,

the [Relevant Authority][10] shall, after giving the body at least 14 days' notice, remove it from the register.

(3) In the case of a body which appears to the [Relevant Authority][11] to have ceased to exist or not to operate, notice under subsection (2) shall be deemed to be given to the body if it is served at the address last known to the [Relevant Authority][12] to be the principal place of business of the body.

(4) A body which is registered as a social landlord may request the [Relevant Authority][13] to remove it from the register and the [Relevant Authority][14] may do so, subject to the following provisions.

(5) Before removing a body from the register of social landlords under subsection (4) the [Relevant Authority][15] shall consult the local authorities in whose area the body operates; and the [Relevant Authority][16] shall also inform those authorities of its decision.

(6) As soon as may be after removing a body from the register of social landlords the [Relevant Authority][17] shall give notice of the removal—

(a) in the case of a registered charity, to the Charity Commissioners,

(b) in the case of an industrial and provident society, to the [Financial Services Authority][18], and

(c) in the case of a company registered under the Companies Act 1985 (including such a company which is also a registered charity), to the registrar of companies,

who shall record the removal.

5 Criteria for registration or removal from register.

(1) The [Relevant Authority][19] shall establish (and may from time to time vary) criteria which should be satisfied by a body seeking registration as a social landlord; and in deciding whether to register a body the [Relevant Authority][20] shall have regard to whether those criteria are met.

(2) The [Relevant Authority][21] shall establish (and may from time to time vary) criteria which should be satisfied where such a body seeks to be removed from the register of social landlords; and in deciding whether to remove a body from the register the [Relevant Authority][22] shall have regard to whether those criteria are met.

(3) Before establishing or varying any such criteria the [Relevant Authority][23] shall consult such bodies

representative of registered social landlords, and such bodies representative of local authorities, as it thinks fit.

(4) The [Relevant Authority][24] shall publish the criteria for registration and the criteria for removal from the register in such manner as the [Relevant Authority][25] considers appropriate for bringing the criteria to the notice of bodies representative of registered social landlords and bodies representative of local authorities.

6 Appeal against decision on removal.

(1) A body which is aggrieved by a decision of the [Relevant Authority][26]—

(a) not to register it as a social landlord, or

(b) to remove or not to remove it from the register of social landlords,

may appeal against the decision to the High Court.

(2) If an appeal is brought against a decision relating to the removal of a body from the register, the [Relevant Authority][27] shall not remove the body from the register until the appeal has been finally determined or is withdrawn.

(3) As soon as may be after an appeal is brought against a decision relating to the removal of a body from the register, the [Relevant Authority][28] shall give notice of the appeal—

(a) in the case of a registered charity, to the Charity Commissioners,

(b) in the case of an industrial and provident society, to the [Financial Services Authority][29], and

(c) in the case of a company registered under the Companies Act 1985 (including such a company which is also a registered charity), to the registrar of companies.

Regulation of registered social landlords

7 Regulation of registered social landlords.

Schedule 1 has effect for the regulation of registered social landlords.

Part I relates to the control of payments to members and similar matters.

Part II relates to the constitution, change of rules, amalgamation or dissolution of a registered social landlord.

Part III relates to accounts and audit.

Part IV relates to inquiries into the affairs of a registered social landlord.

Chapter II Disposal of land and related matters

Power of registered social landlord to dispose of land

8 Power of registered social landlord to dispose of land.

(1) A registered social landlord has power by virtue of this section and not otherwise to dispose, in such manner as it thinks fit, of land held by it.

(2) Section 39 of the Settled Land Act 1925 (disposal of land by trustees) does not apply to the disposal of land by a registered social landlord; and accordingly the disposal need not be for the best consideration in money that can reasonably be obtained.

Nothing in this subsection shall be taken to authorise any action on the part of a charity which would conflict with the trusts of the charity.

(3) This section has effect subject to section 9 (control by [Relevant Authority][30] of land transactions).

Control by [Relevant Authority][31] of land transactions

9 Consent required for disposal of land by registered social landlord.

(1) The consent of the [Relevant Authority][32]. . ., is required for any disposal of land by a registered social landlord under section 8.

[(1A) The consent—

(a) if given by the Housing Corporation, shall be given by order under its seal, and

(b) if given by the Secretary of State, shall be given by order in writing.][33]

(2) The consent of the [Relevant Authority][34] may be so given—

(a) generally to all registered social landlords or to a particular landlord or description of landlords;

(b) in relation to particular land or in relation to a particular description of land,

and may be given subject to conditions.

(3) Before giving any consent other than a consent in relation to a particular landlord or particular land, the [Relevant Authority][35] shall consult such bodies representative of registered social landlords as it

thinks fit.

(4) A disposal of a house by a registered social landlord made without the consent required by this section is void unless—

(a) the disposal is to an individual (or to two or more individuals),

(b) the disposal does not extend to any other house, and

(c) the landlord reasonably believes that the individual or individuals intend to use the house as their principal dwelling.

(5) Any other disposal by a registered social landlord which requires consent under this section is valid in favour of a person claiming under the landlord notwithstanding that that consent has not been given; and a person dealing with a registered social landlord, or with a person claiming under such a landlord, shall not be concerned to see or inquire whether any such consent has been given.

(6) Where at the time of its removal from the register of social landlords a body owns land, this section continues to apply to that land after the removal as if the body concerned continued to be a registered social landlord.

(7) For the purposes of this section "disposal" means sale, lease, mortgage, charge or any other disposition.

(8) This section has effect subject to section 10 (lettings and other disposals not requiring consent of [Relevant Authority][36]).

10 Lettings and other disposals not requiring consent of [Relevant Authority][37].

(1) A letting by a registered social landlord does not require consent under section 9 if it is—

(a) a letting of land under an assured tenancy or an assured agricultural occupancy, or what would be an assured tenancy or an assured agricultural occupancy but for any of paragraphs 4 to 8, or paragraph 12(1)(h), of Schedule 1 to the Housing Act 1988, or

(b) a letting of land under a secure tenancy or what would be a secure tenancy but for any of paragraphs 2 to 12 of Schedule 1 to the Housing Act 1985.

(2) Consent under section 9 is not required in the case of a disposal to which section 81 or 133 of the Housing Act 1988 applies (certain disposals for which the consent of the Secretary of State is required).

(3) Consent under section 9 is not required for a disposal under Part V of the Housing Act 1985 (the right to buy) or under the right conferred by section 16 below (the right to acquire).

11 Covenant for repayment of discount on disposal.

(1) Where on a disposal of a house by a registered social landlord, in accordance with a consent given by the [Relevant Authority][38] under section 9, a discount has been given to the purchaser, and the consent does not provide otherwise, the conveyance, grant or assignment shall contain a covenant binding on the purchaser and his successors in title to the following effect.

(2) The covenant shall be to pay to the landlord on demand, if within a period of three years there is a relevant disposal which is not an exempted disposal (but if there is more than one such disposal then only on the first of them), an amount equal to the discount reduced by one-third for each complete year which has elapsed after the conveyance, grant or assignment and before the further disposal.

(3) The liability that may arise under the covenant is a charge on the house, taking effect as if it had been created by deed expressed to be by way of legal mortgage.

(4) A charge taking effect by virtue of this section is a land charge for the purposes of section 59 of the Land Registration Act 1925 notwithstanding subsection (5) of that section (exclusion of mortgages), and subsection (2) of that section applies accordingly with respect to its protection and realisation.

(5) Where there is a relevant disposal which is an exempted disposal by virtue of section 15(4)(d) or (e) (compulsory disposal or disposal of yard, garden, &c.)—

(a) the covenant required by this section is not binding on the person to whom the disposal is made or any successor in title of his, and

(b) the covenant and the charge taking effect by virtue of this section ceases to apply in relation to the property disposed of.

12 Priority of charge for repayment of discount.

(1) The charge taking effect by virtue of section 11 (charge for repayment of discount) has priority immediately after any legal charge securing an amount—

(a) left outstanding by the purchaser, or

(b) advanced to him by an approved lending institution for the purpose of enabling him to acquire the interest disposed of on the first disposal,

subject to the following provisions.

(2) An advance which is made for a purpose other than that mentioned in subsection (1)(b) and which is secured by a legal charge having priority to the charge taking effect by virtue of section 11, and any further advance which is so secured, shall rank in priority to that charge if, and only if, the registered social landlord by notice served on the institution concerned gives consent.

The landlord shall give consent if the purpose of the advance or further advance is an approved purpose.

(3) The registered social landlord may at any time by notice served on an approved lending institution postpone the charge taking effect by virtue of section 11 to an advance or further advance which—

(a) is made to the purchaser by that institution, and

(b) is secured by a legal charge not having priority to that charge;

and the landlord shall serve such a notice if the purpose of the advance or further advance is an approved purpose.

(4) The covenant required by section 11 does not, by virtue of its binding successors in title of the purchaser, bind a person exercising rights under a charge having priority over the charge taking effect by virtue of that section, or a person deriving title under him.

A provision of the conveyance, grant or assignment, or of a collateral agreement, is void in so far as it purports to authorise a forfeiture, or to impose a penalty or disability, in the event of any such person failing to comply with that covenant.

(5) In this section "approved lending institution" means—

(a) a building society, bank, insurance company or friendly society,

(b) the [Relevant Authority][39], or

(c) any body specified, or of a class or description specified, in an order made under section 156 of the Housing Act 1985 (which makes corresponding provision in relation to disposals in pursuance of the right to buy).

(6) The following are "approved purposes" for the purposes of this section—

(a) to enable the purchaser to defray, or to defray on his behalf, any of the following—

(i) the cost of any works to the house,

(ii) any service charge payable in respect of the house for works, whether or not to the house, and

(iii) any service charge or other amount payable in respect of the house for insurance, whether or not of the house, and

(b) to enable the purchaser to discharge, or to discharge on his behalf, any of the following—

(i) so much as is still outstanding of any advance or further advance which ranks in priority to the charge taking effect by virtue of section 11,

(ii) any arrears of interest on such an advance or further advance, and

(iii) any costs and expenses incurred in enforcing payment of any such interest, or repayment (in whole or in part) of any such advance or further advance.

In this subsection "service charge" has the meaning given by section 621A of the Housing Act 1985.

(7) Where different parts of an advance or further advance are made for different purposes, each of those parts shall be regarded as a separate advance or further advance for the purposes of this section.

13 Restriction on disposal of houses in National Parks, &c.

(1) On the disposal by a registered social landlord, in accordance with a consent given by the [Relevant Authority][40] under section 9, of a house situated in—

(a) a National Park,

(b) an area designated under [section 82 of the Countryside and Rights of Way Act 2000][41] as an area of outstanding natural beauty, or

(c) an area designated as a rural area by order under section 157 of the Housing Act 1985,

the conveyance, grant or assignment may (unless it contains a condition of a kind mentioned in section 33(2)(b) or (c) of the Housing Act 1985 (right of pre-emption or restriction on assignment)) contain a covenant to the following effect limiting the freedom of the purchaser (including any

successor in title of his and any person deriving title under him or such a successor) to dispose of the house.

(2) The limitation is that until such time (if any) as may be notified in writing by the registered social landlord to the purchaser or a successor in title of his, there will be no relevant disposal which is not an exempted disposal without the written consent of the landlord.

(3) That consent shall not be withheld if the person to whom the disposal is made (or, if it is made to more than one person, at least one of them) has, throughout the period of three years immediately preceding the application for consent—

(a) had his place of work in a region designated by order under section 157(3) of the Housing Act 1985 which, or part of which, is comprised in the National Park or area concerned, or

(b) had his only or principal home in such a region,

or if he has had the one in part or parts of that period and the other in the remainder.

The region need not have been the same throughout the period.

(4) A disposal in breach of such a covenant as is mentioned above is void.

(5) The limitation imposed by such a covenant is a local land charge and, if the land is registered under the Land Registration Act 1925, the Chief Land Registrar shall enter the appropriate restriction on the register of title as if an application to that effect had been made under section 58 of that Act.

(6) In this section "purchaser" means the person acquiring the interest disposed of by the first disposal.

(7) Where there is a relevant disposal which is an exempted disposal by virtue of section 15(4)(d) or (e) (compulsory disposal or disposal of yard, garden, &c.), any such covenant as is mentioned in this section ceases to apply in relation to the property disposed of.

14 Treatment of options.

(1) For the purposes of sections 9 to 13 the grant of an option enabling a person to call for a relevant disposal which is not an exempted disposal shall be treated as such a disposal made to him.

(2) For the purposes of section 13(2) (requirement of consent to disposal of house in National Park, &c.) consent to such a grant shall be treated as consent to a disposal made in pursuance of the option.

15 Relevant and exempted disposals.

(1) In sections 11 to 14 the expression "relevant disposal which is not an exempted disposal" shall be construed as follows.

(2) A disposal, whether of the whole or part of the house, is a relevant disposal if it is—

(a) a conveyance of the freehold or an assignment of the lease, or

(b) the grant of a lease or sub-lease (other than a mortgage term) for a term of more than 21 years otherwise than at a rack-rent.

(3) For the purposes of subsection (2)(b) it shall be assumed—

(a) that any option to renew or extend a lease or sub-lease, whether or not forming part of a series of options, is exercised, and

(b) that any option to terminate a lease or sub-lease is not exercised.

(4) A disposal is an exempted disposal if—

(a) it is a disposal of the whole of the house and a conveyance of the freehold or an assignment of the lease and the person or each of the persons to whom it is made is a qualifying person (as defined in subsection (5));

(b) it is a vesting of the whole of the house in a person taking under a will or on an intestacy;

(c) it is a disposal of the whole of the house in pursuance of any such order as is mentioned in subsection (6);

(d) it is a compulsory disposal (as defined in subsection (7));

(e) the property disposed of is a yard, garden, outhouses or appurtenances belonging to a house or usually enjoyed with it.

(5) For the purposes of subsection (4)(a) a person is a qualifying person in relation to a disposal if—

(a) he is the person or one of the persons by whom the disposal is made,

(b) he is the spouse or a former spouse of that person or one of those persons, or

(c) he is a member of the family of that person or one of those persons and has resided with him throughout the period of twelve months ending with the disposal.

(6) The orders referred to in subsection (4)(c) are orders under—

(a) section 24 or 24A of the Matrimonial Causes Act 1973 (property adjustment orders or orders for

the sale of property in connection with matrimonial proceedings);

(b) section 2 of the Inheritance (Provision for Family and Dependants) Act 1975 (orders as to financial provision to be made from estate);

(c) section 17 of the Matrimonial and Family Proceedings Act 1984 (property adjustment orders or orders for the sale of property after overseas divorce, &c.); or

(d) paragraph 1 of Schedule 1 to the Children Act 1989 (orders for financial relief against parents).

(7) For the purposes of subsection (4)(d) a compulsory disposal is a disposal of property which is acquired compulsorily, or is acquired by a person who has made or would have made, or for whom another person has made or would have made, a compulsory purchase order authorising its compulsory purchase for the purposes for which it is acquired.

Right of tenant to acquire dwelling

16 Right of tenant to acquire dwelling.

(1) A tenant of a registered social landlord has the right to acquire the dwelling of which he is a tenant if—

(a) he is a tenant under an assured tenancy, other than an assured shorthold tenancy or a long tenancy, or under a secure tenancy,

(b) the dwelling was provided with public money and has remained in the social rented sector, and

(c) he satisfies any further qualifying conditions applicable under Part V of the Housing Act 1985 (the right to buy) as it applies in relation to the right conferred by this section.

(2) For this purpose a dwelling shall be regarded as provided with public money if—

(a) it was provided or acquired wholly or in part by means of a grant under section 18 (social housing grant),

(b) it was provided or acquired wholly or in part by applying or appropriating sums standing in the disposal proceeds fund of a registered social landlord (see section 25), or

(c) it was acquired by a registered social landlord after the commencement of this paragraph on a disposal by a public sector landlord at a time when it was capable of being let as a separate dwelling.

(3) A dwelling shall be regarded for the purposes of this section as having remained within the social rented sector if, since it was so provided or acquired—

(a) the person holding the freehold interest in the dwelling has been either a registered social landlord or a public sector landlord; and

(b) any person holding an interest as lessee (otherwise than as mortgagee) in the dwelling has been—

(i) an individual holding otherwise than under a long tenancy; or

(ii) a registered social landlord or a public sector landlord.

(4) A dwelling shall be regarded for the purposes of this section as provided by means of a grant under section 18 (social housing grant) if, and only if, the [Relevant Authority][42] when making the grant notified the recipient that the dwelling was to be so regarded.

The [Relevant Authority][43] shall before making the grant inform the applicant that it proposes to give such a notice and allow him an opportunity to withdraw his application within a specified time.

[(5) But notice must be taken to be given to a registered social landlord under subsection (4) by the Housing Corporation if it is sent using electronic communications to such number or address as the registered social landlord has for the time being notified to the Housing Corporation for that purpose.

(6) The means by which notice is sent by virtue of subsection (5) must be such as to enable the registered social landlord to reproduce the notice by electronic means in a form which is visible and legible.

(7) An electronic communication is a communication transmitted (whether from one person to another, from one device to another, or from a person to a device or vice versa)—

(a) by means of a telecommunications system (within the meaning of the Telecommunications Act 1984[44]; or

(b) by other means but while in an electronic form.][45]

17 Right of tenant to acquire dwelling: supplementary provisions.

(1) The Secretary of State may by order—

(a) specify the amount or rate of discount to be given on the exercise of the right conferred by section 16; and

(b) designate rural areas in relation to dwellings in which the right conferred by that section does not arise.

(2) The provisions of Part V of the Housing Act 1985 apply in relation to the right to acquire under section 16—

(a) subject to any order under subsection (1) above, and

(b) subject to such other exceptions, adaptations and other modifications as may be specified by regulations made by the Secretary of State.

(3) The regulations may provide—

(a) that the powers of the Secretary of State under sections 164 to 170 of that Act (powers to intervene, give directions or assist) do not apply,

(b) that paragraphs 1 and 3 (exceptions for charities and certain housing associations), and paragraph 11 (right of appeal to Secretary of State), of Schedule 5 to that Act do not apply,

(c) that the provisions of Part V of that Act relating to the right to acquire on rent to mortgage terms do not apply,

(d) that the provisions of that Part relating to restrictions on disposals in National Parks, &c. do not apply, and

(e) that the provisions of that Part relating to the preserved right to buy do not apply.

Nothing in this subsection affects the generality of the power conferred by subsection (2).

(4) The specified exceptions, adaptations and other modifications shall take the form of textual amendments of the provisions of Part V of that Act as they apply in relation to the right to buy under that Part; and the first regulations, and any subsequent consolidating regulations, shall set out the provisions of Part V as they so apply.

(5) An order or regulations under this section—

(a) may make different provision for different cases or classes of case including different areas, and

(b) may contain such incidental, supplementary and transitional provisions as the Secretary of State considers appropriate.

(6) Before making an order which would have the effect that an area ceased to be designated under subsection (1)(b), the Secretary of State shall consult—

(a) the local housing authority or authorities in whose district the area or any part of it is situated or, if the order is general in its effect, local housing authorities in general, and

(b) such bodies appearing to him to be representative of registered social landlords as he considers appropriate.

(7) An order or regulations under this section shall be made by statutory instrument which shall be subject to annulment in pursuance of a resolution of either House of Parliament.

Chapter III Grants and other financial matters

Grants and other financial assistance

18 Social housing grants.

(1) The [Relevant Authority][46] may make grants to registered social landlords in respect of expenditure incurred or to be incurred by them in connection with their housing activities.

(2) The [Relevant Authority][47], acting in accordance with such principles as it may from time to time determine, shall specify in relation to grants under this section—

(a) the procedure to be followed in relation to applications for grant,

(b) the circumstances in which grant is or is not to be payable,

(c) the method for calculating, and any limitations on, the amount of grant, and

(d) the manner in which, and time or times at which, grant is to be paid.

(3) In making a grant under this section, the [Relevant Authority][48] may provide that the grant is conditional on compliance by the landlord with such conditions as the [Relevant Authority][49] may specify.

(4) The [Relevant Authority][50] may, with the agreement of a local housing authority, appoint the authority to act as its agent in connection with the assessment and payment of grant under this section.

[(5) The appointment—

(a) if made by the Housing Corporation, shall be on such terms as the Housing Corporation may, with the approval of the Secretary of State given with the consent of the Treasury, specify, and

(b) if made by the Secretary of State, shall be on such terms as the Secretary of State may, with the consent of the Treasury, specify;

and, in either case, the authority shall act in accordance with those terms.][51]

(6) Where—

(a) a grant under this section is payable to a registered social landlord, and

(b) at any time property to which the grant relates becomes vested in, or is leased for a term of years to, or reverts to, another registered social landlord, or trustees for another such landlord,

this section (including this subsection) shall have effect after that time as if the grant, or such proportion of it as is specified or determined under subsection (7), were payable to the other landlord.

(7) The proportion mentioned in subsection (6) is that which, in the circumstances of the particular case—

(a) the [Relevant Authority][52], acting in accordance with such principles as it may from time to time determine, may specify as being appropriate, or

(b) the [Relevant Authority][53] may determine to be appropriate.

(8) Where one of the landlords mentioned in subsection (6) is registered by the Housing Corporation and another is registered by [the Secretary of State][54], the determination mentioned in subsection (7) shall be such as shall be agreed between the [Housing Corporation and the Secretary of State][55].

19 Land subject to housing management agreement.

A registered social landlord is not entitled to a grant under section 18 (social housing grant) in respect of land comprised in a management agreement within the meaning of the Housing Act 1985 (see sections 27(2) and 27B(4) of that Act: delegation of housing management functions by certain authorities).

20 Purchase grant where right to acquire exercised.

(1) The [Relevant Authority][56] shall make grants to registered social landlords in respect of discounts given by them to persons exercising the right to acquire conferred by section 16.

(2) The amount of the grant for any year shall be the aggregate value of the discounts given in that year.

(3) The [Relevant Authority][57], acting in accordance with such principles as it may from time to time determine, shall specify in relation to grants under this section—

(a) the procedure to be followed in relation to applications for grant,

(b) the manner in which, and time or times at which, grant is to be paid.

(4) In making a grant the [Relevant Authority][58] may provide that the grant is conditional on compliance by the registered social landlord with such conditions as the [Relevant Authority][59] may specify.

21 Purchase grant in respect of other disposals.

(1) The [Relevant Authority][60] may make grants to registered social landlords in respect of discounts on disposals by them of dwellings to tenants otherwise than in pursuance of the right conferred by section 16.

(2) The [Relevant Authority][61] shall make such a grant if the tenant was entitled to exercise the right conferred by section 16 in relation to another dwelling of the landlord's.

The amount of the grant in such a case shall not exceed the amount of the discount to which the tenant would have been entitled in respect of the other dwelling.

(3) The [Relevant Authority][62], acting in accordance with such principles as it may from time to time determine, shall specify in relation to grants under this section—

(a) the procedure to be followed in relation to applications for grant;

(b) the circumstances in which grant is or is not to be payable;

(c) the method for calculating, and any limitations on, the amount of grant; and

(d) the manner in which, and time or times at which, grant is to be paid.

(4) In making a grant under this section, the [Relevant Authority][63] may provide that the grant is conditional on compliance by the registered social landlord with such conditions as the [Relevant Authority][64] may specify.

22 Assistance from local authorities.

(1) A local authority may promote—

(a) the formation of bodies to act as registered social landlords, and

(b) the extension of the objects or activities of registered social landlords.

(2) A local authority may for the assistance of any registered social landlord subscribe for share or loan capital of the landlord.

(3) A local authority may for the assistance of a registered social landlord—

(a) make grants or loans to the landlord, or

(b) guarantee or join in guaranteeing the payment of the principal of, and interest on, money borrowed by the landlord (including money borrowed by the issue of loan capital) or of interest on share capital issued by the landlord.

(4) A local housing authority may sell or supply under a hire-purchase agreement furniture to the occupants of houses provided by a registered social landlord, and may buy furniture for that purpose.

In this subsection "hire-purchase agreement" means a hire-purchase agreement or conditional sale agreement within the meaning of the Consumer Credit Act 1974.

23 Loans by Public Works Loans Commissioners.

(1) The Public Works Loans Commissioners may lend money to a registered social landlord—

(a) for the purpose of constructing or improving, or facilitating or encouraging the construction or improvement, of dwellings,

(b) for the purchase of dwellings which the landlord desires to purchase with a view to their improvement, and

(c) for the purchase and development of land.

(2) A loan for any of those purposes, and interest on the loan, shall be secured by a mortgage of—

(a) the land in respect of which that purpose is to be carried out, and

(b) such other lands (if any) as may be offered as security for the loan;

and the money lent shall not exceed three-quarters (or, if the payment of the principal of, and interest on, the loan is guaranteed by a local authority, nine-tenths) of the value, to be ascertained to the satisfaction of the Public Works Commissioners, of the estate or interest in the land proposed to be so mortgaged.

(3) Loans may be made by instalments as the building of dwellings or other work on the land mortgaged under subsection (2) progresses (so, however, that the total amount lent does not at any time exceed the amount specified in that subsection); and a mortgage may accordingly be made to secure such loans to be so made.

(4) If the loan exceeds two-thirds of the value referred to in subsection (2), and is not guaranteed as to principal and interest by a local authority, the Public Works Loans Commissioners shall require, in addition to such a mortgage as is mentioned in that subsection, such further security as they think fit.

(5) Subject to subsection (6), the period for repayment of a loan under this section shall not exceed 40 years, and no money shall be lent on mortgage of any land unless the estate proposed to be mortgaged is either an estate in fee simple absolute in possession or an estate for a term of years absolute of which not less than 50 years are unexpired at the date of the loan.

(6) Where a loan under this section is made for the purpose of carrying out a scheme for the provision of houses approved by the Secretary of State, the maximum period for the repayment of the loan is 50 instead of 40 years, and money may be lent on the mortgage of an estate for a term of years absolute of which a period of not less than ten years in excess of the period fixed for the repayment of the sums advanced remains unexpired at the date of the loan.

Treatment of disposal proceeds

24 The disposal proceeds fund.

(1) A registered social landlord shall show separately in its accounts for any period ending after the coming into force of this section its net disposal proceeds.

(2) The net disposal proceeds of a registered social landlord are—

(a) the net proceeds of sale received by it in respect of any disposal of land to a tenant—

(i) in pursuance of the right conferred by section 16 (right of tenant to acquire dwelling), or

(ii) in respect of which a grant was made under section 21 (purchase grant in respect of other disposals);

(b) payments of grant received by it under section 20 or 21 (purchase grant);

(c) where any such grant has been paid to it, any repayments of discount in respect of which the grant was given; and

(d) such other proceeds of sale or payments of grant (if any) as the [Relevant Authority][65] may from time to time determine.

(3) The net proceeds of sale means the proceeds of sale less an amount calculated in accordance with a determination by the [Relevant Authority][66].

(4) The disposal proceeds shall be shown in a fund to be known as a disposal proceeds fund.

(5) The method of constituting the fund and showing it in the landlord's accounts shall be as required by determination of the [Relevant Authority][67] under paragraph 16 of Schedule 1 (general requirements as to accounts).

(6) Interest shall be added to the fund in accordance with a determination made by the [Relevant Authority][68].

(7) Where this section applies in relation to the proceeds of sale arising on a disposal, section 27 below (recovery, &c. of social housing grants) and section 52 of the Housing Act 1988 (recovery, &c. of grants under that Act and earlier enactments) do not apply.

25 Application or appropriation of disposal proceeds.

(1) The sums standing in the disposal proceeds account of a registered social landlord ("disposal proceeds") may only be applied or appropriated by it for such purposes and in such manner as the [Relevant Authority][69] may determine.

(2) If any disposal proceeds are not applied or appropriated as mentioned in subsection (1) within such time as is specified by determination of the [Relevant Authority][70], the [Relevant Authority][71] may direct that the whole or part of them shall be paid to it.

26 Disposal proceeds: power to require information.

(1) The [Relevant Authority][72] may give notice—

(a) to all registered social landlords,

(b) to registered social landlords of a particular description, or

(c) to particular registered social landlords,

requiring them to furnish it with such information as it may reasonably require in connection with the exercise of its functions under sections 24 and 25 (treatment of disposal proceeds).

(2) A notice under subsection (1)(a) or (b) may be given by publication in such manner as the [Relevant Authority][73] considers appropriate for bringing it to the attention of the landlords concerned.

Recovery, &c. of social housing grants

27 Recovery, &c. of social housing grants.

(1) Where a registered social landlord has received a grant under section 18 (social housing grant), the following powers are exercisable in such events as the [Relevant Authority][74] may from time to time determine.

(2) The [Relevant Authority][75] may, acting in accordance with such principles as it has determined—

(a) reduce any grant payable by it, or suspend or cancel any instalment of any such grant, or

(b) direct the registered social landlord to apply or appropriate for such purposes as the [Relevant Authority] may specify, or to pay to the [Relevant Authority][76], such amount as the [Relevant Authority][77] may specify.

(3) A direction by the [Relevant Authority][78] under subsection (2)(b) may require the application, appropriation or payment of an amount with interest.

(4) Any such direction shall specify—

(a) the rate or rates of interest (whether fixed or variable) which is or are applicable,

(b) the date from which interest is payable, and

(c) any provision for suspended or reduced interest which is applicable.

The date from which interest is payable must not be earlier than the date of the event giving rise to the exercise of the [Relevant Authority][79] powers under this section.

(5) In subsection (4)(c)—

(a) provision for suspended interest means provision to the effect that if the principal amount is applied, appropriated or paid before a date specified in the direction, no interest will be payable for any period after the date of the direction; and

(b) provision for reduced interest means provision to the effect that if the principal amount is so applied, appropriated or paid, any interest payable will be payable at a rate or rates lower than the rate or rates which would otherwise be applicable.

(6) Where—

(a) a registered social landlord has received a payment in respect of a grant under section 18, and

(b) at any time property to which the grant relates becomes vested in, or is leased for a term of years to, or reverts to, some other registered social landlord,

this section (including this subsection) shall have effect in relation to periods after that time as if the grant, or such proportion of it as may be determined by the [Relevant Authority][80] to be appropriate, had been made to that other registered social landlord.

(7) The matters specified in a direction under subsection (4)(a) to (c), and the proportion mentioned in subsection (6), shall be—

(a) such as the [Relevant Authority][81], acting in accordance with such principles as it may from time to time determine, may specify as being appropriate, or

(b) such as the [Relevant Authority][82] may determine to be appropriate in the particular case.

Grants, &c. under earlier enactments

28 Grants under ss.50 to 55 of the Housing Act 1988.

(1) No application for a grant under section 50 of the Housing Act 1988 (housing association grant) may be made after the commencement of this subsection.

(2) No application for a grant under section 51 of that Act (revenue deficit grant) may be made after the commencement of this subsection except by an association which had such a deficit as is mentioned in that section for any of the years beginning 1st April 1994, 1st April 1995 or 1st April 1996.

(3) Section 52 of that Act (recovery, &c. of grants) is amended as follows—

(a) in subsection (2)(c), for "to pay to it" substitute " to apply or appropriate for such purposes as the [Relevant Authority][83] may specify, or to pay to the [Relevant Authority][84],";

(b) in the closing words of subsection (2), for the words from "requiring" to "interest on that amount" substitute " may require the application, appropriation or payment of an amount with interest ";

(c) in subsection (7), for the words from "requiring" to "to the [Relevant Authority][85]" substitute " requiring the application, appropriation or payment of an amount with interest ";

(d) in subsection (8)(a), for the words from "the amount" to "is paid" substitute " the principal amount is applied, appropriated or paid ";

(e) in subsection (8)(b), for "that amount is so paid" substitute " the principal amount is so applied, appropriated or paid ".

(4) In section 53 of that Act (determinations by [Relevant Authority][86]), for subsection (2) (requirement of approval of Secretary of State and, in the case of a general determination, consent of the Treasury) substitute—

"(2) The [Relevant Authority][87] shall not make a general determination under the foregoing provisions of this Part except with the approval of the Secretary of State.".

(5) In section 55(1) of that Act (surplus rental income: cases in which section applies), omit paragraph (a).

(6) Any reference in sections 50 to 55 of that Act to registration as a housing association shall be construed after the commencement of section 1 of this Act (the register of social landlords) as a reference to registration as a social landlord.

29 Commutation of payments of special residual subsidy.

(1) The Secretary of State may, after consultation with a housing association, determine to commute any payments of special residual subsidy payable to the association under paragraph 2 of Part I of Schedule 5 to the Housing Associations Act 1985 for the financial year 1998-99 and subsequent years.

(2) Where the Secretary of State makes such a determination the payments of special residual subsidy payable to a housing association shall be commuted into a single sum calculated in such manner, and payable on such date, as the Secretary of State may consider appropriate.

(3) If after a commuted payment has been made to a housing association it appears to the Secretary of State that the payment was smaller or greater than it should have been, the Secretary of State may make a further payment to the association or require the association to repay to him such sum as he may direct.

(4) The Secretary of State may delegate to the Housing Corporation, to such extent and subject to such conditions as he may specify, any of his functions under this section and, where he does so, references to him in this section shall be construed accordingly.

Chapter IV General powers of the [Relevant Authority][88]

Information

30 General power to obtain information.

(1) The [Relevant Authority][89] may for any purpose connected with the discharge of any of its functions in relation to registered social landlords serve a notice on a person requiring him—

(a) to give to the [Relevant Authority][90], at a time and place and in the form and manner specified in the notice, such information relating to the affairs of a registered social landlord as may be specified or described in the notice, or

(b) to produce to the [Relevant Authority] [91]or a person authorised by the [Relevant Authority][92], at a time and place specified in the notice, any documents relating to the affairs of the registered social landlord which are specified or described in the notice and are in his custody or under his control.

(2) A notice under this section may be served on—

(a) a registered social landlord,

(b) any person who is, or has been, an officer, member, employee or agent of a registered social landlord,

(c) a subsidiary or associate of a registered social landlord,

(d) any person who is, or has been, an officer, member, employee or agent of a subsidiary or associate of a registered social landlord, or

(e) any other person whom the [Relevant Authority][93] has reason to believe is or may be in possession of relevant information.

In this section "agent" includes banker, solicitor and auditor.

(3) No notice shall be served on a person within paragraphs (b) to (e) of subsection (2) unless—

(a) a notice has been served on the registered social landlord and has not been complied with, or

(b) the [Relevant Authority][94] believes that the information or documents in question are not in the possession of the landlord.

(4) Nothing in this section authorises the [Relevant Authority][95] to require—

(a) the disclosure of anything which a person would be entitled to refuse to disclose on grounds of legal professional privilege in proceedings in the High Court, or

(b) the disclosure by a banker of anything in breach of any duty of confidentiality owed by him to a person other than a registered social landlord or a subsidiary or associate of a registered social landlord.

[(5) a notice under this section—

(a) if given by the Housing Corporation, shall be given under its seal, and

(b) if given by the Secretary of State, shall be given in writing.][96]

(6) References in this section to a document are to anything in which information of any description is recorded; and in relation to a document in which information is recorded otherwise than in legible form, references to producing it are to producing it in legible form.

(7) Where by virtue of this section documents are produced to any person, he may take copies of or make extracts from them.

31 Enforcement of notice to provide information, &c.

(1) A person who without reasonable excuse fails to do anything required of him by a notice under section 30 commits an offence and is liable on summary conviction to a fine not exceeding level 5 on the standard scale.

(2) A person who intentionally alters, suppresses or destroys a document which he has been required by a notice under section 30 to produce commits an offence and is liable—

(a) on summary conviction, to a fine not exceeding the statutory maximum,

(b) on conviction on indictment, to a fine.

(3) Proceedings for an offence under subsection (1) or (2) may be brought only by or with the consent of the [Relevant Authority][97] or the Director of Public Prosecutions.

(4) If a person makes default in complying with a notice under section 30, the High Court may, on the application of the [Relevant Authority][98], make such order as the court thinks fit for requiring the default to be made good.

Any such order may provide that all the costs or expenses of and incidental to the application shall be borne by the person in default or by any officers of a body who are responsible for its default.

32 Disclosure of information to the [Relevant Authority][99].

(1) A body or person to whom this section applies may, subject to the following provisions, disclose to the [Relevant Authority][100], for the purpose of enabling the [Relevant Authority][101] to discharge any of its functions relating to registered social landlords, any information received by that body or person under or for the purposes of any enactment.

(2) This section applies to the following bodies and persons—

(a) any government department (including a Northern Ireland department);

(b) any local authority;

(c) any constable; and

(d) any other body or person discharging functions of a public nature (including a body or person discharging regulatory functions in relation to any description of activities).

(3) This section has effect subject to any express restriction on disclosure imposed by or under any other enactment.

(4) Nothing in this section shall be construed as affecting any power of disclosure exercisable apart from this section.

33 Disclosure of information by the [Relevant Authority][102].

(1) The [Relevant Authority][103] may disclose to a body or person to whom this section applies any information received by it relating to a registered social landlord—

(a) for any purpose connected with the discharge of the functions of the [Relevant Authority][104] in relation to such landlords, or

(b) for the purpose of enabling or assisting that body or person to discharge any of its or his functions.

(2) This section applies to the following bodies and persons—

(a) any government department (including a Northern Ireland department);

(b) any local authority;

(c) any constable; and

(d) any other body or person discharging functions of a public nature (including a body or person discharging regulatory functions in relation to any description of activities).

Paragraph (d) extends to any such body or person in a country or territory outside the United Kingdom.

(3) Where any information disclosed to the [Relevant Authority][105] under section 32 is so disclosed subject to any express restriction on the further disclosure of the information, the [Relevant Authority's][106] power of disclosure under this section is exercisable subject to that restriction.

A person who discloses information in contravention of any such restriction commits an offence and is liable on summary conviction to a fine not exceeding level 3 on the standard scale.

(4) Any information disclosed by the [Relevant Authority][107] under this section may be subject by the [Relevant Authority][108] to any express restriction on the further disclosure of the information.

(5) A person who discloses information in contravention of any such restriction commits an offence and is liable on summary conviction to a fine not exceeding level 3 on the standard scale.

Proceedings for such an offence may be brought only by or with the consent of the [Relevant Authority][109] or the Director of Public Prosecutions.

(6) Nothing in this section shall be construed as affecting any power of disclosure exercisable apart from this section.

Standards of performance

34 Standards of performance.

The [Relevant Authority][110] may, after consultation with persons or bodies appearing to it to be representative of registered social landlords, from time to time—

(a) determine such standards of performance in connection with the provision of housing as, in its opinion, ought to be achieved by such landlords, and

(b) arrange for the publication, in such form and in such manner as it considers appropriate, of the standards so determined.

35 Information as to levels of performance.

(1) The [Relevant Authority][111] shall from time to time collect information as to the levels of performance achieved by registered social landlords in connection with the provision of housing.

(2) On or before such date in each year as may be specified in a direction given by the [Relevant Authority][112], each registered social landlord shall provide the [Relevant Authority][113], as respects each standard determined under section 34, with such information as to the level of performance achieved by him as may be so specified.

(3) A registered social landlord who without reasonable excuse fails to do anything required of him by a direction under subsection (2) commits an offence and is liable on summary conviction to a fine not exceeding level 5 on the standard scale.

Proceedings for such an offence may be brought only by or with the consent of the [Relevant Authority][114] or the Director of Public Prosecutions.

(4) The [Relevant Authority] shall at least once in every year arrange for the publication, in such form and in such manner as it considers appropriate, of such of the information collected by or provided to it under this section as appears to it expedient to give to tenants or potential tenants of registered social landlords.

(5) In arranging for the publication of any such information the [Relevant Authority][115] shall have regard to the need for excluding, so far as that is practicable—

(a) any matter which relates to the affairs of an individual, where publication of that matter would or might, in the opinion of the [Relevant Authority][116], seriously and prejudicially affect the interests of that individual; and

(b) any matter which relates specifically to the affairs of a particular body of persons, whether corporate or unincorporate, where publication of that matter would or might, in the opinion of the [Relevant Authority][117], seriously and prejudicially affect the interests of that body.

Housing management

36 Issue of guidance by the [Relevant Authority][118].

(1) The [Relevant Authority][119] may issue guidance with respect to the management of housing accommodation by registered social landlords.

(2) Guidance under this section may, in particular, be issued with respect to—

(a) the housing demands for which provision should be made and the means of meeting those demands;

(b) the allocation of housing accommodation between individuals;

(c) the terms of tenancies and the principles upon which levels of rent should be determined;

(d) standards of maintenance and repair and the means of achieving those standards;

(e) the services to be provided to tenants;

(f) the procedures to be adopted to deal with complaints by tenants against a landlord;

(g) consultation and communication with tenants;

(h) the devolution to tenants of decisions concerning the management of housing accommodation.

[(3) Before issuing any guidance under this section the Relevant Authority shall consult such bodies appearing to the Relevant Authority to be representative of registered social landlords as the Relevant Authority considers appropriate; and where the Relevant Authority issues guidance under this section it shall be issued in such manner as the Relevant Authority considers appropriate for bringing it to the notice of the landlords concerned.

(4) The Housing Corporation shall not issue guidance under this section unless—

(a) it has been submitted in draft to the Secretary of State for his approval, and

(b) the Secretary of State has given his approval to the draft.][120]

(5) Guidance issued under this section may be revised or withdrawn; and subsections (3) and (4) apply in relation to the revision of guidance as in relation to its issue.

(6) Guidance under this section may make different provision in relation to different cases and, in particular, in relation to different areas, different descriptions of housing accommodation and different descriptions of registered social landlord.

(7) In considering whether action needs to be taken to secure the proper management of the affairs of a registered social landlord or whether there has been mismanagement, the [Relevant Authority][121] may have regard (among other matters) to the extent to which any guidance under this section is being or has been followed.

37 Powers of entry.

(1) This section applies where it appears to the [Relevant Authority][122] that a registered social landlord may be failing to maintain or repair any premises in accordance with guidance issued under section 36.

(2) A person authorised by the [Relevant Authority][123] may at any reasonable time, on giving not less than 28 days' notice of his intention to the landlord concerned, enter any such premises for the purpose of survey and examination.

(3) Where such notice is given to the landlord, the landlord shall give the occupier or occupiers of the premises not less than seven days' notice of the proposed survey and examination.

A landlord who fails to do so commits an offence and is liable on summary conviction to a fine not exceeding level 3 on the standard scale.

(4) Proceedings for an offence under subsection (3) may be brought only by or with the consent of the [Relevant Authority][124] or the Director of Public Prosecutions.

(5) An authorisation for the purposes of this section shall be in writing stating the particular purpose or purposes for which the entry is authorised and shall, if so required, be produced for inspection by the occupier or anyone acting on his behalf.

(6) The [Relevant Authority][125] shall give a copy of any survey carried out in exercise of the powers conferred by this section to the landlord concerned.

(7) The [Relevant Authority] may require the landlord concerned to pay to it such amount as the [Relevant Authority][126] may determine towards the costs of carrying out any survey under this section.

38 Penalty for obstruction of person exercising power of entry.

(1) It is an offence for a registered social landlord or any of its officers or employees to obstruct a person authorised under section 37 (powers of entry) to enter premises in the performance of anything which he is authorised by that section to do.

(2) A person who commits such an offence is liable on summary conviction to a fine not exceeding level 3 on the standard scale.

(3) Proceedings for such an offence may be brought only by or with the consent of the [Relevant Authority][127] or the Director of Public Prosecutions.

Insolvency, &c. of registered social landlord

39 Insolvency, &c. of registered social landlord: scheme of provisions.

(1) The following sections make provision—

(a) for notice to be given to the [Relevant Authority][128] of any proposal to take certain steps in relation to a registered social landlord (section 40), and for further notice to be given when any such step is taken (section 41),

(b) for a moratorium on the disposal of land, and certain other assets, held by the registered social landlord (sections 42 and 43),

(c) for proposals by the [Relevant Authority][129] as to the future ownership and management of the land held by the landlord (section 44), which are binding if agreed (section 45),

(d) for the appointment of a manager to implement agreed proposals (section 46) and as to the powers of such a manager (sections 47 and 48),

(e) for the giving of assistance by the [Relevant Authority][130] (section 49), and

(f) for application to the court to secure compliance with the agreed proposals (section 50).

(2) In those sections—

"disposal" means sale, lease, mortgage, charge or any other disposition, and includes the grant of an option;

"secured creditor" means a creditor who holds a mortgage or charge (including a floating charge) over land held by the landlord or any existing or future interest of the landlord in rents or other receipts from land; and

"security" means any mortgage, charge or other security.

(3) The Secretary of State may make provision by order defining for the purposes of those sections what is meant by a step to enforce security over land.

Any such order shall be made by statutory instrument which shall be subject to annulment in pursuance of a resolution of either House of Parliament.

40 Initial notice to be given to the [Relevant Authority][131].

(1) Notice must be given to the [Relevant Authority][132] before any of the steps mentioned below is taken in relation to a registered social landlord.

The person by whom the notice must be given is indicated in the second column.

(2) Where the registered social landlord is an industrial and provident society, the steps and the person by whom notice must be given are—

Any step to enforce any security over land held by the landlord.	The person proposing to take the step.
Presenting a petition for the winding up of the landlord.	The petitioner.
Passing a resolution for the winding up of the landlord.	The landlord.

(3) Where the registered social landlord is a company registered under the Companies Act 1985 (including a registered charity), the steps and the person by whom notice must be given are—

Any step to enforce any security over land held by the landlord.	The person proposing to take the step.
Applying for an administration order.	The applicant.
Presenting a petition for the winding up of the landlord.	The petitioner.
Passing a resolution for the winding up of the landlord.	The landlord.

(4) Where the registered social landlord is a registered charity (other than a company registered under the Companies Act 1985), the steps and the person by whom notice must be given are—

Any step to enforce any security over land held by the landlord.	The person proposing to take the step.

(5) Notice need not be given under this section in relation to a resolution for voluntary winding up where the consent of the [Relevant Authority][133] is required (see paragraphs 12(4) and 13(6) of Schedule 1).

(6) Any step purportedly taken without the requisite notice being given under this section is ineffective.

Further notice to be given to the [Relevant Authority][134].

(1) Notice must be given to the [Relevant Authority][135] as soon as may be after any of the steps mentioned below is taken in relation to a registered social landlord.

The person by whom the notice must be given is indicated in the second column.

(2) Where the registered social landlord is an industrial and provident society, the steps and the person by whom notice must be given are—

The taking of a step to enforce any security over land held by the landlord.	The person taking the step.
The making of an order for the winding up of the landlord.	The petitioner.
The passing of a resolution for the winding up of the landlord.	The landlord.

(3) Where the registered social landlord is a company registered under the Companies Act 1985 (including a registered charity), the steps and the person by whom notice must be given are—

The taking of a step to enforce any security over land held by the landlord.	The person taking the step.
The making of an administration order.	The person who applied for the order.
The making of an order for the winding up of the landlord.	The petitioner.

The passing of a resolution for the winding up of the landlord.	The landlord.

(4) Where the registered social landlord is a registered charity (other than a company registered under the Companies Act 1985), the steps and the person by whom notice must be given are—

The taking of a step to enforce any security over land held by the landlord.	The person taking the step.

(5) Failure to give notice under this section does not affect the validity of any step taken; but the period of 28 days mentioned in section 43(1) (period after which moratorium on disposal of land, &c. ends) does not begin to run until any requisite notice has been given under this section.

42 Moratorium on disposal of land, &c.

(1) Where any of the steps mentioned in section 41 is taken in relation to a registered social landlord, there is a moratorium on the disposal of land held by the landlord.

(2) During the moratorium the consent of the [Relevant Authority][136] under this section is required (except as mentioned below) for any disposal of land held by the landlord, whether by the landlord itself or any person having a power of disposal in relation to the land.

Consent under this section may be given in advance and may be given subject to conditions.

(3) Consent is not required under this section for any such disposal as is mentioned in section 10(1), (2) or (3) (lettings and other disposals not requiring consent under section 9).

(4) A disposal made without the consent required by this section is void.

(5) Nothing in this section prevents a liquidator from disclaiming any land held by the landlord as onerous property.

(6) The provisions of this section apply in relation to any existing or future interest of the landlord in rent or other receipts arising from land as they apply to an interest in land.

43 Period of moratorium.

(1) The moratorium in consequence of the taking of any step as mentioned in section 41—

(a) begins when the step is taken, and

(b) ends at the end of the period of 28 days beginning with the day on which notice of its having been taken was given to the [Relevant Authority][137] under that section,

subject to the following provisions.

(2) The taking of any further step as mentioned in section 41 at a time when a moratorium is already in force does not start a further moratorium or affect the duration of the existing one.

(3) A moratorium may be extended from time to time with the consent of all the landlord's secured creditors.

Notice of any such extension shall be given by the [Relevant Authority][138] to—

(a) the landlord, and

(b) any liquidator, administrative receiver, receiver or administrator appointed in respect of the landlord or any land held by it.

(4) If during a moratorium the [Relevant Authority][139] considers that the proper management of the landlord's land can be secured without making proposals under section 44 (proposals as to ownership and management of landlord's land), the [Relevant Authority][140] may direct that the moratorium shall cease to have effect.

Before making any such direction the [Relevant Authority][141] shall consult the person who took the step which brought about the moratorium.

(5) When a moratorium comes to an end, or ceases to have effect under subsection (4), the [Relevant Authority][142] shall give notice of that fact to the landlord and the landlord's secured creditors.

(6) When a moratorium comes to an end (but not when it ceases to have effect under subsection (4)), the following provisions of this section apply.

The [Relevant Authority's][143] notice shall, in such a case, inform the landlord and the landlord's secured creditors of the effect of those provisions.

(7) If any further step as mentioned in section 41 is taken within the period of three years after the end of the original period of the moratorium, the moratorium may be renewed with the consent of all the landlord's secured creditors (which may be given before or after the step is taken).

Notice of any such renewal shall be given by the [Relevant Authority][144] to the persons to whom notice of an extension is required to be given under subsection (3).

(8) If a moratorium ends without any proposals being agreed, then, for a period of three years the taking of any further step as mentioned in section 41 does not start a further moratorium except with the consent of the landlord's secured creditors as mentioned in subsection (7) above.

44 Proposals as to ownership and management of landlord's land.

(1) During the moratorium (see sections 42 and 43) the [Relevant Authority][145] may make proposals as to the future ownership and management of the land held by the registered social landlord, designed to secure the continued proper management of the landlord's land by a registered social landlord.

(2) In drawing up its proposals the [Relevant Authority][146]—

(a) shall consult the landlord and, so far as is practicable, its tenants, and

(b) shall have regard to the interests of all the landlord's creditors, both secured and unsecured.

(3) The [Relevant Authority][147] shall also consult—

(a) where the landlord is an industrial and provident society, the appropriate registrar, and

(b) where the landlord is a registered charity, the Charity Commissioners.

(4) No proposals shall be made under which—

(a) a preferential debt of the landlord is to be paid otherwise than in priority to debts which are not preferential debts, or

(b) a preferential creditor is to be paid a smaller proportion of his preferential debt than another preferential creditor, except with the concurrence of the creditor concerned.

In this subsection references to preferential debts and preferential creditors have the same meaning as in the Insolvency Act 1986.

(5) So far as practicable no proposals shall be made which have the effect that unsecured creditors of the landlord are in a worse position than they would otherwise be.

(6) Where the landlord is a charity the proposals shall not require the landlord to act outside the terms of its trusts, and any disposal of housing accommodation occupied under a tenancy or licence from the landlord must be to another charity whose objects appear to the [Relevant Authority][148] to be, as nearly as practicable, akin to those of the landlord.

(7) The [Relevant Authority][149] shall serve a copy of its proposals on—

(a) the landlord and its officers,

(b) the secured creditors of the landlord, and

(c) any liquidator, administrator, administrative receiver or receiver appointed in respect of the landlord or its land;

and it shall make such arrangements as it considers appropriate to see that the members, tenants and unsecured creditors of the landlord are informed of the proposals.

45 Effect of agreed proposals.

(1) The following provisions apply if proposals made by the [Relevant Authority][150] under section 44 are agreed, with or without modifications, by all the secured creditors of the registered social landlord.

(2) Once agreed the proposals are binding on the [Relevant Authority][151], the landlord, all the landlord's creditors (whether secured or unsecured) and any liquidator, administrator, administrative receiver or receiver appointed in respect of the landlord or its land.

(3) It is the duty of—

(a) the members of the committee where the landlord is an industrial and provident society,

(b) the directors where the landlord is a company registered under the Companies Act 1985 (including a company which is a registered charity), and

(c) the trustees where the landlord is a charitable trust,

to co-operate in the implementation of the proposals.

This does not mean that they have to do anything contrary to any fiduciary or other duty owed by them.

(4) The [Relevant Authority][152] shall serve a copy of the agreed proposals on—

(a) the landlord and its officers,

(b) the secured creditors of the landlord, and

(c) any liquidator, administrator, administrative receiver or receiver appointed in respect of the landlord or its land, and

(d) where the landlord is an industrial and provident society or registered charity, the [Financial

Services Authority][153] or the Charity Commissioners, as the case may be;

and it shall make such arrangements as it considers appropriate to see that the members, tenants and unsecured creditors of the landlord are informed of the proposals.

(5) The proposals may subsequently be amended with the consent of the [Relevant Authority][154] and all the landlord's secured creditors.

Section 44(2) to (7) and subsections (2) to (4) above apply in relation to the amended proposals as in relation to the original proposals.

46 Appointment of manager to implement agreed proposals.

(1) Where proposals agreed as mentioned in section 45 so provide, the [Relevant Authority][155] may by order. . .[156] appoint a manager to implement the proposals or such of them as are specified in the order.

(2) If the landlord is a registered charity, the [Relevant Authority][157] shall give notice to the Charity Commissioners of the appointment.

(3) Where proposals make provision for the appointment of a manager, they shall also provide for the payment of his reasonable remuneration and expenses.

(4) The [Relevant Authority][158] may give the manager directions in relation to the carrying out of his functions.

(5) The manager may apply to the High Court for directions in relation to any particular matter arising in connection with the carrying out of his functions.

A direction of the court supersedes any direction of the [Relevant Authority][159] in respect of the same matter.

(6) If a vacancy occurs by death, resignation or otherwise in the office of manager, the [Relevant Authority][160] may by further order . . . fill the vacancy.

[(7) An order under this section—

(a) if made by the Housing Corporation, shall be made under its seal, and

(b) if made by the Secretary of State, shall be made in writing.][161]

47 Powers of the manager.

(1) An order under section 46(1) shall confer on the manager power generally to do all such things as are necessary for carrying out his functions.

(2) The order may include the following specific powers—

1. Power to take possession of the land held by the landlord and for that purpose to take any legal proceedings which seem to him expedient.
2. Power to sell or otherwise dispose of the land by public auction or private contract.
3. Power to raise or borrow money and for that purpose to grant security over the land.
4. Power to appoint a solicitor or accountant or other professionally qualified person to assist him in the performance of his functions.
5. Power to bring or defend legal proceedings relating to the land in the name and on behalf of the landlord.
6. Power to refer to arbitration any question affecting the land.
7. Power to effect and maintain insurance in respect of the land.
8. Power where the landlord is a body corporate to use the seal of the body corporate for purposes relating to the land.
9. Power to do all acts and to execute in the name and on behalf of the landlord any deed, receipt or other document relating to the land.
10. Power to appoint an agent to do anything which he is unable to do for himself or which can more conveniently be done by an agent, and power to employ and dismiss any employees.
11. Power to do all such things (including the carrying out of works) as may be necessary in connection with the management or transfer of the land.
12. Power to make any payment which is necessary or incidental to the performance of his functions.
13. Power to carry on the business of the landlord so far as relating to the management or transfer of the land.
14. Power to grant or accept a surrender of a lease or tenancy of any of the land, and to take a lease or tenancy of any property required or convenient for the landlord's housing activities.
15. Power to make any arrangement or compromise on behalf of the landlord in relation to the

management or transfer of the land.

16. Power to do all other things incidental to the exercise of any of the above powers.

(3) In carrying out his functions the manager acts as the landlord's agent and he is not personally liable on a contract which he enters into as manager.

(4) A person dealing with the manager in good faith and for value is not concerned to inquire whether the manager is acting within his powers.

(5) The manager shall, so far as practicable, consult the landlord's tenants about any exercise of his powers which is likely to affect them and inform them about any such exercise of his powers.

48 Powers of the manager: transfer of engagements.

(1) An order under section 46(1) may, where the landlord is an industrial and provident society, give the manager power to make and execute on behalf of the society an instrument transferring the engagements of the society.

(2) Any such instrument has the same effect as a transfer of engagements under section 51 or 52 of the Industrial and Provident Societies Act 1965 (transfer of engagements by special resolution to another society or a company).

In particular, its effect is subject to section 54 of that Act (saving for rights of creditors).

(3) A copy of the instrument, signed by the manager, shall be sent to the [Financial Services Authority and registered by it][162]; and until that copy is so registered the instrument shall not take effect.

(4) It is the duty of the manager to send a copy for registration within 14 days from the day on which the instrument is executed; but this does not invalidate registration after that time.

49 Assistance by the [Relevant Authority][163].

(1) The [Relevant Authority][164] may give such assistance as it thinks fit—

(a) to the landlord, for the purpose of preserving the position pending the making of and agreement to proposals;

(b) to the landlord or a manager appointed under section 46, for the purpose of carrying out any agreed proposals.

(2) The [Relevant Authority][165] may, in particular—

(a) lend staff;

(b) pay or secure payment of the manager's reasonable remuneration and expenses;

(c) give such financial assistance as appears to the [Relevant Authority][166] to be appropriate.

(3) The [giving by the Housing Corporation of the following forms of assistance requires][167] the consent of the Secretary of State—

(a) making grants or loans;

(b) agreeing to indemnify the manager in respect of liabilities incurred or loss or damage sustained by him in connection with his functions;

(c) paying or guaranteeing the repayment of the principal of, the payment of interest on and the discharge of any other financial obligation in connection with any sum borrowed (before or after the making of the order) and secured on any land disposed of.

50 Application to court to secure compliance with agreed proposals.

(1) The landlord or any creditor of the landlord may apply to the High Court on the ground that an action of the manager appointed under section 46 is not in accordance with the agreed proposals.

On such an application the court may confirm, reverse or modify any act or decision of the manager, give him directions or make such other order as it thinks fit.

(2) The [Relevant Authority][168] or any other person bound by agreed proposals may apply to the High Court on the ground that any action, or proposed action, by another person bound by the proposals is not in accordance with those proposals.

On such an application the court may—

(a) declare any such action to be ineffective, and

(b) grant such relief by way of injunction, damages or otherwise as appears to the court appropriate.

Chapter V Miscellaneous and general provisions

Housing complaints

51 Schemes for investigation of complaints.

(1) The provisions of Schedule 2 have effect for the purpose of enabling tenants and other individuals to

have complaints against social landlords investigated by a housing ombudsman in accordance with a scheme approved by the Secretary of State.

(2) For the purposes of that Schedule a "social landlord" means—

(a) a registered social landlord [or a body which was at any time a registered social landlord][169];

(b) a transferee of housing pursuant to a qualifying disposal under section 135 of the Leasehold Reform, Housing and Urban Development Act 1993;

(c) a body which has acquired dwellings under Part IV of the Housing Act 1988 (change of landlord: secure tenants); or

(d) any other body which was at any time registered with the [Housing Corporation, or with Housing for Wales,][170] and which owns or manages publicly-funded dwellings.

(3) In subsection (2)(d) a "publicly-funded dwelling" means a dwelling which was—

(a) provided by means of a grant under—

section 18 of this Act (social housing grant), or

section 50 of the Housing Act 1988, section 41 of the Housing Associations Act 1985, or section 29 or 29A of the Housing Act 1974 (housing association grant); or

(b) acquired on a disposal by a public sector landlord.

(4) The Secretary of State may by order add to or amend the descriptions of landlords who are to be treated as social landlords for the purposes of Schedule 2.

(5) Before making any such order the Secretary of State shall consult such persons as he considers appropriate.

(6) Any such order shall be made by statutory instrument which shall be subject to annulment in pursuance of a resolution of either House of Parliament.

Orders and determinations

52 General provisions as to orders.

(1) The following provisions apply to any power of the Secretary of State under [section 2, 17, 39, 51 or 55 or Schedule 2][171] to make an order.

(2) An order may make different provision for different cases or descriptions of case.

This includes power to make different provision for different bodies or descriptions of body, different provision for different housing activities and different provision for different areas.

(3) An order may contain such supplementary, incidental, consequential or transitional provisions and savings as the Secretary of State considers appropriate.

53 General provisions as to determinations.

(1) The following provisions apply to determinations of the [Housing Corporation][172] or the Secretary of State under this Part.

(2) A determination may make different provision for different cases or descriptions of case.

This includes power to make—

(a) different provision for different registered social landlords or descriptions of registered social landlord, and

(b) different provision for different housing activities and different provision for different areas;

and for the purposes of paragraph (b) descriptions may be framed by reference to any matters whatever, including in particular, in the case of housing activities, the manner in which they are financed.

(3) In this Part a general determination means a determination which does not relate solely to a particular case.

(4) Before making a general determination, the [Housing Corporation][173] or the Secretary of State shall consult such bodies appearing to them to be representative of registered social landlords as they consider appropriate.

(5) After making a general determination, the [Housing Corporation][174] or the Secretary of State shall publish the determination in such manner as they consider appropriate for bringing the determination to the notice of the landlords concerned.

54 Determinations of the [Housing Corporation] requiring approval.

The [Housing Corporation][175] shall not make—

(a) a general determination under paragraph 16 of Schedule 1 (accounting and audit requirements for

registered social landlords) or section 18 (social housing grant), or

(b) any determination under section 27 (recovery, &c. of social housing grants),

except with the approval of the Secretary of State.

Minor and consequential amendments

55 Minor and consequential amendments: Part I.

(1) The enactments mentioned in Schedule 3 have effect with the minor amendments specified there.

(2) The Secretary of State may by order make such amendments or repeals of any enactment as appear to him necessary or expedient in consequence of the provisions of this Part.

(3) Any such order shall be made by statutory instrument which shall be subject to annulment in pursuance of a resolution of either House of Parliament.

Interpretation

56 Meaning of "the [Relevant Authority][176]".

(1) In this Part "theRelevant Authority" means the Housing Corporation or [the Secretary of State][177], as follows.

(2) In relation to a registered social landlord, or a body applying for such registration, which is—

(a) a registered charity which has its address for the purposes of registration by the Charity Commissioners in Wales,

(b) an industrial and provident society which has its registered office for the purposes of the Industrial and Provident Societies Act 1965 in Wales, or

(c) a company registered under the Companies Act 1985 which has its registered office for the purposes of that Act in Wales,

"the Relevant Authority" means [the Secretary of State][178].

(3) In relation to any other registered social landlord or body applying for such registration, "the Relevant Authority" means the Housing Corporation.

(4) Nothing in this Part shall be construed as requiring the Housing Corporation and [the Secretary of State][179] to establish the same criteria for registration as a social landlord, or otherwise to act on the same principles in respect of any matter in relation to which they have functions under this Part.

57 Definitions relating to industrial and provident societies.

(1) In this Part, in relation to an industrial and provident society—

. . .[180]

"committee" means the committee of management or other directing body of the society; and

"co-opted member", in relation to the committee, includes any person co-opted to serve on the committee, whether he is a member of the society or not.

(2) Any reference in this Part to a member of the committee of an industrial and provident society includes a co-opted member.

58 Definitions relating to charities.

(1) In this Part—

(a) "charity" and "trusts", in relation to a charity, have the same meaning as in the Charities Act 1993, and "trustee" means a charitable trustee within the meaning of that Act; and

(b) "registered charity" means a charity which is registered under section 3 of that Act and is not an exempt charity within the meaning of that Act.

(2) References in this Part to a company registered under the Companies Act 1985 do not include a company which is a registered charity, except where otherwise provided.

59 Meaning of "officer" of registered social landlord.

(1) References in this Part to an officer of a registered social landlord are—

(a) in the case of a registered charity which is not a company registered under the Companies Act 1985, to any trustee, secretary or treasurer of the charity;

(b) in the case of an industrial and provident society, to any officer of the society as defined in section 74 of the Industrial and Provident Societies Act 1965; and

(c) in the case of a company registered under the Companies Act 1985 (including such a company which is also a registered charity), to any director or other officer of the company within the meaning of that Act.

(2) Any such reference includes, in the case of an industrial and provident society, a co-opted member of the committee of the society.

60 Meaning of "subsidiary".

(1) In this Part "subsidiary", in relation to a registered social landlord, means a company with respect to which one of the following conditions is fulfilled—

(a) the landlord is a member of the company and controls the composition of the board of directors;

(b) the landlord holds more than half in nominal value of the company's equity share capital; or

(c) the company is a subsidiary, within the meaning of the Companies Act 1985 or the Friendly and Industrial and Provident Societies Act 1968, of another company which, by virtue of paragraph (a) or paragraph (b), is itself a subsidiary of the landlord.

(2) For the purposes of subsection (1)(a), the composition of a company's board of directors shall be deemed to be controlled by a registered social landlord if, but only if, the landlord, by the exercise of some power exercisable by him without the consent or concurrence of any other person, can appoint or remove the holders of all or a majority of the directorships.

(3) In relation to a company which is an industrial and provident society—

(a) any reference in this section to the board of directors is a reference to the committee of management of the society; and

(b) the reference in subsection (2) to the holders of all or a majority of the directorships is a reference—

(i) to all or a majority of the members of the committee, or

(ii) if the landlord is himself a member of the committee, such number as together with him would constitute a majority.

(4) In the case of a registered social landlord which is a body of trustees, references in this section to the landlord are to the trustees acting as such.

61 Meaning of "associate".

(1) In this Part "associate", in relation to a registered social landlord, means—

(a) any body of which the landlord is a subsidiary, and

(b) any other subsidiary of such a body.

(2) In this section "subsidiary" has the same meaning as in the Companies Act 1985 or the Friendly and Industrial and Provident Societies Act 1968 or, in the case of a body which is itself a registered social landlord, has the meaning given by section 60.

62 Members of a person's family: Part I.

(1) A person is a member of another's family within the meaning of this Part if—

(a) he is the spouse of that person, or he and that person live together as husband and wife, or

(b) he is that person's parent, grandparent, child, grandchild, brother, sister, uncle, aunt, nephew or niece.

(2) For the purpose of subsection (1)(b)—

(a) a relationship by marriage shall be treated as a relationship by blood,

(b) a relationship of the half-blood shall be treated as a relationship of the whole blood, and

(c) the stepchild of a person shall be treated as his child.

63 Minor definitions: Part I.

(1) In this Part—

"dwelling" means a building or part of a building occupied or intended to be occupied as a separate dwelling, together with any yard, garden, outhouses and appurtenances belonging to it or usually enjoyed with it;

"fully mutual", in relation to a housing association, and "co-operative housing association" have the same meaning as in the Housing Associations Act 1985 (see section 1(2) of that Act);

"hostel" means a building in which is provided for persons generally or for a class or classes of persons—

(a) residential accommodation otherwise than in separate and self-contained premises, and

(b) either board or facilities for the preparation of food adequate to the needs of those persons, or both;

"house" includes—

(a) any part of a building occupied or intended to be occupied as a separate dwelling, and

(b) any yard, garden, outhouses and appurtenances belonging to it or usually enjoyed with it;

"housing accommodation" includes flats, lodging-houses and hostels;

"housing activities" means, in relation to a registered social landlord, all its activities in pursuance of the purposes, objects and powers mentioned in or specified under section 2;

"information" includes accounts, estimates and returns;

"local authority" has the same meaning as in the Housing Associations Act 1985;

"long tenancy" has the same meaning as in Part V of the Housing Act 1985;

"modifications" includes additions, alterations and omissions and cognate expressions shall be construed accordingly;

"notice" means notice in writing;

"public sector landlord" means any of the authorities or bodies within section 80(1) of the Housing Act 1985 (the landlord condition for secure tenancies);

"registrar of companies" has the same meaning as in the Companies Act 1985;

"statutory tenancy" has the same meaning as in the Housing Act 1985.

(2) References in this Part to the provision of a dwelling or house include the provision of a dwelling or house—

(a) by erecting the dwelling or house, or converting a building into dwellings or a house, or

(b) by altering, enlarging, repairing or improving an existing dwelling or house;

and references to a dwelling or house provided by means of a grant or other financial assistance are to its being so provided directly or indirectly.

64 Index of defined expressions: Part I.

The following Table shows provisions defining or otherwise explaining expressions used in this Part (other than provisions defining or explaining an expression used in the same section)—

appointed person (in relation to inquiry into affairs of registered social landlord)	paragraph 20 of Schedule 1
. . .	. . .[181]
associate (in relation to a registered social landlord)	section 61(1)
assured tenancy	section 230
assured agricultural occupancy	section 230
assured shorthold tenancy	section 230
charity	section 58(1)(a)
committee member (in relation to an industrial and provident society)	section 57(2)
company registered under the Companies Act 1985	section 58(2)
co-operative housing association	section 63
co-opted member (of committee of industrial and provident society)	section 57(1)
. . .	. . .[182]
disposal proceeds fund	section 24
dwelling	section 63
enactment	section 230
fully mutual housing association	section 63
hostel	section 63
house	section 63
housing accommodation	section 63
housing activities	section 63
housing association	section 230
industrial and provident society	section 2(1)(b)
information	section 63
lease	section 229
local authority	section 63
long tenancy	section 63
member of family	section 62
modifications	section 63
notice	section 63

officer of registered social landlord	section 59
provision (in relation to dwelling or house)	section 63(2)
public sector landlord	section 63
register, registered and registration (in relation to social landlords)	section 1
registered charity	section 58(1)(b)
registrar of companies	section 63
[the Relevant Authority	section 56][183]
relevant disposal which is not an exempted disposal (in sections 11 to 14)	section 15
secure tenancy	section 230
social housing grant	section 18(1)
statutory tenancy	section 63
subsidiary (in relation to a registered social landlord)	section 60(1)
trustee and trusts (in relation to a charity)	section 58(1)(a)

...

232 Commencement.

(1) The following provisions of this Act come into force on Royal Assent—

section 110 (new leases: valuation principles),

section 120 (payment of housing benefit to third parties), and

sections 223 to 226 and 228 to 233 (general provisions).

(2) The following provisions of this Act come into force at the end of the period of two months beginning with the date on which this Act is passed—

sections 81 and 82 (restriction on termination of tenancy for failure to pay service charge),

section 85 (appointment of manager by the court),

section 94 (provision of general legal advice about residential tenancies),

section 95 (jurisdiction of county courts),

section 221 (exercise of compulsory purchase powers in relation to Crown land),

paragraph 24 (powers of local housing authorities to acquire land for housing purposes), paragraph 26 (preserved right to buy) and paragraphs 27 to 29 of Schedule 18 (local authority assistance in connection with mortgages), and

sections 222 and 227, and Schedule 19 (consequential repeals), in so far as they relate to those paragraphs.

(3) The other provisions of this Act come into force on a day appointed by order of the Secretary of State, and different days may be appointed for different areas and different purposes.

(4) An order under subsection (3) shall be made by statutory instrument and may contain such transitional provisions and savings as appear to the Secretary of State to be appropriate.

233 Short title.

This Act may be cited as the Housing Act 1996.

Section 7.

SCHEDULE 1 REGISTERED SOCIAL LANDLORDS: REGULATION

Part I Control of payments to members, &c

Payments by way of gift, dividend or bonus

1(1) A registered social landlord shall not make a gift or pay a sum by way of dividend or bonus to—

(a) a person who is or has been a member of the body,

(b) a person who is a member of the family of a person within paragraph (a), or

(c) a company of which a person within paragraph (a) or (b) is a director,

except as permitted by this paragraph.

(2) The following are permitted—

(a) the payment of a sum which, in accordance with the constitution or rules of the body, is paid as interest on capital lent to the body or subscribed by way of shares in the body;

(b) the payment by a fully mutual housing association to a person who has ceased to be a member of the association of a sum which is due to him either under his tenancy agreement with the association or under the terms of the agreement under which he became a member of the association.

(3) Where an industrial and provident society or a company registered under the Companies Act 1985 pays a sum or makes a gift in contravention of this paragraph, the society or company may recover the sum or the value of the gift, and proceedings for its recovery shall be taken if the [Relevant Authority][184] so directs.

Payments and benefits to officers and employees, &c.

2(1) A registered social landlord which is an industrial and provident society or a company registered under the Companies Act 1985 shall not make a payment or grant a benefit to—

(a) an officer or employee of the society or company,

(b) a person who at any time within the preceding twelve months has been a person within paragraph (a),

(c) a close relative of a person within paragraph (a) or (b), or

(d) a business trading for profit of which a person falling within paragraph (a), (b) or (c) is a principal proprietor or in the management of which such a person is directly concerned,

except as permitted by this paragraph.

(2) The following are permitted—

(a) payments made or benefits granted to an officer or employee of the society or company under his contract of employment with the society or company;

(b) the payment of remuneration or expenses to an officer of the society or company who does not have a contract of employment with the society or company;

(c) any such payment as may be made in accordance with paragraph 1(2) (interest payable in accordance with the rules and certain sums payable by a fully mutual housing association to a person who has ceased to be a member);

(d) the grant or renewal of a tenancy by a co-operative housing association;

(e) where a tenancy of a house has been granted to, or to a close relative of, a person who later became an officer or employee, the grant to that tenant of a new tenancy whether of the same or another house;

(f) payments made or benefits granted in accordance with any determination made by the [Relevant Authority][185].

(3) A determination for the purposes of sub-paragraph (2)(f) may specify the class or classes of case in which a payment may be made or benefit granted and specify the maximum amount.

(4) Where a society or company pays a sum or grants a benefit in contravention of this paragraph, the society or company may recover the sum or value of the benefit; and proceedings for its recovery shall be taken if the [Relevant Authority][186] so directs.

Maximum amounts payable by way of fees, expenses, &c.

3(1) The [Relevant Authority][187] may from time to time specify the maximum amounts which may be paid by a registered social landlord which is an industrial and provident society or a company registered under the Companies Act 1985—

(a) by way of fees or other remuneration, or by way of expenses, to a member of the society or company who is not an officer or employee of the society or company, or

(b) by way of remuneration or expenses to an officer of the society or company who does not have a contract of employment with the society or company.

(2) Different amounts may be so specified for different purposes.

(3) Where a society or company makes a payment in excess of the maximum permitted under this paragraph, the society or company may recover the excess, and proceedings for its recovery shall be taken if the [Relevant Authority][188] so directs.

Part II Constitution, change of rules, amalgamation and dissolution

General power to remove director, trustee, &c.

4(1) The [Relevant Authority][189] may, in accordance with the following provisions, by order remove—

(a) a director or trustee of a registered social landlord which is a registered charity,

(b) a committee member of a registered social landlord which is an industrial and provident society, or

(c) a director of a registered social landlord which is a company registered under the Companies Act 1985.

(2) The [Relevant Authority][190] may make an order removing any such person if—

(a) he has been adjudged bankrupt or has made an arrangement with his creditors;

(b) he is subject to a disqualification order [or disqualification undertaking][191] under the Company Directors Disqualification Act 1986 [or to a disqualification order under Part II of the companies (Northern Ireland) order 1989][192];

(c) he is subject to an order under section 429(2) of the Insolvency Act 1986 (failure to pay under county court administration order);

(d) he is disqualified under section 72 of the Charities Act 1993 from being a charity trustee;

(e) he is incapable of acting by reason of mental disorder;

(f) he has not acted; or

(g) he cannot be found or does not act and his absence or failure to act is impeding the proper management of the registered social landlord's affairs.

(3) Before making an order the [Relevant Authority][193] shall give at least 14 days' notice of its intention to do so to the person whom it intends to remove, and to the registered social landlord.

(4) That notice may be given by post, and if so given to the person whom the [Relevant Authority][194] intend to remove may be addressed to his last known address in the United Kingdom.

(5) A person who is ordered to be removed under this paragraph may appeal against the order to the High Court.

Restriction on power of removal in case of registered charity

5(1) The [Relevant Authority][195] may make an order under paragraph 4 removing a director or trustee of a registered charity only if the charity has, at any time before the power is exercised—

(a) received financial assistance under section 24 of the Local Government Act 1988 (assistance for privately let housing accommodation),

(b) had property transferred to it on a qualifying disposal under section 135 of the Leasehold Reform, Housing and Urban Development Act 1993, or

(c) received a grant or loan under any of the following provisions.

(2) The provisions are—

section 18 of this Act (social housing grants),

section 22 of this Act or section 58 of the Housing Associations Act 1985 (grants or loans by local authorities),

section 50 of the Housing Act 1988, section 41 of the Housing Associations Act 1985 or any enactment replaced by that section (housing association grant),

section 51 of the Housing Act 1988 or section 54 or 55 of the Housing Associations Act 1985 (revenue deficit grant or hostel deficit grant),

section 79 of the Housing Associations Act 1985 (loans by Housing Corporation),

section 31 of the Housing Act 1974 (management grants), or

any enactment mentioned in paragraph 2 or 3 of Schedule 1 to the Housing Associations Act 1985 (pre-1974 grants and certain loans).

Registered charity: power to appoint new director or trustee

6(1) The [Relevant Authority][196] may by order appoint a person to be a director or trustee of a registered social landlord which is a registered charity—

(a) in place of a person removed by the [Relevant Authority][197],

(b) where there are no directors or no trustees, or

(c) where the [Relevant Authority][198] is of the opinion that it is necessary for the proper management of the charity's affairs to have an additional director or trustee.

The power conferred by paragraph (c) may be exercised notwithstanding that it will cause the maximum number of directors or trustees permissible under the charity's constitution to be exceeded.

(2) The [Relevant Authority][199] shall only exercise its power under sub-paragraph (1) if—

(a) the charity has, at any time before the power is exercised, received financial assistance, had property transferred to it, or received a grant or loan as mentioned in paragraph 5, and

(b) the [Relevant Authority][200] has consulted the Charity Commissioners.

(3) A person may be so appointed notwithstanding any restrictions on appointment in the charity's constitution or rules.

(4) A person appointed under this paragraph shall hold office for such period and on such terms as the [Relevant Authority][201] may specify; and on the expiry of the appointment the [Relevant Authority][202] may renew the appointment for such period as it may specify.

This does not prevent a person appointed under this paragraph from retiring in accordance with the charity's constitution or rules.

(5) A person appointed under this paragraph as director or trustee of a registered charity is entitled—

(a) to attend, speak and vote at any general meeting of the charity and to receive all notices of and other communications relating to any such meeting which a member is entitled to receive,

(b) to move a resolution at any general meeting of the charity, and

(c) to require a general meeting of the charity to be convened within 21 days of a request to that effect made in writing to the directors or trustees.

Company: power to appoint new director

7(1) The [Relevant Authority][203] may by order appoint a person to be a director of a registered social landlord which is a company registered under the Companies Act 1985—

(a) in place of a director removed by the [Relevant Authority][204],

(b) where there are no directors, or

(c) where the [Relevant Authority][205] is of the opinion that it is necessary for the proper management of the company's affairs to have an additional director.

(2) A person may be so appointed whether or not he is a member of the company and notwithstanding anything in the company's articles of association.

(3) Where a person is appointed under this paragraph—

(a) he shall hold office for such period and on such terms as the [Relevant Authority][206] may specify, and

(b) on the expiry of the appointment the [Relevant Authority][207] may renew the appointment for such period as it may specify.

This does not prevent a person from retiring in accordance with the company's articles of association.

(4) A person appointed under this paragraph is entitled—

(a) to attend, speak and vote at any general meeting of the company and to receive all notices of and other communications relating to any general meeting which a member of the company is entitled to receive,

(b) to move a resolution at any general meeting of the company, and

(c) to require an extraordinary general meeting of the company to be convened within 21 days of a request to that effect made in writing to the directors of the company.

Industrial and provident society: power to appoint new committee member

8(1) The [Relevant Authority][208] may by order appoint a person to be a committee member of a registered social landlord which is an industrial and provident society—

(a) in place of a person removed by the [Relevant Authority][209],

(b) where there are no members of the committee, or

(c) where the [Relevant Authority][210] is of the opinion that it is necessary for the proper management of the society's affairs to have an additional committee member.

The power conferred by paragraph (c) may be exercised notwithstanding that it will cause the maximum number of committee members permissible under the society's constitution to be exceeded.

(2) A person may be so appointed whether or not he is a member of the society and, if he is not, notwithstanding that the rules of the society restrict appointment to members.

(3) A person appointed under this paragraph shall hold office for such period and on such terms as the [Relevant Authority][211] may specify; and on the expiry of the appointment the [Relevant Authority][212] may renew the appointment for such period as it may specify.

This does not prevent a person appointed under this paragraph from retiring in accordance with the rules of the society.

(4) A person appointed under this paragraph is entitled—

(a) to attend, speak and vote at any general meeting of the society and to receive all notices of and other communications relating to any general meeting which a member of the society is entitled

to receive,

(b) to move a resolution at any general meeting of the society, and

(c) to require a general meeting of the society to be convened within 21 days of a request to that effect made in writing to the committee of the society.

Change of rules, &c. by industrial and provident society

9(1) This paragraph applies to an industrial and provident society whose registration as a social landlord has been recorded by the [Financial Services Authority][213].

(2) Notice shall be sent to the [Relevant Authority][214] of any change of the society's name or of the situation of its registered office.

(3)..............................[215]

[(3A) Consent under sub-paragraph (3)—

(a) if given by the Housing Corporation, shall be given by order under its seal, and

(b) if given by the Secretary of State, shall be given by order in writing.][216]

(4) A copy of that consent shall be sent with the copies of the amendment required by section 10(1) of the Industrial and Provident Societies Act 1965 to be sent to the [Financial Services Authority][217].

(5) The Industrial and Provident Societies Act 1965 applies in relation to the provisions of this paragraph as if they were contained in section 10 of that Act (amendment of registered rules).

Change of objects by certain charities

10(1) This paragraph applies to a registered social landlord—

(a) which is a registered charity and is not a company incorporated under the Companies Act 1985, and

(b) whose registration under this Part of this Act has been recorded by the Charity Commissioners in accordance with section 3(3).

(2) No power contained in the provisions establishing the registered social landlord as a charity, or regulating its purposes or administration, to vary or add to its objects may be exercised without the consent of the Charity Commissioners.

Before giving their consent the Charity Commissioners shall consult the [Relevant Authority][218].

Change of memorandum or articles of association of company

11(1) This paragraph applies to a company registered under the Companies Act 1985 (including such a company which is also a registered charity) whose registration as a social landlord has been recorded by the registrar of companies.

(2) Notice shall be sent to the [Relevant Authority][219] of any change of the company's name or of the address of its registered office.

(3)..............................[220]

[(3A) Consent under sub-paragraph (3)—

(a) if given by the Housing Corporation, shall be given by order under its seal, and

(b) if given by the Secretary of State, shall be given by order in writing.][221]

(4) a copy of that consent shall be sent with any copy of the alterations required to be sent to the registrar of companies under the Companies Act 1985.

Amalgamation and dissolution &c. of industrial and provident society

12(1) This paragraph applies to an industrial and provident society whose registration as a social landlord has been recorded by the [Financial Services Authority][222].

(2) The [Financial Services Authority][223] shall not register a special resolution which is passed for the purposes of—

(a) section 50 of the Industrial and Provident Societies Act 1965 (amalgamation of societies),

(b) section 51 of that Act (transfer of engagements between societies), or

(c) section 52 of that Act (power of a society to convert itself into, amalgamate with or transfer its engagements to a company registered under the Companies Act 1985),

unless, together with the copy of the resolution, there is sent to [it][224] a copy of the [Relevant Authority's][225] consent to the amalgamation, transfer or conversion.

(3) Any new body created by the amalgamation or conversion or, in the case of a transfer of engagements, the transferee, shall be deemed to be registered as a social landlord forthwith upon the amalgamation, conversion or transfer taking effect.

(4) If the society resolves by special resolution that it be wound up voluntarily under the Insolvency Act 1986, the resolution has no effect unless—

(a) before the resolution was passed the [Relevant Authority][226] gave its consent to its passing, and

(b) a copy of the consent is forwarded to the [Financial Services Authority][227] together with a copy of the resolution required to be so forwarded in accordance with the Companies Act 1985.

(5) If the society is to be dissolved by instrument of dissolution, the [Financial Services Authority][228] shall not—

(a) register the instrument in accordance with section 58(5) of the Industrial and Provident Societies Act 1965, or

(b) cause notice of the dissolution to be advertised in accordance with section 58(6) of that Act,

unless together with the instrument there is sent to [it][229] a copy of the [Relevant Authority's][230] consent to its making.

(6) The references in this paragraph to the [Relevant Authority's][231] consent [are—

(a) if it is given by the Housing Corporation, to consent given by order under its seal, and

(b) if it is given by the Secretary of State, to consent given by order in writing.][232]

Arrangement, reconstruction, &c. of company

13(1) This paragraph applies to a company registered under the Companies Act 1985 whose registration as a social landlord has been recorded by the registrar of companies.

(2) An order of the court given for the purposes of section 425 of the Companies Act 1985 (compromise or arrangement with creditors or members) is not effective unless the [Relevant Authority][233] has given its consent.

A copy of the consent shall be sent to the registrar of companies along with the office copy of the order delivered to him under that section.

(3) An order of the court given for the purposes of section 427 of the Companies Act 1985 (transfer of undertaking or property for purposes of reconstruction or amalgamation) is not effective unless the [Relevant Authority][234] has given its consent.

A copy of the consent shall be sent to the registrar of companies along with the office copy of the order delivered to him under that section.

(4) The registrar of companies shall not register any resolution under section 53 of the Industrial and Provident Societies Act 1965 (conversion of company into industrial and provident society), unless, together with the copy of the resolution, there is sent to him a copy of the [Relevant Authority's][235] consent to the conversion.

(5) Where a director, administrator or liquidator of the company proposes to make a voluntary arrangement with the company's creditors under section 1 of the Insolvency Act 1986, the arrangement shall not take effect under section 5 (effect of approval by members and creditors) of that Act unless the [Relevant Authority][236] has given its consent to the voluntary arrangement.

(6) If the company resolves by special resolution that it be wound up voluntarily under the Insolvency Act 1986, the resolution has no effect unless—

(a) before the resolution was passed the [Relevant Authority][237] gave its consent to its passing, and

(b) a copy of the consent is forwarded to the registrar of companies together with a copy of the resolution required to be so forwarded in accordance with section 380 of the Companies Act 1985.

(7) The references in this paragraph to the [Relevant Authority's][238] consent [are—

(a) if it is given by the Housing Corporation, to consent given by order under its seal, and

(b) if it is given by the Secretary of State, to consent given by order in writing.][239]

(8) Where sub-paragraph (3) or (4) applies, the transferee or, as the case may be, any new body created by the conversion shall be deemed to be registered as a social landlord forthwith upon the transfer or conversion taking effect.

[Relevant Authority's][240] power to petition for winding up

14(1) The [Relevant Authority][241] may present a petition for the winding up under the Insolvency Act 1986 of a registered social landlord which is—

(a) a company incorporated under the Companies Act 1985 (including such a company which is also a registered charity), or

(b) an industrial and provident society (to which the winding up provisions of the Insolvency Act

1986 apply in accordance with section 55(a) of the Industrial and Provident Societies Act 1965), on either of the following grounds.

(2) The grounds are—

(a) that the landlord is failing properly to carry out its purposes or objects, or

(b) that the landlord is unable to pay its debts within the meaning of section 123 of the Insolvency Act 1986.

Transfer of net assets on dissolution or winding up

15(1) This paragraph applies—

(a) where a registered social landlord which is an industrial and provident society is dissolved as mentioned in section 55(a) or (b) of the Industrial and Provident Societies Act 1965 (winding-up under the Insolvency Act 1986 or by instrument of dissolution), and

(b) where a registered social landlord which is a company registered under the Companies Act 1985 is wound up under the Insolvency Act 1986.

(2) On such a dissolution or winding-up, so much of the property of the society or company as remains after meeting the claims of its creditors and any other liabilities arising on or before the dissolution or winding-up shall be transferred to the [Relevant Authority][242] or, if the [Relevant Authority][243] so directs, to a specified registered social landlord.

The above provision has effect notwithstanding anything in the Industrial and Provident Societies Act 1965, the Companies Act 1985 or the Insolvency Act 1986, or in the rules of the society or, as the case may be, in the memorandum or articles of association of the company.

(3) In order to avoid the necessity for the sale of land belonging to the registered social landlord and thereby secure the transfer of the land under this paragraph, the [Relevant Authority][244] may, if it appears to it appropriate to do so, make payments to discharge such claims or liabilities as are referred to in sub-paragraph (2).

(4) Where the registered social landlord which is dissolved or wound up is a charity, the [Relevant Authority][245] may dispose of property transferred to it by virtue of this paragraph only to another registered social landlord—

(a) which is also a charity, and

(b) the objects of which appear to the [Relevant Authority][246] to be, as nearly as practicable, akin to those of the body which is dissolved or wound up.

[(5) In any other case—

(a) the Relevant Authority may dispose of property transferred to it by virtue of this paragraph to a registered social landlord, and

(b) the Housing Corporation may dispose of property transferred to it by virtue of this paragraph to any of its subsidiaries.][247]

(6) Where property transferred to the [Relevant Authority][248] by virtue of this paragraph includes land subject to an existing mortgage or charge (whether in favour of the [Relevant Authority][249] or not), the [Relevant Authority][250] may, in exercise of its powers under Part III of the Housing Associations Act 1985, dispose of the land either—

(a) subject to that mortgage or charge, or

(b) subject to a new mortgage or charge in favour of the [Relevant Authority][251] securing such amount as appears to the [Relevant Authority][252] to be appropriate in the circumstances.

Part III Accounts and audit

General requirements as to accounts and audit

16(1) The [Relevant Authority][253] may from time to time determine accounting requirements for registered social landlords with a view to ensuring that the accounts of every registered social landlord—

(a) are prepared in a proper form, and

(b) give a true and fair view of—

(i) the state of affairs of the landlord, so far as its housing activities are concerned, and

(ii) the disposition of funds and assets which are, or at any time have been, in its hands in connection with those activities.

(2) The [Relevant Authority][254] by a determination under sub-paragraph (1) may lay down a method by which a registered charity is to distinguish in its accounts between its housing activities and other

activities.

(3) The accounts of every registered social landlord shall comply with the requirements laid down under this paragraph.

(4) The auditor's report shall state, in addition to any other matters which it is required to state, whether in the auditor's opinion the accounts do so comply.

(5) Every registered social landlord shall furnish to the [Relevant Authority][255] a copy of its accounts and auditor's report within six months of the end of the period to which they relate.

Appointment of auditors by industrial and provident societies

17 Section 4 of the Friendly and Industrial and Provident Societies Act 1968 (obligation to appoint qualified auditors to audit accounts and balance sheet for each year of account) applies to every industrial and provident society which is a registered social landlord, without regard to the volume of its receipts and payments, the number of its members or the value of its assets.

Accounting and audit requirements for charities

18(1) A registered social landlord which is a registered charity shall, in respect of its housing activities (and separately from its other activities, if any), be subject to the following provisions (which impose accounting and audit requirements corresponding to those imposed by the Friendly and Industrial and Provident Societies Act 1968).

This does not affect any obligation of the charity under sections 41 to 45 of the Charities Act 1993 (charity accounts).

(2) The charity shall in respect of its housing activities—

(a) cause to be kept properly books of account showing its transactions and its assets and liabilities, and

(b) establish and maintain a satisfactory system of control of its books of accounts, its cash holdings and all its receipts and remittances.

The books of account must be such as to enable a true and fair view to be given of the state of affairs of the charity in respect of its housing activities, and to explain its transactions in the course of those activities.

(3) The charity shall for each period of account prepare—

(a) a revenue account giving a true and fair view of the charity's income and expenditure in the period, so far as arising in connection with its housing activities, and

(b) a balance sheet giving a true and fair view as at the end of the period of the state of the charity's affairs.

The revenue account and balance sheet must be signed by at least two directors or trustees of the charity.

(4) The charity shall in each period of account appoint a qualified auditor to audit the accounts prepared in accordance with sub-paragraph (3).

A qualified auditor means a person who is eligible for appointment as auditor of the charity under Part II of the Companies Act 1989 or who would be so eligible if the charity were a company registered under the Companies Act 1985.

(5) The auditor shall make a report to the charity on the accounts audited by him, stating whether in his opinion—

(a) the revenue account gives a true and fair view of the state of income and expenditure of the charity in respect of its housing activities and of any other matters to which it relates, and

(b) the balance sheet gives a true and fair view of the state of affairs of the charity as at the end of the period of account.

(6) The auditor in preparing his report shall carry out such investigations as will enable him to form an opinion as to the following matters—

(a) whether the association has kept, in respect of its housing activities, proper books of account in accordance with the requirements of this paragraph,

(b) whether the charity has maintained a satisfactory system of control over its transactions in accordance with those requirements, and

(c) whether the accounts are in agreement with the charity's books;

and if he is of opinion that the charity has failed in any respect to comply with this paragraph, or if the accounts are not in agreement with the books, he shall state that fact in his report.

(7) The auditor—

(a) has a right of access at all times to the books, deeds and accounts of the charity, so far as relating to its housing activities, and to all other documents relating to those activities, and

(b) is entitled to require from officers of the charity such information and explanations as he thinks necessary for the performance of his duties;

and if he fails to obtain all the information and explanations which, to the best of his knowledge and belief, are necessary for the purposes of his audit, he shall state that fact in his report.

(8) A period of account for the purposes of this paragraph is twelve months or such other period not less than six months or more than 18 months as the charity may, with the consent of the [Relevant Authority][256], determine.

Responsibility for securing compliance with accounting requirements

19(1) Every responsible person, that is to say, every person who—

(a) is directly concerned with the conduct and management of the affairs of a registered social landlord, and

(b) is in that capacity responsible for the preparation and audit of accounts,

shall ensure that paragraph 16 (general requirements as to accounts and audit) and, where applicable, paragraph 18 (accounting and audit requirements for charities) are complied with by the registered social landlord.

(2) If—

(a) paragraph 16(5) (furnishing of accounts and auditor's report) is not complied with,

(b) the accounts furnished to the [Relevant Authority][257] under that provision do not comply with the accounting requirements laid down under paragraph 16(1),

(c) paragraph 18 (accounting and audit requirements for charities), where applicable, is not complied with,

(d) section 55(9) of the Housing Act 1988 (surplus rental income: power to require information) is not complied with, or

(e) any notice under section 26 (information relating to disposal proceeds fund) is not complied with,

every responsible person, and the registered social landlord itself, commits a summary offence and is liable on conviction to a fine not exceeding level 3 on the standard scale.

(3) In proceedings for an offence under this paragraph it is a defence—

(a) for a responsible person to prove that he did everything that could reasonably have been expected of him by way of discharging the relevant duty;

(b) for a registered social landlord to prove that every responsible person did everything that could reasonably have been expected of him by way of discharging the relevant duty in relation to the registered social landlord.

(4) Proceedings for an offence under this paragraph may be brought only by or with the consent of the [Relevant Authority][258] or the Director of Public Prosecutions.

Part IV Inquiry into affairs of registered social landlords

Inquiry

20(1) The [Relevant Authority][259] may direct an inquiry into the affairs of a registered social landlord if it appears to the [Relevant Authority][260] that there may have been misconduct or mismanagement.

For this purpose "misconduct" includes any failure to comply with the requirements of this Part of this Act.

(2) Any such inquiry shall be conducted by one or more persons appointed by the [Relevant Authority][261].

(3) If one person is appointed [by the Housing Corporation to conduct an inquiry][262] he must be a person who is not a member or an employee of the [Housing Corporation][263] and has not been such a member or employee within the previous five years; and if more than one person is [so][264] appointed at least one of them must be such a person.

(4) If the [Relevant Authority][265] so directs, or if during the course of the inquiry the person or persons conducting the inquiry consider it necessary, the inquiry shall extend to the affairs of any other body which at any material time is or was a subsidiary or associate of the registered social landlord.

(5) The person or persons conducting the inquiry may, if they think fit during the course of the inquiry,

make one or more interim reports on such matters as appear to them to be appropriate.

(6) On completion of the inquiry the person or persons conducting the inquiry shall make a final report on such matters as the [Relevant Authority][266] may specify.

(7) An interim or final report shall be in such form as the [Relevant Authority][267] may specify.

Power of appointed person to obtain information

21(1) A person appointed by the [Relevant Authority][268] under paragraph 20 to conduct an inquiry (or, if more than one person is so appointed, each of those persons) has, for the purposes of the inquiry, the same powers as are conferred on the [Relevant Authority][269] by section 30 (general power to obtain information).

(2) Where by virtue of a notice under that section given by an appointed person any documents are produced to any person, the person to whom they are produced may take copies of or make extracts from them.

(3) Section 31 (enforcement of notice to provide information, &c.) applies in relation to a notice given under this paragraph by an appointed person as it applies in relation to a notice given under section 30 by the [Relevant Authority][270].

Extraordinary audit for purposes of inquiry

22(1) For the purposes of an inquiry under paragraph 20 the [Relevant Authority][271] may require the accounts and balance sheet of the registered social landlord concerned, or such of them as the [Relevant Authority][272] may specify, to be audited by a qualified auditor appointed by the [Relevant Authority][273].

(2) A person is a qualified auditor for this purpose if he would be eligible for appointment as auditor of the ordinary accounts of the registered social landlord.

(3) On completion of the audit the appointed auditor shall make a report to the [Relevant Authority][274] on such matters and in such form as the [Relevant Authority][275] may specify.

(4) The expenses of the audit, including the remuneration of the auditor, shall be paid by the [Relevant Authority][276].

(5) An audit under this paragraph is additional to, and does not affect, any audit made or to be made under any other enactment.

Powers exercisable on interim basis

23(1) The [Relevant Authority][277] may make an order under this paragraph—

(a) where an inquiry has been directed under paragraph 20 and the [Relevant Authority][278] has reasonable grounds to believe—

(i) that there has been misconduct or mismanagement in the affairs of the registered social landlord, and

(ii) that immediate action is needed to protect the interests of the tenants of the registered social landlord or to protect the assets of the landlord; or

(b) where an interim report has been made under paragraph 20(5) as a result of which the [Relevant Authority][279] is satisfied that there has been misconduct or mismanagement in the affairs of a registered social landlord.

(2) The orders that may be made under this paragraph are—

(a) an order suspending any officer, employee or agent of the registered social landlord who appears to the [Relevant Authority][280] to have been responsible for or privy to the misconduct or mismanagement or by his conduct to have contributed to or facilitated it;

(b) an order directing any bank or other person who holds money or securities on behalf of the registered social landlord not to part with the money or securities without the approval of the [Relevant Authority][281];

(c) an order restricting the transactions which may be entered into, or the nature or amount of the payments which may be made, by the registered social landlord without the approval of the [Relevant Authority][282].

(3) An order under this paragraph, if not previously revoked by the [Relevant Authority][283], shall cease to have effect six months after the making of the final report under paragraph 20(6) unless the [Relevant Authority][284] renews it, which it may do for a further period of up to six months.

(4) A person suspended by an order under sub-paragraph (2)(a) may appeal against the order to the High Court.

(5) Where a person is suspended by such an order, the [Relevant Authority][285] may give directions with respect to the performance of his functions and otherwise as to matters arising from his suspension. The [Relevant Authority][286] may, in particular, appoint a named person to perform his functions.

(6) A person who contravenes an order under sub-paragraph (2)(b) commits an offence and is liable on summary conviction to a fine not exceeding level 5 on the standard scale or imprisonment for a term not exceeding three months, or both.

Proceedings for such an offence may be brought only by or with the consent of the [Relevant Authority][287] or the Director of Public Prosecutions.

Powers exercisable as a result of final report or audit

24(1) Where the [Relevant Authority][288] is satisfied, as the result of an inquiry under paragraph 20 or an audit under paragraph 22, that there has been misconduct or mismanagement in the affairs of a registered social landlord, it may make an order under this paragraph.

(2) The orders that may be made under this paragraph are—

(a) an order removing any officer, employee or agent of the registered social landlord who appears to the [Relevant Authority][289] to have been responsible for or privy to the misconduct or mismanagement or by his conduct to have contributed to or facilitated it;

(b) An order suspending any such person for up to six months, pending determination whether he should be removed;

(c) an order directing any bank or other person who holds money or securities on behalf of the registered social landlord not to part with the money or securities without the approval of the [Relevant Authority][290];

(d) an order restricting the transactions which may be entered into, or the nature or amount of the payments which may be made, by the registered social landlord without the approval of the [Relevant Authority][291].

(3) Before making an order under sub-paragraph (2)(a) the [Relevant Authority][292] shall give at least 14 days' notice of its intention to do so—

(a) to the person it intends to remove, and

(b) to the registered social landlord concerned.

Notice under this sub-paragraph may be given by post, and if so given to the person whom the [Relevant Authority][293] intends to remove may be addressed to his last known address in the United Kingdom.

(4) A person who is ordered to be removed under sub-paragraph (2)(a) or suspended under sub-paragraph (2)(b) may appeal against the order to the High Court.

(5) Where a person is suspended under sub-paragraph (2)(b), the [Relevant Authority][294] may give directions with respect to the performance of his functions and otherwise as to matters arising from the suspension.

The [Relevant Authority][295] may, in particular, appoint a named person to perform his functions.

(6) A person who contravenes an order under sub-paragraph (2)(c) commits an offence and is liable on summary conviction to a fine not exceeding level 5 on the standard scale or imprisonment for a term not exceeding three months, or both.

Proceedings for such an offence may be brought only by or with the consent of the [Relevant Authority][296] or the Director of Public Prosecutions.

Disqualification as officer of registered social landlord.

25(1) A person is disqualified from being an officer of a registered social landlord if the [Relevant Authority][297] has made an order against him under—

(a) paragraph 24(2)(a) (removal for misconduct or mismanagement), or

(b) section 30(1)(a) of the Housing Associations Act 1985 or section 20(1)(a) of the Housing Act 1974 (corresponding earlier provisions).

(2) The [Relevant Authority][298] may, on the application of any such person, waive his disqualification either generally or in relation to a particular registered social landlord or particular class of registered social landlord.

(3) Any waiver shall be notified in writing to the person concerned.

(4) For the purposes of this paragraph the [Relevant Authority][299] shall keep, in such manner as it thinks fit, a register of all persons who have been removed from office by the [Relevant Authority] under

the provisions mentioned in sub-paragraph (1).

(5) The register shall be available for public inspection at all reasonable times.

Persons acting as officer while disqualified.

26(1) A person who acts as an officer of a registered social landlord while he is disqualified under paragraph 25(1) commits an offence.

A person guilty of such an offence is liable—

(a) on summary conviction, to imprisonment for a term not exceeding six months or to a fine not exceeding the statutory maximum, or both;

(b) on conviction on indictment, to imprisonment for a term not exceeding two years or to a fine, or both.

(2) Proceedings for an offence under sub-paragraph (1) may be brought only by or with the consent of the [Relevant Authority][300] or the Director of Public Prosecutions.

(3) Acts done as an officer of a registered social landlord by a person who is disqualified under paragraph 25(1) are not invalid by reason only of that disqualification.

(4) Where the [Relevant Authority][301] is satisfied—

(a) that a person has acted as an officer of a registered social landlord while disqualified under paragraph 25(1), and

(b) that while so acting he has received from the registered social landlord any payments or benefits in connection with his so acting,

it may by order direct him to repay to the registered social landlord the whole or part of any such sums or, as the case may be, to pay to it the whole or part of the monetary value (as determined by it) of any such benefit.

Power to direct transfer of land

27(1) Where as a result of an inquiry under paragraph 20 or an audit under paragraph 22 the [Relevant Authority][302] is satisfied as regards a registered social landlord—

(a) that there has been misconduct or mismanagement in its administration, or

(b) that the management of its land would be improved if its land were transferred in accordance with the provisions of this paragraph,

the [Relevant Authority][303] may,. . .[304] direct the registered social landlord to make such a transfer. [The consent of the Secretary of State is required for the giving of directions by the Housing Corporation.][305]

(2) Where the registered social landlord concerned is a charity, the [Relevant Authority][306] may only direct a transfer to be made to another registered social landlord—

(a) which is also a charity, and

(b) the objects of which appear to the [Relevant Authority][307] to be, as nearly as practicable, akin to those of the registered social landlord concerned.

(3) In any other case the [Relevant Authority][308] may direct a transfer to be made to the [Relevant Authority][309] or to another registered social landlord.

(4) The transfer shall be on such terms as the [Relevant Authority][310] may direct on the basis of principles determined by it.

[If the transfer is directed by the Housing Corporation, the consent][311] of the Secretary of State is required both for the terms of the transfer and for the determination of the principles on which it is based.

(5) The price shall not be less than the amount certified by the district valuer to be the amount the property would command if sold by a willing seller to another registered social landlord.

(6) The terms shall include provision as to the payment of debts and liabilities (including debts and liabilities secured on the land).

Availability of powers in relation to registered charities.

28(1) The [Relevant Authority][312] may exercise its powers under paragraphs 20 to 26 in relation to a registered charity only if the charity has, at any time before the powers are exercised—

(a) received financial assistance under section 24 of the Local Government Act 1988 (assistance for privately let housing accommodation),

(b) had property transferred to it on a qualifying disposal under section 135 of the Leasehold Reform, Housing and Urban Development Act 1993, or

(c) received a grant or loan under any of the following provisions.

(2) The provisions are—

section 18 of this Act (social housing grant),

section 22 of this Act or section 58 of the Housing Associations Act 1985 (grants or loans by local authorities),

section 50 of the Housing Act 1988, section 41 of the Housing Associations Act 1985 or any enactment replaced by that section (housing association grant),

section 51 of the Housing Act 1988 or section 54 or 55 of the Housing Associations Act 1985 (revenue deficit grant or hostel deficit grant),

section 79 of the Housing Associations Act 1985 (loans by [Relevant Authority][313]),

section 31 of the Housing Act 1974 (management grants), or

any enactment mentioned in paragraph 2 or 3 of Schedule 1 to the Housing Associations Act 1985 (pre-1974 grants and certain loans).

(3) In relation to a registered charity paragraphs 20 to 26 have effect with the following adaptations—

(a) references to its affairs are confined to its housing activities and such other activities (if any) as are incidental to or connected with its housing activities;

(b) references to its accounts do not include revenue accounts which do not relate to its housing activities, except so far as such accounts are necessary for the auditing of revenue accounts which do so relate or of the balance sheet;

(c) a person is a qualified auditor for the purpose of paragraph 22 (extraordinary audit) only if he is an auditor qualified for the purposes of paragraph 18 (accounting and audit requirements for charities).

(4) The [Relevant Authority][314] shall notify the Charity Commissioners upon the exercise in relation to a registered charity of its powers under—

(a) paragraph 20(1) (inquiry into affairs of registered social landlord),

(b) paragraph 23(2)(a) (interim suspension of person in connection with misconduct or mismanagement), or

(c) paragraph 24(2)(a) or (b) (removal of person in connection with misconduct or mismanagement or suspension with a view to removal).

29 The [Relevant Authority][315] may not exercise its powers under paragraph 27 in relation to a registered charity.

Section 51.

SCHEDULE 2 SOCIAL RENTED SECTOR: HOUSING COMPLAINTS

Social landlords required to be member of approved scheme

1(1) A social landlord must be a member of an approved scheme covering, or more than one approved scheme which together cover, all his housing activities.

(2) If a social landlord fails to comply with the duty imposed by this paragraph, the Secretary of State may apply to the High Court for an order directing him to comply within a specified period and the High Court may, if it thinks fit, make such an order.

(3) Nothing in this Schedule shall be construed as restricting membership of an approved scheme to social landlords.

Matters for which scheme must provide

2(1) A scheme shall not be approved for the purposes of this Schedule unless it makes provision for—

1.The establishment or appointment of an independent person to administer the scheme.

2.The criteria for membership for—

(a) social landlords under a duty to be members of an approved scheme, and

(b) other persons.

3.The manner of becoming or ceasing to be a member.

4.The matters about which complaints may be made under the scheme.

5.The grounds on which a matter may be excluded from investigation, including that the matter is the subject of court proceedings or was the subject of court proceedings where judgment on the merits was given.

6.The descriptions of individual who may make a complaint under the scheme.

7.The appointment of an independent individual to be the housing ombudsman under the scheme.

8.The appointment of staff to administer the scheme and to assist the housing ombudsman and the terms upon which they are appointed.

9.A duty of the housing ombudsman to investigate any complaint duly made and not withdrawn, and a power to investigate any complaint duly made but withdrawn, and where he investigates to make a determination.

10.A power of the housing ombudsman to propose alternative methods of resolving a dispute.

11.The powers of the housing ombudsman for the purposes of his investigations, and the procedure to be followed in the conduct of investigations.

12.The powers of the housing ombudsman on making a determination.

13.The making and publication of annual reports by the housing ombudsman on the discharge of his functions.

14.The manner in which determinations are to be—

(a) communicated to the complainant and the person against whom the complaint was made, and

(b) published.

15.The manner in which the expenses of the scheme are to be defrayed by the members.

16.The keeping and auditing of accounts and the submission of accounts to the Secretary of State.

17.The making of annual reports on the administration of the scheme.

18.The manner of amending the scheme.

(2) The Secretary of State may by order amend sub-paragraph (1) by adding to or deleting from it any item or by varying any item for the time being contained in it.

(3) An order under sub-paragraph (2) shall be made by statutory instrument which shall be subject to annulment in pursuance of a resolution of either House of Parliament.

Approval of scheme, or amendment, and withdrawal of approval

3(1) An application to the Secretary of State for approval of a scheme shall be made in such manner as the Secretary of State may determine, and shall be accompanied by such information as the Secretary of State may require.

(2) If it appears to the Secretary of State that the scheme—

(a) provides for the matters specified in paragraph 2, and

(b) is a satisfactory scheme for the purposes of this Schedule,

he shall approve the scheme.

(3) An amendment of an approved scheme is not effective unless approved by the Secretary of State.

Sub-paragraph (1) applies in relation to an application for approval of an amendment as it applies to an application for approval of a scheme; and the Secretary of State shall approve the amendment if it appears to him that the scheme as amended meets the conditions in sub-paragraph (2).

(4) The Secretary of State may withdraw his approval of a scheme.

(5) If the Secretary of State proposes to withdraw his approval of a scheme, he shall serve on the person administering the scheme and on the housing ombudsman under the scheme, a notice stating—

(a) that he proposes to withdraw his approval,

(b) the grounds for the proposed withdrawal of his approval, and

(c) that the person receiving the notice may make representations with respect to the proposed withdrawal of approval within such period of not less than 14 days as is specified in the notice;

and he shall, before reaching a decision on whether to withdraw approval, consider any representations duly made to him.

(6) The Secretary of State shall give notice of his decision on a proposal to withdraw approval of a scheme, together with his reasons, to every person on whom he served a notice under sub-paragraph (5).

(7) Withdrawal of approval by the Secretary of State has effect from such date as is specified in the notice of his decision.

(8) Where the person administering a scheme is given notice of a decision to withdraw approval of the scheme, he shall give notice of the decision to every member of the scheme.

Notice to be given of becoming a member of an approved scheme

4(1) A social landlord who—

(a) becomes a member of an approved scheme, or

(b) is a member of a scheme which becomes an approved scheme,

shall, within the period of 21 days beginning with the date of becoming a member or, as the case may be, of being informed of the Secretary of State's approval of the scheme, give notice of that fact to the [Relevant Authority][316].

(2) The [Relevant Authority][317], on receiving the notice, shall record his membership of an approved scheme.

(3) A person who fails to comply with sub-paragraph (1) commits an offence and is liable on summary conviction to a fine not exceeding level 4 on the standard scale.

Proceedings for such an offence may be brought only by or with the consent of the [Relevant Authority][318] or the Director of Public Prosecutions.

Withdrawal from approved scheme

5(1) A social landlord wishing to withdraw from membership of an approved scheme shall send notice of his proposed withdrawal to the [Relevant Authority][319].

(2) The notice shall specify—

(a) the housing activities in relation to which he is subject to investigation under the scheme,

(b) the approved scheme or schemes of which he is also a member or will, on his withdrawal, become a member, and

(c) under which scheme or schemes the housing activities mentioned in paragraph (a) will be subject to investigation after his withdrawal.

(3) If the [Relevant Authority][320] is satisfied that withdrawal by the landlord from the scheme will not result in a failure to comply with his duty under paragraph 1, it shall confirm the landlord's withdrawal from the scheme.

(4) If the [Relevant Authority][321] is not so satisfied, it shall withhold confirmation of the landlord's withdrawal from the scheme; and the landlord shall continue to be a member of the scheme and bound and entitled under the scheme accordingly.

Register of approved schemes

6(1) The [Relevant Authority][322] shall maintain a register of schemes approved by the Secretary of State for the purposes of this Schedule and of the social landlords who are members of those schemes.

(2) The Secretary of State shall give notice to the [Housing Corporation][323]—

(a) when he grants or withdraws his approval of a scheme, and

(b) when he approves an amendment of a scheme,

and he shall supply the [Housing Corporation][324] with copies of any approved scheme or any amendment to a scheme.

(3) A member of the public shall be entitled, upon payment of such fees as the [Relevant Authority][325] may determine, to receive a copy of an approved scheme and a list of the social landlords who are members of it.

Determinations by housing ombudsman

7(1) A housing ombudsman under an approved scheme shall investigate any complaint duly made to him and not withdrawn, and may investigate any complaint duly made but withdrawn, and where he investigates a complaint he shall determine it by reference to what is, in his opinion, fair in all the circumstances of the case.

(2) He may in his determination—

(a) order the member of a scheme against whom the complaint was made to pay compensation to the complainant, and

(b) order that the member or the complainant shall not exercise or require the performance of any of the contractual or other obligations or rights existing between them.

(3) If the member against whom the complaint was made fails to comply with the determination within a reasonable time, the housing ombudsman may order him to publish in such manner as the ombudsman sees fit that he has failed to comply with the determination.

(4) Where the member is not a social landlord, the housing ombudsman may also order that the member—

(a) be expelled from the scheme, and

(b) publish in such manner as the housing ombudsman sees fit that he has been expelled and the reasons for his expulsion.

(5) If a person fails to comply with an order under sub-paragraph (3) or (4)(b), the housing ombudsman may take such steps as he thinks appropriate to publish what the member ought to have published and recover from the member the costs of doing so.

(6) A member who is ordered by the housing ombudsman to pay compensation or take any other steps has power to do so, except that a member which is also a charity shall not do anything contrary to its trusts.

Publication of determinations, &c.

8(1) A housing ombudsman under an approved scheme may publish—

(a) his determination on any complaint, and

(b) such reports as he thinks fit on the discharge of his functions.

(2) He may include in any such determination or report statements, communications, reports, papers or other documentary evidence obtained in the exercise of his functions.

(3) In publishing any determination or report, a housing ombudsman shall have regard to the need for excluding so far as practicable—

(a) any matter which relates to the private affairs of an individual, where publication would seriously and prejudicially affect the interests of that individual, and

(b) any matter which relates specifically to the affairs of a member of an approved scheme, where publication would seriously and prejudicially affect its interests, unless the inclusion of that matter is necessary for the purposes of the determination or report.

Absolute privilege for communications, &c.

9 For the purposes of the law of defamation absolute privilege attaches to—

(a) any communication between a housing ombudsman under an approved scheme and any person by or against whom a complaint is made to him,

(b) any determination by such an ombudsman, and

(c) the publication of such a determination or any report under paragraph 8.

Appointment and status of housing ombudsman

10(1) Where an approved scheme provides that it shall be administered by a body corporate, that body shall appoint on such terms as it thinks fit the housing ombudsman for the purposes of the scheme and the appointment and its terms shall be subject to the approval of the Secretary of State.

(2) Where an approved scheme does not so provide—

(a) the housing ombudsman for the purposes of the scheme shall be appointed by the Secretary of State on such terms as the Secretary of State thinks fit,

(b) the Secretary of State may by order provide that the housing ombudsman for the purposes of the scheme shall be a corporation sole, and

(c) the staff to administer the scheme and otherwise assist the ombudsman in the discharge of his functions shall be appointed and employed by him.

(3) The Secretary of State may at any time remove from office a housing ombudsman (whether appointed by him or otherwise).

(4) A housing ombudsman appointed by the Secretary of State or otherwise shall not be regarded as the servant or agent of the Crown or as enjoying any status, privilege or immunity of the Crown or as exempt from any tax, duty, rate, levy or other charge whatsoever, whether general or local, and any property held by him shall not be regarded as property of, or held on behalf of, the Crown.

Subscriptions payable in respect of approved schemes

11(1) Members of an approved scheme shall pay a subscription, calculated as set out in the scheme, to the person administering the scheme.

(2) If a social landlord fails to comply with his duty under paragraph 1, the Secretary of State may determine—

(a) which approved scheme or schemes he should have joined, and

(b) what sums by way of subscription he should have paid,

and may require him to pay those amounts to the person administering the scheme or schemes.

(3) The person administering an approved scheme may recover sums payable under sub-paragraph (1) or (2) as if they were debts due to him.

(4) The Secretary of State or the [Housing Corporation][326] may pay grant and provide other financial

assistance to—

(a) a body corporate administering an approved scheme, or

(b) in a case where paragraph 10(2) applies, to the housing ombudsman under an approved scheme,

for such purposes and upon such terms as the Secretary of State or, as the case may be, the [Housing Corporation][327] thinks fit.

---

[1] Words in Pt. 1 substituted (1.11.1998) by 1998 c. 38, s. 140, Sch. 16 para. 82(1)(2) (with ss. 139(2), 141(1), 143(2)); S.I. 1998/2244, art.5.

[2] Words in s. 1(1) repealed (1.11.1998) by 1998 c. 38, ss. 140, 152, Sch. 16 para. 83(2), Sch. 18 Pt.VI (with ss. 137(1), 139(2), 141(1), 143(2)); S.I. 1998/2244, art.5.

[3] S. 1(1A)(1B) inserted (1.11.1998) by 1998 c. 38, s. 140, Sch. 16 para. 83(3) (with ss. 139(2), 141(1), 143(2)); S.I. 1998/2244, art.5.

[4] S. 1(2) repealed (1.11.1998) by 1998 c. 38, ss. 140, 152, Sch. 16 para. 83(4), Sch. 18 Pt.VI (with ss. 137(1), 139(2), 141(1), 143(2)); S.I. 1998/2244, art.5.

[5] Words in Pt. 1 substituted (1.11.1998) by 1998 c. 38, s. 140, Sch. 16 para. 82(1)(2) (with ss. 139(2), 141(1), 143(2)); S.I. 1998/2244, art. 5.

[6] Words in Pt. 1 substituted (1.11.1998) by 1998 c. 38, s. 140, Sch. 16 para. 82(1)(2) (with ss. 139(2), 141(1), 143(2)); S.I. 1998/2244, art. 5.

[7] Words in Pt. 1 substituted (1.11.1998) by 1998 c. 38, s. 140, Sch. 16 para. 82(1)(2) (with ss. 139(2), 141(1), 143(2)); S.I. 1998/2244, art. 5.

[8] Words in s. 3(3)(b) substituted (1.12.2001) by S.I. 2001/3649, arts. 1, 351

[9] Words in Pt. I substituted (1.11.1998) by 1998 c. 38, s. 140, Sch. 16 para. 82(1)(2) (with ss. 139(2), 141(1), 143(2)); S.I. 1998/2244, art. 5.

[10] Words in Pt. I substituted (1.11.1998) by 1998 c. 38, s. 140, Sch. 16 para. 82(1)(2) (with ss. 139(2), 141(1), 143(2)); S.I. 1998/2244, art. 5.

[11] Words in Pt. I substituted (1.11.1998) by 1998 c. 38, s. 140, Sch. 16 para. 82(1)(2) (with ss. 139(2), 141(1), 143(2)); S.I. 1998/2244, art. 5.

[12] Words in Pt. I substituted (1.11.1998) by 1998 c. 38, s. 140, Sch. 16 para. 82(1)(2) (with ss. 139(2), 141(1), 143(2)); S.I. 1998/2244, art. 5.

[13] Words in Pt. I substituted (1.11.1998) by 1998 c. 38, s. 140, Sch. 16 para. 82(1)(2) (with ss. 139(2), 141(1), 143(2)); S.I. 1998/2244, art. 5.

[14] Words in Pt. I substituted (1.11.1998) by 1998 c. 38, s. 140, Sch. 16 para. 82(1)(2) (with ss. 139(2), 141(1), 143(2)); S.I. 1998/2244, art. 5.

[15] Words in Pt. I substituted (1.11.1998) by 1998 c. 38, s. 140, Sch. 16 para. 82(1)(2) (with ss. 139(2), 141(1), 143(2)); S.I. 1998/2244, art. 5.

[16] Words in Pt. I substituted (1.11.1998) by 1998 c. 38, s. 140, Sch. 16 para. 82(1)(2) (with ss. 139(2), 141(1), 143(2)); S.I. 1998/2244, art. 5.

[17] Words in Pt. I substituted (1.11.1998) by 1998 c. 38, s. 140, Sch. 16 para. 82(1)(2) (with ss. 139(2), 141(1), 143(2)); S.I. 1998/2244, art. 5.

[18] Words in s. 4(6)(b) substituted (1.12.2001) by S.I. 2001/3649, arts. 1, 352

[19] Words in Pt. I substituted (1.11.1998) by 1998 c. 38, s. 140, Sch. 16 para. 82(1)(2) (with ss. 139(2), 141(1), 143(2)); S.I. 1998/2244, art.5.

[20] Words in Pt. I substituted (1.11.1998) by 1998 c. 38, s. 140, Sch. 16 para. 82(1)(2) (with ss. 139(2), 141(1), 143(2)); S.I. 1998/2244, art.5.

[21] Words in Pt. I substituted (1.11.1998) by 1998 c. 38, s. 140, Sch. 16 para. 82(1)(2) (with ss. 139(2), 141(1), 143(2)); S.I. 1998/2244, art.5.

[22] Words in Pt. I substituted (1.11.1998) by 1998 c. 38, s. 140, Sch. 16 para. 82(1)(2) (with ss. 139(2), 141(1), 143(2)); S.I. 1998/2244, art.5.

[23] Words in Pt. I substituted (1.11.1998) by 1998 c. 38, s. 140, Sch. 16 para. 82(1)(2) (with ss. 139(2), 141(1), 143(2)); S.I. 1998/2244, art.5.

[24] Words in Pt. I substituted (1.11.1998) by 1998 c. 38, s. 140, Sch. 16 para. 82(1)(2) (with ss. 139(2), 141(1), 143(2)); S.I. 1998/2244, art.5.

[25] Words in Pt. I substituted (1.11.1998) by 1998 c. 38, s. 140, Sch. 16 para. 82(1)(2) (with ss. 139(2), 141(1), 143(2)); S.I. 1998/2244, art.5.

[26] Words in Pt. I substituted (1.11.1998) by 1998 c. 38, s. 140, Sch. 16 para. 82(1)(2) (with ss. 139(2), 141(1), 143(2)); S.I. 1998/2244, art. 5.

[27] Words in Pt. I substituted (1.11.1998) by 1998 c. 38, s. 140, Sch. 16 para. 82(1)(2) (with ss. 139(2), 141(1), 143(2)); S.I. 1998/2244, art. 5.

[28] Words in Pt. I substituted (1.11.1998) by 1998 c. 38, s. 140, Sch. 16 para. 82(1)(2) (with ss. 139(2), 141(1), 143(2)); S.I. 1998/2244, art. 5.

[29] Words in s. 6(3)(b) substituted (1.12.2001) by S.I. 2001/3649, arts. 1, 353

30 Words in Pt. I substituted (1.11.1998) by 1998 c. 38, s. 140, Sch. 16 para. 82(1)(2) (with ss. 139(2), 141(1), 143(2)); S.I. 1998/2244, art.5.

31 Words in Pt. I substituted (1.11.1998) by 1998 c. 38, s. 140, Sch. 16 para. 82(1)(2) (with ss. 139(2), 141(1), 143(2)); S.I. 1998/2244, art.5.

32 Words in Pt. I substituted (1.11.1998) by 1998 c. 38, s. 140, Sch. 16 para. 82(1)(2) (with ss. 139(2), 141(1), 143(2)); S.I. 1998/2244, art.5.

33 S. 9(1A) inserted (1.11.1998) by 1998 c. 38, s. 140, Sch. 16 para. 84(3) (with ss. 139(2), 141(1), 143(2)); S.I. 1998/2244, art.5.

34 Words in Pt. I substituted (1.11.1998) by 1998 c. 38, s. 140, Sch. 16 para. 82(1)(2) (with ss. 139(2), 141(1), 143(2)); S.I. 1998/2244, art.5.

35 Words in Pt. I substituted (1.11.1998) by 1998 c. 38, s. 140, Sch. 16 para. 82(1)(2) (with ss. 139(2), 141(1), 143(2)); S.I. 1998/2244, art.5.

36 Words in Pt. I substituted (1.11.1998) by 1998 c. 38, s. 140, Sch. 16 para. 82(1)(2) (with ss. 139(2), 141(1), 143(2)); S.I. 1998/2244, art.5.

37 Words in Pt. I substituted (1.11.1998) by 1998 c. 38, s. 140, Sch. 16 para. 82(1)(2) (with ss. 139(2), 141(1), 143(2)); S.I. 1998/2244, art.5.

38 Words in Pt. I substituted (1.11.1998) by 1998 c. 38, s. 140, Sch. 16 para. 82(1)(2) (with ss. 139(2), 141(1), 143(2)); S.I. 1998/2244, art.5.

39 Words in Pt. I substituted (1.11.1998) by 1998 c. 38, s. 140, Sch. 16 para. 82(1)(2) (with ss. 139(2), 141(1), 143(2)); S.I. 1998/2244, art.5.

40 Words in Pt. I substituted (1.11.1998) by 1998 c. 38, s. 140, Sch. 16 para. 82(1)(2) (with ss. 139(2), 141(1), 143(2)); S.I. 1998/2244, art. 5.

41 Words in s. 13(1)(b) substituted (1.4.2001 for E. and 1.5.2001 for W.) by 2000 C. 37, s. 93, Sch. 15 Pt. I para. 14; S.I. 2001/114, art. 2(2)(e); S.I. 2001/1410, art. 2(g)

42 Words in Pt. I substituted (1.11.1998) by 1998 c. 38, s. 140, Sch. 16 para. 82(1)(2) (with ss. 139(2), 141(1), 143(2)); S.I. 1998/2244, art. 5.

43 Words in Pt. I substituted (1.11.1998) by 1998 c. 38, s. 140, Sch. 16 para. 82(1)(2) (with ss. 139(2), 141(1), 143(2)); S.I. 1998/2244, art. 5.

44 1984 c. 12.

45 S. 16(5)-(7) added (E.) (24.10.2001) by S.I. 2001/3257, art. 2

46 Words in Pt. I substituted (1.11.1998) by 1998 c. 38, s. 140, Sch. 16 para. 82(1)(2) (with ss. 139(2), 141(1), 143(2)); S.I. 1998/2244, art.5.

47 Words in Pt. I substituted (1.11.1998) by 1998 c. 38, s. 140, Sch. 16 para. 82(1)(2) (with ss. 139(2), 141(1), 143(2)); S.I. 1998/2244, art.5.

48 Words in Pt. I substituted (1.11.1998) by 1998 c. 38, s. 140, Sch. 16 para. 82(1)(2) (with ss. 139(2), 141(1), 143(2)); S.I. 1998/2244, art.5.

49 Words in Pt. I substituted (1.11.1998) by 1998 c. 38, s. 140, Sch. 16 para. 82(1)(2) (with ss. 139(2), 141(1), 143(2)); S.I. 1998/2244, art.5.

50 Words in Pt. I substituted (1.11.1998) by 1998 c. 38, s. 140, Sch. 16 para. 82(1)(2) (with ss. 139(2), 141(1), 143(2)); S.I. 1998/2244, art.5.

51 S. 18(5) substituted (1.11.1998) by 1998 c. 38, s. 140, Sch. 16 para. 85(2) (with ss. 139(2), 141(1), 143(2)); S.I. 1998/2244, art.5.

52 Words in Pt. I substituted (1.11.1998) by 1998 c. 38, s. 140, Sch. 16 para. 82(1)(2) (with ss. 139(2), 141(1), 143(2)); S.I. 1998/2244, art.5.

53 Words in Pt. I substituted (1.11.1998) by 1998 c. 38, s. 140, Sch. 16 para. 82(1)(2) (with ss. 139(2), 141(1), 143(2)); S.I. 1998/2244, art.5.

54 Words in s. 18(8) substituted (1.11.1998) by 1998 c. 38, s. 140, Sch. 16 para. 85(3) (with ss. 139(2), 141(1), 143(2)); S.I. 1998/2244, art.5.

55 Words in s. 18(8) substituted (1.11.1998) by 1998 c. 38, s. 140, Sch. 16 para. 85(3) (with ss. 139(2), 141(1), 143(2)); S.I. 1998/2244, art.5.

56 Words in Pt. I substituted (1.11.1998) by 1998 c. 38, s. 140, Sch. 16 para. 82(1)(2) (with ss. 139(2), 141(1), 143(2)); S.I. 1998/2244, art.5

57 Words in Pt. I substituted (1.11.1998) by 1998 c. 38, s. 140, Sch. 16 para. 82(1)(2) (with ss. 139(2), 141(1), 143(2)); S.I. 1998/2244, art.5

58 Words in Pt. I substituted (1.11.1998) by 1998 c. 38, s. 140, Sch. 16 para. 82(1)(2) (with ss. 139(2), 141(1), 143(2)); S.I. 1998/2244, art.5

59 Words in Pt. I substituted (1.11.1998) by 1998 c. 38, s. 140, Sch. 16 para. 82(1)(2) (with ss. 139(2), 141(1), 143(2)); S.I. 1998/2244, art.5

60 Words in Pt. I substituted (1.11.1998) by 1998 c. 38, s. 140, Sch. 16 para. 82(1)(2) (with ss. 139(2), 141(1), 143(2)); S.I. 1998/2244, art.5.

61 Words in Pt. I substituted (1.11.1998) by 1998 c. 38, s. 140, Sch. 16 para. 82(1)(2) (with ss. 139(2), 141(1), 143(2)); S.I.

1998/2244, art.5.

62 Words in Pt. I substituted (1.11.1998) by 1998 c. 38, s. 140, Sch. 16 para. 82(1)(2) (with ss. 139(2), 141(1), 143(2)); S.I. 1998/2244, art.5.

63 Words in Pt. I substituted (1.11.1998) by 1998 c. 38, s. 140, Sch. 16 para. 82(1)(2) (with ss. 139(2), 141(1), 143(2)); S.I. 1998/2244, art.5.

64 Words in Pt. I substituted (1.11.1998) by 1998 c. 38, s. 140, Sch. 16 para. 82(1)(2) (with ss. 139(2), 141(1), 143(2)); S.I. 1998/2244, art.5.

65 Words in Pt. I substituted (1.11.1998) by 1998 c. 38, s. 140, Sch. 16 para. 82(1)(2) (with ss. 139(2), 141(1), 143(2)); S.I. 1998/2244, art.5.

66 Words in Pt. I substituted (1.11.1998) by 1998 c. 38, s. 140, Sch. 16 para. 82(1)(2) (with ss. 139(2), 141(1), 143(2)); S.I. 1998/2244, art.5.

67 Words in Pt. I substituted (1.11.1998) by 1998 c. 38, s. 140, Sch. 16 para. 82(1)(2) (with ss. 139(2), 141(1), 143(2)); S.I. 1998/2244, art.5.

68 Words in Pt. I substituted (1.11.1998) by 1998 c. 38, s. 140, Sch. 16 para. 82(1)(2) (with ss. 139(2), 141(1), 143(2)); S.I. 1998/2244, art.5.

69 Words in Pt. I substituted (1.11.1998) by 1998 c. 38, s. 140, Sch. 16 para. 82(1)(2) (with ss. 139(2), 141(1), 143(2)); S.I. 1998/2244, art.5.

70 Words in Pt. I substituted (1.11.1998) by 1998 c. 38, s. 140, Sch. 16 para. 82(1)(2) (with ss. 139(2), 141(1), 143(2)); S.I. 1998/2244, art.5.

71 Words in Pt. I substituted (1.11.1998) by 1998 c. 38, s. 140, Sch. 16 para. 82(1)(2) (with ss. 139(2), 141(1), 143(2)); S.I. 1998/2244, art.5.

72 Words in Pt. I substituted (1.11.1998) by 1998 c. 38, s. 140, Sch. 16 para. 82(1)(2) (with ss. 139(2), 141(1), 143(2)); S.I. 1998/2244, art.5.

73 Words in Pt. I substituted (1.11.1998) by 1998 c. 38, s. 140, Sch. 16 para. 82(1)(2) (with ss. 139(2), 141(1), 143(2)); S.I. 1998/2244, art.5.

74 Words in Pt. I substituted (1.11.1998) by 1998 c. 38, s. 140, Sch. 16 para. 82(1)(2) (with ss. 139(2), 141(1), 143(2)); S.I. 1998/2244, art.5.

75 Words in Pt. I substituted (1.11.1998) by 1998 c. 38, s. 140, Sch. 16 para. 82(1)(2) (with ss. 139(2), 141(1), 143(2)); S.I. 1998/2244, art.5.

76 Words in Pt. I substituted (1.11.1998) by 1998 c. 38, s. 140, Sch. 16 para. 82(1)(2) (with ss. 139(2), 141(1), 143(2)); S.I. 1998/2244, art.5.

77 Words in Pt. I substituted (1.11.1998) by 1998 c. 38, s. 140, Sch. 16 para. 82(1)(2) (with ss. 139(2), 141(1), 143(2)); S.I. 1998/2244, art.5.

78 Words in Pt. I substituted (1.11.1998) by 1998 c. 38, s. 140, Sch. 16 para. 82(1)(2) (with ss. 139(2), 141(1), 143(2)); S.I. 1998/2244, art.5.

79 Words in Pt. I substituted (1.11.1998) by 1998 c. 38, s. 140, Sch. 16 para. 82(1)(2) (with ss. 139(2), 141(1), 143(2)); S.I. 1998/2244, art.5.

80 Words in Pt. I substituted (1.11.1998) by 1998 c. 38, s. 140, Sch. 16 para. 82(1)(2) (with ss. 139(2), 141(1), 143(2)); S.I. 1998/2244, art.5.

81 Words in Pt. I substituted (1.11.1998) by 1998 c. 38, s. 140, Sch. 16 para. 82(1)(2) (with ss. 139(2), 141(1), 143(2)); S.I. 1998/2244, art.5.

82 Words in Pt. I substituted (1.11.1998) by 1998 c. 38, s. 140, Sch. 16 para. 82(1)(2) (with ss. 139(2), 141(1), 143(2)); S.I. 1998/2244, art.5.

83 Words in Pt. I substituted (1.11.1998) by 1998 c. 38, s. 140, Sch. 16 para. 82(1)(2) (with ss. 139(2), 141(1), 143(2)); S.I. 1998/2244, art.5.

84 Words in Pt. I substituted (1.11.1998) by 1998 c. 38, s. 140, Sch. 16 para. 82(1)(2) (with ss. 139(2), 141(1), 143(2)); S.I. 1998/2244, art.5.

85 Words in Pt. I substituted (1.11.1998) by 1998 c. 38, s. 140, Sch. 16 para. 82(1)(2) (with ss. 139(2), 141(1), 143(2)); S.I. 1998/2244, art.5.

86 Words in Pt. I substituted (1.11.1998) by 1998 c. 38, s. 140, Sch. 16 para. 82(1)(2) (with ss. 139(2), 141(1), 143(2)); S.I. 1998/2244, art.5.

87 Words in Pt. I substituted (1.11.1998) by 1998 c. 38, s. 140, Sch. 16 para. 82(1)(2) (with ss. 139(2), 141(1), 143(2)); S.I. 1998/2244, art.5.

88 Words in Pt. I substituted (1.11.1998) by 1998 c. 38, s. 140, Sch. 16 para. 82(1)(2) (with ss. 139(2), 141(1), 143(2)); S.I. 1998/2244, art.5.

89 Words in Pt. I substituted (1.11.1998) by 1998 c. 38, s. 140, Sch. 16 para. 82(1)(2) (with ss. 139(2), 141(1), 143(2)); S.I. 1998/2244, art.5.

90 Words in Pt. I substituted (1.11.1998) by 1998 c. 38, s. 140, Sch. 16 para. 82(1)(2) (with ss. 139(2), 141(1), 143(2)); S.I. 1998/2244, art.5.

91 Words in Pt. I substituted (1.11.1998) by 1998 c. 38, s. 140, Sch. 16 para. 82(1)(2) (with ss. 139(2), 141(1), 143(2)); S.I. 1998/2244, art.5.

[92] Words in Pt. I substituted (1.11.1998) by 1998 c. 38, s. 140, Sch. 16 para. 82(1)(2) (with ss. 139(2), 141(1), 143(2)); S.I. 1998/2244, art.5.

[93] Words in Pt. I substituted (1.11.1998) by 1998 c. 38, s. 140, Sch. 16 para. 82(1)(2) (with ss. 139(2), 141(1), 143(2)); S.I. 1998/2244, art.5.

[94] Words in Pt. I substituted (1.11.1998) by 1998 c. 38, s. 140, Sch. 16 para. 82(1)(2) (with ss. 139(2), 141(1), 143(2)); S.I. 1998/2244, art.5.

[95] Words in Pt. I substituted (1.11.1998) by 1998 c. 38, s. 140, Sch. 16 para. 82(1)(2) (with ss. 139(2), 141(1), 143(2)); S.I. 1998/2244, art.5.

[96] S. 30(5) substituted (1.11.1998) by 1998 c. 38, s. 140, Sch. 16 para.86 (with ss. 139(2), 141(1), 143(2)); S.I. 1998/2244, art.5.

[97] Words in Pt. I substituted (1.11.1998) by 1998 c. 38, s. 140, Sch. 16 para. 82(1)(2) (with ss. 139(2), 141(1), 143(2)); S.I. 1998/2244, art.5.

[98] Words in Pt. I substituted (1.11.1998) by 1998 c. 38, s. 140, Sch. 16 para. 82(1)(2) (with ss. 139(2), 141(1), 143(2)); S.I. 1998/2244, art.5.

[99] Words in Pt. I substituted (1.11.1998) by 1998 c. 38, s. 140, Sch. 16 para. 82(1)(2) (with ss. 139(2), 141(1), 143(2)); S.I. 1998/2244, art.5.

[100] Words in Pt. I substituted (1.11.1998) by 1998 c. 38, s. 140, Sch. 16 para. 82(1)(2) (with ss. 139(2), 141(1), 143(2)); S.I. 1998/2244, art.5.

[101] Words in Pt. I substituted (1.11.1998) by 1998 c. 38, s. 140, Sch. 16 para. 82(1)(2) (with ss. 139(2), 141(1), 143(2)); S.I. 1998/2244, art.5.

[102] Words in Pt. I substituted (1.11.1998) by 1998 c. 38, s. 140, Sch. 16 para. 82(1)(2) (with ss. 139(2), 141(1), 143(2)); S.I. 1998/2244, art.5.

[103] Words in Pt. I substituted (1.11.1998) by 1998 c. 38, s. 140, Sch. 16 para. 82(1)(2) (with ss. 139(2), 141(1), 143(2)); S.I. 1998/2244, art.5.

[104] Words in Pt. I substituted (1.11.1998) by 1998 c. 38, s. 140, Sch. 16 para. 82(1)(2) (with ss. 139(2), 141(1), 143(2)); S.I. 1998/2244, art.5.

[105] Words in Pt. I substituted (1.11.1998) by 1998 c. 38, s. 140, Sch. 16 para. 82(1)(2) (with ss. 139(2), 141(1), 143(2)); S.I. 1998/2244, art.5.

[106] Words in Pt. I substituted (1.11.1998) by 1998 c. 38, s. 140, Sch. 16 para. 82(1)(2) (with ss. 139(2), 141(1), 143(2)); S.I. 1998/2244, art.5.

[107] Words in Pt. I substituted (1.11.1998) by 1998 c. 38, s. 140, Sch. 16 para. 82(1)(2) (with ss. 139(2), 141(1), 143(2)); S.I. 1998/2244, art.5.

[108] Words in Pt. I substituted (1.11.1998) by 1998 c. 38, s. 140, Sch. 16 para. 82(1)(2) (with ss. 139(2), 141(1), 143(2)); S.I. 1998/2244, art.5.

[109] Words in Pt. I substituted (1.11.1998) by 1998 c. 38, s. 140, Sch. 16 para. 82(1)(2) (with ss. 139(2), 141(1), 143(2)); S.I. 1998/2244, art.5.

[110] Words in Pt. I substituted (1.11.1998) by 1998 c. 38, s. 140, Sch. 16 para. 82(1)(2) (with ss. 139(2), 141(1), 143(2)); S.I. 1998/2244, art.5.

[111] Words in Pt. I substituted (1.11.1998) by 1998 c. 38, s. 140, Sch. 16 para. 82(1)(2) (with ss. 139(2), 141(1), 143(2)); S.I. 1998/2244, art.5.

[112] Words in Pt. I substituted (1.11.1998) by 1998 c. 38, s. 140, Sch. 16 para. 82(1)(2) (with ss. 139(2), 141(1), 143(2)); S.I. 1998/2244, art.5.

[113] Words in Pt. I substituted (1.11.1998) by 1998 c. 38, s. 140, Sch. 16 para. 82(1)(2) (with ss. 139(2), 141(1), 143(2)); S.I. 1998/2244, art.5.

[114] Words in Pt. I substituted (1.11.1998) by 1998 c. 38, s. 140, Sch. 16 para. 82(1)(2) (with ss. 139(2), 141(1), 143(2)); S.I. 1998/2244, art.5.

[115] Words in Pt. I substituted (1.11.1998) by 1998 c. 38, s. 140, Sch. 16 para. 82(1)(2) (with ss. 139(2), 141(1), 143(2)); S.I. 1998/2244, art.5.

[116] Words in Pt. I substituted (1.11.1998) by 1998 c. 38, s. 140, Sch. 16 para. 82(1)(2) (with ss. 139(2), 141(1), 143(2)); S.I. 1998/2244, art.5.

[117] Words in Pt. I substituted (1.11.1998) by 1998 c. 38, s. 140, Sch. 16 para. 82(1)(2) (with ss. 139(2), 141(1), 143(2)); S.I. 1998/2244, art.5.

[118] Words in Pt. I substituted (1.11.1998) by 1998 c. 38, s. 140, Sch. 16 para. 82(1)(2) (with ss. 139(2), 141(1), 143(2)); S.I. 1998/2244, art.5.

[119] Words in Pt. I substituted (1.11.1998) by 1998 c. 38, s. 140, Sch. 16 para. 82(1)(2) (with ss. 139(2), 141(1), 143(2)); S.I. 1998/2244, art.5.

[120] S. 36(3)(4) substituted (1.11.1998) by 1998 c. 38, s. 140, Sch. 16 para.87 (with ss. 139(2), 141(1), 143(2)); S.I. 1998/2244, art.5.

[121] Words in Pt. I substituted (1.11.1998) by 1998 c. 38, s. 140, Sch. 16 para. 82(1)(2) (with ss. 139(2), 141(1), 143(2)); S.I. 1998/2244, art.5.

[122] Words in Pt. I substituted (1.11.1998) by 1998 c. 38, s. 140, Sch. 16 para. 82(1)(2) (with ss. 139(2), 141(1), 143(2)); S.I. 1998/2244, art.5.

123 Words in Pt. I substituted (1.11.1998) by 1998 c. 38, s. 140, Sch. 16 para. 82(1)(2) (with ss. 139(2), 141(1), 143(2)); S.I. 1998/2244, art.5.

124 Words in Pt. I substituted (1.11.1998) by 1998 c. 38, s. 140, Sch. 16 para. 82(1)(2) (with ss. 139(2), 141(1), 143(2)); S.I. 1998/2244, art.5.

125 Words in Pt. I substituted (1.11.1998) by 1998 c. 38, s. 140, Sch. 16 para. 82(1)(2) (with ss. 139(2), 141(1), 143(2)); S.I. 1998/2244, art.5.

126 Words in Pt. I substituted (1.11.1998) by 1998 c. 38, s. 140, Sch. 16 para. 82(1)(2) (with ss. 139(2), 141(1), 143(2)); S.I. 1998/2244, art.5.

127 Words in Pt. I substituted (1.11.1998) by 1998 c. 38, s. 140, Sch. 16 para. 82(1)(2) (with ss. 139(2), 141(1), 143(2)); S.I. 1998/2244, art.5.

128 Words in Pt. I substituted (1.11.1998) by 1998 c. 38, s. 140, Sch. 16 para. 82(1)(2) (with ss. 139(2), 141(1), 143(2)); S.I. 1998/2244, art.5.

129 Words in Pt. I substituted (1.11.1998) by 1998 c. 38, s. 140, Sch. 16 para. 82(1)(2) (with ss. 139(2), 141(1), 143(2)); S.I. 1998/2244, art.5.

130 Words in Pt. I substituted (1.11.1998) by 1998 c. 38, s. 140, Sch. 16 para. 82(1)(2) (with ss. 139(2), 141(1), 143(2)); S.I. 1998/2244, art.5.

131 Words in Pt. I substituted (1.11.1998) by 1998 c. 38, s. 140, Sch. 16 para. 82(1)(2) (with ss. 139(2), 141(1), 143(2)); S.I. 1998/2244, art.5.

132 Words in Pt. I substituted (1.11.1998) by 1998 c. 38, s. 140, Sch. 16 para. 82(1)(2) (with ss. 139(2), 141(1), 143(2)); S.I. 1998/2244, art.5.

133 Words in Pt. I substituted (1.11.1998) by 1998 c. 38, s. 140, Sch. 16 para. 82(1)(2) (with ss. 139(2), 141(1), 143(2)); S.I. 1998/2244, art.5.

134 Words in Pt. I substituted (1.11.1998) by 1998 c. 38, s. 140, Sch. 16 para. 82(1)(2) (with ss. 139(2), 141(1), 143(2)); S.I. 1998/2244, art.5.

135 Words in Pt. I substituted (1.11.1998) by 1998 c. 38, s. 140, Sch. 16 para. 82(1)(2) (with ss. 139(2), 141(1), 143(2)); S.I. 1998/2244, art.5.

136 Words in Pt. I substituted (1.11.1998) by 1998 c. 38, s. 140, Sch. 16 para. 82(1)(2) (with ss. 139(2), 141(1), 143(2)); S.I. 1998/2244, art.5.

137 Words in Pt. I substituted (1.11.1998) by 1998 c. 38, s. 140, Sch. 16 para. 82(1)(2) (with ss. 139(2), 141(1), 143(2)); S.I. 1998/2244, art.5.

138 Words in Pt. I substituted (1.11.1998) by 1998 c. 38, s. 140, Sch. 16 para. 82(1)(2) (with ss. 139(2), 141(1), 143(2)); S.I. 1998/2244, art.5.

139 Words in Pt. I substituted (1.11.1998) by 1998 c. 38, s. 140, Sch. 16 para. 82(1)(2) (with ss. 139(2), 141(1), 143(2)); S.I. 1998/2244, art.5.

140 Words in Pt. I substituted (1.11.1998) by 1998 c. 38, s. 140, Sch. 16 para. 82(1)(2) (with ss. 139(2), 141(1), 143(2)); S.I. 1998/2244, art.5.

141 Words in Pt. I substituted (1.11.1998) by 1998 c. 38, s. 140, Sch. 16 para. 82(1)(2) (with ss. 139(2), 141(1), 143(2)); S.I. 1998/2244, art.5.

142 Words in Pt. I substituted (1.11.1998) by 1998 c. 38, s. 140, Sch. 16 para. 82(1)(2) (with ss. 139(2), 141(1), 143(2)); S.I. 1998/2244, art.5.

143 Words in Pt. I substituted (1.11.1998) by 1998 c. 38, s. 140, Sch. 16 para. 82(1)(2) (with ss. 139(2), 141(1), 143(2)); S.I. 1998/2244, art.5.

144 Words in Pt. I substituted (1.11.1998) by 1998 c. 38, s. 140, Sch. 16 para. 82(1)(2) (with ss. 139(2), 141(1), 143(2)); S.I. 1998/2244, art.5.

145 Words in Pt. I substituted (1.11.1998) by 1998 c. 38, s. 140, Sch. 16 para. 82(1)(2) (with ss. 139(2), 141(1), 143(2)); S.I. 1998/2244, art.5.

146 Words in Pt. I substituted (1.11.1998) by 1998 c. 38, s. 140, Sch. 16 para. 82(1)(2) (with ss. 139(2), 141(1), 143(2)); S.I. 1998/2244, art.5.

147 Words in Pt. I substituted (1.11.1998) by 1998 c. 38, s. 140, Sch. 16 para. 82(1)(2) (with ss. 139(2), 141(1), 143(2)); S.I. 1998/2244, art.5.

148 Words in Pt. I substituted (1.11.1998) by 1998 c. 38, s. 140, Sch. 16 para. 82(1)(2) (with ss. 139(2), 141(1), 143(2)); S.I. 1998/2244, art.5.

149 Words in Pt. I substituted (1.11.1998) by 1998 c. 38, s. 140, Sch. 16 para. 82(1)(2) (with ss. 139(2), 141(1), 143(2)); S.I. 1998/2244, art.5.

150 Words in Pt. I substituted (1.11.1998) by 1998 c. 38, s. 140, Sch. 16 para. 82(1)(2) (with ss. 139(2), 141(1), 143(2)); S.I. 1998/2244, art.5.

151 Words in Pt. I substituted (1.11.1998) by 1998 c. 38, s. 140, Sch. 16 para. 82(1)(2) (with ss. 139(2), 141(1), 143(2)); S.I. 1998/2244, art.5.

152 Words in Pt. I substituted (1.11.1998) by 1998 c. 38, s. 140, Sch. 16 para. 82(1)(2) (with ss. 139(2), 141(1), 143(2)); S.I. 1998/2244, art.5.

153 Words in s. 45(4)(d) substituted (1.12.2001) by S.I. 2001/3649, arts. 1, 354

[154] Words in Pt. I substituted (1.11.1998) by 1998 c. 38, s. 140, Sch. 16 para. 82(1)(2) (with ss. 139(2), 141(1), 143(2)); S.I. 1998/2244, art.5.

[155] Words in Pt. I substituted (1.11.1998) by 1998 c. 38, s. 140, Sch. 16 para. 82(1)(2) (with ss. 139(2), 141(1), 143(2)); S.I. 1998/2244, art.5.

[156] Words in s. 46(1)(6) repealed (1.11.1998) by 1998 c. 38, ss. 140, 152, Sch. 16 para. 88(2), Sch. 18 Pt.VI (with ss. 137(1), 139(2), 141(1), 143(2)); S.I. 1998/2244, art.5.

[157] Words in Pt. I substituted (1.11.1998) by 1998 c. 38, s. 140, Sch. 16 para. 82(1)(2) (with ss. 139(2), 141(1), 143(2)); S.I. 1998/2244, art.5.

[158] Words in Pt. I substituted (1.11.1998) by 1998 c. 38, s. 140, Sch. 16 para. 82(1)(2) (with ss. 139(2), 141(1), 143(2)); S.I. 1998/2244, art.5.

[159] Words in Pt. I substituted (1.11.1998) by 1998 c. 38, s. 140, Sch. 16 para. 82(1)(2) (with ss. 139(2), 141(1), 143(2)); S.I. 1998/2244, art.5.

[160] Words in Pt. I substituted (1.11.1998) by 1998 c. 38, s. 140, Sch. 16 para. 82(1)(2) (with ss. 139(2), 141(1), 143(2)); S.I. 1998/2244, art.5.

[161] S. 46(7) inserted (1.11.1998) by 1998 c. 38, s. 140, Sch. 16 para. 88(3) (with ss. 139(2), 141(1), 143(2)); S.I. 1998/2244, art.5.

[162] Words in s. 48(3) substituted (1.12.2001) by S.I. 2001/3649, arts. 1, 355

[163] Words in Pt. I substituted (1.11.1998) by 1998 c. 38, s. 140, Sch. 16 para. 82(1)(2) (with ss. 139(2), 141(1), 143(2)); S.I. 1998/2244, art.5.

[164] Words in Pt. I substituted (1.11.1998) by 1998 c. 38, s. 140, Sch. 16 para. 82(1)(2) (with ss. 139(2), 141(1), 143(2)); S.I. 1998/2244, art.5.

[165] Words in Pt. I substituted (1.11.1998) by 1998 c. 38, s. 140, Sch. 16 para. 82(1)(2) (with ss. 139(2), 141(1), 143(2)); S.I. 1998/2244, art.5.

[166] Words in Pt. I substituted (1.11.1998) by 1998 c. 38, s. 140, Sch. 16 para. 82(1)(2) (with ss. 139(2), 141(1), 143(2)); S.I. 1998/2244, art.5.

[167] Words in s. 49(3) substituted (1.11.1998) by 1998 c. 38, s. 140, Sch. 16 para.89 (with ss. 139(2), 141(1), 143(2)); S.I. 1998/2244, art.5.

[168] Words in Pt. I substituted (1.11.1998) by 1998 c. 38, s. 140, Sch. 16 para. 82(1)(2) (with ss. 139(2), 141(1), 143(2)); S.I. 1998/2244, art.5.

[169] Words in s. 51(2)(a) inserted (1.11.1998) by 1998 c. 38, s. 140, Sch. 16 para. 90(a) (with ss. 139(2), 141(1), 143(2)); S.I. 1998/2244, art.5.

[170] Words in s. 51(2)(d) substituted (1.11.1998) by 1998 c. 38, s. 140, Sch. 16 para. 90(b) (with ss. 139(2), 141(1), 143(2)); S.I. 1998/2244, art.5.

[171] Words in s. 52(1) substituted (1.11.1998) by 1998 c. 38, s. 140, Sch. 16 para.91 (with ss. 139(2), 141(1), 143(2)); S.I. 1998/2244, art.5.

[172] Words in s. 53(1)(4)(5) substituted (1.11.1998) by 1998 c. 38, s. 140, Sch. 16 para.92 (with ss. 139(2), 141(1), 143(2)); S.I. 1998/2244, art.5

[173] Words in s. 53(1)(4)(5) substituted (1.11.1998) by 1998 c. 38, s. 140, Sch. 16 para.92 (with ss. 139(2), 141(1), 143(2)); S.I. 1998/2244, art.5

[174] Words in s. 53(1)(4)(5) substituted (1.11.1998) by 1998 c. 38, s. 140, Sch. 16 para.92 (with ss. 139(2), 141(1), 143(2)); S.I. 1998/2244, art.5

[175] Words in s. 54 substituted (1.11.1998) by 1998 c. 38, s. 140, Sch. 16 para.93 (with ss. 139(2), 141(1), 143(2)); S.I. 1998/2244, art.5.

[176] Words in Pt. I substituted (1.11.1998) by 1998 c. 38, s. 140, Sch. 16 para. 82(1)(2) (with ss. 139(2), 141(1), 143(2)); S.I. 1998/2244, art.5.

[177] Words in s. 56(1)(2)(4) substituted (1.11.1998) by 1998 c. 38, s. 140, Sch. 16 para.94 (with ss. 139(2), 141(1), 143(2)); S.I. 1998/2244, art.5.

[178] Words in s. 56(1)(2)(4) substituted (1.11.1998) by 1998 c. 38, s. 140, Sch. 16 para.94 (with ss. 139(2), 141(1), 143(2)); S.I. 1998/2244, art.5.

[179] Words in s. 56(1)(2)(4) substituted (1.11.1998) by 1998 c. 38, s. 140, Sch. 16 para.94 (with ss. 139(2), 141(1), 143(2)); S.I. 1998/2244, art.5.

[180] Definition of "appropriate registrar" in s. 57(1) repealed (1.12.2001) by S.I. 2001/3649, arts. 1, 356(1)

[181] S. 64: Entry relating to "appropriate registrar" in the Table repealed (1.12.2001) by S.I. 2001/3649, arts. 1, 356(2)

[182] Entry in s. 64 repealed (1.11.1998) by 1998 c. 38, ss. 140, 152, Sch. 16 para. 95(a), Sch. 18 Pt. VI (with ss. 137(1), 139(2), 141(1), 143(2)); S.I. 1998/2244, art. 5.

[183] Entry in s. 64 inserted (1.11.1998) by 1998 c. 38, s. 140, Sch. 16 para. 95(b) (with ss. 139(2), 141(1), 143(2)); S.I. 1998/2244, art. 5.

[184] Words in Pt. I substituted (1.11.1998) by 1998 c. 38, s. 140, Sch. 16 para. 82(1)(2) (with ss. 139(2), 141(1), 143(2)); S.I. 1998/2244, art.5.

[185] Words in Pt. I substituted (1.11.1998) by 1998 c. 38, s. 140, Sch. 16 para. 82(1)(2) (with ss. 139(2), 141(1), 143(2)); S.I. 1998/2244, art.5.

186 Words in Pt. I substituted (1.11.1998) by 1998 c. 38, s. 140, Sch. 16 para. 82(1)(2) (with ss. 139(2), 141(1), 143(2)); S.I. 1998/2244, art.5.
187 Words in Pt. I substituted (1.11.1998) by 1998 c. 38, s. 140, Sch. 16 para. 82(1)(2) (with ss. 139(2), 141(1), 143(2)); S.I. 1998/2244, art.5.
188 Words in Pt. I substituted (1.11.1998) by 1998 c. 38, s. 140, Sch. 16 para. 82(1)(2) (with ss. 139(2), 141(1), 143(2)); S.I. 1998/2244, art.5.
189 Words in Pt. I substituted (1.11.1998) by 1998 c. 38, s. 140, Sch. 16 para. 82(1)(2) (with ss. 139(2), 141(1), 143(2)); S.I. 1998/2244, art.5.
190 Words in Pt. I substituted (1.11.1998) by 1998 c. 38, s. 140, Sch. 16 para. 82(1)(2) (with ss. 139(2), 141(1), 143(2)); S.I. 1998/2244, art.5.
191 Words in Sch. 1 para. 4(2)(b) inserted (2.4.2001) by 2000 c. 39, s. 8, Sch. 4 Pt. II para. II para. 21; S.I. 2001/766, art. 2(1)(a)
192 Words in Sch. 1 para. 4(2)(b) inserted (2.4.2001) by 2000 c. 39, s. 8, Sch. 4 Pt. II para. 21; S.I. 2001/766, art. 2(1)(a)
193 Words in Pt. I substituted (1.11.1998) by 1998 c. 38, s. 140, Sch. 16 para. 82(1)(2) (with ss. 139(2), 141(1), 143(2)); S.I. 1998/2244, art.5.
194 Words in Pt. I substituted (1.11.1998) by 1998 c. 38, s. 140, Sch. 16 para. 82(1)(2) (with ss. 139(2), 141(1), 143(2)); S.I. 1998/2244, art.5.
195 Words in Pt. I substituted (1.11.1998) by 1998 c. 38, s. 140, Sch. 16 para. 82(1)(2) (with ss. 139(2), 141(1), 143(2)); S.I. 1998/2244, art.5.
196 Words in Pt. I substituted (1.11.1998) by 1998 c. 38, s. 140, Sch. 16 para. 82(1)(2) (with ss. 139(2), 141(1), 143(2)); S.I. 1998/2244, art. 5.
197 Words in Pt. I substituted (1.11.1998) by 1998 c. 38, s. 140, Sch. 16 para. 82(1)(2) (with ss. 139(2), 141(1), 143(2)); S.I. 1998/2244, art. 5.
198 Words in Pt. I substituted (1.11.1998) by 1998 c. 38, s. 140, Sch. 16 para. 82(1)(2) (with ss. 139(2), 141(1), 143(2)); S.I. 1998/2244, art. 5.
199 Words in Pt. I substituted (1.11.1998) by 1998 c. 38, s. 140, Sch. 16 para. 82(1)(2) (with ss. 139(2), 141(1), 143(2)); S.I. 1998/2244, art. 5.
200 Words in Pt. I substituted (1.11.1998) by 1998 c. 38, s. 140, Sch. 16 para. 82(1)(2) (with ss. 139(2), 141(1), 143(2)); S.I. 1998/2244, art. 5.
201 Words in Pt. I substituted (1.11.1998) by 1998 c. 38, s. 140, Sch. 16 para. 82(1)(2) (with ss. 139(2), 141(1), 143(2)); S.I. 1998/2244, art. 5.
202 Words in Pt. I substituted (1.11.1998) by 1998 c. 38, s. 140, Sch. 16 para. 82(1)(2) (with ss. 139(2), 141(1), 143(2)); S.I. 1998/2244, art. 5.
203 Words in Pt. I substituted (1.11.1998) by 1998 c. 38, s. 140, Sch. 16 para. 82(1)(2) (with ss. 139(2), 141(1), 143(2)); S.I. 1998/2244, art. 5.
204 Words in Pt. I substituted (1.11.1998) by 1998 c. 38, s. 140, Sch. 16 para. 82(1)(2) (with ss. 139(2), 141(1), 143(2)); S.I. 1998/2244, art. 5.
205 Words in Pt. I substituted (1.11.1998) by 1998 c. 38, s. 140, Sch. 16 para. 82(1)(2) (with ss. 139(2), 141(1), 143(2)); S.I. 1998/2244, art. 5.
206 Words in Pt. I substituted (1.11.1998) by 1998 c. 38, s. 140, Sch. 16 para. 82(1)(2) (with ss. 139(2), 141(1), 143(2)); S.I. 1998/2244, art. 5.
207 Words in Pt. I substituted (1.11.1998) by 1998 c. 38, s. 140, Sch. 16 para. 82(1)(2) (with ss. 139(2), 141(1), 143(2)); S.I. 1998/2244, art. 5.
208 Words in Pt. I substituted (1.11.1998) by 1998 c. 38, s. 140, Sch. 16 para. 82(1)(2) (with ss. 139(2), 141(1), 143(2)); S.I. 1998/2244, art. 5.
209 Words in Pt. I substituted (1.11.1998) by 1998 c. 38, s. 140, Sch. 16 para. 82(1)(2) (with ss. 139(2), 141(1), 143(2)); S.I. 1998/2244, art. 5.
210 Words in Pt. I substituted (1.11.1998) by 1998 c. 38, s. 140, Sch. 16 para. 82(1)(2) (with ss. 139(2), 141(1), 143(2)); S.I. 1998/2244, art. 5.
211 Words in Pt. I substituted (1.11.1998) by 1998 c. 38, s. 140, Sch. 16 para. 82(1)(2) (with ss. 139(2), 141(1), 143(2)); S.I. 1998/2244, art. 5.
212 Words in Pt. I substituted (1.11.1998) by 1998 c. 38, s. 140, Sch. 16 para. 82(1)(2) (with ss. 139(2), 141(1), 143(2)); S.I. 1998/2244, art. 5.
213 Words in Sch. 1 para. 9(1)(4) substituted (1.12.2001) by S.I. 2001/3649, arts. 1, 357(2)
214 Words in Pt. I substituted (1.11.1998) by 1998 c. 38, s. 140, Sch. 16 para. 82(1)(2) (with ss. 139(2), 141(1), 143(2)); S.I. 1998/2244, art. 5.
215 Sch. 1 para. 9(3) repealed (1.11.1998) by 1998 c. 38, ss. 140, 152, Sch. 16 para. 96(2)(a), Sch. 18 Pt. VI (with ss. 137(1), 139(2), 141(1), 143(2)); S.I. 1998/2244, art. 5.
216 Sch. 1 para. 9(3A) inserted (1.11.1998) by 1998 c. 38, s. 140, Sch. 16 para. 96(2)(b) (with ss. 139(2), 141(1), 143(2)); S.I. 1998/2244, art. 5.
217 Words in Sch. 1 para. 9(1)(4) substituted (1.12.2001) by S.I. 2001/3649, arts. 1, 357(2)

[218] Words in Pt. I substituted (1.11.1998) by 1998 c. 38, s. 140, Sch. 16 para. 82(1)(2) (with ss. 139(2), 141(1), 143(2)); S.I. 1998/2244, art.5.

[219] Words in Pt. I substituted (1.11.1998) by 1998 c. 38, s. 140, Sch. 16 para. 82(1)(2) (with ss. 139(2), 141(1), 143(2)); S.I. 1998/2244, art.5.

[220] Sch. 1 para. 11(3) repealed (1.11.1998) by 1998 c. 38, ss. 140, 152, Sch. 16 para. 96(2)(a), Sch. 18 Pt.VI (with ss. 137(1), 139(2), 141(1), 143(2)); S.I. 1998/2244, art.5.

[221] Sch. 1 para. 11(3A) inserted (1.11.1998) by 1998 c. 38, s. 140, Sch. 16 para. 96(2)(b) (with ss. 139(2), 141(1), 143(2)); S.I. 1998/2244, art.5.

[222] Words in Sch. 1 para. 12(1) substituted (1.12.2001) by S.I. 2001/3649, arts. 1, 357(3)(a)

[223] Words in Sch. 1 para. 12(2) substituted (1.12.2001) by S.I. 2001/3649, arts. 1, 357(3)(b)(i)

[224] Word in Sch. 1 para. 12(2) substituted (1.12.2001) by S.I. 2001/3649, arts. 1, 357(3)(b)(ii)

[225] Words in Pt. I substituted (1.11.1998) by 1998 c. 38, s. 140, Sch. 16 para. 82(1)(2) (with ss. 139(2), 141(1), 143(2)); S.I. 1998/2244, art. 5.

[226] Words in Pt. I substituted (1.11.1998) by 1998 c. 38, s. 140, Sch. 16 para. 82(1)(2) (with ss. 139(2), 141(1), 143(2)); S.I. 1998/2244, art. 5.

[227] Words in Sch. 1 para. 12(4)(b) substituted (1.12.2001) by S.I. 2001/3649, arts. 1, 357(3)(c)

[228] Words in Sch. 1 para. 12(5) substituted (1.12.2001) by S.I. 2001/3649, arts. 1, 357(3)(d)(i)

[229] Word in Sch. 1 para. 12(5) substituted (1.12.2001) by S.I. 2001/3649, arts. 1, 357(3)(d)(ii)

[230] Words in Pt. I substituted (1.11.1998) by 1998 c. 38, s. 140, Sch. 16 para. 82(1)(2) (with ss. 139(2), 141(1), 143(2)); S.I. 1998/2244, art. 5.

[231] Words in Pt. I substituted (1.11.1998) by 1998 c. 38, s. 140, Sch. 16 para. 82(1)(2) (with ss. 139(2), 141(1), 143(2)); S.I. 1998/2244, art. 5.

[232] Sch. 1 para. 12(6)(a)(b) and the word "are" immediately preceding substituted (1.11.1998) by 1998 c. 38, s. 140, Sch. 16 para. 96(3) (with ss. 139(2), 141(1), 143(2)); S.I. 1998/2244, art. 5.

[233] Words in Pt. I substituted (1.11.1998) by 1998 c. 38, s. 140, Sch. 16 para. 82(1)(2) (with ss. 139(2), 141(1), 143(2)); S.I. 1998/2244, art.5.

[234] Words in Pt. I substituted (1.11.1998) by 1998 c. 38, s. 140, Sch. 16 para. 82(1)(2) (with ss. 139(2), 141(1), 143(2)); S.I. 1998/2244, art.5.

[235] Words in Pt. I substituted (1.11.1998) by 1998 c. 38, s. 140, Sch. 16 para. 82(1)(2) (with ss. 139(2), 141(1), 143(2)); S.I. 1998/2244, art.5.

[236] Words in Pt. I substituted (1.11.1998) by 1998 c. 38, s. 140, Sch. 16 para. 82(1)(2) (with ss. 139(2), 141(1), 143(2)); S.I. 1998/2244, art.5.

[237] Words in Pt. I substituted (1.11.1998) by 1998 c. 38, s. 140, Sch. 16 para. 82(1)(2) (with ss. 139(2), 141(1), 143(2)); S.I. 1998/2244, art.5.

[238] Words in Pt. I substituted (1.11.1998) by 1998 c. 38, s. 140, Sch. 16 para. 82(1)(2) (with ss. 139(2), 141(1), 143(2)); S.I. 1998/2244, art.5.

[239] Sch. 1 para. 13(7)(a)(b) and the word "are" immediately preceding substituted (1.11.1998) by 1998 c. 38, s. 140, Sch. 16 para. 96(3) (with ss. 139(2), 141(1), 143(2)); S.I. 1998/2244, art.5.

[240] Words in Pt. I substituted (1.11.1998) by 1998 c. 38, s. 140, Sch. 16 para. 82(1)(2) (with ss. 139(2), 141(1), 143(2)); S.I. 1998/2244, art.5.

[241] Words in Pt. I substituted (1.11.1998) by 1998 c. 38, s. 140, Sch. 16 para. 82(1)(2) (with ss. 139(2), 141(1), 143(2)); S.I. 1998/2244, art.5.

[242] Words in Pt. I substituted (1.11.1998) by 1998 c. 38, s. 140, Sch. 16 para. 82(1)(2) (with ss. 139(2), 141(1), 143(2)); S.I. 1998/2244, art.5.

[243] Words in Pt. I substituted (1.11.1998) by 1998 c. 38, s. 140, Sch. 16 para. 82(1)(2) (with ss. 139(2), 141(1), 143(2)); S.I. 1998/2244, art.5.

[244] Words in Pt. I substituted (1.11.1998) by 1998 c. 38, s. 140, Sch. 16 para. 82(1)(2) (with ss. 139(2), 141(1), 143(2)); S.I. 1998/2244, art.5.

[245] Words in Pt. I substituted (1.11.1998) by 1998 c. 38, s. 140, Sch. 16 para. 82(1)(2) (with ss. 139(2), 141(1), 143(2)); S.I. 1998/2244, art.5.

[246] Words in Pt. I substituted (1.11.1998) by 1998 c. 38, s. 140, Sch. 16 para. 82(1)(2) (with ss. 139(2), 141(1), 143(2)); S.I. 1998/2244, art.5.

[247] Sch. 1 para. 15(5) substituted (1.11.1998) by 1998 c. 38, s. 140, Sch. 16 para. 96(4) (with ss. 139(2), 141(1), 143(2)); S.I. 1998/2244, art.5

[248] Words in Pt. I substituted (1.11.1998) by 1998 c. 38, s. 140, Sch. 16 para. 82(1)(2) (with ss. 139(2), 141(1), 143(2)); S.I. 1998/2244, art.5.

[249] Words in Pt. I substituted (1.11.1998) by 1998 c. 38, s. 140, Sch. 16 para. 82(1)(2) (with ss. 139(2), 141(1), 143(2)); S.I. 1998/2244, art.5.

[250] Words in Pt. I substituted (1.11.1998) by 1998 c. 38, s. 140, Sch. 16 para. 82(1)(2) (with ss. 139(2), 141(1), 143(2)); S.I. 1998/2244, art.5.

[251] Words in Pt. I substituted (1.11.1998) by 1998 c. 38, s. 140, Sch. 16 para. 82(1)(2) (with ss. 139(2), 141(1), 143(2)); S.I.

1998/2244, art.5.

[252] Words in Pt. I substituted (1.11.1998) by 1998 c. 38, s. 140, Sch. 16 para. 82(1)(2) (with ss. 139(2), 141(1), 143(2)); S.I. 1998/2244, art.5.

[253] Words in Pt. I substituted (1.11.1998) by 1998 c. 38, s. 140, Sch. 16 para. 82(1)(2) (with ss. 139(2), 141(1), 143(2)); S.I. 1998/2244, art.5.

[254] Words in Pt. I substituted (1.11.1998) by 1998 c. 38, s. 140, Sch. 16 para. 82(1)(2) (with ss. 139(2), 141(1), 143(2)); S.I. 1998/2244, art.5.

[255] Words in Pt. I substituted (1.11.1998) by 1998 c. 38, s. 140, Sch. 16 para. 82(1)(2) (with ss. 139(2), 141(1), 143(2)); S.I. 1998/2244, art.5.

[256] Words in Pt. I substituted (1.11.1998) by 1998 c. 38, s. 140, Sch. 16 para. 82(1)(2) (with ss. 139(2), 141(1), 143(2)); S.I. 1998/2244, art.5.

[257] Words in Pt. I substituted (1.11.1998) by 1998 c. 38, s. 140, Sch. 16 para. 82(1)(2) (with ss. 139(2), 141(1), 143(2)); S.I. 1998/2244, art.5.

[258] Words in Pt. I substituted (1.11.1998) by 1998 c. 38, s. 140, Sch. 16 para. 82(1)(2) (with ss. 139(2), 141(1), 143(2)); S.I. 1998/2244, art.5.

[259] Words in Pt. I substituted (1.11.1998) by 1998 c. 38, s. 140, Sch. 16 para. 82(1)(2) (with ss. 139(2), 141(1), 143(2)); S.I. 1998/2244, art.5.

[260] Words in Pt. I substituted (1.11.1998) by 1998 c. 38, s. 140, Sch. 16 para. 82(1)(2) (with ss. 139(2), 141(1), 143(2)); S.I. 1998/2244, art.5.

[261] Words in Pt. I substituted (1.11.1998) by 1998 c. 38, s. 140, Sch. 16 para. 82(1)(2) (with ss. 139(2), 141(1), 143(2)); S.I. 1998/2244, art.5.

[262] Words in Sch. 1 para. 20(3) inserted (1.11.1998) by 1998 c. 38, s. 140, Sch. 16 para. 96(5)(a)(c) (with ss. 139(2), 141(1), 143(2)); S.I. 1998/2244, art.5.

[263] Words in Sch. 1 para. 20(3) substituted (1.11.1998) by 1998 c. 38, s. 140, Sch. 16 para. 96(5)(b) (with ss. 139(2), 141(1), 143(2)); S.I. 1998/2244, art.5.

[264] Words in Sch. 1 para. 20(3) inserted (1.11.1998) by 1998 c. 38, s. 140, Sch. 16 para. 96(5)(a)(c) (with ss. 139(2), 141(1), 143(2)); S.I. 1998/2244, art.5.

[265] Words in Pt. I substituted (1.11.1998) by 1998 c. 38, s. 140, Sch. 16 para. 82(1)(2) (with ss. 139(2), 141(1), 143(2)); S.I. 1998/2244, art.5.

[266] Words in Pt. I substituted (1.11.1998) by 1998 c. 38, s. 140, Sch. 16 para. 82(1)(2) (with ss. 139(2), 141(1), 143(2)); S.I. 1998/2244, art.5.

[267] Words in Pt. I substituted (1.11.1998) by 1998 c. 38, s. 140, Sch. 16 para. 82(1)(2) (with ss. 139(2), 141(1), 143(2)); S.I. 1998/2244, art.5.

[268] Words in Pt. I substituted (1.11.1998) by 1998 c. 38, s. 140, Sch. 16 para. 82(1)(2) (with ss. 139(2), 141(1), 143(2)); S.I. 1998/2244, art.5.

[269] Words in Pt. I substituted (1.11.1998) by 1998 c. 38, s. 140, Sch. 16 para. 82(1)(2) (with ss. 139(2), 141(1), 143(2)); S.I. 1998/2244, art.5.

[270] Words in Pt. I substituted (1.11.1998) by 1998 c. 38, s. 140, Sch. 16 para. 82(1)(2) (with ss. 139(2), 141(1), 143(2)); S.I. 1998/2244, art.5.

[271] Words in Pt. I substituted (1.11.1998) by 1998 c. 38, s. 140, Sch. 16 para. 82(1)(2) (with ss. 139(2), 141(1), 143(2)); S.I. 1998/2244, art.5.

[272] Words in Pt. I substituted (1.11.1998) by 1998 c. 38, s. 140, Sch. 16 para. 82(1)(2) (with ss. 139(2), 141(1), 143(2)); S.I. 1998/2244, art.5.

[273] Words in Pt. I substituted (1.11.1998) by 1998 c. 38, s. 140, Sch. 16 para. 82(1)(2) (with ss. 139(2), 141(1), 143(2)); S.I. 1998/2244, art.5.

[274] Words in Pt. I substituted (1.11.1998) by 1998 c. 38, s. 140, Sch. 16 para. 82(1)(2) (with ss. 139(2), 141(1), 143(2)); S.I. 1998/2244, art.5.

[275] Words in Pt. I substituted (1.11.1998) by 1998 c. 38, s. 140, Sch. 16 para. 82(1)(2) (with ss. 139(2), 141(1), 143(2)); S.I. 1998/2244, art.5.

[276] Words in Pt. I substituted (1.11.1998) by 1998 c. 38, s. 140, Sch. 16 para. 82(1)(2) (with ss. 139(2), 141(1), 143(2)); S.I. 1998/2244, art.5.

[277] Words in Pt. I substituted (1.11.1998) by 1998 c. 38, s. 140, Sch. 16 para. 82(1)(2) (with ss. 139(2), 141(1), 143(2)); S.I. 1998/2244, art.5.

[278] Words in Pt. I substituted (1.11.1998) by 1998 c. 38, s. 140, Sch. 16 para. 82(1)(2) (with ss. 139(2), 141(1), 143(2)); S.I. 1998/2244, art.5.

[279] Words in Pt. I substituted (1.11.1998) by 1998 c. 38, s. 140, Sch. 16 para. 82(1)(2) (with ss. 139(2), 141(1), 143(2)); S.I. 1998/2244, art.5.

[280] Words in Pt. I substituted (1.11.1998) by 1998 c. 38, s. 140, Sch. 16 para. 82(1)(2) (with ss. 139(2), 141(1), 143(2)); S.I. 1998/2244, art.5.

[281] Words in Pt. I substituted (1.11.1998) by 1998 c. 38, s. 140, Sch. 16 para. 82(1)(2) (with ss. 139(2), 141(1), 143(2)); S.I. 1998/2244, art.5.

[282] Words in Pt. I substituted (1.11.1998) by 1998 c. 38, s. 140, Sch. 16 para. 82(1)(2) (with ss. 139(2), 141(1), 143(2)); S.I. 1998/2244, art.5.

[283] Words in Pt. I substituted (1.11.1998) by 1998 c. 38, s. 140, Sch. 16 para. 82(1)(2) (with ss. 139(2), 141(1), 143(2)); S.I. 1998/2244, art.5.

[284] Words in Pt. I substituted (1.11.1998) by 1998 c. 38, s. 140, Sch. 16 para. 82(1)(2) (with ss. 139(2), 141(1), 143(2)); S.I. 1998/2244, art.5.

[285] Words in Pt. I substituted (1.11.1998) by 1998 c. 38, s. 140, Sch. 16 para. 82(1)(2) (with ss. 139(2), 141(1), 143(2)); S.I. 1998/2244, art.5.

[286] Words in Pt. I substituted (1.11.1998) by 1998 c. 38, s. 140, Sch. 16 para. 82(1)(2) (with ss. 139(2), 141(1), 143(2)); S.I. 1998/2244, art.5.

[287] Words in Pt. I substituted (1.11.1998) by 1998 c. 38, s. 140, Sch. 16 para. 82(1)(2) (with ss. 139(2), 141(1), 143(2)); S.I. 1998/2244, art.5.

[288] Words in Pt. I substituted (1.11.1998) by 1998 c. 38, s. 140, Sch. 16 para. 82(1)(2) (with ss. 139(2), 141(1), 143(2)); S.I. 1998/2244, art.5.

[289] Words in Pt. I substituted (1.11.1998) by 1998 c. 38, s. 140, Sch. 16 para. 82(1)(2) (with ss. 139(2), 141(1), 143(2)); S.I. 1998/2244, art.5.

[290] Words in Pt. I substituted (1.11.1998) by 1998 c. 38, s. 140, Sch. 16 para. 82(1)(2) (with ss. 139(2), 141(1), 143(2)); S.I. 1998/2244, art.5.

[291] Words in Pt. I substituted (1.11.1998) by 1998 c. 38, s. 140, Sch. 16 para. 82(1)(2) (with ss. 139(2), 141(1), 143(2)); S.I. 1998/2244, art.5.

[292] Words in Pt. I substituted (1.11.1998) by 1998 c. 38, s. 140, Sch. 16 para. 82(1)(2) (with ss. 139(2), 141(1), 143(2)); S.I. 1998/2244, art.5.

[293] Words in Pt. I substituted (1.11.1998) by 1998 c. 38, s. 140, Sch. 16 para. 82(1)(2) (with ss. 139(2), 141(1), 143(2)); S.I. 1998/2244, art.5.

[294] Words in Pt. I substituted (1.11.1998) by 1998 c. 38, s. 140, Sch. 16 para. 82(1)(2) (with ss. 139(2), 141(1), 143(2)); S.I. 1998/2244, art.5.

[295] Words in Pt. I substituted (1.11.1998) by 1998 c. 38, s. 140, Sch. 16 para. 82(1)(2) (with ss. 139(2), 141(1), 143(2)); S.I. 1998/2244, art.5.

[296] Words in Pt. I substituted (1.11.1998) by 1998 c. 38, s. 140, Sch. 16 para. 82(1)(2) (with ss. 139(2), 141(1), 143(2)); S.I. 1998/2244, art.5.

[297] Words in Pt. I substituted (1.11.1998) by 1998 c. 38, s. 140, Sch. 16 para. 82(1)(2) (with ss. 139(2), 141(1), 143(2)); S.I. 1998/2244, art.5.

[298] Words in Pt. I substituted (1.11.1998) by 1998 c. 38, s. 140, Sch. 16 para. 82(1)(2) (with ss. 139(2), 141(1), 143(2)); S.I. 1998/2244, art.5.

[299] Words in Pt. I substituted (1.11.1998) by 1998 c. 38, s. 140, Sch. 16 para. 82(1)(2) (with ss. 139(2), 141(1), 143(2)); S.I. 1998/2244, art.5.

[300] Words in Pt. I substituted (1.11.1998) by 1998 c. 38, s. 140, Sch. 16 para. 82(1)(2) (with ss. 139(2), 141(1), 143(2)); S.I. 1998/2244, art.5.

[301] Words in Pt. I substituted (1.11.1998) by 1998 c. 38, s. 140, Sch. 16 para. 82(1)(2) (with ss. 139(2), 141(1), 143(2)); S.I. 1998/2244, art.5.

[302] Words in Pt. I substituted (1.11.1998) by 1998 c. 38, s. 140, Sch. 16 para. 82(1)(2) (with ss. 139(2), 141(1), 143(2)); S.I. 1998/2244, art.5.

[303] Words in Pt. I substituted (1.11.1998) by 1998 c. 38, s. 140, Sch. 16 para. 82(1)(2) (with ss. 139(2), 141(1), 143(2)); S.I. 1998/2244, art.5.

[304] Words in Sch. 1 para. 27(1) repealed (1.11.1998) by 1998 c. 38, ss. 140, 152, Sch. 16 para. 96(6)(a), Sch. 18 Pt.VI (with ss. 137(1), 139(2), 141(1), 143(2)); S.I. 1998/2244, art.5.

[305] Words in Sch. 1 para. 27(1) inserted (1.11.1998) by 1998 c. 38, s. 140, Sch. 16 para. 96(6)(b) (with ss. 139(2), 141(1), 143(2)); S.I. 1998/2244, art.5.

[306] Words in Pt. I substituted (1.11.1998) by 1998 c. 38, s. 140, Sch. 16 para. 82(1)(2) (with ss. 139(2), 141(1), 143(2)); S.I. 1998/2244, art.5.

[307] Words in Pt. I substituted (1.11.1998) by 1998 c. 38, s. 140, Sch. 16 para. 82(1)(2) (with ss. 139(2), 141(1), 143(2)); S.I. 1998/2244, art.5.

[308] Words in Pt. I substituted (1.11.1998) by 1998 c. 38, s. 140, Sch. 16 para. 82(1)(2) (with ss. 139(2), 141(1), 143(2)); S.I. 1998/2244, art.5.

[309] Words in Pt. I substituted (1.11.1998) by 1998 c. 38, s. 140, Sch. 16 para. 82(1)(2) (with ss. 139(2), 141(1), 143(2)); S.I. 1998/2244, art.5.

[310] Words in Pt. I substituted (1.11.1998) by 1998 c. 38, s. 140, Sch. 16 para. 82(1)(2) (with ss. 139(2), 141(1), 143(2)); S.I. 1998/2244, art.5.

[311] Words in Sch. 1 para. 27(4) substituted (1.11.1998) by 1998 c. 38, s. 140, Sch. 16 para. 96(7) (with ss. 139(2), 141(1), 143(2)); S.I. 1998/2244, art.5.

[312] Words in Pt. I substituted (1.11.1998) by 1998 c. 38, s. 140, Sch. 16 para. 82(1)(2) (with ss. 139(2), 141(1), 143(2)); S.I.

1998/2244, art.5.

313 Words in Sch. 1 para. 28(2) substituted (1.11.1998) by 1998 c. 38, s. 140, Sch. 16 para. 96(8) (with ss. 139(2), 141(1), 143(2)); S.I. 1998/2244, art.5.

314 Words in Pt. I substituted (1.11.1998) by 1998 c. 38, s. 140, Sch. 16 para. 82(1)(2) (with ss. 139(2), 141(1), 143(2)); S.I. 1998/2244, art.5.

315 Words in Pt. I substituted (1.11.1998) by 1998 c. 38, s. 140, Sch. 16 para. 82(1)(2) (with ss. 139(2), 141(1), 143(2)); S.I. 1998/2244, art.5.

316 Words in Pt. I substituted (1.11.1998) by 1998 c. 38, s. 140, Sch. 16 para. 82(1)(2) (with ss. 139(2), 141(1), 143(2)); S.I. 1998/2244, art.5.

317 Words in Pt. I substituted (1.11.1998) by 1998 c. 38, s. 140, Sch. 16 para. 82(1)(2) (with ss. 139(2), 141(1), 143(2)); S.I. 1998/2244, art.5.

318 Words in Pt. I substituted (1.11.1998) by 1998 c. 38, s. 140, Sch. 16 para. 82(1)(2) (with ss. 139(2), 141(1), 143(2)); S.I. 1998/2244, art.5.

319 Words in Pt. I substituted (1.11.1998) by 1998 c. 38, s. 140, Sch. 16 para. 82(1)(2) (with ss. 139(2), 141(1), 143(2)); S.I. 1998/2244, art.5.

320 Words in Pt. I substituted (1.11.1998) by 1998 c. 38, s. 140, Sch. 16 para. 82(1)(2) (with ss. 139(2), 141(1), 143(2)); S.I. 1998/2244, art.5.

321 Words in Pt. I substituted (1.11.1998) by 1998 c. 38, s. 140, Sch. 16 para. 82(1)(2) (with ss. 139(2), 141(1), 143(2)); S.I. 1998/2244, art.5.

322 Words in Pt. I substituted (1.11.1998) by 1998 c. 38, s. 140, Sch. 16 para. 82(1)(2) (with ss. 139(2), 141(1), 143(2)); S.I. 1998/2244, art.5.

323 Words in Sch. 2 para. 6(2) substituted (1.11.1998) by 1998 c. 38, s. 140, Sch. 16 para. 97(2) (with ss. 139(2), 141(1), 143(2)); S.I. 1998/2244, art.5.

324 Words in Sch. 2 para. 6(2) substituted (1.11.1998) by 1998 c. 38, s. 140, Sch. 16 para. 97(2) (with ss. 139(2), 141(1), 143(2)); S.I. 1998/2244, art.5.

325 Words in Pt. I substituted (1.11.1998) by 1998 c. 38, s. 140, Sch. 16 para. 82(1)(2) (with ss. 139(2), 141(1), 143(2)); S.I. 1998/2244, art.5.

326 Words in Sch. 2 para. 11(4) substituted (1.11.1998) by 1998 c. 38, s. 140, Sch. 16 para. 97(3) (with ss. 139(2), 141(1), 143(2)); S.I. 1998/2244, art.5.

327 Words in Sch. 2 para. 11(4) substituted (1.11.1998) by 1998 c. 38, s. 140, Sch. 16 para. 97(3) (with ss. 139(2), 141(1), 143(2)); S.I. 1998/2244, art.5.

Trusts of Land and Appointment of Trustees Act 1996

1996 CHAPTER 47

An Act to make new provision about trusts of land including provision phasing out the Settled Land Act 1925, abolishing the doctrine of conversion and otherwise amending the law about trusts for sale of land; to amend the law about the appointment and retirement of trustees of any trust; and for connected purposes.

[24th July 1996]

Part I TRUSTS OF LAND

Introductory

1 Meaning of "trust of land".

(1) In this Act—

(a) "trust of land" means (subject to subsection (3)) any trust of property which consists of or includes land, and

(b) "trustees of land" means trustees of a trust of land.

(2) The reference in subsection (1)(a) to a trust—

(a) is to any description of trust (whether express, implied, resulting or constructive), including a trust for sale and a bare trust, and

(b) includes a trust created, or arising, before the commencement of this Act.

(3) The reference to land in subsection (1)(a) does not include land which (despite section 2) is settled land or which is land to which the Universities and College Estates Act 1925 applies.

Settlements and trusts for sale as trusts of land

2 Trusts in place of settlements.

(1) No settlement created after the commencement of this Act is a settlement for the purposes of the Settled Land Act 1925; and no settlement shall be deemed to be made under that Act after that

commencement.

(2) Subsection (1) does not apply to a settlement created on the occasion of an alteration in any interest in, or of a person becoming entitled under, a settlement which—

(a) is in existence at the commencement of this Act, or

(b) derives from a settlement within paragraph (a) or this paragraph.

(3) But a settlement created as mentioned in subsection (2) is not a settlement for the purposes of the Settled Land Act 1925 if provision to the effect that it is not is made in the instrument, or any of the instruments, by which it is created.

(4) Where at any time after the commencement of this Act there is in the case of any settlement which is a settlement for the purposes of the Settled Land Act 1925 no relevant property which is, or is deemed to be, subject to the settlement, the settlement permanently ceases at that time to be a settlement for the purposes of that Act.

In this subsection "relevant property" means land and personal chattels to which section 67(1) of the Settled Land Act 1925 (heirlooms) applies.

(5) No land held on charitable, ecclesiastical or public trusts shall be or be deemed to be settled land after the commencement of this Act, even if it was or was deemed to be settled land before that commencement.

(6) Schedule 1 has effect to make provision consequential on this section (including provision to impose a trust in circumstances in which, apart from this section, there would be a settlement for the purposes of the Settled Land Act 1925 (and there would not otherwise be a trust)).

3 Abolition of doctrine of conversion.

(1) Where land is held by trustees subject to a trust for sale, the land is not to be regarded as personal property; and where personal property is subject to a trust for sale in order that the trustees may acquire land, the personal property is not to be regarded as land.

(2) Subsection (1) does not apply to a trust created by a will if the testator died before the commencement of this Act.

(3) Subject to that, subsection (1) applies to a trust whether it is created, or arises, before or after that commencement.

4 Express trusts for sale as trusts of land.

(1) In the case of every trust for sale of land created by a disposition there is to be implied, despite any provision to the contrary made by the disposition, a power for the trustees to postpone sale of the land; and the trustees are not liable in any way for postponing sale of the land, in the exercise of their discretion, for an indefinite period.

(2) Subsection (1) applies to a trust whether it is created, or arises, before or after the commencement of this Act.

(3) Subsection (1) does not affect any liability incurred by trustees before that commencement.

5 Implied trusts for sale as trusts of land.

(1) Schedule 2 has effect in relation to statutory provisions which impose a trust for sale of land in certain circumstances so that in those circumstances there is instead a trust of the land (without a duty to sell).

(2) Section 1 of the Settled Land Act 1925 does not apply to land held on any trust arising by virtue of that Schedule (so that any such land is subject to a trust of land).

Functions of trustees of land

6 General powers of trustees.

(1) For the purpose of exercising their functions as trustees, the trustees of land have in relation to the land subject to the trust all the powers of an absolute owner.

(2) Where in the case of any land subject to a trust of land each of the beneficiaries interested in the land is a person of full age and capacity who is absolutely entitled to the land, the powers conferred on the trustees by subsection (1) include the power to convey the land to the beneficiaries even though they have not required the trustees to do so; and where land is conveyed by virtue of this subsection—

(a) the beneficiaries shall do whatever is necessary to secure that it vests in them, and

(b) if they fail to do so, the court may make an order requiring them to do so.

(3) The trustees of land have power to [acquire land under the power conferred by section 8 of the Trustee Act 2000.][1]

(4). . . . .[2]

(5) In exercising the powers conferred by this section trustees shall have regard to the rights of the beneficiaries.

(6) The powers conferred by this section shall not be exercised in contravention of, or of any order made in pursuance of, any other enactment or any rule of law or equity.

(7) The reference in subsection (6) to an order includes an order of any court or of the Charity Commissioners.

(8) Where any enactment other than this section confers on trustees authority to act subject to any restriction, limitation or condition, trustees of land may not exercise the powers conferred by this section to do any act which they are prevented from doing under the other enactment by reason of the restriction, limitation or condition.

[(9) The duty of care under section 1 of the Trustee Act 2000 applies to trustees of land when exercising the powers conferred by this section.][3]

7 Partition by trustees.

(1) The trustees of land may, where beneficiaries of full age are absolutely entitled in undivided shares to land subject to the trust, partition the land, or any part of it, and provide (by way of mortgage or otherwise) for the payment of any equality money.

(2) The trustees shall give effect to any such partition by conveying the partitioned land in severalty (whether or not subject to any legal mortgage created for raising equality money), either absolutely or in trust, in accordance with the rights of those beneficiaries.

(3) Before exercising their powers under subsection (2) the trustees shall obtain the consent of each of those beneficiaries.

(4) Where a share in the land is affected by an incumbrance, the trustees may either give effect to it or provide for its discharge from the property allotted to that share as they think fit.

(5) If a share in the land is absolutely vested in a minor, subsections (1) to (4) apply as if he were of full age, except that the trustees may act on his behalf and retain land or other property representing his share in trust for him.

8 Exclusion and restriction of powers.

(1) Sections 6 and 7 do not apply in the case of a trust of land created by a disposition in so far as provision to the effect that they do not apply is made by the disposition.

(2) If the disposition creating such a trust makes provision requiring any consent to be obtained to the exercise of any power conferred by section 6 or 7, the power may not be exercised without that consent.

(3) Subsection (1) does not apply in the case of charitable, ecclesiastical or public trusts.

(4) Subsections (1) and (2) have effect subject to any enactment which prohibits or restricts the effect of provision of the description mentioned in them.

9 Delegation by trustees.

(1) The trustees of land may, by power of attorney, delegate to any beneficiary or beneficiaries of full age and beneficially entitled to an interest in possession in land subject to the trust any of their functions as trustees which relate to the land.

(2) Where trustees purport to delegate to a person by a power of attorney under subsection (1) functions relating to any land and another person in good faith deals with him in relation to the land, he shall be presumed in favour of that other person to have been a person to whom the functions could be delegated unless that other person has knowledge at the time of the transaction that he was not such a person.

And it shall be conclusively presumed in favour of any purchaser whose interest depends on the validity of that transaction that that other person dealt in good faith and did not have such knowledge if that other person makes a statutory declaration to that effect before or within three months after the completion of the purchase.

(3) A power of attorney under subsection (1) shall be given by all the trustees jointly and (unless expressed to be irrevocable and to be given by way of security) may be revoked by any one or more of them; and such a power is revoked by the appointment as a trustee of a person other than those

by whom it is given (though not by any of those persons dying or otherwise ceasing to be a trustee).

(4) Where a beneficiary to whom functions are delegated by a power of attorney under subsection (1) ceases to be a person beneficially entitled to an interest in possession in land subject to the trust—

(a) if the functions are delegated to him alone, the power is revoked,

(b) if the functions are delegated to him and to other beneficiaries to be exercised by them jointly (but not separately), the power is revoked if each of the other beneficiaries ceases to be so entitled (but otherwise functions exercisable in accordance with the power are so exercisable by the remaining beneficiary or beneficiaries), and

(c) if the functions are delegated to him and to other beneficiaries to be exercised by them separately (or either separately or jointly), the power is revoked in so far as it relates to him.

(5) A delegation under subsection (1) may be for any period or indefinite.

(6) A power of attorney under subsection (1) cannot be an enduring power within the meaning of the Enduring Powers of Attorney Act 1985.

(7) Beneficiaries to whom functions have been delegated under subsection (1) are, in relation to the exercise of the functions, in the same position as trustees (with the same duties and liabilities); but such beneficiaries shall not be regarded as trustees for any other purposes (including, in particular, the purposes of any enactment permitting the delegation of functions by trustees or imposing requirements relating to the payment of capital money).

(8) ....[4]

(9) Neither this section nor the repeal by this Act of section 29 of the Law of Property Act 1925 (which is superseded by this section) affects the operation after the commencement of this Act of any delegation effected before that commencement.

[9A

(1) The duty of care under section 1 of the Trustee Act 2000 applies to trustees of land in deciding whether to delegate any of their functions under section 9.

(2) Subsection (3) applies if the trustees of land—

(a) delegate any of their functions under section 9, and

(b) the delegation is not irrevocable.

(3) While the delegation continues, the trustees—

(a) must keep the delegation under review,

(b) if circumstances make it appropriate to do so, must consider whether there is a need to exercise any power of intervention that they have, and

(c) if they consider that there is a need to exercise such a power, must do so.

(4) "Power of intervention" includes—

(a) a power to give directions to the beneficiary;

(b) a power to revoke the delegation.

(5) The duty of care under section 1 of the 2000 Act applies to trustees in carrying out any duty under subsection (3).

(6) A trustee of land is not liable for any act or default of the beneficiary, or beneficiaries, unless the trustee fails to comply with the duty of care in deciding to delegate any of the trustees' functions under section 9 or in carrying out any duty under subsection (3).

(7) Neither this section nor the repeal of section 9(8) by the Trustee Act 2000 affects the operation after the commencement of this section of any delegation effected before that commencement.][5]

Consents and consultation

10 Consents.

(1) If a disposition creating a trust of land requires the consent of more than two persons to the exercise by the trustees of any function relating to the land, the consent of any two of them to the exercise of the function is sufficient in favour of a purchaser.

(2) Subsection (1) does not apply to the exercise of a function by trustees of land held on charitable, ecclesiastical or public trusts.

(3) Where at any time a person whose consent is expressed by a disposition creating a trust of land to be required to the exercise by the trustees of any function relating to the land is not of full age—

(a) his consent is not, in favour of a purchaser, required to the exercise of the function, but

(b) the trustees shall obtain the consent of a parent who has parental responsibility for him (within

the meaning of the Children Act 1989) or of a guardian of his.

11 Consultation with beneficiaries.

(1) The trustees of land shall in the exercise of any function relating to land subject to the trust—

(a) so far as practicable, consult the beneficiaries of full age and beneficially entitled to an interest in possession in the land, and

(b) so far as consistent with the general interest of the trust, give effect to the wishes of those beneficiaries, or (in case of dispute) of the majority (according to the value of their combined interests).

(2) Subsection (1) does not apply—

(a) in relation to a trust created by a disposition in so far as provision that it does not apply is made by the disposition,

(b) in relation to a trust created or arising under a will made before the commencement of this Act, or

(c) in relation to the exercise of the power mentioned in section 6(2).

(3) Subsection (1) does not apply to a trust created before the commencement of this Act by a disposition, or a trust created after that commencement by reference to such a trust, unless provision to the effect that it is to apply is made by a deed executed—

(a) in a case in which the trust was created by one person and he is of full capacity, by that person, or

(b) in a case in which the trust was created by more than one person, by such of the persons who created the trust as are alive and of full capacity.

(4) A deed executed for the purposes of subsection (3) is irrevocable.

Right of beneficiaries to occupy trust land

12 The right to occupy.

(1) A beneficiary who is beneficially entitled to an interest in possession in land subject to a trust of land is entitled by reason of his interest to occupy the land at any time if at that time—

(a) the purposes of the trust include making the land available for his occupation (or for the occupation of beneficiaries of a class of which he is a member or of beneficiaries in general), or

(b) the land is held by the trustees so as to be so available.

(2) Subsection (1) does not confer on a beneficiary a right to occupy land if it is either unavailable or unsuitable for occupation by him.

(3) This section is subject to section 13.

13 Exclusion and restriction of right to occupy.

(1) Where two or more beneficiaries are (or apart from this subsection would be) entitled under section 12 to occupy land, the trustees of land may exclude or restrict the entitlement of any one or more (but not all) of them.

(2) Trustees may not under subsection (1)—

(a) unreasonably exclude any beneficiary's entitlement to occupy land, or

(b) restrict any such entitlement to an unreasonable extent.

(3) The trustees of land may from time to time impose reasonable conditions on any beneficiary in relation to his occupation of land by reason of his entitlement under section 12.

(4) The matters to which trustees are to have regard in exercising the powers conferred by this section include—

(a) the intentions of the person or persons (if any) who created the trust,

(b) the purposes for which the land is held, and

(c) the circumstances and wishes of each of the beneficiaries who is (or apart from any previous exercise by the trustees of those powers would be) entitled to occupy the land under section 12.

(5) The conditions which may be imposed on a beneficiary under subsection (3) include, in particular, conditions requiring him—

(a) to pay any outgoings or expenses in respect of the land, or

(b) to assume any other obligation in relation to the land or to any activity which is or is proposed to be conducted there.

(6) Where the entitlement of any beneficiary to occupy land under section 12 has been excluded or restricted, the conditions which may be imposed on any other beneficiary under subsection (3)

include, in particular, conditions requiring him to—

(a) make payments by way of compensation to the beneficiary whose entitlement has been excluded or restricted, or

(b) forgo any payment or other benefit to which he would otherwise be entitled under the trust so as to benefit that beneficiary.

(7) The powers conferred on trustees by this section may not be exercised—

(a) so as prevent any person who is in occupation of land (whether or not by reason of an entitlement under section 12) from continuing to occupy the land, or

(b) in a manner likely to result in any such person ceasing to occupy the land,

unless he consents or the court has given approval.

(8) The matters to which the court is to have regard in determining whether to give approval under subsection (7) include the matters mentioned in subsection (4)(a) to (c).

Powers of court

14 Applications for order.

(1) Any person who is a trustee of land or has an interest in property subject to a trust of land may make an application to the court for an order under this section.

(2) On an application for an order under this section the court may make any such order—

(a) relating to the exercise by the trustees of any of their functions (including an order relieving them of any obligation to obtain the consent of, or to consult, any person in connection with the exercise of any of their functions), or

(b) declaring the nature or extent of a person's interest in property subject to the trust,

as the court thinks fit.

(3) The court may not under this section make any order as to the appointment or removal of trustees.

(4) The powers conferred on the court by this section are exercisable on an application whether it is made before or after the commencement of this Act.

15 Matters relevant in determining applications.

(1) The matters to which the court is to have regard in determining an application for an order under section 14 include—

(a) the intentions of the person or persons (if any) who created the trust,

(b) the purposes for which the property subject to the trust is held,

(c) the welfare of any minor who occupies or might reasonably be expected to occupy any land subject to the trust as his home, and

(d) the interests of any secured creditor of any beneficiary.

(2) In the case of an application relating to the exercise in relation to any land of the powers conferred on the trustees by section 13, the matters to which the court is to have regard also include the circumstances and wishes of each of the beneficiaries who is (or apart from any previous exercise by the trustees of those powers would be) entitled to occupy the land under section 12.

(3) In the case of any other application, other than one relating to the exercise of the power mentioned in section 6(2), the matters to which the court is to have regard also include the circumstances and wishes of any beneficiaries of full age and entitled to an interest in possession in property subject to the trust or (in case of dispute) of the majority (according to the value of their combined interests).

(4) This section does not apply to an application if section 335A of the Insolvency Act 1986 (which is inserted by Schedule 3 and relates to applications by a trustee of a bankrupt) applies to it.

Purchaser protection

16 Protection of purchasers.

(1) A purchaser of land which is or has been subject to a trust need not be concerned to see that any requirement imposed on the trustees by section 6(5), 7(3) or 11(1) has been complied with.

(2) Where—

(a) trustees of land who convey land which (immediately before it is conveyed) is subject to the trust contravene section 6(6) or (8), but

(b) the purchaser of the land from the trustees has no actual notice of the contravention,

the contravention does not invalidate the conveyance.

(3) Where the powers of trustees of land are limited by virtue of section 8—

(a) the trustees shall take all reasonable steps to bring the limitation to the notice of any purchaser of the land from them, but

(b) the limitation does not invalidate any conveyance by the trustees to a purchaser who has no actual notice of the limitation.

(4) Where trustees of land convey land which (immediately before it is conveyed) is subject to the trust to persons believed by them to be beneficiaries absolutely entitled to the land under the trust and of full age and capacity—

(a) the trustees shall execute a deed declaring that they are discharged from the trust in relation to that land, and

(b) if they fail to do so, the court may make an order requiring them to do so.

(5) A purchaser of land to which a deed under subsection (4) relates is entitled to assume that, as from the date of the deed, the land is not subject to the trust unless he has actual notice that the trustees were mistaken in their belief that the land was conveyed to beneficiaries absolutely entitled to the land under the trust and of full age and capacity.

(6) Subsections (2) and (3) do not apply to land held on charitable, ecclesiastical or public trusts.

(7) This section does not apply to registered land.

Supplementary

17 Application of provisions to trusts of proceeds of sale.

(1)...............................[6]

(2) Section 14 applies in relation to a trust of proceeds of sale of land and trustees of such a trust as in relation to a trust of land and trustees of land.

(3) In this section "trust of proceeds of sale of land" means (subject to subsection (5)) any trust of property (other than a trust of land) which consists of or includes—

(a) any proceeds of a disposition of land held in trust (including settled land), or

(b) any property representing any such proceeds.

(4) The references in subsection (3) to a trust—

(a) are to any description of trust (whether express, implied, resulting or constructive), including a trust for sale and a bare trust, and

(b) include a trust created, or arising, before the commencement of this Act.

(5) A trust which (despite section 2) is a settlement for the purposes of the Settled Land Act 1925 cannot be a trust of proceeds of sale of land.

(6) In subsection (3)—

(a) "disposition" includes any disposition made, or coming into operation, before the commencement of this Act, and

(b) the reference to settled land includes personal chattels to which section 67(1) of the Settled Land Act 1925 (heirlooms) applies.

18 Application of Part to personal representatives.

(1) The provisions of this Part relating to trustees, other than sections 10, 11 and 14, apply to personal representatives, but with appropriate modifications and without prejudice to the functions of personal representatives for the purposes of administration.

(2) The appropriate modifications include—

(a) the substitution of references to persons interested in the due administration of the estate for references to beneficiaries, and

(b) the substitution of references to the will for references to the disposition creating the trust.

(3) Section 3(1) does not apply to personal representatives if the death occurs before the commencement of this Act.

Part II APPOINTMENT AND RETIRMENT OF TRUSTEES

19 Appointment and retirement of trustee at instance of beneficiaries.

(1) This section applies in the case of a trust where—

(a) there is no person nominated for the purpose of appointing new trustees by the instrument, if any, creating the trust, and

(b) the beneficiaries under the trust are of full age and capacity and (taken together) are absolutely entitled to the property subject to the trust.

(2) The beneficiaries may give a direction or directions of either or both of the following descriptions—

(a) a written direction to a trustee or trustees to retire from the trust, and

(b) a written direction to the trustees or trustee for the time being (or, if there are none, to the personal representative of the last person who was a trustee) to appoint by writing to be a trustee or trustees the person or persons specified in the direction.

(3) Where—

(a) a trustee has been given a direction under subsection (2)(a),

(b) reasonable arrangements have been made for the protection of any rights of his in connection with the trust,

(c) after he has retired there will be either a trust corporation or at least two persons to act as trustees to perform the trust, and

(d) either another person is to be appointed to be a new trustee on his retirement (whether in compliance with a direction under subsection (2)(b) or otherwise) or the continuing trustees by deed consent to his retirement,

he shall make a deed declaring his retirement and shall be deemed to have retired and be discharged from the trust.

(4) Where a trustee retires under subsection (3) he and the continuing trustees (together with any new trustee) shall (subject to any arrangements for the protection of his rights) do anything necessary to vest the trust property in the continuing trustees (or the continuing and new trustees).

(5) This section has effect subject to the restrictions imposed by the Trustee Act 1925 on the number of trustees.

20 Appointment of substitute for incapable trustee.

(1) This section applies where—

(a) a trustee is incapable by reason of mental disorder of exercising his functions as trustee,

(b) there is no person who is both entitled and willing and able to appoint a trustee in place of him under section 36(1) of the Trustee Act 1925, and

(c) the beneficiaries under the trust are of full age and capacity and (taken together) are absolutely entitled to the property subject to the trust.

(2) The beneficiaries may give to—

(a) a receiver of the trustee,

(b) an attorney acting for him under the authority of a power of attorney created by an instrument which is registered under section 6 of the Enduring Powers of Attorney Act 1985, or

(c) a person authorised for the purpose by the authority having jurisdiction under Part VII of the Mental Health Act 1983,

a written direction to appoint by writing the person or persons specified in the direction to be a trustee or trustees in place of the incapable trustee.

21 Supplementary.

(1) For the purposes of section 19 or 20 a direction is given by beneficiaries if—

(a) a single direction is jointly given by all of them, or

(b)(subject to subsection (2)) a direction is given by each of them (whether solely or jointly with one or more, but not all, of the others),

and none of them by writing withdraws the direction given by him before it has been complied with.

(2) Where more than one direction is given each must specify for appointment or retirement the same person or persons.

(3) Subsection (7) of section 36 of the Trustee Act 1925 (powers of trustees appointed under that section) applies to a trustee appointed under section 19 or 20 as if he were appointed under that section.

(4) A direction under section 19 or 20 must not specify a person or persons for appointment if the appointment of that person or those persons would be in contravention of section 35(1) of the Trustee Act 1925 or section 24(1) of the Law of Property Act 1925 (requirements as to identity of trustees).

(5) Sections 19 and 20 do not apply in relation to a trust created by a disposition in so far as provision that they do not apply is made by the disposition.

(6) Sections 19 and 20 do not apply in relation to a trust created before the commencement of this Act by

a disposition in so far as provision to the effect that they do not apply is made by a deed executed—

(a) in a case in which the trust was created by one person and he is of full capacity, by that person, or

(b) in a case in which the trust was created by more than one person, by such of the persons who created the trust as are alive and of full capacity.

(7) A deed executed for the purposes of subsection (6) is irrevocable.

(8) Where a deed is executed for the purposes of subsection (6)—

(a) it does not affect anything done before its execution to comply with a direction under section 19 or 20, but

(b) a direction under section 19 or 20 which has been given but not complied with before its execution shall cease to have effect.

Part III SUPPLEMENTARY

22 Meaning of "beneficiary".

(1) In this Act "beneficiary", in relation to a trust, means any person who under the trust has an interest in property subject to the trust (including a person who has such an interest as a trustee or a personal representative).

(2) In this Act references to a beneficiary who is beneficially entitled do not include a beneficiary who has an interest in property subject to the trust only by reason of being a trustee or personal representative.

(3) For the purposes of this Act a person who is a beneficiary only by reason of being an annuitant is not to be regarded as entitled to an interest in possession in land subject to the trust.

23 Other interpretation provisions.

(1) In this Act "purchaser" has the same meaning as in Part I of the Law of Property Act 1925.

(2) Subject to that, where an expression used in this Act is given a meaning by the Law of Property Act 1925 it has the same meaning as in that Act unless the context otherwise requires.

(3) In this Act "the court" means—

(a) the High Court, or

(b) a county court.

24 Application to Crown.

(1) Subject to subsection (2), this Act binds the Crown.

(2) This Act (except so far as it relates to undivided shares and joint ownership) does not affect or alter the descent, devolution or nature of the estates and interests of or in—

(a) land for the time being vested in Her Majesty in right of the Crown or of the Duchy of Lancaster, or

(b) land for the time being belonging to the Duchy of Cornwall and held in right or respect of the Duchy.

25 Amendments, repeals etc.

(1) The enactments mentioned in Schedule 3 have effect subject to the amendments specified in that Schedule (which are minor or consequential on other provisions of this Act).

(2) The enactments mentioned in Schedule 4 are repealed to the extent specified in the third column of that Schedule.

(3) Neither section 2(5) nor the repeal by this Act of section 29 of the Settled Land Act 1925 applies in relation to the deed of settlement set out in the Schedule to the Chequers Estate Act 1917 or the trust instrument set out in the Schedule to the Chevening Estate Act 1959.

(4) The amendments and repeals made by this Act do not affect any entailed interest created before the commencement of this Act.

(5) The amendments and repeals made by this Act in consequence of section 3—

(a) do not affect a trust created by a will if the testator died before the commencement of this Act, and

(b) do not affect personal representatives of a person who died before that commencement;

and the repeal of section 22 of the Partnership Act 1890 does not apply in any circumstances involving the personal representatives of a partner who died before that commencement.

26 Power to make consequential provision.

(1) The Lord Chancellor may by order made by statutory instrument make any such supplementary,

transitional or incidental provision as appears to him to be appropriate for any of the purposes of this Act or in consequence of any of the provisions of this Act.

(2) An order under subsection (1) may, in particular, include provision modifying any enactment contained in a public general or local Act which is passed before, or in the same Session as, this Act.

(3) A statutory instrument made in the exercise of the power conferred by this section is subject to annulment in pursuance of a resolution of either House of Parliament.

27 Short title, commencement and extent.

(1) This Act may be cited as the Trusts of Land and Appointment of Trustees Act 1996.

(2) This Act comes into force on such day as the Lord Chancellor appoints by order made by statutory instrument.

(3) Subject to subsection (4), the provisions of this Act extend only to England and Wales.

(4) The repeal in section 30(2) of the Agriculture Act 1970 extends only to Northern Ireland.

SCHEDULES

Section 2.

SCHEDULE 1 PROVISIONS CONSEQUENTIAL ON SECTION 2

Minors

1(1) Where after the commencement of this Act a person purports to convey a legal estate in land to a minor, or two or more minors, alone, the conveyance—

(a) is not effective to pass the legal estate, but

(b) operates as a declaration that the land is held in trust for the minor or minors (or if he purports to convey it to the minor or minors in trust for any persons, for those persons).

(2) Where after the commencement of this Act a person purports to convey a legal estate in land to—

(a) a minor or two or more minors, and

(b) another person who is, or other persons who are, of full age,

the conveyance operates to vest the land in the other person or persons in trust for the minor or minors and the other person or persons (or if he purports to convey it to them in trust for any persons, for those persons).

(3) Where immediately before the commencement of this Act a conveyance is operating (by virtue of section 27 of the Settled Land Act 1925) as an agreement to execute a settlement in favour of a minor or minors—

(a) the agreement ceases to have effect on the commencement of this Act, and

(b) the conveyance subsequently operates instead as a declaration that the land is held in trust for the minor or minors.

2 Where after the commencement of this Act a legal estate in land would, by reason of intestacy or in any other circumstances not dealt with in paragraph 1, vest in a person who is a minor if he were a person of full age, the land is held in trust for the minor.

Family charges

3 Where, by virtue of an instrument coming into operation after the commencement of this Act, land becomes charged voluntarily (or in consideration of marriage) or by way of family arrangement, whether immediately or after an interval, with the payment of—

(a) a rentcharge for the life of a person or a shorter period, or

(b) capital, annual or periodical sums for the benefit of a person,

the instrument operates as a declaration that the land is held in trust for giving effect to the charge.

Charitable, ecclesiastical and public trusts

4(1) This paragraph applies in the case of land held on charitable, ecclesiastical or public trusts (other than land to which the Universities and College Estates Act 1925 applies).

(2) Where there is a conveyance of such land—

(a) if neither section 37(1) nor section 39(1) of the Charities Act 1993 applies to the conveyance, it shall state that the land is held on such trusts, and

(b) if neither section 37(2) nor section 39(2) of that Act has been complied with in relation to the conveyance and a purchaser has notice that the land is held on such trusts, he must see that any consents or orders necessary to authorise the transaction have been obtained.

(3) Where any trustees or the majority of any set of trustees have power to transfer or create any legal

estate in the land, the estate shall be transferred or created by them in the names and on behalf of the persons in whom it is vested.

Entailed interests

5(1) Where a person purports by an instrument coming into operation after the commencement of this Act to grant to another person an entailed interest in real or personal property, the instrument—

(a) is not effective to grant an entailed interest, but

(b) operates instead as a declaration that the property is held in trust absolutely for the person to whom an entailed interest in the property was purportedly granted.

(2) Where a person purports by an instrument coming into operation after the commencement of this Act to declare himself a tenant in tail of real or personal property, the instrument is not effective to create an entailed interest.

Property held on settlement ceasing to exist

6 Where a settlement ceases to be a settlement for the purposes of the Settled Land Act 1925 because no relevant property (within the meaning of section 2(4)) is, or is deemed to be, subject to the settlement, any property which is or later becomes subject to the settlement is held in trust for the persons interested under the settlement.

Section 5.

SCHEDULE 2 AMENDMENTS OF STATUTORY PROVISIONS IMPOSING TRUST FOR SALE

Mortgaged property held by trustees after redemption barred

1(1) Section 31 of the Law of Property Act 1925 (implied trust for sale of mortgaged property where right of redemption is barred) is amended as follows.

(2) In subsection (1), for the words "on trust for sale." substitute "in trust—

(a) to apply the income from the property in the same manner as interest paid on the mortgage debt would have been applicable; and

(b) if the property is sold, to apply the net proceeds of sale, after payment of costs and expenses, in the same manner as repayment of the mortgage debt would have been applicable."

(3) In subsection (2), for the words from the beginning to "this subsection" substitute—

"(2) Subsection (1) of this section".

(4) Omit subsection (3).

(5) For subsection (4) substitute—

"(4) Where—

(a) the mortgage money is capital money for the purposes of the Settled Land Act 1925;

(b) land other than any forming the whole or part of the property mentioned in subsection (1) of this section is, or is deemed to be, subject to the settlement; and

(c) the tenant for life or statutory owner requires the trustees to execute with respect to land forming the whole or part of that property a vesting deed such as would have been required in relation to the land if it had been acquired on a purchase with capital money,

the trustees shall execute such a vesting deed."

(6) In accordance with the amendments made by sub-paragraphs (2) to (5), in the sidenote of section 31 for the words "Trust for sale" substitute " Trust ".

(7) The amendments made by this paragraph—

(a) apply whether the right of redemption is discharged before or after the commencement of this Act, but

(b) are without prejudice to any dealings or arrangements made before the commencement of this Act.

Land purchased by trustees of personal property etc.

2(1) Section 32 of the Law of Property Act 1925 (implied trust for sale of land acquired by trustees of personal property or of land held on trust for sale) is omitted.

(2) The repeal made by this paragraph applies in relation to land purchased after the commencement of this Act whether the trust or will in pursuance of which it is purchased comes into operation before or after the commencement of this Act.

Dispositions to tenants in common

3(1) Section 34 of the Law of Property Act 1925 is amended as follows.

(2) In subsection (2) (conveyance of land in undivided shares to operate as conveyance to grantees on trust for sale), for the words from "upon the statutory trusts" to "those shares" substitute " in trust for the persons interested in the land ".

(3) In subsection (3) (devise etc. of land in undivided shares to operate as devise etc. to trustees of will etc. on trust for sale)—

(a) omit the words from "the trustees (if any) " to "then to" and the words "in each case", and

(b) for the words "upon the statutory trusts hereinafter mentioned" substitute " in trust for the persons interested in the land ".

(4) After that subsection insert—

"(3A) In subsections (2) and (3) of this section references to the persons interested in the land include persons interested as trustees or personal representatives (as well as persons beneficially interested)."

(5) Omit subsection (4) (settlement of undivided shares in land to operate only as settlement of share of profits of sale and rents and profits).

(6) The amendments made by this paragraph apply whether the disposition is made, or comes into operation, before or after the commencement of this Act.

Joint tenancies

4(1) Section 36 of the Law of Property Act 1925 is amended as follows.

(2) In subsection (1) (implied trust for sale applicable to land held for persons as joint tenants), for the words "on trust for sale" substitute " in trust ".

(3) In subsection (2) (severance of beneficial joint tenancy)—

(a) in the proviso, for the words "under the trust for sale affecting the land the net proceeds of sale, and the net rents and profits until sale, shall be held upon the trusts" substitute " the land shall be held in trust on terms ", and

(b) in the final sentence, for the words "on trust for sale" substitute " in trust ".

(4) The amendments made by this paragraph apply whether the legal estate is limited, or becomes held in trust, before or after the commencement of this Act.

Intestacy

5(1) Section 33 of the Administration of Estates Act 1925 (implied trust for sale on intestacy) is amended as follows.

(2) For subsection (1) substitute—

"(1) On the death of a person intestate as to any real or personal estate, that estate shall be held in trust by his personal representatives with the power to sell it."

(3) In subsection (2), for the words from the beginning to "pay all" substitute—

"(2) The personal representatives shall pay out of—

(a) the ready money of the deceased (so far as not disposed of by his will, if any); and

(b) any net money arising from disposing of any other part of his estate (after payment of costs), all".

(4) In subsection (4), for the words from "including" to "retained" substitute " and any part of the estate of the deceased which remains ".

(5) The amendments made by this paragraph apply whether the death occurs before or after the commencement of this Act.

Reverter of sites

6(1) Section 1 of the Reverter of Sites Act 1987 (right of reverter replaced by trust for sale) is amended as follows.

(2) In subsection (2)—

(a) after "a trust" insert "for the persons who (but for this Act) would from time to time be entitled to the ownership of the land by virtue of its reverter with a power, without consulting them,", and

(b) for the words "upon trust" onwards substitute "in trust for those persons; but they shall not be entitled by reason of their interest to occupy the land."

(3) In subsection (3), for the words "trustees for sale" substitute "trustees".

(4) In subsection (4), for the words "on trust for sale" substitute "in trust".

(5) In accordance with the amendments made by this paragraph, in the sidenote, for "trust for sale" substitute " trust ".

(6) The amendments made by this paragraph apply whether the trust arises before or after the commencement of this Act.

Trusts deemed to arise in 1926

7 Where at the commencement of this Act any land is held on trust for sale, or on the statutory trusts, by virtue of Schedule 1 to the Law of Property Act 1925 (transitional provisions), it shall after that commencement be held in trust for the persons interested in the land; and references in that Schedule to trusts for sale or trustees for sale or to the statutory trusts shall be construed accordingly.

Section 25(1).

SCHEDULE 3 MINOR AND CONSEQUENTIAL AMENDMENTS

The Law of Property Act 1922 (c.16)

1 In paragraph 17(3) and (4) of Schedule 15 to the Law of Property Act 1922, for the words "held on trust for sale" substitute " subject to a trust of land ".

The Settled Land Act 1925 (c.18)

2(1) The Settled Land Act 1925 is amended as follows.

(2) In section 1(1)(ii)(c), after the word "fee" insert " (other than a fee which is a fee simple absolute by virtue of section 7 of the Law of Property Act 1925) ".

(3) In section 3, for the words "not held upon trust for sale which has been subject to a settlement" substitute "which has been subject to a settlement which is a settlement for the purposes of this Act".

(4) In section 7(5), for the words "trustee for sale" substitute " trustee of land ".

(5) In section 12(1), for the words "trustee for sale" substitute " trustee of land ".

(6) In section 17—

(a) in subsection (1)—

(i) for the words "trust for sale", in the first three places, substitute " trust of land", and

(ii) for the words "held on trust for sale" substitute " subject to a trust of land",

(b) in subsection (2)(c), for the words "a conveyance on trust for sale" substitute " land", and

(c) in subsection (3), for the words "any trust for sale" substitute "a trust of land ".

(7) In section 18(2)(b), for the words "trustee for sale" substitute "trustee of land".

(8) In section 20(1)(viii), for the words "an immediate binding trust for sale" substitute "a trust of land".

(9) In section 30(1)—

(a) in paragraph (iii), for the words "power of or upon trust for sale of" substitute " a power or duty to sell ", and

(b) in paragraph (iv)—

(i) for the words "future power of sale, or under a future trust for sale of" substitute " a future power or duty to sell ", and

(ii) for the words "or trust" substitute " or duty ".

(10) In section 33(1), for the words "any power of sale, or trust for sale" substitute "a power or duty to sell".

(11) In section 36—

(a) for the words—

(i) "upon the statutory trusts" in subsection (2), and

(ii) "on the statutory trusts" in subsection (3),

substitute "in trust for the persons interested in the land",

(b) in subsection (4), for the words "trust for sale" substitute "trust of land",

(c) for subsection (6) substitute—

"(6) In subsections (2) and (3) of this section references to the persons interested in the land include persons interested as trustees or personal representatives (as well as persons beneficially interested).", and

(d) in accordance with the amendments made by paragraphs (a) to (c), in the sidenote, for the words "trust for sale of the land" substitute " trust of land ".

(12) In section 110(5), for the words "trustee for sale" substitute " trustee of land ".

(13) In section 117(1)—

(a) in paragraph (ix), for the words "not being" substitute " , but does not (except in the phrase "trust of land") include ", and

(b) in paragraph (xxx), for the words " "trustees for sale" and "power to postpone a sale" have the same meanings" substitute " has the same meaning".

The Trustee Act 1925 (c.19)

3(1) The Trustee Act 1925 is amended as follows.

(2) In section 12—

(a) in subsection (1), for the words "a trust for sale or a power of sale of property is vested in a trustee" substitute " a trustee has a duty or power to sell property ", and

(b) in subsection (2), for the word "trust", in both places, substitute " duty ".

(3) In section 14(2), for paragraph (a) substitute—

"(a) proceeds of sale or other capital money arising under a trust of land;".

(4)...............................[7]

(5) In section 20(3)(c), for the words "property held upon trust for sale" substitute " land subject to a trust of land or personal property held on trust for sale ".

(6) In section 24—

(a) for the words "the proceeds of sale of land directed to be sold, or in any other" substitute " any ",

(b) for the words "trust for sale" substitute " trust ",

(c) for the words "trustees for sale" substitute " trustees ", and

(d) for the words "trust or" substitute " duty or ".

(7) In section 27(1), for the words "or of a disposition on trust for sale" substitute " , trustees of land, trustees for sale of personal property ".

(8) In section 32, for subsection (2) substitute—

"(2) This section does not apply to capital money arising under the Settled Land Act 1925."

(9) In section 34(2), for the words "on trust for sale of land" substitute " creating trusts of land ".

(10) In section 35—

(a) for subsection (1) substitute—

"(1) appointments of new trustees of land and of new trustees of any trust of the proceeds of sale of the land shall, subject to any order of the court, be effected by separate instruments, but in such manner as to secure that the same persons become trustees of land and trustees of the trust of the proceeds of sale.",

(b) for subsection (3) substitute—

"(3) Where new trustees of land are appointed, a memorandum of the persons who are for the time being the trustees of the land shall be endorsed on or annexed to the conveyance by which the land was vested in trustees of land; and that conveyance shall be produced to the persons who are for the time being the trustees of the land by the person in possession of it in order for that to be done when the trustees require its production.", and

(c) in accordance with the amendments made by paragraphs (a) and (b), in the sidenote, for the words "dispositions on trust for sale of land" substitute " and trustees of land ".

(11) In section 36(6), for the words before paragraph (a) substitute—

"(6) Where, in the case of any trust, there are not more than three trustees—".

(12) In section 37(1)(c), for the word "individuals" substitute " persons ".

(13) In section 39(1), for the word "individuals" substitute " persons ".

(14) In section 40(2), for the words "the statutory power" substitute " section 39 of this Act or section 19 of the Trusts of Land and Appointment of Trustees Act 1996 ".

The Law of Property Act 1925 (c.20)

4(1) The Law of Property Act 1925 is amended as follows.

(2) In section 2—

(a) in subsection (1), in paragraph (ii)—

(i) for the words "trustees for sale" substitute " trustees of land ", and

(ii) for the words "the statutory requirements respecting the payment of capital money arising under a disposition upon trust for sale" substitute " the requirements of section 27 of this Act

respecting the payment of capital money arising on such a conveyance ",

(b) after that subsection insert—

"(1A) an equitable interest in land subject to a trust of land which remains in, or is to revert to, the settlor shall (subject to any contrary intention) be overreached by the conveyance if it would be so overreached were it an interest under the trust.", and

(c) in subsection (2)—

(i) for the words "a trust for sale" substitute " a trust of land ",

(ii) for the words "under the trust for sale or the powers conferred on the trustees for sale" substitute " by the trustees ", and

(iii) for the words "to the trust for sale" substitute " to the trust ".

(3) In section 3(1)(c), for the words "Where the legal estate affected is neither settled land nor vested in trustees for sale" substitute " In any other case ".

(4) In section 16—

(a) in subsection (2), for the words "pursuant to a trust for sale" substitute " by trustees of land ", and

(b) in subsection (6), for the words "trustee for sale" substitute " trustee of land ".

(5) In section 18—

(a) in subsection (1)—

(i) after the word "settled" insert " or held subject to a trust of land ", and

(ii) for the words "trustee for sale" substitute " trustee of land ", and

(b) in subsection (2)(b), for the words "of the land or of the proceeds of sale" substitute " or trust ".

(6) In section 22(2)—

(a) for the words "held on trust for sale" substitute " subject to a trust of land ", and

(b) for the words "under the trust for sale or under the powers vested in the trustees for sale" substitute " by the trustees ",

and, in accordance with the amendments made by paragraphs (a) and (b), in the sidenote of section 22, for the words "on trust for sale" substitute " in trust ".

(7) For section 24 substitute—

"Trusts of land

24 Appointment of trustees of land.

(1) The persons having power to appoint new trustees of land shall be bound to appoint the same persons (if any) who are for the time being trustees of any trust of the proceeds of sale of the land.

(2) A purchaser shall not be concerned to see that subsection (1) of this section has been complied with.

(3) This section applies whether the trust of land and the trust of proceeds of sale are created, or arise, before or after the commencement of this Act."

(8) In section 27—

(a) for subsection (1) substitute—

"(1) a purchaser of a legal estate from trustees of land shall not be concerned with the trusts affecting the land, the net income of the land or the proceeds of sale of the land whether or not those trusts are declared by the same instrument as that by which the trust of land is created.", and

(b) in subsection (2)—

(i) for the words "trust for sale" substitute " trust ",

(ii) for the words "the settlement of the net proceeds" substitute " any trust affecting the net proceeds of sale of the land if it is sold ", and

(iii) for the words "trustees for sale" substitute " trustees ".

(9) In section 33—

(a) for the words "trustees for sale" substitute " trustees of land ", and

(b) for the words "on trust for sale" substitute " land in trust ".

(10) In section 39(4), for the words "trusts for sale" substitute " trusts ".

(11) In section 42—

(a) in subsection (1)(a), for the words "trust for sale" substitute " trust of land ", and

(b) in subsection (2)—

(i) in paragraph (a), for the words "a conveyance on trust for sale" substitute " land ", and

(ii) in paragraph (b), for the words "on trust for sale" substitute " in trust ".

(12) In section 66(2), for the words "trustee for sale" substitute " trustee of land ".

(13) In section 102(1)—

(a) for the words "share in the proceeds of sale of the land and in the rents and profits thereof until sale" substitute " interest under the trust to which the land is subject ", and

(b) for the words "trustees for sale" substitute " trustees ".

(14) In section 131, after the words "but for this section" insert " (and paragraph 5 of Schedule 1 to the Trusts of Land and Appointment of Trustees Act 1996) ".

(15) In section 137—

(a) in subsection (2)(ii), for the words "the proceeds of sale of land" onwards substitute " land subject to a trust of land, or the proceeds of the sale of such land, the persons to be served with notice shall be the trustees. ", and

(b) in subsection (5), for the words "held on trust for sale" substitute " subject to a trust of land ".

(16) In section 153(6)(ii), for the words "in trust for sale" substitute " as a trustee of land ".

The Land Registration Act 1925 (c.21)

5(1) The Land Registration Act 1925 is amended as follows.

(2) In section 3(xv)(a)—

(a) for the words "held on trust for sale" substitute "subject to a trust of land", and

(b) for the words "trustees for sale" substitute " trustees ".

(3) In section 4, for the words "trustee for sale" substitute "trustee of land".

(4) In section 8(1), for the words "trustee for sale" substitute "trustee of land".

(5) In section 49—

(a) in subsection (1)(d)—

(i) for the words "the proceeds of sale of land held on trust for sale" substitute "land subject to a trust of land", and

(ii) for the words "disposition on trust for sale or of the" substitute " trust or ",

(b) in subsection (2), for the words "trust for sale" substitute "trust of land",

(c) in the proviso to that subsection, for the words "a disposition on trust for sale or" substitute " land, or trustees of ", and

(d) in subsection (3), for the words "on trust for sale" substitute "subject to a trust of land".

(6) In section 78(4), at the end insert "registered at the commencement of this Act".

(7) In section 83, in paragraph (b) of the proviso to subsection (11), for the words "held on trust for sale" substitute "subject to a trust of land".

(8) In section 94—

(a) for subsection (1) substitute—

"(1) Where registered land is subject to a trust of land, the land shall be registered in the names of the trustees.",

(b) in subsection (3), for the words "trust for sale, the trustees for sale" substitute " trust of land, the trustees ",

(c) after that subsection insert—

"(4) There shall also be entered on the register such restrictions as may be prescribed, or may be expedient, for the protection of the rights of the persons beneficially interested in the land.

(5) Where a deed has been executed under section 16(4) of the Trusts of Land and Appointment of Trustees Act 1996 by trustees of land the registrar is entitled to assume that, as from the date of the deed, the land to which the deed relates is not subject to the trust unless he has actual notice that the trustees were mistaken in their belief that the land was conveyed to beneficiaries absolutely entitled to the land under the trust and of full age and capacity.", and

(d) in accordance with the amendments made by paragraphs (a) to (c), in the sidenote, for the words "on trust for sale" substitute " in trust ".

(9) In section 95, for the words "on trust for sale" substitute " subject to a trust of land ".

(10) In paragraph (b) of the proviso to section 103(1)—

(a) for the words "on trust for sale" substitute "subject to a trust of land", and

(b) for the words "the execution of the trust for sale" substitute "a sale of the land by the trustees".

(11) In section 111(1), for the words "trustees for sale" substitute "trustees of land".

The Administration of Estates Act 1925 (c.23)

6(1) The Administration of Estates Act 1925 is amended as follows.

(2) In section 39(1)—

(a) in paragraph (i), at the beginning insert "as respects the personal estate,",

(b) for paragraph (ii) substitute—

"(ii) as respects the real estate, all the functions conferred on them by Part I of the Trusts of Land and Appointment of Trustees Act 1996;", and

(c) in paragraph (iii), for the words "conferred by statute on trustees for sale, and" substitute " necessary ".

(3) In section 41(6), for the words "trusts for sale" substitute "trusts".

(4) In section 51(3)—

(a) after the word "married" insert " and without issue ",

(b) before the word "settlement", in both places, insert " trust or ", and

(c) for the words "an entailed interest" substitute " a life interest ".

(5) In section 55(1), after paragraph (vi) insert—

"(via) "Land" has the same meaning as in the Law of Property Act 1925;".

The Green Belt (London and Home Counties) Act 1938 (c.xciii)

7 In section 19(1) of the Green Belt (London and Home Counties) Act 1938—

(a) for the words "trustee for sale within the meaning of the Law of Property Act 1925" substitute "trustee of land", and

(b) for the words "of a trustee for sale" substitute "of a trustee of land".

The Settled Land and Trustee Acts (Court's General Powers) Act 1943 (c.25)

8 In section 1 of the Settled Land and Trustee Acts (Court's General Powers) Act 1943—

(a) in subsection (1)—

(i) for the words "trustees for sale of land" substitute " trustees of land ", and

(ii) for the words "land held on trust for sale" substitute " land subject to a trust of land ", and

(b) in subsections (2) and (3), for the words "trust for sale" substitute " trust of land ".

The Historic Buildings and Ancient Monuments Act 1953 (c.49)

9 In sections 8(3), 8A(3) and 8B(3) of the Historic Buildings and Ancient Monuments Act 1953, for the words from "held on" to "thereof" substitute " subject to a trust of land, are conferred by law on the trustees of land in relation to the land and to the proceeds of its sale ".

The Leasehold Reform Act 1967 (c.88)

10 In the Leasehold Reform Act 1967—

(a) in section 6(1), for the words "the statutory trusts arising by virtue of sections 34 to 36" substitute "a trust arising under section 34 or section 36",

(b) in section 24(1)(a), for the words "held on trust for sale" substitute "subject to a trust of land", and

(c) in paragraph 7 of Schedule 2—

(i) in sub-paragraph (1), for the words "a disposition on trust for sale" substitute "trust of land", and

(ii) in sub-paragraph (3), for the words "held on trust for sale" substitute "subject to a trust of land".

The Agriculture Act 1970 (c.40)

11 In section 33(2) of the Agriculture Act 1970—

(a) for the words "held under a trust for sale" substitute "subject to a trust of land", and

(b) for the words "the trustees for sale" substitute "the trustees of land".

The Land Charges Act 1972 (c.61)

12(1) The Land Charges Act 1972 is amended as follows.

(2) In section 2(4)(iii)(b), for the words "trust for sale" substitute " trust of land ".

(3) In section 6, after subsection (1) insert—

"(1A) No writ or order affecting an interest under a trust of land may be registered under subsection (1) above."

The Land Compensation Act 1973 (c.26)

13 In subsection (2) of section 10 of the Land Compensation Act 1973, for the words "held on trust for sale" substitute " subject to a trust of land " and, in accordance with that amendment, in the sidenote of that section, for the words "trusts for sale" substitute " trusts of land ".

The Local Land Charges Act 1975 (c.76)

14 In section 11(2) of the Local Land Charges Act 1975, for the words "held on trust for sale" substitute "subject to a trust of land".

The Rentcharges Act 1977 (c.30)

15(1) The Rentcharges Act 1977 is amended as follows.

(2) In section 2(3), for paragraphs (a) and (b) substitute—

"(a) in the case of which paragraph 3 of Schedule 1 to the Trusts of Land and Appointment of Trustees Act 1996 (trust in case of family charge) applies to the land on which the rent is charged;

(b) in the case of which paragraph (a) above would have effect but for the fact that the land on which the rent is charged is settled land or subject to a trust of land;".

(3) In section 10(2)(b), for the words "trust for sale" substitute "trust of land".

The Interpretation Act 1978 (c.30)

16 In Schedule 1 to the Interpretation Act 1978, after the definition of "The Treasury" insert—

""Trust of land" and "trustees of land", in relation to England and Wales, have the same meanings as in the Trusts of Land and Appointment of Trustees Act 1996."

The Ancient Monuments and Archaeological Areas Act 1979 (c.46)

17 In the Ancient Monuments and Archaeological Areas Act 1979—

(a) in section 12(3), for the words "trust for sale" substitute "trust of land", and

(b) in section 18(4), for paragraph (b) substitute—

"(b) as trustees of land;".

The Limitation Act 1980 (c.58)

18 In paragraph 9 of Schedule 1 to the Limitation Act 1980, for the words "held on trust for sale" substitute "subject to a trust of land".

The Highways Act 1980 (c.66)

19 In section 87(4)(b) of the Highways Act 1980, for the words from "and section 28" to "apply" substitute "applies".

. . .[8]

20. . . . .[9]

The Health and Social Services and Social Security Adjudications Act 1983 (c.41)

21 In section 22 of the Health and Social Services and Social Security Adjudications Act 1983—

(a) in subsection (5)—

(i) for the words "a joint tenant in the proceeds of sale of land held upon trust for sale" substitute "an equitable joint tenant in land", and

(ii) for the words "those proceeds" substitute "the land",

(b) in subsection (6)—

(i) for the words "a joint tenant in the proceeds of sale of land held upon trust for sale" substitute "an equitable joint tenant in land",

(ii) for the words "proceeds is" substitute "land is", and

(iii) for the words "interests in the proceeds" substitute "interests in the land", and

(c) in subsection (8), for the words "an interest in the proceeds of sale of land" substitute "the interest of an equitable joint tenant in land".

The Telecommunications Act 1984 (c.12)

22 In paragraph 4(10) of Schedule 2 to the Telecommunications Act 1984, for the words "trusts for sale" substitute "trusts of land".

The Insolvency Act 1986 (c.45)

23 At the beginning of Chapter V of Part IX of the Insolvency Act 1986 insert—

"Rights under trusts of land

335A Rights under trusts of land.

(1) Any application by a trustee of a bankrupt's estate under section 14 of the Trusts of Land and Appointment of Trustees Act 1996 (powers of court in relation to trusts of land) for an order under that section for the sale of land shall be made to the court having jurisdiction in relation to the bankruptcy.

(2) On such an application the court shall make such order as it thinks just and reasonable having regard to—

(a) the interests of the bankrupt's creditors;

(b) where the application is made in respect of land which includes a dwelling house which is or has been the home of the bankrupt or the bankrupt's spouse or former spouse—

(i) the conduct of the spouse or former spouse, so far as contributing to the bankruptcy,

(ii) the needs and financial resources of the spouse or former spouse, and

(iii) the needs of any children; and

(c) all the circumstances of the case other than the needs of the bankrupt.

(3) Where such an application is made after the end of the period of one year beginning with the first vesting under Chapter IV of this Part of the bankrupt's estate in a trustee, the court shall assume, unless the circumstances of the case are exceptional, that the interests of the bankrupt's creditors outweigh all other considerations.

(4) The powers conferred on the court by this section are exercisable on an application whether it is made before or after the commencement of this section."

The Patronage (Benifices) Measure 1986 (No.3)

24 In section 33 of the Patronage (Benifices) Measure 1986—

(a) in subsection (1), for the words from "held by any trustee" to "capable of sale" substitute "subject to a trust of land", and

(b) in subsection (2), for the words "section 26(1) and (2) of the Law of Property Act 1925 (consents to the execution of a trust for sale) " substitute " section 10 of the Trusts of Land and Appointment of Trustees Act 1996 (consents) ".

The Family Law Reform Act 1987 (c.42)

25 In section 19(2) of the Family Law Reform Act 1987, for the words "which is used to create" substitute "purporting to create".

The Charities Act 1993 (c.10)

26 In section 23 of the Charities Act 1993—

(a) in subsection (1)(b), for the words "trust for sale" substitute "trust",

(b) in subsection (5), for the words "trustee for sale" substitute "trustee",

(c) in subsection (7), for the words "trustees for sale" substitute " trustees ", and

(d) in subsection (9), for the words "trust for sale" substitute " trust ".

The Leasehold Reform, Housing and Urban Development Act 1993 (c.28)

27(1) The Leasehold Reform, Housing and Urban Development Act 1993 is amended as follows.

(2) In Schedule 2—

(a) in paragraph 5(1) and (2), for the words "held on trust for sale" substitute " subject to a trust of land " (and, accordingly, in the heading immediately preceding paragraph 5 for the words "on trust for sale" substitute " in trust "),

(b) in paragraph 6, for the words "as mentioned in paragraph 5(2)(b) above" substitute " by the landlord on the termination of a new lease granted under Chapter II or section 93(4) (whether the payment is made in pursuance of an order under section 61 or in pursuance of an agreement made in conformity with paragraph 5 of Schedule 14 without an application having been made under that section) ", and

(c) in paragraphs 7(2)(b) and 8(3)(b) and (4)(c), for "5(2)(b) " substitute " 6 ".

(3) In Schedule 14—

(a) in paragraph 7(1), for the words "disposition on trust for sale" substitute " trust of land ", and

(b) in paragraph 9(a), for the words "held on trust for sale" substitute " subject to a trust of land ".

Section 25(2).

SCHEDULE 4 REPEALS

Chapter	Short title	Extent of repeal
3 & 4 Will.4 c. 74.	The Fines and Recoveries Act 1833.	In section 1, the words ", and any undivided share thereof", in both places.
7 Will.4 & 1 Vict. c. 26.	The Wills Act 1837.	In section 1, the words "and to any undivided share thereof,".
		Section 32.
53 & 54 Vict. c. 39.	The Partnership Act 1890.	Section 22.
12 & 13 Geo.5 c. 16.	The Law of Property Act 1922.	In section 188— in subsection (1), the words "but not an undivided share in land;" and the words "but not an undivided share thereof", and subsection (30).
15 & 16 Geo.5 c. 18.	The Settled Land Act 1925.	Section 27.
		Section 29.
15 & 16 Geo.5 c. 19.	The Trustee Act 1925.	In section 10(2)— in the first paragraph, the words "by trustees or" and the words "the trustees, or", and in the second paragraph, the words from the beginning to "mortgage; and". In section 19(1), the words "building or", in the second place. In section 68— in subsection (6), the words ", but not an undivided share in land" and the words ", but not an undivided share thereof", and in subsection (19), the word "binding", the words ", and with or without power at discretion to postpone the sale" and the definition of "trustees for sale".
15 & 16 Geo.5 c. 20.	The Law of Property Act 1925.	In section 3— subsections (1)(b) and (2), and in subsection (5), the words "trustees for sale or other". In section 7(3), the second paragraph. In section 18— in subsection (1), the words from ", and personal estate" to "payable", in the second place, and the words "or is capable of being", and in subsection (2), the words "of the settlement or the trustees for sale", in both places. Section 19. Section 23 (and the heading immediately preceding it). Sections 25 and 26. Sections 28 to 30. Section 31(3). Section 32. In section 34— in subsection (3), the words from "the trustees (if any) " to "then to" and the words "in each case", and subsection (4). Section 35. Section 42(6). In section 60, paragraphs (b) and (c) of the proviso to subsection (4). In section 130, subsections (1) to (3) and (6) (and the words "Creation of" in the sidenote).

		Section 201(3). In section 205(1)— in paragraph (ix), the words "but not an undivided share in land;" and the words "but not an undivided share thereof", in paragraph (x), the words "or in the proceeds of sale thereof", and in paragraph (xxix), the word "binding", the words ", and with or without a power at discretion to postpone the sale" and the words "and "power"" onwards.
15 & 16 Geo.5 c. 21.	The Land Registration Act 1925.	In section 3— in paragraph (viii), the words "but not an undivided share in land;", in paragraph (xi), the words "or in the proceeds of sale thereof", in paragraph (xiv), the words ", but not an undivided share thereof", and paragraphs (xxviii) and (xxix).
15 & 16 Geo.5 c. 23.	The Administration of Estates Act 1925.	In section 3(1)(ii), the words "money to arise under a trust for sale of land, nor".
		In section 39(1)(i), the words from ", and such power" to "legal mortgage". In section 51— in subsection (3), the word "settled", and subsection (4). In section 55(1)— in paragraph (vii), the words "or in the proceeds of sale thereof", in paragraph (xxiv), the word " "land"", and paragraph (xxvii).
15 & 16 Geo.5 c. 24.	The Universities and College Estates Act 1925.	In section 43(iv), the words ", but not an undivided share in land".
16 & 17 Geo.5 c. 11.	The Law of Property (Amendment) Act 1926.	In the Schedule, the entries relating to section 3 of the Settled Land Act 1925 and sections 26, 28 and 35 of the Law of Property Act 1925.
17 & 18 Geo.5 c. 36.	The Landlord and Tenant Act 1927.	In section 13— in subsection (1), the words from "(either" to "Property Act, 1925) ", in subsection (2), the words ", trustee for sale, or personal representative", and in subsection (3), the words ", and "settled land"" onwards.
22 & 23 Geo.5 c. 27.	The Law of Property (Entailed Interests) Act 1932.	Section 1.
2 & 3 Geo.6 c. 72.	The Landlord and Tenant (War Damage) Act 1939.	Section 3(c).
9 & 10 Geo.6 c. 73.	The Hill Farming Act 1946.	Section 11(2).
12 & 13 Geo.6 c. 74.	The Coast Protection Act 1949.	In section 11(2)(a)— the words ", by that section as applied by section twenty-eight of the Law of Property Act, 1925, in relation to trusts for sale,", and the words ", by that section as applied as aforesaid,".
2 & 3 Eliz.2 c. 56.	The Landlord and Tenant Act 1954.	In the Second Schedule, in paragraph 6— the words ", by that section as applied by section twenty-eight of the Law of Property Act, 1925, in relation to trusts for sale,", and the words ", by that section as applied as aforesaid,".

7 & 8 Eliz.2 c. 72.	The Mental Health Act 1959.	In Schedule 7, in Part I, the entries relating to sections 26 and 28 of the Law of Property Act 1925.
1964 No. 2.	The Incumbents and Churchwardens (Trusts) Measure 1964.	In section 1, in the definition of "land", the words "nor an undivided share in land".
1967 c. 10.	The Forestry Act 1967.	In Schedule 2, paragraph 1(4).
1967 c. 88.	The Leasehold Reform Act 1967.	In section 6(5)— the words ", or by that section as applied by section 28 of the Law of Property Act 1925 in relation to trusts for sale,", the words "or by that section as applied as aforesaid", and the words "or by trustees for sale". In Schedule 2, in paragraph 9(1)— the words ", or by that section as applied by section 28 of the Law of Property Act 1925 in relation to trusts for sale", and the words "or by that section as applied as aforesaid".
1969 c. 10.	The Mines and Quarries (Tips) Act 1969.	In section 32(2)(a) and (b), the words ", by that section as applied by section 28 of the Law of Property Act 1925 in relation to trusts for sale".
1970 c. 40.	The Agriculture Act 1970.	In section 30— in subsection (1), the words "(including those provisions as extended to trusts for sale by section 28 of the Law of Property Act 1925) ", and in subsection (2), the words "the words from "(including those provisions" to "Law of Property Act 1925) " and".
1972 c. 61.	The Land Charges Act 1972.	In section 17(1), the definition of "trust for sale".
1976 c. 31.	The Legitimacy Act 1976.	Section 10(4).
1976 c. 36.	The Adoption Act 1976.	Section 46(5).
1977 c. 42.	The Rent Act 1977.	In Schedule 2, in Part I, in paragraph 2(b), the words "or, if it is held on trust for sale, the proceeds of its sale are".
1980 c. 58.	The Limitation Act 1980.	In section 18— in subsection (1), the words ", including interests in the proceeds of the sale of land held upon trust for sale,", and in subsections (3) and (4), the words "(including a trust for sale) " and the words "or in the proceeds of sale". In section 38(1)— in the definition of "land", the words ", including an interest in the proceeds of the sale of land held upon trust for sale,", and the definition of "trust for sale". In Schedule 1, in Part I, in paragraph 9— the words "or in the proceeds of sale", the words "or the proceeds", and the words "or the proceeds of sale".
1981 c. 54.	The Supreme Court Act 1981.	In section 128, in the definition of "real estate", in paragraph (b), the words "money to arise under a trust for sale of land, nor".
1983 c. 41.	The Health and Social Services and Social	Section 22(3).

	Security Adjudications Act 1983.	
1984 c. 28.	The County Courts Act 1984.	In Schedule 2, in Part II, in paragraph 2— in sub-paragraph (1), the entry relating to section 30 of the Law of Property Act 1925, sub-paragraph (2), and in sub-paragraph (3), "30(2),".
1984 c. 51.	The Inheritance Tax Act 1984.	In section 237(3), the words "and undivided shares in land held on trust for sale, whether statutory or not,".
1986 c. 5.	The Agricultural Holdings Act 1986.	In section 89(1), the words "or the Law of Property Act 1925".
1986 c. 45.	The Insolvency Act 1986.	In section 336— subsection (3), and in subsection (4), the words "or (3) " and the words "or section 30 of the Act of 1925".
1988 c. 50.	The Housing Act 1988.	In Schedule 1, in Part III, in paragraph 18(1)(b), the words "or, if it is held on trust for sale, the proceeds of its sale are".
1989 c. 34.	The Law of Property (Miscellaneous Provisions) Act 1989.	In sections 1(6) and 2(6), the words "or in or over the proceeds of sale of land".
1990 c. 8.	The Town and Country Planning Act 1990.	In section 328— in subsection (1)(a), the words "and by that section as applied by section 28 of the Law of Property Act 1925 in relation to trusts for sale", and in subsection (2)(a), the words "and by that section as so applied".
1991 c. 31.	The Finance Act 1991.	Section 110(5)(b).
1993 c. 10.	The Charities Act 1993.	Section 37(6).
		Section 39(5).
1993 c. 28.	The Leasehold Reform, Housing and Urban Development Act 1993.	In section 93A(4)— the words ", or by that section as applied by section 28 of the Law of Property Act 1925 in relation to trusts for sale", the words ", or by that section as so applied,", and the words "or by trustees for sale". In Schedule 2, paragraph 5(2)(b) and the word "and" immediately preceding it.
1994 c. 36.	The Law of Property (Miscellaneous Provisions) Act 1994.	In section 16— subsection (2), and in subsection (3), the words "; and subsection (2) " onwards.
1995 c. 8.	The Agricultural Tenancies Act 1995.	In section 33— in subsections (1) and (2), the words from "(either" to "Property Act 1925) ", and in subsection (4), the definition of "settled land" and the word "and" immediately preceding it.
1996 c. 53.	The Housing Grants, Construction and Regeneration Act 1996.	Section 55(4)(b).
		Section 73(3)(b). In section 98(2)(a), the words "or to the proceeds of sale of the dwelling".

[1] Words in s. 6(3) substituted (1.2.2001) by 2000 c. 29, s. 40(1), Sch. 2 Pt. II para. 45(1) (with s. 35); S.I. 2001/49, art. 2
[2] S. 6(4) repealed (1.2.2001) by 2000 c. 29, s. 40(1)(3), Sch. 2 Pt. II para. 45(2), Sch. 4 Pt. II (with s. 35); S.I. 2001/49, art. 2
[3] S. 6(9) inserted (1.2.2001) by 2000 c. 29, s. 40(1), Sch. 2 Pt. II para. 45(3) (with s. 35); S.I. 2001/49, art. 2
[4] S. 9(8) repealed (1.2.2001) by 2000 c. 29, s. 40(1)(3), Sch. 2 Pt. II para. 46, Sch. 4 Pt. II (with s. 35); S.I. 2001/49, art. 2

[5] S. 9A inserted (1.2.2001) by 2000 c. 29, s. 40(2), Sch. 2 Pt. II para. 47 (with s. 35); S.I. 2001/49, art. 2
[6] S. 17(1) repealed (1.2.2001) by 2000 c. 29, s. 40(1)(3), Sch. 2 Pt. II para. 48, Sch. 4 Pt. II (with s. 35); S.I. 2001/49, art. 2
[7] Sch. 3 para. 3(4) repealed (1.2.2001) by 2000 c. 29, s. 40, Sch. 2 Pt. II para. 49, Sch. 4 Pt. II (with s. 35); S.I. 2001/49, art. 2
[8] Sch. 3 para. 20 and the cross-heading preceding it repealed (30.1.2001 for E. and 1.5.2001 for W.) by 2000 c. 37, ss. 102, Sch. 16 Pt. III; S.I. 2001/114, art. 2(1)(d)(ii); S.I. 2001/1410, art. 2(i)(p)
[9] Sch. 3 para. 20 and the cross-heading preceding it repealed (30.1.2001 for E. amd 1.5.2001 for W.) by 2000 c. 37, ss. 102, 103(2), Sch. 16 Pt. III; S.I. 2001/114, art. 2(1)(d)(ii); S.I. 2001/1410, art. 2(i)(p)

Education Act 1997

1997 CHAPTER 44

An Act to amend the law relating to education in schools and further education in England and Wales; to make provision for the supervision of the awarding of external academic and vocational qualifications in England, Wales and Northern Ireland; and for connected purposes.

[21st March 1997]

Part I Assisted places scheme

1. . . . .[1]

Part II School discipline

Responsibility for discipline

[2. . . . .
3. . . . .].[2]

Power to restrain pupils

4 Power of members of staff to restrain pupils.

After section 550 of the Education Act 1996 there shall be inserted—

" **Power to restrain pupils**

550A Power of members of staff to restrain pupils.

(1) A member of the staff of a school may use, in relation to any pupil at the school, such force as is reasonable in the circumstances for the purpose of preventing the pupil from doing (or continuing to do) any of the following, namely—

(a) committing any offence,

(b) causing personal injury to, or damage to the property of, any person (including the pupil himself), or

(c) engaging in any behaviour prejudicial to the maintenance of good order and discipline at the school or among any of its pupils, whether that behaviour occurs during a teaching session or otherwise.

(2) Subsection (1) applies where a member of the staff of a school is—

(a) on the premises of the school, or

(b) elsewhere at a time when, as a member of its staff, he has lawful control or charge of the pupil concerned;

but it does not authorise anything to be done in relation to a pupil which constitutes the giving of corporal punishment within the meaning of section 548.

(3) Subsection (1) shall not be taken to prevent any person from relying on any defence available to him otherwise than by virtue of this section.

(4) In this section—

"member of the staff", in relation to a school, means any teacher who works at the school and any other person who, with the authority of the head teacher, has lawful control or charge of pupils at the school;

"offence" includes anything that would be an offence but for the operation of any presumption that a person under a particular age is incapable of committing an offence."

Detention

5 Detention outside school hours lawful despite absence of parental consent.

After the section 550A inserted in the Education Act 1996 by section 4 of this Act there shall be

inserted—

" **Detention**

550B Detention outside school hours lawful despite absence of parental consent.

(1) Where a pupil to whom this section applies is required on disciplinary grounds to spend a period of time in detention at his school after the end of any school session, his detention shall not be rendered unlawful by virtue of the absence of his parent's consent to it if the conditions set out in subsection (3) are satisfied.

(2) This section applies to any pupil who has not attained the age of 18 and is attending—

(a) a school maintained by a local education authority;

(b) a grant-maintained or grant-maintained special school; or

(c) a city technology college or city college for the technology of the arts.

(3) The conditions referred to in subsection (1) are as follows—

(a) the head teacher of the school must have previously determined, and have—

(i) made generally known within the school, and

(ii) taken steps to bring to the attention of the parent of every person who is for the time being a registered pupil there,

that the detention of pupils after the end of a school session is one of the measures that may be taken with a view to regulating the conduct of pupils;

(b) the detention must be imposed by the head teacher or by another teacher at the school specifically or generally authorised by him for the purpose;

(c) the detention must be reasonable in all the circumstances; and

(d) the pupil's parent must have been given at least 24 hours' notice in writing that the detention was due to take place.

(4) In determining for the purposes of subsection (3)(c) whether a pupil's detention is reasonable, the following matters in particular shall be taken into account—

(a) whether the detention constitutes a proportionate punishment in the circumstances of the case; and

(b) any special circumstances relevant to its imposition on the pupil which are known to the person imposing it (or of which he ought reasonably to be aware) including in particular—

(i) the pupil's age,

(ii) any special educational needs he may have,

(iii) any religious requirements affecting him, and

(iv) where arrangements have to be made for him to travel from the school to his home, whether suitable alternative arrangements can reasonably be made by his parent.

(5) Section 572, which provides for the methods by which notices may be served under this Act, does not preclude a notice from being given to a pupil's parent under this section by any other effective method."

Exclusion of pupils from school

[6. . . . .

7. . . . .

8. . . . .][3]

LEA plans

9 LEA plans relating to children with behavioural difficulties.

After section 527 of the Education Act 1996 there shall be inserted—

" **Plans relating to children with behavioural difficulties**

527A Duty of LEA to prepare plan relating to children with behavioural difficulties.

(1) Every local education authority shall prepare, and from time to time review, a statement setting out the arrangements made or proposed to be made by the authority in connection with the education of children with behavioural difficulties.

(2) The arrangements to be covered by the statement include in particular—

(a) the arrangements made or to be made by the authority for the provision of advice and resources to relevant schools, and other arrangements made or to be made by them, with a view to—

(i) meeting requests by such schools for support and assistance in connection with the

promotion of good behaviour and discipline on the part of their pupils, and

(ii) assisting such schools to deal with general behavioural problems and the behavioural difficulties of individual pupils;

(b) the arrangements made or to be made by the authority in pursuance of section 19(1) (exceptional provision of education for children not receiving education by reason of being excluded or otherwise); and

(c) any other arrangements made or to be made by them for assisting children with behavioural difficulties to find places at suitable schools.

(3) The statement shall also deal with the interaction between the arrangements referred to in subsection (2) and those made by the authority in relation to pupils with behavioural difficulties who have special educational needs.

(4) In the course of preparing the statement required by this section or any revision of it the authority shall carry out such consultation as may be prescribed.

(5) The authority shall—

(a) publish the statement in such manner and by such date, and

(b) publish revised statements in such manner and at such intervals,

as may be prescribed, and shall provide such persons as may be prescribed with copies of the statement or any revised statement.

(6) In discharging their functions under this section a local education authority shall have regard to any guidance given from time to time by the Secretary of State.

(7) In this section "relevant school", in relation to a local education authority, means—

(a) a school maintained by the authority (whether situated in their area or not), or

(b) a grant-maintained or grant-maintained special school situated in their area."

Part III School admissions

Chapter I County and voluntary schools

Partially-selective schools

[10. . . . .

Children permanently excluded from two or more schools

11. . . . .

12. . . . .

13. . . . .

Chapter II Grant-maintained schools

14. . . . .][4]

Part IV Baseline assessments and pupils' performance

Chapter I[5]

15. . . . .

16. . . . .

17. . . . .

18. . . . .

Chapter II Pupils' performance

19 School performance targets.

(1) The Secretary of State may by regulations make such provision as the Secretary of State considers appropriate for requiring the governing bodies of maintained schools to secure that annual targets are set in respect of the performance of pupils—

(a) in public examinations or in assessments for the purposes of the National Curriculum, in the case of pupils of compulsory school age; or

(b) in public examinations or in connection with the attainment of other external qualifications, in the case of pupils of any age over that age.

(2) Regulations under this section may require—

(a) such targets, and

(b) the past performance of pupils in the particular examinations or assessments, or in connection

with the attainment of the particular qualifications, to which such targets relate,

to be published in such manner as is specified in the regulations.

[(3) In this section "maintained school" means—

(a) a community, foundation or voluntary school, or

(b) a community or foundation special school (other than one established in a hospital).][6]

20 Provision of information about individual pupils' performance.

After section 537 of the Education Act 1996 there shall be inserted—

"537A Provision of information about individual pupils' performance.

(1) The Secretary of State may by regulations make provision requiring—

(a) the governing body of every school which is—

(i) maintained by a local education authority, or

(ii) a grant-maintained school, or

(iii) a special school which is not maintained by a local education authority, and

(b) the proprietor of each independent school,

to provide to the Secretary of State such individual performance information relating to pupils or former pupils at the school as may be prescribed.

(2) In this section "individual performance information" means information about the performance of individual pupils (identified in the prescribed manner)—

(a) in any assessment made for the purposes of the National Curriculum or in accordance with a baseline assessment scheme (within the meaning of Chapter I of Part IV of the Education Act 1997);

(b) in any prescribed public examination;

(c) in connection with the attainment of any vocational qualification; or

(d) in any such other assessment or examination, or in connection with the attainment of any such other qualification, as may be prescribed.

(3) The Secretary of State may provide any information received by him by virtue of subsection (1)—

(a) to any prescribed body or person, or

(b) to any body or person falling within a prescribed category.

(4) Any body or person holding any individual performance information may provide that information to any body to which this subsection applies; and any body to which this subsection applies—

(a) may provide any information received by it under this subsection—

(i) to the Secretary of State, or

(ii) to the governing body or proprietor of the school attended by the pupil or pupils to whom the information relates; and

(b) may, at such times as the Secretary of State may determine, provide to any prescribed body such information received by it under this subsection as may be prescribed.

(5) Subsection (4) applies to any body which, for the purposes of or in connection with the functions of the Secretary of State relating to education, is responsible for collating or checking information relating to the performance of pupils—

(a) in any assessment or examination falling within subsection (2)(a), (b) or (d), or

(b) in connection with the attainment of any qualification falling within subsection (2)(c) or (d).

(6) No individual performance information received under or by virtue of this section shall be published in any form which includes the name of the pupil or pupils to whom it relates.

(7) References in this section to the attainment of a qualification of any description include references to the completion of any module or part of a course leading to any such qualification."

Part V Supervision of curriculum for schools and external qualifications

Chapter I The Qualifications and Curriculum Authority

Establishment of the Authority

21 The Qualifications and Curriculum Authority.

(1) There shall be a body corporate known as the Qualifications and Curriculum Authority.

(2) The Authority shall consist of not less than 8 nor more than 13 members appointed by the Secretary of State.

(3) Of the members of the Authority, the Secretary of State—

(a) shall appoint one as chairman, and

(b) may appoint another as deputy chairman.

(4) The Secretary of State shall include among the members of the Authority—

(a) persons who appear to him to have experience of, and to have shown capacity in, the provision of education, or to have held, and to have shown capacity in, any position carrying responsibility for the provision of education;

(b) persons who appear to him to have experience of, and to have shown capacity in, the provision of training or to have held, and to have shown capacity in, any position carrying responsibility for the provision of training; and

(c) persons who appear to him to have experience of, and to have shown capacity in, industrial, commercial or financial matters or the practice of any profession.

(5) Schedule 4 has effect in relation to the Authority.

Functions of the Authority

22 General function of Authority to advance education and training.

(1) The functions conferred on the Qualifications and Curriculum Authority by this Part shall be exercised by the Authority for the purpose of advancing education and training in England and (so far as such functions are exercisable there) in Wales and in Northern Ireland.

(2) The Authority shall exercise their functions under this Part with a view to promoting quality and coherence in education and training in relation to which they have functions under this Part.

23 Functions of the Authority in relation to curriculum and assessment.

(1) The Qualifications and Curriculum Authority shall have the functions set out in subsection (2) [with respect to—

(a) pupils at maintained schools in England who have not ceased to be of compulsory school age,

(b) pupils at maintained nursery schools in England, and

(c) children for whom funded nursery education is provided in England otherwise than at a maintained school or maintained nursery school.][7]

(2) The functions are—

(a) to keep under review all aspects of the curriculum for [maintained schools or maintained nursery schools][8] and all aspects of school examinations and assessment;

(b) to advise the Secretary of State on such matters concerned with the curriculum for such schools or with school examinations and assessment as he may refer to them or as they may see fit;

(c) to advise the Secretary of State on, and if so requested by him assist him to carry out, programmes of research and development for purposes connected with the curriculum for such schools or with school examinations and assessment;

(d) to publish and disseminate, and assist in the publication and dissemination of, information relating to the curriculum for such schools or to school examinations and assessment;

(e) to make arrangements with appropriate bodies for auditing the quality of assessments made in pursuance of assessment arrangements;...[9]

(f)................................

[(2A) In subsection (2) references to the curriculum for a maintained nursery school include references to the curriculum for any funded nursery education provided as mentioned in subsection (1)(c); and references to assessment in schools include references to assessment in funded nursery education.][10]

(3)...............................[11]

(4)................................

(5) In this section—

"assessment" includes examination and test;

["funded nursery education" has the meaning given by section 77 of the Education Act 2002;][12] and "maintained school" means—

(a) [any community, foundation or voluntary school, and

(b) any community or foundation special school.][13]

24 Functions of the Authority in relation to external vocational and academic qualifications.

(1) The Qualifications and Curriculum Authority shall have, in relation to England, the functions set out

in subsection (2) with respect to external qualifications.

(2) The functions are—

(a) to keep under review all aspects of such qualifications;

(b) to advise the Secretary of State on such matters concerned with such qualifications as he may refer to them or as they may see fit;

(c) to advise the Secretary of State on, and if so requested by him assist him to carry out, programmes of research and development for purposes connected with such qualifications;

(d) to provide support and advice to persons providing courses leading to such qualifications with a view to establishing and maintaining high standards in the provision of such courses;

(e) to publish and disseminate, and assist in the publication and dissemination of, information relating to such qualifications;

(f) to develop and publish criteria for the accreditation of such qualifications;

(g) to accredit, where they meet such criteria, any such qualifications submitted for accreditation;

[(gg) to make arrangements (whether or not with others) for the development, setting or administration of tests or tasks which fall to be undertaken with a view to obtaining such qualifications and which fall within a prescribed description.][14]

[(2A) In paragraph (f) of subsection (2) "criteria" includes criteria that are to be applied for the purpose of ensuring that the number of different accredited qualifications in similar subject areas or serving similar functions is not excessive; and paragraph (g) of that subsection is to be construed accordingly.][15]

(3) Except to the extent that, by virtue of an order under section 30(1), they are for the time being exercisable with respect to such qualifications solely by the Qualifications, Curriculum and Assessment Authority for Wales, the functions set out in subsection (2)(a) to [(gg)][16] shall be so exercisable in relation to Wales by the Qualifications and Curriculum Authority, and shall be so exercisable either—

(a) solely by the Authority, or

(b) if an order under section 30(1) so provides, by the Authority concurrently with the Qualifications, Curriculum and Assessment Authority for Wales.

(4) The functions set out in subsection (2)(a) to (g) shall also be exercisable by the Qualifications and Curriculum Authority in relation to Northern Ireland but only with respect to National Vocational Qualifications.

(5) Subsection (2)(a) to (e) do not apply to qualifications awarded or authenticated by institutions within the higher education sector other than those which have been submitted for accreditation under subsection (2)(g).

(6) In this section "external qualification" means—

(a) any academic or vocational qualification authenticated or awarded by an outside person, except an academic qualification at first degree level or any comparable or higher level; or

(b)(whether within paragraph (a) or not) any National Vocational Qualification.

(7) For the purposes of this section—

(a) a qualification is awarded by an outside person if the course of education or training leading to the qualification is provided by an institution or an employer and it is awarded by a person other than the institution or employer or a member of its or his staff; and

(b) a qualification is authenticated by an outside person if it is awarded by an institution or employer and is authenticated by a person other than the institution or employer or a member of its or his staff.

25 Other functions of the Authority.

(1) The Qualifications and Curriculum Authority shall advise the Secretary of State on such matters connected with the provision of education or training in England as the Secretary of State may specify by order.

(2) The Authority shall carry out such ancillary activities as the Secretary of State may direct.

(3) For the purposes of subsection (2) activities are ancillary activities in relation to the Authority if the Secretary of State considers it is appropriate for the Authority to carry out those activities for the purposes of or in connection with the carrying out by the Authority of any of their other functions under this Part.

(4) The Authority shall supply the Secretary of State with such reports and other information with respect to the carrying out of their functions as the Secretary of State may require.

[(5) The Authority may supply any person designated by the Secretary of State with such information as the Authority thinks fit about any matter in relation to which it has a function.][17]

26 Supplementary provisions relating to discharge by Authority of their functions.

(1) In carrying out their functions under this Part the Qualifications and Curriculum Authority shall—

(a) comply with any directions given by the Secretary of State; and

(b) act in accordance with any plans approved by him; and

(c) so far as relevant, have regard to—

(i) the requirements of [section 78 of the Education Act 2002][18](general duties in respect of curriculum),

(ii) the requirements of industry, commerce, finance and the professions regarding education and training (including required standards of practical competence), and

(iii) the requirements of persons with special learning needs.

(2) In carrying out those functions the Authority shall in addition have regard to information supplied to them by Her Majesty's Chief Inspector of Schools in England or by any body designated by the Secretary of State for the purposes of this section.

(3) Where in carrying out any of their functions under this Part the Authority accredit...[19] any qualification, they may do so on such terms (including terms as to payment) ... as they may determine.

[(3A) Where in carrying out those functions the Authority accredit any qualification, they may, at the time of accreditation or later, impose such conditions on accreditation or continued accreditation as they may determine.][20]

(4) Those conditions may in particular include conditions—

(a) placing a limit on the amount of the fee that can be demanded in respect of any award or authentication of the qualification in question; and

[(b) requiring rights of entry to premises and to inspect and copy documents so far as necessary for the Authority—

(i) to satisfy themselves that the appropriate standards are being maintained, in relation to the award or authentication of the qualification in question, by the persons receiving the accreditation, or

(ii) to determine whether to impose a condition falling within paragraph (a) and if so what that condition should be.][21]

(5) Before exercising on any occasion their power to impose conditions falling within subsection (4)(a) the Authority shall obtain the consent of the Secretary of State as to such matters relating to the exercise of that power as he may determine.

(6) In this section "persons with special learning needs" means—

(a) children with special educational needs (as defined in section 312 of the Education Act 1996); or

(b) persons (other than children as so defined) who—

(i) have a significantly greater difficulty in learning than the majority of persons of their age, or

(ii) have a disability which either prevents or hinders them from making use of educational facilities of a kind generally provided for persons of their age.

[26A Power of Authority to give directions

(1) If it appears to the Qualifications and Curriculum Authority—

(a) that any person (in this section referred to as "the awarding body") who, either alone or jointly with others, awards or authenticates any qualification accredited by the Authority has failed or is likely to fail to comply with any condition subject to which the accreditation has effect, and

(b) that the failure—

(i) prejudices or would be likely to prejudice the proper award or authentication of the qualification, or

(ii) prejudices or would be likely to prejudice persons who might reasonably be expected to seek to obtain the qualification,

the Authority may direct the awarding body to take or refrain from taking specified steps with a view to securing compliance with the conditions subject to which the accreditation has effect.

(2) It shall be the duty of the awarding body to comply with any direction under this section.

(3) Any direction under this section is enforceable, on the application of the Qualifications and Curriculum Authority—

(a) in England and Wales, by a mandatory order, or

(b) in Northern Ireland, by an order of mandamus.][22]

Chapter II The Qualifications, Curriculum and Assessment Authority for Wales

Renaming of the Authority

27 The Qualifications, Curriculum and Assessment Authority for Wales.

(1) The body corporate known as Awdurdod Cwricwlwm ac Asesu Cymru shall continue in existence but, as from the commencement of this section, shall be known as Awdurdod Cymwysterau, Cwricwlwm ac Asesu Cymru or the Qualifications, Curriculum and Assessment Authority for Wales.

(2) The Authority shall consist of not less than 10 nor more than 15 members appointed by the Secretary of State.

(3) Of the members of the Authority, the Secretary of State—

(a) shall appoint one as chairman, and

(b) may appoint another as deputy chairman.

(4) The Secretary of State—

(a) shall include among the members of the Authority—

(i) persons who appear to him to have relevant knowledge or experience in education, and

(ii) persons who appear to him to have relevant knowledge or experience in training; and

(b) may include among those members persons who appear to him to have experience of occupations, trades or professions having an interest in education or training.

(5) Schedule 5 to this Act, which replaces Schedule 30 to the Education Act 1996, has effect in relation to the Authority.

Functions of the Authority

28 General function of Authority to advance education and training.

(1) The functions conferred on the Qualifications, Curriculum and Assessment Authority for Wales by this Part shall be exercised by the Authority for the purpose of advancing education and training in Wales.

(2) The Authority shall exercise their functions under this Part with a view to promoting quality and coherence in education and training in relation to which they have functions under this Part.

29 Functions of the Authority in relation to curriculum and assessment.

(1) The Qualifications, Curriculum and Assessment Authority for Wales shall have the functions set out in subsection (2) [with respect to—

(a) pupils at maintained schools in Wales who have not ceased to be of compulsory school age,

(b) pupils at maintained nursery schools in Wales, and

(c) children for whom funded nursery education is provided in Wales otherwise than at a maintained school or maintained nursery school.][23]

(2) The functions are—

(a) to keep under review all aspects of the curriculum for [maintained schools or maintained nursery schools][24] and all aspects of school examinations and assessment;

(b) to advise the Secretary of State on such matters concerned with the curriculum for such schools or with school examinations and assessment as he may refer to them or as they may see fit;

(c) to advise the Secretary of State on, and if so requested by him assist him to carry out, programmes of research and development for purposes connected with the curriculum for such schools or with school examinations and assessment;

(d) to publish and disseminate, and assist in the publication and dissemination of, information relating to the curriculum for such schools or to school examinations and assessment;

(e) to make arrangements with appropriate bodies for auditing the quality of assessments made in pursuance of assessment arrangements;...[25]

(f)...............................

[(2A) In subsection (2) references to the curriculum for a maintained nursery school include references

to the curriculum for any funded nursery education provided asmentioned in subsection (1)(c); and references to assessment in schools include references to assessment in funded nursery education.][26]

(3) The Authority shall have, in relation to Wales, the function of developing learning goals and related materials for children who are [under compulsory school age.][27]

(4) The Authority shall have, in relation to Wales, the following functions in connection with baseline assessment schemes (within the meaning of Chapter I of Part IV), namely—

(a) if designated by the Secretary of State for the purpose, any function of a designated body under that Chapter; and

(b) any other function which may be conferred on the Authority by the Secretary of State.

(5) In this section "assessment" and "maintained school" have the same meaning as in section 23[; and "funded nursery education" has the meaning given by section 98 of the Education Act 2002;][28]

30 Functions of the Authority in relation to external vocational and academic qualifications.

(1) The Qualifications, Curriculum and Assessment Authority for Wales shall have, in relation to Wales, such functions with respect to external qualifications as are for the time being conferred on the Authority by an order made by the Secretary of State under this subsection [or by subsection (3)][29].

(2) The functions with respect to external qualifications which may be conferred on the Authority by an order under subsection (1) are functions falling within paragraphs (a) to [(gg)][30] of section 24(2), and the functions in question may be so conferred so as to be exercisable either—

(a) solely by the Authority, or

(b) by the Authority concurrently with the Qualifications and Curriculum Authority.

[(3) The Authority shall have, in relation to Wales, the following functions with respect to external qualifications, namely—

(a) if designated by the Secretary of State for the purpose, to advise the Secretary of State on the exercise of his powers under section 37 (approval of external qualifications); and

(b) if designated by the Secretary of State for the purpose, to exercise any functions conferred on a designated body by regulations under that section.][31]

(4) Where an order under subsection (1) is made so as to come into force at any time after the day on which that subsection comes into force, the order may include provisions—

(a) for the transfer of staff, and

(b) for the transfer of property, rights and liabilities held, enjoyed or incurred in connection with any function which, as a result of the order, is to be exercisable by the Authority (whether solely or concurrently).

(5) In this section "external qualification" has the same meaning as in section 24.

31 Other functions of the Authority.

(1) The Qualifications, Curriculum and Assessment Authority for Wales shall advise the Secretary of State on such matters connected with the provision of education or training in Wales as the Secretary of State may specify by order.

(2) The Authority shall carry out such ancillary activities as the Secretary of State may direct.

(3) For the purposes of subsection (2) activities are ancillary activities in relation to the Authority if the Secretary of State considers it is appropriate for the Authority to carry out those activities for the purposes of or in connection with the carrying out by the Authority of any of their other functions under this Part.

(4) The Authority shall supply the Secretary of State with such reports and other information with respect to the carrying out of their functions as the Secretary of State may require.

[(5) The Authority may supply any person designated by the National Assembly for Wales with such information as the Authority thinks fit about any matter in relation to which it has a function.][32]

32 Supplementary provisions relating to discharge by Authority of their functions.

(1) In carrying out their functions under this Part the Qualifications, Curriculum and Assessment Authority for Wales shall—

(a) comply with any directions given by the Secretary of State; and

(b) act in accordance with any plans approved by him; and

(c) so far as relevant, have regard to—

(i) the requirements of [section 99 of the Education Act 2002][33](general duties in respect of curriculum),

(ii) the requirements of industry, commerce, finance and the professions regarding education and training (including required standards of practical competence), and

(iii) the requirements of persons with special learning needs.

(2) In carrying out those functions the Authority shall in addition have regard to information supplied to them by [Her Majesty's Chief Inspector of Education and Training in Wales or Prif Arolygydd Ei Mawrhydi dros Addysg a Hyfforddiant yng Nghymru][34] or by any body designated by the Secretary of State for the purposes of this section.

(3) Where in carrying out any of their functions under this Part the Authority accredit...[35] any qualification, they may do so on such terms (including terms as to payment) ... as they may determine.

[(3A) Where in carrying out those functions the Authority accredit any qualification, they may, at the time of accreditation or later, impose such conditions on accreditation or continued accreditation as they may determine.][36]

(4) Those conditions may in particular include conditions—

(a) placing a limit on the amount of the fee that can be demanded in respect of any award or authentication of the qualification in question; and

[(b) requiring rights of entry to premises and to inspect and copy documents so far as necessary for the Authority—

(i) to satisfy themselves that the appropriate standards are being maintained, in relation to the award or authentication of the qualification in question, by the persons receiving the accreditation, or

(ii) to determine whether to impose a condition falling within paragraph (a) and if so what that condition should be.][37]

(5) Before exercising on any occasion their power to impose conditions falling within subsection (4)(a) the Authority shall obtain the consent of the Secretary of State as to such matters relating to the exercise of that power as he may determine.

(6) In this section "persons with special learning needs" has the same meaning as in section 26.

[32A Power of Authority to give directions

(1) If it appears to the Qualifications, Curriculum and Assessment Authority for Wales—

(a) that any person (in this section referred to as "the awarding body") who, either alone or jointly with others, awards or authenticates any qualification accredited by the Authority has failed or is likely to fail to comply with any condition subject to which the accreditation has effect, and

(b) that the failure—

(i) prejudices or would be likely to prejudice the proper award or authentication of the qualification, or

(ii) prejudices or would be likely to prejudice persons who might reasonably be expected to seek to obtain the qualification,

the Authority may direct the awarding body to take or refrain from taking specified steps with a view to securing compliance with the conditions subject to which the accreditation has effect.

(2) It shall be the duty of the awarding body to comply with any direction under this section.

(3) Any direction under this section is enforceable, on the application of the Qualifications, Curriculum and Assessment Authority for Wales, by a mandatory order.][38]

Chapter III Provisions supplementary to Chapters I and II

Dissolution of existing bodies

33 Dissolution of existing bodies.

The National Council for Vocational Qualifications and the School Curriculum and Assessment Authority are hereby dissolved.

Transfer of property and staff

34 Transfer of property.

(1) The Secretary of State may by order provide for the transfer to the Qualifications and Curriculum Authority, or (as the case may be) to the Qualifications, Curriculum and Assessment Authority for Wales, of—

(a) such of the land or other property of the National Council for Vocational Qualifications or the

School Curriculum and Assessment Authority, and

(b) such of the rights and liabilities of either of those bodies (other than rights and liabilities arising under contracts of employment),

as, in his opinion, need to be transferred to enable the transferee Authority to carry out their functions properly.

(2) No order under subsection (1) may be made after the end of the period of six months beginning with the day on which section 21 comes into force.

(3) Any order under subsection (1) made before the day on which section 21 comes into force shall come into force on that day.

(4) Where, immediately after the end of the period within which an order under subsection (1) may be made, any property, rights or liabilities remain vested in the National Council for Vocational Qualifications or the School Curriculum and Assessment Authority, they shall forthwith vest in the Secretary of State.

(5) The Secretary of State may by order provide that there shall be substituted for the period mentioned in subsection (2) such shorter period as he may specify in the order, being a period ending no earlier than the day on which the order comes into force.

35 Transfer of staff.

(1) This section applies to any person who—

(a) is employed by the National Council for Vocational Qualifications ("the NCVQ") or the School Curriculum and Assessment Authority ("the SCAA") immediately before section 21 comes into force, and

(b) is designated as respects the Qualifications and Curriculum Authority, or (as the case may be) the Qualifications, Curriculum and Assessment Authority for Wales, by order of the Secretary of State;

and in this section "the relevant Authority" means, in relation to any such person, the Authority as respects which he is designated by the order.

(2) A contract of employment between a person to whom this section applies and the NCVQ or the SCAA shall have effect, from the day on which the order under subsection (1)(b) comes into force, as if originally made between him and the relevant Authority.

(3) Without prejudice to subsection (2)—

(a) all the rights, powers, duties and liabilities of the NCVQ or the SCAA under or in connection with a contract to which that subsection applies shall by virtue of that subsection be transferred to the relevant Authority on the day on which the order under subsection (1)(b) comes into force, and

(b) anything done before that day by or in relation to the NCVQ or the SCAA in respect of that contract or the employee shall be deemed from that day to have been done by or in relation to the relevant Authority.

(4) Subsections (2) and (3) are without prejudice to any right of an employee to terminate his contract of employment if his working conditions are changed substantially to his detriment; but such a change shall not be taken to have occurred by reason only of the change in employer effected by subsection (2).

(5) In subsection (4) the reference to an employee's working conditions includes a reference to any rights (whether accrued or contingent) under any pension or superannuation scheme of which he was a member by virtue of his employment with the NCVQ or the SCAA (as the case may be).

(6) An order under subsection (1)(b) may designate a person either individually or as falling within a class or description of employee.

(7) No order under subsection (1)(b) may be made after the end of the period of six months beginning with the day on which section 21 comes into force.

(8) any order under subsection (1)(b) made before the day on which section 21 comes into force shall come into force on that day.

(9) The Secretary of State may by order provide that there shall be substituted for the period mentioned in subsection (7) such shorter period as he may specify in the order, being a period ending no earlier than the day on which the order comes into force.

Levy on bodies awarding accredited qualifications

36 Levy on bodies awarding qualifications accredited by relevant Authority.

(1) The Secretary of State may by regulations provide for a levy to be payable to the relevant Authority by persons who award vocational qualifications accredited by that Authority.

(2) Regulations under this section shall—

(a) specify the rate of the levy or the method by which it is to be calculated (and, without prejudice to the generality of section 54(3), may make different provision in relation to different cases);

(b) make provision as to the times when, and the manner in which, payments are to be made in respect of the levy;

(c) provide for the relevant Authority to withdraw their accreditation of a qualification in cases of non-payment of the levy.

(3) Any sums received by the relevant Authority in respect of the levy shall be applied by them in giving such financial assistance to other bodies as the Secretary of State may specify with a view to assisting that Authority to secure the development and improvement of standards in relation to vocational qualifications.

(4) In this section "the relevant Authority" means—

(a) the Qualifications and Curriculum Authority in the case of a qualification accredited by that Authority; and

(b) the Qualifications, Curriculum and Assessment Authority for Wales in the case of a qualification accredited by that Authority.

Chapter IV Control of certain courses leading to external qualifications

37 Requirement for approval of certain publicly-funded and school courses leading to external qualifications.

(1). . . . .[39]

(2). . . . .

(3). . . . .

(4). . . . .

(5) Sections 400 and 401 of the Education Act 1996 (courses leading to external qualifications provided at schools and further education institutions). . .[40] shall cease to have effect.

Part VI Inspection of local education authorities and school inspections

Chapter I Inspection of local education authorities

38 Inspection of LEAs.

(1) The Chief Inspector—

(a) may, and

(b) if requested to do so by the Secretary of State, shall,

arrange for any local education authority to be inspected under this section.

(2) An inspection of a local education authority under this section shall consist of a review of the way in which the authority are performing any function of theirs (of whatever nature) which relates to the provision of education—

(a) for persons of compulsory school age (whether at school or otherwise), or

(b) for persons of any age above or below that age who are registered as pupils at schools maintained by the authority.

(3) A request by the Secretary of State under this section may relate to one or more local education authorities, and shall specify both—

(a) the local education authority or authorities concerned, and

(b) the functions of theirs to which the inspection is to relate.

(4) Before making any such request the Secretary of State shall consult the Chief Inspector as to the matters to be specified in the request in accordance with subsection (3).

(5) Any inspection under this section shall be conducted—

(a) by one of Her Majesty's Inspectors of Schools in England or (as the case may require) Wales, or

(b) by any additional inspector authorised under paragraph 2 of Schedule 1 to the School Inspections Act 1996;

but he may be assisted by such other persons (whether or not members of the Chief Inspector's staff)

as the Chief Inspector thinks fit.

(6) For the purposes of this section a local education authority shall provide the Chief Inspector with such information as may be prescribed, and shall do so in such form and—

(a) within such period following a request made by the Chief Inspector in any prescribed circumstances, or

(b) at such other times,

as regulations may provide.

(7) In this section and sections 39 to 41 "the Chief Inspector" means—

(a) in relation to a local education authority in England, Her Majesty's Chief Inspector of Schools in England; and

(b) in relation to a local education authority in Wales, [Her Majesty's Chief Inspector of Education and Training in Wales or Prif Arolygydd Ei Mawrhydi dros Addysg a Hyfforddiant yng Nghymru][41];

and in those sections references to "the inspector" in relation to an inspection under this section are references to the person conducting the inspection.

39 Reports of inspections under s. 38 and action plan by LEA.

(1) Where an inspection under section 38 has been completed, the inspector shall make a written report on the matters reviewed in the course of the inspection, and shall send copies of the report to—

(a) any local education authority to which the inspection relates; and

(b) the Secretary of State.

(2) Where a local education authority receive a copy of a report under this section, they shall prepare a written statement of the action which they propose to take in the light of the report and the period within which they propose to take it.

(3) The authority shall publish—

(a) the report, and

(b) the statement prepared under subsection (2),

within such period, and in such manner, as may be prescribed.

(4) The Chief Inspector may arrange for any report under this section to be published in such manner as he considers appropriate [; and section 42A(2) to (4) of the School Inspections Act 1996 shall apply in relation to the publication of any such report as they apply in relation to the publication of a report under any of the provisions mentioned in section 42A(2).][42]

[40 Inspector's rights of entry etc.

(1) This section applies where a local education authority are inspected under section 38.

(2) The inspector, and any person assisting him, shall have at all reasonable times a right of entry to—

(a) the premises of the local education authority,

(b) the premises of any school maintained by the authority, and

(c) any other premises at which relevant section 19 education is provided, other than premises which are or form part of a private dwelling house but are not a school.

(3) The inspector, and any person assisting him, shall also have at all reasonable times a right to inspect and take copies of—

(a) any records kept by, and any other documents containing information relating to, the local education authority or any school maintained by the authority, and

(b) any records kept by a person who provides relevant section 19 education that relate to the provision of that education, and any other documents containing information that so relates;

which he considers relevant to the exercise of his functions.

(4) Section 42 of the School Inspections Act 1996 (inspection of computer records) shall apply for the purposes of subsection (3) as it applies for the purposes of Part 1 of that Act.

(5) Without prejudice to subsections (2) and (3), the local education authority and the governing body of any school maintained by the authority—

(a) shall give the inspector and any person assisting him, all assistance in connection with the exercise of his functions which they are reasonably able to give, and

(b) shall secure that all such assistance is also given by persons who work at the school.

(6) It shall be an offence wilfully to obstruct the inspector or any person assisting him in the exercise of his functions in relation to the inspection.

(7) A person guilty of an offence under subsection (6) shall be liable on summary conviction to a fine not exceeding level 4 on the standard scale.

(8) In this section—

"document" and "records" each include information recorded in any form; and

"relevant section 19 education" means education provided to a child by virtue of arrangements made by the local education authority under section 19 of the Education Act 1996 (exceptional provision of education at schools or otherwise).][43]

41 Inspections involving collaboration of Audit Commission.

(1) If requested to do so by the Chief Inspector, the Audit Commission may assist with any inspection under section 38; and subsections (2) to (5) below have effect where the Commission assist with any such inspection.

(2) Section 40 shall apply to the Commission and to any authorised person as it applies to the inspector.

(3) Any information obtained by virtue of section 40 by a person falling within one of the categories mentioned in subsection (4) may be disclosed for the purposes of the inspection, or the preparation or making of the report under section 39(1), to a person falling within the other category.

(4) Those categories are—

(a) the Commission and any authorised person; and

(b) the inspector and any person assisting him.

(5) Any report prepared under section 39(1) shall be prepared by the inspector acting in conjunction with the Commission.

(6) The Commission shall not provide assistance under this section unless, before it does so, the Chief Inspector has agreed to pay the Commission an amount equal to the full costs incurred by the Commission in providing the assistance.

(7) In this section—

"the Audit Commission" means the Audit Commission for Local Authorities and the National Health Service in England and Wales; and

"authorised person" means a person authorised by the Audit Commission for the purposes of this section.

Chapter II School Inspections

42 Miscellaneous amendments relating to school inspections.

Schedule 6 (which contains amendments relating to inspections under the School Inspections Act 1996...[44]) shall have effect.

Part VII Careers education and guidance

43 Provision of careers education in schools.

(1) All registered pupils at a school to which this section applies must be provided, during the relevant phase of their education, with a programme of careers education.

(2) This section applies to—

[(a) community, foundation and voluntary schools;][45]

(b)...............................[46]

[(c) community or foundation special schools (other than those established in hospitals);][47]

(d) city technology colleges [, city colleges for the technology of the arts and [Academies][48]][49]; and

(e) pupil referral units.

(3) It is the duty of each of the following to secure that subsection (1) is complied with, namely—

(a) in the case of a school falling within subsection (2)(a) to (c), the governing body of the school and its head teacher,

(b) in the case of a school falling within subsection (2)(d), the proprietors of the school and its head teacher, and

(c) in the case of a pupil referral unit, the local education authority maintaining the unit and the teacher in charge of it.

(4) Each of sections 496 and 497 of the Education Act 1996 (default powers of Secretary of State) shall, in relation to the duty imposed by subsection (3) above, have effect as if any reference to a body to which that section applies included a reference to the proprietors of a school falling within subsection (2)(d) above.

(5) For the purposes of this section the relevant phase of a pupil's education is the period—

(a) beginning at the same time as the school year in which the majority of pupils in his class attain the age of 14; and

(b) ending with the expiry of the school year in which the majority of pupils in his class attain the age of 16.

(6) In this section—

"career" includes the undertaking of any training, employment or occupation or any course of education;

"careers education" means education designed to prepare persons for taking decisions about their careers and to help them implement such decisions;

"class", in relation to a particular pupil, means—

(a) the teaching group in which he is regularly taught, or

(b) if he is taught in different groups for different subjects, such one of those groups as is designated by the head teacher of the school or, in the case of a pupil at a pupil referral unit, by the teacher in charge of the unit.

44 Schools and other institutions to co-operate with careers advisers.

(1) Where a careers adviser has responsibilities in relation to persons attending an educational institution to which this section applies, he shall on request be provided with—

(a) the name and address of every relevant pupil or student at the institution; and

(b) any information in the institution's possession about any such pupil or student which the careers adviser needs in order to be able to provide him with advice and guidance on decisions about his career or with other information relevant to such decisions.

(2) If the registered address of a parent of any such pupil is different from the pupil's registered address, subsection (1)(a) requires the parent's address to be provided as well.

(3) Paragraph (a) or (as the case may be) paragraph (b) of subsection (1) does not, however, apply to any pupil or student to the extent that—

(a)(where he is under [the age of 16][50]) a parent of his, or

(b)(where he has attained that age) he himself,

has indicated that any information falling within that paragraph should not be provided to the careers adviser.

(4) Where a careers adviser has responsibilities in relation to persons attending an educational institution to which this section applies, he shall on request be permitted to have, in the case of any relevant pupil or student specified by him, access to that person—

(a) on the institution's premises, and

(b) at a reasonable time agreed by or on behalf of the head teacher, principal or other head of the institution,

for the purpose of enabling him to provide that person with advice and guidance on decisions about his career and with any other information relevant to such decisions.

(5) Such access shall include an opportunity for the careers adviser to interview that person about his career, if he agrees to be so interviewed.

(6) Where a careers adviser has responsibilities in relation to persons attending an educational institution to which this section applies, he shall on request be permitted to have, in the case of any group of relevant pupils or students specified by him, access—

(a) to that group of persons in the manner specified in subsection (4)(a) and (b), and

(b) to such of the institution's facilities as can conveniently be made available for his use,

for the purpose of enabling him to provide those persons with group sessions on any matters relating to careers or to advice or guidance about careers.

(7) Any request made for the purposes of subsection (1), (4) or (6) must be made in writing to the head teacher, principal or other head of the institution in question.

(8) This section applies to—

(a) the schools listed in section 43(2)(a) to (d); and

(b) institutions within the further education sector.

(9) It is the duty of each of the following to secure that subsections (1), (4) and (6) are complied with, namely—

(a) in the case of a school falling within section 43(2)(a) to (c) or an institution within the further education sector, the governing body of the school or institution and its head teacher, principal or other head, and

(b) in the case of a school falling within section 43(2)(d), the proprietors of the school and its head teacher;

and section 43(4) shall apply in relation to that duty as it applies in relation to the duty imposed by section 43(3).

(10) For the purposes of this section—

(a) a pupil at a school is a relevant pupil—

(i) at any time during the period which is the relevant phase of his education for the purposes of section 43, or

(ii) if he is over compulsory school age and receiving secondary education; and

(b) a person is a relevant student at an institution within the further education sector if he is receiving at the institution either—

(i) full-time education, or

(ii) part-time education of a description commonly undergone by persons in order to fit them for employment.

(11) For the purposes of this section—

(a) "careers adviser" means a person who is employed by a body providing services in pursuance of arrangements made or directions given under section 10 of the Employment and Training Act 1973 and who is acting, in the course of his employment by that body, for the purposes of the provision of any such services; and

(b) a careers adviser has responsibilities for any persons if his employment by that body includes the provision of any such services for them.

(12) In this section "career" has the same meaning as in section 43.

45 Provision of careers information at schools and other institutions.

(1) Persons attending an educational institution to which this section applies must be provided with access to both—

(a) guidance materials, and

(b) a wide range of up-to-date reference materials,

relating to careers education and career opportunities.

(2) This section applies to—

(a) the schools listed in section 43(2)(a) to (d); and

(b) institutions within the further education sector.

(3) It is the duty of each of the following to secure that subsection (1) is complied with, namely—

(a) in the case of a school falling within section 43(2)(a) to (c) or an institution within the further education sector, the governing body of the school or institution and its head teacher, principal or other head, and

(b) in the case of a school falling within section 43(2)(d), the proprietors of the school and its head teacher;

and section 43(4) shall apply in relation to that duty as it applies in relation to the duty imposed by section 43(3).

(4) The persons who under subsection (3) above are responsible for discharging that duty in relation to an institution shall seek assistance with discharging it from a body providing services in pursuance of arrangements made or directions given under section 10 of the Employment and Training Act 1973.

(5) In this section "career" and "careers education" have the same meaning as in section 43.

(6) Nothing in this section applies to any primary school.

46 Extension or modification of provisions of ss. 43 to 45.

(1) The Secretary of State may by regulations extend the scope of operation of section 43 or section 44 by substituting for the period specified in section 43(5) or section 44(10)(a)(i) such other period as is specified.

(2) The Secretary of State may by regulations make provision for extending the scope of operation of section 43, 44 or 45 to primary schools or to any specified description of such schools.

(3) The Secretary of State may by regulations make provision for requiring—

(a) the governing bodies of institutions within the further education sector, and

(b) the principals or other heads of such institutions,

to secure that a programme of careers education is provided for any specified description of persons attending such institutions.

(4) The Secretary of State may by regulations amend the definition of "careers adviser" set out in section 44(11)(a).

(5) In this section—

"careers education" has the same meaning as in section 43;

"specified" means specified in the regulations in question.

Part VIII Miscellaneous and general

Exceptional educational provision

47 Functions of LEAs as regards exceptional educational provision.

(1) Section 19 of the Education Act 1996 (exceptional provision of education in pupil referral units or elsewhere) shall be amended as follows.

(2) In subsection (1) (duty of local education authority to make arrangements for provision of suitable full-time or part-time education, at school or otherwise, for excluded children etc.), the words "full-time or part-time" shall be omitted.

(3) In subsection (4) (power of local education authority to make arrangements for provision of suitable full-time or part-time education, otherwise than at school, for excluded young persons etc.), the words "full-time or part-time" shall be omitted.

(4) After that subsection there shall be inserted—

"(4A) In determining what arrangements to make under subsection (1) or (4) in the case of any child or young person a local education authority shall have regard to any guidance given from time to time by the Secretary of State."

Management committees for pupil referral units

48 Management committees for pupil referral units.

At the end of Schedule 1 to the Education Act 1996 (pupil referral units) there shall be added—

" Management committees

15(1) Regulations may make provision—

(a) for requiring any local education authority who maintain a pupil referral unit to establish a committee to act as the management committee for the unit; and

(b) for that committee to discharge on behalf of the authority such of their functions in connection with the unit as are delegated by them to the committee in accordance with the regulations.

(2) Regulations under this paragraph may in particular make provision—

(a) for enabling a local education authority to establish a joint committee to act as the management committee for two or more pupil referral units maintained by the authority;

(b) for requiring the approval of the Secretary of State to be obtained before any such joint committee is established;

(c) as to the composition of a management committee established under the regulations and—

(i) the appointment and removal of its members, and

(ii) their terms of office,

and in particular for requiring such a committee to include persons representing schools (including grant-maintained schools) situated in the area from which the unit or units in question may be expected to draw pupils;

(d) for requiring or (as the case may be) prohibiting the delegation by a local education authority to a management committee of such functions in connection with pupil referral units as are specified in the regulations;

(e) for authorising a management committee to establish sub-committees;

(f) for enabling (subject to any provisions of the regulations) a local education authority or a management committee to determine to any extent the committee's procedure and that of any sub-committee;

(g) for limiting the personal liability of members of any such committee or sub-committee in respect of their acts or omissions as such members;

(h) for applying to any such committee or sub-committee, with or without modification—

(i) any provision of the Education Acts, or

(ii) any provision made by or under any other enactment and relating to committees or (as the case may be) sub-committees of a local authority."

Teachers not under contract of employment and persons having access to those under 19

49 Power to make regulations: teachers not under contract of employment and persons having access to those under 19.

[(1) Section 218 of the Education Reform Act 1988 (power of Secretary of State to make regulations in respect of schools and further and higher education institutions) shall be amended as follows.

(2) After subsection (6) there shall be inserted—

"(6A) The Secretary of State may by regulations impose requirements on—

(a) local education authorities,

(b) the governing bodies of schools or institutions falling within subsection (10) below, or

(c) the proprietors of independent schools,

for the purpose of prohibiting or restricting, on medical grounds or in cases of misconduct, access to persons who have not attained the age of nineteen years by persons (not falling within subsection (6) above) who provide services falling within subsection (6B).

(6B) Those services are services provided in relation to the school or institution or persons attending it which—

(a) are provided by whatever means and whether under contract or otherwise, and

(b) bring the persons providing them regularly into contact with persons who have not attained the age of nineteen years."

(3) In subsection (12) (definition of "school"), after "(6)(d) " there shall be inserted " or (6A) ".

(4) After subsection (12) there shall be inserted—

"(13) For the purposes of this section—

(a) any reference to persons employed as teachers includes a reference to persons engaged to provide their services as teachers otherwise than under contracts of employment; and

(b) any reference to teachers or other persons employed by local education authorities or by any description of governing bodies or proprietors includes a reference to teachers or other persons engaged to provide their services for such authorities, governing bodies or proprietors (as the case may be) otherwise than under contracts of employment;

and any reference to employment (or further employment) shall be construed accordingly."][51]

Costs of teachers' premature retirement

50. . . . .[52]

Definition of "school"

51 Definition of "school".

In section 4 of the Education Act 1996 (definition of "school"), for subsection (1) there shall be substituted—

"(1) In this Act "school" means an educational institution which is outside the further education sector and the higher education sector and is an institution for providing—

(a) primary education,

(b) secondary education, or

(c) both primary and secondary education,

whether or not the institution also provides part-time education suitable to the requirements of junior pupils or further education."

Compulsory school age

52 Commencement of compulsory school age.

(1) Section 8 of the Education Act 1996 (compulsory school age) shall be amended in accordance with subsections (2) and (3).

(2) For subsection (2) there shall be substituted—

"(2) A person begins to be of compulsory school age—

(a) when he attains the age of five, if he attains that age on a prescribed day, and

(b) otherwise at the beginning of the prescribed day next following his attaining that age."

(3) For subsection (4) there shall be substituted—

"(4) The Secretary of State may by order—

(a) provide that such days in the year as are specified in the order shall be, for each calendar year, prescribed days for the purposes of subsection (2);

(b) determine the day in any calendar year which is to be the school leaving date for that year."

(4). . . . .[53]

(5). . . . .

General provisions

53 Stamp duty.

(1) Subject to subsection (2), stamp duty shall not be chargeable in respect of any transfer effected by virtue of section 30 or 34.

(2) No instrument (other than a statutory instrument) made or executed in pursuance of either of the provisions mentioned in subsection (1) shall be treated as duly stamped unless it is stamped with the duty to which it would, but for this section (and, if applicable, section 129 of the Finance Act 1982), be liable or it has, in accordance with the provisions of section 12 of the Stamp Act 1891, been stamped with a particular stamp denoting that it is not chargeable with any duty or that it has been duly stamped.

54 Orders and regulations.

(1) Any power of the Secretary of State to make orders or regulations under this Act, except an order under section 25 or 31, shall be exercised by statutory instrument.

(2) A statutory instrument containing any order or regulations under this Act, except an order under section 58, shall be subject to annulment in pursuance of a resolution of either House of Parliament.

(3) Any order or regulations under this Act may make different provision for different cases, circumstances or areas and may contain such incidental, supplemental, saving or transitional provisions as the Secretary of State thinks fit.

(4) Without prejudice to the generality of subsection (3), any order or regulations under this Act may make in relation to Wales provision different from that made in relation to England.

55 Financial provisions.

There shall be paid out of money provided by Parliament—

(a) any sums required for the payment by the Secretary of State of grants under this Act;

(b) any administrative expenses incurred by the Secretary of State in consequence of this Act; and

(c) any increase attributable to this Act in the sums so payable under any other Act.

56 Construction.

(1) In this Act—

"prescribed" means prescribed by regulations; and

"regulations" means regulations made by the Secretary of State under this Act.

(2) This Act shall be construed as one with the Education Act 1996.

(3) Where, however, an expression is given for the purposes of any provision of this Act a meaning different from that given to it for the purposes of that Act, the meaning given for the purposes of that provision shall apply instead of the one given for the purposes of that Act.

57 Minor and consequential amendments, repeals etc.

(1) The minor and consequential amendments set out in Schedule 7 shall have effect.

(2). . . . .[54]

(3). . . . .[55]

(4) The enactments specified in Schedule 8 are repealed to the extent specified.

58 Short title, commencement and extent etc.

(1) This Act may be cited as the Education Act 1997.

(2) This Act shall be included in the list of Education Acts set out in section 578 of the Education Act 1996.

(3) Subject to subsection (4), this Act shall come into force on such day as the Secretary of State may by order appoint, and different days may be appointed for different provisions and for different purposes.

(4) The following provisions come into force on the day on which this Act is passed—

. . .[56]

section 54,

paragraph 48(2) of Schedule 7 and section 57(1) so far as relating thereto, and

this section.

(5) Subject to subsections (6) and (7), this Act extends to England and Wales only.

(6) The following provisions extend to Northern Ireland—

sections 21 and 22,

section 24(4),

[sections 26 and 26A][57],

sections 34 to 36,

section 53,

section 54,

this section, and

Schedule 4.

(7) The amendment or repeal by this Act of an enactment extending to Scotland or Northern Ireland extends also to Scotland or, as the case may be, Northern Ireland.

SCHEDULES

SCHEDULE 1[58]

SCHEDULE 2[59]

SCHEDULE 3[60]

Section 21.

SCHEDULE 4 The Qualifications and Curriculum Authority

Status

1 The Authority shall not be regarded as a servant or agent of the Crown or as enjoying any status, immunity or privilege of the Crown; and the Authority's property shall not be regarded as property of, or property held on behalf of, the Crown.

Powers

2(1) The Authority may do anything which is calculated to facilitate, or is incidental or conducive to, the carrying out of any of their functions.

(2) In particular, the Authority may—

(a) acquire or dispose of land or other property,

(b) enter into contracts,

(c) form bodies corporate or associated or other bodies which are not bodies corporate,

(d) enter into joint ventures with other persons,

(e) subscribe for shares or stock,

(f) invest any sums not immediately required for the purpose of carrying out their functions,

(g) accept gifts of money, land or other property, and

(h) borrow money.

(3) The Authority may authorise the Qualifications, Curriculum and Assessment Authority for Wales to act as agent for the Authority in connection with the exercise of any of the Authority's functions in relation to Wales.

(4) The consent of the Secretary of State is required for the exercise of any power conferred by sub-paragraph (2)(c) or (d) or sub-paragraph (3).

3(1) The Authority may give to any person or body (whether or not in the United Kingdom) such assistance as they may determine.

(2) Assistance may be provided on such terms and subject to such conditions (if any) as the Authority may determine.

(3) In particular, assistance may be provided free of charge or on such terms as to payment as the

Authority may determine.

(4) The power conferred by this paragraph does not extend to the giving of financial assistance; and the consent of the Secretary of State is required for any exercise of that power.

Chief officer

4(1) The Authority shall have a chief officer.

(2) The first chief officer shall be appointed by the Secretary of State on such terms and conditions as the Secretary of State may determine.

(3) Each subsequent chief officer shall be appointed by the Authority with the approval of the Secretary of State on such terms and conditions as the Authority may with the approval of the Secretary of State determine.

(4) The chief officer shall be an ex officio member of the Authority.

Chairman and chief officer: division of functions

5(1) The Secretary of State may, on appointing a person to be the chairman of the Authority, confer on him such additional functions in relation to the Authority as may be specified in the appointment.

(2) The functions for the time being conferred by virtue of appointment as chief officer of the Authority shall not include any function for the time being conferred under sub-paragraph (1) on the chairman of the Authority.

Tenure of office

6(1) a person shall hold and vacate office as a member or as chairman or deputy chairman of the Authority in accordance with the terms of his appointment and shall, on ceasing to be a member, be eligible for re-appointment.

(2) A person may at any time by notice in writing to the Secretary of State resign his office as a member or as chairman or deputy chairman of the Authority.

7 The Secretary of State may, if satisfied that a member of the Authority—

(a) has been absent from meetings of the Authority for a continuous period of more than six months without the permission of the Authority, or

(b) is unable or unfit to discharge the functions of a member,

remove him from office by giving him notice in writing and thereupon the office shall become vacant.

8 If the chairman or deputy chairman of the Authority ceases to be a member of the Authority, he shall also cease to be chairman or deputy chairman.

Payments to members

9(1) The Authority shall pay to their members such salaries or fees, and such travelling, subsistence or other allowances, as the Secretary of State may determine.

(2) The Authority shall, as regards any member in whose case the Secretary of State may so determine, pay, or make provision for the payment of, such sums by way of pension, allowances and gratuities to or in respect of him as the Secretary of State may determine.

(3) If a person ceases to be a member of the Authority and it appears to the Secretary of State that there are special circumstances which make it right that he should receive compensation, the Secretary of State may direct the Authority to make to that person a payment of such amount as the Secretary of State may determine.

Staff

10 Subject to the approval of the Secretary of State, the Authority—

(a) may appoint such number of employees, on such terms and conditions, as they may determine; and

(b) shall pay to their employees such remuneration and allowances as they may determine.

11(1) Employment with the Authority shall be included among the kinds of employment to which a scheme under section 1 of the Superannuation Act 1972 can apply.

(2) The Authority shall pay to the Minister for the Civil Service, at such times as he may direct, such sums as he may determine in respect of the increase attributable to this paragraph in the sums payable under the Superannuation Act 1972 out of money provided by Parliament.

(3) Where an employee of the Authority is (by reference to that employment) a participant in a scheme under section 1 of that Act and is also a member of the Authority, the Secretary of State may

determine that his service as such a member shall be treated for the purposes of the scheme as service as an employee of the Authority (whether or not any benefits are payable to or in respect of him by virtue of paragraph 9).

Finance

12(1) The Secretary of State may make grants to the Authority of such amount as he thinks fit in respect of expenses incurred or to be incurred by the Authority in carrying out their functions.

(2) The payment of grant under this paragraph shall be subject to the fulfilment of such conditions as the Secretary of State may determine.

(3) The Secretary of State may also impose such requirements as he thinks fit in connection with the payment of grant under this paragraph.

Committees

13(1) The Authority—

(a) may establish a committee for any purpose; and

(b) if so directed by the Secretary of State, shall establish a committee for such purpose as is specified in the direction.

(2) The Authority shall determine the number of members which a committee established under this paragraph shall have, and the terms on which they are to hold and vacate office.

(3) Subject to such conditions as the Secretary of State may determine, a committee may include persons who are not members of the Authority.

(4) The Authority shall keep under review the structure of committees established under this paragraph and the scope of each committee's activities.

Delegation of functions

14(1) The Authority may authorise the chairman, the deputy chairman, the chief officer or any committee established under paragraph 13 to carry out such of the Authority's functions as the Authority may determine.

(2) The Secretary of State may authorise any committee established under paragraph 13(1)(b) to carry out such of the Authority's functions as are specified in the direction given under that provision.

(3) Sub-paragraph (1) has effect without prejudice to any power to authorise an employee of the Authority to carry out any of the Authority's activities on behalf of the Authority.

Proceedings

15(1) The following persons, namely—

(a) a representative of the Secretary of State,

(b) the chairman of the Qualifications, Curriculum and Assessment Authority for Wales, or a representative of his,

(c) a representative of such other body as the Secretary of State may designate, and

(d) Her Majesty's Chief Inspector of Schools in England, or a representative of his,

shall be entitled to attend and take part in deliberations (but not in decisions) at meetings of the Authority or of any committee of the Authority.

(2) The Authority shall provide the Secretary of State, the chairman of the Qualifications, Curriculum and Assessment Authority for Wales, any person falling within sub-paragraph (1)(c) and Her Majesty's Chief Inspector of Schools in England with such copies of any documents distributed to members of the Authority or of any such committee as each of those persons may require.

16 The validity of the Authority's proceedings shall not be affected by a vacancy among the members or any defect in the appointment of a member.

17 Subject to the preceding provisions of this Schedule, the Authority may regulate their own procedure and that of any of their committees.

Accounts

18(1) The Authority shall—

(a) keep proper accounts and proper records in relation to the accounts;

(b) prepare a statement of accounts in respect of each financial year of the Authority; and

(c) send copies of the statement to the Secretary of State and to the Comptroller and Auditor General before the end of the month of August next following the financial year to which the statement relates.

(2) The statement of accounts shall comply with any directions given by the Secretary of State with the approval of the Treasury as to—

(a) the information to be contained in it;

(b) the manner in which the information contained in it is to be presented; or

(c) the methods and principles according to which the statement is to be prepared.

(3) The Comptroller and Auditor General shall examine, certify and report on each statement received by him in pursuance of this paragraph and shall lay copies of each statement and of his report before each House of Parliament.

Documents

19 The application of the seal of the Authority shall be authenticated by the signature—

(a) of the chairman or some other person authorised either generally or specially by the Authority to act for that purpose, and

(b) of one other member.

20 Any document purporting to be an instrument made or issued by or on behalf of the Authority, and to be duly executed by a person authorised by the Authority in that behalf, shall be received in evidence and be treated, without further proof, as being so made or issued unless the contrary is shown.

Section 27.

SCHEDULE 5 The Qualifications, Curriculum and Assessment Authority for Wales

Status

1 The Authority shall not be regarded as a servant or agent of the Crown or as enjoying any status, immunity or privilege of the Crown; and the Authority's property shall not be regarded as property of, or property held on behalf of, the Crown.

Powers

2(1) The Authority may do anything which is calculated to facilitate, or is incidental or conducive to, the carrying out of any of their functions.

(2) In particular, the Authority may—

(a) acquire or dispose of land or other property,

(b) enter into contracts,

(c) form bodies corporate or associated or other bodies which are not bodies corporate,

(d) enter into joint ventures with other persons,

(e) subscribe for shares or stock,

(f) invest any sums not immediately required for the purpose of carrying out their functions,

(g) accept gifts of money, land or other property, and

(h) borrow money.

(3) Where authorised to do so under paragraph 2(3) of Schedule 4, the Authority may act as agent for the Qualifications and Curriculum Authority in connection with the exercise of any of that Authority's functions in relation to Wales.

(4) The consent of the Secretary of State is required for the exercise of any power conferred by sub-paragraph (2)(c) or (d).

3(1) The Authority may give to any person or body (whether or not in the United Kingdom) such assistance as they may determine.

(2) Assistance may be provided on such terms and subject to such conditions (if any) as the Authority may determine.

(3) In particular, assistance may be provided free of charge or on such terms as to payment as the Authority may determine.

(4) The power conferred by this paragraph does not extend to the giving of financial assistance; and the consent of the Secretary of State is required for any exercise of that power.

Chief officer

4(1) The Authority shall have a chief officer who shall be appointed—

(a) in the case of a person who is also chairman of the Authority, by the Secretary of State, and

(b) in any other case, by the Authority with the approval of the Secretary of State.

(2) The appointment of the chief officer shall be on such terms and conditions as the Secretary of State,

or (as the case may be) the Authority with the approval of the Secretary of State, may determine.

(3) The Secretary of State may appoint the chief officer (if appointed under sub-paragraph (1)(b)) to be a member of the Authority.

Tenure of office

5(1) A person shall hold and vacate office as a member or as chairman or deputy chairman of the Authority in accordance with the terms of his appointment and shall, on ceasing to be a member, be eligible for re-appointment.

(2) A person may at any time by notice in writing to the Secretary of State resign his office as a member or as chairman or deputy chairman of the Authority.

6The Secretary of State may, if satisfied that a member of the Authority—

(a) has been absent from meetings of the Authority for a continuous period of more than six months without the permission of the Authority, or

(b) is unable or unfit to discharge the functions of a member,

remove him from office by giving him notice in writing and thereupon the office shall become vacant.

7 If the chairman or deputy chairman of the Authority ceases to be a member of the Authority, he shall also cease to be chairman or deputy chairman.

Payments to members

8(1) The Authority shall pay to their members such salaries or fees, and such travelling, subsistence or other allowances, as the Secretary of State may determine.

(2) The Authority shall, as regards any member in whose case the Secretary of State may so determine, pay, or make provision for the payment of, such sums by way of pension, allowances and gratuities to or in respect of him as the Secretary of State may determine.

(3) If a person ceases to be a member of the Authority and it appears to the Secretary of State that there are special circumstances which make it right that he should receive compensation, the Secretary of State may direct the Authority to make to that person a payment of such amount as the Secretary of State may determine.

Staff

9 Subject to the approval of the Secretary of State, the Authority—

(a) may appoint such number of employees, on such terms and conditions, as they may determine; and

(b) shall pay to their employees such remuneration and allowances as they may determine.

10(1) Employment with the Authority shall continue to be included among the kinds of employment to which a scheme under section 1 of the Superannuation Act 1972 can apply.

(2) The Authority shall pay to the Minister for the Civil Service, at such times as he may direct, such sums as he may determine in respect of the increase attributable to this paragraph in the sums payable under the Superannuation Act 1972 out of money provided by Parliament.

(3) Where an employee of the Authority is (by reference to that employment) a participant in a scheme under section 1 of that Act and is also a member of the Authority, the Secretary of State may determine that his service as such a member shall be treated for the purposes of the scheme as service as an employee of the Authority (whether or not any benefits are payable to or in respect of him by virtue of paragraph 8).

Finance

11(1) The Secretary of State may make grants to the Authority of such amount as he thinks fit in respect of expenses incurred or to be incurred by the Authority in carrying out their functions.

(2) The payment of grant under this paragraph shall be subject to the fulfilment of such conditions as the Secretary of State may determine.

(3) The Secretary of State may also impose such requirements as he thinks fit in connection with the payment of grant under this paragraph.

Committees

12(1) The Authority—

(a) may establish a committee for any purpose; and

(b) if so directed by the Secretary of State, shall establish a committee for such purpose as is specified

in the direction.

(2) The Authority shall determine the number of members which a committee established under this paragraph shall have, and the terms on which they are to hold and vacate office.

(3) Subject to such conditions as the Secretary of State may determine, a committee may include persons who are not members of the Authority.

(4) The Authority shall keep under review the structure of committees established under this paragraph and the scope of each committee's activities.

Delegation of functions

13(1) The Authority may authorise the chairman, the deputy chairman, the chief officer or any committee established under paragraph 12 to carry out such of the Authority's functions as the Authority may determine.

(2) The Secretary of State may authorise any committee established under paragraph 12(1)(b) to carry out such of the Authority's functions as are specified in the direction given under that provision.

(3) Sub-paragraph (1) has effect without prejudice to any power to authorise an employee of the Authority to carry out any of the Authority's activities on behalf of the Authority.

Proceedings

14(1) The following persons, namely—

(a) a representative of the Secretary of State,

(b) the chairman of the Qualifications and Curriculum Authority, or a representative of his, and

(c)[Her Majesty's Chief Inspector of Education and Training in Wales or Prif Arolygydd Ei Mawrhydi dros Addysg a Hyfforddiant yng Nghymru][61], or a representative of his,

shall be entitled to attend and take part in deliberations (but not in decisions) at meetings of the Authority or of any committee of the Authority.

(2) The Authority shall provide the Secretary of State, the chairman of the Qualifications and Curriculum Authority and [Her Majesty's Chief Inspector of Education and Training in Wales or Prif Arolygydd Ei Mawrhydi dros Addysg a Hyfforddiant yng Nghymru][62] with such copies of any documents distributed to members of the Authority or of any such committee as each of those persons may require.

15 The validity of the Authority's proceedings shall not be affected by a vacancy among the members or any defect in the appointment of a member.

16 Subject to the preceding provisions of this Schedule, the Authority may regulate their own procedure and that of any of their committees.

Accounts

17(1) The Authority shall—

(a) keep proper accounts and proper records in relation to the accounts;

(b) prepare a statement of accounts in respect of each financial year of the Authority; and

(c) send copies of the statement to the Secretary of State and to the Comptroller and Auditor General before the end of the month of August next following the financial year to which the statement relates.

(2) The statement of accounts shall comply with any directions given by the Secretary of State with the approval of the Treasury as to—

(a) the information to be contained in it;

(b) the manner in which the information contained in it is to be presented; or

(c) the methods and principles according to which the statement is to be prepared.

(3) The Comptroller and Auditor General shall examine, certify and report on each statement received by him in pursuance of this paragraph and shall lay copies of each statement and of his report before each House of Parliament.

Documents

18 The application of the Authority's seal shall be authenticated by the signature of the chairman or deputy chairman and that of one other member.

19 Any document purporting to be an instrument made or issued by or on behalf of the Authority and to be—

(a) duly executed under the Authority's seal, or

(b) signed or executed by a person authorised by the Authority to act in that behalf,

shall be received in evidence and be treated, without further proof, as being so made or issued unless the contrary is shown.

Section 42.

SCHEDULE 6 School inspections

Introductory

1 In this Schedule "the 1996 Act" means the School Inspections Act 1996.

Rights of entry etc. for Chief Inspectors

2 For subsections (8) and (9) of section 2 of the 1996 Act (functions of Chief Inspector for England) there shall be substituted—

"(8) For the purposes of the exercise of any function conferred by or under this section the Chief Inspector for England shall have at all reasonable times, in relation to any school in England—

(a) a right of entry to the premises of the school; and

(b) a right to inspect, and take copies of, any records kept by the school, and any other documents containing information relating to the school, which he requires for those purposes.

(9) It shall be an offence wilfully to obstruct the Chief Inspector for England—

(a) in the exercise of his functions in relation to the inspection of a school for the purposes of subsection (2)(b); or

(b) in the exercise of any right under subsection (8) for the purposes of the exercise of any other function."

3 For subsections (8) and (9) of section 5 of the 1996 Act (functions of Chief Inspector for Wales) there shall be substituted—

"(8) For the purposes of the exercise of any function conferred by or under this section the Chief Inspector for Wales shall have at all reasonable times, in relation to any school in Wales—

(a) a right of entry to the premises of the school; and

(b) a right to inspect, and take copies of, any records kept by the school, and any other documents containing information relating to the school, which he requires for those purposes.

(9) It shall be an offence wilfully to obstruct the Chief Inspector for Wales—

(a) in the exercise of his functions in relation to the inspection of a school for the purposes of subsection (2)(b); or

(b) in the exercise of any right under subsection (8) for the purposes of the exercise of any other function."

Removal of inspectors from register

4 In subsection (2)(d) of section 8 of the 1996 Act (removal from register and imposition or variation of conditions to be satisfied by registered inspector) for "knowingly or recklessly" there shall be substituted " , without reasonable explanation, ".

5. . . . .[63]

Inspections of closing schools

6(1) Section 10 of the 1996 Act (inspections by registered inspectors) shall be amended as follows.

(2) In subsection (3) (schools to which the section applies) after "subsection (4) " there shall be inserted " or (4A) ".

(3) After subsection (4) there shall be inserted—

"(4A) This section does not apply to any school—

(a) which is a closing school (as defined by subsection (4B)), and

(b) in respect of which the Chief Inspector has decided, having regard to the date on which the closure is to take effect, that no useful purpose would be served by the school being inspected under this section.

(4B) In subsection (4A) a "closing school" means—

(a) a county, voluntary or maintained nursery school in respect of which the Secretary of State has under section 169 of the Education Act 1996 approved proposals by the local education authority to cease to maintain the school;

(b) a voluntary school in respect of which the governing body have given notice of their intention to discontinue the school under section 173 of that Act;

(c) a grant-maintained school in respect of which—

(i) the Secretary of State has under section 269 of that Act approved proposals for the discontinuance of the school, or

(ii) the funding authority have made a determination under that section to adopt proposals for the discontinuance of the school;

(d) a maintained or grant-maintained special school in respect of which the Secretary of State has under section 340 of that Act approved proposals for the discontinuance of the school;

(e) a city technology college or city college for the technology of the arts in respect of which notice of termination of an agreement made under section 482 of that Act has been given; or

(f) an independent school falling within subsection (3)(e) which the proprietor has decided to close."

Publication of inspection reports

7 In each of sections 16(4)(c) and 20(4)(c) of the 1996 Act (appropriate authority to take steps to secure that registered parents receive copies of the summary of the inspection report) for "as soon as is reasonably practicable" there shall be substituted " within such period following receipt of the report by the authority as may be prescribed ".

Computer records

8 In section 42 of the 1996 Act (inspection of computer records for the purposes of Part I)—

(a) after "records" (in both places) there shall be inserted " or other documents "; and

(b) at the end there shall be added " (including, in particular, the making of information available for inspection or copying in a legible form) ".

Delegation of functions of Chief Inspectors

9 In paragraph 5(3) of Schedule 1 to the 1996 Act (performance of functions of Chief Inspectors), for "in conducting an inspection under section 2(2)(b) or section 5(2)(b) " there shall be substituted " under sub-paragraph (1) or (2) ".

Tenders and consultation

10 For paragraph 2 of Schedule 3 to the 1996 Act (selection of registered inspectors) there shall be substituted—

"2(1) Before entering into any arrangement for an inspection, the Chief Inspector shall invite tenders from at least two persons who can reasonably be expected to tender for the proposed inspection and to do so at arm's length from each other, and each of whom is either—

(a) a registered inspector, or

(b) a person who the Chief Inspector is satisfied would, if his tender were successful, arrange with a registered inspector for the inspection to be carried out.

(2) before an inspection takes place the Chief Inspector shall consult the appropriate authority about the inspection."

Inspection teams

11 For paragraph 3(1) of Schedule 3 to the 1996 Act (inspection teams) there shall be substituted—

"(1) Every inspection shall be conducted by a registered inspector with the assistance of a team (an "inspection team") consisting of persons who—

(a) are fit and proper persons for carrying out the inspection; and

(b) will be capable of assisting in the inspection competently and effectively."

Rights of entry etc. for registered inspectors

12(1) The existing provisions of paragraph 7 of Schedule 3 to the 1996 Act (rights of entry) shall become sub-paragraph (1) of that paragraph.

(2) After that sub-paragraph there shall be inserted—

"(2) Where—

(a) pupils registered at the school concerned are, by arrangement with another school, receiving part of their education at the other school, and

(b) the inspector is satisfied that he cannot properly discharge his duty under section 10(5) in relation to the school concerned without inspecting the provision made for those pupils at

that other school,

sub-paragraph (1) shall apply in relation to that other school as it applies in relation to the school concerned."

Section 57(1).

SCHEDULE 7 Minor and consequential amendments

Public Records Act 1958 (c. 51)

1 In Part II of the Table at the end of paragraph 3 of Schedule 1 to the Public Records Act 1958 (organisations whose records are public records), insert at the appropriate places—

"Qualifications, Curriculum and Assessment Authority for Wales",

"Qualifications and Curriculum Authority".

Local Authorities (Goods and Services) Act 1970 (c. 39)

2(1) Subject to sub-paragraph (2), in the Local Authorities (Goods and Services) Act 1970 (supply of goods and services by local authorities to public bodies), "public body"—

(a) shall include the Qualifications and Curriculum Authority and the Qualifications, Curriculum and Assessment Authority for Wales; and

(b) shall cease to include the School Curriculum and Assessment Authority and the Curriculum and Assessment Authority for Wales.

(2) The provision in sub-paragraph (1) shall have effect as if made by an order under section 1(5) of that Act (power to provide that a person shall be a public body for the purposes of the Act).

Superannuation Act 1972 (c. 11)

3(1) In Schedule 1 to the Superannuation Act 1972, in the list of Other Bodies (bodies in respect of which there are superannuation schemes)—

(a) omit the entries relating to the Curriculum and Assessment Authority for Wales and the School Curriculum and Assessment Authority; and

(b) insert at the appropriate places—

"the Qualifications, Curriculum and Assessment Authority for Wales",

"the Qualifications and Curriculum Authority".

(2) Section 1 of that Act (persons to or in respect of whom benefits may be provided by schemes under that section) shall apply to persons who at any time before the coming into force of section 21 of this Act have ceased to serve in employment with the National Council for Vocational Qualifications.

House of Commons Disqualification Act 1975 (c. 24)

4(1) Part III of Schedule 1 to the House of Commons Disqualification Act 1975 (disqualifying offices) shall be amended as follows.

(2) Omit the entries relating to the Curriculum and Assessment Authority for Wales and the School Curriculum and Assessment Authority.

(3) Insert at the appropriate places—

"Any member of the Qualifications, Curriculum and Assessment Authority for Wales constituted under section 27 of the Education Act 1997 in receipt of remuneration."

"Any member of the Qualifications and Curriculum Authority constituted under section 21 of the Education Act 1997 in receipt of remuneration."

(4) Omit the entry relating to the National Council for Vocational Qualifications.

Local Government Finance Act 1982 (c. 32)

5. . . . .[64]

Finance Act 1991 (c. 31)

6. . . . .[65]

Charities Act 1993 (c. 10)

7 In Schedule 2 to the Charities Act 1993 (exempt charities)—

(a) for paragraph (da) substitute—

"(da) the Qualifications and Curriculum Authority;"; and

(b) for paragraph (f) substitute—

"(f) the Qualifications, Curriculum and Assessment Authority for Wales;".

Nursery Education and Grant-Maintained Schools Act 1996 (c. 50)

8 In section 1(2) of the Nursery Education and Grant-Maintained Schools Act 1996 (arrangements for making grants in respect of nursery education), for paragraph (a) substitute—

"(a) before they begin to be of compulsory school age; but".

Education Act 1996 (c. 56)

9(1) Section 3 of the Education Act 1996 (definition of pupil etc.) shall be amended as follows.

(2) at the end of subsection (1) insert—

"and references to pupils in the context of the admission of pupils to, or the exclusion of pupils from, a school are references to persons who following their admission will be, or (as the case may be) before their exclusion were, pupils as defined by this subsection."

(3). . . . .[66]

10 In section 4(2) of that Act (schools: general)—

(a) for "For" substitute " Nothing in subsection (1) shall be taken to preclude the making of arrangements under section 19(1) (exceptional educational provision) under which part-time education is to be provided at a school; and for "; and

(b) omit "(pupil referral units) ".

11 In section 6(1) of that Act (nursery schools), for "the age of five" substitute " compulsory school age ".

12 In section 14(4) of that Act (functions of LEA in respect of provision of primary and secondary schools), for "the age of five" substitute " compulsory school age ".

13 In section 17(2) of that Act (powers of LEA in respect of nursery education), for "the age of five", in both places, substitute " compulsory school age ".

14 In section 29(6)(b) of that Act (requirement of LEA to publish information as to their policy and arrangements for primary or secondary education not to apply in relation to nursery schools, etc.), for "the age of five" substitute " compulsory school age ".

15. . . . .[67]

16. . . . .[68]

17. . . . .[69]

18. . . . .[70]

19. . . . .[71]

20. . . . .[72]

21. . . . .[73]

22. . . . .[74]

23 In section 312(2)(c) of that Act (meaning of "learning difficulty" for the purposes of the Act)—

(a) for "the age of five" substitute " compulsory school age ", and

(b) omit "or over".

24 In section 332(1) of that Act (duty of Health Authority or National Health Service Trust to notify parent where child has special educational needs), for "the age of five" substitute " compulsory school age ".

25. . . . .[75]

26 Omit sections 358 to 361 of that Act (provisions about Curriculum Authorities).

27 [In section 362(7) of that Act (development work and experiments)—

(a) for "the School Curriculum and Assessment Authority" substitute " the Qualifications and Curriculum Authority "; and

(b) for "the Curriculum and Assessment Authority for Wales" substitute " the Qualifications, Curriculum and Assessment Authority for Wales ".][76]

28 [In section 368(10) of that Act (procedure for making certain orders and regulations)—

(a) for "the School Curriculum and Assessment Authority" substitute " the Qualifications and Curriculum Authority "; and

(b) for "the Curriculum and Assessment Authority for Wales" substitute " the Qualifications, Curriculum and Assessment Authority for Wales ".][77]

29 In section 391(10) of that Act (functions of advisory councils)—

(a) for "the School Curriculum and Assessment Authority" substitute " the Qualifications and Curriculum Authority "; and

(b) for "the Curriculum and Assessment Authority for Wales" substitute " the Qualifications,

Curriculum and Assessment Authority for Wales ".

30 In section 408 of that Act (provision of information)—

(a) in subsection (1)(a), after "this Part" insert " or Part V of the Education Act 1997 "; and

(b) in subsection (4)(f), omit ", 400, 401".

31. . . . .[78]

32. . . . .[79]

33. . . . .[80]

34. . . . .[81]

35. . . . .[82]

36 In section 492(2) of that Act (adjustment of amounts eligible for recoupment as between local education authorities), for "the age of five" substitute " compulsory school age ".

37 In section 537(4) of that Act (power of Secretary of State to require information from governing bodies etc.), at the end add " ; and regulations under this section may provide that, in such circumstances as may be prescribed, the provision of information to a person other than the Secretary of State is to be treated, for the purposes of any provision of such regulations or this section, as compliance with any requirement of such regulations relating to the provision of information to the Secretary of State. "

38 For the cross-heading "CORPORAL PUNISHMENT" preceding section 548 of that Act substitute—

" **PUNISHMENT AND RESTRAINT OF PUPILS**

Corporal punishment".

39 In section 551 of that Act (regulations as to the duration of the school day, etc.), after subsection (1) insert—

"(1A) In subsection (1) the reference to the duration of the school year at any such schools is a reference to the number of school sessions that must be held during any such year."

40. . . . .[83]

41 In section 571 of that Act (publication of guidance)—

(a) in subsection (1) for "of the provisions mentioned in subsection (2) below" substitute " provision of this Act "; and

(b) omit subsection (2).

42 At the end of section 578 of that Act ("the Education Acts") add—

"the Education Act 1997."

43 In section 579(1) of that Act (general interpretation), after the definition of "school day" insert—

""school year", in relation to a school, means the period beginning with the first school term to begin after July and ending with the beginning of the first such term to begin after the following July;".

44In section 580 of that Act (the index) at the appropriate places insert—

(in the entry relating to "child")

"(in Chapter I of Part VI except sections 431 to 433)	section 411(8) ".
"school year	section 579(1) ".
"wholly based on selection by reference to ability or aptitude (in Chapter I of Part VI)	section 411(9) ".

45. . . . .[84]

47. . . . .[85]

48. . . . .[86]

49. . . . .[87]

50. . . . .[88]

School Inspections Act 1996 (c. 57)

51. . . . .[89]

Section 57(4).

SCHEDULE 8 Repeals

Chapter	Short title	Extent of repeal
1972 c.11.	Superannuation Act 1972.	In Schedule 1, in the list of Other Bodies, the entries relating to the Curriculum and Assessment Authority for Wales and the School Curriculum and Assessment Authority.

1975 c.24.	House of Commons Disqualification Act 1975.	In Part III of Schedule 1, the entries relating to the Curriculum and Assessment Authority for Wales, the National Council for Vocational Qualifications and the School Curriculum and Assessment Authority.
1996 c.56.	Education Act 1996.	In section 4(2), the words "(pupil referral units) ". In section 19(1) and (4), the words "full-time or part-time". In section 312(2)(c), the words "or over". In section 355(5), the definition of "school year" and the "and" preceding it. Sections 358 to 361. Sections 400 and 401. In section 408(4)(f), ", 400, 401". Section 423(6). In section 479(2), the words "providing secondary education". Section 571(2). In Schedule 16, in paragraph 15(1), the words from " ,including" to "brought,". In Schedule 23, in paragraph 4(1) ", 400". Schedules 29 and 30. In Schedule 37, paragraph 17, in paragraph 21 the words in sub-paragraph (1)(a) from "the entry" to "1993) and" and sub-paragraph (1)(b) and the "and" preceding it and sub-paragraph (2), in paragraph 30 sub-paragraphs (1)(a), (2) and (3), and paragraph 120.

---

[1] S. 1 repealed (1.9.1997) by 1997 c. 59, ss. 6(3), 7(3)(a), Sch. Pt.I (with s. 1(3))

[2] Ss. 2-3 repealed (1.9.1999) by 1998 c. 31, s. 140(1)(3), Sch. 30 para. 208(a), Sch.31 (with ss. 138(9), 144(6)); S.I. 1999/2323, art. 2(1), Sch.1

[3] Ss. 6-8 repealed (1.9.1999) by 1998 c. 31, s. 140(1)(3), Sch. 30 para. 208(b), Sch.31 (with ss. 138(9), 144(6)); S.I. 1999/2323, art. 2(1), Sch.1

[4] Pt. III (ss. 10-14) repealed (1.9.1999) by 1998 c. 31, s.140(1)(3), Sch. 30 para. 208(c), Sch.31 (with ss. 138(9), 144(6)); S.I. 1999/2323, art. 2(1), Sch.1

[5] Pt. IV Ch. I repealed (2.9.2002 except in relation to W.) by Education Act 2002 (c. 32), ss. 204, 215(2), 216, Sch. 22 Pt. 3 (with ss. 210(8), 214(4)); S.I. 2002/2002, art. 4

[6] S. 19(3) substituted (1.9.1999) by 1998 c. 31, s. 140(1), Sch. 30 para.213 (with ss. 138(9), 144(6)); S.I. 1999/2323, art. 2(1), Sch.1

[7] Words in s. 23(1) substituted (1.10.2002) by Education Act 2002 (c. 32), s. 189, Sch. 17 para. 1(2) (with ss. 210(8), 214(4)); S.I. 2002/2439, art. 2

[8] Words in s. 23(2)(a) substituted (1.10.2002) by Education Act 2002 (c. 32), s. 189, Sch. 17 para. 1(3)(a) (with ss. 210(8), 214(4)); S.I. 2002/2439, art. 2

[9] S. 23(2)(f) and preceding word repealed (1.10.2002) by Education Act 2002 (c. 32), ss. 189, 215(2), Sch. 17 para. 1(3)(b) , Sch. 22 Pt. 1 (with ss. 210(8), 214(4)); S.I. 2002/2439, art. 2

[10] S. 23(2A) inserted (1.10.2002) by Education Act 2002 (c. 32), s. 189, Sch. 17 para. 1(4) (with ss. 210(8), 214(4)); S.I. 2002/2439, art. 2

[11] S. 23(3)(4) repealed (1.10.2002) by Education Act 2002 (c. 32), ss. 189, 215(2), Sch. 17 para. 1(5), Sch. 22 Pt. 1 (with ss. 210(8), 214(4)); S.I. 2002/2439, art. 2

[12] Words in s. 23(5) inserted (1.10.2002) by Education Act 2002 (c. 32), s. 189, Sch. 17 para. 1(6) (with ss. 210(8), 214(4)); S.I. 2002/2439, art. 2

[13] S. 23(5): in definition of "maintained school" paras. (a)(b) substituted (1.9.1999) for paras. (a)-(c) by 1998 c. 31, s. 140(1), Sch. 30 para. 214 (b) (with ss. 138(9), 144(6)); S.I. 1999/2323, art. 2(1), Sch. 1

[14] S. 24(2)(gg) substituted (1.4.2001 for W. for specified purposes, 1.4.2002 for E. and otherwise prosp.) for s. 24(2)(h)(i) by 2000 c. 21, ss. 103(2), 154; S.I. 2001/1274, art. 2, Sch. Pt. I; S.I. 2002/279, art. 2(2)(a) (with art. 3)

[15] S. 24(2A) inserted (1.10.2002) by Education Act 2002 (c. 32), s. 189, Sch. 17 para. 2 (with ss. 210(8), 214(4)); S.I. 2002/2439, art. 2

[16] Word in s. 24(3) substituted (1.4.2001 for W. for specified purposes, 1.4.2002 for E. and otherwise prosp.) by 2000 c. 21, ss. 103(3), 154; S.I. 2001/1274, art. 2, Sch. Pt. I; S.I. 2002/279, art. 2(2)(a) (with art. 3)

[17] S. 25(5) inserted (28.7.2000 for specified purposes and 1.9.2000 insofar as it relates to England and otherwiseprosp.) by 2000 c. 21, ss. 149, 154, Sch. 9 para. 69; S.I. 2000/2114, art. 2(3), Sch. Pt. III

[18] Words in s. 26(1)(c)(i) substituted (1.10.2002 except in relation to W.) by Education Act 2002 (c. 32), ss. 215(1), 216, Sch. 21 para. 69 (with ss. 210(8), 214(4)); S.I. 2002/2439, art. 3

[19] Words in s. 26(3) repealed (1.10.2002) by Education Act 2002 (c. 32), s. 215(2), Sch. 22 Pt. 1 (with ss. 210(8), 214(4)); S.I. 2002/2439, art. 2

[20] S. 26(3A) inserted (1.10.2002) by Education Act 2002 (c. 32), s. 189, Sch. 17 para. 3(3) (with ss. 210(8), 214(4)); S.I. 2002/2439, art. 2

[21] S. 26(4)(b) substituted (1.10.2002) by Education Act 2002 (c. 32), s. 189, Sch. 17 para. 3(4) (with ss. 210(8), 214(4)); S.I. 2002/2439, art. 2

[22] S. 26A inserted (1.10.2002) by Education Act 2002 (c. 32), s. 189, Sch. 17 para. 4 (with ss. 210(8), 214(4)); S.I. 2002/2439, art. 2

[23] Words in s. 29(1) substituted (19.12.2002) by Education Act 2002 (c. 32), Sch. 17 para. 5(2) (with ss. 210(8), 214(4)); S.I. 2002/3185, arts. 2, 4, Sch. Pt. 1

[24] Words in s. 29(2)(a) substituted (19.12.2002) by Education Act 2002 (c. 32), s. 189, Sch. 17 para. 5(3)(a) (with ss. 210(8), 214(4)); S.I. 2002/3185, arts. 2, 4, Sch. Pt. 1

[25] S. 29(2)(f) and preceding word repealed (19.12.2002) by Education Act 2002 (c. 32), ss. 189, 215(2), Sch. 17 para. 5(3)(b), Sch. 22 Pt. 2 (with ss. 210(8), 214(4)); S.I. 2002/3185, arts. 2, 4, Sch. Pt. 1

[26] S. 29(2A) inserted (19.12.2002) by Education Act 2002 (c. 32), s. 189, Sch. 17 para. 5(4) (with ss. 210(8), 214(4)); S.I. 2002/3185, arts. 2, 4, Sch. Pt. 1

[27] Words in s. 29(3) substituted (1.9.1999) by 1998 c. 31, s. 140(1), Sch. 30 para. 215 (with ss. 138(9), 144(6)); S.I. 1999/2323, art. 2(1), Sch. 1

[28] Words in s. 29(5) inserted (19.12.2002) by virtue of Education Act 2002 (c. 32), s. 189, Sch. 17 para. 5(6) (with ss. 210(8), 214(4)); S.I. 2002/3185, arts. 2, 4, Sch. Pt. 1

[29] Words in s. 30(1) repealed (in force for specified purposes on 28.7.2000 and for W. on 1.4.2001 and otherwiseprosp.) by 2000 c. 21, ss. 103(4)(a), 153, 154, Sch. 11; S.I. 2001/1274, art. 2, Sch. Pt. I

[30] Word in s. 30(2) substituted (1.4.2001 for W. and otherwiseprosp.) by 2000 c. 21, ss. 103(4)(b), 154; S.I. 2001/1274, art. 2, Sch. Pt. I

[31] S. 30(3) repealed (1.4.2001 for W. and otherwiseprosp.) by 2000 c. 21, ss. 103(4)(c), 153, 154, Sch. 11; S.I. 2001/1274, art. 2, Sch. Pt. I

[32] S. 31(5) inserted (in force for specified purposes on 28.7.2000 and 1.1.2001 for W. and 1.9.2001 for E.) by 2000 c. 21, s. 149, Sch. 9 para. 70; S.I. 2000/3230, art. 2, Sch.; S.I. 2001/654, art. 2, Sch. Pt. III

[33] Words in s. 32(1)(c)(i) substituted (19.12.2002) by Education Act 2002 (c. 32), s. 215(1), Sch. 21 para. 70 (with ss. 210(8), 214(4)); S.I. 2002/3185, arts. 2, 4, Sch. Pt. 1

[34] Words in s. 32(2) substituted (1.1.2001) by 2000 c. 21, s. 73(a); S.I. 2000/3230, art. 2, Sch.

[35] Words in s. 32(3) repealed (19.12.2002) by Education Act 2002 (c. 32), ss. 189, 215(2), Sch. 17 para. 7(2), Sch. 22 Pt. 2 (with ss. 210(8), 214(4)); S.I. 2002/3185, arts. 2, 4, Sch. Pt. 1

[36] S. 32(3A) inserted (19.12.2002) by Education Act 2002 (c. 32), s. 189, Sch. 17 para. 7(3) (with ss. 210(8), 214(4)); S.I. 2002/3185, arts. 2, 4, Sch. Pt. 1

[37] S. 32(4)(b) substituted (19.12.2002) by Education Act 2002 (c. 32), s. 189, Sch. 17 para. 7(4) (with ss. 210(8), 214(4)); S.I. 2002/3185, arts. 2, 4, Sch. Pt. 1

[38] S. 32A inserted (19.12.2002) by Education Act 2002 (c. 32), s. 189, Sch. 17 para. 8 (with ss. 210(8), 214(4)); S.I. 2002/3185, arts. 2, 4, Sch. Pt. 1

[39] S. 37(1)-(4) repealed (in force for specified purposes on 28.7.2000 and 1.9.2001 for E. and W.) by 2000 c. 21, ss. 103(5), 153, Sch. 11; S.I. 2001/654, art. 2, Sch. Pt. III; S.I. 2001/1274, art. 2, Sch. Pt. II

[40] Words in s. 37(5) repealed (in force for specified purposes on 28.7.2000 and 1.9.2001 for E. and W.) by 2000 c. 21, ss. 103(5), 153, Sch. 11; S.I. 2001/654, art. 2, Sch. Pt. III; S.I. 2001/1274, art. 2, Sch. Pt. II

[41] Words in s. 38(7)(a) substituted (1.1.2001) by 2000 c. 21, s. 73(a); S.I. 2000/3230, art. 2, Sch.

[42] Words in s. 39(4) inserted (1.10.1998) by 1998 c. 31, s. 134(3) (with ss. 138(9), 144(6)); S.I. 1998/2212, art. 2, Sch.1 Pt. I

[43] S. 40 substituted (1.10.2002 except in relation to W. and 19.12.2002 otherwise) by Education Act 2002 (c. 32), ss. 180, 216, (with ss. 210(8), 214(4)); S.I. 2002/2439, art. 3; S.I. 2002/3185, art. 4

[44] Words in s. 42 repealed (1.10.1998) by 1998 c. 31, s. 140(1)(3), Sch. 30 para.216, Sch. 31 (with ss. 138(9), 144(6)); S.I. 1998/2212, art. 2, Sch.1 Pt. I

[45] S. 43(2)(a) substituted (1.9.1999) by 1998 c. 31, s. 140(1), Sch. 30 para. 217(a) (with ss. 138(9), 144(6)); S.I. 1999/2323, art. 2(1), Sch. 1

[46] S. 43(2)(b) repealed (1.9.1999) by 1998 c. 31, s. 140(1)(3), Sch. 30 para. 217(b), Sch. 31 (with ss. 138(9), 144(6)); S.I. 1999/2323, art. 2(1), Sch. 1

[47] S. 43(2)(c) substituted (1.9.1999) by 1998 c. 31, s. 140(1), Sch. 30 para. 217(c) (with ss. 138(9), 144(6)); S.I. 1999/2323, art. 2(1), Sch. 1

[48] Words in s. 43(2)(d) substituted (26.7.2002) by Education Act 2002 (c. 32), s. 65(3), Sch. 7 Pt. 2 para. 8 (with ss. 210(8), 214(4)); S.I. 2002/2002, art. 2

[49] Words in s. 43(2)(d) substituted (28.7.2000 and 1.9.2001 for E. for specified purposes and otherwise prosp.) by 2000 c. 21, ss. 149, 154, Sch. 9 para. 71; S.I. 2001/654, art. 2, Sch. Pt. III

[50] Words in s. 43(3)(a) substituted (in force for specified purposes on 28.7.2000 and 1.4.2001 for E. and W.) by 2000 c. 21, s. 149, Sch. 9 para. 72; S.I. 2001/654, art. 2, Sch. Pt. I; S.I. 2001/1274, art. 2, Sch. Pt. I

[51] S. 49 repealed (31.3.2003 for W. for s. 49(2)(3) and otherwise prosp.) by Education Act 2002 (c. 32), ss. 215, 216, Sch. 21 para. 71, Sch. 22 Pt. 3 (with ss. 210(8), 214(4)); S.I. 2002/3185, art. 5, Sch. Pt. II

[52] S. 50 repealed (1.4.1999) by 1998 c. 31, s. 140(1)(3), Sch. 30 para.218, Sch. 31 (with ss. 138(9), 144(6)); S.I. 1999/1016, art. 2(1), Sch.1

[53] S. 52(4)(5) repealed (1.10.1998) by 1998 c. 31, ss. 140(1)(3), Sch. 30 para.218, Sch. 31 (with ss. 138(9), 144(6)); S.I. 1998/2212, art. 2, Sch.1, Pt. I

[54] S. 57(2) repealed (1.9.1999) by 1998 c. 31, s. 140(1)(3), Sch. 30 para.220, Sch. 31 (with ss. 138(9), 144(6)); S.I. 1999/1016, art. 2(3), Sch.3

[55] S. 57(3) repealed (1.9.1999) by 1998 c. 31, s. 140(1)(3), Sch. 30 para.220, Sch. 31 (with ss. 138(9), 144(6)); S.I. 1999/1016, art. 2(3), Sch.3

[56] Words in s. 58(4) repealed (1.9.1999) by 1998 c. 31, s. 140(1)(3), Sch. 30 para.221, Sch. 31 (with ss. 138(9), 144(6)); S.I. 1999/2323, art. 2(1), Sch.1

[57] Words in s. 58(6) substituted (1.10.2002) by Education Act 2002 (c. 32), s. 189, Sch. 17 para. 9 (with ss. 210(8), 214(4)); S.I. 2002/2439, art. 2

[58] Sch. 1 repealed (1.9.1999) by 1998 c. 31, s. 140(1)(3), Sch. 30 para. 222(a), Sch. 31 (with ss. 138(9), 144(6); S.I. 1999/2323, art. 2(1), Sch.1

[59] Sch. 2 repealed (1.9.1999) by 1998 c. 31, s. 140(1)(3), Sch. 30 para. 222(a), Sch. 31 (with ss. 138(9), 144(6)); S.I. 1999/2323, art. 2(1), Sch.1

[60] Sch. 3 repealed (1.2.1999 to the extent that it relates to the repeal of paragraphs 1 and 2 of the Schedule inserted as Schedule 33B to the 1996 Act set out in Sch. 3, and wholly repealed (1.9.1999)) by 1998 c. 31, s. 140(1)(3), Sch. 30 para. 222(a), Sch. 31 (with ss. 138(9), 144(6)); S.I. 1998/2212, art. 2, Sch.1 Pt. III and S.I. 1999/2323, art. 2(1), Sch.1

[61] Words in Sch. 5 para. 14(1)(c)(2) substituted (1.1.2001) by 2000 c. 21, s. 73(a); S.I. 2000/3230, art. 2, Sch.

[62] Words in Sch. 5 para. 14(1)(c)(2) substituted (1.1.2001) by 2000 c. 21, s. 73(a); S.I. 2000/3230, art. 2, Sch.

[63] Sch. 6 para. 5 repealed (1.10.1998) by 1998 c. 31, s. 140(1)(3), Sch. 30 para. 222(b), Sch. 31 (with ss. 138(9), 144(6)); S.I. 1998/2212, art. 2, Sch.1 Pt. I

[64] Sch. 7 para. 5 repealed (11.9.1998) by 1998 c. 18, ss. 54(3), 55(2), Sch.5

[65] Sch. 7 para. 6 repealed (27.7.1999 with effect as mentioned in s. 59(3)(b) of the repealing Act) by 1999 c. 16, s. 139, Sch. 20 Pt. III(15)

[66] Sch. 7 para. 9(3) repealed (1.10.2002 except in relation to W.) by Education Act 2002 (c. 32), ss. 215(2), 216, Sch. 22 Pt. 3 (with ss. 210(8), 214(4)); S.I. 2002/2439, art. 3

[67] Sch. 7 paras. 15-22, 25, 31-35, 40, 45-51 repealed (1.9.1999) by 1998 c. 31, s. 140(1)(3), Sch. 30 para.223, Sch. 31 (with ss. 138(9), 144(6)); S.I. 1999/2323, art. 2(1), Sch.1

[68] Sch. 7 paras. 15-22, 25, 31-35, 40, 45-51 repealed (1.9.1999) by 1998 c. 31, s. 140(1)(3), Sch. 30 para.223, Sch. 31 (with ss. 138(9), 144(6)); S.I. 1999/2323, art. 2(1), Sch.1

[69] Sch. 7 paras. 15-22, 25, 31-35, 40, 45-51 repealed (1.9.1999) by 1998 c. 31, s. 140(1)(3), Sch. 30 para.223, Sch. 31 (with ss. 138(9), 144(6)); S.I. 1999/2323, art. 2(1), Sch.1

[70] Sch. 7 paras. 15-22, 25, 31-35, 40, 45-51 repealed (1.9.1999) by 1998 c. 31, s. 140(1)(3), Sch. 30 para.223, Sch. 31 (with ss. 138(9), 144(6)); S.I. 1999/2323, art. 2(1), Sch.1

[71] Sch. 7 paras. 15-22, 25, 31-35, 40, 45-51 repealed (1.9.1999) by 1998 c. 31, s. 140(1)(3), Sch. 30 para.223, Sch. 31 (with ss. 138(9), 144(6)); S.I. 1999/2323, art. 2(1), Sch.1

[72] Sch. 7 paras. 15-22, 25, 31-35, 40, 45-51 repealed (1.9.1999) by 1998 c. 31, s. 140(1)(3), Sch. 30 para.223, Sch. 31 (with ss. 138(9), 144(6)); S.I. 1999/2323, art. 2(1), Sch.1

[73] Sch. 7 paras. 15-22, 25, 31-35, 40, 45-51 repealed (1.9.1999) by 1998 c. 31, s. 140(1)(3), Sch. 30 para.223, Sch. 31 (with ss. 138(9), 144(6)); S.I. 1999/2323, art. 2(1), Sch.1

[74] Sch. 7 paras. 15-22, 25, 31-35, 40, 45-51 repealed (1.9.1999) by 1998 c. 31, s. 140(1)(3), Sch. 30 para.223, Sch. 31 (with ss. 138(9), 144(6)); S.I. 1999/2323, art. 2(1), Sch.1

[75] Sch. 7 paras. 15-22, 25, 31-35, 40, 45-51 repealed (1.9.1999) by 1998 c. 31, s. 140(1)(3), Sch. 30 para.223, Sch. 31 (with ss. 138(9), 144(6)); S.I. 1999/2323, art. 2(1), Sch.1

[76] Sch. 7 para. 27 repealed (1.10.2002 for Sch. 7 para. 27(a) and otherwise 20.1.2003 except in relation to W.) by Education Act 2002 (c. 32), ss. 215(2), 216, Sch. 22 Pt. 3 (with ss. 210(8), 214(4)); S.I. 2002/2439, art. 3; S.I. 2002/2952, art. 2

[77] Sch. 7 para. 28 repealed (1.10.2002 for Sch. 7 para. 28(b) and otherwise 20.1.2003 except in relation to W.) by Education Act 2002 (c. 32), ss. 215(2), 216, Sch. 22 Pt. 3 (with ss. 210(8), 214(4)); S.I. 2002/2439, art. 3; S.I. 2002/2952, art. 2

[78] Sch. 7 paras. 15-22, 25, 31-35, 40, 45-51 repealed (1.9.1999) by 1998 c. 31, s. 140(1)(3), Sch. 30 para.223, Sch. 31 (with ss. 138(9), 144(6)); S.I. 1999/2323, art. 2(1), Sch.1

[79] Sch. 7 paras. 15-22, 25, 31-35, 40, 45-51 repealed (1.9.1999) by 1998 c. 31, s. 140(1)(3), Sch. 30 para.223, Sch. 31 (with ss. 138(9), 144(6)); S.I. 1999/2323, art. 2(1), Sch.1

[80] Sch. 7 paras. 15-22, 25, 31-35, 40, 45-51 repealed (1.9.1999) by 1998 c. 31, s. 140(1)(3), Sch. 30 para.223, Sch. 31 (with ss.

138(9), 144(6)); S.I. 1999/2323, art. 2(1), Sch.1

[81] Sch. 7 paras. 15-22, 25, 31-35, 40, 45-51 repealed (1.9.1999) by 1998 c. 31, s. 140(1)(3), Sch. 30 para.223, Sch. 31 (with ss. 138(9), 144(6)); S.I. 1999/2323, art. 2(1), Sch. 1

[82] Sch. 7 paras. 15-22, 25, 31-35, 40, 45-51 repealed (1.9.1999) by 1998 c. 31, s. 140(1)(3), Sch. 30 para.223, Sch. 31 (with ss. 138(9), 144(6)); S.I. 1999/2323, art. 2(1), Sch.1

[83] Sch. 7 paras. 15-22, 25, 31-35, 40, 45-51 repealed (1.9.1999) by 1998 c. 31, s. 140(1)(3), Sch. 30 para.223, Sch. 31 (with ss. 138(9), 144(6)); S.I. 1999/2323, art. 2(1), Sch.1

[84] Sch. 7 paras. 15-22, 25, 31-35, 40, 45-51 repealed (1.9.1999) by 1998 c. 31, s. 140(1)(3), Sch. 30 para.223, Sch. 31 (with ss. 138(9), 144(6)); S.I. 1999/2323, art. 2(1), Sch.1

[85] Sch. 7 paras. 15-22, 25, 31-35, 40, 45-51 repealed (1.9.1999) by 1998 c. 31, s. 140(1)(3), Sch. 30 para. 223, Sch.31 (with ss. 138(9), 144(6)); S.I. 1999/2323, art. 2(1), Sch.1

[86] Sch. 7 paras. 15-22, 25, 31-35, 40, 45-51 repealed (1.9.1999) by 1998 c. 31, s. 140(1)(3), Sch. 30 para.223, Sch. 31 (with ss. 138(9), 144(6)); S.I. 1999/2323, art. 2(1), Sch.1

[87] Sch. 7 paras. 15-22, 25, 31-35, 40, 45-51 repealed (1.9.1999) by 1998 c. 31, s. 140(1)(3), Sch. 30 para.223, Sch. 31 (with ss. 138(9), 144(6)); S.I. 1999/2323, art. 2(1), Sch.1

[88] Sch. 7 paras. 15-22, 25, 31-35, 40, 45-51 repealed (1.9.1999) by 1998 c. 31, s. 140(1)(3), Sch. 30 para.223, Sch. 31 (with ss. 138(9), 144(6)); S.I. 1999/2323, art. 2(1), Sch.1

[89] Sch. 7 paras. 15-22, 25, 31-35, 40, 45-51 repealed (1.9.1999) by 1998 c. 31, s. 140(1)(3), Sch. 30 para.223, Sch. 31 (with ss. 138(9), 144(6)); S.I. 1999/2323, art. 2(1), Sch.1

Data Protection Act 1998

1998 CHAPTER 29

An Act to make new provision for the regulation of the processing of information relating to individuals, including the obtaining, holding, use or disclosure of such information.

[16th July 1998]

Part I Preliminary

1 Basic interpretative provisions.

(1) In this Act, unless the context otherwise requires—

"data" means information which—

(a) is being processed by means of equipment operating automatically in response to instructions given for that purpose,

(b) is recorded with the intention that it should be processed by means of such equipment,

(c) is recorded as part of a relevant filing system or with the intention that it should form part of a relevant filing system, . . .[1]

(d) does not fall within paragraph (a), (b) or (c) but forms part of an accessible record as defined by section 68; [or

(e) is recorded information held by a public authority and does not fall within any of paragraphs (a) to (d);][2]

"data controller" means, subject to subsection (4), a person who (either alone or jointly or in common with other persons) determines the purposes for which and the manner in which any personal data are, or are to be, processed;

"data processor", in relation to personal data, means any person (other than an employee of the data controller) who processes the data on behalf of the data controller;

"data subject" means an individual who is the subject of personal data;

"personal data" means data which relate to a living individual who can be identified—

(a) from those data, or

(b) from those data and other information which is in the possession of, or is likely to come into the possession of, the data controller,

and includes any expression of opinion about the individual and any indication of the intentions of the data controller or any other person in respect of the individual;

"processing", in relation to information or data, means obtaining, recording or holding the information or data or carrying out any operation or set of operations on the information or data, including—

(a) organisation, adaptation or alteration of the information or data,

(b) retrieval, consultation or use of the information or data,

(c) disclosure of the information or data by transmission, dissemination or otherwise making available, or

(d) alignment, combination, blocking, erasure or destruction of the information or data;

["public authority" means a public authority as defined by the Freedom of Information Act 2000 or a Scottish public authority as defined by the Freedom of Information (Scotland) Act 2002;][3]

"relevant filing system" means any set of information relating to individuals to the extent that, although the information is not processed by means of equipment operating automatically in response to instructions given for that purpose, the set is structured, either by reference to individuals or by reference to criteria relating to individuals, in such a way that specific information relating to a particular individual is readily accessible.

(2) In this Act, unless the context otherwise requires—

(a) "obtaining" or "recording", in relation to personal data, includes obtaining or recording the information to be contained in the data, and

(b) "using" or "disclosing", in relation to personal data, includes using or disclosing the information contained in the data.

(3) In determining for the purposes of this Act whether any information is recorded with the intention—

(a) that it should be processed by means of equipment operating automatically in response to instructions given for that purpose, or

(b) that it should form part of a relevant filing system,

it is immaterial that it is intended to be so processed or to form part of such a system only after being transferred to a country or territory outside the European Economic Area.

(4) Where personal data are processed only for purposes for which they are required by or under any enactment to be processed, the person on whom the obligation to process the data is imposed by or under that enactment is for the purposes of this Act the data controller.

[(5) In paragraph (e) of the definition of "data" in subsection (1), the reference to information "held" by a public authority shall be construed in accordance with section 3(2) of the Freedom of Information Act 2000 [or section 3(2), (4) and (5) of the Freedom of Information (Scotland) Act 2002.][4]

(6) Where

[(a)]section 7 of the Freedom of Information Act 2000 prevents Parts I to V of that Act[or][5]

[(b) section 7(1) of the Freedom of Information (Scotland) Act 2002 prevents that Act,][6]

from applying to certain information held by a public authority, that information is not to be treated for the purposes of paragraph (e) of the definition of "data" in subsection (1) as held by a public authority.][7]][8]

2 Sensitive personal data.

In this Act "sensitive personal data" means personal data consisting of information as to—

(a) the racial or ethnic origin of the data subject,

(b) his political opinions,

(c) his religious beliefs or other beliefs of a similar nature,

(d) whether he is a member of a trade union (within the meaning of the Trade Union and Labour Relations (Consolidation) Act 1992),

(e) his physical or mental health or condition,

(f) his sexual life,

(g) the commission or alleged commission by him of any offence, or

(h) any proceedings for any offence committed or alleged to have been committed by him, the disposal of such proceedings or the sentence of any court in such proceedings.

3 The special purposes.

In this Act "the special purposes" means any one or more of the following—

(a) the purposes of journalism,

(b) artistic purposes, and

(c) literary purposes.

4 The data protection principles.

(1) References in this Act to the data protection principles are to the principles set out in Part I of Schedule 1.

(2) Those principles are to be interpreted in accordance with Part II of Schedule 1.

(3) Schedule 2 (which applies to all personal data) and Schedule 3 (which applies only to sensitive personal data) set out conditions applying for the purposes of the first principle; and Schedule 4 sets out cases in which the eighth principle does not apply.

(4) Subject to section 27(1), it shall be the duty of a data controller to comply with the data protection principles in relation to all personal data with respect to which he is the data controller.

5 Application of Act.

(1) Except as otherwise provided by or under section 54, this Act applies to a data controller in respect of any data only if—

(a) the data controller is established in the United Kingdom and the data are processed in the context of that establishment, or

(b) the data controller is established neither in the United Kingdom nor in any other EEA State but uses equipment in the United Kingdom for processing the data otherwise than for the purposes of transit through the United Kingdom.

(2) a data controller falling within subsection (1)(b) must nominate for the purposes of this Act a representative established in the United Kingdom.

(3) For the purposes of subsections (1) and (2), each of the following is to be treated as established in the United Kingdom—

(a) an individual who is ordinarily resident in the United Kingdom,

(b) a body incorporated under the law of, or of any part of, the United Kingdom,

(c) a partnership or other unincorporated association formed under the law of any part of the United Kingdom, and

(d) any person who does not fall within paragraph (a), (b) or (c) but maintains in the United Kingdom—

(i) an office, branch or agency through which he carries on any activity, or

(ii) a regular practice;

and the reference to establishment in any other EEA State has a corresponding meaning.

6 The Commissioner....[9]

[(1) For the purposes of this Act and of the Freedom of Information Act 2000 there shall be an officer known as the Information Commissioner (in this Act referred to as "the Commissioner").][10]

(2) The Commissioner shall be appointed by Her Majesty by Letters Patent.

(3. . . . .[11]

(4). . . . .

(5). . . . .

(6). . . . .

(7) Schedule 5 has effect in relation to the Commissioner....[12]

Part II Rights of data subjects and others

7 Right of access to personal data.

(1) Subject to the following provisions of this section and to [sections 8, 9 and 9A][13], an individual is entitled—

(a) to be informed by any data controller whether personal data of which that individual is the data subject are being processed by or on behalf of that data controller,

(b) if that is the case, to be given by the data controller a description of—

(i) the personal data of which that individual is the data subject,

(ii) the purposes for which they are being or are to be processed, and

(iii) the recipients or classes of recipients to whom they are or may be disclosed,

(c) to have communicated to him in an intelligible form—

(i) the information constituting any personal data of which that individual is the data subject, and

(ii) any information available to the data controller as to the source of those data, and

(d) where the processing by automatic means of personal data of which that individual is the data subject for the purpose of evaluating matters relating to him such as, for example, his performance at work, his creditworthiness, his reliability or his conduct, has constituted or is likely to constitute the sole basis for any decision significantly affecting him, to be informed by

the data controller of the logic involved in that decision-taking.

(2) A data controller is not obliged to supply any information under subsection (1) unless he has received—

(a) a request in writing, and

(b) except in prescribed cases, such fee (not exceeding the prescribed maximum) as he may require.

[(3) Where a data controller—

(a) reasonably requires further information in order to satisfy himself as to the identity of the person making a request under this section and to locate the information which that person seeks, and

(b) has informed him of that requirement,

the data controller is not obliged to comply with the request unless he is supplied with that further information.][14]

(4) Where a data controller cannot comply with the request without disclosing information relating to another individual who can be identified from that information, he is not obliged to comply with the request unless—

(a) the other individual has consented to the disclosure of the information to the person making the request, or

(b) it is reasonable in all the circumstances to comply with the request without the consent of the other individual.

(5) In subsection (4) the reference to information relating to another individual includes a reference to information identifying that individual as the source of the information sought by the request; and that subsection is not to be construed as excusing a data controller from communicating so much of the information sought by the request as can be communicated without disclosing the identity of the other individual concerned, whether by the omission of names or other identifying particulars or otherwise.

(6) In determining for the purposes of subsection (4)(b) whether it is reasonable in all the circumstances to comply with the request without the consent of the other individual concerned, regard shall be had, in particular, to—

(a) any duty of confidentiality owed to the other individual,

(b) any steps taken by the data controller with a view to seeking the consent of the other individual,

(c) whether the other individual is capable of giving consent, and

(d) any express refusal of consent by the other individual.

(7) An individual making a request under this section may, in such cases as may be prescribed, specify that his request is limited to personal data of any prescribed description.

(8) Subject to subsection (4), a data controller shall comply with a request under this section promptly and in any event before the end of the prescribed period beginning with the relevant day.

(9) If a court is satisfied on the application of any person who has made a request under the foregoing provisions of this section that the data controller in question has failed to comply with the request in contravention of those provisions, the court may order him to comply with the request.

(10) In this section—

"prescribed" means prescribed by the [Secretary of State][15] by regulations;

"the prescribed maximum" means such amount as may be prescribed;

"the prescribed period" means forty days or such other period as may be prescribed;

"the relevant day", in relation to a request under this section, means the day on which the data controller receives the request or, if later, the first day on which the data controller has both the required fee and the information referred to in subsection (3).

(11) Different amounts or periods may be prescribed under this section in relation to different cases.

[(12) A person is a relevant person for the purposes of subsection (4)(c) if he—

(a) is a person referred to in paragraph 4(a) or (b) or paragraph 8(a) or (b) of Schedule 11;

(b) is employed by an education authority (within the meaning of paragraph 6 of Schedule 11) in pursuance of its functions relating to education and the information relates to him, or he supplied the information in his capacity as such an employee; or

(c) is the person making the request.][16]

[(12) A person is a relevant person for the purposes of subsection (4)(c) if he—

(a) is a person referred to in paragraph 1(p) or (q) of the Schedule to the Data Protection (Subject

Access Modification) (Social Work) Order 2000; or

(b) is or has been employed by any person or body referred to in paragraph 1 of that Schedule in connection with functions which are or have been exercised in relation to the data consisting of the information; or

(c) has provided for reward a service similar to a service provided in the exercise of any functions specified in paragraph 1(a)(i), (b), (c) or (d) of that Schedule,

and the information relates to him or he supplied the information in his official capacity or, as the case may be, in connection with the provision of that service.][17]

8 Provisions supplementary to section 7.

(1) The [Secretary of State][18] may by regulations provide that, in such cases as may be prescribed, a request for information under any provision of subsection (1) of section 7 is to be treated as extending also to information under other provisions of that subsection.

(2) The obligation imposed by section 7(1)(c)(i) must be complied with by supplying the data subject with a copy of the information in permanent form unless—

(a) the supply of such a copy is not possible or would involve disproportionate effort, or

(b) the data subject agrees otherwise;

and where any of the information referred to in section 7(1)(c)(i) is expressed in terms which are not intelligible without explanation the copy must be accompanied by an explanation of those terms.

(3) Where a data controller has previously complied with a request made under section 7 by an individual, the data controller is not obliged to comply with a subsequent identical or similar request under that section by that individual unless a reasonable interval has elapsed between compliance with the previous request and the making of the current request.

(4) In determining for the purposes of subsection (3) whether requests under section 7 are made at reasonable intervals, regard shall be had to the nature of the data, the purpose for which the data are processed and the frequency with which the data are altered.

(5) Section 7(1)(d) is not to be regarded as requiring the provision of information as to the logic involved in any decision-taking if, and to the extent that, the information constitutes a trade secret.

(6) The information to be supplied pursuant to a request under section 7 must be supplied by reference to the data in question at the time when the request is received, except that it may take account of any amendment or deletion made between that time and the time when the information is supplied, being an amendment or deletion that would have been made regardless of the receipt of the request.

(7) For the purposes of section 7(4) and (5) another individual can be identified from the information being disclosed if he can be identified from that information, or from that and any other information which, in the reasonable belief of the data controller, is likely to be in, or to come into, the possession of the data subject making the request.

9 Application of section 7 where data controller is credit reference agency.

(1) Where the data controller is a credit reference agency, section 7 has effect subject to the provisions of this section.

(2) An individual making a request under section 7 may limit his request to personal data relevant to his financial standing, and shall be taken to have so limited his request unless the request shows a contrary intention.

(3) Where the data controller receives a request under section 7 in a case where personal data of which the individual making the request is the data subject are being processed by or on behalf of the data controller, the obligation to supply information under that section includes an obligation to give the individual making the request a statement, in such form as may be prescribed by the [Secretary of State][19] by regulations, of the individual's rights—

(a) under section 159 of the Consumer Credit Act 1974 , and

(b) to the extent required by the prescribed form, under this Act.

[9A Unstructured personal data held by public authorities.

(1) In this section "unstructured personal data" means any personal data falling within paragraph (e) of the definition of "data" in section 1(1), other than information which is recorded as part of, or with the intention that it should form part of, any set of information relating to individuals to the extent that the set is structured by reference to individuals or by reference to criteria relating to individuals.

(2) A public authority is not obliged to comply with subsection (1) of section 7 in relation to any

unstructured personal data unless the request under that section contains a description of the data.

(3) Even if the data are described by the data subject in his request, a public authority is not obliged to comply with subsection (1) of section 7 in relation to unstructured personal data if the authority estimates that the cost of complying with the request so far as relating to those data would exceed the appropriate limit.

(4) Subsection (3) does not exempt the public authority from its obligation to comply with paragraph (a) of section 7(1) in relation to the unstructured personal data unless the estimated cost of complying with that paragraph alone in relation to those data would exceed the appropriate limit.

(5) In subsections (3) and (4) "the appropriate limit" means such amount as may be prescribed by the [Secretary of State][20] by regulations, and different amounts may be prescribed in relation to different cases.

(6) Any estimate for the purposes of this section must be made in accordance with regulations under section 12(5) of the Freedom of Information Act 2000.][21]

10 Right to prevent processing likely to cause damage or distress.

(1) Subject to subsection (2), an individual is entitled at any time by notice in writing to a data controller to require the data controller at the end of such period as is reasonable in the circumstances to cease, or not to begin, processing, or processing for a specified purpose or in a specified manner, any personal data in respect of which he is the data subject, on the ground that, for specified reasons—

(a) the processing of those data or their processing for that purpose or in that manner is causing or is likely to cause substantial damage or substantial distress to him or to another, and

(b) that damage or distress is or would be unwarranted.

(2) Subsection (1) does not apply—

(a) in a case where any of the conditions in paragraphs 1 to 4 of Schedule 2 is met, or

(b) in such other cases as may be prescribed by the [Secretary of State][22] by order.

(3) The data controller must within twenty-one days of receiving a notice under subsection (1) ("the data subject notice") give the individual who gave it a written notice—

(a) stating that he has complied or intends to comply with the data subject notice, or

(b) stating his reasons for regarding the data subject notice as to any extent unjustified and the extent (if any) to which he has complied or intends to comply with it.

(4) If a court is satisfied, on the application of any person who has given a notice under subsection (1) which appears to the court to be justified (or to be justified to any extent), that the data controller in question has failed to comply with the notice, the court may order him to take such steps for complying with the notice (or for complying with it to that extent) as the court thinks fit.

(5) The failure by a data subject to exercise the right conferred by subsection (1) or section 11(1) does not affect any other right conferred on him by this Part.

11 Right to prevent processing for purposes of direct marketing.

(1) An individual is entitled at any time by notice in writing to a data controller to require the data controller at the end of such period as is reasonable in the circumstances to cease, or not to begin, processing for the purposes of direct marketing personal data in respect of which he is the data subject.

(2) If the court is satisfied, on the application of any person who has given a notice under subsection (1), that the data controller has failed to comply with the notice, the court may order him to take such steps for complying with the notice as the court thinks fit.

[(2A) This section shall not apply in relation to the processing of such data as are mentioned in paragraph (1) of regulation 8 of the Telecommunications (Data Protection and Privacy) Regulations 1999 (processing of telecommunications billing data for certain marketing purposes) for the purposes mentioned in paragraph (2) of that regulation.][23]

(3) In this section "direct marketing" means the communication (by whatever means) of any advertising or marketing material which is directed to particular individuals.

12 Rights in relation to automated decision-taking.

(1) An individual is entitled at any time, by notice in writing to any data controller, to require the data controller to ensure that no decision taken by or on behalf of the data controller which significantly affects that individual is based solely on the processing by automatic means of personal data in respect of which that individual is the data subject for the purpose of evaluating matters relating to

him such as, for example, his performance at work, his creditworthiness, his reliability or his conduct.

(2) Where, in a case where no notice under subsection (1) has effect, a decision which significantly affects an individual is based solely on such processing as is mentioned in subsection (1)—

(a) the data controller must as soon as reasonably practicable notify the individual that the decision was taken on that basis, and

(b) the individual is entitled, within twenty-one days of receiving that notification from the data controller, by notice in writing to require the data controller to reconsider the decision or to take a new decision otherwise than on that basis.

(3) The data controller must, within twenty-one days of receiving a notice under subsection (2)(b) ("the data subject notice") give the individual a written notice specifying the steps that he intends to take to comply with the data subject notice.

(4) A notice under subsection (1) does not have effect in relation to an exempt decision; and nothing in subsection (2) applies to an exempt decision.

(5) In subsection (4) "exempt decision" means any decision—

(a) in respect of which the condition in subsection (6) and the condition in subsection (7) are met, or

(b) which is made in such other circumstances as may be prescribed by the [Secretary of State][24] by order.

(6) The condition in this subsection is that the decision—

(a) is taken in the course of steps taken—

(i) for the purpose of considering whether to enter into a contract with the data subject,

(ii) with a view to entering into such a contract, or

(iii) in the course of performing such a contract, or

(b) is authorised or required by or under any enactment.

(7) The condition in this subsection is that either—

(a) the effect of the decision is to grant a request of the data subject, or

(b) steps have been taken to safeguard the legitimate interests of the data subject (for example, by allowing him to make representations).

(8) If a court is satisfied on the application of a data subject that a person taking a decision in respect of him ("the responsible person") has failed to comply with subsection (1) or (2)(b), the court may order the responsible person to reconsider the decision, or to take a new decision which is not based solely on such processing as is mentioned in subsection (1).

(9) An order under subsection (8) shall not affect the rights of any person other than the data subject and the responsible person.

[12A. . . . .[25]

13 Compensation for failure to comply with certain requirements.

(1) An individual who suffers damage by reason of any contravention by a data controller of any of the requirements of this Act is entitled to compensation from the data controller for that damage.

(2) An individual who suffers distress by reason of any contravention by a data controller of any of the requirements of this Act is entitled to compensation from the data controller for that distress if—

(a) the individual also suffers damage by reason of the contravention, or

(b) the contravention relates to the processing of personal data for the special purposes.

(3) In proceedings brought against a person by virtue of this section it is a defence to prove that he had taken such care as in all the circumstances was reasonably required to comply with the requirement concerned.

14 Rectification, blocking, erasure and destruction.

(1) If a court is satisfied on the application of a data subject that personal data of which the applicant is the subject are inaccurate, the court may order the data controller to rectify, block, erase or destroy those data and any other personal data in respect of which he is the data controller and which contain an expression of opinion which appears to the court to be based on the inaccurate data.

(2) Subsection (1) applies whether or not the data accurately record information received or obtained by the data controller from the data subject or a third party but where the data accurately record such information, then—

(a) if the requirements mentioned in paragraph 7 of Part II of Schedule 1 have been complied with,

the court may, instead of making an order under subsection (1), make an order requiring the data to be supplemented by such statement of the true facts relating to the matters dealt with by the data as the court may approve, and

(b) if all or any of those requirements have not been complied with, the court may, instead of making an order under that subsection, make such order as it thinks fit for securing compliance with those requirements with or without a further order requiring the data to be supplemented by such a statement as is mentioned in paragraph (a).

(3) Where the court—

(a) makes an order under subsection (1), or

(b) is satisfied on the application of a data subject that personal data of which he was the data subject and which have been rectified, blocked, erased or destroyed were inaccurate,

it may, where it considers it reasonably practicable, order the data controller to notify third parties to whom the data have been disclosed of the rectification, blocking, erasure or destruction.

(4) If a court is satisfied on the application of a data subject—

(a) that he has suffered damage by reason of any contravention by a data controller of any of the requirements of this Act in respect of any personal data, in circumstances entitling him to compensation under section 13, and

(b) that there is a substantial risk of further contravention in respect of those data in such circumstances,

the court may order the rectification, blocking, erasure or destruction of any of those data.

(5) Where the court makes an order under subsection (4) it may, where it considers it reasonably practicable, order the data controller to notify third parties to whom the data have been disclosed of the rectification, blocking, erasure or destruction.

(6) In determining whether it is reasonably practicable to require such notification as is mentioned in subsection (3) or (5) the court shall have regard, in particular, to the number of persons who would have to be notified.

15 Jurisdiction and procedure.

(1) The jurisdiction conferred by sections 7 to 14 is exercisable by the High Court or a county court or, in Scotland, by the Court of Session or the sheriff.

(2) For the purpose of determining any question whether an applicant under subsection (9) of section 7 is entitled to the information which he seeks (including any question whether any relevant data are exempt from that section by virtue of Part IV) a court may require the information constituting any data processed by or on behalf of the data controller and any information as to the logic involved in any decision-taking as mentioned in section 7(1)(d) to be made available for its own inspection but shall not, pending the determination of that question in the applicant's favour, require the information sought by the applicant to be disclosed to him or his representatives whether by discovery (or, in Scotland, recovery) or otherwise.

Part III Notification by data controllers

16 Preliminary.

(1) In this Part "the registrable particulars", in relation to a data controller, means—

(a) his name and address,

(b) if he has nominated a representative for the purposes of this Act, the name and address of the representative,

(c) a description of the personal data being or to be processed by or on behalf of the data controller and of the category or categories of data subject to which they relate,

(d) a description of the purpose or purposes for which the data are being or are to be processed,

(e) a description of any recipient or recipients to whom the data controller intends or may wish to disclose the data,

(f) the names, or a description of, any countries or territories outside the European Economic Area to which the data controller directly or indirectly transfers, or intends or may wish directly or indirectly to transfer, the data,

[(ff) where the data controller is a public authority, a statement of that fact,]...[26]

(g) in any case where—

(i) personal data are being, or are intended to be, processed in circumstances in which the

prohibition in subsection (1) of section 17 is excluded by subsection (2) or (3) of that section, and

(ii) the notification does not extend to those data,

a statement of that fact.[, and

(h) such information about the data controller as may be prescribed under section 18(5A).][27]

(2) In this Part—

"fees regulations" means regulations made by the [Secretary of State][28] under section 18(5) or 19(4) or (7);

"notification regulations" means regulations made by the [Secretary of State][29] under the other provisions of this Part;

"prescribed", except where used in relation to fees regulations, means prescribed by notification regulations.

(3) For the purposes of this Part, so far as it relates to the addresses of data controllers—

(a) the address of a registered company is that of its registered office, and

(b) the address of a person (other than a registered company) carrying on a business is that of his principal place of business in the United Kingdom.

17 Prohibition on processing without registration.

(1) Subject to the following provisions of this section, personal data must not be processed unless an entry in respect of the data controller is included in the register maintained by the Commissioner under section 19 (or is treated by notification regulations made by virtue of section 19(3) as being so included).

(2) Except where the processing is assessable processing for the purposes of section 22, subsection (1) does not apply in relation to personal data consisting of information which falls neither within paragraph (a) of the definition of "data" in section 1(1) nor within paragraph (b) of that definition.

(3) If it appears to the [Secretary of State][30] that processing of a particular description is unlikely to prejudice the rights and freedoms of data subjects, notification regulations may provide that, in such cases as may be prescribed, subsection (1) is not to apply in relation to processing of that description.

(4) Subsection (1) does not apply in relation to any processing whose sole purpose is the maintenance of a public register.

18 Notification by data controllers.

(1) Any data controller who wishes to be included in the register maintained under section 19 shall give a notification to the Commissioner under this section.

(2) A notification under this section must specify in accordance with notification regulations—

(a) the registrable particulars, and

(b) a general description of measures to be taken for the purpose of complying with the seventh data protection principle.

(3) Notification regulations made by virtue of subsection (2) may provide for the determination by the Commissioner, in accordance with any requirements of the regulations, of the form in which the registrable particulars and the description mentioned in subsection (2)(b) are to be specified, including in particular the detail required for the purposes of section 16(1)(c), (d), (e) and (f) and subsection (2)(b).

(4) Notification regulations may make provision as to the giving of notification—

(a) by partnerships, or

(b) in other cases where two or more persons are the data controllers in respect of any personal data.

(5) The notification must be accompanied by such fee as may be prescribed by fees regulations.

[(5A) Notification regulations may prescribe the information about the data controller which is required for the purpose of verifying the fee payable under subsection (5).][31]

(6) Notification regulations may provide for any fee paid under subsection (5) or section 19(4) to be refunded in prescribed circumstances.

19 Register of notifications.

(1) The Commissioner shall—

(a) maintain a register of persons who have given notification under section 18, and

(b) make an entry in the register in pursuance of each notification received by him under that section from a person in respect of whom no entry as data controller was for the time being included in

the register.

(2) Each entry in the register shall consist of—

(a) the registrable particulars notified under section 18 or, as the case requires, those particulars as amended in pursuance of section 20(4), and

(b) such other information as the Commissioner may be authorised or required by notification regulations to include in the register.

(3) Notification regulations may make provision as to the time as from which any entry in respect of a data controller is to be treated for the purposes of section 17 as having been made in the register.

(4) No entry shall be retained in the register for more than the relevant time except on payment of such fee as may be prescribed by fees regulations.

(5) In subsection (4) "the relevant time" means twelve months or such other period as may be prescribed by notification regulations; and different periods may be prescribed in relation to different cases.

(6) The Commissioner—

(a) shall provide facilities for making the information contained in the entries in the register available for inspection (in visible and legible form) by members of the public at all reasonable hours and free of charge, and

(b) may provide such other facilities for making the information contained in those entries available to the public free of charge as he considers appropriate.

(7) The Commissioner shall, on payment of such fee, if any, as may be prescribed by fees regulations, supply any member of the public with a duly certified copy in writing of the particulars contained in any entry made in the register.

[(8) Nothing in subsection (6) or (7) applies to information which is included in an entry in the register only by reason of it falling within section 16(1)(h).][32]

20 Duty to notify changes.

(1) For the purpose specified in subsection (2), notification regulations shall include provision imposing on every person in respect of whom an entry as a data controller is for the time being included in the register maintained under section 19 a duty to notify to the Commissioner, in such circumstances and at such time or times and in such form as may be prescribed, such matters relating to the registrable particulars and measures taken as mentioned in section 18(2)(b) as may be prescribed.

(2) The purpose referred to in subsection (1) is that of ensuring, so far as practicable, that at any time—

(a) the entries in the register maintained under section 19 contain current names and addresses and describe the current practice or intentions of the data controller with respect to the processing of personal data, and

(b) the Commissioner is provided with a general description of measures currently being taken as mentioned in section 18(2)(b).

(3) Subsection (3) of section 18 has effect in relation to notification regulations made by virtue of subsection (1) as it has effect in relation to notification regulations made by virtue of subsection (2) of that section.

(4) On receiving any notification under notification regulations made by virtue of subsection (1), the Commissioner shall make such amendments of the relevant entry in the register maintained under section 19 as are necessary to take account of the notification.

21 Offences.

(1) If section 17(1) is contravened, the data controller is guilty of an offence.

(2) Any person who fails to comply with the duty imposed by notification regulations made by virtue of section 20(1) is guilty of an offence.

(3) It shall be a defence for a person charged with an offence under subsection (2) to show that he exercised all due diligence to comply with the duty.

22 Preliminary assessment by Commissioner.

(1) In this section "assessable processing" means processing which is of a description specified in an order made by the [Secretary of State][33] as appearing to him to be particularly likely—

(a) to cause substantial damage or substantial distress to data subjects, or

(b) otherwise significantly to prejudice the rights and freedoms of data subjects.

(2) On receiving notification from any data controller under section 18 or under notification regulations

made by virtue of section 20 the Commissioner shall consider—

(a) whether any of the processing to which the notification relates is assessable processing, and

(b) if so, whether the assessable processing is likely to comply with the provisions of this Act.

(3) Subject to subsection (4), the Commissioner shall, within the period of twenty-eight days beginning with the day on which he receives a notification which relates to assessable processing, give a notice to the data controller stating the extent to which the Commissioner is of the opinion that the processing is likely or unlikely to comply with the provisions of this Act.

(4) Before the end of the period referred to in subsection (3) the Commissioner may, by reason of special circumstances, extend that period on one occasion only by notice to the data controller by such further period not exceeding fourteen days as the Commissioner may specify in the notice.

(5) No assessable processing in respect of which a notification has been given to the Commissioner as mentioned in subsection (2) shall be carried on unless either—

(a) the period of twenty-eight days beginning with the day on which the notification is received by the Commissioner (or, in a case falling within subsection (4), that period as extended under that subsection) has elapsed, or

(b) before the end of that period (or that period as so extended) the data controller has received a notice from the Commissioner under subsection (3) in respect of the processing.

(6) Where subsection (5) is contravened, the data controller is guilty of an offence.

(7) The [Secretary of State][34] may by order amend subsections (3), (4) and (5) by substituting for the number of days for the time being specified there a different number specified in the order.

23 Power to make provision for appointment of data protection supervisors.

(1) The [Secretary of State][35] may by order—

(a) make provision under which a data controller may appoint a person to act as a data protection supervisor responsible in particular for monitoring in an independent manner the data controller's compliance with the provisions of this Act, and

(b) provide that, in relation to any data controller who has appointed a data protection supervisor in accordance with the provisions of the order and who complies with such conditions as may be specified in the order, the provisions of this Part are to have effect subject to such exemptions or other modifications as may be specified in the order.

(2) An order under this section may—

(a) impose duties on data protection supervisors in relation to the Commissioner, and

(b) confer functions on the Commissioner in relation to data protection supervisors.

24 Duty of certain data controllers to make certain information available.

(1) Subject to subsection (3), where personal data are processed in a case where—

(a) by virtue of subsection (2) or (3) of section 17, subsection (1) of that section does not apply to the processing, and

(b) the data controller has not notified the relevant particulars in respect of that processing under section 18,

the data controller must, within twenty-one days of receiving a written request from any person, make the relevant particulars available to that person in writing free of charge.

(2) In this section "the relevant particulars" means the particulars referred to in paragraphs (a) to (f) of section 16(1).

(3) This section has effect subject to any exemption conferred for the purposes of this section by notification regulations.

(4) Any data controller who fails to comply with the duty imposed by subsection (1) is guilty of an offence.

(5) It shall be a defence for a person charged with an offence under subsection (4) to show that he exercised all due diligence to comply with the duty.

25 Functions of Commissioner in relation to making of notification regulations.

(1) As soon as practicable after the passing of this Act, the Commissioner shall submit to the Secretary of State proposals as to the provisions to be included in the first notification regulations.

(2) The Commissioner shall keep under review the working of notification regulations and may from time to time submit to the [Secretary of State][36] proposals as to amendments to be made to the regulations.

(3) The [Secretary of State][37] may from time to time require the Commissioner to consider any matter relating to notification regulations and to submit to him proposals as to amendments to be made to the regulations in connection with that matter.

(4) Before making any notification regulations, the [Secretary of State][38] shall—

(a) consider any proposals made to him by the Commissioner under [subsection (2) or (3)][39], and

(b) consult the Commissioner.

26 Fees regulations.

(1) Fees regulations prescribing fees for the purposes of any provision of this Part may provide for different fees to be payable in different cases.

(2) In making any fees regulations, the [Secretary of State][40] shall have regard to the desirability of securing that the fees payable to the Commissioner are sufficient to offset—

[(a) the expenses incurred by the Commissioner in discharging his functions under this Act and any expenses of the Secretary of State in respect of the Commissioner so far as attributable to those functions; and][41]

(b) to the extent that the Secretary of State considers appropriate—

(i) any deficit previously incurred (whether before or after the passing of this Act) in respect of the expenses mentioned in paragraph (a), and

(ii) expenses incurred or to be incurred by the Secretary of State in respect of the inclusion of any officers or staff of the Commissioner in any scheme under section 1 of the Superannuation Act 1972.

Part IV Exemptions

27 Preliminary.

(1) References in any of the data protection principles or any provision of Parts II and III to personal data or to the processing of personal data do not include references to data or processing which by virtue of this Part are exempt from that principle or other provision.

(2) In this Part "the subject information provisions" means—

(a) the first data protection principle to the extent to which it requires compliance with paragraph 2 of Part II of Schedule 1, and

(b) section 7.

(3) In this Part "the non-disclosure provisions" means the provisions specified in subsection (4) to the extent to which they are inconsistent with the disclosure in question.

(4) The provisions referred to in subsection (3) are—

(a) the first data protection principle, except to the extent to which it requires compliance with the conditions in Schedules 2 and 3,

(b) the second, third, fourth and fifth data protection principles, and

(c) sections 10 and 14(1) to (3).

(5) Except as provided by this Part, the subject information provisions shall have effect notwithstanding any enactment or rule of law prohibiting or restricting the disclosure, or authorising the withholding, of information.

28 National security.

(1) Personal data are exempt from any of the provisions of—

(a) the data protection principles,

(b) Parts II, III and V, and

(c)[sections 54A and][42] 55,

if the exemption from that provision is required for the purpose of safeguarding national security.

(2) Subject to subsection (4), a certificate signed by a Minister of the Crown certifying that exemption from all or any of the provisions mentioned in subsection (1) is or at any time was required for the purpose there mentioned in respect of any personal data shall be conclusive evidence of that fact.

(3) A certificate under subsection (2) may identify the personal data to which it applies by means of a general description and may be expressed to have prospective effect.

(4) Any person directly affected by the issuing of a certificate under subsection (2) may appeal to the Tribunal against the certificate.

(5) If on an appeal under subsection (4), the Tribunal finds that, applying the principles applied by the

court on an application for judicial review, the Minister did not have reasonable grounds for issuing the certificate, the Tribunal may allow the appeal and quash the certificate.

(6) Where in any proceedings under or by virtue of this Act it is claimed by a data controller that a certificate under subsection (2) which identifies the personal data to which it applies by means of a general description applies to any personal data, any other party to the proceedings may appeal to the Tribunal on the ground that the certificate does not apply to the personal data in question and, subject to any determination under subsection (7), the certificate shall be conclusively presumed so to apply.

(7) On any appeal under subsection (6), the Tribunal may determine that the certificate does not so apply.

(8) A document purporting to be a certificate under subsection (2) shall be received in evidence and deemed to be such a certificate unless the contrary is proved.

(9) A document which purports to be certified by or on behalf of a Minister of the Crown as a true copy of a certificate issued by that Minister under subsection (2) shall in any legal proceedings be evidence (or, in Scotland, sufficient evidence) of that certificate.

(10) The power conferred by subsection (2) on a Minister of the Crown shall not be exercisable except by a Minister who is a member of the Cabinet or by the Attorney General or the Lord Advocate.

(11) No power conferred by any provision of Part V may be exercised in relation to personal data which by virtue of this section are exempt from that provision.

(12) Schedule 6 shall have effect in relation to appeals under subsection (4) or (6) and the proceedings of the Tribunal in respect of any such appeal.

29 Crime and taxation.

(1) Personal data processed for any of the following purposes—

(a) the prevention or detection of crime,

(b) the apprehension or prosecution of offenders, or

(c) the assessment or collection of any tax or duty or of any imposition of a similar nature,

are exempt from the first data protection principle (except to the extent to which it requires compliance with the conditions in Schedules 2 and 3) and section 7 in any case to the extent to which the application of those provisions to the data would be likely to prejudice any of the matters mentioned in this subsection.

(2) Personal data which—

(a) are processed for the purpose of discharging statutory functions, and

(b) consist of information obtained for such a purpose from a person who had it in his possession for any of the purposes mentioned in subsection (1),

are exempt from the subject information provisions to the same extent as personal data processed for any of the purposes mentioned in that subsection.

(3) Personal data are exempt from the non-disclosure provisions in any case in which—

(a) the disclosure is for any of the purposes mentioned in subsection (1), and

(b) the application of those provisions in relation to the disclosure would be likely to prejudice any of the matters mentioned in that subsection.

(4) Personal data in respect of which the data controller is a relevant authority and which—

(a) consist of a classification applied to the data subject as part of a system of risk assessment which is operated by that authority for either of the following purposes—

(i) the assessment or collection of any tax or duty or any imposition of a similar nature, or

(ii) the prevention or detection of crime, or apprehension or prosecution of offenders, where the offence concerned involves any unlawful claim for any payment out of, or any unlawful application of, public funds, and

(b) are processed for either of those purposes,

are exempt from section 7 to the extent to which the exemption is required in the interests of the operation of the system.

(5) In subsection (4)— "public funds" includes funds provided by any Community institution; "relevant authority" means—

(a) a government department,

(b) a local authority, or

(c) any other authority administering housing benefit or council tax benefit.

30 Health, education and social work.

(1) The [Secretary of State][43] may by order exempt from the subject information provisions, or modify those provisions in relation to, personal data consisting of information as to the physical or mental health or condition of the data subject.

(2) The [Secretary of State][44] may by order exempt from the subject information provisions, or modify those provisions in relation to—

(a) personal data in respect of which the data controller is the proprietor of, or a teacher at, a school, and which consist of information relating to persons who are or have been pupils at the school, or

(b) personal data in respect of which the data controller is an education authority in Scotland, and which consist of information relating to persons who are receiving, or have received, further education provided by the authority.

(3) The [Secretary of State][45] may by order exempt from the subject information provisions, or modify those provisions in relation to, personal data of such other descriptions as may be specified in the order, being information—

(a) processed by government departments or local authorities or by voluntary organisations or other bodies designated by or under the order, and

(b) appearing to him to be processed in the course of, or for the purposes of, carrying out social work in relation to the data subject or other individuals;

but the [Secretary of State][46] shall not under this subsection confer any exemption or make any modification except so far as he considers that the application to the data of those provisions (or of those provisions without modification) would be likely to prejudice the carrying out of social work.

(4) An order under this section may make different provision in relation to data consisting of information of different descriptions.

(5) In this section—

"education authority" and "further education" have the same meaning as in the Education (Scotland) Act 1980 ("the 1980 Act"), and

"proprietor"—

(a) in relation to a school in England or Wales, has the same meaning as in the Education Act 1996,

(b) in relation to a school in Scotland, means—

(b)(i) [in the case of a self-governing school, the board of management within the meaning of the Self-Governing Schools etc. (Scotland) Act 1989,][47]

(ii) in the case of an independent school, the proprietor within the meaning of the 1980 Act,

(iii) in the case of a grant-aided school, the managers within the meaning of the 1980 Act, and

(iv) in the case of a public school, the education authority within the meaning of the 1980 Act, and

(c) in relation to a school in Northern Ireland, has the same meaning as in the Education and Libraries (Northern Ireland) Order 1986 and includes, in the case of a controlled school, the Board of Governors of the school.

31 Regulatory activity.

(1) Personal data processed for the purposes of discharging functions to which this subsection applies are exempt from the subject information provisions in any case to the extent to which the application of those provisions to the data would be likely to prejudice the proper discharge of those functions.

(2) Subsection (1) applies to any relevant function which is designed—

(a) for protecting members of the public against—

(i) financial loss due to dishonesty, malpractice or other seriously improper conduct by, or the unfitness or incompetence of, persons concerned in the provision of banking, insurance, investment or other financial services or in the management of bodies corporate,

(ii) financial loss due to the conduct of discharged or undischarged bankrupts, or

(iii) dishonesty, malpractice or other seriously improper conduct by, or the unfitness or incompetence of, persons authorised to carry on any profession or other activity,

(b) for protecting charities [or community interest companies][48] against misconduct or mismanagement (whether by trustees [, directors][49] or other persons) in their administration,

(c) for protecting the property of charities [or community interest companies][50] from loss or misapplication,

(d) for the recovery of the property of charities [or community interest companies][51] ,

(e) for securing the health, safety and welfare of persons at work, or

(f) for protecting persons other than persons at work against risk to health or safety arising out of or in connection with the actions of persons at work.

(3) In subsection (2) "relevant function" means—

(a) any function conferred on any person by or under any enactment,

(b) any function of the Crown, a Minister of the Crown or a government department, or

(c) any other function which is of a public nature and is exercised in the public interest.

(4) Personal data processed for the purpose of discharging any function which—

(a) is conferred by or under any enactment on—

(i) the Parliamentary Commissioner for Administration,

(ii) the Commission for Local Administration in England [...[or][52] , the Commission for Local Administration in Wales][53]......[54] ,

(iii) the Health Service Commissioner for England [...[or][55] , the Health Service Commissioner for Wales][56]......[57] ,

[(iv) the Public Services Ombudsman for Wales,] [58]

(v) the Assembly Ombudsman for Northern Ireland,...[59]

(vi) the Northern Ireland Commissioner for Complaints, [or][60]

[(vii) the Scottish Public Services Ombudsman, and][61]

(b) is designed for protecting members of the public against—

(i) maladministration by public bodies,

(ii) failures in services provided by public bodies, or

(iii) a failure of a public body to provide a service which it was a function of the body to provide,

are exempt from the subject information provisions in any case to the extent to which the application of those provisions to the data would be likely to prejudice the proper discharge of that function.

[(4A) Personal data processed for the purpose of discharging any function which is conferred by or under Part XVI of the Financial Services and Markets Act 2000 on the body established by the Financial Services Authority for the purposes of that Part are exempt from the subject information provisions in any case to the extent to which the application of those provisions to the data would be likely to prejudice the proper discharge of the function.][62]

[(4B) Personal data processed for the purposes of discharging any function of the Legal Services Board are exempt from the subject information provisions in any case to the extent to which the application of those provisions to the data would be likely to prejudice the proper discharge of the function.][63]

[(4C) Personal data processed for the purposes of the function of considering a complaint under the scheme established under Part 6 of the Legal Services Act 2007 (legal complaints) are exempt from the subject information provisions in any case to the extent to which the application of those provisions to the data would be likely to prejudice the proper discharge of the function.][64]

(5) Personal data processed for the purpose of discharging any function which—

(a) is conferred by or under any enactment on the [the Office of Fair Trading][65] , and

(b) is designed—

(i) for protecting members of the public against conduct which may adversely affect their interests by persons carrying on a business,

(ii) for regulating agreements or conduct which have as their object or effect the prevention, restriction or distortion of competition in connection with any commercial activity, or

(iii) for regulating conduct on the part of one or more undertakings which amounts to the abuse of a dominant position in a market,

are exempt from the subject information provisions in any case to the extent to which the application of those provisions to the data would be likely to prejudice the proper discharge of that function.

[(5A) Personal data processed by a CPC enforcer for the purpose of discharging any function conferred on such a body by or under the CPC Regulation are exempt from the subject information provisions in any case to the extent to which the application of those provisions to the data would be likely to

prejudice the proper discharge of that function.

(5B) In subsection (5A)—

(a) "CPC enforcer" has the meaning given to it in section 213(5A) of the Enterprise Act 2002 but does not include the Office of Fair Trading;

(b) "CPC Regulation" has the meaning given to it in section 235A of that Act.][66]

[(6) Personal data processed for the purpose of the function of considering a complaint under section 113(1) or (2) or 114(1) or (3) of the Health and Social Care (Community Health and Standards) Act 2003, or section 24D, 26...[67] or 26ZB of the Children Act 1989, are exempt from the subject information provisions in any case to the extent to which the application of those provisions to the data would be likely to prejudice the proper discharge of that function.][68]

[(7) Personal data processed for the purpose of discharging any function which is conferred by or under Part 3 of the Local Government Act 2000 on—

(a) the monitoring officer of a relevant authority,

(b) an ethical standards officer, or

(c) the Public Services Ombudsman for Wales,

are exempt from the subject information provisions in any case to the extent to which the application of those provisions to the data would be likely to prejudice the proper discharge of that function.

(8) In subsection (7)—

(a) "relevant authority" has the meaning given by section 49(6) of the Local Government Act 2000, and

(b) any reference to the monitoring officer of a relevant authority, or to an ethical standards officer, has the same meaning as in Part 3 of that Act.][69]

32 Journalism, literature and art.

(1) Personal data which are processed only for the special purposes are exempt from any provision to which this subsection relates if—

(a) the processing is undertaken with a view to the publication by any person of any journalistic, literary or artistic material,

(b) the data controller reasonably believes that, having regard in particular to the special importance of the public interest in freedom of expression, publication would be in the public interest, and

(c) the data controller reasonably believes that, in all the circumstances, compliance with that provision is incompatible with the special purposes.

(2) Subsection (1) relates to the provisions of—

(a) the data protection principles except the seventh data protection principle,

(b) section 7,

(c) section 10,

(d) section 12, and

(e) section 14(1) to (3).

(3) In considering for the purposes of subsection (1)(b) whether the belief of a data controller that publication would be in the public interest was or is a reasonable one, regard may be had to his compliance with any code of practice which—

(a) is relevant to the publication in question, and

(b) is designated by the [Secretary of State][70] by order for the purposes of this subsection.

(4) Where at any time ("the relevant time") in any proceedings against a data controller under section 7(9), 10(4), 12(8) or 14 or by virtue of section 13 the data controller claims, or it appears to the court, that any personal data to which the proceedings relate are being processed—

(a) only for the special purposes, and

(b) with a view to the publication by any person of any journalistic, literary or artistic material which, at the time twenty-four hours immediately before the relevant time, had not previously been published by the data controller,

the court shall stay the proceedings until either of the conditions in subsection (5) is met.

(5) Those conditions are—

(a) that a determination of the Commissioner under section 45 with respect to the data in question takes effect, or

(b) in a case where the proceedings were stayed on the making of a claim, that the claim is

withdrawn.

(6) For the purposes of this Act "publish", in relation to journalistic, literary or artistic material, means make available to the public or any section of the public.

33 Research, history and statistics.

(1) In this section— "research purposes" includes statistical or historical purposes; "the relevant conditions", in relation to any processing of personal data, means the conditions—

(a) that the data are not processed to support measures or decisions with respect to particular individuals, and

(b) that the data are not processed in such a way that substantial damage or substantial distress is, or is likely to be, caused to any data subject.

(2) For the purposes of the second data protection principle, the further processing of personal data only for research purposes in compliance with the relevant conditions is not to be regarded as incompatible with the purposes for which they were obtained.

(3) Personal data which are processed only for research purposes in compliance with the relevant conditions may, notwithstanding the fifth data protection principle, be kept indefinitely.

(4) Personal data which are processed only for research purposes are exempt from section 7 if—

(a) they are processed in compliance with the relevant conditions, and

(b) the results of the research or any resulting statistics are not made available in a form which identifies data subjects or any of them.

(5) For the purposes of subsections (2) to (4) personal data are not to be treated as processed otherwise than for research purposes merely because the data are disclosed—

(a) to any person, for research purposes only,

(b) to the data subject or a person acting on his behalf,

(c) at the request, or with the consent, of the data subject or a person acting on his behalf, or

(d) in circumstances in which the person making the disclosure has reasonable grounds for believing that the disclosure falls within paragraph (a), (b) or (c).

[33A Manual data held by public authorities.

(1) Personal data falling within paragraph (e) of the definition of "data" in section 1(1) are exempt from—

(a) the first, second, third, fifth, seventh and eighth data protection principles,

(b) the sixth data protection principle except so far as it relates to the rights conferred on data subjects by sections 7 and 14,

(c) sections 10 to 12,

(d) section 13, except so far as it relates to damage caused by a contravention of section 7 or of the fourth data protection principle and to any distress which is also suffered by reason of that contravention,

(e) Part III, and

(f) section 55.

(2) Personal data which fall within paragraph (e) of the definition of "data" in section 1(1) and relate to appointments or removals, pay, discipline, superannuation or other personnel matters, in relation to—

(a) service in any of the armed forces of the Crown,

(b) service in any office or employment under the Crown or under any public authority, or

(c) service in any office or employment, or under any contract for services, in respect of which power to take action, or to determine or approve the action taken, in such matters is vested in Her Majesty, any Minister of the Crown, the National Assembly for Wales, any Northern Ireland Minister (within the meaning of the Freedom of Information Act 2000) or any public authority,

are also exempt from the remaining data protection principles and the remaining provisions of Part II.][71]

34 Information available to the public by or under enactment.

Personal data are exempt from—

(a) the subject information provisions,

(b) the fourth data protection principle and section 14(1) to (3), and

(c) the non-disclosure provisions,

if the data consist of information which the data controller is obliged by or under any enactment [other than an enactment contained in the Freedom of Information Act 2000][72] to make available to the public, whether by publishing it, by making it available for inspection, or otherwise and whether gratuitously or on payment of a fee.

35 Disclosures required by law or made in connection with legal proceedings etc.

(1) Personal data are exempt from the non-disclosure provisions where the disclosure is required by or under any enactment, by any rule of law or by the order of a court.

(2) Personal data are exempt from the non-disclosure provisions where the disclosure is necessary—

(a) for the purpose of, or in connection with, any legal proceedings (including prospective legal proceedings), or

(b) for the purpose of obtaining legal advice,

or is otherwise necessary for the purposes of establishing, exercising or defending legal rights.

[35A Parliamentary privilege.

Personal data are exempt from—

(a) the first data protection principle, except to the extent to which it requires compliance with the conditions in Schedules 2 and 3,

(b) the second, third, fourth and fifth data protection principles,

(c) section 7, and

(d) sections 10 and 14(1) to (3),

if the exemption is required for the purpose of avoiding an infringement of the privileges of either House of Parliament.][73]

36 Domestic purposes.

Personal data processed by an individual only for the purposes of that individual's personal, family or household affairs (including recreational purposes) are exempt from the data protection principles and the provisions of Parts II and III.

37 Miscellaneous exemptions.

Schedule 7 (which confers further miscellaneous exemptions) has effect.

38 Powers to make further exemptions by order.

(1) The [Secretary of State][74] may by order exempt from the subject information provisions personal data consisting of information the disclosure of which is prohibited or restricted by or under any enactment if and to the extent that he considers it necessary for the safeguarding of the interests of the data subject or the rights and freedoms of any other individual that the prohibition or restriction ought to prevail over those provisions.

(2) The [Secretary of State][75] may by order exempt from the non-disclosure provisions any disclosures of personal data made in circumstances specified in the order, if he considers the exemption is necessary for the safeguarding of the interests of the data subject or the rights and freedoms of any other individual.

39 Transitional relief.

Schedule 8 (which confers transitional exemptions) has effect.

Part V Enforcement

40 Enforcement notices.

(1) If the Commissioner is satisfied that a data controller has contravened or is contravening any of the data protection principles, the Commissioner may serve him with a notice (in this Act referred to as "an enforcement notice") requiring him, for complying with the principle or principles in question, to do either or both of the following—

(a) to take within such time as may be specified in the notice, or to refrain from taking after such time as may be so specified, such steps as are so specified, or

(b) to refrain from processing any personal data, or any personal data of a description specified in the notice, or to refrain from processing them for a purpose so specified or in a manner so specified, after such time as may be so specified.

(2) In deciding whether to serve an enforcement notice, the Commissioner shall consider whether the contravention has caused or is likely to cause any person damage or distress.

(3) An enforcement notice in respect of a contravention of the fourth data protection principle which requires the data controller to rectify, block, erase or destroy any inaccurate data may also require the data controller to rectify, block, erase or destroy any other data held by him and containing an expression of opinion which appears to the Commissioner to be based on the inaccurate data.

(4) An enforcement notice in respect of a contravention of the fourth data protection principle, in the case of data which accurately record information received or obtained by the data controller from the data subject or a third party, may require the data controller either—

(a) to rectify, block, erase or destroy any inaccurate data and any other data held by him and containing an expression of opinion as mentioned in subsection (3), or

(b) to take such steps as are specified in the notice for securing compliance with the requirements specified in paragraph 7 of Part II of Schedule 1 and, if the Commissioner thinks fit, for supplementing the data with such statement of the true facts relating to the matters dealt with by the data as the Commissioner may approve.

(5) Where—

(a) an enforcement notice requires the data controller to rectify, block, erase or destroy any personal data, or

(b) the Commissioner is satisfied that personal data which have been rectified, blocked, erased or destroyed had been processed in contravention of any of the data protection principles,

an enforcement notice may, if reasonably practicable, require the data controller to notify third parties to whom the data have been disclosed of the rectification, blocking, erasure or destruction; and in determining whether it is reasonably practicable to require such notification regard shall be had, in particular, to the number of persons who would have to be notified.

(6) An enforcement notice must contain—

(a) a statement of the data protection principle or principles which the Commissioner is satisfied have been or are being contravened and his reasons for reaching that conclusion, and

(b) particulars of the rights of appeal conferred by section 48.

(7) Subject to subsection (8), an enforcement notice must not require any of the provisions of the notice to be complied with before the end of the period within which an appeal can be brought against the notice and, if such an appeal is brought, the notice need not be complied with pending the determination or withdrawal of the appeal.

(8) If by reason of special circumstances the Commissioner considers that an enforcement notice should be complied with as a matter of urgency he may include in the notice a statement to that effect and a statement of his reasons for reaching that conclusion; and in that event subsection (7) shall not apply but the notice must not require the provisions of the notice to be complied with before the end of the period of seven days beginning with the day on which the notice is served.

(9) Notification regulations (as defined by section 16(2)) may make provision as to the effect of the service of an enforcement notice on any entry in the register maintained under section 19 which relates to the person on whom the notice is served.

(10) This section has effect subject to section 46(1).

41 Cancellation of enforcement notice.

(1) If the Commissioner considers that all or any of the provisions of an enforcement notice need not be complied with in order to ensure compliance with the data protection principle or principles to which it relates, he may cancel or vary the notice by written notice to the person on whom it was served.

(2) A person on whom an enforcement notice has been served may, at any time after the expiry of the period during which an appeal can be brought against that notice, apply in writing to the Commissioner for the cancellation or variation of that notice on the ground that, by reason of a change of circumstances, all or any of the provisions of that notice need not be complied with in order to ensure compliance with the data protection principle or principles to which that notice relates.

[41AAssessment notices

(1) The Commissioner may serve a data controller within subsection (2) with a notice (in this Act referred to as an "assessment notice") for the purpose of enabling the Commissioner to determine whether the data controller has complied or is complying with the data protection principles.

(2) A data controller is within this subsection if the data controller is—

(a) a government department,

(b) a public authority designated for the purposes of this section by an order made by the Secretary of State, or

(c) a person of a description designated for the purposes of this section by such an order.

(3) An assessment notice is a notice which requires the data controller to do all or any of the following—

(a) permit the Commissioner to enter any specified premises;

(b) direct the Commissioner to any documents on the premises that are of a specified description;

(c) assist the Commissioner to view any information of a specified description that is capable of being viewed using equipment on the premises;

(d) comply with any request from the Commissioner for—

(i) a copy of any of the documents to which the Commissioner is directed;

(ii) a copy (in such form as may be requested) of any of the information which the Commissioner is assisted to view;

(e) direct the Commissioner to any equipment or other material on the premises which is of a specified description;

(f) permit the Commissioner to inspect or examine any of the documents, information, equipment or material to which the Commissioner is directed or which the Commissioner is assisted to view;

(g) permit the Commissioner to observe the processing of any personal data that takes place on the premises;

(h) make available for interview by the Commissioner a specified number of persons of a specified description who process personal data on behalf of the data controller (or such number as are willing to be interviewed).

(4) In subsection (3) references to the Commissioner include references to the Commissioner's officers and staff.

(5) An assessment notice must, in relation to each requirement imposed by the notice, specify—

(a) the time at which the requirement is to be complied with, or

(b) the period during which the requirement is to be complied with.

(6) An assessment notice must also contain particulars of the rights of appeal conferred by section 48.

(7) The Commissioner may cancel an assessment notice by written notice to the data controller on whom it was served.

(8) Where a public authority has been designated by an order under subsection (2)(b) the Secretary of State must reconsider, at intervals of no greater than 5 years, whether it continues to be appropriate for the authority to be designated.

(9) The Secretary of State may not make an order under subsection (2)(c) which designates a description of persons unless—

(a) the Commissioner has made a recommendation that the description be designated, and

(b) the Secretary of State has consulted—

(i) such persons as appear to the Secretary of State to represent the interests of those that meet the description;

(ii) such other persons as the Secretary of State considers appropriate.

(10) The Secretary of State may not make an order under subsection (2)(c), and the Commissioner may not make a recommendation under subsection (9)(a), unless the Secretary of State or (as the case may be) the Commissioner is satisfied that it is necessary for the description of persons in question to be designated having regard to—

(a) the nature and quantity of data under the control of such persons, and

(b) any damage or distress which may be caused by a contravention by such persons of the data protection principles.

(11) Where a description of persons has been designated by an order under subsection (2)(c) the Secretary of State must reconsider, at intervals of no greater than 5 years, whether it continues to be necessary for the description to be designated having regard to the matters mentioned in subsection (10).

(12) In this section—

"public authority" includes any body, office-holder or other person in respect of which—

(a) an order may be made under section 4 or 5 of the Freedom of Information Act 2000, or

(b) an order may be made under section 4 or 5 of the Freedom of Information (Scotland) Act 2002;

"specified" means specified in an assessment notice.

41BAssessment notices: limitations

(1) A time specified in an assessment notice under section 41A(5) in relation to a requirement must not fall, and a period so specified must not begin, before the end of the period within which an appeal can be brought against the notice, and if such an appeal is brought the requirement need not be complied with pending the determination or withdrawal of the appeal.

(2) If by reason of special circumstances the Commissioner considers that it is necessary for the data controller to comply with a requirement in an assessment notice as a matter of urgency, the Commissioner may include in the notice a statement to that effect and a statement of the reasons for that conclusion; and in that event subsection (1) applies in relation to the requirement as if for the words from "within" to the end there were substituted of 7 days beginning with the day on which the notice is served.

(3) A requirement imposed by an assessment notice does not have effect in so far as compliance with it would result in the disclosure of—

(a) any communication between a professional legal adviser and the adviser's client in connection with the giving of legal advice with respect to the client's obligations, liabilities or rights under this Act, or

(b) any communication between a professional legal adviser and the adviser's client, or between such an adviser or the adviser's client and any other person, made in connection with or in contemplation of proceedings under or arising out of this Act (including proceedings before the Tribunal) and for the purposes of such proceedings.

(4) In subsection (3) references to the client of a professional legal adviser include references to any person representing such a client.

(5) Nothing in section 41A authorises the Commissioner to serve an assessment notice on—

(a) a judge,

(b) a body specified in section 23(3) of the Freedom of Information Act 2000 (bodies dealing with security matters), or

(c) the Office for Standards in Education, Children's Services and Skills in so far as it is a data controller in respect of information processed for the purposes of functions exercisable by Her Majesty's Chief Inspector of Eduction, Children's Services and Skills by virtue of section 5(1)(a) of the Care Standards Act 2000.

(6) In this section "judge" includes —

(a) a justice of the peace (or, in Northern Ireland, a lay magistrate),

(b) a member of a tribunal, and

(c) a clerk or other officer entitled to exercise the jurisdiction of a court or tribunal;

and in this subsection "tribunal" means any tribunal in which legal proceedings may be brought.

41CCode of practice about assessment notices

(1) The Commissioner must prepare and issue a code of practice as to the manner in which the Commissioner's functions under and in connection with section 41A are to be exercised.

(2) The code must in particular—

(a) specify factors to be considered in determining whether to serve an assessment notice on a data controller;

(b) specify descriptions of documents and information that—

(i) are not to be examined or inspected in pursuance of an assessment notice, or

(ii) are to be so examined or inspected only by persons of a description specified in the code;

(c) deal with the nature of inspections and examinations carried out in pursuance of an assessment notice;

(d) deal with the nature of interviews carried out in pursuance of an assessment notice;

(e) deal with the preparation, issuing and publication by the Commissioner of assessment reports in respect of data controllers that have been served with assessment notices.

(3) The provisions of the code made by virtue of subsection (2)(b) must, in particular, include provisions

that relate to—

(a) documents and information concerning an individual's physical or mental health;

(b) documents and information concerning the provision of social care for an individual.

(4) an assessment report is a report which contains—

(a) a determination as to whether a data controller has complied or is complying with the data protection principles,

(b) recommendations as to any steps which the data controller ought to take, or refrain from taking, to ensure compliance with any of those principles, and

(c) such other matters as are specified in the code.

(5) The Commissioner may alter or replace the code.

(6) If the code is altered or replaced, the Commissioner must issue the altered or replacement code.

(7) The Commissioner may not issue the code (or an altered or replacement code) without the approval of the Secretary of State.

(8) The Commissioner must arrange for the publication of the code (and any altered or replacement code) issued under this section in such form and manner as the Commissioner considers appropriate.

(9) In this section "social care" has the same meaning as in Part 1 of the Health and Social Care Act 2008 (see section 9(3) of that Act).][76]

42 Request for assessment.

(1) A request may be made to the Commissioner by or on behalf of any person who is, or believes himself to be, directly affected by any processing of personal data for an assessment as to whether it is likely or unlikely that the processing has been or is being carried out in compliance with the provisions of this Act.

(2) On receiving a request under this section, the Commissioner shall make an assessment in such manner as appears to him to be appropriate, unless he has not been supplied with such information as he may reasonably require in order to—

(a) satisfy himself as to the identity of the person making the request, and

(b) enable him to identify the processing in question.

(3) The matters to which the Commissioner may have regard in determining in what manner it is appropriate to make an assessment include—

(a) the extent to which the request appears to him to raise a matter of substance,

(b) any undue delay in making the request, and

(c) whether or not the person making the request is entitled to make an application under section 7 in respect of the personal data in question.

(4) Where the Commissioner has received a request under this section he shall notify the person who made the request—

(a) whether he has made an assessment as a result of the request, and

(b) to the extent that he considers appropriate, having regard in particular to any exemption from section 7 applying in relation to the personal data concerned, of any view formed or action taken as a result of the request.

43 Information notices.

(1) If the Commissioner—

(a) has received a request under section 42 in respect of any processing of personal data, or

(b) reasonably requires any information for the purpose of determining whether the data controller has complied or is complying with the data protection principles,

he may serve the data controller with a notice (in this Act referred to as "an information notice") requiring the data controller, [to furnish the Commissioner with specified information relating to the request or to compliance with the principles.][77]

[(1A) In subsection (1) "specified information" means information—

(a) specified, or described, in the information notice, or

(b) falling within a category which is specified, or described, in the information notice.

(1B) The Commissioner may also specify in the information notice—

(a) the form in which the information must be furnished;

(b) the period within which, or the time and place at which, the information must be furnished.][78]

(2) An information notice must contain—

(a) in a case falling within subsection (1)(a), a statement that the Commissioner has received a request under section 42 in relation to the specified processing, or

(b) in a case falling within subsection (1)(b), a statement that the Commissioner regards the specified information as relevant for the purpose of determining whether the data controller has complied, or is complying, with the data protection principles and his reasons for regarding it as relevant for that purpose.

(3) An information notice must also contain particulars of the rights of appeal conferred by section 48.

(4) Subject to subsection (5), [a period specified in an information notice under subsection (1B)(b) must not end, and a time so specified must not fall,][79] before the end of the period within which an appeal can be brought against the notice and, if such an appeal is brought, the information need not be furnished pending the determination or withdrawal of the appeal.

(5) If by reason of special circumstances the Commissioner considers that the information is required as a matter of urgency, he may include in the notice a statement to that effect and a statement of his reasons for reaching that conclusion; and in that event subsection (4) shall not apply, but the notice shall not require the information to be furnished before the end of the period of seven days beginning with the day on which the notice is served.

(6) A person shall not be required by virtue of this section to furnish the Commissioner with any information in respect of—

(a) any communication between a professional legal adviser and his client in connection with the giving of legal advice to the client with respect to his obligations, liabilities or rights under this Act, or

(b) any communication between a professional legal adviser and his client, or between such an adviser or his client and any other person, made in connection with or in contemplation of proceedings under or arising out of this Act (including proceedings before the Tribunal) and for the purposes of such proceedings.

(7) In subsection (6) references to the client of a professional legal adviser include references to any person representing such a client.

(8) A person shall not be required by virtue of this section to furnish the Commissioner with any information if the furnishing of that information would, by revealing evidence of the commission of any offence [, other than an offence under this Act or an offence within subsection (8A),][80] expose him to proceedings for that offence.

[(8A) The offences mentioned in subsection (8) are—

(a) an offence under section 5 of the Perjury Act 1911 (false statements made otherwise than on oath),

(b) an offence under section 44(2) of the Criminal Law (Consolidation) (Scotland) Act 1995 (false statements made otherwise than on oath), or

(c) an offence under Article 10 of the Perjury (Northern Ireland) Order 1979 (false statutory declarations and other false unsworn statements).

(8B) Any relevant statement provided by a person in response to a requirement under this section may not be used in evidence against that person on a prosecution for any offence under this Act (other than an offence under section 47) unless in the proceedings—

(a) in giving evidence the person provides information inconsistent with it, and

(b) evidence relating to it is adduced, or a question relating to it is asked, by that person or on that person's behalf.

(8C) In subsection (8B) "relevant statement", in relation to a requirement under this section, means—

(a) an oral statement, or

(b) a written statement made for the purposes of the requirement.][81]

(9) The Commissioner may cancel an information notice by written notice to the person on whom it was served.

(10) This section has effect subject to section 46(3).

40 Enforcement notices.

(1) If the Commissioner is satisfied that a data controller has contravened or is contravening any of the data protection principles, the Commissioner may serve him with a notice (in this Act referred to as

"an enforcement notice") requiring him, for complying with the principle or principles in question, to do either or both of the following—

(a) to take within such time as may be specified in the notice, or to refrain from taking after such time as may be so specified, such steps as are so specified, or

(b) to refrain from processing any personal data, or any personal data of a description specified in the notice, or to refrain from processing them for a purpose so specified or in a manner so specified, after such time as may be so specified.

(2) In deciding whether to serve an enforcement notice, the Commissioner shall consider whether the contravention has caused or is likely to cause any person damage or distress.

(3) An enforcement notice in respect of a contravention of the fourth data protection principle which requires the data controller to rectify, block, erase or destroy any inaccurate data may also require the data controller to rectify, block, erase or destroy any other data held by him and containing an expression of opinion which appears to the Commissioner to be based on the inaccurate data.

(4) An enforcement notice in respect of a contravention of the fourth data protection principle, in the case of data which accurately record information received or obtained by the data controller from the data subject or a third party, may require the data controller either—

(a) to rectify, block, erase or destroy any inaccurate data and any other data held by him and containing an expression of opinion as mentioned in subsection (3), or

(b) to take such steps as are specified in the notice for securing compliance with the requirements specified in paragraph 7 of Part II of Schedule 1 and, if the Commissioner thinks fit, for supplementing the data with such statement of the true facts relating to the matters dealt with by the data as the Commissioner may approve.

(5) Where—

(a) an enforcement notice requires the data controller to rectify, block, erase or destroy any personal data, or

(b) the Commissioner is satisfied that personal data which have been rectified, blocked, erased or destroyed had been processed in contravention of any of the data protection principles,

an enforcement notice may, if reasonably practicable, require the data controller to notify third parties to whom the data have been disclosed of the rectification, blocking, erasure or destruction; and in determining whether it is reasonably practicable to require such notification regard shall be had, in particular, to the number of persons who would have to be notified.

(6) an enforcement notice must contain—

(a) a statement of the data protection principle or principles which the Commissioner is satisfied have been or are being contravened and his reasons for reaching that conclusion, and

(b) particulars of the rights of appeal conferred by section 48.

(7) Subject to subsection (8), an enforcement notice must not require any of the provisions of the notice to be complied with before the end of the period within which an appeal can be brought against the notice and, if such an appeal is brought, the notice need not be complied with pending the determination or withdrawal of the appeal.

(8) If by reason of special circumstances the Commissioner considers that an enforcement notice should be complied with as a matter of urgency he may include in the notice a statement to that effect and a statement of his reasons for reaching that conclusion; and in that event subsection (7) shall not apply but the notice must not require the provisions of the notice to be complied with before the end of the period of seven days beginning with the day on which the notice is served.

(9) Notification regulations (as defined by section 16(2)) may make provision as to the effect of the service of an enforcement notice on any entry in the register maintained under section 19 which relates to the person on whom the notice is served.

(10) This section has effect subject to section 46(1).

41 Cancellation of enforcement notice.

(1) If the Commissioner considers that all or any of the provisions of an enforcement notice need not be complied with in order to ensure compliance with the data protection principle or principles to which it relates, he may cancel or vary the notice by written notice to the person on whom it was served.

(2) A person on whom an enforcement notice has been served may, at any time after the expiry of the

period during which an appeal can be brought against that notice, apply in writing to the Commissioner for the cancellation or variation of that notice on the ground that, by reason of a change of circumstances, all or any of the provisions of that notice need not be complied with in order to ensure compliance with the data protection principle or principles to which that notice relates.

[41A Assessment notices

(1) The Commissioner may serve a data controller within subsection (2) with a notice (in this Act referred to as an "assessment notice") for the purpose of enabling the Commissioner to determine whether the data controller has complied or is complying with the data protection principles.

(2) A data controller is within this subsection if the data controller is—

(a) a government department,

(b) a public authority designated for the purposes of this section by an order made by the Secretary of State, or

(c) a person of a description designated for the purposes of this section by such an order.

(3) an assessment notice is a notice which requires the data controller to do all or any of the following—

(a) permit the Commissioner to enter any specified premises;

(b) direct the Commissioner to any documents on the premises that are of a specified description;

(c) assist the Commissioner to view any information of a specified description that is capable of being viewed using equipment on the premises;

(d) comply with any request from the Commissioner for—

(i) a copy of any of the documents to which the Commissioner is directed;

(ii) a copy (in such form as may be requested) of any of the information which the Commissioner is assisted to view;

(e) direct the Commissioner to any equipment or other material on the premises which is of a specified description;

(f) permit the Commissioner to inspect or examine any of the documents, information, equipment or material to which the Commissioner is directed or which the Commissioner is assisted to view;

(g) permit the Commissioner to observe the processing of any personal data that takes place on the premises;

(h) make available for interview by the Commissioner a specified number of persons of a specified description who process personal data on behalf of the data controller (or such number as are willing to be interviewed).

(4) In subsection (3) references to the Commissioner include references to the Commissioner's officers and staff.

(5) An assessment notice must, in relation to each requirement imposed by the notice, specify—

(a) the time at which the requirement is to be complied with, or

(b) the period during which the requirement is to be complied with.

(6) an assessment notice must also contain particulars of the rights of appeal conferred by section 48.

(7) The Commissioner may cancel an assessment notice by written notice to the data controller on whom it was served.

(8) Where a public authority has been designated by an order under subsection (2)(b) the Secretary of State must reconsider, at intervals of no greater than 5 years, whether it continues to be appropriate for the authority to be designated.

(9) The Secretary of State may not make an order under subsection (2)(c) which designates a description of persons unless—

(a) the Commissioner has made a recommendation that the description be designated, and

(b) the Secretary of State has consulted—

(i) such persons as appear to the Secretary of State to represent the interests of those that meet the description;

(ii) such other persons as the Secretary of State considers appropriate.

(10) The Secretary of State may not make an order under subsection (2)(c), and the Commissioner may not make a recommendation under subsection (9)(a), unless the Secretary of State or (as the case may be) the Commissioner is satisfied that it is necessary for the description of persons in question to be designated having regard to—

(a) the nature and quantity of data under the control of such persons, and

(b) any damage or distress which may be caused by a contravention by such persons of the data protection principles.

(11) Where a description of persons has been designated by an order under subsection (2)(c) the Secretary of State must reconsider, at intervals of no greater than 5 years, whether it continues to be necessary for the description to be designated having regard to the matters mentioned in subsection (10).

(12) In this section—

"public authority" includes any body, office-holder or other person in respect of which—

(a) an order may be made under section 4 or 5 of the Freedom of Information Act 2000, or

(b) an order may be made under section 4 or 5 of the Freedom of Information (Scotland) Act 2002;

"specified" means specified in an assessment notice.

41B Assessment notices: limitations

(1) a time specified in an assessment notice under section 41A(5) in relation to a requirement must not fall, and a period so specified must not begin, before the end of the period within which an appeal can be brought against the notice, and if such an appeal is brought the requirement need not be complied with pending the determination or withdrawal of the appeal.

(2) If by reason of special circumstances the Commissioner considers that it is necessary for the data controller to comply with a requirement in an assessment notice as a matter of urgency, the Commissioner may include in the notice a statement to that effect and a statement of the reasons for that conclusion; and in that event subsection (1) applies in relation to the requirement as if for the words from "within" to the end there were substituted of 7 days beginning with the day on which the notice is served.

(3) A requirement imposed by an assessment notice does not have effect in so far as compliance with it would result in the disclosure of—

(a) any communication between a professional legal adviser and the adviser's client in connection with the giving of legal advice with respect to the client's obligations, liabilities or rights under this Act, or

(b) any communication between a professional legal adviser and the adviser's client, or between such an adviser or the adviser's client and any other person, made in connection with or in contemplation of proceedings under or arising out of this Act (including proceedings before the Tribunal) and for the purposes of such proceedings.

(4) In subsection (3) references to the client of a professional legal adviser include references to any person representing such a client.

(5) Nothing in section 41A authorises the Commissioner to serve an assessment notice on—

(a) a judge,

(b) a body specified in section 23(3) of the Freedom of Information Act 2000 (bodies dealing with security matters), or

(c) the Office for Standards in Education, Children's Services and Skills in so far as it is a data controller in respect of information processed for the purposes of functions exercisable by Her Majesty's Chief Inspector of Eduction, Children's Services and Skills by virtue of section 5(1)(a) of the Care Standards Act 2000.

(6) In this section "judge" includes —

(a) a justice of the peace (or, in Northern Ireland, a lay magistrate),

(b) a member of a tribunal, and

(c) a clerk or other officer entitled to exercise the jurisdiction of a court or tribunal;

and in this subsection "tribunal" means any tribunal in which legal proceedings may be brought.

41C Code of practice about assessment notices

(1) The Commissioner must prepare and issue a code of practice as to the manner in which the Commissioner's functions under and in connection with section 41A are to be exercised.

(2) The code must in particular—

(a) specify factors to be considered in determining whether to serve an assessment notice on a data controller;

(b) specify descriptions of documents and information that—

(i) are not to be examined or inspected in pursuance of an assessment notice, or

(ii) are to be so examined or inspected only by persons of a description specified in the code;

(c) deal with the nature of inspections and examinations carried out in pursuance of an assessment notice;

(d) deal with the nature of interviews carried out in pursuance of an assessment notice;

(e) deal with the preparation, issuing and publication by the Commissioner of assessment reports in respect of data controllers that have been served with assessment notices.

(3) The provisions of the code made by virtue of subsection (2)(b) must, in particular, include provisions that relate to—

(a) documents and information concerning an individual's physical or mental health;

(b) documents and information concerning the provision of social care for an individual.

(4) An assessment report is a report which contains—

(a) a determination as to whether a data controller has complied or is complying with the data protection principles,

(b) recommendations as to any steps which the data controller ought to take, or refrain from taking, to ensure compliance with any of those principles, and

(c) such other matters as are specified in the code.

(5) The Commissioner may alter or replace the code.

(6) If the code is altered or replaced, the Commissioner must issue the altered or replacement code.

(7) The Commissioner may not issue the code (or an altered or replacement code) without the approval of the Secretary of State.

(8) The Commissioner must arrange for the publication of the code (and any altered or replacement code) issued under this section in such form and manner as the Commissioner considers appropriate.

(9) In this section "social care" has the same meaning as in Part 1 of the Health and Social Care Act 2008 (see section 9(3) of that Act).][82]

42 Request for assessment.

(1) A request may be made to the Commissioner by or on behalf of any person who is, or believes himself to be, directly affected by any processing of personal data for an assessment as to whether it is likely or unlikely that the processing has been or is being carried out in compliance with the provisions of this Act.

(2) On receiving a request under this section, the Commissioner shall make an assessment in such manner as appears to him to be appropriate, unless he has not been supplied with such information as he may reasonably require in order to—

(a) satisfy himself as to the identity of the person making the request, and

(b) enable him to identify the processing in question.

(3) The matters to which the Commissioner may have regard in determining in what manner it is appropriate to make an assessment include—

(a) the extent to which the request appears to him to raise a matter of substance,

(b) any undue delay in making the request, and

(c) whether or not the person making the request is entitled to make an application under section 7 in respect of the personal data in question.

(4) Where the Commissioner has received a request under this section he shall notify the person who made the request—

(a) whether he has made an assessment as a result of the request, and

(b) to the extent that he considers appropriate, having regard in particular to any exemption from section 7 applying in relation to the personal data concerned, of any view formed or action taken as a result of the request.

43 Information notices.

(1) If the Commissioner—

(a) has received a request under section 42 in respect of any processing of personal data, or

(b) reasonably requires any information for the purpose of determining whether the data controller has complied or is complying with the data protection principles,

he may serve the data controller with a notice (in this Act referred to as "an information notice") requiring the data controller, [to furnish the Commissioner with specified information relating to the request or to compliance with the principles.][83]

[(1A) In subsection (1) "specified information" means information—

(a) specified, or described, in the information notice, or

(b) falling within a category which is specified, or described, in the information notice.

(1B) The Commissioner may also specify in the information notice—

(a) the form in which the information must be furnished;

(b) the period within which, or the time and place at which, the information must be furnished.][84]

(2) An information notice must contain—

(a) in a case falling within subsection (1)(a), a statement that the Commissioner has received a request under section 42 in relation to the specified processing, or

(b) in a case falling within subsection (1)(b), a statement that the Commissioner regards the specified information as relevant for the purpose of determining whether the data controller has complied, or is complying, with the data protection principles and his reasons for regarding it as relevant for that purpose.

(3) An information notice must also contain particulars of the rights of appeal conferred by section 48.

(4) Subject to subsection (5), [a period specified in an information notice under subsection (1B)(b) must not end, and a time so specified must not fall,][85] before the end of the period within which an appeal can be brought against the notice and, if such an appeal is brought, the information need not be furnished pending the determination or withdrawal of the appeal.

(5) If by reason of special circumstances the Commissioner considers that the information is required as a matter of urgency, he may include in the notice a statement to that effect and a statement of his reasons for reaching that conclusion; and in that event subsection (4) shall not apply, but the notice shall not require the information to be furnished before the end of the period of seven days beginning with the day on which the notice is served.

(6) A person shall not be required by virtue of this section to furnish the Commissioner with any information in respect of—

(a) any communication between a professional legal adviser and his client in connection with the giving of legal advice to the client with respect to his obligations, liabilities or rights under this Act, or

(b) any communication between a professional legal adviser and his client, or between such an adviser or his client and any other person, made in connection with or in contemplation of proceedings under or arising out of this Act (including proceedings before the Tribunal) and for the purposes of such proceedings.

(7) In subsection (6) references to the client of a professional legal adviser include references to any person representing such a client.

(8) A person shall not be required by virtue of this section to furnish the Commissioner with any information if the furnishing of that information would, by revealing evidence of the commission of any offence [, other than an offence under this Act or an offence within subsection (8A),][86] expose him to proceedings for that offence.

[(8A) The offences mentioned in subsection (8) are—

(a) an offence under section 5 of the Perjury Act 1911 (false statements made otherwise than on oath),

(b) an offence under section 44(2) of the Criminal Law (Consolidation) (Scotland) Act 1995 (false statements made otherwise than on oath), or

(c) an offence under Article 10 of the Perjury (Northern Ireland) Order 1979 (false statutory declarations and other false unsworn statements).

(8B) Any relevant statement provided by a person in response to a requirement under this section may not be used in evidence against that person on a prosecution for any offence under this Act (other than an offence under section 47) unless in the proceedings—

(a) in giving evidence the person provides information inconsistent with it, and

(b) evidence relating to it is adduced, or a question relating to it is asked, by that person or on that person's behalf.

(8C) In subsection (8B) "relevant statement", in relation to a requirement under this section, means—

(a) an oral statement, or

(b) a written statement made for the purposes of the requirement.][87]

(9) The Commissioner may cancel an information notice by written notice to the person on whom it was served.

(10) This section has effect subject to section 46(3).

50 Powers of entry and inspection.

Schedule 9 (powers of entry and inspection) has effect.

Part VI Miscellaneous and General

Functions of Commissioner

51 General duties of Commissioner.

(1) It shall be the duty of the Commissioner to promote the following of good practice by data controllers and, in particular, so to perform his functions under this Act as to promote the observance of the requirements of this Act by data controllers.

(2) The Commissioner shall arrange for the dissemination in such form and manner as he considers appropriate of such information as it may appear to him expedient to give to the public about the operation of this Act, about good practice, and about other matters within the scope of his functions under this Act, and may give advice to any person as to any of those matters.

(3) Where—

(a) the [Secretary of State][88] so directs by order, or

(b) the Commissioner considers it appropriate to do so,

the Commissioner shall, after such consultation with trade associations, data subjects or persons representing data subjects as appears to him to be appropriate, prepare and disseminate to such persons as he considers appropriate codes of practice for guidance as to good practice.

(4) The Commissioner shall also—

(a) where he considers it appropriate to do so, encourage trade associations to prepare, and to disseminate to their members, such codes of practice, and

(b) where any trade association submits a code of practice to him for his consideration, consider the code and, after such consultation with data subjects or persons representing data subjects as appears to him to be appropriate, notify the trade association whether in his opinion the code promotes the following of good practice.

(5) An order under subsection (3) shall describe the personal data or processing to which the code of practice is to relate, and may also describe the persons or classes of persons to whom it is to relate.

[(5A) In determining the action required to discharge the duties imposed by subsections (1) to (4), the Commissioner may take account of any action taken to discharge the duty imposed by section 52A (data-sharing code).][89]

(6) The Commissioner shall arrange for the dissemination in such form and manner as he considers appropriate of—

(a) any Community finding as defined by paragraph 15(2) of Part II of Schedule 1,

(b) any decision of the European Commission, under the procedure provided for in Article 31(2) of the Data Protection Directive, which is made for the purposes of Article 26(3) or (4) of the Directive, and

(c) such other information as it may appear to him to be expedient to give to data controllers in relation to any personal data about the protection of the rights and freedoms of data subjects in relation to the processing of personal data in countries and territories outside the European Economic Area.

(7) The Commissioner may, with the consent of the data controller, assess any processing of personal data for the following of good practice and shall inform the data controller of the results of the assessment.

(8) The Commissioner may charge such sums as he may with the consent of the [Secretary of State][90] determine for any services provided by the Commissioner by virtue of this Part.

(9) In this section—

"good practice" means such practice in the processing of personal data as appears to the

Commissioner to be desirable having regard to the interests of data subjects and others, and includes (but is not limited to) compliance with the requirements of this Act;

"trade association" includes any body representing data controllers.

52 Reports and codes of practice to be laid before Parliament.

(1) The Commissioner shall lay annually before each House of Parliament a general report on the exercise of his functions under this Act.

(2) The Commissioner may from time to time lay before each House of Parliament such other reports with respect to those functions as he thinks fit.

(3) The Commissioner shall lay before each House of Parliament any code of practice prepared under section 51(3) for complying with a direction of the [Secretary of State][91] , unless the code is included in any report laid under subsection (1) or (2).

[52AData-sharing code

(1) The Commissioner must prepare a code of practice which contains—

(a) practical guidance in relation to the sharing of personal data in accordance with the requirements of this Act, and

(b) such other guidance as the Commissioner considers appropriate to promote good practice in the sharing of personal data.

(2) For this purpose "good practice" means such practice in the sharing of personal data as appears to the Commissioner to be desirable having regard to the interests of data subjects and others, and includes (but is not limited to) compliance with the requirements of this Act.

(3) Before a code is prepared under this section, the Commissioner must consult such of the following as the Commissioner considers appropriate—

(a) trade associations (within the meaning of section 51);

(b) data subjects;

(c) persons who appear to the Commissioner to represent the interests of data subjects.

(4) In this section a reference to the sharing of personal data is to the disclosure of the data by transmission, dissemination or otherwise making it available.

52BData-sharing code: procedure

(1) When a code is prepared under section 52A, it must be submitted to the Secretary of State for approval.

(2) Approval may be withheld only if it appears to the Secretary of State that the terms of the code could result in the United Kingdom being in breach of any of its Community obligations or any other international obligation.

(3) The Secretary of State must—

(a) if approval is withheld, publish details of the reasons for withholding it;

(b) if approval is granted, lay the code before Parliament.

(4) If, within the 40-day period, either House of Parliament resolves not to approve the code, the code is not to be issued by the Commissioner.

(5) If no such resolution is made within that period, the Commissioner must issue the code.

(6) Where—

(a) the Secretary of State withholds approval, or

(b) such a resolution is passed,

the Commissioner must prepare another code of practice under section 52A.

(7) Subsection (4) does not prevent a new code being laid before Parliament.

(8) A code comes into force at the end of the period of 21 days beginning with the day on which it is issued.

(9) A code may include transitional provision or savings.

(10) In this section "the 40-day period" means the period of 40 days beginning with the day on which the code is laid before Parliament (or, if it is not laid before each House of Parliament on the same day, the later of the 2 days on which it is laid).

(11) In calculating the 40-day period, no account is to be taken of any period during which Parliament is dissolved or prorogued or during which both Houses are adjourned for more than 4 days.

52CAlteration or replacement of data-sharing code

(1) The Commissioner—

(a) must keep the data-sharing code under review, and

(b) may prepare an alteration to that code or a replacement code.

(2) Where, by virtue of a review under subsection (1)(a) or otherwise, the Commissioner becomes aware that the terms of the code could result in the United Kingdom being in breach of any of its Community obligations or any other international obligation, the Commissioner must exercise the power under subsection (1)(b) with a view to remedying the situation.

(3) Before an alteration or replacement code is prepared under subsection (1), the Commissioner must consult such of the following as the Commissioner considers appropriate—

(a) trade associations (within the meaning of section 51);

(b) data subjects;

(c) persons who appear to the Commissioner to represent the interests of data subjects.

(4) Section 52B (other than subsection (6)) applies to an alteration or replacement code prepared under this section as it applies to the code as first prepared under section 52A.

(5) In this section "the data-sharing code" means the code issued under section 52B(5) (as altered or replaced from time to time).

52DPublication of data-sharing code

(1) The Commissioner must publish the code (and any replacement code) issued under section 52B(5).

(2) Where an alteration is so issued, the Commissioner must publish either—

(a) the alteration, or

(b) the code or replacement code as altered by it.

52EEffect of data-sharing code

(1) A failure on the part of any person to act in accordance with any provision of the data-sharing code does not of itself render that person liable to any legal proceedings in any court or tribunal.

(2) The data-sharing code is admissible in evidence in any legal proceedings.

(3) If any provision of the data-sharing code appears to—

(a) the Tribunal or a court conducting any proceedings under this Act,

(b) a court or tribunal conducting any other legal proceedings, or

(c) the Commissioner carrying out any function under this Act,

to be relevant to any question arising in the proceedings, or in connection with the exercise of that jurisdiction or the carrying out of those functions, in relation to any time when it was in force, that provision of the code must be taken into account in determining that question.

(4) In this section "the data-sharing code" means the code issued under section 52B(5) (as altered or replaced from time to time).][92]

53 Assistance by Commissioner in cases involving processing for the special purposes.

(1) An individual who is an actual or prospective party to any proceedings under section 7(9), 10(4), 12(8) or 14 or by virtue of section 13 which relate to personal data processed for the special purposes may apply to the Commissioner for assistance in relation to those proceedings.

(2) The Commissioner shall, as soon as reasonably practicable after receiving an application under subsection (1), consider it and decide whether and to what extent to grant it, but he shall not grant the application unless, in his opinion, the case involves a matter of substantial public importance.

(3) If the Commissioner decides to provide assistance, he shall, as soon as reasonably practicable after making the decision, notify the applicant, stating the extent of the assistance to be provided.

(4) If the Commissioner decides not to provide assistance, he shall, as soon as reasonably practicable after making the decision, notify the applicant of his decision and, if he thinks fit, the reasons for it.

(5) In this section—

(a) references to "proceedings" include references to prospective proceedings, and

(b) "applicant", in relation to assistance under this section, means an individual who applies for assistance.

(6) Schedule 10 has effect for supplementing this section.

54 International co-operation.

(1) The Commissioner—

(a) shall continue to be the designated authority in the United Kingdom for the purposes of Article 13 of the Convention, and

(b) shall be the supervisory authority in the United Kingdom for the purposes of the Data Protection Directive.

(2) The [Secretary of State][93] may by order make provision as to the functions to be discharged by the Commissioner as the designated authority in the United Kingdom for the purposes of Article 13 of the Convention.

(3) The [Secretary of State][94] may by order make provision as to co-operation by the Commissioner with the European Commission and with supervisory authorities in other EEA States in connection with the performance of their respective duties and, in particular, as to—

(a) the exchange of information with supervisory authorities in other EEA States or with the European Commission, and

(b) the exercise within the United Kingdom at the request of a supervisory authority in another EEA State, in cases excluded by section 5 from the application of the other provisions of this Act, of functions of the Commissioner specified in the order.

(4) The Commissioner shall also carry out any data protection functions which the [Secretary of State][95] may by order direct him to carry out for the purpose of enabling Her Majesty's Government in the United Kingdom to give effect to any international obligations of the United Kingdom.

(5) The Commissioner shall, if so directed by the [Secretary of State][96] , provide any authority exercising data protection functions under the law of a colony specified in the direction with such assistance in connection with the discharge of those functions as the [Secretary of State][97] may direct or approve, on such terms (including terms as to payment) as the [Secretary of State][98] may direct or approve.

(6) Where the European Commission makes a decision for the purposes of Article 26(3) or (4) of the Data Protection Directive under the procedure provided for in Article 31(2) of the Directive, the Commissioner shall comply with that decision in exercising his functions under paragraph 9 of Schedule 4 or, as the case may be, paragraph 8 of that Schedule.

(7) The Commissioner shall inform the European Commission and the supervisory authorities in other EEA States—

(a) of any approvals granted for the purposes of paragraph 8 of Schedule 4, and

(b) of any authorisations granted for the purposes of paragraph 9 of that Schedule.

(8) In this section—

"the Convention" means the Convention for the Protection of Individuals with regard to Automatic Processing of Personal Data which was opened for signature on 28th January 1981;

"data protection functions" means functions relating to the protection of individuals with respect to the processing of personal information.

[54AInspection of overseas information systems

(1) The Commissioner may inspect any personal data recorded in—

(a) the Schengen information system,

(b) the Europol information system,

(c) the Customs information system.

(2) The power conferred by subsection (1) is exercisable only for the purpose of assessing whether or not any processing of the data has been or is being carried out in compliance with this Act.

(3) The power includes power to inspect, operate and test equipment which is used for the processing of personal data.

(4) Before exercising the power, the Commissioner must give notice in writing of his intention to do so to the data controller.

(5) But subsection (4) does not apply if the Commissioner considers that the case is one of urgency.

(6) Any person who—

(a) intentionally obstructs a person exercising the power conferred by subsection (1), or

(b) fails without reasonable excuse to give any person exercising the power any assistance he may reasonably require,

is guilty of an offence.

(7) In this section—

"the Customs information system" means the information system established under Chapter II of

the Convention on the Use of Information Technology for Customs Purposes,

"the Europol information system" means the information system established under Title II of the Convention on the Establishment of a European Police Office,

"the Schengen information system" means the information system established under Title IV of the Convention implementing the Schengen Agreement of 14th June 1985, or any system established in its place in pursuance of any Community obligation.][99]

Unlawful obtaining etc. of personal data

55 Unlawful obtaining etc. of personal data.

(1) A person must not knowingly or recklessly, without the consent of the data controller—

(a) obtain or disclose personal data or the information contained in personal data, or

(b) procure the disclosure to another person of the information contained in personal data.

(2) Subsection (1) does not apply to a person who shows—

(a) that the obtaining, disclosing or procuring—

(i) was necessary for the purpose of preventing or detecting crime, or

(ii) was required or authorised by or under any enactment, by any rule of law or by the order of a court,

(b) that he acted in the reasonable belief that he had in law the right to obtain or disclose the data or information or, as the case may be, to procure the disclosure of the information to the other person,

(c) that he acted in the reasonable belief that he would have had the consent of the data controller if the data controller had known of the obtaining, disclosing or procuring and the circumstances of it, or

(d) that in the particular circumstances the obtaining, disclosing or procuring was justified as being in the public interest.

(3) A person who contravenes subsection (1) is guilty of an offence.

(4) A person who sells personal data is guilty of an offence if he has obtained the data in contravention of subsection (1).

(5) A person who offers to sell personal data is guilty of an offence if—

(a) he has obtained the data in contravention of subsection (1), or

(b) he subsequently obtains the data in contravention of that subsection.

(6) For the purposes of subsection (5), an advertisement indicating that personal data are or may be for sale is an offer to sell the data.

(7) Section 1(2) does not apply for the purposes of this section; and for the purposes of subsections (4) to (6), "personal data" includes information extracted from personal data.

(8) References in this section to personal data do not include references to personal data which by virtue of section 28 [or 33A][100] are exempt from this section.

[Monetary penalties][101]

[55APower of Commissioner to impose monetary penalty

(1) The Commissioner may serve a data controller with a monetary penalty notice if the Commissioner is satisfied that—

(a) there has been a serious contravention of section 4(4) by the data controller,

(b) the contravention was of a kind likely to cause substantial damage or substantial distress, and

(c) subsection (2) or (3) applies.

(2) This subsection applies if the contravention was deliberate.

(3) This subsection applies if the data controller—

(a) knew or ought to have known —

(i) that there was a risk that the contravention would occur, and

(ii) that such a contravention would be of a kind likely to cause substantial damage or substantial distress, but

(b) failed to take reasonable steps to prevent the contravention.

[(3A) The Commissioner may not be satisfied as mentioned in subsection (1) by virtue of any matter which comes to the Commissioner's attention as a result of anything done in pursuance of—

(a) An assessment notice;

(b) An assessment under section 51(7).][102]

(4) A monetary penalty notice is a notice requiring the data controller to pay to the Commissioner a monetary penalty of an amount determined by the Commissioner and specified in the notice.

(5) The amount determined by the Commissioner must not exceed the prescribed amount.

(6) The monetary penalty must be paid to the Commissioner within the period specified in the notice.

(7) The notice must contain such information as may be prescribed.

(8) Any sum received by the Commissioner by virtue of this section must be paid into the Consolidated Fund.

(9) In this section—

"data controller" does not include the Crown Estate Commissioners or a person who is a data controller by virtue of section 63(3);

"prescribed" means prescribed by regulations made by the Secretary of State.][103]

[55BMonetary penalty notices: procedural rights

(1) Before serving a monetary penalty notice, the Commissioner must serve the data controller with a notice of intent.

(2) A notice of intent is a notice that the Commissioner proposes to serve a monetary penalty notice.

(3) A notice of intent must—

(a) inform the data controller that he may make written representations in relation to the Commissioner's proposal within a period specified in the notice, and

(b) contain such other information as may be prescribed.

(4) The Commissioner may not serve a monetary penalty notice until the time within which the data controller may make representations has expired.

(5) A person on whom a monetary penalty notice is served may appeal to the Tribunal against—

(a) the issue of the monetary penalty notice;

(b) the amount of the penalty specified in the notice.

(6) In this section, "prescribed" means prescribed by regulations made by the Secretary of State.][104]

[55CGuidance about monetary penalty notices

(1) The Commissioner must prepare and issue guidance on how he proposes to exercise his functions under sections 55A and 55B.

(2) The guidance must, in particular, deal with—

(a) the circumstances in which he would consider it appropriate to issue a monetary penalty notice, and

(b) how he will determine the amount of the penalty.

(3) The Commissioner may alter or replace the guidance.

(4) If the guidance is altered or replaced, the Commissioner must issue the altered or replacement guidance.

(5) The Commissioner may not issue guidance under this section without the approval of the Secretary of State.

(6) The Commissioner must lay any guidance issued under this section before each House of Parliament.

(7) The Commissioner must arrange for the publication of any guidance issued under this section in such form and manner as he considers appropriate.

(8) In subsections (5) to (7), "guidance" includes altered or replacement guidance.][105]

[55DMonetary penalty notices: enforcement

(1) This section applies in relation to any penalty payable to the Commissioner by virtue of section 55A.

(2) In England and Wales, the penalty is recoverable—

(a) if a county court so orders, as if it were payable under an order of that court;

(b) if the High Court so orders, as if it were payable under an order of that court.

(3) In Scotland, the penalty may be enforced in the same manner as an extract registered decree arbitral bearing a warrant for execution issued by the sheriff court of any sheriffdom in Scotland.

(4) In Northern Ireland, the penalty is recoverable—

(a) if a county court so orders, as if it were payable under an order of that court;

(b) if the High Court so orders, as if it were payable under an order of that court.][106]

[55ENotices under sections 55A and 55B: supplemental

(1) The Secretary of State may by order make further provision in connection with monetary penalty notices and notices of intent.

(2) An order under this section may in particular—

(a) provide that a monetary penalty notice may not be served on a data controller with respect to the processing of personal data for the special purposes except in circumstances specified in the order;

(b) make provision for the cancellation or variation of monetary penalty notices;

(c) confer rights of appeal to the Tribunal against decisions of the Commissioner in relation to the cancellation or variation of such notices;

(d). . . . .[107]

(e) make provision for the determination of [appeals made by virtue of paragraph (c)][108];

(f). . . . .[109]

(3) An order under this section may apply any provision of this Act with such modifications as may be specified in the order.

(4) An order under this section may amend this Act.][110]

Records obtained under data subject's right of access

56 Prohibition of requirement as to production of certain records.

(1) A person must not, in connection with—

(a) the recruitment of another person as an employee,

(b) the continued employment of another person, or

(c) any contract for the provision of services to him by another person,

require that other person or a third party to supply him with a relevant record or to produce a relevant record to him.

(2) A person concerned with the provision (for payment or not) of goods, facilities or services to the public or a section of the public must not, as a condition of providing or offering to provide any goods, facilities or services to another person, require that other person or a third party to supply him with a relevant record or to produce a relevant record to him.

(3) Subsections (1) and (2) do not apply to a person who shows—

(a) that the imposition of the requirement was required or authorised by or under any enactment, by any rule of law or by the order of a court, or

(b) that in the particular circumstances the imposition of the requirement was justified as being in the public interest.

(4) Having regard to the provisions of Part V of the Police Act 1997 (certificates of criminal records etc.), the imposition of the requirement referred to in subsection (1) or (2) is not to be regarded as being justified as being in the public interest on the ground that it would assist in the prevention or detection of crime.

(5) A person who contravenes subsection (1) or (2) is guilty of an offence.

(6) In this section "a relevant record" means any record which—

(a) has been or is to be obtained by a data subject from any data controller specified in the first column of the Table below in the exercise of the right conferred by section 7, and

(b) contains information relating to any matter specified in relation to that data controller in the second column,

and includes a copy of such a record or a part of such a record.

TABLE

Data controller	Subject-matter
1. Any of the following persons—	(a) Convictions.
(a) a chief officer of police of a police force in England and Wales.	(b) Cautions.
(b) a chief constable of a police force in Scotland.	
(c) the Chief Constable of the Royal Ulster Constabulary.	
[(d) the Director General of the	

Serious Organised Crime Agency.][111]	
2. The Secretary of State.	(a) Convictions. (b) Cautions. (c) His functions under [section 92 of the Powers of Criminal Courts (Sentencing) Act 2000][112], section 205(2) or 208 of the Criminal Procedure (Scotland) Act 1995 or section 73 of the Children and Young Persons Act (Northern Ireland) 1968 in relation to any person sentenced to detention. (d) His functions under the Prison Act 1952, the Prisons (Scotland) Act 1989 or the Prison Act (Northern Ireland) 1953 in relation to any person imprisoned or detained. (e) His functions under the Social Security Contributions and Benefits Act 1992, the Social Security Administration Act 1992 or the Jobseekers Act 1995. (f) His functions under Part V of the Police Act 1997. [(g) His functions under the Safeguarding Vulnerable Groups Act 2006][113][or the Safeguarding Vulnerable Groups (Northern Ireland) Order 2007][114].
3. The Department of Health and Social Services for Northern Ireland.	Its functions under the Social Security Contributions and Benefits (Northern Ireland) Act 1992, the Social Security Administration (Northern Ireland) Act 1992 or the Jobseekers (Northern Ireland) Order 1995.
[The [Independent Safeguarding Authority][115]	Its functions under the Safeguarding Vulnerable Groups Act 2006][116][or the Safeguarding Vulnerable Groups (Northern Ireland) Order 2007][117] .

[(6A) A record is not a relevant record to the extent that it relates, or is to relate, only to personal data falling within paragraph (e) of the definition of "data" in section 1(1).][118]

(7) In the Table in subsection (6)—

"caution" means a caution given to any person in England and Wales or Northern Ireland in respect of an offence which, at the time when the caution is given, is admitted;

"conviction" has the same meaning as in the Rehabilitation of Offenders Act 1974 or the Rehabilitation of Offenders (Northern Ireland) Order 1978.

(8) The [Secretary of State][119] may by order amend—

(a) the Table in subsection (6), and

(b) subsection (7).

(9) For the purposes of this section a record which states that a data controller is not processing any personal data relating to a particular matter shall be taken to be a record containing information relating to that matter.

(10) In this section "employee" means an individual who—

(a) works under a contract of employment, as defined by section 230(2) of the Employment Rights Act 1996, or

(b) holds any office,

whether or not he is entitled to remuneration; and "employment" shall be construed accordingly.

57 Avoidance of certain contractual terms relating to health records.

(1) Any term or condition of a contract is void in so far as it purports to require an individual—

(a) to supply any other person with a record to which this section applies, or with a copy of such a record or a part of such a record, or

(b) to produce to any other person such a record, copy or part.

(2) This section applies to any record which—

(a) has been or is to be obtained by a data subject in the exercise of the right conferred by section 7, and

(b) consists of the information contained in any health record as defined by section 68(2).

Information provided to Commissioner or Tribunal

58 Disclosure of information.

No enactment or rule of law prohibiting or restricting the disclosure of information shall preclude a person from furnishing the Commissioner or the Tribunal with any information necessary for the discharge of their functions under this Act [or the Freedom of Information Act 2000][120].

59 Confidentiality of information.

(1) No person who is or has been the Commissioner, a member of the Commissioner's staff or an agent of the Commissioner shall disclose any information which—

(a) has been obtained by, or furnished to, the Commissioner under or for the purposes of [the information Acts][121],

(b) relates to an identified or identifiable individual or business, and

(c) is not at the time of the disclosure, and has not previously been, available to the public from other sources,

unless the disclosure is made with lawful authority.

(2) For the purposes of subsection (1) a disclosure of information is made with lawful authority only if, and to the extent that—

(a) the disclosure is made with the consent of the individual or of the person for the time being carrying on the business,

(b) the information was provided for the purpose of its being made available to the public (in whatever manner) under any provision of [the information Acts][122],

(c) the disclosure is made for the purposes of, and is necessary for, the discharge of—

(i) any functions under [the information Acts][123], or

(ii) any Community obligation,

(d) the disclosure is made for the purposes of any proceedings, whether criminal or civil and whether arising under, or by virtue of, [the information Acts][124] or otherwise, or

(e) having regard to the rights and freedoms or legitimate interests of any person, the disclosure is necessary in the public interest.

(3) Any person who knowingly or recklessly discloses information in contravention of subsection (1) is guilty of an offence.

[(4) In this section "the information Acts" means this Act and the Freedom of Information Act 2000.][125]

General provisions relating to offences

60 Prosecutions and penalties.

(1) No proceedings for an offence under this Act shall be instituted—

(a) in England or Wales, except by the Commissioner or by or with the consent of the Director of Public Prosecutions;

(b) in Northern Ireland, except by the Commissioner or by or with the consent of the Director of Public Prosecutions for Northern Ireland.

(2) A person guilty of an offence under any provision of this Act other than [section 54A and][126] paragraph 12 of Schedule 9 is liable—

(a) on summary conviction, to a fine not exceeding the statutory maximum, or

(b) on conviction on indictment, to a fine.

(3) A person guilty of an offence under [section 54A and][127] paragraph 12 of Schedule 9 is liable on summary conviction to a fine not exceeding level 5 on the standard scale.

(4) Subject to subsection (5), the court by or before which a person is convicted of—

(a) an offence under section 21(1), 22(6), 55 or 56,

(b) an offence under section 21(2) relating to processing which is assessable processing for the purposes of section 22, or

(c) an offence under section 47(1) relating to an enforcement notice,

may order any document or other material used in connection with the processing of personal data and appearing to the court to be connected with the commission of the offence to be forfeited, destroyed or erased.

(5) The court shall not make an order under subsection (4) in relation to any material where a person (other than the offender) claiming to be the owner of or otherwise interested in the material applies

to be heard by the court, unless an opportunity is given to him to show cause why the order should not be made.

61 Liability of directors etc.

(1) Where an offence under this Act has been committed by a body corporate and is proved to have been committed with the consent or connivance of or to be attributable to any neglect on the part of any director, manager, secretary or similar officer of the body corporate or any person who was purporting to act in any such capacity, he as well as the body corporate shall be guilty of that offence and be liable to be proceeded against and punished accordingly.

(2) Where the affairs of a body corporate are managed by its members subsection (1) shall apply in relation to the acts and defaults of a member in connection with his functions of management as if he were a director of the body corporate.

(3) Where an offence under this Act has been committed by a Scottish partnership and the contravention in question is proved to have occurred with the consent or connivance of, or to be attributable to any neglect on the part of, a partner, he as well as the partnership shall be guilty of that offence and shall be liable to be proceeded against and punished accordingly.

Amendments of Consumer Credit Act 1974

62 Amendments of Consumer Credit Act 1974.

(1) In section 158 of the Consumer Credit Act 1974 (duty of agency to disclose filed information)—

(a) in subsection (1)—

(i) in paragraph (a) for "individual" there is substituted " partnership or other unincorporated body of persons not consisting entirely of bodies corporate ", and

(ii) for "him" there is substituted " it ",

(b) in subsection (2), for "his" there is substituted " the consumer's ", and

(c) in subsection (3), for "him" there is substituted " the consumer ".

(2) In section 159 of that Act (correction of wrong information) for subsection (1) there is substituted—

"(1) any individual (the "objector") given—

(a) information under section 7 of the Data Protection Act 1998 by a credit reference agency, or

(b) information under section 158,

who considers that an entry in his file is incorrect, and that if it is not corrected he is likely to be prejudiced, may give notice to the agency requiring it either to remove the entry from the file or amend it."

(3) In subsections (2) to (6) of that section—

(a) for "consumer", wherever occurring, there is substituted " objector ", and

(b) for "Director", wherever occurring, there is substituted " the relevant authority ".

(4) After subsection (6) of that section there is inserted—

"(7) The Data Protection Commissioner may vary or revoke any order made by him under this section.

(8) In this section "the relevant authority" means—

(a) where the objector is a partnership or other unincorporated body of persons, the Director, and

(b) in any other case, the Data Protection Commissioner."

(5) In section 160 of that Act (alternative procedure for business consumers)—

(a) in subsection (4)—

(i) for "him" there is substituted " to the consumer ", and

(ii) in paragraphs (a) and (b) for "he" there is substituted " the consumer " and for "his" there is substituted " the consumer's ", and

(b) after subsection (6) there is inserted—

"(7) In this section "consumer" has the same meaning as in section 158."

General

63 Application to Crown.

(1) This Act binds the Crown.

(2) For the purposes of this Act each government department shall be treated as a person separate from any other government department.

(3) Where the purposes for which and the manner in which any personal data are, or are to be,

processed are determined by any person acting on behalf of the Royal Household, the Duchy of Lancaster or the Duchy of Cornwall, the data controller in respect of those data for the purposes of this Act shall be—

(a) in relation to the Royal Household, the Keeper of the Privy Purse,

(b) in relation to the Duchy of Lancaster, such person as the Chancellor of the Duchy appoints, and

(c) in relation to the Duchy of Cornwall, such person as the Duke of Cornwall, or the possessor for the time being of the Duchy of Cornwall, appoints.

(4) Different persons may be appointed under subsection (3)(b) or (c) for different purposes.

(5) Neither a government department nor a person who is a data controller by virtue of subsection (3) shall be liable to prosecution under this Act, but [sections 54A and][128] 55 and paragraph 12 of Schedule 9 shall apply to a person in the service of the Crown as they apply to any other person.

[63A Application to Parliament.

(1) Subject to the following provisions of this section and to section 35A, this Act applies to the processing of personal data by or on behalf of either House of Parliament as it applies to the processing of personal data by other persons.

(2) Where the purposes for which and the manner in which any personal data are, or are to be, processed are determined by or on behalf of the House of Commons, the data controller in respect of those data for the purposes of this Act shall be the Corporate Officer of that House.

(3) Where the purposes for which and the manner in which any personal data are, or are to be, processed are determined by or on behalf of the House of Lords, the data controller in respect of those data for the purposes of this Act shall be the Corporate Officer of that House.

(4) Nothing in subsection (2) or (3) is to be taken to render the Corporate Officer of the House of Commons or the Corporate Officer of the House of Lords liable to prosecution under this Act, but section 55 and paragraph 12 of Schedule 9 shall apply to a person acting on behalf of either House as they apply to any other person.][129]

64 Transmission of notices etc. by electronic or other means.

(1) This section applies to—

(a) a notice or request under any provision of Part II,

(b) a notice under subsection (1) of section 24 or particulars made available under that subsection, or

(c) an application under section 41(2),

but does not apply to anything which is required to be served in accordance with rules of court.

(2) The requirement that any notice, request, particulars or application to which this section applies should be in writing is satisfied where the text of the notice, request, particulars or application—

(a) is transmitted by electronic means,

(b) is received in legible form, and

(c) is capable of being used for subsequent reference.

(3) The [Secretary of State][130] may by regulations provide that any requirement that any notice, request, particulars or application to which this section applies should be in writing is not to apply in such circumstances as may be prescribed by the regulations.

65 Service of notices by Commissioner.

(1) Any notice authorised or required by this Act to be served on or given to any person by the Commissioner may—

(a) if that person is an individual, be served on him—

(i) by delivering it to him, or

(ii) by sending it to him by post addressed to him at his usual or last-known place of residence or business, or

(iii) by leaving it for him at that place;

(b) if that person is a body corporate or unincorporate, be served on that body—

(i) by sending it by post to the proper officer of the body at its principal office, or

(ii) by addressing it to the proper officer of the body and leaving it at that office;

(c) if that person is a partnership in Scotland, be served on that partnership—

(i) by sending it by post to the principal office of the partnership, or

(ii) by addressing it to that partnership and leaving it at that office.

(2) In subsection (1)(b) "principal office", in relation to a registered company, means its registered office

and "proper officer", in relation to any body, means the secretary or other executive officer charged with the conduct of its general affairs.

(3) This section is without prejudice to any other lawful method of serving or giving a notice.

66 Exercise of rights in Scotland by children.

(1) Where a question falls to be determined in Scotland as to the legal capacity of a person under the age of sixteen years to exercise any right conferred by any provision of this Act, that person shall be taken to have that capacity where he has a general understanding of what it means to exercise that right.

(2) Without prejudice to the generality of subsection (1), a person of twelve years of age or more shall be presumed to be of sufficient age and maturity to have such understanding as is mentioned in that subsection.

67 Orders, regulations and rules.

(1) Any power conferred by this Act on the [Secretary of State][131] to make an order, regulations or rules shall be exercisable by statutory instrument.

(2) Any order, regulations or rules made by the [Secretary of State][132] under this Act may—

(a) make different provision for different cases, and

(b) make such supplemental, incidental, consequential or transitional provision or savings as the [Secretary of State][133] considers appropriate;

and nothing in section 7(11), 19(5), 26(1) or 30(4) limits the generality of paragraph (a).

(3) Before making—

(a) an order under any provision of this Act other than section 75(3),

(b) any regulations under this Act other than notification regulations (as defined by section 16(2)),

the [Secretary of State][134] shall consult the Commissioner.

(4) A statutory instrument containing (whether alone or with other provisions) an order under—

section 10(2)(b),

section 12(5)(b),

section 22(1),

section 30,

section 32(3),

section 38,

[section 41A(2)(c),][135]

[section 55E(1),][136]

section 56(8),

paragraph 10 of Schedule 3, or

paragraph 4 of Schedule 7,

shall not be made unless a draft of the instrument has been laid before and approved by a resolution of each House of Parliament.

(5) A statutory instrument which contains (whether alone or with other provisions)—

(a) an order under—

section 22(7),

section 23,

[section 41A(2)(b),][137]

section 51(3),

section 54(2), (3) or (4),

paragraph 3, 4 or 14 of Part II of Schedule 1,

paragraph 6 of Schedule 2,

paragraph 2, 7 or 9 of Schedule 3,

paragraph 4 of Schedule 4,

paragraph 6 of Schedule 7,

(b) regulations under section 7 which—

(i) prescribe cases for the purposes of subsection (2)(b),

(ii) are made by virtue of subsection (7), or

(iii) relate to the definition of "the prescribed period",

(c) regulations under section 8(1) [, 9(3) or 9A(5)][138],

[(ca) regulations under section 55A(5) or (7) or 55B(3)(b),][139]

(d) regulations under section 64,

(e) notification regulations (as defined by section 16(2)), or

(f) rules under paragraph 7 of Schedule 6,

and which is not subject to the requirement in subsection (4) that a draft of the instrument be laid before and approved by a resolution of each House of Parliament, shall be subject to annulment in pursuance of a resolution of either House of Parliament.

(6) A statutory instrument which contains only—

(a) regulations prescribing fees for the purposes of any provision of this Act, or

(b) regulations under section 7 prescribing fees for the purposes of any other enactment,

shall be laid before Parliament after being made.

68 Meaning of "accessible record".

(1) In this Act "accessible record" means—

(a) a health record as defined by subsection (2),

(b) an educational record as defined by Schedule 11, or

(c) an accessible public record as defined by Schedule 12.

(2) In subsection (1)(a) "health record" means any record which—

(a) consists of information relating to the physical or mental health or condition of an individual, and

(b) has been made by or on behalf of a health professional in connection with the care of that individual.

69 Meaning of "health professional".

(1) In this Act "health professional" means any of the following—

(a) a registered medical practitioner,

(b) a registered dentist as defined by section 53(1) of the Dentists Act 1984,

[(c) a registered dispensing optician or a registered optometrist within the meaning of the Opticians Act 1989,][140]

(d)[a registered pharmacist or a registered pharmacy technician within the meaning of article 3(1) of the Pharmacy Order 2010][141] or a registered person as defined by Article 2(2) of the Pharmacy (Northern Ireland) Order 1976,

[(e) a registered nurse or midwife][142]

(f) a registered osteopath as defined by section 41 of the Osteopaths Act 1993,

(g) a registered chiropractor as defined by section 43 of the Chiropractors Act 1994,

(h) any person who is registered as a member of a profession to which [the Health Professions Order 2001][143] for the time being extends,

(i) a...[144][child psychotherapist][145] ,

(j)................................[146]

(k) a scientist employed by such a body as head of a department.

(2) In subsection (1)(a) "registered medical practitioner" includes any person who is provisionally registered under section 15 or 21 of the Medical Act 1983 and is engaged in such employment as is mentioned in subsection (3) of that section.

(3) In subsection (1) "health service body" means—

(a) a [Strategic Health Authority][147][established under section 13 of the National Health Service Act 2006][148] ,

(b) a Special Health Authority established under [section 28 of that Act, or section 22 of the National Health Service (Wales) Act 2006][149] ,

[(bb) a Primary Care Trust established under [section 18 of the National Health Service Act 2006][150],][151]

[(bbb) a Local Health Board established under [section 11 of the National Health Service (Wales) Act 2006][152] ,][153]

(c) a Health Board within the meaning of the National Health Service (Scotland) Act 1978,

(d) a Special Health Board within the meaning of that Act,

(e) the managers of a State Hospital provided under section 102 of that Act,

(f) a National Health Service trust first established under section 5 of the National Health Service

and Community Care Act 1990 [, section 25 of the National Health Service Act 2006, section 18 of the National Health Service (Wales) Act 2006][154] or section 12A of the National Health Service (Scotland) Act 1978,

[(fa) an NHS foundation trust;][155]

(g) a Health and Social Services Board established under Article 16 of the Health and Personal Social Services (Northern Ireland) Order 1972,

(h) a special health and social services agency established under the Health and Personal Social Services (Special Agencies) (Northern Ireland) Order 1990, or

(i) a Health and Social Services trust established under Article 10 of the Health and Personal Social Services (Northern Ireland) Order 1991.

70 Supplementary definitions.

(1) In this Act, unless the context otherwise requires—

"business" includes any trade or profession;

"the Commissioner" means [the Information Commissioner][156];

"credit reference agency" has the same meaning as in the Consumer Credit Act 1974;

"the Data Protection Directive" means Directive 95/46/EC on the protection of individuals with regard to the processing of personal data and on the free movement of such data;

"EEA State" means a State which is a contracting party to the Agreement on the European Economic Area signed at Oporto on 2nd May 1992 as adjusted by the Protocol signed at Brussels on 17th March 1993;

"enactment" includes an enactment passed after this Act [and any enactment comprised in, or in any instrument made under, an Act of the Scottish Parliament][157];

["government department"includes—

(a) any part of the Scottish Administration;

(b) a Northern Ireland department;

(c) the Welsh Assembly Government;

(d) any body or authority exercising statutory functions on behalf of the Crown.][158]

"Minister of the Crown" has the same meaning as in the Ministers of the Crown Act 1975;

"public register" means any register which pursuant to a requirement imposed—

(a) by or under any enactment, or

(b) in pursuance of any international agreement,

is open to public inspection or open to inspection by any person having a legitimate interest;

"pupil"—

(a) in relation to a school in England and Wales, means a registered pupil within the meaning of the Education Act 1996,

(b) in relation to a school in Scotland, means a pupil within the meaning of the Education (Scotland) Act 1980, and

(c) in relation to a school in Northern Ireland, means a registered pupil within the meaning of the Education and Libraries (Northern Ireland) Order 1986;

"recipient", in relation to any personal data, means any person to whom the data are disclosed, including any person (such as an employee or agent of the data controller, a data processor or an employee or agent of a data processor) to whom they are disclosed in the course of processing the data for the data controller, but does not include any person to whom disclosure is or may be made as a result of, or with a view to, a particular inquiry by or on behalf of that person made in the exercise of any power conferred by law;

"registered company" means a company registered under the enactments relating to companies for the time being in force in the United Kingdom;

"school"—

(a) in relation to England and Wales, has the same meaning as in the Education Act 1996,

(b) in relation to Scotland, has the same meaning as in the Education (Scotland) Act 1980, and

(c) in relation to Northern Ireland, has the same meaning as in the Education and Libraries (Northern Ireland) Order 1986;

"teacher" includes—

(a) in Great Britain, head teacher, and

(b) in Northern Ireland, the principal of a school;

"third party", in relation to personal data, means any person other than—

(a) the data subject,

(b) the data controller, or

(c) any data processor or other person authorised to process data for the data controller or processor;

["the Tribunal", in relation to any appeal under this Act, means—

(a) the Upper Tribunal, in any case where it is determined by or under Tribunal Procedure Rules that the Upper Tribunal is to hear the appeal; or

(b) the First-tier Tribunal, in any other case;][159]

(2) For the purposes of this Act data are inaccurate if they are incorrect or misleading as to any matter of fact.

71 Index of defined expressions.

The following Table shows provisions defining or otherwise explaining expressions used in this Act (other than provisions defining or explaining an expression only used in the same section or Schedule)—

accessible record	section 68
address (in Part III)	section 16(3)
business	section 70(1)
the Commissioner	section 70(1)
credit reference agency	section 70(1)
data	section 1(1)
data controller	sections 1(1) and (4) and 63(3)
data processor	section 1(1)
the Data Protection Directive	section 70(1)
data protection principles	section 4 and Schedule 1
data subject	section 1(1)
disclosing (of personal data)	section 1(2)(b)
EEA State	section 70(1)
enactment	section 70(1)
enforcement notice	section 40(1)
fees regulations (in Part III)	section 16(2)
government department	section 70(1)
health professional	section 69
inaccurate (in relation to data)	section 70(2)
information notice	section 43(1)
Minister of the Crown	section 70(1)
the non-disclosure provisions (in Part IV)	section 27(3)
notification regulations (in Part III)	section 16(2)
obtaining (of personal data)	section 1(2)(a)
personal data	section 1(1)
prescribed (in Part III)	section 16(2)
processing (of information or data)	section 1(1) and paragraph 5 of Schedule 8
[public authority	section 1(1)][160]
public register	section 70(1)
publish (in relation to journalistic, literary or artistic material)	section 32(6)
pupil (in relation to a school)	section 70(1)
recipient (in relation to personal data)	section 70(1)
recording (of personal data)	section 1(2)(a)
registered company	section 70(1)
registrable particulars (in Part III)	section 16(1)
relevant filing system	section 1(1)
school	section 70(1)

sensitive personal data	section 2
special information notice	section 44(1)
the special purposes	section 3
the subject information provisions (in Part IV)	section 27(2)
teacher	section 70(1)
third party (in relation to processing of personal data)	section 70(1)
the Tribunal	section 70(1)
using (of personal data)	section 1(2)(b).

72 Modifications of Act.

During the period beginning with the commencement of this section and ending with 23rd October 2007, the provisions of this Act shall have effect subject to the modifications set out in Schedule 13.

73 Transitional provisions and savings.

Schedule 14 (which contains transitional provisions and savings) has effect.

74 Minor and consequential amendments and repeals and revocations.

(1) Schedule 15 (which contains minor and consequential amendments) has effect.

(2) The enactments and instruments specified in Schedule 16 are repealed or revoked to the extent specified.

75 Short title, commencement and extent.

(1) This Act may be cited as the Data Protection Act 1998.

(2) The following provisions of this Act—

(a) sections 1 to 3,

(b) section 25(1) and (4),

(c) section 26,

(d) sections 67 to 71,

(e) this section,

(f) paragraph 17 of Schedule 5,

(g) Schedule 11,

(h) Schedule 12, and

(i) so much of any other provision of this Act as confers any power to make subordinate legislation, shall come into force on the day on which this Act is passed.

(3) The remaining provisions of this Act shall come into force on such day as the [Secretary of State][161] may by order appoint; and different days may be appointed for different purposes.

(4) The day appointed under subsection (3) for the coming into force of section 56 must not be earlier than the first day on which sections 112, 113 and 115 of the Police Act 1997 (which provide for the issue by the Secretary of State of criminal conviction certificates, criminal record certificates and enhanced criminal record certificates) are all in force.

[(4A) Subsection (4) does not apply to section 56 so far as that section relates to a record containing information relating to—

(a) the Secretary of State's functions under the Safeguarding Vulnerable Groups Act 2006 [or the Safeguarding Vulnerable Groups (Northern Ireland) Order 2007][162] , or

(b) the ["Independent Safeguarding Authority's"][163] functions under that Act [or that Order][164] .][165]

(5) Subject to subsection (6), this Act extends to Northern Ireland.

(6) Any amendment, repeal or revocation made by Schedule 15 or 16 has the same extent as that of the enactment or instrument to which it relates.

SCHEDULES

Section 4(1) and (2).

SCHEDULE 1 The data protection principles

Part I The principles

1 Personal data shall be processed fairly and lawfully and, in particular, shall not be processed unless—

(a) at least one of the conditions in Schedule 2 is met, and

(b) in the case of sensitive personal data, at least one of the conditions in Schedule 3 is also met.

2 Personal data shall be obtained only for one or more specified and lawful purposes, and shall not be

further processed in any manner incompatible with that purpose or those purposes.

3 Personal data shall be adequate, relevant and not excessive in relation to the purpose or purposes for which they are processed.

4 Personal data shall be accurate and, where necessary, kept up to date.

5 Personal data processed for any purpose or purposes shall not be kept for longer than is necessary for that purpose or those purposes.

6 Personal data shall be processed in accordance with the rights of data subjects under this Act.

7 Appropriate technical and organisational measures shall be taken against unauthorised or unlawful processing of personal data and against accidental loss or destruction of, or damage to, personal data.

8 Personal data shall not be transferred to a country or territory outside the European Economic Area unless that country or territory ensures an adequate level of protection for the rights and freedoms of data subjects in relation to the processing of personal data.

Part II Interpretation of the principles in Part I

The first principle

1(1) In determining for the purposes of the first principle whether personal data are processed fairly, regard is to be had to the method by which they are obtained, including in particular whether any person from whom they are obtained is deceived or misled as to the purpose or purposes for which they are to be processed.

(2) Subject to paragraph 2, for the purposes of the first principle data are to be treated as obtained fairly if they consist of information obtained from a person who—

(a) is authorised by or under any enactment to supply it, or

(b) is required to supply it by or under any enactment or by any convention or other instrument imposing an international obligation on the United Kingdom.

2(1) Subject to paragraph 3, for the purposes of the first principle personal data are not to be treated as processed fairly unless—

(a) in the case of data obtained from the data subject, the data controller ensures so far as practicable that the data subject has, is provided with, or has made readily available to him, the information specified in sub-paragraph (3), and

(b) in any other case, the data controller ensures so far as practicable that, before the relevant time or as soon as practicable after that time, the data subject has, is provided with, or has made readily available to him, the information specified in sub-paragraph (3).

(2) In sub-paragraph (1)(b) "the relevant time" means—

(a) the time when the data controller first processes the data, or

(b) in a case where at that time disclosure to a third party within a reasonable period is envisaged—

(i) if the data are in fact disclosed to such a person within that period, the time when the data are first disclosed,

(ii) if within that period the data controller becomes, or ought to become, aware that the data are unlikely to be disclosed to such a person within that period, the time when the data controller does become, or ought to become, so aware, or

(iii) in any other case, the end of that period.

(3) The information referred to in sub-paragraph (1) is as follows, namely—

(a) the identity of the data controller,

(b) if he has nominated a representative for the purposes of this Act, the identity of that representative,

(c) the purpose or purposes for which the data are intended to be processed, and

(d) any further information which is necessary, having regard to the specific circumstances in which the data are or are to be processed, to enable processing in respect of the data subject to be fair.

3(1) Paragraph 2(1)(b) does not apply where either of the primary conditions in sub-paragraph (2), together with such further conditions as may be prescribed by the [Secretary of State][166] by order, are met.

(2) The primary conditions referred to in sub-paragraph (1) are—

(a) that the provision of that information would involve a disproportionate effort, or

(b) that the recording of the information to be contained in the data by, or the disclosure of the data

by, the data controller is necessary for compliance with any legal obligation to which the data controller is subject, other than an obligation imposed by contract.

4(1) Personal data which contain a general identifier falling within a description prescribed by the [Secretary of State][167] by order are not to be treated as processed fairly and lawfully unless they are processed in compliance with any conditions so prescribed in relation to general identifiers of that description.

(2) In sub-paragraph (1) "a general identifier" means any identifier (such as, for example, a number or code used for identification purposes) which—

(a) relates to an individual, and

(b) forms part of a set of similar identifiers which is of general application.

The second principle

5 The purpose or purposes for which personal data are obtained may in particular be specified—

(a) in a notice given for the purposes of paragraph 2 by the data controller to the data subject, or

(b) in a notification given to the Commissioner under Part III of this Act.

6 In determining whether any disclosure of personal data is compatible with the purpose or purposes for which the data were obtained, regard is to be had to the purpose or purposes for which the personal data are intended to be processed by any person to whom they are disclosed.

The fourth principle

7 The fourth principle is not to be regarded as being contravened by reason of any inaccuracy in personal data which accurately record information obtained by the data controller from the data subject or a third party in a case where—

(a) having regard to the purpose or purposes for which the data were obtained and further processed, the data controller has taken reasonable steps to ensure the accuracy of the data, and

(b) if the data subject has notified the data controller of the data subject's view that the data are inaccurate, the data indicate that fact.

The sixth principle

8 A person is to be regarded as contravening the sixth principle if, but only if—

(a) he contravenes section 7 by failing to supply information in accordance with that section,

(b) he contravenes section 10 by failing to comply with a notice given under subsection (1) of that section to the extent that the notice is justified or by failing to give a notice under subsection (3) of that section,

(c) he contravenes section 11 by failing to comply with a notice given under subsection (1) of that section, or

(d) he contravenes section 12 by failing to comply with a notice given under subsection (1) or (2)(b) of that section or by failing to give a notification under subsection (2)(a) of that section or a notice under subsection (3) of that section.

The seventh principle

9 Having regard to the state of technological development and the cost of implementing any measures, the measures must ensure a level of security appropriate to—

(a) the harm that might result from such unauthorised or unlawful processing or accidental loss, destruction or damage as are mentioned in the seventh principle, and

(b) the nature of the data to be protected.

10 The data controller must take reasonable steps to ensure the reliability of any employees of his who have access to the personal data.

11 Where processing of personal data is carried out by a data processor on behalf of a data controller, the data controller must in order to comply with the seventh principle—

(a) choose a data processor providing sufficient guarantees in respect of the technical and organisational security measures governing the processing to be carried out, and

(b) take reasonable steps to ensure compliance with those measures.

12 Where processing of personal data is carried out by a data processor on behalf of a data controller, the data controller is not to be regarded as complying with the seventh principle unless—

(a) the processing is carried out under a contract—

(i) which is made or evidenced in writing, and

(ii) under which the data processor is to act only on instructions from the data controller, and

(b) the contract requires the data processor to comply with obligations equivalent to those imposed on a data controller by the seventh principle.

The eighth principle

13 An adequate level of protection is one which is adequate in all the circumstances of the case, having regard in particular to—

(a) the nature of the personal data,

(b) the country or territory of origin of the information contained in the data,

(c) the country or territory of final destination of that information,

(d) the purposes for which and period during which the data are intended to be processed,

(e) the law in force in the country or territory in question,

(f) the international obligations of that country or territory,

(g) any relevant codes of conduct or other rules which are enforceable in that country or territory (whether generally or by arrangement in particular cases), and

(h) any security measures taken in respect of the data in that country or territory.

14 The eighth principle does not apply to a transfer falling within any paragraph of Schedule 4, except in such circumstances and to such extent as the [Secretary of State][168] may by order provide.

15 (1) Where—

(a) in any proceedings under this Act any question arises as to whether the requirement of the eighth principle as to an adequate level of protection is met in relation to the transfer of any personal data to a country or territory outside the European Economic Area, and

(b) a Community finding has been made in relation to transfers of the kind in question,

that question is to be determined in accordance with that finding.

(2) In sub-paragraph (1) "Community finding" means a finding of the European Commission, under the procedure provided for in Article 31(2) of the Data Protection Directive, that a country or territory outside the European Economic Area does, or does not, ensure an adequate level of protection within the meaning of Article 25(2) of the Directive.

Section 4(3).

SCHEDULE 2 Conditions relevant for purposes of the first principle: processing of any personal data

1 The data subject has given his consent to the processing.

2 The processing is necessary—

(a) for the performance of a contract to which the data subject is a party, or

(b) for the taking of steps at the request of the data subject with a view to entering into a contract.

3 The processing is necessary for compliance with any legal obligation to which the data controller is subject, other than an obligation imposed by contract.

4 The processing is necessary in order to protect the vital interests of the data subject.

5 The processing is necessary—

(a) for the administration of justice,

[(aa) for the exercise of any functions of either House of Parliament,][169]

(b) for the exercise of any functions conferred on any person by or under any enactment,

(c) for the exercise of any functions of the Crown, a Minister of the Crown or a government department, or

(d) for the exercise of any other functions of a public nature exercised in the public interest by any person.

6(1) The processing is necessary for the purposes of legitimate interests pursued by the data controller or by the third party or parties to whom the data are disclosed, except where the processing is unwarranted in any particular case by reason of prejudice to the rights and freedoms or legitimate interests of the data subject.

(2) The [Secretary of State][170] may by order specify particular circumstances in which this condition is, or is not, to be taken to be satisfied.

Section 4(3).

SCHEDULE 3 Conditions relevant for purposes of the first principle: processing of sensitive personal data

1 The data subject has given his explicit consent to the processing of the personal data.

2(1) The processing is necessary for the purposes of exercising or performing any right or obligation which is conferred or imposed by law on the data controller in connection with employment.

(2) The [Secretary of State][171] may by order—

(a) exclude the application of sub-paragraph (1) in such cases as may be specified, or

(b) provide that, in such cases as may be specified, the condition in sub-paragraph (1) is not to be regarded as satisfied unless such further conditions as may be specified in the order are also satisfied.

3 The processing is necessary—

(a) in order to protect the vital interests of the data subject or another person, in a case where—

(i) consent cannot be given by or on behalf of the data subject, or

(ii) the data controller cannot reasonably be expected to obtain the consent of the data subject, or

(b) in order to protect the vital interests of another person, in a case where consent by or on behalf of the data subject has been unreasonably withheld.

4The processing—

(a) is carried out in the course of its legitimate activities by any body or association which—

(i) is not established or conducted for profit, and

(ii) exists for political, philosophical, religious or trade-union purposes,

(b) is carried out with appropriate safeguards for the rights and freedoms of data subjects,

(c) relates only to individuals who either are members of the body or association or have regular contact with it in connection with its purposes, and

(d) does not involve disclosure of the personal data to a third party without the consent of the data subject.

5 The information contained in the personal data has been made public as a result of steps deliberately taken by the data subject.

6 The processing—

(a) is necessary for the purpose of, or in connection with, any legal proceedings (including prospective legal proceedings),

(b) is necessary for the purpose of obtaining legal advice, or

(c) is otherwise necessary for the purposes of establishing, exercising or defending legal rights.

7(1) The processing is necessary—

(a) for the administration of justice,

[(aa) for the exercise of any functions of either House of Parliament,][172]

(b) for the exercise of any functions conferred on any person by or under an enactment, or

(c) for the exercise of any functions of the Crown, a Minister of the Crown or a government department.

(2) The [Secretary of State][173] may by order—

(a) exclude the application of sub-paragraph (1) in such cases as may be specified, or

(b) provide that, in such cases as may be specified, the condition in sub-paragraph (1) is not to be regarded as satisfied unless such further conditions as may be specified in the order are also satisfied.

[7A(1) The processing—

(a) is either—

(i) the disclosure of sensitive personal data by a person as a member of an anti-fraud organisation or otherwise in accordance with any arrangements made by such an organisation; or

(ii) any other processing by that person or another person of sensitive personal data so disclosed; and

(b) is necessary for the purposes of preventing fraud or a particular kind of fraud.

(2) In this paragraph "an anti-fraud organisation" means any unincorporated association, body corporate or other person which enables or facilitates any sharing of information to prevent fraud or a particular kind of fraud or which has any of these functions as its purpose or one of its purposes.][174]

8(1) The processing is necessary for medical purposes and is undertaken by—

(a) a health professional, or

(b) a person who in the circumstances owes a duty of confidentiality which is equivalent to that which would arise if that person were a health professional.

(2) In this paragraph "medical purposes" includes the purposes of preventative medicine, medical diagnosis, medical research, the provision of care and treatment and the management of healthcare services.

9(1) The processing—

(a) is of sensitive personal data consisting of information as to racial or ethnic origin,

(b) is necessary for the purpose of identifying or keeping under review the existence or absence of equality of opportunity or treatment between persons of different racial or ethnic origins, with a view to enabling such equality to be promoted or maintained, and

(c) is carried out with appropriate safeguards for the rights and freedoms of data subjects.

(2) The [Secretary of State][175] may by order specify circumstances in which processing falling within sub-paragraph (1)(a) and (b) is, or is not, to be taken for the purposes of sub-paragraph (1)(c) to be carried out with appropriate safeguards for the rights and freedoms of data subjects.

10 The personal data are processed in circumstances specified in an order made by the [Secretary of State][176] for the purposes of this paragraph.

Section 4(3).

SCHEDULE 4 Cases where the eighth principle does not apply

1 The data subject has given his consent to the transfer.

2 The transfer is necessary—

(a) for the performance of a contract between the data subject and the data controller, or

(b) for the taking of steps at the request of the data subject with a view to his entering into a contract with the data controller.

3The transfer is necessary—

(a) for the conclusion of a contract between the data controller and a person other than the data subject which—

(i) is entered into at the request of the data subject, or

(ii) is in the interests of the data subject, or

(b) for the performance of such a contract.

4(1) The transfer is necessary for reasons of substantial public interest.

(2) The [Secretary of State][177] may by order specify—

(a) circumstances in which a transfer is to be taken for the purposes of sub-paragraph (1) to be necessary for reasons of substantial public interest, and

(b) circumstances in which a transfer which is not required by or under an enactment is not to be taken for the purpose of sub-paragraph (1) to be necessary for reasons of substantial public interest.

5 The transfer—

(a) is necessary for the purpose of, or in connection with, any legal proceedings (including prospective legal proceedings),

(b) is necessary for the purpose of obtaining legal advice, or

(c) is otherwise necessary for the purposes of establishing, exercising or defending legal rights.

6 The transfer is necessary in order to protect the vital interests of the data subject.

7 The transfer is of part of the personal data on a public register and any conditions subject to which the register is open to inspection are complied with by any person to whom the data are or may be disclosed after the transfer.

8 The transfer is made on terms which are of a kind approved by the Commissioner as ensuring adequate safeguards for the rights and freedoms of data subjects.

9 The transfer has been authorised by the Commissioner as being made in such a manner as to ensure adequate safeguards for the rights and freedoms of data subjects.

Section 6(7).

SCHEDULE 5 The Data Protection Commissioner...[178]

Part I The Commissioner

Status and capacity

1(1) The corporation sole by the name of the Data Protection Registrar established by the Data Protection Act 1984 shall continue in existence by the name of the [Information Commissioner][179].

(2) The Commissioner and his officers and staff are not to be regarded as servants or agents of the Crown.

Tenure of office

2(1) Subject to the provisions of this paragraph, the Commissioner shall hold office for such term not exceeding five years as may be determined at the time of his appointment.

(2) The Commissioner may be relieved of his office by Her Majesty at his own request.

(3) The Commissioner may be removed from office by Her Majesty in pursuance of an Address from both Houses of Parliament.

(4) The Commissioner shall in any case vacate his office—

(a) on completing the year of service in which he attains the age of sixty-five years, or

(b) if earlier, on completing his fifteenth year of service.

(5) Subject to sub-paragraph (4), a person who ceases to be Commissioner on the expiration of his term of office shall be eligible for re-appointment, but a person may not be re-appointed for a third or subsequent term as Commissioner unless, by reason of special circumstances, the person's re-appointment for such a term is desirable in the public interest.

Salary etc.

3(1) There shall be paid—

(a) to the Commissioner such salary, and

(b) to or in respect of the Commissioner such pension,

as may be specified by a resolution of the House of Commons.

(2) A resolution for the purposes of this paragraph may—

(a) specify the salary or pension,

(b) provide that the salary or pension is to be the same as, or calculated on the same basis as, that payable to, or to or in respect of, a person employed in a specified office under, or in a specified capacity in the service of, the Crown, or

(c) specify the salary or pension and provide for it to be increased by reference to such variables as may be specified in the resolution.

(3) A resolution for the purposes of this paragraph may take effect from the date on which it is passed or from any earlier or later date specified in the resolution.

(4) A resolution for the purposes of this paragraph may make different provision in relation to the pension payable to or in respect of different holders of the office of Commissioner.

(5) Any salary or pension payable under this paragraph shall be charged on and issued out of the Consolidated Fund.

(6) In this paragraph "pension" includes an allowance or gratuity and any reference to the payment of a pension includes a reference to the making of payments towards the provision of a pension.

Officers and staff

4(1) The Commissioner—

(a) shall appoint a deputy commissioner [or two deputy commissioners][180], and

(b) may appoint such number of other officers and staff as he may determine.

[(1A) The Commissioner shall, when appointing any second deputy commissioner, specify which of the Commissioner's functions are to be performed, in the circumstances referred to in paragraph 5(1), by each of the deputy commissioners.][181]

(2) The remuneration and other conditions of service of the persons appointed under this paragraph shall be determined by the Commissioner.

(3) The Commissioner may pay such pensions, allowances or gratuities to or in respect of the persons appointed under this paragraph, or make such payments towards the provision of such pensions, allowances or gratuities, as he may determine.

(4) The references in sub-paragraph (3) to pensions, allowances or gratuities to or in respect of the

persons appointed under this paragraph include references to pensions, allowances or gratuities by way of compensation to or in respect of any of those persons who suffer loss of office or employment.

(5) Any determination under sub-paragraph (1)(b), (2) or (3) shall require the approval of the [Secretary of State][182] .

(6) The Employers' Liability (Compulsory Insurance) Act 1969 shall not require insurance to be effected by the Commissioner.

5(1) The deputy commissioner [or deputy commissioners][183] shall perform the functions conferred by this Act [or the Freedom of Information Act 2000][184] on the Commissioner during any vacancy in that office or at any time when the Commissioner is for any reason unable to act.

(2) Without prejudice to sub-paragraph (1), any functions of the Commissioner under this Act [or the Freedom of Information Act 2000][185] may, to the extent authorised by him, be performed by any of his officers or staff.

Authentication of seal of the Commissioner

6 The application of the seal of the Commissioner shall be authenticated by his signature or by the signature of some other person authorised for the purpose.

Presumption of authenticity of documents issued by the Commissioner

7 Any document purporting to be an instrument issued by the Commissioner and to be duly executed under the Commissioner's seal or to be signed by or on behalf of the Commissioner shall be received in evidence and shall be deemed to be such an instrument unless the contrary is shown.

Money

8 The [Secretary of State][186] may make payments to the Commissioner out of money provided by Parliament.

9(1) All fees and other sums received by the Commissioner in the exercise of his functions under this Act [, under section 159 of the Consumer Credit Act 1974 or under the Freedom of Information Act 2000][187] shall be paid by him to the [Secretary of State][188].

(2) Sub-paragraph (1) shall not apply where the [Secretary of State][189], with the consent of the Treasury, otherwise directs.

(3) Any sums received by the [Secretary of State][190] under sub-paragraph (1) shall be paid into the Consolidated Fund.

Accounts

10(1) It shall be the duty of the Commissioner—

(a) to keep proper accounts and other records in relation to the accounts,

(b) to prepare in respect of each financial year a statement of account in such form as the [Secretary of State][191] may direct, and

(c) to send copies of that statement to the Comptroller and Auditor General on or before 31st August next following the end of the year to which the statement relates or on or before such earlier date after the end of that year as the Treasury may direct.

(2) The Comptroller and Auditor General shall examine and certify any statement sent to him under this paragraph and lay copies of it together with his report thereon before each House of Parliament.

(3) In this paragraph "financial year" means a period of twelve months beginning with 1st April.

Application of Part I in Scotland

11 Paragraphs 1(1), 6 and 7 do not extend to Scotland.

Part II The Tribunal[192]

....

[Part III][193]

....

SCHEDULE 6 Appeal proceedings

Hearing of appeals

1................................[194]

Constitution of Tribunal in national security cases

2................................[195]

3. . . . .[196]

Constitution of Tribunal in other cases

4. . . . .[197]

Determination of questions by full Tribunal

5. . . . .[198]

Ex parte proceedings

6. . . . .[199]

[Tribunal Procedure Rules][200]

7[(1) Tribunal Procedure Rules may make provision for regulating the exercise of the rights of appeal conferred—

(a) by sections 28(4) and (6) and 48 of this Act, and

(b) by sections 47(1) and (2) and 60(1) and (4) of the Freedom of Information Act 2000.

(2) In the case of appeals under this Act and the Freedom of Information Act 2000, Tribunal Procedure Rules may make provision—

(a) for securing the production of material used for the processing of personal data;

(b) for the inspection, examination, operation and testing of any equipment or material used in connection with the processing of personal data;

(c) for hearing an appeal in the absence of the appellant or for determining an appeal without a hearing.][201]

(3). . . . .[202]

Obstruction etc.

8(1) If any person is guilty of any act or omission in relation to proceedings before the Tribunal which, if those proceedings were proceedings before a court having power to commit for contempt, would constitute contempt of court, the Tribunal may certify the offence to the High Court or, in Scotland, the Court of Session.

(2) Where an offence is so certified, the court may inquire into the matter and, after hearing any witness who may be produced against or on behalf of the person charged with the offence, and after hearing any statement that may be offered in defence, deal with him in any manner in which it could deal with him if he had committed the like offence in relation to the court.

Section 37.

SCHEDULE 7 Miscellaneous exemptions

Confidential references given by the data controller

1 Personal data are exempt from section 7 if they consist of a reference given or to be given in confidence by the data controller for the purposes of—

(a) the education, training or employment, or prospective education, training or employment, of the data subject,

(b) the appointment, or prospective appointment, of the data subject to any office, or

(c) the provision, or prospective provision, by the data subject of any service.

Armed forces

2 Personal data are exempt from the subject information provisions in any case to the extent to which the application of those provisions would be likely to prejudice the combat effectiveness of any of the armed forces of the Crown.

Judicial appointments and honours

3 Personal data processed for the purposes of—

(a) assessing any person's suitability for judicial office or the office of Queen's Counsel, or

(b) the conferring by the Crown of any honour [or dignity][203],

are exempt from the subject information provisions.

Crown employment and Crown or Ministerial appointments

4(1)[204] The [Secretary of State][205] may by order exempt from the subject information provisions personal data processed for the purposes of assessing any person's suitability for—

(a) employment by or under the Crown, or

(b) any office to which appointments are made by Her Majesty, by a Minister of the Crown or by a

[Northern Ireland authority][206].

[(2) In this paragraph "Northern Ireland authority" means the First Minister, the deputy First Minister, a Northern Ireland Minister or a Northern Ireland department.][207]

Management forecasts etc.

5 Personal data processed for the purposes of management forecasting or management planning to assist the data controller in the conduct of any business or other activity are exempt from the subject information provisions in any case to the extent to which the application of those provisions would be likely to prejudice the conduct of that business or other activity.

Corporate finance

6(1) Where personal data are processed for the purposes of, or in connection with, a corporate finance service provided by a relevant person—

(a) the data are exempt from the subject information provisions in any case to the extent to which either—

(i) the application of those provisions to the data could affect the price of any instrument which is already in existence or is to be or may be created, or

(ii) the data controller reasonably believes that the application of those provisions to the data could affect the price of any such instrument, and

(b) to the extent that the data are not exempt from the subject information provisions by virtue of paragraph (a), they are exempt from those provisions if the exemption is required for the purpose of safeguarding an important economic or financial interest of the United Kingdom.

(2) For the purposes of sub-paragraph (1)(b) the [Secretary of State][208] may by order specify—

(a) matters to be taken into account in determining whether exemption from the subject information provisions is required for the purpose of safeguarding an important economic or financial interest of the United Kingdom, or

(b) circumstances in which exemption from those provisions is, or is not, to be taken to be required for that purpose.

(3) In this paragraph—

"corporate finance service" means a service consisting in—

(a) underwriting in respect of issues of, or the placing of issues of, any instrument,

(b) advice to undertakings on capital structure, industrial strategy and related matters and advice and service relating to mergers and the purchase of undertakings, or

(c) services relating to such underwriting as is mentioned in paragraph (a);

"instrument" means any instrument listed in [section C of Annex I to Directive 2004/39/EC of the European Parliament and of the Council of 21 April 2004 on markets in financial instruments][209]...[210] ;

"price" includes value;

"relevant person" means—

(a) [any person who, by reason of any permission he has under Part IV of the Financial Services and Markets Act 2000, is ableto carry on a corporate finance service without contravening the general prohibition, within the meaning of section 19 of that Act;

(b) an EEA firm of the kind mentioned in paragraph 5(a) or (b) of Schedule 3 to that Act which hasqualified for authorisation under paragraph 12 of that Schedule, and may lawfully carry on a corporate finance service;

(c) any person who is exempt from the general prohibition in respect of any corporate finance service—

(c)(i) as a result of an exemption order made under section 38(1) of that Act, or

(ii) by reason of section 39(1) of that Act (appointed representatives);

(cc) any person, not falling within paragraph (a), (b) or (c) who may lawfully carry on acorporate finance service without contravening the general prohibition;][211]

(d) any person who, in the course of his employment, provides to his employer a service falling within paragraph (b) or (c) of the definition of "corporate finance service", or

(e) any partner who provides to other partners in the partnership a service falling within either of those paragraphs.

Negotiations

7 Personal data which consist of records of the intentions of the data controller in relation to any negotiations with the data subject are exempt from the subject information provisions in any case to the extent to which the application of those provisions would be likely to prejudice those negotiations.

Examination marks

8(1) Section 7 shall have effect subject to the provisions of sub-paragraphs (2) to (4) in the case of personal data consisting of marks or other information processed by a data controller—

(a) for the purpose of determining the results of an academic, professional or other examination or of enabling the results of any such examination to be determined, or

(b) in consequence of the determination of any such results.

(2) Where the relevant day falls before the day on which the results of the examination are announced, the period mentioned in section 7(8) shall be extended until—

(a) the end of five months beginning with the relevant day, or

(b) the end of forty days beginning with the date of the announcement,

whichever is the earlier.

(3) Where by virtue of sub-paragraph (2) a period longer than the prescribed period elapses after the relevant day before the request is complied with, the information to be supplied pursuant to the request shall be supplied both by reference to the data in question at the time when the request is received and (if different) by reference to the data as from time to time held in the period beginning when the request is received and ending when it is complied with.

(4) For the purposes of this paragraph the results of an examination shall be treated as announced when they are first published or (if not published) when they are first made available or communicated to the candidate in question.

(5) In this paragraph— "examination" includes any process for determining the knowledge, intelligence, skill or ability of a candidate by reference to his performance in any test, work or other activity; "the prescribed period" means forty days or such other period as is for the time being prescribed under section 7 in relation to the personal data in question; "relevant day" has the same meaning as in section 7.

Examination scripts etc.

9(1) Personal data consisting of information recorded by candidates during an academic, professional or other examination are exempt from section 7.

(2) In this paragraph "examination" has the same meaning as in paragraph 8.

Legal professional privilege

10 Personal data are exempt from the subject information provisions if the data consist of information in respect of which a claim to legal professional privilege [or, in Scotland, to confidentiality of communications][212] could be maintained in legal proceedings.

Self-incrimination

11(1) a person need not comply with any request or order under section 7 to the extent that compliance would, by revealing evidence of the commission of any offence [, other than an offence under this Act or an offence within sub-paragraph (1A),][213] expose him to proceedings for that offence.

[(1A) The offences mentioned in sub-paragraph (1) are—

(a) an offence under section 5 of the Perjury Act 1911 (false statements made otherwise than on oath),

(b) an offence under section 44(2) of the Criminal Law (Consolidation) (Scotland) Act 1995 (false statements made otherwise than on oath), or

(c) an offence under Article 10 of the Perjury (Northern Ireland) Order 1979 (false statutory declarations and other false unsworn statements).][214]

(2) Information disclosed by any person in compliance with any request or order under section 7 shall not be admissible against him in proceedings for an offence under this Act.

Section 39.

SCHEDULE 8 Transitional relief

Part I Interpretation of Schedule

1(1) For the purposes of this Schedule, personal data are "eligible data" at any time if, and to the extent that, they are at that time subject to processing which was already under way immediately before 24th October 1998.

(2) In this Schedule— "eligible automated data" means eligible data which fall within paragraph (a) or (b) of the definition of "data" in section 1(1); "eligible manual data" means eligible data which are not eligible automated data; "the first transitional period" means the period beginning with the commencement of this Schedule and ending with 23rd October 2001; "the second transitional period" means the period beginning with 24th October 2001 and ending with 23rd October 2007.

Part II Exemptions available before 24th October 2001

Manual data

2(1) Eligible manual data, other than data forming part of an accessible record, are exempt from the data protection principles and Parts II and III of this Act during the first transitional period.

(2) This paragraph does not apply to eligible manual data to which paragraph 4 applies.

3(1) This paragraph applies to—

(a) eligible manual data forming part of an accessible record, and

(b) personal data which fall within paragraph (d) of the definition of "data" in section 1(1) but which, because they are not subject to processing which was already under way immediately before 24th October 1998, are not eligible data for the purposes of this Schedule.

(2) during the first transitional period, data to which this paragraph applies are exempt from—

(a) the data protection principles, except the sixth principle so far as relating to sections 7 and 12A,

(b) Part II of this Act, except—

(i) section 7 (as it has effect subject to section 8) and section 12A, and

(ii) section 15 so far as relating to those sections, and

(c) Part III of this Act.

4(1) This paragraph applies to eligible manual data which consist of information relevant to the financial standing of the data subject and in respect of which the data controller is a credit reference agency.

(2) during the first transitional period, data to which this paragraph applies are exempt from—

(a) the data protection principles, except the sixth principle so far as relating to sections 7 and 12A,

(b) Part II of this Act, except—

(i) section 7 (as it has effect subject to sections 8 and 9) and section 12A, and

(ii) section 15 so far as relating to those sections, and

(c) Part III of this Act.

Processing otherwise than by reference to the data subject

5 During the first transitional period, for the purposes of this Act (apart from paragraph 1), eligible automated data are not to be regarded as being "processed" unless the processing is by reference to the data subject.

Payrolls and accounts

6(1) Subject to sub-paragraph (2), eligible automated data processed by a data controller for one or more of the following purposes—

(a) calculating amounts payable by way of remuneration or pensions in respect of service in any employment or office or making payments of, or of sums deducted from, such remuneration or pensions, or

(b) keeping accounts relating to any business or other activity carried on by the data controller or keeping records of purchases, sales or other transactions for the purpose of ensuring that the requisite payments are made by or to him in respect of those transactions or for the purpose of making financial or management forecasts to assist him in the conduct of any such business or activity,

are exempt from the data protection principles and Parts II and III of this Act during the first transitional period.

(2) It shall be a condition of the exemption of any eligible automated data under this paragraph that the

data are not processed for any other purpose, but the exemption is not lost by any processing of the eligible data for any other purpose if the data controller shows that he had taken such care to prevent it as in all the circumstances was reasonably required.

(3) data processed only for one or more of the purposes mentioned in sub-paragraph (1)(a) may be disclosed—

(a) to any person, other than the data controller, by whom the remuneration or pensions in question are payable,

(b) for the purpose of obtaining actuarial advice,

(c) for the purpose of giving information as to the persons in any employment or office for use in medical research into the health of, or injuries suffered by, persons engaged in particular occupations or working in particular places or areas,

(d) if the data subject (or a person acting on his behalf) has requested or consented to the disclosure of the data either generally or in the circumstances in which the disclosure in question is made, or

(e) if the person making the disclosure has reasonable grounds for believing that the disclosure falls within paragraph (d).

(4) data processed for any of the purposes mentioned in sub-paragraph (1) may be disclosed—

(a) for the purpose of audit or where the disclosure is for the purpose only of giving information about the data controller's financial affairs, or

(b) in any case in which disclosure would be permitted by any other provision of this Part of this Act if sub-paragraph (2) were included among the non-disclosure provisions.

(5) In this paragraph "remuneration" includes remuneration in kind and "pensions" includes gratuities or similar benefits.

Unincorporated members' clubs and mailing lists

7 Eligible automated data processed by an unincorporated members' club and relating only to the members of the club are exempt from the data protection principles and Parts II and III of this Act during the first transitional period.

8 Eligible automated data processed by a data controller only for the purposes of distributing, or recording the distribution of, articles or information to the data subjects and consisting only of their names, addresses or other particulars necessary for effecting the distribution, are exempt from the data protection principles and Parts II and III of this Act during the first transitional period.

9 Neither paragraph 7 nor paragraph 8 applies to personal data relating to any data subject unless he has been asked by the club or data controller whether he objects to the data relating to him being processed as mentioned in that paragraph and has not objected.

10 It shall be a condition of the exemption of any data under paragraph 7 that the data are not disclosed except as permitted by paragraph 11 and of the exemption under paragraph 8 that the data are not processed for any purpose other than that mentioned in that paragraph or as permitted by paragraph 11, but—

(a) the exemption under paragraph 7 shall not be lost by any disclosure in breach of that condition, and

(b) the exemption under paragraph 8 shall not be lost by any processing in breach of that condition,

if the data controller shows that he had taken such care to prevent it as in all the circumstances was reasonably required.

11 Data to which paragraph 10 applies may be disclosed—

(a) if the data subject (or a person acting on his behalf) has requested or consented to the disclosure of the data either generally or in the circumstances in which the disclosure in question is made,

(b) if the person making the disclosure has reasonable grounds for believing that the disclosure falls within paragraph (a), or

(c) in any case in which disclosure would be permitted by any other provision of this Part of this Act if paragraph 8 were included among the non-disclosure provisions.

Back-up data

12 Eligible automated data which are processed only for the purpose of replacing other data in the event of the latter being lost, destroyed or impaired are exempt from section 7 during the first transitional period.

Exemption of all eligible automated data from certain requirements

13(1) During the first transitional period, eligible automated data are exempt from the following provisions—

(a) the first data protection principle to the extent to which it requires compliance with—

(i) paragraph 2 of Part II of Schedule 1,

(ii) the conditions in Schedule 2, and

(iii) the conditions in Schedule 3,

(b) the seventh data protection principle to the extent to which it requires compliance with paragraph 12 of Part II of Schedule 1;

(c) the eighth data protection principle,

(d) in section 7(1), paragraphs (b), (c)(ii) and (d),

(e) sections 10 and 11,

(f) section 12, and

(g) section 13, except so far as relating to—

(i) any contravention of the fourth data protection principle,

(ii) any disclosure without the consent of the data controller,

(iii) loss or destruction of data without the consent of the data controller, or

(iv) processing for the special purposes.

(2) The specific exemptions conferred by sub-paragraph (1)(a), (c) and (e) do not limit the data controller's general duty under the first data protection principle to ensure that processing is fair.

Part III Exemptions available after 23rd October 2001 but before 24th October 2007

14(1) This paragraph applies to—

(a) eligible manual data which were held immediately before 24th October 1998, and

(b) personal data which fall within paragraph (d) of the definition of "data" in section 1(1) but do not fall within paragraph (a) of this sub-paragraph,

but does not apply to eligible manual data to which the exemption in paragraph 16 applies.

(2) During the second transitional period, data to which this paragraph applies are exempt from the following provisions—

(a) the first data protection principle except to the extent to which it requires compliance with paragraph 2 of Part II of Schedule 1,

(b) the second, third, fourth and fifth data protection principles, and

(c) section 14(1) to (3).

[14A(1) This paragraph applies to personal data which fall within paragraph (e) of the definition of "data" in section 1(1) and do not fall within paragraph 14(1)(a), but does not apply to eligible manual data to which the exemption in paragraph 16 applies.

(2) During the second transitional period, data to which this paragraph applies are exempt from—

(a) the fourth data protection principle, and

(b) section 14(1) to (3).][215]

Part IV Exemptions after 23rd October 2001 for historical research

15 In this Part of this Schedule "the relevant conditions" has the same meaning as in section 33.

16(1) Eligible manual data which are processed only for the purpose of historical research in compliance with the relevant conditions are exempt from the provisions specified in sub-paragraph (2) after 23rd October 2001.

(2) The provisions referred to in sub-paragraph (1) are—

(a) the first data protection principle except in so far as it requires compliance with paragraph 2 of Part II of Schedule 1,

(b) the second, third, fourth and fifth data protection principles, and

(c) section 14(1) to (3).

17(1) After 23rd October 2001 eligible automated data which are processed only for the purpose of historical research in compliance with the relevant conditions are exempt from the first data protection principle to the extent to which it requires compliance with the conditions in Schedules 2 and 3.

(2) Eligible automated data which are processed—

(a) only for the purpose of historical research,

(b) in compliance with the relevant conditions, and

(c) otherwise than by reference to the data subject,

are also exempt from the provisions referred to in sub-paragraph (3) after 23rd October 2001.

(3) The provisions referred to in sub-paragraph (2) are—

(a) the first data protection principle except in so far as it requires compliance with paragraph 2 of Part II of Schedule 1,

(b) the second, third, fourth and fifth data protection principles, and

(c) section 14(1) to (3).

18 For the purposes of this Part of this Schedule personal data are not to be treated as processed otherwise than for the purpose of historical research merely because the data are disclosed—

(a) to any person, for the purpose of historical research only,

(b) to the data subject or a person acting on his behalf,

(c) at the request, or with the consent, of the data subject or a person acting on his behalf, or

(d) in circumstances in which the person making the disclosure has reasonable grounds for believing that the disclosure falls within paragraph (a), (b) or (c).

Part V Exemption from section 22

19 Processing which was already under way immediately before 24th October 1998 is not assessable processing for the purposes of section 22.

Section 50.

SCHEDULE 9 Powers of entry and inspection

Issue of warrants

1(1) If a circuit judge [or a District Judge (Magistrates' Courts)][216] is satisfied by information on oath supplied by the Commissioner that there are reasonable grounds for suspecting—

(a) that a data controller has contravened or is contravening any of the data protection principles, or

(b) that an offence under this Act has been or is being committed,

and that evidence of the contravention or of the commission of the offence is to be found on any premises specified in the information, he may, subject to sub-paragraph (2) and paragraph 2, grant a warrant to the Commissioner.

[(1A) Sub-paragraph (1B) applies if a circuit judge or a District Judge (Magistrates' Courts) is satisfied by information on oath supplied by the Commissioner that a data controller has failed to comply with a requirement imposed by an assessment notice.

(1B) The judge may, for the purpose of enabling the Commissioner to determine whether the data controller has complied or is complying with the data protection principles, grant a warrant to the Commissioner in relation to any premises that were specified in the assessment notice; but this is subject to sub-paragraph (2) and paragraph 2.][217]

(2) A judge shall not issue a warrant under this Schedule in respect of any personal data processed for the special purposes unless a determination by the Commissioner under section 45 with respect to those data has taken effect.

(3) A warrant issued under [this Schedule][218] shall authorise the Commissioner or any of his officers or staff at any time within seven days of the date of the warrant

[(a) to enter the premises;

(b) to search the premises;

(c) to inspect, examine, operate and test any equipment found on the premises which is used or intended to be used for the processing of personal data;

(d) to inspect and seize any documents or other material found on the premises which—

(i) in the case of a warrant issued under sub-paragraph (1), may be such evidence as is mentioned in that paragraph;

(ii) in the case of a warrant issued under sub-paragraph (1B), may enable the Commissioner to determine whether the data controller has complied or is complying with the data protection principles;

(e) to require any person on the premises to provide an explanation of any document or other material found on the premises;

(f) to require any person on the premises to provide such other information as may reasonably be required for the purpose of determining whether the data controller has contravened, or is

contravening, the data protection principles.][219]

2(1) A judge shall not issue a warrant under this Schedule unless he is satisfied—

(a) that the Commissioner has given seven days' notice in writing to the occupier of the premises in question demanding access to the premises, and

(b) that either—

(i) access was demanded at a reasonable hour and was unreasonably refused, or

(ii) although entry to the premises was granted, the occupier unreasonably refused to comply with a request by the Commissioner or any of the Commissioner's officers or staff to permit the Commissioner or the officer or member of staff to do any of the things referred to in paragraph 1(3), and

(c) that the occupier, has, after the refusal, been notified by the Commissioner of the application for the warrant and has had an opportunity of being heard by the judge on the question whether or not it should be issued.

[(1A) In determining whether the Commissioner has given an occupier the seven days' notice referred to in sub-paragraph (1)(a) any assessment notice served on the occupier is to be disregarded.][220]

(2) Sub-paragraph (1) shall not apply if the judge is satisfied that the case is one of urgency or that compliance with those provisions would defeat the object of the entry.

3 A judge who issues a warrant under this Schedule shall also issue two copies of it and certify them clearly as copies.

Execution of warrants

4 A person executing a warrant issued under this Schedule may use such reasonable force as may be necessary.

5 A warrant issued under this Schedule shall be executed at a reasonable hour unless it appears to the person executing it that there are grounds for suspecting that the [object of the warrant would be defeated][221] if it were so executed.

6 If the person who occupies the premises in respect of which a warrant is issued under this Schedule is present when the warrant is executed, he shall be shown the warrant and supplied with a copy of it; and if that person is not present a copy of the warrant shall be left in a prominent place on the premises.

7(1) A person seizing anything in pursuance of a warrant under this Schedule shall give a receipt for it if asked to do so.

(2) Anything so seized may be retained for so long as is necessary in all the circumstances but the person in occupation of the premises in question shall be given a copy of anything that is seized if he so requests and the person executing the warrant considers that it can be done without undue delay.

Matters exempt from inspection and seizure

8 The powers of inspection and seizure conferred by a warrant issued under this Schedule shall not be exercisable in respect of personal data which by virtue of section 28 are exempt from any of the provisions of this Act.

9(1) Subject to the provisions of this paragraph, the powers of inspection and seizure conferred by a warrant issued under this Schedule shall not be exercisable in respect of—

(a) any communication between a professional legal adviser and his client in connection with the giving of legal advice to the client with respect to his obligations, liabilities or rights under this Act, or

(b) any communication between a professional legal adviser and his client, or between such an adviser or his client and any other person, made in connection with or in contemplation of proceedings under or arising out of this Act (including proceedings before the Tribunal) and for the purposes of such proceedings.

(2) Sub-paragraph (1) applies also to—

(a) any copy or other record of any such communication as is there mentioned, and

(b) any document or article enclosed with or referred to in any such communication if made in connection with the giving of any advice or, as the case may be, in connection with or in contemplation of and for the purposes of such proceedings as are there mentioned.

(3) This paragraph does not apply to anything in the possession of any person other than the professional legal adviser or his client or to anything held with the intention of furthering a criminal

purpose.

(4) In this paragraph references to the client of a professional legal adviser include references to any person representing such a client.

10 If the person in occupation of any premises in respect of which a warrant is issued under this Schedule objects to the inspection or seizure under the warrant of any material on the grounds that it consists partly of matters in respect of which those powers are not exercisable, he shall, if the person executing the warrant so requests, furnish that person with a copy of so much of the material as is not exempt from those powers.

Return of warrants

11 A warrant issued under this Schedule shall be returned to the court from which it was issued—

(a) after being executed, or

(b) if not executed within the time authorised for its execution;

and the person by whom any such warrant is executed shall make an endorsement on it stating what powers have been exercised by him under the warrant.

Offences

12 Any person who—

(a) intentionally obstructs a person in the execution of a warrant issued under this Schedule,...[222]

(b) fails without reasonable excuse to give any person executing such a warrant such assistance as he may reasonably require for the execution of the warrant,

[(c) makes a statement in response to a requirement under paragraph (e) or (f) of paragraph 1(3) which that person knows to be false in a material respect, or

(d) recklessly makes a statement in response to such a requirement which is false in a material respect,][223]

is guilty of an offence.

Vessels, vehicles etc.

13 In this Schedule "premises" includes any vessel, vehicle, aircraft or hovercraft, and references to the occupier of any premises include references to the person in charge of any vessel, vehicle, aircraft or hovercraft.

Scotland and Northern Ireland

14 In the application of this Schedule to Scotland—

(a) for any reference to a circuit judge there is substituted a reference to the sheriff,

(b) for any reference to information on oath there is substituted a reference to evidence on oath, and

(c) for the reference to the court from which the warrant was issued there is substituted a reference to the sheriff clerk.

15 In the application of this Schedule to Northern Ireland—

(a) for any reference to a circuit judge there is substituted a reference to a county court judge, and

(b) for any reference to information on oath there is substituted a reference to a complaint on oath.

[Self-incrimination

16 An explanation given, or information provided, by a person in response to a requirement under paragraph (e) or (f) of paragraph 1(3) may only be used in evidence against that person—

(a) on a prosecution for an offence under—

(i) paragraph 12,

(ii) section 5 of the Perjury Act 1911 (false statements made otherwise than on oath),

(iii) section 44(2) of the Criminal Law (Consolidation) (Scotland) Act 1995 (false statements made otherwise than on oath), or

(iv) article 10 of the Perjury (Northern Ireland) Order 1979 (false statutory declarations and other false unsworn statements), or

(b) on a prosecution for any other offence where—

(i) in giving evidence that person makes a statement inconsistent with that explanation or information, and

(ii) evidence relating to that explanation or information is adduced, or a question relating to it is asked, by that person or on that person's behalf.][224]

Section 53(6).

SCHEDULE 10 Further provisions relating to assistance under section 53

1 In this Schedule "applicant" and "proceedings" have the same meaning as in section 53.

2 The assistance provided under section 53 may include the making of arrangements for, or for the Commissioner to bear the costs of—

(a) the giving of advice or assistance by a solicitor or counsel, and

(b) the representation of the applicant, or the provision to him of such assistance as is usually given by a solicitor or counsel—

(i) in steps preliminary or incidental to the proceedings, or

(ii) in arriving at or giving effect to a compromise to avoid or bring an end to the proceedings.

3 Where assistance is provided with respect to the conduct of proceedings—

(a) it shall include an agreement by the Commissioner to indemnify the applicant (subject only to any exceptions specified in the notification) in respect of any liability to pay costs or expenses arising by virtue of any judgment or order of the court in the proceedings,

(b) it may include an agreement by the Commissioner to indemnify the applicant in respect of any liability to pay costs or expenses arising by virtue of any compromise or settlement arrived at in order to avoid the proceedings or bring the proceedings to an end, and

(c) it may include an agreement by the Commissioner to indemnify the applicant in respect of any liability to pay damages pursuant to an undertaking given on the grant of interlocutory relief (in Scotland, an interim order) to the applicant.

4 Where the Commissioner provides assistance in relation to any proceedings, he shall do so on such terms, or make such other arrangements, as will secure that a person against whom the proceedings have been or are commenced is informed that assistance has been or is being provided by the Commissioner in relation to them.

5 In England and Wales or Northern Ireland, the recovery of expenses incurred by the Commissioner in providing an applicant with assistance (as taxed or assessed in such manner as may be prescribed by rules of court) shall constitute a first charge for the benefit of the Commissioner—

(a) on any costs which, by virtue of any judgment or order of the court, are payable to the applicant by any other person in respect of the matter in connection with which the assistance is provided, and

(b) on any sum payable to the applicant under a compromise or settlement arrived at in connection with that matter to avoid or bring to an end any proceedings.

6 In Scotland, the recovery of such expenses (as taxed or assessed in such manner as may be prescribed by rules of court) shall be paid to the Commissioner, in priority to other debts—

(a) out of any expenses which, by virtue of any judgment or order of the court, are payable to the applicant by any other person in respect of the matter in connection with which the assistance is provided, and

(b) out of any sum payable to the applicant under a compromise or settlement arrived at in connection with that matter to avoid or bring to an end any proceedings.

Section 68(1)(6).

SCHEDULE 11 Educational records

Meaning of "educational record"

1 For the purposes of sec tion 68 "educational record" means any record to which paragraph 2, 5 or 7 applies.

England and Wales

2 This paragraph applies to any record of information which—

(a) is processed by or on behalf of the governing body of, or a teacher at, any school in England and Wales specified in paragraph 3,

(b) relates to any person who is or has been a pupil at the school, and

(c) originated from or was supplied by or on behalf of any of the persons specified in paragraph 4, other than information which is processed by a teacher solely for the teacher's own use.

3 The schools referred to in paragraph 2(a) are—

(a) a school maintained by a [local authority][225], and

(b) a special school, as defined by section 6(2) of the Education Act 1996, which is not so maintained.

4 The persons referred to in paragraph 2(c) are—

(a) an employee of the [local authority][226] which maintains the school,

(b) in the case of—

(i) a voluntary aided, foundation or foundation special school (within the meaning of the School Standards and Framework Act 1998), or

(ii) a special school which is not maintained by a [local authority][227],

a teacher or other employee at the school (including an educational psychologist engaged by the governing body under a contract for services),

(c) the pupil to whom the record relates, and

(d) a parent, as defined by section 576(1) of the Education Act 1996, of that pupil.

[4A In paragraphs 3 and 4 "local authority" has the meaning given by section 579(1) of the Education Act 1996.][228]

Scotland

5 This paragraph applies to any record of information which is processed—

(a) by an education authority in Scotland, and

(b) for the purpose of the relevant function of the authority,

other than information which is processed by a teacher solely for the teacher's own use.

6 For the purposes of paragraph 5—

(a) "education authority" means an education authority within the meaning of the Education (Scotland) Act 1980 ("the 1980 Act") [or, in relation to a self-governing school, the board of management within the meaning of the Self-Governing Schools etc. (Scotland) Act 1989 ("the 1989 Act")][229],

(b) "the relevant function" means, in relation to each of those authorities, their function under section 1 of the 1980 Act and section 7(1) of the 1989 Act, and

(c) information processed by an education authority is processed for the purpose of the relevant function of the authority if the processing relates to the discharge of that function in respect of a person—

(i) who is or has been a pupil in a school provided by the authority, or

(ii) who receives, or has received, further education (within the meaning of the 1980 Act) so provided.

Northern Ireland

7(1) This paragraph applies to any record of information which—

(a) is processed by or on behalf of the Board of Governors of, or a teacher at, any grant-aided school in Northern Ireland,

(b) relates to any person who is or has been a pupil at the school, and

(c) originated from or was supplied by or on behalf of any of the persons specified in paragraph 8,

other than information which is processed by a teacher solely for the teacher's own use.

(2) In sub-paragraph (1) "grant-aided school" has the same meaning as in the Education and Libraries (Northern Ireland) Order 1986.

8 The persons referred to in paragraph 7(1) are—

(a) a teacher at the school,

(b) an employee of an education and library board, other than such a teacher,

(c) the pupil to whom the record relates, and

(d) a parent (as defined by Article 2(2) of the Education and Libraries (Northern Ireland) Order 1986) of that pupil.

England and Wales: transitory provisions

9(1) Until the appointed day within the meaning of section 20 of the School Standards and Framework Act 1998, this Schedule shall have effect subject to the following modifications.

(2) Paragraph 3 shall have effect as if for paragraph (b) and the "and" immediately preceding it there were substituted—

"(aa) a grant-maintained school, as defined by section 183(1) of the Education Act 1996,

(ab) a grant-maintained special school, as defined by section 337(4) of that Act, and

(b) a special school, as defined by section 6(2) of that Act, which is neither a maintained special school, as defined by section 337(3) of that Act, nor a grant-maintained special school."

(3) Paragraph 4(b)(i) shall have effect as if for the words from "foundation", in the first place where it

occurs, to "1998) " there were substituted " or grant-maintained school ".

Section 68(1)(c).

SCHEDULE 12 Accessible public records

Meaning of "accessible public record"

1 For the purposes of section 68 "accessible public record" means any record which is kept by an authority specified—

(a) as respects England and Wales, in the Table in paragraph 2,

(b) as respects Scotland, in the Table in paragraph 4, or

(c) as respects Northern Ireland, in the Table in paragraph 6,

and is a record of information of a description specified in that Table in relation to that authority.

Housing and social services records: England and Wales

2The following is the Table referred to in paragraph 1(a).

TABLE OF AUTHORITIES AND INFORMATION

The authorities	The accessible information
Housing Act local authority.	Information held for the purpose of any of the authority's tenancies.
Local social services authority.	Information held for any purpose of the authority's social services functions.

3(1) The following provisions apply for the interpretation of the Table in paragraph 2.

(2) any authority which, by virtue of section 4(e) of the Housing Act 1985, is a local authority for the purpose of any provision of that Act is a "Housing Act local authority" for the purposes of this Schedule, and so is any housing action trust established under Part III of the Housing Act 1988.

(3) Information contained in records kept by a Housing Act local authority is "held for the purpose of any of the authority's tenancies" if it is held for any purpose of the relationship of landlord and tenant of a dwelling which subsists, has subsisted or may subsist between the authority and any individual who is, has been or, as the case may be, has applied to be, a tenant of the authority.

(4) any authority which, by virtue of section 1 or 12 of the Local Authority Social Services Act 1970, is or is treated as a local authority for the purposes of that Act is a "local social services authority" for the purposes of this Schedule; and information contained in records kept by such an authority is "held for any purpose of the authority's social services functions" if it is held for the purpose of any past, current or proposed exercise of such a function in any case.

(5) any expression used in paragraph 2 or this paragraph and in Part II of the Housing Act 1985 or the Local Authority Social Services Act 1970 has the same meaning as in that Act.

Housing and social services records: Scotland

4 The following is the Table referred to in paragraph 1(b).

TABLE OF AUTHORITIES AND INFORMATION

The authorities	The accessible information
Local authority. Scottish Homes.	Information held for the purpose of any of the body's tenancies.
Social work authority.	Information held for any purpose of the authority's functions under the Social Work (Scotland) Act 1968 and the enactments referred to in section 5(1B) of that Act.

5(1) The following provisions apply for the interpretation of the Table in paragraph 4.

(2) "Local authority" means—

(a) a council constituted under section 2 of the Local Government etc. (Scotland) Act 1994,

(b) a joint board or joint committee of two or more of those councils, or

(c) any trust under the control of such a council.

(3) Information contained in records kept by a local authority or Scottish Homes is held for the purpose of any of their tenancies if it is held for any purpose of the relationship of landlord and tenant of a dwelling-house which subsists, has subsisted or may subsist between the authority or, as the case may be, Scottish Homes and any individual who is, has been or, as the case may be, has applied to be a tenant of theirs.

(4) "Social work authority" means a local authority for the purposes of the Social Work (Scotland) Act

1968; and information contained in records kept by such an authority is held for any purpose of their functions if it is held for the purpose of any past, current or proposed exercise of such a function in any case.

Housing and social services records: Northern Ireland

6 The following is the Table referred to in paragraph 1(c).

TABLE OF AUTHORITIES AND INFORMATION

The authorities	The accessible information
The Northern Ireland Housing Executive.	Information held for the purpose of any of the Executive's tenancies.
A Health and Social Services Board.	Information held for the purpose of any past, current or proposed exercise by the Board of any function exercisable, by virtue of directions under Article 17(1) of the Health and Personal Social Services (Northern Ireland) Order 1972, by the Board on behalf of the Department of Health and Social Services with respect to the administration of personal social services under— (a) the Children and Young Persons Act (Northern Ireland) 1968; (b) the Health and Personal Social Services (Northern Ireland) Order 1972; (c) Article 47 of the Matrimonial Causes (Northern Ireland) Order 1978; (d) Article 11 of the Domestic Proceedings (Northern Ireland) Order 1980; (e) the Adoption (Northern Ireland) Order 1987; or (f) the Children (Northern Ireland) Order 1995.
An HSS trust	Information held for the purpose of any past, current or proposed exercise by the trust of any function exercisable, by virtue of an authorisation under Article 3(1) of the Health and Personal Social Services (Northern Ireland) Order 1994, by the trust on behalf of a Health and Social Services Board with respect to the administration of personal social services under any statutory provision mentioned in the last preceding entry.

7(1) This paragraph applies for the interpretation of the Table in paragraph 6.

(2) Information contained in records kept by the Northern Ireland Housing Executive is "held for the purpose of any of the Executive's tenancies" if it is held for any purpose of the relationship of landlord and tenant of a dwelling which subsists, has subsisted or may subsist between the Executive and any individual who is, has been or, as the case may be, has applied to be, a tenant of the Executive.

Section 72.

SCHEDULE 13 Modifications of Act having effect before 24th October 2007

1 After section 12 there is inserted—

"12A Rights of data subjects in relation to exempt manual data.

(1) A data subject is entitled at any time by notice in writing—

(a) to require the data controller to rectify, block, erase or destroy exempt manual data which are inaccurate or incomplete, or

(b) to require the data controller to cease holding exempt manual data in a way incompatible with the legitimate purposes pursued by the data controller.

(2) A notice under subsection (1)(a) or (b) must state the data subject's reasons for believing that the data are inaccurate or incomplete or, as the case may be, his reasons for believing that they are held in a way incompatible with the legitimate purposes pursued by the data controller.

(3) If the court is satisfied, on the application of any person who has given a notice under subsection (1) which appears to the court to be justified (or to be justified to any extent) that the data controller in question has failed to comply with the notice, the court may order him to take such steps for complying with the notice (or for complying with it to that extent) as the court thinks fit.

(4) In this section "exempt manual data" means—

(a) in relation to the first transitional period, as defined by paragraph 1(2) of Schedule 8, data to which paragraph 3 or 4 of that Schedule applies, and

(b) in relation to the second transitional period, as so defined, data to which paragraph 14 [or 14A][230] of that Schedule applies.

(5) For the purposes of this section personal data are incomplete if, and only if, the data, although not inaccurate, are such that their incompleteness would constitute a contravention of the third or fourth data protection principles, if those principles applied to the data."

2 In section 32—

(a) in subsection (2) after "section 12" there is inserted—

"(dd) section 12A,", and

(b) in subsection (4) after "12(8) " there is inserted " , 12A(3) ".

3 In section 34 for "section 14(1) to (3) " there is substituted " sections 12A and 14(1) to (3). "

4 In section 53(1) after "12(8) " there is inserted " , 12A(3) ".

5 In paragraph 8 of Part II of Schedule 1, the word "or" at the end of paragraph (c) is omitted and after paragraph (d) there is inserted "or

(e) he contravenes section 12A by failing to comply with a notice given under subsection (1) of that section to the extent that the notice is justified."

Section 73.

SCHEDULE 14 Transitional provisions and savings

Interpretation

1 In this Schedule— "the 1984 Act" means the Data Protection Act 1984; "the old principles" means the data protection principles within the meaning of the 1984 Act; "the new principles" means the data protection principles within the meaning of this Act.

Effect of registration under Part II of 1984 Act

2(1) Subject to sub-paragraphs (4) and (5) any person who, immediately before the commencement of Part III of this Act—

(a) is registered as a data user under Part II of the 1984 Act, or

(b) is treated by virtue of section 7(6) of the 1984 Act as so registered,

is exempt from section 17(1) of this Act until the end of the registration period. . ..[231]

(2) In sub-paragraph (1) "the registration period", in relation to a person, means—

(a) where there is a single entry in respect of that person as a data user, the period at the end of which, if section 8 of the 1984 Act had remained in force, that entry would have fallen to be removed unless renewed, and

(b) where there are two or more entries in respect of that person as a data user, the period at the end of which, if that section had remained in force, the last of those entries to expire would have fallen to be removed unless renewed.

(3) Any application for registration as a data user under Part II of the 1984 Act which is received by the Commissioner before the commencement of Part III of this Act (including any appeal against a refusal of registration) shall be determined in accordance with the old principles and the provisions of the 1984 Act.

(4) If a person falling within paragraph (b) of sub-paragraph (1) receives a notification under section 7(1) of the 1984 Act of the refusal of his application, sub-paragraph (1) shall cease to apply to him—

(a) if no appeal is brought, at the end of the period within which an appeal can be brought against the refusal, or

(b) on the withdrawal or dismissal of the appeal.

(5) If a data controller gives a notification under section 18(1) at a time when he is exempt from section 17(1) by virtue of sub-paragraph (1), he shall cease to be so exempt.

(6) The Commissioner shall include in the register maintained under section 19 an entry in respect of each person who is exempt from section 17(1) by virtue of sub-paragraph (1); and each entry shall consist of the particulars which, immediately before the commencement of Part III of this Act, were included (or treated as included) in respect of that person in the register maintained under section 4 of the 1984 Act.

(7) Notification regulations under Part III of this Act may make provision modifying the duty referred to in section 20(1) in its application to any person in respect of whom an entry in the register maintained under section 19 has been made under sub-paragraph (6).

(8) Notification regulations under Part III of this Act may make further transitional provision in connection with the substitution of Part III of this Act for Part II of the 1984 Act (registration), including provision modifying the application of provisions of Part III in transitional cases.

Rights of data subjects

3(1) The repeal of section 21 of the 1984 Act (right of access to personal data) does not affect the application of that section in any case in which the request (together with the information referred to in paragraph (a) of subsection (4) of that section and, in a case where it is required, the consent referred to in paragraph (b) of that subsection) was received before the day on which the repeal comes into force.

(2) Sub-paragraph (1) does not apply where the request is made by reference to this Act.

(3) Any fee paid for the purposes of section 21 of the 1984 Act before the commencement of section 7 in a case not falling within sub-paragraph (1) shall be taken to have been paid for the purposes of section 7.

4 The repeal of section 22 of the 1984 Act (compensation for inaccuracy) and the repeal of section 23 of that Act (compensation for loss or unauthorised disclosure) do not affect the application of those sections in relation to damage or distress suffered at any time by reason of anything done or omitted to be done before the commencement of the repeals.

5 The repeal of section 24 of the 1984 Act (rectification and erasure) does not affect any case in which the application to the court was made before the day on which the repeal comes into force.

6 Subsection (3)(b) of section 14 does not apply where the rectification, blocking, erasure or destruction occurred before the commencement of that section.

Enforcement and transfer prohibition notices served under Part V of 1984 Act

7(1) If, immediately before the commencement of section 40—

(a) an enforcement notice under section 10 of the 1984 Act has effect, and

(b) either the time for appealing against the notice has expired or any appeal has been determined,

then, after that commencement, to the extent mentioned in sub-paragraph (3), the notice shall have effect for the purposes of sections 41 and 47 as if it were an enforcement notice under section 40.

(2) Where an enforcement notice has been served under section 10 of the 1984 Act before the commencement of section 40 and immediately before that commencement either—

(a) the time for appealing against the notice has not expired, or

(b) an appeal has not been determined,

the appeal shall be determined in accordance with the provisions of the 1984 Act and the old principles and, unless the notice is quashed on appeal, to the extent mentioned in sub-paragraph (3) the notice shall have effect for the purposes of sections 41 and 47 as if it were an enforcement notice under section 40.

(3) An enforcement notice under section 10 of the 1984 Act has the effect described in sub-paragraph (1) or (2) only to the extent that the steps specified in the notice for complying with the old principle or principles in question are steps which the data controller could be required by an enforcement notice under section 40 to take for complying with the new principles or any of them.

8(1) If, immediately before the commencement of section 40—

(a) a transfer prohibition notice under section 12 of the 1984 Act has effect, and

(b) either the time for appealing against the notice has expired or any appeal has been determined,

then, on and after that commencement, to the extent specified in sub-paragraph (3), the notice shall have effect for the purposes of sections 41 and 47 as if it were an enforcement notice under section 40.

(2) Where a transfer prohibition notice has been served under section 12 of the 1984 Act and immediately before the commencement of section 40 either—

(a) the time for appealing against the notice has not expired, or

(b) an appeal has not been determined,

the appeal shall be determined in accordance with the provisions of the 1984 Act and the old principles and, unless the notice is quashed on appeal, to the extent mentioned in sub-paragraph (3) the notice shall have effect for the purposes of sections 41 and 47 as if it were an enforcement notice under section 40.

(3) A transfer prohibition notice under section 12 of the 1984 Act has the effect described in sub-paragraph (1) or (2) only to the extent that the prohibition imposed by the notice is one which could be imposed by an enforcement notice under section 40 for complying with the new principles or any of them.

Notices under new law relating to matters in relation to which 1984 Act had effect

9 The Commissioner may serve an enforcement notice under section 40 on or after the day on which that section comes into force if he is satisfied that, before that day, the data controller contravened the old principles by reason of any act or omission which would also have constituted a contravention of the new principles if they had applied before that day.

10 Subsection (5)(b) of section 40 does not apply where the rectification, blocking, erasure or destruction occurred before the commencement of that section.

11 The Commissioner may serve an information notice under section 43 on or after the day on which that section comes into force if he has reasonable grounds for suspecting that, before that day, the data controller contravened the old principles by reason of any act or omission which would also have constituted a contravention of the new principles if they had applied before that day.

12 Where by virtue of paragraph 11 an information notice is served on the basis of anything done or omitted to be done before the day on which section 43 comes into force, subsection (2)(b) of that section shall have effect as if the reference to the data controller having complied, or complying, with the new principles were a reference to the data controller having contravened the old principles by reason of any such act or omission as is mentioned in paragraph 11.

Self-incrimination, etc.

13(1) In section 43(8), section 44(9) and paragraph 11 of Schedule 7, any reference to an offence under this Act includes a reference to an offence under the 1984 Act.

(2) In section 34(9) of the 1984 Act, any reference to an offence under that Act includes a reference to an offence under this Act.

Warrants issued under 1984 Act

14 The repeal of Schedule 4 to the 1984 Act does not affect the application of that Schedule in any case where a warrant was issued under that Schedule before the commencement of the repeal.

Complaints under section 36(2) of 1984 Act and requests for assessment under section 42

15 The repeal of section 36(2) of the 1984 Act does not affect the application of that provision in any case where the complaint was received by the Commissioner before the commencement of the repeal.

16 In dealing with a complaint under section 36(2) of the 1984 Act or a request for an assessment under section 42 of this Act, the Commissioner shall have regard to the provisions from time to time applicable to the processing, and accordingly—

(a) in section 36(2) of the 1984 Act, the reference to the old principles and the provisions of that Act includes, in relation to any time when the new principles and the provisions of this Act have effect, those principles and provisions, and

(b) in section 42 of this Act, the reference to the provisions of this Act includes, in relation to any time when the old principles and the provisions of the 1984 Act had effect, those principles and provisions.

Applications under Access to Health Records Act 1990 or corresponding Northern Ireland legislation

17(1) The repeal of any provision of the Access to Health Records Act 1990 does not affect—

(a) the application of section 3 or 6 of that Act in any case in which the application under that section was received before the day on which the repeal comes into force, or

(b) the application of section 8 of that Act in any case in which the application to the court was made before the day on which the repeal comes into force.

(2) Sub-paragraph (1)(a) does not apply in relation to an application for access to information which was made by reference to this Act.

18(1) The revocation of any provision of the Access to Health Records (Northern Ireland) Order 1993 does not affect—

(a) the application of Article 5 or 8 of that Order in any case in which the application under that Article was received before the day on which the repeal comes into force, or

(b) the application of Article 10 of that Order in any case in which the application to the court was made before the day on which the repeal comes into force.

(2) Sub-paragraph (1)(a) does not apply in relation to an application for access to information which was made by reference to this Act.

Applications under regulations under Access to Personal Files Act 1987 or corresponding Northern Ireland legislation

19(1) The repeal of the personal files enactments does not affect the application of regulations under those enactments in relation to—

(a) any request for information,

(b) any application for rectification or erasure, or

(c) any application for review of a decision,

which was made before the day on which the repeal comes into force.

(2) Sub-paragraph (1)(a) does not apply in relation to a request for information which was made by reference to this Act.

(3) In sub-paragraph (1) "the personal files enactments" means—

(a) in relation to Great Britain, the Access to Personal Files Act 1987, and

(b) in relation to Northern Ireland, Part II of the Access to Personal Files and Medical Reports (Northern Ireland) Order 1991.

Applications under section 158 of Consumer Credit Act 1974

20 Section 62 does not affect the application of section 158 of the Consumer Credit Act 1974 in any case where the request was received before the commencement of section 62, unless the request is made by reference to this Act.

Section 74(1).

SCHEDULE 15 Minor and consequential amendments

Public Records Act 1958 (c. 51)

1(1). . . . .[232]

(2). . . . .[233]

(3). . . . .

Parliamentary Commissioner Act 1967 (c. 13)

2. . . . .[234]

3. . . . .[235]

Superannuation Act 1972 (c. 11)

4. . . . .[236]

House of Commons Disqualification Act 1975 (c. 24)

5 (1). . . . .[237]

(2). . . . .[238]

Northern Ireland Assembly Disqualification Act 1975 (c. 25)

6 (1). . . . .[239]

(2). . . . .[240]

Representation of the People Act 1983 (c. 2)

7 In Schedule 2 of the Representation of the People Act 1983 (provisions which may be included in regulations as to registration etc), in paragraph 11A(2)—

(a) for "data user" there is substituted " data controller ", and

(b) for "the Data Protection Act 1984" there is substituted " the Data Protection Act 1998 ".

Access to Medical Reports Act 1988 (c. 28)

8 In section 2(1) of the Access to Medical Reports Act 1988 (interpretation), in the definition of "health professional", for "the Data Protection (Subject Access Modification) Order 1987" there is substituted " the Data Protection Act 1998 ".

Football Spectators Act 1989 (c. 37)

9. . . . .[241]

Education (Student Loans) Act 1990 (c. 6)

10 Schedule 2 to the Education (Student Loans) Act 1990 (loans for students) so far as that Schedule continues in force shall have effect as if the reference in paragraph 4(2) to the Data Protection Act 1984 were a reference to this Act.

Access to Health Records Act 1990 (c. 23)

11 For section 2 of the Access to Health Records Act 1990 there is substituted—

"2 Health professionals.

In this Act "health professional" has the same meaning as in the Data Protection Act 1998."

12 In section 3(4) of that Act (cases where fee may be required) in paragraph (a), for "the maximum prescribed under section 21 of the Data Protection Act 1984" there is substituted " such maximum as may be prescribed for the purposes of this section by regulations under section 7 of the Data Protection Act 1998 ".

13 In section 5(3) of that Act (cases where right of access may be partially excluded) for the words from the beginning to "record" in the first place where it occurs there is substituted " Access shall not be given under section 3(2) to any part of a health record ".

Access to Personal Files and Medical Reports (Northern Ireland) Order 1991 (1991/1707 (N.I. 14))

14 In Article 4 of the Access to Personal Files and Medical Reports (Northern Ireland) Order 1991 (obligation to give access), in paragraph (2) (exclusion of information to which individual entitled under section 21 of the Data Protection Act 1984) for "section 21 of the Data Protection Act 1984" there is substituted " section 7 of the Data Protection Act 1998 ".

15 In Article 6(1) of that Order (interpretation), in the definition of "health professional", for "the Data Protection (Subject Access Modification) (Health) Order 1987" there is substituted " the Data Protection Act 1998 ".

Tribunals and Inquiries Act 1992 (c. 53)

16 In Part 1 of Schedule 1 to the Tribunals and Inquiries Act 1992 (tribunals under direct supervision of Council on Tribunals), for paragraph 14 there is substituted—

"Data protection	14. (a) The Data Protection Commissioner appointed under section 6 of the Data Protection Act 1998; (b) the Data Protection Tribunal constituted under that section, in respect of its jurisdiction under section 48 of that Act."

Access to Health Records (Northern Ireland) Order 1993 (1993/1250 (N.I. 4))

17 For paragraphs (1) and (2) of Article 4 of the Access to Health Records (Northern Ireland) Order 1993 there is substituted—

"(1) In this Order "health professional" has the same meaning as in the Data Protection Act 1998."

18 In Article 5(4) of that Order (cases where fee may be required) in sub-paragraph (a), for "the maximum prescribed under section 21 of the Data Protection Act 1984" there is substituted " such maximum as may be prescribed for the purposes of this Article by regulations under section 7 of the Data Protection Act 1998 ".

19 In Article 7 of that Order (cases where right of access may be partially excluded) for the words from the beginning to "record" in the first place where it occurs there is substituted " Access shall not be given under Article 5(2) to any part of a health record ".

Section 74(2).

SCHEDULE 16 Repeals and revocations

Part I Repeals

Repeals

Chapter	**Short title**	**Extent of repeal**
1984 c. 35.	The Data Protection Act 1984.	The whole Act.
1986 c. 60.	The Financial Services Act 1986.	Section 190.
1987 c. 37.	The Access to Personal Files Act 1987.	The whole Act.
1988 c. 40.	The Education Reform Act 1988.	Section 223.
1988 c. 50.	The Housing Act 1988.	In Schedule 17, paragraph 80.
1990 c. 23.	The Access to Health Records Act 1990.	In section 1(1), the words from "but does not" to the end. In section 3, subsection (1)(a) to (e) and, in subsection (6)(a), the words "in the case of an application made otherwise than by the

		patient". Section 4(1) and (2). In section 5(1)(a)(i), the words "of the patient or" and the word "other". In section 10, in subsection (2) the words "or orders" and in subsection (3) the words "or an order under section 2(3) above". In section 11, the definitions of "child" and "parental responsibility".
1990 c. 37.	The Human Fertilisation and Embryology Act 1990.	Section 33(8).
1990 c. 41.	The Courts and Legal Services Act 1990.	In Schedule 10, paragraph 58.
1992 c. 13.	The Further and Higher Education Act 1992.	Section 86.
1992 c. 37.	The Further and Higher Education (Scotland) Act 1992.	Section 59.
1993 c. 8.	The Judicial Pensions and Retirement Act 1993.	In Schedule 6, paragraph 50.
1993 c. 10.	The Charities Act 1993.	Section 12.
1993 c. 21.	The Osteopaths Act 1993.	Section 38.
1994 c. 17.	The Chiropractors Act 1994.	Section 38.
1994 c. 19.	The Local Government (Wales) Act 1994.	In Schedule 13, paragraph 30.
1994 c. 33.	The Criminal Justice and Public Order Act 1994.	Section 161.
1994 c. 39.	The Local Government etc. (Scotland) Act 1994.	In Schedule 13, paragraph 154.

Part II Revocations

Number	Title	Extent of revocation
S.I. 1991/1142.	The Data Protection Registration Fee Order 1991.	The whole Order.
S.I. 1991/1707 (N.I. 14).	The Access to Personal Files and Medical Reports (Northern Ireland) Order 1991.	Part II. The Schedule.
S.I. 1992/3218.	The Banking Co-ordination (Second Council Directive) Regulations 1992.	In Schedule 10, paragraphs 15 and 40.
S.I. 1993/1250 (N.I. 4).	The Access to Health Records (Northern Ireland) Order 1993.	In Article 2(2), the definitions of "child" and "parental responsibility". In Article 3(1), the words from "but does not include" to the end. In Article 5, paragraph (1)(a) to (d) and, in paragraph (6)(a), the words "in the case of an application made otherwise than by the patient". Article 6(1) and (2). In Article 7(1)(a)(i), the words "of the patient or" and the word "other".
S.I. 1994/429 (N.I. 2).	The Health and Personal Social Services (Northern Ireland) Order 1994.	In Schedule 1, the entries relating to the Access to Personal Files and Medical Reports (Northern Ireland) Order 1991.
S.I.	The Insurance Companies (Third	In Schedule 8, paragraph 8.

1994/1696.	Insurance Directives) Regulations 1994.	
S.I. 1995/755 (N.I. 2).	The Children (Northern Ireland) Order 1995.	In Schedule 9, paragraphs 177 and 191.
S.I. 1995/3275.	The Investment Services Regulations 1995.	In Schedule 10, paragraphs 3 and 15.
S.I. 1996/2827.	The Open-Ended Investment Companies (Investment Companies with Variable Capital) Regulations 1996.	In Schedule 8, paragraphs 3 and 26.

---

[1] In s. 1(1) in definition of "data" word repealed (1.1.2005) by 2000 c. 36, ss. 68(2)(a), 86, 87(3), Sch. 8 Pt. III (with ss. 56, 78); S.I. 2004/1909, art. 2; S.I. 2004/3122, art. 2

[2] In s. 1(1) in definition of "data" paragraph (e) and preceding word inserted (1.1.2005) by 2000 c. 36, ss. 68(2)(a), 87(3) (with ss. 56, 78); S.I. 2004/1909, art. 2; S.I. 2004/3122, art. 2

[3] In s. 1(1) definition of "public authority" inserted (1.1.2005) by 2000 c. 36, ss. 68(2)(b), 87(3) (with ss. 56, 78); S.I. 2004/1909, art. 2; S.I. 2004/3122, art. 2; and this same definition substituted (1.1.2005) by The Freedom of Information (Scotland) Act 2002 (Consequential Modifications) Order 2004 (S.I. 2004/3089), art. 2(2)(a)

[4] Words in s. 1(5) inserted (1.1.2005) by The Freedom of Information (Scotland) Act 2002 (Consequential Modifications) Order 2004 (S.I. 2004/3089), art. 2(2)(b)

[5] S. 1(6)(b) and preceding word inserted (1.1.2005) by The Freedom of Information (Scotland) Act 2002 (Consequential Modifications) Order 2004 (S.I. 2004/3089), art. 2(2)(c)

[6] S. 1(6)(b) and preceding word inserted (1.1.2005) by The Freedom of Information (Scotland) Act 2002 (Consequential Modifications) Order 2004 (S.I. 2004/3089), art. 2(2)(c)

[7] Words in s. 1(6) renumbered (1.1.2005) as s. 1(6)(a) by The Freedom of Information (Scotland) Act 2002 (Consequential Modifications) Order 2004 (S.I. 2004/3089), art. 2(2)(c)

[8] S. 1(5)(6) inserted (1.1.2005) by 2000 c. 36, ss. 68(3), 87(3) (with ss. 56, 78); S.I. 2004/1909, art. 2; S.I. 2004/3122, art. 2

[9] S. 6: words in heading omitted (18.1.2010) by virtue of The Transfer of Tribunal Functions Order 2010 (S.I. 2010/22), arts. 1(1), 5(1), Sch. 2 para. 25(a)

[10] S. 6(1) substituted (30.1.2001) by 2000 c. 36, ss. 18(4), 87(2)(c), Sch. 2 Pt. I para. 13(2) (with ss. 7(1)(7), 56, 78)

[11] S. 6(3)-(6) omitted (18.1.2010) by virtue of The Transfer of Tribunal Functions Order 2010 (S.I. 2010/22) , arts. 1(1), 5(1), Sch. 2 para. 25(b)

[12] Words in s. 6(7) omitted (18.1.2010) by virtue of The Transfer of Tribunal Functions Order 2010 (S.I. 2010/22), arts. 1(1), 5(1), Sch. 2 para. 25(c)

[13] Words in s. 7(1) substituted (30.11.2000 for certain purposes and otherwise 1.1.2005) by 2000 c. 36, ss. 69(1), 87(1)(3) (with ss. 7(1)(7), 56, 78); S.I. 2004/1909, art. 2; S.I. 2004/3122, art. 2

[14] S. 7(3) substituted (14.5.2001) by 2000 c. 36, s. 73, Sch. 6 para. 1 (with ss. 56, 78); S.I. 2001/1637, art. 2(d)

[15] Words in s. 7 substituted (19.8.2003) by The Secretary of State for Constitutional Affairs Order 2003 (S.I. 2003/1887), art. 9, Sch. 2 para. 9(1)(a)

[16] S. 7(12) inserted after s. 7(11) (1.3.2000) by virtue of S.I. 2000/414, art. 7(2)

[17] S. 7(12) inserted (1.3.2000) by S.I. 2000/415, art. 7(2)

[18] Words in s. 8 substituted (19.8.2003) by The Secretary of State for Constitutional Affairs Order 2003 (S.I. 2003/1887), art. 9, Sch. 2 para. 9(1)(a)

[19] Words in s. 9 substituted (19.8.2003) by The Secretary of State for Constitutional Affairs Order 2003 (S.I. 2003/1887), art. 9, Sch. 2 para. 9(1)(a)

[20] Words in s. 9A substituted (19.8.2003) by The Secretary of State for Constitutional Affairs Order 2003 (S.I. 2003/1887), art. 9, Sch. 2 paras. 9(1)(a), 12(1)(b)

[21] S. 9A inserted (30.11.2000 for certain purposes and otherwise 1.1.2005) by 2000 c. 36, ss. 69(2), 87(1)(3) (with ss. 56, 78); S.I. 2004/1909, art. 2; S.I. 2004/3122, art. 2 (s. 69(2) of the amending Act was itself amended (19.8.2003) by S.I. 2003/1887, art. 9, Sch. 2 para. 12(1)(b))

[22] Words in s. 10 substituted (19.8.2003) by The Secretary of State for Constitutional Affairs Order 2003 (S.I. 2003/1887), art. 9, Sch. 2 para. 9(1)(a)

[23] S. 11(2A) inserted (1.3.2000) by S.I. 1999/2093, reg. 3(3), Sch. 1 Pt. II para. 3

[24] Words in s. 12 substituted (19.8.2003) by The Secretary of State for Constitutional Affairs Order 2003 (S.I. 2003/1887), art. 9, Sch. 2 para. 9(1)(a)

[25] S. 12A inserted (temp. from 1.3.2000 to 23.10.2007) by 1998 c. 29, s. 72, Sch. 13 para. 1; S.I. 2000/183, art. 2(1)

[26] S. 16(1)(ff) inserted (1.1.2005) by 2000 c. 36, ss. 71, 87(3) (with ss. 56, 78); S.I. 2004/1909, art. 2; S.I. 2004/3122, art. 2

[27] S. 16(1)(h) and word inserted (1.2.2010) by Coroners and Justice Act 2009 (c. 25), ss. 175, 182, Sch. 20 para. 1(b) (with s. 180); S.I. 2010/145, art. 2(2), Sch. para. 24

[28] Words in s. 16 substituted (19.8.2003) by The Secretary of State for Constitutional Affairs Order 2003 (S.I. 2003/1887),

art. 9, Sch. 2 para. 9(1)(a)

[29] Words in s. 16 substituted (19.8.2003) by The Secretary of State for Constitutional Affairs Order 2003 (S.I. 2003/1887), art. 9, Sch. 2 para. 9(1)(a)

[30] Words in s. 17 substituted (19.8.2003) by The Secretary of State for Constitutional Affairs Order 2003 (S.I. 2003/1887), art. 9, Sch. 2 para. 9(1)(a)

[31] S. 18(5A) inserted (1.2.2010) by Coroners and Justice Act 2009 (c. 25), ss. 175, 182, Sch. 20 para. 2 (with s. 180); S.I. 2010/145, art. 2, Sch. para. 24

[32] S. 19(8) added (1.2.2010) by Coroners and Justice Act 2009 (c. 25), ss. 175, 182, Sch. 20 para. 3 (with s. 180); S.I. 2010/145, art. 2, Sch. para. 24

[33] Words in s. 22 substituted (19.8.2003) by The Secretary of State for Constitutional Affairs Order 2003 (S.I. 2003/1887), art. 9, Sch. 2 para. 9(1)(a)

[34] Words in s. 22 substituted (19.8.2003) by The Secretary of State for Constitutional Affairs Order 2003 (S.I. 2003/1887), art. 9, Sch. 2 para. 9(1)(a)

[35] Words in s. 23 substituted (19.8.2003) by The Secretary of State for Constitutional Affairs Order 2003 (S.I. 2003/1887), art. 9, Sch. 2 para. 9(1)(a)

[36] Words in s. 25 substituted (19.8.2003) by The Secretary of State for Constitutional Affairs Order 2003 (S.I. 2003/1887), art. 9, Sch. 2 para. 9(1)(a)

[37] Words in s. 25 substituted (19.8.2003) by The Secretary of State for Constitutional Affairs Order 2003 (S.I. 2003/1887), art. 9, Sch. 2 para. 9(1)(a)

[38] Words in s. 25 substituted (19.8.2003) by The Secretary of State for Constitutional Affairs Order 2003 (S.I. 2003/1887), art. 9, Sch. 2 para. 9(1)(a)

[39] Words in s. 25(4)(a) substituted (26.11.2001) by S.I. 2001/3500, art. 8, Sch. 2 Pt. I para. 6(2)

[40] Words in s. 26 substituted (19.8.2003) by The Secretary of State for Constitutional Affairs Order 2003 (S.I. 2003/1887) , art. 9, Sch. 2 para. 9(1)(a)

[41] S. 26(2)(a) and following word substituted (18.1.2010) by The Transfer of Tribunal Functions Order 2010 (S.I. 2010/22), arts. 1(1), 5(1), Sch. 2 para. 26

[42] Words in s. 28(1)(c) substituted (26.4.2004) by Crime (International Co-operation) Act 2003 (c. 32), ss. 91, 94, Sch. 5 para. 69; S.I. 2004/786, art. 3

[43] Words in s. 30 substituted (19.8.2003) by The Secretary of State for Constitutional Affairs Order 2003 (S.I. 2003/1887), art. 9 {Sch. 2 para. 9(1)(a)}

[44] Words in s. 30 substituted (19.8.2003) by The Secretary of State for Constitutional Affairs Order 2003 (S.I. 2003/1887), art. 9 {Sch. 2 para. 9(1)(a)}

[45] Words in s. 30 substituted (19.8.2003) by The Secretary of State for Constitutional Affairs Order 2003 (S.I. 2003/1887), art. 9 {Sch. 2 para. 9(1)(a)}

[46] Words in s. 30 substituted (19.8.2003) by The Secretary of State for Constitutional Affairs Order 2003 (S.I. 2003/1887), art. 9 {Sch. 2 para. 9(1)(a)}

[47] S. 30(5)(b)(i) repealed (S.) (31.12.2004) by 2000 asp 6, ss. 60(2), 61(2), Sch. 3; S.S.I. 2004/528, art. 2

[48] Words in s. 31(2)(b)(c)(d) inserted (1.7.2005) by Companies (Audit, Investigations and Community Enterprise) Act 2004 (c. 27), ss. 59(3)(a), 65; S.I. 2004/3322, art. 2(3), Sch. 3

[49] Words in s. 31(2)(b) inserted (1.7.2005) by Companies (Audit, Investigations and Community Enterprise) Act 2004 (c. 27), ss. 59(3)(b), 65; S.I. 2004/3322, art. 2(3), Sch. 3

[50] Words in s. 31(2)(b)(c)(d) inserted (1.7.2005) by Companies (Audit, Investigations and Community Enterprise) Act 2004 (c. 27), ss. 59(3)(a), 65; S.I. 2004/3322, art. 2(3), Sch. 3

[51] Words in s. 31(2)(b)(c)(d) inserted (1.7.2005) by Companies (Audit, Investigations and Community Enterprise) Act 2004 (c. 27), ss. 59(3)(a), 65; S.I. 2004/3322, art. 2(3), Sch. 3

[52] Word in s. 31(4)(a)(ii) inserted (14.7.2004) by The Scottish Public Services Ombudsman Act 2002 (Consequential Provisions and Modifications) Order 2004 (S.I. 2004/1823), art. 19(a)(i)

[53] Words in s. 31(4)(a)(ii) repealed (1.4.2006 for W) by Public Services Ombudsman (Wales) Act 2005 (c. 10), ss. 39, 40, Sch. 6 para. 60(a), Sch. 7; S.I. 2005/2800, art. 5

[54] Words in s. 31(4)(a)(ii) omitted (14.7.2004) by virtue of The Scottish Public Services Ombudsman Act 2002 (Consequential Provisions and Modifications) Order 2004 (S.I. 2004/1823), art. 19(a)(ii)

[55] Word in s. 31(4)(a)(iii) inserted (14.7.2004) by The Scottish Public Services Ombudsman Act 2002 (Consequential Provisions and Modifications) Order 2004 (S.I. 2004/1823), art. 19(b)(i)

[56] Words in s. 31(4)(a)(iii) repealed (1.4.2006 for W.) by Public Services Ombudsman (Wales) Act 2005 (c. 10), ss. 39, 40, Sch. 6 para. 60(b), Sch. 7; S.I. 2005/2800, art. 5

[57] Words in s. 31(4)(a)(iii) omitted (14.7.2004) by virtue of The Scottish Public Services Ombudsman Act 2002 (Consequential Provisions and Modifications) Order 2004 (S.I. 2004/1823), art. 19(b)(ii)

[58] S. 31(4)(a)(iv) substituted (1.4.2006 for W.) by Public Services Ombudsman (Wales) Act 2005 (c. 10), ss. 39, 40, Sch. 6 para. 60(c), Sch. 7; S.I. 2005/2800, art. 5

[59] Word in s. 31(4)(a)(v) omitted (14.7.2004) by virtue of The Scottish Public Services Ombudsman Act 2002 (Consequential Provisions and Modifications) Order 2004 (S.I. 2004/1823), art. 19(c)

[60] Word in s. 31(4)(a)(vi) substituted (14.7.2004) by The Scottish Public Services Ombudsman Act 2002 (Consequential Provisions and Modifications) Order 2004 (S.I. 2004/1823), art. 19(d)

[61] S. 31(4)(a)(vii) inserted (14.7.2004) by The Scottish Public Services Ombudsman Act 2002 (Consequential Provisions and Modifications) Order 2004 (S.I. 2004/1823), art. 19(e)

[62] S. 31(4A) inserted (1.12.2001) by 2000 c. 8, s. 233; S.I. 2001/3538, art. 2(1)

[63] S. 31(4B) inserted (1.1.2010) by Legal Services Act 2007 (c. 29), ss. 170, 211 (with ss. 29, 192, 193); S.I. 2009/3250, art. 2(e) (with art. 9)

[64] S. 31(4C) inserted (6.10.2010) by Legal Services Act 2007 (c. 29), ss. 153, 211 (with ss. 29, 192, 193); S.I. 2010/2089, art. 2(a)

[65] Words in s. 31(5)(a) substituted (1.4.2003) by Enterprise Act 2002 (c. 40), ss. 278(1), 279, Sch. 25 para. 37; S.I. 2003/766, art. 2, Sch. (with art. 3)

[66] S. 31(5A)(5B) inserted (8.1.2007) by The Enterprise Act 2002 (Amendment) Regulations 2006 (S.I. 2006/3363), reg. 29

[67] Words in s. 31(6) repealed (1.4.2007) by Education and Inspections Act 2006 (c. 40), ss. 157, 184, 188, Sch. 14 para. 32, Sch. 18 Pt. 5; S.I. 2007/935, art. 5(gg)(ii)

[68] S. 31(6) inserted (1.6.2004) by Health and Social Care (Community Health and Standards) Act 2003 (c. 43), ss. 119, 199; S.I. 2004/759, art. 8

[69] S. 31(7)(8) inserted (E.W.) (1.4.2008) by Local Government and Public Involvement in Health Act 2007 (c. 28), ss. 200, 245 (with s. 201); S.I. 2008/172, art. 4(k)

[70] Words in s. 32 substituted (19.8.2003) by The Secretary of State for Constitutional Affairs Order 2003 (S.I. 2003/1887), art. 9, Sch. 2 para. 9(1)(a)

[71] S. 33A inserted (1.1.2005) by 2000 c. 36, ss. 70(1), 87(3) (with ss. 56, 78); S.I. 2004/1909, art. 2; S.I. 2004/3122, art. 2

[72] Words in s. 34 inserted (30.11.2002) by 2000 c. 36, ss. 72, 87(3) (with ss. 56, 78); S.I. 2002/2812, art. 2

[73] S. 35A inserted (1.1.2005) by 2000 c. 36, ss. 73, 87(3), Sch. 6 para. 2 (with ss. 56, 78); S.I. 2004/1909, art. 2; S.I. 2004/3122, art. 2

[74] Words in s. 38 substituted (19.8.2003) by The Secretary of State for Constitutional Affairs Order 2003 (S.I. 2003/1887), art. 9, Sch. 2 para. 9(1)(a)

[75] Words in s. 38 substituted (19.8.2003) by The Secretary of State for Constitutional Affairs Order 2003 (S.I. 2003/1887), art. 9, Sch. 2 para. 9(1)(a)

[76] Ss. 41A-41C inserted (1.2.2010 as regards s. 41C and 6.4.2010 as regards ss. 41A, 41B) by Coroners and Justice Act 2009 (c. 25), ss. 173, 182 (with s. 180); S.I. 2010/145, art. 2, Sch. para. 15; S.I. 2010/816, art. 2, Sch. para. 12

[77] Words in s. 43(1) substituted 6.4.2010) by Coroners and Justice Act 2009 (c. 25), ss. 175, 182, Sch. 20 para. 8(2) (with s. 180); S.I. 2010/816, art. 2, Sch. para. 19

[78] S. 43(1A)(1B) inserted (6.4.2010) by Coroners and Justice Act 2009 (c. 25), ss. 175, 182, Sch. 20 para. 8(3) (with s. 180); S.I. 2010/816, art. 2, Sch. para. 19

[79] Words in s. 43(4) substituted (6.4.2010) by Coroners and Justice Act 2009 (c. 25), ss. 175, 182, Sch. 20 para. 8(4) (with s. 180); S.I. 2010/816, art. 2, Sch. para. 19

[80] Words in s. 43(8) substituted (6.4.2010) by Coroners and Justice Act 2009 (c. 25), ss. 175, 182, Sch. 20 para. 10(2) (with s. 180); S.I. 2010/816, art. 2, Sch. para. 19

[81] S. 43(8A)-(8C) inserted (6.4.2010) by Coroners and Justice Act 2009 (c. 25), ss. 175, 182, Sch. 20 para. 10(3) (with s. 180); S.I. 2010/816, art. 2, Sch. para. 19

[82] Ss. 41A-41C inserted (1.2.2010 as regards s. 41C and 6.4.2010 as regards ss. 41A, 41B) by Coroners and Justice Act 2009 (c. 25), ss. 173, 182 (with s. 180); S.I. 2010/145, art. 2, Sch. para. 15; S.I. 2010/816, art. 2, Sch. para. 12

[83] Words in s. 43(1) substituted 6.4.2010) by Coroners and Justice Act 2009 (c. 25), ss. 175, 182, Sch. 20 para. 8(2) (with s. 180); S.I. 2010/816, art. 2, Sch. para. 19

[84] S. 43(1A)(1B) inserted (6.4.2010) by Coroners and Justice Act 2009 (c. 25), ss. 175, 182, Sch. 20 para. 8(3) (with s. 180); S.I. 2010/816, art. 2, Sch. para. 19

[85] Words in s. 43(4) substituted (6.4.2010) by Coroners and Justice Act 2009 (c. 25), ss. 175, 182, Sch. 20 para. 8(4) (with s. 180); S.I. 2010/816, art. 2, Sch. para. 19

[86] Words in s. 43(8) substituted (6.4.2010) by Coroners and Justice Act 2009 (c. 25), ss. 175, 182, Sch. 20 para. 10(2) (with s. 180); S.I. 2010/816, art. 2, Sch. para. 19

[87] S. 43(8A)-(8C) inserted (6.4.2010) by Coroners and Justice Act 2009 (c. 25), ss. 175, 182, Sch. 20 para. 10(3) (with s. 180); S.I. 2010/816, art. 2, Sch. para. 19

[88] Words in s. 51 substituted (19.8.2003) by The Secretary of State for Constitutional Affairs Order 2003 (S.I. 2003/1887), art. 9, Sch. 2 para. 9(1)(a)

[89] S. 51(5A) inserted (1.2.2010) by Coroners and Justice Act 2009 (c. 25), ss. 174(2), 175, 182 (with s. 180); S.I. 2010/145, art. 2, Sch. para. 16

[90] Words in s. 51 substituted (19.8.2003) by The Secretary of State for Constitutional Affairs Order 2003 (S.I. 2003/1887), art. 9, Sch. 2 para. 9(1)(a)

[91] Words in s. 52 substituted (19.8.2003) by The Secretary of State for Constitutional Affairs Order 2003 (S.I. 2003/1887), art. 9, Sch. 2 para. 9(1)(a)

[92] Ss. 52A-52E inserted (1.2.2010) by Coroners and Justice Act 2009 (c. 25), ss. 174(1), 175, 182 (with s. 180); S.I. 2010/145,

art. 2, Sch. para. 16

[93] Words in s. 54 substituted (19.8.2003) by The Secretary of State for Constitutional Affairs Order 2003 (S.I. 2003/1887), art. 9, Sch. 2 para. 9(1)(a)

[94] Words in s. 54 substituted (19.8.2003) by The Secretary of State for Constitutional Affairs Order 2003 (S.I. 2003/1887), art. 9, Sch. 2 para. 9(1)(a)

[95] Words in s. 54 substituted (19.8.2003) by The Secretary of State for Constitutional Affairs Order 2003 (S.I. 2003/1887), art. 9, Sch. 2 para. 9(1)(a)

[96] Words in s. 54 substituted (19.8.2003) by The Secretary of State for Constitutional Affairs Order 2003 (S.I. 2003/1887), art. 9, Sch. 2 para. 9(1)(a)

[97] Words in s. 54 substituted (19.8.2003) by The Secretary of State for Constitutional Affairs Order 2003 (S.I. 2003/1887), art. 9, Sch. 2 para. 9(1)(a)

[98] Words in s. 54 substituted (19.8.2003) by The Secretary of State for Constitutional Affairs Order 2003 (S.I. 2003/1887), art. 9, Sch. 2 para. 9(1)(a)

[99] S. 54A inserted (26.4.2004) by Crime (International Co-operation) Act 2003 (c. 32), ss. 81, 94; S.I. 2004/786, art. 3

[100] Words in s. 55(8) inserted (1.1.2005) by 2000 c. 36, ss. 70(2), 87(3) (with ss. 56, 78); S.I. 2004/1909, art. 2; S.I. 2004/3122, art. 2

[101] Ss. 55A - 55E and cross-heading inserted (1.10.2009 for certain purposes and 1.4.2010 to the extent that it is not already in force) by Criminal Justice and Immigration Act 2008 (c. 4), ss. 144(1), 153; S.I. 2009/2606, art. 2(n); S.I. 2010/712, art. 4

[102] S. 55(3A) inserted (6.4.2010) by Coroners and Justice Act 2009 (c. 25), ss. 175, 182, Sch. 20 para. 13 (with s. 180); S.I. 2010/816, art. 2, Sch. para. 19

[103] S. 55A inserted (1.10.2009 for certain purposes and 6.4.2010 to the extent that it is not already in force) by Criminal Justice and Immigration Act 2008 (c. 4), ss. 144(1), 153; S.I. 2009/2606, art. 2(n); S.I. 2010/712, art. 4

[104] S. 55B inserted (1.10.2009 for certain purposes and 6.4.2010 to the extent that it is not already in force) by Criminal Justice and Immigration Act 2008 (c. 4), ss. 144(1), 153; S.I. 2009/2606, art. 2(n); S.I. 2010/712, art. 4

[105] S. 55C inserted (1.10.2009) by Criminal Justice and Immigration Act 2008 (c. 4), ss. 144(1), 153; S.I. 2009/2606, art. 2(n)

[106] S. 55D inserted (6.4.2010) by Criminal Justice and Immigration Act 2008 (c. 4), ss. 144(1), 153; S.I. 2010/712, art. 4

[107] S. 55E(2)(d) omitted (18.1.2010) by virtue of The Transfer of Tribunal Functions Order 2010 (S.I. 2010/22), arts. 1(1), 5(1), Sch. 2 para. 28(a)

[108] Words in s. 55E(2)(e) substituted (18.1.2010) by The Transfer of Tribunal Functions Order 2010 (S.I. 2010/22), arts. 1(1), 5(1), Sch. 2 para. 28(b)

[109] S. 55E(2)(f) omitted (18.1.2010) by virtue of The Transfer of Tribunal Functions Order 2010 (S.I. 2010/22), arts. 1(1), 5(1), Sch. 2 para. 28(c)

[110] S. 55E inserted (1.10.2009) by Criminal Justice and Immigration Act 2008 (c. 4), ss. 144(1), 153; S.I. 2009/2606, art. 2(n)

[111] S. 56(6) Table: para. (d) in first entry substituted (1.4.2005) for paras. (d)(e) by Serious Organised Crime and Police Act 2005 (c. 15), ss. 59, 178, Sch. 4 para. 112; S.I. 2006/378, art. 4, Sch.

[112] S. 56(6) Table: words in entry 2 substituted (25.8.2000) by 2000 c. 6, ss. 165, 168, Sch. 9 para. 191

[113] S. 56(6) Table: in entry relating to the Secretary of State para. (g) inserted (19.5.2008) by Safeguarding Vulnerable Groups Act 2006 (c. 47), ss. 63, 65, Sch. 9 para. 15(2)(a) (with ss. 51, 57(3), 60(4), 64(5)); S.I. 2008/1320, art. 3

[114] S. 56(6) Table: words inserted (N.I.) (29.5.2008) by The Safeguarding Vulnerable Groups (Northern Ireland) Order 2007 (S.I. 2007/1351 (N.I. 11)), art. 60, Sch. 7 para. 4(1) (with arts. 2(4), 53, 57(3), 61(4)); S.R. 2008/233, art. 3(c)

[115] Words in s. 56 substituted (12.11.2009) by Policing and Crime Act 2009 (c. 26), ss. 81(2)(3)(i), 116

[116] S. 56(6) Table: entry inserted (19.5.2008) by Safeguarding Vulnerable Groups Act 2006 (c. 47), ss. 63, 65, Sch. 9 para. 15(2)(b) (with ss. 51, 57(3), 60(4), 64(5)); S.I. 2008/1320, art. 3

[117] S. 56(6) Table: words inserted (N.I.) (29.5.2008) by The Safeguarding Vulnerable Groups (Northern Ireland) Order 2007 (S.I. 2007/1351 (N.I. 11)), art. 60, Sch. 7 para. 4(1) (with arts. 2(4), 53, 57(3), 61(4)); S.R. 2008/233, art. 3(c)

[118] S. 56(6A) inserted (1.1.2005) by 2000 c. 36, ss. 68(4), 87(3) (with ss. 56, 78); S.I. 2004/1909, art. 2; S.I. 2004/3122, art. 2

[119] Words in s. 56 substituted (19.8.2003) by The Secretary of State for Constitutional Affairs Order 2003 (S.I. 2003/1887), art. 9, Sch. 2 para. 9(1)(a

[120] Words in s. 58 inserted (30.11.2000) by 2000 c. 36, ss. 18(4), 87(1)(i), Sch. 2 Pt. II para. 18 (with ss. 7(1)(7), 56, 78)

[121] Words in s. 59(1)(a)(2)(b)(c)(i)(d) substituted (30.11.2000) by 2000 c. 36, ss. 18(4), 87(1)(i), Sch. 2 Pt. II para. 19(2) (with ss. 7(1)(7), 56, 78)

[122] Words in s. 59(1)(a)(2)(b)(c)(i)(d) substituted (30.11.2000) by 2000 c. 36, ss. 18(4), 87(1)(i), Sch. 2 Pt. II para. 19(2) (with ss. 7(1)(7), 56, 78)

[123] Words in s. 59(1)(a)(2)(b)(c)(i)(d) substituted (30.11.2000) by 2000 c. 36, ss. 18(4), 87(1)(i), Sch. 2 Pt. II para. 19(2) (with ss. 7(1)(7), 56, 78)

[124] Words in s. 59(1)(a)(2)(b)(c)(i)(d) substituted (30.11.2000) by 2000 c. 36, ss. 18(4), 87(1)(i), Sch. 2 Pt. II para. 19(2) (with ss. 7(1)(7), 56, 78)

[125] S. 59(4) inserted (30.11.2000) by 2000 c. 36, ss. 18(4), 87(1)(i), Sch. 2 Pt. II para. 19(3) (with ss. 7(1)(7), 56, 78)

[126] Words in s. 60(2)(3) inserted (26.4.2004) by Crime (International Co-operation) Act 2003 (c. 32), ss. 91, 94, Sch. 5 para. 70, S.I. 2004/786, {art. 3}

127 Words in s. 60(2)(3) inserted (26.4.2004) by Crime (International Co-operation) Act 2003 (c. 32), ss. 91, 94, Sch. 5 para. 70, S.I. 2004/786, {art. 3}
128 Words in s. 63(5) inserted (26.4.2004) by Crime (International Co-operation) Act 2003 (c. 32), ss. 91, 94, Sch. 5 para. 71; S.I. 2004/786, art. 3
129 S. 63A inserted (1.1.2005) by 2000 c. 36, ss. 73, 87(3), Sch. 6 para. 3 (with ss. 56, 78); S.I. 2004/1909, art. 2; S.I. 2004/3122, art. 2
130 Words in s. 64 substituted (19.8.2003) by The Secretary of State for Constitutional Affairs Order 2003 (S.I. 2003/1887), art. 9, Sch. 2 para. 9(1)(a)
131 Words in s. 67 substituted (19.8.2003) by The Secretary of State for Constitutional Affairs Order 2003 (S.I. 2003/1887), art. 9, Sch. 2 para. 9(1)(a)
132 Words in s. 67 substituted (19.8.2003) by The Secretary of State for Constitutional Affairs Order 2003 (S.I. 2003/1887), art. 9, Sch. 2 para. 9(1)(a)
133 Words in s. 67 substituted (19.8.2003) by The Secretary of State for Constitutional Affairs Order 2003 (S.I. 2003/1887), art. 9, Sch. 2 para. 9(1)(a)
134 Words in s. 67 substituted (19.8.2003) by The Secretary of State for Constitutional Affairs Order 2003 (S.I. 2003/1887), art. 9, Sch. 2 para. 9(1)(a)
135 Words in s. 67(4) inserted (6.4.2010) by Coroners and Justice Act 2009 (c. 25), ss. 175, 182, Sch. 20 para. 6(a) (with s. 180)); S.I. 2010/816, art. 2, Sch. para. 19
136 Words in s. 67(4) inserted (1.10.2009) by Criminal Justice and Immigration Act 2008 (c. 4), ss. 144(2)(a), 153; S.I. 2009/2606, art. 2(o)
137 Words in s. 67(5)(a) inserted (6.4.2010) by Coroners and Justice Act 2009 (c. 25), ss. 175, 182, Sch. 20 para. 6(b) (with s. 180); S.I. 2010/816, art. 2, Sch. para. 19
138 Words in s. 67(5)(c) substituted (30.11.2000 for certain purposes and otherwise 1.1.2005) by 2000 c. 36, ss. 69(3), 87(1)(3) (with ss. 56, 78); S.I. 2004/1909, art. 2; S.I. 2004/3122, art. 2
139 S. 67(5)(ca) inserted (1.10.2009) by Criminal Justice and Immigration Act 2008 (c. 4), ss. 144(2)(b), 153; S.I. 2009/2606, art. 2(o)
140 S. 69(1)(c) substituted by The Opticians Act 1989 (Amendment) Order 2005 (S.I. 2005/848), art. 28, Sch. 1 para. 12 (with art. 29, Sch. 2) (the amendment coming into force in accordance with art. 1(2)-(6))
141 S. 69(1)(d): words in definition of "health professional" substituted (27.9.2010) by The Pharmacy Order 2010 (S.I. 2010/231), arts. 1, 68, Sch. 4 para. 6; S.I. 2010/1621, art. 2(1), Sch.
142 S. 69(1)(e) substituted by The Nursing and Midwifery Order 2001 (S.I. 2002/253), art. 54(3), Sch. 5 para. 14 (with art. 3(18)) (the amendment coming into force in accordance with art. 1(2)(3) of the amending S.I.)
143 Words in s. 69(1)(h) substituted by The Health Professions Order 2001 (S.I. 2002/254), art. 48(3), Sch. 4 para. 7 (with art. 3(19)) (the amendment coming into force in accordance with art. 1(2)(3) of the amending S.I.)
144 Words in s. 69(1)(i) omitted (1.7.2009) by virtue of The Health Care and Associated Professions (Miscellaneous Amendments and Practitioner Psychologists) Order 2009 (S.I. 2009/1182, art. 4(2), Sch. 5 para. 4 (with arts. 9, 10); S.I. 2009/1357, art. 2(1)(d)
145 Words in s. 69(1)(i) substituted (9.7.2003) by The Health Professions Order 2001 (Consequential Amendments) Order 2003 (S.I. 2003/1590), art. 3, Sch. para. 1(a)
146 S. 69(1)(j) omitted (9.7.2003) by virtue of The Health Professions Order 2001 (Consequential Amendments) Order 2003 (S.I. 2003/1590), art. 3, Sch. para. 1(b)
147 Words in s. 69(3)(a) inserted (1.10.2002) by The National Health Service Reform and Health Care Professions Act 2002 (Supplementary, Consequential etc. Provisions) Regulations 2002 (S.I. 2002/2469), reg. 4, Sch. 1 para. 24
148 Words in s. 69(3)(a) substituted (1.3.2007) by National Health Service (Consequential Provisions) Act 2006 (c. 43), ss. 2, 8, Sch. 1 para. 191(a)
149 Words in s. 69(3)(b) substituted (1.3.2007) by National Health Service (Consequential Provisions) Act 2006 (c. 43), ss. 2, 8, Sch. 1 para. 191(b)
150 Words in s. 69(3)(bb) substituted (1.3.2007) by National Health Service (Consequential Provisions) Act 2006 (c. 43), ss. 2, 8, Sch. 1 para. 191(c)
151 S. 69(3)(bb) inserted (8.2.2000) by S.I. 2000/90, art. 3(1), Sch. 1 para. 33
152 Words in s. 69(3)(bbb) substituted (1.3.2007) by National Health Service (Consequential Provisions) Act 2006 (c. 43), ss. 2, 8, Sch. 1 para. 191(d)
153 S. 69(3)(bbb) inserted (10.10.2002 for W. and 1.3.2007 otherwise for E.W.) by National Health Service Reform and Health Care Professions Act 2002 (c. 17), ss. 6(2), 42(3), Sch. 5 para. 41; S.I. 2002/2532, art. 2, Sch.; S.I. 2006/1407, arts. 1, 2, Sch. 1 Pt. 2 para. 12
154 Words in s. 69(3)(f) inserted (1.3.2007) by National Health Service (Consequential Provisions) Act 2006 (c. 43), ss. 2, 8, Sch. 1 para. 191(e)
155 S. 69(3)(fa) inserted (1.4.2004) by Health and Social Care (Community Health and Standards) Act 2003 (c. 43), ss. 34, 199, Sch. 4 para. 107; S.I. 2004/759, art. 2
156 Words in s. 70(1) substituted (30.1.2001) by 2000 c. 36, ss. 18(4), 87(2)(c), Sch. 2 Pt. I para. 14(a) (with ss. 7(1)(7), 56, 78)
157 Words inserted (1.7.1999) in definition of "enactment" in s. 70(1) by S.I. 1999/1820, arts. 1(2), 4, Sch. 2 Pt. I para. 133;

S.I. 1999/3178, art. 3

[158] S. 70(1): the definition of "government department" substituted (6.4.2010) by Coroners and Justice Act 2009 (c. 25), ss. 175, 182, Sch. 20 para. 7 (with s. 180); S.I. 2010/816, art. 2, Sch. para. 19

[159] S. 70(1): definition of "the Tribunal" substituted (18.1.2010) by The Transfer of Tribunal Functions Order 2010 (S.I. 2010/22), arts. 1(1), 5(1), Sch. 2 para. 29

[160] S. 71 Table: entry inserted (1.1.2005) by 2000 c. 36, ss. 68(5), 87(3) (with ss. 56, 78); S.I. 2004/1909, art. 2; S.I. 2004/3122, art. 2

[161] Words in s. 75 substituted (19.8.2003) by The Secretary of State for Constitutional Affairs Order 2003 (S.I. 2003/1887), art. 9, Sch. 2 para. 9(1)(a)

[162] Words in s. 75(4A)(a) inserted (N.I.) (29.5.2008) by The Safeguarding Vulnerable Groups (Northern Ireland) Order 2007 (S.I. 2007/1351 (N.I. 11)), art. 60, Sch. 7 para. 4(2)(a); S.R. 2008/233, art. 3(c)

[163] Words in s. 75 substituted (12.11.2009) by Policing and Crime Act 2009 (c. 26), ss. 81(2)(3)(i), 116

[164] Words in s. 75(4A)(b) inserted (N.I.) (29.5.2008) by The Safeguarding Vulnerable Groups (Northern Ireland) Order 2007 (S.I. 2007/1351 (N.I. 11)), art. 60, Sch. 7 para. 4(2)(b); S.R. 2008/233, art. 3(c)

[165] S. 75(4A) inserted (19.5.2008) by Safeguarding Vulnerable Groups Act 2006 (c. 47), ss. 63, 65, Sch. 9 para. 15(3) (with ss. 51, 57(3), 60(4), 64(5)); S.I. 2008/1320, art. 3

[166] Words in Sch. 1 Pt. 2 para. 3 substituted (19.8.2003) by The Secretary of State for Constitutional Affairs Order 2003 (S.I. 2003/1887), art. 9, Sch. 2 para. 9(1)(b)

[167] Words in Sch. 1 Pt. 2 para. 4 substituted (19.8.2003) by The Secretary of State for Constitutional Affairs Order 2003 (S.I. 2003/1887), art. 9, Sch. 2 para. 9(1)(b)

[168] Words in Sch. 1 Pt. 2 para. 14 substituted (19.8.2003) by The Secretary of State for Constitutional Affairs Order 2003 (S.I. 2003/1887), art. 9, Sch. 2 para. 9(1)(b)

[169] Sch. 2 para. 5(aa) inserted (1.1.2005) by 2000 c. 36, ss. 73, 87(3), Sch. 6 para. 4 (with ss. 56, 78); S.I. 2004/1909, art. 2; S.I. 2004/3122, art. 2

[170] Words in Sch. 2 para. 6 substituted (19.8.2003) by The Secretary of State for Constitutional Affairs Order 2003 (S.I. 2003/1887), art. 9, Sch. 2 para. 9(1)(b)

[171] Words in Sch. 3 para. 2 substituted (19.8.2003) by The Secretary of State for Constitutional Affairs Order 2003 (S.I. 2003/1887), art. 9, Sch. 2 para. 9(1)(b)

[172] Sch. 3 para. 7(1)(aa) inserted (1.1.2005) by 2000 c. 36, ss. 73, 87(3), Sch. 6 para. 4 (with ss. 56, 78); S.I. 2004/1909, art. 2; S.I. 2004/3122, art. 2

[173] Words in Sch. 3 para. 7 substituted (19.8.2003) by The Secretary of State for Constitutional Affairs Order 2003 (S.I. 2003/1887), art. 9, Sch. 2 para. 9(1)(b)

[174] Sch. 3 para. 7A inserted (1.10.2008) by Serious Crime Act 2007 (c. 27), ss. 72, 94; S.I. 2008/2504, art. 2(e)

[175] Words in Sch. 3 para. 9 substituted (19.8.2003) by The Secretary of State for Constitutional Affairs Order 2003 (S.I. 2003/1887), art. 9, Sch. 2 para. 9(1)(b)

[176] Words in Sch. 3 para. 10 substituted (19.8.2003) by The Secretary of State for Constitutional Affairs Order 2003 (S.I. 2003/1887), art. 9, Sch. 2 para. 9(1)(b)

[177] Words in Sch. 4 para. 4 substituted (19.8.2003) by The Secretary of State for Constitutional Affairs Order 2003 (S.I. 2003/1887), art. 9, Sch. 2 para. 9(1)(b)

[178] Sch. 5: words in heading omitted (18.1.2010) by virtue of The Transfer of Tribunal Functions Order 2010 (S.I. 2010/22), arts. 1(1), 5(1), Sch. 2 para. 30(a)

[179] Words in Sch. 5 para. 1(2) substituted (30.1.2001) by 2000 c. 36, ss. 18(4), 87(2)(c), Sch. 2 Pt. I para. 15(2) (with ss. 7(1)(7), 56, 78)

[180] Words in Sch. 5 para. 4(1)(a) inserted (30.11.2000) by 2000 c. 36, ss. 18(4), 87(1)(i), Sch. 2 Pt. II para. 20(2) (with ss. 7(1)(7), 56, 78)

[181] Sch. 5 para. 4(1A) inserted (30.11.2000) by 2000 c. 36, ss. 18(4), 87(1)(i), Sch. 2 Pt. II para. 20(3) (with s. 7(1)(7), 56, 78)

[182] Words in Sch. 5 para. 4 substituted (19.8.2003) by The Secretary of State for Constitutional Affairs Order 2003 (S.I. 2003/1887), art. 9, Sch. 2 para. 9(1)(c)

[183] Words in Sch. 5 para. 5(1) inserted (30.11.2000) by 2000 c. 36, ss. 18(4), 87(1)(i), Sch. 2 Pt. II para. 21(2)(a) (with ss. 7(1)(7), 56, 78)

[184] Words in Sch. 5 para. 5(1) inserted (30.11.2000) by 2000 c. 36, ss. 18(4), 87(1)(i), Sch. 2 Pt. II para. 21(2)(b) (with ss. 7(1)(7), 56, 78)

[185] Words in Sch. 5 para. 5(2) inserted (30.11.2000) by 2000 c. 36, ss. 18(4), 87(1)(i), Sch. 2 Pt. II para. 21(3) (with ss. 7(1)(7), 56, 78)

[186] Words in Sch. 5 para. 8 substituted (19.8.2003) by The Secretary of State for Constitutional Affairs Order 2003 (S.I. 2003/1887), art. 9, Sch. 2 para. 9(1)(c)

[187] Words in Sch. 5 para. 9(1) substituted (30.11.2000) by 2000 c. 36, ss. 18(4), 87(1)(i), Sch. 2 Pt. II para. 22 (with ss. 7(1)(7), 56, 78)

[188] Words in Sch. 5 para. 9 substituted (19.8.2003) by The Secretary of State for Constitutional Affairs Order 2003 (S.I. 2003/1887), art. 9, Sch. 2 para. 9(1)(c)

[189] Words in Sch. 5 para. 9 substituted (19.8.2003) by The Secretary of State for Constitutional Affairs Order 2003 (S.I.

2003/1887), art. 9, Sch. 2 para. 9(1)(c)

190 Words in Sch. 5 para. 9 substituted (19.8.2003) by The Secretary of State for Constitutional Affairs Order 2003 (S.I. 2003/1887), art. 9, Sch. 2 para. 9(1)(c)

191 Words in Sch. 5 para. 10 substituted (19.8.2003) by The Secretary of State for Constitutional Affairs Order 2003 (S.I. 2003/1887), art. 9, Sch. 2 para. 9(1)(c)

192 Sch. 5 Pt. 2 omitted (18.1.2010) by virtue of The Transfer of Tribunal Functions Order 2010 (S.I. 2010/22), arts. 1(1), 5(1), Sch. 2 para. 30(b)

193 Sch. 5 Pt. III (ss. 16-17) repealed (30.1.2001) by 2000 c. 36, ss. 86, 87(3), Sch. 8 Pt. II (with ss. 56, 78) Sections 28(12), 48(5).

194 Sch. 6 paras. 1-6 omitted (18.1.2010) by virtue of The Transfer of Tribunal Functions Order 2010 (S.I. 2010/22), arts. 1(1), 5(1), Sch. 2 para. 31(a)

195 Sch. 6 paras. 1-6 omitted (18.1.2010) by virtue of The Transfer of Tribunal Functions Order 2010 (S.I. 2010/22), arts. 1(1), 5(1), Sch. 2 para. 31(a)

196 Sch. 6 paras. 1-6 omitted (18.1.2010) by virtue of The Transfer of Tribunal Functions Order 2010 (S.I. 2010/22), arts. 1(1), 5(1), Sch. 2 para. 31(a)

197 Sch. 6 paras. 1-6 omitted (18.1.2010) by virtue of The Transfer of Tribunal Functions Order 2010 (S.I. 2010/22), arts. 1(1), 5(1), Sch. 2 para. 31(a)

198 Sch. 6 paras. 1-6 omitted (18.1.2010) by virtue of The Transfer of Tribunal Functions Order 2010 (S.I. 2010/22), arts. 1(1), 5(1), Sch. 2 para. 31(a)

199 Sch. 6 paras. 1-6 omitted (18.1.2010) by virtue of The Transfer of Tribunal Functions Order 2010 (S.I. 2010/22), arts. 1(1), 5(1), Sch. 2 para. 31(a)

200 Sch. 6 para. 7: heading substituted (18.1.2010) by The Transfer of Tribunal Functions Order 2010 (S.I. 2010/22), arts. 1(1), 5(1), Sch. 2 para. 31(b)(i)

201 Sch. 6 para. 7(1)(2) substituted (18.1.2010) by The Transfer of Tribunal Functions Order 2010 (S.I. 2010/22), arts. 1(1), 5(1), Sch. 2 para. 31(b)(ii)

202 Sch. 6 para. 7(3) omitted (18.1.2010) by virtue of The Transfer of Tribunal Functions Order 2010 (S.I. 2010/22), arts. 1(1), 5(1), Sch. 2 para. 31(b)(iii)

203 Words in Sch. 7 para. 3(b) inserted (14.5.2001) by 2000 c. 36, s. 73, Sch. 6 para. 6 (with ss. 56, 78); S.I. 2001/1637, art. 2(d)

204 Sch. 7 para. 4 renumbered as Sch. 7 para. 4(1) (2.12.1999) by 1998 c. 47, s. 99, Sch. 13 para. 21(1) (with s. 95); S.I. 1999/3209, art. 2, Sch.

205 Words in Sch. 7 para. 4 substituted (19.8.2003) by The Secretary of State for Constitutional Affairs Order 2003 (S.I. 2003/1887), art. 9, Sch. 2 para. 9(1)(e)

206 Words in Sch. 7 para. 4 substituted (2.12.1999) by 1998 c. 47, s. 99, Sch. 13 para. 21(1) (with s. 95); S.I. 1999/3209, art. 2, Sch.

207 Sch. 7 para. 4(2) inserted (as renumbered) (2.12.1999) by 1998 c. 47, s. 99, Sch. 13 para. 21(2) (with s. 95); S.I. 1999/3209, art. 2, Sch.

208 Words in Sch. 7 para. 6 substituted (19.8.2003) by The Secretary of State for Constitutional Affairs Order 2003 S.I. 2003/1887), art. 9, {Sch. 2 para. 9(1)(e)}

209 Sch. 7 para. 6(3): words in definition of "instrument" substituted (1.4.2007 for certain purposes and 1.11.2007 in so far as not already in force) by The Financial Services and Markets Act 2000 (Markets in Financial Instruments) Regulations 2007 (S.I. 2007/126), art. 3(6), Sch. 6 para. 12

210 Sch. 7 para. 6(3): words in definition of "instrument" omitted (3.7.2002) by virtue of The Financial Services and Markets Act 2000 (Consequential Amendments) Order 2002 (S.I. 2002/1555), art. 25(2)

211 Sch. 7 para. 6(3): in definition of "relevant person" paragraphs (a)-(cc) substituted (3.7.2002) for (a)-(c) by The Financial Services and Markets Act 2000 (Consequential Amendments) Order 2002 (S.I. 2002/1555), art. 25(3)

212 Words in Sch. 7 para. 10 substituted (14.5.2001) by 2000 c. 36, s. 73, Sch. 6 para. 7 (with ss. 56, 78); S.I. 2001/1637, art. 2(d)

213 Words in Sch. 7 para. 11(1) substituted (6.4.2010) by Coroners and Justice Act 2009 (c. 25), ss. 175, 182, Sch. 20 para. 12(2) (with s. 180); S.I. 2010/816, art. 2, Sch. para. 19

214 Sch. 7 para. 11(1A) inserted (6.4.2010) by Coroners and Justice Act 2009 (c. 25), ss. 175, 182, Sch. 20 para. 12(3) (with s. 180); S.I. 2010/816, art. 2, Sch. para. 19

215 Sch. 8 Pt. III para. 14A inserted (1.1.2005) by 2000 c. 36, ss. 70(3), 87(3) (with ss. 56, 78); S.I. 2004/1909, art. 2; S.I. 2004/3122, art. 2

216 Words in Sch. 9 para. 1(1) inserted (1.4.2005) by Courts Act 2003 (c. 39), ss. 65, 110, Sch. 4 para. 8; S.I. 2005/910, art. 3(u)

217 Sch. 9 para. 1(1A)(1B) inserted (6.4.2010) by Coroners and Justice Act 2009 (c. 25), ss. 175, 182, Sch. 20 para. 14(2) (with s. 180 Sch. 22 para. 46); S.I. 2010/816, art. 2, Sch. para. 19

218 Words in Sch. 9 para. 1(3) substituted (6.4.2010) by Coroners and Justice Act 2009 (c. 25), ss. 175, 182, Sch. 20 para. 14(3)(a) (with s. 180); S.I. 2010/816, art. 2, Sch. para. 19

219 Words in Sch. 9 para. 1(3) substituted (6.4.2010) by Coroners and Justice Act 2009 (c. 25), ss. 175, 182, Sch. 20 para.

14(3)(b) (with s. 180); S.I. 2010/816, art. 2, Sch. para. 19

[220] Sch. 9 para. 2(1A) inserted (6.4.2010) by Coroners and Justice Act 2009 (c. 25), ss. 175, 182, Sch. 20 para. 14(4) (with s. 180); S.I. 2010/816, art. 2, Sch. para. 19

[221] Words in Sch. 9 para. 5 substituted (6.4.2010) by Coroners and Justice Act 2009 (c. 25), ss. 175, 182, Sch. 20 para. 14(5) (with s. 180); S.I. 2010/816, art. 2, Sch. para. 19

[222] Word in Sch. 9 para. 12 repealed (6.4.2010) by Coroners and Justice Act 2009 (c. 25), ss. 178, 182, Sch. 23 Pt. 8 (with s. 180); S.I. 2010/816, art. 2, Sch. para. 22

[223] Sch. 9 para. 12(c)(d) inserted (6.4.2010) by Coroners and Justice Act 2009 (c. 25), ss. 175, 182, Sch. 20 para. 14(6) (with s. 180); S.I. 2010/816, art. 2, Sch. para. 19

[224] Sch. 9 para. 16 and cross-heading inserted (6.4.2010) by Coroners and Justice Act 2009 (c. 25), ss. 175, 182, Sch. 20 para. 14(7) (with s. 180); S.I. 2010/816, art. 2, Sch. para. 19

[225] Words in Sch. 11 para. 3 substituted (5.5.2010) by The Local Education Authorities and Children's Services Authorities (Integration of Functions) Order 2010 (S.I. 2010/1158), arts. 1, 5(1), Sch. 2 para. 42(2)

[226] Words in Sch. 11 para. 4 substituted (5.5.2010) by The Local Education Authorities and Children's Services Authorities (Integration of Functions) Order 2010 (S.I. 2010/1158), arts. 1, 5(1), Sch. 2 para. 42(2)

[227] Words in Sch. 11 para. 4 substituted (5.5.2010) by The Local Education Authorities and Children's Services Authorities (Integration of Functions) Order 2010 (S.I. 2010/1158), arts. 1, 5(1), Sch. 2 para. 42(2)

[228] Sch. 11 para. 4A inserted (5.5.2010) by The Local Education Authorities and Children's Services Authorities (Integration of Functions) Order 2010 (S.I. 2010/1158), arts. 1, 5(1), Sch. 2 para. 42(3)

[229] Words in Sch. 11 para. 6(a) repealed (S.) (31.12.2004) by 2000 asp 6, ss. 60(2), 61(2), Sch. 3; S.S.I. 2004/528, art. 2

[230] Words in Sch. 13 para. 1 inserted (1.1.2005) by 2000 c. 36, ss. 70(4), 87(3) (with ss. 56, 78); S.I. 2004/1909, art. 2; S.I. 2004/3122, art. 2

[231] Words in Sch. 14 para. 2(1) repealed (30.11.2000) by 2000 c. 36, ss. 73, 86, 87(1)(k)(l), Sch. 6 para. 8, Sch. 8 Pt. I (with ss. 56, 78)

[232] Sch. 15 para. 1(1) repealed (30.1.2001) by 2000 c. 36, ss. 86, 87(2)(d), Sch. 8 Pt. II (with ss. 56, 78)

[233] Sch. 15 para. 1(2)(3) repealed (1.1.2005) by 2000 c. 36, ss. 86, 87(3), Sch. 8 Pt. III (with ss. 56, 78); S.I. 2004/3122, art. 2

[234] Sch. 15 para. 2 repealed (30.1.2001) by 2000 c. 36, ss. 86, 87(2)(d), Sch. 8 Pt. II (with ss. 56, 78)

[235] Sch. 15 para. 3 repealed (1.1.2005) by 2000 c. 36, ss. 86, 87(3), Sch. 8 Pt. III (with ss. 56, 78); S.I. 2004/3122, art. 2

[236] Sch. 15 para. 4 repealed (30.1.2001) by 2000 c. 36, ss. 86, 87(2)(d), Sch. 8 Pt. II (with ss. 56, 78)

[237] Sch. 15 para. 5(1) repealed (1.1.2005) by 2000 c. 36, ss. 86, 87(3), Sch. 8 Pt. III (with ss. 56, 78); S.I. 2004/3122, art. 2

[238] Sch. 15 para. 5(2) repealed (30.1.2001) by 2000 c. 36, ss. 86, 87(2)(d), Sch. 8 Pt. II (with ss. 56, 78)

[239] Sch. 15 para. 6(1) repealed (1.1.2005) by 2000 c. 36, ss. 86, 87(3), Sch. 8 Pt. III (with ss. 56, 78); S.I. 2004/3122, art. 2

[240] Sch. 15 para. 6(2) repealed (30.1.2001) by 2000 c. 36, ss. 86, 87(2)(d), Sch. 8 Pt. II (with ss. 56, 78)

[241] Sch. 15 para. 9 repealed (6.4.2007) by Violent Crime Reduction Act 2006 (c. 38), ss. 65, 66(2), Sch. 5; S.I. 2007/858, {art. (m)(n)(vii)}

Human Rights Act 1998

1998 CHAPTER 42

An Act to give further effect to rights and freedoms guaranteed under the European Convention on Human Rights; to make provision with respect to holders of certain judicial offices who become judges of the European Court of Human Rights; and for connected purposes.

[9th November 1998]

Introduction

1 The Convention Rights.

(1) In this Act "the Convention rights" means the rights and fundamental freedoms set out in—

(a) articles 2 to 12 and 14 of the Convention,

(b) articles 1 to 3 of the First Protocol, and

(c)[Article 1 of the Thirteenth Protocol][1],

as read with Articles 16 to 18 of the Convention.

(2) Those Articles are to have effect for the purposes of this Act subject to any designated derogation or reservation (as to which see sections 14 and 15).

(3) The Articles are set out in Schedule 1.

(4) The [Secretary of State][2] may by order make such amendments to this Act as he considers appropriate to reflect the effect, in relation to the United Kingdom, of a protocol.

(5) In subsection (4) "protocol" means a protocol to the Convention—

(a) which the United Kingdom has ratified; or

(b) which the United Kingdom has signed with a view to ratification.

(6) No amendment may be made by an order under subsection (4) so as to come into force before the protocol concerned is in force in relation to the United Kingdom.

2 Interpretation of Convention rights.

(1) A court or tribunal determining a question which has arisen in connection with a Convention right must take into account any—

(a) judgment, decision, declaration or advisory opinion of the European Court of Human Rights,

(b) opinion of the Commission given in a report adopted under Article 31 of the Convention,

(c) decision of the Commission in connection with Article 26 or 27(2) of the Convention, or

(d) decision of the Committee of Ministers taken under Article 46 of the Convention,

whenever made or given, so far as, in the opinion of the court or tribunal, it is relevant to the proceedings in which that question has arisen.

(2) Evidence of any judgment, decision, declaration or opinion of which account may have to be taken under this section is to be given in proceedings before any court or tribunal in such manner as may be provided by rules.

(3) In this section "rules" means rules of court or, in the case of proceedings before a tribunal, rules made for the purposes of this section—

(a) by...[3][the Lord Chancellor or][4] the Secretary of State, in relation to any proceedings outside Scotland;

(b) by the Secretary of State, in relation to proceedings in Scotland; or

(c) by a Northern Ireland department, in relation to proceedings before a tribunal in Northern Ireland—

(i) which deals with transferred matters; and

(ii) for which no rules made under paragraph (a) are in force.

Legislation

3 Interpretation of legislation.

(1) So far as it is possible to do so, primary legislation and subordinate legislation must be read and given effect in a way which is compatible with the Convention rights.

(2) This section—

(a) applies to primary legislation and subordinate legislation whenever enacted;

(b) does not affect the validity, continuing operation or enforcement of any incompatible primary legislation; and

(c) does not affect the validity, continuing operation or enforcement of any incompatible subordinate legislation if (disregarding any possibility of revocation) primary legislation prevents removal of the incompatibility.

4 Declaration of incompatibility.

(1) Subsection (2) applies in any proceedings in which a court determines whether a provision of primary legislation is compatible with a Convention right.

(2) If the court is satisfied that the provision is incompatible with a Convention right, it may make a declaration of that incompatibility.

(3) Subsection (4) applies in any proceedings in which a court determines whether a provision of subordinate legislation, made in the exercise of a power conferred by primary legislation, is compatible with a Convention right.

(4) If the court is satisfied—

(a) that the provision is incompatible with a Convention right, and

(b) that (disregarding any possibility of revocation) the primary legislation concerned prevents removal of the incompatibility,

it may make a declaration of that incompatibility.

(5) In this section "court" means—

[(a) the Supreme Court;][5]

(b) the Judicial Committee of the Privy Council;

(c) the [Court Martial Appeal Court][6] ;

(d) in Scotland, the High Court of Justiciary sitting otherwise than as a trial court or the Court of Session;

(e) in England and Wales or Northern Ireland, the High Court or the Court of Appeal.

[(f) the Court of Protection, in any matter being dealt with by the President of the Family Division, the Vice-Chancellor or a puisne judge of the High Court.][7]

(6) A declaration under this section ("a declaration of incompatibility")—

(a) does not affect the validity, continuing operation or enforcement of the provision in respect of which it is given; and

(b) is not binding on the parties to the proceedings in which it is made.

5 Right of Crown to intervene.

(1) Where a court is considering whether to make a declaration of incompatibility, the Crown is entitled to notice in accordance with rules of court.

(2) In any case to which subsection (1) applies—

(a) a Minister of the Crown (or a person nominated by him),

(b) a member of the Scottish Executive,

(c) a Northern Ireland Minister,

(d) a Northern Ireland department,

is entitled, on giving notice in accordance with rules of court, to be joined as a party to the proceedings.

(3) Notice under subsection (2) may be given at any time during the proceedings.

(4) A person who has been made a party to criminal proceedings (other than in Scotland) as the result of a notice under subsection (2) may, with leave, appeal to the [Supreme Court][8] against any declaration of incompatibility made in the proceedings.

(5) In subsection (4)—

"criminal proceedings" includes all proceedings before the [Court Martial Appeal Court][9]; and

"leave" means leave granted by the court making the declaration of incompatibility or by the [Supreme Court][10]

Public authorities

6 Acts of public authorities.

(1) It is unlawful for a public authority to act in a way which is incompatible with a Convention right.

(2) Subsection (1) does not apply to an act if—

(a) as the result of one or more provisions of primary legislation, the authority could not have acted differently; or

(b) in the case of one or more provisions of, or made under, primary legislation which cannot be read or given effect in a way which is compatible with the Convention rights, the authority was acting so as to give effect to or enforce those provisions.

(3) In this section "public authority" includes—

(a) a court or tribunal, and

(b) any person certain of whose functions are functions of a public nature,

but does not include either House of Parliament or a person exercising functions in connection with proceedings in Parliament.

(4)..............................[11]

(5) In relation to a particular act, a person is not a public authority by virtue only of subsection (3)(b) if the nature of the act is private.

(6) "An act" includes a failure to act but does not include a failure to—

(a) introduce in, or lay before, Parliament a proposal for legislation; or

(b) make any primary legislation or remedial order.

7 Proceedings.

(1) A person who claims that a public authority has acted (or proposes to act) in a way which is made unlawful by section 6(1) may—

(a) bring proceedings against the authority under this Act in the appropriate court or tribunal, or

(b) rely on the Convention right or rights concerned in any legal proceedings,

but only if he is (or would be) a victim of the unlawful act.

(2) In subsection (1)(a) "appropriate court or tribunal" means such court or tribunal as may be determined in accordance with rules; and proceedings against an authority include a counterclaim

or similar proceeding.

(3) If the proceedings are brought on an application for judicial review, the applicant is to be taken to have a sufficient interest in relation to the unlawful act only if he is, or would be, a victim of that act.

(4) If the proceedings are made by way of a petition for judicial review in Scotland, the applicant shall be taken to have title and interest to sue in relation to the unlawful act only if he is, or would be, a victim of that act.

(5) Proceedings under subsection (1)(a) must be brought before the end of—

(a) the period of one year beginning with the date on which the act complained of took place; or

(b) such longer period as the court or tribunal considers equitable having regard to all the circumstances,

but that is subject to any rule imposing a stricter time limit in relation to the procedure in question.

(6) In subsection (1)(b) "legal proceedings" includes—

(a) proceedings brought by or at the instigation of a public authority; and

(b) an appeal against the decision of a court or tribunal.

(7) For the purposes of this section, a person is a victim of an unlawful act only if he would be a victim for the purposes of Article 34 of the Convention if proceedings were brought in the European Court of Human Rights in respect of that act.

(8) Nothing in this Act creates a criminal offence.

(9) In this section "rules" means—

(a) in relation to proceedings before a court or tribunal outside Scotland, rules made by...[12][the Lord Chancellor or][13] the Secretary of State for the purposes of this section or rules of court,

(b) in relation to proceedings before a court or tribunal in Scotland, rules made by the Secretary of State for those purposes,

(c) in relation to proceedings before a tribunal in Northern Ireland—

(i) which deals with transferred matters; and

(ii) for which no rules made under paragraph (a) are in force,

rules made by a Northern Ireland department for those purposes,

and includes provision made by order under section 1 of the Courts and Legal Services Act 1990.

(10) In making rules, regard must be had to section 9.

(11) The Minister who has power to make rules in relation to a particular tribunal may, to the extent he considers it necessary to ensure that the tribunal can provide an appropriate remedy in relation to an act (or proposed act) of a public authority which is (or would be) unlawful as a result of section 6(1), by order add to—

(a) the relief or remedies which the tribunal may grant; or

(b) the grounds on which it may grant any of them.

(12) An order made under subsection (11) may contain such incidental, supplemental, consequential or transitional provision as the Minister making it considers appropriate.

(13) "The Minister" includes the Northern Ireland department concerned.

8 Judicial remedies.

(1) In relation to any act (or proposed act) of a public authority which the court finds is (or would be) unlawful, it may grant such relief or remedy, or make such order, within its powers as it considers just and appropriate.

(2) But damages may be awarded only by a court which has power to award damages, or to order the payment of compensation, in civil proceedings.

(3) No award of damages is to be made unless, taking account of all the circumstances of the case, including—

(a) any other relief or remedy granted, or order made, in relation to the act in question (by that or any other court), and

(b) the consequences of any decision (of that or any other court) in respect of that act,

the court is satisfied that the award is necessary to afford just satisfaction to the person in whose favour it is made.

(4) In determining—

(a) whether to award damages, or

(b) the amount of an award,

the court must take into account the principles applied by the European Court of Human Rights in relation to the award of compensation under Article 41 of the Convention.

(5) A public authority against which damages are awarded is to be treated—

(a) in Scotland, for the purposes of section 3 of the Law Reform (Miscellaneous Provisions) (Scotland) Act 1940 as if the award were made in an action of damages in which the authority has been found liable in respect of loss or damage to the person to whom the award is made;

(b) for the purposes of the Civil Liability (Contribution) Act 1978 as liable in respect of damage suffered by the person to whom the award is made.

(6) In this section—

"court" includes a tribunal;

"damages" means damages for an unlawful act of a public authority; and

9 Judicial acts.

(1) Proceedings under section 7(1)(a) in respect of a judicial act may be brought only—

(a) by exercising a right of appeal;

(b) on an application (in Scotland a petition) for judicial review; or

(c) in such other forum as may be prescribed by rules.

(2) That does not affect any rule of law which prevents a court from being the subject of judicial review.

(3) In proceedings under this Act in respect of a judicial act done in good faith, damages may not be awarded otherwise than to compensate a person to the extent required by Article 5(5) of the Convention.

(4) an award of damages permitted by subsection (3) is to be made against the Crown; but no award may be made unless the appropriate person, if not a party to the proceedings, is joined.

(5) In this section—

"appropriate person" means the Minister responsible for the court concerned, or a person or government department nominated by him;

"court" includes a tribunal;

"judge" includes a member of a tribunal, a justice of the peace [(or, in Northern Ireland, a lay magistrate)][14] and a clerk or other officer entitled to exercise the jurisdiction of a court;

"judicial act" means a judicial act of a court and includes an act done on the instructions, or on behalf, of a judge; and

"rules" has the same meaning as in section 7(9).

Remedial action

10 Power to take remedial action.

(1) This section applies if—

(a) a provision of legislation has been declared under section 4 to be incompatible with a Convention right and, if an appeal lies—

(i) all persons who may appeal have stated in writing that they do not intend to do so;

(ii) the time for bringing an appeal has expired and no appeal has been brought within that time; or

(iii) an appeal brought within that time has been determined or abandoned; or

(b) it appears to a Minister of the Crown or Her Majesty in Council that, having regard to a finding of the European Court of Human Rights made after the coming into force of this section in proceedings against the United Kingdom, a provision of legislation is incompatible with an obligation of the United Kingdom arising from the Convention.

(2) If a Minister of the Crown considers that there are compelling reasons for proceeding under this section, he may by order make such amendments to the legislation as he considers necessary to remove the incompatibility.

(3) If, in the case of subordinate legislation, a Minister of the Crown considers—

(a) that it is necessary to amend the primary legislation under which the subordinate legislation in question was made, in order to enable the incompatibility to be removed, and

(b) that there are compelling reasons for proceeding under this section,

he may by order make such amendments to the primary legislation as he considers necessary.

(4) This section also applies where the provision in question is in subordinate legislation and has been quashed, or declared invalid, by reason of incompatibility with a Convention right and the Minister

proposes to proceed under paragraph 2(b) of Schedule 2.

(5) If the legislation is an Order in Council, the power conferred by subsection (2) or (3) is exercisable by Her Majesty in Council.

(6) In this section "legislation" does not include a Measure of the Church Assembly or of the General Synod of the Church of England.

(7) Schedule 2 makes further provision about remedial orders.

Other rights and proceedings

11 Safeguard for existing human rights.

A person's reliance on a Convention right does not restrict—

(a) any other right or freedom conferred on him by or under any law having effect in any part of the United Kingdom; or

(b) his right to make any claim or bring any proceedings which he could make or bring apart from sections 7 to 9.

12 Freedom of expression.

(1) This section applies if a court is considering whether to grant any relief which, if granted, might affect the exercise of the Convention right to freedom of expression.

(2) If the person against whom the application for relief is made ("the respondent") is neither present nor represented, no such relief is to be granted unless the court is satisfied—

(a) that the applicant has taken all practicable steps to notify the respondent; or

(b) that there are compelling reasons why the respondent should not be notified.

(3) No such relief is to be granted so as to restrain publication before trial unless the court is satisfied that the applicant is likely to establish that publication should not be allowed.

(4) The court must have particular regard to the importance of the Convention right to freedom of expression and, where the proceedings relate to material which the respondent claims, or which appears to the court, to be journalistic, literary or artistic material (or to conduct connected with such material), to—

(a) the extent to which—

(i) the material has, or is about to, become available to the public; or

(ii) it is, or would be, in the public interest for the material to be published;

(b) any relevant privacy code.

(5) In this section—

"court" includes a tribunal; and

"relief" includes any remedy or order (other than in criminal proceedings).

13 Freedom of thought, conscience and religion.

(1) If a court's determination of any question arising under this Act might affect the exercise by a religious organisation (itself or its members collectively) of the Convention right to freedom of thought, conscience and religion, it must have particular regard to the importance of that right.

(2) In this section "court" includes a tribunal.

Derogations and reservations

14 Derogations.

(1) In this Act "designated derogation" means—

.................................[15]

any derogation by the United Kingdom from an Article of the Convention, or of any protocol to the Convention, which is designated for the purposes of this Act in an order made by the [Secretary of State][16]

(2)..................................[17]

(3) If a designated derogation is amended or replaced it ceases to be a designated derogation.

(4) but subsection (3) does not prevent the [Secretary of State][18] from exercising his power under subsection (1)...[19] to make a fresh designation order in respect of the Article concerned.

(5) The [Secretary of State][20] must by order make such amendments to Schedule 3 as he considers appropriate to reflect—

(a) any designation order; or

(b) the effect of subsection (3).

(6) A designation order may be made in anticipation of the making by the United Kingdom of a proposed derogation.

15 Reservations.

(1) In this Act "designated reservation" means—

(a) the United Kingdom's reservation to Article 2 of the First Protocol to the Convention; and

(b) any other reservation by the United Kingdom to an Article of the Convention, or of any protocol to the Convention, which is designated for the purposes of this Act in an order made by the [Secretary of State][21] .

(2) The text of the reservation referred to in subsection (1)(a) is set out in Part II of Schedule 3.

(3) If a designated reservation is withdrawn wholly or in part it ceases to be a designated reservation.

(4) But subsection (3) does not prevent the [Secretary of State][22] from exercising his power under subsection (1)(b) to make a fresh designation order in respect of the Article concerned.

(5)[Secretary of State][23] must by order make such amendments to this Act as he considers appropriate to reflect—

(a) any designation order; or

(b) the effect of subsection (3).

16 Period for which designated derogations have effect.

(1) If it has not already been withdrawn by the United Kingdom, a designated derogation ceases to have effect for the purposes of this Act—

...............................[24]

. . ., at the end of the period of five years beginning with the date on which the order designating it was made.

(2) At any time before the period—

(a) fixed by subsection (1). . .[25], or

(b) extended by an order under this subsection,

comes to an end, the [Secretary of State][26] may by order extend it by a further period of five years.

(3) An order under section 14(1) . . . [27] ceases to have effect at the end of the period for consideration, unless a resolution has been passed by each House approving the order.

(4) Subsection (3) does not affect—

(a) anything done in reliance on the order; or

(b) the power to make a fresh order under section 14(1) . . ..

(5) In subsection (3) "period for consideration" means the period of forty days beginning with the day on which the order was made.

(6) In calculating the period for consideration, no account is to be taken of any time during which—

(a) Parliament is dissolved or prorogued; or

(b) both Houses are adjourned for more than four days.

(7) If a designated derogation is withdrawn by the United Kingdom, the [Secretary of State][28] must by order make such amendments to this Act as he considers are required to reflect that withdrawal.

17 Periodic review of designated reservations.

(1) The appropriate Minister must review the designated reservation referred to in section 15(1)(a)—

(a) before the end of the period of five years beginning with the date on which section 1(2) came into force; and

(b) if that designation is still in force, before the end of the period of five years beginning with the date on which the last report relating to it was laid under subsection (3).

(2) The appropriate Minister must review each of the other designated reservations (if any)—

(a) before the end of the period of five years beginning with the date on which the order designating the reservation first came into force; and

(b) if the designation is still in force, before the end of the period of five years beginning with the date on which the last report relating to it was laid under subsection (3).

(3) The Minister conducting a review under this section must prepare a report on the result of the review and lay a copy of it before each House of Parliament.

Judges of the European Court of Human Rights

18 Appointment to European Court of Human Rights.

(1) In this section "judicial office" means the office of—

(a) Lord Justice of Appeal, Justice of the High Court or Circuit judge, in England and Wales;

(b) judge of the Court of Session or sheriff, in Scotland;

(c) Lord Justice of Appeal, judge of the High Court or county court judge, in Northern Ireland.

(2) The holder of a judicial office may become a judge of the European Court of Human Rights ("the Court") without being required to relinquish his office.

(3) But he is not required to perform the duties of his judicial office while he is a judge of the Court.

(4) In respect of any period during which he is a judge of the Court—

(a) a Lord Justice of Appeal or Justice of the High Court is not to count as a judge of the relevant court for the purposes of section 2(1) or 4(1) of the [Senior Courts Act 1981][29] (maximum number of judges) nor as a judge of the [Senior Courts][30] for the purposes of section 12(1) to (6) of that Act (salaries etc.);

(b) a judge of the Court of Session is not to count as a judge of that court for the purposes of section 1(1) of the Court of Session Act 1988 (maximum number of judges) or of section 9(1)(c) of the Administration of Justice Act 1973 ("the 1973 Act") (salaries etc.);

(c) a Lord Justice of Appeal or judge of the High Court in Northern Ireland is not to count as a judge of the relevant court for the purposes of section 2(1) or 3(1) of the Judicature (Northern Ireland) Act 1978 (maximum number of judges) nor as a judge of the [Court of Judicature][31] of Northern Ireland for the purposes of section 9(1)(d) of the 1973 Act (salaries etc.);

(d) a Circuit judge is not to count as such for the purposes of section 18 of the Courts Act 1971 (salaries etc.);

(e) a sheriff is not to count as such for the purposes of section 14 of the Sheriff Courts (Scotland) Act 1907 (salaries etc.);

(f) a county court judge of Northern Ireland is not to count as such for the purposes of section 106 of the County Courts Act Northern Ireland) 1959 (salaries etc.).

(5) If a sheriff principal is appointed a judge of the Court, section 11(1) of the Sheriff Courts (Scotland) Act 1971 (temporary appointment of sheriff principal) applies, while he holds that appointment, as if his office is vacant.

(6) Schedule 4 makes provision about judicial pensions in relation to the holder of a judicial office who serves as a judge of the Court.

(7) The Lord Chancellor or the Secretary of State may by order make such transitional provision (including, in particular, provision for a temporary increase in the maximum number of judges) as he considers appropriate in relation to any holder of a judicial office who has completed his service as a judge of the Court.

[(7A) The following paragraphs apply to the making of an order under subsection (7) in relation to any holder of a judicial office listed in subsection (1)(a)—

(a) before deciding what transitional provision it is appropriate to make, the person making the order must consult the Lord Chief Justice of England and Wales;

(b) before making the order, that person must consult the Lord Chief Justice of England and Wales.

(7B) The following paragraphs apply to the making of an order under subsection (7) in relation to any holder of a judicial office listed in subsection (1)(c)—

(a) before deciding what transitional provision it is appropriate to make, the person making the order must consult the Lord Chief Justice of Northern Ireland;

(b) before making the order, that person must consult the Lord Chief Justice of Northern Ireland.

(7C) The Lord Chief Justice of England and Wales may nominate a judicial office holder (within the meaning of section 109(4) of the Constitutional Reform Act 2005) to exercise his functions under this section.

(7D) The Lord Chief Justice of Northern Ireland may nominate any of the following to exercise his functions under this section—

(a) the holder of one of the offices listed in Schedule 1 to the Justice (Northern Ireland) Act 2002;

(b) a Lord Justice of Appeal (as defined in section 88 of that Act).][32]

Supplemental

20 Orders etc. under this Act.

(1) Any power of a Minister of the Crown to make an order under this Act is exercisable by statutory instrument.

(2) The power of... [33] [the Lord Chancellor or][34] the Secretary of State to make rules (other than rules of court) under section 2(3) or 7(9) is exercisable by statutory instrument.

(3) Any statutory instrument made under section 14, 15 or 16(7) must be laid before Parliament.

(4) No order may be made by ...[35][the Lord Chancellor or][36] the Secretary of State under section 1(4), 7(11) or 16(2) unless a draft of the order has been laid before, and approved by, each House of Parliament.

(5) Any statutory instrument made under section 18(7) or Schedule 4, or to which subsection (2) applies, shall be subject to annulment in pursuance of a resolution of either House of Parliament.

(6) The power of a Northern Ireland department to make—

(a) rules under section 2(3)(c) or 7(9)(c), or

(b) an order under section 7(11),

is exercisable by statutory rule for the purposes of the Statutory Rules (Northern Ireland) Order 1979.

(7) Any rules made under section 2(3)(c) or 7(9)(c) shall be subject to negative resolution; and section 41(6) of the Interpretation Act Northern Ireland) 1954 (meaning of "subject to negative resolution") shall apply as if the power to make the rules were conferred by an Act of the Northern Ireland Assembly.

(8) No order may be made by a Northern Ireland department under section 7(11) unless a draft of the order has been laid before, and approved by, the Northern Ireland Assembly.

21 Interpretation, etc.

(1) In this Act—

"amend" includes repeal and apply (with or without modifications);

"the appropriate Minister" means the Minister of the Crown having charge of the appropriate authorised government department (within the meaning of the Crown Proceedings Act 1947);

"the Commission" means the European Commission of Human Rights;

"the Convention" means the Convention for the Protection of Human Rights and Fundamental Freedoms, agreed by the Council of Europe at Rome on 4th November 1950 as it has effect for the time being in relation to the United Kingdom;

"declaration of incompatibility" means a declaration under section 4;

"Minister of the Crown" has the same meaning as in the Ministers of the Crown Act 1975;

"Northern Ireland Minister" includes the First Minister and the deputy First Minister in Northern Ireland;

"primary legislation" means any—

(a) public general Act;

(b) local and personal Act;

(c) private Act;

(d) Measure of the Church Assembly;

(e) Measure of the General Synod of the Church of England;

(f) Order in Council—

(i) made in exercise of Her Majesty's Royal Prerogative;

(ii) made under section 38(1)(a) of the Northern Ireland Constitution Act 1973 or the corresponding provision of the Northern Ireland Act 1998; or

(iii) amending an Act of a kind mentioned in paragraph (a), (b) or (c);

and includes an order or other instrument made under primary legislation (otherwise than by the [Welsh Ministers, the First Minister for Wales, the Counsel General to the Welsh Assembly Government,][37] a member of the Scottish Executive, a Northern Ireland Minister or a Northern Ireland department) to the extent to which it operates to bring one or more provisions of that legislation into force or amends any primary legislation;

"the First Protocol" means the protocol to the Convention agreed at Paris on 20th March 1952;

...[38]

"the Eleventh Protocol" means the protocol to the Convention (restructuring the control machinery established by the Convention) agreed at Strasbourg on 11th May 1994;

["the Thirteenth Protocol" means the protocol to the Convention (concerning the abolition of the death penalty in all circumstances) agreed at Vilnius on 3rd May 2002;][39]

"remedial order" means an order under section 10;

"subordinate legislation" means any—

(a) Order in Council other than one—

(i) made in exercise of Her Majesty's Royal Prerogative;

(ii) made under section 38(1)(a) of the Northern Ireland Constitution Act 1973 or the corresponding provision of the Northern Ireland Act 1998; or

(iii) amending an Act of a kind mentioned in the definition of primary legislation;

(b) act of the Scottish Parliament;

(ba)[Measure of the National Assembly for Wales;

(bb) act of the National Assembly for Wales;][40]

(c) act of the Parliament of Northern Ireland;

(d) Measure of the Assembly established under section 1 of the Northern Ireland Assembly Act 1973;

(e) act of the Northern Ireland Assembly;

(f) order, rules, regulations, scheme, warrant, byelaw or other instrument made under primary legislation (except to the extent to which it operates to bring one or more provisions of that legislation into force or amends any primary legislation);

(g) order, rules, regulations, scheme, warrant, byelaw or other instrument made under legislation mentioned in paragraph (b), (c), (d) or (e) or made under an Order in Council applying only to Northern Ireland;

(h) order, rules, regulations, scheme, warrant, byelaw or other instrument made by a member of the Scottish Executive [, Welsh Ministers, the First Minister for Wales, the Counsel General to the Welsh Assembly Government,][41] a Northern Ireland Minister or a Northern Ireland department in exercise of prerogative or other executive functions of Her Majesty which are exercisable by such a person on behalf of Her Majesty;

"transferred matters" has the same meaning as in the Northern Ireland Act 1998; and

"tribunal" means any tribunal in which legal proceedings may be brought.

(2) The references in paragraphs (b) and (c) of section 2(1) to Articles are to Articles of the Convention as they had effect immediately before the coming into force of the Eleventh Protocol.

(3) The reference in paragraph (d) of section 2(1) to Article 46 includes a reference to Articles 32 and 54 of the Convention as they had effect immediately before the coming into force of the Eleventh Protocol.

(4) The references in section 2(1) to a report or decision of the Commission or a decision of the Committee of Ministers include references to a report or decision made as provided by paragraphs 3, 4 and 6 of Article 5 of the Eleventh Protocol (transitional provisions).

(5)................................[42]

22 Short title, commencement, application and extent.

(1) This Act may be cited as the Human Rights Act 1998.

(2) Sections 18, 20 and 21(5) and this section come into force on the passing of this Act.

(3) The other provisions of this Act come into force on such day as the Secretary of State may by order appoint; and different days may be appointed for different purposes.

(4) Paragraph (b) of subsection (1) of section 7 applies to proceedings brought by or at the instigation of a public authority whenever the act in question took place; but otherwise that subsection does not apply to an act taking place before the coming into force of that section.

(5) This Act binds the Crown.

(6) This Act extends to Northern Ireland.

(7)................................[43]

Section 1(3).

SCHEDULE 1 The Articles

PART I The Convention Rights and Freedoms

Article 2 Right to life

1 Everyone's right to life shall be protected by law. No one shall be deprived of his life intentionally save in the execution of a sentence of a court following his conviction of a crime for which this penalty is provided by law.

2 Deprivation of life shall not be regarded as inflicted in contravention of this Article when it results from the use of force which is no more than absolutely necessary:

(a) in defence of any person from unlawful violence;

(b) in order to effect a lawful arrest or to prevent the escape of a person lawfully detained;

(c) in action lawfully taken for the purpose of quelling a riot or insurrection.

Article 3 Prohibition of torture

No one shall be subjected to torture or to inhuman or degrading treatment or punishment.

Article 4 Prohibition of slavery and forced labour

1 No one shall be held in slavery or servitude.

2 No one shall be required to perform forced or compulsory labour.

3 For the purpose of this Article the term "forced or compulsory labour" shall not include:

(a) any work required to be done in the ordinary course of detention imposed according to the provisions of Article 5 of this Convention or during conditional release from such detention;

(b) any service of a military character or, in case of conscientious objectors in countries where they are recognised, service exacted instead of compulsory military service;

(c) any service exacted in case of an emergency or calamity threatening the life or well-being of the community;

(d) any work or service which forms part of normal civic obligations.

Article 5 Right to liberty and security

1 Everyone has the right to liberty and security of person. No one shall be deprived of his liberty save in the following cases and in accordance with a procedure prescribed by law:

(a) the lawful detention of a person after conviction by a competent court;

(b) the lawful arrest or detention of a person for non-compliance with the lawful order of a court or in order to secure the fulfilment of any obligation prescribed by law;

(c) the lawful arrest or detention of a person effected for the purpose of bringing him before the competent legal authority on reasonable suspicion of having committed an offence or when it is reasonably considered necessary to prevent his committing an offence or fleeing after having done so;

(d) the detention of a minor by lawful order for the purpose of educational supervision or his lawful detention for the purpose of bringing him before the competent legal authority;

(e) the lawful detention of persons for the prevention of the spreading of infectious diseases, of persons of unsound mind, alcoholics or drug addicts or vagrants;

(f) the lawful arrest or detention of a person to prevent his effecting an unauthorised entry into the country or of a person against whom action is being taken with a view to deportation or extradition.

2 Everyone who is arrested shall be informed promptly, in a language which he understands, of the reasons for his arrest and of any charge against him.

3 Everyone arrested or detained in accordance with the provisions of paragraph 1(c) of this Article shall be brought promptly before a judge or other officer authorised by law to exercise judicial power and shall be entitled to trial within a reasonable time or to release pending trial. Release may be conditioned by guarantees to appear for trial.

4 Everyone who is deprived of his liberty by arrest or detention shall be entitled to take proceedings by which the lawfulness of his detention shall be decided speedily by a court and his release ordered if the detention is not lawful.

5 Everyone who has been the victim of arrest or detention in contravention of the provisions of this Article shall have an enforceable right to compensation.

Article 6 Right to a fair trial

1 In the determination of his civil rights and obligations or of any criminal charge against him, everyone is entitled to a fair and public hearing within a reasonable time by an independent and impartial tribunal established by law. Judgment shall be pronounced publicly but the press and public may be excluded from all or part of the trial in the interest of morals, public order or national security in a democratic society, where the interests of juveniles or the protection of the private life of the parties so require, or to the extent strictly necessary in the opinion of the court in special circumstances where publicity would prejudice the interests of justice.

2 Everyone charged with a criminal offence shall be presumed innocent until proved guilty according to law.

3 Everyone charged with a criminal offence has the following minimum rights:

(a) to be informed promptly, in a language which he understands and in detail, of the nature and cause of the accusation against him;

(b) to have adequate time and facilities for the preparation of his defence;

(c) to defend himself in person or through legal assistance of his own choosing or, if he has not sufficient means to pay for legal assistance, to be given it free when the interests of justice so require;

(d) to examine or have examined witnesses against him and to obtain the attendance and examination of witnesses on his behalf under the same conditions as witnesses against him;

(e) to have the free assistance of an interpreter if he cannot understand or speak the language used in court.

Article 7 No punishment without law

1 No one shall be held guilty of any criminal offence on account of any act or omission which did not constitute a criminal offence under national or international law at the time when it was committed. Nor shall a heavier penalty be imposed than the one that was applicable at the time the criminal offence was committed.

2 This Article shall not prejudice the trial and punishment of any person for any act or omission which, at the time when it was committed, was criminal according to the general principles of law recognised by civilised nations.

Article 8 Right to respect for private and family life

1 Everyone has the right to respect for his private and family life, his home and his correspondence.

2 There shall be no interference by a public authority with the exercise of this right except such as is in accordance with the law and is necessary in a democratic society in the interests of national security, public safety or the economic well-being of the country, for the prevention of disorder or crime, for the protection of health or morals, or for the protection of the rights and freedoms of others.

Article 9 Freedom of thought, conscience and religion

1 Everyone has the right to freedom of thought, conscience and religion; this right includes freedom to change his religion or belief and freedom, either alone or in community with others and in public or private, to manifest his religion or belief, in worship, teaching, practice and observance.

2 Freedom to manifest one's religion or beliefs shall be subject only to such limitations as are prescribed by law and are necessary in a democratic society in the interests of public safety, for the protection of public order, health or morals, or for the protection of the rights and freedoms of others.

Article 10 Freedom of expression

1 Everyone has the right to freedom of expression. This right shall include freedom to hold opinions and to receive and impart information and ideas without interference by public authority and regardless of frontiers. This Article shall not prevent States from requiring the licensing of broadcasting, television or cinema enterprises.

2 The exercise of these freedoms, since it carries with it duties and responsibilities, may be subject to such formalities, conditions, restrictions or penalties as are prescribed by law and are necessary in a democratic society, in the interests of national security, territorial integrity or public safety, for the prevention of disorder or crime, for the protection of health or morals, for the protection of the reputation or rights of others, for preventing the disclosure of information received in confidence, or for maintaining the authority and impartiality of the judiciary.

Article 11 Freedom of assembly and association

1 Everyone has the right to freedom of peaceful assembly and to freedom of association with others, including the right to form and to join trade unions for the protection of his interests.

2 No restrictions shall be placed on the exercise of these rights other than such as are prescribed by law and are necessary in a democratic society in the interests of national security or public safety, for the prevention of disorder or crime, for the protection of health or morals or for the protection of the rights and freedoms of others. This Article shall not prevent the imposition of lawful restrictions on the exercise of these rights by members of the armed forces, of the police or of the administration of the State.

Article 12 Right to marry

Men and women of marriageable age have the right to marry and to found a family, according to the national laws governing the exercise of this right.

Article 14 Prohibition of discrimination

The enjoyment of the rights and freedoms set forth in this Convention shall be secured without discrimination on any ground such as sex, race, colour, language, religion, political or other opinion, national or social origin, association with a national minority, property, birth or other status.

Article 16 Restrictions on political activity of aliens

Nothing in Articles 10, 11 and 14 shall be regarded as preventing the High Contracting Parties from imposing restrictions on the political activity of aliens.

Article 17 Prohibition of abuse of rights

Nothing in this Convention may be interpreted as implying for any State, group or person any right to engage in any activity or perform any act aimed at the destruction of any of the rights and freedoms set forth herein or at their limitation to a greater extent than is provided for in the Convention.

Article 18 Limitation on use of restrictions on rights

The restrictions permitted under this Convention to the said rights and freedoms shall not be applied for any purpose other than those for which they have been prescribed.

Part II The First Protocol

Article 1 Protection of property

Every natural or legal person is entitled to the peaceful enjoyment of his possessions. No one shall be deprived of his possessions except in the public interest and subject to the conditions provided for by law and by the general principles of international law.

The preceding provisions shall not, however, in any way impair the right of a State to enforce such laws as it deems necessary to control the use of property in accordance with the general interest or to secure the payment of taxes or other contributions or penalties.

Article 2 Right to education

No person shall be denied the right to education. In the exercise of any functions which it assumes in relation to education and to teaching, the State shall respect the right of parents to ensure such education and teaching in conformity with their own religious and philosophical convictions.

Article 3 Right to free elections

The High Contracting Parties undertake to hold free elections at reasonable intervals by secret ballot, under conditions which will ensure the free expression of the opinion of the people in the choice of the legislature.

[PART 3 ARTICLE 1 OF THE THIRTEENTH PROTOCOLAbolition of the death penalty

The death penalty shall be abolished. No one shall be condemned to such penalty or executed.][44]

Part III The Sixth Protocol

. . . .

Section 10.

SCHEDULE 2 Remedial Orders

Orders

1(1) A remedial order may—

(a) contain such incidental, supplemental, consequential or transitional provision as the person making it considers appropriate;

(b) be made so as to have effect from a date earlier than that on which it is made;

(c) make provision for the delegation of specific functions;

(d) make different provision for different cases.

(2) The power conferred by sub-paragraph (1)(a) includes—

(a) power to amend primary legislation (including primary legislation other than that which contains the incompatible provision); and

(b) power to amend or revoke subordinate legislation (including subordinate legislation other than that which contains the incompatible provision).

(3) A remedial order may be made so as to have the same extent as the legislation which it affects.

(4) No person is to be guilty of an offence solely as a result of the retrospective effect of a remedial order.

Procedure

2 No remedial order may be made unless—

(a) a draft of the order has been approved by a resolution of each House of Parliament made after the end of the period of 60 days beginning with the day on which the draft was laid; or

(b) it is declared in the order that it appears to the person making it that, because of the urgency of the matter, it is necessary to make the order without a draft being so approved.

Orders laid in draft

3(1) No draft may be laid under paragraph 2(a) unless—

(a) the person proposing to make the order has laid before Parliament a document which contains a draft of the proposed order and the required information; and

(b) the period of 60 days, beginning with the day on which the document required by this sub-paragraph was laid, has ended.

(2) If representations have been made during that period, the draft laid under paragraph 2(a) must be accompanied by a statement containing—

(a) a summary of the representations; and

(b) if, as a result of the representations, the proposed order has been changed, details of the changes.

Urgent cases

4(1) If a remedial order ("the original order") is made without being approved in draft, the person making it must lay it before Parliament, accompanied by the required information, after it is made.

(2) If representations have been made during the period of 60 days beginning with the day on which the original order was made, the person making it must (after the end of that period) lay before Parliament a statement containing—

(a) a summary of the representations; and

(b) if, as a result of the representations, he considers it appropriate to make changes to the original order, details of the changes.

(3) If sub-paragraph (2)(b) applies, the person making the statement must—

(a) make a further remedial order replacing the original order; and

(b) lay the replacement order before Parliament.

(4) If, at the end of the period of 120 days beginning with the day on which the original order was made, a resolution has not been passed by each House approving the original or replacement order, the order ceases to have effect (but without that affecting anything previously done under either order or the power to make a fresh remedial order).

Definitions

5 In this Schedule—

"representations" means representations about a remedial order (or proposed remedial order) made to the person making (or proposing to make) it and includes any relevant Parliamentary report or resolution; and

"required information" means—

(a) an explanation of the incompatibility which the order (or proposed order) seeks to remove, including particulars of the relevant declaration, finding or order; and

(b) a statement of the reasons for proceeding under section 10 and for making an order in those terms.

Calculating periods

6 In calculating any period for the purposes of this Schedule, no account is to be taken of any time during which—

(a) Parliament is dissolved or prorogued; or

(b) both Houses are adjourned for more than four days.

[7(1) This paragraph applies in relation to–

(a) any remedial order made, and any draft of such an order proposed to be made,–

(i) by the Scottish Ministers; or

(ii) within devolved competence (within the meaning of the Scotland Act 1998) by Her Majesty in Council; and

(b) any document or statement to be laid in connection with such an order (or proposed order).

(2) This Schedule has effect in relation to any such order (or proposed order), document or statement subject to the following modifications.

(3) Any reference to Parliament, each House of Parliament or both Houses of Parliament shall be construed as a reference to the Scottish Parliament.

(4) Paragraph 6 does not apply and instead, in calculating any period for the purposes of this Schedule, no account is to be taken of any time during which the Scottish Parliament is dissolved or is in recess for more than four days.][45]

Sections 14 and 15.

SCHEDULE 3 Derogation and Reservation

Part I[46]

....

PART I DEROGATION[47]

....

Part II Reservation

At the time of signing the present (First) Protocol, I declare that, in view of certain provisions of the Education Acts in the United Kingdom, the principle affirmed in the second sentence of Article 2 is accepted by the United Kingdom only so far as it is compatible with the provision of efficient instruction and training, and the avoidance of unreasonable public expenditure.

Dated 20 March 1952

Made by the United Kingdom Permanent Representative to the Council of Europe.

Section 18(6).

SCHEDULE 4 Judicial Pensions

Duty to make orders about pensions

1(1) The appropriate Minister must by order make provision with respect to pensions payable to or in respect of any holder of a judicial office who serves as an ECHR judge.

(2) A pensions order must include such provision as the Minister making it considers is necessary to secure that—

(a) an ECHR judge who was, immediately before his appointment as an ECHR judge, a member of a judicial pension scheme is entitled to remain as a member of that scheme;

(b) the terms on which he remains a member of the scheme are those which would have been applicable had he not been appointed as an ECHR judge; and

(c) entitlement to benefits payable in accordance with the scheme continues to be determined as if, while serving as an ECHR judge, his salary was that which would (but for section 18(4)) have been payable to him in respect of his continuing service as the holder of his judicial office.

Contributions

2 A pensions order may, in particular, make provision—

(a) for any contributions which are payable by a person who remains a member of a scheme as a result of the order, and which would otherwise be payable by deduction from his salary, to be made otherwise than by deduction from his salary as an ECHR judge; and

(b) for such contributions to be collected in such manner as may be determined by the administrators of the scheme.

Amendments of other enactments

3 A pensions order may amend any provision of, or made under, a pensions Act in such manner and to such extent as the Minister making the order considers necessary or expedient to ensure the proper administration of any scheme to which it relates.

Definitions

4 In this Schedule—

"appropriate Minister" means—

(a) in relation to any judicial office whose jurisdiction is exercisable exclusively in relation to Scotland, the Secretary of State; and

(b) otherwise, the Lord Chancellor;

"ECHR judge" means the holder of a judicial office who is serving as a judge of the Court;

"judicial pension scheme" means a scheme established by and in accordance with a pensions Act;

"pensions Act" means—

(a) the County Courts Act Northern Ireland) 1959;

(b) the Sheriffs' Pensions (Scotland) Act 1961;

(c) the Judicial Pensions Act 1981; or

(d) the Judicial Pensions and Retirement Act 1993; and

"pensions order" means an order made under paragraph 1.

---

1 Words in s. 1(1)(c) substituted (22.6.2004) by The Human Rights Act 1998 (Amendment) Order 2004 (S. I. 2004/1574), art. 2(1)

2 Words in s. 1 substituted (19.8.2003) by The Secretary of State for Constitutional Affairs Order 2003 (S. I. 2003/1887), art. 9, Sch. 2 para. 10(1)

3 Words in s. 2(3)(a) repealed (19.8.2003) by The Secretary of State for Constitutional Affairs Order 2003 (S. I. 2003/1887), art. 9, Sch. 2 para. 10(2)

4 Words in s. 2(3)(a) inserted (12.1.2006) by The Transfer of Functions (Lord Chancellor and Secretary of State) Order 2005 (S.I. 2005/3429), art. 8, Sch. para. 3

5 S. 4(5)(a) substituted (1.10.2009) by Constitutional Reform Act 2005 (c. 4), ss. 40, 148, Sch. 9 para. 66(2); S.I. 2009/1604, art. 2(d)

6 Words in s. 4(5)(c) substituted (28.3.2009 for certain purposes and 31.10.2009 otherwise) by Armed Forces Act 2006 (c. 52), ss. 378, 383, Sch. 16 para. 156; S.I. 2009/812, art. 3 (with transitional provisions in S.I. 2009/1059); S.I. 2009/1167, art. 4

7 S. 4(5)(f) inserted (1.10.2007) by Mental Capacity Act 2005 (c. 9), ss. 67(1), 68(1)-(3), Sch. 6 para. 43 (with ss. 27, 28, 29, 62); S.I. 2007/1897, art. 2(1)(c)(d)

8 Words in s. 5(4) substituted (1.10.2009) by Constitutional Reform Act 2005 (c. 4), ss. 40, 148, Sch. 9 para. 66(3); S.I. 2009/1604, art. 2(d)

9 Words in s. 5(5) substituted (28.3.2009 for certain purposes and 31.10.2009 otherwise) by Armed Forces Act 2006 (c. 52), ss. 378, 383, Sch. 16 para. 157; S.I. 2009/812, art. 3 (with transitional provisions in S.I. 2009/1059); S.I. 2009/1167, art. 4

10 Words in s. 5(5) substituted (1.10.2009) by Constitutional Reform Act 2005 (c. 4), ss. 40, 148, Sch. 9 para. 66(3); S.I. 2009/1604, art. 2(d)

11 S. 6(4) repealed (1.10.2009) by Constitutional Reform Act 2005 (c. 4), ss. 40, 146, 148, Sch. 9 para. 66(4), Sch. 18 Pt. 5; S.I. 2009/1604, art. 2(d)(f)

12 Words in s. 7(9)(a) repealed (19.8.2003) by The Secretary of State for Constitutional Affairs Order 2003 (S. I. 2003/1887), art. 9, Sch. 2 para. 10(2)

13 Words in s. 7(9)(a) inserted (12.1.2006) by The Transfer of Functions (Lord Chancellor and Secretary of State) Order 2005 (S.I. 2005/3429), art. 8, Sch. para. 3,

14 Words in definition s. 9(5) inserted (N.I.)(1.4.2005) by 2002 c. 26, s. 10(6), Sch. 4 para. 39; S.R. 2005/109, art. 2 Sch.

15 S. 14(1): from "(a) " to "(b) " repealed (1.4.2001) by S.I. 2001/1216, art. 2(a)

16 Words in s. 14 substituted (19.8.2003) by The Secretary of State for Constitutional Affairs Order 2003 (S. I. 2003/1887), art. 9, Sch. 2 para. 10(1)

17 S. 14(2) repealed (1.4.2001) by S.I. 2001/1216, art. 2(b)

18 Words in s. 14 substituted (19.8.2003) by The Secretary of State for Constitutional Affairs Order 2003 (S. I. 2003/1887), art. 9, Sch. 2 para. 10(1)

19 S. 14(4): "(b) " repealed (1.4.2001) by S.I. 2001/1216, art. 2(c)

20 Words in s. 14 substituted (19.8.2003) by The Secretary of State for Constitutional Affairs Order 2003 (S. I. 2003/1887), art. 9, Sch. 2 para. 10(1)

21 Words in s. 15 substituted (19.8.2003) by The Secretary of State for Constitutional Affairs Order 2003 (S. I. 2003/1887), art. 9, Sch. 2 para. 10(1)

[22] Words in s. 15 substituted (19.8.2003) by The Secretary of State for Constitutional Affairs Order 2003 (S. I. 2003/1887), art. 9, Sch. 2 para. 10(1)

[23] Words in s. 15 substituted (19.8.2003) by The Secretary of State for Constitutional Affairs Order 2003 (S. I. 2003/1887), art. 9, Sch. 2 para. 10(1)

[24] S. 16(1): words from "(a) " to "any other derogation" repealed (1.4.2001) by S.I. 2001/1216, art. 3(a)

[25] Words in s. 16(2)(a) repealed (1.4.2001) by S.I. 2001/1216, art. 3(b)

[26] Words in s. 16 substituted (19.8.2003) by The Secretary of State for Constitutional Affairs Order 2003 (S. I. 2003/1887), art. 9, Sch. 2 para. 10(1)

[27] S. 16(3)(4)(b): "(b) " repealed (1.4.2001) by S.I. 2001/1216, art. 3(c)(d)

[28] Words in s. 16 substituted (19.8.2003) by The Secretary of State for Constitutional Affairs Order 2003 (S. I. 2003/1887), art. 9, Sch. 2 para. 10(1)

[29] Words in s. 18(4)(a) substituted (1.10.2009) by Constitutional Reform Act 2005 (c. 4), ss. 59, 148, Sch. 11 para. 4; S.I. 2009/1604, art. 2(d)

[30] Words in s. 18(4)(a) substituted (1.10.2009) by Constitutional Reform Act 2005 (c. 4), ss. 59, 148, Sch. 11 para. 4; S.I. 2009/1604, art. 2(d)

[31] Words in s. 18(4)(c) substituted (1.10.2009) by Constitutional Reform Act 2005 (c. 4), ss. 59, 148, Sch. 11 para. 6; S.I. 2009/1604, art. 2(d)

[32] S. 18(7A)-(7D) inserted (3.4.2006) by Constitutional Reform Act 2005 (c. 4), ss. 15, 148, Sch. 4 para. 278; S.I. 2006/1014, art. 2, Sch. 1 para. 11(v)

[33] Words in s. 20(2) repealed (19.8.2003) by The Secretary of State for Constitutional Affairs Order 2003 (S. I. 2003/1887), art. 9, Sch. 2 para. 10(2)

[34] Words in s. 20(2) inserted (12.1.2006) by The Transfer of Functions (Lord Chancellor and Secretary of State) Order 2005 (S.I. 2005/3429), art. 8, Sch. para. 3

[35] Words in s. 20(4) repealed (19.8.2003) by The Secretary of State for Constitutional Affairs Order 2003 (S. I. 2003/1887), art. 9, Sch. 2 para. 10(2)

[36] Words in s. 20(4) inserted (12.1.2006) by The Transfer of Functions (Lord Chancellor and Secretary of State) Order 2005 (S.I. 2005/3429), art. 8, Sch. para. 3

[37] Words in the definition of "primary legislation" in s. 21(1) substituted by Government of Wales Act 2006 (c. 32), s. 160(1), Sch. 10 para.56(2) (with Sch. 11 para. 22) the amending provision coming into force immediately after "the 2007 election" (held on 3.5.2007) subject to s. 161(4)(5) of the amending Act, which provides for certain provisions to come into force for specified purposes immediately after the end of "the initial period" (which ended with the day of the first appointment of a First Minister on 25.5.2007) - see ss. 46, 161(1)(4)(5) of the amending Act.

[38] S. 21(1): definition of "the Sixth Protocol" omitted (22.6.2004) by virtue of The Human Rights Act 1998 (Amendment) Order 2004 (S.I. 2004/1574), art. 2(2)

[39] S. 21(1): definition of "the Thirteenth Protocol" inserted (22.6.2004) by virtue of The Human Rights Act 1998 (Amendment) Order 2004 (S.I. 2004/1574), art. 2(2)

[40] Words in the definition of "subordinate legislation" in s. 21(1) substituted by Government of Wales Act 2006 (c. 32), s. 160(1), Sch. 10 para.56(3) (with Sch. 11 para. 22) the amending provision coming into force immediately after "the 2007 election" (held on 3.5.2007) subject to s. 161(4)(5) of the amending Act, which provides for certain provisions to come into force for specified purposes immediately after the end of "the initial period" (which ended with the day of the first appointment of a First Minister on 25.5.2007) - see ss. 46, 161(1)(4)(5) of the amending Act.

[41] Words in the definition of "subordinate legislation" in s. 21(1) substituted by Government of Wales Act 2006 (c. 32), s. 160(1), Sch. 10 para.56(4) (with Sch. 11 para. 22) the amending provision coming into force immediately after "the 2007 election" (held on 3.5.2007) subject to s. 161(4)(5) of the amending Act, which provides for certain provisions to come into force for specified purposes immediately after the end of "the initial period" (which ended with the day of the first appointment of a First Minister on 25.5.2007) - see ss. 46, 161(1)(4)(5) of the amending Act.

[42] S. 21(5) repealed (28.3.2009 for certain purposes and 31.10.2009 otherwise) by Armed Forces Act 2006 (c. 52), ss. 378, 383, Sch. 17; S.I. 2009/812, art. 3 (with transitional provisions in S.I. 2009/1059); S.I. 2009/1167, art. 4

[43] S. 22(7) repealed (28.3.2009 for certain purposes and 31.10.2009 otherwise) by Armed Forces Act 2006 (c. 52), ss. 378, 383, Sch. 17; S.I. 2009/812, art. 3 (with transitional provisions in S.I. 2009/1059); S.I. 2009/1167, art. 4

[44] Sch. 1 Pt. 3 substituted (22.6.2004) by The Human Rights Act 1998 (Amendment) Order 2004 (S.I. 2004/1574), art. 2(3)

[45] Sch. 2 para. 7 inserted (27.7.2000) by S.I. 2000/2040, art. 2, Sch. Pt. I para. 21 (with art. 3)

[46] Sch. 3 Pt. I repealed (1.4.2001) by S.I. 2001/1216, art. 4

[47] Sch. 3 Pt. I repealed (8.4.2005) by The Human Rights Act 1998 (Amendment) Order 2005 (S.I. 2005/1071), art. 2

National Lottery Act 1998

1998 CHAPTER 22

An Act to make further provision in relation to the National Lottery; to make provision for and in connection with the establishment of a body corporate to be endowed out of the National Lottery Distribution Fund and to be known as the National Endowment for Science, Technology and the Arts;

and for connected purposes.

[2nd July 1998]

Part I Provisions relating to the National Lottery

The Director General and the National Lottery Commission

1 Replacement of Director General by National Lottery Commission.

(1) There shall cease to be an office of Director General of the National Lottery.

(2) In consequence of subsection (1) above, in the National Lottery etc. Act 1993 (in this Act referred to as "the 1993 Act") section 3 and Schedule 2 (which relate to the Director General of the National Lottery) shall cease to have effect.

(3) After section 3 of the 1993 Act there shall be inserted—

"3A The National Lottery Commission.

(1) There shall be a body corporate known as the National Lottery Commission.

(2) Schedule 2A makes provision in relation to the Commission."

(4) On the day on which this subsection comes into force under section 27(3) below, the functions conferred or imposed on the Director General of the National Lottery by or under the 1993 Act (including any functions so conferred or imposed by virtue of this Act) shall, by virtue of this subsection, be transferred to the National Lottery Commission.

(5) Schedule 1 to this Act (which makes provision supplemental to, or consequential on, this section) shall have effect.

...

Part II The National Endowment for Science, Technology and the Arts

16 The National Endowment for Science, Technology and the Arts.

(1) There shall be a body corporate known as the National Endowment for Science, Technology and the Arts (in this Part of this Act referred to as "NESTA").

(2) Schedule 4 to this Act makes provision in relation to NESTA.

...

Part III Supplemental provisions

...

27 Short title, interpretation, commencement and extent.

(1) This Act may be cited as the National Lottery Act 1998.

(2) In this Act "the 1993 Act" means the National Lottery etc. Act 1993.

(3) The following provisions of this Act, namely—

(a) section 1,

(b) Schedule 1, and

(c) Part I of Schedule 5 and section 26 so far as relating to that Part of that Schedule,

shall come into force on such day as the Secretary of State may appoint by order made by statutory instrument; and different days may be so appointed for different purposes.

(4) The following provisions of this Act, namely—

(a) this section,

(b) sections 6 to 12 and 15 to 25,

(c) Schedules 2 to 4, and

(d) section 26 and Part II of Schedule 5, so far as relating to the repeals in section 22 of, and paragraphs 2, 3 and 6 of Schedule 5 to, the 1993 Act,

shall come into force on the day on which this Act is passed.

(5) The remaining provisions of this Act shall come into force at the end of the period of two months beginning with the day on which this Act is passed.

(6) The power conferred by subsection (3) above to make an order includes power to make incidental, consequential, supplemental or transitional provision or savings (including power to amend enactments).

(7) This Act extends to Northern Ireland.

...

SCHEDULES

Section 1.

SCHEDULE 1 Replacement of Director General by Commission: supplementary provisions

Part II Constitution of the Commission

7 After Schedule 2 to the 1993 Act there shall be inserted—

Section 3A.

"Schedule 2A The National Lottery Commission

Status and capacity

1(1) The Commission shall not be regarded as the servant or agent of the Crown or as enjoying any status, immunity or privilege of the Crown.

(2) The members and employees of the Commission shall not be regarded as civil servants and the Commission's property shall not be regarded as property of, or held on behalf of, the Crown.

(3) The Commission may for the purpose of enabling them to exercise their functions acquire and dispose of land.

(4) It shall be within the capacity of the Commission as a body corporate created by statute to do such things and enter into such transactions as are incidental or conducive to the discharge of their functions under this Act.

Membership

2(1) The Commission shall consist of five members, all of whom shall be appointed by the Secretary of State.

(2) Before appointing a person to be a member, the Secretary of State shall satisfy himself that that person will have no such financial or other interest as is likely to affect prejudicially the discharge by him of his functions as a member.

(3) The Secretary of State shall also satisfy himself from time to time with respect to every member that he has no such interest as is mentioned in sub-paragraph (2).

(4) Any person who is, or whom the Secretary of State proposes to appoint to be, a member shall, whenever requested by the Secretary of State to do so, furnish him with such information as the Secretary of State considers necessary for the performance by him of his duties under sub-paragraphs (2) and (3).

Tenure of office

3(1) Members shall hold and vacate office in accordance with their terms of appointment, subject to the following provisions.

(2) Any appointment of a member shall be for a term no longer than five years.

(3) A member may resign his membership by giving written notice to the Secretary of State.

(4) A person who ceases to be a member shall be eligible for re-appointment.

(5) The Secretary of State may by notice in writing to the member concerned remove from office a member who—

(a) has been absent from three or more consecutive meetings of the Commission without their prior approval,

(b) has become bankrupt, has made an arrangement with his creditors, has had his estate sequestrated, has granted a trust deed for his creditors or has made a composition contract with his creditors, or

(c) is, in the opinion of the Secretary of State, unable or unfit to perform his duties as a member.

Chairman

4(1) The members of the Commission shall select one of their number to be the chairman of the Commission.

(2) A person's term of office as chairman shall be no longer than twelve months.

(3) A person may resign as chairman by giving written notice to the other members.

(4) If the chairman ceases to be a member he shall also cease to be chairman.

(5) A member who ceases to be the chairman shall again become eligible for selection as chairman after the expiration of a period equal to that for which he was last chairman.

Remuneration and allowances

5(1) The Commission may pay such remuneration, and such travelling and other allowances, to a member of the Commission as the Secretary of State may determine in the case of the member.

(2) Where the Secretary of State so determines in the case of a member of the Commission, the Commission shall—

(a) pay to or in respect of him such pension, allowances or gratuities, or

(b) make such payments towards the provision of a pension, allowances or gratuities to or in respect of him,

as the Secretary of State may determine.

(3) If the Secretary of State determines that there are special circumstances that make it right for a person ceasing to be a member of the Commission to receive compensation, the Commission may pay to him such compensation as the Secretary of State may determine.

Staff

6(1) There shall be a Chief Executive of the Commission, who shall be appointed by the Commission as an employee of theirs.

(2) The Chief Executive shall be responsible to the Commission for the general exercise of the Commission's functions.

(3) Subject to any directions given to them by the Secretary of State with respect to the number of persons who may be employed by the Commission, the Commission may appoint such other employees as they think fit.

(4) Subject to any directions given to the Commission by the Secretary of State, the Chief Executive and any other employees shall be employed on such terms and conditions (including terms and conditions as to remuneration) as the Commission think fit.

(5) Service as an employee of the Commission shall be included in the kinds of employment to which a scheme under section 1 of the Superannuation Act 1972 can apply.

(6) Accordingly, in the Superannuation Act 1972, in Schedule 1 (kinds of employment etc referred to in section 1) the following entry shall be inserted at the appropriate place among the entries under the heading "*Royal Commissions and other Commissions*"—

"National Lottery Commission".

(7) The Commission shall pay to the Minister for the Civil Service, at such times as that Minister may direct, such sums as that Minister may determine in respect of the increase attributable to sub-paragraphs (5) and (6) in the sums payable out of money provided by Parliament under the Superannuation Act 1972.

Proceedings

7(1) The Commission may regulate their own procedure and that of any of their committees (and in particular may specify a quorum for meetings).

(2) The validity of any proceedings of the Commission shall not be affected—

(a) by any vacancy among the members or in the office of chairman, or

(b) by any defect in the appointment or selection of any person as a member or as chairman of the Commission.

Delegation

8(1) Anything authorised or required by or under any enactment to be done by the Commission may be done—

(a) by any member or employee of the Commission who has been authorised for the purpose, whether generally or specially, by the Commission; or

(b) by any committee of the Commission which has been so authorised and whose membership consists of—

(i) members of the Commission; or

(ii) one or more members of the Commission and one or more employees of the Commission.

(2) In exercising their functions under sub-paragraph (1), the Commission shall comply with any directions given to them by the Secretary of State.

Duty to give reasons for decisions

9(1) It shall be the duty of the Commission to give to any person affected a written statement of their reasons for any decisions which they may make in the exercise of their functions under sections 5 to 10 or Schedule 3.

(2) It shall be the duty of the Commission to arrange for the publication, in such manner as they think fit, of a written statement of their reasons—

(a) for any decision which they may make to grant, or not to grant, to any particular applicant a licence under section 5;

(b) for any decision which they may make to revoke a licence granted under section 5; and

(c) for any other decision which they may make in the exercise of their functions under sections 5 to 10A or Schedule 3 and which they consider likely to be of interest to the public.

(3) Sub-paragraphs (1) and (2) do not apply if or to the extent that the giving, or (as the case may be) the publication, of reasons would involve disclosure of information in breach of—

(a) a restriction imposed by or under any other enactment; or

(b) an obligation of confidence.

Finance

10 There shall be paid out of money provided by Parliament such sums as are necessary to defray any expenditure of the Commission.

Accounts

11(1) The Commission shall—

(a) keep proper accounts and proper records in relation to the accounts, and

(b) prepare a statement of accounts in respect of each financial year.

(2) The statement shall comply with any directions that may be given by the Secretary of State as to the information to be contained in such a statement, the manner in which such information is to be presented or the methods and principles according to which such a statement is to be prepared.

(3) Copies of the statement shall be sent to the Secretary of State and the Comptroller and Auditor General within such period after the end of the financial year to which the statement relates as the Secretary of State may direct.

(4) The Comptroller and Auditor General shall examine, certify and report on the statement and shall lay copies of the statement and of his report before Parliament.

(5) The Secretary of State shall not give a direction under this paragraph without the Treasury's approval.

(6) In this paragraph "financial year" means—

(a) the period beginning with the coming into force of section 3A and ending with the next 31st March, and

(b) each successive period of twelve months ending with 31st March.

Application of seal and evidence

12 The application of the seal of the Commission shall be authenticated by the signature—

(a) of any member of the Commission, or

(b) of any other person who has been authorised by the Commission (whether generally or specially) for that purpose.

13 A document purporting to be duly executed under the seal of the Commission, or to be signed on behalf of the Commission, shall be received in evidence and, unless the contrary is proved, taken to be so executed or signed.

14 Paragraphs 12 and 13 do not extend to Scotland."

Section 16.

SCHEDULE 4 The National Endowment for Science, Technology and the Arts

Membership

1(1) NESTA shall consist of not more than 15 members (in this Schedule referred to as "trustees")—

(a) all of whom shall be appointed by the Secretary of State; and

(b) one of whom shall be so appointed as chairman.

(2) before making any appointment under this paragraph, the Secretary of State shall consult such persons as appear to him to be representative of those engaged in the fields of science, technology and the arts.

(3) The Secretary of State may by order amend sub-paragraph (1) above so as to increase the number for the time being specified in that sub-paragraph.

(4) An order under this paragraph shall be made by statutory instrument which shall be subject to annulment in pursuance of a resolution of either House of Parliament.

Delegation of functions

2(1) NESTA may appoint any other body or person to exercise on their behalf any of their functions under this Part of this Act—

(a) in any particular case, or

(b) in cases of any particular description.

(2) The persons who may be appointed by NESTA under sub-paragraph (1) above include a trustee, member of staff or committee of NESTA.

(3) NESTA may establish a committee for the purpose of exercising on behalf of NESTA any such function as is mentioned in sub-paragraph (1) above.

(4) A committee established under sub-paragraph (3) above—

(a) may consist of or include persons who are trustees of NESTA;

(b) may consist of or include persons who are members of staff of NESTA; and

(c) may consist of or include persons who are neither trustees nor members of staff of NESTA.

(5) Any reference in this paragraph to a trustee of NESTA includes a reference to the chairman of NESTA.

Tenure of office

3(1) Subject to the following provisions of this paragraph, a person shall hold and vacate office as chairman or trustee of NESTA in accordance with the terms of his appointment.

(2) The Secretary of State shall not appoint a person to hold office as a trustee of NESTA for a term of more than five years.

(3) A chairman or trustee of NESTA may at any time resign his office by notice in writing addressed to the Secretary of State.

(4) A trustee of NESTA may be removed from office by the Secretary of State on the ground that—

(a) he has been absent for a period longer than three consecutive months from meetings of NESTA, or of any committee of NESTA, without NESTA's consent,

(b) a bankruptcy order has been made against him, or his estate has been sequestrated, or he has made a composition or arrangement with, or granted a trust deed for, his creditors, or

(c) he is unable or unfit to discharge the functions of his office.

(5) If a chairman of NESTA ceases to be a trustee of NESTA he shall also cease to be chairman.

(6) A person who ceases, otherwise than by virtue of sub-paragraph (4) above, to be a trustee or chairman of NESTA shall be eligible for re-appointment.

Remuneration and allowances

4(1) If the Secretary of State so determines, NESTA may pay such remuneration to their chairman or any other trustee of NESTA as the Secretary of State may determine.

(2) NESTA may, in accordance with any scheme for the time being approved by the Secretary of State, pay travelling and other allowances to their chairman, to any other trustee of NESTA, to any member of a committee of theirs or to any person who, by virtue of paragraph 2 above, exercises on behalf of NESTA any of their functions under this Part of this Act.

(3) Where the Secretary of State so determines in the case of a holder of the office of chairman of NESTA, or in the case of any other trustee of NESTA, NESTA shall—

(a) pay to or in respect of him such pension, allowances or gratuities, or

(b) make such payments towards the provision of a pension, allowances or gratuities to or in respect of him,

as the Secretary of State may determine.

(4) If the Secretary of State determines that there are special circumstances that make it right for a person ceasing to hold office as chairman of NESTA, or ceasing to be a trustee of NESTA, to receive compensation, NESTA may pay to him such compensation as the Secretary of State may determine.

Staff

5 Subject to any directions under section 21 of this Act, NESTA may appoint such staff as they think fit, on such terms (including terms as to remuneration and pensions) as they think fit.

Proceedings

6(1) NESTA may regulate their own procedure and that of any of their committees (and in particular may specify a quorum for meetings).

(2) The validity of any proceedings of NESTA shall not be affected by any vacancy among their trustees, or by any defect in the appointment of any person as chairman or a trustee.

Application of seal and evidence

7The application of the seal of NESTA shall be authenticated by the signature—

(a) of any trustee of NESTA, or

(b) of any other person who has been authorised by NESTA (whether generally or specially) for that purpose.

8 A document purporting to be duly executed under the seal of NESTA or to be signed on their behalf shall be received in evidence and, unless the contrary is proved, taken to be so executed or signed.

Status of NESTA

9NESTA shall not be regarded as the servant or agent of the Crown or as enjoying any status, immunity or privilege of the Crown.

Parliamentary disqualification

10(1) In the House of Commons Disqualification Act 1975, in Part III of Schedule 1 (other disqualifying offices) the following entry shall be inserted at the appropriate place—

"Chairman of the National Endowment for Science, Technology and the Arts ("NESTA") and, if in receipt of remuneration, any other member of NESTA;".

(2) The same entry shall be inserted at the appropriate place in Part III of Schedule 1 to the Northern Ireland Assembly Disqualification Act 1975.

Reimbursement

11 The payments which may be made under section 31 of the 1993 Act (payments from Distribution Fund into Consolidated Fund in respect of expenses) shall include a payment of such amount as the Secretary of State with the approval of the Treasury determines to be appropriate for defraying expenses incurred by the Secretary of State before the commencement of this Part of this Act for the purpose of facilitating the establishment of NESTA.

Prior consultation

12 Any consultation undertaken before the commencement of this Schedule in connection with any appointments under paragraph 1 above shall be as effective, in relation to those appointments, as if this Schedule had been in force at the time the consultation was undertaken.

Application to Scotland

13Paragraphs 7 and 8 above do not extend to Scotland.

National Minimum Wage Act 1998

1998 CHAPTER 39

An Act to make provision for and in connection with a national minimum wage; to provide for the amendment of certain enactments relating to the remuneration of persons employed in agriculture; and for connected purposes.

[31st July 1998]

Entitlement to the national minimum wage

1 Workers to be paid at least the national minimum wage.

(1) A person who qualifies for the national minimum wage shall be remunerated by his employer in respect of his work in any pay reference period at a rate which is not less than the national minimum wage.

(2) A person qualifies for the national minimum wage if he is an individual who—

(a) is a worker;

(b) is working, or ordinarily works, in the United Kingdom under his contract; and

(c) has ceased to be of compulsory school age.

(3) The national minimum wage shall be such single hourly rate as the Secretary of State may from time to time prescribe.

(4) For the purposes of this Act a "pay reference period" is such period as the Secretary of State may prescribe for the purpose.

(5) Subsections (1) to (4) above are subject to the following provisions of this Act.

Exclusions

44 Voluntary workers.

(1) A worker employed by a charity, a voluntary organisation, an associated fund-raising body or a statutory body does not qualify for the national minimum wage in respect of that employment if he receives, and under the terms of his employment (apart from this Act) is entitled to,—

(a) no monetary payments of any description, or no monetary payments except in respect of expenses—

(i) actually incurred in the performance of his duties; or

(ii) reasonably estimated as likely to be or to have been so incurred; and

(b) no benefits in kind of any description, or no benefits in kind other than the provision of some or all of his subsistence or of such accommodation as is reasonable in the circumstances of the employment.

(2) A person who would satisfy the conditions in subsection (1) above but for receiving monetary payments made solely for the purpose of providing him with means of subsistence shall be taken to satisfy those conditions if—

(a) he is employed to do the work in question as a result of arrangements made between a charity acting in pursuance of its charitable purposes and the body for which the work is done; and

(b) the work is done for a charity, a voluntary organisation, an associated fund-raising body or a statutory body.

(3) For the purposes of subsection (1)(b) above—

(a) any training (other than that which a person necessarily acquires in the course of doing his work) shall be taken to be a benefit in kind; but

(b) there shall be left out of account any training provided for the sole or main purpose of improving the worker's ability to perform the work which he has agreed to do.

(4) In this section—

"associated fund-raising body" means a body of persons the profits of which are applied wholly for the purposes of a charity or voluntary organisation;

"charity" means a body of persons, or the trustees of a trust, established for charitable purposes only;

"receive", in relation to a monetary payment or a benefit in kind, means receive in respect of, or otherwise in connection with, the employment in question (whether or not under the terms of the employment);

"statutory body" means a body established by or under an enactment (including an enactment comprised in Northern Ireland legislation);

"subsistence" means such subsistence as is reasonable in the circumstances of the employment in question, and does not include accommodation;

"voluntary organisation" means a body of persons, or the trustees of a trust, which is established only for charitable purposes (whether or not those purposes are charitable within the meaning of any rule of law), benevolent purposes or philanthropic purposes, but which is not a charity.

[44A Religious and other communities: resident workers.

(1) A residential member of a community to which this section applies does not qualify for the national minimum wage in respect of employment by the community.

(2) Subject to subsection (3), this section applies to a community if—

(a) it is a charity or is established by a charity,

(b) a purpose of the community is to practise or advance a belief of a religious or similar nature, and

(c) all or some of its members live together for that purpose.

(3) This section does not apply to a community which—

(a) is an independent school, or

(b) provides a course of further or higher education.

(4) The residential members of a community are those who live together as mentioned in subsection (2)(c).

(5) In this section—

(a) "charity" has the same meaning as in section 44, and

(b) "independent school" has the same meaning as in section 463 of the Education Act 1996 (in

England and Wales), section 135 of the Education (Scotland) Act 1980 (in Scotland) and Article 2 of the Education and Libraries (Northern Ireland) Order 1986 (in Northern Ireland).

(6) In this section "course of further or higher education" means—

(a) in England and Wales, a course of a description referred to in Schedule 6 to the Education Reform Act 1988 or Schedule 2 to the Further and Higher Education Act 1992;

(b) in Scotland, a course or programme of a description mentioned in or falling within section 6(1) or 38 of the Further and Higher Education (Scotland) Act 1992;

(c) in Northern Ireland, a course of a description referred to in Schedule 1 to the Further Education (Northern Ireland) Order 1997 or a course providing further education within the meaning of Article 3 of that Order.][1]

54 Meaning of "worker", "employee" etc.

(1) In this Act "employee" means an individual who has entered into or works under (or, where the employment has ceased, worked under) a contract of employment.

(2) In this Act "contract of employment" means a contract of service or apprenticeship, whether express or implied, and (if it is express) whether oral or in writing.

(3) In this Act "worker" (except in the phrases "agency worker" and "home worker") means an individual who has entered into or works under (or, where the employment has ceased, worked under)—

(a) a contract of employment; or

(b) any other contract, whether express or implied and (if it is express) whether oral or in writing, whereby the individual undertakes to do or perform personally any work or services for another party to the contract whose status is not by virtue of the contract that of a client or customer of any profession or business undertaking carried on by the individual;

and any reference to a worker's contract shall be construed accordingly.

(4) In this Act "employer", in relation to an employee or a worker, means the person by whom the employee or worker is (or, where the employment has ceased, was) employed.

(5) In this Act "employment"—

(a) in relation to an employee, means employment under a contract of employment; and

(b) in relation to a worker, means employment under his contract;

and "employed" shall be construed accordingly.

...

56 Short title, commencement and extent.

(1) This Act may be cited as the National Minimum Wage Act 1998.

(2) Apart from this section and any powers to make an Order in Council or regulations or an order (which accordingly come into force on the day on which this Act is passed) the provisions of this Act shall come into force on such day or days as the Secretary of State may by order appoint; and different days may be appointed for different purposes.

(3) This Act extends to Northern Ireland

---

[1] S. 44A inserted (25.10.1999) by 1999 c. 26, s. 22; S.I. 1999/2830, art. 2(1)(2), Sch. 1 Pt. I

Trustee Delegation Act 1999

1999 CHAPTER 15

An Act to amend the law relating to the delegation of trustee functions by power of attorney and the exercise of such functions by the donee of a power of attorney; and to make provision about the authority of the donee of a power of attorney to act in relation to land.

[15th July 1999]

Attorney of trustee with beneficial interest in land

1 Exercise of trustee functions by attorney.

(1) The donee of a power of attorney is not prevented from doing an act in relation to—

(a) land,

(b) capital proceeds of a conveyance of land, or

(c) income from land,

by reason only that the act involves the exercise of a trustee function of the donor if, at the time when the act is done, the donor has a beneficial interest in the land, proceeds or income.

(2) In this section—

(a) "conveyance" has the same meaning as in the Law of Property Act 1925, and

(b) references to a trustee function of the donor are to a function which the donor has as trustee (either alone or jointly with any other person or persons).

(3) Subsection (1) above—

(a) applies only if and so far as a contrary intention is not expressed in the instrument creating the power of attorney, and

(b) has effect subject to the terms of that instrument.

(4) The donor of the power of attorney—

(a) is liable for the acts or defaults of the donee in exercising any function by virtue of subsection (1) above in the same manner as if they were acts or defaults of the donor, but

(b) is not liable by reason only that a function is exercised by the donee by virtue of that subsection.

(5) Subsections (1) and (4) above—

(a) apply only if and so far as a contrary intention is not expressed in the instrument (if any) creating the trust, and

(b) have effect subject to the terms of such an instrument.

(6) The fact that it appears that, in dealing with any shares or stock, the donee of the power of attorney is exercising a function by virtue of subsection (1) above does not affect with any notice of any trust a person in whose books the shares are, or stock is, registered or inscribed.

(7) In any case where (by way of exception to section 3(1) of the Trusts of Land and Appointment of Trustees Act 1996) the doctrine of conversion continues to operate, any person who, by reason of the continuing operation of that doctrine, has a beneficial interest in the proceeds of sale of land shall be treated for the purposes of this section and section 2 below as having a beneficial interest in the land.

(8) The donee of a power of attorney is not to be regarded as exercising a trustee function by virtue of subsection (1) above if he is acting under a trustee delegation power; and for this purpose a trustee delegation power is a power of attorney given under—

(a) a statutory provision, or

(b) a provision of the instrument (if any) creating a trust,

under which the donor of the power is expressly authorised to delegate the exercise of all or any of his trustee functions by power of attorney.

(9) Subject to section 4(6) below, this section applies only to powers of attorney created after the commencement of this Act.

2 Evidence of beneficial interest.

(1) This section applies where the interest of a purchaser depends on the donee of a power of attorney having power to do an act in relation to any property by virtue of section 1(1) above.

In this subsection "purchaser" has the same meaning as in Part I of the Law of Property Act 1925.

(2) Where this section applies an appropriate statement is, in favour of the purchaser, conclusive evidence of the donor of the power having a beneficial interest in the property at the time of the doing of the act.

(3) In this section "an appropriate statement" means a signed statement made by the donee—

(a) when doing the act in question, or

(b) at any other time within the period of three months beginning with the day on which the act is done,

that the donor has a beneficial interest in the property at the time of the donee doing the act.

(4) If an appropriate statement is false, the donee is liable in the same way as he would be if the statement were contained in a statutory declaration.

3 General powers in specified form.

In section 10(2) of the Powers of Attorney Act 1971 (which provides that a general power of attorney in the form set out in Schedule 1 to that Act, or a similar form, does not confer on the donee of the power any authority to exercise functions of the donor as trustee etc.), for the words "This section" substitute " Subject to section 1 of the Trustee Delegation Act 1999, this section ".

4 Enduring powers.

(1) Section 3(3) of the Enduring Powers of Attorney Act 1985 (which entitles the donee of an enduring power to exercise any of the donor's functions as trustee and to give receipt for capital money etc.) does

not apply to enduring powers created after the commencement of this Act.

(2) Section 3(3) of the Enduring Powers of Attorney Act 1985 ceases to apply to enduring powers created before the commencement of this Act—

(a) where subsection (3) below applies, in accordance with that subsection, and

(b) otherwise, at the end of the period of one year from that commencement.

(3) Where an application for the registration of the instrument creating such an enduring power is made before the commencement of this Act, or during the period of one year from that commencement, section 3(3) of the Enduring Powers of Attorney Act 1985 ceases to apply to the power—

(a) if the instrument is registered pursuant to the application (whether before commencement or during or after that period), when the registration of the instrument is cancelled, and

(b) if the application is finally refused during or after that period, when the application is finally refused.

(4) In subsection (3) above—

(a) "registration" and "registered" mean registration and registered under section 6 of the Enduring Powers of Attorney Act 1985, and

(b) "cancelled" means cancelled under section 8(4) of that Act.

(5) For the purposes of subsection (3)(b) above an application is finally refused—

(a) if the application is withdrawn or any appeal is abandoned, when the application is withdrawn or the appeal is abandoned, and

(b) otherwise, when proceedings on the application (including any proceedings on, or in consequence of, an appeal) have been determined and any time for appealing or further appealing has expired.

(6) Section 1 above applies to an enduring power created before the commencement of this Act from the time when (in accordance with subsections (2) to (5) above) section 3(3) of the Enduring Powers of Attorney Act 1985 ceases to apply to it.

Trustee delegation under section 25 of the Trustee Act 1925

5 Delegation under section 25 of the Trustee Act 1925.

(1) For section 25 of the Trustee Act 1925 substitute—

"25 Delegation of trustee's functions by power of attorney.

(1) Notwithstanding any rule of law or equity to the contrary, a trustee may, by power of attorney, delegate the execution or exercise of all or any of the trusts, powers and discretions vested in him as trustee either alone or jointly with any other person or persons.

(2) A delegation under this section—

(a) commences as provided by the instrument creating the power or, if the instrument makes no provision as to the commencement of the delegation, with the date of the execution of the instrument by the donor; and

(b) continues for a period of twelve months or any shorter period provided by the instrument creating the power.

(3) The persons who may be donees of a power of attorney under this section include a trust corporation.

(4) Before or within seven days after giving a power of attorney under this section the donor shall give written notice of it (specifying the date on which the power comes into operation and its duration, the donee of the power, the reason why the power is given and, where some only are delegated, the trusts, powers and discretions delegated) to—

(a) each person (other than himself), if any, who under any instrument creating the trust has power (whether alone or jointly) to appoint a new trustee; and

(b) each of the other trustees, if any;

but failure to comply with this subsection shall not, in favour of a person dealing with the donee of the power, invalidate any act done or instrument executed by the donee.

(5) A power of attorney given under this section by a single donor—

(a) in the form set out in subsection (6) of this section; or

(b) in a form to the like effect but expressed to be made under this subsection,

shall operate to delegate to the person identified in the form as the single donee of the power the execution and exercise of all the trusts, powers and discretions vested in the donor as trustee (either alone or jointly with any other person or persons) under the single trust so identified.

(6) The form referred to in subsection (5) of this section is as follows—

"THIS GENERAL TRUSTEE POWER OF ATTORNEY is made on [*date*] by [*name of one donor*] of [*address of donor*] as trustee of [*name or details of one trust*].

I appoint [*name of one donee*] of [*address of donee*] to be my attorney [*if desired, the date on which the delegation commences or the period for which it continues (or both)*] in accordance with section 25(5) of the Trustee Act 1925.

[*To be executed as a deed*]".

(7) The donor of a power of attorney given under this section shall be liable for the acts or defaults of the donee in the same manner as if they were the acts or defaults of the donor.

(8) For the purpose of executing or exercising the trusts or powers delegated to him, the donee may exercise any of the powers conferred on the donor as trustee by statute or by the instrument creating the trust, including power, for the purpose of the transfer of any inscribed stock, himself to delegate to an attorney power to transfer, but not including the power of delegation conferred by this section.

(9) The fact that it appears from any power of attorney given under this section, or from any evidence required for the purposes of any such power of attorney or otherwise, that in dealing with any stock the donee of the power is acting in the execution of a trust shall not be deemed for any purpose to affect any person in whose books the stock is inscribed or registered with any notice of the trust.

(10) This section applies to a personal representative, tenant for life and statutory owner as it applies to a trustee except that subsection (4) shall apply as if it required the notice there mentioned to be given—

(a) in the case of a personal representative, to each of the other personal representatives, if any, except any executor who has renounced probate;

(b) in the case of a tenant for life, to the trustees of the settlement and to each person, if any, who together with the person giving the notice constitutes the tenant for life; and

(c) in the case of a statutory owner, to each of the persons, if any, who together with the person giving the notice constitute the statutory owner and, in the case of a statutory owner by virtue of section 23(1)(a) of the Settled Land Act 1925, to the trustees of the settlement."

(2) Subsection (1) above has effect in relation to powers of attorney created after the commencement of this Act.

(3) In section 34(2)(b) of the Pensions Act 1995 (delegation by trustees of trustee scheme under section 25 of the Trustee Act 1925), for "during absence abroad" substitute " for period not exceeding twelve months ".

6 Section 25 powers as enduring powers.

Section 2(8) of the Enduring Powers of Attorney Act 1985 (which prevents a power of attorney under section 25 of the Trustee Act 1925 from being an enduring power) does not apply to powers of attorney created after the commencement of this Act.

Miscellaneous provisions about attorney acting for trustee

7 Two-trustee rules.

(1) A requirement imposed by an enactment—

(a) that capital money be paid to, or dealt with as directed by, at least two trustees or that a valid receipt for capital money be given otherwise than by a sole trustee, or

(b) that, in order for an interest or power to be overreached, a conveyance or deed be executed by at least two trustees,

is not satisfied by money being paid to or dealt with as directed by, or a receipt for money being given by, a relevant attorney or by a conveyance or deed being executed by such an attorney.

(2) In this section "relevant attorney" means a person (other than a trust corporation within the meaning of the Trustee Act 1925) who is acting either—

(a) both as a trustee and as attorney for one or more other trustees, or

(b) as attorney for two or more trustees,

and who is not acting together with any other person or persons.

(3) This section applies whether a relevant attorney is acting under a power created before or after the commencement of this Act (but in the case of such an attorney acting under an enduring power created before that commencement is without prejudice to any continuing application of section 3(3) of the Enduring Powers of Attorney Act 1985 to the enduring power after that commencement in accordance

with section 4 above).

8 Appointment of additional trustee by attorney.

(1) In section 36 of the Trustee Act 1925 (appointment of trustees), after subsection (6) (additional trustees) insert—

"(6A) a person who is either—

(a) both a trustee and attorney for the other trustee (if one other), or for both of the other trustees (if two others), under a registered power; or

(b) attorney under a registered power for the trustee (if one) or for both or each of the trustees (if two or three),

may, if subsection (6B) of this section is satisfied in relation to him, make an appointment under subsection (6)(b) of this section on behalf of the trustee or trustees.

(6B) This subsection is satisfied in relation to an attorney under a registered power for one or more trustees if (as attorney under the power)—

(a) he intends to exercise any function of the trustee or trustees by virtue of section 1(1) of the Trustee Delegation Act 1999; or

(b) he intends to exercise any function of the trustee or trustees in relation to any land, capital proceeds of a conveyance of land or income from land by virtue of its delegation to him under section 25 of this Act or the instrument (if any) creating the trust.

(6C) In subsections (6A) and (6B) of this section "registered power" means a power of attorney created by an instrument which is for the time being registered under section 6 of the Enduring Powers of Attorney Act 1985.

(6D) Subsection (6A) of this section—

(a) applies only if and so far as a contrary intention is not expressed in the instrument creating the power of attorney (or, where more than one, any of them) or the instrument (if any) creating the trust; and

(b) has effect subject to the terms of those instruments."

(2) The amendment made by subsection (1) above has effect only where the power, or (where more than one) each of them, is created after the commencement of this Act.

9 Attorney acting for incapable trustee.

(1) In section 22 of the Law of Property Act 1925 (requirement, before dealing with legal estate vested in trustee who is incapable by reason of mental disorder, to appoint new trustee or discharge incapable trustee), after subsection (2) insert—

"(3) Subsection (2) of this section does not prevent a legal estate being dealt with without the appointment of a new trustee, or the discharge of the incapable trustee, at a time when the donee of an enduring power (within the meaning of the Enduring Powers of Attorney Act 1985) is entitled to act for the incapable trustee in the dealing."

(2) The amendment made by subsection (1) above has effect whether the enduring power was created before or after the commencement of this Act.

Authority of attorney to act in relation to land

10 Extent of attorney's authority to act in relation to land.

(1) Where the donee of a power of attorney is authorised by the power to do an act of any description in relation to any land, his authority to do an act of that description at any time includes authority to do it with respect to any estate or interest in the land which is held at that time by the donor (whether alone or jointly with any other person or persons).

(2) Subsection (1) above—

(a) applies only if and so far as a contrary intention is not expressed in the instrument creating the power of attorney, and

(b) has effect subject to the terms of that instrument.

(3) This section applies only to powers of attorney created after the commencement of this Act.

Supplementary

11 Interpretation.

(1) In this Act—

"land" has the same meaning as in the Trustee Act 1925, and

"enduring power" has the same meaning as in the Enduring Powers of Attorney Act 1985.

(2) References in this Act to the creation of a power of attorney are to the execution by the donor of the instrument creating it.

12 Repeals.

The enactments specified in the Schedule to this Act are repealed to the extent specified in the third column, but subject to the note at the end.

13 Commencement, extent and short title.

(1) The preceding provisions of this Act shall come into force on such day as the Lord Chancellor may by order made by statutory instrument appoint.

(2) This Act extends to England and Wales only.

(3) This Act may be cited as the Trustee Delegation Act 1999.

SCHEDULE

Repeals

Chapter	Short title	Extent of repeal
1971 c. 27.	The Powers of Attorney Act 1971.	Section 9.
1985 c. 29.	The Enduring Powers of Attorney Act 1985.	Section 2(8). Section 3(3).

The repeal of section 3(3) of the Enduring Powers of Attorney Act 1985 has effect in accordance with section 4 of this Act and the remaining repeals have effect in relation to powers of attorney created after the commencement of this Act.

Financial Services and Markets Act 2000

2000 CHAPTER 8

Part XXI Mutual Societies

Industrial and provident societies and credit unions

...

338 Industrial and provident societies and credit unions.

(1) The Treasury may by order provide for the transfer to the Authority of any functions conferred by—

(a) the Industrial and Provident Societies Act 1965;

(b) the Industrial and Provident Societies Act 1967;

(c) the Friendly and Industrial and Provident Societies Act 1968;

(d) the Industrial and Provident Societies Act 1975;

(e) the Industrial and Provident Societies Act 1978;

(f) the Credit Unions Act 1979.

(2) The Treasury may by order provide for the transfer to the Treasury of any functions under those enactments which have not been, or are not being, transferred to the Authority.

(3) The enactments relating to industrial and provident societies which are mentioned in Part IV of Schedule 18 are amended as set out in that Part.

(4) The enactments relating to credit unions which are mentioned in Part V of Schedule 18 are amended as set out in that Part.

...

Part XXX Supplemental

430 Extent.

(1) This Act, except Chapter IV of Part XVII, extends to Northern Ireland.

(2) Except where Her Majesty by Order in Council provides otherwise, the extent of any amendment or repeal made by or under this Act is the same as the extent of the provision amended or repealed.

(3) Her Majesty may by Order in Council provide for any provision of or made under this Act relating to a matter which is the subject of other legislation which extends to any of the Channel Islands or the Isle of Man to extend there with such modifications (if any) as may be specified in the Order.

431 Commencement.

(1) The following provisions come into force on the passing of this Act—

(a) this section;

(b) sections 428, 430 and 433;

(c) paragraphs 1 and 2 of Schedule 21.

(2) The other provisions of this Act come into force on such day as the Treasury may by order appoint; and different days may be appointed for different purposes.

...

433 Short title.

This Act may be cited as the Financial Services and Markets Act 2000.

Finance Act 2000

2000 CHAPTER 17

Chapter II Other provisions

Giving to charity

38 Payroll deduction scheme.

(1) Where in accordance with a scheme approved under section 202 of the Taxes Act 1988 (donations to charity: payroll deduction scheme) an agent is to pay to a charity any sum which—

(a) is withheld by an employer from a payment which an employee is entitled to receive; and

(b) is paid by the employer to the agent,

the agent shall, within a period prescribed by regulations made by the Treasury, pay a supplement equal to 10% of that sum to the charity.

(2) On a claim made by an agent in such form as the Board may prescribe, the Board shall pay to the agent out of money provided by Parliament—

(a) such amounts as are required—

(i) to fund the payment of supplements falling to be paid by him; or

(ii) to reimburse him for supplements paid by him the payment of which has not been so funded; and

(b) in the case of an agent which is a charity, an amount which is equal to 10% of the aggregate of sums which—

(i) are withheld and paid as mentioned in paragraphs (a) and (b) of subsection (1) above; and

(ii) are sums to which the agent is itself entitled in its capacity as a charity.

(3) The Treasury may by regulations make provision—

(a) requiring agents to notify the Board of any failures of theirs to comply with subsection (1) above, and of the reasons for those failures;

(b) requiring agents to keep records of supplements paid by them under that subsection; and

(c) for the assessment and recovery under the Taxes Acts of amounts paid to agents under subsection (2) above which ought not to have been so paid.

The regulations may contain such supplementary and incidental provision as appears to the Treasury necessary or expedient.

(4) In this section—

"agent" means any such person or charity as is mentioned in subsection (4) of section 202 of the Taxes Act 1988;

"employee" and "employer" shall be construed in accordance with subsection (1) of that section;

"charity" has the same meaning as in section 506 of that Act and includes each of the bodies mentioned in section 507 of that Act;

"the Taxes Acts" has the same meaning as in the Taxes Management Act 1970.

(5) In section 202 of the Taxes Act 1988—

(a) in subsection (6), the words "must not be paid by the employee under a covenant" shall cease to have effect;

(b) subsection (7) shall cease to have effect; and

(c) in subsection (11), in the definition of "charity", after "section 506" there shall be inserted " and includes each of the bodies mentioned in section 507 ".

(6) Subsections (1) to (4) above shall have effect in relation to supplements or other amounts payable in respect of sums withheld on or after 6th April 2000 and before 6th April 2003; and no claim under

subsection (2) above shall be entertained if made on or after 6th April 2004.

(7) Subsection (5) above shall have effect in relation to sums withheld on or after 6th April 2000.

39 Gift aid payments by individuals.

(1) Section 25 of the Finance Act 1990 (donations to charity by individuals) shall be amended in accordance with subsections (2) to (7) below.

(2) In subsection (1)(c), for "an appropriate certificate" there shall be substituted " an appropriate declaration ".

(3) In subsection (2)—

(a) paragraphs (c) and (g) shall cease to have effect;

(b) in paragraph (e), for "two and a half per cent of the amount of the gift" there shall be substituted " the limit imposed by subsection (5A) below "; and

(c) for paragraph (i) there shall be substituted—

"(i) either—

(i) at the time the gift is made, the donor is resident in the United Kingdom or performs duties which by virtue of section 132(4)(a) of the Taxes Act 1988 (Crown employees serving overseas) are treated as being performed in the United Kingdom; or

(ii) the grossed up amount of the gift would, if in fact made, be payable out of profits or gains brought into charge to income tax or capital gains tax.".

(4) For subsection (3) there shall be substituted—

"(3) The reference in subsection (1)(c) above to an appropriate declaration is a reference to a declaration which—

(a) is given in such manner as may be prescribed by regulations made by the Board; and

(b) contains such information and such statements as may be so prescribed.

(3A) Regulations made for the purposes of subsection (3) above may—

(a) provide for declarations to have effect, to cease to have effect or to be deemed never to have had effect in such circumstances and for such purposes as may be prescribed by the regulations;

(b) require charities to keep records with respect to declarations given to them by donors; and

(c) make different provision for declarations made in a different manner.".

(5) After subsection (5) there shall be inserted—

"(5A) The limit imposed by this subsection is—

(a) where the amount of the gift does not exceed £100, 25 per cent of the amount of the gift;

(b) where the amount of the gift exceeds £100 but does not exceed £1,000, £25;

(c) where the amount of the gift exceeds £1,000, 2.5 per cent of the amount of the gift.

(5B) Where a benefit received in consequence of making a gift—

(a) consists of the right to receive benefits at intervals over a period of less than twelve months;

(b) relates to a period of less than twelve months; or

(c) is one of a series of benefits received at intervals in consequence of making a series of gifts at intervals of less than twelve months,

the value of the benefit shall be adjusted for the purposes of subsection (4) above and the amount of the gift shall be adjusted for the purposes of subsection (5A) above.

(5C) Where a benefit, other than a benefit which is one of a series of benefits received at intervals, is received in consequence of making a gift which is one of a series of gifts made at intervals of less than twelve months, the amount of the gift shall be adjusted for the purposes of subsection (5A) above.

(5D) Where the value of a benefit, or the amount of a gift, falls to be adjusted under subsection (5B) or (5C) above, the value or amount shall be multiplied by 365 and the result shall be divided by—

(a) in a case falling within subsection (5B)(a) or (b) above, the number of days in the period of less than twelve months;

(b) in a case falling within subsection (5B)(c) or (5C) above, the average number of days in the intervals of less than twelve months;

and the reference in subsection (5B) above to subsection (4) above is a reference to that subsection as it applies for the purposes of subsection (2)(e) above.

(5E) In determining whether a gift to a charity falling within subsection (5F) below is a qualifying donation, there shall be disregarded the benefit of any right of admission received in consequence of

the making of the gift—

(a) to view property the preservation of which is the sole or main purpose of the charity; or

(b) to observe wildlife the conservation of which is the sole or main purpose of the charity;

but this subsection shall not apply unless the opportunity to make gifts which attract such a right is available to members of the public.

(5F) A charity falls within this subsection if its sole or main purpose is the preservation of property, or the conservation of wildlife, for the public benefit.

(5G) In subsection (5E) above "right of admission" refers to admission of the person making the gift (or any member of his family who may be admitted because of the gift) either free of the charges normally payable for admission by members of the public, or on payment of a reduced charge."

(6) For subsections (6) to (9) there shall be substituted—

"(6) Where any gift made by the donor in a year of assessment is a qualifying donation, then, for that year—

(a) the Income Tax Acts and the Taxation of Chargeable Gains Act 1992 shall have effect, in their application to him, as if—

(i) the gift had been made after deduction of income tax at the basic rate; and

(ii) the basic rate limit were increased by an amount equal to the grossed up amount of the gift;

(b) the provisions mentioned in subsection (7) below shall have effect, in their application to him, as if any reference to income tax which he is entitled to charge against any person included a reference to the tax treated as deducted from the gift; and

(c) to the extent, if any, necessary to ensure that he is charged to an amount of income tax and capital gains tax equal to the tax treated as deducted from the gift, he shall not be entitled to relief under Chapter I of Part VII of the Taxes Act 1988;

but paragraph (a)(ii) above shall not apply for the purposes of any computation under section 550(2)(a) or (b) of that Act (relief where gain charged at a higher rate).

(7) The provisions referred to in subsection (6)(b) above are—

(a) section 289A(5)(e) of the Taxes Act 1988 (relief under enterprise investment scheme);

(b) section 796(3) of that Act (credit for foreign tax); and

(c) paragraph 1(6)(f) of Schedule 15B to that Act (venture capital trusts).

(8) Where the tax treated as deducted from a gift by virtue of subsection (6) above exceeds the amount of income tax and capital gains tax with which the donor is charged for the year of assessment, the donor shall be assessable and chargeable with income tax at the basic rate on so much of the gift as is necessary to recover an amount of tax equal to the excess.

(9) In determining for the purposes of subsection (8) above the total amount of income tax and capital gains tax with which the donor is charged for the year of assessment, there shall be disregarded—

(a) any tax charged at the basic rate by virtue of—

(i) section 348 of the Taxes Act 1988 (read with section 3 of that Act); or

(ii) section 349 of that Act (read with section 350 of that Act);

(b) any tax treated as having been paid under—

(i) section 233(1)(a) of that Act (taxation of certain recipients of distributions);

(ii) section 249(4)(a) of that Act (stock dividends treated as income); or

(iii) section 547(5)(a) of that Act (method of charging life policy gain to tax);

(c) any relief to which section 256(2) of that Act applies (relief by way of income tax reduction);

(d) any relief under—

(i) section 347B of that Act (relief for maintenance payments);

(ii) section 788 of that Act (relief by agreement with other countries); or

(iii) section 790(1) of that Act (unilateral relief);

(e) any set off of tax deducted, or treated as deducted, from income other than—

(i) tax treated as deducted from income by virtue of section 421(1)(a) of that Act (taxation of borrower when loan released etc); or

(ii) tax treated as deducted from a relevant amount within the meaning of section 699A of that Act (untaxed sums comprised in the income of an estate) except to the extent that the relevant amount is or would be paid in respect of a distribution chargeable under Schedule F; and

(f) any set off of tax credits.

(9A) For the purposes of sections 257(5) and 257A(5) of the Taxes Act 1988 (age related allowances), the donor's total income shall be treated as reduced by the aggregate amount of gifts from which tax is treated as deducted by virtue of subsection (6) above."

(7) In subsection (12), paragraphs (b) and (e) and the word "and" immediately preceding paragraph (e) shall cease to have effect.

(8) In subsections (1)(b) and (3)(b) of section 257BB of the Taxes Act 1988 (transfer of relief under section 257A where relief exceeds income), after "section 256(2)(b)" there shall be inserted "(read with section 25(6)(c) of the Finance Act 1990 where applicable) ".

(9) In paragraph 4(1)(b) of Schedule 13B to that Act (children's tax credit), after "section 256(2)(b)" there shall be inserted " (read with section 25(6)(c) of the Finance Act 1990 where applicable) ".

(10) This section has effect in relation to—

(a) gifts made on or after 6th April 2000 which are not covenanted payments; and

(b) covenanted payments falling to be made on or after that date;

and any regulations made under subsection (3) of section 25 of the Finance Act 1990 (as substituted by subsection (4) above) within three months of the passing of this Act may be so made as to apply to any payments in relation to which this section has effect.

40 Gift aid payments by companies.

(1) Section 339 of the Taxes Act 1988 (charges on income: donations to charity) shall be amended in accordance with subsections (2) to (8) below.

(2) In subsection (1), for paragraph (a) there shall be substituted—

"(a) a payment which, by reason of any provision of the Taxes Acts (within the meaning of the Management Act) except section 209(4), is to be regarded as a distribution; and".

(3) Subsections (2), (3), (3A), (3F), (6), (7) and (8) shall cease to have effect.

(4) In subsection (3B)(b), for "two and a half per cent. of the amount given after deducting tax under section 339(3)" there shall be substituted " the limit imposed by subsection (3DA) below ".

(5) After subsection (3D) there shall be inserted—

"(3DA) The limit imposed by this subsection is—

(a) where the amount of the payment does not exceed £100, 25 per cent of the amount of the payment;

(b) where the amount of the payment exceeds £100 but does not exceed £1,000, £25;

(c) where the amount of the payment exceeds £1,000, 2.5 per cent of the amount of the payment.

(3DB) Where a benefit received in consequence of making a payment—

(a) consists of the right to receive benefits at intervals over a period of less than twelve months;

(b) relates to a period of less than twelve months; or

(c) is one of a series of benefits received at intervals in consequence of making a series of payments at intervals of less than twelve months,

the value of the benefit shall be adjusted for the purposes of subsection (3C) above and the amount of the payment shall be adjusted for the purposes of subsection (3DA) above.

(3DC) Where a benefit, other than a benefit which is one of a series of benefits received at intervals, is received in consequence of making a payment which is one of a series of payments made at intervals of less than twelve months, the amount of the payment shall be adjusted for the purposes of subsection (3DA) above.

(3DD) Where the value of a benefit, or the amount of a payment, falls to be adjusted under subsection (3DB) or (3DC) above, the value or amount shall be multiplied by 365 and the result shall be divided by—

(a) in a case falling within subsection (3DB)(a) or (b) above, the number of days in the period of less than twelve months;

(b) in a case falling within subsection (3DB)(c) or (3DC) above, the average number of days in the intervals of less than twelve months;

and the reference in subsection (3DB) to subsection (3C) above is a reference to that subsection as it applies for the purposes of subsection (3B) above."

(6) For subsection (4) there shall be substituted—

"(4) Where a company gives a sum of money to a charity, the gift shall in the hands of the charity be treated for the purposes of this Act as if it were an annual payment.".

(7) For subsection (7AA) there shall be substituted—

"(7AA) Where—

(a) a qualifying donation to a charity is made by a company which is wholly owned by a charity, and

(b) the company makes a claim for the donation, or any part of it, to be deemed for the purposes of section 338 to be a charge on income paid in an accounting period falling wholly or partly within the period of nine months ending with the date of the making of the donation,

the donation or part shall be deemed for those purposes to be a charge on income paid in that accounting period, and not in any later period.

A claim under this subsection must be made within the period of two years immediately following the accounting period in which the donation is made, or such longer period as the Board may allow."

(8) In subsection (9), the words "in subsections (1) to (4) above includes" shall cease to have effect.

(9) In subsection (1) of section 209 of the Taxes Act 1988 (meaning of "distribution"), for "section 339(6) and any other express exceptions" there shall be substituted " any express exceptions ".

(10) In subsection (2)(a) of section 338 of that Act (allowance of charges on income and capital), after "company" there shall be inserted " or payments falling within paragraph (b) below ".

(11) This section has effect in relation to payments made on or after 1st April 2000; and—

(a) so much of an accounting period as falls before that date; and

(b) so much of it as falls after 31st March 2000,

shall be treated as separate accounting periods for the purposes of the amendment made by subsection (5) above.

41 Covenanted payments to charities.

(1) In subsection (5)(b) of section 338 of the Taxes Act 1988 (allowances of charges on income and capital), for "a covenanted donation to charity" there shall be substituted " a qualifying donation".

(2) In section 347A of that Act (annual payments and interest: general rule), subsections (2)(b), (7) and (8) shall cease to have effect.

(3) In subsection (3) of section 348 of that Act (payments out of profits or gains brought into charge to income tax: deductions of tax), at the end there shall be inserted " or to any payment which is a qualifying donation for the purposes of section 25 of the Finance Act 1990 ".

(4) In subsection (1) of section 349 of that Act (payments not out of profits or gains brought into charge to income tax, and annual interest), at the end there shall be inserted " or to any payment which is a qualifying donation (within the meaning of section 339) or a qualifying donation for the purposes of section 25 of the Finance Act 1990 ".

(5) In subsection (6) of section 505 of that Act (charities: general), the words "and, for this purpose, all covenanted payments to charity (within the meaning of section 347A(7)) shall be treated as a single item" shall cease to have effect.

(6) In subsection (9) of section 660A of that Act (income arising under a settlement where settlor retains an interest), for paragraph (b) there shall be substituted—

"(b) qualifying donations for the purposes of section 25 of the Finance Act 1990."

(7) Section 59 of the Finance Act 1989 (covenanted subscriptions) shall cease to have effect.

(8) Where a deed of covenant executed by an individual before 6th April 2000 provides for the payment of specified amounts, any amount payable under the deed on or after that date shall be determined as if the individual were entitled to deduct tax from that amount at the basic rate.

(9) This section shall have effect in relation to covenanted payments—

(a) falling to be made by individuals on or after 6th April 2000; or

(b) made by companies on or after 1st April 2000.

...

44 Gifts to charity from certain trusts.

(1) Chapter IA of Part XV of the Taxes Act 1988 (liability of settlors) shall not apply to any qualifying income which arises under a trust the trustees of which are resident in the United Kingdom (a "UK trust") if—

(a) it is given by the trustees to a charity in the year of assessment in which it arises; or

(b) it is income to which a charity is entitled under the terms of the trust.

(2) Subject to subsection (3) below, where in any year of assessment qualifying income arising under a UK trust from different sources exceeds the amount of that income falling within subsection (1) above, that amount shall be rateably apportioned between those sources.

(3) Nothing in subsection (2) above shall affect the operation of any requirement that the whole, or any specified part, of the income from a particular source be given to a charity.

(4) Where in any year of assessment qualifying income arising under a UK trust exceeds the amount of that income falling within subsection (1) above, any management expenses for that year shall be rateably apportioned between—

(a) so much of that income as is equal to that amount; and

(b) so much of that income as exceeds that amount.

(5) In this section—

"charity" has the same meaning as in section 506 of the Taxes Act 1988 and includes each of the bodies mentioned in section 507 of that Act;

"qualifying income" means—

(i) income which is to be accumulated;

(ii) income which is payable at the discretion of the trustees or any other person (whether or not the trustees have power to accumulate it); or

(iii) income which (before being distributed) is income of any person other than the trustees;

"resident", in relation to the trustees of a trust, shall be construed in accordance with section 110 of the Finance Act 1989;

and the reference to Chapter IA of Part XV of the Taxes Act 1988 includes a reference to that Chapter as it has effect by virtue of section 660E of that Act (application to settlements by two or more settlors).

(6) This section has effect in relation to qualifying income arising to a UK trust on or after 6th April 2000.

...

157 Short title.

This Act may be cited as the Finance Act 2000.

Freedom of Information Act 2000

2000 CHAPTER 36

An Act to make provision for the disclosure of information held by public authorities or by persons providing services for them and to amend the Data Protection Act 1998 and the Public Records Act 1958; and for connected purposes.

[30th November 2000]

Part I Access to information held by public authorities

Right to information

1 General right of access to information held by public authorities.

(1) Any person making a request for information to a public authority is entitled—

(a) to be informed in writing by the public authority whether it holds information of the description specified in the request, and

(b) if that is the case, to have that information communicated to him.

(2) Subsection (1) has effect subject to the following provisions of this section and to the provisions of sections 2, 9, 12 and 14.

(3) Where a public authority—

(a) reasonably requires further information in order to identify and locate the information requested, and

(b) has informed the applicant of that requirement,

the authority is not obliged to comply with subsection (1) unless it is supplied with that further information.

(4) The information—

(a) in respect of which the applicant is to be informed under subsection (1)(a), or

(b) which is to be communicated under subsection (1)(b),

is the information in question held at the time when the request is received, except that account may be taken of any amendment or deletion made between that time and the time when the information is

to be communicated under subsection (1)(b), being an amendment or deletion that would have been made regardless of the receipt of the request.

(5) A public authority is to be taken to have complied with subsection (1)(a) in relation to any information if it has communicated the information to the applicant in accordance with subsection (1)(b).

(6) In this Act, the duty of a public authority to comply with subsection (1)(a) is referred to as "the duty to confirm or deny".

2 Effect of the exemptions in Part II.

(1) Where any provision of Part II states that the duty to confirm or deny does not arise in relation to any information, the effect of the provision is that where either—

(a) the provision confers absolute exemption, or

(b) in all the circumstances of the case, the public interest in maintaining the exclusion of the duty to confirm or deny outweighs the public interest in disclosing whether the public authority holds the information,

section 1(1)(a) does not apply.

(2) In respect of any information which is exempt information by virtue of any provision of Part II, section 1(1)(b) does not apply if or to the extent that—

(a) the information is exempt information by virtue of a provision conferring absolute exemption, or

(b) in all the circumstances of the case, the public interest in maintaining the exemption outweighs the public interest in disclosing the information.

(3) For the purposes of this section, the following provisions of Part II (and no others) are to be regarded as conferring absolute exemption—

(a) section 21,

(b) section 23,

(c) section 32,

(d) section 34,

(e) section 36 so far as relating to information held by the House of Commons or the House of Lords,

(f) in section 40—

(i) subsection (1), and

(ii) subsection (2) so far as relating to cases where the first condition referred to in that subsection is satisfied by virtue of subsection (3)(a)(i) or (b) of that section,

(g) section 41, and

(h) section 44.

3 Public authorities.

(1) In this Act "public authority" means—

(a) subject to section 4(4), any body which, any other person who, or the holder of any office which—

(i) is listed in Schedule 1, or

(ii) is designated by order under section 5, or

(b) a publicly-owned company as defined by section 6.

(2) For the purposes of this Act, information is held by a public authority if—

(a) it is held by the authority, otherwise than on behalf of another person, or

(b) it is held by another person on behalf of the authority.

4 Amendment of Schedule 1.

(1) The [Secretary of State][1] may by order amend Schedule 1 by adding to that Schedule a reference to any body or the holder of any office which (in either case) is not for the time being listed in that Schedule but as respects which both the first and the second conditions below are satisfied.

(2) The first condition is that the body or office—

(a) is established by virtue of Her Majesty's prerogative or by an enactment or by subordinate legislation, or

(b) is established in any other way by a Minister of the Crown in his capacity as Minister, by a government department or by [the Welsh Ministers, the First Minister for Wales or the Counsel General to the Welsh Assembly Government][2].

(3) The second condition is—

(a) in the case of a body, that the body is wholly or partly constituted by appointment made by the Crown, by a Minister of the Crown, by a government department or by [the Welsh Ministers, the

First Minister for Wales or the Counsel General to the Welsh Assembly Government][3], or

(b) in the case of an office, that appointments to the office are made by the Crown, by a Minister of the Crown, by a government department or by [the Welsh Ministers, the First Minister for Wales or the Counsel General to the Welsh Assembly Government][4].

(4) If either the first or the second condition above ceases to be satisfied as respects any body or office which is listed in Part VI or VII of Schedule 1, that body or the holder of that office shall cease to be a public authority by virtue of the entry in question.

(5) The [Secretary of State][5] may by order amend Schedule 1 by removing from Part VI or VII of that Schedule an entry relating to any body or office—

(a) which has ceased to exist, or

(b) as respects which either the first or the second condition above has ceased to be satisfied.

(6) An order under subsection (1) may relate to a specified person or office or to persons or offices falling within a specified description.

(7) Before making an order under subsection (1), the [Secretary of State][6] shall—

(a) if the order adds to Part II, III, IV or VI of Schedule 1 a reference to—

(i) a body whose functions are exercisable only or mainly in or as regards Wales, or

(ii) the holder of an office whose functions are exercisable only or mainly in or as regards Wales,

consult [the Welsh Ministers][7], and

(b) if the order relates to a body which, or the holder of any office who, if the order were made, would be a Northern Ireland public authority, consult the First Minister and deputy First Minister in Northern Ireland.

(8) This section has effect subject to section 80.

(9) In this section "Minister of the Crown" includes a Northern Ireland Minister.

5 Further power to designate public authorities.

(1) The [Secretary of State][8] may by order designate as a public authority for the purposes of this Act any person who is neither listed in Schedule 1 nor capable of being added to that Schedule by an order under section 4(1), but who—

(a) appears to the Secretary of State to exercise functions of a public nature, or

(b) is providing under a contract made with a public authority any service whose provision is a function of that authority.

(2) An order under this section may designate a specified person or office or persons or offices falling within a specified description.

(3) Before making an order under this section, the [Secretary of State] shall consult every person to whom the order relates, or persons appearing to him to represent such persons.

(4) This section has effect subject to section 80.

6 Publicly-owned companies.

(1) A company is a "publicly-owned company" for the purposes of section 3(1)(b) if—

(a) it is wholly owned by the Crown, or

(b) it is wholly owned by any public authority listed in Schedule 1 other than—

(i) a government department, or

(ii) any authority which is listed only in relation to particular information.

(2) For the purposes of this section—

(a) a company is wholly owned by the Crown if it has no members except—

(i) Ministers of the Crown, government departments or companies wholly owned by the Crown, or

(ii) persons acting on behalf of Ministers of the Crown, government departments or companies wholly owned by the Crown, and

(b) a company is wholly owned by a public authority other than a government department if it has no members except—

(i) that public authority or companies wholly owned by that public authority, or

(ii) persons acting on behalf of that public authority or of companies wholly owned by that public authority.

(3) In this section—

"company" includes any body corporate;

"Minister of the Crown" includes a Northern Ireland Minister.

7 Public authorities to which Act has limited application.

(1) Where a public authority is listed in Schedule 1 only in relation to information of a specified description, nothing in Parts I to V of this Act applies to any other information held by the authority.

(2) An order under section 4(1) may, in adding an entry to Schedule 1, list the public authority only in relation to information of a specified description.

(3) The [Secretary of State][9] may by order amend Schedule 1—

(a) by limiting to information of a specified description the entry relating to any public authority, or

(b) by removing or amending any limitation to information of a specified description which is for the time being contained in any entry.

(4) Before making an order under subsection (3), the [Secretary of State][10] shall

[(a) if the order relates to the National Assembly for Wales or a Welsh public authority referred to in section 83(1)(b)(ii) (subsidiary of the Assembly Commission), consult the Presiding Officer of the National Assembly for Wales,

(aa) if the order relates to the Welsh Assembly Government or a Welsh public authority other than one referred to in section 83(1)(b)(ii), consult the First Minister for Wales,][11]

(b) if the order relates to the Northern Ireland Assembly, consult the Presiding Officer of that Assembly, and

(c) if the order relates to a Northern Ireland department or a Northern Ireland public authority, consult the First Minister and deputy First Minister in Northern Ireland.

(5) An order under section 5(1)(a) must specify the functions of the public authority designated by the order with respect to which the designation is to have effect; and nothing in Parts I to V of this Act applies to information which is held by the authority but does not relate to the exercise of those functions.

(6) An order under section 5(1)(b) must specify the services provided under contract with respect to which the designation is to have effect; and nothing in Parts I to V of this Act applies to information which is held by the public authority designated by the order but does not relate to the provision of those services.

(7) Nothing in Parts I to V of this Act applies in relation to any information held by a publicly-owned company which is excluded information in relation to that company.

(8) In subsection (7) "excluded information", in relation to a publicly-owned company, means information which is of a description specified in relation to that company in an order made by the [Secretary of State][12] for the purposes of this subsection.

(9) In this section "publicly-owned company" has the meaning given by section 6.

8 Request for information.

(1) In this Act any reference to a "request for information" is a reference to such a request which—

(a) is in writing,

(b) states the name of the applicant and an address for correspondence, and

(c) describes the information requested.

(2) For the purposes of subsection (1)(a), a request is to be treated as made in writing where the text of the request—

(a) is transmitted by electronic means,

(b) is received in legible form, and

(c) is capable of being used for subsequent reference.

9 Fees.

(1) A public authority to whom a request for information is made may, within the period for complying with section 1(1), give the applicant a notice in writing (in this Act referred to as a "fees notice") stating that a fee of an amount specified in the notice is to be charged by the authority for complying with section 1(1).

(2) Where a fees notice has been given to the applicant, the public authority is not obliged to comply with section 1(1) unless the fee is paid within the period of three months beginning with the day on which the fees notice is given to the applicant.

(3) Subject to subsection (5), any fee under this section must be determined by the public authority in accordance with regulations made by the [Secretary of State][13].

(4) Regulations under subsection (3) may, in particular, provide—

(a) that no fee is to be payable in prescribed cases,

(b) that any fee is not to exceed such maximum as may be specified in, or determined in accordance with, the regulations, and

(c) that any fee is to be calculated in such manner as may be prescribed by the regulations.

(5) Subsection (3) does not apply where provision is made by or under any enactment as to the fee that may be charged by the public authority for the disclosure of the information.

10 Time for compliance with request.

(1) Subject to subsections (2) and (3), a public authority must comply with section 1(1) promptly and in any event not later than the twentieth working day following the date of receipt.

(2) Where the authority has given a fees notice to the applicant and the fee is paid in accordance with section 9(2), the working days in the period beginning with the day on which the fees notice is given to the applicant and ending with the day on which the fee is received by the authority are to be disregarded in calculating for the purposes of subsection (1) the twentieth working day following the date of receipt.

(3) If, and to the extent that—

(a) section 1(1)(a) would not apply if the condition in section 2(1)(b) were satisfied, or

(b) section 1(1)(b) would not apply if the condition in section 2(2)(b) were satisfied,

the public authority need not comply with section 1(1)(a) or (b) until such time as is reasonable in the circumstances; but this subsection does not affect the time by which any notice under section 17(1) must be given.

(4) The [Secretary of State][14] may by regulations provide that subsections (1) and (2) are to have effect as if any reference to the twentieth working day following the date of receipt were a reference to such other day, not later than the sixtieth working day following the date of receipt, as may be specified in, or determined in accordance with, the regulations.

(5) Regulations under subsection (4) may—

(a) prescribe different days in relation to different cases, and

(b) confer a discretion on the Commissioner.

(6) In this section—

"the date of receipt" means—

(a) the day on which the public authority receives the request for information, or

(b) if later, the day on which it receives the information referred to in section 1(3);

"working day" means any day other than a Saturday, a Sunday, Christmas Day, Good Friday or a day which is a bank holiday under the Banking and Financial Dealings Act 1971 in any part of the United Kingdom.

11 Means by which communication to be made.

(1) Where, on making his request for information, the applicant expresses a preference for communication by any one or more of the following means, namely—

(a) the provision to the applicant of a copy of the information in permanent form or in another form acceptable to the applicant,

(b) the provision to the applicant of a reasonable opportunity to inspect a record containing the information, and

(c) the provision to the applicant of a digest or summary of the information in permanent form or in another form acceptable to the applicant,

the public authority shall so far as reasonably practicable give effect to that preference.

(2) In determining for the purposes of this section whether it is reasonably practicable to communicate information by particular means, the public authority may have regard to all the circumstances, including the cost of doing so.

(3) Where the public authority determines that it is not reasonably practicable to comply with any preference expressed by the applicant in making his request, the authority shall notify the applicant of the reasons for its determination.

(4) Subject to subsection (1), a public authority may comply with a request by communicating information by any means which are reasonable in the circumstances.

12 Exemption where cost of compliance exceeds appropriate limit.

(1) Section 1(1) does not oblige a public authority to comply with a request for information if the authority

estimates that the cost of complying with the request would exceed the appropriate limit.

(2) Subsection (1) does not exempt the public authority from its obligation to comply with paragraph (a) of section 1(1) unless the estimated cost of complying with that paragraph alone would exceed the appropriate limit.

(3) In subsections (1) and (2) "the appropriate limit" means such amount as may be prescribed, and different amounts may be prescribed in relation to different cases.

(4) The [Secretary of State][15] may by regulations provide that, in such circumstances as may be prescribed, where two or more requests for information are made to a public authority—

(a) by one person, or

(b) by different persons who appear to the public authority to be acting in concert or in pursuance of a campaign,

the estimated cost of complying with any of the requests is to be taken to be the estimated total cost of complying with all of them.

(5) The [Secretary of State][16] may by regulations make provision for the purposes of this section as to the costs to be estimated and as to the manner in which they are to be estimated.

13 Fees for disclosure where cost of compliance exceeds appropriate limit.

(1) A public authority may charge for the communication of any information whose communication—

(a) is not required by section 1(1) because the cost of complying with the request for information exceeds the amount which is the appropriate limit for the purposes of section 12(1) and (2), and

(b) is not otherwise required by law,

such fee as may be determined by the public authority in accordance with regulations made by the [Secretary of State][17] .

(2) Regulations under this section may, in particular, provide—

(a) that any fee is not to exceed such maximum as may be specified in, or determined in accordance with, the regulations, and

(b) that any fee is to be calculated in such manner as may be prescribed by the regulations.

(3) Subsection (1) does not apply where provision is made by or under any enactment as to the fee that may be charged by the public authority for the disclosure of the information.

14 Vexatious or repeated requests.

(1) Section 1(1) does not oblige a public authority to comply with a request for information if the request is vexatious.

(2) Where a public authority has previously complied with a request for information which was made by any person, it is not obliged to comply with a subsequent identical or substantially similar request from that person unless a reasonable interval has elapsed between compliance with the previous request and the making of the current request.

15 Special provisions relating to public records transferred to Public Record Office, etc.

(1) Where—

(a) the appropriate records authority receives a request for information which relates to information which is, or if it existed would be, contained in a transferred public record, and

(b) either of the conditions in subsection (2) is satisfied in relation to any of that information,

that authority shall, within the period for complying with section 1(1), send a copy of the request to the responsible authority.

(2) The conditions referred to in subsection (1)(b) are—

(a) that the duty to confirm or deny is expressed to be excluded only by a provision of Part II not specified in subsection (3) of section 2, and

(b) that the information is exempt information only by virtue of a provision of Part II not specified in that subsection.

(3) On receiving the copy, the responsible authority shall, within such time as is reasonable in all the circumstances, inform the appropriate records authority of the determination required by virtue of subsection (3) or (4) of section 66.

(4) In this Act "transferred public record" means a public record which has been transferred—

(a) to the Public Record Office,

(b) to another place of deposit appointed by the Lord Chancellor under the Public Records Act 1958, or

(c) to the Public Record Office of Northern Ireland.

(5) In this Act—

"appropriate records authority", in relation to a transferred public record, means—

(a) in a case falling within subsection (4)(a), the Public Record Office,

(b) in a case falling within subsection (4)(b), the Lord Chancellor, and

(c) in a case falling within subsection (4)(c), the Public Record Office of Northern Ireland;

"responsible authority", in relation to a transferred public record, means—

(a) in the case of a record transferred as mentioned in subsection (4)(a) or (b) from a government department in the charge of a Minister of the Crown, the Minister of the Crown who appears to the Lord Chancellor to be primarily concerned,

(b) in the case of a record transferred as mentioned in subsection (4)(a) or (b) from any other person, the person who appears to the Lord Chancellor to be primarily concerned,

(c) in the case of a record transferred to the Public Record Office of Northern Ireland from a government department in the charge of a Minister of the Crown, the Minister of the Crown who appears to the appropriate Northern Ireland Minister to be primarily concerned,

(d) in the case of a record transferred to the Public Record Office of Northern Ireland from a Northern Ireland department, the Northern Ireland Minister who appears to the appropriate Northern Ireland Minister to be primarily concerned, or

(e) in the case of a record transferred to the Public Record Office of Northern Ireland from any other person, the person who appears to the appropriate Northern Ireland Minister to be primarily concerned.

16 Duty to provide advice and assistance.

(1) It shall be the duty of a public authority to provide advice and assistance, so far as it would be reasonable to expect the authority to do so, to persons who propose to make, or have made, requests for information to it.

(2) Any public authority which, in relation to the provision of advice or assistance in any case, conforms with the code of practice under section 45 is to be taken to comply with the duty imposed by subsection (1) in relation to that case.

Refusal of request

17 Refusal of request.

(1) A public authority which, in relation to any request for information, is to any extent relying on a claim that any provision of Part II relating to the duty to confirm or deny is relevant to the request or on a claim that information is exempt information must, within the time for complying with section 1(1), give the applicant a notice which—

(a) states that fact,

(b) specifies the exemption in question, and

(c) states (if that would not otherwise be apparent) why the exemption applies.

(2) Where—

(a) in relation to any request for information, a public authority is, as respects any information, relying on a claim—

(i) that any provision of Part II which relates to the duty to confirm or deny and is not specified in section 2(3) is relevant to the request, or

(ii) that the information is exempt information only by virtue of a provision not specified in section 2(3), and

(b) at the time when the notice under subsection (1) is given to the applicant, the public authority (or, in a case falling within section 66(3) or (4), the responsible authority) has not yet reached a decision as to the application of subsection (1)(b) or (2)(b) of section 2,

the notice under subsection (1) must indicate that no decision as to the application of that provision has yet been reached and must contain an estimate of the date by which the authority expects that such a decision will have been reached.

(3) A public authority which, in relation to any request for information, is to any extent relying on a claim that subsection (1)(b) or (2)(b) of section 2 applies must, either in the notice under subsection (1) or in a separate notice given within such time as is reasonable in the circumstances, state the reasons for claiming—

(a) that, in all the circumstances of the case, the public interest in maintaining the exclusion of the duty

to confirm or deny outweighs the public interest in disclosing whether the authority holds the information, or

(b) that, in all the circumstances of the case, the public interest in maintaining the exemption outweighs the public interest in disclosing the information.

(4) A public authority is not obliged to make a statement under subsection (1)(c) or (3) if, or to the extent that, the statement would involve the disclosure of information which would itself be exempt information.

(5) A public authority which, in relation to any request for information, is relying on a claim that section 12 or 14 applies must, within the time for complying with section 1(1), give the applicant a notice stating that fact.

(6) Subsection (5) does not apply where—

(a) the public authority is relying on a claim that section 14 applies,

(b) the authority has given the applicant a notice, in relation to a previous request for information, stating that it is relying on such a claim, and

(c) it would in all the circumstances be unreasonable to expect the authority to serve a further notice under subsection (5) in relation to the current request.

(7) A notice under subsection (1), (3) or (5) must—

(a) contain particulars of any procedure provided by the public authority for dealing with complaints about the handling of requests for information or state that the authority does not provide such a procedure, and

(b) contain particulars of the right conferred by section 50.

The Information Commissioner and the Information Tribunal

18 The Information Commissioner and the Information Tribunal.

(1) The Data Protection Commissioner shall be known instead as the Information Commissioner.

(2) The Data Protection Tribunal shall be known instead as the Information Tribunal.

(3) In this Act—

(a) the Information Commissioner is referred to as "the Commissioner", and

(b) the Information Tribunal is referred to as "the Tribunal".

(4) Schedule 2 (which makes provision consequential on subsections (1) and (2) and amendments of the Data Protection Act 1998 relating to the extension by this Act of the functions of the Commissioner and the Tribunal) has effect.

(5) If the person who held office as Data Protection Commissioner immediately before the day on which this Act is passed remains in office as Information Commissioner at the end of the period of two years beginning with that day, he shall vacate his office at the end of that period.

(6) Subsection (5) does not prevent the re-appointment of a person whose appointment is terminated by that subsection.

(7) In the application of paragraph 2(4)(b) and (5) of Schedule 5 to the Data Protection Act 1998 (Commissioner not to serve for more than fifteen years and not to be appointed, except in special circumstances, for a third or subsequent term) to anything done after the passing of this Act, there shall be left out of account any term of office served by virtue of an appointment made before the passing of this Act.

Publication schemes

19 Publication schemes.

(1) It shall be the duty of every public authority—

(a) to adopt and maintain a scheme which relates to the publication of information by the authority and is approved by the Commissioner (in this Act referred to as a "publication scheme"),

(b) to publish information in accordance with its publication scheme, and

(c) from time to time to review its publication scheme.

(2) A publication scheme must—

(a) specify classes of information which the public authority publishes or intends to publish,

(b) specify the manner in which information of each class is, or is intended to be, published, and

(c) specify whether the material is, or is intended to be, available to the public free of charge or on payment.

(3) In adopting or reviewing a publication scheme, a public authority shall have regard to the public interest—

(a) in allowing public access to information held by the authority, and

(b) in the publication of reasons for decisions made by the authority.

(4) A public authority shall publish its publication scheme in such manner as it thinks fit.

(5) The Commissioner may, when approving a scheme, provide that his approval is to expire at the end of a specified period.

(6) Where the Commissioner has approved the publication scheme of any public authority, he may at any time give notice to the public authority revoking his approval of the scheme as from the end of the period of six months beginning with the day on which the notice is given.

(7) Where the Commissioner—

(a) refuses to approve a proposed publication scheme, or

(b) revokes his approval of a publication scheme,

he must give the public authority a statement of his reasons for doing so.

20 Model publication schemes.

(1) The Commissioner may from time to time approve, in relation to public authorities falling within particular classes, model publication schemes prepared by him or by other persons.

(2) Where a public authority falling within the class to which an approved model scheme relates adopts such a scheme without modification, no further approval of the Commissioner is required so long as the model scheme remains approved; and where such an authority adopts such a scheme with modifications, the approval of the Commissioner is required only in relation to the modifications.

(3) The Commissioner may, when approving a model publication scheme, provide that his approval is to expire at the end of a specified period.

(4) Where the Commissioner has approved a model publication scheme, he may at any time publish, in such manner as he thinks fit, a notice revoking his approval of the scheme as from the end of the period of six months beginning with the day on which the notice is published.

(5) Where the Commissioner refuses to approve a proposed model publication scheme on the application of any person, he must give the person who applied for approval of the scheme a statement of the reasons for his refusal.

(6) Where the Commissioner refuses to approve any modifications under subsection (2), he must give the public authority a statement of the reasons for his refusal.

(7) Where the Commissioner revokes his approval of a model publication scheme, he must include in the notice under subsection (4) a statement of his reasons for doing so.

Part II Exempt information

21 Information accessible to applicant by other means.

(1) Information which is reasonably accessible to the applicant otherwise than under section 1 is exempt information.

(2) For the purposes of subsection (1)—

(a) information may be reasonably accessible to the applicant even though it is accessible only on payment, and

(b) information is to be taken to be reasonably accessible to the applicant if it is information which the public authority or any other person is obliged by or under any enactment to communicate (otherwise than by making the information available for inspection) to members of the public on request, whether free of charge or on payment.

(3) For the purposes of subsection (1), information which is held by a public authority and does not fall within subsection (2)(b) is not to be regarded as reasonably accessible to the applicant merely because the information is available from the public authority itself on request, unless the information is made available in accordance with the authority's publication scheme and any payment required is specified in, or determined in accordance with, the scheme.

22 Information intended for future publication.

(1) Information is exempt information if—

(a) the information is held by the public authority with a view to its publication, by the authority or any other person, at some future date (whether determined or not),

(b) the information was already held with a view to such publication at the time when the request for information was made, and

(c) it is reasonable in all the circumstances that the information should be withheld from disclosure until the date referred to in paragraph (a).

(2) The duty to confirm or deny does not arise if, or to the extent that, compliance with section 1(1)(a) would involve the disclosure of any information (whether or not already recorded) which falls within subsection (1).

23 Information supplied by, or relating to, bodies dealing with security matters.

(1) Information held by a public authority is exempt information if it was directly or indirectly supplied to the public authority by, or relates to, any of the bodies specified in subsection (3).

(2) A certificate signed by a Minister of the Crown certifying that the information to which it applies was directly or indirectly supplied by, or relates to, any of the bodies specified in subsection (3) shall, subject to section 60, be conclusive evidence of that fact.

(3) The bodies referred to in subsections (1) and (2) are—

(a) the Security Service,

(b) the Secret Intelligence Service,

(c) the Government Communications Headquarters,

(d) the special forces,

(e) the Tribunal established under section 65 of the Regulation of Investigatory Powers Act 2000,

(f) the Tribunal established under section 7 of the Interception of Communications Act 1985,

(g) the Tribunal established under section 5 of the Security Service Act 1989,

(h) the Tribunal established under section 9 of the Intelligence Services Act 1994,

(i) the Security Vetting Appeals Panel,

(j) the Security Commission,

(k) the National Criminal Intelligence Service,...[18]

(l) the Service Authority for the National Criminal Intelligence Service.

[(m) the Serious Organised Crime Agency.]

(4) In subsection (3)(c) "the Government Communications Headquarters" includes any unit or part of a unit of the armed forces of the Crown which is for the time being required by the Secretary of State to assist the Government Communications Headquarters in carrying out its functions.

(5) The duty to confirm or deny does not arise if, or to the extent that, compliance with section 1(1)(a) would involve the disclosure of any information (whether or not already recorded) which was directly or indirectly supplied to the public authority by, or relates to, any of the bodies specified in subsection (3).

24 National security.

(1) Information which does not fall within section 23(1) is exempt information if exemption from section 1(1)(b) is required for the purpose of safeguarding national security.

(2) The duty to confirm or deny does not arise if, or to the extent that, exemption from section 1(1)(a) is required for the purpose of safeguarding national security.

(3) a certificate signed by a Minister of the Crown certifying that exemption from section 1(1)(b), or from section 1(1)(a) and (b), is, or at any time was, required for the purpose of safeguarding national security shall, subject to section 60, be conclusive evidence of that fact.

(4) A certificate under subsection (3) may identify the information to which it applies by means of a general description and may be expressed to have prospective effect.

25 Certificates under ss. 23 and 24: supplementary provisions.

(1) A document purporting to be a certificate under section 23(2) or 24(3) shall be received in evidence and deemed to be such a certificate unless the contrary is proved.

(2) A document which purports to be certified by or on behalf of a Minister of the Crown as a true copy of a certificate issued by that Minister under section 23(2) or 24(3) shall in any legal proceedings be evidence (or, in Scotland, sufficient evidence) of that certificate.

(3) The power conferred by section 23(2) or 24(3) on a Minister of the Crown shall not be exercisable except by a Minister who is a member of the Cabinet or by the Attorney General, the Advocate General for Scotland or the Attorney General for Northern Ireland.

26 Defence.

(1) Information is exempt information if its disclosure under this Act would, or would be likely to, prejudice—

(a) the defence of the British Islands or of any colony, or

(b) the capability, effectiveness or security of any relevant forces.

(2) In subsection (1)(b) "relevant forces" means—

(a) the armed forces of the Crown, and

(b) any forces co-operating with those forces,

or any part of any of those forces.

(3) The duty to confirm or deny does not arise if, or to the extent that, compliance with section 1(1)(a) would, or would be likely to, prejudice any of the matters mentioned in subsection (1).

27 International relations.

(1) Information is exempt information if its disclosure under this Act would, or would be likely to, prejudice—

(a) relations between the United Kingdom and any other State,

(b) relations between the United Kingdom and any international organisation or international court,

(c) the interests of the United Kingdom abroad, or

(d) the promotion or protection by the United Kingdom of its interests abroad.

(2) Information is also exempt information if it is confidential information obtained from a State other than the United Kingdom or from an international organisation or international court.

(3) For the purposes of this section, any information obtained from a State, organisation or court is confidential at any time while the terms on which it was obtained require it to be held in confidence or while the circumstances in which it was obtained make it reasonable for the State, organisation or court to expect that it will be so held.

(4) The duty to confirm or deny does not arise if, or to the extent that, compliance with section 1(1)(a)—

(a) would, or would be likely to, prejudice any of the matters mentioned in subsection (1), or

(b) would involve the disclosure of any information (whether or not already recorded) which is confidential information obtained from a State other than the United Kingdom or from an international organisation or international court.

(5) In this section—

"international court" means any international court which is not an international organisation and which is established—

(a) by a resolution of an international organisation of which the United Kingdom is a member, or

(b) by an international agreement to which the United Kingdom is a party;

"international organisation" means any international organisation whose members include any two or more States, or any organ of such an organisation;

"State" includes the government of any State and any organ of its government, and references to a State other than the United Kingdom include references to any territory outside the United Kingdom.

28 Relations within the United Kingdom.

(1) Information is exempt information if its disclosure under this Act would, or would be likely to, prejudice relations between any administration in the United Kingdom and any other such administration.

(2) In subsection (1) "administration in the United Kingdom" means—

(a) the government of the United Kingdom,

(b) the Scottish Administration,

(c) the Executive Committee of the Northern Ireland Assembly, or

[(d) the Welsh Assembly Government.][19]

(3) The duty to confirm or deny does not arise if, or to the extent that, compliance with section 1(1)(a) would, or would be likely to, prejudice any of the matters mentioned in subsection (1).

29 The economy.

(1) Information is exempt information if its disclosure under this Act would, or would be likely to, prejudice—

(a) the economic interests of the United Kingdom or of any part of the United Kingdom, or

(b) the financial interests of any administration in the United Kingdom, as defined by section 28(2).

(2) The duty to confirm or deny does not arise if, or to the extent that, compliance with section 1(1)(a) would, or would be likely to, prejudice any of the matters mentioned in subsection (1).

30 Investigations and proceedings conducted by public authorities.

(1) Information held by a public authority is exempt information if it has at any time been held by the authority for the purposes of—

(a) any investigation which the public authority has a duty to conduct with a view to it being ascertained—

(i) whether a person should be charged with an offence, or

(ii) whether a person charged with an offence is guilty of it,

(b) any investigation which is conducted by the authority and in the circumstances may lead to a decision by the authority to institute criminal proceedings which the authority has power to conduct, or

(c) any criminal proceedings which the authority has power to conduct.

(2) Information held by a public authority is exempt information if—

(a) it was obtained or recorded by the authority for the purposes of its functions relating to—

(i) investigations falling within subsection (1)(a) or (b),

(ii) criminal proceedings which the authority has power to conduct,

(iii) investigations (other than investigations falling within subsection (1)(a) or (b)) which are conducted by the authority for any of the purposes specified in section 31(2) and either by virtue of Her Majesty's prerogative or by virtue of powers conferred by or under any enactment, or

(iv) civil proceedings which are brought by or on behalf of the authority and arise out of such investigations, and

(b) it relates to the obtaining of information from confidential sources.

(3) The duty to confirm or deny does not arise in relation to information which is (or if it were held by the public authority would be) exempt information by virtue of subsection (1) or (2).

(4) In relation to the institution or conduct of criminal proceedings or the power to conduct them, references in subsection (1)(b) or (c) and subsection (2)(a) to the public authority include references—

(a) to any officer of the authority,

(b) in the case of a government department other than a Northern Ireland department, to the Minister of the Crown in charge of the department, and

(c) in the case of a Northern Ireland department, to the Northern Ireland Minister in charge of the department.

[(5) In this section—

"criminal proceedings" includes service law proceedings (as defined by section 324(5) of the Armed Forces Act 2006);

"offence" includes a service offence (as defined by section 50 of that Act).][20]

(6) In the application of this section to Scotland—

(a) in subsection (1)(b), for the words from "a decision" to the end there is substituted " a decision by the authority to make a report to the procurator fiscal for the purpose of enabling him to determine whether criminal proceedings should be instituted ",

(b) in subsections (1)(c) and (2)(a)(ii) for "which the authority has power to conduct" there is substituted " which have been instituted in consequence of a report made by the authority to the procurator fiscal ", and

(c) for any reference to a person being charged with an offence there is substituted a reference to the person being prosecuted for the offence.

31 Law enforcement.

(1) Information which is not exempt information by virtue of section 30 is exempt information if its disclosure under this Act would, or would be likely to, prejudice—

(a) the prevention or detection of crime,

(b) the apprehension or prosecution of offenders,

(c) the administration of justice,

(d) the assessment or collection of any tax or duty or of any imposition of a similar nature,

(e) the operation of the immigration controls,

(f) the maintenance of security and good order in prisons or in other institutions where persons are

lawfully detained,

(g) the exercise by any public authority of its functions for any of the purposes specified in subsection (2),

(h) any civil proceedings which are brought by or on behalf of a public authority and arise out of an investigation conducted, for any of the purposes specified in subsection (2), by or on behalf of the authority by virtue of Her Majesty's prerogative or by virtue of powers conferred by or under an enactment, or

(i) any inquiry held under the Fatal Accidents and Sudden Deaths Inquiries (Scotland) Act 1976 to the extent that the inquiry arises out of an investigation conducted, for any of the purposes specified in subsection (2), by or on behalf of the authority by virtue of Her Majesty's prerogative or by virtue of powers conferred by or under an enactment.

(2) The purposes referred to in subsection (1)(g) to (i) are—

(a) the purpose of ascertaining whether any person has failed to comply with the law,

(b) the purpose of ascertaining whether any person is responsible for any conduct which is improper,

(c) the purpose of ascertaining whether circumstances which would justify regulatory action in pursuance of any enactment exist or may arise,

(d) the purpose of ascertaining a person's fitness or competence in relation to the management of bodies corporate or in relation to any profession or other activity which he is, or seeks to become, authorised to carry on,

(e) the purpose of ascertaining the cause of an accident,

(f) the purpose of protecting charities against misconduct or mismanagement (whether by trustees or other persons) in their administration,

(g) the purpose of protecting the property of charities from loss or misapplication,

(h) the purpose of recovering the property of charities,

(i) the purpose of securing the health, safety and welfare of persons at work, and

(j) the purpose of protecting persons other than persons at work against risk to health or safety arising out of or in connection with the actions of persons at work.

(3) The duty to confirm or deny does not arise if, or to the extent that, compliance with section 1(1)(a) would, or would be likely to, prejudice any of the matters mentioned in subsection (1).

32 Court records, etc.

(1) Information held by a public authority is exempt information if it is held only by virtue of being contained in—

(a) any document filed with, or otherwise placed in the custody of, a court for the purposes of proceedings in a particular cause or matter,

(b) any document served upon, or by, a public authority for the purposes of proceedings in a particular cause or matter, or

(c) any document created by—

(i) a court, or

(ii) a member of the administrative staff of a court,

for the purposes of proceedings in a particular cause or matter.

(2) Information held by a public authority is exempt information if it is held only by virtue of being contained in—

(a) any document placed in the custody of a person conducting an inquiry or arbitration, for the purposes of the inquiry or arbitration, or

(b) any document created by a person conducting an inquiry or arbitration, for the purposes of the inquiry or arbitration.

(3) The duty to confirm or deny does not arise in relation to information which is (or if it were held by the public authority would be) exempt information by virtue of this section.

(4) In this section—

(a)"court" includes any tribunal or body exercising the judicial power of the State,

(b)"proceedings in a particular cause or matter" includes any inquest or post-mortem examination,

(c)"inquiry" means any inquiry or hearing held under any provision contained in, or made under, an enactment, and

(d) except in relation to Scotland, "arbitration" means any arbitration to which Part I of the Arbitration

Act 1996 applies.

33 Audit functions.

(1) This section applies to any public authority which has functions in relation to—

(a) the audit of the accounts of other public authorities, or

(b) the examination of the economy, efficiency and effectiveness with which other public authorities use their resources in discharging their functions.

(2) Information held by a public authority to which this section applies is exempt information if its disclosure would, or would be likely to, prejudice the exercise of any of the authority's functions in relation to any of the matters referred to in subsection (1).

(3) The duty to confirm or deny does not arise in relation to a public authority to which this section applies if, or to the extent that, compliance with section 1(1)(a) would, or would be likely to, prejudice the exercise of any of the authority's functions in relation to any of the matters referred to in subsection (1).

34 Parliamentary privilege.

(1) Information is exempt information if exemption from section 1(1)(b) is required for the purpose of avoiding an infringement of the privileges of either House of Parliament.

(2) The duty to confirm or deny does not apply if, or to the extent that, exemption from section 1(1)(a) is required for the purpose of avoiding an infringement of the privileges of either House of Parliament.

(3) A certificate signed by the appropriate authority certifying that exemption from section 1(1)(b), or from section 1(1)(a) and (b), is, or at any time was, required for the purpose of avoiding an infringement of the privileges of either House of Parliament shall be conclusive evidence of that fact.

(4) In subsection (3) "the appropriate authority" means—

(a) in relation to the House of Commons, the Speaker of that House, and

(b) in relation to the House of Lords, the Clerk of the Parliaments.

35 Formulation of government policy, etc.

(1) Information held by a government department or by [the Welsh Assembly Government][21] is exempt information if it relates to—

(a) the formulation or development of government policy,

(b) Ministerial communications,

(c) the provision of advice by any of the Law Officers or any request for the provision of such advice, or

(d) the operation of any Ministerial private office.

(2) Once a decision as to government policy has been taken, any statistical information used to provide an informed background to the taking of the decision is not to be regarded—

(a) for the purposes of subsection (1)(a), as relating to the formulation or development of government policy, or

(b) for the purposes of subsection (1)(b), as relating to Ministerial communications.

(3) The duty to confirm or deny does not arise in relation to information which is (or if it were held by the public authority would be) exempt information by virtue of subsection (1).

(4) In making any determination required by section 2(1)(b) or (2)(b) in relation to information which is exempt information by virtue of subsection (1)(a), regard shall be had to the particular public interest in the disclosure of factual information which has been used, or is intended to be used, to provide an informed background to decision-taking.

(5) In this section—

"government policy" includes the policy of the Executive Committee of the Northern Ireland Assembly and the policy of [the Welsh Assembly Government][22];

"the Law Officers" means the Attorney General, the Solicitor General, the Advocate General for Scotland, the Lord Advocate, the Solicitor General for Scotland [, the Counsel General to the Welsh Assembly Government][23] and the Attorney General for Northern Ireland;

"Ministerial communications" means any communications—

(a) between Ministers of the Crown,

(b) between Northern Ireland Ministers, including Northern Ireland junior Ministers, or

(c)[between members of the Welsh Assembly Government][24]

and includes, in particular, proceedings of the Cabinet or of any committee of the Cabinet, proceedings of the Executive Committee of the Northern Ireland Assembly, and proceedings of [the Cabinet or any committee of the Cabinet of the Welsh Assembly Government][25];

"Ministerial private office" means any part of a government department which provides personal administrative support to a Minister of the Crown, to a Northern Ireland Minister or a Northern Ireland junior Minister or [any part of the administration of the Welsh Assembly Government providing personal administrative support to the members of the Welsh Assembly Government][26];

"Northern Ireland junior Minister" means a member of the Northern Ireland Assembly appointed as a junior Minister under section 19 of the Northern Ireland Act 1998.

36 Prejudice to effective conduct of public affairs.

(1) This section applies to—

(a) information which is held by a government department or by [the Welsh Assembly Government][27] and is not exempt information by virtue of section 35, and

(b) information which is held by any other public authority.

(2) Information to which this section applies is exempt information if, in the reasonable opinion of a qualified person, disclosure of the information under this Act—

(a) would, or would be likely to, prejudice—

(i) the maintenance of the convention of the collective responsibility of Ministers of the Crown, or

(ii) the work of the Executive Committee of the Northern Ireland Assembly, or

[(iii) the work of the Cabinet of the Welsh Assembly Government.][28]

(b) would, or would be likely to, inhibit—

(i) the free and frank provision of advice, or

(ii) the free and frank exchange of views for the purposes of deliberation, or

(c) would otherwise prejudice, or would be likely otherwise to prejudice, the effective conduct of public affairs.

(3) The duty to confirm or deny does not arise in relation to information to which this section applies (or would apply if held by the public authority) if, or to the extent that, in the reasonable opinion of a qualified person, compliance with section 1(1)(a) would, or would be likely to, have any of the effects mentioned in subsection (2).

(4) In relation to statistical information, subsections (2) and (3) shall have effect with the omission of the words "in the reasonable opinion of a qualified person".

(5) In subsections (2) and (3) "qualified person"—

(a) in relation to information held by a government department in the charge of a Minister of the Crown, means any Minister of the Crown,

(b) in relation to information held by a Northern Ireland department, means the Northern Ireland Minister in charge of the department,

(c) in relation to information held by any other government department, means the commissioners or other person in charge of that department,

(d) in relation to information held by the House of Commons, means the Speaker of that House,

(e) in relation to information held by the House of Lords, means the Clerk of the Parliaments,

(f) in relation to information held by the Northern Ireland Assembly, means the Presiding Officer,

[(g) in relation to information held by the Welsh Assembly Government, means the Welsh Ministers or the Counsel General to the Welsh Assembly Government,

(ga) in relation to information held by the National Assembly for Wales, means the Presiding Officer of the National Assembly for Wales,

(gb) in relation to information held by any Welsh public authority (other than one referred to in section 83(1)(b)(ii) (subsidiary of the Assembly Commission), the Auditor General for Wales or the Public Services Ombudsman for Wales), means—

(i) the public authority, or

(ii) any officer or employee of the authority authorised by the Welsh Ministers or the Counsel General to the Welsh Assembly Government",

(gc) in relation to information held by a Welsh public authority referred to in section 83(1)(b)(ii), means—

(i) the public authority, or

(ii) any officer or employee of the authority authorised by the Presiding Officer of the National Assembly for Wales,][29]

(i) in relation to information held by the National Audit Office, means the Comptroller and Auditor

General,

(j) in relation to information held by the Northern Ireland Audit Office, means the Comptroller and Auditor General for Northern Ireland,

(k) in relation to information held by the Auditor General for Wales, means the Auditor General for Wales,

[(ka) in relation to information held by the Public Services Ombudsman for Wales, means the Public Services Ombudsman for Wales,][30]

(l) in relation to information held by any Northern Ireland public authority other than the Northern Ireland Audit Office, means—

(i) the public authority, or

(ii) any officer or employee of the authority authorised by the First Minister and deputy First Minister in Northern Ireland acting jointly,

(m) in relation to information held by the Greater London Authority, means the Mayor of London,

(n) in relation to information held by a functional body within the meaning of the Greater London Authority Act 1999, means the chairman of that functional body, and

(o) in relation to information held by any public authority not falling within any of paragraphs (a) to (n), means—

(i) a Minister of the Crown,

(ii) the public authority, if authorised for the purposes of this section by a Minister of the Crown, or

(iii) any officer or employee of the public authority who is authorised for the purposes of this section by a Minister of the Crown.

(6) Any authorisation for the purposes of this section—

(a) may relate to a specified person or to persons falling within a specified class,

(b) may be general or limited to particular classes of case, and

(c) may be granted subject to conditions.

(7) A certificate signed by the qualified person referred to in subsection (5)(d) or (e) above certifying that in his reasonable opinion—

(a) disclosure of information held by either House of Parliament, or

(b) compliance with section 1(1)(a) by either House,

would, or would be likely to, have any of the effects mentioned in subsection (2) shall be conclusive evidence of that fact.

37 Communications with Her Majesty, etc. and honours.

(1) Information is exempt information if it relates to—

(a) communications with Her Majesty, with other members of the Royal Family or with the Royal Household, or

(b) the conferring by the Crown of any honour or dignity.

(2) The duty to confirm or deny does not arise in relation to information which is (or if it were held by the public authority would be) exempt information by virtue of subsection (1).

38 Health and safety.

(1) Information is exempt information if its disclosure under this Act would, or would be likely to—

(a) endanger the physical or mental health of any individual, or

(b) endanger the safety of any individual.

(2) The duty to confirm or deny does not arise if, or to the extent that, compliance with section 1(1)(a) would, or would be likely to, have either of the effects mentioned in subsection (1).

39 Environmental information.

(1) Information is exempt information if the public authority holding it—

(a) is obliged by [environmental information regulations][31] to make the information available to the public in accordance with the regulations, or

(b) would be so obliged but for any exemption contained in the regulations.

[(1A) In subsection (1) "environmental information regulations" means—

(a) regulations made under section 74, or

(b) regulations made under section 2(2) of the European Communities Act 1972 for the purpose of implementing any Community obligation relating to public access to, and the dissemination of, information on the environment.][32]

(2) The duty to confirm or deny does not arise in relation to information which is (or if it were held by the public authority would be) exempt information by virtue of subsection (1).

(3) Subsection (1)(a) does not limit the generality of section 21(1).

40 Personal information.

(1) Any information to which a request for information relates is exempt information if it constitutes personal data of which the applicant is the data subject.

(2) Any information to which a request for information relates is also exempt information if—

(a) it constitutes personal data which do not fall within subsection (1), and

(b) either the first or the second condition below is satisfied.

(3) The first condition is—

(a) in a case where the information falls within any of paragraphs (a) to (d) of the definition of "data" in section 1(1) of the Data Protection Act 1998, that the disclosure of the information to a member of the public otherwise than under this Act would contravene—

(i) any of the data protection principles, or

(ii) section 10 of that Act (right to prevent processing likely to cause damage or distress), and

(b) in any other case, that the disclosure of the information to a member of the public otherwise than under this Act would contravene any of the data protection principles if the exemptions in section 33A(1) of the Data Protection Act 1998 (which relate to manual data held by public authorities) were disregarded.

(4) The second condition is that by virtue of any provision of Part IV of the Data Protection Act 1998 the information is exempt from section 7(1)(c) of that Act (data subject's right of access to personal data).

(5) The duty to confirm or deny—

(a) does not arise in relation to information which is (or if it were held by the public authority would be) exempt information by virtue of subsection (1), and

(b) does not arise in relation to other information if or to the extent that either—

(i) the giving to a member of the public of the confirmation or denial that would have to be given to comply with section 1(1)(a) would (apart from this Act) contravene any of the data protection principles or section 10 of the Data Protection Act 1998 or would do so if the exemptions in section 33A(1) of that Act were disregarded, or

(ii) by virtue of any provision of Part IV of the Data Protection Act 1998 the information is exempt from section 7(1)(a) of that Act (data subject's right to be informed whether personal data being processed).

(6) In determining for the purposes of this section whether anything done before 24th October 2007 would contravene any of the data protection principles, the exemptions in Part III of Schedule 8 to the Data Protection Act 1998 shall be disregarded.

(7) In this section—

"the data protection principles" means the principles set out in Part I of Schedule 1 to the Data Protection Act 1998, as read subject to Part II of that Schedule and section 27(1) of that Act;

"data subject" has the same meaning as in section 1(1) of that Act;

"personal data" has the same meaning as in section 1(1) of that Act.

41 Information provided in confidence.

(1) Information is exempt information if—

(a) it was obtained by the public authority from any other person (including another public authority), and

(b) the disclosure of the information to the public (otherwise than under this Act) by the public authority holding it would constitute a breach of confidence actionable by that or any other person.

(2) The duty to confirm or deny does not arise if, or to the extent that, the confirmation or denial that would have to be given to comply with section 1(1)(a) would (apart from this Act) constitute an actionable breach of confidence.

42 Legal professional privilege.

(1) Information in respect of which a claim to legal professional privilege or, in Scotland, to confidentiality of communications could be maintained in legal proceedings is exempt information.

(2) The duty to confirm or deny does not arise if, or to the extent that, compliance with section 1(1)(a) would involve the disclosure of any information (whether or not already recorded) in respect of which

such a claim could be maintained in legal proceedings.

43 Commercial interests.

(1) Information is exempt information if it constitutes a trade secret.

(2) Information is exempt information if its disclosure under this Act would, or would be likely to, prejudice the commercial interests of any person (including the public authority holding it).

(3) The duty to confirm or deny does not arise if, or to the extent that, compliance with section 1(1)(a) would, or would be likely to, prejudice the interests mentioned in subsection (2).

44 Prohibitions on disclosure.

(1) Information is exempt information if its disclosure (otherwise than under this Act) by the public authority holding it—

(a) is prohibited by or under any enactment,

(b) is incompatible with any Community obligation, or

(c) would constitute or be punishable as a contempt of court.

(2) The duty to confirm or deny does not arise if the confirmation or denial that would have to be given to comply with section 1(1)(a) would (apart from this Act) fall within any of paragraphs (a) to (c) of subsection (1).

Part III General functions of Secretary of State, Lord Chancellor and Information Commissioner

45 Issue of code of practice by Secretary of State.

(1) The [Secretary of State][33] shall issue, and may from time to time revise, a code of practice providing guidance to public authorities as to the practice which it would, in his opinion, be desirable for them to follow in connection with the discharge of the authorities' functions under Part I.

(2) The code of practice must, in particular, include provision relating to—

(a) the provision of advice and assistance by public authorities to persons who propose to make, or have made, requests for information to them,

(b) the transfer of requests by one public authority to another public authority by which the information requested is or may be held,

(c) consultation with persons to whom the information requested relates or persons whose interests are likely to be affected by the disclosure of information,

(d) the inclusion in contracts entered into by public authorities of terms relating to the disclosure of information, and

(e) the provision by public authorities of procedures for dealing with complaints about the handling by them of requests for information.

(3) The code may make different provision for different public authorities.

(4) Before issuing or revising any code under this section, the [Secretary of State][34] shall consult the Commissioner.

(5) The [Secretary of State][35] shall lay before each House of Parliament any code or revised code made under this section.

46 Issue of code of practice by Lord Chancellor.

(1) The Lord Chancellor shall issue, and may from time to time revise, a code of practice providing guidance to relevant authorities as to the practice which it would, in his opinion, be desirable for them to follow in connection with the keeping, management and destruction of their records.

(2) For the purpose of facilitating the performance by the Public Record Office, the Public Record Office of Northern Ireland and other public authorities of their functions under this Act in relation to records which are public records for the purposes of the Public Records Act 1958 or the Public Records Act (Northern Ireland) 1923, the code may also include guidance as to—

(a) the practice to be adopted in relation to the transfer of records under section 3(4) of the Public Records Act 1958 or section 3 of the Public Records Act (Northern Ireland) 1923, and

(b) the practice of reviewing records before they are transferred under those provisions.

(3) In exercising his functions under this section, the Lord Chancellor shall have regard to the public interest in allowing public access to information held by relevant authorities.

(4) The code may make different provision for different relevant authorities.

(5) Before issuing or revising any code under this section the Lord Chancellor shall consult—

[(a) the Secretary of State,][36]

(b) the Commissioner, and

(c) in relation to Northern Ireland, the appropriate Northern Ireland Minister.

(6) The Lord Chancellor shall lay before each House of Parliament any code or revised code made under this section.

(7) In this section "relevant authority" means—

(a) any public authority, and

(b) any office or body which is not a public authority but whose administrative and departmental records are public records for the purposes of the Public Records Act 1958 or the Public Records Act (Northern Ireland) 1923.

47 General functions of Commissioner.

(1) It shall be the duty of the Commissioner to promote the following of good practice by public authorities and, in particular, so to perform his functions under this Act as to promote the observance by public authorities of—

(a) the requirements of this Act, and

(b) the provisions of the codes of practice under sections 45 and 46.

(2) The Commissioner shall arrange for the dissemination in such form and manner as he considers appropriate of such information as it may appear to him expedient to give to the public—

(a) about the operation of this Act,

(b) about good practice, and

(c) about other matters within the scope of his functions under this Act,

and may give advice to any person as to any of those matters.

(3) The Commissioner may, with the consent of any public authority, assess whether that authority is following good practice.

(4) The Commissioner may charge such sums as he may with the consent of the [Secretary of State][37] determine for any services provided by the Commissioner under this section.

(5) The Commissioner shall from time to time as he considers appropriate—

(a) consult the Keeper of Public Records about the promotion by the Commissioner of the observance by public authorities of the provisions of the code of practice under section 46 in relation to records which are public records for the purposes of the Public Records Act 1958, and

(b) consult the Deputy Keeper of the Records of Northern Ireland about the promotion by the Commissioner of the observance by public authorities of those provisions in relation to records which are public records for the purposes of the Public Records Act (Northern Ireland) 1923.

(6) In this section "good practice", in relation to a public authority, means such practice in the discharge of its functions under this Act as appears to the Commissioner to be desirable, and includes (but is not limited to) compliance with the requirements of this Act and the provisions of the codes of practice under sections 45 and 46.

48 Recommendations as to good practice.

(1) If it appears to the Commissioner that the practice of a public authority in relation to the exercise of its functions under this Act does not conform with that proposed in the codes of practice under sections 45 and 46, he may give to the authority a recommendation (in this section referred to as a "practice recommendation") specifying the steps which ought in his opinion to be taken for promoting such conformity.

(2) A practice recommendation must be given in writing and must refer to the particular provisions of the code of practice with which, in the Commissioner's opinion, the public authority's practice does not conform.

(3) Before giving to a public authority other than the Public Record Office a practice recommendation which relates to conformity with the code of practice under section 46 in respect of records which are public records for the purposes of the Public Records Act 1958, the Commissioner shall consult the Keeper of Public Records.

(4) Before giving to a public authority other than the Public Record Office of Northern Ireland a practice recommendation which relates to conformity with the code of practice under section 46 in respect of records which are public records for the purposes of the Public Records Act (Northern Ireland) 1923, the Commissioner shall consult the Deputy Keeper of the Records of Northern Ireland.

49 Reports to be laid before Parliament.

(1) The Commissioner shall lay annually before each House of Parliament a general report on the exercise of his functions under this Act.

(2) The Commissioner may from time to time lay before each House of Parliament such other reports with respect to those functions as he thinks fit.

Part IV Enforcement

50 Application for decision by Commissioner.

(1) Any person (in this section referred to as "the complainant") may apply to the Commissioner for a decision whether, in any specified respect, a request for information made by the complainant to a public authority has been dealt with in accordance with the requirements of Part I.

(2) On receiving an application under this section, the Commissioner shall make a decision unless it appears to him—

(a) that the complainant has not exhausted any complaints procedure which is provided by the public authority in conformity with the code of practice under section 45,

(b) that there has been undue delay in making the application,

(c) that the application is frivolous or vexatious, or

(d) that the application has been withdrawn or abandoned.

(3) Where the Commissioner has received an application under this section, he shall either—

(a) notify the complainant that he has not made any decision under this section as a result of the application and of his grounds for not doing so, or

(b) serve notice of his decision (in this Act referred to as a "decision notice") on the complainant and the public authority.

(4) Where the Commissioner decides that a public authority—

(a) has failed to communicate information, or to provide confirmation or denial, in a case where it is required to do so by section 1(1), or

(b) has failed to comply with any of the requirements of sections 11 and 17,

the decision notice must specify the steps which must be taken by the authority for complying with that requirement and the period within which they must be taken.

(5) A decision notice must contain particulars of the right of appeal conferred by section 57.

(6) Where a decision notice requires steps to be taken by the public authority within a specified period, the time specified in the notice must not expire before the end of the period within which an appeal can be brought against the notice and, if such an appeal is brought, no step which is affected by the appeal need be taken pending the determination or withdrawal of the appeal.

(7) This section has effect subject to section 53.

51 Information notices.

(1) If the Commissioner—

(a) has received an application under section 50, or

(b) reasonably requires any information—

(i) for the purpose of determining whether a public authority has complied or is complying with any of the requirements of Part I, or

(ii) for the purpose of determining whether the practice of a public authority in relation to the exercise of its functions under this Act conforms with that proposed in the codes of practice under sections 45 and 46,

he may serve the authority with a notice (in this Act referred to as "an information notice") requiring it, within such time as is specified in the notice, to furnish the Commissioner, in such form as may be so specified, with such information relating to the application, to compliance with Part I or to conformity with the code of practice as is so specified.

(2) An information notice must contain—

(a) in a case falling within subsection (1)(a), a statement that the Commissioner has received an application under section 50, or

(b) in a case falling within subsection (1)(b), a statement—

(i) that the Commissioner regards the specified information as relevant for either of the purposes referred to in subsection (1)(b), and

(ii) of his reasons for regarding that information as relevant for that purpose.

(3) An information notice must also contain particulars of the right of appeal conferred by section 57.

(4) The time specified in an information notice must not expire before the end of the period within which an appeal can be brought against the notice and, if such an appeal is brought, the information need not be furnished pending the determination or withdrawal of the appeal.

(5) An authority shall not be required by virtue of this section to furnish the Commissioner with any information in respect of—

(a) any communication between a professional legal adviser and his client in connection with the giving of legal advice to the client with respect to his obligations, liabilities or rights under this Act, or

(b) any communication between a professional legal adviser and his client, or between such an adviser or his client and any other person, made in connection with or in contemplation of proceedings under or arising out of this Act (including proceedings before the Tribunal) and for the purposes of such proceedings.

(6) In subsection (5) references to the client of a professional legal adviser include references to any person representing such a client.

(7) The Commissioner may cancel an information notice by written notice to the authority on which it was served.

(8) In this section "information" includes unrecorded information.

52 Enforcement notices.

(1) If the Commissioner is satisfied that a public authority has failed to comply with any of the requirements of Part I, the Commissioner may serve the authority with a notice (in this Act referred to as "an enforcement notice") requiring the authority to take, within such time as may be specified in the notice, such steps as may be so specified for complying with those requirements.

(2) An enforcement notice must contain—

(a) a statement of the requirement or requirements of Part I with which the Commissioner is satisfied that the public authority has failed to comply and his reasons for reaching that conclusion, and

(b) particulars of the right of appeal conferred by section 57.

(3) An enforcement notice must not require any of the provisions of the notice to be complied with before the end of the period within which an appeal can be brought against the notice and, if such an appeal is brought, the notice need not be complied with pending the determination or withdrawal of the appeal.

(4) The Commissioner may cancel an enforcement notice by written notice to the authority on which it was served.

(5) This section has effect subject to section 53.

53 Exception from duty to comply with decision notice or enforcement notice.

(1) This section applies to a decision notice or enforcement notice which—

(a) is served on—

(i) a government department,

[(ii) the Welsh Assembly Government, or][38]

(iii) any public authority designated for the purposes of this section by an order made by the [Secretary of State][39], and

(b) relates to a failure, in respect of one or more requests for information—

(i) to comply with section 1(1)(a) in respect of information which falls within any provision of Part II stating that the duty to confirm or deny does not arise, or

(ii) to comply with section 1(1)(b) in respect of exempt information.

(2) A decision notice or enforcement notice to which this section applies shall cease to have effect if, not later than the twentieth working day following the effective date, the accountable person in relation to that authority gives the Commissioner a certificate signed by him stating that he has on reasonable grounds formed the opinion that, in respect of the request or requests concerned, there was no failure falling within subsection (1)(b).

(3) Where the accountable person gives a certificate to the Commissioner under subsection (2) he shall as soon as practicable thereafter lay a copy of the certificate before—

(a) each House of Parliament,

(b) the Northern Ireland Assembly, in any case where the certificate relates to a decision notice or enforcement notice which has been served on a Northern Ireland department or any Northern Ireland public authority, or

[(c) the National Assembly for Wales, in any case where the certificate relates to a decision notice or enforcement notice which has been served on—

(i) the Welsh Assembly Government,

(ii) the National Assembly for Wales, or

(iii) any Welsh public authority.][40]

(4) In subsection (2) "the effective date", in relation to a decision notice or enforcement notice, means—

(a) the day on which the notice was given to the public authority, or

(b) where an appeal under section 57 is brought, the day on which that appeal (or any further appeal arising out of it) is determined or withdrawn.

(5) Before making an order under subsection (1)(a)(iii), the [Secretary of State][41] shall—

(a) if the order relates to a Welsh public authority, consult [the Welsh Ministers][42],

[(aa) if the order relates to the National Assembly for Wales, consult the Presiding Officer of that Assembly,][43]

(b) if the order relates to the Northern Ireland Assembly, consult the Presiding Officer of that Assembly, and

(c) if the order relates to a Northern Ireland public authority, consult the First Minister and deputy First Minister in Northern Ireland.

(6) Where the accountable person gives a certificate to the Commissioner under subsection (2) in relation to a decision notice, the accountable person shall, on doing so or as soon as reasonably practicable after doing so, inform the person who is the complainant for the purposes of section 50 of the reasons for his opinion.

(7) The accountable person is not obliged to provide information under subsection (6) if, or to the extent that, compliance with that subsection would involve the disclosure of exempt information.

(8) In this section "the accountable person"—

(a) in relation to a Northern Ireland department or any Northern Ireland public authority, means the First Minister and deputy First Minister in Northern Ireland acting jointly,

[(b) in relation the Welsh Assembly Government, the National Assembly for Wales or any Welsh public authority, means the First Minister for Wales, and][44]

(c) in relation to any other public authority, means—

(i) a Minister of the Crown who is a member of the Cabinet, or

(ii) the Attorney General, the Advocate General for Scotland or the Attorney General for Northern Ireland.

(9) In this section "working day" has the same meaning as in section 10.

54 Failure to comply with notice.

(1) If a public authority has failed to comply with—

(a) so much of a decision notice as requires steps to be taken,

(b) an information notice, or

(c) an enforcement notice,

the Commissioner may certify in writing to the court that the public authority has failed to comply with that notice.

(2) For the purposes of this section, a public authority which, in purported compliance with an information notice—

(a) makes a statement which it knows to be false in a material respect, or

(b) recklessly makes a statement which is false in a material respect,

is to be taken to have failed to comply with the notice.

(3) Where a failure to comply is certified under subsection (1), the court may inquire into the matter and, after hearing any witness who may be produced against or on behalf of the public authority, and after hearing any statement that may be offered in defence, deal with the authority as if it had committed a contempt of court.

(4) In this section "the court" means the High Court or, in Scotland, the Court of Session.

55 Powers of entry and inspection.

Schedule 3 (powers of entry and inspection) has effect.

56 No action against public authority.

(1) This Act does not confer any right of action in civil proceedings in respect of any failure to comply with

any duty imposed by or under this Act.

(2) Subsection (1) does not affect the powers of the Commissioner under section 54.

Part V Appeals

57 Appeal against notices served under Part IV.

(1) Where a decision notice has been served, the complainant or the public authority may appeal to the Tribunal against the notice.

(2) A public authority on which an information notice or an enforcement notice has been served by the Commissioner may appeal to the Tribunal against the notice.

(3) In relation to a decision notice or enforcement notice which relates—

(a) to information to which section 66 applies, and

(b) to a matter which by virtue of subsection (3) or (4) of that section falls to be determined by the responsible authority instead of the appropriate records authority,

subsections (1) and (2) shall have effect as if the reference to the public authority were a reference to the public authority or the responsible authority.

58 Determination of appeals.

(1) If on an appeal under section 57 the Tribunal considers—

(a) that the notice against which the appeal is brought is not in accordance with the law, or

(b) to the extent that the notice involved an exercise of discretion by the Commissioner, that he ought to have exercised his discretion differently,

the Tribunal shall allow the appeal or substitute such other notice as could have been served by the Commissioner; and in any other case the Tribunal shall dismiss the appeal.

(2) On such an appeal, the Tribunal may review any finding of fact on which the notice in question was based.

59 Appeals from decision of Tribunal.

Any party to an appeal to the Tribunal under section 57 may appeal from the decision of the Tribunal on a point of law to the appropriate court; and that court shall be—

(a) the High Court of Justice in England if the address of the public authority is in England or Wales,

(b) the Court of Session if that address is in Scotland, and

(c) the High Court of Justice in Northern Ireland if that address is in Northern Ireland.

60 Appeals against national security certificate.

(1) Where a certificate under section 23(2) or 24(3) has been issued—

(a) the Commissioner, or

(b) any applicant whose request for information is affected by the issue of the certificate,

may appeal to the Tribunal against the certificate.

(2) If on an appeal under subsection (1) relating to a certificate under section 23(2), the Tribunal finds that the information referred to in the certificate was not exempt information by virtue of section 23(1), the Tribunal may allow the appeal and quash the certificate.

(3) If on an appeal under subsection (1) relating to a certificate under section 24(3), the Tribunal finds that, applying the principles applied by the court on an application for judicial review, the Minister did not have reasonable grounds for issuing the certificate, the Tribunal may allow the appeal and quash the certificate.

(4) Where in any proceedings under this Act it is claimed by a public authority that a certificate under section 24(3) which identifies the information to which it applies by means of a general description applies to particular information, any other party to the proceedings may appeal to the Tribunal on the ground that the certificate does not apply to the information in question and, subject to any determination under subsection (5), the certificate shall be conclusively presumed so to apply.

(5) On any appeal under subsection (4), the Tribunal may determine that the certificate does not so apply.

61 Appeal proceedings.

(1) Schedule 4 (which contains amendments of Schedule 6 to the Data Protection Act 1998 relating to appeal proceedings) has effect.

(2) Accordingly, the provisions of Schedule 6 to the Data Protection Act 1998 have effect (so far as applicable) in relation to appeals under this Part.

Part VI Historical records and records in Public Record Office or Public Record Office of Northern Ireland

62 Interpretation of Part VI.

(1) For the purposes of this Part, a record becomes a "historical record" at the end of the period of thirty years beginning with the year following that in which it was created.

(2) Where records created at different dates are for administrative purposes kept together in one file or other assembly, all the records in that file or other assembly are to be treated for the purposes of this Part as having been created when the latest of those records was created.

(3) In this Part "year" means a calendar year.

63 Removal of exemptions: historical records generally.

(1) Information contained in a historical record cannot be exempt information by virtue of section 28, 30(1), 32, 33, 35, 36, 37(1)(a), 42 or 43.

(2) Compliance with section 1(1)(a) in relation to a historical record is not to be taken to be capable of having any of the effects referred to in section 28(3), 33(3), 36(3), 42(2) or 43(3).

(3) Information cannot be exempt information by virtue of section 37(1)(b) after the end of the period of sixty years beginning with the year following that in which the record containing the information was created.

(4) Information cannot be exempt information by virtue of section 31 after the end of the period of one hundred years beginning with the year following that in which the record containing the information was created.

(5) Compliance with section 1(1)(a) in relation to any record is not to be taken, at any time after the end of the period of one hundred years beginning with the year following that in which the record was created, to be capable of prejudicing any of the matters referred to in section 31(1).

64 Removal of exemptions: historical records in public record offices.

(1) Information contained in a historical record in the Public Record Office or the Public Record Office of Northern Ireland cannot be exempt information by virtue of section 21 or 22.

(2) In relation to any information falling within section 23(1) which is contained in a historical record in the Public Record Office or the Public Record Office of Northern Ireland, section 2(3) shall have effect with the omission of the reference to section 23.

65 Decisions as to refusal of discretionary disclosure of historical records.

(1) Before refusing a request for information relating to information which is contained in a historical record and is exempt information only by virtue of a provision not specified in section 2(3), a public authority shall—

(a) if the historical record is a public record within the meaning of the Public Records Act 1958, consult the Lord Chancellor, or

(b) if the historical record is a public record to which the Public Records Act (Northern Ireland) 1923 applies, consult the appropriate Northern Ireland Minister.

(2) This section does not apply to information to which section 66 applies.

66 Decisions relating to certain transferred public records.

(1) This section applies to any information which is (or, if it existed, would be) contained in a transferred public record, other than information which the responsible authority has designated as open information for the purposes of this section.

(2) Before determining whether—

(a) information to which this section applies falls within any provision of Part II relating to the duty to confirm or deny, or

(b) information to which this section applies is exempt information,

the appropriate records authority shall consult the responsible authority.

(3) Where information to which this section applies falls within a provision of Part II relating to the duty to confirm or deny but does not fall within any of the provisions of that Part relating to that duty which are specified in subsection (3) of section 2, any question as to the application of subsection (1)(b) of that section is to be determined by the responsible authority instead of the appropriate records authority.

(4) Where any information to which this section applies is exempt information only by virtue of any provision of Part II not specified in subsection (3) of section 2, any question as to the application of

subsection (2)(b) of that section is to be determined by the responsible authority instead of the appropriate records authority.

(5) Before making by virtue of subsection (3) or (4) any determination that subsection (1)(b) or (2)(b) of section 2 applies, the responsible authority shall consult—

(a) where the transferred public record is a public record within the meaning of the Public Records Act 1958, the Lord Chancellor, and

(b) where the transferred public record is a public record to which the Public Records Act (Northern Ireland) 1923 applies, the appropriate Northern Ireland Minister.

(6) Where the responsible authority in relation to information to which this section applies is not (apart from this subsection) a public authority, it shall be treated as being a public authority for the purposes of Parts III, IV and V of this Act so far as relating to—

(a) the duty imposed by section 15(3), and

(b) the imposition of any requirement to furnish information relating to compliance with Part I in connection with the information to which this section applies.

67 Amendments of public records legislation.

Schedule 5 (which amends the Public Records Act 1958 and the Public Records Act (Northern Ireland) 1923) has effect.

Part VII Amendments of Data Protection Act 1998

Amendments relating to personal information held by public authorities

68 Extension of meaning of "data".

(1) Section 1 of the Data Protection Act 1998 (basic interpretative provisions) is amended in accordance with subsections (2) and (3).

(2) In subsection (1)—

(a) in the definition of "data", the word "or" at the end of paragraph (c) is omitted and after paragraph

(d) there is inserted "or

(e) is recorded information held by a public authority and does not fall within any of paragraphs (a) to (d);", and

(b) after the definition of "processing" there is inserted—

""public authority" has the same meaning as in the Freedom of Information Act 2000;".

(3) After subsection (4) there is inserted—

"(5) In paragraph (e) of the definition of "data" in subsection (1), the reference to information "held" by a public authority shall be construed in accordance with section 3(2) of the Freedom of Information Act 2000.

(6) Where section 7 of the Freedom of Information Act 2000 prevents Parts I to V of that Act from applying to certain information held by a public authority, that information is not to be treated for the purposes of paragraph (e) of the definition of "data" in subsection (1) as held by a public authority."

(4) In section 56 of that Act (prohibition of requirement as to production of certain records), after subsection (6) there is inserted—

"(6A) a record is not a relevant record to the extent that it relates, or is to relate, only to personal data falling within paragraph (e) of the definition of "data" in section 1(1)."

(5) In the Table in section 71 of that Act (index of defined expressions) after the entry relating to processing there is inserted—

"public authority section 1(1).".

69 Right of access to unstructured personal data held by public authorities.

(1) In section 7(1) of the Data Protection Act 1998 (right of access to personal data), for "sections 8 and 9" there is substituted " sections 8, 9 and 9A".

(2) After section 9 of that Act there is inserted—[45]

"9A Unstructured personal data held by public authorities.

(1) In this section "unstructured personal data" means any personal data falling within paragraph (e) of the definition of "data" in section 1(1), other than information which is recorded as part of, or with the intention that it should form part of, any set of information relating to individuals to the extent that the set is structured by reference to individuals or by reference to criteria relating to individuals.

(2) A public authority is not obliged to comply with subsection (1) of section 7 in relation to any unstructured personal data unless the request under that section contains a description of the data.

(3) Even if the data are described by the data subject in his request, a public authority is not obliged to comply with subsection (1) of section 7 in relation to unstructured personal data if the authority estimates that the cost of complying with the request so far as relating to those data would exceed the appropriate limit.

(4) Subsection (3) does not exempt the public authority from its obligation to comply with paragraph (a) of section 7(1) in relation to the unstructured personal data unless the estimated cost of complying with that paragraph alone in relation to those data would exceed the appropriate limit.

(5) In subsections (3) and (4) "the appropriate limit" means such amount as may be prescribed by the Secretary of State by regulations, and different amounts may be prescribed in relation to different cases.

(6) Any estimate for the purposes of this section must be made in accordance with regulations under section 12(5) of the Freedom of Information Act 2000."

(3) In section 67(5) of that Act (statutory instruments subject to negative resolution procedure), in paragraph (c), for "or 9(3)" there is substituted ", 9(3) or 9A(5)".

70 Exemptions applicable to certain manual data held by public authorities.

(1) after section 33 of the Data Protection Act 1998 there is inserted—

"33A Manual data held by public authorities.

(1) Personal data falling within paragraph (e) of the definition of "data" in section 1(1) are exempt from—

(a) the first, second, third, fifth, seventh and eighth data protection principles,

(b) the sixth data protection principle except so far as it relates to the rights conferred on data subjects by sections 7 and 14,

(c) sections 10 to 12,

(d) section 13, except so far as it relates to damage caused by a contravention of section 7 or of the fourth data protection principle and to any distress which is also suffered by reason of that contravention,

(e) Part III, and

(f) section 55.

(2) Personal data which fall within paragraph (e) of the definition of "data" in section 1(1) and relate to appointments or removals, pay, discipline, superannuation or other personnel matters, in relation to—

(a) service in any of the armed forces of the Crown,

(b) service in any office or employment under the Crown or under any public authority, or

(c) service in any office or employment, or under any contract for services, in respect of which power to take action, or to determine or approve the action taken, in such matters is vested in Her Majesty, any Minister of the Crown, the National Assembly for Wales, any Northern Ireland Minister (within the meaning of the Freedom of Information Act 2000) or any public authority,

are also exempt from the remaining data protection principles and the remaining provisions of Part II."

(2) In section 55 of that Act (unlawful obtaining etc. of personal data) in subsection (8) after "section 28" there is inserted " or 33A ".

(3) In Part III of Schedule 8 to that Act (exemptions available after 23rd October 2001 but before 24th October 2007) after paragraph 14 there is inserted—

"14A(1) This paragraph applies to personal data which fall within paragraph (e) of the definition of "data" in section 1(1) and do not fall within paragraph 14(1)(a), but does not apply to eligible manual data to which the exemption in paragraph 16 applies.

(2) during the second transitional period, data to which this paragraph applies are exempt from—

(a) the fourth data protection principle, and

(b) section 14(1) to (3)."

(4) In Schedule 13 to that Act (modifications of Act having effect before 24th October 2007) in subsection (4)(b) of section 12A to that Act as set out in paragraph 1, after "paragraph 14" there is inserted " or 14A ".

71 Particulars registrable under Part III of Data Protection Act 1998.

In section 16(1) of the Data Protection Act 1998 (the registrable particulars), before the word "and" at the end of paragraph (f) there is inserted—

"(ff) where the data controller is a public authority, a statement of that fact,".

72 Availability under Act disregarded for purpose of exemption.

In section 34 of the Data Protection Act 1998 (information available to the public by or under enactment), after the word "enactment" there is inserted " other than an enactment contained in the Freedom of Information Act 2000 ".

Other amendments

73 Further amendments of Data Protection Act 1998.

Schedule 6 (which contains further amendments of the Data Protection Act 1998) has effect.

Part VIII Miscellaneous and supplemental

74 Power to make provision relating to environmental information.

(1) In this section "the Aarhus Convention" means the Convention on Access to Information, Public Participation in Decision-making and Access to Justice in Environmental Matters signed at Aarhus on 25th June 1998.

(2) For the purposes of this section "the information provisions" of the Aarhus Convention are Article 4, together with Articles 3 and 9 so far as relating to that Article.

(3) The Secretary of State may by regulations make such provision as he considers appropriate—

(a) for the purpose of implementing the information provisions of the Aarhus Convention or any amendment of those provisions made in accordance with Article 14 of the Convention, and

(b) for the purpose of dealing with matters arising out of or related to the implementation of those provisions or of any such amendment.

(4) Regulations under subsection (3) may in particular—

(a) enable charges to be made for making information available in accordance with the regulations,

(b) provide that any obligation imposed by the regulations in relation to the disclosure of information is to have effect notwithstanding any enactment or rule of law,

(c) make provision for the issue by the Secretary of State of a code of practice,

(d) provide for sections 47 and 48 to apply in relation to such a code with such modifications as may be specified,

(e) provide for any of the provisions of Parts IV and V to apply, with such modifications as may be specified in the regulations, in relation to compliance with any requirement of the regulations, and

(f) contain such transitional or consequential provision (including provision modifying any enactment) as the Secretary of State considers appropriate.

(5) This section has effect subject to section 80.

75 Power to amend or repeal enactments prohibiting disclosure of information.

(1) If, with respect to any enactment which prohibits the disclosure of information held by a public authority, it appears to the [Secretary of State][46] that by virtue of section 44(1)(a) the enactment is capable of preventing the disclosure of information under section 1, he may by order repeal or amend the enactment for the purpose of removing or relaxing the prohibition.

(2) In subsection (1)—

"enactment" means—

(a) any enactment contained in an Act passed before or in the same Session as this Act, or

(b) any enactment contained in Northern Ireland legislation or subordinate legislation passed or made before the passing of this Act;

"information" includes unrecorded information.

(3) An order under this section may do all or any of the following—

(a) make such modifications of enactments as, in the opinion of the [Secretary of State][47], are consequential upon, or incidental to, the amendment or repeal of the enactment containing the prohibition;

(b) contain such transitional provisions and savings as appear to the [Secretary of State][48] to be appropriate;

(c) make different provision for different cases.

76 Disclosure of information between Commissioner and ombudsmen.

(1) The Commissioner may disclose to a person specified in the first column of the Table below any

information obtained by, or furnished to, the Commissioner under or for the purposes of this Act or the Data Protection Act 1998 if it appears to the Commissioner that the information relates to a matter which could be the subject of an investigation by that person under the enactment specified in relation to that person in the second column of that Table.

TABLE

Ombudsman	**Enactment**
The Parliamentary Commissioner for Administration.	The Parliamentary Commissioner Act 1967 (c. 13).
The Health Service Commissioner for England.	The Health Service Commissioners Act 1993 (c. 46).
....	................................[49]
[The Health Service Commissioner for Scotland.	The Health Service Commissioners Act 1993 (c. 46).][50]
A Local Commissioner as defined by section 23(3) of the Local Government Act 1974. The Scottish Public Services Ombudsman	Part III of the Local Government Act 1974 (c. 7).
[The Scottish Public Services Ombudsman	The Scottish Public Services Ombudsman Act 2002 (asp 11)][51]
[The Commissioner for Local Administration in Scotland.	Part II of the Local Government (Scotland) Act 1975 (c. 30).][52]
[The Scottish Parliamentary Commissioner for Administration.	The Scotland Act 1998 (Transitory and Transitional Provisions)(Complaints of Maladministration) Order 1999 (S.I. 1999/1351).][53]
[The Public Services Ombudsman for Wales	Part 2 of the Public Services Ombudsman (Wales) Act 2005][54]
....	................................[55]
The Northern Ireland Commissioner for Complaints.	The Commissioner for Complaints (Northern Ireland) Order 1996 (S.I. 1996/1297 (N.I. 7)).
The Assembly Ombudsman for Northern Ireland.	The Ombudsman (Northern Ireland) Order 1996 (S.I. 1996/1298 (N.I. 8)).
[The Commissioner for Older People in Wales	The Commissioner for Older People (Wales) Act 2006][56]

(2) Schedule 7 (which contains amendments relating to information disclosed to ombudsmen under subsection (1) and to the disclosure of information by ombudsmen to the Commissioner) has effect.

[76A Disclosure between Commissioner and Scottish Information Commissioner

The Commissioner may disclose to the Scottish Information Commissioner any information obtained or furnished as mentioned in section 76(1) of this Act if it appears to the Commissioner that the information is of the same type that could be obtained by, or furnished to, the Scottish Information Commissioner under or for the purposes of the Freedom of Information (Scotland) Act 2002.][57]

77 Offence of altering etc. records with intent to prevent disclosure.

(1) Where—

(a) a request for information has been made to a public authority, and

(b) under section 1 of this Act or section 7 of the Data Protection Act 1998, the applicant would have been entitled (subject to payment of any fee) to communication of any information in accordance with that section,

any person to whom this subsection applies is guilty of an offence if he alters, defaces, blocks, erases, destroys or conceals any record held by the public authority, with the intention of preventing the disclosure by that authority of all, or any part, of the information to the communication of which the applicant would have been entitled.

(2) Subsection (1) applies to the public authority and to any person who is employed by, is an officer of, or is subject to the direction of, the public authority.

(3) A person guilty of an offence under this section is liable on summary conviction to a fine not exceeding level 5 on the standard scale.

(4) No proceedings for an offence under this section shall be instituted—

(a) in England or Wales, except by the Commissioner or by or with the consent of the Director of Public Prosecutions;

(b) in Northern Ireland, except by the Commissioner or by or with the consent of the Director of Public Prosecutions for Northern Ireland.

78 Saving for existing powers.

Nothing in this Act is to be taken to limit the powers of a public authority to disclose information held by it.

79 Defamation.

Where any information communicated by a public authority to a person ("the applicant") under section 1 was supplied to the public authority by a third person, the publication to the applicant of any defamatory matter contained in the information shall be privileged unless the publication is shown to have been made with malice.

80 Scotland.

(1) No order may be made under section 4(1) or 5 in relation to any of the bodies specified in subsection (2); and the power conferred by section 74(3) does not include power to make provision in relation to information held by any of those bodies.

(2) The bodies referred to in subsection (1) are—

(a) the Scottish Parliament,

(b) any part of the Scottish Administration,

(c) the Scottish Parliamentary Corporate Body, or

(d) any Scottish public authority with mixed functions or no reserved functions (within the meaning of the Scotland Act 1998).

[(3) Section 50 of the Copyright, Designs and Patents Act 1988 and paragraph 6 of Schedule 1 to the Copyright and Rights in Databases Regulations 1997 apply in relation to the Freedom of Information (Scotland) Act 2002 as they apply in relation to this Act.][58]

81 Application to government departments, etc.

(1) For the purposes of this Act each government department is to be treated as a person separate from any other government department.

(2) Subsection (1) does not enable—

(a) a government department which is not a Northern Ireland department to claim for the purposes of section 41(1)(b) that the disclosure of any information by it would constitute a breach of confidence actionable by any other government department (not being a Northern Ireland department), or

(b) a Northern Ireland department to claim for those purposes that the disclosure of information by it would constitute a breach of confidence actionable by any other Northern Ireland department.

(3) A government department [or the Welsh Assembly Government][59] is not liable to prosecution under this Act, but section 77 and paragraph 12 of Schedule 3 apply to a person in the public service of the Crown as they apply to any other person.

(4) The provisions specified in subsection (3) also apply to a person acting on behalf of either House of Parliament or on behalf of the Northern Ireland Assembly [or the National Assembly for Wales][60] as they apply to any other person.

82 Orders and regulations.

(1) Any power of the... [61] Secretary of State to make an order or regulations under this Act shall be exercisable by statutory instrument.

(2) A statutory instrument containing (whether alone or with other provisions)—

(a) an order under section 5, 7(3) or (8), 53(1)(a)(iii) or 75, or

(b) regulations under section 10(4) or 74(3),

shall not be made unless a draft of the instrument has been laid before, and approved by a resolution of, each House of Parliament.

(3) A statutory instrument which contains (whether alone or with other provisions)—

(a) an order under section 4(1), or

(b) regulations under any provision of this Act not specified in subsection (2)(b),

and which is not subject to the requirement in subsection (2) that a draft of the instrument be laid before and approved by a resolution of each House of Parliament, shall be subject to annulment in pursuance

of a resolution of either House of Parliament.

(4) An order under section 4(5) shall be laid before Parliament after being made.

(5) If a draft of an order under section 5 or 7(8) would, apart from this subsection, be treated for the purposes of the Standing Orders of either House of Parliament as a hybrid instrument, it shall proceed in that House as if it were not such an instrument.

83 Meaning of "Welsh public authority".

(1) In this Act "Welsh public authority" means—

(a) any public authority which is listed in Part II, III, IV or VI of Schedule 1 and whose functions are exercisable only or mainly in or as regards Wales, other than an excluded authority, or

[(b) any public authority which is—

(i) a subsidiary of the Welsh Ministers (as defined by section 134(4) of the Government of Wales Act 2006), or

(ii) a subsidiary of the Assembly Commission (as defined by section 139(4) of that Act).][62]

(2) In paragraph (a) of subsection (1) "excluded authority" means a public authority which is designated by the [Secretary of State][63] by order as an excluded authority for the purposes of that paragraph.

(3) Before making an order under subsection (2), the [Secretary of State][64] shall consult [the First Minister for Wales][65].

84 Interpretation.

In this Act, unless the context otherwise requires—

"applicant", in relation to a request for information, means the person who made the request;

"appropriate Northern Ireland Minister" means the Northern Ireland Minister in charge of the Department of Culture, Arts and Leisure in Northern Ireland;

"appropriate records authority", in relation to a transferred public record, has the meaning given by section 15(5);

"body" includes an unincorporated association;

"the Commissioner" means the Information Commissioner;

"decision notice" has the meaning given by section 50;

"the duty to confirm or deny" has the meaning given by section 1(6);

"enactment" includes an enactment contained in Northern Ireland legislation;

"enforcement notice" has the meaning given by section 52;

. . . .[66]

"exempt information" means information which is exempt information by virtue of any provision of Part II;

"fees notice" has the meaning given by section 9(1);

"government department" includes a Northern Ireland department, the Northern Ireland Court Service and any other body or authority exercising statutory functions on behalf of the Crown, but does not include—

(a) any of the bodies specified in section 80(2),

(b) the Security Service, the Secret Intelligence Service or the Government Communications Headquarters, or

(c)[the Welsh Assembly Government][67]

"information" (subject to sections 51(8) and 75(2)) means information recorded in any form;

"information notice" has the meaning given by section 51;

"Minister of the Crown" has the same meaning as in the Ministers of the Crown Act 1975;

"Northern Ireland Minister" includes the First Minister and deputy First Minister in Northern Ireland;

"Northern Ireland public authority" means any public authority, other than the Northern Ireland Assembly or a Northern Ireland department, whose functions are exercisable only or mainly in or as regards Northern Ireland and relate only or mainly to transferred matters;

"prescribed" means prescribed by regulations made by the [Secretary of State][68];

"public authority" has the meaning given by section 3(1);

"public record" means a public record within the meaning of the Public Records Act 1958 or a public record to which the Public Records Act (Northern Ireland) 1923 applies;

"publication scheme" has the meaning given by section 19;

"request for information" has the meaning given by section 8;

"responsible authority", in relation to a transferred public record, has the meaning given by section 15(5);

"the special forces" means those units of the armed forces of the Crown the maintenance of whose capabilities is the responsibility of the Director of Special Forces or which are for the time being subject to the operational command of that Director;

"subordinate legislation" has the meaning given by subsection (1) of section 21 of the Interpretation Act 1978, except that the definition of that term in that subsection shall have effect as if "Act" included Northern Ireland legislation;

"transferred matter", in relation to Northern Ireland, has the meaning given by section 4(1) of the Northern Ireland Act 1998;

"transferred public record" has the meaning given by section 15(4);

"the Tribunal" means the Information Tribunal;

"Welsh public authority" has the meaning given by section 83.

85 Expenses.

There shall be paid out of money provided by Parliament—

(a) any increase attributable to this Act in the expenses of the [Secretary of State][69] in respect of the Commissioner, the Tribunal or the members of the Tribunal,

(b) any administrative expenses of the [Secretary of State][70] attributable to this Act,

(c) any other expenses incurred in consequence of this Act by a Minister of the Crown or government department or by either House of Parliament, and

(d) any increase attributable to this Act in the sums which under any other Act are payable out of money so provided.

86 Repeals.

Schedule 8 (repeals) has effect.

87 Commencement.

(1) The following provisions of this Act shall come into force on the day on which this Act is passed—

(a) sections 3 to 8 and Schedule 1,

(b) section 19 so far as relating to the approval of publication schemes,

(c) section 20 so far as relating to the approval and preparation by the Commissioner of model publication schemes,

(d) section 47(2) to (6),

(e) section 49,

(f) section 74,

(g) section 75,

(h) sections 78 to 85 and this section,

(i) paragraphs 2 and 17 to 22 of Schedule 2 (and section 18(4) so far as relating to those paragraphs),

(j) paragraph 4 of Schedule 5 (and section 67 so far as relating to that paragraph),

(k) paragraph 8 of Schedule 6 (and section 73 so far as relating to that paragraph),

(l) Part I of Schedule 8 (and section 86 so far as relating to that Part), and

(m) so much of any other provision of this Act as confers power to make any order, regulations or code of practice.

(2) The following provisions of this Act shall come into force at the end of the period of two months beginning with the day on which this Act is passed—

(a) section 18(1),

(b) section 76 and Schedule 7,

(c) paragraphs 1(1), 3(1), 4, 6, 7, 8(2), 9(2), 10(a), 13(1) and (2), 14(a) and 15(1) and (2) of Schedule 2 (and section 18(4) so far as relating to those provisions), and

(d) Part II of Schedule 8 (and section 86 so far as relating to that Part).

(3) Except as provided by subsections (1) and (2), this Act shall come into force at the end of the period of five years beginning with the day on which this Act is passed or on such day before the end of that period as the [Secretary of State][71] may by order appoint; and different days may be appointed for different purposes.

(4) An order under subsection (3) may contain such transitional provisions and savings (including provisions capable of having effect after the end of the period referred to in that subsection) as the

[Secretary of State][72] considers appropriate.

(5) During the twelve months beginning with the day on which this Act is passed, and during each subsequent complete period of twelve months in the period beginning with that day and ending with the first day on which all the provisions of this Act are fully in force, the [Secretary of State][73] shall—

(a) prepare a report on his proposals for bringing fully into force those provisions of this Act which are not yet fully in force, and

(b) lay a copy of the report before each House of Parliament.

88 Short title and extent.

(1) This Act may be cited as the Freedom of Information Act 2000.

(2) Subject to subsection (3), this Act extends to Northern Ireland.

(3) The amendment or repeal of any enactment by this Act has the same extent as that enactment.

SCHEDULES

Section 3(1)(a)(i).

SCHEDULE 1 Public authorities

Part I General

1 Any government department [other than the Office for Standards in Education, Children's Services and Ski][74] .

[1AThe Office for Standards in Education, Children's Services and Skills, in respect of information held for purposes other than those of the functions exercisable by Her Majesty's Chief Inspector of Education, Children's Services and Skills by virtue of section 5(1)(a)(iii) of the Care Standards Act 2000.][75]

2 The House of Commons [, in respect of information other than—

(a) information relating to any residential address of a member of either House of Parliament,

(b) information relating to travel arrangements of a member of either House of Parliament, where the arrangements relate to travel that has not yet been undertaken or is regular in nature,

(c) information relating to the identity of any person who delivers or has delivered goods, or provides or has provided services, to a member of either House of Parliament at any residence of the member,

(d) information relating to expenditure by a member of either House of Parliament on security arrangements.

Paragraph (b) does not except information relating to the total amount of expenditure incurred on regular travel during any month.][76]

3 The House of Lords [, in respect of information other than—

(a) information relating to any residential address of a member of either House of Parliament,

(b) information relating to travel arrangements of a member of either House of Parliament, where the arrangements relate to travel that has not yet been undertaken or is regular in nature,

(c) information relating to the identity of any person who delivers or has delivered goods, or provides or has provided services, to a member of either House of Parliament at any residence of the member,

(d) information relating to expenditure by a member of either House of Parliament on security arrangements.

Paragraph (b) does not except information relating to the total amount of expenditure incurred on regular travel during any month.][77]

4 The Northern Ireland Assembly.

5 The National Assembly for Wales[, in respect of information other than—

(a) information relating to any residential address of a member of the Assembly,

(b) information relating to travel arrangements of a member of the Assembly, where the arrangements relate to travel that has not yet been undertaken or is regular in nature,

(c) information relating to the identity of any person who delivers or has delivered goods, or provides or has provided services, to a member of the Assembly at any residence of the member,

(d) information relating to expenditure by a member of the Assembly on security arrangements.

Paragraph (b) does not except information relating to the total amount of expenditure incurred on regular travel during any month.][78]

[5Athe Welsh Assembly Government.][79]

6 The armed forces of the Crown, except—

(a) the special forces, and

(b) any unit or part of a unit which is for the time being required by the Secretary of State to assist the Government Communications Headquarters in the exercise of its functions.

Part II Local government

England and Wales

7 A local authority within the meaning of the Local Government Act 1972, namely—

(a) in England, a county council, a London borough council, a district council or a parish council,

(b) in Wales, a county council, a county borough council or a community council.

8 The Greater London Authority.

9 The Common Council of the City of London, in respect of information held in its capacity as a local authority, police authority or port health authority.

10 The Sub-Treasurer of the Inner Temple or the Under-Treasurer of the Middle Temple, in respect of information held in his capacity as a local authority.

11 The Council of the Isles of Scilly.

12 A parish meeting constituted under section 13 of the Local Government Act 1972.

13 Any charter trustees constituted under section 246 of the Local Government Act 1972.

[14 A fire and rescue authority constituted by a scheme under section 2 of the Fire and Rescue Services Act 2004 or a scheme to which section 4 of that Act applies.][80]

15A waste disposal authority established by virtue of an order under section 10(1) of the Local Government Act 1985.

[15 AAn authority established for an area in England by an order under section 207 of the Local Government and Public Involvement in Health Act 2007 (joint waste authorities).][81]

16 A port health authority constituted by an order under section 2 of the Public Health (Control of Disease) Act 1984.

17. . . . .[82]

18 An internal drainage board which is continued in being by virtue of section 1 of the Land Drainage Act 1991.

19 A joint authority established under Part IV of the Local Government Act 1985 [(fire and rescue services and transport)][83].

[19AAn economic prosperity board established under section 88 of the Local Democracy, Economic Development and Construction Act 2009.

19BA combined authority established under section 103 of that Act.][84]

20The London Fire and Emergency Planning Authority.

21 A joint fire authority established by virtue of an order under section 42(2) of the Local Government Act 1985 (reorganisation of functions).

22 A body corporate established pursuant to an order under section 67 of the Local Government Act 1985 (transfer of functions to successors of residuary bodies, etc.).

23 A body corporate established pursuant to an order under [section 17 of the Local Government and Public Involvement in Health Act 2007][85] (residuary bodies).

24 The Broads Authority established by section 1 of the Norfolk and Suffolk Broads Act 1988.

25 A joint committee constituted in accordance with section 102(1)(b) of the Local Government Act 1972.

26 A joint board which is continued in being by virtue of section 263(1) of the Local Government Act 1972.

27 A joint authority established under section 21 of the Local Government Act 1992.

[28A Passenger Transport Executive for an integrated transport area for the purposes of Part 2 of the Transport Act 1968.][86]

29 Transport for London.

30 The London Transport Users Committee.

31 A joint board the constituent members of which consist of any of the public authorities described in paragraphs 8, 9, 10, 12, 15, 16, 20 to 31, 57 and 58.

32 A National Park authority established by an order under section 63 of the Environment Act 1995.

33 A joint planning board constituted for an area in Wales outside a National Park by an order under section 2(1B) of the Town and Country Planning Act 1990.

34. . . . .[87]

35 The London Development Agency.

[35A A local fisheries committee for a sea fisheries district established under section 1 of the Sea Fisheries

Regulation Act 1966[88].][89]

Northern Ireland

36A district council within the meaning of the Local Government Act (Northern Ireland) 1972.

Part III The National Health Service

England and Wales

[36AA Strategic Health Authority established under [section 13 of the National Health Service Act 2006][90].][91]

37.............................[92]

38A special health authority established under [section 28 of the National Health Service Act 2006 or section 22 of the National Health Service (Wales) Act 2006][93].

39 A primary care trust established under [section 18 of the National Health Service Act 2006][94].

[39AA Local Health Board established under [section 11 of the National Health Service (Wales) Act 2006][95].][96]

40 A National Health Service trust established under [section 25 of the National Health Service Act 2006 or section 18 of the National Health Service (Wales) Act 2006][97].

[40AAn NHS foundation trust.][98]

41 A Community Health Council [established under section 182 of the National Health Service (Wales) Act 2006][99].

[41A.............................[100]][101]

42.............................[102]

43.............................[103]

[43AAny person providing primary medical services [, primary dental services or primary ophthalmic services][104]—

(a) in accordance with arrangements made under [section 92 or 107 of the National Health Service Act 2006, or section 50 or 64 of the National Health Service (Wales) Act 2006][105]; or

(b) under a contract under [section 84 or 100 of the National Health Service Act 2006 or section 42 or 57 of the National Health Service (Wales) Act 2006][106];

in respect of information relating to the provision of those services.][107]

44 Any person providing [...general medical services, general dental services,][108]... general ophthalmic services or pharmaceutical services under [the National Health Service Act 2006 or the National Health Service (Wales) Act 2006][109], in respect of information relating to the provision of those services.

45 [Any person providing personal medical services or personal dental services under arrangements made under section 28C of the National Health Service Act 1977, in respect of information relating to the provision of those services.][110]

[45 Any person providing local pharmaceutical services under—

(a) a pilot scheme established under [section 134 of the National Health Service Act 2006 or section 92 of the National Health Service (Wales) Act 2006][111]; or

(b) an LPS scheme established under [Schedule 12 to the National Health Service Act 2006 or Schedule 7 to the National Health Service (Wales) Act 2006][112],

in respect of information relating to the provision of those services.][113]

[45B[114].............................][115]

Northern Ireland

46 [A Health and Social Services Board established under Article 16 of the Health and Personal Social Services (Northern Ireland) Order 1972.][116]

47 A Health and Social Services Council established under Article 4 of the Health and Personal Social Services (Northern Ireland) Order 1991.

48 A Health and Social Services Trust established under Article 10 of the Health and Personal Social Services (Northern Ireland) Order 1991.

49 A special agency established under Article 3 of the Health and Personal Social Services (Special Agencies) (Northern Ireland) Order 1990.

50 [The Northern Ireland Central Services Agency for the Health and Social Services established under Article 26 of the Health and Personal Social Services (Northern Ireland) Order 1972.][117]

51 Any person providing [primary medical services][118], general dental services, general ophthalmic

services or pharmaceutical services under Part VI of the Health and Personal Social Services (Northern Ireland) Order 1972, in respect of information relating to the provision of those services.

[51A The Regional Business Services Organisation established under section 14 of the Health and Social Services (Reform) Act (Northern Ireland) 2009.

51B The Patient and Client Council established under section 16 of the Health and Social Care (Reform) Act (Northern Ireland) 2009.

51C The Regional Health and Social Care Board established under section 7 of the Health and Social Care (Reform) Act (Northern Ireland) 2009.

51D The Regional Agency for Public Health and Social Well-being established under section 12 of the Health and Social Care (Reform) Act (Northern Ireland) 2009.][119]

Part IV Maintained schools and other educational institutions

England and Wales

[52 The governing body of—

(a) a maintained school, as defined by section 20(7) of the School Standards and Framework Act 1998, or

(b) a maintained nursery school, as defined by section 22(9) of that Act.][120]

53(1) The governing body of—

(a) an institution within the further education sector,

(b) a university receiving financial support under section 65 of the Further and Higher Education Act 1992,

(c) an institution conducted by a higher education corporation,

(d) a designated institution for the purposes of Part II of the Further and Higher Education Act 1992 as defined by section 72(3) of that Act, or

(e) any college, school, hall or other institution of a university which falls within paragraph (b).

(2) In sub-paragraph (1)—

(a) "governing body" is to be interpreted in accordance with subsection (1) of section 90 of the Further and Higher Education Act 1992 but without regard to subsection (2) of that section,

(b) in paragraph (a), the reference to an institution within the further education sector is to be construed in accordance with section 91(3) of the Further and Higher Education Act 1992,

(c) in paragraph (c), "higher education corporation" has the meaning given by section 90(1) of that Act, and

(d) in paragraph (e) "college" includes any institution in the nature of a college.

Northern Ireland

54(1) The managers of—

(a) a controlled school, voluntary school or grant-maintained integrated school within the meaning of Article 2(2) of the Education and Libraries (Northern Ireland) Order 1986, or

(b) a pupil referral unit as defined by Article 87(1) of the Education (Northern Ireland) Order 1998.

(2) In sub-paragraph (1) "managers" has the meaning given by Article 2(2) of the Education and Libraries (Northern Ireland) Order 1986.

55(1) The governing body of—

(a) a university receiving financial support under Article 30 of the Education and Libraries (Northern Ireland) Order 1993,

(b) a college of education...[121] or in respect of which grants are paid under Article 66(2) or (3) of the Education and Libraries (Northern Ireland) Order 1986, or

(c) an institution of further education within the meaning of the Further Education (Northern Ireland) Order 1997.

(2) In sub-paragraph (1) "governing body" has the meaning given by Article 30(3) of the Education and Libraries (Northern Ireland) Order 1993.

56 Any person providing further education to whom grants, loans or other payments are made under Article 5(1)(b) of the Further Education (Northern Ireland) Order 1997.

Part V Police

England and Wales

57 A police authority established under section 3 of the Police Act 1996.

58 The Metropolitan Police Authority established under section 5B of the Police Act 1996.

59 A chief officer of police of a police force in England or Wales.

Northern Ireland

60 The [Northern Ireland Policing Board][122].

61 The Chief Constable of the [Police Service of Northern Ireland][123].

Miscellaneous

62 The British Transport Police.

63 The Ministry of Defence Police established by section 1 of the Ministry of Defence Police Act 1987.

[63A The Civil Nuclear Police Authority.

63B The chief constable of the Civil Nuclear Constabulary.][124]

64 Any person who—

(a) by virtue of any enactment has the function of nominating individuals who may be appointed as special constables by justices of the peace, and

(b) is not a public authority by virtue of any other provision of this Act,

in respect of information relating to the exercise by any person appointed on his nomination of the functions of a special constable.

Part VI Other public bodies and offices: general

[The Adjudication Panel for Wales.][125]

The Adjudicator for the Inland Revenue and Customs and Excise.

The Administration of Radioactive Substances Advisory Committee.

[The Administrative Justice and Tribunals Council.][126]

[[The Adult Learning Inspectorate.][127]][128]

[...The Advisory Board on Family Law][129]...

The Advisory Board on Restricted Patients.

The Advisory Board on the Registration of Homoeopathic Products.

[The Advisory Committee for Cleaner Coal Technology.][130]

The Advisory Committee for Disabled People in Employment and Training.

The Advisory Committee for the Public Lending Right.

[...The Advisory Committee for Wales (in relation to the Environment Agency).][131]...

The Advisory Committee on Advertising.

The Advisory Committee on Animal Feedingstuffs.

The Advisory Committee on Borderline Substances.

The Advisory Committee on Business and the Environment.

The Advisory Committee on Business Appointments.

The Advisory Committee on Conscientious Objectors.

The Advisory Committee on Consumer Products and the Environment.

The Advisory Committee on Dangerous Pathogens.

The Advisory Committee on Distinction Awards.

[An Advisory Committee on General Commissioners of Income Tax.][132]

The Advisory Committee on the Government Art Collection

The Advisory Committee on Hazardous Substances.

The Advisory Committee on Historic Wreck Sites.

An Advisory Committee on Justices of the Peace in England and Wales.

The Advisory Committee on the Microbiological Safety of Food.

[...The Advisory Committee on NHS Drugs][133]...

The Advisory Committee on Novel Foods and Processes.

[The Advisory Committee on Organic Standards.][134]

The Advisory Committee on Overseas Economic and Social Research.

The Advisory Committee on Packaging.

The Advisory Committee on Pesticides.

The Advisory Committee on Releases to the Environment.

[The Advisory Committee on Statute Law.][135]

[The Advisory Committee on Telecommunications for the Disabled and Elderly.][136]

The Advisory Council on Libraries.

The Advisory Council on the Misuse of Drugs.

The Advisory Council on Public Records.

The Advisory Group on Hepatitis.

[The Advisory Council on Historical Manuscripts.][137]

[The Advisory Council on National Records and Archives.][138]

[The Advisory Group on Medical Countermeasures.][139]

[The Advisory Panel on Beacon Councils.][140]

[The Advisory Panel on Public Sector Information.][141]

The Advisory Panel on Standards for the Planning Inspectorate.

The Aerospace Committee.

An Agricultural Dwelling House Advisory Committee.

An Agricultural Wages Board for England and Wales.

An Agricultural Wages Committee.

The Agriculture and Environment Biotechnology Commission.

[The Agriculture and Horticulture Development Board.][142]

The Airborne Particles Expert Group.

[The Air Quality Expert Group.][143]

The Alcohol Education and Research Council.

[The All-Wales Medicines Strategy Group.][144]

[The Ancient Monuments Board for Wales.][145]

The Animal Procedures Committee.

The Animal Welfare Advisory Committee.

[...The Apple and Pear Research Council.][146]...

[The Appointments Commission.][147]

[The Architects Registration Board.][148]

The Armed Forces Pay Review Body.

[The Arts and Humanities Research Council.][149]

The Arts Council of England.

The Arts Council of Wales.

The Audit Commission for Local Authorities and the National Health Service in England and Wales.

The Auditor General for Wales.

[The Authorised Conveyancing Practitioners Board.][150]

The Bank of England, in respect of information held for purposes other than those of its functions with respect to—

(a) monetary policy,

(b) financial operations intended to support financial institutions for the purposes of maintaining stability, and

(c) the provision of private banking services and related services.

The Better Regulation Task Force.

[The Big Lottery Fund][151]

The Biotechnology and Biological Sciences Research Council.

[The Board of the Pension Protection Fund.][152]

[Any Board of Visitors established under section 6(2) of the Prison Act 1952.][153]

The Britain-Russia Centre and East-West Centre.

The British Association for Central and Eastern Europe.

The British Broadcasting Corporation, in respect of information held for purposes other than those of journalism, art or literature.

The British Coal Corporation.

The British Council.

The British Educational Communications and Technology Agency.

The British Hallmarking Council.

The British Library.

The British Museum.

The British Pharmacopoeia Commission.

[The British Potato Council.][154]

The British Railways Board[155].
British Shipbuilders.
The British Tourist Authority.
[The British Transport Police Authority.][156]
The British Waterways Board.
The British Wool Marketing Board.
The Broadcasting Standards Commission.
The Building Regulations Advisory Committee.
[[The Business Incubation Fund Investment Panel.][157]][158]
[The Care Council for Wales.][159]
[The Care Quality Commission.][160]
The Central Advisory Committee on War Pensions.
[...The Central Council for Education and Training in Social Work (UK).][161]...
[[The Central Police Training and Development Authority.][162]][163]
The Central Rail Users' Consultative Committee.
[The Certification Officer.][164]
The Channel Four Television Corporation, in respect of information held for purposes other than those of journalism, art or literature.
[The Chemical Weapons Convention National Authority Advisory Committee.][165]
[The Child Maintenance and Enforcement Commission.][166]
The Children and Family Court Advisory and Support Service.
[The Children's Commissioner.][167]
[The Children's Commissioner for Wales.][168]
The Civil Aviation Authority.
The Civil Justice Council.
The Civil Procedure Rule Committee.
The Civil Service Appeal Board.
The Civil Service Commissioners.
The Coal Authority.
The Commission for Architecture and the Built Environment.
[The Commission for Equality and Human Rights.][169]
[...The Commission for Health Improvement.][170]...
[[...Commission for Healthcare Audit and Inspection, in respect of information held for purposes other than those of its functions exercisable by virtue of paragraph 5(a)(i) of the Care Standards Act 2000.][171]...][172]
[The Commission for Integrated Transport.][173]
The Commission for Local Administration in England.
[The Commission for Local Administration in Wales.][174]
[...The Commission for the New Towns.][175]...
[The Commission for Racial Equality.][176]
[Commission for Rural Communities.][177]
[[...Commission for Social Care Inspection, in respect of information held for purposes other than those of its functions exercisable by virtue of paragraph 5(a)(ii) of the Care Standards Act 2000.]...][178]
[The Commissioner for Integrated Transport.][179]
[The Commissioner for Older People in Wales][180]
The Commissioner for Public Appointments.
[Commissioner for Parliamentary Investigations.][181]
[The Commissioners of Northern Lighthouses.][182]
The Committee for Monitoring Agreements on Tobacco Advertising and Sponsorship.
[The Committee of Investigation for Great Britain.][183]
The Committee on Agricultural Valuation.
The Committee on Carcinogenicity of Chemicals in Food, Consumer Products and the Environment.
The Committee on Chemicals and Materials of Construction For Use in Public Water Supply and Swimming Pools.

[The Committee on Climate Change.][184]
The Committee on Medical Aspects of Food and Nutrition Policy.
The Committee on Medical Aspects of Radiation in the Environment.
The Committee on Mutagenicity of Chemicals in Food, Consumer Products and the Environment.
[The Committee on Radioactive Waste Management.][185]
[The Committee on Safety of Devices.][186]
The Committee on Standards in Public Life.
The Committee on Toxicity of Chemicals in Food, Consumer Products and the Environment.
The Committee on the Medical Effects of Air Pollutants.
The Committee on the Safety of Medicines.
The Commonwealth Scholarship Commission in the United Kingdom.
[Communications for Business.][187]
The Community Development Foundation.
The Competition Commission, in relation to information held by it otherwise than as a tribunal.
[The Competition Service.][188]
[A conservation board established under section 86 of the Countryside and Rights of Way Act 2000.][189]
The Construction Industry Training Board.
Consumer Communications for England.
[The Consumer Council for Postal Services.][190]
[The Consumer Council for Water][191]
[...The Consumer Panel.][192]...
[The Consumer Panel established under section 16 of the Communications Act 2003.][193]
[The consumers' committee for Great Britain appointed under section 19 of the Agricultural Marketing Act 1958.][194]
[...The Council for Professions Supplementary to Medicine.][195]...
The Council for the Central Laboratory of the Research Councils.
[[The Council for Healthcare Regulatory Excellence][196].][197]
The Council for Science and Technology.
[The Council on Tribunals.][198]
[The Countryside Agency.][199]
The Countryside Council for Wales.
[A courts board established under section 4 of the Courts Act 2003.][200]
The Covent Garden Market Authority.
The Criminal Cases Review Commission.
[[The Criminal Injuries Compensation Appeals Panel, in relation to information held by it otherwise than as a tribunal.][201]][202]
[The Criminal Injuries Compensation Authority.][203]
The Criminal Justice Consultative Council.
[The Criminal Procedure Rule Committee.][204]
The Crown Court Rule Committee.
The Dartmoor Steering Group and Working Party.
The Darwin Advisory Committee.
The Defence Nuclear Safety Committee.
The Defence Scientific Advisory Council.
The Design Council.
[...The Development Awareness Working Group.]...[205]
The Diplomatic Service Appeal Board.
[The Director of Fair Access to Higher Education.][206]
[The Disability Employment Advisory Committee.][207]
The Disability Living Allowance Advisory Board.
[The Disability Rights Commission.][208]
The Disabled Persons Transport Advisory Committee.
[The Distributed Generation Co-Ordinating Group.][209]
[The East of England Industrial Development Board.][210]

The Economic and Social Research Council.
[...The Education Transfer Council.]...[211]
[The Electoral Commission.][212]
[...The Energy Advisory Panel]...[213]
The Engineering Construction Industry Training Board.
The Engineering and Physical Sciences Research Council.
[The English National Board for Nursing, Midwifery and Health Visiting.][214]
[English Nature.][215]
The English Sports Council.
The English Tourist Board.
The Environment Agency.
[The Equal Opportunities Commission.][216]
[The Ethnic Minority Business Forum.][217]
The Expert Advisory Group on AIDS.
The Expert Group on Cryptosporidium in Water Supplies.
An Expert Panel on Air Quality Standards.
The Export Guarantees Advisory Council.
[The Family Justice Council.][218]
[The Family Procedure Rule Committee.][219]
The Family Proceedings Rules Committee.
The Farm Animal Welfare Council.
[The Financial Reporting Advisory Board.][220]
[The Financial Services Authority.][221]
The Fire Services Examination Board.
The Firearms Consultative Committee.
The Food Advisory Committee.
Food from Britain.
The Football Licensing Authority.
The Fuel Cell Advisory Panel.
[The Fuel Poverty Advisory Group.][222]
[...The Further Education Funding Council For Wales][223]...
[The Gaelic Media Service, in respect of information held for purposes other than those of journalism, art or literature.][224]
[Gambling Commission][225]
[Gangmasters Licensing Authority][226]
[The Gas and Electricity Consumer Council.][227]
[...The Gas Consumers Council][228]...
The Gene Therapy Advisory Committee.
The General Chiropractic Council.
The General Dental Council.
The General Medical Council.
[The General Optical Council.][229]
The General Osteopathic Council.
[The General Social Care Council.][230]
[The General Teaching Council for England.][231]
[The General Teaching Council for Wales.][232]
The Genetic Testing and Insurance Committee.
The Government Hospitality Advisory Committee for the Purchase of Wine.
The Government Chemist.
[The Government-Industry Forum on Non-Food Use of Crops.][233]
The Great Britain-China Centre.
The Health and Safety Commission.
[The Health and Safety Executive.][234]
[The Health Professions Council][235]

[The Health Protection Agency.][236]

The Health Service Commissioner for England.

[The Health Service Commissioner for Wales.][237]

[[...The Hearing Aid Council.][238]...][239]

[Her Majesty's Chief Inspector of Education and Training in Wales or Prif Arolygydd Ei Mawrhydi dros Addysg a Hyfforddiant yng Nghymru][240].

[Her Majesty's Commissioners for Judicial Appointments.][241]

The Higher Education Funding Council for England.

The Higher Education Funding Council for Wales.

[The Hill Farming Advisory Committee.][242]

[The Hill Farming Advisory Sub-committee for Wales.][243]

[The Historic Buildings Council for Wales.][244]

The Historic Buildings and Monuments Commission for England.

The Historic Royal Palaces Trust.

[The Home-Grown Cereals Authority.][245]

[The Homes and Communities Agency.][246]

[...The Honorary Investment Advisory Committee.]...[247]

The Horserace Betting Levy Board.

The Horserace Totalisator Board.

[The Horticultural Development Council.][248]

Horticulture Research International.

The House of Lords Appointments Commission.

Any housing action trust established under Part III of the Housing Act 1988.

[...The Housing Corporation.]...[249]

The Human Fertilisation and Embryology Authority.

The Human Genetics Commission.

[The Human Tissue Authority.][250]

The Immigration Services Commissioner.

The Imperial War Museum.

[The Independent Advisory Group on Teenage Pregnancy.][251]

The Independent Board of Visitors for Military Corrective Training Centres.

The Independent Case Examiner for the Child Support Agency.

[The Independent Groundwater Complaints Administrator.][252]

The Independent Living Funds.

[Any Independent Monitoring Board established under section 6(2) of the Prison Act 1952.][253]

[The Independent Parliamentary Standards Authority.][254]

[The Independent Police Complaints Commission.][255]

[The Independent Regulator of NHS Foundation Trusts.][256]

[The Independent Review Panel for Advertising.][257]

[The Independent Review Panel for Borderline Products.][258]

[The Independent Scientific Group on Cattle Tuberculosis.][259]

The Independent Television Commission.

[...The Indian Family Pensions Funds Body of Commissioners.]...[260]

The Industrial Development Advisory Board.

The Industrial Injuries Advisory Council.

The Information Commissioner.

[The Infrastructure Planning Commission.][261]

[Inland Waterways Advisory Council][262]

The Insolvency Rules Committee.

[The Insurance Brokers Registration Council.][263]

[The Integrated Administration and Controls System Appeals Panel.][264]

[The Intellectual Property Advisory Committee.][265]

Investors in People UK.

The Joint Committee on Vaccination and Immunisation.

The Joint Nature Conservation Committee.
The Joint Prison/Probation Accreditation Panel.
[The Judicial Appointments and Conduct Ombudsman.][266]
[The Judicial Appointments Commission.][267]
The Judicial Studies Board.
The Know-How Fund Advisory Board.
The Land Registration Rule Committee.
The Law Commission.
[The Learning and Skills Council for England.][268]
[The Legal Deposit Advisory Panel][269]
[The Legal Services Board.][270]
The Legal Services Commission.
[[...The Legal Services Complaints Commissioner.][271]...][272]
[...The Legal Services Consultative Panel.]...[273]
[...The Legal Services Ombudsman.]...[274]
[...The Library and Information Services Council (Wales).]...[275]
[The Local Better Regulation Office.][276]
[The Local Government Boundary Commission for England.][277]
The Local Government Boundary Commission for Wales.
[... The Local Government Commission for England.]...[278]
A local probation board established under section 4 of the Criminal Justice and Court Services Act 2000.
[The London and South East Industrial Development Board.][279]
The London Pensions Fund Authority.
The Low Pay Commission.
The Magistrates' Courts Rules Committee.
[The Marine Management Organisation.][280]
The Marshall Aid Commemoration Commission.
The Measurement Advisory Committee.
[The Meat and Livestock Commission.][281]
[...The Medical Practices Committee.]...[282]
The Medical Research Council.
[...The Medical Workforce Standing Advisory Committee.]...[283]
The Medicines Commission.
[The Milk Development Council.][284]
[The Millennium Commission.][285]
The Museum of London.
The National Army Museum.
The National Audit Office.
[...The National Biological Standards Board (UK).]...[286]
[The National Care Standards Commission.][287]
The National Consumer Council.
[The National Consumer Council.][288]
[[The National Council for Education and Training for Wales.][289]][290]
[The National Crime Squad.][291]
The National Employers' Liaison Committee.
[The National Employment Panel.][292]
The National Endowment for Science, Technology and the Arts.
[The National Expert Group on Transboundary Air Pollution.][293]
[The National Forest Company.][294]
The National Gallery.
The National Heritage Memorial Fund.
[The National Identity Scheme Commissioner.][295]
[The National Information Governance Board for Health and Social Care.][296]
The National Library of Wales.

[The National Lottery Charities Board.][297]
The National Lottery Commission.
The National Maritime Museum.
The National Museum of Science and Industry.
The National Museums and Galleries of Wales.
The National Museums and Galleries on Merseyside.
[The National Policing Improvement Agency.][298]
The National Portrait Gallery.
[The National Radiological Protection Board.][299]
[Natural England.][300]
The Natural Environment Research Council.
The Natural History Museum.
The New Deal Task Force.
[The New Opportunities Fund.][301]
[The North East Industrial Development Board.][302]
[The Northern Ireland Judicial Appointments Ombudsman.][303]
[The North West Industrial Development Board.][304]
[The Nuclear Decommissioning Authority.][305]
[The Nuclear Research Advisory Council.][306]
[The Nursing and Midwifery Council.][307]
[The Occupational Pensions Regulatory Authority.][308]
[The Office of Communications.][309]
[The Office of the Health Professions Adjudicator.][310]
[The Office of Government Commerce.][311]
[The Office for Legal Complaints.][312]
[The Office of Manpower Economics.][313]
[Office for Tenants and Social Landlords.][314]
The Oil and Pipelines Agency.
[The Olympic Delivery Authority.][315]
[The Olympic Lottery Distributor][316]
[The Ombudsman for the Board of the Pension Protection Fund.][317]
The OSO Board.
The Overseas Service Pensions Scheme Advisory Board.
The Panel on Standards for the Planning Inspectorate.
The Parliamentary Boundary Commission for England.
The Parliamentary Boundary Commission for Scotland.
The Parliamentary Boundary Commission for Wales.
The Parliamentary Commissioner for Administration.
The Parole Board.
The Particle Physics and Astronomy Research Council.
[[...The Patient Information Advisory Group.]...[318]][319]
[The Pensions Compensation Board.][320]
The Pensions Ombudsman.
[The Pensions Regulator.][321]
[The Personal Accounts Delivery Authority][322]
[The Pesticide Residues Committee.][323]
[The Pesticides Forum.][324]
[The Pharmacists' Review Panel.][325]
[...The Place Names Advisory Committee]...[326]
The Poisons Board.
[The Police Advisory Board for England and Wales.][327]
[The Police Complaints Authority.][328]
[The Police Information Technology Organisation.][329]
The Police Negotiating Board.

[The Police Senior Appointments Panel][330]

The Political Honours Scrutiny Committee.

The Post Office.

[...The Post Office Users Councils for Scotland, Wales and Northern Ireland.]...[331]

[...The Post Office Users National Council.]...[332]

[The Postgraduate Medical Education and Training Board.][333]

[The Prison Service Pay Review Body.][334]

[A probation trust.][335]

[The Property Advisory Group.][336]

[The Public Private Partnership Agreement Arbiter.][337]

[The Public Services Ombudsman for Wales][338]

[The Qualifications, Curriculum and Assessment Authority for Wales.][339]

[The Qualifications and Curriculum Development Agency][340]

The Race Education and Employment Forum.

The Race Relations Forum.

The Radio Authority.

The Radioactive Waste Management Advisory Committee.

[[Any Rail Passengers' Committee established under section 2(2) of the Railways Act 1993.][341]][342]

A Regional Cultural Consortium.

Any regional development agency established under the Regional Development Agencies Act 1998, other than the London Development Agency.

Any regional flood defence committee.

[The Registrar General for England and Wales.][343]

[The Registrar of Occupational and Personal Pension Schemes.][344]

The Registrar of Public Lending Right.

Remploy Ltd.

The Renewable Energy Advisory Committee.

[The Renewables Advisory Board.][345]

Resource: The Council for Museums, Archives and Libraries.

The Review Board for Government Contracts.

The Review Body for Nursing Staff, Midwives, Health Visitors and Professions Allied to Medicine.

The Review Body on Doctors and Dentists Remuneration.

The Reviewing Committee on the Export of Works of Art.

The Royal Air Force Museum.

The Royal Armouries.

The Royal Botanic Gardens, Kew.

[The Royal College of Veterinary Surgeons, in respect of information held by it otherwise than as a tribunal.][346]

The Royal Commission on Ancient and Historical Monuments of Wales.

The Royal Commission on Environmental Pollution.

The Royal Commission on Historical Manuscripts.

[The Royal Hospital at Chelsea.][347]

[The Royal Military College of Science Advisory Council.][348]

The Royal Mint Advisory Committee on the Design of Coins, Medals, Seals and Decorations.

[The Royal Pharmaceutical Society of Great Britain, in respect of information held by it otherwise than as a tribunal.][349]

The School Teachers' Review Body.

[The Scientific Advisory Committee on Nutrition.][350]

The Scientific Committee on Tobacco and Health.

[...The Scottish Advisory Committee on Telecommunications.]...[351]

[The Scottish Committee of the Administrative Justice and Tribunals Council.][352]

[The Scottish Committee of the Council on Tribunals.][353]

The Sea Fish Industry Authority.

[The Security Industry Authority][354]

The Senior Salaries Review Body.
[The Sentencing Council for England and Wales.][355]
[The Sentencing Advisory Panel][356]
[[The Sentencing Guidelines Council.][357]][358]
[The Service Authority for the National Crime Squad.][359]
Sianel Pedwar Cymru, in respect of information held for purposes other than those of journalism, art or literature.
Sir John Soane's Museum.
[The Skills Task Force.] [360]
[The Small Business Council.][361]
[The Small Business Investment Task Force.][362]
[The Social Care Institute for Excellence.][363]
The social fund Commissioner appointed under section 65 of the Social Security Administration Act 1992.
The Social Security Advisory Committee.
The Social Services Inspectorate for Wales Advisory Group.
[The South West Industrial Development Board.][364]
[The Specialist Advisory Committee on Antimicrobial Research.][365]
The Spongiform Encephalopathy Advisory Committee.
The Sports Council for Wales.
[The Standards Board for England.][366]
The Standing Advisory Committee on Industrial Property.
The Standing Advisory Committee on Trunk Road Assessment.
The Standing Dental Advisory Committee.
[The Standing Medical Advisory Committee.][367]
[The Standing Nursing and Midwifery Advisory Committee.][368]
[The Standing Pharmaceutical Advisory Committee.][369]
[The Statistics Commission.][370]
The Steering Committee on Pharmacy Postgraduate Education.
[The Strategic Investment Board.][371]
[[The Strategic Rail Authority.][372]][373]
The subsidence adviser appointed under section 46 of the Coal Industry Act 1994.
The Substance Misuse Advisory Panel.
The Sustainable Development Commission.
[...The Sustainable Development Education Panel.]..[374].
[The Sustainable Energy Policy Advisory Board.][375]
The Tate Gallery.
[The TB Advisory Group][376]
[The Teacher Training Agency.][377]
[The Technical Advisory Board.][378]
The Theatres Trust.
The Traffic Commissioners, in respect of information held by them otherwise than as a tribunal.
[The Training and Development Agency for Schools.][379]
The Treasure Valuation Committee.
[The trustee corporation established by section 75 of the Pensions Act 2008.][380]
The UK Advisory Panel for Health Care Workers Infected with Bloodborne Viruses.
[The UK Chemicals Stakeholder Forum.][381]
[The UK Commission for Employment and Skills][382]
The UK Sports Council.
The United Kingdom Atomic Energy Authority.
[...The United Kingdom Central Council for Nursing, Midwifery and Health Visiting.]...[383]
[The United Kingdom Register of Organic Food Standards.][384]
The United Kingdom Xenotransplantation Interim Regulatory Authority.
[The University for Industry.][385]
The Unlinked Anonymous Serosurveys Steering Group.

The Unrelated Live Transplant Regulatory Authority.
[...The Urban Regeneration Agency.]...[386]
[The Valuation Tribunal Service.][387]
[The verderers of the New Forest, in respect of information held by them otherwise than as a tribunal.][388]
The Veterinary Products Committee.
[The Veterinary Residues Committee.][389]
The Victoria and Albert Museum.
[The Wales Centre for Health.][390]
[...The Wales New Deal Advisory Task Force.].[391]..
[The Wales Tourist Board.][392]
The Wallace Collection.
The War Pensions Committees.
The Water Regulations Advisory Committee.
[The Welsh Administration Ombudsman.][393]
[...The Welsh Advisory Committee on Telecommunications.]...[394]
The Welsh Committee for Professional Development of Pharmacy.
[The Welsh Committee of the Administrative Justice and Tribunals Council.][395]
The Welsh Dental Committee.
[The Welsh Development Agency.][396]
The Welsh Industrial Development Advisory Board.
The Welsh Language Board.
The Welsh Medical Committee.
[...The Welsh National Board for Nursing, Midwifery and Health Visiting.]...[397]
The Welsh Nursing and Midwifery Committee.
The Welsh Optometric Committee.
The Welsh Pharmaceutical Committee.
The Welsh Scientific Advisory Committee.
The Westminster Foundation for Democracy.
[The West Midlands Industrial Development Board.][398]
The Wilton Park Academic Council.
The Wine Standards Board of the Vintners' Company.
The Women's National Commission.
[The Yorkshire and the Humber and the East Midlands Industrial Development Board.][399]
The Youth Justice Board for England and Wales.
The Zoos Forum.

Part VII Other public bodies and offices: Northern Ireland

[An advisory committee established under paragraph 25 of the Health and Personal Social Services (Northern Ireland) Order 1972.][400]
[An Advisory Committee on General Commissioners of Income Tax (Northern Ireland).][401]
The Advisory Committee on Justices of the Peace in Northern Ireland.
[...The Advisory Committee on Juvenile Court Lay Panel (Northern Ireland).]...[402]
The Advisory Committee on Pesticides for Northern Ireland.
[...The Agricultural Research Institute of Northern Ireland.]...[403]
The Agricultural Wages Board for Northern Ireland.
[The Agri-food and Biosciences Institute][404]
The Arts Council of Northern Ireland.
The Assembly Ombudsman for Northern Ireland.
[The Attorney General for Northern Ireland.][405]
[The Belfast Harbour Commissioners.][406]
The Board of Trustees of National Museums and Galleries of Northern Ireland.
[...Boards of Visitors and Visiting Committees.]...[407]
The Boundary Commission for Northern Ireland.
[A central advisory committee established under paragraph 24 of the Health and Personal Social Services (Northern Ireland) Order 1972.][408]

[The Certification Officer for Northern Ireland.][409]

The Charities Advisory Committee.

[The Charity Commission for Northern Ireland][410]

The Chief Electoral Officer for Northern Ireland.

[The Chief Inspector of Criminal Justice in Northern Ireland.][411]

The Civil Service Commissioners for Northern Ireland.

[Comhairle na Gaelscolaíochta.][412]

[The Commission for Victims and Survivors for Northern Ireland][413]

[The Commissioner for Children and Young People for Northern Ireland][414]

The Commissioner for Public Appointments for Northern Ireland.

[[The Commissioner for Victims and Survivors for Northern Ireland][415]][416]

The Construction Industry Training Board.

The consultative Civic Forum referred to in section 56(4) of the Northern Ireland Act 1998.

The Council for Catholic Maintained Schools.

The Council for Nature Conservation and the Countryside.

The County Court Rules Committee (Northern Ireland).

[The Criminal Injuries Compensation Appeals Panel for Northern Ireland, in relation to information held by it otherwise than as a tribunal.][417]

[A development corporation established under Part III of the Strategic Investment and Regeneration of Sites (Northern Ireland) Order 2003][418]

[The Disability Living Allowance Advisory Board for Northern Ireland.][419]

The Distinction and Meritorious Service Awards Committee.

[A district policing partnership.][420]

The Drainage Council for Northern Ireland.

An Education and Library Board established under Article 3 of the Education and Libraries (Northern Ireland) Order 1986.

[Enterprise Ulster.][421]

The Equality Commission for Northern Ireland.

The Family Proceedings Rules Committee (Northern Ireland).

[...The Fire Authority for Northern Ireland.]...[422]

[...The Fisheries Conservancy Board for Northern Ireland.]...[423]

The General Consumer Council for Northern Ireland.

[The General Teaching Council for Northern Ireland.][424]

[The Governors of the Armargh Observatory and Planetarium.][425]

[The Harbour of Donaghadee Commissioners.][426]

The Health and Safety Agency for Northern Ireland.

The Historic Buildings Council.

The Historic Monuments Council.

The Independent Assessor of Military Complaints Procedures in Northern Ireland.

The Independent Commissioner for Holding Centres.

[An independent monitoring board appointed under section 10 of the Prison Act (Northern Ireland) 1953.][427]

The Independent Reviewer of the Northern Ireland (Emergency Provisions) Act.

[...The Industrial Development Board for Northern Ireland.]...[428]

[...The Industrial Research and Technology Unit.]...[429]

[Invest Northern Ireland][430]

[...The Juvenile Justice Board.]...[431]

The Labour Relations Agency.

[...The Laganside Corporation.]...[432]

[...The Law Reform Advisory Committee for Northern Ireland.]...[433]

The Lay Observer for Northern Ireland.

[[...The Learning and Skills Advisory Board.]...[434]][435]

The Legal Aid Advisory Committee (Northern Ireland).

[[... The Life Sentence Review Commissioners appointed under Article 3 of the Life Sentences (Northern

Ireland) Order 2001.]...[436]][437]
The Livestock & Meat Commission for Northern Ireland.
[...The Local Enterprise Development Unit.]...[438]
The Local Government Staff Commission.
[The Londonderry Port and Harbour Commissioners.][439]
The Magistrates' Courts Rules Committee (Northern Ireland).
[... The Mental Health Commission for Northern Ireland.]...[440]
[...The Northern Ireland Advisory Committee on Telecommunications.]...[441]
The Northern Ireland Audit Office.
[The Northern Ireland Authority for Utility Regulation.][442]
The Northern Ireland Building Regulations Advisory Committee.
The Northern Ireland Civil Service Appeal Board.
The Northern Ireland Commissioner for Complaints.
The Northern Ireland Community Relations Council.
[...The Northern Ireland Consumer Committee for Electricity.]...[443]
The Northern Ireland Council for the Curriculum, Examinations and Assessment.
[...The Northern Ireland Council for Postgraduate Medical and Dental Education.]...[444]
[The Northern Ireland Court of Judicature Rules Committee.][445]
The Northern Ireland Crown Court Rules Committee.
[...The Northern Ireland Economic Council.]...[446]
[The Northern Ireland Events Company.][447]
[The Northern Ireland Fire and Rescue Service Board][448]
The Northern Ireland Fishery Harbour Authority.
[The Northern Ireland Health and Personal Social Services Regulation and Improvement Authority.][449]
The Northern Ireland Higher Education Council.
The Northern Ireland Housing Executive.
The Northern Ireland Human Rights Commission.
The Northern Ireland Insolvency Rules Committee.
[The Northern Ireland Judicial Appointments Commission.][450]
[The Northern Ireland Law Commission.][451]
[The Northern Ireland Legal Services Commission.][452]
[The Northern Ireland Library Authority][453]
The Northern Ireland Local Government Officers' Superannuation Committee.
The Northern Ireland Museums Council.
[...The Northern Ireland Pig Production Development Committee.]...[454]
[The Northern Ireland Practice and Education Council for Nursing and Midwifery.][455]
[The Northern Ireland Social Care Council.][456]
[... The Northern Ireland Supreme Court Rules Committee.]...[457]
The Northern Ireland Tourist Board.
The Northern Ireland Transport Holding Company.
[...The Northern Ireland Water Council.]...[458]
[[...Obstetrics Committee.]...[459]][460]
The Parades Commission.
[Parole Commissioners for Northern Ireland][461]
[The Pharmaceutical Society of Northern Ireland, in respect of information held by it otherwise than as a tribunal.][462]
[The Poisons Board (Northern Ireland).][463]
The Police Ombudsman for Northern Ireland.
The Probation Board for Northern Ireland.
The Rural Development Council for Northern Ireland.
The Sentence Review Commissioners appointed under section 1 of the Northern Ireland (Sentences) Act 1998.
The social fund Commissioner appointed under Article 37 of the Social Security (Northern Ireland) Order 1998.

The Sports Council for Northern Ireland.
The Staff Commission for Education and Library Boards.
The Statistics Advisory Committee.
The Statute Law Committee for Northern Ireland.
[A sub-group established under section 21 of the Police (Northern Ireland) Act 2000.][464]
[...The Training and Employment Agency.]...[465]
Ulster Supported Employment Ltd.
[The Warrenpoint Harbour Authority.][466]
[The Waste Management Advisory Board.][467]
The Youth Council for Northern Ireland.

SCHEDULE 2 The Commissioner and the Tribunal

Part I Provision consequential on s. 18(1) and (2)

General

1(1) any reference in any enactment, instrument or document to the Data Protection Commissioner or the Data Protection Registrar shall be construed, in relation to any time after the commencement of section 18(1), as a reference to the Information Commissioner.

(2) Any reference in any enactment, instrument or document to the Data Protection Tribunal shall be construed, in relation to any time after the commencement of section 18(2), as a reference to the Information Tribunal.

[1AThe Office for Standards in Education, Children's Services and Skills, in respect of information held for purposes other than those of the functions exercisable by Her Majesty's Chief Inspector of Education, Children's Services and Skills by virtue of section 5(1)(a)(iii) of the Care Standards Act 2000.][468]

2(1) Any reference in this Act or in any instrument under this Act to the Commissioner shall be construed, in relation to any time before the commencement of section 18(1), as a reference to the Data Protection Commissioner.

(2) Any reference in this Act or in any instrument under this Act to the Tribunal shall be construed, in relation to any time before the commencement of section 18(2), as a reference to the Data Protection Tribunal.

Public Records Act 1958 (c. 51)

3(1) In Part II of the Table in paragraph 3 of Schedule 1 to the Public Records Act 1958 (definition of public records), the entry relating to the Data Protection Commissioner is omitted and there is inserted at the appropriate place—
"Information Commissioner."

(2) In paragraph 4(1) of that Schedule, for paragraph (nn) there is substituted—
"(nn) records of the Information Tribunal;".

Parliamentary Commissioner Act 1967 (c. 13)

4 In Schedule 2 to the Parliamentary Commissioner Act 1967 (departments etc. subject to investigation), the entry relating to the Data Protection Commissioner is omitted and there is inserted at the appropriate place—
"Information Commissioner".

5 In Schedule 4 to that Act (tribunals exercising administrative functions), for the entry relating to the Data Protection Tribunal there is substituted—
"Information Tribunal constituted under section 6 of the Data Protection Act 1998."

Superannuation Act 1972 (c. 11)

6 In Schedule 1 to the Superannuation Act 1972 (employment with superannuation scheme), for "Data Protection Commissioner" there is substituted " Information Commissioner ".

Consumer Credit Act 1974 (c. 39)

7 In section 159 of the Consumer Credit Act 1974 (correction of wrong information), in subsections (7) and (8)(b), for "Data Protection Commissioner", in both places where it occurs, there is substituted "Information Commissioner".

House of Commons Disqualification Act 1975 (c. 24)

8(1) In Part II of Schedule 1 to the House of Commons Disqualification Act 1975 (bodies whose members

are disqualified), the entry relating to the Data Protection Tribunal is omitted and there is inserted at the appropriate place—

"The Information Tribunal".

(2) In Part III of that Schedule (disqualifying offices), the entry relating to the Data Protection Commissioner is omitted and there is inserted at the appropriate place—

"The Information Commissioner".

Northern Ireland Assembly Disqualification Act 1975 (c. 25)

9(1) In Part II of Schedule 1 to the Northern Ireland Assembly Disqualification Act 1975 (bodies whose members are disqualified), the entry relating to the Data Protection Tribunal is omitted and there is inserted at the appropriate place—

"The Information Tribunal".

(2) In Part III of that Schedule (disqualifying offices), the entry relating to the Data Protection Commissioner is omitted and there is inserted at the appropriate place—

"The Information Commissioner".

Tribunals and Inquiries Act 1992 (c. 53)

10 In paragraph 14 of Part I of Schedule 1 to the Tribunals and Inquiries Act 1992 (tribunals under direct supervision of Council on Tribunals)—

(a) in sub-paragraph (a), for "The Data Protection Commissioner" there is substituted " The Information Commissioner ", and

(b) for sub-paragraph (b) there is substituted—

"(b) the Information Tribunal constituted under that section, in respect of its jurisdiction under—

(i) section 48 of that Act, and

(ii) section 57 of the Freedom of Information Act 2000."

Judicial Pensions and Retirement Act 1993 (c. 8)

11 In Schedule 5 to the Judicial Pensions and Retirement Act 1993 (retirement provisions: the relevant offices), in the entry relating to the chairman and deputy chairman of the Data Protection Tribunal, for "the Data Protection Tribunal" there is substituted " the Information Tribunal ".

12 In Schedule 7 to that Act (retirement dates: transitional provisions), in paragraph 5(5)(xxvi) for "the Data Protection Tribunal" there is substituted " the Information Tribunal ".

Data Protection Act 1998 (c. 29)

13(1) Section 6 of the Data Protection Act 1998 (the Data Protection Commissioner and the Data Protection Tribunal) is amended as follows.

(2) For subsection (1) there is substituted—

"(1) For the purposes of this Act and of the Freedom of Information Act 2000 there shall be an officer known as the Information Commissioner (in this Act referred to as "the Commissioner")."

(3) For subsection (3) there is substituted—

"(3) For the purposes of this Act and of the Freedom of Information Act 2000 there shall be a tribunal known as the Information Tribunal (in this Act referred to as "the Tribunal")."

14 In section 70(1) of that Act (supplementary definitions)—

(a) in the definition of "the Commissioner", for "the Data Protection Commissioner" there is substituted " the Information Commissioner ", and

(b) in the definition of "the Tribunal", for "the Data Protection Tribunal" there is substituted " the Information Tribunal ".

15(1) Schedule 5 to that Act (the Data Protection Commissioner and the Data Protection Tribunal) is amended as follows.

(2) In paragraph 1(1), for "Data Protection Commissioner" there is substituted " Information Commissioner ".

(3) Part III shall cease to have effect.

Part II Amendments relating to extension of functions of Commissioner and Tribunal

Interests represented by lay members of Tribunal

16 In section 6(6) of the Data Protection Act 1998 (lay members of Tribunal)—

(a) for the word "and" at the end of paragraph (a) there is substituted—

"(aa) persons to represent the interests of those who make requests for information under the

Freedom of Information Act 2000,", and

(b) after paragraph (b) there is inserted "and

(bb) persons to represent the interests of public authorities."

Expenses incurred under this Act excluded in calculating fees

17 In section 26(2) of that Act (fees regulations), in paragraph (a)—

(a) after "functions" there is inserted "under this Act", and

(b) after "Tribunal" there is inserted "so far as attributable to their functions under this Act".

Information provided to Commissioner or Tribunal

18 In section 58 of that Act (disclosure of information to Commissioner or Tribunal), after "this Act" there is inserted "or the Freedom of Information Act 2000".

19(1) Section 59 of that Act (confidentiality of information) is amended as follows.

(2) In subsections (1) and (2), for "this Act", wherever occurring, there is substituted " the information Acts ".

(3) After subsection (3) there is inserted—

"(4) In this section "the information Acts" means this Act and the Freedom of Information Act 2000."

Deputy commissioners

20(1) Paragraph 4 of Schedule 5 to that Act (officers and staff) is amended as follows.

(2) In sub-paragraph (1)(a), after "a deputy commissioner" there is inserted " or two deputy commissioners ".

(3) After sub-paragraph (1) there is inserted—

"(1A) The Commissioner shall, when appointing any second deputy commissioner, specify which of the Commissioner's functions are to be performed, in the circumstances referred to in paragraph 5(1), by each of the deputy commissioners."

Exercise of Commissioner's functions by others

21(1) Paragraph 5 of Schedule 5 to that Act (exercise of functions of Commissioner during vacancy etc.) is amended as follows.

(2) In sub-paragraph (1)—

(a) after "deputy commissioner" there is inserted " or deputy commissioners ", and

(b) after "this Act" there is inserted " or the Freedom of Information Act 2000 ".

(3) In sub-paragraph (2) after "this Act" there is inserted " or the Freedom of Information Act 2000 ".

Money

22 In paragraph 9(1) of Schedule 5 to that Act (money) for "or section 159 of the Consumer Credit Act 1974" there is substituted " , under section 159 of the Consumer Credit Act 1974 or under the Freedom of Information Act 2000 ".

Section 55

SCHEDULE 3 Powers of entry and inspection

Issue of warrants

1(1) If a circuit judge [or a District Judge (Magistrates' Courts)][469] is satisfied by information on oath supplied by the Commissioner that there are reasonable grounds for suspecting—

(a) that a public authority has failed or is failing to comply with—

(i) any of the requirements of Part I of this Act,

(ii) so much of a decision notice as requires steps to be taken, or

(iii) an information notice or an enforcement notice, or

(b) that an offence under section 77 has been or is being committed,

and that evidence of such a failure to comply or of the commission of the offence is to be found on any premises specified in the information, he may, subject to paragraph 2, grant a warrant to the Commissioner.

(2) A warrant issued under sub-paragraph (1) shall authorise the Commissioner or any of his officers or staff at any time within seven days of the date of the warrant—

(a) to enter and search the premises,

(b) to inspect and seize any documents or other material found there which may be such evidence as is mentioned in that sub-paragraph, and

(c) to inspect, examine, operate and test any equipment found there in which information held by the public authority may be recorded.

2(1) A judge shall not issue a warrant under this Schedule unless he is satisfied—

(a) that the Commissioner has given seven days' notice in writing to the occupier of the premises in question demanding access to the premises, and

(b) that either—

(i) access was demanded at a reasonable hour and was unreasonably refused, or

(ii) although entry to the premises was granted, the occupier unreasonably refused to comply with a request by the Commissioner or any of the Commissioner's officers or staff to permit the Commissioner or the officer or member of staff to do any of the things referred to in paragraph 1(2), and

(c) that the occupier, has, after the refusal, been notified by the Commissioner of the application for the warrant and has had an opportunity of being heard by the judge on the question whether or not it should be issued.

(2) Sub-paragraph (1) shall not apply if the judge is satisfied that the case is one of urgency or that compliance with those provisions would defeat the object of the entry.

3 A judge who issues a warrant under this Schedule shall also issue two copies of it and certify them clearly as copies.

Execution of warrants

4 A person executing a warrant issued under this Schedule may use such reasonable force as may be necessary.

5 A warrant issued under this Schedule shall be executed at a reasonable hour unless it appears to the person executing it that there are grounds for suspecting that the evidence in question would not be found if it were so executed.

6(1) If the premises in respect of which a warrant is issued under this Schedule are occupied by a public authority and any officer or employee of the authority is present when the warrant is executed, he shall be shown the warrant and supplied with a copy of it; and if no such officer or employee is present a copy of the warrant shall be left in a prominent place on the premises.

(2) If the premises in respect of which a warrant is issued under this Schedule are occupied by a person other than a public authority and he is present when the warrant is executed, he shall be shown the warrant and supplied with a copy of it; and if that person is not present a copy of the warrant shall be left in a prominent place on the premises.

7(1) A person seizing anything in pursuance of a warrant under this Schedule shall give a receipt for it if asked to do so.

(2) Anything so seized may be retained for so long as is necessary in all the circumstances but the person in occupation of the premises in question shall be given a copy of anything that is seized if he so requests and the person executing the warrant considers that it can be done without undue delay.

Matters exempt from inspection and seizure

8 The powers of inspection and seizure conferred by a warrant issued under this Schedule shall not be exercisable in respect of information which is exempt information by virtue of section 23(1) or 24(1).

9(1) Subject to the provisions of this paragraph, the powers of inspection and seizure conferred by a warrant issued under this Schedule shall not be exercisable in respect of—

(a) any communication between a professional legal adviser and his client in connection with the giving of legal advice to the client with respect to his obligations, liabilities or rights under this Act, or

(b) any communication between a professional legal adviser and his client, or between such an adviser or his client and any other person, made in connection with or in contemplation of proceedings under or arising out of this Act (including proceedings before the Tribunal) and for the purposes of such proceedings.

(2) Sub-paragraph (1) applies also to—

(a) any copy or other record of any such communication as is there mentioned, and

(b) any document or article enclosed with or referred to in any such communication if made in connection with the giving of any advice or, as the case may be, in connection with or in contemplation of and for the purposes of such proceedings as are there mentioned.

(3) This paragraph does not apply to anything in the possession of any person other than the professional

legal adviser or his client or to anything held with the intention of furthering a criminal purpose.

(4) In this paragraph references to the client of a professional legal adviser include references to any person representing such a client.

10 If the person in occupation of any premises in respect of which a warrant is issued under this Schedule objects to the inspection or seizure under the warrant of any material on the grounds that it consists partly of matters in respect of which those powers are not exercisable, he shall, if the person executing the warrant so requests, furnish that person with a copy of so much of the material in relation to which the powers are exercisable.

Return of warrants

11 A warrant issued under this Schedule shall be returned to the court from which it was issued—

(a) after being executed, or

(b) if not executed within the time authorised for its execution;

and the person by whom any such warrant is executed shall make an endorsement on it stating what powers have been exercised by him under the warrant.

Offences

12 Any person who—

(a) intentionally obstructs a person in the execution of a warrant issued under this Schedule, or

(b) fails without reasonable excuse to give any person executing such a warrant such assistance as he may reasonably require for the execution of the warrant,

is guilty of an offence.

Vessels, vehicles etc.

13 In this Schedule "premises" includes any vessel, vehicle, aircraft or hovercraft, and references to the occupier of any premises include references to the person in charge of any vessel, vehicle, aircraft or hovercraft.

Scotland and Northern Ireland

14 In the application of this Schedule to Scotland—

(a) for any reference to a circuit judge there is substituted a reference to the sheriff, and

(b) for any reference to information on oath there is substituted a reference to evidence on oath.

15 In the application of this Schedule to Northern Ireland—

(a) for any reference to a circuit judge there is substituted a reference to a county court judge, and

(b) for any reference to information on oath there is substituted a reference to a complaint on oath.

Section 61(1).

SCHEDULE 4 Appeal proceedings: amendments of Schedule 6 to Data Protection Act 1998

Constitution of Tribunal in national security cases

1 In paragraph 2(1) of Schedule 6 to the Data Protection Act 1998 (constitution of Tribunal in national security cases), at the end there is inserted " or under section 60(1) or (4) of the Freedom of Information Act 2000 ".

2 For paragraph 3 of that Schedule there is substituted—

"3 The Tribunal shall be duly constituted—

(a) for an appeal under section 28(4) or (6) in any case where the application of paragraph 6(1) is excluded by rules under paragraph 7, or

(b) for an appeal under section 60(1) or (4) of the Freedom of Information Act 2000,

if it consists of three of the persons designated under paragraph 2(1), of whom one shall be designated by the Lord Chancellor to preside."

Constitution of Tribunal in other cases

3(1) Paragraph 4 of that Schedule (constitution of Tribunal in other cases) is amended as follows.

(2) After sub-paragraph (1) there is inserted—

"(1A) Subject to any rules made under paragraph 7, the Tribunal shall be duly constituted for an appeal under section 57(1) or (2) of the Freedom of Information Act 2000 if it consists of—

(a) the chairman or a deputy chairman (who shall preside), and

(b) an equal number of the members appointed respectively in accordance with paragraphs (aa) and (bb) of section 6(6)."

(3) In sub-paragraph (2), after "(1)" there is inserted " or (1A) ".

Rules of procedure

4(1) Paragraph 7 of that Schedule (rules of procedure) is amended as follows.

(2) In sub-paragraph (1), for the words from "regulating" onwards there is substituted "regulating—

(a) the exercise of the rights of appeal conferred—

(i) by sections 28(4) and (6) and 48, and

(ii) by sections 57(1) and (2) and section 60(1) and (4) of the Freedom of Information Act 2000, and

(b) the practice and procedure of the Tribunal."

(3) In sub-paragraph (2), after paragraph (a) there is inserted—

"(aa) for the joinder of any other person as a party to any proceedings on an appeal under the Freedom of Information Act 2000,

(ab) for the hearing of an appeal under this Act with an appeal under the Freedom of Information Act 2000,".

Section 67

SCHEDULE 5 Amendments of public records legislation

Part I Amendments of Public Records Act 1958

Functions of Advisory Council on Public Records

1 In section 1 of the Public Records Act 1958 (general responsibility of the Lord Chancellor for public records), after subsection (2) there is inserted—

"(2A) The matters on which the Advisory Council on Public Records may advise the Lord Chancellor include matters relating to the application of the Freedom of Information Act 2000 to information contained in public records which are historical records within the meaning of Part VI of that Act."

Access to public records

2(1) Section 5 of that Act (access to public records) is amended in accordance with this paragraph.

(2) Subsections (1) and (2) are omitted.

(3) For subsection (3) there is substituted—

"(3) It shall be the duty of the Keeper of Public Records to arrange that reasonable facilities are available to the public for inspecting and obtaining copies of those public records in the Public Record Office which fall to be disclosed in accordance with the Freedom of Information Act 2000."

(4) Subsection (4) and, in subsection (5), the words from "and subject to" to the end are omitted.

3 Schedule 2 of that Act (enactments prohibiting disclosure of information obtained from the public) is omitted.

Power to extend meaning of "public records"

4 In Schedule 1 to that Act (definition of public records) after the Table at the end of paragraph 3 there is inserted—

"3A(1) Her Majesty may by Order in Council amend the Table at the end of paragraph 3 of this Schedule by adding to either Part of the Table an entry relating to any body or establishment—

(a) which, at the time when the Order is made, is specified in Schedule 2 to the Parliamentary Commissioner Act 1967 (departments, etc. subject to investigation), or

(b) in respect of which an entry could, at that time, be added to Schedule 2 to that Act by an Order in Council under section 4 of that Act (which confers power to amend that Schedule).

(2) An Order in Council under this paragraph may relate to a specified body or establishment or to bodies or establishments falling within a specified description.

(3) An Order in Council under this paragraph shall be subject to annulment in pursuance of a resolution of either House of Parliament."

Part II Amendment of Public Records Act (Northern Ireland) 1923

5 After section 5 of the Public Records Act (Northern Ireland) 1923 (deposit of documents in Record Office by trustees or other persons) there is inserted—

"5A Access to public records

It shall be the duty of the Deputy Keeper of the Records of Northern Ireland to arrange that reasonable facilities are available to the public for inspecting and obtaining copies of those public records in the Public Record Office of Northern Ireland which fall to be disclosed in accordance with

the Freedom of Information Act 2000."

Section 73

SCHEDULE 6 Further amendments of Data Protection Act 1998

Request by data controller for further information

1 In section 7 of the Data Protection Act 1998 (right of access to personal data), for subsection (3) there is substituted—

"(3) Where a data controller—

(a) reasonably requires further information in order to satisfy himself as to the identity of the person making a request under this section and to locate the information which that person seeks, and

(b) has informed him of that requirement,

the data controller is not obliged to comply with the request unless he is supplied with that further information."

Parliament

2 After section 35 of that Act there is inserted—

"35A Parliamentary privilege

Personal data are exempt from—

(a) the first data protection principle, except to the extent to which it requires compliance with the conditions in Schedules 2 and 3,

(b) the second, third, fourth and fifth data protection principles,

(c) section 7, and

(d) sections 10 and 14(1) to (3),

if the exemption is required for the purpose of avoiding an infringement of the privileges of either House of Parliament."

3 After section 63 of that Act there is inserted—

"63A Application to Parliament

(1) Subject to the following provisions of this section and to section 35A, this Act applies to the processing of personal data by or on behalf of either House of Parliament as it applies to the processing of personal data by other persons.

(2) Where the purposes for which and the manner in which any personal data are, or are to be, processed are determined by or on behalf of the House of Commons, the data controller in respect of those data for the purposes of this Act shall be the Corporate Officer of that House.

(3) Where the purposes for which and the manner in which any personal data are, or are to be, processed are determined by or on behalf of the House of Lords, the data controller in respect of those data for the purposes of this Act shall be the Corporate Officer of that House.

(4) Nothing in subsection (2) or (3) is to be taken to render the Corporate Officer of the House of Commons or the Corporate Officer of the House of Lords liable to prosecution under this Act, but section 55 and paragraph 12 of Schedule 9 shall apply to a person acting on behalf of either House as they apply to any other person."

4 In Schedule 2 to that Act (conditions relevant for the purposes of the first data protection principle: processing of any personal data) in paragraph 5 after paragraph (a) there is inserted—

"(aa) for the exercise of any functions of either House of Parliament,".

5 In Schedule 3 to that Act (conditions relevant for the purposes of the first data protection principle: processing of sensitive personal data) in paragraph 7 after paragraph (a) there is inserted—

"(aa) for the exercise of any functions of either House of Parliament,".

Honours

6 In Schedule 7 to that Act (miscellaneous exemptions) in paragraph 3(b) (honours) after "honour" there is inserted "or dignity".

Legal professional privilege

7 In paragraph 10 of that Schedule (legal professional privilege), for the words "or, in Scotland, to confidentiality as between client and professional legal adviser," there is substituted " or, in Scotland, to confidentiality of communications ".

Extension of transitional exemption

8 In Schedule 14 to that Act (transitional provisions), in paragraph 2(1) (which confers transitional

exemption from the prohibition on processing without registration on those registered under the Data Protection Act 1984) the words "or, if earlier, 24th October 2001" are omitted.

Section 76(2).

SCHEDULE 7 Disclosure of information by ombudsmen

The Parliamentary Commissioner for Administration

1 At the end of section 11 of the Parliamentary Commissioner Act 1967 (provision for secrecy of information) there is inserted—

"(5) Information obtained from the Information Commissioner by virtue of section 76(1) of the Freedom of Information Act 2000 shall be treated for the purposes of subsection (2) of this section as obtained for the purposes of an investigation under this Act and, in relation to such information, the reference in paragraph (a) of that subsection to the investigation shall have effect as a reference to any investigation."

2 After section 11A of that Act there is inserted—

"11AA Disclosure of information by Parliamentary Commissioner to Information Commissioner.

(1) The Commissioner may disclose to the Information Commissioner any information obtained by, or furnished to, the Commissioner under or for the purposes of this Act if the information appears to the Commissioner to relate to—

(a) a matter in respect of which the Information Commissioner could exercise any power conferred by—

(i) Part V of the Data Protection Act 1998 (enforcement),

(ii) section 48 of the Freedom of Information Act 2000 (practice recommendations), or

(iii) Part IV of that Act (enforcement), or

(b) the commission of an offence under—

(i) any provision of the Data Protection Act 1998 other than paragraph 12 of Schedule 9 (obstruction of execution of warrant), or

(ii) section 77 of the Freedom of Information Act 2000 (offence of altering etc. records with intent to prevent disclosure).

(2) Nothing in section 11(2) of this Act shall apply in relation to the disclosure of information in accordance with this section."

The Commissions for Local Administration in England and Wales

3 In section 32 of the Local Government Act 1974 (law of defamation, and disclosure of information) after subsection (6) there is inserted—

"(7) Information obtained from the Information Commissioner by virtue of section 76 of the Freedom of Information Act 2000 shall be treated for the purposes of subsection (2) above as obtained for the purposes of an investigation under this Part of this Act and, in relation to such information, the reference in paragraph (a) of that subsection to the investigation shall have effect as a reference to any investigation."

4 After section 33 of that Act there is inserted—

"33A Disclosure of information by Local Commissioner to Information Commissioner.

(1) a Local Commissioner may disclose to the Information Commissioner any information obtained by, or furnished to, the Local Commissioner under or for the purposes of this Part of this Act if the information appears to the Local Commissioner to relate to—

(a) a matter in respect of which the Information Commissioner could exercise any power conferred by—

(i) Part V of the Data Protection Act 1998 (enforcement),

(ii) section 48 of the Freedom of Information Act 2000 (practice recommendations), or

(iii) Part IV of that Act (enforcement), or

(b) the commission of an offence under—

(i) any provision of the Data Protection Act 1998 other than paragraph 12 of Schedule 9 (obstruction of execution of warrant), or

(ii) section 77 of the Freedom of Information Act 2000 (offence of altering etc. records with intent to prevent disclosure).

(2) Nothing in section 32(2) of this Act shall apply in relation to the disclosure of information in accordance with this section."

The Health Service Commissioners

5 At the end of section 15 of the Health Service Commissioners Act 1993 (confidentiality of information) there is inserted—

"(4) Information obtained from the Information Commissioner by virtue of section 76 of the Freedom of Information Act 2000 shall be treated for the purposes of subsection (1) as obtained for the purposes of an investigation and, in relation to such information, the reference in paragraph (a) of that subsection to the investigation shall have effect as a reference to any investigation."

6 After section 18 of that Act there is inserted—

"18A Disclosure of information to Information Commissioner.

(1) The Health Service Commissioner for England or the Health Service Commissioner for Wales may disclose to the Information Commissioner any information obtained by, or furnished to, the Health Service Commissioner under or for the purposes of this Act if the information appears to the Health Service Commissioner to relate to—

(a) a matter in respect of which the Information Commissioner could exercise any power conferred by—

(i) Part V of the Data Protection Act 1998 (enforcement),

(ii) section 48 of the Freedom of Information Act 2000 (practice recommendations), or

(iii) Part IV of that Act (enforcement), or

(b) the commission of an offence under—

(i) any provision of the Data Protection Act 1998 other than paragraph 12 of Schedule 9 (obstruction of execution of warrant), or

(ii) section 77 of the Freedom of Information Act 2000 (offence of altering etc. records with intent to prevent disclosure).

(3) Nothing in section 15 (confidentiality of information) applies in relation to the disclosure of information in accordance with this section."

The Welsh Administration Ombudsman

7. . . . .[470]

8. . . . .[471]

The Northern Ireland Commissioner for Complaints

9 At the end of Article 21 of the Commissioner for Complaints (Northern Ireland) Order 1996 (disclosure of information by Commissioner) there is inserted—

"(5) Information obtained from the Information Commissioner by virtue of section 76 of the Freedom of Information Act 2000 shall be treated for the purposes of paragraph (1) as obtained for the purposes of an investigation under this Order and, in relation to such information, the reference in paragraph (1)(a) to the investigation shall have effect as a reference to any investigation."

10 After that Article there is inserted—

"21A Disclosure of information to Information Commissioner

(1) The Commissioner may disclose to the Information Commissioner any information obtained by, or furnished to, the Commissioner under or for the purposes of this Order if the information appears to the Commissioner to relate to—

(a) a matter in respect of which the Information Commissioner could exercise any power conferred by—

(i) Part V of the Data Protection Act 1998 (enforcement),

(ii) section 48 of the Freedom of Information Act 2000 (practice recommendations), or

(iii) Part IV of that Act (enforcement), or

(b) the commission of an offence under—

(i) any provision of the Data Protection Act 1998 other than paragraph 12 of Schedule 9 (obstruction of execution of warrant), or

(ii) section 77 of the Freedom of Information Act 2000 (offence of altering etc. records with intent to prevent disclosure).

(2) Nothing in Article 21(1) applies in relation to the disclosure of information in accordance with this Article."

The Assembly Ombudsman for Northern Ireland

11 At the end of Article 19 of the Ombudsman (Northern Ireland) Order 1996 there is inserted—

"(5) Information obtained from the Information Commissioner by virtue of section 76 of the Freedom of Information Act 2000 shall be treated for the purposes of paragraph (1) as obtained for the purposes of an investigation under this Order and, in relation to such information, the reference in paragraph (1)(a) to the investigation shall have effect as a reference to any investigation."

12 After that Article there is inserted—

"19A Disclosure of information to Information Commissioner

(1) The Ombudsman may disclose to the Information Commissioner any information obtained by, or furnished to, the Ombudsman under or for the purposes of this Order if the information appears to the Ombudsman to relate to—

(a) a matter in respect of which the Information Commissioner could exercise any power conferred by—

(i) Part V of the Data Protection Act 1998 (enforcement),

(ii) section 48 of the Freedom of Information Act 2000 (practice recommendations), or

(iii) Part IV of that Act (enforcement), or

(b) the commission of an offence under—

(i) any provision of the Data Protection Act 1998 other than paragraph 12 of Schedule 9 (obstruction of execution of warrant), or

(ii) section 77 of the Freedom of Information Act 2000 (offence of altering etc. records with intent to prevent disclosure).

(2) Nothing in Article 19(1) applies in relation to the disclosure of information in accordance with this Article."

The Commissioner for Local Administration in Scotland

13 [In section 30 of the Local Government (Scotland) Act 1975 (limitation on disclosure of information), after subsection (5) there is inserted—

"(5A) Information obtained from the Information Commissioner by virtue of section 76 of the Freedom of Information Act 2000 shall be treated for the purposes of subsection (2) as obtained for the purposes of an investigation under this Part of this Act and, in relation to such information, the reference in subsection (2)(a) to the investigation shall have effect as a reference to any investigation."][472]

Section 86

SCHEDULE 8 Repeals

Part I Repeal coming into force on passing of Act

Chapter	Short title	Extent of repeal
1998 c. 29.	The Data Protection Act 1998.	In Schedule 14, in paragraph 2(1), the words "or, if earlier, 24th October 2001".

Part II Repeals coming into force in accordance with section 87(2)

Chapter	Short title	Extent of repeal
1958 c. 51.	The Public Records Act 1958.	In Schedule 1, in Part II of the Table in paragraph 3, the entry relating to the Data Protection Commissioner.
1967 c. 13.	The Parliamentary Commissioner Act 1967.	In Schedule 2, the entry relating to the Data Protection Commissioner.
1975 c. 24.	The House of Commons Disqualification Act 1975.	In Schedule 1, in Part III, the entry relating to the Data Protection Commissioner.
1975 c. 25.	The Northern Ireland Assembly Disqualification Act 1975.	In Schedule 1, in Part III, the entry relating to the Data Protection Commissioner.
1998 c. 29.	The Data Protection Act 1998.	In Schedule 5, Part III. In Schedule 15, paragraphs 1(1), 2, 4, 5(2) and 6(2)

Part III Repeals coming into force in accordance with section 87(3)

Chapter	Short title	Extent of repeal
1958 c. 51.	The Public Records Act 1958.	In section 5, subsections (1), (2) and (4) and, in subsection (5), the words from "and subject to" to the end.

		Schedule 2.
1975 c. 24.	The House of Commons Disqualification Act 1975.	In Schedule 1, in Part II, the entry relating to the Data Protection Tribunal.
1975 c. 25.	The Northern Ireland Assembly Disqualification Act 1975.	In Schedule 1, in Part II, the entry relating to the Data Protection Tribunal.
1998 c. 29.	The Data Protection Act 1998.	In section 1(1), in the definition of "data", the word "or" at the end of paragraph (c). In Schedule 15, paragraphs 1(2) and (3), 3, 5(1) and 6(1).

---

1 Words in s. 4 substituted (19.8.2003) by The Secretary of State for Constitutional Affairs Order 2003 (S.I. 2003/1887), art. 9, Sch. 2 para. 12(1)(a)

2 Words in s. 4(2)(b) substituted by The Government of Wales Act 2006 (Consequential Modifications and Transitional Provisions) Order 2007 (S.I. 2007/1388), art. 3, Sch. 1 para. 78(2) (the amendment coming into force immediately after the end of "the initial period" (which ended with the day of the first appointment of a First Minister on 25.5.2007) in accordance with art. 1(2)(3) of the amending S.I. and see ss. 46, 161(5) of Government of Wales Act 2006 (c. 32))

3 Words in s. 4(3)(a)(b) substituted by The Government of Wales Act 2006 (Consequential Modifications and Transitional Provisions) Order 2007 (S.I. 2007/1388), art. 3, Sch. 1 para. 78(3) (the amendment coming into force immediately after the end of "the initial period" (which ended with the day of the first appointment of a First Minister on 25.5.2007) in accordance with art. 1(2)(3) of the amending S.I. and see ss. 46, 161(5) of Government of Wales Act 2006 (c. 32))

4 Words in s. 4(3)(a)(b) substituted by The Government of Wales Act 2006 (Consequential Modifications and Transitional Provisions) Order 2007 (S.I. 2007/1388), art. 3, Sch. 1 para. 78(3) (the amendment coming into force immediately after the end of "the initial period" (which ended with the day of the first appointment of a First Minister on 25.5.2007) in accordance with art. 1(2)(3) of the amending S.I. and see ss. 46, 161(5) of Government of Wales Act 2006 (c. 32))

5 Words in s. 4 substituted (19.8.2003) by The Secretary of State for Constitutional Affairs Order 2003 (S.I. 2003/1887), art. 9, Sch. 2 para. 12(1)(a)

6 Words in s. 4 substituted (19.8.2003) by The Secretary of State for Constitutional Affairs Order 2003 (S.I. 2003/1887), art. 9, Sch. 2 para. 12(1)(a)

7 Words in s. 4(7)(a)(ii) substituted by The Government of Wales Act 2006 (Consequential Modifications and Transitional Provisions) Order 2007 (S.I. 2007/1388), art. 3, Sch. 1 para. 78(4) (the amendment coming into force immediately after the end of "the initial period" (which ended with the day of the first appointment of a First Minister on 25.5.2007) in accordance with art. 1(2)(3) of the amending S.I. and see ss. 46, 161(5) of Government of Wales Act 2006 (c. 32))

8 Words in s. 5 substituted (19.8.2003) by The Secretary of State for Constitutional Affairs Order 2003 (S.I. 2003/1887), art. 9, Sch. 2 para. 12(1)(a)

9 Words in s. 7 substituted (19.8.2003) by The Secretary of State for Constitutional Affairs Order 2003 (S.I. 2003/1887), art. 9, Sch. 2 para. 12(1)(a)

10 Words in s. 7 substituted (19.8.2003) by The Secretary of State for Constitutional Affairs Order 2003 (S.I. 2003/1887), art. 9, Sch. 2 para. 12(1)(a)

11 S. 7(4)(a)(aa) substituted for s. 7(4)(a) by The Government of Wales Act 2006 (Consequential Modifications and Transitional Provisions) Order 2007 (S.I. 2007/1388), art. 3, Sch. 1 para. 79 (the amendment coming into force immediately after the end of "the initial period" (which ended with the day of the first appointment of a First Minister on 25.5.2007) in accordance with art. 1(2)(3) of the amending S.I. and see ss. 46, 161(5) of Government of Wales Act 2006 (c. 32))

12 Words in s. 7 substituted (19.8.2003) by The Secretary of State for Constitutional Affairs Order 2003 (S.I. 2003/1887), art. 9, Sch. 2 para. 12(1)(a)

13 Words in s. 9 substituted (19.8.2003) by The Secretary of State for Constitutional Affairs Order 2003 (S.I. 2003/1887), art. 9, Sch. 2 para. 12(1)(a)

14 Words in s. 10 substituted (19.8.2003) by The Secretary of State for Constitutional Affairs Order 2003 (S.I. 2003/1887), art. 9, Sch. 2 para. 12(1)(a)

15 Words in s. 12 substituted (19.8.2003) by The Secretary of State for Constitutional Affairs Order 2003 (S.I. 2003/1887), art. 9, Sch. 2 para. 12(1)(a)

16 Words in s. 12 substituted (19.8.2003) by The Secretary of State for Constitutional Affairs Order 2003 (S.I. 2003/1887), art. 9, Sch. 2 para. 12(1)(a)

17 Words in s. 13 substituted (19.8.2003) by The Secretary of State for Constitutional Affairs Order 2003 (S.I. 2003/1887), art. 9, Sch. 2 para. 12(1)(a)

18 Word in s. 23(3)(k) repealed (1.4.2006) by Serious Organised Crime and Police Act 2005 (c. 15), ss. 59, 174, 178, Sch. 4 para. 159, Sch. 17; S.I. 2006/378, art. 4(1), Sch. para. 10 (subject to art. 4(2)-(7))

19 S. 28(2)(d) substituted by The Government of Wales Act 2006 (Consequential Modifications and Transitional Provisions) Order 2007 (S.I. 2007/1388), art. 3, Sch. 1 para. 80 (the amendment coming into force immediately after the end of "the initial period" (which ended with the day of the first appointment of a First Minister on 25.5.2007) in accordance with art. 1(2)(3) of the amending S.I. and see ss. 46, 161(5) of Government of Wales Act 2006 (c. 32))

[20] S. 30(5) substituted (28.3.2009 for certain purposes and 31.10.2009 otherwise) by Armed Forces Act 2006 (c. 52), ss. 378(1), 383(2), Sch. 16 para. 176; S.I. 2009/812, art. 3; S.I. 2009/1167, art. 4

[21] Words in s. 35(1) substituted by The Government of Wales Act 2006 (Consequential Modifications and Transitional Provisions) Order 2007 (S.I. 2007/1388), art. 3, Sch. 1 para. 81(2) (the amendment coming into force immediately after the end of "the initial period" (which ended with the day of the first appointment of a First Minister on 25.5.2007) in accordance with art. 1(2)(3) of the amending S.I. and see ss. 46, 161(5) of Government of Wales Act 2006 (c. 32))

[22] S. 35(5): words in definition of "government policy" substituted by The Government of Wales Act 2006 (Consequential Modifications and Transitional Provisions) Order 2007 (S.I. 2007/1388), art. 3, Sch. 1 para. 81(3)(a) (the amendment coming into force immediately after the end of "the initial period" (which ended with the day of the first appointment of a First Minister on 25.5.2007) in accordance with art. 1(2)(3) of the amending S.I. and see ss. 46, 161(5) of Government of Wales Act 2006 (c. 32))

[23] S. 35(5): words in definition of "the Law Officers" substituted by The Government of Wales Act 2006 (Consequential Modifications and Transitional Provisions) Order 2007 (S.I. 2007/1388), art. 3, Sch. 1 para. 81(3)(b) (the amendment coming into force immediately after the end of "the initial period" (which ended with the day of the first appointment of a First Minister on 25.5.2007) in accordance with art. 1(2)(3) of the amending S.I. and see ss. 46, 161(5) of Government of Wales Act 2006 (c. 32))

[24] S. 35(5): para. (c) in definition of "Ministerial communications" substituted by The Government of Wales Act 2006 (Consequential Modifications and Transitional Provisions) Order 2007 (S.I. 2007/1388), art. 3, Sch. 1 para. 81(c)(i) (the amendment coming into force immediately after the end of "the initial period" (which ended with the day of the first appointment of a First Minister on 25.5.2007) in accordance with art. 1(2)(3) of the amending S.I. and see ss. 46, 161(5) of Government of Wales Act 2006 (c. 32))

[25] S. 35(5): words in definition of "Ministerial communications" substituted by The Government of Wales Act 2006 (Consequential Modifications and Transitional Provisions) Order 2007 (S.I. 2007/1388), art. 3, Sch. 1 para. 81(c)(ii) (the amendment coming into force immediately after the end of "the initial period" (which ended with the day of the first appointment of a First Minister on 25.5.2007) in accordance with art. 1(2)(3) of the amending S.I. and see ss. 46, 161(5) of Government of Wales Act 2006 (c. 32))

[26] S. 35(5): words in definition of "Ministerial private office" substituted by The Government of Wales Act 2006 (Consequential Modifications and Transitional Provisions) Order 2007 (S.I. 2007/1388), art. 3, Sch. 1 para. 81(d) (the amendment coming into force immediately after the end of "the initial period" (which ended with the day of the first appointment of a First Minister on 25.5.2007) in accordance with art. 1(2)(3) of the amending S.I. and see ss. 46, 161(5) of Government of Wales Act 2006 (c. 32))

[27] Words in s. 36(1)(a) substituted by The Government of Wales Act 2006 (Consequential Modifications and Transitional Provisions) Order 2007 (S.I. 2007/1388), art. 3, Sch. 1 para. 82(2) (the amendment coming into force immediately after the end of "the initial period" (which ended with the day of the first appointment of a First Minister on 25.5.2007) in accordance with art. 1(2)(3) of the amending S.I. and see ss. 46, 161(5) of Government of Wales Act 2006 (c. 32))

[28] S.36(2)(a)(iii) substituted by The Government of Wales Act 2006 (Consequential Modifications and Transitional Provisions) Order 2007 (S.I. 2007/1388), art.3, Sch.1 para. 82(3) (the amendment coming into force immediately after the end of "the initial period" (which ended with the day of the first appointment of a First Minister on 25.5.2007) in accordance with art.1(2)(3) of the amending S.I. and see ss.46, 161(5) of Government of Wales Act 2006 (c.32))

[29] S.36(5)(g)-(gc) substituted for s. 36(g)(h) by The Government of Wales Act 2006 (Consequential Modifications and Transitional Provisions) Order 2007 (S.I. 2007/1388), art.3, Sch.1 para.82(4)(a) (the amendment coming into force immediately after the end of "the initial period" (which ended with the day of the first appointment of a First Minister on 25.5.2007) in accordance with art.1(2)(3) of the amending S.I. and see ss.46, 161(5) of Government of Wales Act 2006 (c.32))

[30] S.36(5)(ka) inserted by The Government of Wales Act 2006 (Consequential Modifications and Transitional Provisions) Order 2007 (S.I.2007/1388), art.3, Sch.1 para.82(4)(b)(the amendment coming into force immediately after the end of "the initial period" (which ended with the day of the first appointment of a First Minister on 25.5.2007) in accordance with art.1(2)(3) of the amending S.I. and see ss.46, 161(5) of Government of Wales Act 2006 (c.32))

[31] Words in s. 39(1)(a) substituted (1.1.2005) by The Environmental Information Regulations 2004 (S.I. 2004/3391), reg. 20(2) (with reg. 3)

[32] S.39(1A) inserted (1.1.2005) by The Environmental Information Regulations 2004 (S.I.2004/3391), reg.20(3) (with reg.3)

[33] Words in s.45 substituted (19.8.2003) by The Secretary of State for Constitutional Affairs Order 2003 (S.I.2003/1887), art.9, Sch.2 para.12(1)(a)

[34] Words in s. 45 substituted (19.8.2003) by The Secretary of State for Constitutional Affairs Order 2003 (S.I. 2003/1887), art. 9, Sch. 2 para. 12(1)(a)

[35] Words in s. 45 substituted (19.8.2003) by The Secretary of State for Constitutional Affairs Order 2003 (S.I. 2003/1887), art. 9, Sch. 2 para. 12(1)(a)

[36] S. 46(5)(a) inserted (19.8.2003) by The Secretary of State for Constitutional Affairs Order 2003 (S.I. 2003/1887), art. 9, Sch. 2 para. 12(2)

[37] Words in s. 47 substituted (19.8.2003) by The Secretary of State for Constitutional Affairs Order 2003 (S.I. 2003/1887), art. 9, Sch. 2 para. 12(1)(a)

[38] S. 53(1)(a)(ii) substituted by The Government of Wales Act 2006 (Consequential Modifications and Transitional Provisions) Order 2007 (S.I. 2007/1388), art. 3, Sch. 1 para. 83(2) (the amendment coming into force immediately after the end of "the initial period" (which ended with the day of the first appointment of a First Minister on 25.5.2007) in accordance with art. 1(2)(3) of the amending S.I. and see ss. 46, 161(5) of Government of Wales Act 2006 (c. 32))

[39] Words in s. 53 substituted (19.8.2003) by The Secretary of State for Constitutional Affairs Order 2003 (S.I. 2003/1887), art. 9, Sch. 2 para. 12(1)(a)

[40] S. 53(3)(c) substituted by The Government of Wales Act 2006 (Consequential Modifications and Transitional Provisions) Order 2007 (S.I. 2007/1388), art. 3, Sch. 1 para. 83(3) (the amendment coming into force immediately after the end of "the initial period" (which ended with the day of the first appointment of a First Minister on 25.5.2007) in accordance with art. 1(2)(3) of the amending S.I. and see ss. 46, 161(5) of Government of Wales Act 2006 (c. 32))

[41] Words in s. 53 substituted (19.8.2003) by The Secretary of State for Constitutional Affairs Order 2003 (S.I. 2003/1887), art. 9, Sch. 2 para. 12(1)(a)

[42] Words in s. 53(5)(a) substituted by The Government of Wales Act 2006 (Consequential Modifications and Transitional Provisions) Order 2007 (S.I. 2007/1388), art. 3, Sch. 1 para. 83(4)(a) (the amendment coming into force immediately after the end of "the initial period" (which ended with the day of the first appointment of a First Minister on 25.5.2007) in accordance with art. 1(2)(3) of the amending S.I. and see ss. 46, 161(5) of Government of Wales Act 2006 (c. 32))

[43] S. 53(5)(aa) inserted by The Government of Wales Act 2006 (Consequential Modifications and Transitional Provisions) Order 2007 (S.I. 2007/1388), art. 3, Sch. 1 para. 83(4)(b) (the amendment coming into force immediately after the end of "the initial period" (which ended with the day of the first appointment of a First Minister on 25.5.2007) in accordance with art. 1(2)(3) of the amending S.I. and see ss. 46, 161(5) of Government of Wales Act 2006 (c. 32))

[44] S. 53(8)(b) substituted by The Government of Wales Act 2006 (Consequential Modifications and Transitional Provisions) Order 2007 (S.I. 2007/1388), art. 3, Sch. 1 para. 83(5) (the amendment coming into force immediately after the end of "the initial period" (which ended with the day of the first appointment of a First Minister on 25.5.2007) in accordance with art. 1(2)(3) of the amending S.I. and see ss. 46, 161(5) of Government of Wales Act 2006 (c. 32))

[45] By The Secretary of State for Constitutional Affairs Order 2003 (S.I. 2003/1887), art. 9, Sch. 2 para. 12(1)(b), it is provided (19.8.2003) that in s. 69(2), in the inserted s. 9A of the Data Protection Act 1998, in each place for the words "Lord Chancellor" there be substituted the words "Secretary of State"

[46] Words in s. 75 substituted (19.8.2003) by The Secretary of State for Constitutional Affairs Order 2003 (S.I. 2003/1887) , art. 9, Sch. 2 para. 12(1)(c)

[47] Words in s. 75 substituted (19.8.2003) by The Secretary of State for Constitutional Affairs Order 2003 (S.I. 2003/1887) , art. 9, Sch. 2 para. 12(1)(c)

[48] Words in s. 75 substituted (19.8.2003) by The Secretary of State for Constitutional Affairs Order 2003 (S.I. 2003/1887) , art. 9, Sch. 2 para. 12(1)(c)

[49] S. 76(1): entry relating to Health Service Commisioner for Wales repealed (1.4.2006) by Public Services Ombudsman (Wales) Act 2005 (c. 10), ss. 39, 40, Sch. 6 para. 71(a), Sch. 7; S.I. 2005/2800, art. 5(1) (with art. 5(2), Sch. 2)

[50] S. 76(1): entry repealed (S.) (23.10.2002) by Scottish Public Services Ombudsman Act 2002 (asp 11), s. 25, Sch. 6 para. 23(2)(a); S.S.I. 2002/467, art. 2

[51] S. 76(1): entry inserted (S.) (23.10.2002) by Scottish Public Services Ombudsman Act 2002 (asp 11), s. 25, Sch. 6 para. 23(2)(b); S.S.I. 2002/467, art. 2

[52] S. 76(1): entry repealed (S.) (23.10.2002) by Scottish Public Services Ombudsman Act 2002 (asp 11), s. 25, Sch. 6 para. 23(2)(a); S.S.I. 2002/467, art. 2

[53] S. 76(1): entry repealed (S.) (23.10.2002) by Scottish Public Services Ombudsman Act 2002 (asp 11), s. 25, Sch. 6 para. 23(2)(a); S.S.I. 2002/467, art. 2

[54] S. 76(1): entry substituted (1.4.2006) by Public Services Ombudsman (Wales) Act 2005 (c. 10), ss. 39(1), 40, Sch. 6 para. 71(b); S.I. 2005/2800, art. 5(1) (with art. 5(2), Sch. 2)

[55] S. 76(1): entry relating to Social Housing Ombudsman for Wales repealed (1.4.2006) by Public Services Ombudsman (Wales) Act 2005 (c. 10), ss. 39, 40, Sch. 6 para. 71(a), Sch. 7; S.I. 2005/2800, art. 5(1) (with art. 5(2), Sch. 2)

[56] S. 76(1): entry inserted (14.10.2006 for W.) by Commissioner for Older People (Wales) Act 2006 (c. 30), ss. 1(2), 23, Sch. 1 para. 21(a); S.I. 2006/2699, art. 2

[57] S. 76A inserted (1.1.2005) by The Freedom of Information (Scotland) Act 2002 (Consequential Modifications) Order 2004 (S.I. 2004/3089), art. 3(2)

[58] S. 80(3) added (1.1.2005) by The Freedom of Information (Scotland) Act 2002 (Consequential Modifications) Order 2004 (S.I. 2004/3089), art. 3(3)

[59] Words in s. 81(3) inserted by The Government of Wales Act 2006 (Consequential Modifications and Transitional Provisions) Order 2007 (S.I. 2007/1388), art. 3, Sch. 1 para. 84(2) (the amendment coming into force immediately after the end of "the initial period" (which ended with the day of the first appointment of a First Minister on 25.5.2007) in accordance with art. 1(2)(3) of the amending S.I. and see ss. 46, 161(5) of Government of Wales Act 2006 (c. 32))

[60] Words in s. 81(4) inserted by The Government of Wales Act 2006 (Consequential Modifications and Transitional Provisions) Order 2007 (S.I. 2007/1388), art. 3, Sch. 1 para. 84(3) (the amendment coming into force immediately after the end of "the initial period" (which ended with the day of the first appointment of a First Minister on 25.5.2007) in accordance with art. 1(2)(3) of the amending S.I. and see ss. 46, 161(5) of Government of Wales Act 2006 (c. 32))

[61] Words in s. 82(1) repealed (19.8.2003) by The Secretary of State for Constitutional Affairs Order 2003 (S.I. 2003/1887), art. 9, Sch. 2 para. 12(3)

[62] S. 83(1)(b) substituted by The Government of Wales Act 2006 (Consequential Modifications and Transitional Provisions) Order 2007 (S.I.2007/1388), art. 3, Sch.1 para. 85(2) (the amendment coming into force immediately after the end of "the initial period" (which ended with the day of the first appointment of a First Minister on 25.5.2007) in accordance with art. 1(2)(3) of the amending S.I. and see ss. 46,161(5) of Government of Wales Act 2006 (c.32))

[63] Words in s. 83 substituted (19.8.2003) by The Secretary of State for Constitutional Affairs Order 2003 (S.I. 2003/1887), art. 9, Sch. 2 para. 12(1)(c)

[64] Words in s. 83 substituted (19.8.2003) by The Secretary of State for Constitutional Affairs Order 2003 (S.I. 2003/1887), art. 9, Sch. 2 para. 12(1)(c)

[65] Words in s. 83(3) substituted by The Government of Wales Act 2006 (Consequential Modifications and Transitional Provisions) Order 2007 (S.I. 2007/1388), art.3, Sch.1 para. 85(3) (the amendment coming into force immediately after the end of "the initial period" (which ended with the day of the first appointment of a First Minister on 25.5.2007) in accordance with art.1(2)(3) of the amending S.I. and see ss.46, 161(5) of Government of Wales Act 2006 (c.32))

[66] S. 84: definition of "executive committee" omitted by virtue of The Government of Wales Act 2006 (Consequential Modifications and Transitional Provisions) Order 2007 (S.I. 2007/1388), art. 3, Sch. 1 para. 86(2) (the amendment coming into force immediately after the end of "the initial period" (which ended with the day of the first appointment of a First Minister on 25.5.2007) in accordance with art. 1(2)(3) of the amending S.I. and see ss. 46, 161(5) of Government of Wales Act 2006 (c. 32))

[67] S. 84: in definition of "government department" para. (c) substituted by The Government of Wales Act 2006 (Consequential Modifications and Transitional Provisions) Order 2007 (S.I. 2007/1388), art. 3, Sch. 1 para. 86(3) (the amendment coming into force immediately after the end of "the initial period" (which ended with the day of the first appointment of a First Minister on 25.5.2007) in accordance with art. 1(2)(3) of the amending S.I. and see ss. 46, 161(5) of Government of Wales Act 2006 (c. 32))

[68] Words in s. 84 substituted (19.8.2003) by The Secretary of State for Constitutional Affairs Order 2003 (S.I. 2003/1887), art. 9, Sch. 2 para. 12(1)(c)

[69] Words in s. 85 substituted (19.8.2003) by The Secretary of State for Constitutional Affairs Order 2003 (S.I. 2003/1887), art. 9, Sch. 2 para. 12(1)(c)

[70] Words in s. 85 substituted (19.8.2003) by The Secretary of State for Constitutional Affairs Order 2003 (S.I. 2003/1887), art. 9, Sch. 2 para. 12(1)(c)

[71] Words in s. 87 substituted (19.8.2003) by The Secretary of State for Constitutional Affairs Order 2003 (S.I. 2003/1887), art. 9, Sch. 2 para. 12(1)(c)

[72] Words in s. 87 substituted (19.8.2003) by The Secretary of State for Constitutional Affairs Order 2003 (S.I. 2003/1887), art. 9, Sch. 2 para. 12(1)(c)

[73] Words in s. 87 substituted (19.8.2003) by The Secretary of State for Constitutional Affairs Order 2003 (S.I. 2003/1887), art. 9, Sch. 2 para. 12(1)(c)

[74] Words in Sch. 1 para. 1 inserted (1.4.2007) by Education and Inspections Act 2006 (c. 40), ss. 157, 188(3), Sch. 14 para. 69(2)(a); S.I. 2007/935, art. 5(w)(gg)

[75] Sch. 1 para. 1A inserted (1.4.2007) by Education and Inspections Act 2006 (c. 40), ss. 157, 188(3), Sch. 14 para. 69(2)(b); S.I. 2007/935, art. 5(w)(gg)

[76] Words in Sch. 1 para. 2 inserted (23.7.2008) by The Freedom of Information (Parliament and National Assembly for Wales) Order 2008 (S.I. 2008/1967), art. 2(2)

[77] Words in Sch. 1 para. 3 inserted (23.7.2008) by The Freedom of Information (Parliament and National Assembly for Wales) Order 2008 (S.I. 2008/1967), art. 2(3)

[78] Words in Sch. 1 para. 5 inserted (23.7.2008) by The Freedom of Information (Parliament and National Assembly for Wales) Order 2008 (S.I. 2008/1967), art. 2(4)

[79] Sch. 1 para. 5A inserted by The Government of Wales Act 2006 (Consequential Modifications and Transitional Provisions) Order 2007 (S.I. 2007/1388), art. 3, Sch. 1 para. 87 (the amendment coming into force immediately after the end of "the initial period" (which ended with the day of the first appointment of a First Minister on 25.5.2007) in accordance with art. 1(2)(3) of the amending S.I. and see ss. 46, 161(5) of Government of Wales Act 2006 (c. 32))

[80] Sch. 1 para. 14 substituted (E.W.) (1.10.2004 for E. and 10.11.2004 for W.) by Fire and Rescue Services Act 2004 (c. 21) , ss. 53(1), 61, Sch. 1 para. 95; S.I. 2004/2304, art. 2(2) (subject to art. 3); S.I. 2004/2917, art. 2

[81] Sch. 1 para. 15A inserted (1.4.2008) by Local Government and Public Involvement in Health Act 2007 (c. 28), ss. 209(2), 245, Sch. 13 para. 54; S.I. 2008/917, art. 2(1)(o)(p)

[82] Sch. 1 para. 17 repealed (24.11.2005) by Licensing Act 2003 (c. 17), ss. 199, 201(2), Sch. 7 (with ss. 2(3), 15(2), 195); S.I. 2005/3056, arts. 1(2), 2(2)

[83] Words in Sch. 1 para. 19 substituted (1.4.2005) by Civil Contingencies Act 2004 (c. 36), ss. 32(1), 34, Sch. 2 para. 10(3)(d); S.I. 2005/772, art. 2(b)

[84] Sch. 1 paras. 19A, 19B inserted (17.12.2009) by Local Democracy, Economic Development and Construction Act 2009 (c. 20), ss. 119, 149, Sch. 6 para. 94; S.I. 2009/3318, art. 2(b)

[85] Words in Sch. 1 para. 23 substituted (1.11.2007 with application as mentioned in art. 1(1) of the commencing S.I.) by

Local Government and Public Involvement in Health Act 2007 (c. 28), ss. 22, 245, Sch. 1 para. 20; S.I. 2007/3136, art. 2 (subject to art. 3)

[86] Sch. 1 para. 28 substituted (E.W.) (9.2.2009) by Local Transport Act 2008 (c. 26), ss. 77, 134, Sch. 4 para. 64(2); S.I. 2009/107, art. 2(1), Sch. 1 Pt. 1 (subject to transitional provisions in Sch. 1 Pt. II)

[87] Sch. 1 para. 34 repealed (1.4.2005) by Courts Act 2003 (c. 39), ss. 109(1)(3), 110(1), Sch. 8 para. 392, Sch. 10; S.I. 2005/910, art. 3

[88] 1966 c. 38.

[89] Sch. 1 Pt. 2 para. 35A added (19.4.2004) by The Freedom of Information (Additional Public Authorities) Order 2004 (S.I. 2004/938), art. 2, Sch. 1 (as amended (10.8.2004) by Freedom of Information (Additional Public Authorities) (Amendment) Order (S.I. 2004/1870), art. 2)

[90] Words in Sch. 1 para. 36A substituted (1.3.2007) by National Health Service (Consequential Provisions) Act 2006 (c. 43), ss. 2, 5, 8, Sch. 1 para. 211(a) (with Sch. 3 Pt. 1)

[91] Sch. 1 para. 36A inserted (1.10.2002) by The National Health Service Reform and Health Care Professions Act 2002 (Supplementary, Consequential etc. Provisions) Regulations 2002 (S.I. 2002/2469), reg. 4, Sch. 1 Pt. 1 para. 29

[92] Sch. 1 para. 37 repealed (1.3.2007) by National Health Service (Consequential Provisions) Act 2006 (c. 43), ss. 2, 4-6, 8, Sch. 1 para. 211(b), Sch. 4 (with Sch.2 Pt. 1, Sch. 3 Pt. 1)

[93] Words in Sch. 1 para. 38 substituted (1.3.2007) by National Health Service (Consequential Provisions) Act 2006 (c. 43), ss. 2, 5, 8, Sch. 1 para. 211(c) (with Sch. 3 Pt. 1)

[94] Words in Sch. 1 para. 39 substituted (1.3.2007) by National Health Service (Consequential Provisions) Act 2006 (c. 43), ss. 2, 5, 8, Sch. 1 para. 211(d) (with Sch. 3 Pt. 1)

[95] Words in Sch. 1 para. 39A substituted (1.3.2007) by National Health Service (Consequential Provisions) Act 2006 (c. 43), ss. 2, 5, 8, Sch. 1 para. 211(e) (with Sch. 3 Pt. 1)

[96] Sch. 1 para. 39A inserted (10.10.2002 for W. and 1.3.2007 for E.) by National Health Service Reform and Health Care Professions Act 2002 (c. 17), s. 6(2), Sch. 5 para. 48; S.I. 2002/2532, art. 2; S.I. 2006/1407, art. 2, Sch. 1 Pt. 2 para. 12

[97] Words in Sch. 1 para. 40 substituted (1.3.2007) by National Health Service (Consequential Provisions) Act 2006 (c. 43), ss. 2, 5, 8, Sch. 1 para. 211(f) (with Sch. 3 Pt. 1)

[98] Sch. 1 para. 40A inserted (1.4.2004 for E.W.) by Health and Social Care (Community Health and Standards) Act 2003 (c. 43), ss. 34, 199, Sch. 4 para. 114, S.I. 2004/759, {art. 2}

[99] Words in Sch. 1 para. 41 substituted (1.3.2007) by National Health Service (Consequential Provisions) Act 2006 (c. 43), ss. 2, 5, 8, Sch. 1 para. 211(g) (with Sch. 3 Pt. 1)

[100] Sch. 1 para. 41A repealed (1.4.2008) by Local Government and Public Involvement in Health Act 2007 (c. 28), ss. 241, 245, Sch. 18 Pt. 18; S.I. 2008/461, art. 2(3), Sch.

[101] Sch. 1 para. 41A inserted (1.9.2003) by National Health Service Reform and Health Care Professions Act 2002 (c. 17), ss. 19(7), 42(3); S.I. 2003/2246, art. 2

[102] Sch. 1 para. 42 repealed (1.4.2006) by Health and Social Care (Community Health and Standards) Act 2003 (c. 43), ss. 196, 199, Sch. 14 Pt. 4, S.I. 2005/2925, arts. 1(3)(4)(c), {11}

[103] Sch. 1 para. 43 repealed (1.4.2005 for E.W.) by Health and Social Care (Community Health and Standards) Act 2003 (c. 43), ss. 190, 196, 199, Sch. 13 para. 10, Sch. 14 Pt. 7; S.I. 2005/457, art. 2(a)(b)

[104] Words in Sch. 1 para. 43A substituted (1.8.2008) by Health Act 2006 (c. 28), ss. 80(1), 83, Sch. 8 para. 45(2)(a); S.I. 2008/1972, art. 2(b)

[105] Words in Sch. 1 para. 43A(a) substituted (1.3.2007) by National Health Service (Consequential Provisions) Act 2006 (c. 43), ss. 2, 5, 8, Sch. 1 para. 211(i) (with Sch. 3 Pt. 1)

[106] Words in Sch. 1 para. 43A(b) substituted (1.3.2007) by National Health Service (Consequential Provisions) Act 2006 (c. 43), ss. 2, 5, 8, Sch. 1 para. 211(j) (with Sch. 3 Pt. 1)

[107] Sch. 1 para. 43A inserted (17.1.2005 for E., 1.4.2006 for W. for certain purposes and 1.3.2007 otherwise) by Health and Social Care (Community Health and Standards) Act 2003 (c. 43), ss. 184, 199, Sch. 11 para. 68; S.I. 2005/38, art. 2(c) (with art. 3); S.I. 2006/345, art. 6; S.I. 2006/1407, arts. 1(1), 2, Sch. 1 Pt. 2 para. 13(b)

[108] Words in Sch. 1 para. 44 repealed (17.1.2005 for E., 1.4.2006 for W. for certain purposes and otherwise prosp.) by Health and Social Care (Community Health and Standards) Act 2003 (c. 43), ss. 196, 199, Sch. 14 Pt. 4; S.I. 2005/38, art. 2(d)(i) (with art. 3); S.I. 2005/2925, arts. 1(3), 11; S.I. 2006/345, art. 7

[109] Words in Sch. 1 para. 44 substituted (1.3.2007) by National Health Service (Consequential Provisions) Act 2006 (c. 43), ss. 2, 5, 8, Sch. 1 para. 211(k) (with Sch. 3 Pt. 1)

[110] Sch. 1 para. 45 repealed (17.1.2005 for E. for certain purposes, 1.4.2006 for E. otherwise, 1.4.2006 for W. for certain purposes and otherwise prosp.) by Health and Social Care (Community Health and Standards) Act 2003 (c. 43), ss. 196, 199, Sch. 14 Pt. 4; SI 2005/38, {art. 2(d)(ii)}; S.I. 2005/2925, arts. 1(3), 11; SI 2006/345, {art. 7}

[111] Words in Sch. 1 para. 45A(a) substituted (1.3.2007) by National Health Service (Consequential Provisions) Act 2006 (c. 43), ss. 2, 5, 8, Sch. 1 para. 211(l) (with Sch. 3 Pt. 1)

[112] Words in Sch. 1 para. 45A(b) substituted (1.3.2007) by virtue of National Health Service (Consequential Provisions) Act 2006 (c. 43), ss. 2, 5, 8, Sch. 1 para. 211(m) (with Sch. 3 Pt. 1)

[113] Sch. 1 para. 45A inserted (1.7.2002 for W. and 1.1.2003 for E.) by 2001 c. 15, ss. 67, 70, Sch. 5 Pt. 1 para. 14 (with ss. 64(9), 65(4)); S.I. 2002/1475, art. 2(1), Sch. Pt. 1; S.I. 2003/53, art. 2(a)

[114] Sch. 1 para. 45B repealed (30.6.2008) by Local Government and Public Involvement in Health Act 2007 (c. 28), ss. 241, 245, Sch. 18 Pt. 18; S.I. 2008/461, art. 2(4)(b)(c)

[115] Sch. 1 para. 45B inserted (1.1.2003 for E. and otherwise prosp.) by National Health Service Reform and Health Care Professions Act 2002 (c. 17), s. 20(11), Sch. 6 para. 19; S. I. 2002/3190, art. 2

[116] Sch. 1 para. 46 repealed (N.I.) (1.4.2009) by Health and Social Care (Reform) Act (Northern Ireland) 2009 (c. 1), ss. 32, 33, 34, Sch. 6 para. 17(2)(a), Sch. 7; S.R. 2009/114, art. 2

[117] Sch. 1 para. 50 repealed (N.I.) (1.4.2009) by Health and Social Care (Reform) Act (Northern Ireland) 2009 (c. 1), ss. 32, 33, 34, Sch. 6 para. 17(2)(a), Sch. 7; S.R. 2009/114, art. 2

[118] Words in Sch. 1 para. 51 substituted (N.I.) (1.4.2004) by The Primary Medical Services (Northern Ireland) Order 2004 (S.I. 2004/311 (N.I. 2)), art. 10, Sch. 1 para. 18; S.R. 2004/123, art. 2(2)

[119] Sch. 1 paras. 51A-51D inserted (N.I.) (1.4.2009) by Health and Social Care (Reform) Act (Northern Ireland) 2009 (c. 1), ss. 32, 34, Sch. 6 para. 17(2)(b); S.R. 2009/114, art. 2

[120] Sch. 1 para. 52 substituted (1.9.2003 except in relation to W. and otherwise 31.10.2005) by Education Act 2002 (c. 32), ss. 215(1), 216, Sch. 21 para. 127 (with ss. 210(8), 214(4)); S.I. 2003/1667, art. 4; S.I. 2005/2910, art. 4, Sch.

[121] Words in Sch.1 para.55(1)(b) repealed (N.I.) (1.10.2005 or such later date as the Department may by order appoint) by The Colleges of Education (Northern Ireland) Order 2005 (S.I. 2005/1963 (N.I. 13)), arts.1(3), 2(2), 14, Sch.3 para. 4, Sch. 4

[122] Words in entry in Sch. 1 Pt. V para. 60 substituted (4.11.2001) by virtue of 2000 c. 32, s. 74, Sch. 6 para. 25(2)(a); S.R. 2001/396, art. 2, Sch.

[123] Words in entry in Sch. 1 Pt. V para. 61 substituted (4.11.2001) by 2000 c. 32, s. 74, Sch. 6 para. 25(2)(b); S.R. 2001/396, art. 2, Sch.

[124] Sch. 1 paras. 63A, 63B inserted (E.W.S.) (1.3.2005) by Energy Act 2004 (c. 20), ss. 51(2), 198(2), Sch. 10 para. 18; S.I. 2005/442, art. 2(1), Sch. 1

[125] Sch. 1 Pt. VI: entry added (11.11.2002) by The Freedom of Information (Additional Public Authorities) Order 2002 (S.I. 2002/2623), art. 2, Sch. 1

[126] Sch. 1 Pt. VI: entry added (11.11.2002) by The Freedom of Information (Additional Public Authorities) Order 2002 (S.I. 2002/2623), art. 2, Sch. 1

Sch. 1 Pt. VI: entry repealed (1.4.2007) by Education and Inspections Act 2006 (c. 40), ss. 157, 184, 188(3), Sch. 14 para. 69(3), Sch. 18 Pt. 5; S.I. 2007/935, art. 5(w)(z)(gg)(ii)

[127] Sch. 1 Pt. VI: entry inserted (11.8.2003) by The Freedom of Information (Additional Public Authorities) Order 2003 (S.I. 2003/1882), art. 2, Sch. 1

[128] Sch. 1 Pt. VI: entry inserted (1.11.2007) by Tribunals, Courts and Enforcement Act 2007 (c. 15), ss. 48(1), 148(5), Sch. 8 para. 53; S.I. 2007/2709, art. 3(b)(ii)

[129] Sch. 1 Pt. VI: entry removed (11.8.2003) by virtue of The Freedom of Information (Removal of References to Public Authorities) Order 2003 (S.I. 2003/1883), art. 2, Sch.

[130] Sch. 1 Pt. VI: entries removed (29.6.2004) by virtue of The Freedom of Information (Removal of References to Public Authorities) Order 2004 (S.I. 2004/1641), art. 2, Sch. 1

[131] Sch. 1 Pt. VI: entry removed (11.8.2003) by virtue of The Freedom of Information (Removal of References to Public Authorities) Order 2003 (S.I. 2003/1883), art. 2, Sch.

[132] Sch. 1 Pt. 6: entry omitted (1.4.2009) by virtue of The Transfer of Tribunal Functions and Revenue and Customs Appeals Order 2009 (S.I. 2009/56), art. 3, Sch. 1 para. 296(a)

[133] Sch. 1 Pt. VI: entry removed (11.8.2003) by virtue of The Freedom of Information (Removal of References to Public Authorities) Order 2003 (S.I. 2003/1883), art. 2, Sch.

[134] Sch. 1 Pt. VI: entry added (19.4.2004) by The Freedom of Information (Additional Public Authorities) Order 2004 (S.I. 2004/938), art. 3, Sch. 2

[135] Sch. 1 Pt. VI: entry added (19.4.2004) by The Freedom of Information (Additional Public Authorities) Order 2004 (S.I. 2004/938), art. 3, Sch. 2

[136] Sch. 1 Pt. VI: entry inserted (11.8.2003) by The Freedom of Information (Additional Public Authorities) Order 2003 (S.I. 2003/1882), art. 2, Sch. 1

[137] Sch. 1 Pt. VI: entry inserted (11.8.2003) by The Freedom of Information (Additional Public Authorities) Order 2003 (S.I. 2003/1882), art. 2, Sch. 1

[138] Sch. 1 Pt. VI: entry inserted (11.8.2003) by The Freedom of Information (Additional Public Authorities) Order 2003 (S.I. 2003/1882), art. 2, Sch. 1

[139] Sch. 1 Pt. VI: entry inserted (11.8.2003) by The Freedom of Information (Additional Public Authorities) Order 2003 (S.I. 2003/1882), art. 2, Sch. 1

[140] Sch. 1 Pt. VI: entry inserted (11.8.2003) by The Freedom of Information (Additional Public Authorities) Order 2003 (S.I. 2003/1882), art. 2, Sch. 1

[141] Sch. 1 Pt. VI: entry inserted (7.2.2006) by The Freedom of Information (Additional Public Authorities) Order 2005 (S.I. 2005/3593), art. 2, Sch. 1

[142] Sch. 1 Pt. VI: entry inserted (29.2.2008) by The Agriculture and Horticulture Development Board Order 2008 (S.I. 2008/576), art. 18, Sch. 5 para. 5

[143] Sch. 1 Pt. VI: entry inserted (11.8.2003) by The Freedom of Information (Additional Public Authorities) Order 2003 (S.I. 2003/1882), art. 2, Sch. 1

[144] Sch. 1 Pt. VI: entry added (11.11.2002) by The Freedom of Information (Additional Public Authorities) Order 2002 (S.I. 2002/2623), art. 2, Sch. 1

[145] Sch. 1 Pt. VI: entry repealed (1.4.2006) by The Ancient Monuments Board for Wales (Abolition) Order 2006 (S.I. 2006/64), art. 3(1)(b)(iii)

[146] Sch. 1 Pt. VI: entry removed (11.8.2003) by virtue of The Freedom of Information (Removal of References to Public Authorities) Order 2003 (S.I. 2003/1883), art. 2, Sch.

[147] Sch. 1 Pt. VI: entry inserted (1.10.2006) by Health Act 2006 (c. 28), ss. 80(1), 83, Sch. 8 para. 45(3); S.I. 2006/2603, art. 4(5)(c)(ii)

[148] Sch. 1 Pt. VI: entry added (19.4.2004) by The Freedom of Information (Additional Public Authorities) Order 2004 (S.I. 2004/938), art. 3, Sch. 2

[149] Sch. 1 Pt. VI: entry inserted (16.12.2004) by Higher Education Act 2004 (c. 8), ss. 49, 52(2), Sch. 6 para. 10; S.I. 2004/3255, art. 2

[150] Sch. 1 Pt. VI: entry repealed (31.3.2009) by Legal Services Act 2007 (c. 29), ss. 210, 211(2), Sch. 23 (with ss. 29, 192, 193); S.I. 2009/503, art. 2(f)(vii)

[151] Sch. 1 Pt. VI: entry inserted (2.6.2008) by The Freedom of Information (Additional Public Authorities) Order 2008 (S.I. 2008/1271), art. 2, Sch.

[152] Sch. 1 Pt. VI: entry inserted (6.4.2005) by Pensions Act 2004 (c. 35), ss. 319(1), 322, Sch. 12 para. 79; S.I. 2005/275, art. 2(7), Sch. Pt. 7 (subject to art. 2(12))

[153] Sch. 1 Pt. VI: entry repealed (1.11.2007) by Offender Management Act 2007 (c. 21), ss. 39, 41(1), Sch. 5 Pt. 2; S.I. 2007/3001, art. 2(1)(p)(t)(v)

[154] Sch. 1 Pt. VI: entries repealed (1.4.2008) by The Agriculture and Horticulture Development Board Order 2008 (S.I. 2008/576), art. 18, Sch. 5 para. 7 (with Sch. 4 para. 10)

[155] Sch. 1 Pt. VI entry repealed (prosp.) by 2000 c. 38. ss. 274, 275(1), Sch. 31 Pt. IV

[156] Sch. 1 Pt. VI: entry inserted (7.2.2006) by The Freedom of Information (Additional Public Authorities) Order 2005 (S.I. 2005/3593), art. 2, Sch. 1

[157] Sch. 1 Pt. VI: entry removed (7.2.2006) by virtue of The Freedom of Information (Removal of References to Public Authorities) Order 2005 (S.I. 2005/3594), art. 2, Sch. 1

[158] Sch. 1 Pt. VI: entry inserted (11.8.2003) by The Freedom of Information (Additional Public Authorities) Order 2003 (S.I. 2003/1882), art. 2, Sch. 1

[159] Sch. 1 Pt. VI: entry added (11.11.2002) by The Freedom of Information (Additional Public Authorities) Order 2002 (S.I. 2002/2623), art. 2, Sch. 1

[160] Sch. 1 Pt. VI: entry inserted (1.10.2008) by Health and Social Care Act 2008 (c. 14), ss. 95, 170, Sch. 5 para. 73(b); S.I. 2008/2497, art. 2(q)(viii)

[161] Sch. 1 Pt. VI: entry repealed (1.4.2002) by The Abolition of the Central Council for Education and Training in Social Work Order 2002 (S.I. 2002/797), art. 2(c)

[162] Sch. 1 Pt. VI: entry repealed (1.4.2007) by Police and Justice Act 2006 (c. 48), ss. 52, 53, Sch. 15 Pt. 1(A); S.I. 2007/709, art. 3(o)(q) (subject to arts. 6, 7)

[163] Entry in Sch. 1 Pt. VI inserted (1.4.2002) by 2001 c. 16, s. 102, Sch. 4 para. 8; S. I. 2002/533, art. 2

[164] Sch. 1 Pt. VI: entry added (11.11.2002) by The Freedom of Information (Additional Public Authorities) Order 2002 (S.I. 2002/2623), art. 2, Sch. 1

[165] Sch. 1 Pt. VI: entry added (19.4.2004) by The Freedom of Information (Additional Public Authorities) Order 2004 (S.I. 2004/938), art. 3, Sch. 2

[166] Words in Sch. 1 Pt. VI inserted (10.6.2008 for specified purposes and 24.7.2008 otherwise) by Child Maintenance and Oth er Payments Act 2008 (c. 6), ss. 1, 62, Sch. 1 para. 29; S.I. 2008/1476, art. 2(1); S.I. 2008/2033, art. 2(1)

[167] Sch. 1 Pt. VI: entry inserted (1.6.2006) by The Freedom of Information (Additional Public Authorities) Order 2005 (S.I. 2005/3593), art. 3, Sch. 2

[168] Sch. 1 Pt. VI: entry added (11.11.2002) by The Freedom of Information (Additional Public Authorities) Order 2002 (S.I. 2002/2623), art. 2, Sch. 1

[169] Sch. 1 Pt. VI: entry inserted (18.4.2006) by Equality Act 2006 (c. 3), ss. 2, 93, Sch. 1 para. 48 (with s. 92); S.I. 2006/1082, art. 2(a)(l)

[170] Sch. 1 Pt. VI: entry repealed (1.4.2004 for E.W.) by Health and Social Care (Community Health and Standards) Act 2003 (c. 43), ss. 196, 199, Sch. 14 Pt. 2; S.I. 2004/759, art. 13

[171] Sch. 1 Pt. VI: entry repealed (1.4.2009) by Health and Social Care Act 2008 (c. 14), ss. 95, 166, 170, Sch. 5 para. 73(a), Sch. 15 Pt. 1; S.I. 2009/462, art. 2, Sch. 1 para. 36

[172] Sch. 1 Pt. VI: entry inserted (8.1.2004) by Health and Social Care (Community Health and Standards) Act 2003 (c. 43), ss. 147, 199, Sch. 9 para. 31; S.I. 2003/3346, art. 5(b)

[173] Sch. 1 Pt. VI: entry inserted (7.2.2006) by The Freedom of Information (Additional Public Authorities) Order 2005 (S.I. 2005/3593), art. 2, Sch. 1

[174] Sch. 1 Pt. VI: entry repealed (1.4.2006) by Public Services Ombudsman (Wales) Act 2005 (c. 10), ss. 39, 40, Sch. 6 para.

71(a), Sch. 7; S.I. 2005/2800, art. 5(1) (with art. 5(2), Sch. 2)

[175] Sch. 1 Pt. 6: entry repealed (1.4.2009) by Housing and Regeneration Act 2008 (c. 17), ss. 56, 321(1), 325, Sch. 8 para. 77(3), Sch. 16; S.I. 2009/803, arts. 1(2), 3(2)(3), 10

[176] Sch. 1 Pt. VI: entry repealed (1.10.2007) by Equality Act 2006 (c. 3), ss. 40, 91, 93(1), Sch. 3 para. 60, Sch. 4 (with s. 92); S.I. 2007/2603, art. 2(a)(d) (subject to art. 3)

[177] Sch. 1 Pt. VI: entry inserted (2.5.2006 for E.W. and 1.10.2006 otherwise) by Natural Environment and Rural Communities Act 2006 c. 16), ss. 105(1), 107, {Sch. 11 para. 153(2)}; S.I. 2006/1176, art. 4; S.I. 2006/2541, art. 2

[178] Sch. 1 Pt. VI: entry inserted (1.1.2004 for E.) by Health and Social Care (Community Health and Standards) Act 2003 (c. 43), ss.147, 199, Sch. 9 para. 31; S.I. 2003/3346, art. 3(b)

[179] Sch. 1 Pt. VI: entry removed (7.2.2006) by virtue of The Freedom of Information (Removal of References to Public Authorities) Order 2005 (S.I. 2005/3594), art. 2, Sch. 1

[180] Sch. 1 Pt. VI: entry inserted (14.10.2006) by Commissioner for Older People (Wales) Act 2006 (c. 30), ss. 1(2), 23, Sch. 1 para. 21(b); S.I. 2006/2699, art. 2

[181] Sch. 1 Pt. VI: entry inserted (prosp.) by Parliamentary Standards Act 2009 (c. 13), ss. 3, 14(2)(3), Sch. 2 para. 10 (with ss. 1, 2(1))

[182] Sch. 1 Pt. VI: entry added (11.11.2002) by The Freedom of Information (Additional Public Authorities) Order 2002 (S.I. 2002/2623), art. 2, Sch. 1

[183] Sch. 1 Pt. VI: entry repealed (1.10.2006) by Natural Environment and Rural Communities Act 2006 c. 16), ss. 105, 107, Sch. 11 para. 153(3), {Sch. 12}; S.I. 2006/2541, art. 2

[184] Sch. 1 Pt. VI: entry inserted (26.11.2008) by Climate Change Act 2008 (c. 27), ss. 32, 100, Sch. 1 para. 33

[185] Sch. 1 Pt. VI: entry added (19.4.2004) by The Freedom of Information (Additional Public Authorities) Order 2004 (S.I. 2004/938), art. 3, Sch. 2

[186] Sch. 1 Pt. VI: entry inserted (11.8.2003) by The Freedom of Information (Additional Public Authorities) Order 2003 (S.I. 2003/1882), art. 2, Sch. 1

[187] Sch. 1 Pt. VI: entry inserted (11.8.2003) by The Freedom of Information (Additional Public Authorities) Order 2003 (S.I. 2003/1882), art. 2, Sch. 1

[188] Sch. 1 Pt. VI: entry inserted (11.8.2003) by The Freedom of Information (Additional Public Authorities) Order 2003 (S.I. 2003/1882), art. 2, Sch. 1

[189] Sch. 1 Pt. VI: entry inserted (1.6.2006) by The Freedom of Information (Additional Public Authorities) Order 2005 (S.I. 2005/3593), art. 3, Sch. 2

[190] Sch. 1 Pt. VI: entry added (11.11.2002) by The Freedom of Information (Additional Public Authorities) Order 2002 (S.I. 2002/2623), art. 2, Sch. 1

[191] Sch. 1 Pt. VI: entry inserted (2.6.2008) by The Freedom of Information (Additional Public Authorities) Order 2008 (S.I. 2008/1271), art. 2, Sch.

[192] Sch. 1 Pt. VI: entry removed (11.8.2003) by virtue of The Freedom of Information (Removal of References to Public Authorities) Order 2003 (S.I. 2003/1883), art. 2, Sch.

[193] Sch. 1 Pt. VI: entry inserted (29.12.2003) by Communications Act 2003 (c. 21), ss. 406(1)(7), 411(2), Sch. 17 para. 164 (with Sch. 18); S.I. 2003/3142, art. 3(1), Sch. 1 (subject to art. 3(3) and with art. 11)

[194] Sch. 1 Pt. VI: entry repealed (1.10.2006) by Natural Environment and Rural Communities Act 2006 c. 16), ss. 105, 107, Sch. 11 para. 153(3), {Sch. 12}; S.I. 2006/2541, art. 2

[195] Sch. 1 Pt. VI: entry omitted by virtue of The Health Professions Order 2001 (S.I. 2002/254), art. 48(3), Sch. 4 para. 9 (with art. 3(19)) (the amendment coming into force in accordance with art. 1(2)(3) of the amending S.I.)

[196]Words in Sch. 1 Pt. 6 substituted (1.1.2009) by Health and Social Care Act 2008 (c. 14), ss. 127, 170, Sch. 10 para. 13(a); S.I. 2008/3244, art. 2(i)(x)

[197]Sch. 1 Pt. VI: entry inserted (1.12.2002) by National Health Service Reform and Health Care Professions Act 2002 (c. 17), s. 25(4), Sch. 7 para. 24; S.I. 2002/2202, art. 2(2)(b)

[198] Sch. 1 Pt. VI: entry repealed (1.11.2007) by Tribunals, Courts and Enforcement Act 2007 (c. 15), ss. 146, 148, Sch. 23 Pt. 1; S.I. 2007/2709, art. 3(d)(vii)

[199] Sch. 1 Pt. VI: entry repealed (1.10.2006) by Natural Environment and Rural Communities Act 2006 c. 16), ss. 105, 107, Sch. 11 para. 153(3), {Sch. 12}; S.I. 2006/2541, art. 2

[200] Sch. 1 Pt. VI: entry inserted (7.2.2006) by The Freedom of Information (Additional Public Authorities) Order 2005 (S.I. 2005/3593), art. 2, Sch. 1

[201]Sch. 1 Pt. VI: entry omitted (3.11.2008) by virtue of The Transfer of Tribunal Functions Order 2008 (S.I. 2008/2833), art. 9(1), Sch. 3 para. 188

[202]Sch. 1 Pt. VI: entry added (11.11.2002) by The Freedom of Information (Additional Public Authorities) Order 2002 (S.I. 2002/2623), art. 2, Sch. 1

[203]Sch. 1 Pt. VI: entry added (11.11.2002) by The Freedom of Information (Additional Public Authorities) Order 2002 (S.I. 2002/2623), art. 2, Sch. 1

[204] Sch. 1 Pt. VI: entry inserted (7.2.2006) by The Freedom of Information (Additional Public Authorities) Order 2005 (S.I. 2005/3593), art. 2, Sch. 1

[205] Sch. 1 Pt. VI: entry removed (11.8.2003) by virtue of The Freedom of Information (Removal of References to Public

Authorities) Order 2003 (S.I. 2003/1883), art. 2, Sch.

206 Sch. 1 Pt. VI: entry inserted (1.7.2004) by Higher Education Act 2004 (c. 8), ss. 49, 52(1), Sch. 6 para. 10

207 Sch. 1 Pt. VI: entry inserted (11.8.2003) by The Freedom of Information (Additional Public Authorities) Order 2003 (S.I. 2003/1882), art. 2, Sch. 1

208 Sch. 1 Pt. VI: entry repealed (1.10.2007) by Equality Act 2006 (c. 3), ss. 40, 91, 93(1), Sch. 3 para. 60, Sch. 4 (with s. 92); S.I. 2007/2603, art. 2(a)(d) (subject to art. 3)

209 Sch. 1 Pt. VI: entry added (19.4.2004) by The Freedom of Information (Additional Public Authorities) Order 2004 (S.I. 2004/938), art. 3, Sch. 2

210 Sch. 1 Pt. VI: entry added (19.4.2004) by The Freedom of Information (Additional Public Authorities) Order 2004 (S.I. 2004/938), art. 3, Sch. 2

211 Sch. 1 Pt. VI: entry removed (11.8.2003) by virtue of The Freedom of Information (Removal of References to Public Authorities) Order 2003 (S.I. 2003/1883), art. 2, Sch.

212 Sch. 1 Pt. VI: entry added (11.11.2002) by The Freedom of Information (Additional Public Authorities) Order 2002 (S.I. 2002/2623), art. 2, Sch. 1

213 Sch. 1 Pt. VI: entry removed (11.8.2003) by virtue of The Freedom of Information (Removal of References to Public Authorities) Order 2003 (S.I. 2003/1883), art. 2, Sch.

214 Sch. 1 Pt. VI: entry omitted (coming into force in accordance with art. 1(2)(3)) by virtue of The Nursing and Midwifery Order 2001 (S.I. 2002/253), art. 54(3), Sch. 5 para. 17(a) (with art. 3(18))

215 Sch. 1 Pt. VI: entry repealed (1.10.2006) by Natural Environment and Rural Communities Act 2006 c. 16), ss. 105, 107, Sch. 11 para. 153(3), {Sch. 12}; S.I. 2006/2541, art. 2

216 Sch. 1 Pt. VI: entry repealed (1.10.2007) by Equality Act 2006 (c. 3), ss. 40, 91, 93(1), Sch. 3 para. 60, Sch. 4 (with s. 92); S.I. 2007/2603, art. 2(a)(d) (subject to art. 3)

217 Sch. 1 Pt. VI: entry inserted (11.8.2003) by The Freedom of Information (Additional Public Authorities) Order 2003 (S.I. 2003/1882), art. 2, Sch. 1

218 Sch. 1 Pt. VI: entry inserted (7.2.2006) by The Freedom of Information (Additional Public Authorities) Order 2005 (S.I. 2005/3593), art. 2, Sch. 1

219 Sch. 1 Pt. VI: entry inserted (7.2.2006) by The Freedom of Information (Additional Public Authorities) Order 2005 (S.I. 2005/3593), art. 2, Sch. 1

220 Sch. 1 Pt. VI: entry inserted (11.8.2003) by The Freedom of Information (Additional Public Authorities) Order 2003 (S.I. 2003/1882), art. 2, Sch. 1

221 Sch. 1 Pt. VI: entry inserted (11.8.2003) by The Freedom of Information (Additional Public Authorities) Order 2003 (S.I. 2003/1882), art. 2, Sch. 1

222 Sch. 1 Pt. VI: entry added (19.4.2004) by The Freedom of Information (Additional Public Authorities) Order 2004 (S.I. 2004/938), art. 3, Sch. 2

223 Sch. 1 Pt. VI: entry removed (11.8.2003) by virtue of The Freedom of Information (Removal of References to Public Authorities) Order 2003 (S.I. 2003/1883), art. 2, Sch.

224 Sch. 1 Pt. VI: entry inserted (7.2.2006) by The Freedom of Information (Additional Public Authorities) Order 2005 (S.I. 2005/3593), art. 2, Sch. 1

225 Sch. 1 Pt. VI: entry for "Gambling Commission" substituted (1.10.2005) for entry for "Gaming Board of Great Britain" by Gambling Act 2005 (c. 19), ss. 356(1), 358(1), Sch. 16 para. 16 (with ss. 352, 354, Sch. 16 para. 21); S.I. 2005/2455, art. 2(1), Sch.

226 Sch. 1 Pt. VI: entry inserted (1.12.2004) by Gangmasters (Licensing) Act 2004 (c. 11), ss. 1(6), 29(1), Sch. 1 para. 6; S.I. 2004/2857, arts. 1(1), 2(a)(l)

227 Sch. 1 Pt. VI: entry added (11.11.2002) by The Freedom of Information (Additional Public Authorities) Order 2002 (S.I. 2002/2623), art. 2, Sch. 1

228 Sch. 1 Pt. VI: entry removed (11.8.2003) by virtue of The Freedom of Information (Removal of References to Public Authorities) Order 2003 (S.I. 2003/1883), art. 2, Sch.

229 Sch. 1 Pt. VI: entry inserted (7.2.2006) by The Freedom of Information (Additional Public Authorities) Order 2005 (S.I. 2005/3593), art. 2, Sch. 1

230 Sch. 1 Pt. VI: entry added (11.11.2002) by The Freedom of Information (Additional Public Authorities) Order 2002 (S.I. 2002/2623), art. 2, Sch. 1

231 Sch. 1 Pt. VI: entry inserted (11.8.2003) by The Freedom of Information (Additional Public Authorities) Order 2003 (S.I. 2003/1882), art. 2, Sch. 1

232 Sch. 1 Pt. VI: entry added (11.11.2002) by The Freedom of Information (Additional Public Authorities) Order 2002 (S.I. 2002/2623), art. 2, Sch. 1

233 Sch. 1 Pt. VI: entry inserted (11.8.2003) by The Freedom of Information (Additional Public Authorities) Order 2003 (S.I. 2003/1882), art. 2, Sch. 1

234 Sch. 1 Pt. VI: entry omitted (1.4.2008) by virtue of The Legislative Reform (Health and Safety Executive) Order 2008 (S.I. 2008/960), art. 22, Sch. 3

235 Sch. 1 Pt. VI: entry inserted (coming into force in accordance with art. 1(2)(3)) by The Health Professions Order 2001 (2002/254), art. 48(3), {Sch. 4 para. 9} (with art. 3(19))

[236] Sch. 1 Pt. VI: entry inserted (1.4.2005) by Health Protection Agency Act 2004 (c. 17), ss. 11(1), 12, Sch. 3 para. 15; S.I. 2005/121, art. 2(2)

[237] Sch. 1 Pt. VI: entry repealed (1.4.2006) by Public Services Ombudsman (Wales) Act 2005 (c. 10), ss. 39, 40, Sch. 6 para. 71(a), Sch. 7; S.I. 2005/2800, art. 5(1) (with art. 5(2), Sch. 2)

[238] Sch. 1 Pt. VI: entry repealed (prosp.) by Health and Social Care Act 2008 (c. 14), ss. 166, 170, Sch. 15 Pt. 2

[239] Sch. 1 Pt. VI: entry inserted (11.8.2003) by The Freedom of Information (Additional Public Authorities) Order 2003 (S.I. 2003/1882), art. 2, Sch. 1

[240] Sch. 1 Pt. VI: entry substituted (1.1.2001) by virtue of 2000 c. 21, s. 73(3)(a); S.I. 2000/3230, art. 2, Sch.

[241] Sch. 1 Pt. VI: entry added (19.4.2004) by The Freedom of Information (Additional Public Authorities) Order 2004 (S.I. 2004/938), art. 3, Sch. 2

[242] Sch. 1 Pt. VI: entries removed (29.6.2004) by virtue of The Freedom of Information (Removal of References to Public Authorities) Order 2004 (S.I. 2004/1641), art. 2, Sch. 1

[243] Sch. 1 Pt. VI: entries removed (29.6.2004) by virtue of The Freedom of Information (Removal of References to Public Authorities) Order 2004 (S.I. 2004/1641), art. 2, Sch. 1

[244] Sch. 1 Pt. VI: entry repealed (1.4.2006) by The Historic Buildings Council for Wales (Abolition) Order 2006 (S.I. 2006/63), art. 3(1)(c)(iii)

[245] Sch. 1 Pt. VI: entries repealed (1.4.2008) by The Agriculture and Horticulture Development Board Order 2008 (S.I. 2008/576), art. 18, Sch. 5 para. 7 (with Sch. 4 para. 10)

[246] Sch. 1 Pt. VI: entry inserted (8.9.2008) by Housing and Regeneration Act 2008 (c. 17), ss. 56, 325, Sch. 8 para. 77(2); S.I. 2008/2358, art. 2(1)(2)

[247] Sch. 1 Pt. VI: entry removed (11.8.2003) by virtue of The Freedom of Information (Removal of References to Public Authorities) Order 2003 (S.I. 2003/1883), art. 2, Sch.

[248] Sch. 1 Pt. VI: entries repealed (1.4.2008) by The Agriculture and Horticulture Development Board Order 2008 (S.I. 2008/576), art. 18, Sch. 5 para. 7 (with Sch. 4 para. 10)

[249] Sch. 1 Pt. 6: entry repealed (1.4.2009) by Housing and Regeneration Act 2008 (c. 17), ss. 277, 321(1), 325, Sch. 9 para. 28(3), Sch. 16; S.I. 2009/803, arts. 1(2), 8(1)(2), 10

[250] Sch. 1 Pt. VI: entry inserted (1.4.2005) by Human Tissue Act 2004 (c. 30), ss. 13(2), 60(2), Sch. 2 para. 27 (with s. 37(7)); S.I. 2005/919, art. 3, Sch. (with art. 2)

[251] Sch. 1 Pt. VI: entry inserted (11.8.2003) by The Freedom of Information (Additional Public Authorities) Order 2003 (S.I. 2003/1882), art. 2, Sch. 1

[252] Sch. 1 Pt. VI: entry inserted (7.2.2006) by The Freedom of Information (Additional Public Authorities) Order 2005 (S.I. 2005/3593), art. 2, Sch. 1

[253] Sch. 1 Pt. VI: entry inserted (1.11.2007) by Offender Management Act 2007 (c. 21), ss. 39, 41(1), Sch. 3 para. 10; S.I. 2007/3001, art. 2(1)(p)(r)

[254] Sch. 1 Pt. VI: entry inserted (12.10.2009) by Parliamentary Standards Act 2009 (c. 13), ss. 3, 14(2)(3), Sch. 1 para. 27(1) (with ss. 1, 2(1)); S.I. 2009/2500, art. 2(d)

[255] Sch. 1 Pt. VI: entry inserted (1.4.2004) by Police Reform Act 2002 (c. 30), ss. 107, 108(2)-(5), Sch. 7 para. 23(a); S.I. 2004/913, art. 2(e)

[256] Sch. 1 Pt. VI: entry inserted (7.2.2006) by The Freedom of Information (Additional Public Authorities) Order 2005 (S.I. 2005/3593), art. 2, Sch. 1

[257] Sch. 1 Pt. VI: entry added (19.4.2004) by The Freedom of Information (Additional Public Authorities) Order 2004 (S.I. 2004/938), art. 3, Sch. 2

[258] Sch. 1 Pt. VI: entry added (19.4.2004) by The Freedom of Information (Additional Public Authorities) Order 2004 (S.I. 2004/938), art. 3, Sch. 2

[259] Sch. 1 Pt. VI: entry inserted (11.8.2003) by The Freedom of Information (Additional Public Authorities) Order 2003 (S.I. 2003/1882), art. 2, Sch. 1

[260] Sch. 1 Pt. VI: entry removed (11.8.2003) by virtue of The Freedom of Information (Removal of References to Public Authorities) Order 2003 (S.I. 2003/1883), art. 2, Sch.

[261] Sch. 1 Pt. VI: entry inserted (1.10.2009) by Planning Act 2008 (c. 29), ss. 1(3), 241, Sch. 1 para. 27 (with s. 226); S.I. 2009/2260, art. 2(a); S.I. 2009/2573, art. 2

[262] Sch. 1 Pt. VI: entry substituted (1.4.2007) by Natural Environment and Rural Communities Act 2006 (c. 16), ss. 105(1), 107, Sch. 11 para. 175; S.I. 2007/816, art. 2(b)

[263] Sch. 1 Pt. VI: entry omitted (30.4.2001) by virtue of S.I. 2001/1283, art. 3(7)

[264] Sch. 1 Pt. VI: entry inserted (11.8.2003) by The Freedom of Information (Additional Public Authorities) Order 2003 (S.I. 2003/1882), art. 2, Sch. 1

[265] Sch. 1 Pt. VI: entry inserted (11.8.2003) by The Freedom of Information (Additional Public Authorities) Order 2003 (S.I. 2003/1882), art. 2, Sch. 1

[266] Sch. 1 Pt. VI: entry inserted (3.4.2006) by Constitutional Reform Act 2005 (c. 4), ss. 62(2), 148, Sch. 13 para. 17(3); S.I. 2006/1014, art. 2(a), Sch. 1 para. 16

[267] Sch. 1 Pt. VI: entry inserted (3.4.2006) by Constitutional Reform Act 2005 (c. 4), ss. 61(2), 148, Sch. 12 para. 36(3); S.I. 2006/1014, art. 2(a), Sch. 1 para. 15

268 Sch. 1 Pt. VI: entry inserted (11.8.2003) by The Freedom of Information (Additional Public Authorities) Order 2003 (S.I. 2003/1882), art. 2, Sch. 1

269 Sch. 1 Pt. VI: entry inserted (2.6.2008) by The Freedom of Information (Additional Public Authorities) Order 2008 (S.I. 2008/1271), art. 2, Sch.

270 Sch. 1 Pt. VI: entry inserted (7.3.2008) by Legal Services Act 2007 (c. 29), ss. 2(2), 211(2), Sch. 1 para. 31 (with ss. 29, 192, 193); S.I. 2008/222, art. 2(h)

271 Sch. 1 Pt. VI: entry repealed (prosp.) by Legal Services Act 2007 (c. 29), ss. 210, 211(2), Sch. 23 (with ss. 29, 192, 193)

272 Sch. 1 Pt. VI: entry added (19.4.2004) by The Freedom of Information (Additional Public Authorities) Order 2004 (S.I. 2004/938), art. 3, Sch. 2

273 Sch. 1 Pt. VI: entry repealed (prosp.) by Legal Services Act 2007 (c. 29), ss. 210, 211(2), Sch. 23 (with ss. 29, 192, 193)

274 Sch. 1 Pt. VI: entry repealed (prosp.) by Legal Services Act 2007 (c. 29), ss. 210, 211(2), Sch. 23 (with ss. 29, 192, 193)

275 Sch. 1 Pt. VI: entry repealed (W.) (1.4.2004) by The Library Advisory Council for Wales Abolition and Consequential Amendments Order 2004 (S.I. 2004/803), art. 3(3)

276 Sch. 1 Pt. VI: entry inserted (1.10.2008) by Regulatory Enforcement and Sanctions Act 2008 (c. 13), ss. 1, 76, Sch. 1 para. 19; S.I. 2008/2371, art. 2(a)

277 Sch. 1 Pt. 6: entry inserted (1.4.2010) by Local Democracy, Economic Development and Construction Act 2009 (c. 20), ss. 55, 148, Sch. 1 para. 21; S.I. 2009/3318, art. 4(d)(dd)

278 Sch. 1 Pt. 6: entry repealed (1.4.2010) by Local Democracy, Economic Development and Construction Act 2009 (c. 20), ss. 146, 148, Sch. 7 Pt. 3; S.I. 2009/3318, art. 4(hh)

279 Sch. 1 Pt. VI: entry added (19.4.2004) by The Freedom of Information (Additional Public Authorities) Order 2004 (S.I. 2004/938), art. 3, Sch. 2

280 Sch. 1 Pt. 6: entry inserted (12.1.2010) by Marine and Coastal Access Act 2009 (c. 23), ss. 1, 324, Sch. 2 para. 6; S.I. 2009/3345, art. 2, Sch. para. 1

281 Sch. 1 Pt. VI: entries repealed (1.4.2008) by The Agriculture and Horticulture Development Board Order 2008 (S.I. 2008/576), art. 18, Sch. 5 para. 7 (with Sch. 4 para. 10)

282 Sch. 1 Pt. VI: entry removed (11.8.2003) by virtue of The Freedom of Information (Removal of References to Public Authorities) Order 2003 (S.I. 2003/1883), art. 2, Sch.

283 Sch. 1 Pt. VI: entry removed (11.8.2003) by virtue of The Freedom of Information (Removal of References to Public Authorities) Order 2003 (S.I. 2003/1883), art. 2, Sch.

284 Sch. 1 Pt. VI: entries repealed (1.4.2008) by The Agriculture and Horticulture Development Board Order 2008 (S.I. 2008/576), art. 18, Sch. 5 para. 7 (with Sch. 4 para. 10)

285 Sch. 1 Pt. VI: entry repealed (1.12.2006) by National Lottery Act 2006 (c. 23), ss. 21, 22, Sch. 3; S.I. 2006/3201, art. 2(e)

286 Sch. 1 Pt. VI: entry repealed (1.4.2009) by Health and Social Care Act 2008 (c. 14), ss. 166, 170, Sch. 15 Pt. 7; S.I. 2009/270, art. 2(2)(b)

287 Sch. 1 Pt. VI: entry added (11.11.2002) by The Freedom of Information (Additional Public Authorities) Order 2002 (S.I. 2002/2623), art. 2, Sch. 1

288 Sch. 1 Pt. VI: entry inserted (21.12.2007) by Consumers, Estate Agents and Redress Act 2007 (c. 17), ss. 1(4), 66(2), Sch. 1 para. 35 (with s. 6(9)); S.I. 2007/3546, art. 3, Sch.

289 Sch. 1 Pt. VI: entry omitted (1.4.2006) by virtue of The National Council for Education and Training for Wales (Transfer of Functions to the National Assembly for Wales and Abolition) Order 2005 (S.I. 2005/3238), art. 9(1), Sch. 1 para. 85 (with art. 7)

290 Sch. 1 Pt. VI: entry added (11.11.2002) by The Freedom of Information (Additional Public Authorities) Order 2002 (S.I. 2002/2623), art. 2, Sch. 1

291 Sch. 1 Pt. VI: entry repealed (1.4.2006) by Serious Organised Crime and Police Act 2005 (c. 15), ss. 59, 174(2), 178, Sch. 4 para. 160, Sch. 17 Pt. 2; S.I. 2006/378, art. 4(1), Sch. para. 13(kk) (subject to art. 4(2)-(7))

292 Sch. 1 Pt. VI: entry inserted (11.8.2003) by The Freedom of Information (Additional Public Authorities) Order 2003 (S.I. 2003/1882), art. 2, Sch. 1

293 Sch. 1 Pt. VI: entry removed (7.2.2006) by virtue of The Freedom of Information (Removal of References to Public Authorities) Order 2005 (S.I. 2005/3594), art. 2, Sch. 1

294 Sch. 1 Pt. VI: entry inserted (11.8.2003) by The Freedom of Information (Additional Public Authorities) Order 2003 (S.I. 2003/1882), art. 2, Sch. 1

295 Sch. 1 Pt. VI: entry inserted (1.10.2009) by Identity Cards Act 2006 (c. 15), ss. 22(8), 44(3); S.I. 2009/2303, art. 2(a)

296 Sch. 1 Pt. VI: entry inserted (1.10.2008) by Health and Social Care Act 2008 (c. 14), ss. 160, 170, Sch. 14 para. 4; S.I. 2008/2497, art. 7(1)(b)

297 Sch. 1 Pt. VI: entry repealed (1.12.2006) by National Lottery Act 2006 (c. 23), ss. 21, 22, Sch. 3; S.I. 2006/3201, art. 2(e)

298 Sch. 1 Pt. VI: entry inserted (1.4.2007) by Police and Justice Act 2006 (c. 48), ss. 1(3), 53, Sch. 1 para. 74; S.I. 2007/709, art. 3(a) (subject to arts. 6, 7)

299 Sch. 1 Pt. VI: entry repealed (1.4.2005) by Health Protection Agency Act 2004 (c. 17), ss. 11(2), 12, Sch. 4; S.I. 2005/121, art. 2(2)

300 Sch. 1 Pt. VI: entry inserted (2.5.2006 for E.W. and 1.10.2006 otherwise) by Natural Environment and Rural Communities Act 2006 (c. 16), ss. 105(1), 107, Sch. 11 para. 153(2); S.I. 2006/1176, art. 4; S.I. 2006/2541, art. 2

[301] Sch. 1 Pt. VI: entry repealed (1.12.2006) by National Lottery Act 2006 (c. 23), ss. 21, 22, Sch. 3; S.I. 2006/3201, art. 2(e)

[302] Sch. 1 Pt. VI: entry added (19.4.2004) by The Freedom of Information (Additional Public Authorities) Order 2004 (S.I. 2004/938), art. 3, Sch. 2

[303] Sch. 1 Pt. VI: entry inserted by Justice (Northern Ireland) Act 2002 (c. 26), Sch. 3A para. 17(3) (as inserted (25.9.2006) by Constitutional Reform Act 2005 (c. 4), ss. 124(3), 148, Sch. 15; S.I. 2006/1537, art. 3(d))

[304] Sch. 1 Pt. VI: entry added (19.4.2004) by The Freedom of Information (Additional Public Authorities) Order 2004 (S.I. 2004/938), art. 3, Sch. 2

[305] Sch.1 Pt.VI: entry inserted (27.7.2004) by Energy Act 2004 (c.20), ss.2(10), 198(2), Sch.1 para.18; S.I. 2004/1973, art.2,Sch.

[306] Sch. 1 Pt. VI: entry inserted (11.8.2003) by The Freedom of Information (Additional Public Authorities) Order 2003 (S.I. 2003/1882), art. 2, Sch. 1

[307] Sch. 1 Pt. VI: entry inserted (coming into force in accordance with art. 1(2)(3)) by The Nursing and Midwifery Order 2001 (S.I. 2002/253), art. 54(3), Sch. 5 para. 17(b) (with art. 3(18))

[308] Sch. 1 Pt. VI: entry repealed (6.4.2005) by Pensions Act 2004 (c. 35), ss. 320, 322, Sch. 13 Pt. 1; S.I. 2005/275, art. 2(7), Sch. Pt. 7 (subject to art. 2(12))

[309] Sch. 1 Pt. VI: entry inserted (1.7.2002) by Office of Communications Act 2002 (c. 11), s. 1(10), Sch. para. 22; S.I. 2002/1483, art. 2

[310] Sch. 1 Pt. VI: entry inserted (prosp.) by Health and Social Care Act 2008 (c. 14), ss. 127, 170, Sch. 10 para. 13(b)

[311] Sch. 1 Pt. VI: entry inserted (11.8.2003) by The Freedom of Information (Additional Public Authorities) Order 2003 (S.I. 2003/1882), art. 2, Sch. 1

[312] Sch. 1 Pt. VI: entry inserted (1.1.2009) by Legal Services Act 2007 (c. 29), ss. 114(2), 211(2), Sch. 15 para. 32 (with ss. 29, 192, 193); S.I. 2008/3149, art. 2(e)(ii)

[313] Sch. 1 Pt. VI: entry inserted (11.8.2003) by The Freedom of Information (Additional Public Authorities) Order 2003 (S.I. 2003/1882), art. 2, Sch. 1

[314]Sch. 1 Pt. VI: entry inserted (8.9.2008) by Housing and Regeneration Act 2008 (c. 17), ss. 277, 325, Sch. 9 para. 28(2); S.I. 2008/2358, art. 3(1)(2)

[315] Sch. 1 Pt. VI: entry inserted (30.3.2006) by London Olympic Games and Paralympic Games Act 2006 (c. 12), ss. 3(2), 40(1)(b), Sch. 1 para. 23

[316] Sch. 1 Pt. VI: entry inserted (2.6.2008) by The Freedom of Information (Additional Public Authorities) Order 2008 (S.I. 2008/1271), art. 2, Sch.

[317] Sch. 1 Pt. VI: entry inserted (6.4.2005) by Pensions Act 2004 (c. 35), ss. 319(1), 322, Sch. 12 para. 79; S.I. 2005/275, art. 2(7), Sch. Pt. 7 (subject to art. 2(12))

[318] Sch. 1 Pt. VI: entry repealed (1.1.2009) by Health and Social Care Act 2008 (c. 14), ss. 166, 170, Sch. 15 Pt. 6; S.I. 2008/2497, art. 7(2)(d)

[319] Sch. 1 Pt. VI: entry inserted (11.5.2001) by 2001 c. 15, s. 67, Sch. 5 Pt. 3 para. 18 (with ss. 64(9), 65(4))

[320] Sch. 1 Pt. VI: entry repealed (1.9.2005) by Pensions Act 2004 (c. 35), ss. 320, 322, Sch. 13 Pt. 1; S.I. 2005/1720, art. 2(16), Sch. Pt. 3 (with arts. 4, 5)

[321] Sch. 1 Pt. VI: entry inserted (6.4.2005) by Pensions Act 2004 (c. 35), ss. 319(1), 322, Sch. 12 para. 79; S.I. 2005/275, art. 2(7), Sch. Pt. 7 (subject to art. 2(12))

[322] Sch. 1 Pt. VI: entry inserted (26.7.2007) by Pensions Act 2007 (c. 22), ss. 20, 30(1)(c), Sch. 6 para. 23

[323] Sch. 1 Pt. VI: entry inserted (11.8.2003) by The Freedom of Information (Additional Public Authorities) Order 2003 (S.I. 2003/1882), art. 2, Sch. 1

[324] Sch. 1 Pt. VI: entry added (19.4.2004) by The Freedom of Information (Additional Public Authorities) Order 2004 (S.I. 2004/938), art. 3, Sch. 2

[325] Sch. 1 Pt. VI: entry removed (7.2.2006) by virtue of The Freedom of Information (Removal of References to Public Authorities) Order 2005 (S.I. 2005/3594), art. 2, Sch. 1

[326] Sch. 1 Pt. VI: entry removed (11.8.2003) by virtue of The Freedom of Information (Removal of References to Public Authorities) Order 2003 (S.I. 2003/1883), art. 2, Sch.

[327] Sch. 1 Pt. VI: entry added (19.4.2004) by The Freedom of Information (Additional Public Authorities) Order 2004 (S.I. 2004/938), art. 3, Sch. 2

[328] Sch. 1 Pt. VI: entry repealed (1.4.2004) by Police Reform Act 2002 (c. 30), ss. 107, 108(2), Sch. 7 para. 23(b), Sch. 8; S.I. 2004/913, art. 2(c)(e)(f)(ix)

[329] Sch. 1 Pt. VI: entry repealed (1.4.2007) by Police and Justice Act 2006 (c. 48), ss. 52, 53, Sch. 15 Pt. 1(A); S.I. 2007/709, art. 3(o)(q) (subject to arts. 6, 7)

[330] Sch. 1 Pt. 6: entry inserted (prosp.) by Policing and Crime Act 2009 (c. 26), ss. 2(4), 116

[331] Sch. 1 Pt. VI: entry removed (11.8.2003) by virtue of The Freedom of Information (Removal of References to Public Authorities) Order 2003 (S.I. 2003/1883), art. 2, Sch.

[332] Sch. 1 Pt. VI: entry removed (11.8.2003) by virtue of The Freedom of Information (Removal of References to Public Authorities) Order 2003 (S.I. 2003/1883), art. 2, Sch.

[333] Sch. 1 Pt. VI: entry added (19.4.2004) by The Freedom of Information (Additional Public Authorities) Order 2004 (S.I. 2004/938), art. 3, Sch. 2

[334] Sch. 1 Pt. VI: entry added (19.4.2004) by The Freedom of Information (Additional Public Authorities) Order 2004 (S.I.

2004/938), art. 3, Sch. 2

335 Sch. 1 Pt. VI: entry inserted (1.4.2008) by The Offender Management Act 2007 (Consequential Amendments) Order 2008 (S.I. 2008/912), art. 3, Sch. 1 para. 17(2)

336 Sch. 1 Pt. VI: entries removed (29.6.2004) by virtue of The Freedom of Information (Removal of References to Public Authorities) Order 2004 (S.I. 2004/1641), art. 2, Sch. 1

337 Sch. 1 Pt. VI: entry added (19.4.2004) by The Freedom of Information (Additional Public Authorities) Order 2004 (S.I. 2004/938), art. 3, Sch. 2

338 Sch. 1 Pt. VI: entry inserted (1.4.2006) by Public Services Ombudsman (Wales) Act 2005 (c. 10), ss. 39(1), 40, Sch. 6 para. 71(b); S.I. 2005/2800, art. 5(1) (with art. 5(2), Sch. 2)

339 Sch. 1 Pt. VI: entry omitted (1.4.2006) by virtue of The Qualifications, Curriculum and Assessment Authority for Wales (Transfer of Functions to the National Assembly for Wales and Abolition) Order 2005 (S.I. 2005/3239), art. 9(1), Sch. 1 para. 31 (with art. 7)

340 Sch. 1 Pt. 6: entry substituted (prosp.) by Apprenticeships, Skills, Children and Learning Act 2009 (c. 22), ss. 174, 192, 269, Sch. 12 para. 30

341 Sch. 1 Pt. VI: entry repealed (24.7.2005) by Railways Act 2005 (c. 14), ss. 59(6)(7), 60, Sch. 13 (with s. 14(4)(5), Sch. 11 para. 11(2)); S.I. 2005/1909, art. 2, Sch.

342 Sch. 1 Pt. VI: entry added (11.11.2002) by The Freedom of Information (Additional Public Authorities) Order 2002 (S.I. 2002/2623), art. 2, Sch. 1

343 Sch. 1 Pt. VI: entry inserted (7.2.2006) by The Freedom of Information (Additional Public Authorities) Order 2005 (S.I. 2005/3593), art. 2, Sch. 1

344 Sch. 1 Pt. VI: entry repealed (6.4.2005) by Pensions Act 2004 (c. 35), ss. 320, 322, Sch. 13 Pt. 1; S.I. 2005/275, art. 2(7), Sch. Pt. 7 (subject to art. 2(12))

345 Sch. 1 Pt. VI: entry added (19.4.2004) by The Freedom of Information (Additional Public Authorities) Order 2004 (S.I. 2004/938), art. 3, Sch. 2

346 Sch. 1 Pt. VI: entry inserted (1.6.2006) by The Freedom of Information (Additional Public Authorities) Order 2005 (S.I. 2005/3593), art. 3, Sch. 2

347 Sch. 1 Pt. VI: entry added (19.4.2004) by The Freedom of Information (Additional Public Authorities) Order 2004 (S.I. 2004/938), art. 3, Sch. 2

348 Sch. 1 Pt. VI: entries removed (29.6.2004) by virtue of The Freedom of Information (Removal of References to Public Authorities) Order 2004 (S.I. 2004/1641), art. 2, Sch. 1

349 Sch. 1 Pt. VI: entry inserted (1.6.2006) by The Freedom of Information (Additional Public Authorities) Order 2005 (S.I. 2005/3593), art. 3, Sch. 2

350 Sch. 1 Pt. VI: entry inserted (11.8.2003) by The Freedom of Information (Additional Public Authorities) Order 2003 (S.I. 2003/1882), art. 2, Sch. 1

351 Sch. 1 Pt. VI: entry repealed (29.12.2003) by Communications Act 2003 (c. 21), ss. 406(6)(7), 411(2), Sch. 19(1) (with Sch. 18, Sch. 19(1) Note 1); S.I. 2003/3142, art. 3(1), Sch. 1 (subject to art. 3(3) and with art. 11)

352 Sch. 1 Pt. VI: entry inserted (1.11.2007) by Tribunals, Courts and Enforcement Act 2007 (c. 15), ss. 48(1), 148(5), Sch. 8 para. 53; S.I. 2007/2709, art. 3(b)(ii)

353 Sch. 1 Pt. VI: entry repealed (1.11.2007) by Tribunals, Courts and Enforcement Act 2007 (c. 15), ss. 146, 148(5), Sch. 23 Pt. 1; S.I. 2007/2709, art. 3(d)(vii)

354 Sch. 1 Pt. VI: entry inserted (1.4.2003) by 2001 c. 12, ss. 1, 26, Sch. 1 para. 23; S.I. 2002/3125, art. 3(d)

355 Sch. 1 Pt. 6: entry inserted (prosp.) by Coroners and Justice Act 2009 (c. 25), ss. 177, 182, Sch. 21 para. 82

356 Sch. 1 Pt. 6: entry repealed (prosp.) by Coroners and Justice Act 2009 (c. 25), ss. 178, 182, Sch. 23 Pt. 4

357 Sch. 1 Pt. 6: entry repealed (prosp.) by Coroners and Justice Act 2009 (c. 25), ss. 178, 182, Sch. 23 Pt. 4

358 Sch. 1 Pt. VI: entry inserted (7.2.2006) by The Freedom of Information (Additional Public Authorities) Order 2005 (S.I. 2005/3593), art. 2, Sch. 1

359 Sch. 1 Pt. VI: entry repealed (1.4.2006) by Serious Organised Crime and Police Act 2005 (c. 15), ss. 59, 174(2), 178, Sch. 4 para. 160, Sch. 17 Pt. 2; S.I. 2006/378, art. 4(1), Sch. para. 13(kk) (subject to art. 4(2)-(7))

360 Sch. 1 Pt. VI: entries removed (29.6.2004) by virtue of The Freedom of Information (Removal of References to Public Authorities) Order 2004 (S.I. 2004/1641), art. 2, Sch. 1

361 Sch. 1 Pt. VI: entry inserted (11.8.2003) by The Freedom of Information (Additional Public Authorities) Order 2003 (S.I. 2003/1882), art. 2, Sch. 1

362 Sch. 1 Pt. VI: entry inserted (11.8.2003) by The Freedom of Information (Additional Public Authorities) Order 2003 (S.I. 2003/1882), art. 2, Sch. 1

363 Sch. 1 Pt. VI: entry inserted (11.8.2003) by The Freedom of Information (Additional Public Authorities) Order 2003 (S.I. 2003/1882), art. 2, Sch. 1

364 Sch. 1 Pt. VI: entry added (19.4.2004) by The Freedom of Information (Additional Public Authorities) Order 2004 (S.I. 2004/938), art. 3, Sch. 2

365 Sch. 1 Pt. VI: entry inserted (11.8.2003) by The Freedom of Information (Additional Public Authorities) Order 2003 (S.I. 2003/1882), art. 2, Sch. 1

366 Sch. 1 Pt. VI: entry added (11.11.2002) by The Freedom of Information (Additional Public Authorities) Order 2002 (S.I.

2002/2623), art. 2, Sch. 1

[367] Sch. 1 Pt. VI: entry removed (7.2.2006) by virtue of The Freedom of Information (Removal of References to Public Authorities) Order 2005 (S.I. 2005/3594), art. 2, Sch. 1

[368] Sch. 1 Pt. VI: entry removed (7.2.2006) by virtue of The Freedom of Information (Removal of References to Public Authorities) Order 2005 (S.I. 2005/3594), art. 2, Sch. 1

[369] Sch. 1 Pt. VI: entry removed (7.2.2006) by virtue of The Freedom of Information (Removal of References to Public Authorities) Order 2005 (S.I. 2005/3594), art. 2, Sch. 1

[370] Sch. 1 Pt. VI: entry inserted (11.8.2003) by The Freedom of Information (Additional Public Authorities) Order 2003 (S.I. 2003/1882), art. 2, Sch. 1

[371] Sch. 1 Pt. VI: entry inserted (11.8.2003) by The Freedom of Information (Additional Public Authorities) Order 2003 (S.I. 2003/1882), art. 2, Sch. 1

[372] Sch. 1 Pt. VI: entry repealed (1.12.2006) by Railways Act 2005 (c. 14), ss. 59(6)(7), 60, Sch. 13 (with s. 14(4)(5), Sch. 11 para. 11(2)); S.I. 2006/2911, art. 2, Sch. (subject to arts. 3-7)

[373] Sch. 1 Pt. VI: entry inserted (15.1.2001) by Transport Act 2000 (c. 38), s. 204, Sch. 14 para. 30; S.I. 2000/3376, art. 2; and expressed to be added (11.11.2002) by The Freedom of Information (Additional Public Authorities) Order 2002 (S.I. 2002/2623), art. 2, Sch. 1

[374] Sch. 1 Pt. VI: entry removed (11.8.2003) by virtue of The Freedom of Information (Removal of References to Public Authorities) Order 2003 (S.I. 2003/1883), art. 2, Sch.

[375] Sch. 1 Pt. VI: entry added (19.4.2004) by The Freedom of Information (Additional Public Authorities) Order 2004 (S.I. 2004/938), art. 3, Sch. 2

[376] Sch. 1 Pt. VI: entry inserted (2.6.2008) by The Freedom of Information (Additional Public Authorities) Order 2008 (S.I. 2008/1271), art. 2, Sch.

[377] Sch. 1 Pt. VI: entry repealed (1.9.2005) by Education Act 2005 (c. 18), ss. 123, 125(3)(b), Sch. 19 Pt. 3

[378] Sch. 1 Pt. VI: entry inserted (11.8.2003) by The Freedom of Information (Additional Public Authorities) Order 2003 (S.I. 2003/1882), art. 2, Sch. 1

[379] Sch. 1 Pt. VI: entry inserted (1.9.2005) by Education Act 2005 (c. 18), ss. 98, 125(3), Sch. 14 para. 22

[380] Sch. 1 Pt. VI: entry inserted (prosp.) by Pensions Act 2008 (c. 30), ss. 75, 149, Sch. 1 para. 24

[381] Sch. 1 Pt. VI: entry inserted (11.8.2003) by The Freedom of Information (Additional Public Authorities) Order 2003 (S.I. 2003/1882), art. 2, Sch. 1

[382] Sch. 1 Pt. VI: entry inserted (2.6.2008) by The Freedom of Information (Additional Public Authorities) Order 2008 (S.I. 2008/1271), art. 2, Sch.

[383] Sch. 1 Pt. VI: entry omitted by virtue of The Nursing and Midwifery Order 2001 (S.I. 2002/253), art. 54(3), Sch. 5 para. 17(b) (with art. 3(18)) (the amendment coming into force in accordance with art. 1(2)(3) of the amending S.I.)

[384] Sch. 1 Pt. VI: entries removed (29.6.2004) by virtue of The Freedom of Information (Removal of References to Public Authorities) Order 2004 (S.I. 2004/1641), art. 2, Sch. 1

[385] Sch. 1 Pt. VI: entry inserted (1.6.2006) by The Freedom of Information (Additional Public Authorities) Order 2005 (S.I. 2005/3593), art. 3, Sch. 2

[386] Sch. 1 Pt. 6: entry repealed (1.4.2009) by Housing and Regeneration Act 2008 (c. 17), ss. 56, 321(1), 325, Sch. 8 para. 77(3), Sch. 16; S.I. 2009/803, arts. 1(2), 3(2)(3), 10

[387] Sch. 1 Pt. VI: entry inserted (1.4.2004) by Local Government Act 2003 (c. 26), ss. 105(9), 128, Sch. 4 para. 24; S.I. 2003/2938, art. 6(a) (subject to art. 8, Sch.)

[388] Sch. 1 Pt. VI: entry inserted (1.6.2006) by The Freedom of Information (Additional Public Authorities) Order 2005 (S.I. 2005/3593), art. 3, Sch. 2

[389] Sch. 1 Pt. VI: entry inserted (11.8.2003) by The Freedom of Information (Additional Public Authorities) Order 2003 (S.I. 2003/1882), art. 2, Sch. 1

[390] Sch. 1 Pt. VI: entry inserted (1.4.2005) by Health (Wales) Act 2003 (c. 4), ss. 7(1), 10(2), Sch. 3 para. 15; S.I. 2003/2660, art. 3(2)

[391] Sch. 1 Pt. VI: entry removed (11.8.2003) by virtue of The Freedom of Information (Removal of References to Public Authorities) Order 2003 (S.I. 2003/1883), art. 2, Sch.

[392] Sch. 1 Pt. VI: entry omitted (1.4.2006) by virtue of The Wales Tourist Board (Transfer of Functions to the National Assembly for Wales and Abolition) Order 2005 (S.I. 2005/3225), arts. 1(2), 2, 6(2), Sch. 2 Pt. 1 para. 5 (with art. 3(1))

[393] Sch. 1 Pt. VI: entry repealed (1.4.2006) by Public Services Ombudsman (Wales) Act 2005 (c. 10), ss. 39, 40, Sch. 6 para. 71(a), Sch. 7; S.I. 2005/2800, art. 5(1) (with art. 5(2), Sch. 2)

[394] Sch. 1 Pt. VI: entry repealed (29.12.2003) by Communications Act 2003 (c. 21), ss. 406(6)(7), 411(2), Sch. 19(1) (with Sch. 18, Sch. 19(1) Note 1); S.I. 2003/3142, art. 3(1), Sch. 1 (subject to art. 3(3) and with art. 11)

[395] FSch. 1 Pt. VI: entry inserted (1.6.2008) by Tribunals, Courts and Enforcement Act 2007 (c. 15), ss. 48(1), 148(5), Sch. 8 para. 53; S.I. 2007/2709, art. 6(b)(ii)

[396] Sch.1 Pt.VI: entry repealed (1.4.2006) by The Welsh Development Agency (Transfer of Functions to the National Assembly for Wales and Abolition) Order 2005 (S.I.2005/3226), arts.1(2), 2, 7(1)(b), Sch. 2 Pt. 1 para.13 (with art.3(1))

[397] Sch. 1 Pt. VI: entry omitted by virtue of The Nursing and Midwifery Order 2001 (S.I. 2002/253), art. 54(3), Sch. 5 para. 17 (with art. 3(18)) (the amendment coming into force in accordance with art. 1(2)(3) of the amending S.I.)

398 Sch. 1 Pt. VI: entry added (19.4.2004) by The Freedom of Information (Additional Public Authorities) Order 2004 (S.I. 2004/938), art. 3, Sch. 2

399 Sch. 1 Pt. VI: entry added (19.4.2004) by The Freedom of Information (Additional Public Authorities) Order 2004 (S.I. 2004/938), art. 3, Sch. 2

400 Sch. 1 Pt. VII: entry added (19.4.2004) by The Freedom of Information (Additional Public Authorities) Order 2004 (S.I. 2004/938), art. 4, Sch. 3

401 Sch. 1 Pt. VII: entry omitted (1.4.2009) by virtue of The Transfer of Tribunal Functions and Revenue and Customs Appeals Order 2009 (S.I. 2009/56), art. 3, Sch. 1 para. 296(b)

402 Sch. 1 Pt. VII: entry repealed (1.4.2005) by Justice (Northern Ireland) Act 2002 (c. 26), ss. 86, 87(1), Sch. 13; S.R. 2005/109, art. 2, Sch.

403 Sch. 1 Pt. VII: entry repealed (N.I.) (1.4.2006) by The Agriculture (Northern Ireland) Order 2004 (S.I. 2004/3327 (N.I. 23)), arts. 1(3), 13, Sch. 4; S.R. 2006/172, art. 2

404 Sch. 1 Pt. VII: entry inserted (N.I.) (1.4.2006) by The Agriculture (Northern Ireland) Order 2004 (S.I. 2004/3327 (N.I. 23)), arts. 1(3), 3(5), Sch. 1 para. 21; S.R. 2006/172, art. 2

405 Sch. 1 Pt. VII: entry inserted (prosp.) by Justice (Northern Ireland) Act 2002 (c. 26), ss. 23(9), 87(1)

406 Sch. 1 Pt. VII: entry added (11.11.2002) by The Freedom of Information (Additional Public Authorities) Order 2002 (S.I. 2002/2623), art. 3, Sch. 2

407 Sch. 1Pt. VII: entry repealed (prosp.) by The Criminal Justice (Northern Ireland) Order 2005 (S.I. 2005/1965 (N.I. 15)), arts. 1(4), 10(2), 27, Sch. 1 para. 10(a), Sch. 2

408 Sch. 1 Pt. VII: entry added (19.4.2004) by The Freedom of Information (Additional Public Authorities) Order 2004 (S.I. 2004/938), art. 4, Sch. 3

409 Sch. 1 Pt. VII: entry added (11.11.2002) by The Freedom of Information (Additional Public Authorities) Order 2002 (S.I. 2002/2623), art. 3, Sch. 2

410 Sch. 1 Pt. VII: entry inserted (N.I.) (27.3.2009) by Charities Act (Northern Ireland) 2008 (c. 12), ss. 6(7), 185, Sch. 1 para. 14; S.R. 2009/138, art. 2, Sch.

411 Sch. 1 Pt. VII: entry inserted (26.5.2003) by Justice (Northern Ireland) Act 2002 (c. 26), ss. 45(3), 87, Sch. 8 para. 16; S.R. 2003/265, art. 2

412 Sch. 1 Pt. VII: entry inserted (11.8.2003) by The Freedom of Information (Additional Public Authorities) Order 2003 (S.I. 2003/1882), art. 3, Sch. 2

413 Sch. 1 Pt. VII: entry inserted (N.I.) by The Victims and Survivors (Northern Ireland) Order 2006 (S.I. 2006/2953 (N.I. 17)), Sch. para. 19 (as substituted (23.5.2008) by Commission for Victims and Survivors Act (Northern Ireland) 2008 (c. 6), s. 1(2), Sch. 1)

414 Sch. 1 Pt. VII: entry inserted (N.I.) (14.3.2003) by The Commissioner for Children and Young People (Northern Ireland) Order 2003 (S.I. 2003/439 (N.I. 11)), arts. 1(2)(b), 5(3), Sch. 2 para. 15

415 Sch. 1 Pt. VII: entry inserted (N.I.) (15.2.2007) by The Victims and Survivors (Northern Ireland) Order 2006 (S.I. 2006/2953 (N.I. 17)), arts. 1(3), 4(3), Sch. para. 15; S.R. 2007/96, art. 2

416 Sch. 1 Pt. VII: entry repealed (N.I.) (23.5.2008) by Commission for Victims and Survivors Act (Northern Ireland) 2008 (c. 6), s. 1, Sch. 2

417 Sch. 1 Pt. VII: entry inserted (11.8.2003) by The Freedom of Information (Additional Public Authorities) Order 2003 (S.I. 2003/1882), art. 3, Sch. 2

418 Sch. 1 Pt. VII: entry inserted (N.I.) (7.3.2003) by The Strategic Investment and Regeneration of Sites (Northern Ireland) Order 2003 (S.I. 2003/410 (N.I. 1)), arts. 1(2), 15(3), Sch. 1 para. 23

419 Sch. 1 Pt. VII: entry repealed (N.I.) (prosp.) by Public Authorities (Reform) Act (Northern Ireland) 2009 (c. 3), ss. 2, 7, Sch. 2 para. 4, Sch. 3

420 Sch. 1 Pt. VII: entry inserted (4.11.2001) by 2000 c. 32, s. 74, Sch. 6 para. 25(3); S.R. 2001/396, art. 2, Sch.

421 Sch.1 Pt.VII: entry repealed (N.I.)(prosp) by Public Authorities (Reform) Act (Northern Ireland) 2009 (c.3), ss.6,7,Sch.3

422 Sch. 1 Pt. VII: entry repealed (N.I.) (1.7.2006) by The Fire and Rescue Services (Northern Ireland) Order 2006 (S.I. 2006/1254 (N.I. 9)), arts. 1(3), 63(2), Sch. 4 (with art. 49); S.R. 2006/257, art. 2(b)(e)(v)

423 Sch. 1 Pt. VII: entry repealed (N.I.) (1.6.2009) by Public Authorities (Reform) Act (Northern Ireland) 2009 (c. 3), ss. 1, 7, Sch. 1 para. 13, Sch. 3; S.R. 2009/172, art. 2(e)

424 Sch. 1 Pt. VII: entry inserted (11.8.2003) by The Freedom of Information (Additional Public Authorities) Order 2003 (S.I. 2003/1882), art. 3, Sch. 2

425 Sch. 1 Pt. VII: entry inserted (11.8.2003) by The Freedom of Information (Additional Public Authorities) Order 2003 (S.I. 2003/1882), art. 3, Sch. 2

426 Sch. 1 Pt. VII: entry inserted (11.8.2003) by The Freedom of Information (Additional Public Authorities) Order 2003 (S.I. 2003/1882), art. 3, Sch. 2

427 Sch. 1Pt. VII: entry inserted (prosp.) by The Criminal Justice (Northern Ireland) Order 2005 (S.I. 2005/1965 (N.I. 15)), arts. 1(4), 10(2), Sch. 1 para. 10(b)

428 Sch. 1 Pt. VII: entries repealed (N.I.) (1.4.2002) by Industrial Development Act (Northern Ireland) 2002 (c. 1 (N.I.)), s. 5(4), Sch. 4 (with Sch. 2 paras. 1(4), 4(4), 6(4)); S.R. 2002/134, art. 2

429 Sch. 1 Pt. VII: entries repealed (N.I.) (1.4.2002) by Industrial Development Act (Northern Ireland) 2002 (c. 1 (N.I.)), s.

5(4), Sch. 4 (with Sch. 2 paras. 1(4), 4(4), 6(4)); S.R. 2002/134, art. 2

430 Sch. 1 Pt. VII: entry inserted (N.I.) (1.4.2002) by Industrial Development Act (Northern Ireland) 2002 (c. 1 (N.I.)), s. 1(2), Sch. 1 para. 21 (with Sch. 2 paras. 1(4), 4(4), 6(4)); S.R. 2002/134, art. 2

431 Sch. 1 Pt. VII: entries removed (29.6.2004) by virtue of The Freedom of Information (Removal of References to Public Authorities) Order 2004 (S.I. 2004/1641), art. 3, Sch. 2

432 Sch. 1 Pt. VII: entry repealed (N.I.) (1.6.2009) by Public Authorities (Reform) Act (Northern Ireland) 2009 (c. 3), ss. 5(1)(a)(iii), 6, 7, Sch. 3; S.R. 2009/172, art. 2(e)

433 Sch. 1 Pt. VII: entry repealed (prosp.) by Justice (Northern Ireland) Act 2002 (c. 26), ss. 86, 87(1), Sch. 13

434 Sch. 1 Pt. VII: entries removed (29.6.2004) by virtue of The Freedom of Information (Removal of References to Public Authorities) Order 2004 (S.I. 2004/1641), art. 3, Sch. 2

435 Sch. 1 Pt. VII: entry inserted (11.8.2003) by The Freedom of Information (Additional Public Authorities) Order 2003 (S.I. 2003/1882), art. 3, Sch. 2

436 Sch. 1 Pt. VII: entry omitted (15.5.2008) by virtue of The Criminal Justice (Northern Ireland Consequential Amendments) Order 2008 (S.I. 2008/1241), art. 4(a)

437 Entry in Sch. 1 Pt. VII inserted (8.10.2001) by S.I. 2001/2565, arts. 1(2), 4; S.R. 2001/337, art. 2

438 Sch. 1 Pt. VII: entries repealed (N.I.) (1.4.2002) by Industrial Development Act (Northern Ireland) 2002 (c. 1 (N.I.)), s. 5(4), Sch. 4 (with Sch. 2 paras. 1(4), 4(4), 6(4)); S.R. 2002/134, art. 2

439 Sch. 1 Pt. VII: entry added (11.11.2002) by The Freedom of Information (Additional Public Authorities) Order 2002 (S.I. 2002/2623), art. 3, Sch. 2

440 Sch. 1 Pt. VII: entry repealed (N.I.) (1.4.2009) by Health and Social Care (Reform) Act (Northern Ireland) 2009 (c. 1), ss. 32, 33, 34, Sch. 6 para. 17(3), Sch. 7; S.R. 2009/114, art. 2

441 Sch. 1 Pt. VII: entry repealed (29.12.2003) by Communications Act 2003 (c. 21), ss. 406(6)(7), 411(2), Sch. 19(1) (with Sch 18, Sch. 19(1) Note 1); S.I. 2003/3142, art. 3(1), Sch. 1 (subject to art. 3(3) and with art. 11)

442 Sch.1 Pt.VII: entry inserted (N.I.)(1.4.2007) by The Water and Sewerage Services (Northern Ireland) Order 2006 (S.I.2006/3336 (N.I. 21)), arts.1(2), 308(1), Sch.12 para. 43 (with art. 307); S.R. 2007/194, art.2(2), Sch.1 Pt.2 (subject to art.3)

443 Sch. 1 Pt. VII: entries removed (29.6.2004) by virtue of The Freedom of Information (Removal of References to Public Authorities) Order 2004 (S.I. 2004/1641), art. 3, Sch. 2

444 Sch. 1 Pt. VII: entries removed (29.6.2004) by virtue of The Freedom of Information (Removal of References to Public Authorities) Order 2004 (S.I. 2004/1641), art. 3, Sch. 2

445 Sch. 1 Pt. VII: entry inserted (1.10.2009) by Constitutional Reform Act 2005 (c. 4), ss. 59(5), 148(1), Sch. 11 para. 34(b); S.I. 2009/1604, art. 2(d)

446 Sch. 1 Pt. VII: entries removed (7.2.2006) by virtue of The Freedom of Information (Removal of References to Public Authorities) Order 2005 (S.I. 2005/3594), art. 2, Sch. 1

447 Sch. 1 Pt. VII: entry added (1.6.2006) by The Freedom of Information (Additional Public Authorities) Order 2005 (S.I. 2005/3593), art. 5, Sch. 4

448 Sch. 1 Pt. VII: entry inserted (N.I.) (1.7.2006) by The Fire and Rescue Services (Northern Ireland) Order 2006 (S.I. 2006/1254 (N.I. 9)), arts. 1(3), 3(3), Sch. 1 para. 19 (with art. 49); S.R. 2006/257, art. 2(a)(c)

449 Sch. 1 Pt. VII: entry added (7.2.2006) by The Freedom of Information (Additional Public Authorities) Order 2005 (S.I. 2005/3593), art. 4, Sch. 3

450 Sch. 1 Pt. VII: entry inserted (15.6.2005) by Justice (Northern Ireland) Act 2002 (c. 26), ss. 3(3), 87(1), Sch. 2 para. 20; S.R. 2005/281, art. 3(1), Sch. 2 paras. 2, 6 (subject to art. 3(2)(3))

451 Sch. 1 Pt. VII: entry inserted (16.4.2007) by Justice (Northern Ireland) Act 2002 (c. 26), ss. 50(7), 87(1), Sch. 9 para. 15; S.R. 2007/237, art. 2, Sch. paras. 1, 5

452 Sch. 1 Pt. VII: entry inserted (N.I.) (20.3.2006) by Access to Justice (Northern Ireland) Order 2003 (S.I. 2003/435 (N.I. 10)), arts. 1(2), 49(1), Sch. 4 para. 15 (with arts. 45, 48(2)(3), Sch. 3); S.R. 2006/27, arts. 1, 2

453 Sch. 1 Pt. VII: entry inserted (N.I.) (1.10.2008) by Libraries Act (Northern Ireland) 2008 (c. 8), ss. 10, 12, Sch. 3 para. 6; S.R. 2008/396, art. 2(h)

454 Sch. 1 Pt. VII: entry repealed (N.I.) (1.6.2009) by Public Authorities (Reform) Act (Northern Ireland) 2009 (c. 3), ss. 6, 7, Sch. 3; S.R. 2009/172, art. 2(e)

455 Sch. 1 Pt. VII: entry inserted (11.8.2003) by The Freedom of Information (Additional Public Authorities) Order 2003 (S.I. 2003/1882), art. 3, Sch. 2

456 Sch. 1 Pt. VII: entry inserted (11.8.2003) by The Freedom of Information (Additional Public Authorities) Order 2003 (S.I. 2003/1882), art. 3, Sch. 2

457 Sch. 1 Pt. VII: entry repealed (1.10.2009) by Constitutional Reform Act 2005 (c. 4), ss. 59(5), 148(1), Sch. 11 para. 34(a), Sch. 18 Pt. 5; S.I. 2009/1604, art. 2(f)

458 Sch. 1 Pt. VII: entry repealed (N.I.) (1.4.2007) by The Water and Sewerage Services (Northern Ireland) Order 2006 (S.I. 2006/3336 (N.I. 21)), arts. 1(2), 308(2), Sch. 13 (with art. 307); S.R. 2007/194, art. 2(2), Sch. 1 Pt. 2 (subject to art. 3)

459 Sch. 1 Pt. VII: entries removed (7.2.2006) by virtue of The Freedom of Information (Removal of References to Public Authorities) Order 2005 (S.I. 2005/3594), art. 2, Sch. 1

460 Sch. 1 Pt. VII: entry added (19.4.2004) by The Freedom of Information (Additional Public Authorities) Order 2004 (S.I.

2004/938), art. 4, Sch. 3

461 Sch. 1 Pt. VII: entry inserted (15.5.2008) by virtue of The Criminal Justice (Northern Ireland Consequential Amendments) Order 2008 (S.I. 2008/1241), art. 4(b)

462 Sch. 1 Pt. VII: entry added (1.6.2006) by The Freedom of Information (Additional Public Authorities) Order 2005 (S.I. 2005/3593), art. 5, Sch. 4

463 Sch. 1 Pt. VII: entry added (7.2.2006) by The Freedom of Information (Additional Public Authorities) Order 2005 (S.I. 2005/3593), art. 4, Sch. 3

464 Sch. 1 Pt. VII: entry inserted (N.I.) (4.9.2007) by Police (Northern Ireland) Act 2003 (c. 6), s. 19, Sch. 1 para. 15; S.R. 2007/371, art. 2(c)

465 Sch. 1 Pt. VII: entries removed (29.6.2004) by virtue of The Freedom of Information (Removal of References to Public Authorities) Order 2004 (S.I. 2004/1641), art. 3, Sch. 2

466 Sch. 1 Pt. VII: entry added (11.11.2002) by The Freedom of Information (Additional Public Authorities) Order 2002 (S.I. 2002/2623), art. 3, Sch. 2

467 Sch. 1 Pt. VII: entry inserted (11.8.2003) by The Freedom of Information (Additional Public Authorities) Order 2003 (S.I. 2003/1882), art. 3, Sch. 2

468 Sch. 1 Pt. 1 para. 1A inserted (1.4.2007) by Education and Inspections Act 2006 (c. 40), ss. 157, 188, Sch. 14 para. 69(2)(b); S.I. 2007/935, art. 5(gg)

469 Words in Sch. 3 para. 1(1) inserted (1.4.2005) by Courts Act 2003 (c. 39), ss. 65(2), 110(1), Sch. 4 para. 13; S.I. 2005/910, art. 3(u)

470 Sch. 7 para. 7 repealed (1.4.2006 for W.) by Public Services Ombudsman (Wales) Act 2005 (c. 10), ss. 39, 40, Sch. 7; S.I. 2005/2800, art. 5

471 Sch. 7 para. 8 repealed (1.4.2006 for W.) by Public Services Ombudsman (Wales) Act 2005 (c. 10), ss. 39, 40, Sch. 7; S.I. 2005/2800, art. 5

472 Sch. 7 para. 13 repealed (S.) (23.10.2002) by Scottish Public Services Ombudsman Act 2002 (asp 11), s. 26, Sch. 6 para. 23(3); S.S.I. 2002/467, art. 2

Trustee Act 2000

2000 CHAPTER 29

An Act to amend the law relating to trustees and persons having the investment powers of trustees; and for connected purposes.

[23rd November 2000]

Part I The Duty of Care

1 The duty of care

(1) Whenever the duty under this subsection applies to a trustee, he must exercise such care and skill as is reasonable in the circumstances, having regard in particular—

(a) to any special knowledge or experience that he has or holds himself out as having, and

(b) if he acts as trustee in the course of a business or profession, to any special knowledge or experience that it is reasonable to expect of a person acting in the course of that kind of business or profession.

(2) In this Act the duty under subsection (1) is called "the duty of care".

2 Application of duty of care

Schedule 1 makes provision about when the duty of care applies to a trustee.

Part II Investment

3 General power of investment

(1) Subject to the provisions of this Part, a trustee may make any kind of investment that he could make if he were absolutely entitled to the assets of the trust.

(2) In this Act the power under subsection (1) is called "the general power of investment".

(3) The general power of investment does not permit a trustee to make investments in land other than in loans secured on land (but see also section 8).

(4) A person invests in a loan secured on land if he has rights under any contract under which—

(a) one person provides another with credit, and

(b) the obligation of the borrower to repay is secured on land.

(5) "Credit" includes any cash loan or other financial accommodation.

(6) "Cash" includes money in any form.

4 Standard investment criteria

(1) In exercising any power of investment, whether arising under this Part or otherwise, a trustee must have regard to the standard investment criteria.

(2) A trustee must from time to time review the investments of the trust and consider whether, having regard to the standard investment criteria, they should be varied.

(3) The standard investment criteria, in relation to a trust, are—

(a) the suitability to the trust of investments of the same kind as any particular investment proposed to be made or retained and of that particular investment as an investment of that kind, and

(b) the need for diversification of investments of the trust, in so far as is appropriate to the circumstances of the trust.

5 Advice

(1) Before exercising any power of investment, whether arising under this Part or otherwise, a trustee must (unless the exception applies) obtain and consider proper advice about the way in which, having regard to the standard investment criteria, the power should be exercised.

(2) When reviewing the investments of the trust, a trustee must (unless the exception applies) obtain and consider proper advice about whether, having regard to the standard investment criteria, the investments should be varied.

(3) The exception is that a trustee need not obtain such advice if he reasonably concludes that in all the circumstances it is unnecessary or inappropriate to do so.

(4) Proper advice is the advice of a person who is reasonably believed by the trustee to be qualified to give it by his ability in and practical experience of financial and other matters relating to the proposed investment.

6 Restriction or exclusion of this Part etc.

(1) The general power of investment is—

(a) in addition to powers conferred on trustees otherwise than by this Act, but

(b) subject to any restriction or exclusion imposed by the trust instrument or by any enactment or any provision of subordinate legislation.

(2) For the purposes of this Act, an enactment or a provision of subordinate legislation is not to be regarded as being, or as being part of, a trust instrument.

(3) In this Act "subordinate legislation" has the same meaning as in the Interpretation Act 1978.

7 Existing trusts

(1) This Part applies in relation to trusts whether created before or after its commencement.

(2) No provision relating to the powers of a trustee contained in a trust instrument made before 3rd August 1961 is to be treated (for the purposes of section 6(1)(b)) as restricting or excluding the general power of investment.

(3) A provision contained in a trust instrument made before the commencement of this Part which—

(a) has effect under section 3(2) of the Trustee Investments Act 1961 as a power to invest under that Act, or

(b) confers power to invest under that Act,

is to be treated as conferring the general power of investment on a trustee.

Part III Acquisition of Land

8 Power to acquire freehold and leasehold land

(1) A trustee may acquire freehold or leasehold land in the United Kingdom—

(a) as an investment,

(b) for occupation by a beneficiary, or

(c) for any other reason.

(2) "Freehold or leasehold land" means—

(a) in relation to England and Wales, a legal estate in land,

(b) in relation to Scotland—

(i) the estate or interest of the proprietor of the dominium utile or, in the case of land not held on feudal tenure, the estate or interest of the owner, or

(ii) a tenancy, and

(c) in relation to Northern Ireland, a legal estate in land, including land held under a fee farm grant.

(3) For the purpose of exercising his functions as a trustee, a trustee who acquires land under this section has all the powers of an absolute owner in relation to the land.

9 Restriction or exclusion of this Part etc.

The powers conferred by this Part are—

(a) in addition to powers conferred on trustees otherwise than by this Part, but

(b) subject to any restriction or exclusion imposed by the trust instrument or by any enactment or any provision of subordinate legislation.

10 Existing trusts

(1) This Part does not apply in relation to—

(a) a trust of property which consists of or includes land which (despite section 2 of the Trusts of Land and Appointment of Trustees Act 1996) is settled land, or

(b) a trust to which the Universities and College Estates Act 1925 applies.

(2) Subject to subsection (1), this Part applies in relation to trusts whether created before or after its commencement.

Part IV Agents, nominees and custodians

Agents

11 Power to employ agents

(1) Subject to the provisions of this Part, the trustees of a trust may authorise any person to exercise any or all of their delegable functions as their agent.

(2) In the case of a trust other than a charitable trust, the trustees' delegable functions consist of any function other than—

(a) any function relating to whether or in what way any assets of the trust should be distributed,

(b) any power to decide whether any fees or other payment due to be made out of the trust funds should be made out of income or capital,

(c) any power to appoint a person to be a trustee of the trust, or

(d) any power conferred by any other enactment or the trust instrument which permits the trustees to delegate any of their functions or to appoint a person to act as a nominee or custodian.

(3) In the case of a charitable trust, the trustees' delegable functions are—

(a) any function consisting of carrying out a decision that the trustees have taken;

(b) any function relating to the investment of assets subject to the trust (including, in the case of land held as an investment, managing the land and creating or disposing of an interest in the land);

(c) any function relating to the raising of funds for the trust otherwise than by means of profits of a trade which is an integral part of carrying out the trust's charitable purpose;

(d) any other function prescribed by an order made by the Secretary of State.

(4) For the purposes of subsection (3)(c) a trade is an integral part of carrying out a trust's charitable purpose if, whether carried on in the United Kingdom or elsewhere, the profits are applied solely to the purposes of the trust and either—

(a) the trade is exercised in the course of the actual carrying out of a primary purpose of the trust, or

(b) the work in connection with the trade is mainly carried out by beneficiaries of the trust.

(5) The power to make an order under subsection (3)(d) is exercisable by statutory instrument which shall be subject to annulment in pursuance of a resolution of either House of Parliament.

12 Persons who may act as agents

(1) Subject to subsection (2), the persons whom the trustees may under section 11 authorise to exercise functions as their agent include one or more of their number.

(2) The trustees may not authorise two (or more) persons to exercise the same function unless they are to exercise the function jointly.

(3) The trustees may not under section 11 authorise a beneficiary to exercise any function as their agent (even if the beneficiary is also a trustee).

(4) The trustees may under section 11 authorise a person to exercise functions as their agent even though he is also appointed to act as their nominee or custodian (whether under section 16, 17 or 18 or any other power).

13 Linked functions etc.

(1) Subject to subsections (2) and (5), a person who is authorised under section 11 to exercise a function is (whatever the terms of the agency) subject to any specific duties or restrictions attached to the function.

For example, a person who is authorised under section 11 to exercise the general power of investment is subject to the duties under section 4 in relation to that power.

(2) A person who is authorised under section 11 to exercise a power which is subject to a requirement to obtain advice is not subject to the requirement if he is the kind of person from whom it would have been proper for the trustees, in compliance with the requirement, to obtain advice.

(3) Subsections (4) and (5) apply to a trust to which section 11(1) of the Trusts of Land and Appointment of Trustees Act 1996 (duties to consult beneficiaries and give effect to their wishes) applies.

(4) The trustees may not under section 11 authorise a person to exercise any of their functions on terms that prevent them from complying with section 11(1) of the 1996 Act.

(5) a person who is authorised under section 11 to exercise any function relating to land subject to the trust is not subject to section 11(1) of the 1996 Act.

14 Terms of agency

(1) Subject to subsection (2) and sections 15(2) and 29 to 32, the trustees may authorise a person to exercise functions as their agent on such terms as to remuneration and other matters as they may determine.

(2) The trustees may not authorise a person to exercise functions as their agent on any of the terms mentioned in subsection (3) unless it is reasonably necessary for them to do so.

(3) The terms are—

(a) a term permitting the agent to appoint a substitute;

(b) a term restricting the liability of the agent or his substitute to the trustees or any beneficiary;

(c) a term permitting the agent to act in circumstances capable of giving rise to a conflict of interest.

15 Asset management: special restrictions

(1) The trustees may not authorise a person to exercise any of their asset management functions as their agent except by an agreement which is in or evidenced in writing.

(2) The trustees may not authorise a person to exercise any of their asset management functions as their agent unless—

(a) they have prepared a statement that gives guidance as to how the functions should be exercised ("a policy statement"), and

(b) the agreement under which the agent is to act includes a term to the effect that he will secure compliance with—

(i) the policy statement, or

(ii) if the policy statement is revised or replaced under section 22, the revised or replacement policy statement.

(3) The trustees must formulate any guidance given in the policy statement with a view to ensuring that the functions will be exercised in the best interests of the trust.

(4) The policy statement must be in or evidenced in writing.

(5) The asset management functions of trustees are their functions relating to—

(a) the investment of assets subject to the trust,

(b) the acquisition of property which is to be subject to the trust, and

(c) managing property which is subject to the trust and disposing of, or creating or disposing of an interest in, such property.

Nominees and custodians

16 Power to appoint nominees

(1) Subject to the provisions of this Part, the trustees of a trust may—

(a) appoint a person to act as their nominee in relation to such of the assets of the trust as they determine (other than settled land), and

(b) take such steps as are necessary to secure that those assets are vested in a person so appointed.

(2) An appointment under this section must be in or evidenced in writing.

(3) This section does not apply to any trust having a custodian trustee or in relation to any assets vested

in the official custodian for charities.

17 Power to appoint custodians

(1) Subject to the provisions of this Part, the trustees of a trust may appoint a person to act as a custodian in relation to such of the assets of the trust as they may determine.

(2) For the purposes of this Act a person is a custodian in relation to assets if he undertakes the safe custody of the assets or of any documents or records concerning the assets.

(3) An appointment under this section must be in or evidenced in writing.

(4) This section does not apply to any trust having a custodian trustee or in relation to any assets vested in the official custodian for charities.

18 Investment in bearer securities

(1) If trustees retain or invest in securities payable to bearer, they must appoint a person to act as a custodian of the securities.

(2) Subsection (1) does not apply if the trust instrument or any enactment or provision of subordinate legislation contains provision which (however expressed) permits the trustees to retain or invest in securities payable to bearer without appointing a person to act as a custodian.

(3) An appointment under this section must be in or evidenced in writing.

(4) This section does not apply to any trust having a custodian trustee or in relation to any securities vested in the official custodian for charities.

19 Persons who may be appointed as nominees or custodians

(1) A person may not be appointed under section 16, 17 or 18 as a nominee or custodian unless one of the relevant conditions is satisfied.

(2) The relevant conditions are that—

(a) the person carries on a business which consists of or includes acting as a nominee or custodian;

(b) the person is a body corporate which is controlled by the trustees;

(c) the person is a body corporate recognised under section 9 of the Administration of Justice Act 1985.

(3) The question whether a body corporate is controlled by trustees is to be determined in accordance with section 840 of the Income and Corporation Taxes Act 1988.

(4) The trustees of a charitable trust which is not an exempt charity must act in accordance with any guidance given by the Charity Commissioners concerning the selection of a person for appointment as a nominee or custodian under section 16, 17 or 18.

(5) Subject to subsections (1) and (4), the persons whom the trustees may under section 16, 17 or 18 appoint as a nominee or custodian include—

(a) one of their number, if that one is a trust corporation, or

(b) two (or more) of their number, if they are to act as joint nominees or joint custodians.

(6) The trustees may under section 16 appoint a person to act as their nominee even though he is also—

(a) appointed to act as their custodian (whether under section 17 or 18 or any other power), or

(b) authorised to exercise functions as their agent (whether under section 11 or any other power).

(7) Likewise, the trustees may under section 17 or 18 appoint a person to act as their custodian even though he is also—

(a) appointed to act as their nominee (whether under section 16 or any other power), or

(b) authorised to exercise functions as their agent (whether under section 11 or any other power).

20 Terms of appointment of nominees and custodians

(1) Subject to subsection (2) and sections 29 to 32, the trustees may under section 16, 17 or 18 appoint a person to act as a nominee or custodian on such terms as to remuneration and other matters as they may determine.

(2) The trustees may not under section 16, 17 or 18 appoint a person to act as a nominee or custodian on any of the terms mentioned in subsection (3) unless it is reasonably necessary for them to do so.

(3) The terms are—

(a) a term permitting the nominee or custodian to appoint a substitute;

(b) a term restricting the liability of the nominee or custodian or his substitute to the trustees or to any beneficiary;

(c) a term permitting the nominee or custodian to act in circumstances capable of giving rise to a

conflict of interest.

Review of and liability for agents, nominees and custodians etc.

21 Application of sections 22 and 23

(1) Sections 22 and 23 apply in a case where trustees have, under section 11, 16, 17 or 18—

(a) authorised a person to exercise functions as their agent, or

(b) appointed a person to act as a nominee or custodian.

(2) Subject to subsection (3), sections 22 and 23 also apply in a case where trustees have, under any power conferred on them by the trust instrument or by any enactment or any provision of subordinate legislation—

(a) authorised a person to exercise functions as their agent, or

(b) appointed a person to act as a nominee or custodian.

(3) If the application of section 22 or 23 is inconsistent with the terms of the trust instrument or the enactment or provision of subordinate legislation, the section in question does not apply.

22 Review of agents, nominees and custodians etc.

(1) While the agent, nominee or custodian continues to act for the trust, the trustees—

(a) must keep under review the arrangements under which the agent, nominee or custodian acts and how those arrangements are being put into effect,

(b) if circumstances make it appropriate to do so, must consider whether there is a need to exercise any power of intervention that they have, and

(c) if they consider that there is a need to exercise such a power, must do so.

(2) If the agent has been authorised to exercise asset management functions, the duty under subsection (1) includes, in particular—

(a) a duty to consider whether there is any need to revise or replace the policy statement made for the purposes of section 15,

(b) if they consider that there is a need to revise or replace the policy statement, a duty to do so, and

(c) a duty to assess whether the policy statement (as it has effect for the time being) is being complied with.

(3) Subsections (3) and (4) of section 15 apply to the revision or replacement of a policy statement under this section as they apply to the making of a policy statement under that section.

(4) "Power of intervention" includes—

(a) a power to give directions to the agent, nominee or custodian;

(b) a power to revoke the authorisation or appointment.

23 Liability for agents, nominees and custodians etc.

(1) a trustee is not liable for any act or default of the agent, nominee or custodian unless he has failed to comply with the duty of care applicable to him, under paragraph 3 of Schedule 1—

(a) when entering into the arrangements under which the person acts as agent, nominee or custodian, or

(b) when carrying out his duties under section 22.

(2) If a trustee has agreed a term under which the agent, nominee or custodian is permitted to appoint a substitute, the trustee is not liable for any act or default of the substitute unless he has failed to comply with the duty of care applicable to him, under paragraph 3 of Schedule 1—

(a) when agreeing that term, or

(b) when carrying out his duties under section 22 in so far as they relate to the use of the substitute.

Supplementary

24 Effect of trustees exceeding their powers

A failure by the trustees to act within the limits of the powers conferred by this Part—

(a) in authorising a person to exercise a function of theirs as an agent, or

(b) in appointing a person to act as a nominee or custodian,

does not invalidate the authorisation or appointment.

25 Sole trustees

(1) Subject to subsection (2), this Part applies in relation to a trust having a sole trustee as it applies in relation to other trusts (and references in this Part to trustees—except in sections 12(1) and (3) and

19(5)—are to be read accordingly).

(2) Section 18 does not impose a duty on a sole trustee if that trustee is a trust corporation.

26 Restriction or exclusion of this Part etc.

The powers conferred by this Part are—

(a) in addition to powers conferred on trustees otherwise than by this Act, but

(b) subject to any restriction or exclusion imposed by the trust instrument or by any enactment or any provision of subordinate legislation.

27 Existing trusts

This Part applies in relation to trusts whether created before or after its commencement.

Part V Remuneration

28 Trustee's entitlement to payment under trust instrument

(1) Except to the extent (if any) to which the trust instrument makes inconsistent provision, subsections (2) to (4) apply to a trustee if—

(a) there is a provision in the trust instrument entitling him to receive payment out of trust funds in respect of services provided by him to or on behalf of the trust, and

(b) the trustee is a trust corporation or is acting in a professional capacity.

(2) The trustee is to be treated as entitled under the trust instrument to receive payment in respect of services even if they are services which are capable of being provided by a lay trustee.

(3) Subsection (2) applies to a trustee of a charitable trust who is not a trust corporation only—

(a) if he is not a sole trustee, and

(b) to the extent that a majority of the other trustees have agreed that it should apply to him.

(4) Any payments to which the trustee is entitled in respect of services are to be treated as remuneration for services (and not as a gift) for the purposes of—

(a) section 15 of the Wills Act 1837 (gifts to an attesting witness to be void), and

(b) section 34(3) of the Administration of Estates Act 1925 (order in which estate to be paid out).

(5) For the purposes of this Part, a trustee acts in a professional capacity if he acts in the course of a profession or business which consists of or includes the provision of services in connection with—

(a) the management or administration of trusts generally or a particular kind of trust, or

(b) any particular aspect of the management or administration of trusts generally or a particular kind of trust,

and the services he provides to or on behalf of the trust fall within that description.

(6) For the purposes of this Part, a person acts as a lay trustee if he—

(a) is not a trust corporation, and

(b) does not act in a professional capacity.

29 Remuneration of certain trustees

(1) Subject to subsection (5), a trustee who—

(a) is a trust corporation, but

(b) is not a trustee of a charitable trust,

is entitled to receive reasonable remuneration out of the trust funds for any services that the trust corporation provides to or on behalf of the trust.

(2) Subject to subsection (5), a trustee who—

(a) acts in a professional capacity, but

(b) is not a trust corporation, a trustee of a charitable trust or a sole trustee,

is entitled to receive reasonable remuneration out of the trust funds for any services that he provides to or on behalf of the trust if each other trustee has agreed in writing that he may be remunerated for the services.

(3) "Reasonable remuneration" means, in relation to the provision of services by a trustee, such remuneration as is reasonable in the circumstances for the provision of those services to or on behalf of that trust by that trustee and for the purposes of subsection (1) includes, in relation to the provision of services by a trustee who is an authorised institution under the Banking Act 1987 and provides the services in that capacity, the institution's reasonable charges for the provision of such services.

(4) A trustee is entitled to remuneration under this section even if the services in question are capable of

being provided by a lay trustee.

(5) a trustee is not entitled to remuneration under this section if any provision about his entitlement to remuneration has been made—

(a) by the trust instrument, or

(b) by any enactment or any provision of subordinate legislation.

(6) This section applies to a trustee who has been authorised under a power conferred by Part IV or the trust instrument—

(a) to exercise functions as an agent of the trustees, or

(b) to act as a nominee or custodian,

as it applies to any other trustee.

30 Remuneration of trustees of charitable trusts

(1) The Secretary of State may by regulations make provision for the remuneration of trustees of charitable trusts who are trust corporations or act in a professional capacity.

(2) The power under subsection (1) includes power to make provision for the remuneration of a trustee who has been authorised under a power conferred by Part IV or any other enactment or any provision of subordinate legislation, or by the trust instrument—

(a) to exercise functions as an agent of the trustees, or

(b) to act as a nominee or custodian.

(3) Regulations under this section may—

(a) make different provision for different cases;

(b) contain such supplemental, incidental, consequential and transitional provision as the Secretary of State considers appropriate.

(4) The power to make regulations under this section is exercisable by statutory instrument, but no such instrument shall be made unless a draft of it has been laid before Parliament and approved by a resolution of each House of Parliament.

31 Trustees' expenses

(1) a trustee—

(a) is entitled to be reimbursed from the trust funds, or

(b) may pay out of the trust funds,

expenses properly incurred by him when acting on behalf of the trust.

(2) This section applies to a trustee who has been authorised under a power conferred by Part IV or any other enactment or any provision of subordinate legislation, or by the trust instrument—

(a) to exercise functions as an agent of the trustees, or

(b) to act as a nominee or custodian,

as it applies to any other trustee.

32 Remuneration and expenses of agents, nominees and custodians

(1) This section applies if, under a power conferred by Part IV or any other enactment or any provision of subordinate legislation, or by the trust instrument, a person other than a trustee has been—

(a) authorised to exercise functions as an agent of the trustees, or

(b) appointed to act as a nominee or custodian.

(2) The trustees may remunerate the agent, nominee or custodian out of the trust funds for services if—

(a) he is engaged on terms entitling him to be remunerated for those services, and

(b) the amount does not exceed such remuneration as is reasonable in the circumstances for the provision of those services by him to or on behalf of that trust.

(3) The trustees may reimburse the agent, nominee or custodian out of the trust funds for any expenses properly incurred by him in exercising functions as an agent, nominee or custodian.

33 Application

(1) Subject to subsection (2), sections 28, 29, 31 and 32 apply in relation to services provided to or on behalf of, or (as the case may be) expenses incurred on or after their commencement on behalf of, trusts whenever created.

(2) Nothing in section 28 or 29 is to be treated as affecting the operation of—

(a) section 15 of the Wills Act 1837, or

(b) section 34(3) of the Administration of Estates Act 1925,

in relation to any death occurring before the commencement of section 28 or (as the case may be) section 29.

Part VI Miscellaneous and Supplementary

34 Power to insure

(1) For section 19 of the Trustee Act 1925 (power to insure) substitute—

"**19 Power to insure.**

(1) a trustee may—

(a) insure any property which is subject to the trust against risks of loss or damage due to any event, and

(b) pay the premiums out of the trust funds.

(2) In the case of property held on a bare trust, the power to insure is subject to any direction given by the beneficiary or each of the beneficiaries—

(a) that any property specified in the direction is not to be insured;

(b) that any property specified in the direction is not to be insured except on such conditions as may be so specified.

(3) Property is held on a bare trust if it is held on trust for—

(a) a beneficiary who is of full age and capacity and absolutely entitled to the property subject to the trust, or

(b) beneficiaries each of whom is of full age and capacity and who (taken together) are absolutely entitled to the property subject to the trust.

(4) If a direction under subsection (2) of this section is given, the power to insure, so far as it is subject to the direction, ceases to be a delegable function for the purposes of section 11 of the Trustee Act 2000 (power to employ agents).

(5) In this section "trust funds" means any income or capital funds of the trust."

(2) In section 20(1) of the Trustee Act 1925 (application of insurance money) omit "whether by fire or otherwise".

(3) The amendments made by this section apply in relation to trusts whether created before or after its commencement.

35 Personal representatives

(1) Subject to the following provisions of this section, this Act applies in relation to a personal representative administering an estate according to the law as it applies to a trustee carrying out a trust for beneficiaries.

(2) For this purpose this Act is to be read with the appropriate modifications and in particular—

(a) references to the trust instrument are to be read as references to the will,

(b) references to a beneficiary or to beneficiaries, apart from the reference to a beneficiary in section 8(1)(b), are to be read as references to a person or the persons interested in the due administration of the estate, and

(c) the reference to a beneficiary in section 8(1)(b) is to be read as a reference to a person who under the will of the deceased or under the law relating to intestacy is beneficially interested in the estate.

(3) Remuneration to which a personal representative is entitled under section 28 or 29 is to be treated as an administration expense for the purposes of—

(a) section 34(3) of the Administration of Estates Act 1925 (order in which estate to be paid out), and

(b) any provision giving reasonable administration expenses priority over the preferential debts listed in Schedule 6 to the Insolvency Act 1986.

(4) Nothing in subsection (3) is to be treated as affecting the operation of the provisions mentioned in paragraphs (a) and (b) of that subsection in relation to any death occurring before the commencement of this section.

36 Pension schemes

(1) In this section "pension scheme" means an occupational pension scheme (within the meaning of the Pension Schemes Act 1993) established under a trust and subject to the law of England and Wales.

(2) Part I does not apply in so far as it imposes a duty of care in relation to—

(a) the functions described in paragraphs 1 and 2 of Schedule 1, or

(b) the functions described in paragraph 3 of that Schedule to the extent that they relate to trustees—

(i) authorising a person to exercise their functions with respect to investment, or

(ii) appointing a person to act as their nominee or custodian.

(3) Nothing in Part II or III applies to the trustees of any pension scheme.

(4) Part IV applies to the trustees of a pension scheme subject to the restrictions in subsections (5) to (8).

(5) The trustees of a pension scheme may not under Part IV authorise any person to exercise any functions relating to investment as their agent.

(6) The trustees of a pension scheme may not under Part IV authorise a person who is—

(a) an employer in relation to the scheme, or

(b) connected with or an associate of such an employer,

to exercise any of their functions as their agent.

(7) For the purposes of subsection (6)—

(a) "employer", in relation to a scheme, has the same meaning as in the Pensions Act 1995;

(b) sections 249 and 435 of the Insolvency Act 1986 apply for the purpose of determining whether a person is connected with or an associate of an employer.

(8) Sections 16 to 20 (powers to appoint nominees and custodians) do not apply to the trustees of a pension scheme.

37 Authorised unit trusts

(1) Parts II to IV do not apply to trustees of authorised unit trusts.

(2)"Authorised unit trust" means a unit trust scheme in the case of which an order under section 78 of the Financial Services Act 1986 is in force.

38 Common investment schemes for charities etc.

Parts II to IV do not apply to—

(a) trustees managing a fund under a common investment scheme made, or having effect as if made, under section 24 of the Charities Act 1993, other than such a fund the trusts of which provide that property is not to be transferred to the fund except by or on behalf of a charity the trustees of which are the trustees appointed to manage the fund, or

(b) trustees managing a fund under a common deposit scheme made, or having effect as if made, under section 25 of that Act.

39 Interpretation

(1) In this Act—

"asset" includes any right or interest;

"charitable trust" means a trust under which property is held for charitable purposes and "charitable purposes" has the same meaning as in the Charities Act 1993;

"custodian trustee" has the same meaning as in the Public Trustee Act 1906;

"enactment" includes any provision of a Measure of the Church Assembly or of the General Synod of the Church of England;

"exempt charity" has the same meaning as in the Charities Act 1993;

"functions" includes powers and duties;

"legal mortgage" has the same meaning as in the Law of Property Act 1925;

"personal representative" has the same meaning as in the Trustee Act 1925;

"settled land" has the same meaning as in the Settled Land Act 1925;

"trust corporation" has the same meaning as in the Trustee Act 1925;

"trust funds" means income or capital funds of the trust.

(2) In this Act the expressions listed below are defined or otherwise explained by the provisions indicated—

asset management functions	section 15(5)
custodian	section 17(2)
the duty of care	section 1(2)
the general power of investment	section 3(2)
lay trustee	section 28(6)
power of intervention	section 22(4)
the standard investment criteria	section 4(3)
subordinate legislation	section 6(3)

trustee acting in a professional capacity	section 28(5)
trust instrument	sections 6(2) and 35(2)(a)

40 Minor and consequential amendments etc.

(1) Schedule 2 (minor and consequential amendments) shall have effect.

(2) Schedule 3 (transitional provisions and savings) shall have effect.

(3) Schedule 4 (repeals) shall have effect.

41 Power to amend other Acts

(1) A Minister of the Crown may by order make such amendments of any Act, including an Act extending to places outside England and Wales, as appear to him appropriate in consequence of or in connection with Part II or III.

(2) Before exercising the power under subsection (1) in relation to a local, personal or private Act, the Minister must consult any person who appears to him to be affected by any proposed amendment.

(3) An order under this section may—

(a) contain such transitional provisions and savings as the Minister thinks fit;

(b) make different provision for different purposes.

(4) The power to make an order under this section is exercisable by statutory instrument which shall be subject to annulment in pursuance of a resolution of either House of Parliament.

(5) "Minister of the Crown" has the same meaning as in the Ministers of the Crown Act 1975.

42 Commencement and extent

(1) Section 41, this section and section 43 shall come into force on the day on which this Act is passed.

(2) The remaining provisions of this Act shall come into force on such day as the Lord Chancellor may appoint by order made by statutory instrument; and different days may be so appointed for different purposes.

(3) An order under subsection (2) may contain such transitional provisions and savings as the Lord Chancellor considers appropriate in connection with the order.

(4) Subject to section 41(1) and subsection (5), this Act extends to England and Wales only.

(5) An amendment or repeal in Part II or III of Schedule 2 or Part II of Schedule 4 has the same extent as the provision amended or repealed.

43 Short title

This Act may be cited as the Trustee Act 2000.

SCHEDULES

Section 2.

SCHEDULE 1 Application of duty of care

Investment

1 The duty of care applies to a trustee—

(a) when exercising the general power of investment or any other power of investment, however conferred;

(b) when carrying out a duty to which he is subject under section 4 or 5 (duties relating to the exercise of a power of investment or to the review of investments).

Acquisition of land

2 The duty of care applies to a trustee—

(a) when exercising the power under section 8 to acquire land;

(b) when exercising any other power to acquire land, however conferred;

(c) when exercising any power in relation to land acquired under a power mentioned in sub-paragraph (a) or (b).

Agents, nominees and custodians

3(1) The duty of care applies to a trustee—

(a) when entering into arrangements under which a person is authorised under section 11 to exercise functions as an agent;

(b) when entering into arrangements under which a person is appointed under section 16 to act as a nominee;

(c) when entering into arrangements under which a person is appointed under section 17 or 18 to act

as a custodian;

(d) when entering into arrangements under which, under any other power, however conferred, a person is authorised to exercise functions as an agent or is appointed to act as a nominee or custodian;

(e) when carrying out his duties under section 22 (review of agent, nominee or custodian, etc.).

(2) For the purposes of sub-paragraph (1), entering into arrangements under which a person is authorised to exercise functions or is appointed to act as a nominee or custodian includes, in particular—

(a) selecting the person who is to act,

(b) determining any terms on which he is to act, and

(c) if the person is being authorised to exercise asset management functions, the preparation of a policy statement under section 15.

Compounding of liabilities

4 The duty of care applies to a trustee—

(a) when exercising the power under section 15 of the Trustee Act 1925 to do any of the things referred to in that section;

(b) when exercising any corresponding power, however conferred.

Insurance

5 The duty of care applies to a trustee—

(a) when exercising the power under section 19 of the Trustee Act 1925 to insure property;

(b) when exercising any corresponding power, however conferred.

Reversionary interests, valuations and audit

6 The duty of care applies to a trustee—

(a) when exercising the power under section 22(1) or (3) of the Trustee Act 1925 to do any of the things referred to there;

(b) when exercising any corresponding power, however conferred.

Exclusion of duty of care

7 The duty of care does not apply if or in so far as it appears from the trust instrument that the duty is not meant to apply.

Section 40.

SCHEDULE 2 Minor and consequential amendments

Part I The Trustee Investments Act 1961 and the Charities Act 1993

The Trustee Investments Act 1961 (c.62)

1(1) Sections 1, 2, 5, 6, 12, 13 and 15 shall cease to have effect, except in so far as they are applied by or under any other enactment.

(2) Section 3 and Schedules 2 and 3 shall cease to have effect, except in so far as they relate to a trustee having a power of investment conferred on him under an enactment—

(a) which was passed before the passing of the 1961 Act, and

(b) which is not amended by this Schedule.

(3) Omit—

(a) sections 8 and 9,

(b) paragraph 1(1) of Schedule 4, and

(c) section 16(1), in so far as it relates to paragraph 1(1) of Schedule 4.

The Charities Act 1993 (c.10)

2(1) Omit sections 70 and 71.

(2) In section 86(2) in paragraph (a)—

(a) omit "70", and

(b) at the end insert "or".

(3) Omit section 86(2)(b).

Part II Other Public General Acts

The Places of Worship Sites Act 1873 (c.50)

3 In section 2 (payment of purchase money, etc.) for "shall be invested upon such securities or

investments as would for the time being be authorised by statute or the Court of Chancery" substitute " shall be invested under the general power of investment in section 3 of the Trustee Act 2000".

The Technical and Industrial Institutions Act 1892 (c.29)

4 In section 9 (investment powers relating to proceeds of sale of land acquired under the Act) for subsection (5) substitute—

"(5) Money arising by sale may, until reinvested in the purchase of land, be invested—

(a) in the names of the governing body, in any investments in which trustees may invest under the general power of investment in section 3 of the Trustee Act 2000 (as restricted by sections 4 and 5 of that Act), or

(b) under the general power of investment in section 3 of that Act, by trustees for the governing body or by a person authorised by the trustees under that Act to invest as an agent of the trustees.

(6) Any profits from investments under subsection (5) shall be invested in the same way and added to capital until the capital is reinvested in the purchase of land."

The Duchy of Cornwall Management Act 1893 (c.20)

5 The 1893 Act is hereby repealed.

The Duchy of Lancaster Act 1920 (c.51)

6 In section 1 (extension of powers of investment of funds of Duchy of Lancaster) for "in any of the investments specified in paragraph (a) of section one of the Trustees Act 1893 and any enactment amending or extending that paragraph" substitute " under the general power of investment in section 3 of the Trustee Act 2000 (as restricted by sections 4 and 5 of that Act)".

The Settled Land Act 1925 (c.18)

7 In section 21 (absolute owners subject to certain interests to have the powers of tenant for life), in subsection (1)(d) for "income thereof" substitute " resultant profits ".

8 In section 39 (regulations respecting sales), in subsection (2), in the proviso, for the words from "accumulate" to the end of the subsection substitute " accumulate the profits from the capital money by investing them and any resulting profits under the general power of investment in section 3 of the Trustee Act 2000 and shall add the accumulations to capital. "

9 In section 73 (modes of investment or application), in subsection (1) for paragraph (i) substitute—

"(i) In investment in securities either under the general power of investment in section 3 of the Trustee Act 2000 or under a power to invest conferred on the trustees of the settlement by the settlement;".

10(1) In section 75 (regulations respecting investment, devolution, and income of securities etc.), for subsection (2) substitute—

"(2) Subject to Part IV of the Trustee Act 2000, to section 75A of this Act and to the following provisions of this section—

(a) the investment or other application by the trustees shall be made according to the discretion of the trustees, but subject to any consent required or direction given by the settlement with respect to the investment or other application by the trustees of trust money of the settlement, and

(b) any investment shall be in the names or under the control of the trustees."

(2) For subsection (4) of that section substitute—

"(4) The trustees, in exercising their power to invest or apply capital money, shall—

(a) so far as practicable, consult the tenant for life; and

(b) so far as consistent with the general interest of the settlement, give effect to his wishes.

(4A) Any investment or other application of capital money under the direction of the court shall not during the subsistence of the beneficial interest of the tenant for life be altered without his consent.

(4B) The trustees may not under section 11 of the Trustee Act 2000 authorise a person to exercise their functions with respect to the investment or application of capital money on terms that prevent them from complying with subsection (4) of this section.

(4C) A person who is authorised under section 11 of the Trustee Act 2000 to exercise any of their

functions with respect to the investment or application of capital money is not subject to subsection (4) of this section."

(3) Nothing in this paragraph affects the operation of section 75 in relation to directions of the tenant for life given, but not acted upon by the trustees, before the commencement of this paragraph.

11 After section 75 insert—

"75A Power to accept charge as security for part payment for land sold.

(1) Where—

(a) land subject to the settlement is sold by the tenant for life or statutory owner, for an estate in fee simple or a term having at least five hundred years to run, and

(b) the proceeds of sale are liable to be invested,

the tenant for life or statutory owner may, with the consent of the trustees of the settlement, contract that the payment of any part, not exceeding two-thirds, of the purchase money shall be secured by a charge by way of legal mortgage of the land sold, with or without the security of any other property.

(2) If any buildings are comprised in the property secured by the charge, the charge must contain a covenant by the mortgagor to keep them insured for their full value against loss or damage due to any event.

(3) A person exercising the power under subsection (1) of this section, or giving consent for the purposes of that subsection—

(a) is not required to comply with section 5 of the Trustee Act 2000 before giving his consent, and

(b) is not liable for any loss incurred merely because the security is insufficient at the date of the charge.

(4) The power under subsection (1) of this section is exercisable subject to the consent of any person whose consent to a change of investment is required by the instrument, if any, creating the trust.

(5) Where the sale referred to in subsection (1) of this section is made under the order of the court, the power under that subsection applies only if and as far as the court may by order direct."

12 Omit section 96 (protection of each trustee individually).

13 In section 98 (protection of trustees in particular cases), omit subsections (1) and (2).

14 Omit section 100 (trustees' reimbursements).

15 In section 102 (management of land during minority or pending contingency), in subsection (2) for paragraph (e) substitute—

"(e) to insure against risks of loss or damage due to any event under section 19 of the Trustee Act 1925;".

16(1) In section 104 (powers of tenant for life not assignable etc.)—

(a) in subsection (3)(b) omit "authorised by statute for the investment of trust money", and

(b) in subsection (4)(b) for the words from "no investment" to "trust money;" substitute "the consent of the assignee shall be required to an investment of capital money for the time being affected by the assignment in investments other than securities, and to any application of such capital money;".

(2) Sub-paragraph (1) applies to the determination on or after the commencement of that sub-paragraph of whether an assignee's consent is required to the investment or application of capital money.

17 In section 107 (tenant for life deemed to be in the position and to have the duties and liabilities of a trustee, etc.) after subsection (1) insert—

"(1A) The following provisions apply to the tenant for life as they apply to the trustees of the settlement—

(a) sections 11, 13 to 15 and 21 to 23 of the Trustee Act 2000 (power to employ agents subject to certain restrictions),

(b) section 32 of that Act (remuneration and expenses of agents etc.),

(c) section 19 of the Trustee Act 1925 (power to insure), and

(d) in so far as they relate to the provisions mentioned in paragraphs (a) and (c), Part I of, and Schedule 1 to, the Trustee Act 2000 (the duty of care)."

The Trustee Act 1925 (c.19)

18 Omit Part I (investments).

19 In section 14 (power of trustees to give receipts) in subsection (1) after "securities," insert

"investments".

20 In section 15 (power to compound liabilities), for "in good faith" substitute " if he has or they have discharged the duty of care set out in section 1(1) of the Trustee Act 2000 ".

21 Omit section 21 (deposit of documents for safe custody).

22 In section 22 (reversionary interests, valuations, and audit)—

(a) in subsection (1), for "in good faith" substitute " if they have discharged the duty of care set out in section 1(1) of the Trustee Act 2000 ", and

(b) in subsection (3), omit "in good faith" and at the end insert " if the trustees have discharged the duty of care set out in section 1(1) of the Trustee Act 2000 ".

23 Omit section 23 (power to employ agents).

24 Omit section 30 (implied indemnity of trustees).

25 In section 31(2) (power to invest income during minority) for "in the way of compound interest by investing the same and the resulting income thereof" substitute " by investing it, and any profits from so investing it ".

The Land Registration Act 1925 (c.21)

26 In section 94(1) (registered land subject to a trust to be registered in the names of the trustees), at the end insert "or in the name of a nominee appointed under section 16 of the Trustee Act 2000".

The Administration of Estates Act 1925 (c.23)

27 In section 33, in subsection (3) (investment during minority of beneficiary or the subsistence of a life interest) for the words from "in any investments for the time being authorised by statute" to the end of the subsection substitute "under the Trustee Act 2000."

28 In section 39 (powers of management) after subsection (1) insert—

"(1A) Subsection (1) of this section is without prejudice to the powers conferred on personal representatives by the Trustee Act 2000."

The Universities and College Estates Act 1925 (c.24)

29 In section 26 (modes of application of capital money) in subsection (1) for paragraph (i) substitute—

"(i) In investments in which trustees may invest under the general power of investment in section 3 of the Trustee Act 2000 (as restricted by sections 4 and 5 of that Act);".

The Regimental Charitable Funds Act 1935 (c.11)

30 In section 2(1) (application of funds held on account of regimental charitable funds)—

(a) in paragraph (a) for "in some manner" to "trusts" substitute " under the general power of investment in section 3 of the Trustee Act 2000 ";

(b) in paragraph (b) after "the income" insert " or the other profits ".

The Agricultural Marketing Act 1958 (c.47)

31(1) In section 16 (investment of surplus funds of boards) for paragraph (a) substitute—

"(a) the moneys of the board not for the time being required by them for the purposes of their functions are not, except with the approval of the Minister, invested otherwise than in investments in which trustees may invest under the general power of investment in section 3 of the Trustee Act 2000 (as restricted by sections 4 and 5 of that Act); and".

(2) Any scheme made under the 1958 Act and in effect before the day on which sub-paragraph (1) comes into force shall be treated, in relation to the making of investments on and after that day, as including provision permitting investment by the board in accordance with section 16(a) of the 1958 Act as amended by sub-paragraph (1).

The Horticulture Act 1960 (c.22)

32 In section 13 (miscellaneous financial powers of organisations promoting home-grown produce) for subsection (3) substitute—

"(3) A relevant organisation may invest any of its surplus money which is not for the time being required for any other purpose in any investments in which trustees may invest under the general power of investment in section 3 of the Trustee Act 2000 (as restricted by sections 4 and 5 of that Act)".

The House of Commons Members' Fund Act 1962 (c.53)

33(1) In section 1 (powers of investment of trustees of House of Commons Members' Fund)—

(a) in subsection (2) omit "Subject to the following provisions of this section";

(b) omit subsections (3) to (5).

(2) In section 2 (interpretation etc.) omit subsection (1).

The Betting, Gaming and Lotteries Act 1963 (c.2)

34 In section 25(1) (general powers and duties of the Horserace Betting Levy Board) for paragraph (e) substitute—

"(e) to make such other investments as—

(i) they judge desirable for the proper conduct of their affairs, and

(ii) a trustee would be able to make under the general power of investment in section 3 of the Trustee Act 2000 (as restricted by sections 4 and 5 of that Act);".

The Cereals Marketing Act 1965 (c.14)

35(1) In section 18, in subsection (2) (Home-Grown Cereals Authority's power to invest reserve funds) for "in accordance with the next following subsection" substitute " in any investments in which trustees may invest under the general power of investment in section 3 of the Trustee Act 2000 (as restricted by sections 4 and 5 of that Act). "

(2) Omit section 18(3).

The Agriculture Act 1967 (c.22)

36(1) In section 18, in subsection (2) (Meat and Livestock Commission's power to invest reserve fund) for "in accordance with the next following subsection" substitute " in any investments in which trustees may invest under the general power of investment in section 3 of the Trustee Act 2000 (as restricted by sections 4 and 5 of that Act). "

(2) Omit section 18(3).

The Solicitors Act 1974 (c.47)

37 In Schedule 2, for paragraph 3 (power of Law Society to invest) substitute—

"3 The Society may invest any money which forms part of the fund in any investments in which trustees may invest under the general power of investment in section 3 of the Trustee Act 2000 (as restricted by sections 4 and 5 of that Act)."

The Policyholders Protection Act 1975 (c.75)

38 In Schedule 1, in paragraph 7, for sub-paragraph (1) (power of Policyholders Protection Board to invest) substitute—

"(1) The Board may invest any funds held by them which appear to them to be surplus to their requirements for the time being—

(a) in any investments in which trustees may invest under the general power of investment in section 3 of the Trustee Act 2000 (as restricted by sections 4 and 5 of that Act); or

(b) in any investment approved for the purpose by the Treasury."

The National Heritage Act 1980 (c.17)

39 In section 6 for subsection (3) (powers of investment of Trustees of National Heritage Memorial Fund) substitute—

"(3) The Trustees may invest any sums to which subsection (2) does not apply in any investments in which trustees may invest under the general power of investment in section 3 of the Trustee Act 2000 (as restricted by sections 4 and 5 of that Act)."

The Licensing (Alcohol Education and Research) Act 1981 (c.28)

40 In section 7 (powers of investment of Alcohol Education and Research Council) for subsection (5) substitute—

"(5) Any sums in the Fund which are not immediately required for any other purpose may be invested by the Council in any investments in which trustees may invest under the general power of investment in section 3 of the Trustee Act 2000 (as restricted by sections 4 and 5 of that Act)."

The Fisheries Act 1981 (c.29)

41 For section 10 (powers of investment of Sea Fish Industry Authority) substitute—

"10 Investment of reserve funds

Any money of the Authority which is not immediately required for any other purpose may be

invested by the Authority in any investments in which trustees may invest under the general power of investment in section 3 of the Trustee Act 2000 (as restricted by sections 4 and 5 of that Act)".

The Duchy of Cornwall Management Act 1982 (c.47)

42 For section 1 (powers of investment of Duchy property) substitute—

"1 Powers of investment of Duchy property.

The power of investment conferred by the Duchy of Cornwall Management Act 1863 includes power to invest in any investments in which trustees may invest under the general power of investment in section 3 of the Trustee Act 2000 (as restricted by sections 4 and 5 of that Act)."

43 In—

(a) section 6(3) (Duchy of Cornwall Management Acts extended in relation to banking), and

(b) section 11(2) (collective citation of Duchy of Cornwall Management Acts),

for "Duchy of Cornwall Management Acts 1868 to 1893" substitute " Duchy of Cornwall Management Acts 1863 to 1868 ".

The Administration of Justice Act 1982 (c.53)

44 In section 42 (common investment schemes) in subsection (6) for paragraph (a) substitute—

"(a) he may invest trust money in shares in the fund without obtaining and considering advice on whether to make such an investment; and".

The Trusts of Land and Appointment of Trustees Act 1996 (c.47)

45(1) In section 6 (general powers of trustees), in subsection (3) for "purchase a legal estate in any land in England and Wales" substitute " acquire land under the power conferred by section 8 of the Trustee Act 2000. "

(2) Omit subsection (4) of that section.

(3) After subsection (8) of that section insert—

"(9) The duty of care under section 1 of the Trustee Act 2000 applies to trustees of land when exercising the powers conferred by this section."

46 In section 9 (delegation by trustees) omit subsection (8).

47 After section 9 insert—

"9A Duties of trustees in connection with delegation etc.

(1) The duty of care under section 1 of the Trustee Act 2000 applies to trustees of land in deciding whether to delegate any of their functions under section 9.

(2) Subsection (3) applies if the trustees of land—

(a) delegate any of their functions under section 9, and

(b) the delegation is not irrevocable.

(3) While the delegation continues, the trustees—

(a) must keep the delegation under review,

(b) if circumstances make it appropriate to do so, must consider whether there is a need to exercise any power of intervention that they have, and

(c) if they consider that there is a need to exercise such a power, must do so.

(4) "Power of intervention" includes—

(a) a power to give directions to the beneficiary;

(b) a power to revoke the delegation.

(5) The duty of care under section 1 of the 2000 Act applies to trustees in carrying out any duty under subsection (3).

(6) A trustee of land is not liable for any act or default of the beneficiary, or beneficiaries, unless the trustee fails to comply with the duty of care in deciding to delegate any of the trustees' functions under section 9 or in carrying out any duty under subsection (3).

(7) Neither this section nor the repeal of section 9(8) by the Trustee Act 2000 affects the operation after the commencement of this section of any delegation effected before that commencement."

48 Omit section 17(1) (application of section 6(3) in relation to trustees of proceeds of sale of land).

49 In Schedule 3 (consequential amendments) omit paragraph 3(4) (amendment of section 19(1) and (2) of Trustee Act 1925).

Part III Measures

The Ecclesiastical Dilapidations Measure 1923 (No.3)

50 In section 52, in subsection (5) (investment of sums held in relation to repair of chancels)—

(a) for "in any investment permitted by law for the investment of trust funds, and the yearly income resulting therefrom shall be applied," substitute " in any investments in which trustees may invest under the general power of investment in section 3 of the Trustee Act 2000, and the annual profits from the investments shall be applied "; and

(b) in paragraph (iii) for "any residue of the said income not applied as aforesaid in any year" substitute " any residue of the profits from the investments not applied in any year. "

The Diocesan Stipends Funds Measure 1953 (No.2)

51 In section 4 (application of moneys credited to capital accounts) in subsection (1) for paragraph (bc) substitute—

"(bc) investment in any investments in which trustees may invest under the general power of investment in section 3 of the Trustee Act 2000 (as restricted by sections 4 and 5 of that Act);".

The Church Funds Investment Measure 1958 (No.1)

52 In the Schedule, in paragraph 21 (range of investments of deposit fund) for paragraphs (a) to (d) of sub-paragraph (1) substitute—

"(aa) In any investments in which trustees may invest under the general power of investment in section 3 of the Trustee Act 2000 (as restricted by sections 4 and 5 of that Act);".

The Clergy Pensions Measure 1961 (No.3)

53(1) In section 32 (investment powers of Board), in subsection (1), for paragraph (a) substitute—

"(a) in any investments in which trustees may invest under the general power of investment in section 3 of the Trustee Act 2000 (as restricted by sections 4 and 5 of that Act);".

(2) Omit subsection (3) of that section.

The Repair of Benefice Buildings Measure 1972 (No.2)

54 In section 17, in subsection (2) (diocesan parsonages fund's power of investment), for "who shall have the same powers of investment as trustees of trust funds:" substitute " who shall have the same power as trustees to invest in any investments in which trustees may invest under the general power of investment in section 3 of the Trustee Act 2000 (as restricted by sections 4 and 5 of that Act). "

The Pastoral Measure 1983 (No.1)

55 In section 44, for subsection (6) (Redundant Churches Fund's power of investment) substitute—

"(6) The powers to invest any such sums are—

(a) power to invest in investments in which trustees may invest under the general power of investment in section 3 of the Trustee Act 2000 (as restricted by sections 4 and 5 of that Act); and

(b) power to invest in the investments referred to in paragraph 21(1)(e) and (f) of the Schedule to the Church Funds Investment Measure 1958."

The Church of England (Pensions) Measure 1988 (No.4)

56 Omit section 14(b) (amendment of section 32(3) of the Clergy Pensions Measure 1961).

The Cathedrals Measure 1999 (No.1)

57 In section 16 (cathedral moneys: investment powers, etc.), in subsection (1)—

(a) for paragraph (c) substitute—

"(c) power to invest in any investments in which trustees may invest under the general power of investment in section 3 of the Trustee Act 2000 (as restricted by sections 4 and 5 of that Act),",and

(b) omit the words from "and the powers" to the end of the subsection.

Section 40.

SCHEDULE 3 Transitional provisions and savings

The Trustee Act 1925 (c.19)

1(1) Sub-paragraph (2) applies if, immediately before the day on which Part IV of this Act comes into force, a banker or banking company holds any bearer securities deposited with him under section

7(1) of the 1925 Act (investment in bearer securities).

(2) On and after the day on which Part IV comes into force, the banker or banking company shall be treated as if he had been appointed as custodian of the securities under section 18.

2 The repeal of section 8 of the 1925 Act (loans and investments by trustees not chargeable as breaches of trust) does not affect the operation of that section in relation to loans or investments made before the coming into force of that repeal.

3 The repeal of section 9 of the 1925 Act (liability for loss by reason of improper investment) does not affect the operation of that section in relation to any advance of trust money made before the coming into force of that repeal.

4(1) Sub-paragraph (2) applies if, immediately before the day on which Part IV of this Act comes into force, a banker or banking company holds any documents deposited with him under section 21 of the 1925 Act (deposit of documents for safe custody).

(2) On and after the day on which Part IV comes into force, the banker or banking company shall be treated as if he had been appointed as custodian of the documents under section 17.

5(1) Sub-paragraph (2) applies if, immediately before the day on which Part IV of this Act comes into force, a person has been appointed to act as or be an agent or attorney under section 23(1) or (3) of the 1925 Act (general power to employ agents etc.).

(2) On and after the day on which Part IV comes into force, the agent shall be treated as if he had been authorised to exercise functions as an agent under section 11 (and, if appropriate, as if he had also been appointed under that Part to act as a custodian or nominee).

6 The repeal of section 23(2) of the 1925 Act (power to employ agents in respect of property outside the United Kingdom) does not affect the operation after the commencement of the repeal of an appointment made before that commencement.

The Trustee Investments Act 1961 (c.62)

7(1) A trustee shall not be liable for breach of trust merely because he continues to hold an investment acquired by virtue of paragraph 14 of Part II of Schedule 1 to the 1961 Act (perpetual rent-charges etc.).

(2) A person who—

(a) is not a trustee,

(b) before the commencement of Part II of this Act had powers to invest in the investments described in paragraph 14 of Part II of Schedule 1 to the 1961 Act, and

(c) on that commencement acquired the general power of investment,

shall not be treated as exceeding his powers of investment merely because he continues to hold an investment acquired by virtue of that paragraph.

The Cathedrals Measure 1963 (No.2)

8 While section 21 of the Cathedrals Measure 1963 (investment powers, etc. of capitular bodies) continues to apply in relation to any cathedral, that section shall have effect as if—

(a) in subsection (1), for paragraph (c) and the words from "and the powers" to the end of the subsection there were substituted—

"(c) power to invest in any investments in which trustees may invest under the general power of investment in section 3 of the Trustee Act 2000 (as restricted by sections 4 and 5 of that Act).", and

(b) in subsection (5), for "subsections (2) and (3) of section six of the Trustee Investments Act 1961" there were substituted " section 5 of the Trustee Act 2000 ".

Section 40.

SCHEDULE 4 Repeals

Part I The Trustee Investments Act 1961 and the Charities Act 1993

Chapter	**Short title**	**Extent of repeal**
1961 c. 62.	The Trustee Investments Act 1961.	Sections 1 to 3, 5, 6, 8, 9, 12, 13, 15 and 16(1). Schedules 2 and 3. In Schedule 4, paragraph 1(1).
1993 c. 10.	The Charities Act 1993.	Sections 70 and 71. In section 86(2) in paragraph (a), "70" and

paragraph (b).

Note: the repeals in this Part of this Schedule have effect in accordance with Part I of Schedule 2.

Part II Other repeals

Chapter	Short title	Extent of repeal
1893 c. 20.	The Duchy of Cornwall Management Act 1893.	The whole Act.
1925 c. 18.	The Settled Land Act 1925.	Section 96. Section 98(1) and (2). Section 100. In section 104(3)(b) the words "authorised by statute for the investment of trust money".
1925 c. 19.	The Trustee Act 1925.	Part I. In section 20(1) the words "whether by fire or otherwise". Sections 21, 23 and 30.
1961 No. 3.	The Clergy Pensions Measure 1961.	Section 32(3).
1962 c. 53.	The House of Commons Members' Fund Act 1962.	In section 1, in subsection (2) the words "Subject to the following provisions of this section" and subsections (3) to (5). Section 2(1).
1965 c. 14.	The Cereals Marketing Act 1965.	Section 18(3).
1967 c. 22.	The Agriculture Act 1967.	Section 18(3).
1988 No. 4.	The Church of England (Pensions) Measure 1988.	Section 14(b).
1996 c. 47.	The Trusts of Land and Appointment of Trustees Act 1996.	Section 6(4). Section 9(8). Section 17(1). In Schedule 3, paragraph 3(4).
1999 No. 1.	The Cathedrals Measure 1999.	In section 16(1), the words from "and the powers" to the end of the subsection.